Renaissance Literature

$\mathscr{B}$LACKWELL $\mathscr{A}$NTHOLOGIES

Editorial Advisers

Blackwell Anthologies are a series of extensive and comprehensive volumes designed to address the numerous issues raised by recent debates regarding the literary canon, value, text, context, gender, genre, and period. While providing the reader with key canonical writings in their entirety, the series is also ambitious in its coverage of hitherto marginalized texts and flexible in the overall variety of its approaches to periods and movements. Each volume has been thoroughly researched to meet the current needs of teachers and students.

Victorian Women Poets: An Anthology
edited by Angela Leighton and Margaret Reynolds

Romanticism: An Anthology. Second Edition
edited by Duncan Wu

Romantic Women Poets: An Anthology
edited by Duncan Wu

British Literature 1640–1789: An Anthology.
Second Edition
edited by Robert DeMaria, Jr

Chaucer to Spenser: An Anthology of English
Writing 1375–1575
edited by Derek Pearsall

Renaissance Drama: An Anthology of Plays
and Entertainments
edited by Arthur Kinney

Old and Middle English: An Anthology
edited by Elaine Treharne

Restoration Drama: An Anthology
edited by David Womersley

The Victorians: An Anthology of Poetry and Poetics
edited by Valentine Cunningham

Medieval Drama: An Anthology
edited by Greg Walker

Nineteenth-Century American Women Writers:
An Anthology
edited by Karen L. Kilcup

Nineteenth-Century American Women Poets:
An Anthology
edited by Paula Bernat Bennett

American Gothic: An Anthology 1787–1916
edited by Charles L. Crow

Native American Women Writers: An Anthology of
Works c.1800–1924
edited by Karen L. Kilcup

Children's Literature: An Anthology 1801–1902
edited by Peter Hunt

The Literatures of Colonial America: An Anthology
edited by Susan Castillo and Ivy T. Schweitzer

Renaissance Literature: An Anthology
edited by Michael Payne and John Hunter

RENAISSANCE LITERATURE

AN ANTHOLOGY

EDITED BY **MICHAEL PAYNE** AND **JOHN HUNTER**

Blackwell
Publishing

Editorial material and organization © 2003 by Blackwell Publishing Ltd

350 Main Street, Malden, MA 02148-5018, USA
108 Cowley Road, Oxford OX4 1JF, UK
550 Swanston Street, Carlton South, Melbourne, Victoria 3053, Australia
Kurfürstendamm 57, 10707 Berlin, Germany

First published 2003 by Blackwell Publishing Ltd

Library of Congress Cataloging-in-Publication Data

Renaissance literature : an anthology / edited by Michael Payne and John Hunter.
p.   cm. – (Blackwell anthologies)
Includes bibliographical references (p.) and indexes.
ISBN 0-631-19897-0 (alk. paper) – ISBN 0-631-19898-9 (pbk. : alk. paper)
1. English literature–Early modern, 1500–1700.   2. Renaissance–England.
I. Payne, Micheal, 1941–   II. Hunter, John.   III. Series.

PR1121 .R36 2003
820.8′003–dc21   2002074763

A catalogue record for this title is available from the British Library.

Typeset in Garamond 3 on 9.5/11 pt
by SNP Best-set Typesetter Ltd., Hong Kong
Printed and bound in the United Kingdom
by T.J. International, Padstow, Cornwall

For further information on
Blackwell Publishing, visit our website:
http://www.blackwellpublishing.com

Contents

(os = texts in original spelling)

Alphabetical List of Authors

Preface

This anthology is intended as a pleasurable and informative survey of English Renaissance poetry and prose for students and general readers. Although the concept of the Renaissance as a meaningful historical designation has long been disputed, for the purposes of this volume it refers simply to writing published or circulated between the accession of Henry VIII in 1509 and the English Civil War of 1641. We are mindful of the fact that the term "Early Modern" has come to replace both "Renaissance" and "Medieval" in literary studies and of the scholarly consensus about the increasing difficulty in drawing absolute distinctions between these two eras. We have chosen to retain the word "Renaissance," however, for the sake of chronological specificity and because most of the writers included in this anthology believed in the distinctiveness of their historical moment from the "Middle Ages." Our hope is that readers will read in a spirit of curious skepticism about this claim of uniqueness, and explore the implications of this overdetermined term for themselves.

The arrangement of the collection is chronological, based usually on the date of birth of the author, and, following that, on the date of publication of individual texts (where known). Although this is principally an anthology of prose and poetry originally written in English during the sixteenth and early seventeenth centuries, some translations are also included because of their cultural importance. Every effort has been made to produce a coherent book that nonetheless tells at least two discontinuous stories. The first records the response of English literary culture to the challenges and transformations embodied by humanism as an intellectual, historical, and socio-political movement. The second traces the critical and sometimes suspicious assessments of humanist commonplaces that appeared at the same time, often produced by women and others who felt alienated from its restrictive ideological assumptions. Both of these stories are, of course, as much products of centuries of Renaissance scholarship as they are of their own time, and this anthology also hopes to expose some of the ideological processes by which texts are edited and taught as representatives of the "Renaissance world." After much debate, we decided not to try to cover the literature surrounding the exploration of the New World in great detail, simply because we could not do this important theme full justice.

The task of selecting texts for a period anthology has been completely revolutionized by the rise of the World Wide Web. Fifty years ago, historical anthology editors were conscious of the fact that their selection decisions had a decisive impact on what was available for students and the general public to read. Scholarly editions of specific writers were (and still are) expensive and intimidating to the non-specialist, and editors had to create their teaching anthologies with the heavy responsibility of embodying an entire historical period. Over the past twenty years, however, scholars have come to recognize the essential arbitrariness of all period classifications and of all attempts to try to represent a historical epoch. With the World Wide Web freely available in most schools, colleges, and universities (and in many public libraries), on-line editions of any literary text can be mounted and circulated with minimal cost. The past ten years have seen an enormous proliferation of sites devoted to Early Modern literary study and many feature editions of previously unavailable authors. The Brown University Women Writers Project, for example, is a remarkable trove of texts that would have been very difficult for a general reader to obtain or even learn about twenty years ago. Not all websites are as editorially scrupulous as this one, but the quality and quantity of online editions have relieved printed anthologies of some of the more intractable problems of working with a literary canon. More and more, it is readers and instructors who decide what to read, and this is as it should be.

The selections included in this book have been made on the basis of three principles. One has been unabashedly *canonical*. Writing by figures such as Sidney, Spenser, Marlowe, Shakespeare, and

Jonson is given considerable space because their work has been crucial for all formulations of English Renaissance culture and because of their impact on the subsequent history of English poetry and prose. Equally important, they were all recognized as important writers in their own day, so they can help us to understand what Renaissance England valued about itself, as opposed to what we value about it. A second principle might loosely be called *non-canonical*, even though secular literary canons are remarkably fluid, often incorporating and celebrating in a succeeding generation what was excluded previously. In this anthology writing by women whom Virginia Woolf might have called "Shakespeare's sisters" is given considerable attention. Although such names as Anne Askew, Elizabeth Cary, Æmilia Lanyer, Martha Moulsworth, and Mary Wroth have recently become increasingly familiar to students of the English Renaissance, their work can profitably be read not only as previously marginalized women's writing but also, as here, in the context of writing by their male contemporaries, whose texts they often openly or ironically subvert. We have also included texts that are rarely anthologized but were very influential during the period, such as the extracts from the *Book of Homilies*, and texts that contravene many received ideas about the Renaissance, such as Nashe's "Choice of Valentines." A third principle is *scholarly currency*, or the importance of certain authors and texts for current critical and scholarly debates about the Renaissance, literary history, critical theory, and cultural studies. Head notes to individual authors give a brief sense of such debates, along with references to relevant items in the critical bibliography.

The form of the texts in this anthology reflects an important change that has been taking place during the past twenty years in editing practice. Based on the assumptions of the New Criticism and related nineteenth-century conceptions of lyric poetry, the editing of Renaissance texts once assumed that it was the editor's task to recover from the vicissitudes of textual transmission as pure and accessible a form of an aesthetically unified original as possible. The unstated and often un-reflective assumption was that literature – or at least the greatest literature – begins with an act of free, imaginative creation that has the power unproblematically to transcend its age and to speak to all time. This assumption has been systematically challenged by New-Historicist and cultural-materialist critique, which emphasizes instead the inescapable connections between social power, the economic conditions of cultural production, and artistic processes (see especially Greenblatt 1980 and Dollimore 1989). Thus, literary texts are now rarely seen as sites where aesthetic unity ultimately triumphs over all forms of human conflict, but rather as scenes of eruption in discourse of both the personal and social forms of that conflict.

This change in assumptions underlying editing practice has important but somewhat untidy implications for the modernization of Renaissance texts. On the one hand, the practice of modernization has been seriously questioned on the grounds that it substitutes a twentieth-century set of presuppositions concerning spelling, punctuation, and grammar for the more fluid conditions of textual production during the Renaissance, when spelling, punctuation, and the rules of grammar were not standardized, when poetry was closer to oral rhetoric, and when "publication" often meant that an author (such as Wyatt, Lady Mary Wroth, or Donne) circulated manuscripts among his or her friends, who were then free to copy and to alter what their authors had written. On the other hand, a unilateral retreat from the problems of modernization, back to old spelling and irregular punctuation, puts obstacles in the way of modern readers, often simply perpetuating printers' or copyists' practices that have nothing to do with authorial composition. The protocols of textual emendation also have a long history of controversy. In his "Preface to Shakespeare," Samuel Johnson warned against succumbing to the temptation of editorial "licentiousness," by which he meant an editor's leaping from the margins into the text in order to emend it. There are no tidy compro-mises that solve these dilemmas, but it seems clear that the literary academy as a whole is coming more and more to accept that every edition of a text is, in effect, a performance of it and that no one performance can ever be definitive.

Rather than imposing a uniform system of modernization, this anthology opts for a more strate-gic procedure that responds to the conditions of each text. Sometimes this results in inconsistent editorial practice between different authors in order, for example, to avoid losing a syllable and thus a rhythmic poetic pattern by changing from old to new spelling. Prose selections here tend to be more heavily modernized than the poetic ones, except when brief prose passages in old spelling provide a more immediate sense of an author's prose style. The salient modernization problem with Renaissance texts is punctuation, however, because Renaissance punctuation is typically more a rhetorical than a syntactic marker, and punctuation changes often impose a resolution of ambiguity. We have tried to be as sensitive as possible to this problem, while recognizing that our readers are (in the main) non-specialists. The best reading procedure, where possible, is always to look at facsimile or scholarly editions of the works in this book in comparison with what we present here. Doing so illustrates the performative nature of all literary texts and the material processes that make possible the imaginative work of reading.

Proper names are usually glossed only when they first appear in a given text, unless they are subsequently used in a different sense. The Index to Introductions and Notes lists glosses of all proper names, and a gazetteer is included for commonly used names and texts.

Whenever possible, complete texts have been chosen over excerpts, even when the consequence, because of space limitations, has been that a less familiar text is included. Considerable attention has also been given to relationships or parallels between selections. The sequence of prose selections provides in miniature a history of English prose style over a century and a half of major syntactic and rhetorical change. The poetic selections can sustain the conventional observation that two potentially complementary styles – one sensuous, the other witty – are epitomized respectively by Spenser and by Donne, but also include rarely taught texts that subvert or complicate this convention. Few undergraduates today are encouraged to read Ben Jonson' s "On the Famous Voyage" or Marston's satires, but they are just as much part of the Renaissance as Shakespeare. Several other poetic forms and traditions are also given space in this book, which includes such musical forms as carols, hymns, ballads, and lyrics; visual forms related to the emblem tradition; and genres yet to be named, such as that represented by Martha Moulsworth's autobiographical poem. The editorial apparatus as a whole is intended to reflect the mercurial state of current scholarly work on English Renaissance literature, including materials now readily available on the Internet. Such websites as Renascence Editions, the Brown University Women Writers Project, Mr. William Shakespeare on the Internet, Luminarium, and the Spenser homepage are highly recommended.

We are very grateful to Kevin Kuck and Matthew Perakovich for their help in checking the proofs of this book. For their patience and support during all phases of this project, we also thank Andrew McNeillie, Alison Dunnett, and Sandra Raphael, whose good sense and sharp eyes have been invaluable to us. We dedicate this book to our children with love and with the hope that they might discover in it what their fathers find endlessly fascinating about the literature of the English Renaissance.

READING

Jonathan Dollimore, *Radical Tragedy: Religion, Ideology, and Power in the Drama of Shakespeare and his Contemporaries.*

Wallace K. Ferguson, *The Renaissance in Historical Thought: Five Centuries of Interpretation.*

Anthony Grafton and Lisa Jardine, *From Humanism to the Humanities.*

Stephen Greenblatt, *Renaissance Self-Fashioning: From More to Shakespeare.*

William Kerrigan and Gorden Braden, *The Idea of the Renaissance.*

Andrew Murphy (ed.) *The Renaissance Text: Theory, Editing, Textuality.*

David Norbrook and H. R. Woudhuysen (eds.), *The Penguin Book of Renaissance Verse, 1509–1659.*

Erwin Panofsky, *Renaissance and Renascences in Western Art.*

E. M. W. Tillyard, *The English Renaissance: Fact or Fiction?*

Virginia Woolf, *A Room of One's Own.*

M. P. and J. H.

Introduction
The Renaissance in Cultural and Critical Theory

"This age, like a golden age, has restored to light the liberal arts that were almost extinct." Ficino

"Those arts that are closest to the liberal arts . . . (which) were first so long and so greatly denigrated and almost perished with letters themselves {are} now being reawakened and revived." Valla

"Since in our age we see letters restored to life, what prevents us from seeing among us a new Demosthenes, Plato, Thucydides, Cicero?" Budé

"We would have woes in abundance, even if no more were added. For some time now we have been infected with the plague, which does not come to an end. The high cost of living continues to go up. God only knows what is to follow. . . . If the sword is the means of solving the situation, then the biggest share of calamities will fall upon the innocent, and under the guise of defending religion the world will be filled with robbers. . . . This whole sea of filth will first engulf Germany, then the rest of the world." Erasmus

During the past five centuries the concept of the Renaissance, with its broad sense of intellectual and artistic rebirth, has had a major role in the development of the idea of Western European culture itself. In part this is because history as an intellectual and academic discipline began to assume its distinctive identity, in contrast to poetry and philosophy, as a consequence of the humanist intellectual and academic reforms of the sixteenth century. Thus, to inquire into the nature of the Renaissance is simultaneously to inquire into the nature of history as a mode of thought and into the nature of Western European culture, the origins of which modern historical writing first set out to describe and to celebrate. Whether there was in fact such a thing as the Renaissance, and if so what it was and when it occurred, have been matters of continuous interest and debate.

BURCKHARDT'S IDEA OF THE RENAISSANCE

One of the most influential definitions of the Renaissance appears in Jacob Burckhardt's *The Civilization of the Renaissance in Italy*, which has continued to be a powerfully influential book since its publication in 1860.

"In the Middle Ages," Burckhardt wrote,

> both sides of human consciousness – that which was turned within as that which was turned without – lay dreaming or half awake beneath a common veil. The veil was woven of faith, illusion, and child-ish prepossession, through which the world and history were seen clad in strange hues. Man was con-scious of himself only as a member of a race, people, party, family, or corporation – only through some general category. In Italy this veil first melted into air; an *objective* treatment and consideration of the State and of all the things of this world became possible. The *subjective* side at the same time asserted itself with corresponding emphasis; man became a spiritual *individual*, and recognized himself as such. (Burckhardt, p. 100)

Here Burckhardt sounds several themes that have been constantly replayed in accounts of the Renaissance: that it was a reaction against the Middle Ages, that it replaced faith and illusion with reason and truth, that it was mature where the Middle Ages were childish, that it gave birth to individual self-consciousness where before there was but a vague sense of general humanity, and that it gave sharp definition to the objectivity of the world and to the subjectivity of the human spirit. Although Burckhardt is unequivocal in his conviction that the Renaissance began in Italy, he is understandably less definite about the time of its advent. He claims it manifested itself when the spirit of patriotism began to be felt, not as an achievement but as a longing, in the city-states of Venice and Florence in the fifteenth century; or when the revival of antiquity began to be united (by the beginning of the sixteenth century) with the "genius of the Italian people." Another possible date is 1390, when "there was no longer any prevailing fashion of dress for men at Florence, each preferring to clothe himself in his own way" (p. 101n). Such self-fashioning marks for Burckhardt and for later historians the emergence of individualism as a form of Renaissance cultural expression.

The past twenty years of scholarship on this period have left few, if any, of Burckhardt's large claims unqualified. Many have been proved demonstrably wrong. Nevertheless, it was his vision of the Renaissance that set the terms for all discussions from his day to our own, and its hold on the cultural imagination of the West is still very strong. What he is obviously right about is his view that many Renaissance artists and scholars were reacting strongly against some medieval conventions in writing, philosophy, art, and history and defined themselves in opposition to things medieval in general. The extent to which their self-declared revolution actually constituted a revolution is a matter for ongoing debate, and the continuities within Early Modern culture are just as productive and interesting as the differences between the "medieval" and the "Renaissance." The appeal of the idea of a rebirth of learning is a powerful one and, as terms like "the Harlem Renaissance" show, it continues to influence how we think about the past and contemporary life.

The Multiplicity of the Renaissance

Despite the continuing appeal of Burckhardt's unified image of the Renaissance, several features of the age, which have been variously emphasized by modern historians, have contributed to the sense that it constituted a multiplicitous culture. These features include humanism, the Protestant Reformation, the invention of the printing press, the New Philosophy, the Hermetic tradition, perspective in the visual arts, and harmony in music. It is the influence of humanism, however, and its stress on a return to classical standards in grammar, literature, philosophy, plastic arts, and science which did the most to foment the sense that a new era in human history was under way.

Although the term "humanism" did not come into general use before the nineteenth century, it has its roots in the Latin *humanitas* which refers to certain broad cultural values, including reasonableness, open-mindedness, magnanimity, and refinement, that since classical times have been thought to be the outcome of the *studia humanitatis*, which would now be called the humanities or the human sciences. Of these disciplines, literature, language (especially rhetoric), history, and philosophy were considered the most important during the Renaissance. Humanism is further – and perhaps more specifically – associated with the critical study of texts of ancient Greece and Rome. During the Latin Middle Ages, the study of Greek and Hebrew was often neglected, with the consequence that writing in those languages was either ignored or mediated by Latin translations and scholarly authority, which usually deprived students of the means to read and assess much of ancient literary, philosophical, and religious writing for themselves. Above all, Renaissance humanism was a return to texts, which simultaneously promoted the importance of individual critical judgment and significantly changed the power of institutional authority. As an intellectual and academic movement, humanism became closely associated with the Protestant Reformation, which placed great emphasis on the dissemination of Scripture in vernacular languages, and with the development of the printing press, which was the technological advance that rapidly spread the effects of humanism and Reformation thought throughout Europe.

If a single symbolic act can be isolated as the focal point of the Protestant Reformation, it would be Martin Luther's nailing of his 95 *Theses* to the door of the Schlosskirche in Wittenberg on October

31, 1517. (Philipp Melanchthon, who wrote an early sketch of Luther's life a few months after Luther died, is the source of this story.) Luther was an Augustinian monk and a professor of theology. Far from wishing to remove himself from the established Church, Luther was calling for a debate on the commercial and political worldliness of its practices. He was, nevertheless, excommunicated four years later. Although it was in some ways much more dramatic than the humanist reforms, the Protestant Reformation constituted a similar challenge to institutional authority and promoted the importance of individual critical judgment. Calvinist ideas took hold quickly in England during the 1520s, largely because a way had been prepared for them by the teachings of Wycliffe in the fourteenth century and by the activities of such proletarian religious groups as the Lollards, who began to be organized from about 1390.

A. G. Dickens has usefully summarized the chief characteristics of the Protestant Reformation under six points: (1) the affirmation of the authority of the biblical texts in place of ecclesiastical custom; (2) the elucidation of the biblical texts by modern scholarship, which looked beyond the Latin Vulgate to the earliest surviving Greek and Hebrew texts; (3) the emphasis on the Gospels and the Pauline Epistles, which stress justification by means of faith and grace as a receptive trust in Christ as the medium of salvation; (4) the concentration on the central importance of Christ instead of the Virgin Mary or the saints as mediators between human beings and God; (5) the insistence, therefore, on the omnipotence of God alone, rather than on the merit of human beings, as the means of salvation; and (6) the rejection of the concept of transubstantiation, which was the belief that during the Mass the bread and wine became in fact the body and blood of Christ, rather than their symbolic representations. This change was enhanced also by Luther's translation of the Bible into German, which in part inspired Tyndale's English translation, as well as by the publication of Lutheran teaching in pamphlets and the introduction of congregational hymn-singing into Lutheran worship. Taken together, these principles greatly increased the spiritual authority and responsibility of the individual Christian at the expense of the power of the Church, at least theoretically. In practice, however, Protestant rulers and state Churches were as intolerant of dissent and individual claims of divine authority as their Catholic counterparts. The selection from the Elizabethan *Book of Homilies* in this anthology illustrates this point very forcefully.

No doubt the single most important technological development during the Renaissance was the invention of printing from movable type, which made possible the rapid transmission of humanist and Reformation ideas. By 1450 Johann Gutenberg had developed the three essential features of printing that were used for the next five centuries: oil-based ink, metal prisms used to mold the faces of letters, and a press that incorporated features also used in wine-making and book-binding. Gutenberg's 42-line Bible appeared in Mainz in 1455, and in less than ten years two German printers had set up shops in Rome, where they sold Cicero's Latin grammar, along with other important humanist texts. The first printer's shop opened in Venice in 1469, which led to a flourishing book trade in that city. Renaissance printed books were not always vehicles of humanism, however. For example, William Caxton published the medieval *Morte d'Arthur* by Malory in 1485, which was sold in England alongside collections of the sayings of the Greek philosophers and the retelling of the story of Troy. New printing techniques began to be introduced into the production of musical texts by Ottaviano Petrucci as early as 1501, although single-impression printing of music did not become widespread until 1528. The advantages of printed books were enormous: Not only could they be produced more rapidly and cheaply than scribal copies, they also provided standardized reference texts in hundreds of identical copies. For the first time editors' textual improvements were reasonably permanent and cumulative in a way that was not possible in manuscript books.

An important consequence of the rapid advancement of new learning that was facilitated by the availability of printed books during the sixteenth and seventeenth centuries was an inevitable conflict between traditional learning and what came to be called the New Philosophy. Four versions of this conflict that have had a major influence on Renaissance studies during the past half-century are Theodore Spencer's *Shakespeare and the Nature of Man* (1942), E. M. W. Tillyard's *The Elizabethan World Picture* (1943), Hardin Craig's *The Enchanted Glass* (1950), and C. S. Lewis's *The Discarded Image* (1964). According to Theodore Spencer's lucid formulation, the traditional, or "optimistic theory" held that "order is behind everything" in the universe, and "this order reveals the interdependence of everything, the essential unity of creation" (p. 6). Among the chief proponents of this cosmic theory in England were Sir Thomas Elyot, Richard Hooker, and Sir John Davies. In his influential summary, Tillyard argues that this order consisted of a hierarchal structure and sets of correspondences. The basic hierarchy, or Great Chain of Being, included God, the angels, man, animals, plants, and inanimate objects, with each of the orders below God subdivided into its constituent hierarchies as well. These other hierarchies related to each other and to the whole of creation in terms of correspondence (or analogy). Thus, reason rules the mind as the king rules the state, the father the family, the lion the beasts, and God the universe. When all of these orders are in harmony, the subtle music of the spheres can be heard. The most comprehensive, succinct state-ment of this optimist theory is Ulysses' speech on order and degree in Shakespeare's *Troilus and Cressida*:

> The heavens themselves, the planets, and this centre
> Observe degree, priority, and place,
> Insisture, course, proportion, season, form,
> Office, and custom, in all line of order.
> And therefore is the glorious planet Sol
> In noble eminence enthroned and sphered
> Amidst the other; whose med'cinable eye
> Corrects the influence of evil planets,
> And posts like the commandment of a king,
> Sans check to good and bad. But when the planets
> In evil mixture to disorder wander,
> What plagues, and what portents, what mutiny,
> What raging of the sea, shaking of earth,
> Commotion in the winds, frights, changes, horrors,
> Divert and crack, rend and deracinate
> The unity and married calm of states
> Quite from their fixure! O, when degree is shaked,
> Which is the ladder of all high designs,
> The enterprise is sick! How could communities,
> Degrees in schools, and brotherhoods in cities,
> Peaceful commerce from dividable shores,
> The primogeniture and due of birth,
> Prerogative of age, crowns, sceptres, laurels,
> But by degree stand in authentic place?
> Take but degree away, untune that string,
> And hark what discord follows. Each thing meets
> In mere oppugnancy. The bounded waters
> Should lift their bosoms higher than the shores,
> And make a sop of all this solid globe;
> Strength should be lord of imbecility,
> And the rude son should strike his father dead.
> Force should be right; or rather, right and wrong,
> Between whose endless jar justice resides,
> Should lose their names, and so should justice too.
> Then everything includes itself in power,
> Power into will, will into appetite;
> And appetite, an universal wolf,
> So doubly seconded with will and power,
> Must make perforce an universal prey,
> And last eat up himself. (I.iii.84–123)

The fundamental challenge to this optimistic theory was the composite impact of three books – Machiavelli's *The Prince* (1513), Copernicus's *On the Revolution of the Celestial Spheres* (1543), and

Montaigne's *Apology for Raymond Sebond* (1569) – which came to be called the New Philosophy. Instead of depicting the state in terms of social justice and human rights, Machiavelli advised new princes to ignore the Great Chain of Being, to imitate the fox for cunning and the lion for ferocity, and to care more for the strategic appearance of virtue than for its universal application. In his challenge to the Ptolemaic, earth-centered model of the universe, Copernicus displaced human beings from the center of creation with his image of the sun as a virile man who holds the planets in their surrounding orbits by the strength of his arms. But even more important than the details of this mathematically based replacement of an older cosmology was the cultural impact of the realization that knowledge advances with the disrupting power of such paradigm shifts. (Copernicus's theoretical work was soon confirmed and developed by Galileo's use of the telescope.) In his ironic apology for an outmoded thinker, Montaigne called into question all of the essential features of the optimistic theory, especially in his idea that culture alienates human beings from the vital dynamics of nature and produces a life of dull, mechanistic routine. Just as Shakespeare's Ulysses spoke eloquently for the optimistic model, John Donne's "An Anatomy of the World" succinctly captures the pessimism of the New Philosophy:

> . . . New philosophy calls all in doubt,
> The element of fire is quite put out;
> The sun is lost, and th' earth, and no man's wit
> Can well direct him, where to look for it.
> And freely men confess, that this world's spent,
> When in the planets, and the firmament
> They seek so many new; they see that this
> Is crumbled out again to his atomies.
> 'Tis all in pieces, all coherence gone;
> All just supply, and all relation:
> Prince, subject, father, son, are things forgot,
> For every man alone thinks he hath got
> To be a phoenix, and that there can be
> None of that kind, of which he is, but he.

Here the newly felt weight of the responsibility for fashioning oneself is initially felt to be crushing. Renaissance literature is full of characters, most famously Hamlet, for whom the burden is simply too much.

Serving in some ways as a mediator between the old optimism and the new skepticism, the Hermetic tradition aspired to create a productive unity out of the many opposing currents that charged through Renaissance culture. The work of Frances Yates, however, has brilliantly shown that that tradition, too, was a multiplicity rather than a unified force of ideas. The heterogeneous texts that composed this tradition were erroneously thought during the Renaissance to be the work of Hermes Trismegistus, a thrice-great polymath (possibly Egyptian) whose learning could not only unify religion, philosophy, and science but also overcome the conflicts between Christianity, Judaism, and Islam; idealism and skepticism; and science and magic. Pico's great text, "The Oration on the Dignity of Man," captures the exhilarating intellectual ambition of this project, which was nothing less than the full achievement of the divine potential that was thought to be in the mind of every human being. In *The Tempest* Shakespeare sketches a benevolently comic outcome of this ambition, just as Marlowe in *Dr. Faustus* portrays its darkly tragic potential. The appeal of the Hermetic tradition is still very much alive in Milton's work, which, like Dürer's great engraving on this topic, associates it with creative (or divine) melancholy.

The Hermetic tradition both absorbed and contributed to the theory and practice of the visual arts, which included such now seemingly esoteric techniques as the art of memory. Initially a procedure for mentally storing and recalling vast amounts of verbal material, the art of memory was an important component of rhetorical instruction. According to this system, a verbal or musical text would be divided into its constituent parts, such as the seven portions of the classical oration; each of those parts would be imaginatively transformed into a mental picture; these mnemonic images would then be stored in an imaginary building (a memory theater or temple of music, for example); an actual paneled room, library, or theater would then be used as a screen for projecting the stored images when they were needed in a speech, sermon, legal defense, or dramatic performance. The art of memory thus combined visual and verbal materials, promoted the techniques of imaginative projection, and profoundly influenced such architectural developments as the evolution of the English public theaters.

In his Sonnet 24 Shakespeare declares that "perspective it is best painter's art." Indeed, the art of perspective, which was the discovery of Brunelleschi, is one of the most important achievements of Renaissance culture. Although the two demonstration pieces in which Brunelleschi presented his invention of mathematically based perspective are lost, his biographer Antonio Manetti has left a vivid account of his master's work and a lucid description of his discovery:

> [Brunelleschi] himself proposed and practiced what painters today call perspective; for it is part of that science, which is in effect to put down well and with reason the diminutions and enlargements which appear to the eyes of men from things far away or close at hand: buildings, plains and mountains and countrysides of every kind and in every part, the figures and the other objects, in that measurement which corresponds to that distance away which they show themselves to be: and from him is born the rule, which is the basis of all that has been done of that kind from that day to this. (White, p. 113)

In 1435 Alberti's *Della Pittura* gave Brunelleschi's discovery its theoretical formulation, which was later elaborated by Ghiberti's *Third Commentary*. The most important point in these Renaissance discourses on perspective is the insistence that visible objects are not comprehended by the visual sense alone. Vision requires the active operations of the intellect. The lighting, color, remoteness, and parts of an object, together with the magnitude of the intervening distance between it and its observer must be perceived, according to Ghiberti, in order to comprehend that object. Manetti, Alberti, and Ghiberti share a fundamentally humanist approach to perspective in their attention to the essential but ultimately relative position of the spectator in determining the appearance of things.

Roughly analogous to the development of artificial (or mathematical) perspective in painting is the emergence of the simultaneous conception of harmony and of polyphony in Renaissance musical composition. Although the change from medieval to Renaissance music occurred gradually during the period 1450 to 1600, the dominance of two distinctive features of medieval music – first, the reliance on preexisting melodies (*cantus firmus*), preexisting formal schemes, and preexisting rhythmic forms; and, second, successive rather than simultaneous voice harmony – eventually gave way to innovative conceptions and techniques. Edward E. Lowinsky has convincingly argued that these innovations were possible only when Renaissance composers began to think in terms of simultaneous harmonies instead of gradual, successive layering of different voices, which was characteristic of medieval polyphony (Lowinsky, p. 357). By 1480 Italian composers were producing four-part harmony in which the melody was in the highest and the root of the harmony in the lowest part. Josquin des Prez (1450–1521) appears to have been the first composer to use this new technique as the formal basis for a series of major compositions. "Here a number of subjects are taken up by one voice after another resulting in a free, unified, and yet complex contrapuntal organism: free because it is not tied to a *cantus firmus*, unified because the same thematic substance penetrates all parts, complex because each part presents the theme at a different time while the other voices go against it contrapuntally, avoiding simultaneity in rhythm and meter" (Lowinsky, pp. 358–9). Such was the cultural power of harmony that it was thought to be the divine condition at the time of the creation of the world but only rarely heard since the fall of Adam and Eve. Whether this sound was thought to be produced by a siren on the upper surface of each heavenly sphere (as in Plato's myth of Er in *The Republic*), by the glassy celestial spheres rubbing against each other (as in Aristotle's *De Caelo*), by the rush and motion of the spheres themselves (as in Cicero's *Somnium Scipionis*), or by an angelic choir, it was commonly thought during the Renaissance to represent the perfection of the ordered universe as it was related to human lives.

THE RENAISSANCE AT THE PRESENT TIME

The intellectual and artistic history of the Renaissance – which can only be sketchily glimpsed through such concepts as humanism, Reformation, the New Philosophy, Hermeticism, perspective, and harmony – constitutes only one dimension of the cultural structure of the age. Beginning with the so-called *Annales* historians in France in the 1930s and continuing in the work of scholars such as Fernand Braudel, scholars began to look past political history and such canonical cultural products as literary texts and to emphasize what was "beneath" this superstructure in the material details of everyday life. Here we find recorded the waves of disease and famine; the production and use of wheat, rice, and maize; the appetite for sugar; the consumption of wine, beer, cider, and tobacco; the circulation of wealth as goods, labor, and money; the size, structure, and population of cities; the construction of floors, walls, ceilings, doors, windows, chimneys, fireplaces, and stoves – all of the details that contribute to make the culture of the Renaissance what it was.

This reorientation of scholarly focus reminds us again that all conceptions of the Renaissance are the products of historical thought, and it is not surprising that they change just as rapidly as the discipline of history itself. During the past twenty years what is called "New Historicism" in America, or "Historical Materialism" in Britain, has found its center of gravity in Renaissance studies. One of the most important foundational texts of New Historicism is Stephen Greenblatt's *Renaissance Self-Fashioning: From More to Shakespeare* (1980), a book partly indebted to Burckhardt but even more significantly influenced by the work of Michel Foucault and Clifford Geertz. Foucault, by way of Nietzsche, called into question two recurring mirages of historical investigation: origin and outcome, which uncritically assume continuity, stability, and unity in human action and agency. In place of the historical pursuit of definitive origins and outcomes, Foucault proposes a genealogical focus on descent, which deals with the multiplicity of an "exteriority of accidents" that has produced what continues to exist in the present. Genealogy does not assume a unity of the past with the present, nor does it presume to map the destiny of a people. Instead, the structure of descent is a highly "unstable assemblage of faults, fissures, and heterogeneous layers that threaten the fragile inheritor from within or from underneath" (Foucault 1977, p. 146). Thus, a genealogical history of the Renaissance would recognize the ecclesiastical politics involved in the Protestant promotion of science against magic, the reluctant acceptance of the skeptical freedom initiated by the New Philosophy, and the efforts of printers to make their first products look like manuscripts. Foucault's genealogical history and the New Historicism look on the darker side of the Renaissance as well as on its golden achievements (see, for example, Kinsman).

In his most important book, *The Order of Things* (1966), Foucault takes a long view of the descent of the cultural legacy of the Renaissance. Until the end of the sixteenth century, he argues, resemblance (or representation) played a central, constructive role in Western knowledge. In such rhetorical forms as juxtaposition and analogy, the world during the Renaissance came to be seen as a world of signs. As the author of the universe, God was thought to have produced two books, Scripture and the Book of Nature. It is not surprising, therefore (Foucault observes), that the Renaissance produced the sciences of hermeneutics and semiology, the first to interpret the meaning of signs and the second to discover the location, definition, and links between signs. According to this scheme, nature is trapped in a dark space between the layers of hermeneutics and semiology. Because language has the power to proliferate itself, knowledge consisted largely of commentary, by which one form of language was related to another with no need to justify claims of truth by other means (Foucault 1970, pp. 17–40).

The continuing controversies concerning the character and dynamics of the Renaissance make it a fascinating and virtually inexhaustible subject of study. As we write this introduction, it seems that New Historicism may have lost some of its original energy, but it is unclear what will replace it. Foucault and other thinkers associated with the period of "high theory" (roughly 1968–2000) are being dismissed by some historians who have been longing for an excuse to ignore theory's achievements and reading techniques. The work of scholars such as Lisa Jardine and Anthony Grafton has reminded us that the humanists were not disinterested bearers of intellectual ideals, but ambitious promoters of a cultural and political agenda that served the interests of absolutist rulers very handily. And beyond all of the debates about what the Renaissance was really like, we must now examine the possibility that the modern concept of discrete historical periods, which dates back only as far as the nineteenth century, might itself be giving way to other models of charting the past. Whether one agrees with Foucault's apocalyptic conclusion that the tide of skepticism released by the Renaissance will eventually wash away the very concept of man or whether one continues to affirm the optimism of Burckhardt – that the creative achievements of Renaissance culture made it possible for human beings to comprehend their internal and external worlds for the first time – it seems inevitable that such final judgments will rest on a critical examination of the texts and material relics which that culture produced.

READING

General Studies of the Renaissance:

Jacob Burckhardt, *The Civilization of the Renaissance in Italy*.
Wallace K. Ferguson, *The Renaissance in Historical Thought: Five Centuries of Interpretation*.
John Hale, *The Civilization of Europe in the Renaissance*.
William Kerrigan and Gordon Braden, *The Idea of the Renaissance*.
Robert S. Kinsman (ed.), *The Darker Vision of the Renaissance*.

Humanism

Anthony Grafton and Lisa Jardine, *From Humanism to the Humanities*.
Charles Garfield Nauert, *Humanism and the Culture of Renaissance Europe*.
L. D. Reynolds and N. G. Wilson, *Scribes and Scholars: A Guide to the Transmission of Greek and Latin Literature*.

Reformation

Richard Marius, *Martin Luther: The Christian Between God and Death*.
A. G. Dickens, *The English Reformation*.

Printing

Elizabeth Eisenstein, *The Printing Press as an Agent of Change*; *The Printing Revolution in Early Modern Europe*.
Iain Fenlon, "Music and Society."

New Philosophy

Theodore Spencer, *Shakespeare and the Nature of Man*.
E. M. W. Tillyard, *The Elizabethan World Picture*.

Hermetic Tradition

Frances Yates, *The Art of Memory*; *Giordano Bruno and the Hermetic Tradition*; *The Theatre of the World*.

Perspective

John White, *The Birth and Rebirth of Pictorial Space*.

Harmony

John Hollander, *The Untuning of the Sky: Ideas of Music in English Poetry 1500–1700*.
Edward E. Lowinsky, "Music in the Culture of the Renaissance."

New Historicism

Michel Foucault, *The Order of Things*.
Stephen Greenblatt, *Renaissance Self-Fashioning: From More to Shakespeare*.

M. P. and J. H.

John Skelton (1460?–1529)

Although there is little reliable information about Skelton's early life, he appears to have studied at both Cambridge and Oxford, where he was installed as poet laureate, apparently by Henry VII himself in 1488. The wonderful, dramatic hymn "Woefully Arrayed," addressed as though by Christ to humanity, was most likely written during this period. In 1498 Skelton took holy orders and soon after became the tutor of Prince Henry, who would become king Henry VIII. When Erasmus visited England in 1499, he paid Skelton the lavish compliment of claiming that what Homer was to Greece and Virgil to Rome, Skelton was to Britain. Although this estimate may be extravagant, Skelton was doubtless the most important English poet of the generation before Wyatt. In recognition of his royal service, he was made rector of Diss, near the border of Suffolk and Norfolk. His tenure there was, to say the least, controversial, in that his parishioners thought him more fit for the stage than the pulpit. According to a legend preserved in the jest book entitled *Merie Tales* (c.1567), in response to their complaint to the Bishop of Norwich that he kept a wench who was the mother of his child, Skelton delivered a sermon proclaiming his own humanity, during which he proudly displayed his naked infant son from the pulpit. During his rectorship he also wrote two comic Latin epitaphs on members of his congregation: "Epitaph for Adam Udersall" and "A Devout Trental for Old John Clarke," which anticipate the satirical vein of his later poetry.

The remarkable poem "Philip Sparrow" is a fine example of Skelton's determination to experiment with new verse forms (now called Skeltonics) at a time when the English language was changing rapidly. Like the best of his writing, this poem is a superb accommodation between the traditional and the new. The poem celebrates a mock mass – much as children sometimes elaborately bury their dead pets – for Jane Scrope's sparrow, killed by a Carrow Abbey cat. The poem is in two parts: the first is the girl's lament, in her own voice, for Philip; and the second is the poet's commendation of Jane's beauty. Fifteen years after composing the poem, Skelton wrote an additional section, replying to those, possibly including Jane's gentrified family, who raised moral objections about part two. Taken together, parts one and two have been rightly called a comparative study of innocence and experience (Fish, p. 99). While part two is an intricately sensual application of the art of rhetoric, which makes explicit use of rhetorical terminology from such handbooks as the anonymous *Ad herennium*, its learning is undercut in part one by the girl's polymathic knowledge, which weaves together bird lore, musicology, the language of the Bible and the Office for the Dead, English literary history, and classical learning. The meshing of pagan mythology and Christianity is a hallmark of Renaissance culture (see Seznec). Because of its complex treatment of female sexuality, from the fictionalized points of view of Jane and the poet himself, the poem and the history of its reception have recently received sustained attention from feminist critics (see Schibanoff and Daileader).

With Henry VIII's accession to the throne in 1509, Skelton celebrated the occasion in "A Laud and Praise Made for Our Sovereign Lord and King." Most of Skelton's political poems, which include "Speak, Parrot" and "Colin Clout," are bitingly satirical, his attack on corruption in Church and State culminating (dangerously) in a magnificent assault on Cardinal Wolsey in "Why come ye not to Court?" There is, however, another voice in his political poems, which can be heard early in his lament for the death of the Earl of Northumberland and later in his celebration of Henry VIII. In such poems as these, Skelton gathers together some important pieces of the ideological mythology of the Tudors, where the political and religious orders are inextricably linked, where the Tudor rose – "both White and Red / In one Rose now doth grow" – puts symbolically to rest the long dispute between Lancastrians and Yorkists, and where there is a Renaissance hope that the great figures of the classical age – Alexander, Adrastus, Astraea, Priam, Mars, and even Christ himself – will be re-embodied in Henry's reign. In his last major poem – "A Replication Against Certain Young Scholars Abjured of Late" (1528) – Skelton put aside his old conflicts with Wolsey to join him in combatting what both men thought to be the heresy of Lutheranism, which was beginning to take root at Cambridge in the mid-1520s (see Waller).

READING

Stanley Fish, *John Skelton's Poetry*.
Maurice Pollet, *John Skelton: Poet of Tudor England*, trans. John Warington.
Greg Waller, *John Skelton and the Politics of the 1520s*.

M. P.

WOEFULLY ARRAYED

Woefully arrayed,
   My blood, man,
   For thee ran,
  It may not be nay'd:
   My body blo and wan,
  Woefully arrayed.

Behold me, I pray thee, with all thy whole reason,
And be not so hard-hearted, and for this encheason,   *occasion*
Sith I for thy soul sake was slain in good season,
Beguiled and betrayed by Judas' false treason:
   Unkindly entreated,
   With sharp cord sore freted,
   The Jewes me threted:
  They mowed, they grinned, they scorned me,
  Condemned to death, as thou mayest see,
   Woefully arrayed.

Thus naked am I nailed, O man, for thy sake!
I love thee, then love me; why sleepest thou? awake!
Remember my tender heart-root for thee brake,
With paines my veines constrained to crake:
   Thus tugged to and fro,
   Thus wrapped all in woe,
   Whereas never man was so,
  Entreated thus in most cruel wise,
  Was like a lamb offered in sacrifice,
   Woefully arrayed.

Of sharp thorn I have worn a crown on my head,
So pained, so strained, so rueful, so red,
Thus bobbed, thus robbed, thus for thy love dead,
Unfeigned I deigned my blood for to shed:
   My feet and handes sore
   The sturdy nailes bore:
   What might I suffer more
  Than I have done, O man, for thee?
  Come when thou list, welcome to me,
   Woefully arrayed.

Of record thy good Lord I have been and shall be:
I am thine, thou art mine, my brother I call thee.
Thee love I entirely—see what is befall'n me!
Sore beating, sore threating, to make thee, man, all free: *threatening*
   Why art thou unkind?
   Why hast not me in mind?
   Come yet and thou shalt find
  Mine endless mercy and grace—
  See how a spear my heart did race,
   Woefully arrayed.

Dear brother, no other thing I of thee desire
But give me thine heart free to reward mine hire:
I wrought thee, I bought thee from eternal fire:
I pray thee array thee toward my high empire
   Above the orient,
   Whereof I am regent,
   Lord God omnipotent,

With me to reign in endless wealth:
Remember, man, thy soules health.

Woefully arrayed,
My blood, man,
For thee ran,
It may not be nay'd:
60   My body blo and wan,
Woefully arrayed.

PHILIP SPARROW [PART I]

Pla ce bo![1]
Who is there, who?
Di le xi![1]
Dame Margery.
Fa, re, my, my.
Wherefore and why, why?
For the soul of Philip Sparrow
That was late slain at Carrow,[2]
Among the Nunes Black.
10   For that sweet soules sake,
And for all sparrows' souls
Set in our bead-rolls,[3]
Pater noster qui,[4]
With an *Ave Mari,*[5]
And with the corner of a Creed,
The more shall be your meed.

When I remember again
How my Philip was slain,
Never half the pain
20   Was between you twain,
Pyramus and Thisbe,[6]
As then befell to me.
I wept and I wailed,
The teares down hailed,
But nothing it availed
To call Philip again,
Whom Gib, our cat, hath slain.

Gib, I say, our cat
Worrowed her on that   *bit*
30   Which I loved best.
It cannot be exprest
My sorrowful heaviness,
But all without redress!
For within that stound,   *moment*
Half slumbering, in a sound
I fell downe to the ground.

Unneth I cast mine eyes   *barely*
Toward the cloudy skies.
But when I did behold

PHILIP SPARROW [PART I]
1 From the opening of the antiphon and the Psalm of the Vespers for the Office of the Dead. The syllabic divisions suggest plainsong.
2 A nunnery outside Norwich.
3 Lists of those for whom prayers were to be offered.
4 "Our Father which . . ."
5 "Hail Mary."
6 Tragic lovers in a tale by Ovid.

40   My sparrow dead and cold,
No creature but that wold
Have rued upon me,   *pitied*
To behold and see
What heaviness did me pang:
Wherewith my hands I wrang,
That my sinews cracked,
As though I had been racked,
So pained and so strained
That no life wellnigh remained.

50   I sighed and I sobbed,
For that I was robbed
Of my sparrow's life.
O maiden, widow, and wife,
Of what estate ye be,
Of high or low degree,
Great sorrow then ye might see,
And learn to weep at me!
Such paines did me frete
That mine heart did beat,
60   My visage pale and dead,
Wan, and blue as lead:
The pangs of hateful death
Wellnigh had stopped my breath.

        Heu, heu, me,
That I am woe for thee!
Ad Dominum, cum tribularer, clamavi.[7]
Of God nothing else crave I
But Philip's soul to keep
From the marees deep   *marsh*
70   Of Acheronte's[8] well,
That is a flood of hell;
And from the great Pluto,[9]
The prince of endless woe;
And from foul Alecto,[10]
With visage black and blo;
And from Medusa,[11] that mare,   *hag*
That like a fiend doth stare;
And from Megaera's[12] adders
For ruffling of Philip's feathers,
80   And from her fiery sparklings
For burning of his wings;
And from the smokes sour
Of Proserpina's[13] bower;
And from the denes dark
Where Cerberus[14] doth bark,
Whom Theseus[15] did affray,
Whom Hercules[16] did outray,   *vanquish*
As famous poetes say;
From that hell-hound

7   "Woe, woe is me . . . In my distress, I cried unto the Lord" (second antiphon and Psalm of the Vespers).

8   Acheron, one of the rivers of the Underworld in Greek myth.

9   God of the Underworld, whose other name is Dis. There is a pun running through this section on Diss, where Skelton was rector. In Roman literature Dis was a symbol of death.

10   One of the Furies, or avenging spirits.

11   A female monster whose hideous head turned to stone anyone who looked at it.

12   One of the Furies.

13   Goddess of the Underworld.

14   A monstrous dog who guarded the entrance to the Underworld.

15   A mythical king of Athens.

16   A mythical Greek hero.

90 That lieth in chaines bound,
With ghastly heades three;
To Jupiter pray we
That Philip preserved may be!
Amen, say ye with me!

   Do mi nus,
Help now, sweet Jesus!
Levavi oculos meos in montes.[17]
Would God I had Zenophontes,[18]
Or Socrates the wise,
100 To shew me their device
Moderately to take
This sorrow that I make
For Philip Sparrow's sake!
So fervently I shake,
I feel my body quake;
So urgently I am brought
Into careful thought.
Like Andromach, Hector's[19] wife,   *Andromache*
Was weary of her life,
110 When she had lost her joy,
Noble Hector of Troy;
In like manner also
Increaseth my deadly woe,
For my sparrow is go.

   It was so pretty a fool,
It would sit on a stool,
And learned after my school
For to keep his cut,   *place*
With 'Philip, keep your cut!'

120   It had a velvet cap,
And would sit upon my lap,
And seek after small wormes,
And sometime white bread-crumbes;
And many times and oft
Between my breastes soft
It woulde lie and rest;
It was proper and prest.

   Sometime he would gasp
When he saw a wasp;
130 A fly or a gnat,
He would fly at that;
And prettily he would pant
When he saw an ant.
Lord, how he would pry
After the butterfly!
Lord, how he would hop
After the gressop!   *grasshopper*
And when I said, 'Phip, Phip!'
Then he would leap and skip,

---

17 "Lord . . . I lifted up my eyes unto the hills" (third antiphon and Psalm of the Vespers).

18 Xenophon, disciple of Socrates.

19 Eldest son of King Priam and bravest of the Trojans; killed by Achilles.

140
And take me by the lip.
Alas, it will me slo
That Philip is gone me fro!

Si in i qui ta tes . . .
Alas, I was evil at ease!
De pro fun dis cla ma vi[20]
When I saw my sparrow die!

Now, after my dome,   *judgment*
Dame Sulpicia[21] at Rome,
Whose name registered was
150
For ever in tables of brass,
Because that she did pass
In poesy to indite
And eloquently to write,
Though she would pretend
My sparrow to commend,
I trow she could not amend
Reporting the virtues all
Of my sparrow royal.

For it would come and go,
160
And fly so to and fro;
And on me it would leap
When I was asleep,
And his feathers shake,
Wherewith he would make
Me often for to wake,
And for to take him in
Upon my naked skin.
God wot, we thought no sin:
What though he crept so low?
170
It was no hurt, I trow
He did nothing, perde,   *truly*
But sit upon my knee.
Philip, though he were nice,
In him it was no vice.
Philip had leave to go
To pick my little toe,
Philip might be bold
And do what he wold:
Philip would seek and take
180
All the fleas black
That he could there espy
With his wanton eye.

O pe ra:[22]
La, sol, fa, fa,
Confitebor tibi, Domine, in toto corde meo![23]
Alas, I would ride and go
A thousand mile of ground!
If any such might be found
It were worth an hundred pound

---

20   "If iniquities . . . Out of the depths have I cried" (fourth antiphon
and Psalm of the Vespers).
21   Niece of Messala and author of six elegies.

22   "The works [of the Lord are great]" (Psalm 90:2, Vulgate).
23   "I will confess to thee, Lord, with my whole heart" (Psalm 90:1,
Vulgate).

190 Of King Croesus'[24] gold,
Or of Attalus the old,
The rich prince of Pergame,[25]
Whoso list the story to see.
Cadmus,[26] that his sister sought,
An he should be bought
For gold and fee,
He should over the sea
To weet if he could bring
Any of the offspring,
200 Or any of the blood.
But whoso understood
Of Medea's[27] art,
I would I had a part
Of her crafty magic!
My sparrow then should be quick
With a charm or twain,
And play with me again.
But all this is in vain
Thus for to complain.

210   I took my sampler once
Of purpose, for the nonce,
To sew with stitches of silk
My sparrow white as milk,
That by representation
Of his image and fashion
To me it might import
Some pleasure and comfort,
For my solace and sport.
But when I was sewing his beak,
220 Methought my sparrow did speak,
And opened his pretty bill,
Saying, 'Maid, ye are in will
Again me for to kill,
Ye prick me in the head!'
With that my needle waxed red,
Methought, of Philip's blood;
Mine hair right upstood,
I was in such a fray
My speech was taken away.
230 I cast down that there was,
And said, 'Alas, alas,
How cometh this to pass?'
My fingers, dead and cold,
Could not my sampler hold:
My needle and thread
I threw away for dread.
The best now that I may
Is for his soul to pray:
A porta inferi . . .[28]

---

24   King of Lydia, known for his great wealth.
25   Pergamum, city in Asia Minor, which reached the height of its splendor under the Attalids.
26   Legendary founder of Thebes, who searched for his sister Europa, who had been carried off by Zeus in the form of a bull.
27   Her magic helped Jason take the golden fleece.
28   "From the gate of hell" (antiphon).

<pre>
240   Good Lord, have mercy
            Upon my sparrow's soul,
            Written in my bead-roll!

                Au di vi vo cem,²⁹
            Japhet, Ham, and Shem,³⁰
            Ma gni fi cat,³¹
            Shew me the right path
            To the hills of Armony,³²
            Whereon the boards yet lie
            Of your father's boat,
250   That was sometime afloat,
            And now they lie and rot;
            Let some poetes write
            Deucalion's³³ flood it hight.
            But as verily as ye be
            The natural sonnes three
            Of Noe the patriarch,   Noah
            That made that great ark,
            Wherein he had apes and owls,
            Beasts, birds, and fowls,
260   That if ye can find
            Any of my sparrow's kind
            (God send the soul good rest!)
            I would have yet a nest
            As pretty and as prest
            As my sparrow was.
            But my sparrow did pass
            All sparrows of the wood
            That were since Noe's flood,
            Was never none so good.
270   King Philip of Macedony³⁴
            Had no such Philip as I,
            No, no, sir, hardely!

                That vengeance I ask and cry,
            By way of exclamation,
            On all the whole nation
            Of cattes wild and tame:
            God send them sorrow and shame!
            That cat specially
            That slew so cruelly
280   My little pretty sparrow
            That I brought up at Carrow.

                O cat of carlish kind,
            The fiend was in thy mind
            When thou my bird untwined!
            I would thou hadst been blind!
            The leopards savage,
            The lions in their rage
            Might catch thee in their paws,
</pre>

---

29   "I heard a voice" (antiphon, Rev. 14:12).
30   Sons of Noah.
31   "Magnify," as in "My soul magnifies the Lord" (Luke 1:46).
32   Aremenius, birthplace of Armenius, who was one of the Argonauts.
Noah's ark came to rest at Ararat in the Armenian mountains.

33   The equivalent of Noah in Greek mythology.
34   Philip II, King of Macedon.

And gnaw thee in their jaws!
290   The serpents of Libany[35]
Might sting thee venomously!
The dragons with their tongues
Might poison thy liver and lungs!
The manticors of the mountains
Might feed them on thy brains!

    Melanchaetes, that hound
That plucked Actacon to the ground,[36]
Gave him his mortal wound,
Changed to a deer,
300   The story doth appear,
Was changed to an hart:
So thou, foul cat that thou art,
The selfsame hound
Might thee confound,
That his own lorde bote,
Might bite asunder thy throat!

    Of Ind the greedy grypes   *India/griffins*
Might tear out all thy tripes!
Of Arcady the bears
310   Might pluck away thine ears!
The wild wolf Lycaon[37]
Bite asunder thy backbone!
Of Etna[38] the burning hill,
That day and night burneth still,
Set in thy tail a blaze
That all the world may gaze
And wonder upon thee,
From Ocean the great sea
Unto the Isles of Orcady,[39]
320   From Tilbury Ferry
To the plain of Salisbury!
So traitorously my bird to kill
That never ought thee evil will!

    Was never bird in cage
More gentle of courage
In doing his homage
Unto his sovereign.
Alas, I say again,
Death hath departed us twain!
330   The false cat hath thee slain:
Farewell, Philip, adew!
Our Lord, thy soul rescue!
Farewell, without restore,
Farewell, for evermore!

    An it were a Jew,
It would make one rue,
To see my sorrow new.
These villainous false cats
Were made for mice and rats,

---

35   Libya, or Africa as a whole.
36   While hunting, Actaeon was changed by Artemis into a stag and then was torn to pieces by his own hounds.
37   According to Ovid, Lycaon of Arcadia was transformed into a wolf.
38   Etna, Europe's highest active volcano, located in Sicily.
39   Orkney Islands.

340
And not for birdes smale.
Alas, my face waxeth pale,
Telling this piteous tale,
How my bird so fair,
That was wont to repair,
And go in at my spare,[40]
And creep in at my gore
Of my gown before,
Flickering with his wings!
Alas, my heart it stings,

350
Remembering pretty things!
Alas, mine heart it sleth,
My Philip's doleful death!
When I remember it,
How prettily it would sit,
Many times and oft,
Upon my finger aloft!
I played with him tittle-tattle,
And fed him with my spittle,
With his bill between my lips,

360
It was my pretty Phips!
Many a pretty kiss
Had I of his sweet muss!
And now the cause is thus,
That he is slain me fro,
To my great pain and woe.

Of fortune this the chance
Standeth on variance:
Oft time after pleasance,
Trouble and grievance.

370
No man can be sure
Alway to have pleasure:
As well perceive ye may
How my disport and play
From me was taken away
By Gib, our cat savage,
That in a furious rage
Caught Philip by the head
And slew him there stark dead!
            Kyrie, eleison,

380
            Christe, eleison,
            Kyrie, eleison![41]
For Philip Sparrow's soul,
Set in our bead-roll,
Let us now whisper
A *Paternoster.*[42]

Lauda, anima mea, Dominum![43]
To weep with me look that ye come
All manner of birdes in your kind;
See none be left behind.

---

40 An opening or slit in a gown.
41 Lord, have mercy,
    Christ, have mercy,
    Lord, have mercy.

42 Our Father.
43 "Praise the Lord, O my soul!" (Psalm 145:1, Vulgate). Skelton puns on the word "anima" (soul) here.

390 To mourning looke that ye fall
With dolorous songes funerall,
Some to sing, and some to say,
Some to weep, and some to pray,
Every birde in his lay.
The goldfinch, the wagtail;
The jangling jay to rail,
The flecked pie to chatter   *magpie*
Of this dolorous matter;
And robin redbreast,
400 He shall be the priest
The requiem mass to sing,
Softly warbeling,
With help of the reed sparrow,
And the chatteringe swallow,
This hearse for to hallow;
The lark with his long toe;
The spink, and the martinet also;   *chaffinch/martin*
The shoveller with his broad beak;   *spoonbill*
The dotterel, that foolish peke,   *plover/dolt*
410 And also the mad coot,
With balde face to toot;   *pry*
The fieldfare and the snite;   *snipe*
The crow and the kite;
The raven, called Rolfe,
His plain-song to sol-fa;
The partridge, the quail;
The plover with us to wail;
The woodhack, that singeth 'chur'   *woodpecker*
Hoarsely, as he had the mur;   *catarrh*
420 The lusty chanting nightingale;
The popinjay to tell her tale,
That toteth oft in a glass,   *looks*
Shall read the Gospel at mass;
The mavis with her whistle   *song-thrush*
Shall read there the Epistle.
But with a large and a long
To keep just plain-song,
Our chanters shall be the cuckoo,
The culver, the stockdowe,   *dove/wild pigeon*
430 With 'peewit' the lapwing,
The Versicles shall sing.

The bittern with his bumpe,   *loud call*
The crane with his trumpe,
The swan of Maeander,
The goose and the gander,
The duck and the drake,
Shall watch at this wake;
The peacock so proud,
Because his voice is loud,
440 And hath a glorious tail,
He shall sing the Grail;   *Gradual*
The owl, that is so foul,
Must help us to howl;
The heron so gaunt,
And the cormorant,
With the pheasant,

And the gaggling gant,   *gannet*
And the churlish chough;
The knot and the ruff;
450   The barnacle, the buzzard,   *wild goose*
With the wild mallard;
The divendop to sleep;   *dabchick*
The water-hen to weep;
The puffin and the teal
Money they shall deal
To poore folk at large,
That shall be their charge;
The seamew and the titmouse;   *gull*
The woodcock with the longe nose;
460   The throstle with her warbling;   *song-thrush*
The starling with her brabling;
The rook, with the osprey
That putteth fishes to a fray;
And the dainty curlew,
With the turtle most true.

At this *Placebo*
We may not well forgo
The countering of the coe;   *counterpoint/jackdaw*
The stork also,
470   That maketh his nest
In chimneys to rest;
Within those walls
No broken galls
May there abide
Of cuckoldry side,
Or else philosophy
Maketh a great lie.
The ostrich, that will eat
An horseshoe so great,
480   In the stead of meat,
Such fervent heat
His stomach doth frete;   *digest*
He cannot well fly,
Nor sing tunably,
Yet at a brayd   *suddenly*
He hath well assayed
To sol-fa above E-la.
Fa, lorell, fa, fa!
Ne quando
490   *Male cantando,*[44]
The best that we can,
To make him our bell-man,
And let him ring the bells.
He can do nothing else.

Chanticleer, our cock,
Must tell what is of the clock
By the astrology
That he hath naturally
Conceived and caught,

---

44   Lest ever by singing badly.

500   And was never taught
By Albumazer
The astronomer,
Nor by Ptolomy   *Ptolemy*
Prince of astronomy,
Nor yet by Haly;
And yet he croweth daily
And nightly the tides
That no man abides,
With Partlot his hen,
510   Whom now and then
He pluckcth by the head
When he doth her tread.

      The bird of Araby,
That potentially
May never die,
And yet there is none
But one alone;
A phoenix it is
This hearse that must bless
520   With aromatic gums
That cost great sums,
The way of thurification[45]
To make a fumigation,
Sweete of reflare,
And redolent of aire,
This corse for to cense
With greate reverence,
As patriarch or pope
In a blacke cope.
530   Whiles he censeth the hearse,
He shall sing the verse,
Libera me,[46]
In de la, sol, re,
Softly B molle
For my sparrow's soul.
Pliny[47] sheweth all
In his *Story Natural*
What he doth find
Of the phoenix kind;
540   Of whose incineration
There riseth a new creation
Of the same fashion
Without alteration,
Saving that olde age
Is turned into corage
Of freshe youth again;
This matter true and plain,
Plain matter indeed,
Who so list to read.

550   But for the eagle doth fly
Highest in the sky,
He shall be the sub-dean,

---

45   Burning of incense.
46   "Deliver me" (opening of the Responsory).
47   Pliny the Elder, Roman author of the *Natural History*.

The choir to demean,   *conduct*
As provost principal,
To teach them their Ordinal;
Also the noble falcon,
With the ger-falcon,
The tarsel gentil,[48]
They shall mourn soft and still
In their amice of gray;
560   The saker with them shall say   *lanner falcon*
Dirige[49] for Philip's soul;
The goshawk shall have a roll
The choristers to control;
The lanners and the merlions   *merlins*
Shall stand in their mourning-gowns;
The hobby[50] and the musket
The censers and the cross shall fet;   *fetch*
The kestrel in all this wark
570   Shall be holy water clerk.

    And now the dark cloudy night
Chaseth away Phoebus bright,
Taking his course toward the west,
God send my sparrow's soul good rest!
Requiem aeternam dona eis, Domine![51]
Fa, fa, fa, mi, re, re,
A por ta in fe ri,[52]
Fa, fa, fa, mi, mi.

    Credo videre bona Domini,[53]
580   I pray God, Philip to heaven may fly!
Domine, exaudi orationem meam![54]
To heaven he shall, from heaven he came!
    Do mi nus vo bis cum![55]
Of all good prayers God send him some!
    Oremus,
Deus, cui proprium est misereri et parcere,[56]
On Philip's soul have pity!
For he was a pretty cock,
And came of a gentle stock,
590   And wrapt in a maiden's smock,
And cherished full daintily,
Till cruel fate made him to die:
Alas, for doleful destiny!
But whereto should I
Longer mourn or cry?
To Jupiter I call,
Of heaven imperial,
That Philip may fly
Above the starry sky,
600   To tread the pretty wren,
That is our Lady's hen.
Amen, amen, amen!

48   Male peregrine falcon.
49   "Direct [my steps]."
50   A male sparrowhawk.
51   "Grant them eternal rest, O Lord!"
52   "From the gates of hell."
53   "I had thought to see the goodness of the Lord" (Psalm 26:13, Vulgate).
54   "Lord, hear my prayer" (Psalm 102:2, Vulgate).
55   "The Lord be with you."
56   "O God, whose property it is to be merciful and to spare."

Yet one thing is behind,
That now cometh to mind;
An epitaph I would have
For Philippes grave:
But for I am a maid,
Timorous, half afraid,
That never yet assayed
610 Of Helicones[57] well,
Where the Muses dwell;
Though I can read and spell,
Recount, report, and tell
Of the *Tales of Canterbury*,
Some sad stories, some merry;
As Palamon and Arcet,
Duke Theseus, and Partelet;
And of the Wife of Bath,[58]
That worketh much scath
620 When her tale is told
Among housewives bold,
How she controlled
Her husbands as she wold,
And them to despise
In the homeliest wise,
Bring other wives in thought
Their husbands to set at nought.
And though that read have I
Of Gawain and Sir Guy,
630 And tell can a great piece
Of the Golden Fleece,
How Jason it wan,
Like a valiant man;
Of Arthur's Round Table,
With his knights commendable,
And Dame Gaynour, his queen,
Was somewhat wanton, I ween;
How Sir Lancelot de Lake
Many a spear brake
640 For his lady's sake;
Of Tristram, and King Mark,
And all the whole wark
Of Belle Isold his wife,
For whom was much strife;
Some say she was light,
And made her husband knight
Of the common hall,
That cuckolds men call;
And of Sir Lybius,
650 Named Dysconius;[59]
Of Quater Fylz Amund,[60]
And how they were summoned
To Rome, to Charlemagne,
Upon a great pain,

---

57 Helicon, a favorite haunt of the Muses.
58 Characters in Chaucer's *Canterbury Tales*.
59 *Lybeau's Disconus* in Ritson's *Met. Rom.*, 2.
60 Caxton, *The Four Sons of Aymon*.

And how they rode each one
On Bayard Mountalbon;[61]
Men see him now and then
In the forest of Arden.
What though I can frame
660   The stories by name
Of Judas Maccabeus,[62]
And of Caesar Julius;
And of the love between
Paris and Vienne;
And of the duke Hannibal,
That made the Romans all
Fordread and to quake;
How Scipion[63] did wake
The city of Carthage,
670   Which by his unmerciful rage
He beat down to the ground.
And though I can expound
Of Hector of Troy,
That was all their joy,
Whom Achilles slew,
Wherefore all Troy did rue;
And of the love so hot
That made Troilus to dote
Upon fair Cresseid;[64]
680   And what they wrote and said,
And of their wanton willes
Pander bare the billes   *love letters*
From one to the other;
His master's love to further,
Sometime a precious thing,
A brooch or else a ring;
From her to him again
Sometime a pretty chain,
Or a bracelet of her hair,
690   Prayed Troilus for to wear
That token for her sake;
How heartily he did it take,
And much thereof did make;
And all that was in vain,
For she did but feign;
The story telleth plain,
He could not obtain,
Though his father were a king,
Yet there was a thing
700   That made the male to wring;[65]
She made him to sing
The song of lover's lay;
Musing night and day,
Mourning all alone,
Comfort had he none,
For she was quite gone.

---

61   French chivalric hero.
62   Jewish hero in 2 Maccabees.
63   Publius Cornelius Scipio Aemilianus (c.185–129 BC); destroyed the city of Carthage.
64   Troilus and Criseyde are lovers in a poem by Chaucer; their love letters are delivered by Pandarus.
65   Wrung his withers.

Thus in conclusion,
She brought him in abusion;
In earnest and in game
710   She was much to blame;
Disparaged is her fame,
And blemished is her name,
In manner half with shame;
Troilus also hath lost
On her much love and cost,
And now must kiss the post;
Pandarus, that went between,
Hath won nothing, I ween,
But light for summer green;
720   Yet for a special laud
He is named Troilus' bawd;
Of that name he is sure
Whiles the world shall 'dure.

Though I remember the fable
Of Penelope[66] most stable,
To her husband most true,
Yet long-time she ne knew
Whether he were live or dead;
Her wit stood her in stead,
730   That she was true and just
For any bodily lust
To Ulysses her make,
And never would him forsake.

Of Marcus Marcellus[67]
A process I could tell us;
And of Antiochus,[68]
And of Josephus[69]
De Antiquitatibus;
And of Mardocheus,[70]
740   And of great Ahasuerus,
And of Vesca his queen,
Whom he forsook with teen,
And of Esther his other wife,
With whom he led a pleasant life;
Of King Alexander;[71]
And of King Evander;[72]
And of Porsena the great,[73]
That made the Romans to sweat.

Though I have enrolled
750   A thousand new and old
Of these historious tales,
To fill budgets and males
With books that I have read,

---

66 Faithful wife of Ulysses in Homer's *Odyssey*.
67 Conqueror of Syracuse in the second Punic War.
68 Name of several of the Seleucid kings of Asia.
69 Flavius Josephus, author of *Antiquitates Iudaicae*.
70 Mordecai, the hero of the Book of Esther, enabled his orphaned cousin Esther to marry King Ahasuerus of Persia.

71 Alexander the Great.
72 Legendary founder of Rome.
73 Thought by the Romans to be an Etruscan chieftain who once was master of Rome.

Yet I am nothing sped,
And can but little skill
Of Ovid or Virgil,[74]
Or of Plutarch,
Or Francis Petrarch,
Alcaeus or Sappho,
760 Or such other poets mo,
As Linus and Homerus,
Euphorion and Theocritus,
Anacreon and Arion,
Sophocles and Philemon,
Pindarus and Simonides,
Philistion and Pherecydes;
These poets of anciente,
They are too diffuse for me:

For, as I tofore have said,
770 I am but a young maid,
And cannot in effect
My style as yet direct
With English words elect.
Our natural tongue is rude,
And hard to be ennewed
With polished termes lusty;
Our language is so rusty,
So cankered, and so full
Of frowards, and so dull,
780 That if I would apply
To write ornately,
I wot not where to find
Terms to serve my mind.

Gower's[75] English is old,
And of no value told;
His matter is worth gold,
And worthy to be enrolled.

In Chaucer I am sped,
His *Tales* I have read:
790 His matter is delectable,
Solacious, and commendable;
His English well allowed,
So as it is enprowed,
For as it is employed,
There is no English void,
At those days much commended;
And now men would have amended
His English, whereat they bark,
And mar all they wark.
800 Chaucer, that famous clerk,
His termes were not dark,
But pleasant, easy, and plain;
No word he wrote in vain.

---

74 There follows a catalogue of Greek, Roman, and Italian poets, some
perhaps legendary.

75 John Gower, medieval English poet, author of *Confessio Amantis*.

Also John Lydgate[76]
Writeth after an higher rate;
It is diffuse to find
The sentence of his mind,
Yet writeth he in his kind,
No man that can amend
810   Those matters that he hath penned;
Yet some men find a faute,
And say he writeth too haut.

Wherefore hold me excused
If I have not well perused
Mine English half abused;
Though it be refused,
In worth I shall it take,
And fewer wordes make.

But, for my sparrow's sake,
820   Yet as a woman may,
My wit I shall assay
An epitaph to write
In Latin plain and light,
Whereof the elegy
Followeth by and by:
Flos volucrum formose, vale!
Philippe, sub isto
Marmore jam recubas,
Qui mihi carus eras.
830   *Semper erunt nitido*
Radiantia sidera cœlo;
Impressusque meo
Pectore semper eris.[77]

A LAUD AND PRAISE MADE FOR OUR SOVEREIGN LORD THE KING

THE Rose both White and Red
In one Rose now doth grow:
Thus thorough every stead
Thereof the fame doth blow.
Grace the seed did sow:
England, now gather floures,
Exclude now all doloures.

Noble Henry the Eight,
Thy loving sovereign lord,
10   Of kinges line most straight
His title doth record:
In whom doth well accord
Alexis[1] young of age,
Adrastus[2] wise and sage,

---

76   Medieval English poet reputed to be the dullest writer in the
language, author of the 36,000 line poem, *The Fall of Princes*.
77   Farewell, sweet bird. Philip, beneath that marble you lie; you who
were dear to me. So long as the stars shine in the sky will your image
be graven on my heart.

A LAUD AND PRAISE MADE FOR OUR SOVEREIGN LORD
THE KING
1   Alexander the Great.
2   Mythical king of Argos.

Astraea,[3] Justice hight,
  That from the starry sky
Shall now come and do right.
  This hundred year scantly
  A man could not espy
That Right dwelt us among,
And that was the more wrong.

Right shall the foxes chare,
  The wolves, the bearès also,
That wrought have muché care,
  And brought Engeland in woe:
  They shall worry no mo,
Nor root the Rosary
By extort treachery.

Of this our noble king
  The law they shall not break;
They shall come to reckoning;
  No man for them will speak:
  The people durst not creke
Their griefes to complain,
They brought them in such pain.

Therefore no more they shall
  The commons overbace,
That wont were over all
  Both lord and knight to face:
  For now the years of grace
And wealth are come again,
That maketh England fain.

Adonis[4] of fresh colour,
  Of youth the goodly floure,
Our prince of high honour,
  Our paves, our succour,
  Our king, our emperour,
Our Priamus of Troy,[5]
Our wealth, our worldly joy:

Upon us he doth reign,
  That maketh our heartes glad,
As king most sovereign
  That ever England had;
  Demure, sober, and sad,
And Mars's lusty knight;
God save him in his right!

       Amen.

20

30

40

50

---

3   Mythical figure of justice who fled to heaven during the wicked Bronze Age, awaiting her return to earth at a more auspicious time.

4   Beautiful youth loved by Aphrodite.

5   King of Troy during the Trojan War.

Sir Thomas More (1477/8–1535)

One of the most fascinating and controversial figures in English history, Sir Thomas More was a humanist, statesman, and martyr, as well as a prolific writer. Because of his key role in the controversies surrounding Henry VIII's divorce from Catherine of Aragon and subsequent marriage to Anne Boleyn, More was the subject of several sixteenth-century biographies, including one by his son-in-law William Roper (written 1555–7). His English writings were published by his nephew William Rastell in 1557, followed by his Latin works in 1565, Ralph Robinson's English translation of *Utopia* having appeared in 1551.

Born in London, More was educated at St. Anthony's School, where his chief subject was Latin. From 1492–4 he attended Canterbury College, Oxford, studying the trivium (grammar, rhetoric, logic), as well as Latin and basic Greek. He left Oxford to study law at New Inn and Lincoln's Inn, London, where he met Erasmus on the occasion of his first visit to England in 1499. More was called to the bar in 1501, when he also began a three-year lectureship on law. Most of his English poetry, including "A Lament of Queen Elizabeth," dates from this period. In 1504, with his election to Parliament, More began his career as a politician. He married Jane Colt the following year, and they had four children: Margaret (later Margaret Roper), Elizabeth, Cecily, and John. (Jane was to die in 1511, and More subsequently married Alice Middleton.) In 1506 he and Erasmus collaborated in translating some of the dialogues of Lucian from Greek into Latin, which is an important indication both of the limited knowledge of Greek in Europe at this time and of the commitment by such humanists as Erasmus and More to promoting the study of Greek literature and culture. In 1513 he was at work on the *History of Richard III*, which he wrote both in Latin and in English; and in 1516 he published the Latin text of *Utopia*.

Although *Utopia* is More's most familiar work, it is often misread as though it were an unironic vision of an ideal society. The text to which it is a distant response is Plato's *Republic*, a no less problematic work in terms of its multiple ironies, many of which flow from that master of understatement, Socrates. During the earliest Christian centuries, Plato was regarded as the most important of the pagan philosophers and a key precursor of Christianity. In *The City of God*, however, St. Augustine insisted that Plato's thought is a product of reason without faith. A fundamental concept in Christian theology and philosophy is the idea that the illusion of self-sufficiency deprives a person of the ability to love and to accept love, especially to accept the love of God in the form of divine grace that is necessary for salvation. More's utopian commonwealth is a society without Christian revelation. It is a world of reason without faith that is so well constructed as to appeal to those for whom the claims of faith are meaningless. More, however, thought that the proof of reason's limitation could be discovered in the mind's capacity to make a convincing case for what is both false and impossible (see Ackroyd, pp. 172–4). Perhaps this is where the ambiguity of the word "utopia" is most significant: is it the good place or is it nowhere? As an abstract construction of reason without faith (or love) it may have been a nowhere for More.

At last persuaded to enter the King's service, despite his early premonitions of disaster, More was made Privy Councilor in 1517 and advanced rapidly. He was knighted in 1521, elected Speaker of the House of Commons in 1523, and made Lord Chancellor in 1529, following the dismissal of Wolsey, who had failed in the divorce negotiations with Rome. During the last years of his life More defied the tides of the English Reformation on two fronts: first, in his opposition to the King's bid for divorce and to his eventual declaration of himself as supreme head of the Church "so far as the law of Christ allows," and second, in his opposition to what he considered the heresy of Protestantism, especially in the form of Tyndale's unsanctioned biblical translations, which More attacked in *Dialogue Concerning Tyndale* (1529). Following Tyndale's response (*An Answer Unto More's Dialogue* [1531]), More wrote *The Confutation to Tyndale's Answer* (1532–3), his longest and least attractive work.

A year after becoming Lord Chancellor, More refused to sign the King's latest divorce appeal to the Pope. In 1532 he at last resigned the Chancellorship. Events of 1533 moved rapidly. In January Henry married Anne Boleyn, who was then pregnant; in May Archbishop Cranmer nullified the previous marriage to Catherine (she was the widow of Henry's brother Arthur); in June More refused to attend the coronation of Anne Boleyn; in September the Pope excommunicated the King. The following March Parliament passed the Act of Succession, which required all subjects to take an Oath of Allegiance. Refusal to do so was declared an act of treason, punishable by imprisonment and the confiscation of property for the Crown. Arguing that it repudiated papal supremacy, More refused to take the Oath on April 13th. Four days later he began a fifteen-month imprisonment in the Tower of London, during which he wrote the *Dialogue of Comfort against Tribulation* (published in 1553), in anticipation of his execution. Five days after his trial at Westminster, More was executed and his head exhibited on London Bridge until it was recovered by his daughter Margaret, to whom he had written a farewell letter on the day before his death.

Perhaps it is not surprising that the stylistic assessment of a man who lived such a life amidst controversy should also be a matter of controversy. As might be expected, More's biographer R. W. Chambers, in *The Contintuity of English Prose from Alfred to More and His School*, ranks his achievement as an English prose stylist very high:

> More brings English eloquence from the cloister where it had taken refuge, and applies it to the needs of Sixteenth-Century England. Thereby he deserves the title . . . of restorer of political eloquence. He knows all the tricks. He couples synonyms together when it suits his purpose; but he does not do it with the maddening persistency which . . . had become a real danger to English style. In the same way More uses balanced sentences, and sometimes emphasizes the balance with alliteration, sometimes even with cross-alliteration; the most characteristic cadences of Lyly's *Euphues* are anticipated. But when More has once achieved them, he goes on and tries something else, instead of repeating the trick with the reiterated folly of Lyly. (pp. clv–clvi)

Given his lifelong study of Latin and the fact that most of his professional writing was in that language, More's English prose style is predictably Latinate. However, to specify in what sense it is Latinate is not an easy task because of More's own participation, along with Erasmus, in the anti-Ciceronian disputes of the 1520s. The fundamental distinction here is between advocates of the sole persuasiveness of rational argumentation and those who see a greater (or different) power in rhetorical ornamentation, which can appeal to other than rational faculties, analogous to the persuasiveness of poetry. Although this is not his own position, Cicero gives a clear account of what he calls the Attic stylist's preference for plain, clear, and rational argumentation:

> He is restrained and plain, he follows the ordinary usage . . . and is loose but not rambling. . . . His very freedom from periodic structure obliges him to see that his short and concise clauses are not handled carelessly, for there is such a thing even as a careful negligence. . . . All noticeable ornament will be excluded. . . . only elegance and neatness will remain. The language will be pure Latin, plain and clear . . . (*Orator* 75–90)

Like the Greek writer Isocrates, Cicero approved of ornamentation as a persuasive means of appealing to the emotions, and in this respect he could claim the authority of Aristotle's *Rhetoric*. Isocrates had promoted three forms of parallelism: a parallelism of sense (antithesis), a parallelism

in form and size between two or more clauses or sentences (parisosis), and a parallelism of sound when the second of two clauses gives to the ear an echo of the former (paromoiosis). Erasmus and More objected to what were then fashionable imitators of the Ciceronian style in English, based on Isocrates, which would eventually reach its ultimate extreme in Lyly's euphuism. In the meantime, however, a different model of parallelism was emerging in the English language, based on the model of biblical Hebrew. Tyndale's superb biblical translations cut through the opposition of Attic and Ciceronian style in a way that More was not in a position to anticipate. When he opposed Tyndale on theological grounds, More did so in a prose unequal to what might be called Tyndale's middle style, which was somewhere between plainness and Ciceronian ornamentation. Tyndale believed that Greek agreed more with the English tongue than did Latin, but that Hebrew agreed a thousand times more. For all his great learning and intellectual integrity, this was an argument More appears never to have considered.

Because he wrote mostly in Latin, More's contribution to English literature rests largely on his *History of Richard III* and *A Dialogue of Comfort Against Tribulation*. The textual history of both works is complex but for quite different reasons. It appears that More carefully revised portions of the *History*, preparing the English version of the text himself; while the *Dialogue* was written in prison during the last months of his life, without the aid of a library or even adequate writing materials. Despite its Christian argument, this powerful text is in the form of a Platonic dialogue; but it is set as though in the context of the impending Turkish invasion of Hungary in 1528. The speakers are Vincent, a terrified young man, and his uncle, Anthony, to whom he turns for advice on how to face the crisis that is about to occur. Anthony, then, might be read as the spokesman for More, while Henry VIII is the Grand Turk, who has besieged Budapest. The allegorical setting of the *Dialogue* is, therefore, an early example of what Edward Said has called "Orientalism": the European invention of an idea of the Orient as an indispensable, but fictional, image of cultural otherness.

READING

Peter Ackroyd, *The Life of Thomas More.*
R. W. Chambers, *On the Continuity of English Prose from Alfred to More and His School.*
Alistair Fox, *Thomas More: History and Providence.*
Richard Marius, *Thomas More: A Biography.*
Edward Said, *Orientalism.*
George Williamson, *The Senecan Amble.*

M. P.

A LAMENTATION OF QUEEN ELIZABETH[1]

O YE that put your trust and confidence
  In worldly joy and frail prosperity,
That so live here as ye should never hence,
  Remember death and look here upon me.
  Ensample I think there may no better be.
    Your self wot well that in this realm was I
    Your queen but late, and lo now here I lie.

Was I not born of old worthy lineage?
  Was not my mother queen, my father king?
Was I not a king's fere in marriage?   *wife*
  Had I not plenty of every pleasant thing?
  Merciful God, this is a strange reckoning:
    Riches, honour, wealth and ancestry
    Hath me forsaken, and lo now here I lie.

If worship might have kept me, I had not gone.
  If wit might have me saved, I needed not fear.
If money might have holp, I lacked none.
  But O good God what vaileth all this gear?   *avails/possessions*
  When death is come, thy mighty messenger,
    Obey we must, there is no remedy:
    Me hath he summoned, and lo here I lie.

Yet was I late promised otherwise,
  This year to live in wealth and delice.
Lo whereto cometh thy blandishing promise.
  O false astrology and divinatrice,
  Of God's secrets making thy self so wise!
    How true is for this year thy prophecy!
    The year yet lasteth and lo now here I lie.

O brittle wealth, aye full of bitterness,
  Thy single pleasure doubled is with pain.
Account my sorrow first and my distress,
  In sundry wise, and reckon there again
  The joy that I have had, and I dare sayn,
    For all my honour, endured yet have I
    More woe than wealth, and lo now here I lie.

Where are our castles now, where are our towers?
  Goodly Richmond, soon art thou gone from me;
At Westminster that costly work of yours,
  Mine own dear lord, now shall I never see.
  Almighty God vouchsafe to grant that ye

10

20

30

40

A LAMENTATION OF QUEEN ELIZABETH
1   Elizabeth of York (1465–1503), Queen Consort of Henry VII and
mother of Henry VIII.

For you and your children well may edify.
My palace builded is, and lo now here I lie.

Adieu, mine own dear spouse, my worthy lord.
The faithful love that did us both combine
In marriage and peaceable concord
Into your hands here I clean resign
To be bestowed upon your children and mine.
Erst were you father, and now must ye supply
The mother's part also, for lo now here I lie.

50   Farewell, my daughter lady Margaret.
God wot full oft it grieved hath my mind
That ye should go where we should seldom meet.
Now am I gone, and have left you behind.
O mortal folk, that we be very blind;
That we least fear, full oft it is most nigh:
From you depart I first, and lo now here I lie.

Farewell, madame, my lord's worthy mother,
Comfort your son, and be ye of good cheer.
Take all a worth, for it will be no nother.
60   Farewell, my daughter Katherine late the fere
To prince Arthur, mine own child so dear.
It booteth not for me to weep or cry;
Pray for my soul, for lo now here I lie,

Adieu, Lord Henry, my loving son, adieu.
Our Lord increase your honour and estate.
Adieu, my daughter Mary, bright of hue.
God make you virtuous, wise, and fortunate.
Adieu, sweet heart, my little daughter Kate;
Thou shalt, sweet babe, such is thy destiny,
70   Thy mother never know, for lo now here I lie.

Lady Cecily, Anne, and Katherine,
Farewell my well-beloved sisters three;
O Lady Bridget, other sister mine.
Lo here the end of worldly vanity.
Now well are ye that earthly folly flee,
And heavenly things love and magnify.
Farewell and pray for me, for lo now here I lie.

Adieu my lords, adieu my ladies all,
Adieu my faithful servants every chone.
80   Adieu my commons whom I never shall
See in this world, wherefore to Thee alone,
Immortal God verily three and one,
I me commend Thy infinite mercy
Show to Thy servant, for lo now here I lie.

[From] *Utopia*[1]

A FRUITFUL, PLEASANT, AND WITTY WORK, OF THE BEST STATE OF A PUBLIC WEAL AND OF THE NEW ISLE CALLED UTOPIA, WRITTEN IN LATIN BY THE RIGHT WORTHY AND FAMOUS SIR THOMAS MORE, KNIGHT, AND TRANSLATED INTO ENGLISH BY RALPH ROBYNSON . . .

THE TRANSLATOR TO THE GENTLE READER[2]

Thou shalt understand, gentle reader, that though this work of Utopia in English come now the second time forth in print, yet was it never my mind nor intent that it should ever have been imprinted at all, as who for no such purpose took upon me at the first the translation thereof, but did it only at the request of a friend for his own private use, upon hope that he would have kept it secret to himself alone. Whom though I knew to be a man indeed, both very witty and also skillful, yet was I certain that, in the knowledge of the Latin tongue, he was not so well seen as to be able to judge of the fineness or coarseness of my translation. Wherefore, I went the more slightly through with it, propounding to myself therein, rather to please my said friend's judgment than mine own. To the meanness of whose learning I thought it my part to submit and attemper my style. Lightly, therefore, I overran the whose work and in short time, with more haste than good speed, I brought it to an end. But as the Latin proverb saith; the hasty bitch bringeth forth blind whelps, for, when this my work was finished, the rudeness thereof showed it to be done in posthaste. Howbeit, rude and base though it were, yet fortune so ruled the matter that to imprinting it came, and that partly against my will. Howbeit, not being able in this behalf to resist the pithy persuasions of my friends, and perceiving, therefore, none other remedy but that forth it should, I comforted myself for the time only with this notable saying of Terence:

> *Ita vita est hominum, quasi quum ludas tesseris*
> *Si illud, quod est maxume opus, iactu non cadit:*
> *Illud, quod cecidit forte, id arte ut corrigas.*[3]

In which verses the poet likeneth or compareth the life of man to a dice playing or a game at the tables. Meaning therein, if that chance rise not, which is most for the players' advantage, that then the chance which fortune hath sent ought so cunningly to be played, as may be to the player least damage. By the which worthy similitude surely the witty poet giveth us to understand that though in any of our acts and doings (as it oft chanceth), we happen to fail and miss of our good pretensed purpose so that the success and our intent prove things far odd, yet so we ought with witty circumspection to handle the matter that no evil or incommodity, as far forth as may be, and as in us lieth, do thereof ensue. According to the which counsel, though I am, indeed, in comparison of an expert gamester and a cunning player but a very bungler, yet have I in this by chance that on my side unawares hath fallen, so (I suppose) behaved myself that, as doubtless it might have been of me much more cunningly handled had I forethought so much, or doubted any such request at the beginning of my play, so I am sure it had been much worse than it is if I had not in the end looked somewhat earnestly to my game. For though this work came not from me so fine, so perfect, and so exact that at first, as surely for my small learning it should have done, if I had then meant the publishing thereof in print. Yet I trust I have now in this second edition taken about it such pains that very few great faults and notable errors are in it to be found. Now, therefore, most gentle reader, the meanness of this simple translation and the faults that be therein (as I fear much there

---

[From] UTOPIA

1   According to the *OED*, this word first enters the English language with the publication of More's text. One meaning of "utopia," as derived from the Greek, means "no place," although there is also a lingering suggestion of "beautiful, or ideal place."

2   Ralph Robynson's preface to the second edition of 1556.

3   From Terence's *Adelphi*: "Human life is like a game with dice; if you don't get the throw you most want, you must show your skill in making the best throw which you can get" (lines 739–41).

be some), I doubt not but thou wilt, in just consideration of the premises, gently and favorably wink at them. So doing you shall minister unto my good cause to think my labor and pains herein not altogether bestowed in vain.

Vale

THE EPISTLE

Thomas More to Peter Giles[4] sendeth greeting.

I am almost ashamed, right well-beloved Peter Giles, to send unto you this book of the Utopian commonwealth well nigh after a year's space, which I am sure you looked for within a month and a half. And no marvel. For you knew well enough that I was already disburdened of all the labor and study belonging to the invention of this work, and that I had no need at all to trouble my brains about the disposition or conveyance of the matter, and therefore had herein nothing else to do, but only to rehearse those things which you and I together heard Master Raphael tell and declare. Wherefore, there was no cause why I should study to set forth the matter with eloquence. Forasmuch as his talk could not be fine and eloquent, being first not studied for, but sudden and unpremeditate and then, as you know, of a man better seen in the Greek language than in the Latin tongue. And my writing, the nigher[5] it should approach to his homely, plain, and *Truth loveth simplicity* simple speech, so much the nigher should it go to the truth, which is the only *and plainness.*[6] mark whereunto I do and ought to direct all my travail and study herein. I grant and confess, friend Peter, myself discharged of so much labor, having all these things ready done to my hand, that almost there was nothing left for me to do, else either the invention or the disposition of his matter might have required of a wit neither base, neither at all unlearned, both some time and leisure and also some study. But if it were requisite and necessary that the matter should also have been written eloquently and not alone truly, of a surety that thing could I have performed by no time nor study. But now, seeing all these cares, stays, and lets were taken away, wherein else so much labor and study should have been employed, and that there remained no other thing for me to do but only to write plainly the matter as I hath it spoken, that, indeed, was a thing light and to be done.

Howbeit, to the dispatching of this so little business, my other cares and troubles did leave almost less than no leisure. Whiles I do daily bestow my time about law matters: some to plead, some to hear, some as an arbitrator with mine award to determine, some as an *The author's business* umpire or a judge with mine sentence finally to discuss. Whiles I go one way to *and lets.*[7] see and visit my friend; another way about mine own private affairs. Whiles I spend almost all the day abroad amongst others and the residue at home among mine own, I leave to myself, I mean to my book, no time. For when I am come home, I must common with my wife, chat with my children, and talk with my servants, all the which things I reckon and account among business, for as much as they must of necessity be done, and done must they needs be unless a man will be stranger in his own house. And in any wise, a man must so fashion and order his conditions and so appoint and dispose himself that he be merry, jocund, and pleasant among them whom either nature hath provided or chance hath made or he himself hath chosen to be the fellows and companions of his life. So that with too much gentle behavior and familiarity, he do not mar them and, by too much sufferance of his servants, make them his masters. Among these things now rehearsed stealeth away the day, the month, the year. When do I write then? And all this while have I spoken no word of sleep, neither yet of meat, which among a great number doth waste no less time *Meat & sleep: great* than doth sleep, wherein almost half the lifetime of man creepeth away. I, there- *wasters of time.*

---

4 Peter Giles (1486–1533) was a fellow humanist in Antwerp. 7 *debts.*
5 *nearer.*
6 These marginal notes are Robynson's equivalents for those by Erasmus and Peter Giles in the Latin editions.

fore, do win and get only that time which I steal from sleep and meat. Which time, because it is very little, and yet somewhat it is, therefore, have I once at the last, though it be long first, finished *Utopia* and have sent it to you, friend Peter, to read and peruse to the intent that if anything have escaped me, you might put me in remembrance of it.

For though in this behalf I do not greatly mistrust myself (which would God I were somewhat in wit and learning, as I am not all of the worst and dullest memory), yet have I not so great trust and confidence in it that I think nothing could fall out of my mind. For John Clement,[8] *John Clement.* my boy, who as you know was there present with us, whom I suffer to be away from no talk wherein may be any profit or goodness (for out of this young-bladed and new-shot-up corn, which hath already begun to spring up both in Latin and Greek learning, I look for plentiful increase at length of goodly ripe grain), he, I say, hath brought me into a great doubt. For, whereas Hythloday[9] (unless my memory fail me) said that the bridge of Amaurote[10] which goeth over the river of Anyder is 500 paces, that is to say half mile in length, my John saith that 200 of those paces must be plucked away, for that the river containeth there not above 300 paces in breadth. I pray you heartily call the matter to your remembrance, for if you agree with him, I also *A diversity between mak-* will say as you say and confess myself deceived. But if you cannot remember *ing a lie and telling a lie.* the thing, then surely I will write as I have done and as mine own remembrance serveth me. For as I will take good heed that there be in my book nothing false, so if there be anything doubtful, I will rather tell a lie than make a lie, because I had rather be good than wily. Howbeit, this matter may easily be remedied if you will take the pains to ask the question of Raphael himself by word of mouth if he be now with you, or else by your letters, *In what part of the world* which you must needs do for another doubt also that hath chanced, through *Utopia standeth it is un-* whose fault I cannot tell, whether through mine or yours or Raphael's. For *known.*[11] neither we remembered to inquire of him nor he to tell us in what part of the new world Utopia is situate, the which thing I had rather have spent no small sum of money than that it should thus have escaped us, as well for that I am ashamed to be ignorant in what sea that *It is thought of some that* island standeth, whereof I write so long a treatise, as also because there be with *here is unfainedly meant* us certain men, and especially one virtuous and godly man, and a professor of *the late famous vicar of* divinity, who is exceeding desirous to go unto Utopia, not for a vain and curious *Croydon in Surrey.*[12] desire to see news, but to the intent he may further and increase our religion, which is there already luckily begun. And that he may the better accomplish and perform this his good intent, he is minded to procure that he may be sent thither by the high bishop. Yea, and that he *A godly suit.* himself may be made Bishop of Utopia, being nothing scrupulous herein, that he must obtain this bishopric with suit. For he counteth that a godly suit, which proceedeth not of the desire of honor or lucre, but only of a godly zeal. Wherefore, I most earnestly desire you, friend Peter, to talk with Hythloday, if you can face to face, or else to write your letters to him, and so to work in this matter, that in this my book there may neither anything be found which is untrue, neither anything be lacking which is true. And I think, verily, it shall be well done that you show unto him the book itself, for if I have missed or failed in any point, or if any fault have escaped me, no man can so well correct and amend it as he can, and, yet, that can he not do unless he peruse and read over my book written. Moreover, by this means shall you perceive whether he be well willing and content that I should undertake to put this work in writing, for if he be minded to publish and put forth his own labors and travails himself, perchance he would be loathe, and so would I also, that in publishing the Utopian weal public[13] I should prevent him and take from him the flower and grace of the novelty of this his history.

Howbeit, to say the very truth, I am not yet fully determined with myself whether I will put forth my book or no, for the natures of men be so divers, the fantasies of some so wayward, their

8 John Clement was a young humanist and a member of More's household.

9 The name is Latin, derived from the Greek, meaning something like "an expert in nonsense."

10 This name is also Latin, derived from the Greek, meaning "dark place."

11 No doubt a play on the primary meaning of "utopia."

12 Rowland Phillips.

13 commonwealth.

minds so unkind, their judgments so corrupt that they which lead a merry and a jocund life, following their own sensual pleasures and carnal lusts, may seem to be in a much better state or case
than they that vex and unquiet themselves with cares and study for the putting   *The unkind judgments of*
forth and publishing of something that may be either profit or pleasure to   *men.*
others, which others nevertheless will disdainfully, scornfully, and unkindly accept the same. The
most part of all be unlearned, and a great number hath learning in contempt. The rude and barbarous alloweth nothing but that which is very barbarous indeed. If it be one that hath a little
smack of learning, he rejecteth as homely gear and common ware whatsoever is not stuffed full of
old moth-eaten terms and that be worn out of use. Some there be that have pleasure only in old
rusty antiquities, and some only in their own doings. One is so sour, so crabbed, and so unpleasant that he can away with no mirth nor sport; another is so narrow between the shoulders that he
can bear no jests nor taunts. Some silly poor souls be so afraid that at every snappish word their
nose shall be bitten off that they stand in no less dread of every quick and sharp word than he that
is bitten of a mad dog feareth water. Some be so mutable and wavering that every hour they be in
a new mind, saying one thing sitting and another thing standing. Another sort sitteth upon their
ale benches, and there among their cups they give judgment of the wits of writers, and with great
authority they condemn even as pleaseth them, every writer according to his writing, in most spiteful manner mocking, louting, and flouting them, being themselves in the mean season safe and, as
saith the proverb, out of all danger of gunshot. For why they be so smug and smooth that they
have not so much as one hair of an honest man whereby one may take hold of them. There be,
moreover, some so unkind and ungentle that though they take great pleasure and   *A fit similitude.*
delectation in the work, yet for all that they cannot find in their hearts to love the
author thereof, nor to afford him a good word, being much like the uncourteous, unthankful, and
churlish guests which, when they have with good and dainty meats well-filled their bellies, depart
home, giving no thanks to the feast maker. Go your ways now and make a costly feast at your own
charges for guests so dainty-mouthed, so divers in taste, and, besides that, of so unkind and unthankful natures. But nevertheless (friend Peter) do, I pray you, with Hythloday as I willed you before,
and as for this matter I shall be at my liberty afterwards to take new advisement. Howbeit, seeing
I have taken great pains and labor in writing this matter, if it may stand with his mind and pleasure, I will, as touching the edition or publishing of the book, follow the counsel and advice of my
friends, and especially yours. Thus, fare you well right heartily beloved friend Peter, with your gentle
wife, and love me as you have ever done for I love you better than ever I did.

THE CONFUTATION OF TYNDALE'S ANSWER

[FROM] THE PREFACE TO THE CHRISTIAN READER

Our Lord send us now some years as plenteous of good corn as we have had some years of late plenteous of evil books. For they have grown so fast and sprung up so thick, full of pestilent errors and
pernicious heresies, that they have infected and killed, I fear me, more silly simple souls than the
famine of the dire years have destroyed bodies.[1] And surely no little cause there is to dread that
the great abundance and plenty of the one is no little cause and occasion of the great dearth and
scarcity of the other. For since that our Lord of his especial providence useth temporally to punish
the whole people for the sins of some part, to compel the good folk to forbear and abhor the naughty,
whereby they may bring them to amendment and avoid themself the contagion of their company:
wisdom were it for us to perceive it like as folk begin now to delight in feeding their souls of the
venomous carrion of those poisoned heresies, of which may well be verified the words of holy writ:[2]

THE CONFUTATION OF TYNDALE'S ANSWER   2   2 Kings 4:40.
[FROM] THE PREFACE TO THE CHRISTIAN READER
1   The years 1531–2 were lean years for corn production, but there is
also an allusion here to Genesis 41:22.

Death is in the pot; our Lord likewise againward to revenge it withal, beginneth to withdraw his gracious hand from the fruits of the earth, diminishing the fertility both in corn and cattle, and bringing all in dearth much more than men can remedy or fully find out the cause. And yet beside this somewhere he sendeth war, sickness, and mortality to punish in the flesh that odious and hateful sin of the soul, that spoileth the fruit from all manner of virtues, I mean unbelief, false faith, and infidelity, and – to tell you all at once in plain English – heresy. And I say that God now beginneth. For I fear me surely that except folk begin to reform that fault yea sooner God shall not fail in such wise to go forward, that we shall well perceive and feel by the increase of our grief, that all this gere[3] hitherto is but a beginning yet. The prophet Elias, as it is written in the third book of Kings,[4] for the infidelity and idolatry that then was used in Israel, by his hearty prayer made unto God, kept that whole country from rain by the space of three years and a half, not of evil will or malice, but of devotion and pity by the pain and pinching of the bodies, to compel men to remember their souls, which else were in peril of perishing by false idolatry.

Now albeit that these bold shameless heretics have of long while neither letted nor ceased, falsely to insimulate and accuse the church of God, calling all good Christian people idolaters for honoring of saints and reverent behavior used at their images: yet that have they done so far against their own conscience (by which themself well wote that the church useth to saints and images none honor but ordinate, not honoring images but for the saint's sake, nor saints but for the sake of God & neither image as saint, but saint as God) & this knoweth I say Tyndale himself so well, and thereby so far hath railed against his own conscience that now at the last in his answer to my book, he retreateth so far back, that he revoketh almost all that ever he said before & is fain now to grant that Christian men may have images, & kneel before them too, as ye shall hereafter see when we shall come to the place.

But we on the other side say plainly unto them, that the things wherewith they corrupt the world are of infidelity and faithless idolatry, the very most cursed kind. The chief evil in an idol was that it bare the name of God, either itself or the devil that it represented, and being so reputed and worshipped for God, robbed the reverence and devout honor from God.

Now when Tyndale calleth his heresies by the name of faith, and maketh men serve the devil while they wene to serve God: what abominable idolatry is this?

If it be idolatry to put trust in the devil, & serve the devil with faith, it is worse than idolatry to make men wene they serve God with faith while they despise him with a false belief.

And if it be very infidelity to do as the Turks do, bid men believe in Mohammed's Koran, it is more infidelity to do as Tyndale hath done, purposely mistranslate Christ's holy gospel, to set forth heresies as evil as the Koran.

And if it be idolatry to do as the paynims did, make an idol god, it must needs be much worse idolatry to do as these heretics do, that call God the cause of all evil, and thereby make God not a vain idol but a very devil.

And what can be worse kind of infidelity than to make books of heresies and call them the right faith?

And what more abominable infidelity than to abuse the scripture of God to the color of their false belief?

And what can be a worse belief than to believe that the sacraments that God hath ordained by his Holy Spirit be but inventions of man, or as Tyndale saith of confession, but invention of the devil?

And what can be worse belief than to believe that God's word is not to be believed but if it be put in writing?

Or what can be worse belief than to believe that men's good works be they never so well done, be yet nothing worth, nor the man never the better for them, nor no reward for them coming toward man in heaven?[5]

---

3 *fit of passion.*
4 i.e. 1 Kings 18:36.

5 Here is the fundamental issue that divided Protestantism from Catholicism until 1999: whether salvation (or "justification") came by faith or good works. Tyndale's translation of Luther's Prologue to Romans is a full statement of the Protestant position.

Or what can be worse belief than to believe that a man doth wrong to pray for his father's soul?

Or what can be a worse belief than to believe that a man may as slightly regard Whitsun Sunday as Hock Monday and as boldly eat flesh on Good Friday as on Shrove Tuesday?[6]

And what can be a worse belief than to believe that none other sin can damn a man but only lack of belief?

And if it be idolatry to do as the Paynims do, give worship unto an idol, how much is it worse than idolatry to do as Tyndale doth, forbid us to give worship to the very body and blessed blood of God in the holy sacrament of the altar?

These pestilent infidelities and these abominable kinds of idolatries far exceed and pass, and incomparably more offend the majesty of our Lord God, than all the setting up of Bel and Baal and Beelzaebub,[7] and all the devils in hell. Wherefore like as in other places where these heresies have taken deeper root, & been more spread abroad, God hath taken more deep and sore vengeance, not only by dearth and death but also by battle and sword: so is it to be feared that for the receipt of these pestilent books, our Lord sendeth us some lack of corn and cattle for a beginning and will not fail but if our fault be mended to send us as sore punishment as he hath sent already, into such other places as would not be by like warning mended. . . .

[The Princes' Murder from] The History of King Richard III

King Richarde[1] after his coronacion, takyng his way to Gloucester to visit in his newe honor, the towne of which he bare the name of his old, deuised as he roode, to fulfil y^t thing which he before had intended. And forasmuch as his minde gaue him, y^t his nephewes liuing, men woulde not recken that hee could haue right to ye realm, he thought therfore without delay to rid them, as though the killing of his kinsmen, could amend his cause, and make him a kindly king. Whereuppon he sent one Iohn Grene[2] whom he specially trusted, vnto sir Robert Brakenbery[3] constable of the Tower, with a letter and credence also, that the same sir Robert shoulde in any wise put the two children to death. This Iohn Grene did his errande vnto Brakenbery kneling before our Lady in the Tower, who plainely answered that he would neuer putte them to death to dye therfore, with which answer Ihon Grene returning recounted the same to Kynge Richarde at Warwick yet in his way. Wherwith he toke such displeasure and thought, that the same night, he said vnto a secrete page of his: Ah whome shall a man trust? those that I haue broughte vp my selfe, those that I had sent would most surely serue me, euen those fayle me, and at my commaundemente wyll do nothyng for me. Sir quod his page there lyeth one on your paylet without, y^t I dare well say to do your grace pleasure, the thyng were right harde that he wold refuse, meaning this by sir Iames Tyrell,[4] which was a man of right goodlye parsonage, and for natures gyftes, woorthy to haue serued a muche better prince, if he had well serued god, and by grace obtayned as muche trouthe & good wil as he had strength and witte. The man had an high heart, and sore longed vpwarde, not rising yet so fast as he had hoped, being hindered and kept vnder by the meanes of sir Richarde Ratclife[5] and sir William Catesby,[6] which longing for no moo parteners of the princes fauour, and namely

Iohn Grene

Robert Brakenbury constable of the Tower

Syr Iames Tyrell

6   These are, respectively, the seventh Sunday after Easter, the second Monday after Easter, Friday before Easter, and the day before Ash Wednesday.

7   Bel, the subject of the apocryphal book Bel and the Dragon, was an idol roughly equivalent to Baal, the chief god of the Phoenicians. Beelzebub ("the lord of the flies") is "the prince of the devils," according to Matthew 12:24.

History of Richard III

1   Richard III (1452–85), Duke of Gloucester, succeeded his brother King Edward IV in 1483 by setting aside the claims of his nephews. Whether he was in fact responsible for their deaths, as More here relates, has been a matter of great controversy. For example, Paul Murray

Kindall reads More's *History* as a humanist tract in which the characteristics of the Bad Prince are embodied in Richard (*Richard III* [New York, 1956], p. 501).

2   His identity is uncertain, but he may have been the John Green (d. 1486) who was yeoman of the chamber under Edward IV.

3   He was to die with Richard at Bosworth (1485).

4   Sir James Tyrell (1445–1502) was a strong Yorkist and loyal follower of Richard.

5   A Yorkshire knight and brother-in-law of Richard's neighbor Lord Scrope of Bolton.

6   William Catesby (c. 1440–85), one of Richard's favorites and his only follower to be executed after Bosworth.

not for hym, whose pride thei wist would beare no pere, kept him by secrete driftes oute of all secrete trust. Whiche thyng this page wel had marked and knowen. Wherefore thys occasion offered, of very speciall frendship he toke his time to put him forward, & by such wise doe him good, that al the enemies he had except the deuil, could *Authority loueth no partners* neuer haue done him so muche hurte. For vpon this pages wordes king Richard arose. (For this communicacion had he sitting at the draught, a conuenient carpet for such a counsaile) and came out in to the pailet chamber, on which he found in bed sir Iames and sir Thomas Tyrels,[7] of parson like and brethren of blood, but nothing of kin in condicions. Then said the king merely to them: What sirs be ye in bed so soone, and calling vp syr Iames, brake to him secretely his mind in this mischieuous matter. In whiche he founde him nothing strange. Wherfore on the morow he sente him to Brakenbury with a letter, by which he was commaunded to deliuer sir Iames all ye kayes of the Tower for one nyght, to ye ende he might there accomplish the kinges pleasure, in such thing as he had geuen him commaundement. After which letter deliuered and the kayes receiued, sir Iames appointed the night nexte ensuing to destroy them, deuysing before and preparing the meanes. The prince as soone as the protector left that name and toke himself as king, had it shewed vnto him, that he should not reigne, but his vncle should haue the crowne. At which worde the prince sore abashed, began to sigh and said: Alas I woulde my vncle woulde lette me haue my lyfe yet, though I lese my kingdome. Then he y^t tolde him the tale, vsed him with good wordes, and put him in the best comfort he could. But forthwith was the prince and his brother bothe shet vp, and all other remoued from them, onely one called black wil or William slaughter[8] except, set to serue them and see them sure. After whiche time the prince neuer tyed his pointes, nor ought rought of hymselfe, but with that young babe hys brother, lingered in thought and heauines til this tratorous death, deliuered them of that wretchednes. For sir Iames *Miles Forest* Tirel deuised that thei shold be murthered in their beddes. To the execucion wherof, *Ihon Dighton* he appointed Miles Forest one of the foure that kept them, a felowe fleshed in murther before time. To him he ioyned one Iohn Dighton[9] his own horsekeper, a big brode square strong knaue. Then al ye other beeing remoued from them, thys Miles Forest and Iohn Dighton, about midnight (the sely children lying in their beddes) came into the chamber, and sodainly lapped them vp among ye clothes so be wrapped them and entangled them keping down by force the fetherbed and pillowes hard vnto their mouthes, that within a while smored and stifled, theyr breath failing, thei gaue vp to god their innocent soules into the ioyes of heauen, leauing to the tormentors their bodyes dead in the bed. Whiche after that the wretches parceiued, first by ye strugling with the paines of death, and after long lying styll, to be throughly dead: they laide their bodies naked out vppon the bed, and fetched sir Iames to see them. Which vpon the sight of them, caused those murtherers to burye them at the stayre foote, metely depe in the grounde *The yong kyng* vnder a great heape of stones. Than rode sir Iames in great hast to king *and his brother murthered* Richarde, and shewed him al the maner of the murther, who gaue hym gret thanks, and as som say there made him knight. But he allowed not as I haue heard, ye burying in so vile a corner, saying that he woulde haue them buried in a better place, because thei wer a kinges sonnes. Loe the honourable corage of a kynge. Wherupon thei say that a prieste of syr Robert Brakenbury toke vp the bodyes again, and secretely entered them in such place, as by the occasion of his deathe, whiche only knew it could neuer synce come to light. Very trouthe is it & well knowen, that at such time as syr Iames Tirell was in the Tower, for Treason committed agaynste the moste famous prince king Henry the seuenth, bothe Dighton and he were examined, & confessed the murther in maner aboue writen, but whither the bodies were remoued thei could nothing tel. And thus as I haue learned of them that much knew and litle cause had to lye, wer these two noble princes, these innocent tender children, borne of moste royall bloode, brought vp in great wealth, likely long to liue to reigne and rule in the realme, by traytorous tiranny taken, depryued of their estate, shortly shitte vp in prison, and priuily slaine and murthered, theyr bodies cast god wote where by the cruel ambicion of their vnnaturall vncle and his dispiteous tormentors. Which thinges on euery part wel

---

7 Younger brother of James.

8 William Slaughter (or Slatter), bailiff of Chadlington, Oxfordshire.

9 The identities of Forest and Dighton are unknown.

pondered: god neuer gaue this world a more notable example, neither in what vnsuretie standeth this worldly wel, or what mischief worketh the prowde enterprise of an hyghe heart, or finally what wretched end ensueth such dispiteous crueltie. For first to beginne with the ministers, Miles Forest at sainct Martens pecemele rotted away. Dighton in dede yet walketh on a liue in good possibilitie to bee hanged ere he dye. But sir Iames Tirel dyed at Tower hill, beheaded for treason. King Richarde himselfe as ye shal herafter here, slain in the fielde, hacked and hewed of his enemies handes, haryed on horsebacke dead, his here in despite torn and togged lyke a cur dogge. And the mischief that he tooke, within lesse then thre yeares of the mischiefe that he dyd. And yet all the meane time spente in much pain and trouble outward, much feare anguish and sorow within. For I haue heard by credible report of such as wer secrete w^t his chamberers, that after this abhominable deede done, he neuer hadde quiet in his minde, hee neuer thought himself sure. Where he went abrode, his eyen whirled about, *The out & inward troubles of tyrauntes* his body priuily fenced, his hand euer on his dager, his countenance and maner like one alway ready to strike againe, he toke ill rest a nightes, lay long wakyng and musing, sore weried with care & watch, rather slumbred then slept, troubled wyth fearerful dreames, sodainly sommetyme sterte vp, leape out of his bed & runne about the chamber, so was his restles herte continually tossed & tumbled w^t the tedious impression & stormy remembrance of his abominable dede.

[FROM] A DIALOGUE OF COMFORT AGAINST TRIBULATION

{From Part I}

Introduction

VINCENT: Who would have weened, O my good uncle, afore a few years passed, that such as in this country would visit their friends lying in disease and sickness should come, as I do now, to seek and fetch comfort of them? Or in giving comfort to them, use the way that I may well use to you? For albeit that the priests and friars be wont to call upon sick men to remember death, yet we worldly friends, for fear of discomforting them, have ever had a guise in Hungary to lift up their hearts, and put them in good hope of life. But now, good uncle, the world is here waxen such, and so great perils appear to fall at hand, that methinketh the greatest comfort that a man can have is when he may see that he shall soon be gone.

We that are likely long to live here in wretchedness have need of some comfortable counsel against tribulation, to be given by such as you be, good uncle, that have so long lived virtuously and are so learned in the law of God [that] very few be better in this country here. [You] have had of such things as we do now fear good experience and assay in yourself, as he that hath been taken prisoner in Turkey two times in your days, and now likely to depart hence ere long. But that may be your great comfort, good uncle, sith you depart to God. But us here shall you leave of your kindred a sort of sorry comfortless orphans, to all whom your good help, comfort, and counsel hath long been a great stay – not as an uncle unto some and to some as one farther of kin, but as though unto us all you had been a natural father.

ANTHONY: Mine own good cousin, I cannot much say nay but that there is indeed, not here in Hungary only but almost also in all places of Christendom, such a customable[1] manner of unchristian comforting . . . that in any sick man it doth more harm than good, [by] drawing him in time of sickness with looking and longing for life from the meditation of death, judgment, heaven, and hell[2]. . . . Yet is that manner in my mind more than mad, where such kind of comfort is used to a man of mine age. For as we well wot that a young man may die soon, so be we very sure that an old man cannot live long. And yet . . . there is (as Tully saith) no man for all that so old but that

2   These "last things" were the subject of More's unfinished *De quatuor novissimus* (1522).

he hopeth yet that he may live one year more, and of a frail folly delighteth to think thereon.[3] And comforting himself therewith (other men's words of like manner comfort adding more sticks to that fire), [he] shall in a manner burn up quite the pleasant moisture that most should refresh him – the wholesome dew, I mean, of God's grace, by which he should wish with God's will to be hence, and long to be with him in heaven.

Now where you take my departing from you so heavily, as of him whom you recognize of your goodness to have had here before help and comfort, would God I had to you and to other more done half so much as myself reckoneth had been my duty to do. But whensoever God take me hence, to reckon yourselves comfortless, as though your chief comfort stood in me – therein make you, methinketh, a reckoning very much like as though you would cast away a strong staff and lean upon a rotten reed. For God is and must be your comfort, and not I. And He is a sure comforter that, as He said unto His disciples, never leaveth His servants in case of[4] comfortless orphans; not even when He departed from His disciples by death. But both, as He promised, sent them a comforter, the Holy Spirit of His Father and Himself, and made them also sure that to the world's end He would ever dwell with them Himself.[5] And therefore if you be part of His flock and believe His promise, how can you be comfortless in any tribulation, when Christ and His Holy Spirit, and with them their inseparable Father (if you put full trust and confidence in them), be never neither one finger breadth of space nor one minute of time from you?

VINCENT: O my good uncle, even these selfsame words, wherewith you well prove that because of God's own gracious presence we cannot be left comfortless, make me now feel and perceive what a miss of much comfort we shall have when you be gone. For albeit, good uncle, that while you do tell me this I cannot but grant it for true, yet if I now had not heard it of you I had not remembered it, now it had now fallen in my mind. And over that, like as our tribulations shall in weight and number increase, so shall we need not only such good word or twain, but a great heap thereof, to stable and strength[6] the walls of our hearts against the great surges of this tempestuous sea.

ANTHONY: Good cousin, trust well in God and He shall provide you teachers abroad[7] convenient in every time, or else shall Himself sufficiently teach you within.

VINCENT: Very well, good uncle. But yet if we would leave the seeking of outward learning where we may have it, and look to be inwardly taught only by God, then should we thereby tempt God, and displease Him. . . . I now see the likelihood that when you be gone we shall be sore destitute of any such other like. Therefore thinketh me that God of duty bindeth me to sue to you now, good uncle, in this short time that we have you, that . . . against these great storms of tribulation with which both I and all mine are sore beaten already (and now upon the coming of this cruel Turk fear to fall in far more), I may learn of you much plenty of good counsel and comfort. Then I may, with the same laid up in remembrance, govern and stay the ship of our kindred and keep it afloat from peril of spiritual drowning.

You be not ignorant, good uncle, what heaps of heaviness hath of late fallen among us already, with which some of our poor family be fallen into such dumps, that scantily can any such comfort as my poor wit can give them anything assuage their sorrow.[8] And now sith these tidings have come hither so brim[9] of the great Turk's enterprise into these parts here, we can almost neither talk nor think of any other thing else than of his might and our mischief.[10] There falleth so continually before the eyes of our heart a fearful imagination of this terrible thing: his mighty strength and power; his high malice and hatred; and his incomparable cruelty – with robbing, spoiling, burning, and laying waste all the way that his army cometh. Then, killing or carrying away the people far thence from home, and there sever[ing] the couples and the kindred asunder, every one

3   Marcus Tullius Cicero, *On Old Age*, 7:24.
4   *as though they were.*
5   John 14:18–28.
6   *stabilize and strengthen.*
7   *outwardly.*

8   The autobiographical allusion here is to the series of catastrophes More and his family suffered from the time of his resignation of the Lord Chancellorship in May 1532.
9   *full.*
10   *suffering.*

far from other. Some kept in thraldom, and some kept in prison, and some for a triumph[11] tormented and killed in his presence.

Then send his people hither, and his false faith therewith, so that such as are here and remain still shall either both lose all and be lost too, or forced to forsake the faith of our Saviour Christ, and fall to the false sect of Mahomet. And yet (which we more fear than all the remnant), no small part of our own folk that dwell even here about us are, as we fear, falling to him or already confedered with him. . . . If it so be, [it] shall haply keep [t]his quarter from the Turk's incursion. But then shall they that turn to his law leave all their neighbors nothing, but shall have our good[s] given them, and our bodies both, but if we turn as they do, and forsake our Savior too. And then – for there is no born Turk so cruel to Christian folk as is the false Christian that falleth from the faith[12] – we shall stand in peril (if we persevere in the truth) to be more hardly handled and die more cruel death by our own countrymen at home, than if we were taken hence and carried into Turkey.

These fearful heaps of peril lie so heavy at our hearts while we wot not into which we shall fortune to fall (and therefore fear all the worst), that as our Savior prophesied of the people of Jerusalem, many wish among us already, before the peril come, that the mountains would overwhelm them or the valleys open and swallow them up and cover them.[13] Therefore, good uncle, against these horrible fears of these terrible tribulations, of which some, ye wot well, our house already hath and the remnant stand in dread of, give us (while God lendeth you us) such plenty of your comfortable counsel as I may write and keep with us, to stay us when God shall call you hence.

ANTHONY: Ah, my good cousin, this is an heavy hearing, and likewise as we that dwell here in this part fear that thing sore now which, [a] few years past, feared it not at all. So doubt I not that ere it long be, they shall fear it as much that think themself now very sure because they dwell farther off. Greece feared not the Turk when that I was born; and within a while after, that whole empire was his.[14] The great sultan of Syria thought himself more than his match; and long since you were born hath he that empire too.[15] Then hath he taken Belgrade,[16] the fortress of this realm, and since hath he destroyed our noble young goodly king.[17] And now strive there twain for us. Our Lord send the grace that the third dog[18] carry not away the bone from them both.

What should I speak of the noble strong city of the Rhodes, the winning whereof he counted as a victory against the whole corps of Christendom, sith all Christendom was not able to defend that strong town against him? Howbeit, if the princes of Christendom everywhere about would, whereas need was, have set to their hands in time, the Turk had never taken any one place of all those places. But partly [because] dissensions [have] fallen among ourself, partly [because] no man careth what harm other folk feel (but each part suffereth other to shift for itself), the Turk is in few years wonderfully increased, and Christendom on the other side very sore decayed. And all this worketh our wickedness, with which God is not content.

But now, . . . you desire of me some plenty of comfortable things, which ye may put in remembrance and comfort therewith your company. Verily, in the rehearsing and heaping of your manifold fears, myself began to feel that they should much need (against so many troubles) many comfortable counsels! For surely a little before your coming, as I devised with myself upon the Turk's coming, it happed my mind to fall suddenly from that into the devising upon my own departing. . . . I fully put my trust and hope to be a saved soul by the great mercy of God. Yet sith no man is here so sure that without revelation may clean stand out of dread, I bethought me also upon the pain of hell. And after, I bethought me then upon the Turk again. And first methought his terror nothing when I compared with it the joyful hope of heaven. Then compared I it on the

---

11   *triumphant celebration.*

12   One of Henry VIII's titles was "Defender of the Faith."

13   Luke 23:28–30.

14   The Byzantine Empire fell to Muhammad II, who took Constantinople in 1453. This establishes Anthony's age as approximately 78 years.

15   The Sultan of Syria (Ashraf Tuman Bey) lost his empire in 1517.

16   Here More conflates the Sultan with Suleiman I, who captured Belgrade in 1521.

17   Louis II died, aged 20, at the battle of Mohacs in 1526.

18   Suleiman I.

other side with the fearful dread of hell; and therein casting in my mind those terrible devilish tormentors with the deep consideration of that furious endless fire, methought that if the Turk with his whole host and all trumpets and his timbrels too, were (to kill me in my bed) come to my chamber door, in respect of the other reckoning I regard him not a rush.[19]

And yet when I now heard your lamentable words, laying forth as it were present before my face that heap of heavy sorrowful tribulations that, beside those that are already fallen, are in short space like to follow, I waxed therewith myself suddenly somewhat affright. And therefore I will allow your request in this behalf, that would have store of comfort aforehand ready by you, to resort to and to lay up in your heart as a triacle[20] against the poison of all desperate dread that might rise of occasion of sore tribulation. And herein shall I be glad, as my poor wit will serve me, to call to mind with you such things as I before have read, heard, or thought upon, that may conveniently serve us to this purpose.

Chapter 1

[ANTHONY] First shall you, good cousin, understand this, that the natural wise men of this world, the old moral philosophers, labored much in this matter, and many natural reasons have they written, whereby they might encourage men to set little by such goods or such hurts either, the going or the coming whereof are the matter and the cause of tribulation. [Such] are the goods of fortune, riches, favor, friends, fame, worldly worship, and such other things; or of the body, as beauty, strength, agility, quickness, and health. These things (ye wot well) coming to us, are matter of worldly wealth, and taken from us by fortune or by force or the fear of the losing, be matter of adversity and tribulation. For tribulation seemeth generally to signify nothing else but some kind of grief, either pain of the body or heaviness of the mind.

Now the body not to feel that it feeleth, all the wit in the world cannot bring about. But that the mind should not be grieved neither with the pain that the body feeleth, nor with occasions of heaviness offered and given unto the soul itself, this thing labored the philosophers very much about. And many goodly sayings have they toward the strength and comfort against tribulation, exciting men to the full contempt of all worldly loss and despising of sickness, and all bodily grief, painful death, and all.

Howbeit, in very deed, for anything that ever I read in them, I never could yet find that ever those natural reasons were able to give sufficient comfort of themself. For they never stretch so far but that they leave untouched, for lack of necessary knowledge, that special point which is not only the chief comfort of all, but without which also all other comforts are nothing. That is to wit, the referring the final end of their comfort unto God, and to repute and take for the special cause of comfort, that by the patient sufferance of their tribulation they shall attain His favor, and for their pain receiveth reward at His hand in heaven. And for lack of knowledge of this end they did (as they needs must) leave untouched also the very special mean, without which we can never attain to this comfort, that is to wit, the gracious aid and help of God to move, stir, and guide us forward, in the referring all our ghostly comfort, yea, and our worldly comfort too, all unto that heavenly end. And therefore, as I say, for the lack of these things, all their comfortable counsels are very far insufficient.

Howbeit, though they be far unable to cure our disease of themself, and therefore are not sufficient to be taken for our physicians, some good drugs have they yet in their shops for which they may be suffered to dwell among our poticaries[21] – if their medicines be made not of their own brains, but after the bills made by the great physician God, prescribing the medicines Himself, and correcting the faults of their erroneous receipts.[22] For without this way taken with them, they shall not fail to do as many bold blind poticaries do which, either for lucre or of a foolish

---

19 *candle.*
20 *antidote.*

21 *apothecaries.*
22 *prescriptions.*

pride, give sick folk medicines of their own devising, and therewith kill up in corners many such simple folk as they find so foolish to put their lives in such lewd and unlearned blind Bayards' hands.[23]

We shall therefore neither fully receive these philosophers' reasons in this matter, nor yet utterly refuse them. But, using them in such order as shall beseem them, the principal and the effectual medicines against these diseases of tribulation shall we fetch from that high, great, and excellent physician without whom we could never be healed of our very deadly disease of damnation. For our necessity wherein, the Spirit of God spiritually speaketh of Himself to us, and biddeth us of all our health give Him the honor, and therein this saith unto us: "Honor thou the physician, for him hath the high God ordained for thy necessity."[24]

Therefore let us require that high physician, our Blessed Savior Christ, whose holy manhood God ordained for our necessity, to cure our deadly wounds with the medicine made of the most wholesome blood of His own blessed body. . . . Likewise as He cured by the incomparable medicine our mortal malady, it may like Him to send us and put in our minds such medicines at this time, as against the sickness and sorrows of tribulations may . . . comfort and strength us in His grace. So our deadly enemy the devil may never have the power by his poisoned dart of murmur,[25] grudge, and impatience to turn our short sickness of worldly tribulation into the endless everlasting death of infernal damnation.

Chapter 2

[ANTHONY:] Sith all our principal comfort must come of God, we must first presuppose in to whom we shall with any ghostly counsel give any effectual comfort, one ground to begin withal, whereupon all that we shall build must be supported and stand. That is to wit, the ground and foundation of faith, without which had ready before, all the spiritual comfort that any man may speak of can never avail a fly. For likewise as it were utterly vain to lay natural reasons of comfort to him that hath no wit, so were it undoubtedly frustrate to lay spiritual causes of comfort to him that hath no faith. For except a man first believe that Holy Scripture is the word of God, and that the word of God is true, how can a man take any comfort of that the Scripture telleth him therein? Needs must the man take little fruit of the Scripture, if he either believe not that it were the word of God, or else ween that though it were, it might yet be for all that untrue.

This faith as it is more faint or more strong, so shall the comfortable words of Holy Scripture stand the man in more stead or less. This virtue of faith can neither any man give himself nor yet any one man another. . . . Though men may with preaching be ministers unto God therein, and the man with his own free will obeying freely the inward inspiration of God be a weak worker with Almighty God therein, yet is the faith indeed the gracious gift of God himself. For as Saint James saith: "Every good gift and every perfect gift is given from above, descending from the Father of Lights."[26] Therefore, feeling our faith by many tokens very faint, let us pray to Him that giveth it that it may please Him to help and increase it. And let us first say with him in the Gospel: "I believe, good Lord, but help Thou the lack of my belief."[27] And after let us pray with the apostles: "Lord, increase our faith."[28]

And finally, let us . . . not suffer the strength and fervor of our faith to wax lukewarm (or rather key-cold), and in manner lose vigor by scattering our minds abroad about so many trifling things that of the matters of our faith we very seldom think. . . . We would withdraw our thought from the respect and regard of all worldly fantasies, and so gather our faith together into a little narrow room. And like the little grain of mustard seed, which is of nature hot, set it in the garden of our soul, all weeds pulled out for the better feeding of our faith. Then shall it grow, and so spread up in height, that the birds (that is to wit the holy angels of heaven) shall breed in our soul, and bring

23 The proverb "as bold as a blind baynard" refers to those who do not look before they leap.

24 Ecclesiasticus 38:1.

25 *cursing*.

26 James 1:17.

27 Mark 9:23.

28 Luke 17:5.

forth virtues in the branches of our faith.[29] And then with the faithful trust, that through the true belief of God's word we shall put in His promise, we shall be well able to command a great mountain of tribulation to void from the place where he stood in our heart. Whereas with a very feeble faith and a faint we shall be scant able to remove a little hillock. . . .

VINCENT: Forsooth, good uncle, methinketh that this foundation of faith, which, as you say, must be laid first, is so necessarily requisite, that without it all spiritual comfort were utterly given in vain. And therefore now shall we pray God for a full and a fast faith. And I pray you, good uncle, proceed you farther in the process of your matter of spiritual comfort against tribulation.

ANTHONY: That shall I, cousin, with goodwill.

[FROM PART III]

Chapter 19

ANTHONY: If we could consider what thing imprisonment is of his own nature we should not, methinketh, have so great horror thereof. For of itself it is, pardie, but a restraint of liberty which letteth a man from going whither he would.

VINCENT: Yet, by Saint Mary, uncle, methinketh it is much more sorrow than so. For beside the let and restraint of liberty, it hath many more displeasures and very sore griefs knit and adjoined thereto.

ANTHONY: That is, cousin, very true indeed. . . . Howbeit, I purpose now to consider first imprisonment, but as imprisonment only, without any other incommodity beside; for a man may be, pardie, imprisoned and yet not set in the stocks nor collared fast by the neck. . . . Those other kinds of griefs that come with imprisonment are but accidents thereunto. . . . We will, I say, therefore begin with the considering what manner pain or incommodity we should reckon imprisonment to be of himself and of his own nature alone. And then in the course of our communication, you shall as you list increase and aggrieve the cause of your horror with the terror of those painful accidents.

VINCENT: I am sorry that I did interrupt your tale. For you were about (I see well) to take an orderly way therein. And as yourself have devised, so I beseech you proceed. For though I reckon imprisonment much the sorer thing by sore and hard handling therein, yet reckon I not the prisonment of itself any less than a thing very tedious – all were it used in the most favorable manner that it possibly might. For, uncle, [suppose there] were a great prince that were taken prisoner upon the field, and in the hand of a Christian king, which use in such case . . . to shew much humanity to them and in very favorable wise entreat them. . . . (These infidel emperors handle oftentimes the princes that they take more villainously than they do the poorest men. . . . The great Tamburlaine[30] kept the great Turk when he had taken him, to tread on his back alway while he leapt on horseback.)

But as I began to say by the sample of a prince taken prisoner, were the imprisonment never so favorable, yet were it in my mind no little grief in itself for a man to be pinned up, though not in a narrow chamber. But although his walk were right large and right fair gardens too therein, it could not but grieve his heart to be restrained by another man within certain limits and bounds, and lose the liberty to be where him list.

ANTHONY: This is, cousin, well considered of you. For in this you perceive well that imprisonment is of himself and his own very nature alone nothing else but the retaining of a man's person within the circuit of a certain space narrower or larger (as shall be limited to him), restraining his liberty from the further going into any other place.

VINCENT: Very well said, as methinketh.

ANTHONY: Yet forgat I, cousin, to ask you one question.

---

29   Luke 13:18–19.
30   "Timur the Lame" (1336–1405), conqueror of Persia, the subject
of Marlowe's later (1586) tragedy.

VINCENT: What is that, uncle?

ANTHONY: This, lo. If there be two men kept in two several chambers of one great castle, of which two chambers the one is much more large than the other, whether be they prisoners both? Or but the one that hath the less room to walk in?

VINCENT: What question is it, uncle, but that they be prisoners both (as I said myself before), although the one lay fast locked in the stocks and the other had all the whole castle to walk in.

ANTHONY: Me thinketh verily, cousin, that you say the truth. And then if prisonment be such a thing as yourself here agree it is, that is to wit, but a lack of liberty to go whither we list, now would I fain wit of you what any one man you know that is at this day out of prison?

VINCENT: What one man, uncle? Marry, I know almost none other. For surely prisoner am I none acquainted with that I remember.

ANTHONY: Then I see well you visit poor prisoners seld[om].

VINCENT: No, by troth, uncle, I cry God mercy. I send them sometime mine alms, but by my troth I love not to come myself where I should see such misery.

ANTHONY: In good faith, cousin Vincent, . . . I assure you it is hard to tell how much good to a man's soul the personal visiting of poor prisoners doth. But now sith ye can name me none of them that are in prison, I pray you name me some one of all them that you be (as you say) better acquainted with: men (I mean) that are out of prison. For I know, methinketh, as few of them as you know of the other.

VINCENT: That were, uncle, a strange case. For every man is, uncle, out of prison that may go where he will, though he be the poorest beggar in the town. And in good faith, uncle, . . . the poor beggar that is at his liberty and may walk where he will is (as meseemeth) in better case than is a king kept in prison, that cannot go but where men give him leave.

ANTHONY: Well, cousin, whether every waywalking beggar be by this reason out of prison or no we shall consider further when you will. But in the meantime I can by this reason see no prince that seemeth to be out of prison. For if the lack of liberty to go where a man will be imprisonment (as yourself say it is), then is the great Turk by whom we so fear to be put in prison, in prison already himself. For he may not go where he will. For an he might, he would into Portugal, Italy, Spain, France, Almaine, and England, and as far one another quarter too, both Prester John's[31] land and the Grand Khan's[32] too.

Now the beggar that you speak of: If he be [able] . . . to go where he will . . . , then is the beggar in better case not only than a prince in prison, but also than many a prince out of prison too. . . . But . . . neither the beggar nor the prince is at free liberty to walk where they will. . . . If they would walk in some place [where] neither of them both should be suffered, . . . men would withstand them and say them nay. Therefore if imprisonment be (as you grant it is) a lack of liberty to go where we list, I cannot see but (as I say) the beggar and the prince whom you reckon both at liberty be, by your own reason, restrained in prison both.

VINCENT: Yea, but (uncle) both the one and the other have way enough to walk: the one in his own ground, the other in other men's; or in the common highway where they may walk till they be both weary of walking ere any man say them nay.

ANTHONY: So may, cousin, that king that had, as yourself put the case, all the whole castle to walk in. And yet you say not nay but that he is prisoner for all that – though not so straitly kept, yet as verily prisoner as he that lieth in the stocks.

VINCENT: But they may go at the least wise to every place that they need or that is commodious for them. And therefore they do not will to go but where they may go. And therefore be they at liberty to go where they will.

ANTHONY: Me needeth not, cousin, to spend the time about the impugning every part of this answer. For letting pass by that though a prisoner were with his keeper brought into every place

---

31 Legendary Christian conqueror of the Far East, who came to be identified with the King of Ethiopia; see, for example, Francisco Alvares, *The Prester John of the Indies*, ed. C. F. Beckingham and G. W. B. Huntingford (Cambridge, 1961).

32 Medieval ruler of China.

SIR THOMAS MORE 39

where need required, yet sith he might not when he would go where he would for his only pleasure, he were, ye wot well, a prisoner still. . . . Then let us look on our other prisoners enclosed within a castle. And we shall find that the straitest kept of them both . . . get the wisdom and the grace to quiet his own mind and hold himself content with that place, and long not (like a woman with child for her lusts) to be gadding out anywhere else. [Then he] is, by the same reason of yours, . . . at his free liberty to be where he will, and so is out of prison too.

And on the other side, if though his will be not longing to be anywhere else, yet because that if his will so were he should not so be suffered, he is therefore not at his free liberty, but a prisoner still. So your free beggar that you speak of and the prince that you call out of prison too, . . . be (which I ween very few be) by some special wisdom so temperately disposed that they have not the will to be but where they see they may be suffered to be. Yet sith that if they would have that will, they could not then be where they would, they lack the effect of free liberty, and be both twain in prison too.

VINCENT: Well, uncle, if every man universally be by this reason in prison already, . . . yet to be imprisoned in this special manner (which manner is only commonly called imprisonment) is a thing of great horror and fear, both for the straitness of the keeping and the hard handling that many men have therein. Of all which griefs and pains and displeasures in this other general imprisonment that you speak of, we feel nothing at all. And therefore every man abhorreth the one and would be loath to come into it, and no man abhorreth the other. For they feel none harm nor find no fault therein.

Wherefore, uncle, in good faith, though I cannot find answers convenient wherewith to avoid your arguments, yet to be plain with you and tell you the very truth, my mind findeth not itself satisfied in this point. But . . . ever methinketh that these things, wherewith you rather convince and conclude me than induce a credence and persuade me that every man is in prison already, be but sophistical fantasies. Except those that are commonly called prisoners, other men are not in any prison at all.

Chapter 20

ANTHONY: Well fare thine heart, good cousin Vincent. There was, in good faith, no word that you spake since we first talked of these matters that half so well liked me as these that you speak now. For if you had assented in words and in your mind departed unpersuaded, then if the thing be true that I say, yet had you lost the fruit. And if it be peradventure false and myself deceived therein, then while I should ween that it like you too, you should have confirmed me in my folly. For in good faith, cousin, such an old fool am I that this thing, in the persuading [t]hereof unto you, I had weened I had quit me well. And when I have all done, appeareth to your mind but a trifle and a sophistical fantasy. Myself have so many years taken for so very substantial truth, that as yet my mind cannot give me to think it any other.

I play as the French priest played, that had so long used to say *dominus* with the second syllable long, that at last he thought it must needs be so, and was ashamed to say it short. To the intent that you may the better perceive me or I the better myself, we shall here between us a little more consider the thing. And hardly spit well on your hands and take good hold, and give it not over against your own mind. For then were we never the nearer.

VINCENT: Nay by my troth, uncle, that intend I not, nor nothing did yet since we began. And that may you well perceive by some things which without any great cause, save for the further satisfaction of mine own mind, I repeated and debated again.

ANTHONY: That guise, cousin, hold on hardly still. For in this matter I purpose to give over my part, except I make yourself perceive [first] that every man universally is a very prisoner in very prison plainly without any sophistication at all. And that there is also no prince living upon earth but he is in worse case prisoner by this general imprisonment that I speak of, than is many a lewd simple wretch by the special imprisonment that you speak of. And over this, that in this general imprisonment that I speak of, men are for the time that they be therein so sore handled . . . that

men's hearts have with reason great cause as sore to abhor this hard handling that is in this imprisonment, as the other that is in that.

VINCENT: By my troth, uncle, these things would I fain see well proved.

ANTHONY: Tell me then, cousin, first (by your troth), there were a man attainted of treason or
of felony, and after judgment given of his death . . . , only the time of his execution delayed till
the king's further pleasure known. And he there upon delivered to certain keepers and put up in
a sure place out of which he could not scape. Were this man a prisoner or no?

VINCENT: This man, quoth he? Yea, marry, that he were in very deed if ever any man
were!

ANTHONY: But now, what if for the time that were mean between his attainder and his execution, he were so favorably handled that he were suffered to do what he would, as he was while he
was abroad? To have the use of his lands and his goods, and his wife and his children licence to be
with him, and his friends leave at liberty to resort unto him, and his servants not forboden to abide
about him. And add yet thereunto that the place were a great castle royal with parks and other
pleasures therein, a very great circuit about.

Yea, add yet (an ye will) that he were suffered to go and ride also, both when he would and
whither he would, only this one point alway provided and foreseen, that he should ever be surely
seen to and safely kept from scaping. So that took he never so much of his own mind in the meanwhile all other ways save scaping, yet he well knew that scape he could not. And that when he
were called for, to execution and to death he should [come]. Now, cousin Vincent, what would you
call this man? A prisoner because he is kept for execution, or no prisoner because he is in the meanwhile so favorably handled, and suffered to do all that he would save scape? And I bid you not here
be hasty in your answer, but advise it well, that you grant no such thing in haste as you would
after mislike by leisure and think yourself deceived.

VINCENT: Nay, by my troth, uncle, this thing needeth no study at all in my mind. But that for
all this favor shewed him and all this liberty lent him, yet being condemned to death and being
kept therefor, . . . he is all that while a very plain prisoner still.

ANTHONY: In good faith, cousin, methinketh you say very true. But then one thing must I yet
desire you, cousin, to tell me a little further. There were another laid in prison for a fray, and
through the jailer's displeasure were bolted and fettered and laid in a low dungeon in the stocks.
[T]here he might hap to lie peradventure for a while, and abide in the mean season some pain but
no danger of death at all but that out again he should come well enough. Which of these two prisoners stood in worse case? He that hath all this favor or he that is thus hardly handled?

VINCENT: By our Lady, uncle, I ween that most part of men, if they should needs choose, had
liefer[33] be such prisoners in every point as be that so sorely lieth in the stocks, than in every point
such as he that at such liberty walketh about the park.

ANTHONY: Consider then, cousin, whether this thing seem any sophistry to you that I shall
shew you now. For it shall be such as seemeth in good faith substantial true to me. And if it so
happen that you think otherwise, I will be very glad to perceive which of us both is beguiled. For
it seemeth to me, cousin, first, that every man coming into this world here upon earth, as he is
created by God, so cometh he hither by the providence of God. Is this any sophistry first or not?

VINCENT: Nay verily, this is very substantial truth.

ANTHONY: Now take I think this also for very truth in my mind: that there cometh no man
nor woman hither into the earth but that ere ever they come quick[34] into the world out of the
mother's womb, God condemneth them unto death by His own sentence and judgment for the
original sin that they bring with them, contracted in the corrupted stock of our forefather Adam.
Is this, think you, verily thus or not?

VINCENT: This is, uncle, very true indeed.

ANTHONY: Then seemeth this true further unto me: that God hath put every man here upon
the earth under so sure and under so safe keeping, that of all the whole people living in this wide

---

33 *rather.*   34 *alive.*

world there is neither man, woman, nor child . . . that possibly can find any way whereby they may scape from death. Is this, cousin, a fond imagined fantasy or is it very truth indeed?

VINCENT: Nay, this is none imagination, uncle, but a thing so clearly proved true that no man is so mad to say nay.

ANTHONY: Then need I no more, cousin. For then is all the matter plain and open evident truth which I said I took for truth. Which is yet more a little now than I told you before when you took my proof yet but for a sophistical fantasy. [You] said that, for all my reasoning that every man is a prisoner, yet you thought that except these whom the common people call prisoners, there is else no man a very prisoner indeed. And now you grant yourself again for very substantial open truth that every man is here (though he be the greatest king upon earth), set here by the ordinance of God in a place (be it never so large) . . . out of which no man can escape. But that therein is every man put under sure and safe keeping to be readily set forth when God calleth for him. And that then he shall surely die.

And is not then, cousin, by your own granting before, every man a very prisoner when he is put in a place to be kept to be brought forth when he would not, and himself not wot wither?

VINCENT: Yes, in good faith, uncle. I cannot but well perceive this to be so.

ANTHONY: This were (you wot well) true, although a man should be but taken by the arm and in fair manner led out of this world unto his judgment. But now . . . we well know that there is no king so great but that all the while he walketh here, walk he never so loose, ride he with never so strong an army for his defense, yet himself is very sure . . . that escape can be not. And very well he knoweth that he hath already sentence given upon him to die, and that verily die he shall. And that himself, though he hope upon long respite of his execution, yet can he not tell how soon.

And therefore (but if he be a fool) he can never be without fear, . . . either on the morrow or on the selfsame day, [of] the grisly cruel hangman Death. . . . From his first coming in hath [Death] ever hoved aloof and looked toward him and ever lien in a wait on him. [Death] shall amid among all his royalty and all his main strength neither kneel before him nor make him any reverence nor with any good manner desire him to come forth. But rigorously and fiercely grip him by the very breast and make all his bones rattle, and so by long and divers sore torments strike him stark dead in this prison. And then cause his body to be cast into the ground in a foul pit within some corner of the same, there to rot and be eaten with the wretched worms of the earth. . . .

Methinketh therefore, cousin, that (as I told you) this keeping of every man in this wretched world for execution of death is a very plain imprisonment indeed. And that (as I say) such that the greatest king in this prison is in much worse case in all his wealth than many a man is by the other imprisonment, that is therein sore and hardly handled. For where some of those lie not there attainted nor condemned to death, the greatest man of this world and the most wealthy in this universal prison is laid to be kept undoubtedly for death.

VINCENT: But yet, uncle, in that case is the other prisoner too, for he is as sure that he shall die, pardie!

ANTHONY: This is very true, cousin, indeed, and well objected too. But then you must consider that he is not in danger of death by reason of the prison into which he is put peradventure but for a light fray. But his danger of death is by the other imprisonment, by which he is prisoner in the great prison of this whole earth — in which prison all the princes thereof be prisoners as well as he. . . .

Now may you, methinketh, very plainly perceive that this whole earth is . . . for all the whole kind of man a very plain prison indeed. . . . They that ween they stand in great wealth, do stand for all that indeed, by the reason of their imprisonment in this large prison of the whole earth, in the selfsame condition that other do stand which in the narrow prisons . . . [are] condemned already to death. And now, cousin, if this thing that I tell you seem but a sophistical fantasy to your mind, I would be glad to know what moveth you so to think. For in good faith, as I have told you twice, I am no wiser but that I verily ween that the thing is thus of very plain truth in very deed.

Chapter 21

VINCENT: In good faith, uncle, as for thus farforth, I not only can make with any reason no resistance thereagainst; but also [I] see very clearly proved that it can be none otherwise but that every man is in this world a very prisoner—sith we be all put here into a sure hold to be kept till we be put unto execution, as folk already condemned all to death. But yet, uncle, the strait keeping, collaring, bolting, and stocking, with lying in straw or on the cold ground . . . must needs make the imprisonment which only beareth among the people that name, much more odious and dreadful than the general imprisonment. Wherewith we be every man universally prisoned at large, walking where we will round about the wide world. To [that] broad prison out[side] of those narrow prisons, there is with the prisoners no such hard handling used.

ANTHONY: I said (I trow) cousin, that I purposed to prove you further yet that in this general prison—the large prison I mean of this whole world—folk be for the time that they be therein [so] sore handled, . . . that our hearts (save that we consider it not) have with reason . . . as much horror to conceive against the hard handling that is in this prison, as the other that is in that.

VINCENT: Indeed, uncle, truth it is that this you said you would prove.

ANTHONY: Nay, so much said I not, cousin. But I said I would if I could, and if I could not then would I therein give over my part. But that, trust I cousin, I shall not need to do, the thing seemeth me so plain. For, cousin, not only [over] the prince and king, but also (although he have both angels and devils that are jailers under him) yet the chief jailer over this whole broad prison the world is (as I take it) God; and that I suppose ye will grant me too.

VINCENT: That will I not, uncle, deny.

ANTHONY: A man be, cousin, committed unto prison for no cause but to be kept. Though there be never so great charge upon him, yet his keeper (if he be good and honest) is neither so cruel that would pain the man of malice, nor so covetous that would put him to pain to make him seek his friends and to pay for a pennyworth of ease. . . . But, marry, if the place be such as the keeper cannot otherwise be sure, then is he compelled to keep him after the rate the straiter. And also, if the prisoner be unruly and fall to fighting with his fellows or do some other manner of shrewd turns, then useth the keeper to punish him sundry wise in some of such fashions as yourself have spoken of.

So is it now, cousin, that God, the chief jailer, as I say, of this broad prison the world, is neither cruel nor covetous. And this prison is also so sure and so subtly builded that albeit that it lieth open on every side without any wall in the world, yet wander we never so far about therein, the way to get out at shall we never find. So that He neither needeth to collar us nor to stock us for any fear of scaping away. And therefore, except He see some other cause than our only keeping for death, He letteth us in the meanwhile (for as long as He list to respite us) walk about in the prison and do therein what we will, using ourself in such wise as He hath by reason and revelation from time to time told us His pleasure.

And hereof it cometh, lo, that by reason of this favor for a time we wax, as I said, so wanton that we forget where we be, weening that we were lords at large. Whereas we be indeed (if we would consider it) even silly poor wretches in prison. For, of very truth, our very prison this earth is. And yet thereof we cant us out,[35] part by covenants that we make among us and part by fraud and part by violence too, divers parts diversely to ourself, and change the name thereof from the odious name of prison and call it our own land and and our livelihood.

Upon our prison we build. Our prison we garnish with gold and make it glorious; in this prison they buy and sell; in this prison they brawl and chide; in this they run together and fight; in this they dice; in this they card;[36] in this they pipe and revel; in this they sing and dance. And in this prison many a man reputed right honest letteth not for his pleasure in the dark privily to play the knave. And thus while God, our king and our chief jailer too, suffereth us and letteth us alone, we ween ourself at liberty, and we abhor the state of those whom we call prisoners, taking ourself for no prisoners at all. . . .

35 *divide the land.*   36 *play cards.*

We forget with our folly both ourself and our jail and our underjailers, angels and devils both, and our chief jailer God too. [But] God . . . forgetteth not us, but seeth us all the while well enough. And being sore discontent to see so shrewd rule kept in the jail (beside that He sendeth the hangman Death to put to execution here and there sometime by the thousand at once), He handleth many of the remnant, whose execution He forbeareth yet unto a farther time, even as hardly, and punisheth them as sore in this common prison of the world as there are any handled in those special prisons. . . .

VINCENT: The remnant will I not gainsay, for methinketh I see it so indeed. But that God, our chief jailer in this world, useth any such prisonly fashion of punishment, that point must I needs deny. For I neither see Him lay any man in the stocks, or strike fetters on his legs, or so much as shut him up in a chamber either.

ANTHONY: Is he no minstrel, cousin, that playeth not on an harp? Maketh no man melody but he that playeth on a lute? He may be a minstrel and make melody, you wot well, with some other instruments—some strange fashioned [instrument] peradventure that never was seen before. God our chief jailer, as Himself is invisible, so useth He in His punishments invisible instruments, and therefore not of like fashion as the other jailers do, but yet of like effect and as painful in feeling as those.

For He layeth one of His prisoners with an hot fever as evil at his ease in a warm bed, as the other jailer layeth his [prisoner] on the cold ground. He wringeth them by the brows with a megrim.[37] He collareth them by the neck with a quinsy.[38] He bolteth them by the arm with a palsy that they cannot lift their hands to their head. He manacleth their hands with the gout in their fingers. He wringeth them by the legs with the cramp in their shins. He bindeth them to the bed board with the crick in the back, and layeth one there along and as unable to rise as though he lay fast by the feet in the stocks.

Some prisoner of another jail singeth, danceth in his two fetters, and feareth not his feet for stumbling at a stone; while God's prisoner that hath his one foot fettered with the gout lieth groaning on a couch and quaketh, and crieth out if he fear there would fall on his foot no more but a cushion. And therefore, cousin, as I said, if we consider it well, we shall find this general prison of this whole earth a place in which the prisoners be as sore handled as they be in the other. . . .

[Finally, suppose] there were some folk born and brought up in a prison that never came on the wall, nor looked out at the door, nor never heard of other world abroad. But [they] saw some, for shrewd turns done among themself, locked up in straiter room, and heard them only called prisoners that were so served, and themself ever called free folk at large. The like opinion would they have there of themself then, that we have here of ourself now. And when we take ourself for other than prisoners now, as verily be we now deceived as those prisoners should there be then.

VINCENT: I cannot, uncle, in good faith say nay but that you have performed all that you have promised. But . . . we wot well for all this that when we come to those [narrower] prisons, we shall not fail to be in a straiter prison than we be now, and to have a door shut upon us where we have none shut on us now. This shall we be sure of at the least wise, if there come no worse. And then may there come worse, ye wot well, it cometh there so commonly. Wherefore, for all this, it is yet little marvel though men's hearts grudge much thereagainst. . . .

ANTHONY: The incommodities proper to the imprisonment, of their own nature, [are] to have less room to walk in and to have the door shut upon us. These are (methinketh) so very slender and slight, that in so great a cause as to suffer for God's sake, we might be sore ashamed so much as once to think upon them. Many a good man there is, ye wot well, which without any force at all or any necessity wherefore he should so do, suffereth these two things willingly of his own choice with much other hardness more.

Holy monks, I mean, of the Charterhouse[39] order such as never pass their cells but only to the church set fast by their cells, and thence to their cells again. And Saint Bridget's order, and

---

37 *migraine headache.*
38 *sore throat.*

39 The Carthusians were the order with whom More lived in London (1501–5).

Saint Clare's much like, and in a manner all close[40] religious houses. And anchors[41] and anchoresses most especially, all those whose room is less than a meetly large chamber. And yet are they there as well content many long years together as are other men, and better too, that walk about the world.

And therefore you may see that the loathness of less room and the door shut upon us, while so many folk are so well content therewith, and will for God's love choose so to live, is but an horror enhanced of our own fantasy. And indeed I wist a woman once that came into a prison to visit of her charity a poor prisoner there. Whom she found in a chamber to say the truth, meetly fair— and at the least wise it was strong enough! But with mats of straw the prisoner had made it so warm both under the foot and round about the walls, that in these things for the keeping of his health she was on his behalf glad and very well comforted.

But among many other displeasures that for his sake she was sorry for, one she lamented much in her mind, that he should have the chamber door upon him by night made fast by the jailer that should shut him in. "For, by my troth," quoth she, "if the door should be shut upon me I would ween it would stop up my breath." At that word of hers the prisoner laughed in his mind, but he durst not laugh aloud nor say nothing to her, for somewhat indeed he stood in awe of her, and had his finding[42] there much part of her charity for alms. But he could not but laugh inwardly, why he wist well enough, that she used on the inside to shut every night full surely her own chamber to her, both door and windows too, and used not to open them of all the long night. And what difference, then, as to the stopping of the breath, whether they were shut up [from] within or without?[43]

And so surely, cousin, these two things that you speak of are neither other of so great weight that in Christ's cause ought to move a Christian man. And the one of the twain is so very a childish fantasy that in a matter almost of three chips[44] (but if it were in chance of fire), [it] never should move any man. As for those other accidents of hard handling therein, so mad am I not to say they be no grief; but I say that our fear may imagine them much greater grief than they be. And I say that such as they be, many a man endureth them, yea and many a woman too, that after fare full well. . . . In prison was Joseph while his brethren were at large; and yet after were his brethren fain to seek upon him for bread.[45] In prison was Daniel, and the wild lions about him; and yet even there God kept him harmless and brought him safe out again.[46]

If we think that He will not do the like wise for us, let us not doubt but He will do for us either the like or better. For better may He do for us if He suffer us there to die. Saint John the Baptist was, you wot well, in prison while Herod and Herodias sat full merry at the feast, and the daughter of Herodias delighted them with her dancing, till with her dancing she danced off Saint John's head.[47] And now sitteth he with great feast in heaven at God's board, while Herod and Herodias full heavily sit in hell burning both twain. And to make them sport withal, the devil with the damsel dance in the fire afore them!

Finally, cousin, to finish this piece with, our Savior was Himself taken prisoner for our sake. And prisoner was He carried, and prisoner was He kept, and prisoner was He brought forth before Annas, and prisoner from Annas carried unto Caiaphas. Then prisoner was He carried from Caiaphas unto Pilate, and prisoner was He sent from Pilate to King Herod, prisoner from Herod unto Pilate again, and so kept as prisoner to the end of His Passion. The time of His imprisonment, I grant well, was not long; but as for hard handling which our hearts most abhor, He had as much in that short while as many men among them all in much longer time.

And surely then, if we consider of what estate He was and therewith that He was prisoner in such wise for our sake, we shall I trow (but if we be worse than wretched beasts) never so shamefully play the unkind cowards as for fear of imprisonment sinfully to forsake Him. Nor so foolish neither as by forsaking of Him to give Him the occasion again to forsake us, and with the avoiding of an easier prison fall into a worse. Instead of prison that cannot keep us long, fall into that prison out of which we can never come. Where[as] the short prisonment would win us everlasting liberty.

[LETTER] TO MARGARET ROPER[1]

Tower of London
5 July 1535

Our Lord bless you good daughter and your good husband and your little boy and all yours and all my children and all my godchildren and all our friends. Recommend[2] me when you may to my good daughter Cecilye, whom I beseech our Lord to comfort, and I send her my blessing and to all her children and pray her to pray for me. I send her an handekercher and God comfort my good son her husband. My good daughter Daunce hath the picture in parchment that you delivered me from my Lady Coniers; her name is on the back side. Show her that I heartily pray her that you may send it in my name again for a token from me to pray for me.

I like special well Dorothy Coly,[3] I pray you be good unto her. I would wit[4] whether this be she that you wrote me of. If not I pray you be good to the other as you may in her affliction and to my good daughter Joan Aleyn[5] to give her I pray you some kind answer, for she sued[6] hither to me this day so pray you be good to her.

I cumber you good Margaret much, but I would be sorry, if it should be any longer than tomorrow, for it is Saint Thomas even, and the utas of Saint Peter[7] and therefore tomorrow long I to go to God, it were a day very meet[8] and convenient for me. I never liked your manner toward me better than when[9] you kissed me last for I love when daughterly love and dear charity hath no leisure to look to worldly courtesy.

Fare well my dear child and pray for me, and I shall for you and all your friends that we may merrily meet in heaven. I thank you for your great cost.[10]

I send now unto my good daughter Clement[11] her algorism stone[12] and I send her and my good son and all hers God's blessing and mine.

I pray you at time convenient recommend me to my good son John More. I liked well his natural fashion.[13] Our Lord bless him and his good wife my loving daughter,[14] to whom I pray him be good, as he hath great cause, and that if the land of mine come to his hand, he break not my will concerning his sister Daunce. And our Lord bless Thomas and Austen[15] and all that they shall have.

LETTER TO MARGARET ROPER

1 More's eldest daughter.

2 commend.

3 Margaret Roper's maid who visited More daily during his imprisonment. She married More's secretary, John Harris, and they preserved many of More's letters.

4 know.

5 Another of Margaret Roper's maids, whom More had helped to educate.

6 appealed.

7 29 June, the octave of the Feast of St. Peter, and the eve of the translation of the relics of St. Thomas (Becket) of Canterbury.

8 fitting. More sees a certain parallel between his political situation and Becket's.

9 She had embraced him on Tower Wharf after his conviction and sentencing.

10 trouble.

11 Margaret Gyge, wife of John Clement.

12 a slate, possibly for mathematical computation.

13 He had knelt on Tower Wharf and asked for his father's blessing.

14 Anne Cresacre, who had been More's ward.

15 John and Anne's children, More's grandchildren.

Sir Thomas Elyot (1490–1546)

Elyot was born in Wiltshire and received his education at home and at the Middle Temple and Oxford, where he received his BA (1519) in civil law. But even more important to his intellectual development was his association with Sir Thomas More's circle, which included Thomas Linacre, Hans Holbein the Younger, Erasmus, and Colet. It was from this group that he absorbed the New Learning of classical humanism that had not yet reached Oxford and Cambridge. Through Cardinal Wolsey's influence, he became Chief Clerk of the King's Council, a post he held until Wolsey's fall in 1530. The only reward for his service was his knighthood. He wrote *The Book Named the Governor* during his forced retirement from government. Book I sets forth his monarchical political theory, which is addressed more to aristocratic courtiers than to the monarch. The next two books specify the virtues a ruler should cultivate. Probably because of the success of his book, which he dedicated to Henry VIII, he was appointed (1531)

ambassador to the Emperor Charles V, nephew to the King's wife, Catherine of Aragon. Elyot's impossible assignment was to persuade Charles that Henry VIII's divorce case against his Queen, with whom Elyot sympathized, should not be tried in Rome. His most important achievement was to make available in English the best fruits of Renaissance humanist thought. There is, nonetheless, a strange disjunction between his political optimism and the political realities that he witnessed. His paragraph on the order of nature is a classic exposition of the Great Chain of Being.

READING

S. E. Lehmberg, *Sir Thomas Elyot, Tudor Humanist.*
Christopher Morris, *Political Thought in England: Tyndale to Hooker.*

M. P.

[FROM] THE BOOK NAMED THE GOVERNOR

THE FIRST BOOK

1. *The signification of a public weal, and why it is called in Latin* Respublica.

A PUBLIC weal is in sundry wise defined by philosophers; but knowing by experience that the often repetition of anything of grave or sad importance will be tedious to the readers of this work, who perchance for the more part have not been trained in learning containing semblable[1] matter, I have compiled one definition out of many, in as compendious form as my poor wit can devise, trusting that in those few words the true signification of a public weal shall evidently appear to them whom reason can satisfy.

A public weal is a body living, compact or made of sundry estates and degrees of men, which is disposed by the order of equity and governed by the rule and moderation of reason. In the Latin tongue it is called *Respublica,* of the which the word *Res* hath divers significations, and doth not only betoken that that is called a thing which is distinct from a person, but also signifieth estate, condition, substance, and profit. In our old vulgar, profit is called weal. And it is called a wealthy country wherein is all thing that is profitable. And he is a wealthy man that is rich in money and substance. Public (as Varro[2] saith) is derived of people, which in Latin is called *Populus*; wherefore it seemeth that men have been long abused in calling *Respublicam* a common weal. And they which do suppose it so to be called for that, that everything should be to all men in common, without

---

2 Marcus Terentius Varro (116–27 BC). The reference here is to his *De Lingua Latina*, one of the few of his 600 books to survive, if only as a fragment.

discrepance[3] of any estate or condition, be thereto moved more by sensuality than by any good reason or inclination to humanity. And that shall soon appear unto them that will be satisfied either with authority or with natural order and example.

First, the proper and true signification of the words public and common, which be borrowed of the Latin tongue for the insufficiency of our own language, shall sufficiently declare the blindness of them which have hitherto holden and maintained the said opinions. As I have said, public took his beginning of people, which in Latin is *Populus,* in which word is contained all the inhabitants of a realm or city, of what estate or condition so ever they be.

Plebs in English is called the commonalty, which signifieth only the multitude, wherein be contained the base and vulgar inhabitants not advanced to any honour or dignity, which is also used in our daily communication. For in the city of London and other cities they that be none aldermen or sheriffs be called commoners; and in the country, at a sessions or other assembly, if no gentlemen be thereat, the saying is that there was none but the commonalty, which proveth in mine opinion that *Plebs* in Latin is in English commonalty, and *Plebeii* be commoners. And consequently there may appear like diversity to be in English between a public weal and a common weal, as should be in Latin between *Res publica* and *Res plebeia.* And after that signification, if there should be a common weal either the commoners only must be wealthy, and the gentle and noble men needy and miserable, or else, excluding gentility, all men must be of one degree and sort, and a new name provided. For as much as *Plebs* in Latin, and commoners in English, be words only made for the discrepance of degrees, whereof proceedeth order; which in things as well natural as supernatural hath ever had such a pre-eminence that thereby the incomprehensible majesty of God, as it were by a bright leam[4] of a torch or candle, is declared to the blind inhabitants of this world. Moreover take away order from all things, what should then remain? Certes[5] nothing finally, except some man would imagine eftsoons[6] *Chaos,* which of some is expound a confuse mixture. Also where there is any lack of order needs must be perpetual conflict, and in things subject to nature nothing of himself only may be nourished; but when he had destroyed that wherewith he doth participate by the order of his creation, he himself of necessity must then perish, whereof ensueth universal dissolution.

But now to prove, by example of those things that be within only among men but also with God, albeit His wisdom, bounty, and magnificence can be with no tongue or pen sufficiently expressed. Hath not He set degrees and estates in all His glorious works?

First in His heavenly ministers, whom, as the Church affirmeth, He hath constituted to be in divers degrees called hierarchs.

Also Christ saith by His evangelist that in the house of His Father (which is God) be many mansions.[7] But to treat of that which by natural understanding may be comprehended. Behold the four elements whereof the body of man is compact, how they be set in their places called spheres, higher or lower according to the sovereignty of their natures, that is to say, the fire as the most pure element, having in it nothing that is corruptible, in his place is highest and above other elements. The air, which next to the fire is most pure in substance, is in the second sphere or place. The water, which is somewhat consolidate, and approacheth to corruption, is next unto the earth. The earth, which is of substance gross and ponderous, is set of all elements most lowest.

Behold also the order that God hath put generally in all His creatures, beginning at the most inferior or base, and ascending upward. He made not only herbs to garnish the earth, but also trees of a more eminent stature than herbs, and yet in the one and the other be degrees of qualities: some pleasant to behold, some delicate or good in taste, other wholesome and medicinable, some commodious and necessary. Semblably in birds, beasts, and fishes, some be good for the sustenance of man, some bear things profitable to sundry uses, other be apt to occupation and labour; in divers is strength and fierceness only; in many is both strength and commodity; some other serve for pleasure; none of them hath all these qualities; few have the more part or many, specially beauty,

3   *distinction.*
4   *gleam.*
5   *certainly.*

6   *again.*
7   John 14:2.

strength, and profit. But where any is found that hath many of the said properties, he is more set by than all the other, and by that estimation the order of his place and degree evidently appeareth; so that every kind of trees, herbs, birds, beasts, and fishes, beside their diversity of forms, have (as who saith) a peculiar disposition appropered[8] unto them by God their creator: so that in everything is order, and without order may be nothing stable or permanent; and it may not be called order, except it do contain in it degrees, high and base, according to the merit or estimation of the thing that is ordered.

Now to return to the estate of mankind, for whose use all the said creatures were ordained of God, and also excelleth them all by prerogative of knowledge and wisdom. It seemeth that in him should be no less providence of God declared than in the inferior creatures, but rather with a more perfect order and disposition. And therefore it appeareth that God giveth not to every man like gifts of grace, or of nature, but to some more, some less, as it liketh His Divine Majesty.

Ne they be not in common (as fantastical fools would have all things), nor one man hath not all virtues and good qualities. Notwithstanding for as much as understanding is the most excellent gift that man can receive in his creation, whereby he doth approach most nigh unto the similitude of God, which understanding is the principal part of the soul, it is therefore congruent and according that as one excelleth another in that influence, as thereby being next to the similitude of his maker, so should the estate of his person be advanced in degree or place where understanding may profit; which is also distributed into sundry uses, faculties, and offices, necessary for the living and governance of mankind. And like as the angels which be most fervent in contemplation be highest exalted in glory (after the opinion of holy doctors), and also the fire, which is the most pure of elements and also doth clarify the inferior elements, is deputed to the highest sphere or place, so in this world they which excel other in this influence of understanding, and do employ it to the detaining of other within the bounds of reason, and show them how to provide for their necessary living, such ought to be set in a more high place than the residue where they may see and also be seen, that by the beams of their excellent wit, showed through the glass of authority, other of inferior understanding may be directed to the way of virtue and commodious living. And unto men of such virtue by very equity appertaineth honour, as their just reward and duty, which by other men's labours must also be maintained according to their merits. For as much as the said persons, excelling in knowledge whereby other be governed, be ministers for the only profit and commodity of them which have not equal understanding; where they which do exercise artificial science or corporal labour do not travail for their superiors only, but also for their own necessity. So the maker apparelleth himself and the husband; they both succour other artificers; other artificers them; they and other artificers them that be governors. But they that be governors (as I before said) nothing do acquire by the said influence of knowledge for their own necessities, but do employ all the powers of their wits and their diligence to the only preservation of other their inferiors; among which inferiors also behoveth to be a disposition and order according to reason, that is to say, that the slothful or idle person do not participate with him that is industrious and taketh pain, whereby the fruits of his labours should be diminished, wherein should be none equality, but thereof should proceed discourage, and finally dissolution for lack of provision. Wherefore it can none other wise stand with reason but that the estate of the person in pre-eminence of living should be esteemed with his understanding, labour, and policy; whereunto must be added an augmentation of honour and substance, which not only impresseth a reverence, whereof proceedeth due obedience among subjects, but also inflameth men naturally inclined to idleness or sensual appetite to covet like fortune, and for that cause to dispose them to study or occupation. Now to conclude my first assertion or argument: where all thing is common there lacketh order, and where order lacketh there all thing is odious and uncomely. And that have we in daily experience; for the pans and pots garnisheth well the kitchen, and yet should they be to the chamber none ornament. Also the beds, testers, and pillows beseemeth not the hall, no more than the carpets and cushions becometh the stable. Semblably the potter and tinker, only perfect in their craft, shall little do in the ministra-

8   *appropriated.*

tion of justice. A ploughman or carter shall make but a feeble answer to an ambassador. Also a weaver or fuller should be an unmeet captain of an army, or in any other office of a governor. Wherefore, to conclude, it is only a public weal where, like as God hath disposed the said influence of understanding, is also appointed degrees and places according to the excellency thereof; and thereto also would be substance convenient and necessary for the ornament of the same, which also impresseth a reverence and due obedience to the vulgar people or commonalty; and without that, it can be no more said that there is a public weal than it may be affirmed that a house without his proper and necessary ornaments is well and sufficiently furnished.

II. *That one sovereign governor ought to be in a public weal. And what damage hath happened where a multitude hath had equal authority without any sovereign.*

LIKE AS to a castle or fortress sufficeth one owner or sovereign, and where any more be of like power and authority seldom cometh the work to perfection; or being already made, where the one diligently overseeth and the other neglecteth, in that contention all is subverted and cometh to ruin. In semblable wise doth a public weal that hath more chief governors than one. Example we may take of the Greeks, among whom in divers cities were divers forms of public weals governed by multitudes. Wherein one was most tolerable where the governance and rule was always permitted to them which excelled in virtue, and was in the Greek tongue called *Aristocratia*, in Latin *Optimorum Potentia,* in English the rule of men of best disposition, which the Thebans of long time observed.

Another public weal was among the Athenians, where equality was of estate among the people, and only by their whole consent their city and dominions were governed: which might well be called a monster with many heads. Nor never it was certain nor stable; and often times they banished or slew the best citizens, which by their virtue and wisdom had most profited to the public weal. This manner of governance was called in Greek *Democratia*, in Latin *Popularis Potentia*, in English the rule of the commonalty. Of these two governances none of them may be sufficient. For in the first, which consisteth of good men, virtue is not so constant in a multitude, but that some, being once in authority, be incensed with glory, some with ambition, other with covetousness and desire of treasure or possessions. Whereby they fall into contention; and finally, where any achieveth the superiority, the whole governance is reduced unto a few in number, which fearing the multitude and their mutability, to the intent to keep them in dread to rebel, ruleth by terror and cruelty, thinking thereby to keep themselves in surety. Notwithstanding, rancour, coarced[9] and long detained in a narrow room, at the last bursteth out with intolerable violence and bringeth all to confusion. For the power that is practised to the hurt of many cannot continue. The popular estate, if it anything do vary from equality of substance or estimation, or that the multitude of people have over much liberty, of necessity one of these inconveniences must happen: either tyranny, where he that is too much in favour would be elevate and suffer none equality, or else into the rage of a commonalty, which of all rules is most to be feared. For like as the commons, if they feel some severity, they do humbly serve and obey, so where they embracing a license refuse to be bridled, they fling and plunge; and if they once throw down their governor, they order everything without justice, only with vengeance and cruelty, and with incomparable difficulty and unneth[10] by any wisdom be pacified and brought again into order. Wherefore undoubtedly the best and most sure governance is by one king or prince, which ruleth only for the weal of his people to him subject; and that manner at governance is best approved, and hath longest continued, and is most ancient. For who can deny but that all thing in heaven and earth is governed by one God, by one perpetual order, by one providence? One sun ruleth over the day, and one moon over the night; and to descend down to the earth, in a little beast, which of all other is most to be marvelled at, I mean the bee, is left to man by nature, as it seemeth, a perpetual figure of a just governance or rule: who hath among them one principal bee for their governor, who excelleth all other in greatness, yet hath he no prick or sting, but in him is more knowledge than in the residue. For if the day

9 *confined.* 10 *scarcely.*

following shall be fair and dry, and that the bees may issue out of their stalls without peril of rain or vehement wind, in the morning early he calleth them, making a noise as it were the sound of a horn or a trumpet; and with that all the residue prepare them to labour, and flyeth abroad, gathering nothing but that shall be sweet and profitable, although they sit often times on herbs and other things that be venomous and stinking.

The captain himself laboureth not for his sustenance, but all the other for him; he only seeth that if any drone or other unprofitable bee entereth into the hive, and consumeth the honey gathered by other, that he be immediately expelled from that company. And when there is another number of bees increased, they semblably have also a captain, which be not suffered to continue with the other. Wherefore this new company gathered into a swarm, having their captain among them, and environing him to preserve him from harm, they issue forth seeking a new habitation, which they find in some tree, except with some pleasant noise they be lured and conveyed unto another hive. I suppose who seriously beholdeth this example, and hath any commendable wit, shall thereof gather much matter to the forming of a public weal. But because I may not be long therein, considering my purpose, I would that if the reader hereof be learned, that he should repair to the *Georgics* of Virgil, or to Pliny, or Columella,[11] where he shall find the example more ample and better declared. And if any desireth to have the governance of one person proved by histories, let him first resort to the Holy Scripture, where he shall find that Almighty God commanded Moses only to bring his elected people out of captivity, giving only to him that authority without appointing to him any other assistance of equal power or dignity, except in the message to King Pharaoh, wherein Aaron, rather as a minister than a companion, went with Moses. But only Moses conducted the people through the Red Sea; he only governed them forty years in desert. And because Dathan and Abiram disdained his rule and coveted to be equal with him, the earth opened, and fire issued out, and swallowed them in with all their whole family and confederates to the number of 14,700.

And although Jethro, Moses' father-in-law, counselled him to depart[12] his importable[13] labours, in continual judgments, unto the wise men that were in his company, he notwithstanding still retained the sovereignty by God's commandment, until, a little before he died, he resigned it to Joshua, assigned by God to be ruler after him. Semblably after the death of Joshua by the space of 246 years succeeded from time to time one ruler among the Jews, which was chosen for his excellency in virtue and specially justice, wherefore he was called the judge, until the Israelites desired of Almighty God to let them have a king as other people had: who appointed to them Saul to be their king, who exceeded all other in stature.[14] And so successively one king governed all the people of Israel unto the time of Rehoboam, son of the noble King Solomon, who, being unlike to his father in wisdom, practised tyranny among his people, wherefore nine parts of them which they called Tribes forsook him and elected Jeroboam, late servant to Solomon, to be their king, only the tenth part remaining with Rehoboam.

And so in that realm were continually two kings until the King of Mede had depopulated the country and brought the people in captivity to the city of Babylon, so that during the time that two kings reigned over the Jews was ever continual battle among themselves: where if one king had always reigned like to David or Solomon, of likelihood the country should not so soon have been brought in captivity.

Also in the time of the Maccabees,[15] as long as they had but one bishop which was their ruler, and was in the stead of a prince at that day, they valiantly resisted the Gentiles; and as well the Romans, then great lords of the world, as Persians and divers other realms desired to have with them amity and alliance; and all the inhabitants of that country lived in great weal and quietness. But after that by simony and ambition there happened to be two bishops which divided their authorities, and also the Romans had divided the realm of Judea to four princes called *tetrarchas*

11   The references here are to Pliny the Elder's *Naturalis Historia* and Lucius Junius Moderatus' *De Res Rustica*, a treatise on the farmer's life and work.

12   *delegate.*

13   *heavy.*

14   See 1 and 2 Samuel.

15   Second century BC; see the two Books of the Maccabees in the Apocrypha.

and also constituted a Roman captain or president over them, among the heads there never ceased to be sedition and perpetual discord, whereby at the last the people was destroyed and the country brought to desolation and horrible barrenness.

The Greeks, which were assembled to revenge the reproach of Menelaus that he took of the Trojans by the ravishing of Helen, his wife, did not they by one assent elect Agamemnon to be their emperor or captain, obeying him as their sovereign during the siege of Troy?[16] Although that they had divers excellent princes, not only equal to him, but also excelling him: as in prowess, Achilles and Ajax Thelemonius; in wisdom, Nestor and Ulysses, and his own brother Menelaus, to whom they might have given equal authority with Agamemnon; but those wise princes considered that, without a general captain, so many persons as were there of divers realms gathered together, should be by no means well governed: wherefore Homer calleth Agamemnon the shepherd of the people. They rather were contented to be under one man's obedience, than severally to use their authorities or to join in one power and dignity; whereby at the last should have sourded[17] dissension among the people, they being separately inclined toward their natural sovereign lord, as it appeared in the particular contention that was between Achilles and Agamemnon for their concubines, where Achilles, renouncing the obedience that he with all other princes had before promised, at the battle first enterprised against the Trojans. For at that time no little murmur and sedition was moved in the host of the Greeks, which notwithstanding was wonderfully pacified, and the army unscattered by the majesty of Agamemnon, joining to him counsellors Nestor and the witty Ulysses.

But to return again. Athens and other cities of Greece, when they had abandoned kings and concluded to live as it were in a commonalty which abusively they called equality, how long time did any of them continue in peace? Yea what vacation had they from the wars, or what noble man had they which advanced the honour and weal of their city, whom they did not banish or slay in prison? Surely it shall appear to them that will read Plutarch, or Aemilius Probus, in the lives of Milciades, Cimon, Themistocles, Aristides, and divers other noble and valiant captains: which is too long here to rehearse.[18]

In like wise the Romans, during the time that they were under kings, which was by the space of 144 years, were well governed, nor never was among them discord or sedition. But after that by the persuasion of Brutus and Colatinus, whose wife (Lucretia) was ravished by Aruncius, son of Tarquin, King of Romans, not only the said Tarquin and all his posterity were exiled out of Rome for ever, but also it was finally determined amongst the people that never after they would have a king reign over them.

Consquently the commonality more and more encroached a license, and at the last compelled the Senate to suffer them to choose yearly among them governors of their own estate and condition, whom they called Tribunes: under whom they received such audacity and power that they finally obtained the highest authority in the public weal, in so much that often times they did repeal the acts of the Senate, and to those Tribunes might a man appeal from the Senate or any other office or dignity.

But what came thereof in conclusion? Surely when there was any difficult war imminent, then were they constrained to elect one sovereign and chief of all other, whom they named *Dictator*, as it were commander, from whom it was not lawful for any man to appeal. But because there appeared to be in him the pristine authority and majesty of a king, they would no longer suffer him to continue in that dignity than by the space of six months, except he then resigned it, and by the consent of the people eftsoons did resume it. Finally, until Octavius Augustus had destroyed Anthony, and also Brutus, and finished all the Civil Wars (that were so called because they were between the same self Roman citizens), the city of Rome was never long quiet from factions or seditions among the people. And if the nobles of Rome had not been men of excellent learning, wisdom, and prowess, and that the Senate, the most noble council in all the world, which was first ordained by Romulus

---

16 Here follows a summary of the Trojan War as told by Homer.   18 See Plutarch's *Lives*.
17 *incited.*

and increased by Tullus Hostilius, the third King of Romans, had not continued and with great difficulty retained their authority, I suppose verily that the city of Rome had been utterly desolate soon after the expelling of Tarquin; and if it had been eftsoons renewed it should have been twenty times destroyed before the time that Augustus reigned: so much discord was ever in the city for lack of one governor.

But what need we to search so far from us, since we have sufficient examples near unto us? Behold the estate of Florence and Genoa, noble cities of Italy, what calamity have they both sustained by their own factions, for lack of a continual governor. Ferrara and the most excellent city of Venice, the one having a duke, the other an earl, seldom suffereth damage except it happen by outward hostility. We have also an example domestical, which is most necessary to be noted. After that the Saxons by treason had expelled out of England the Britons, which were the ancient inhabitants, this realm was divided into sundry regions or kingdoms. O what misery was the people then in! O how this most noble Isle of the world was decerpt[19] and rent in pieces; the people pursued and hunted like wolves or other beasts savage; none industry availed, no strength defended, no riches profited. Who would then have desired to have been rather a man than a dog, when men either with sword or with hunger perished, having no profit or sustenance of their own corn or cattle, which by mutual war was continually destroyed? Yet the dogs, either taking that that men could not quietly come by or feeding on the dead bodies which on every part lay scattered plenteously, did satisfy their hunger.

Where find ye any good laws that at that time were made and used, or any commendable monument of science or craft in this realm occupied? Such iniquity seemeth to be then, that by the multitude of sovereign governors all things had been brought to confusion, if the noble King Edgar had not reduced the monarch to his pristine estate and figure: which brought to pass, reason was revived, and people came to conformity, and the realm began to take comfort and to show some visage of a public weal, and so (lauded be God) have continued: but not being alway in like estate or condition. Albeit it is not to be despaired, but that the King our sovereign lord now reigning, and this realm alway having one prince like unto his Highness, equal to the ancient princes in virtue and courage, it shall be reduced (God so disposing) unto a public weal excelling all other in pre-eminence of virtue and abundance of things necessary. But for as much as I do well perceive that to write of the office or duty of a sovereign governor or prince far exceedeth the compass of my learning, Holy Scripture affirming that the hearts of princes be in God's own hands and disposition, I will therefore keep my pen within the space that is described to me by the three noble masters, reason, learning, and experience; and by their ensignment or teaching I will ordinately treat of the two parts of a public weal, whereof the one shall be named Due Administration, the other Necessary Occupation, which shall be divided into two volumes. In the first shall be comprehended the best form of education or bringing up of noble children from their nativity, in such manner as they may be found worthy and also able to be governors of a public weal. The second volume, which, God granting me quietness and liberty of mind, I will shortly after send forth, it shall contain all the remnant, which I can either by learning or experience find apt to the perfection of a just public weal: in the which I shall so endeavour myself, that all men, of what estate or condition soever they be, shall find therein occasion to be alway virtuously occupied; and not without pleasure, if they be not of the schools of Aristippus or Apicius,[20] of whom the one supposed felicity to be only in lechery, the other in delicate feeding and gluttony: from whose sharp talons and cruel teeth, I beseech all gentle readers to defend these works, which for their commodity is only compiled.

19   *plucked.*
20   Aristippus, whose writings are lost, was a pupil of Socrates and a predecessor of Epicurus in his advocacy of pleasure as the highest good. Apicius was a gourmet during the reign of Tiberius.

King Henry VIII (1491–1547)

Henry VIII not only surrounded himself with poets and musicians of extraordinary talent but also wrote lyrics and composed music himself. His authorship of individual poems is less certain than that of the musical compositions attributed to him. The texts that carry his name, however, raise the important question of the relationship of music to poetry and make it difficult if not impossible to draw an absolute line between the two. Courtier poets, such as Wyatt, most likely sang at least some of their lyrics to lute accompaniment, although Campion stands alone in having excelled equally in poetic and musical composition.

READING

Noah Greenberg (ed.), *An Anthology of English Medieval and Renaissance Vocal Music*.

M. P.

[WITH OWT DYSCORDE]

With owt dyscorde
and bothe accorde
    now let us be,
Bothe hart a- lone
to set in one
    best semyth me.
For when one sole
ys in the dole
    of loveys payne.
10 Then helpe must have
hym selfe to save
    and love to optayne.
Wher for now we
that lovers be
    let us now pray.
Onys love sure
ffor to procure
    with owt denay.
Wher love so sewith   *sueth*
20 ther no hart rewith   *rueth*
    but condyscend.
Yf contrarye
What remedy
    god yt amend.

[O MY HART]

O my hart and O my hart,
my hart it is so sore,

Sens I must nedys
from my love de- part
and know no cause where- fore.

William Tyndale (1494–1536)

In an age of gifted translators, Tyndale's accomplishments are extraordinary. He was the first to translate the Bible directly from its original languages (Hebrew and Greek) into English. His New Testament, which was published in 1534, may have cost him his life. His work was completed with amazing speed and fidelity to his example by Miles Coverdale, who produced the first complete printed Bible in English in 1535, the year of Tyndale's imprisonment. Although Tyndale was martyred in 1536, before he completed his work on the Old Testament, he managed to change the way the English language has been written and spoken ever since. He introduced especially a simpler use of coordination into English, based on Hebrew practice. Indeed, his impact on English prose is equal in importance to Shakespeare's influence on English poetry. Together Tyndale and Shakespeare are the most important reshapers of the English language for subsequent English literature and for English common speech and writing. Some of Tyndale's sentences, which are often spoken as though by the voice of God or by other definitive speakers, include these:

Let there be light (Genesis 1).
Behold, I stand at the door and knock (Revelation 3).
Am I my brother's keeper? (Genesis 4).
The spirit is willing, but the flesh is weak (Matthew 26).
Eat, drink and be merry (Luke 12).

John Foxe's version of Tyndale's life and death has been an important source of information since the sixteenth century, but not until 1994, on the occasion of the five-hundredth anniversary of his birth, was Tyndale's achievement appropriately celebrated with a major exhibition at the British Library, a definitive biography by David Daniell, and essential editions of his Old and New Testament translations, edited by Daniell and published by Yale University Press.

Born into a prosperous family in Gloucestershire, Tyndale had the advantage of a good local grammar school and an education at Magdalen Hall, Oxford. He completed the long arts course and received his BA degree in 1512 and his MA in philosophy in 1515. John Foxe writes that Tyndale then went on to Cambridge. If so, that would possibly have brought him into contact with Erasmus, whose editions of the Greek New Testament appeared from 1516 to 1535 and who was then teaching Greek at Cambridge as Lady Margaret Professor. Cambridge was also an important center of Lutheran ideas, which were discussed at the White Horse Tavern (now the site of the Cavendish Laboratory) under the direction of Robert Barnes, who, like Luther, was an Augustinian. Tyndale's work was heavily opposed, not least powerfully by Thomas More. Like Luther, whose Prologue to St. Paul's Epistle to the Romans he included in his New Testament translation, Tyndale was committed to the ideas that Scripture provided what the Church could not, and that faith (or grace) was what was essential to salvation, instead of ritual acts, good works, or payments ('indulgences') to the Church.

Tyndale's work was appropriated wholesale into the 1611 Authorized Version of the Bible, but usually without his marginal notes and commentary, some of which is reproduced here. Stephen Greenblatt has observed that Tyndale occupied a liminal cultural space during the English Renaissance, somewhere between the Renaissance sense that a person can – or must – fashion the self and the medieval sense that there were limits on such self-generation. In his address to the reader of his New Testament and in his "Four Senses of the Scripture," Tyndale also demonstrates his genius as a literary theorist. He was strangled and burned in 1536, after sixteen months in a prison near Brussels. Thomas More was at least indirectly involved in his murder.

READING

David Daniell, *William Tyndale: A Biography*.
David Daniell (ed.), *Tyndale's New Testament*.
G. E. Duffield (ed.), *The Work of William Tyndale*.

M. P.

[FROM] THE OBEDIENCE OF A CHRISTIAN MAN

THE INTERPRETATION OF SCRIPTURE

The Four Senses of the Scripture

THEY[1] divide the scripture into four senses, the literal, tropological, allegorical, and anagogical. The literal sense is become nothing at all: for the pope hath taken it clean away, and hath made it his possession.[2] He hath partly locked it up with the false and counterfeited keys of his traditions, ceremonies, and feigned lies; and partly driveth men from it with violence of sword: for no man dare abide by the literal sense of the text, but under a protestation, 'If it shall please the pope.' The tropological sense pertaineth to good manners (say they), and teacheth what we ought to do. The allegory is appropriate to faith; and the anagogical to hope, and things above. Tropological and anagogical are terms of their own feigning, and altogether unnecessary. For they are but allegories, both two of them; and this word allegory comprehendeth them both, and is enough. For tropological is but an allegory of manners; and anagogical, an allegory of hope. And allegory is as much to say as strange speaking, or borrowed speech: as when we say of a wanton child, 'This sheep hath magots in his tail, he must be anointed with birchen salve;' which speech I borrow of the shepherds.

Thou shalt understand, therefore, that the scripture hath but one sense, which is the literal sense. And that literal sense is the root and ground of all, and the anchor that never faileth, whereunto if thou cleave, thou canst never err or go out of the way. And if thou leave the literal sense, thou canst not but go out of the way. Neverthelater, the scripture useth proverbs, similitudes, riddles, or allegories, as all other speeches do; but that which the proverb, similitude, riddle, or allegory signifieth, is ever the literal sense, which thou must seek out diligently: as in the English we borrow words and sentences of one thing, and apply them unto another, and give them new significations. We say, 'Let the sea swell and rise as high as he will, yet hath God appointed how far he shall go:' meaning that the tyrants shall not do what they would, but that only which God hath appointed them to do. 'Look ere thou leap:' whose literal sense is, 'Do nothing suddenly, or without advisement.' 'Cut not the bough that thou standest upon:' whose literal sense is, 'Oppress not the commons;' and is borrowed of hewers. When a thing speedeth not well, we borrow speech, and say, 'The bishop hath blessed it;' because that nothing speedeth well that they meddle withal. If the porridge be burned too, or the meat over roasted, we say, 'The bishop hath put his foot in the pot,' or, 'The bishop hath played the cook;' because the bishops burn whom they lust, and whosoever displeaseth them. 'He is a pontifical fellow;' that is, proud and stately. 'He is popish;' that is, superstitious and faithless. 'It is a pastime for a prelate.' 'It is a pleasure for a pope.' 'He would be free, and yet will not have his head shaven.' 'He would that no man should smite him, and yet hath not the pope's mark.' And of him that is betrayed, and wotteth not how, we say, 'He hath been at shrift.' 'She is master parson's sister's daughter;' 'He is the bishop's sister's son;' 'He hath a cardinal to his uncle;' 'She is a spiritual whore;' 'It is the gentlewoman of the parsonage;' 'He gave me a *Kyrie eleyson*.'[3] And of her that answereth her husband six words for one, we say, 'She is a sister of the Charterhouse:' as who should say, 'She thinketh that she is not bound to keep silence; their silence shall be a satisfaction for her.' And of him that will not be saved by Christ's merits, but by the works of his own imagination, we say, 'It is a holy-work-man.' Thus borrow we,

[FROM] THE OBEDIENCE OF A CHRISTIAN MAN
THE INTERPRETATION OF SCRIPTURE

1   That is, Roman Catholic tradition. From Origen's idea that the scriptures "have two senses, the literal and the hidden" (*De Princip.*, 1, prol.), allegorical tradition developed into the four senses that Tyndale lists. Dante, for example, in his letter to Can Grande about the *Divine Comedy*, explains his poem in terms of these four senses, using biblical examples. Although he does not mention Tyndale, Angus Fletcher, *Allegory: The Theory of a Symbolic Mode*, provides a still excellent theory

of allegory. For a more succinct statement, see Northrop Frye, "Levels of Meaning in Literature."

2   Tyndale may be referring to a papal gloss here on the Gospel of John that leaves out the literal or historical sense when discussing the way to read scripture. For Tyndale, this would be an appropriation of the necessary basis for interpretation by the Church and its loss by the ordinary Christian.

3   "Lord, have mercy."

and feign new speech in every tongue. All fables, prophecies, and riddles, are allegories; as Æsop's fables, and Merlin's prophecies; and the interpretation of them are the literal sense.

So in like manner the scripture borroweth words and sentences of all manner things, and maketh proverbs and similitudes, or allegories. As Christ saith, Luke iv. 'Physician, heal thyself:' whose interpretation is, 'Do that at home, which thou dost in strange places;' and that is the literal sense. So when I say, 'Christ is a lamb;' I mean not a lamb that beareth wool, but a meek and a patient lamb, which is beaten for other men's faults. 'Christ is a vine;' not that beareth grapes; but out of whose root the branches that believe suck the Spirit of life, and mercy, and grace, and power to be the sons of God, and to do his will. The similitudes of the gospel are allegories, borrowed of worldly matters, to express spiritual things.[4] The apocalypse, or revelations of John, are allegories whose literal sense is hard to find in many places.

Beyond all this, when we have found out the literal sense of the scripture by the process of the text, or by a like text of another place, then go we, and as the scripture borroweth similitudes of worldly things, even so we again borrow similitudes or allegories of the scripture, and apply them to our purposes; which allegories are no sense of the scripture, but free things besides the scripture, and altogether in the liberty of the Spirit.[5] Which allegories I may not make at all the wild adventures; but must keep me within the compass of the faith, and ever apply mine allegory to Christ, and unto the faith. Take an ensample: thou hast the story of Peter, how he smote off Malchus's ear, and how Christ healed it again. There hast thou in the plain text great learning, great fruit, and great edifying, which I pass over because of tediousness. Then come I, when I preach of the law and the gospel, and borrow this ensample, to express the nature of the law and of the gospel, and to paint it unto thee before thine eyes. And of Peter and his sword make I the law, and of Christ the gospel; saying, 'As Peter's sword cutteth off the ear, so doth the law: the law damneth, the law killeth, and mangleth the conscience: there is no ear so righteous that can abide the hearing of the law: there is no deed so good but that the law damneth it.[6] But Christ, that is to say, the gospel, the promises and testament that God hath made in Christ, healeth the ear and conscience, which the law hath hurt. The gospel is life, mercy, and forgiveness freely, and altogether an healing plaister. And as Peter doth but hurt and make a wound, where was none before, even so doth the law: for when we think that we are holy and righteous, and full of good deeds; if the law be preached aright; our righteousness and good deeds vanish away, as smoke in the wind, and we are left damnable sinners only. And as thou seest how that Christ healeth not, till Peter had wounded; and as an healing plaister helpeth not, till the corrosive hath troubled the wound; even so the gospel helpeth not, but when the law hath wounded the conscience, and brought the sinner into the knowledge of his sin.' This allegory proveth nothing, neither can do. For it is not the scripture, but an ensample or a similitude borrowed of the scripture, to declare a text or a conclusion of the scripture more expressly, and to root it and grave it in the heart. For a similitude, or an ensample, doth print a thing much deeper in the wits of a man than doth a plain speaking, and leaveth behind him as it were a sting to prick him forward, and to awake him withal. Moreover, if I could not prove with an open text that which the allegory doth express, then were the allegory a thing to he jested at, and of no greater value than a tale of Robin Hood. This allegory, as touching his first part, is proved by Paul in the ivth chapter of his epistle to the Romans, where he saith, 'The law causeth wrath;" and in the viith chapter to the Romans, "When the law or commandment came, sin revived, and I became dead:" and in the iind epistle to the Corinthians, in the third chapter, the law is called "the minister of death and damnation," &c. And as concerning the second part, Paul saith to the Romans in the vth chapter, "In that we are justified by faith we are at peace with

4   W. T. glosses this: "The right use of allegories." Most of his subsequent glosses simply label or repeat what is in the main text. Only the glosses that add to the text are reprinted below, labeled "W. T."
5   W. T.: "Allegories are no sense of scripture."
6   This sentence was cited as Article XIX of the heresy charges against Tyndale. John Foxe wrote replies to some of the articles (see below). About his trial in August 1536, David Daniell writes, "In netting

Tyndale, the heresy-hunters had their largest catch. Tyndale was a particularly learned scholar, and a leader of European Lutherans. He was also extremely important in England – had not Sir Thomas More, no less, expended gallons of ink in attacking him? Tyndale was almost single-handedly spreading the heresy of Lutheranism in London and across England, with his books and especially his translations" (1994: p. 375).

God." And in the iind epistle to the Corinthians, in the third [chapter], the gospel is called "the ministration of justifying and of the Spirit." And, Gal. iii. "The Spirit cometh by preaching of the faith," &c. Thus doth the literal sense prove the allegory, and bear it, as the foundation beareth the house. And because that allegories prove nothing, therefore are they to be used soberly and seldom, and only where the text offereth thee an allegory.

And of this manner (as I above have done) doth Paul borrow a similitude, a figure or allegory, of Genesis, to express the nature of the law and of the gospel;[7] and by Agar and her son declareth the property of the law, and of her bond-children which will be justified by deeds; and by Sarah and her son declareth the property of the gospel, and of her free children which are justified by faith; and how the children of the law, which believe in their works, persecute the children of the gospel, which believe in the mercy and truth of God and in the testament of his Son Jesus our Lord.

And likewise do we borrow likenesses or allegories of the scripture, as of Pharaoh and Herod, and of the scribes and Pharisees, to express our miserable captivity and persecution under antichrist the pope. The greatest cause of which captivity and the decay of the faith, and this blindness wherein we now are, sprang first of allegories.[8] For Origen and the doctors of his time drew all the scripture unto allegories: whose ensample they that came after followed so long, till they at last forgot the order and process of the text, supposing that the scripture served but to feign allegories upon; insomuch that twenty doctors expound one text twenty ways, as children make descant upon plain song. Then came our sophisters with their anagogical and chopological sense, and with an antitheme of half an inch, out of which some of them draw a thread of nine days long. Yea, thou shalt find enough that will preach Christ, and prove whatsoever point of the faith that thou wilt, as well out of a fable of Ovid or any other poet, as out of St John's gospel or Paul's epistles.[9] Yea, they are come unto such blindness, that they not only say the literal sense profiteth not, but also that it is hurtful, and noisome, and killeth the soul. Which damnable doctrine they prove by a text of Paul, 2 Cor. iii. where he saith, "The letter killeth, but the spirit giveth life." Lo, say they, the literal sense killeth, and the spiritual sense giveth life. We must therefore, say they, seek out some chopological sense.

Here learn what sophistry is, and how blind they are, that thou mayest abhor them and spue them out of thy stomach for ever. Paul by the letter meaneth Moses's law; which the process of the text following declareth more bright than the sun. But it is not their guise to look on the order of any text; but as they find it in their doctors, so allege they it, and so understand it. Paul maketh a comparison between the law and the gospel; and calleth the law the letter, because it was but letters graven in two tables of cold stone: for the law doth but kill, and damn the consciences, as long as there is no lust in the heart to do that which the law commandeth. Contrariwise, he calleth the gospel the administration of the Spirit and of righteousness or justifying. For when Christ is preached, and the promises which God hath made in Christ are believed, the Spirit entereth the heart, and looseth the heart, and giveth lust to do the law, and maketh the law a lively thing in the heart.[10] Now as soon as the heart lusteth to do the law, then are we righteous before God, and our sins forgiven. Nevertheless the law of the letter graved in stone, and not in their hearts was as glorious, and Moses's face shone so bright, that the children of Israel could not behold his face for brightness. It was also given in thunder and lightning and terrible signs; so that they for fear came to Moses, and desired him that he would speak to them, and let God speak no more; "Lest we die (said they) if we hear him any more:" as thou mayest see Exod. xx. Whereupon Paul maketh his comparison, saying: "If the ministration of death through the letters figured in stones was glorious, so that the children of Israel could not behold the face of Moses for the glory of his countenance; why shall not the administration of the Spirit be glorious?" And again: "If the administration of damnation be glorious, much more shall the administration of righteousness exceed in glory:"

---

7   W. T.: "They that justify themselves by their works are the bond-children of the law."

8   W. T.: "The faith was lost through allegories."

9   W. T.: "Poetry is as good divinity as the scripture to our schoolmen."

10   W. T.: "To love the law is righteousness."

that is, if the law that killeth sinners, and helpeth them not, be glorious; then the gospel, which pardoneth sinners, and giveth them power to be the sons of God and to overcome sin, is much more glorious.

And the text that goeth before is as clear. For the holy apostle Paul saith: "Ye Corinthians are our epistle, which is understand and read of all men, in that ye are known how that ye are the epistle of Christ ministered by us, and written, not with ink," (as Moses's law,) "but with the Spirit of the living God; not in tables of stone," (as the ten commandments,) "but in the fleshy tables of the heart:" as who should say, "We write not a dead law with ink and in parchment, nor grave that which damned you in tables of stone; but preach you that which bringeth the Spirit of life unto your breasts, which Spirit writeth and graveth the law of love in your hearts, and giveth you lust to do the will of God." And furthermore, saith he, "Our ableness cometh of God, which hath made us able to minister the new Testament, not of the letter," (that is to say, not of the law,) "but of the Spirit: for the letter" (that is to say, the law) "killeth; but the Spirit giveth life;" that is to say, the Spirit of God, which entereth your hearts when ye believe the glad tidings that are preached you in Christ, quickeneth your hearts, and giveth you life and lust, and maketh you to do of love and of your own accord, without compulsion, that which the law compelled you to do, and damned you because ye could not do with love and lust, and naturally. Thus seest thou that the letter signifieth not the literal sense, and the spirit the spiritual sense. And, Rom. ii. Paul useth this term *Litera* for the law; and Rom. vii. where he setteth it so plain, that if the great wrath of God had not blinded them, they could never have stumbled at it.

God is a Spirit, and all his words are spiritual. His literal sense is spiritual, and all his words are spiritual. When thou readest (Matt. i.), "She shall bear a son, and thou shalt call his name Jesus; for he shall save his people from their sins:" this literal sense is spiritual, and everlasting life unto as many as believe it. And the literal sense of these words, (Matt. v.) "Blessed are the merciful, for they shall have mercy," are spiritual and life; whereby they that are merciful may of right, by the truth and promise of God, challenge mercy. And like is it of these words, Matt. vi. "If you forgive other men their sins, your heavenly Father shall forgive you yours." And so is it of all the promises of God. Finally, all God's words are spiritual, if thou have eyes of God to see the right meaning of the text, and whereunto the scripture pertaineth, and the final end and cause thereof.

All the scripture is either the promises and testament of God in Christ, and stories pertaining thereunto, to strength thy faith; either the law, and stories pertaining thereto, to fear thee from evil doing. There is no story nor gest, seem it never so simple or so vile unto the world, but that thou shalt find therein spirit and life and edifying in the literal sense: for it is God's scripture, written for thy learning and comfort. There is no clout or rag there, that hath not precious relics wrapt therein of faith, hope, patience and long suffering, and of the truth of God, and also of his righteousness. Set before thee the story of Reuben, which defiled his father's bed. Mark what a cross God suffered to fall on the neck of his elect Jacob. Consider first the shame among the heathen, when as yet there was no more of the whole world within the testament of God, but he and his household. I report me to our prelates, which swear by their honour, whether it were a cross or no. Seest thou not how our wicked builders rage, because they see their buildings burn, now they are tried by the fire of God's word; and how they stir up the whole world, to quench the word of God, for fear of losing their honour? Then what business had he to pacify his children! Look what ado he had at the defiling of his daughter Dinah. And be thou sure that the brethren there were no more furious for the defiling of their sister, than the sons here for defiling of their mother. Mark what followed Reuben, to fear other, that they shame not their fathers and mothers. He was cursed, and lost the kingdom, and also the priestdom, and his tribe or generation was ever few in number, as it appeareth in the stories of the bible.

The adultery of David with Bathsheba is an ensample, not to move us to evil; but, if (while we follow the way of righteousness) any chance drive us aside, that we despair not. For if we saw not such infirmities in God's elect, we, which are so weak and fall so oft, should utterly despair, and think that God had clean forsaken us. It is therefore a sure and an undoubted conclusion, whether we be holy or unholy, we are all sinners. But the difference is, that God's sinners consent not to their sin. They consent unto the law that is both holy and righteous, and mourn to have their sin taken away. But the devil's sinners consent unto their sin, and would have the law and hell taken away, and are enemies unto the righteousness of God.

Likewise in the homely gest of Noe, when he was drunk, and lay in his tent with his privy members open, hast thou great edifying in the literal sense. Thou seest what became of the cursed children of wicked Ham, which saw his father's privy members, and jested thereof unto his brethren. Thou seest also what blessing fell on Shem and Japhet, which went backward and covered their father's members, and saw them not. And thirdly, thou seest what infirmity accompanieth God's elect, be they never so holy, which yet is not imputed unto them: for the faith and trust they have in God swalloweth up all their sins.

Notwithstanding, this text offers us an apt and an handsome allegory or similitude to describe our wicked Ham, antichrist the pope, which many hundred years hath done all the shame that heart can think unto the word of promise, or the word of faith, as Paul calleth it, Rom. x.; and the gospel and testament of Christ, wherewith we are begotten; as thou seest, I Pet. i. and James i. And as the cursed children of Ham grew into giants, so mighty and great that the children of Israel seemed but grasshoppers in respect of them; so the cursed sons of our Ham, the pope, his cardinals, bishops, abbots, monks, and friars, are become mighty giants above all power and authority; so that the children of faith, in respect of them, are much less than grasshoppers. They heap mountain upon mountain, and will to heaven by their own strength, by a way of their own making, and not by the way Christ. Neverthelater, those giants, for the wickedness and abominations which they had wrought, did God utterly destroy, part of them by the children of Lot, and part by the children of Esau, and seven nations of them by the children of Israel. So no doubt shall he destroy these for like abominations, and that shortly. For their kingdom is but the kingdom of lies and falsehood; which must needs perish at the coming of the truth of God's word, as the night vanisheth away at the presence of day. The children of Israel slew not those giants, but the power of God; God's truth and promises, as thou mayest see in Deuteronomy. So it is not we that shall destroy those giants, as thou mayest see by Paul, (2 Thess. ii.) speaking of our Ham, antichrist: "Whom the Lord shall destroy" (saith he) "with the spirit of his mouth," that is, by the words of truth, "and by the brightness of his coming," that is, by the preaching of his gospel.

And as I have said of allegories, even so it is of worldly similitudes, which we make either when we preach, either when we expound the scripture. The similitudes prove nothing, but are made to express more plainly that which is contained in the scripture, and to lead thee into the spiritual understanding of the text: as the similitude of matrimony is taken to express the marriage that is between Christ and our souls, and what exceeding mercy we have there, whereof all the scriptures make mention; and the similitude of the members, how every one of them careth for other, is taken to make thee feel what it is to love thy neighbour as thyself. That preacher therefore, that bringeth a naked similitude to prove that which is contained in no text of scripture, nor followeth of a text, count a deceiver, a leader out of the way, and a false prophet, and beware of his philosophy and persuasions of man's wisdom, as Paul saith: "My words and my preaching were not with enticing words and persuasions of man's wisdom, but in shewing of the Spirit and power;" (that is, he preached not dreams, confirming them with similitudes; but God's word, confirming it with miracles and with working of the Spirit, the which made them feel every thing in their hearts:) "that your faith," said he, "should not stand in the wisdom of man; but in the power of God." For the reasons and similitudes of man's wisdom make no faith, but wavering and uncertain opinions only: one draweth me this way with his argument, another that way, and of what principle thou provest black, another proveth white: and so am I ever uncertain; as, if thou tell me of a thing done in a far land, and another tell me the contrary, I wot not what to believe. But faith is wrought by the power of God;[11] that is, when God's word is preached, the Spirit entereth thine heart, and maketh thy soul feel it, and maketh thee so sure of it, that neither adversity, nor persecution, nor death,

---

11 W. T.: "God's word maketh sure faith; for God cannot lie."

neither hell, nor the powers of hell, neither yet all the pains of hell could once prevail against thee, or move thee from the sure rock of God's word, that thou shouldst not believe that which God hath sworn.

And Peter saith, "We followed not deceivable fables, when we opened unto you the power and coming of our Lord Jesus Christ; but with our eyes we saw his majesty." And again, "We have" (saith he) "a more sure word of prophecy, whereunto if ye take heed, as unto a light shining in a dark place, ye do well." The word of prophecy was the old Testament, which beareth record unto Christ in every place; without which record the apostles made neither similitudes nor arguments of worldly wit. Hereof seest thou, that all the allegories, similitudes, persuasions and arguments, which they bring without scripture, to prove praying to saints, purgatory, ear-confession; and that God will hear thy prayer more in one place than in another; and that it is more meritorious to eat fish than flesh; and that to disguise thyself, and put on this or that manner coat, is more acceptable than to go as God hath made thee; and that widowhood is better than matrimony, and virginity than widowhood; and to prove the assumption of our lady, and that she was born without original sin, yea, and with a kiss (say some), are but false doctrine.

Take an ensample, how they prove that widowhood and virginity exceed matrimony. They bring this worldly similitude: he that taketh most pain for a man deserveth most, and to him a man is most bound; so likewise must it be with God, and so forth. Now the widow and virgin take more pain in resisting their lusts than the married wife; therefore is their state holier. First, I say, that in their own sophistry a similitude is the worst and feeblest argument that can be, and proveth least, and soonest deceiveth. Though that one son do more service for his father than another, yet is the father free, and may with right reward them all alike. For though I had a thousand brethren, and did more than they all, yet do I not my duty. The fathers and mothers also care most for the least and weakest, and them that can do least: yea, for the worst care they most, and would spend, not their goods only, but also their blood, to bring them to the right way. And even so is it of the kingdom of Christ, as thou mayest well see in the similitude of the riotous son. Moreover Paul saith, (1 Cor. vii.) "It is better to marry than to burn." For the person that burneth cannot quietly serve God, inasmuch as his mind is drawn away, and the thoughts of his heart occupied with wonderful and monstrous imaginations. He can neither see, nor hear, nor read, but that his wits are rapt, and he clean from himself. And again, saith he, "circumcision is nothing, uncircumcision is nothing; but the keeping of the commandments" is all together. Look wherein thou canst best keep the commandments; thither get thyself and therein abide; whether thou be widow, wife, or maid; and then hast thou all with God. If we have infirmities that draw us from the laws of God, let us cure them with the remedies that God hath made. If thou burn, marry: for God hath promised thee no chastity, as long as thou mayest use the remedy that he hath ordained; no more than he hath promised to slake thine hunger without meat. Now, to ask of God more than he hath promised, cometh of a false faith, and is plain idolatry;[12] and to desire a miracle, where there is natural remedy, is tempting of God. And of pains-taking, this-wise understand. He that taketh pains to keep the commandments of God, is sure thereby that he loveth God, and that he hath God's Spirit in him. And the more pain a man taketh (I mean patiently and without grudging), the more he loveth God, and the perfecter he is, and nearer unto that health which the souls of all christian men long for, and the more purged from the infirmity and sin that remaineth in the flesh. But to look for any other reward or promotion in heaven, or in the life to come, than that which God hath promised for Christ's sake, and which Christ hath deserved for us with his pain-taking, is abominable in the sight of God.[13] For Christ only hath purchased the reward; and our pain-taking to keep the commandments doth but purge the sin that remaineth in the flesh, and certify us that we are chosen and sealed with God's Spirit unto the reward that Christ hath purchased for us.

I was once at the creating of doctors of divinity, where the opponent brought the same reason to prove that the widow had more merit than the virgin; because she had greater pain, forasmuch

---

12   Quoted as Article XX against Tyndale.
13   Article XXI against Tyndale reads, "He saith, Our pains-taking in keeping commandments doth nothing but purge the sin that remaineth in the flesh; but to look for any other reward or promotion in heaven than God hath promised for Christ's sake, is abominable in the sight of God."

as she had once proved the pleasures of matrimony. *Ego nego, domine doctor*, said the respondent: 'for though the virgin have not proved, yet she imagineth that the pleasure is greater than it is indeed, and therefore is more moved, and hath greater temptation and greater pain.' Are not these disputers they that Paul speaketh of in the sixth chapter of the first epistle to Timothy? that "they are not content with the wholesome words of our Lord Jesus Christ, and doctrine of godliness; and therefore know nothing, but waste their brains about questions and strife of words, whereof spring envy, strife and railing of men with corrupt minds, destitute of the truth."

As pertaining to our lady's body, where it is, or where the body of Elias, of John the evangelist, and of many other be, pertaineth not to us to know. One thing are we sure of, that they are where God hath laid them. If they be in heaven, we have never the more in Christ: if they be not there, we have never the less. Our duty is to prepare ourselves unto the commandments, and to be thankful for that which is opened unto us; and not to search the unsearchable secrets of God. Of God's secrets can we know no more than he openeth unto us. If God shut, who shall open? How then can natural reason come by the knowledge of that which God hath hid unto himself?

Yet let us see one of their reasons wherewith they prove it. The chief reason is this: Every man doth more for his mother, say they, than for other; in like manner must Christ do for his mother; therefore hath she this pre-eminence, that her body is in heaven. And yet Christ, in the xiith chap. of Matthew knoweth her not for his mother, but as far forth as she kept his Father's commandments. And Paul, in the iind epistle to the Corinthians, chap. v. knoweth not Christ himself fleshly, or after a worldly purpose. Last of all, God is free, and no further bound than he bindeth himself: if he have made her any promise, he is bound; if not, then is he not. Finally, if thou set this above rehearsed chapter of Matthew before thee, where Christ would not know his mother, and the iind of John where he rebuked her, and the iind of Luke where she lost him, and how negligent she was to leave him behind her at Jerusalem unawares, and to go a day's journey ere she sought for him; thou mightest resolve many of their reasons which they make of this matter, and that she was without original sin. Read also Erasmus's Annotations in the said places. And as for me, I commit all such matters unto those idle bellies, which have nought else to do than to move such questions; and give them free liberty to hold what they list, as long as it hurteth not the faith, whether it be so or no: exhorting yet, with Paul, all that will please God, and obtain that salvation that is in Christ, that they give no heed unto unnecessary and brawling disputations, and that they labour for the knowledge of those things without which they cannot be saved. And remember that the sun was given us to guide us in our way and works bodily. Now if thou leave the natural use of the sun, and will look directly on him to see how bright he is, and suchlike curiosity, then will the sun blind thee. So was the scripture given us to guide us in our way and works ghostly. The way is Christ; and the promises in him are our salvation, if we long for them. Now if we shall leave that right use and turn ourselves unto vain questions, and to search the unsearchable secrets of God; then no doubt shall the scripture blind us, as it hath done our schoolmen and our subtle disputers.

And as they are false prophets, which prove with allegories, similitudes, and worldly reasons, that which is no where made mention of in the scripture; even so count them for false prophets which expound the scriptures, drawing them unto a worldly purpose, clean contrary unto the ensample, living, and practising of Christ and of his apostles, and of all the holy prophets. For, saith Peter, (2 Pet. i.) "No prophecy in the scripture hath any private interpretation. For the scripture came not by the will of man; but the holy men of God spake as they were moved by the Holy Ghost." No place of the scripture may have a private exposition; that is, it may not be expounded after the will of man, or after the will of the flesh, or drawn unto a worldly purpose contrary unto the open texts, and the general articles of the faith, and the whole course of the scripture, and contrary to the living and practising of Christ and the apostles and holy prophets. For as they came not by the will of man, so may they not be drawn or expounded after the will of man: but as they came by the Holy Ghost, so must they be expounded and understood by the Holy Ghost. The scripture is that wherewith God draweth us unto him, and not wherewith we should be led from him. The scriptures spring out of God, and flow unto Christ, and were given to lead us to Christ.

Thou must therefore go along by the scripture as by a line, until thou come at Christ, which is the way's end and resting-place. If any man, therefore, use the scripture to draw thee from Christ, and to nosel[14] thee in any thing save in Christ, the same is a false prophet. And that thou mayest perceive what Peter meaneth, it followeth in the text, "There were false prophets among the people" (whose prophecies were belly-wisdom), "as there shall be false teachers among you, which shall privily bring in damnable sects," (as thou seest how we are divided into monstrous sects or orders of religion,) "even denying the Lord that hath bought them." For every one of them taketh on him to sell thee for money that which God in Christ promiseth thee freely. "And many shall follow their damnable ways, by whom the way of truth shall be evil spoken of:" as thou seest how the way of truth is become heresy, seditious, or cause of insurrection, and breaking of the king's peace, and treason unto his highness. "And through covetousness with feigned words shall they make merchandise of you." Covetousness is the conclusion: for covetousness and ambition, that is to say, lucre and desire of honour, is the final end of all false prophets and of all false teachers. Look upon the pope's false doctrine: what is the end thereof, and what seek they thereby? Wherefore serveth purgatory, but to purge thy purse, and to poll thee, and rob both thee and thy heirs of house and lands, and of all thou hast, that they may be in honour? Serve not pardons for the same purpose? Whereto pertaineth praying to saints, but to offer unto their bellies? Wherefore serveth confession, but to sit in thy conscience and to make thee fear and tremble at whatsoever they dream, and that thou worship them as gods? And so forth, in all their traditions, ceremonies, and conjurations, they serve not the Lord, but their bellies.

And of their false expounding the scripture, and drawing it contrary unto the ensample of Christ and the apostles and holy prophets, unto their damnable covetousness and filthy ambition, take an ensample: When Peter saith to Christ, (Matt. xvi.) "Thou art the Son of the living God;" and Christ answered, "Thou art Peter, and upon this rock I will build my congregation;" by the rock interpret they Peter. And then cometh the pope, and will be Peter's successor, whether Peter will or will not; yea, whether God will or will not; and though all the scripture say, "Nay," to any such succession; and saith, "Lo, I am the rock, the foundation, and head of Christ's church." Now saith all the scripture, that the rock is Christ, the faith, and God's word. As Christ saith, (Matt. vii.) "He that heareth my words, and doth thereafter, is like a man that buildeth on a rock."[15] For the house that is built on God's word will stand, though heaven should fall. And, John xv. "Christ is the vine, and we the branches:" so is Christ the rock, the stock, and foundation whereon we be built. And Paul (1 Cor. iii.) calleth Christ our foundation; and all other, whether it be Peter or Paul, he calleth them our servants, to preach Christ, and to build us on him. If therefore the pope be Peter's successor, his duty is to preach Christ only; and other authority hath he none.[16] And (2 Cor. xi.) Paul marrieth us unto Christ, and driveth us from all trust and confidence in man. And, (Eph. ii.) saith Paul, "Ye are built on the foundation of the apostles and prophets;" that is, on the word which they preached; "Christ being, saith he, the head corner-stone, in whom every building coupled together groweth up into an holy temple in the Lord; in whom also ye are built together and made an habitation for God in the Spirit." And Peter, in the iind of his first epistle, buildeth us on Christ; contrary to the pope, which buildeth us on himself. Hell gates shall not prevail against it; that is to say, against the congregation that is built upon Christ's faith, and upon God's word. Now were the pope the rock, hell gates could not prevail against him: for the house could not stand, if the rock and foundation whereon it is built did perish: but the contrary see we in our popes. For hell gates have prevailed against them many hundred years, and have swallowed them up, if God's word be true, and the stories that are written of them; yea, or if it be true that we see with our eyes. "I will give thee the keys of heaven," saith Christ, and not, "I give;" and, John xx. after the resurrection paid it, and gave the keys to them all indifferently.

"Whatsoever thou bindest on earth, it shall be bound in heaven; and whatsoever thou loosest on earth, it shall be loosed in heaven." Of this text maketh the pope what he will; and expoundeth

---

14   *nurse.*

15   W. T.: "Christ, the faith, and God's word is the rock, and not the pope."

16   Article XXII against Tyndale: "He saith, The pope hath no other authority, but to preach only."

it contrary to all the scripture, contrary to Christ's practising, and the apostles', and all the prophets'. Now the scripture giveth record to himself, and ever expaundeth itself by another open text. If the pope then cannot bring for his exposition the practising of Christ, or of the apostles and prophets, or an open text, then is his exposition false doctrine. Christ expoundeth himself, (Matt. xviii.) saying: "If thy brother sin against thee, rebuke him betwixt him and thee alone. If he hear thee, thou hast won thy brother: but if he hear thee not, then take with thee one or two," and so forth, as it standeth in the text. He concludeth, saying to them all: "Whatsoever ye bind in earth, it shall be bound in heaven; and whatsoever ye loose on earth, it shall be loosed in heaven." Where binding is but to rebuke them that sin; and loosing to forgive them that repent. And, "Whose sins ye forgive, they are forgiven; and whose sins ye hold, they are holden." And Paul (1 Cor. v.) bindeth; and (2 Cor. ii.) looseth, after the same manner.

Also this binding and loosing is one power: and as he bindeth, so looseth he; yes, and bindeth first ere he can loose. For who can loose that is not bound? Now whatsoever Peter bindeth, or his successor, (as he will be called and is not, but indeed the very successor of Satan,) is not so to be understood, that Peter, or the pope, hath power to command a man to be in deadly sin, or to be damned, or to go into hell, saying, Be thou in deadly sin; be thou damned; go thou to hell; go thou to purgatory: for that exposition is contrary to the everlasting testament that God hath made unto us in Christ. He sent his Son Christ to loose us from sin, and damnation, and hell; and that to testify unto the world, sent he his disciples. (Acts i.) Paul also hath no power to destroy, but to edify. 2 Cor. x. xiii. How can Christ give his disciples power against himself, and against his everlasting testament? Can he send them to preach salvation, and give them power to damn whom they lust? What mercy and profit have we in Christ's death, and in his gospel, if the pope, which passeth all men in wickedness, hath power to send whom he will to hell, and to damn whom he lusteth? We had then no cause, to call him Jesus, that is to say, Saviour; but might of right call him destroyer. Wherefore, then, this binding is to be understood as Christ interpreteth it in the places above rehearsed, and as the apostles practised it, and is nothing but to rebuke men of their sins by preaching the law. A man must first sin against God's law, ere the pope can bind him: yea, and a man must first sin against God's law, ere he need to fear the pope's curse. For cursing and binding are both one; and nothing, saving to rebuke a man of his sins by God's law. It followeth also, then, that the loosing is of like manner; and is nothing but forgiving of sin to them that repent, through preaching of the promises which God hath made in Christ; in whom only we have all forgiveness of sins, as Christ interpreteth it, and as the apostles and prophets practised it. So is it a false power that the pope taketh on him, to loose God's laws; as to give a man licence to put away his wife to whom God hath bound him, and to bind them to chastity, which God commandeth to marry; that is to wit, them that burn and cannot live chaste. It is also a false power to bind that which God's word maketh free, making sin in the creatures which God hath made for man's use.

The pope, which so fast looseth and purgeth in purgatory, cannot, with all the loosings and purgations that he hath, either loose or purge our appetites, and lust, and rebellion that is in us against the law of God. And yet the purging of them is the right purgatory. if he cannot purge them that are alive, wherewith purgeth he them that are dead? The apostles knew no other ways to purge, but through preaching God's word, which word only is that that purgeth the heart, as thou mayest see, John xv. "Ye are pure," saith Christ, "through the word." Now the pope preacheth not to them whom they feign to lie in purgatory, no more than he doth to us that are alive. How then purgeth he them? The pope is kin to Robin Goodfellow; which sweepeth the house, washeth the dishes, and purgeth all, by night; but when day cometh, there is nothing found clean.[17]

Some man will say, the pope bindeth them not, they bind themselves. I answer, he that bindeth himself to the pope, and had lever have his life and soul ruled by the pope's will than by the will of God, and by the pope's word than by the word of God, is a fool. And he that had lever be bond

---

17   Robin Goodfellow, the other name for Puck in Shakespeare's *A Midsummer Night's Dream*, was a popular figure of the trickster in English folk tradition.

than free, is not wise. And he that will not abide in the freedom wherein Christ hath set us, is also mad. And he that maketh deadly sin where none is, and seeketh causes of hatred between him and God, is not in his right wits. Furthermore, no man can bind himself, further than he hath power over himself. He that is under the power of another man, cannot bind himself without licence, as son, daughter, wife, servant, and subject. Neither canst thou give God that which is not in thy power. Chastity canst thou not give, further than God lendeth it thee: if thou cannot live chaste, thou art bound to marry or to be damned. Last of all, for what purpose thou bindest thyself must be seen. If thou do it to obtain thereby that which Christ hath purchased for thee freely, so art thou an infidel, and hast no part with Christ, and so forth.[18] If thou wilt see more of this matter, look in Deuteronomy, and there shalt thou find it more largely entreated.

Take another ensample of their false expounding the scripture. Christ saith, "The scribes and the Pharisees sit on Moses' seat: whatsoever they bid you observe, that observe and do; but after their works do not." Lo, say our sophisters or hypocrites, live we never so abominably, yet is our authority never the less. Do as we teach therefore, (say they,) and not as we do. And yet Christ saith, they sit on Moses' seat; that is, as long they teach Moses, do as they teach. For the law of Moses is the Law of God. But for their own traditions and false doctrine Christ rebuked them, and disobeyed them, and taught other to beware of their leaven. So if our Pharisees sit on Christ's seat and preach him, we ought to hear them; but when they sit on their own seat, then ought we to beware as well of their pestilent doctrine as of their abominable living.

Likewise where they find mention made of a sword, they turn it unto the pope's power. The disciples said unto Christ, Luke xxii. "Lo, here be two swords." And Christ answered, "Two is enough." Lo, say they, the pope hath two swords, the spiritual sword and the temporal sword. And therefore is it lawful for him to fight and make war.

Christ, a little before he went to his passion, asked his disciples, saying, "When I sent you out without all provision, lacked ye any thing? and they said, Nay. And he answered, But now let him that hath a wallet take it with him, and he that hath a scrip likewise; and let him that hath never a sword, sell his coat and buy one:" as who should say, "It shall go otherwise now than then. Then ye went forth in faith of my word, and my Father's promises; and it fed you and made provision for you, and was your sword, and shield, and defender; but now it shall go as thou readest Zechariah xiii. "I will smite the shepherd, and the sheep of the flock shall be scattered." Now shall my Father leave me in the hands of the wicked; and ye also shall be forsaken and destitute of faith, and shall trust in yourselves, and in your own provision, and in your own defence." Christ gave no commandment; but prophesied what should happen: and they, because they understood him not, answered," Here are two swords." And Christ (to make an end of such babbling) answered, "Two is enough." For if he had commanded every man to buy a sword, how had two been enough? Also, if two were enough, and pertained to the pope only, why are they all commanded to buy every man a sword? By the sword, therefore, Christ prophesied, that they should be left unto their own defence. And two swords were enough; yea, never-a-one had been enough: for if every one of them had had ten swords, they would have fled ere midnight.

In the same chapter of Luke, not twelve lines from the foresaid text, the disciples, even at the last supper, asked who should be the greatest. And Christ rebuked them, and said it was an heathenish thing, and there should be no such thing among them, but that the greatest should be as the smallest, and that to be great was to do service as Christ did.[19] But this text because it is brighter than the sun, that they can make no sophistry of it, therefore will they not hear it, nor let other know it.

Forasmuch now as thou partly seest the falsehood of our prelates, how all their study is to deceive us and to keep us in darkness, to sit as gods in our consciences, and handle us at their pleasure, and to lead us whither they lust; therefore I read thee, get thee to God's word, and thereby try all doctrine, and against that receive nothing; neither any exposition contrary unto the open texts,

18   Article XXIII against Tyndale: "He saith, If thou bind thyself to chastity, to obtain that which Christ purchased for thee, so surely art thou an infidel."

19   W. T.: "Christ rebuketh desire of pre-eminence in his disciples, but the pope challengeth it above all men as his own inheritance."

neither contrary to the general articles of the faith, neither contrary to the living and practising of Christ and his apostles. And when they cry, "Fathers, fathers," remember that it were the fathers that blinded and robbed the whole world, and brought us into this captivity, wherein these enforce to keep us still. Furthermore, as they of the old time are fathers to us, so shall these foul monsters be fathers to them that come after us; and the hypocrites that follow us will cry of these and of their doings, "Fathers, fathers," as these cry "Fathers, fathers," of them that are past. And as we feel our fathers, so did they that are past feel their fathers: neither were there in the world any other fathers than such as we both see and feel this many hundred years; as their decrees bear record, and the stories and chronicles well testify. If God's word appeared any where, they agreed all against it. When they had brought that asleep, then strove they one with another about their own traditions, and one pope condemned another's decrees, and were sometime two, yea, three popes at once.[20] And one bishop went to law with another, and one cursed another for their own fantasies, and such things as they had falsely gotten. And the greatest saints are they that most defended the liberties of the church (as they call it), which they falsely got with blinding kings; neither had the world any rest this many hundred years, for reforming of friars and monks, and ceasing of schisms that were among our clergy. And as for the holy doctors, as Augustine, Hierome, Cyprian, Chrysostomus, and Bede, will they not hear. If they wrote any thing negligently, (as they were men,) that draw they clean contrary to their meaning, and thereof triumph they. Those doctors knew of none authority that one bishop should have above another, neither thought or once dreamed that ever any such should be, or of any such whispering, or of pardons, or scouring of purgatory, as they have feigned.

And when they cry, "Miracles, miracles," remember that God hath made an everlasting testament with us in Christ's blood, against which we may receive no miracles,[21] no, neither the preaching of Paul himself, if he came again, by his own teaching to the Galatians, neither yet the preaching of the angels of heaven. Wherefore either they are no miracles but they have feigned them, (as is the miracle that St Peter hallowed Westminster;) or else if there be miracles that confirm doctrine contrary to God's word, then are they done of the devil, (as the maid of Ipswich and of Kent,) to prove us whether we will cleave fast to God's word, and to deceive them that have no love to the truth of God's word, nor lust to walk in his laws.

And forasmuch as they to deceive withal arm themselves against them with arguments and persuasions of fleshly wisdom, with worldly similitudes, with shadows, with false allegories, with false expositions of the scripture, contrary unto the living and practising of Christ and the apostles, with lies and false miracles, with false names, dumb ceremonies, with disguising of hypocrisy, with the authorities of the fathers, and last of all with the violence of the temporal sword; therefore do thou contrariwise arm thyself to defend thee withal, as Paul teacheth in the last chapter of the Ephesians: "Gird on thee the sword of the Spirit, which is God's word, and take to thee the shield of faith:" which is, not to believe a tale of Robin Hood, or Gesta Romanorum, or of the Chronicles, but to believe God's word that lasteth ever.

And when the pope with his falsehead challengeth temporal authority above king and emperor, set before thee the xxvith chapter of St Matthew, where Christ commandeth Peter to put up his sword. And set before thee Paul, 2 Cor. xth, where he saith, "The weapons of our war are not carnal things, but mighty in God to bring all understanding in captivity under the obedience of Christ;" that is, the weapons are God's word and doctrine, and not swords of iron and steel. And set before thee the doctrine of Christ and of his apostles, and their practice.

And when the pope challengeth authority over his fellow bishops and over all the congregation of Christ by succession of Peter, set before thee the first of the Acts; where Peter, for all his authority, put no man in the room of Judas; but all the apostles chose two indifferently, and cast

20   The references here are to the papal historian Platina concerning Stephen VI, who was elected pope in 897; and John IX, elected in 900. There were rival popes from September 21, 1378 to July 26, 1429.

21   Article XXIV against Tyndale: "He denieth, rebuketh, and damneth miracles." There follows here a gloss by W. T.: "The woman of Lenster was a solemn miracle." This note concerns a woman of Lenster who believed she lived by the food of angels. Sir Thomas More had claimed this was a fraud.

lots, desiring God to temper them, that the lot might fall on the most ablest. And (Acts viii.) the apostles sent Peter; and in the xith call him to reckoning, and to give accounts of that he hath done.

And when the pope's law commandeth, saying, though that the pope live never so wickedly and draw with him through his evil ensample innumerable thousands into hell, yet see that no man presume to rebuke him, for he is head over all, and no man over him; set before thee Galatians iind, where Paul rebuketh Peter openly: and see how both to the Corinthians, and also to the Galatians, he will have no superior but God's word, and he that could teach better by God's word. And because, when he rehearsed his preaching and his doings unto the high apostles, they could improve nothing, therefore will he be equal with the best.

And when the friars say, they do more than their duty when they preach, and more than they are bound to: ("To say our service are we bound, say they, and that is our duty; and to preach is more than we are bound to:") set thou before thee how that Christ's blood-shedding hath bound us to love one another with all our might, and to do the uttermost of our power one to another. And Paul saith, 1 Cor. ix. "Woe be unto me, if I preach not:" yea, woe is unto him that hath wherewith to help his neighbour, and to make him better, and do it not. If they think it more than their duty to preach Christ unto you, then they think it more than their duty to pray that ye should come to the knowledge of Christ. And therefore it is no marvel though they take so great labour, yea, and so great wages also, to keep you still in darkness.

And when they cry furiously, "Hold the heretics unto the wall, and if they will not revoke, burn them without any more ado; reason not with them, it is an article condemned by the fathers;" set thou before thee the saying of Peter, 1 Pet. iii. "To all that ask you be ready to give an answer of the hope that is in you, and that with meekness." The fathers of the Jews and the bishops, which had as great authority over them as ours have over us, condemned Christ and his doctrine. If it be enough to say the fathers have condemned it, then are the Jews to be holden excused; yea, they are yet in the right way, and we in the false. But and if the Jews be bound to look in the scripture, and to see whether their fathers have done right or wrong; then are we likewise bound to look in the scripture, whether our fathers have done right or wrong, and ought to believe nothing without a reason of the scripture and authority of God's word.

And of this manner defend thyself against all manner wickedness of our sprites, armed always with God's word, and with a strong and a stedfast faith thereunto. Without God's word do nothing. And to his word add nothing; neither pull any thing therefrom, as Moses everywhere teacheth thee. Serve God in the spirit, and thy neighbour with all outward service. Serve God as he hath appointed thee; and not with thy good intent and good zeal. Remember Saul was cast away of God for ever for his good intent. God requireth obedience unto his word; and abhorreth all good intents and good zeals which are without God's word: for they are nothing else than plain idolatry, and worshipping of false gods.[22]

And remember that Christ is the end of all things. He only is our resting-place, and he is our peace. For as there is no salvation in any other name, so is there no peace in any other name. Thou shalt never have rest in thy soul, neither shall the worm of conscience ever cease to gnaw thine heart, till thou come at Christ; till thou hear the glad tidings, how that God for his sake hath forgiven thee all freely. If thou trust in thy works, there is no rest. Thou shalt think, I have not done enough. Have I done it with so great love as I should do? Was I so glad in doing, as I would be to receive help at my need? I have left this or that undone: and such like. If thou trust in confession, then shalt thou think, Have I told all? Have I told all the circumstances? Did I repent enough? Had I as great sorrow in my repentance for my sins, as I had pleasure in doing them? Likewise in our holy pardons and pilgrimages gettest thou no rest. For thou seest that the very gods themselves, which sell their pardon so good cheap, or some whiles give them freely for glory sake, trust not therein themselves. They build colleges, and make perpetuities, to be prayed for for

---

22   Article XXV against Tyndale: "He saith that no man should serve God with good intent or zeal; for it is plain idolatry." To all of these charges Foxe replies in his biography of Tyndale. See below.

ever; and lade the lips of their beadmen, or chaplains, with so many masses, and diriges, and so long service, that I have known of some that have bid the devil take their founders' souls, for very impatiency and weariness of so painful labour.

As pertaining to good deeds therefore, do the best thou canst, and desire God to give strength to do better daily; but in Christ put thy trust, and in the pardon and promises that God hath made thee for his sake; and on that rock build thine house, and there dwell. For there only shalt thou be sure from all storms and tempests, and from all wily assaults of our wicked spirits, which study with all falsehead to undermine us. And the God of all mercy give thee grace so to do, unto whom be glory for ever! Amen.

[FROM TYNDALE'S TRANSLATION OF THE NEW TESTAMENT]

W. T. UNTO THE READER

Here thou hast (most dear reader) the new testament or covenant made with us of God in Christ's blood. Which I have looked over again (now at the last) with all diligence, and compared it unto the Greek, and have weeded out of it many faults, which lack of help at the beginning, and over-sight, did sow therein. If ought seem changed, or not altogether agreeing with the Greek, let the finder of the fault consider the Hebrew phrase or manner of speech left in the Greek words. Whose preterperfect tense and present tense is oft both one, and the future tense is the optative mode also, and the future tense is oft the imperative mode in the active voice, and in the passive ever. Like-wise person for person, number for number, and an interrogation for a conditional, and such like is with the Hebrews a common usage.

I have also in many places set light in the margin to understand the text by. If any man find faults either with the translation or ought beside (which is easier for many to do, than so well to have translated it themselves of their own pregnant wits, at the beginning without fore-example) to the same it shall be lawful to translate it themselves and to put what they lust thereto. If I shall perceive either by myself or by the information of other, that ought be escaped me, or might be more plainly translated, I will shortly after, cause it to be mended. Howbeit in many places, me thinketh it better to put a declaration in the margin, than to run too far from the text. And in many places, where the text seemeth at the first chop hard to be understood, yet the circumstances before and after, and often reading together, maketh it plain enough etc.

Moreover, because the kingdom of heaven, which is the scripture and word of God, may be so locked up, that he which readeth or heareth it, cannot understand it: as Christ testifieth how that the scribes and Pharisees had so shut it up (Matt. 23) and had taken away the key of knowledge (Luke 11) that their Jews which thought themselves within, were yet so locked out, and are to this day that they can understand no sentence of the scripture unto their salvation, though they can rehearse the texts everywhere and dispute thereof as subtly as the popish doctors of dunces' dark learning, which with their sophistry, served us, as the Pharisees did the Jews. There-fore (that I might be found faithful to my father and Lord in distributing unto my brethren and fellows of one faith, their due and necessary food: so dressing it and seasoning it, that the weak stomachs may receive it also, and be the better for it) I thought it my duty (most dear reader) to warn thee before, and to shew thee the right way in, and to give thee the true key to open it withal, and to arm thee against false prophets and malicious hypocrites, whose perpetual study is to leaven the scripture with glosses, and there to lock it up where it should save thy soul, and to make us shoot at a wrong mark, to put our trust in those things that profit their bellies only and slay our souls.

The right way: yea and the only way to understand the scripture unto our salvation, is, that we earnestly and above all thing, search for the profession of our baptism or covenants made between God and us. As for an example: Christ saith (Matt. 5) Happy are the merciful, for they shall obtain mercy. Lo, here God hath made a covenant with us, to be merciful unto us, if we will be merciful one to another: so that the man which sheweth mercy unto his neighbour, may be bold to trust in

God for mercy at all needs. And contrary-wise, judgement without mercy, shall be to him that sheweth not mercy (Jas. 2). So now, if he that showeth no mercy, trust in God for mercy, his faith is carnal and worldly, and but vain presumption. For God hath promised mercy only to the merciful. And therefore the merciless have no God's word that they shall have mercy: but contrary-wise, that they shall have judgement without mercy. And (Matt. 6) If ye shall forgive men their faults, your heavenly father shall forgive you: but and if ye shall not forgive men their faults, no more shall your father forgive you your faults. Here also by the virtue and strength of this covenant wherewith God of his mercy hath bound himself to us unworthy, may he that forgiveth his neighbour, be bold when he returneth and amendeth to believe and trust in God for remission of whatsoever he hath done amiss. And contrary-wise, he that will not forgive, cannot but despair of forgiveness in the end, and fear judgement without mercy.

The general covenant wherein all other are comprehended and included, is this. If we meek ourselves to God, to keep all his laws, after the example of Christ: then God hath bound himself unto us to keep and make good all the mercies promised in Christ, throughout all the scripture.

All the whole law which was given to utter our corrupt nature, is comprehended in the ten commandments. And the ten commandments are comprehended in these two: love God and thy neighbour. And he that loveth his neighbour in God and Christ, fulfilleth these two, and consequently the ten, and finally all the other. Now if we love our neighbours in God and Christ: that is to weet, if we be loving, kind and merciful to them, because God hath created them unto his likeness, and Christ hath redeemed them and bought them with his blood, then may we be bold to trust in God through Christ and his deserving, for all mercy. For God hath promised and bound himself to us: to show us all mercy, and to be a father almighty to us, so that we shall not need to fear the power of all our adversaries.

Now if any man that submitteth not himself to keep the commandments, do think that he hath any faith in God: the same man's faith is vain, worldly, damnable, devilish and plain presumption, as it is above said, and is no faith that can justify or be accepted before God. And that is it that James meaneth in his Epistle. For how can a man believe saith Paul, without a preacher (Rom. 10). Now read all the scripture and see where God sent any to preach mercy to any, save unto them only that repent and turn to God with all their hearts, to keep his commandments. Unto the disobedient that will not turn, is threatened wrath, vengeance and damnation, according to all the terrible curses and fearful examples of the Bible.

Faith now in God the father through our Lord Jesus Christ, according to the covenants and appointment made between God and us, is our salvation. Wherefore I have ever noted the covenants in the margins, and also the promises. Moreover where thou findest a promise and no covenant expressed therewith, there must thou understand a covenant. For all the promises of the mercy and grace that Christ hath purchased for us, are made upon the condition that we keep the law. As for an example: when the scripture saith (Matt. 7) Ask and it shall be given you: seek and ye shall find: knock and it shall be opened unto you. It is to be understood, if that when thy neighbour asketh, seeketh or knocketh to thee, thou then shew him the same mercy which thou desirest of God, then hath God bound himself to help thee again, and else not.

Also ye see that two things are required to begin a Christian man. The first is a steadfast faith and trust in almighty God, to obtain all the mercy that he hath promised us, through the deserving and merits of Christ's blood only, without all respect to our own works. And the other is, that we forsake evil and turn to God, to keep his laws and to fight against ourselves and our corrupt nature perpetually, that we may do the will of God every day better and better.

This have I said (most dear reader) to warn thee, lest thou shouldest be deceived, and shouldest not only read the scriptures in vain and to no profit, but also unto thy greater damnation. For the nature of God's word is, that whosoever read it or hear it reasoned and disputed before him, it will begin immediately to make him every day better and better, till he be grown into a perfect man in the knowledge of Christ and love of the law of God: or else make him worse and worse, till he be hardened that he openly resist the spirit of God, and then blaspheme, after the example of Pharaoh, Coza, Abiram, Balaam, Judas, Simon Magus and such other.

This to be even so, the words of Christ (John 3) do well confirm. This is condemnation saith he, the light is come into the world, but the men loved darkness more than light for their deeds were evil. Behold, when the light of God's word cometh to a man, whether he read it or hear it preached and testified, and he yet have no love thereto, to fashion his life thereafter, but consenteth still unto his old deeds of ignorance: then beginneth his just damnation immediately, and he is henceforth without excuse: in that he refused mercy offered him. For God offereth him mercy upon the condition that he will mend his living: but he will not come under the covenant. And from that hour forward he waxeth worse and worse, God taking his spirit of mercy and grace from him for his unthankfulness' sake.

And Paul writeth (Rom. 1) that the heathen because when they knew God, they had no lust to honour him with godly living, therefore God poured his wrath upon them, and took his spirit from them and gave them up unto their hearts' lusts to serve sin, from iniquity to iniquity till they were thoroughly hardened and past repentance.

And Pharaoh, because when the word of God was in his country and God's people scattered throughout all his land, and yet neither loved them or it: therefore God gave him up, and in taking his spirit of grace from him so hardened his heart with covetousness, that afterward no miracle could convert him.

Hereto pertaineth the parable of the talents (Matt. 25). The Lord commandeth the talent to be taken away from the evil and slothful servant and to bind him hand and foot and to cast him into utter darkness, and to give the talent unto him that had ten, saying: to all that have, more shall be given. But from him that hath not, that he hath shall be taken from him. That is to say, he that hath a good heart toward the word of God, and a set purpose to fashion his deeds thereafter and to garnish it with godly living and to testify it to other, the same shall increase more and more daily in the grace of Christ. But he that loveth it not, to live thereafter and to edify other, the same shall lose the grace of true knowledge and be blinded again and every day wax worse and worse and blinder and blinder, till he be an utter enemy of the word of God, and his heart so hardened, that it shall be impossible to convert him.

And (Luke 12) The servant that knoweth his master's will and prepareth not himself, shall be beaten with many stripes: that is, shall have greater damnation. And (Matt. 7) all that hear the word of God and do not, thereafter build on sand: that is, as the foundation laid on sand cannot resist violence of water, but is undermined and overthrown, even so the faith of them that have no lust nor love to the law of God built upon the sand of their own imaginations, and not on the rock of God's word according to his covenants, turneth to desperation in time of tribulation and when God cometh to judge.

And the vineyard (Matt. 21) planted and hired out to the husbandmen that would not render to the Lord, of the fruit in due time, and therefore was taken from them and hired out to other, doth confirm the same. For Christ saith to the Jews, the kingdom of heaven shall be taken from you and given to a nation that will bring forth the fruits thereof, as it is come to pass. For the Jews have lost the spiritual knowledge of God and of his commandments and also of all the scripture, so that they can understand nothing godly. And the door is so locked up that all their knocking is in vain, though many of them take great pain for God's sake. And (Luke 13) the fig tree that beareth no fruit is commanded to be plucked up.

And finally, hereto pertaineth with infinite other, the terrible parable of the unclean spirit (Luke 11) which after he is cast out, when he cometh and findeth his house swept and garnished, taketh to him seven worse than himself, and cometh and entereth in and dwelleth there, and so is the end of the man worse than the beginning. The Jews, they had cleansed themselves with God's word, from all outward idolatry and worshipping of idols. But their hearts remained still faithless to Godward and toward his mercy and truth and therefore without love also and lust to his law, and to their neighbours for his sake, and through false trust in their own works (to which heresy, the child of perdition, the wicked bishop of Rome with his lawyers hath brought us christians) were more abominable idolaters than before, and become ten times worse in the end than at the beginning. For the first idolatry was soon spied and easy to be rebuked of the prophets by the scripture. But the later is more subtle to beguile withal, and an hundred times of more difficulty to be weeded out of men's hearts.

This also is a conclusion, nothing more certain, or more proved by the testimony and examples of the scripture: that if any that favoureth the word of God, be so weak that he cannot chasten his flesh, him will the Lord chastise and scourge every day sharper and sharper, with tribulation and misfortune, that nothing shall prosper with him but all shall go against him, whatsoever he taketh in hand, and shall visit him with poverty, with sicknesses and diseases, and shall plague him with plague upon plague, each more loathsome, terrible and fearful than other, till he be at utter defiance with his flesh.

Let us therefore that have now at this time our eyes opened again through the tender mercy of God, keep a mean. Let us so put our trust in the mercy of God through Christ, that we know it our duty to keep the law of God and to love our neighbours for their fathers' sake which created them and for their lord's sake which redeemed them, and bought them so dearly with his blood. Let us walk in the fear of God, and have our eyes open unto both parts of God's covenants, certified that none shall be partaker of the mercy, save he that will fight against the flesh, to keep the law. And let us arm ourselves with this remembrance, that as Christ's works justify from sin and set us in the favour of God, so our own deeds through working of the spirit of God, help us to continue in the favour and the grace, into which Christ hath brought us; and that we can no longer continue in favour and grace than our hearts are to keep the law.

Furthermore concerning the law of God, this is a general conclusion, that the whole law, whether they be ceremonies, sacrifices, yea or sacraments either, or precepts of equity between man and man throughout all degrees of the world, all were given for our profit and necessity only, and not for any need that God hath of our keeping them, or that his joy is increased thereby or that the deed, for the deed itself, doth please him. That is, all that God requireth of us when we be at one with him and do put our trust in him and love him, is that we love every man his neighbour to pity him and to have compassion on him in all his needs and to be merciful unto him. This to be even so, Christ testifieth (Matt. 7) saying: this is the law and the prophets. That is, to do as thou wouldest be done to (according I mean to the doctrine of the scripture) and not to do that thou wouldest not have done to thee, is all that the law requireth and the prophets. And Paul (to the Romans 13) affirmeth also that love is the fulfilling of the law, and that he which loveth, doth of his own accord all that the law requireth. And (1 Tim. 1) Paul saith that the love of a pure heart and good conscience and faith unfeigned is the end and fulfilling of the law. For faith unfeigned in Christ's blood causeth to love for Christ's sake. Which love is the pure love only and the only cause of a good conscience. For then is the conscience pure, when the eye looketh to Christ in all her deeds, to do them for his sake and not for her own singular advantage or any other wicked purpose. And John both in his gospel and also epistles, speaketh never of any other law than to love one another purely, affirming that we have God himself dwelling in us and all that God desireth, if we love one the other.

Seeing then that faith to God and love and mercifulness to our neighbours, is all that the law requireth, therefore of necessity the law must be understood and interpreted by them. So that all inferior laws are to be kept and observed as long as they be servants to faith and love: and then to be broken immediately, if through any occasion, they hurt either the faith which we should have to Godward in the confidence of Christ's blood or the love which we owe to our neighbours for Christ's sake.

And therefore when the blind Pharisees murmured and grudged at him and his disciples, that they brake the sabbath day and traditions of the elders, and that he himself did eat with publicans and sinners, he answereth (Matt. 9) alleging Esaias the prophet: go rather and learn what this meaneth, I require mercy and not sacrifice. And (Matt. 12) Oh that ye wist what this meaneth, I require mercy and not sacrifice. For only love and mercifulness understandeth the law, and else nothing. And he that hath not that written in his heart, shall never understand the law, no: though all the angels of heaven went about to teach him. And he that hath that graven in his heart, shall not only understand the law but also shall do of his own inclination all that is required of the law, though never law had been given: as all mothers do of themselves without law unto their children, all that can be required by any law, love overcoming all pain, grief, tediousness or loathsomeness:

and even so no doubt if we had continued in our first state of innocency, we should ever have fulfilled the law, without compulsion of the law.

And because the law (which is a doctrine through teaching every man his duty, doth utter our corrupt nature) is sufficiently described by Moses, therefore is little mention made thereof in the new testament, save of love only wherein all the law is included, as seldom mention is made of the new testament in the old law, save here and there are promises made unto them, that Christ should come and bless them and deliver them, and that the gospel and new testament should be preached and published unto all nations.

The gospel is glad tidings of mercy and grace and that our corrupt nature shall be healed again for Christ's sake and for the merits of his deservings only: Yet on the condition that we will turn to God, to learn to keep his laws spiritually, that is to say, of love for his sake, and will also suffer the curing of our infirmities.

The new testament is as much to say as a new covenant. The old testament is an old temporal covenant made between God and the carnal children of Abraham, Isaac and Jacob otherwise called Israel, upon the deeds and the observing of a temporal law. Where the reward of the keeping is temporal life and prosperity in the land of Canaan, and the breaking is rewarded with temporal death and punishment. But the new testament is an everlasting covenant made unto the children of God through faith in Christ, upon the deservings of Christ. Where eternal life is promised to all that believe, and death to all that are unbelieving. My deeds if I keep the law are rewarded with the temporal promises of this life. But if I believe in Christ, Christ's deeds have purchased for me the eternal promise of the everlasting life. If I commit nothing worthy of death, I deserve to my reward that no man kill me: if I hurt no man I am worthy that no man hurt me. If I help my neighbour, I am worthy that he help me again etc. So that with outward deeds with which I serve other men, I deserve that other men do like to me in this world: and they extend no further. But Christ's deeds extend to life everlasting unto all that believe etc. This be sufficient in this place concerning the law and the gospel, new testament and old: so that as there is but one God, one Christ, one faith and one baptism, even so thou understand that there is but one gospel, though many write it and many preach it. For all preach the same Christ and bring the same glad tidings. And thereto Paul's epistles with the gospel of John and his first epistle and the first epistle of saint Peter, are most pure gospel and most plainly and richly described the glory of the grace of Christ: If ye require more of the law, seek in the prologue to the Romans and in other places where it is sufficiently intreated of.

Repentance

Concerning this word repentance or (as they used) penance, the Hebrew hath in the Old Testament generally *Sob* [shub] turn or be converted. For which the translation that we take for saint Jerome's hath most part *converti* to turn or be converted, and sometime yet *agere penitenciam*. And the Greek in the New Testament hath perpetually *metanoeo* to turn in the heart and mind, and to come to the right knowledge, and to a man's right wit again. For which *metanoeo* S. Jerome's translation hath: sometime *ago penetenciam* I do repent: sometime *peniteo* I repent: sometime *peniteor* I am repentant: sometime *habeo penitenciam* I have repentance: sometime *penitet me* it repenteth me. And Erasmus useth much this word *resipisco* I come to myself or to my right mind again. And the very sense and signification both of the Hebrew and also of the Greek word, is, to be converted and to turn to God with all the heart, to know his will and to live according to his laws, and to be cured of our corrupt nature with the oil of his spirit and wine of obedience to his doctrine. Which conversion or turning if it be unfeigned, these four do accompany it and are included therein: Confession, not in the priest's ear, for that is but man's invention, but to God in the heart and before all the congregation of God, how that we be sinners and sinful, and that our whole nature is corrupt and inclined to sin and all unrighteousness, and therefore evil, wicked and damnable, and his law holy and just, by which our sinful nature is rebuked: and also to our neighbours, if we have offended any person particularly. Then contrition, sorrowfulness that we be such, damnable sinners, and not only have sinned but are wholly inclined to sin still. Thirdly faith (of which our old doctors have made no mention at all in the description of their penance) yet God for Christ's sake doth forgive us and receive us to mercy, and is at one with us and will heal our corrupt nature. And fourthly satisfaction or amends-making, not to God with holy works, but to my neighbour whom I have hurt, and the congregation of God whom I have offended, (if any open crime be found in me) and submitting of a man's self unto the congregation or church of Christ, and to the officers of the same, to have his life corrected and governed henceforth of them, according to the true doctrine of the church of Christ. And note this: that as satisfaction or amends-making is counted righteousness before the world and a purging of the sin, so that the world when I have made a full amends, hath no further to complain. Even so faith in Christ's blood is counted righteousness and a purging of all sin before God.

Moreover, he that sinneth against his brother sinneth also against his father almighty God. And as the sin committed against his brother, is purged before the world with making amends or asking forgiveness, even so is the sin committed against God, purged through faith in Christ's blood only. For Christ saith (John 8) except ye believe that I am he, ye shall die in your sins. That is to say, if ye think that there is any other sacrifice or satisfaction to Godward, than me, ye remain ever in sin before God, howsoever righteous ye appear before the world. Wherefore now, whether ye call this *metanoia*, repentance, conversion or turning again to God, either amending and etc. or whether ye say repent, be converted, turn to God, amend your living or what ye lust, I am content so ye understand what is meant thereby, as I have now declared.

Elders

In the Old Testament the temporal heads and rulers of the Jews which had the governance over the lay or common people are called elders, as ye may see in the four evangelists. Out of which custom Paul in his epistle and also Peter, call the prelates and spiritual governors which are bishops and priests, elders. Now whether ye call them elders or priests, it is to me all one: so that ye understand that they be officers and servants of the word of God, unto the which all men both high and low that will not rebel against Christ, must obey as long as they preach and rule truly and no longer.

A prologue into the four Evangelists showing what they were and their authority. And first of

St Matthew

As touching the evangelists: ye see in the New Testament clearly what they were. First Matthew (as ye read Matt. 9, Mark 2, Luke 5) was one of Christ's apostles, and was with Christ all the time of his preaching, and saw and heard his own self almost all that he wrote.

Mark

Of Mark read (Acts 12) how Peter (after he was loosed out of prison by the angel) came to Mark's mother's house, where many of the disciples were praying for his deliverance. And Paul and Barnabas took him with them from Jerusalem and brought him to Antioch, (Acts 12). And (Acts 13) Paul and Barnabas took Mark with them when they were sent out to preach: from whom he also departed, as it apeareth in the said chapter, and returned to Jerusalem again. And (Acts 15) Paul and Barnabas were at variance about him, Paul not willing to take him with them, because he forsook them in their first journey. Notwithstanding yet, when Paul wrote the epistle to the Colossians, Mark was with him, as he saith in the fourth chapter: of whom Paul also testifieth, both that he was Barnabas' sister's son and also his fellow worker in the kingdom of God.

And (2 Tim. 4) Paul commandeth Timothy to bring Mark with him, affirming that he was needful to him, to minister to him. Finally, he was also with Peter when he wrote his first epistle, and so familiar that Peter calleth him his son. Whereof ye see, of whom he learned his gospel, even of the very apostles, with whom he had his continual conversation, and also of what authority his writing is, and how worthy of credence.

Luke

Luke was Paul's companion, at the least way from the 16th chapter of Acts forth and with him in all his tribulation. And he went with Paul at his last going up to Jerusalem. And from thence he followed Paul to Cæsarea, where he lay two years in prison. And from Cæsarea he went with Paul to Rome where he lay two other years in prison. And he was with Paul when he wrote to the Colossians, as he testifieth in the fourth chapter saying: the beloved Luke the physician saluteth you. And he was with Paul when he wrote the second epistle to Timothy. as he saith in the fourth chapter saying: Only Luke is with me. Whereby ye see the authority of the man and of what credence and reverence his writing is worthy of, and thereto of whom he learned the story of his gospel, as he himself saith, how that he learned it and searched it out with all diligence of them that saw it and were also partakers at the doing. And as for the Acts of the Apostles, he himself was at the doing of them (at the least) of the most part, and had his part therein, and therefore wrote of his own experience.

John

John, what he was, is manifest by the three first evangelists. First Christ's apostle, and that one of the chief. Then Christ's nigh kinsman, and for his singular innocency and softness, singularly beloved and of singular familiarity with Christ, and ever one of the three witnesses of most secret things. The cause of his writing was certain heresies that arose in his time, and namely two, of which one denied Christ to be very man and to be come in the very flesh and nature of man. Against which two heresies he wrote both his gospel and also his first epistle, and in the beginning of his gospel saith that the word or thing was at the beginning, and was with God, and was also very God and that all things was created and made by it, and that it was also made flesh: that is to say, became very man. And he dwelt among us (saith he) and we saw his glory.

And in the beginning of his epistle, he saith we shew you of the thing that was from the beginning, which also we heard, saw with our eyes and our hands handled. And again we shew you everlasting life, that was with the father and appeared to us, and we heard and saw, and etc.

In that he saith that it was from the beginning, and that it was eternal life, and that it was with God, he affirmeth him to be very God. And that he saith, we heard, saw and felt, he witnesseth that he was very man also. John also wrote last, and therefore touched not the story that the other had compiled. But writeth most of the faith and promises, and of the sermons of Christ.

This be sufficient concerning the four Evangelists and their authority and worthiness to be believed.

[TYNDALE'S TRANSLATION OF THE SERMON ON THE MOUNT]

MATTHEW 5–7

When he saw the people, he went up into a mountain, and when he was set, his disciples came to him, and he opened his mouth, and taught them saying: Blessed are the poor in spirit: for theirs is the kingdom of heaven. Blessed are they that mourn: for they shall be comforted. Blessed are the meek: for they shall inherit the earth. Blessed are they which hunger and thirst for righteousness: for they shall be filled. Blessed are the merciful: for they shall obtain mercy. Blessed are the pure in heart: for they shall see God. Blessed are the peacemakers: for they shall be called the children of God. Blessed are they which suffer persecution for righteousness' sake: for theirs is the kingdom of heaven. Blessed are ye when men revile you, and persecute you, and shall falsely say all manner of evil sayings against you for my sake. Rejoice, and be glad, for great is your reward in heaven. For so persecuted they the prophets which were before your days.

Ye are the salt of the earth: but and if the salt have lost her saltness, what can be salted therewith? It is thenceforth good for nothing, but to be cast out, and to be trodden under foot of men. Ye are the light of the world. A city that is set on an hill, cannot be hid, neither do men light a candle and put it under a bushel, but on a candlestick, and it lighteth all that are in the house. Let your light so shine before men, that they may see your good works, and glorify your father which is in heaven.

Think not that I am come to destroy the law, or the prophets: no I am not come to destroy them, but to fulfil them. For truly I say unto you, till heaven and earth perish, one jot or one tittle of the law shall not scape, till all be fulfilled.

Whosoever breaketh one of these least commandments, and teacheth men so, he shall be called the least in the kingdom of heaven. But whosoever observeth and teacheth, the same shall be called great in the kingdom of heaven.

For I say unto you, except your righteousness exceed, the righteousness of the scribes and Pharisees, ye cannot enter into the kingdom of heaven.

Ye have heard how it was said unto them of the old time: Thou shalt not kill. For whosoever killeth, shall be in danger of judgement. But I say unto you, whosoever is angry with his brother, shall be in danger of judgement. Whosoever sayeth unto his brother Raca, shall be in danger of a council. But whosoever sayeth thou fool, shall be in danger of hell fire.

Therefore when thou offerest thy gift at the altar, and there rememberest that thy brother hath ought against thee; leave there thine offering before the altar, and go thy way first and be reconciled to thy brother, and then come and offer thy gift.

Agree with thine adversary quickly, whiles thou art in the way with him, lest that adversary deliver thee to the judge, and the judge deliver thee to the minister, and then thou be cast into prison. I say unto thee verily: thou shalt not come out thence till thou have paid the utmost farthing.

Ye have heard how it was said to them of old time: Thou shalt not commit advoutry. But I say unto you, that whosoever looketh on a wife, lusting after her, hath committed advoutry with her already in his heart.

Wherefore if thy right eye offend thee, pluck him out, and cast him from thee. Better it is for thee that one of thy members perish, than that thy whole body should be cast into hell. Also if thy right hand offend thee, cut him off and cast him from thee. Better it is that one of thy members perish, than that all thy body should be cast into hell.

It is said, whosoever put away his wife, let him give her a testimonial also of the divorcement. But I say unto you: whosoever put away his wife, (except it be for fornication) causeth her to break matrimony. And whosoever marrieth her that is divorced, breaketh wedlock.

Again ye have heard how it was said to them of old time, thou shalt not forswear thyself, but shalt perform thine oath to God. But I say unto you, swear not at all: neither by heaven, for it is God's seat: nor yet by the earth, for it is his footstool: neither by Jerusalem, for it is the city of that great king: neither shalt thou swear by thy head, because thou canst not make one white hair, or black: But your communication shall be, yea, yea: nay, nay. For whatsoever is more than that, cometh of evil.

Ye have heard how it is said, an eye for an eye: a tooth for a tooth. But I say to you, that ye resist not wrong. But whosoever give thee a blow on thy right cheek, turn to him the other. And if any man will sue thee at the law, and take away thy coat, let him have thy cloak also. And whosoever will compel thee to go a mile, go with him twain. Give to him that asketh, and from him that would borrow turn not away.

Ye have heard how it is said: thou shalt love thine neighbour, and hate thine enemy. But I say unto you, love your enemies. Bless them that curse you. Do good to them that hate you. Pray for them which do you wrong and persecute you, that ye may be the children of your father that is in heaven: for he maketh his sun to arise on the evil, and on the good, and sendeth his rain on the just and unjust. For if ye love them, which love you: what reward shall ye have? Do not the publicans, even so? And if ye be friendly to your brethren only: what singular thing do ye? Do not the publicans likewise? Ye shall therefore be perfect, even as your father which is in heaven, is perfect.

CHAPTER SIX

Take heed to your alms, that ye give it not in the sight of men, to the intent that ye would be seen of them. Or else ye get no reward of your father which is in heaven. Whensoever therefore thou givest thine alms, thou shalt not make a trumpet to be blown before thee, as the hypocrites do in the synagogues and in the streets, for to be praised of men. Verily I say unto you, they have their reward. But when thou doest thine alms, let not thy left hand know, what thy right hand doth, that thine alms may be secret: and thy father which seeth in secret, shall reward thee openly.

And when thou prayest, thou shalt not be as the hypocrites are. For they love to stand and pray in the synagogues, and in the corners of the streets, because they would be seen of men. Verily I say unto you, they have their reward. But when thou prayest, enter into thy chamber, and shut thy door to thee, and pray to thy father which is in secret: and thy father which seeth in secret, shall reward thee openly.

And when ye pray, babble not much, as the heathen do: for they think that they shall be heard, for their much babbling's sake. Be ye not like them therefore. For your father knoweth whereof ye have need, before ye ask of him. After this manner therefore pray ye.

O our father which art in heaven, hallowed be thy name. Let thy kingdom come. Thy will be fulfilled, as well in earth, as it is in heaven. Give us this day our daily bread. And forgive us our trespasses, even as we forgive our trespassers. And lead us not into temptation: but deliver us from evil. For thine is the kingdom and the power, and the glory for ever. Amen. For and if ye shall forgive other men their trespasses, your heavenly father shall also forgive you. But and ye will not forgive men their trespasses, no more shall your father forgive your trespasses.

Moreover when ye fast, be not sad as the hypocrites are. For they disfigure their faces, that they might be seen of men how they fast. Verily I say unto you, they have their reward. But thou, when thou fastest, anoint thine head, and wash thy face, that it appear not unto men how that thou fastest: but unto thy father which is in secret: and thy father which seeth in secret, shall reward thee openly.

See that ye gather you not treasure upon the earth, where rust and moths corrupt, and where thieves break through and steal. But gather ye treasure together in heaven, where neither rust nor moths corrupt, and where thieves neither break up nor yet steal. For wheresoever your treasure is, there will your hearts be also.

The light of the body is thine eye. Wherefore if thine eye be single, all thy body shall be full of light. But and if thine eye be wicked then all thy body shall be full of darkness. Wherefore if the light that is in thee, be darkness: how great is that darkness.

No man can serve two masters. For either he shall hate the one and love the other: or else he shall lean to the one and despise the other: ye cannot serve God and mammon. Therefore I say unto you, be not careful for your life, what ye shall eat, or what ye shall drink, nor yet for your body, what ye shall put on. Is not the life more worth than meat, and the body more of value than raiment? Behold the fowls of the air: for they sow not, neither reap, nor yet carry into the barns: and yet your heavenly father feedeth them. Are ye not much better than they?

Which of you (though he took thought therefore) could put one cubit unto his stature? And why care ye then for raiment? Consider the lilies of the field, how they grow. They labour not neither spin. And yet for all that I say unto you, that even Solomon in all his royalty was not arrayed like unto one of these.

Wherefore if God so clothe the grass, which is today in the field, and tomorrow shall be cast into the furnace: shall he not much more do the same unto you, o ye of little faith?

Therefore take no thought saying: what shall we eat, or what shall we drink, or wherewith shall we be clothed? After all these things seek the Gentiles. For your heavenly father knoweth that ye have need of all these things. But rather seek ye first the kingdom of heaven and the righteousness thereof, and all these things shall be ministered unto you.

Care not then for the morrow, but let the morrow care for itself: for the day present hath ever enough of his own trouble.

CHAPTER SEVEN

Judge not, that ye be not judged. For as ye judge so shall ye be judged. And with what measure ye mete, with the same shall it be measured to you again. Why seest thou a mote in thy brother's eye, and perceivest not the beam that is in thine own eye? Or why sayest thou to thy brother: suffer me to pluck out the mote out of thine eye, and behold a beam is in thine own eye. Hypocrite, first cast out the beam out of thine own eye, and then shalt thou see clearly to pluck out the mote out of thy brother's eye.

Give not that which is holy, to dogs, neither cast ye your pearls before swine, lest they tread them under their feet, and the other turn again and all to rent you.

Ask and it shall be given you. Seek and ye shall find. Knock and it shall be opened unto you. For whosoever asketh receiveth and he that seeketh findeth, and to him that knocketh, it shall be opened. Is there any man among you which if his son asked him bread, would offer him a stone? Or if he asked fish, would he proffer him a serpent? If ye then which are evil, can give to your children good gifts: how much more shall your father which is in heaven, give good things to them that ask him?

Therefore whatsoever ye would that men should do to you, even so do ye to them. This is the law and the prophets.

Enter in at the strait gate: for wide is the gate, and broad is the way that leadeth to destruction: and many there be which go in thereat. But strait is the gate, and narrow is the way which leadeth unto life: and few there be that find it.

Beware of false prophets, which come to you in sheep's clothing but inwardly they are ravening wolves. Ye shall know them by their fruits. Do men gather grapes of thorns? Or figs of briars? Even so every good tree bringeth forth good fruit. But a corrupt tree, bringeth forth evil fruit. A good tree cannot bring forth bad fruit: nor yet a bad tree can bring forth good fruit. Every tree that bringeth not forth good fruit, shall be hewn down, and cast into the fire. Wherefore by their fruits ye shall know them.

Not all they that say unto me, Master, Master, shall enter in to the kingdom of heaven: but he that doth my father's will which is in heaven. Many will say to me in that day, Master, master, have we not in thy name prophesied? And in thy name have cast out devils? And in thy name have done many miracles? And then will I knowledge unto them, that I never knew them. Depart from me, ye workers of iniquity.

Whosoever heareth of me these sayings and doeth the same, I will liken him unto a wise man which built his house on a rock: and abundance of rain descended, and the floods came, and the winds blew and beat upon that same house, and it fell not, because it was grounded on the rock. And whosoever heareth of me these sayings and doth them not, shall be likened unto a foolish man which built his house upon the sand: and abundance of rain descended, and the floods came, and the winds blew and beat upon that house, and it fell, and great was the fall of it.

And it came to pass, that when Jesus had ended these sayings, the people were astonied at his doctrine. For he taught them as one having power, and not as the scribes.

[TYNDALE'S TRANSLATION OF THE PARABLE OF THE SOWER AND THE SEED]

MARK 4:1–34

And he began again to teach by the sea side. And there gathered together unto him much people, so greatly that he entered into a ship, and sat in the sea, and all the people was by the sea side on the shore. And he taught them many things in similitudes, and said unto them in his doctrine: Hearken to. Behold, There went out a sower to sow. And it fortuned as he sowed, that some fell by the way side, and the fowls of the air came and devoured it up. Some fell on stony ground, where it had not much earth: and by and by sprang up, because it had not depth of earth: but as soon as the sun was up it caught heat, and because it had not rooting, withered away.

And some fell among the thorns, and the thorns grew up and choked it, so that it gave no fruit. And some fell upon good ground and did yield fruit that sprang and grew, and brought forth: some thirty-fold, some sixty-fold and some an hundred-fold. And he said unto them: he that hath ears to hear, let him hear.

And when he was alone, they that were about him with the twelve asked him of the similitude. And he said unto them. To you it is given to know the mystery of the kingdom of God. But unto them that are without, shall all things be done in similitudes: that when they see, they shall see, and not discern: and when they hear they shall hear, and not understand; lest at any time they should turn, and their sins should be forgiven them. And he said unto them: Perceive ye not this similitude? how then should ye understand all other similitudes?

The sower soweth the word. And they that are by the way's side, where the word is sown, are they to whom as soon as they have heard it, Satan cometh immediately, and taketh away the word that was sown in their hearts. And likewise they that are sown on the stony ground, are they: which when they have heard the word, at once receive it with gladness, yet have no roots in themselves, and so endure but a time: and anon as trouble and persecution ariseth for the word's sake, they fall immediately. And they that are sown among the thorns, are such as hear the word: and the care of this world and the deceitfulness of riches and the lusts of other things, enter in and choke the word, and it is made unfruitful. And those that were sown in good ground, are they that hear the word and receive it, and bring forth fruit, some thirty-fold, some sixty-fold, some an hundred-fold.

And he said unto them: is the candle lighted, to be put under a bushel, or under the table, and not rather to be put on a candlestick? For there is nothing so privy, that shall not be opened: neither so secret, but that it shall come abroad. If any man have ears to hear, let him hear. And he said unto them: take heed what ye hear. With what measure ye mete, with the same shall it be measured unto you again. And unto you that hear shall more he given.[1] For unto him that hath, shall it be given: and from him that hath not, shall be taken away, even that he hath.

And he said: so is the kingdom of God, even as if a man should sow seed in the ground, and should sleep and rise up night and day: and the seed should spring and grow up, he not ware. For the earth bringeth forth fruit of herself: first the blade, then the ears, after that full corn in the ears. And as soon as the fruit is brought forth, anon he thrusteth in the sickle, because the harvest is come.

And he said: whereunto shall we liken the kingdom of God? or with what comparison shall we compare it? It is like a grain of mustardseed, which when it is sown in the earth, is the least of all seeds that be in the earth: but after that it is sown, it groweth up, and is greatest of all herbs: and beareth great branches, so that the fowls of the air may dwell under the shadow of it.

And with many such similitudes he preached the word unto them, after as they might hear it. And without similitude spake he nothing unto them. But when they were apart, he expounded all things to his disciples.

[TYNDALE'S TRANSLATION FROM]

THE GOSPEL OF SAINT LUKE, 1–2

Forasmuch as many have taken in hand to compile a treatise of those things, which are surely known among us, even as they declared them unto us, which from the beginning saw them theirselves,

---

[TYNDALE'S TRANSLATION OF THE PARABLE OF THE SOWER AND THE SEED]
MARK 4:1–34

1   W. T.: "A covenant to them that love the word of God to win other with word and deed: and another to them that love it not, that it shall be their destruction."

and were ministers at the doing: I determined also, as soon as I had searched out diligently all things from the beginning, that then I would write unto thee, good Theophilus:[1] that thou mightest know the certainty of those things, whereof thou art informed.

CHAPTER ONE

There was in the days of Herod king of Jewry, a certain priest named Zacharias, of the course of Abia. And his wife was of the daughters of Aaron: And her name was Elizabeth. Both were perfect before God, and walked in all the laws and ordinances of the Lord, that no man could find fault with them. And they had no child, because that Elizabeth was barren and both were well stricken in age.

And it came to pass, as he executed the priest's office before God, as his course came (according to the custom of the priest's office) his lot was to burn incense. And went into the temple of the Lord and the whole multitude of the people were without in prayer while the incense was a-burning. And there appeared unto him an angel of the lord standing on the right side of the altar of incense. And when Zacharias saw him, he was abashed, and fear came on him.

And the angel said unto him: fear not Zachary, for thy prayer is heard: And thy wife Elizabeth shall bear thee a son, and thou shalt call his name John, and thou shalt have joy and gladness, and many shall rejoice at his birth. For he shall be great in the sight of the lord, and shall neither drink wine nor strong drink. And he shall be filled with the holy ghost, even in his mother's womb: and many of the children of Israel shall he turn to their Lord God. And he shall go before him in the spirit and power of Elias to turn the hearts[2] of the fathers to the children, and the unbelievers to the wisdom of the just men: to make the people ready for the Lord.

And Zacharias said unto the angel: Whereby shall I know this? seeing that I am old and my wife well stricken in years. And the angel answered and said unto him: I am Gabriel that stand in the presence of God, and am sent to speak unto thee: and to shew thee these glad tidings. And behold thou shalt be dumb, and not able to speak until the time that these things be performed, because thou believedst not my words which shall be fulfilled in their season.

And the people waited for Zacharias, and marvelled that he tarried in the temple. And when he came out, he could not speak unto them. Whereby they perceived that he had seen some vision in the temple. And he beckoned unto them, and remained speechless.

And it fortuned, as soon as the time of his office was out, he departed home into his own house. And after those days, his wife Elizabeth conceived, and hid herself five months saying: This wise hath God dealt with me in the days when he looked on me, to take from me the rebuke that I suffered among men.

And in the sixth month the angel Gabriel was sent from God unto a city of Galilee, named Nazareth, to a virgin spoused to a man whose name was Joseph, of the house of David, and the virgin's name was Mary. And the angel went in unto her, and said: Hail full of grace, the Lord is with thee: blessed art thou among women.

When she saw him, she was abashed at his saying: and cast in her mind what manner of salutation that should be. And the angel said unto her: fear not Mary: for thou hast found grace with God. Lo: thou shalt conceive in thy womb, and shalt bear a son, and shalt call his name Jesus. He shall be great, and shall be called the son of the highest. And the lord God shall give unto him the seat of his father David, and he shall reign over the house of Jacob for ever, and of his kingdom shall be none end.

Then said Mary unto the angel: How shall this be, seeing I know not a man? And the angel answered and said unto her: The holy ghost shall come upon thee, and the power of the highest shall overshadow thee. Therefore also that holy thing which shall be born, shall be called the son

---

[TYNDALE'S TRANSLATION FROM]
THE GOSPEL OF SAINT LUKE, 1–2

1   Literally, "lover of God," perhaps the name of a Roman convert to Christianity.

2   W. T.: "To make the children have such an heart to God as Abraham and the Fathers had."

of God. And behold thy cousin Elizabeth, she hath also conceived a son in her age. And this is her sixth month, though she be called barren: for with God can nothing be unpossible. And Mary said: behold the handmaiden of the lord, be it unto me even as thou hast said. And the angel departed from her.

And Mary arose in those days, and went into the mountains with haste, into a city of Jewry and entered into the house of Zachary, and saluted Elizabeth. And it fortuned, as Elizabeth heard the salutation of Mary, the babe sprang in her belly. And Elizabeth was filled with the holy ghost, and cried with a loud voice, and said: Blessed art thou among women, and blessed is the fruit of thy womb. And whence happeneth this to me, that the mother of my Lord should come to me? For lo, as soon as the voice of thy salutation sounded in mine ears, the babe sprang in my belly for joy. And blessed art thou that believedst: for those things shall be performed which were told thee from the Lord. And Mary said:

My soul magnifieth the Lord.

And my spirit rejoiceth in God my saviour.

For he hath looked on the poor degree of his handmaiden. Behold now from henceforth shall all generations call me blessed.

For he that is mighty hath done to me great things, and holy is his name.

And his mercy is on them that fear him throughout all generations.

He sheweth strength with his arm, he scattereth them that are proud in the imagination of their hearts.

He putteth down the mighty from their seats, and exalteth them of low degree.

He filleth the hungry with good things: and sendeth away the rich empty.

He remembereth mercy: and helpeth his servant Israel.

Even as he promised to our fathers, Abraham and to his seed for ever.

And Mary abode with her about a three months, and returned again to her own house.

Elizabeth's time was come that she should be delivered, and she brought forth a son. And her neighbours and her cousins heard tell how the Lord had shewed great mercy upon her, and they rejoiced with her.

And it fortuned the eighth day: they came to circumcise the child: and called his name Zacharias, after the name of his father. Howbeit his mother answered, and said: not so, but he shall be called John. And they said unto her: There is none of thy kin, that is named with this name. And they made signs to his father, how he would have him called. And he asked for writing tables and wrote saying: his name is John. And they marvelled all. And his mouth was opened immediately, and his tongue also, and he spake lauding God. And fear came on all them that dwelt nigh unto them. And all these sayings were noised abroad throughout all the hill country of Jewry and all they that heard them laid them up in their hearts saying: What manner child shall this be? And the hand of the Lord was with him.

And his father Zacharias was filled with the holy ghost, and prophesied saying:

Blessed be the Lord God of Israel, for he hath visited and redeemed his people.

And hath raised up an horn of salvation unto us, in the house of his servant David.

Even as he promised by the mouth of his holy prophets which were since the world began,

That we should be saved from our enemies and from the hands of all that hate us:

To fulfil the mercy promised to our fathers, and to remember his holy covenant.

And to perform the oath which he sware to our father Abraham, for to give us.

That we, delivered out of the hands of our enemies, might serve him without fear, all the days of our life, in such holiness and righteousness that are accept before him.

And thou child, shalt be called the prophet of the highest: for thou shalt go before the face of the lord, to prepare his ways:

And to give knowledge of salvation unto his people, for the remission of sins:

Through the tender mercy of our God, whereby the day-spring[3] from on high hath visited us.

---

3   W. T.: "Christ is the day-spring that giveth light to them that sit
in darkness of the ignorance of God."

To give light to them that sat in darkness and in shadow of death, and to guide our feet into the way of peace.

And the child grew and waxed strong in spirit, and was in wilderness, till the day came when he should shew himself unto the Israelites.

CHAPTER TWO

And it chanced in those days: that there went out a commandment from August the Emperor, that all the world should be taxed. And this taxing was the first and executed when Cyrenius was lieutenant in Syria. And every man went unto his own city to be taxed. And Joseph also ascended from Galilee, out of a city called Nazareth, into Jewry: unto the city of David which is called Bethlehem, because he was of the house and lineage of David, to be taxed with Mary his spoused wife which was with child.

And it fortuned while they were there, her time was come that she should be delivered. And she brought forth her first begotten son, and wrapped him in swaddling clothes, and laid him in a manger, because there was no room for them within in the inn.

And there were in the same region shepherds abiding in the field and watching their flock by night. And lo: the angel of the Lord stood hard by them, and the brightness of the Lord shone round about them, and they were sore afraid. But the angel said unto them: Be not afraid. For behold, I bring you tidings of great joy that shall come to all the people: for unto you is born this day in the city of David, a saviour which is Christ the Lord. And take this for a sign: ye shall find the child swaddled and laid in a manger. And straightway there was with the angel a multitude of heavenly soldiers, lauding God and saying: Glory to God on high, and peace on the earth: and unto men rejoicing.

And it fortuned, as soon as the angels were gone away from them into heaven, the shepherds said one to another: let us go even unto Bethlehem, and see this thing that is happened which the Lord hath shewed unto us. And they came with haste, and found Mary and Joseph and the babe laid in a manger. And when they had seen it, they published abroad the saying which was told them of that child. And all that heard it, wondered at those things which were told them of the shepherds. But Mary kept all those sayings, and pondered them in her heart. And the shepherds returned, praising and lauding God for all that they had heard and seen, even as it was told unto them.

And when the eighth day was come that the child should be circumcised, his name was called Jesus, which was named of the angel before he was conceived in the womb.

And when the time of their purification (after the law of Moses) was come, they brought him to Jerusalem, to present him to the Lord (as it is written in the law of the Lord: every man that first openeth the matrix, shall be called holy to the Lord) and to offer (as it is said in the law of the Lord) a pair of turtle-doves or two young pigeons.

And behold there was a man in Jerusalem whose name was Simeon. And the same man was just and feared God, and longed for the consolation of Israel, and the holy ghost was in him. And an answer was given him of the holy ghost, that he should not see death, before he had seen the Lord's Christ. And he came by inspiration into the temple.

And when the father and mother brought in the child Jesus, to do for him after the custom of the law, then took he him up in his arms and said,

Lord, now lettest thou thy servant depart in peace, according to thy promise.

For mine eyes have seen the saviour sent from thee,

Which thou hast prepared before the face of all people.

A light to lighten the gentiles, and the glory of thy people Israel.

And his father and mother marvelled at those things which were spoken of him. And Simeon blessed them, and said unto Mary his mother: behold, this child shall be the fall and resurrection of many in Israel, and a sign which shall be spoken against. And moreover the sword shall pierce thy soul, that the thoughts of many hearts may be opened.

And there was a prophetess, one Anna, the daughter of Phanuel of the tribe of Aser: which was of a great age, and had lived with an husband seven years from her virginity. And she had been a widow about four score and four years, which went never out of the temple, but served God with fasting and prayer night and day. And the same came forth that same hour, and praised the Lord, and spake of him to all that looked for redemption in Jerusalem.

And as soon as they had performed all things according to the law of the Lord, they returned into Galilee to their own city Nazareth. And the child grew and waxed strong in spirit, and was filled with wisdom, and the grace of God was with him.

And his father and mother went to Jerusalem every year at the feast of Easter. And when he was twelve years old, they went up to Jerusalem after the custom of the feast. And when they had ful-filled the days, as they returned home, the child Jesus bode still in Jerusalem, unknowing to his father and mother. For they supposed he had been in the company, and therefore came a day's journey, and sought him among their kinsfolk and acquaintance. And when they found him not, they went back again to Jerusalem, and sought him. And it fortuned after three days, that they found him in the temple, sitting in the midst of the doctors, both hearing them and posing them. And all that heard him, marvelled at his wit and answers.

And when they saw him, they were astonied. And his mother said unto him: son, why hast thou thus dealt with us? Behold thy father and I have sought thee, sorrowing. And he said unto them: how is it that ye sought me? Wist ye not that I must go about my father's business? And they understood not the saying that he spake to them. And he went with them, and came to Nazareth, and was obedient to them. But his mother kept all these things in her heart. And Jesus increased in wisdom and age, and in favour with God and man.

[TYNDALE'S TRANSLATION FROM] THE GOSPEL OF SAINT JOHN, I

In the beginning was the word, and the word was with God: and the word was God. The same was in the beginning with God. All things were made by it, and without it, was made nothing, that was made. In it was life, and the life was the light of men, and the light shineth in the dark-ness, but the darkness comprehended it not.

There was a man sent from God, whose name was John. The same came as a witness to bear witness of the light, that all men through him might believe. He was not that light: but to bear witness of the light. That was a true light, which lighteth all men that come into the world. He was in the world, and the world was made by him: and yet the world knew him not.

He came among his own and his own received him not. But as many as received him, to them he gave power to be the sons of God in that they believed on his name: which were born, not of blood nor of the will of the flesh, nor yet of the will of man: but of God.[1]

And the word was made flesh and dwelt among us, and we saw the glory of it, as the glory of the only begotten son of the father, which word was full of grace and verity.

John bare witness of him and cried saying: This was he of whom I spake, he that cometh after me, was before me, because he was ere than I. And of his fulness have all we received, even grace for grace.[2] For the law was given by Moses, but grace and truth came by Jesus Christ. No man hath seen God at any time. The only begotten son, which is in the bosom of the father, he hath declared him.

And this is the record of John: When the Jews sent priests and Levites from Jerusalem, to ask him, what art thou? And he confessed and denied not, and said plainly: I am not Christ. And they asked him: what then? art thou Elias? And he said: I am not. Art thou a Prophet? And he answered no. Then said they unto him: what art thou that we may give an answer to them that sent us: What

[TYNDALE'S TRANSLATION FROM] THE GOSPEL OF SAINT JOHN, I
1   W. T.: "Faith maketh us the sons of God."

2   W. T.: "Grace: all grace: and all that is pleasant in the sight of God, is given us for Christ's sake only: even out of the fulness and abundance of the favour that he receiveth with his father."

sayest thou of thyself? He said: I am the voice[3] of a crier in the wilderness, make straight the way of the Lord, as said the Prophet Esaias.[4]

And they which were sent, were of the Pharisees. And they asked him, and said unto him: why baptisest thou then, if thou be not Christ nor Elias, neither a Prophet? John answered them saying: I baptise with water: but one is come among you, whom ye know not, he it is that cometh after me, which was before me, whose shoe latchet I am not worthy to unloose. These things were done in Bethabara beyond Jordan. where John did baptise.

The next day, John saw Jesus coming unto him, and said: behold the lamb of God, which taketh away the sin of the world. This is he of whom I said, After me cometh a man, which was before me, for he was ere than I, and I knew him not: but that he should be declared to Israel, therefore am I come baptising with water.

And John bare record saying: I saw the spirit descend from heaven, like unto a dove, and abide upon him, and I knew him not. But he that sent me to baptise in water, the same said unto me: upon whom thou shalt see the spirit descend and tarry still on him, the same is he which baptiseth with the holy ghost. And I saw and bare record, that this is the son of God.

The next day after, John stood again, and two of his disciples. And he beheld Jesus as he walked by, and said: behold the lamb of God. And the two disciples heard him speak, and followed Jesus. And Jesus turned about, and saw them follow, and said unto them: What seek ye? They said unto him: Rabbi (which is to say by interpretation, Master) where dwellest thou? He said unto them: come and see. They came and saw where he dwelt: and abode with him that day. For it was about the tenth hour.

One of the two which heard John speak and followed Jesus was Andrew, Simon Peter's brother. The same found his brother Simon first, and said unto him: we have found Messias, which is by interpretation, anointed: and brought him to Jesus. And Jesus beheld him and said: thou art Simon the son of Jonas, thou shalt be called Cephas: which is by interpretation, a stone.

The day following Jesus would go into Galilee, and found Philip, and said unto him, follow me. Philip was of Bethsaida the city of Andrew and Peter. And Philip found Nathanael, and said unto him. We have found him of whom Moses in the law, and the prophets did write. Jesus the son of Joseph of Nazareth. And Nathanael said unto him: can there any good thing come out of Nazareth? Philip said to him: come and see.

Jesus saw Nathanael coming to him, and said of him: Behold a right Israelite, in whom is no guile. Nathanael said unto him: where knewest thou me? Jesus answered, and said unto him: Before that Philip called thee, when thou wast under the fig tree, I saw thee. Nathanael answered and said unto him: Rabbi, thou art the son of God, thou art the king of Israel. Jesus answered and said unto him: Because I said unto thee, I saw thee under the fig tree, thou believest. Thou shalt see greater things than these. And he said unto him: Verily verily I say unto you: hereafter shall ye see heaven open, and the angels of God ascending and descending over the son of man.

[TYNDALE'S TRANSLATION OF LUTHER]

A PROLOGUE TO THE EPISTLE OF PAUL TO THE ROMANS

Forasmuch as this epistle is the principal and most excellent part of the new testament, and most pure evangelion, that is to say glad tidings and that we call gospel, and also a light and a way in unto the whole scripture, I think it meet, that every Christian man not only know it by rote and without the book, but also exercise himself therein evermore continually, as with the daily bread of the soul. No man verily can read it too oft or study it too well: for the more it

---

3   W. T.: "Voice: that is: I am that I preach. I am sent to prove you   4   Isaiah.
sinners and to cry on you to amend that ye may receive Christ and his
grace."

is studied the easier it is, the more it is chewed the pleasanter it is, and the more groundly it is searched the preciouser things are found in it, so great treasure of spiritual things lieth hid therein.

I will therefore bestow my labour and diligence, through this little preface or prologue, to prepare a way in thereunto, so far forth as God shall give me grace, that it may be the better understood of every man, for it hath been hitherto evil darkened with glosses and wonderful dreams of sophisters, that no man could spy out the intent and meaning of it, which nevertheless of itself, is a bright light, and sufficient to give light unto all the scripture.

First we must mark diligently the manner of speaking of the apostle, and above all things know what Paul meaneth by these words, the law, sin, grace, faith, righteousness, flesh, spirit and such like, or else read thou it never so oft, thou shalt but lose thy labour.[1] This word law may not be understood here after the common manner, and to use Paul's term, after the manner of men or after man's ways, that thou wouldest say the law here in this place were nothing but learning which teacheth what ought to be done and what ought not to be done, as it goeth with man's law where the law is fulfilled with outward works only, though the heart be never so far off. But God judgeth the ground of the heart, yea and the thoughts and the secret movings of the mind, and therefore his law requireth the ground of the heart and love from the bottom thereof, and is not content with the outward work only: but rebuketh those works most of all which spring not of love from the ground and low bottom of the heart, though they appear outward never so honest and good, as Christ in the gospel rebuketh the Pharisees above all other that were open sinners, and calleth them hypocrites, that is to say simulars, and painted sepulchres. Which Pharisees yet lived no men so pure, as pertaining to the outward deeds and works of the law. Yea and Paul in the third chapter of his epistle unto the Philippians confesseth of himself, that as touching the law he was such a one as no man could complain on, and notwithstanding was yet a murderer of the Christians, persecuted them, and tormented them, so sore, that he compelled them to blaspheme Christ, and was altogether merciless, as many which now fain outward good work are.

For this cause the 116th Psalm calleth all men liars, because that no man keepeth the law from the ground of the heart, neither can keep it, though he appear outward full of good works.

For all men are naturally inclined unto evil and hate the law. We find in ourselves unlust and tediousness to do good, but lust and delectation to do evil. Now where no free lust is to do good, there the bottom of the heart fulfilleth not the law, and there no doubt is also sin, and wrath is deserved before God, though there be never so great an outward show and appearance of honest living.

For this cause concludeth saint Paul in the second chapter, that the Jews are all sinners and transgressors of the law, though they make men believe, through hypocrisy of outward works, how that they fulfil the law, and saith that he only which doeth the law, is righteous before God, meaning thereby that no man with outward works, fulfilleth the law.

Thou (saith he to the Jew) teachest, a man should not break wedlock, and yet breakest wedlock thyself. Wherein thou judgest another man, therein condemnest thou thyself, for thou thyself dost even the very same things which thou judgest. As though he would say, thou livest outwardly well in the works of the law, and judgest them that live not so.

Thou teachest other men: and seest a mote in another man's eye, but art not ware of the beam that is in thine own eye. For though thou keep the law outwardly with works for fear of rebuke, shame and punishment, other for love of reward, vantage and vainglory, yet dost thou all without lust and love toward the law, and hadst liefer a great deal otherwise do, if thou didest not fear the law. Yea, inwardly in thine heart, thou wouldest that there were no law, no nor yet God, the author and avenger of the law, if it were possible: so painful it is unto thee to have thine appetites refrained, and to be kept down.

[TYNDALE'S TRANSLATION OF LUTHER]
A PROLOGUE TO THE EPISTLE OF PAUL TO THE ROMANS
1   W. T.: "How Paul useth certain words, must be diligently understood."

Wherefore then it is a plain conclusion, that thou from the ground and bottom of thine heart, art an enemy to the law. What prevaileth it now, that thou teachest another man not to steal, when thou thine own self art a thief in thine heart, and outwardly would fain steal if thou durst? – though that the outward deeds abide not alway behind with such hypocrites and dissemblers, but break forth among, even as an evil scab or a pock cannot always be kept in with violence of medicine.

Thou teachest another man, but teachest not thyself, yea thou wotst not what thou teachest, for thou understandest not the law aright, how that it cannot be fulfilled and satisfied, but with an unfeigned love and affection, so greatly it cannot be fulfilled with outward deeds and works only. Moreover the law increaseth sin, as he saith in the fifth chapter, because that man is an enemy to the law, forasmuch as it requireth so many things clean contrary to his nature, whereof he is not able to fulfil one point or tittle, as the law requireth it. And therefore are we more provoked, and have greater lust to break it.

For which cause's sake he saith in the seventh chapter, that the law is spiritual: as though he would say, if the law were fleshly and but man's doctrine, it might be fulfilled, satisfied and stilled with outward deeds.

But now is the law ghostly, and no man fulfilleth it, except that all that he doth, spring of love from the bottom of the heart. Such a new heart and lusty courage unto the law-ward, canst thou never come by of thine own strength and enforcement, but by the operation and working of the spirit.[2]

For the spirit of God only maketh a man spiritual and like unto the law, so that now hence-forth he doth nothing of fear or for lucre or vantage's sake or of vainglory, but of a free heart, and of inward lust. The law is spiritual and will be both loved and fulfilled of a spiritual heart, and therefore of necessity requireth it the spirit that maketh a man's heart free, and giveth him lust and courage unto the law-ward. Where such a spirit is not, there remaineth sin, grudging and hatred against the law, which law nevertheless is good, righteous and holy.

Acquaint thyself therefore with the manner of speaking of the apostle, and let this now stick fast in thine heart, that it is not both one, to do the deeds and works of the law, and to fulfil the law.[3] The work of the law is, whatsoever a man doth or can do of his own free will, of his own proper strength and enforcing, notwithstanding though there be never so great working, yet as long as there remaineth in the heart unlust, tediousness, grudging, grief, pain, loathsomeness, and compulsion toward the law, so long are all the works unprofitable, lost, yea and damnable in the sight of God. This meaneth Paul in the third chapter where he saith, by the deeds of the law shall no flesh be justified in the sight of God. Hereby perceivest thou, that those sophisters are but deceivers, which teach that a man may, and must prepare himself to grace and to the favour of God, with good works. How can they prepare themselves unto the favour of God, and to that which is good, when they themselves can do no good, no cannot once think a good thought or consent to do good, the devil possessing their hearts, minds and thoughts captive at his pleasure? Can those works please God, thinkest thou, which are done with grief, pain and tediousness, with an evil will, with a contrary and grudging mind?

O holy Saint Prosperus,[4] how mightily with the scripture of Paul, didst thou confound this heresy, about (I trow) a twelve hundred years ago, or thereupon.

To fulfil the law is, to do the work thereof and whatsoever the law cormmandeth, with love, lust and inward affection and delectation: and to live godly and well, freely, willingly, and without compulsion of the law, even as though there were no law at all. Such lust and free liberty to love the law, cometh only by the working of the spirit in the heart, as he saith in the first chapter.

---

2   W. T.: "The spirit is required, ere we can keep the law before God."
3   W. T.: "To do the deeds of the law, and to fulfil the law, are two things."
4   The reference here is to St. Prosper of Aquitaine (c.390–c.463), who sided with Augustine against Pelagius. Pelagianism stressed Jesus' directive "Be ye perfect" in arguing that some dimension of moral achievement must be possible by human effort and not by divine elec-

tion or by grace alone. It is no longer possible to draw a clear distinc-tion here between faith and works or between Pauline and Judeo-Chris-tianity (before his conversion Paul was a Pharisee). However, the epistles in the New Testament also include the Epistle of James, the brother of Jesus and head of the Jerusalem Church. James writes, "Faith, if it hath not works, is dead, being alone" (James 2:17), which seems to continue his controversy with Paul (cf. Galatians 2:12).

Now is the spirit none otherwise given, than by faith only, in that we believe the promises of God, without wavering, how that God is true, and will fulfil all his good promises toward us, for Christ's blood's sake, as it is plain in the first chapter. I am not ashamed saith Paul, of Christ's glad tidings, for it is the power of God, unto salvation to as many as believe. For at once and together even as we believe the glad tidings preached to us, the holy ghost entereth into our hearts, and looseth the bonds of the devil, which before possessed our hearts in captivity, and held them that we could have no lust to the will of God in the law. And as the spirit cometh by faith only, even so faith cometh by hearing the word or glad tidings of God, when Christ is preached, how that he is God's son and man also, dead and risen again for our sakes, as he saith in the third, fourth and tenth chapters. All our justifying then cometh of faith, and faith and the spirit come of God and not of us.

Hereof cometh it, that faith only justifieth, maketh righteous, and fulfilleth the law, for it bringeth the spirit through Christ's deservings, the spirit bringeth lust, looseth the heart, maketh him free, setteth him at liberty, and giveth him strength to work the deeds of the law with love, even as the law requireth. Then at the last out of the same faith so working in the heart, spring all good works by their own accord. That meaneth he in the third chapter: for after he hath cast away the works of the law, so that he soundeth as though he would break and disannul the law through faith: he answereth to that might be laid against, saying: we destroy not the law through faith but maintain, further or establish the law through faith. That is to say, we fulfil the law through faith.

Sin in the scripture is not called that outward work only committed by the body, but all the whole business and whatsoever accompanieth, moveth or strirreth unto the outward deed, and that whence the works spring: as unbelief, proneness and readiness unto the deed in the ground of the heart, with all the powers, affections and appetites wherewith we can but sin. So that we say, that a man then sinneth, when he is carried away headlong into sin, altogether as much as he is, of that poison inclination and corrupt nature wherein he was conceived and born. For there is none outward sin committed, except a man be carried away altogether, with life, soul, heart, body, lust and mind thereunto. The scripture looketh singularly unto the heart, and unto the root and original fountain of all sin, which is unbelief in the bottom of the heart. For as faith only justifieth and bringeth the spirit and lust unto the outward good works,[5] even so unbelief only damneth and keepeth out the spirit, provoketh the flesh and stirreth up lust unto the evil outward works, as happened to Adam and Eve in Paradise (Gen. 3).

For this cause Christ calleth sin unbelief, and that notably in the sixteenth chapter of John. The spirit, saith he, shall rebuke the world of sin, because they believe not in me. And (John 8) he saith: I am the light of the world. And therefore in the twelfth of John he biddeth them, while they have light, to believe in the light, that ye may be the children of light: for he that walketh in darkness wotteth not whither he goeth. Now as Christ is the light, so is the ignorance of Christ that darkness whereof he speaketh, in which he that walketh wotteth not whither he goeth: that is, he knoweth not how to work a good work in the sight of God, or what a good work is. And therefore in the ninth he saith: as long as I am in the world, I am the light of the world: but there cometh night when no man can work. Which night is but the ignorance of Christ in which no man can see to do any work that pleaseth God. And Paul exhorteth (Eph. 4) that they walk not as other heathen which are strangers from the life of God, through the ignorance that is in them. And again in the same chapter, Put off (saith he) the old man which is corrupt through the lusts of error, that is to say ignorance. And (Rom. 13) Let us cast away the deeds of darkness: that is to say of ignorance and unbelief. And (1 Pet. 1) Fashion not yourselves unto your old lusts of ignorance. And (1 John 2) He that loveth his brother dwelleth in light: and he that hateth his brother walketh in darkness, and wotteth not whither he goeth, for darkness hath blinded his eyes. By light he meaneth the knowledge of Christ, and by darkness, the ignorance of Christ. For it is impossible that he that knoweth Christ truly, should hate his brother.

5   W. T.: "Faith is the mother of all good works, and unbelief of evil."

Furthermore, to perceive this thing more clearly, thou shalt understand, that it is impossible to sin any sin at all except a man break the first commandment before. Now is the first commandment divided into two verses. Thy Lord God is one God: and thou shalt love thy Lord God with all thine heart, with all thy soul, with all thy power and with all thy might. And the whole cause why I sin against any inferior precept, is that this love is not in mine heart: for were this law written in my heart and were full and perfect in my soul, it would keep mine heart from consenting unto any sin. And the whole and only cause why this love is written in our hearts, is that we believe not the first part, that our Lord God is one God. For wist I what these words, one Lord and one God meaneth: that is to say, if I understood that he made all, and ruleth all, and that whatsoever is done to me, whether it be good or bad, is yet his will, and that he only is the Lord that ruleth and doth it: and wist I thereto what this word meaneth, that is to say, if mine heart believed and felt the infinite benefits and kindness of God to me-ward, and understood and earnestly believed the manifold covenants of mercy wherewith God hath bound himself to be mine, wholly and altogether, with all his power, love, mercy and might, then should I love him with all mine heart, soul, power and might, and of that love ever keep his commandments. So see ye now that as faith is the mother of all goodness and of all good works, so is unbelief the ground and root of all evil and all evil works.

Finally, if any man hath forsaken sin and is converted to put his trust in Christ and to keep the law of God, doth fall at a time: the cause is, that the flesh through negligence hath choked the spirit and oppressed her and taken from her the food of her strength. Which food is her meditation in God and in his wonderful deeds, and in the manifold covenants of his mercy.

Wherefore then before all good works as good fruits, there must needs be faith in the heart whence they spring. And before all bad deeds as bad fruits, there must needs be unbelief in the heart as in the root, fountain, pith and strength of all sin. Which unbelief and ignorance is called the head of the serpent and of the old dragon, which the woman's seed Christ must tread under foot, as it was promised unto Adam.

Grace and gift have this difference. Grace properly is God's favour, benevolence or kind mind, which of his own self, without deserving of us, he beareth to us, whereby he was moved and inclined to give Christ unto us, with all his other gifts of grace. Gift is the holy ghost and his working whom he poureth into the hearts of them, on whom he hath mercy, and whom he favoureth. Though the gifts of the spirit increase in us daily, and have not yet their full perfection: yea and though there remain in us yet evil lusts and sin which fight against the spirit, as he saith here in the seventh chapter, and in the fifth to the Galatians, and as it was spoken before in the third chapter of Genesis of the debate between the woman's seed and the seed of the serpent: yet nevertheless God's favour is so great, and so strong over us for Christ's sake, that we are counted for full as whole and perfect before God. For God's favour toward us divideth not herself, increasing a little and a little, as do the gifts, but receiveth us whole and altogether in full love for Christ's sake our intercessor and mediator, and because that the gifts of the spirit and the battle between the spirit and evil lusts, are begun in us already.

Of this now understandest thou the seventh chapter where Paul accuseth himself as a sinner and yet in the eighth chapter saith, there is no damnation to them that are in Christ, and that because of the spirit, and because the gifts of the spirit are begun in us. Sinners we are because the flesh is not full killed and mortified. Nevertheless inasmuch as we believe in Christ, and have the earnest and beginning of the spirit, and would fain be perfect, God is so loving and favourable unto us that he will not look on such sin, neither will count it as sin, but will deal with us according to our belief in Christ, and according to his promises which he hath sworn to us, until the sin be full slain and mortified by death.

Faith is not man's opinion and dream,[6] as some imagine and feign when they hear the story of the gospel: but when they see that there follow no good works nor amendment of living, though they hear, and yet can babble many things of faith, then they fall from the right way and say, faith only justifieth not, a man must have good works also, if he will be righteous and safe. The cause

---

6 W. T.: "Faith is not the work of man."

is when they hear the gospel or glad tidings, they fain of their own strength certain imaginations and thoughts in their hearts saying: I have heard the gospel, I remember the story, lo I believe. And that they count right faith, which nevertheless as it is but man's imagination and feigning even so profiteth it not, neither follow there any good works or amendment of living.

But right faith is a thing wrought by the holy ghost in us,[7] which changeth us, turneth us into a new nature and begetteth us anew in God, and maketh us the sons of God, as thou readest in the first of John, and killeth the old Adam, and maketh us altogether new in the heart, mind, will, lust and in all our affections and powers of the soul, and bringeth the holy ghost with her. Faith is a lively thing, mighty in working, valiant and strong, ever doing, ever fruitful, so that it is impossible that he which is endued therewith, should not work always good works without ceasing. He asketh not whether good works are to be done or not, but hath done them already, ere mention be made of them, and is always doing, for such is his nature now: quick faith in his heart and lively moving of the spirit drive him and stir him thereunto. Whosoever doeth not good works, is an unbelieving person and faithless, and looketh round about groping after faith and good works, and wot not what faith or good works mean, though he babble never so many things of faith and good works.

Faith is then a lively and steadfast trust in the favour of God, wherewith we commit ourselves altogether unto God, and that trust is so surely grounded and sticketh so fast in our hearts, that a man would not once doubt of it, though he should die a thousand times therefore. And such trust wrought by the holy ghost through faith, maketh a man glad, lusty, cheerful and true-hearted unto God and to all creatures. By the means whereof, willingly and without compulsion he is glad and ready to do good to every man, to do service to every man, to suffer all things, that God may be loved and praised, which hath given him such grace: so that it is impossible to separate good works from faith, even as it is impossible to separate heat and burning from fire.

Therefore take heed to thyself, and beware of thine own fantasies and imaginations, which to judge of faith and good works will seem wise, when indeed they are stark blind and of all things most foolish. Pray God that he will witesafe to work faith in thine heart, or else shalt thou remain evermore faithless, feign thou, imagine thou: enforce thou, wrestle with thyself, and do what thou wilt or canst.

Righteousness is even such faith, and is called God's righteousness, or righteousness that is of valour before God. For it is God's gift, and it altereth a man and changeth him to a new spiritual nature, and maketh him free and liberal to pay every man his duty. For through faith is a man purged of his sins, and obtaineth lust unto the law of God whereby he giveth God his honour and payeth him that he oweth him, and unto men he doeth service willingly wherewithsoever he can, and payeth every man his duty. Such righteousness can nature, freewill, and our own strength never bring to pass. For as no man can give himself faith, so can he not take away unbelief, how then can he take away any sin at all? Wherefore all is false hypocrisy and sin, whatsoever is done without faith or in unbelief, as it is evident in the fourteenth chapter unto the Romans, though it appear never so glorious or beautiful outwards.

Flesh and spirit mayest thou not here understand, as though flesh were only that which pertaineth unto unchastity, and the spirit that which inwardly pertaineth to the heart: but Paul calleth flesh here as Christ doth (John 3) All that is born of flesh, that is to weet, the whole man with life, soul, body, wit, will, reason and whatsoever he is or doth within and without, because that these all, and all that is in man, study after the world and the flesh. Call flesh therefore whatsoever (as long as we are without the spirit of God) we think or speak of God, of faith of good works and of spiritual matters. Call flesh also all works which are done without grace and without the working of the spirit, howsoever good, holy and spiritual they seem to be, as thou mayest prove by the fifth chapter unto the Galatians, where Paul numbereth worshipping of idols, witchcraft, envy and hate among the deeds of the flesh, and by the eighth unto the Romans, where he saith that the law by the reason of the flesh is weak which is not understood of unchastity only, but of all sins, and most specially, of unbelief which is a vice most spiritual and ground of all sins.

---

7   W. T.: "Right faith is of the working of the spirit of God."

And as thou callest him which is not renewed with the spirit and born again in Christ, flesh, and all his deeds, even the very motions of his heart and mind, his learning, doctrine and contemplation of high things, his preaching, teaching and study in scripture, building of churches, founding of abbeys, giving of alms, mass, matins and whatsoever he doeth, though it seem spiritual and after the law of God: So contrarywise call him spiritual which is renewed in Christ, and all his deeds which spring of faith, seem they never so gross as the washing of the disciples' feet, done by Christ, and Peter's fishing after the resurrection, yea and all the deeds of matrimony are pure spiritual, if they proceed of faith, and whatsoever is done within the laws of God, though it be wrought by the body, as the very wiping of shoes and such like, howsoever gross they appear outward. Without such understanding of these words canst thou never understand this epistle of Paul, neither any other place in the holy scripture. Take heed therefore, for whosoever understandeth these words otherwise, the same understandeth not Paul, whatsoever he be. Now will we prepare ourselves unto the epistle.

Forasmuch as it becometh the preacher of Christ's glad tidings, first through opening of the law, to rebuke all things and to prove all things sin, that proceed not of the spirit and of faith in Christ, and to prove all men sinners and children of wrath by inheritance, and how that to sin is their nature, and that by nature they can none otherwise do than to sin, and therewith to abate the pride of man, and to bring him unto the knowledge of himself, and of his misery and wretchedness, that he might desire help. Even so doeth saint Paul and beginneth in the first chapter to rebuke unbelief and gross sins which all men see, as the idolatry, and as the gross sins of the heathen were and as the sins now are of all them which live in ignorance without faith, and without the favour of God: and saith, the wrath of God of heaven appeareth through the gospel upon all men for their ungodly and unholy living. For though it be known and daily understood by the creatures, that there is but one God, yet is nature of herself without the spirit and grace so corrupt and so poisoned, that men neither can thank him, neither worship him, neither give him his due honour, but blind themselves and fall without ceasing into worse case, even until they come unto worshipping of images and working of shameful sins which are abominable and against nature, and moreover suffer the same unrebuked in other, having delectation and pleasure therein.

In the second chapter he proceedeth further, and rebuketh all those holy people also which without lust and love to the law, live well outwardly in the face of the world and condemn other gladly, as the nature of all hypocrites is, to think themselves pure in respect of open sinners, and yet hate the law inwardly, and are full of covetousness and envy and of all uncleanness, (Matt. 23). These are they which despise the goodness of God, and according to the hardness of their hearts, heap together for themselves the wrath of God. Furthermore saint Paul as a true expounder of the law, suffereth no man to be without sin, but declareth that all they are under sin which of freewill of nature, will live well, and suffereth them not to be better than the open sinners, yea he calleth them hard-hearted and such as cannot repent.

In the third chapter he mingleth both together, both the Jews and the Gentiles, and saith that the one is as the other, both sinners, and no difference between them, save in this only, that the Jews had the word of God committed unto them. And though many of them believed not thereon, yet is God's truth and promise thereby neither hurt nor diminished: And he taketh in his way and allegeth the saying of the fifty-first Psalm that God might abide true in his words and overcome when he is judged. After that he returneth to his purpose again, and proveth by the scripture, that all men without difference or exception are sinners, and that by the works of the law no man is justified: but that the law was given to utter and to declare sin only.[8] Then he beginneth and showeth the right way unto righteousness, by what means men must be made righteous and safe, and saith: They are all sinners and without praise before God, and must without their own deserving be made righteous through faith in Christ, which hath deserved such righteousness for us, and is become unto us God's mercystool for the remission of sins that are past, thereby proving that

---

8　W. T.: "The law justifieth not: but uttereth the sin only and condemneth."

Christ's righteousness which cometh on us through faith, helpeth us only. Which righteousness, saith he, is now declared through the gospel and was testified of before by the law and the prophets. Furthermore (saith he) the law is helped and furthered through faith, though that the works thereof with all their boast are brought to nought and proved not to justify.

In the fourth chapter (after that now by the three first chapters, the sins are opened, and the way of faith unto righteousness laid) he beginneth to answer unto certain objections and cavillations. And first he putteth forth those blind reasons, which commonly they that will be justified by their own works, are wont to make when they hear that faith only without works justifieth, saying, shall men do no good works, yea and if faith only justifieth, what needeth a man to study for to do good works? He putteth forth therefore Abraham for an example, saying: What did Abraham with his works? was all in vain? came his works to no profit? And so concludeth that Abraham without and before all works was justified and made righteous. Insomuch that before the work of circumcision he was praised of the scripture and called righteous by his faith only, (Genesis 15). So that he did not the work of circumcision for to be helped thereby unto righteousness, which yet God commanded him to do, and was a good work of obedience, so in like wise no doubt none other works help anything at all unto a man's justifying: but as Abraham's circumcision was an outward sign whereby he declared his righteousness which he had by faith, and his obedience and readiness unto the will of God, even so are all other good works outward signs and outward fruit of faith and of the spirit,[9] which justify not a man, but that a man is justified already before God inwardly in the heart, through faith and through the spirit purchased by Christ's blood.

Herewith now establisheth saint Paul his doctrine of faith afore rehearsed in the third chapter, and bringeth also testimony of David in the thirty-second Psalm, which calleth a man blessed not of works, but in that his sin is not reckoned and in that faith is imputed for righteousness, though he abide not afterward without good works, when he is once justified.[10]

For we are justified and receive the spirit for to do good works, neither were it otherwise possible to do good works, except we had first the spirit.

For how is it possible to do anything well in the sight of God, while we are yet in captivity and bondage under the devil, and the devil possesseth us altogether and holdeth our hearts, so that we cannot once consent unto the will of God. No man therefore can prevent the spirit in doing good: but the spirit must first come and wake him out of his sleep and with the thunder of the law fear him, and show him his miserable estate and wretchedness, and make him abhor, and hate himself and to desire help, and then comfort him again with the pleasant rain of the gospel, that is to say, with the sweet promises of God in Christ, and stir up faith in him to believe the promises. Then when he believeth the promises, as God was merciful to promise, so is he true to fulfil them, and will give him the spirit and strength, both to love the will of God and to work thereafter. So see we that God only (which according to the scripture worketh all in all things) worketh a man's justifying, salvation and health, yea and poureth faith and belief, lust to love God's will, and strength to fulfil the same, into us, even as water is poured into a vessel, and that of his good will and purpose, and not of our deservings and merits. God's mercy in promising and truth in fulfilling his promises saveth us and not we ourselves. And therefore is all laud, praise and glory, to be given unto God for his mercy and truth, and not unto us for our merits and deservings. After that, he stretcheth his example out against all other good work of the law, and concludeth that the Jews cannot be Abraham's heirs because of blood and kindred only, and much less by the works of the law, but must inherit Abraham's faith, if they will be the right heirs of Abraham forasmuch as Abraham before the law, both of Moses and also of circumcision, was through faith made righteous and called the father of all them that believe, and not of them that work. Moreover the law causeth wrath, inasmuch as no man can fulfil it with love and lust, and as long as such grudging, hate and indignation against the law remaineth in the heart, and is not taken away by the spirit that cometh by faith, so long (no doubt) the works of the law, declare evidently that the wrath of God is upon us and not favour. Wherefore faith only receiveth the grace promised unto Abraham. And these examples were not written for Abraham's sake only (saith he) but for ours also

---

9 W. T.: "Outward works are signs and witnesses of the inward faith."   10 W. T.: "Blessed is he that hath his sins forgiven him."

to whom if we believe, faith shall be reckoned likewise for righteousness, as he saith in the end of the chapter.

In the fifth chapter he commendeth the fruits and works of faith, as are peace, rejoicing in the conscience, inward love, to God and man: moreover, boldness, trust, confidence and a strong and a lusty mind and steadfast hope in tribulation and suffering. For all such follow, where the right faith is, for the abundant grace's sake and gifts of the spirit, which God hath given us in Christ, in that he gave him to die for us yet his enemies. Now have we then that faith only before all works justifieth, and that it followeth not yet therefore that a man should do no good works but that the right shapen works abide not behind, but accompany faith, even as brightness doth the sun, and are called of Paul the fruits of the spirit. Where the spirit is, there it is always summer and there are always good fruits, that is to say: good works. This is Paul's order, that good works spring of the spirit, the spirit cometh by faith and faith cometh by hearing the word of God, when the glad tidings and promises which God hath made to us in Christ, are preached truly, and received in the ground of the heart without wavering or doubting after that the law hath passed upon us and hath damned our consciences. Where the word of God is preached purely and received in the heart, there is faith and the spirit of God, and there are also good works of necessity whensoever occasion is given. Where God's word is not purely preached, but men's dreams, traditions, imaginations, inventions, ceremonies and superstition, there is no faith and consequently no spirit that cometh of God. And where God's spirit is not, there can be no good works, even as where an apple tree is not, there can grow no apples, but there is unbelief, the devil's spirit and evil works. Of this God's spirit and his fruit, have our holy hypocrites not once known, neither yet tasted how sweet they are, though they feign many good works of their own imagination, to be justified withal, in which is not one crumb of true faith or spiritual love, or of inward joy, peace and quietness of conscience, forasmuch as they have not the word of God for them, that such works please God, but they are even the rotten fruits of a rotten tree.

After that he breaketh forth, and runneth at large, and showeth whence both sin and righteousness, death and life come. And he compareth Adam and Christ together, thuswise reasoning and disputing, that Christ must needs come as a second Adam to make us heirs of his righteousness, through a new spiritual birth, without our deservings: even as the first Adam made us heirs of sin, through the bodily generation, without our deserving. Whereby is evidently known and proved to the uttermost, that no man can bring himself out of sin unto rightousness, no more than he could have withstood that he was born bodily. And that is proved herewith, forasmuch as the very law of God, which of right should have helped if anything could have helped, not only came and brought no help with her, but also increased sin, because that the evil and poisoned nature is offended and utterly displeased with the law, and the more she is forced by the law, the more is she provoked and set afire to fulfil and satisfy her lusts. By the law then we see clearly that we must needs have Christ to justify us with his grace, and to help nature.

In the sixth he setteth forth the chief and principal work of faith, the battle of the spirit against the flesh, how the spirit laboureth and enforceth to kill the remnant of sin and lust which remain in the flesh, after our justifying. And this chapter teacheth us, that we are not so free from sin through faith, that we should henceforth go up and down idle careless and sure of ourselves, as though there were now no more sin in us. Yes there is sin remaining in us, but it is not reckoned, because of faith and of the spirit, which fight against it. Wherefore we have enough to do all our lives long, to tame our bodies, and to compel the members to obey the spirit and not the appetites, that thereby we might be like unto Christ's death and resurrection, and might fulfil our baptism, which signifieth the mortifying of sins, and the new life of grace.[11] For this battle ceaseth not in us until the last breath, and until that sin be utterly slain by the death of the body.

This thing (I mean to tame the body and so forth) we are able to do (saith he) seeing we are under grace and not to be under the law, what it is, not to be under the law, he himself expoundeth. For not to be under the law is not so to be understood, that every man may do what him lusteth.

But not to be under the law, is to have a free heart renewed with the spirit, so that thou hast lust inwardly of thine own accord to do that which the law commandeth without compulsion, yea though there were no law. For grace, that is to say God's favour bringeth us the spirit, and maketh us love the law, so is there now no more sin, neither is the law now any more against us, but at one and agreed with us and we with it.

But to be under the law, is to deal with the works of the law, and to work without the spirit and grace: for so long no doubt sin reigneth in us through the law, that is to say, the law declareth that we are under sin and that sin hath power and dominion over us, seeing we cannot fulfil the law, namely within, in the heart, forasmuch as no man of nature favoureth the law, consenteth thereunto and therein. Which thing is exceeding great sin, that we cannot consent to the law which law is nothing else save the will of God.

This is the right freedom and liberty from sin and from the law whereof he writeth unto the end of this chapter, that it is a freedom to do good only with lust, and to live well without compulsion of the law. Wherefore this freedom is a spiritual freedom, which destroyeth not the law, but ministreth that which the law requireth, and wherewith the law is fulfilled, that is to understand, lust and love, wherewith the law is stilled and accuseth us no more, compelleth us no more, neither hath ought to crave of us any more. Even as though thou were in debt to another man, and were not able to pay, two manner ways mightest thou be loosed. One way, if he would require nothing of thee, and break thine obligation. Another way, if some other good man would pay for thee, and give thee as much as thou mightest satisfy thine obligation withal. Of this wise hath Christ made us free from the law: and therefore is this no wild fleshly liberty, that should do nought, but that doeth all things, and is free from the craving and debt of the law.

In the seventh he confirmeth the same with a similitude of the state of matrimony. As when the husband dieth the wife is at her liberty, and the one loosed and departed from the other, not that the woman should not have power to marry unto another man, but rather now first of all is she free and hath power to marry unto another man which she could not do before, till she was loosed from her first husband. Even so are our consciences bound and in danger to the law under old Adam the flesh, as long as he liveth in us. For the law declareth that our hearts are bound and that we cannot disconsent from him. But when he is mortified and killed by the spirit, then is the conscience free and at liberty: not so that the conscience shall now nought do, but now first of all cleaveth unto another, that is to wit Christ, and bringeth forth the fruits of life. So now to be under the law, is not to be able to fulfil the law, but to be debtor to it and not able to pay that which the law requireth. And to be loose from the law, is to fulfil it and to pay that which the law demandeth, so that it can now henceforth ask thee nought.

Consequently Paul declareth more largely the nature of sin and of the law, how that through the law sin reviveth, moveth herself, and gathereth strength. For the old man and corrupt nature, the more he is forbidden and kept under of the law, is the more offended and displeased therewith, forasmuch as he cannot pay that which is required of the law. For sin is his nature and of himself, he cannot but sin. Therefore is the law death to him, torment and martyrdom. Not that the law is evil, but because that the evil nature cannot suffer that which is good, cannot abide that the law should require of him any good thing. Like as a sick man cannot suffer that a man should desire of him to run, to leap and to do other deeds of an whole man.

For which cause Saint Paul concludeth, that where the law is understood and perceived of the best wise, there it doeth no more but utter sin, and bring us unto the knowledge of our selves, and thereby kill us and make us bond unto eternal damnation and debtors of the everlasting wrath of God, even as he well feeleth and understandeth whose conscience is truly touched of the law. In such danger were we ere the law came, that we knew not what sin meant, neither yet know we the wrath of God upon sinners, till the law had uttered it. So seest thou that a man must have some other thing, yea and a greater and a more mighty thing than the law, to make him righteous and safe. They that understand not the law on this wise, are blind and go to work presumptuously, supposing to satisfy the law with works. For they know not that the law requireth a free, a willing, a lusty and a loving heart. Therefore they see not Moses right in the face, the veil hangeth between and hideth his face so that they cannot behold the glory of his countenance, how that the law is spiritual and requireth the heart. I may of mine own strength refrain that I do mine enemy no hurt, but to love him with all mine heart, and to put away wrath clean out of my mind can I not of mine own strength. I may refuse money of mine own strength, but to put away love unto riches out of mine heart can I not do of mine own strength. To abstain from adultery as concerning the deed can I do of mine own strength, but not to desire in mine heart is as unpossible unto me as is to choose whether I will hunger or thirst, and yet so the law requireth. Wherefore of a man's own strength is the law never fulfilled, we must have there unto God's favour and his spirit, purchased by Christ's blood.

Nevertheless when I say a man may do many things outwardly clean against his heart, we must understand that man is but driven of divers appetites, and the greatest appetite overcometh the less and carrieth the man away violently with her.

As when I desire vengeance, and fear also the inconvenience that is like to follow, if fear be greater, I abstain and if the appetite that desireth vengeance be greater, I cannot but prosecute the deed, as we see by experience in many murderers and thieves, which though they be brought into never so great peril of death, yet after they have escaped, do even, the same again. And common women prosecute their lusts because fear and shame are away, when other which have the same appetites in their hearts, abstain at the least way outwardly or work secretly being overcome of fear and of shame, and so likewise is it of all other appetites.

Furthermore he declareth, how the spirit and the flesh fight together in one man, and maketh an example of himself, that we might learn to know that work aright, I mean to kill sin in our-selves. He calleth both the spirit and also the flesh a law, because that like as the nature of God's law is to drive, to compel, and to crave, even so the flesh driveth, compelleth, craveth and rageth, against the spirit, and will have her lusts satisfied.

On the other side driveth the spirit, crieth and fighteth against the flesh, and will have his lust satisfied. And this strife dureth in us, as long as we live: in some more and in some less as the spirit or the flesh is stronger, and the very man his own self is both the spirit and the flesh, which fight-eth with his own self until sin be utterly slain and he altogether spiritual.

In the eighth chapter he comforteth such fighters that they despair not because of such flesh, or think that they are less in favour with God. And he sheweth how that the sin remaining in us, hurteth not, for there is no danger to them that are in Christ which walk not after the flesh, but fight against it. And he expoundeth more largely what the nature of the flesh and of the spirit is, and how the spirit cometh by Christ, which spirit maketh us spiritual, tameth, subdueth and mor-tifieth the flesh, and certifieth us that we are nevertheless the sons of God, and also beloved, though that sin rage never so much in us, so long as we follow the spirit and fight against sin to kill and mortify it. And because the chastising of the cross and suffering are nothing pleasant, he com-forteth us in our passions and afflictions by the assistance of the spirit which maketh intercession to God for us, mightily with groanings that pass man's utterance, so that man's speech cannot com-prehend them, and the creatures mourn also with us of great desire that they have, that we were loosed from sin and corruption of the flesh. So see we that these three chapters, the sixth, seventh and eighth, do none other thing so much as to drive us unto the right work of faith, which is to kill the old man and mortify the flesh.

In the ninth, tenth and eleventh chapters he treateth of God's predestination, whence it springeth altogether, whether we shall believe or not believe, be loosed from sin or not be loosed. By which predestination our justifying and salvation are clean taken out of our hands, and put in the hands of God only, which thing is most necessary of all. For we are so weak and so uncertain, that if it stood in us, there would of a truth no man be saved, the devil no doubt would deceive us. But now is God sure, that his predestination cannot deceive him, neither can any man with-stand or let him, and therefore have we hope and trust against sin.

But here must a mark be set unto those unquiet, busy and high-climbing spirits how far they shall go, which first of all bring hither their high reasons and pregnant wits, and begin first from on high to search the bottomless secrets of God's predestination, whether they be predestinate or not. These must needs either cast themselves down headlong into desperation or else commit them-selves to free chance careless. But follow thou the order of this epistle, and noosell thyself with

Christ, and learn to understand what the law and the gospel mean, and the office of both two, that thou mayst in the one know thyself, and how that thou hast of thyself no strength, but to sin: and in the other the grace of Christ. And then see thou fight against sin and the flesh as the seven first chapters teach thee. After that when thou art come to the eighth chapter, and art under the cross and suffering of tribulation, the necessity of predestination will wax sweet and thou shalt well feel how precious a thing it is. For except thou have borne the cross of adversity and temptation, and hast felt thyself brought unto the very brim of desperation, yea and unto hell gates, thou canst never meddle with the sentence of predestination without thine own harm, and without secret wrath and grudging inwardly against God, for otherwise it shall not be possible for thee to think that God is righteous and just. Therefore must Adam be well mortified and the fleshly wit brought utterly to nought, ere that thou mayst away with this thing, and drink so strong wine. Take heed therefore unto thyself, that thou drink not wine, while thou art yet but a suckling. For every learning hath her time, measure and age, and in Christ is there a certain childhood, in which a man must be content with milk for a season, until he wax strong and grow up unto a perfect man in Christ, and be able to eat of more strong meat.

In the twelfth chapter he giveth exhortations. For this manner observeth Paul in all his epistles, first he teacheth Christ and the faith, then exhorteth he to good works, and unto continual mortifying of the flesh. So here teacheth he good works indeed, and the true serving of God, and maketh all men priests, to offer up not money and beasts, as the manner was in the time of the law, but their own bodies, with killing and mortifying of the lusts of the flesh. After that he describeth the outward conversation of Christian men, how they ought to behave themselves in spiritual things, how to teach, preach and rule in the congregation of Christ, to serve one another, to suffer all things patiently, and to commit the wreak and vengeance to God, in conclusion how a Christian man ought to behave himself unto all men, to friend, foe or whatsoever he be. These are the right works of a Christian man which spring out of faith. For faith keepeth not holiday neither suffereth any man to be idle, wheresoever he dwelleth.

In the thirteenth he teacheth to honour the wordly and temporal sword. For though that man's law and ordinance make not a man good before God, neither justify him in the heart, yet are they ordained for the furtherance of the commonwealth, to maintain peace, to punish the evil and to defend the good. Therefore ought the good to honour the temporal sword and to have it in reverence, though as concerning themselves they need it not, but would abstain from evil of their own accord, yea and do good without man's law, but by the law of the spirit which governeth the heart, and aideth it unto all that is the will of God.[12] Finally he comprehendeth and knitteth up all in love. Love of her own nature bestoweth all that she hath and even her own self on that which is loved. Thou needest not to bid a kind mother to be loving unto her only son. Much less spiritual love. Which hath eyes given her of God, needeth man's law to teach her to do her duty?

And as in the beginning he did put forth Christ as the cause and author of our righteousness and salvation, even so here setteth he him forth as an example to counterfeit that as he hath done to us, even so should we do one to another.

In the fourteenth chapter he teacheth to deal soberly with the consciences of the weak in the faith, which yet understand not the liberty of Christ perfectly enough and to favour them of Christian love, and not to use the liberty of the faith unto hindrance. But unto the furtherance and edifying of the weak. For where such consideration is not, there followeth debate and despising of the gospel. It is better therefore to forbear the weak a while, until they wax strong, than that learning of the gospel should come altogether underfoot. And such work is singular work of love, and where love is perfect, there must needs be such a respect unto the weak, a thing that Christ commanded and charged to be had above all things.

In the fifteenth chapter he setteth forth Christ again to be followed, that we also by his example, should suffer other that are yet weak, as them that are frail, open sinners, unlearned, unexpert, and of loathsome manners, and not to cast them away forthwith, but to suffer them till they wax better and exhort them in the meantime. For so dealt Christ in the gospel and now dealeth with us daily,

12   W. T.: "Love is the fulfilling of the law."

suffering our unperfectness weakness, conversation and manners, not yet fashioned after the doctrine of the gospel, but smell of the flesh, yea and sometime break forth into outward deeds.

After that to conclude withal he wisheth them increase of faith, peace, and joy of conscience, praiseth them and committeth them to God and magnifieth his office and administration in the gospel, and soberly and with great discretion desireth succour and aid of them for the poor saints of Jerusalem, and it is all pure love that he speaketh or dealeth withal. So find we in this epistle plenteously, unto the utmost, whatsoever a Christian man or woman ought to know, that is to wit what the law, the gospel, sin, grace, faith, righteousness, Christ, God, good works, love, hope, and the cross are, and even wherein the pith of all that pertaineth to the Christian faith standeth and how a Christian man ought to behave himself unto every man, be he perfect or a sinner, good or bad, strong or weak, friend or foe, and in conclusion how to behave ourselves both toward God and toward ourselves also. And all things are profoundly grounded in the scriptures, and declared with examples of himself, of the fathers and of the prophets, that a man can here desire no more.

Wherefore it appeareth evidently, that Paul's mind was to comprehend briefly in this epistle all the whole learning of Christ's gospel, and to prepare an introduction unto all the old testament.[13] For without doubt whosoever hath this epistle perfectly in his heart, the same hath the light and the effect of the old testament with him. Wherefore let every man without exception exercise himself therein diligently, and record it night and day continually, until he be full acquainted therewith.

The last chapter is a chapter of recommendation, wherein he yet mingleth a good admonition, that we should beware of the traditions and doctrine of men which beguile the simple with sophistry and learning that is not after the gospel, and draw them from Christ, and noosell them in weak and feeble and (as Paul calleth them in the epistle to the Galatians) in beggarly ceremonies, for the intent that they would live in fat pastures and be in authority, and be taken as Christ, yea and above Christ, and sit in the temple of God, that is to wit in the consciences of men, where God only, his word, and his Christ ought to sit. Compare therefore all manner doctrine of men unto the scripture, and see whether they agree or not. And commit thyself whole and altogether unto Christ, and so shall he with his holy spirit and with all his fulness dwell in thy soul.

The sum and whole cause of the writings of this epistle,[14] is, to prove that a man is justified by faith only: which proposition whoso denieth, to him is not only this epistle and all that Paul writeth, but also the whole scripture so locked up, that he shall never understand it to his soul's health. And to bring a man to the understanding and feeling that faith only justifieth: Paul proveth that the whole nature of man is so poisoned and so corrupt, yea and so dead concerning godly living or godly thinking, that it is impossible for her to keep the law in the sight of God: that is to say, to love it, and of love and lust to do it as naturally as a man eateth or drinketh, until she be quickened again and healed through faith.

And by justifying, understand none other thing than to be reconciled to God and to be restored unto his favour, and to have thy sins forgiven thee. As when I say God justifieth us, understand thereby, that God for Christ's sake, merits and deservings only, receiveth us unto his mercy, favour and grace, and forgiveth us our sins. And when I say Christ justifieth us, understand thereby that Christ only hath redeemed us, bought and delivered us out of the wrath of God and damnation, and hath with his work only, purchased us the mercy, the favour and grace of God, and the forgiveness of our sins. And when I say that faith only justifieth, understand thereby that faith and trust in the truth of God and in the mercy promised us for Christ's sake, and for his deserving and works only, doth quiet the conscience and certify her that our sins be forgiven and we in the full favour of God.

Furthermore, set before thine eyes Christ's works and thine own works. Christ's works only justifieth and make satisfaction for thy sin, and thine own works not: that is to say, quieteth thy conscience and make thee sure that thy sins are forgiven thee, and not thine own works. For the promise of mercy is made thee for Christ's works' sake, and not for thine own works' sake. Wherefore, seeing

---

13   W. T.: "This epistle to the Romans is the door into all the scripture: yea, and the key that openeth it and bringeth men to the true understanding of it."

14   The last five paragraphs are Tyndale's summary of Luther's argument.

God hath not promised that thine own works shall save thee, therefore faith in thine own works can never quiet thy conscience nor certify thee before God (when God cometh to judge and to take a reckoning) that thy sins are forgiven thee. Beyond all this, mine own works can never satisfy the law or pay her that I owe her. For I owe the law to love her with all mine heart, soul, power and might. Which thing to pay I am never able while I am compassed with flesh. No, I cannot once begin to love the law, except I be first sure by faith that God loveth me and forgiveth me.

Finally that we say faith only justifieth, ought to offend no man. For if this be true, that Christ only redeemed us, Christ only bare our sins, made satisfaction for them and purchased us the favour of God, then must it needs be true, that the trust only in Christ's deserving and in the promises of God the father made us for Christ's sake, doth only quiet the conscience and certify her that the sins are forgiven. And when they say, a man must repent, forsake sin, and have a purpose to sin no more as nigh as he can and love the law of God: Ergo faith alone justifieth not: I answer, that and all like arguments are nought, and like to this. I must repent and be sorry, the Gospel must be preached me, and I must believe it or else I cannot be partaker of the mercy which Christ hath deserved for me, Ergo Christ only justifieth me not, or Christ only hath not made satisfaction for my sins. As this is a naughty argument so is the other.

Now go to reader, and according to the order of Paul's writing, even so do thou. First behold thyself diligently in the law of God, and see there thy just damnation. Secondarily turn thine eyes to Christ, and see there the exceeding mercy of thy most kind and loving father. Thirdly remember that Christ made not this atonement that thou shouldest anger God again: neither died he for thy sins, that thou shouldest live still in them: neither cleansed he thee, that thou shouldest return (as a swine) unto thine old puddle again: but that thou shouldest be a new creature and live a new life after the will of God and not of the flesh. And be diligent lest through thine own negligence and unthankfulness thou lose this favour and mercy again.

Farewell.

W.T.

[Tyndale's Translation From]

The Epistle of the Apostle Saint Paul to the Romans, i

CHAPTER ONE

Paul the servant of Jesus Christ, called to be an apostle, put apart to preach the gospel of God, which he promised afore by his prophets, in the holy scriptures that make mention of his son, the which was begotten of the seed of David, as pertaining to the flesh: and declared to be the son of God with power of the holy ghost that sanctifieth, since the time that Jesus Christ our Lord rose again from death, by whom we have received grace and apostleship, to bring all manner heathen people unto obedience of the faith, that is in his name: of the which heathen are ye a part also, which are Jesus Christ's by vocation.

To all you of Rome beloved of God and saints by calling, grace be with you and peace from God our father, and from the Lord Jesus Christ.

First verily I thank my God through Jesus Christ for you all, because your faith is published throughout all the world. For God is my witness, whom I serve with my spirit in the gospel of his son, that without ceasing I make mention of you always in my prayers, beseeching that at one time or another, a prosperous journey (by the will of God) might fortune me, to come unto you. For I long to see you, that I might bestow among you some spiritual gift, to strength you withal: that is, that I might have consolation together with you, through the common faith, which both ye and I have.

I would that ye should know brethren, how that I have often times purposed to come unto you (but have been let hitherto) to have some fruit among you, as I have among other of the gentiles.

For I am debtor both to the Greeks and to them which are no Greeks, unto the learned and also unto the unlearned. Likewise, as much as in me is, I am ready to preach the gospel to you of Rome also.

For I am not ashamed of the gospel of Christ, because it is the power of God unto salvation to all that believe, namely to the Jew, and also to the gentile. For by it the righteousness which cometh of God, is opened, from faith to faith.[1] As it is written: The just shall live by faith.

For the wrath of God appeareth from heaven against all ungodliness and unrighteousness of men which withhold the truth in unrighteousness: seeing, what may be known of God, that same is manifest among them. For God did shew it unto them. So that his invisible things: that is to say, his eternal power and Godhead are understood and seen, by the works from the creation of the world. So that they are without excuse, inasmuch as when they knew God, they glorified him not as God, neither were thankful, but waxed full of vanities in their imaginations, and their foolish hearts were blinded. When they counted themselves wise, they became fools and turned the glory of the immortal God, unto the similitude of the image of mortal man, and of birds, and fourfooted beasts, and of serpents.[2] Wherefore God likewise gave them up unto their heart's lusts, unto uncleanness, to defile their own bodies between themselves: which turned his truth unto a lie, and worshipped and served the creatures more than the maker, which is blessed for ever Amen. For this cause God gave them up unto shameful lusts. For even their women did change the natural use unto the unnatural. And likewise also the men left the natural use of the woman, and burned in their lusts one on another. And man with man wrought filthiness, and received in themselves the reward of their error, as it was according.

And as it seemed not good unto them to be a-known of God, even so God delivered them up unto a lewd mind, that they should do those things which were not comely, being full of all unrighteous doing, of fornication, wickedness, covetousness, maliciousness, full of envy, murder, debate, deceit, evil conditioned, whisperers, backbiters, haters of God, doers of wrong, proud, boasters, bringers-up of evil things, disobedient to father and mother, without understanding, covenant-breakers, unloving, truce-breakers and merciless. Which men though they knew the righteousness of God, how that they which such things commit, are worthy of death, yet not only do the same, but also have pleasure in them that do them.[3]

CHAPTER TWO

Therefore art thou inexcusable o man, whosoever thou be that judgest. For in the same wherein thou judgest another, thou condemnest thyself. For thou that judgest, doest even the same self things. But we are sure that the judgement of God is according to truth, against them which commit such things. Thinkest thou this O thou man that judgest them which do such things and yet doest even the very same, that thou shalt escape the judgement of God? Either despisest thou the riches of his goodness, patience and long-sufferance? and rememberest not how that the kindness of God leadeth thee to repentance?

But thou after thine hard heart that cannot repent, heapest thee together the treasure of wrath against the day of vengeance, when shall be opened the righteous judgement of God, which will reward every man according to his deeds:[4] that is to say, praise, honour and immortality, to them which continue in good doing, and seek eternal life. But unto them that are rebellious and disobey the truth, yet follow iniquity, shall come indignation and wrath, tribulation and anguish, upon the soul of every man that doth evil: of the Jew first, and also of the gentile. To every man that doth good, shall come praise, honour and peace, to the Jew first, and also to the gentile. For there is no

---

[TYNDALE'S TRANSLATION FROM]
THE EPISTLE OF THE APOSTLE SAINT PAUL TO THE ROMANS, 1
1   W. T.: "From faith to faith: that is from a weak faith to a stronger, or from one battle of faith to another, for as we have escaped one jeopardy through faith, another invadeth us, through which we must wade by the help of faith also."

2   W. T.: "What followeth when men know the truth and love it not."
3   W. T.: "To have pleasure in another man's sin is greater wickedness than to sin thyself."
4   W. T.: "The deserving of Christ is promised to be the reward of our good deeds: which reward yet our deeds deserve not."

partiality with God. But whosoever hath sinned without law, shall perish without law. And as many as have sinned under the law, shall be judged by the law. For before God they are not righteous which hear the law: but the doers[5] of the law shall be justified. For if the gentiles which have no law, do of nature the things contained in the law: then they having no law, are a law unto themselves, which shew the deed of the law written in their hearts: while their conscience beareth witness unto them, and also their thoughts, accusing one another or excusing, at the day when God shall judge the secrets of men by Jesus Christ, according to my gospel.

Behold, thou art called a Jew, and trustest in the law, and rejoicest in God, and knowest his will, and hast experience of good and bad, in that thou art informed by the law: and believest that thou thyself art a guide unto the blind, a light to them which are in darkness, an informer of them which lack discretion, a teacher of unlearned, which hast the example of that which ought to be known, and of the truth, in the law. But thou which teachest another teachest not thyself. Thou preachest, a man should not steal: and yet thou stealest. Thou sayest, a man should not commit advoutry: and thou breakest wedlock. Thou abhorrest images, and robbest God of his honour. Thou rejoicest in the law, and through breaking the law dishonourest God. For the name of God is evil spoken of among the gentiles through you, as it is written.

Circumcision[6] verily availeth, if thou keep the law. But if thou break the law, thy circumcision is made uncircumcision. Therefore if the uncircumcised keep the right things contained in the law: shall not his uncircumcision be counted for circumcision? And shall not uncircumcision which is by nature (if it keep the law) judge thee, which being under the letter and circumcision, dost transgress the law? For he is not a Jew, which is a Jew outward. Neither is that thing circumcision, which is outward in the flesh. But he is a Jew which is hid within and the circumcision of the heart is the true circumcision, which is in the spirit, and not in the letter, whose praise is not of men, but of God.

Sir Thomas Wyatt (c.1503–1542)

Wyatt's father, Sir Henry, was Privy Councillor to both Henry VII and Henry VIII and was present at the "Field of Cloth of Gold," the lavish entertainment and meeting of Henry VIII and Francis I of France in 1520. Like his father, Thomas Wyatt spent most of his life in royal service. In 1526 he took part in the diplomatic mission to France that included the negotiation of England's role as "protector" of the alliance among France, Florence, Venice, Milan, and Pope Clement VII, known as the Holy League of Cognac. This and his mission to the papal court in Rome the following year were moves to counter any coalition between Francis I and the emperor Charles V against England. (Wyatt's efforts in this matter were to continue until his death.) His marriage to Elizabeth Brooke (c.1520), with whom he had a son Thomas, ended in separation and in a brief relationship with Anne Boleyn (c.1525). After his return from Rome in 1527 Wyatt probably learned for the first time of Henry VIII's interest in Anne. These dangerous circumstances constitute the background to the sonnet "Whoso list to hunt." Although there are several different

accounts of how Wyatt managed to escape the king's wrath, it appears that he simply confessed his circumstances, either to the king himself or to the Privy Council, once it became clear the king was planning to marry Anne. By 1536, however, Anne had fallen from grace with the king, her husband; and Wyatt found himself in prison, facing for a time the possibility of execution along with others who had been close to her. Understandably, he never forgot this threat to his life from the king to whose service most of his life was dedicated. From 1532 Wyatt enjoyed the friendship and patronage of Thomas Cromwell, Earl of Essex, whose Lutheranism and insistence on a Protestant alliance led eventually to his downfall and execution in 1540. Wyatt mourned his death in the sonnet "The pillar perished" by appropriating a source (in this case Petrarch's *Rime* 269), as he typically does to express – or to mask – deep feeling. In 1541 Wyatt was again arrested, imprisoned in the Tower, and charged with treason, based on the empty accusations of Dr. Edmund Bonner, Archdeacon of Leicester, who had accompanied Wyatt on diplomatic

---

5 W. T.: "Deeds are an outward righteousness before the world and testify what a man is within: but justify not the heart before God: nor certify the conscience that the fore-sins are forgiven."

6 W. T.: "Circumcision was a witness of the covenant between them and God and holp not but after as it put them in remembrance to believe in God and to keep the law."

missions to France and Spain and who was beginning to emerge as the notorious burner of heretics that he was later to become as Bishop of London. Having answered Bonner's charges in "A Declaration of his Innocence," Wyatt was pardoned by the Privy Council at the request of Queen Catherine Howard. He died the following year after a short illness, the Queen herself having lost favor and been executed eight months before his death.

In Wyatt's poetry, as in his life, the public and the private and the secular and the sacred coexist in a creative but uneasy tension that makes his sensibility seem both uncannily modern and specifically Tudor. One of the burdens of recent scholarship on Wyatt has been to read him as a poet of his time rather than as a proto-Elizabethan. It is not surprising, therefore, that the critical procedures known as the "New Historicism" have been particularly fruitful in dealing with his work. For example, in an excellent study of "Power, Sexuality, and Inwardness in Wyatt's Poetry," in *Renaissance Self-Fashioning*, Stephen Greenblatt clearly demonstrates that the striking sense of an intimately reflective, vulnerable inner self that Wyatt's poetry captures is in fact very much a part of the cultural processes of the sixteenth century, when there appeared to be "an increased consciousness about the fashioning of human identity as a manipulable, artful process" (p. 2). Whereas for More and Tyndale self-fashioning was subject to a theology in which the power of the biblical Word shaped the identity of the individual person – a concept for which they literally sacrificed their lives – for Wyatt the institution of the Church had already become absorbed by the political and sexual dynamics of the court of Henry VIII.

Even when he translates and paraphrases the penitential psalms (Psalms 6, 32, 38, 51, 102, 130, and 143), Wyatt sets them in the context of King David's abuse of power, his adultery with Bathsheba, and his responsibility for her husband's death. If indeed Wyatt composed this work while in prison in 1536, at the time of the fall of Anne Boleyn, he may be writing subtle political allegory even here, hidden, as Greenblatt suggests (p. 121), behind the double mask of Old Testament politics and his Italian source in Aretino's translations. Both here and in his masterful lyrics Wyatt can be seen simultaneously forging new aesthetic forms out of traditional materials, responding critically and incisively to the court culture that circumscribed his life, and fashioning an articulate, lyrical self. Whether circulated in manuscript, read at court, or performed by Wyatt to the accompaniment of a lute, these intensely private and inward poems are occasions for the public display of his artful self.

READING

Donald M. Friedman, "The Mind in the Poem: Wyatt's 'They Flee from Me.'"

Stephen Greenblatt, *Renaissance Self-Fashioning: From More to Shakespeare.*

Michael McCanles, "Love and Power in the Poetry of Sir Thomas Wyatt."

Kenneth Muir, *The Life and Letters of Sir Thomas Wyatt.*

Patricia Thomson, *Sir Thomas Wyatt and His Background.*

M. P.

[FROM] *CERTAIN PSALMS*

[PROLOGUE]

Love, to give law unto his subject hearts,[1]
Stood in the eyes of Barsabe[2] the bright,
And in a look anon himself converts
Cruelly pleasant before King David sight;
First dazed his eyes, and further forth he starts
With venomed breath, as softly as he might
Touched his senses, and overruns his bones
With creeping fire sparpled for the nonce.   *scattered*

10   And when he saw that kindled was the flame,
The moist poison in his heart he lanced
So that the soul did tremble with the same.
And in this branle as he stood and tranced,

[FROM] *CERTAIN PSALMS*
[PROLOGUE]
1   The Prologue is a close translation of Pietro Aretino's *I sette salmi de la penitentia di David* (1534), which does not preclude the possibility of its being read as Tudor political allegory.

2   Bathsheba (cf. 2 Samuel 11–12).

Yielding unto the figure and the frame
That those fair eyes had in his presence glanced,
The form that Love had printed in his breast
He honour'th it as thing of things best.

So that forgot the wisdom and forecast
(Which woe to realms when that these kings doth lack)
Forgetting eke God's majesty as fast,
Yea, and his own, forthwith he doth to make
Urie[3] to go into the field in haste –
Urie I say, that was his idol's make –   *husband (mate)*
Under pretence of certain victory,
For en'mies' swords a ready prey to die.

Whereby he may enjoy her out of doubt
Whom more than God or himself he mindeth.
And after he had brought this thing about
And of that lust possessed himself he findeth
That hath and doth reverse and clean turn out
Kings from kingdoms and cities undermineth,
He, blinded, thinks this train so blind and close
To blind all thing, that naught may it disclose.

But Nathan hath spied out this treachery
With rueful cheer and sets afore his face
The great offence, outrage, and injury
That he hath done to God as in this case –
By murder for to cloak adultery.
He shew'th him eke from heaven the threats, alas,
So sternly sore this prophet, this Nathan,
That all amazed this aged woeful man.

Like him that meets with horror and with fear,
The heat doth straight forsake the limbs cold,
The colour eke droopeth down from his cheer,
So doth he feel his fire manifold,
His heat, his lust, and pleasure all in fear
Consume and waste; and straight his crown of gold,
His purple pall, his sceptre he lets fall
And to the ground he throw'th himself withal.

The pompous pride of state and dignity
Forthwith rebates repentant humbleness.
Thinner vile cloth than clotheth poverty
Doth scantly hide and clad his nakedness,
His fair hoar beard of reverent gravity
With ruffled hair knowing his wickedness.
More like was he the selfsame repentance[4]
Than stately prince of worldly governance.

His harp he taketh in hand to be his guide
Wherewith he offer'th his plaints, his soul to save,
That from his heart distils on every side,
Withdrawing him into a dark cave
Within the ground, wherein he might him hide,
Fleeing the light as in prison or grave,

20
30
40
50
60

---

3   Uriah, Bathsheba's Hittite husband.   4   *embodiment (or essence) of repentance.*

In which as soon as David entered had,
The dark horror did make his fault adrad.   *dreaded*

But he, without prolonging or delay,
Rof that⁵ that might his Lord, his God appease,
Fall'th on his knees, and with his harp, I say,
Afore his breast, fraughted with disease
Of stormy sighs, his cheer coloured like clay,
70   Dressed upright, seeking to counterpoise
His song with sighs, and touching of the strings
With tender heart, lo, thus to God he sings.

PSALM 51. *MISERERE MEI DOMINE*

[HAVE MERCY ON ME, O LORD]

Rue¹ on me, Lord, for thy goodness and grace,
    That of thy nature art so bountiful,
    For that goodness that in the world doth brace
Repugnant natures in quiet wonderful.
    And for thy mercies' number without end,
    In heaven and earth perceived so plentiful
That over all they do themselves extend,
    For those mercies much more than man can sin,
    Do way my sins that so thy grace offend.²
10   Again wash me, but wash me well within,
    And from my sin that thus mak'th me afraid
    Make thou me clean as ay thy wont hath been.
For unto thee no number can be laid
    For to prescribe remissions of offence
    In hearts returned, as thou thyself hath said.
And I beknow my fault, my negligence,
    And in my sight my sin is fixed fast,
    Thereof to have more perfect penitence.
To thee alone, to thee have I trespassed
20   For none can measure my fault but thou alone.
    For in thy sight I have not been aghast
For to offend, judging thy sight as none
    So that my fault were hid from sight of man,
    Thy majesty so from my mind was gone.
This know I and repent. Pardon thou then,
    Whereby thou shalt keep still thy word stable,
    Thy justice pure and clean; because that when
I pardoned am, then forthwith justly able,
    Just I am judged by justice of thy grace.³
30   For I myself, lo, thing most unstable,
Formed in offence, conceived in like case,
    Am naught but sin from my nativity.
    Be not this said for my excuse, alas,

---

5   *took the harp.*

PSALM 51. *MISERERE MEI DOMINE*
[HAVE MERCY ON ME, O LORD]
1   *Have pity.*

2   Wyatt's addition here emphasizes God's forgiving grace, which gives
the psalm a Pauline interpretation.
3   David claims he is justified (that is, made just) by God's grace,
according to the argument of Romans 1–5, which was a fundamental
text for Reformers.

But of thy help to show necessity.
    For, lo, thou loves the truth of inward heart
    Which yet doth live in my fidelity
Though I have fallen, by frailty overthwart;   *perverted*
    For wilful malice led me not the way
    So much as hath the flesh drawn me apart.
40   Wherefore, O Lord, as thou hast done alway,
    Teach me the hidden wisdom of thy lore
    Since that my faith doth not yet decay.
And as the Jews to heal the leper sore
    With hyssop cleanse, cleanse me and I am clean.
    Thou shalt me wash and more than snow therefore
I shall be white, how foul my fault hath been.
    Thou of my health shalt gladsome tidings bring
    When from above remission shall be seen
Descend on earth. Then shall for joy upspring
50   The bones that were afore consumed to dust.
    Look not, O Lord, upon mine offending
But do away my deeds that are unjust.
    Make a clean heart in the mids of my breast
    With sprite upright voided from filthy lust.
From thine eyes' cure cast me not in unrest
    Nor take from me thy sprite of holiness.[4]
    Render to me joy of thy help and rest;
My will confirm with sprite of steadfastness.
    And by this shall these goodly things ensue:
60   Sinners I shall into thy ways address,
They shall return to thee and thy grace sue;
    My tongue shall praise thy justification;
    My mouth shall spread thy glorious praises true.
But of thyself, O God, this operation
    It must proceed by purging me from blood,
    Among the just that I may have relation.
And of thy lauds for to let out the flood
    Thou must, O Lord, my lips first unloose.
    For if thou hadst esteemed pleasant good
70   The outward deeds that outward men disclose
    I would have offered unto thee sacrifice.
    But thou delights not in no such gloze   *pretence*
Of outward deed as men dream and devise.
    The sacrifice that the Lord liketh most
    Is sprite contrite; low heart in humble wise
Thou dost accept, O God, for pleasant host.[5]
    Make Zion, Lord, according to thy will,
    Inward Zion, the Zion of the ghost.[6]
Of heart's Jerusalem strength the walls still.
80   Then shalt thou take for good these outward deeds
    As sacrifice thy pleasure to fulfil.
Of thee alone thus all our good proceeds.

               *

Of deep secrets that David here did sing,
Of mercy, of faith, of frailty, of grace,[7]

---

4 *Holy Spirit.*
5 *acceptable sacrifice.*
6 Here Wyatt transforms Zion into the repentant state of the spirit.

7 Throughout this narrative link (lines 509–40), Wyatt departs from his source in order further to emphasize the Reformed view that faith is the necessary condition for redemption.

Of God's goodness, and of justifying,
The greatness did so astone himself a space,
As who might say: 'Who hath expressed this thing?
I, sinner, I! What have I said, alas?
That God's goodness would within my song entreat
90   Let me again consider and repeat.'

And so he doth, but not expressed by word.
But in his heart he turneth and poiseth
Each word that erst his lips might forth afford.
He points, he pauseth, he wonders, he praiseth
The mercy that hides of justice the sword,
The justice that so his promise complisheth
For his words' sake to worthiless desert
That gratis his graces to men doth depart.

Here hath he comfort when he doth measure
100   Measureless mercies to measureless fault,
To prodigal sinners infinite treasure,
Treasure termless that never shall default.
Yea, when that sin shall fail and may not dure,   *endure*
Mercy shall reign, 'gain whom shall no assault
Of hell prevail, by whom, lo, at this day,
Of heaven gates remission is the key.[8]

And when David hath pondered well and tried
And seeth himself not utterly deprived
From light of grace that dark of sin did hide,
110   He finds his hope so much therewith revived
He dare importune the Lord on every side
(For he know'th well to mercy is ascribed
Respectless labour), importune, cry, and call;
And thus begin'th his song therewithal.

PSALM 102. *DOMINE EXAUDI ORATIONEM MEAM*

[LORD, HEAR MY PRAYER]

Lord, hear my prayer and let my cry pass
Unto thee, Lord, without impediment.
Do not from me turn thy merciful face,
Unto myself leaving my government.
In time of trouble and adversity
Incline to me thine ear and thine intent.
And when I call, help my necessity,
Readily grant th'effect of my desire.
These bold demands do please thy majesty
10   And eke my case such haste doth well require.
For like as smoke my days been passed away,
My bones dried up as furnace with the fire.
My heart, my mind is withered up like hay
Because I have forgot to take my bread,
My bread of life, the word of truth, I say.

8 Matthew 16:18–19.

And for my plaintful sighs and my dread,
  My bones, my strength, my very force of mind
  Cleaved to the flesh and from thy sprite were fled
As desperate thy mercy for to find.
20   So made I me the solein pelican'
  And like the owl that fleeth by proper kind
Light of the day and hath herself beta'en
  To ruin life out of all company.
  With waker care that with this woe began,
Like the sparrow was I solitary
  That sits alone under the house's eaves.
  This while my foes conspired continually
And did provoke the harm of my disease.
  Wherefore like ashes my bread did me savour;
30   Of thy just word the taste might not me please.
Wherefore my drink I tempered with liquor
  Of weeping tears that from mine eyes do rain
  Because I know the wrath of thy furor,
Provoked by right, had of my pride disdain
  For thou didst lift me up to throw me down,
  To teach me how to know myself again;
Whereby I know that helpless I should drown.
  My days like shadow decline and I do dry
  And thee forever eternity doth crown;
40 World without end doth last thy memory.
  For this frailty that yoketh all mankind –
  Thou shalt awake and rue this misery,   *regret*
Rue on Zion, Zion that, as I find,
  Is the people that live under thy law.
  For now is time, the time at hand assigned,
The time so long that doth thy servants draw
  In great desire to see that pleasant day,
  Day of redeeming Zion from sin's awe.
For they have ruth to see in such decay,
50   In dust and stones, this wretched Zion lower.
  Then the gentiles shall dread thy name alway;
All earthly kings thy glory shall honour
  Then when thy grace this Zion thus redeemeth,
  When thus thou hast declared thy mighty power.
The Lord his servants' wishes so esteemeth
  That he him turn'th unto the poors' request.
  To our descent this to be written seemeth,
Of all comforts, as consolation best;
  And they that then shall be regenerate
60   Shall praise the Lord therefore, both most and least.
For he hath looked from the height of his estate;
  The Lord from heaven in earth hath looked on us
  To hear the moan of them that are algate   *altogether*
In foul bondage, to loose and to discuss
  The sons of death out from their deadly bond,
  To give thereby occasion gracious

PSALM 102. *DOMINE EXAUDI ORATIONEM MEAM*
[LORD, HEAR MY PRAYER]
1 In this addition to his source, Wyatt compares the fallen state to
the solitary life of the pelican and of the owl, whose nature makes it flee
from light.

In this Zion his holy name to stand
   And in Jerusalem his lauds, lasting ay,
   When in one church the people of the land
70   And realms been gathered to serve, to laud, to pray
     The Lord above so just and merciful.
     But to this sembly running in the way,
My strength faileth to reach it at the full.
   He hath abridged my days; they may not dure
   To see that term, that term so wonderful,
Although I have with hearty will and cure
   Prayed to the Lord: 'Take me not, Lord, away
   In mids of my years, though thine ever sure
Remain eterne, whom time cannot decay.
80   Thou wrought'st the earth; thy hands th'heavens did make:
   They shall perish and thou shalt last alway.
And all things age shall wear and overtake
   Like cloth, and thou shalt change them like apparel,
   Turn and translate, and they in worth it take.
But thou thyself the self remainest well
   That thou wast erst, and shalt thy years extend.
   Then since to this there may nothing rebel
The greatest comfort that I can pretend
   Is that the children of thy servants dear,
90   That in thy word are got, shall without end
Before thy face be stablished all in fere.'

*

When David had perceived in his breast
The sprite of God returned that was exiled,
Because he knew he hath alone expressed
These great things that greater sprite compiled,
As shawm or pipe lets out the sound impressed,
By music's art forged tofore and filed,
I say when David had perceived this
The sprite of comfort in him revived is.

100   For thereupon he maketh argument
Of reconciling unto the Lord's grace,
Although some time to prophesy have lent
Both brute beasts and wicked hearts a place.
But our David judgeth in his intent
Himself by penance clean out of this case,
Whereby he hath remission of offence,
And ginneth to allow his pain and penitence.

But when he weigh'th the fault and recompense,
He damn'th his deed and findeth plain
110   Atween them two no whit equivalence;
Whereby he takes all outward deed in vain
To bear the name of rightful penitence,
Which is alone the heart returned again
And sore contrite that doth his fault bemoan,
And outward deed the sign or fruit alone.

With this he doth defend the sly assault
Of vain allowance of his void desert,
And all the glory of his forgiven fault

120
To God alone he doth it whole convert.
His own merit he findeth in default.
And whilst he pondered these things in his heart,
His knee, his arm, his hand sustained his chin
When he his song again thus did begin.

Psalm 130. *De Profundis Clamavi*

[From the Depths I have Called]

From depth of sin and from a deep despair,
   From depth of death, from depth of heart's sorrow,
   From this deep cave of darkness' deep repair,
Thee have I called, O Lord, to be my borrow.   *ransom*
   Thou in my voice, O Lord, perceive and hear
   My heart, my hope, my plaint, my overthrow,
My will to rise, and let by grant appear
   That to my voice thine ears do well intend.
   No place so far that to thee is not near;
10
No depth so deep that thou ne mayst extend
   Thine ear thereto. Hear then my woeful plaint.
   For, Lord, if thou do observe what men offend
And put thy native mercy in restraint,
   If just exaction demand recompense,
   Who may endure, O Lord? Who shall not faint
At such account? Dread and not reverence
   Should so reign large. But thou seeks rather love
   For in thy hand is mercy's residence
By hope whereof thou dost our hearts move.
20
   I in thee, Lord, have set my confidence;
   My soul such trust doth evermore approve.
Thy holy word of eterne excellence,
   Thy mercy's promise that is alway just,
   Have been my stay, my pillar, and pretence.
My soul in God hath more desirous trust
   Than hath the watchman looking for the day
   By the relief to quench of sleep the thrust.
Let Israel trust unto the Lord alway
   For grace and favour arr his property.   *are*
30
   Plenteous ransom shall come with him, I say,
And shall redeem all our iniquity.
This word 'redeem' that in his mouth did sound
Did put David, it seemeth unto me,
As in a trance to stare upon the ground
And with his thought the height of heaven to see,
Where he beholds the Word that should confound
The sword of death, by humble ear to be
In mortal maid, in mortal habit made,
Eternal life in mortal veil to shade.

40
He seeth that Word, when full ripe time should come,
Do way that veil by fervent affection,
Torn off with death (for death should have her doom),
And leapeth lighter from such corruption
Than glint of light that in the air doth lome.
Man redeemed, death hath her destruction,

That mortal veil hath immortality,
David assurance of his iniquity.

Whereby he frames this reason in his heart:
'That goodness which doth not forbear his son
50   From death for me and can thereby convert
My death to life, my sin to salvation,
Both can and will a smaller grace depart
To him that sueth by humble supplication.
And since I have his larger grace assayed,
To ask this thing why am I then afraid?

'He granteth most to them that most do crave
And be delights in suit without respect.
Alas, my son pursues me to the grave,
Suffered by God my sin for to correct.
60   But of my sin since I my pardon have,
My son's pursuit shall shortly be reject.
Then will I crave with sured confidence.'
And thus begins the suit of his pretence.

POEMS ATTRIBUTED TO WYATT IN THE EGERTON MANUSCRIPT AND IN *TOTTEL'S MISCELLANY*

[THE LONG LOVE][1]

The long love that in my thought doth harbour
And in mine heart doth keep his residence
Into my face presseth with bold pretence
And therein campeth, spreading his banner.
She that me learneth to love and suffer
And will that my trust and lust's negligence
Be reined[2] by reason, shame, and reverence,
With his hardiness taketh displeasure.
Wherewithal unto the heart's forest he fleeth,
10   Leaving his enterprise with pain and cry,
And there him hideth and not appeareth.
What may I do when my master feareth,
But in the field with him to live and die?
For good is the life ending faithfully.

[WHOSO LIST TO HUNT][1]

Whoso list to hunt, I know where is an hind,
But as for me, helas, I may no more.
The vain travail hath wearied me so sore,
I am of them that farthest cometh behind.
Yet may I by no means my wearied mind

POEMS ATTRIBUTED TO WYATT IN THE EGERTON MANUSCRIPT AND
  IN *TOTTEL'S MISCELLANY*
[THE LONG LOVE]
1 Translation of Petrarch's *Rime* 140.
2 The manuscript spelling "rayned" suggests a pun on "rein" and
"reign."

[WHOSO LIST TO HUNT]
1 Based on Petrarch's *Rime* 190.

Draw from the deer, but as she fleeth afore
Fainting I follow. I leave off therefore
Sithens in a net I seek to hold the wind.
Who list her hunt, I put him out of doubt,
As well as I may spend his time in vain.
And graven with diamonds in letters plain
There is written her fair neck round about:
'*Noli me tangere*[2] for Caesar's I am,
And wild for to hold though I seem tame.'

10

[My Galley][1]

My galley charged with forgetfulness
Thorough sharp seas in winter nights doth pass
'Tween rock and rock;[2] and eke mine enemy, alas,
That is my lord, steereth with cruelness;
And every oar a thought in readiness
As though that death were light in such a case.
An endless wind doth tear the sail apace
Of forced sighs and trusty fearfulness.
A rain of tears, a cloud of dark disdain
Hath done the wearied cords great hindrance,
Wreathed with error and eke with ignorance.
The stars be hid that led me to this pain.
Drowned is reason that should me comfort
And I remain despairing of the port.

10

[Unstable Dream]

Unstable dream, according to the place,
Be steadfast once or else at least be true.
By tasted sweetness make me not to rue
The sudden loss of thy false feigned grace.
By good respect in such a dangerous case
Thou brought'st not her into this tossing mew[1]
But madest my sprite live my care to renew,
My body in tempest her succour to embrace.
The body dead, the sprite had his desire;
Painless was th'one, th'other in delight.
Why then, alas, did it not keep it right,
Returning to leap into the fire,
And where it was at wish it could not remain?
Such mocks of dreams they turn to deadly pain.

10

[If Waker Care]

If waker care, if sudden pale colour,   *sleepless*
If many sighs, with little speech to plain,

---

2   *Do not touch me* (cf. John 20:17 and Matthew 22:21).

[My Galley]
1   Translation of Petrarch's *Rime* 189.
2   Scylla and Charybdis in Petrarch.

[Unstable Dream]
1   A holding cage for birds; here a figure for the speaker's bed and/or his restless mind.

Now joy, now woe, if they my cheer distain,
For hope of small, if much to fear therefore,
To haste, to slack my pace less or more
Be sign of love, then do I love again.
If thou ask whom, sure since I did refrain
Brunet[1] that set my wealth in such a roar,
Th'unfeigned cheer of Phyllis[2] hath the place
10   That Brunet had. She hath and ever shall.
She from myself now hath me in her grace.
She hath in hand my wit, my will, and all.
My heart alone well worthy she doth stay
Without whose help scant do I live a day.

[THE PILLAR PERISHED][1]

The pillar perished is whereto I leant,
The strongest stay of mine unquiet mind;
The like of it no man again can find –
From east to west still seeking though be went –
To mine unhap, for hap away hath rent
Of all my joy the very bark and rind,
And I, alas, by chance am thus assigned
Dearly to mourn till death do it relent.
But since that thus it is by destiny,
10   What can I more but have a woeful heart,
My pen in plaint, my voice in woeful cry,
My mind in woe, my body full of smart,
And I myself myself always to hate
Till dreadful death do cease my doleful state?

[FAREWELL, LOVE]

Farewell, Love, and all thy laws forever.
Thy baited hooks shall tangle me no more.
Senec[1] and Plato call me from thy lore
To perfect wealth my wit for to endeavour.
In blind error when I did persevere,
Thy sharp repulse that pricketh ay so sore
Hath taught me to set in trifles no store
And scape forth since liberty is lever.   *preferable*
Therefore farewell. Go trouble younger hearts
10   And in me claim no more authority.
With idle youth go use thy property
And thereon spend thy many brittle darts:
For hitherto though I have lost all my time,
Me lusteth no longer rotten boughs to climb.[2]

[IF WAKER CARE]
1   Probably Anne Boleyn.
2   Possibly Wyatt's mistress, Elizabeth Darrell.

[THE PILLAR PERISHED]
1   Imitation of Petrarch's *Rime* 269. Possibly Wyatt's lament for his
patron, Thomas Cromwell, who was executed on July 28, 1540.

[FAREWELL, LOVE]
1   Seneca (*c.*4 BCE–CE 65), whose writings Wyatt admired and recommended to his son.
2   Allusion to the proverb "Who trusts to rotten boughs may fall"
(Tilley, B557).

[SOMETIME I FLED THE FIRE][1]

Sometime I fled the fire that me brent   *burnt*
By sea, by land, by water, and by wind,
And now I follow the coals that be quent   *quenched*
From Dover to Calais, against my mind.
Lo, how desire is both sprung and spent!
And he may see that whilom was so blind,
And all his labour now he laugh to scorn,
Meshed in the briers that erst was all to-torn.   *shredded*

[TAGUS, FAREWELL][1]

Tagus,[2] farewell, that westward with thy streams
Turns up the grains of gold already tried,
With spur and sail for I go seek the Thames,
Gainward the sun[3] that shew'th her wealthy pride
And, to the town which Brutus sought by dreams,[4]
Like bended moon doth lend her lusty side.
My king, my country, alone for whom I live,
Of mighty love the wings for this me give.

[SIGHS ARE MY FOOD][1]

Sighs are my food, drink are my tears;
Clinking of fetters such music would crave.
Stink and close air away my life wears.
Innocency is all the hope I have.
Rain, wind, or weather I judge by mine ears.
Malice assaulted that righteousness should save.
Sure I am, Brian, this wound shall heal again
But yet, alas, the scar shall still remain.[2]

[LUCKS, MY FAIR FALCON]

Lucks, my fair falcon, and your fellows all,
How well pleasant it were your liberty!
Ye not forsake me that fair might ye befall.
But they that sometime liked my company
Like lice away from dead bodies they crawl.
Lo, what a proof in light adversity!
But ye, my birds, I swear by all your bells,
Ye be my friends and so be but few else.

[SOMETIME I FLED THE FIRE]
1   The occasion for this epigram may have been Anne Boleyn and Henry VIII's visit to Francis I at Calais in October 1532.

[TAGUS, FAREWELL]
1   Entitled "In Spain" in the Egerton manuscript, referring to Wyatt's departure from Spain in June 1539.
2   A river in Spain, whose sand was reputed to be golden.

3   *toward the east.*
4   London, traditionally claimed to have been founded as a new Troy by Brutus, a descendant of Aeneas.

[SIGHS ARE MY FOOD]
1   Probably written during Wyatt's imprisonment between January and March 1541.
2   First recorded use of this proverb (see Tilley, W929).

[THROUGHOUT THE WORLD]

Throughout the world, if it were sought,
Fair words enough a man shall find.
They be good cheap;[1] they cost right naught;
Their substance is but only wind.
But well to say and so to mean –
That sweet accord is seldom seen.

[IN COURT TO SERVE]

In court to serve, decked with fresh array,
Of sugared meats feeling the sweet repast,
The life in banquets and sundry kinds of play
Amid the press of lordly looks to waste,
Hath with it joined oft-times such bitter taste
That whoso joys such kind of life to hold,
In prison joys, fettered with chains of gold.

[THEY FLEE FROM ME]

They flee from me that sometime did me seek
With naked foot stalking in my chamber.
I have seen them gentle, tame, and meek
That now are wild and do not remember
That sometime they put themself in danger
To take bread at my hand; and now they range
Busily seeking with a continual change.

Thanked be fortune it hath been otherwise
Twenty times better, but once in special,
10 In thin array after a pleasant guise,
When her loose gown from her shoulders did fall
And she me caught in her arms long and small,
Therewithal sweetly did me kiss
And softly said, 'Dear heart, how like you this?'

It was no dream: I lay broad waking.
But all is turned thorough my gentleness
Into a strange fashion of forsaking.
And I have leave to go of her goodness
And she also to use newfangleness.
20 But since that I so kindly am served
I would fain know what she hath deserved.

[MADAM, WITHOUTEN MANY WORDS][1]

Madam, withouten many words
Once I am sure ye will or no.

[THROUGHOUT THE WORLD]
1   *of little worth.*

[MADAM, WITHOUTEN MANY WORDS]
1   Translation of a madrigal by Dragonetto Bonifacio (1500–26).

And if ye will then leave your bourds
And use your wit and shew it so

And with a beck ye shall me call.
And if of one that burneth alway
Ye have any pity at all
Answer him fair with yea or nay.

10 If it be yea I shall be fain.
If it be nay friends as before.
Ye shall another man obtain
And I mine own² and yours no more.

[And Wilt Thou Leave Me Thus?]

And wilt thou leave me thus?
Say nay, say nay, for shame,
To save thee from the blame
Of all my grief and grame.   *sorrow*
And wilt thou leave me thus?
    Say nay, say nay.

And wilt thou leave me thus
That hath loved thee so long
In wealth and woe among?
10 And is thy heart so strong
As for to leave me thus?
    Say nay, say nay.

And wilt thou leave me thus
That hath given thee my heart
Never for to depart,
Nother for pain nor smart?   *neither*
And wilt thou leave me thus?
    Say nay, say nay.

And wilt thou leave me thus
20 And have no more pity
Of him that loveth thee?
Helas, thy cruelty!
And wilt thou leave me thus?
    Say nay, say nay!

[My Lute, Awake!]

My lute, awake! Perform the last
Labour that thou and I shall waste,
And end that I have now begun;
For when this song is sung and past,
My lute, be still for I have done.

As to be heard where ear is none,
As lead to grave in marble stone,¹

2   *I will be my own man.*

[My Lute, Awake!]
1   *As soon as (soft) lead is able to engrave marble.*

My song may pierce her heart as soon.
Should we then sigh or sing or moan?
10   No, no, my lute, for I have done.

The rocks do not so cruelly
Repulse the waves continually
As she my suit and affection,
So that I am past remedy,
Whereby my lute and I have done.

Proud of the spoil that thou hast got
Of simple hearts thorough Love's shot
By whom, unkind, thou hast them won,
Think not he hath his bow forgot
20   Although my lute and I have done.

Vengeance shall fall on thy disdain
That makest but game on earnest pain.
Think not alone under the sun
Unquit to cause thy lovers plain   *not repaid*
Although my lute and I have done.

May chance thee lie withered and old
The winter nights that are so cold,
Plaining in vain unto the moon.
Thy wishes then dare not be told.
30   Care then who list for I have done.

And then may chance thee to repent
The time that thou hast lost and spent
To cause thy lovers sigh and swoon.
Then shalt thou know beauty but lent
And wish and want as I have done.

Now cease, my lute. This is the last
Labour that thou and I shall waste
And ended is that we begun.
Now is this song both sung and past.
40   My lute, be still, for I have done.

[MINE OWN JOHN POYNTZ]¹

Mine own John Poyntz, since ye delight to know
          The cause why that homeward I me draw
          (And flee the press of courts whereso they go.
Rather than to live thrall under the awe
          Of lordly looks) wrapped within my cloak,
          To will and lust learning to set a law,
It is not because I scorn or mock
          The power of them to whom Fortune hath lent
          Charge over us, of right to strike the stroke;²

[MINE OWN JOHN POYNTZ]

1   Based on the classical model of Horace and on the works of Luigi Alamanni (1495–1556), the epistolary satire is a form that Wyatt introduced into English poetry. An imitation of Alamanni's *Satira* X, which was published in 1532, this is the best-known example of Wyatt's experimentation in this genre. John Poyntz was a friend of Wyatt's and a member of Henry VIII's court.

2   *right to punish.*

10

But true it is that I have always meant
    Less to esteem them than the common sort,
    Of outward things that judge in their intent
Without regard what doth inward resort.
    I grant sometime that of glory the fire
    Doth touch my heart; me list not to report
Blame by honour and honour to desire.
    But how may I this honour now attain
    That cannot dye the colour black a liar?
My Poyntz, I cannot frame my tune to feign,

20

    To cloak the truth for praise, without desert,
    Of them that list all vice for to retain.
I cannot honour them that sets their part
    With Venus and Bacchus[3] all their life long,
    Nor hold my peace of them although I smart.
I cannot crouch nor kneel to do such wrong
    To worship them like God on earth alone
    That are like wolves these silly lambs among.   *innocent*
I cannot with my words complain and moan
    And suffer naught, nor smart without complaint,

30

    Nor turn the word that from my mouth is gone.
I cannot speak and look like a saint,
    Use wiles for wit and make deceit a pleasure
    And call craft counsel, for profit still to paint.
I cannot wrest the law to fill the coffer,
    With innocent blood to feed myself fat,
    And do most hurt where most help I offer.
I am not he that can allow the state
    Of him Caesar and damn Cato to die,[4]
    That with his death did 'scape out of the gate
From Caesar's hands, if Livy doth not lie,[5]
    And would not live where liberty was lost,
    So did his heart the common wealth apply.
I am not he such eloquence to boast
    To make the crow singing as the swan,
    Nor call 'the lion' of coward beasts the most
That cannot take a mouse as the cat can;
    And he that dieth for hunger of the gold,
    Call him Alexander,[6] and say that Pan
Passeth Apollo in music many fold;[7]

50

    Praise Sir Thopas for a noble tale
    And scorn the story that the knight told;[8]
Praise him for counsel that is drunk of ale;
    Grin when he laugheth that beareth all the sway,
    Frown when he frowneth and groan when he is pale,
On other's lust to hang both night and day.
    None of these points would ever frame in me.
    My wit is naught. I cannot learn the way.
And much the less of things that greater be,
    That asken help of colours of device

60

    To join the mean with each extremity:

3 The god of wine and drunkenness.
4 I am not one who can approve the rule of Caesar and damn Cato.
5 According to Livy's *History* 114, Cato committed suicide to keep
from falling into Caesar's hands.
6 Alexander the Great (356–323 BCE).

7 Ovid tells the story of the musical contest between Pan and Apollo
in *Metamorphoses* 11.
8 Reference to the poetic superiority of the Knight's Tale to that of
Sir Thopas in Chaucer's *Canterbury Tales* I(A) and VII.

With the nearest virtue to cloak alway the vice
        And, as to purpose likewise it shall fall,
        To press the virtue that it may not rise.
As drunkenness good fellowship to call;
        The friendly foe with his double face
        Say he is gentle and courteous therewithal;
And say that Favel[9] hath a goodly grace
        In eloquence; and cruelty to name
        Zeal of justice and change in time and place;
70   And he that suffereth offence without blame
        Call him pitiful, and him true and plain
        That raileth reckless to every man's shame;
Say he is rude that cannot lie and feign,
        The lecher a lover, and tyranny
        To be the right of a prince's reign.
I cannot, I! No, no, it will not be!
        This is the cause that I could never yet
        Hang on their sleeves that weigh, as thou mayst see,
A chip of chance more than a pound of wit.
80   This maketh me at home to hunt and to hawk
        And in foul weather at my book to sit;
In frost and snow then with my bow to stalk.
        No man doth mark whereso I ride or go;
        In lusty leas in liberty I walk.
And of these news I feel nor weal nor woe,
        Save that a clog doth hang yet at my heel.
        No force for that, for it is ordered so
That I may leap both hedge and dike full well.
        I am not now in France to judge the wine,
90   With savoury sauce the delicates to feel;
Nor yet in Spain where one must him incline,
        Rather than to be, outwardly to seem.
        I meddle not with wits that be so fine.
Nor Flander's cheer letteth not my sight to deem
        Of black and white nor taketh my wit away
        With beastliness they, beasts, do so esteem.
Nor I am not where Christ is given in prey
        For money, poison, and treason at Rome –
        A common practice used night and day.
100   But here I am in Kent and Christendom
        Among the Muses where I read and rhyme,
        Where if thou list, my Poyntz, for to come,
Thou shalt be judge how I do spend my time.

John Knox (1505–1572)

A Scottish reformer, Knox was educated at Haddington School and Glasgow University. He began preaching on behalf of the reformed religion in 1547. He met John Calvin in Geneva in 1554. His publications include six tracts on the religious controversy in Scotland, of which "The First Blast of the Trumpet Against the Monstrous Regiment of Women" (1558) is the most famous, having been untimely published in the year of Queen Mary's death (she was the object of his attack) and of Elizabeth I's accession to the throne. This text may have permanently

9   The medieval personification of duplicity.

affected the young queen's attitude toward the Scottish reformation. It was answered the next year by John Aylmer, a Protestant exile who later became Bishop of London, in his *An Harborowe for Faithfull and Trewe Subjects.* Knox had to answer for it himself on September 4, 1558 when Mary Queen of Scots confronted him in a personal interview.

READING

J. W. Allen, *A History of Political Thought in the Sixteenth Century.*
A. G. Dickens, *The English Reformation.*
Eustace Percy, *John Knox.*

M. P.

[From] the First Blast of the Trumpet Against the Monstrous Regiment of Women

To promote a woman to bear rule, superiority, dominion, or empire above any realm, nation, or city, is repugnant to nature, contumely to God, a thing most contrarious to his revealed will and approved ordinance; and finally, it is the subversion of good order, of all equity and justice.

In the probation of this proposition, I will not be so curious as to gather whatsoever may amplify, set forth, or decore the same; but I am purposed, even as I have spoken my conscience in most plain and few words, so to stand content with a simple proof of every member, bringing in for my witness God's ordinance in nature, his plain will revealed in his word, and the minds of such as be most ancient amongst godly writers.

And first, where that I affirm the empire of a woman to be a thing repugnant to nature, I mean not only that God by the order of his creation hath spoiled woman of authority and dominion, but also that man hath seen, proved and pronounced just causes why that it should be. Man, I say, in many other cases blind, doth in this behalf see very clearly. For the causes be so manifest, that they cannot be hid. For who can deny but it repugneth to nature that the blind shall be appointed to lead and conduct such as do see? That the weak, the sick, and impotent persons shall nourish and keep the whole and strong, and finally, that the foolish, mad and phrenetic shall govern the discreet and give counsel to such as be sober of mind? And such be all women, compared unto man in bearing of authority. For their sight in civil regiment is but blindness, their strength weakness, their counsel foolishness, and judgement frenzy, if it be rightly considered.

I except such as God, by singular privilege, and for certain causes known only to himself, hath exempted from the common rank of women, and do speak of women as nature and experience do this day declare them. Nature, I say, doth paint them forth to be weak, frail, impatient, feeble and foolish; and experience hath declared them to be unconstant, variable, cruel and lacking the spirit of counsel and regiment. And these notable faults have men in all ages espied in that kind, for the which not only they have removed women from rule and authority, but also some have thought that men subject to the counsel or empire of their wives were unworthy of all public office . . .

I am not ignorant that the subtle wits of carnal men (which can never be brought under the obedience of God's simple precepts to maintain this monstrous empire) have yet two vain shifts. First, they allege that, albeit women may not absolutely reign by themselves, because they may neither sit in judgement, neither pronounce sentence, neither execute any public office, yet may they do all such things by their lieutenants, deputies and judges substitute. Secondarily, say they, a woman born to rule over any realm may choose her a husband, and to him she may transfer and give her authority and right. To both I answer in few words. First, that from a corrupt and venomed fountain can spring no wholesome water. Secondarily that no person hath power to give the thing which doth not justly appertain to themselves. But the authority of a woman is a corrupted fountain, and therefore from her can never spring any lawful officer. She is not born to rule over men, and therefore she can appoint none by her gift, nor by her power (which she hath not), to the place of a lawful magistrate.

Henry Howard, Earl of Surrey (1517–1547)

Surrey's translations of the *Aeneid* and the Psalms are some of the first experiments in the writing of English blank verse. His significant achievement as a poet lies in this formal innovation and in his creative response to the new humanist way of teaching Latin, which directed attention away from the medieval scholastic emphasis on abstract grammatical rules and toward a careful consideration of the idiom of the best Roman authors, which for him meant especially Virgil. The complex process by which Italian and northern humanists, such as Valla and Erasmus, effected a profound change in the teaching of Latin – and in turn in the understanding of language and of poetry – is captured remarkably well in a single sentence of Colet's contribution to John Lyly's *Grammar* (1527):

> How and in what manner, and with what construction of words, and all the varieties, and diversities, and changes in Latin speech (which be innumerable), if any man will know, and by that knowledge attain to understand Latin books, and to speak and to write the clean Latin: let him above all busily learn and read good Latin authors of chosen poets and orators, and note widely how they wrote, and spoke, and study always to follow them, desiring none other rules but their examples.

By imitating Virgil's syntax and rhythm in his English translations, Surrey introduced a new regularity into English poetry. Like most innovations, however, this one includes some heavy borrowing and considerable uncertainty. Just as Tudor biblical translators worked as much with other existing translations as with ancient sources, so Surrey made heavy use of Gavin Douglas's Scottish rhyming version of the *Aeneid* in producing his own translation. In doing so, however, Surrey (like Chaucer in the *Canterbury Tales* and Wyatt in his sonnets and satires) opted for a ten-syllable line, although his translation of Psalm 55 is an interesting example of unrhyming hexameters.

The two passages below from the *Aeneid* are not only important in the history of English prosody. They are also two powerfully dramatic moments in the history of the tragic depiction of women: the first (from Book II) is the scene in which Aeneas and his wife Creusa are separated during the destruction of Troy, in the course of which she dies and later appears to him in order to prophesy his future; the second (from Book IV) is the scene of the suicide of Dido, following Aeneas' departure from Carthage. These selections reflect Surrey's commitment to render into English Virgil's syntactical and rhetorical virtuosity. Surrey's translations and his love poems were first published in *Tottel's Miscellany* (1557), which was one of the earliest

and most important sixteenth-century collections of English lyric poetry and a major source for English translations of Petrarch, of which Surrey's are among the best. Although Surrey is there represented equally with the works of Nicholas Grimald, who may have served as editor of the collection, his work is more importantly juxtaposed with 96 poems by Wyatt, with whom he has been linked ever since. In his preface Tottel bases his judgment that English has an equal claim to eloquence with Latin and Italian on the achievement of Wyatt and Surrey. In his elegy for Wyatt ("W. Resteth Here"), deservedly one of his most famous poems, Surrey credits Wyatt with teaching "what might be sayd in ryme."

Like Wyatt's – but less politically fortunate than his – Surrey's life was circumscribed by the dangerous dynamics of Henry VIII's court. From 1530 he was a close personal friend of the Duke of Richmond, the king's natural son. Two years later he married Lady Frances Vere, the daughter of the Earl of Oxford. In 1536 he was present at the trial of Anne Boleyn, but in 1540 he gave a distinguished performance in a tournament honoring Anne of Cleves, Henry VIII's new queen. A simple list of a few events in his life during the six years before his death provides an index of his varying fortunes: in 1541 he was made a Knight of the Garter; in 1542 he witnessed the execution of his cousin, Catherine Howard; later the same year he was briefly imprisoned for angrily challenging a courtier, only to join his father, the Duke of Norfolk, soon after in the Scottish campaign; in 1543 he was imprisoned for what was probably drunken behavior in London (eating flesh in Lent and breaking windows); later that year he served in a campaign with the Emperor Charles V; in 1544 he began construction of an elegant house in the classic Italian style, one of the first of its kind in England, of which nothing survives; following several military campaigns in which he was either reckless or chivalrous, he was accused of treason and beheaded on January 19, 1547 at the age of 30.

READING

O. B. Hardison, Jr., *Prosody and Purpose in the English Renaissance*, ch. VI.
Henry Howard, Earl of Surrey, *Poems*, ed. Emrys Jones.
J. W. Lever, *The Elizabethan Love Sonnet*, ch. III.
Elizabeth M. Pomeroy, *The Elizabethan Miscellanies: Their Development and Conventions*, ch. III.
Florence Ridley, *The Aeneid of Henry Howard, Earl of Surrey*.
W. A. Sessions, *Henry Howard, Earl of Surrey*.

M. P.

[Translations From The Aeneid]

[From] Book II [The Death of Creusa]

And now we gan draw nere unto the gate,
Right well escapte the daunger, as me[1] thought,
When that at hand a sound of feet we heard.
My father[2] then, gazing throughout the dark,
Cried on me, 'Flee, son! They ar at hand.'
With that bright shelds and shene armours I saw.
But then I knowe not what unfrendly god
My trobled wit from me biraft for fere.
For while I ran by the most secret stretes,
Eschuing still the common haunted track,
From me catif, alas, bereved was
Creusa then, my spouse, I wot not how,
Whether by fate, or missing of the way,
Or that she was by werinesse reteind.
But never sithe these eies might her behold,
Nor did I yet perceive that she was lost,
Ne never backward turned I my mind,
Till we came to the hill wheras there stood
The old temple dedicate to Ceres.[3]

    And when that we were there assembled all,
She was only away, deceiving us,
Her spouse, her son, and all her compainie.
What god or man did I not then accuse,
Nere wood for ire? or what more cruell chaunce
Did hap to me in all Troies overthrow?
Ascanius[4] to my feeres I then betoke,
With Anchises, and eke the Troian gods,
And left them hid within a valley depe.
And to the town I gan me hye againe,
Clad in bright armes, and bent for to renew
Aventures past, to search throughout the town,
And yeld my hed to perils ones againe.

    And first the walles and dark entrie I sought
Of the same gate wherat I issued out,
Holding backward the steppes where we had come
In the dark night, loking all round about.
In every place the ugsome sightes I saw,
The silence selfe of night agast my sprite.
From hense againe I past unto our house,
If she by chaunce had ben returned home.
The Grekes were there, and had it all beset.
The wasting fire blown up by drift of wind
Above the roofes; the blazing flame sprang up,
The sound wherof with furie pearst the skies.
To Priams[5] palace and the castel then
I made; and there at Junous[6] sanctuair,
In the void porches, Phenix, Ulisses[7] eke,

10

20

30

40

[Translations From The Aeneid]
[From] Book II [The Death of Creusa]
1 Aeneas, prince of Troy.
2 Anchises, his father, whom he rescues from the burning city.
3 Goddess of agriculture.
4 Aeneas' son.
5 King of Troy.
6 Juno, goddess of marriage and the home.
7 Conquering Greeks.

Sterne guardens stood, watching of the spoile.
The richesse here were set, reft from the brent
50   Temples of Troy; the tables of the gods,
The vessells eke that were of massy gold,
And vestures spoild, were gatherd all in heap.
The children orderly and mothers pale for fright
Long ranged on a rowe stode round about.
    So bold was I to showe my voice that night,
With clepes and cries to fill the stretes throughout,
With Creuse name in sorrow, with vain teres,
And often sithes the same for to repete.
The town restlesse with furie as I sought,
60   Th'unlucky figure of Creusaes ghost,
Of stature more than wont, stood fore mine eyen.
Abashed then I woxe. Therwith my heare   *hair*
Gan start right up, my voice stack in my throte.
When with such words she gan my hart remove:
'What helps to yeld unto such furious rage,
Sweet spouse?' quod she. 'Without wil of the gods
This chaunced not; ne lefull was for thee
To lead away Creusa hense with thee:
The king of the hye heven suffreth it not.
70   A long exile thou art assigned to bere,
Long to furrow large space of stormy seas:
So shalt thou reach at last Hesperian land,
Wher Lidian Tiber with his gentle streme
Mildly doth flow along the frutfull felds.
There mirthful wealth, there kingdom is for thee,
There a kinges child preparde to be thy make.
For thy beloved Creusa stint thy teres.
For now shal I not see the proud abodes
Of Myrmidons, nor yet of Dolopes;
80   Ne I, a Troyan lady and the wife
Unto the sonne of Venus the goddesse,
Shall goe a slave to serve the Grekish dames.
Me here the gods great mother holdes.
And now farwell, and kepe in fathers brest
The tender love of thy yong son and myne.'
    This having said, she left me all in teres,
And minding much to speake; but she was gone,
And suttly fled into the weightlesse aire.
Thrise raught I with mine arms t'accoll her neck,
90   Thrise did my handes vaine hold th'image escape,
Like nimble windes, and like the flieng dreame.
So night spent out, returne I to my feers.
And ther wondring I find together swarmd
A new nomber of mates, mothers and men,
A rout exiled, a wreched multitude,
From eche where flockte together, prest to passe,
With hart and goods, to whatsoever land
By sliding seas me listed them to lede.
And now rose Lucifer above the ridge
100   Of lusty Ide, and brought the dawning light.
The Grekes held th'entries of the gates beset;
Of help there was no hope. Then gave I place,
Toke up my sire, and hasted to the hill."

[FROM] BOOK IV [THE SUICIDE OF DIDO]

Aurora[8] now from Titans purple bed
With new day light hath overspred the earth,
When by her windowes the quene the peping day
Espyed, and navie with splaid sailes depart
The shore, and eke the port of vessels voyde.
Her comly brest thrise or foure times she smote
With her own hand, and tore her golden tresse.
'Oh Jove,' quoth she, 'shall he then thus depart
A straunger thus and scorne our kingdom so?
10 Shall not my men do on theyr armure prest,
And eke pursue them throughout all the town?
Out of the rode some shall the vessels warpe?
Hast on, cast flame, set sayle and welde your owers!
What said I? but where am I? what phrensie
Alters thy minde? Unhappy Dido[9] now
Hath thee beset a froward destenie.
Then it behoved, when thou didst geve to him
The scepter. Lo, his faith and his right hand,
That leades with him (they say) his countrie godes,
20 That on his back his aged father bore.
His body might I not have caught and rent?
And in the seas drenched him and his feers?
And from Ascanius his life with iron reft,
And set him on his fathers bord for meate?
Of such debate perchaunce the fortune might
Have bene doubtfull: would God it were assayed!
Whom should I feare, sith I my selfe must die?
Might I have throwen into that navy brandes,
And filled eke their deckes with flaming fire,
30 The father, sonne, and all their nacion
Destroyed, and falln my self ded over al.
Sunne, with thy beames that mortall workes discries,
And thou Juno, that wel these travailes knowest,
Proserpine thou, upon whom folk do use
To houle, and call in forked wayes by night,
Infernal furies, ye wreakers of wrong,
And Didos gods, who standes at point of death,
Receive these wordes, and eke your heavy power
Withdraw from me, that wicked folk deserve,
40 And our request accept, we you beseche.
If so that yonder wicked head must needes
Recover port, and saile to land of force,
And if Joves wil have so resolved it
And such ende set as no wight can fordoe,
Yet at the least asailed mought he be
With armes and warres of hardy nacions,
From the boundes of his kingdom farre exiled,
Iulus eke rashed out of his armes,
Driven to call for helpe, that he may see
50 The giltles corpses of his folke lie dead.
And after hard condicions of peace,

---

8 The dawn.

9 Queen of Carthage and its founder, who has fallen in love with
Aeneas, although he is driven by his destiny to be the founder of Rome.

His realme nor life desired may he brooke,
But fall before his time, ungraved amid the sandes.
This I require, these wordes with blood I shed.
And Tirians, ye his stocke and all his race
Pursue with hate, rewarde our cinders so.
No love nor leage betwixt our peoples be.
And of our bones some wreaker may there spring,
With sword and flame that Troyans may pursue.
60   And from hencefoorth, when that our powr may stretch,
Our costes to them contrary be for aye,
I crave of God, and our streames to their fluddes,
Armes unto armes, and offspring of eche race
With mortal warr eche other may fordoe.'
    This said, her mind she writhed on al sides,
Seking with spede to end her irksome life.
To Sichees nurse Barcen then thus she said
(For hers at home in ashes did remaine):
'Cal unto me, deare nurse, my sister Anne.
70   Bid her in hast in water of the fludde
She sprinckle the body, and bring the beastes
And purging sacrifice I did her shewe.
So let her come; and thou thy temples bind
With sacred garlandes; for the sacrifice
That I to Pluto have begonne, my mind
Is to performe, and geve end to these cares;
And Troyan statue throw into the flame.'
When she had said, redouble gan her nurse
Her steppes, forth on an aged womans trot.
80   But trembling Dido egerly now bent
Upon her sterne determinacion,
Her bloodshot eyes roling within her head,
Her quivering chekes flecked with deadly staine,
Both pale and wan to think on death to come,
Into the inward wardes of her palace
She rusheth in, and clam up as distraught
The buriall stack, and drew the Troyan swerd,
Her gift sometime, but ment to no such use.
Where when she saw his weed and wel knowen bed,
90   Weping a while, in study gan she stay,
Fell on the bed, and these last words she said:
'Swete spoiles, whiles God and destenies it wold,
Receve this sprite, and rid me of these cares.
I lived and ranne the course fortune did graunt,
And under earth my great gost now shall wende.
A goodly town I built, and saw my walles,
Happy, alas to happy, if these costes
The Troyan shippes had never touched aye.'
    This said, she laid her mouth close to the bed.
100   'Why then,' quoth she, 'unwroken shall we die?   *unavenged*
But let us die, for thus and in this sort
It liketh us to seeke the shadowes darck.
And from the seas the cruel Troyans eyes
Shall wel discern this flame, and take with him
Eke these unlucky tokens of my death.'
    As she had said, her damsells might perceve
Her with these wordes fal pearced on a sword,
The blade embrued, an hands besprent with gore.
The clamor rang unto the pallace toppe,

110   The brute ranne throughout al th'astoined towne.
With wailing great and womens shril yelling
The roofes gan roare, the aire resound with plaint,
As though Cartage or th'auncient town of Tyre
With prease of entred enemies swarmed full,
Or when the rage of furious flame doth take
The temples toppes and mansions eke of men.
    Her sister Anne, spritelesse for dread to heare
This fearefull sturre, with nailes gan teare her face.
She smote her brest, and rushed through the rout
120   And her dyeng she cleapes thus by her name:
'Sister, for this with craft did you me bourd?   *deceive*
The stak, the flame, the altars, bred they this?
What shall I first complaine, forsaken wight?
Lothest thou in death thy sisters felowship?
Thou shouldst have calld me to like destiny:
One wo, one sword, one houre mought end us both.
This funerall stak built I with these handes
And with this voice cleped our native gods,
And cruel so absentest me from thy death?
130   Destroyd thou hast, sister, both thee and me,
Thy people eke, and princes borne of Tyre.
Geve here: I shall with water washe her woundes,
And suck with mouth her breath, if ought be left.'
    This said, unto the high degrees shee mounted,
Embracing fast her sister now half dead,
With wailefull plaint, whom in her lap she layd,
The black swart gore wiping dry with her clothes.
But Dido striveth to lift up againe
Her heavy eyen, and hath no power thereto:
140   Deepe in her brest that fixed wound doth gape.
Thrise leaning on her elbow gan she raise
Her self upward, and thrise she overthrewe
Upon the bed, ranging with wandring eyes
The skies for light, and wept when she it found.
    Almighty Juno having ruth by this
Of her long paines and eke her lingring death,
From heaven she sent the goddesse Iris downe,
The throwing sprit and jointed limmes to loose.
For that neither by lot of destiny
150   Nor yet by kindly death she perished,
But wretchedly before her fatall day,
And kindled with a sodein rage of flame;
Prosperpine had not from her head bereft
The golden heare, nor judged her to hell.
The dewye Iris thus with golden wings,
A thousand hues shewing against the sunne,
Amid the skies then did she flye adowne,
On Didos head where as she gan alight:
'This heare,' quod she, 'to Pluto consecrate,
160   Commaunded I reve, and thy spirit unloose
From this body.' And when she thus had said,
With her right hand she cut the heare in twaine,
And therwith al the kindly heat gan quench
And into wind the life foorthwith resolve.

PSALM 55

Give eare to my suit, Lord, fromward hide not thy face.
Beholde, herking in grief, lamenting how I praye.
My fooes they bray so lowde, and eke threpe on so fast,
Buckeled to do me scathe, so is their malice bent.
Care perceth my entrayles and traveyleth my sprite;
The greslye feare of death envyroneth my brest;
A tremblynge cold of dred clene overwhelmeth my hert.
'O', thinke I, 'hadd I wings like to the symple dove,
This peryll myght I flye, and seke some place of rest
10   In wylder woods, where I might dwell farr from these cares.'
What speady way of wing my playnts shold thei lay on,
To skape the stomtye blast that treatned is to me!
Rayne those unbrydled tungs! breake that conjured league!
For I decyphred have amydd our towne the stryfe:
Gyle and wrong kept the walles, they ward both day and night;
And whiles myscheif with care doth kepe the market stede;
Whilst wickidnes with craft in heaps swarme through the strete.
Ne my declared foo wrought me all this reproche;
By harme so loked for, yt wayeth halfe the lesse.
20   For though myne ennemyes happ had byn for to prevaile,
I cold have hidd my face from venym of his eye.
It was a frendly foo, by shadow of good will,
Myne old fere and dere frende, my guyde, that trapped me;
Where I was wont to fetche the cure of all my care,
And in his bosome hyde my secreat zeale to God.
Such soden surprys quicke may them hell devoure,
Whilst I invoke the Lord, whose power shall me defend.
My prayer shall not cease from that the sonne disscends
Till he his haulture wynn and hyde them in the see.   *weight*
30   With words of hott effect, that moveth from hert contryte,
Such humble sute, O Lord, doth perce thy pacyent eare.
It was the Lord that brake the bloody compackts of those
That preloked on with yre to slaughter me and myne.   *anticipated*
The everlasting God whose kingdom hath no end,
Whome, by no tale to dred he cold divert from synne,
The conscyence unquiet he stryks with hevy hand,
And proves their force in fayth whome he sware to defend.
Butter fales not so soft as doth hys pacyence longe,
And over passeth fine oyle, running not halfe so smothe.[1]
40   But when his suffraunce fynds that brydled wrath provoks,
He thretneth wrath, he whets more sharppe then any toole can fyle.
Friowr, whose harme and tounge presents the wicked sort[2]
Of those false wolves, with cootes which doo their ravin hyde,
That sweare to me by heaven, the fotestole of the Lord,
Who though force had hurt my fame, they did not touche my lyfe:
Such patching care I lothe as feeds the welth with lyes.
But in the th'other Psalme of David fynd I ease:
Iacta curam tuam super dominum et ipse te enutriet.[3]

PSALM 55
1   Coverdale's version, to which Surrey may here be alluding, reads,
"Their mouthes are softer then butter, & yet have they batell in their
mynde: their wordes are smoother then oyle, and yet they be very
swerdes."

2   From here on Surrey has abandoned the task of translation.
3   The Authorized Version, based on Coverdale, translates the final
verse as, "But thou, O God, shalt bring them down into the pit of
destruction: bloody and deceitful men shall not live out half their days;
but I will trust in thee."

[WHEN RAGYNG LOVE]

When ragyng love with extreme payne
Most cruelly distrains my hart;
When that my teares, as floudes of rayne,
Beare witnes of my wofull smart;
When sighes have wasted so my breath
That I lye at the poynte of death:

I call to minde the navye greate
That the Grekes brought to Troye towne,
And how the boysteous windes did beate
Their shyps, and rente their sayles adowne,
Till Agamemnons daughters bloode
Appeasde the goddes that them withstode.[1]

And how that in those ten yeres warre
Full manye a bloudye dede was done,
And manye a lord, that came full farre,
There caught his bane, alas, to sone,
And many a good knight overronne,
Before the Grekes had Helene wonne.

Then thinke I thus: sithe suche repayre,
So longe time warre of valiant men,
Was all to winne a ladye fayre,
Shall I not learne to suffer then,
And thinke my life well spent to be
Servyng a worthier wight than she?

Therfore I never will repent,
But paynes contented stil endure:
For like as when, rough winter spent,
The pleasant spring straight draweth in ure,   *arrives*
So after ragyng stormes of care
Joyful at length may be my fare.

[THE SOOTE SEASON]

The soote season, that bud and blome furth bringes,   *spring*
With grene hath clad the hill and eke the vale;
The nightingale with fethers new she singes;
The turtle to her make hath tolde her tale.
Somer is come, for every spray nowe springes;
The hart hath hong his olde hed on the pale;
The buck in brake his winter cote he flinges;
The fishes flote with newe repaired scale;
The adder all her sloughe awaye she slinges;
The swift swalow pursueth the flyes smale;
The busy bee her honye now she minges;   *remembers*

[WHEN RAGYNG LOVE]
1 The allusion here is to Agamemnon's sacrifice of his daughter
Iphigeneia, which made it possible for the Greeks to sail for Troy by
appeasing the goddess Artemis.

Winter is worne that was the flowers bale.
And thus I see among these pleasant thinges
Eche care decayes, and yet my sorow springes.

[SET ME WHERAS THE SONNE][1]

Set me wheras the sonne dothe perche the grene,
Or whear his beames may not dissolve the ise;
In temprat heat wheare he is felt and sene;
With prowde people, in presence sad and wyse;
Set me in base, or yet in highe degree,
In the long night, or in the shortyst day,
In clere weather, or wheat mysts thikest be,
In loste yowthe, or when my heares be grey;
Set me in earthe, in heaven, or yet in hell,
In hill, in dale, or in the fowming floode;
Thrawle, or at large, alive whersoo I dwell,
Sike, or in healthe, in yll fame or in good:
    Yours will I be, and with that onely thought
    Comfort my self when that my hape is nowght.

[LOVE THAT DOTH RAINE][1]

Love that doth raine and live within my thought,
And buylt his seat within my captyve brest,
Clad in the armes wherin with me he fowght
Oft in my face he doth his banner rest.
But she that tawght me love and suffre paine,
My doubtfull hope and eke my hote desire
With shamfast looke to shadoo and refrayne,
Her smyling grace convertyth streight to yre.
And cowarde love than to the hert apace
Taketh his flight where he doth lorke and playne
His purpose lost, and dare not show his face.
For my lordes gylt thus fawtless byde I payine;
    Yet from my lorde shall not my foote remove.
    Sweet is the death that taketh end by love.

[I NEVER SAW YOUE][1]

I never saw youe, madam, laye aparte
Your cornet black in colde nor yet in heate   *head-dress*
Sythe first ye knew of my desire so greate
Which other fances chased cleane from my harte.
Whiles to my self I did the thought reserve
That so unware did wounde my wofull brest

[SET ME WHERAS THE SONNE]

1   The form of this sonnet – in three quatrains and a couplet, rhyming abab cdcd efef gg – is usually called (anachronistically) "Shakespearean," although it was in fact Surrey's invention. Despite this formal innovation, the text of the poem is a translation of Petrarch's *In vita*, 145, which in turn is based on Horace.

[LOVE THAT DOTH RAINE]

1   Translation of Petrarch's *In vita*, 140, which was also translated by Wyatt (see his "[The Long Love]").

[I NEVER SAW YOUE]

1   Translation of Petrarch's *In vita*, 11.

Pytie I saw within your hart dyd rest;
But since ye knew I did youe love and serve
Your golden treese was clad alway in blacke,
10   Your smilyng lokes were hid thus evermore,
All that withdrawne that I did crave so sore.
So doth this cornet governe me alacke,
    In sommere sonne, in winter breath of frost;
    Of your faire eies whereby the light is lost

[ALAS, SO ALL THINGES NOWE DOE HOLDE THEIR PEACE][1]

Alas, so all thinges nowe doe holde their peace,
Heaven and earth disturbed in nothing;
The beastes, the ayer, the birdes their song doe cease;
The nightes chare the starres aboute dothe bring.
Calme is the sea, the waves worke lesse and lesse;
So am not I, whom love alas doth wring,
Bringing before my face the great encrease
Of my desires, whereat I wepe and syng
In joye and wo as in a doutfull ease.
10   For my swete thoughtes sometyme doe pleasure bring,
But by and by the cause of my disease
Geves me a pang that inwardly dothe sting,
    When that I thinke what griefe it is againe
    To live and lacke the thing should ridde my paine.

[FROM TUSCAN CAM]

From Tuscan cam my ladies[1] worthi race;   *Tuscany*
Faire Florence was sometime her auncient seate;
The westorne ile, whose pleasaunt showre doth face
Wylde Chambares cliffes, did geve her lyvely heate.
Fostred she was with mylke of Irishe brest;
Her syer an erle, hir dame of princes bloud;[2]
From tender yeres in Britaine she doth rest,
With a kinges child, where she tastes gostly foode.
Honsdon did furst present her to myn eyen:
10   Bryght ys her hew, and Geraldine she hight;
Hampton me tawght to wishe her furst for myne,
And Windsor, alas, doth chase me from her sight.[3]
    Bewty of kind, her vertues from above;
    Happy ys he that may obtaine her love.

[ALAS, SO ALL THINGES NOWE DOE HOLDE THEIR PEACE]
1 Adapted from Petrarch's *In vita*, 144.

[FROM TUSCAN CAM]
1 The lady referred to is Lady Elizabeth ("Geraldine") Fitzgerald, who married Sir Anthony Browne in 1542. She was then 14 or 15, and her husband was about 60. Surrey's relationship to her has been a continuing source of romantic speculation since Nashe's account in *The*

Unfortunate Traveller (1594). The date of the sonnet, on which speculation continues to rest, remains in doubt, although 1541 is possible.
2 Geraldine was the daughter of Lady Elizabeth Grey, who was a cousin of Henry VIII.
3 The household of the Princesses Mary and Elizabeth, with which Geraldine was associated, moved among Hunsdon, Hampton, and Windsor during 1536–9. Surrey had been confined at Windsor in 1537 for an offense against a courtier.

[The Sonne Hath Twyse Brought Forthe][1]

The sonne hath twyse brought forthe the tender grene,
    And cladd the yerthe in livelye lustynes;
    Ones have the wyndes the trees dispoyled clene,
And now agayne begynnes their cruelnes,
    Sins I have hidd under my brest the harme
    That never shall recover helthfulnes.
The wynters hurt recovers with the warme;
    The perched grene restored is with shade:
    What warmth, alas, may sarve for to disarme
10   The froosyn hart that my inflame hath made?
    What colde agayne is hable to restore
    My freshe grene yeres that wither thus and faade?
Alas, I see nothinge to hurt so sore
    But tyme somtyme reduceth a retourne;
    Yet tyme my harme increseth more and more,
And semes to have my cure allwayes in skorne.
    Straunge kynd of death, in lief that I doo trye:
    At hand to melt, farr of in flame to bourne;
And like as time list to my cure aply,
20   So doth eche place my comfort cleane refuse.
    Eche thing alive that sees the heaven with eye
With cloke of night maye cover and excuse
    Him self from travaile of the dayes unrest,
    Save I, alas, against all others use,
That then sturre upp the torment of my brest

    To curse eche starr as cawser of my faat.
    And when the sonne hath eke the darke represt
And brought the daie, it doth nothing abaat
    The travaile of my endles smart and payne.
30   For then, as one that hath the light in haat,
I wishe for night, more covertlye to playne
    And me withdrawe from everie haunted place,
    Lest in my chere my chaunce should pere to playne;
And with my mynd I measure paas by paas
    To seke that place where I my self hadd lost,
    That daye that I was tangled in that laase,
In seming slacke that knytteth ever most;
    But never yet the trayvaile of my thought
    Of better state could catche a cawse to bost.
40   For yf I fynde somtyme that I have sought,
    Those starres by whome I trusted of the port,
    My sayles do fall, and I advaunce right nought,
As anchord fast; my sprites do all resort
    To stand atgaas, and sinke in more and mote   *gazing*
    The deadlye harme which she doth take in sport.
Loo, yf I seke, how I do fynd my sore!
    And yf I flye, I carrey with me still
    The venymd shaft which dothe his force restore
By hast of flight. And I maye playne my fill

[The Sonne Hath Twyse Brought Forthe]
1   Although not a translation, this poem incorporates many lines from
Petrarch's *In vita.*

50   Unto my self, oneles this carefull song
          Prynt in your hert some percell of my will.
      For I, alas, in sylence all to long
         Of myne old hurt yet fele the wound but grene.
         Rue on my lief, or elles your crewell wrong
      Shall well appeare, and by my deth be sene.

[GEVE PLACE, YE LOVERS]

Geve place, ye lovers, here before
That spent your bostes and bragges in vain:
My ladies beawtie passeth more
The best of yours, I dare well sayen,
Than doth the sonne the candle light
Or brightest day the darkest night.

And thereto hath a trothe as just
As had Penelope the fayre:
For what she saith, ye may it trust
10   As it by writing sealed were.
And vertues hath she many moe
Than I with pen have skill to showe.

I coulde rehearse, if that I wolde,
The whole effect of Natures plaint,
When she had lost the perfit mold,
The like to whom she could not paint;
With wringing handes howe she dyd cry,
And what she said, I know it, I.

I knowe she swore with ragyng mind,
20   Her kingdom onely set apart,
There was no losse, by lawe of kind,
That could have gone so nere her hart.
And this was chiefly all her payne:
She coulde not make the lyke agayne.

Sith Nature thus gave her the prayse
To be the chiefest worke she wrought,
In faith, me thinke some better waies
On your behalfe might well be sought,
Then to compare, as ye have done,
To matche the candle with the sonne.

[SUCH WAIWARDE WAIES]

Suche waiwarde waies hath love that moste parte in discorde;
Our willes do stand wherby our hartes but seldom dooth accorde.
Disceyte is his delight, and to begyle and mocke
The symple hertes which he doth stryke with froward dyvers stroke.
He cawseth hertes to rage with golden burninge darte,
And doth alaye with ledden cold agayne the tothers harte.
Hot gleames of burning fyre and easye sparkes of flame   *slight*
In balaunce of unegall weight he pondereth by ame.
From easye fourde, where I might wade and passe full well,

10 He me withdrawes, and doth me drive into the darke diep well;
    And me withholdes where I am cald and offerd place,
    And wooll that still my mortall foo I do beseche of grace.
    He lettes me to pursue a conquest well nere woon,
    To follow where my paynes were spilt or that my sute begune.
    Lo, by these rules I know how sone a hart can turne
    From warr to peace, from trewce to stryf, and so again returne.
    I know how to convert my will in others lust;
    Of litle stuff unto my self to weyve a webb of trust;
    And how to hide my harme with soft dissembled chere,
20 When in my face the paynted thoughtes wolde owtwardlye appere.
    I know how that the blood forsakes the faas for dredd,
    And how by shame it staynes agayne the cheke with flaming redd.
    I know under the grene the serpent how he lurckes;
    The hamer of the restles forge I know eke how yt workes.
    I know, and can be roote, the tale that I wold tell,
    But ofte the wordes come forth a wrye of hym that loveth well.
    I know in heat and cold the lover how he shakes,
    In singinge how he can complayne, in sleaping how he wakes,
    To languishe without ache, sickles for to consume,
30 A thousand thinges for to devyse resolving all hys fume.
    And thoughe he lyke to see his ladies face full sore,
    Such pleasure as delightes his eye doth not his health restore.
    I know to seke the tracke of my desyred foo,
    And feare to fynd that I do seke; but chefelye this I know,
    That lovers must transforme into the thing beloved,
    And live (alas, who colde beleve?) with spryte from lief removed.
    I know in hartye sighes and lawghters of the splene
    At ones to chaunge my state, my will, and eke my colour clene.
    I know how to disceyve myself withouten helpp,
40 And how the lyon chastysed is by beating of the whelpp.
    In standing nere my fyer, I know how that I frese;
    Farr of, to burn; in both to wast, and so my lief to lese.
    I know how love doth rage uppon the yeldon mynd,
    How small a nett may take and mashe a harte of gentle kynd;
    With seldome tasted swete, to season heaps of gall,
    Revyved with a glyns of grace olde sorowes to let fall.
    The hidden traynes I know, and secret snares of love;
    How sone a loke may prynt a thought that never will remove.
    That slipper state I know, those sodayne tournes from welthe,
50 That doubtfull hope, that certayne woo, and sure dispaire of helthe.

[WRAPT IN MY CARELESSE CLOKE]

    Wrapt in my carelesse cloke, as I walke to and fro,
    I se how love can shew what force there reigneth in his bow;
    And how he shoteth eke, a hardy hart to wound;
    And where he glanceth by agayne, that litle hurt is found.
    For seldom is it sene he woundeth hartes alike;
    The tone may rage, when tothers love is often farre to seke.
    All this I se, with more; and wonder thinketh me
    Howe he can strike the one so sore, and leave the other fre.
    I se that wounded wight that suffreth all this wrong,
10 How he is fed with yeas and nayes, and liveth all to long.
    In silence though I kepe such secretes to my self,
    Yet do I se how she somtime doth yeld a loke by stelth,
    As though it seemd, 'Ywys, I will not lose the so',

When in her hart so swete a thought did never truely go.
  Then say I thus: 'Alas, that man is farre from blisse
That doth receive for his relief none other gayn but this.
  And she that fedes him so, I fele and finde it plain,
Is but to glory in her power, that over such can reign.
  Nor are such graces spent but when she thinkes that he,
20 A weried man, is fully bent such fansies to let flie.
  Then to retain him stil, she wrasteth new her grace,
And smileth, lo, as though she would forthwith the man embrace.
  But when the proofe is made to try such lokes withall,
He findeth then the place all voyde, and fraighted full of gall.
  Lorde, what abuse is this! who can such women praise
That for their glory do devise to use such crafty wayes!
  I that among the rest do sit, and mark the row,
Fynde that in her is greater craft then is in twenty mo,
  Whose tender yeres, alas, with wyles so well are spedde:
What will she do when hory heares are powdred in her hedde!'

[LONDON, HAST THOW ACCUSED ME]

London, hast thow accused me
  Of breche of lawes, the roote of stryfe?
  Within whose brest did boyle to see,
So fervent hotte thy dissolute lief,
  That even the hate of synnes, that groo
  Within thy wicked walles so rife,
For to breake forthe did convert soo
  That terrour colde it not represse.
  The which, by wordes syns prechers knoo
10 What hope is left for to redresse,
  By unknowne meanes it liked me
  My hydden burden to expresse,
Wherby yt might appere to the
  That secret synn hath secret spight;[1]
  From justice rodd no fault is free;
But that all such as wourke unright
  In most quyet are next ill rest.
  In secret sylence of the night
This made me, with a reckles brest,
20 To wake thy sluggardes with my bowe:
  A fygure of the Lordes behest,
Whose scourge for synn the Screptures shew.
  That, as the fearfull thonder clapp
  By soddayne flame at hand we knowe,
Of peoble stones the sowndles rapp
  The dredfull plage might mak the see
  Of Goddes wrath, that doth the enwrapp;
That pryde[2] might know, from conscyence free,
  How loftye workes may her defend;
30 And envy fynd, as her hath sought,
  How other seke hym to offend;
  And wrath tast of eche crewell thought

[LONDON, HAST THOW ACCUSED ME]
1 Here begins an allusion to the Psalms, especially Psalm 19:12. An ongoing controversy about this poem concerns the extent to which it departs from the particular biographical circumstances of 1543 (see headnote) and deals with larger issues of Protestant faith.
2 There follows here a catalogue of the Seven Deadly Sins.

The just shapp hyer[3] in the end;
And ydell slouthe, that never wrought,
To heven hys spirite lift may begyn;
And gredye lucre lyve in drede
To see what haate ill gott goodes wynn;
The lechers, ye that luste do feed,
Perceve what secrecye is in synne;
40   And gluttons hartes for sorow blede,
Awaked when their faulte they fynd.
In lothsome vyce eche dronken wight
To styrr to Godd, this was my mynd.
Thy wyndowes had don me no spight;
But prowd people that drede no fall,
Clothed with falshed and unright
Bred in the closures of thy wall.
But wrested to wrathe in fervent zeale
Thow hast to strief my secret call.
50   Endured hartes no warning feale.
Oh shamles hore! is dred then gone[4]
By suche thy foes as ment thy weale?
Oh membre of false Babylon!
The shopp of craft! the denne of ire!
Thy dredfull dome drawes fast uppon.
Thy martyres blood, by swoord and fyre,[5]
In Heaven and earth for justice call.
The Lord shall here their just desyre;
The flame of wrath shall on the fall;
60   With famyne and pest lamentablie
Stricken shalbe thy lecheres all;
Thy prowd towers and turretes hye,
Enmyes to God, beat stone from stone;
Thyne idolles burnt, that wrought iniquitie;
When none thy ruyne shall bemone,
But render unto the right wise Lord,
That so hath judged Babylon,
Imortall praise with one accord.

[W. RESTETH HERE]

W.[1] resteth here, that quick could never rest;
Whose heavenly giftes encreased by disdayn   *malice*
And vertue sank the deper in his brest:
Such profit he by envy could obtain.

A hed, where wisdom misteries did frame;   *hidden meanings*
Whose hammers bet styll in that lively brayn
As on a stithe, where that some work of fame
Was dayly wrought to turne to Britaines gayn.

A visage stern and myld; where bothe did grow
10   Vice to contemne, in vertue to rejoyce;
Amid great stormes whom grace assured so
To lyve upright and smile at fortunes choyce.

---

3   Justly appointed punishment.
4   Cf. Petrarch, *In vita*, 138. 1–11.
5   The concluding lines of the poem are rich in biblical allusion, e.g.
Revelation 18:24, Ezekiel 5:12–17 and 6:11–14; the poem also echoes
Petrarch's *In vita*, 126, 297.

[W. RESTETH HERE]
1   Sir Thomas Wyatt, who died in October 1542. This poem, perhaps
Surrey's first to be published, appeared in a pamphlet entitled *An excellent Epitaffe of syr Thomas Wyat, With two other compendious dytties, wherin
are touchyd, and set forth the state of mannes lyfe* (1542).

A hand that taught what might be sayd in ryme;
That reft Chaucer the glory of his wit;
A mark the which, unparfited for time,   *for want of time*
Some may approche, but never none shall hit.

A toung that served in forein realmes his king;
Whose courteous talke to vertue did enflame
Eche noble hart; a worthy guide to bring
20   Our English youth by travail unto fame.

An eye, whose judgement none affect could blinde,
Frendes to allure, and foes to reconcile;
Whose persing loke did represent a mynde
With vertue fraught, reposed, voyd of gyle.

A hart, where drede was never so imprest
To hyde the thought that might the trouth avance;
In neyther fortune loft nor yet represt,
To swell in wealth, or yeld unto mischance.

A valiant corps, where force and beawty met;
30   Happy, alas, to happy, but for foes;
Lived and ran the race that nature set;
Of manhodes shape, where she the molde did lose.

But to the heavens that simple soule is fled,
Which left with such as covet Christ to know
Witnesse of faith that never shall be ded;
Sent for our helth, but not received so.

Thus, for our gilte, this jewel have we lost.
The earth his bones, the heavens possesse his gost.

John Foxe (1517–1587)

John Foxe, whose *Acts and Monuments* was one of the most read books of his time, was born in Lincolnshire and went to Brasenose College, Oxford, where he received his BA (1538) and MA (1543) degrees. In that year also he was elected a Fellow of Magdalen College. There is a legend (possibly true) that he began his life as a Papist but abandoned the Roman Catholic Church because his ecclesiastical research into the Church's violence against reformers horrified him, setting him on a zealous course of prosecuting the Church's errors in his writings. The immediate consequence of his conversion, predictably, was ostracism from the University and from friends and family, especially during the reign of Queen Mary. He eventually found a patron in Sir Thomas Lucy, a Warwickshire man. Foxe became a tutor to the Lucy family and later to the children of the Earl of Surrey. Nevertheless, opposition to his work on the Protestant martyrs persisted, and he fled to Basel. After the death of Queen Mary and the accession of Elizabeth, he returned to England (most likely with the active support of the Duke of Norfolk), proceeded for the next eleven years with his work on the Protestant martyrs, and eventually received a prebendary at Salisbury. One of the distinctive features of Foxe's writing is its incorporation of transcriptions of texts by his subjects. Thus, *Acts and Monuments* is the chief source for the writings of Anne Askew and for principal details in the life of William Tyndale, whose works Foxe edited in an edition published in 1573. Chained copies of *Acts and Monuments* were placed in cathedrals, beginning in 1571, to provide general access. His work was a powerful force in securing the ideological dominance of Protestantism in English literature and in forming "the mythology which saw Englishmen as God's chosen people courageously defending His truth through the centuries" (Hill 1972: 179).

READING

A. G. Dickens, *The English Reformation*.
Stephen Greenblatt, *Renaissance Self-Fashioning: From More to Shakespeare*.
Christopher Hill, *The Intellectual Origins of the English Revolution*.
John N. King, *English Reformation Literature: The Tudor Origins of the Protestant Tradition*.
E. G. Rupp, *Studies in the Making of the English Protestant Tradition*.

M. P.

[FROM] ACTS AND MONUMENTS OF THESE LATTER AND PERILOUS DAYS

Story and Martyrdom of Anne Askew

Anne Askew was descended from a good family, and had received an accomplished education: but the reader will best form his judgment of her by what follows, and which was written by herself.

"To satisfy your expectation, good people," said she, "this was my first examination, in the year of our Lord 1545, in the month of March.

"First, Christopher Dare examined me at Sadler's Hall, being one of the quest, and asked if I did not believe that the sacrament hanging over the altar was the very body of Christ really. Then I demanded this question of him: 'Wherefore was St. Stephen stoned to death?' and he said he could not tell. Then answered I that no more would I answer his vain question.

"Then he said he had sent for a priest to examine me, who was at hand.

"The priest asked me what I said to the sacrament of the altar, and required much to know my meaning therein. But I desired him again to hold me excused concerning that matter; no other answer would I make him, because I perceived him to be a papist.

"He asked me if I did not think that private masses helped the departed souls. I said it was great idolatry to believe more in them than in the death which Christ died for us.

"Then they brought me unto my lord mayor, and he examined me as they had before.

"Then the lord mayor commanded me to prison. I asked him if sureties would not serve me; he made me short answer, that he would take none. Then was I forced to the Compter,[1] where I remained eleven days, no friend admitted to speak with me. But in the meantime, there was a priest sent unto me, who said that he was commanded by the bishop to examine me, and to give me good counsel, which he did not. But first he asked me for what cause I was put in the Compter, and I told him I could not tell.

"He said it was told him that I denied the sacrament of the altar. I answered again, 'What I have said I have said.'

"A short time later, the Bishop of London sent for me, and as I came before him, he said he was sorry for my trouble, and desired to know my opinions in such matters as were laid against me.

"In the meanwhile he commanded his archdeacon to commune with me, who said, 'Mistress, wherefore are you accused and thus troubled here before the bishops?'

"I answered, 'Sir, ask my accusers, for I know not as yet.'

"Then he took my hand, and said, 'Such a book as this has brought you to the trouble you are in. Beware!' said he, 'beware! for he that made this book, and was the author thereof, was a heretic and burned in Smithfield.'[2]

"I asked him if he was certain and sure that it was true what he had spoken. He said he knew well the book was of John Frith's making. Then I asked him if he was not ashamed to judge of the book before he saw it within, or yet knew the truth thereof. Then I opened the book and showed it him. He said he thought it had been another, for he could find no fault therein.

"Then inquired the bishop of me, 'What if the Scripture doth say that it is the body of Christ?'

"'I believe,' said I, 'as the Scripture doth teach.'

"Then he asked again, 'What if the Scripture doth say that it is not the body of Christ?'

"My answer was still, 'I believe as the Scripture informeth me.'

"Then he asked me, why I had so few words; and I answered, 'God hath given me the gift of knowledge, but not of utterance.'

[FROM] ACTS AND MONUMENTS OF THESE LATTER AND
PERILOUS DAYES
1   A city prison.

2   This was apparently John Frith's tract on "The Sacrament of the Altar." Frith's works were edited and published in 1573 by Foxe along with other reformist tracts by William Tyndale and Robert Barnes.

"Then my lord went away, and said he would entitle some of my meaning in writing; but what it was I have not in my memory, for he would not suffer me to have the copy thereof, only I remember this small portion of it:—

"'Be it known of all men, that I, Anne Askew, do confess this to be my faith and belief, notwithstanding many reports made afore to the contrary.'

"Then he read it to me, and asked me if I did agree to it.

"And I said again, 'I believe so much thereof as the Holy Scripture doth agree unto; wherefore I desire you that you will add that thereunto.'

"Then he answered that I should not teach him what he should write.

"Then my lord sat down, and gave me the writing to set thereto my hand, and I wrote after this manner: 'I, Anne Askew, do believe all manner of things contained in the faith of the catholic Church.'

"Then because I did add unto it the 'catholic Church,' he went into his chamber in great fury.

"After this we thought that I should be put to bail immediately, according to the order of the law. At the last, after much ado and reasoning to and fro, they took a bond of them of recognisance for my forthcoming: and thus I was at the last delivered.

"Written by me, ANNE ASKEW."

Thus ends her first persecution, from which, for a time, she escaped; but not conforming to the erroneous doctrine of the sacrament,[3] she was, in 1546, again apprehended, of which, before her martyrdom, she wrote as follows:—

"SUM OF MY EXAMINATION BEFORE THE KING'S COUNCIL AT GREENWICH.

"I being before the council, was asked of Mr. Kyme. I answered that my lord chancellor knew already my mind in that matter. Then my lord chancellor asked of me my opinion in the sacrament. My answer was this. 'I believe that so oft as I, in a Christian congregation, do receive the bread in remembrance of Christ's death, and with thanksgiving according to his holy institution, I receive therewith the fruits also of his most glorious passion. The Bishop of Winchester bade me make a direct answer. I said I would not sing a new song of the Lord in a strange land.

"They then drew out a confession respecting the sacrament, urging me to set my hand thereunto; but this I refused. On the following Sunday I was so extremely ill, that I thought death was upon me. In the height of my illness I was conveyed to Newgate, where the Lord was pleased to renew my strength.

"MY FAITH BRIEFLY WRITTEN TO THE KING'S GRACE, AND SENT BY THE HANDS OF THE CHANCELLOR.

"I, Anne Askew, of good memory, although God hath given me the bread of adversity and the water of trouble, yet not so much as my sins have deserved, desire this to be known unto your grace, that forasmuch as I am by the law condemned for an evil doer, here I take heaven and earth to record, that I shall die in my innocency; and according to that I have said first, and will say last, I utterly abhor and detest all heresies. And as concerning the supper of the Lord, I believe so much as Christ hath said therein, which he confirmed with his most blessed blood: I believe so much as he willed me to follow, and believe so much as the catholic Church of him doth teach. For I will not forsake the commandment of his holy lips. But look what God hath charged me with his mouth, that I have shut up in my heart. And thus briefly I end for lack of learning.

"ANNE ASKEW."

3   The dispute here is whether the bread and the wine used in the sacrament of communion become in fact the body and blood of Christ or whether they are, as Anne Askew believed, symbols or "remembrances" of Christ's sacrifice.

"MY EXAMINATION AND TREATMENT AFTER MY DEPARTURE FROM NEWGATE.

"On Tuesday I was sent from Newgate to the sign of the 'Crown,' where Mr. Rich and the Bishop of London, with all their power and flattering words, went about to persuade me from God; but I did not esteem their glossing pretences.

"Then Mr. Rich sent me to the Tower, where I remained till three o'clock, when Rich came and one of the council, charging me upon my obedience to show unto them if I knew any man or woman of my sect. My answer was that I knew none. Then they asked me of Lady Suffolk, Lady Sussex, Lady Hertford, Lady Denny, and Lady Fitzwilliam. To whom I answered, if I should pronounce anything against them, that I was not able to prove it.

"Then they commanded me to show how I was maintained in the Compter, and who willed me to stick to my opinion.

"I said, that there was no creature that therein did strengthen me. And as for the help that I had in the Compter, it was by the means of my maid. For as she went abroad in the streets, she told my case to the apprentices, and they by her did send me money, but who they were I never knew.

"Then they did put me on the rack, because I confessed no ladies or gentlewomen to be of my opinion, and thereon they kept me a long time.

"The lieutenant then caused me to be loosed from the rack. After that I sat two hours reasoning with my lord chancellor upon the bare floor, when he, with many flattering words, tried to persuade me to leave my opinion; but my Lord God, I thank his everlasting goodness, gave me grace to persevere.

"Then was I brought to a house and laid in a bed. Then my lord chancellor sent me word, if I would leave my opinion I should want for nothing; if I would not, I should forthwith to Newgate, and so be burned. I sent him again word that I would rather die than break my faith."

THE CONFESSION OF HER FAITH WHICH SHE MADE IN NEWGATE.

"I, Anne Askew, of good memory, although my merciful Father hath given me the bread of adversity, do confess myself here a sinner before the throne of his heavenly majesty, desiring his forgiveness and mercy. And for so much as I am by the law unrighteously condemned for an evil-doer, concerning opinions, I take the same most merciful God of mine, which hath made both heaven and earth, to record that I hold no opinions contrary to his most holy Word; and I trust in my merciful Lord, which is the giver of all grace, that he will graciously assist me against all evil opinions which are contrary to his blessed verity.

"But this is the heresy which they report me to hold, that after the priest had spoken the words of consecration, there remaineth bread still. They both say and also teach it for a necessary article of faith, that after these words be once spoken, there remaineth no bread, but even the selfsame body that hung upon the cross of Good Friday, both flesh, blood, and bone. To this belief of theirs say I, Nay. For then were our common creed false, which saith, that He sitteth on the right hand of God the Father Almighty, and from thence shall come to judge the quick and the dead. But as touching the holy and blessed supper of the Lord, I believe it to be a most necessary remembrance of his glorious sufferings and death.

"Finally, I believe all those Scriptures to be true which he hath confirmed with his most precious blood; yea, and as St. Paul saith, those Scriptures are sufficient for our learning and salvation, that Christ hath left here with us; so that I believe we need no unwritten verities to rule his Church with.

"There be some that say I deny the eucharist, or sacrament of thanksgiving; but those people untruly report of me, for I both say and believe it, that if it were ordered as Christ instituted and left it, a most singular comfort it were unto us all. But as concerning your mass as it is now used in our days, I say and believe it to be the most abominable idol that is in the world. For my God will not be eaten with teeth, neither yet dieth he again; and upon these words that I have now spoken will I suffer death.

"O Lord, I have more enemies now than there be hairs on my head. Yet, sweet Lord, let me not set by them which are against me, for in thee is my whole delight; and, Lord, I heartily desire of thee that thou wilt, of thy most merciful goodness, forgive them that violence which they do and have done unto me. Open also thou their blind hearts, that they may hereafter do that thing in thy sight which is only acceptable before thee, and set forth thy verity aright, without all vain phantasy of sinful men. So be it, O Lord, so be it.

"ANNE ASKEW."

Hitherto we have given the words of this good lady; now it remains for us to speak of her martyrdom. Being born of such a kindred as would have enabled her to live in wealth and prosperity, if she had chosen rather to have followed the world than Christ, yet she had been so tortured that she could not live long. The day of her execution being appointed, she was brought to Smithfield in a chair, because she could not go on her feet from the cruel effects of the torments. Three others were also brought to suffer with her, and for the same offence these were Nicholas Belenian, a priest, of Shropshire; John Adams, a tailor; and John Lacels, a gentleman of the court and household of King Henry. The martyrs being all chained to the stake, and all things ready for the fire, Dr. Shaxton, then appointed to preach, gave his sermon.

The sermon being finished, the martyrs, standing there, tied at three several stakes ready for their martyrdom, began their prayers. There was a great concourse of people; the place where they stood being railed about to keep out the press. Upon the bench, under St. Bartholomew's Church, sat Wrisley, the Chancellor of England, the old Duke of Norfolk, the old Earl of Bedford, the Lord Mayor, with divers others.

Then the Lord Chancellor sent letters to Anne Askew, offering to her the king's pardon if she would recant, but she refused to look at them, answering again that she came not thither to deny her Lord and Master. Then were the letters likewise offered unto the others, who, in like manner, following the constancy of the woman, refused not only to receive them, but even to look at them; whereon they continued mutually to exhort each other by the glory they were about to enter; after which the Lord Mayor commanded fire to be put to them.

And thus Anne Askew, with these blessed martyrs, were compassed about with flames of fire, as sacrifices unto God.

Life and Martyrdom of William Tyndale

We shall now rehearse the story and martyrdom of William Tyndale, who, although he did not suffer in England, ought to be ranked with the martyrs of our country, of which, from his great zeal, perseverance, and dispersing of truth, he may properly be esteemed the apostle.

William Tyndale was born about the borders of Wales, and brought up in the University of Oxford, where he grew up and increased in the knowledge of the liberal arts, and in his acquaintance with the Scriptures.

After this he removed to Cambridge, and then to Gloucestershire, and engaged himself to a knight, named Welch, as tutor to his children. To this gentleman's table several abbots, deans, and other beneficed men used to resort, with whom Tyndale conversed of learned men, particularly of Luther and Erasmus, and of questions relative to the Scriptures.

In course of time it happened that the bishop's chancellor held a court, at which the priests were summoned to appear, among whom was Tyndale. The latter had his doubts as to the formation of a conspiracy against him; and on his way thither he earnestly prayed to God to enable him to bear witness to the truth of his word. The chancellor reviled him grievously; but no definite accusation could be proved against him.

There dwelt not far off a certain doctor, named Munmouth, who had been an old acquaintance of Tyndale's. Tyndale went to him to disclose his heart. After some discourse, the doctor said –

"Do you not know that the pope is very Antichrist, whom the Scripture speaketh of? But beware what you say: for if you be perceived of that opinion, it will cost you your life. I have been an officer of his; but I have given it up, and defy him and all his works."

Not long after, Tyndale happened to be in company of a certain divine, and in disputing with him he pressed him so hard that the doctor burst out into these blasphemous words: "We were better to be without God's laws than the pope's."

Tyndale full of godly zeal, replied: "I defy the pope and all his laws;" and added, that if God spared him life, ere many years, he would cause a boy that driveth the plough to know more of the Scripture than he did.

After this the priests became more bitter against Tyndale, saying that he was a heretic. Being so molested by the priests, he was obliged to remove from that part. On coming to London he was recommended to Tonstall, Bishop of London, by Sir Henry Guildford. He remained in London almost a year, greatly distressed with the pomp, pride, and ignorance of the clergy, insomuch that he perceived not only no room in the bishop's house for him to translate the New Testament, but also that there was no place for him in all England. He departed to Germany, and studied by what possible means he could bring his countrymen to the understanding of God's Word, and to the possession of the same privileges which he himself enjoyed. He perceived that the cause of the people's blindness, and of the errors and superstitions of the Church, was ignorance of the Scriptures. The truth was entombed in the sepulchre of a dead language; the efforts of the priests were directed to keep men from inquiring of the oracles of God; and when reference was ever made to the sacred text, these doctors of the law did what they could to perplex the inquirers, wresting the Scriptures to suit their own purposes. From these considerations Tyndale felt moved, by the Spirit of God, to translate the Scriptures into his mother tongue, for the benefit of the simple people of England. He first began with the New Testament, which was translated about the year 1527, prefixing a short preface to every book, after which, in like manner, he translated the five books of Moses, and wrote sundry other godly works. His books were published and sent over to England, and became like holy fire from the altar, to give light in the night season.

On Tyndale's departure from England he went to Germany, after which he moved to the Netherlands, and resided principally at Antwerp. Having finished his translation of the five books of Moses, he sailed to Hamburg, intending to print them in that city. On his voyage he was shipwrecked, and lost all his manuscripts, and almost all he possessed. However, with true moral heroism, he proceeded to Hamburg, and began the work again, in company with Mr. Coverdale, in the house of Miss Emmerson, anno 1529. When the translation of the New Testament was first issued, Tyndale appealed to the learned for help, for the correction of accidental errors; but the dignitaries of the Church, indignant that the people should possess the Word of God, clamorously inveighed against it, as being so full of heresy, sedition, and inaccuracies, that its suppression was the duty of the faithful. They scanned it with a microscopic jealousy, and magnified the inadvertent omission of a letter into a flagrant and wilful perversion of the original. The English prelates were filled with wrath, and did not rest until they had persuaded the king to take hostile proceedings in the matter. A proclamation was then issued, under authority, which condemned and prohibited Tyndale's translation of the New Testament. But not content with this, they studied how they might entangle and destroy its author.

Accordingly, after some stratagem and the employment of treachery, Tyndale was betrayed at Antwerp by one Philips, and conveyed to the castle of Filford, eighteen miles from Antwerp, where he remained until his death.

At last, after the lapse of a year and a half, and much fruitless disputation, he was condemned by virtue of the emperor's decree made in the assembly at Augsburg. When he was brought out for execution, and was being tied to the stake, he cried with a loud and earnest voice, "Lord, open the King of England's eyes!" He was then strangled, and his remains burnt to ashes. Such was the power and excellence of this truly good man, that during his imprisonment he converted his keeper, with his daughter, and others of his attendants. Several of those who came in contact with him during his imprisonment reported of him, that if he were not a good Christian, they did not know whom to trust; and the procurator-general left this testimony about him, that he was "a learned, a good, and a godly man."

John Stow (1525?–1605)

Stow's delightful *Survey of London* derives much of its charm from its source: a Londoner who knows the ins and outs of his native city. Although he eventually became a chronicler and antiquary, Stow first adopted the trade of a tailor and was admitted to the Merchant Taylors' Company in 1547. By 1560 he was seriously involved in the collection and transcription of manuscripts. He joined the Society of Antiquaries founded by Archbishop Parker, with whom he stayed in contact, even while charged with popish sentiments from 1568 to 1570. He edited the works of Chaucer (1561), Matthew Paris (1571), and Holinshed (1585–7),

spending what means he had on his literary commitments. Deploring the greedy destruction of the city he loved, Stow ended his long life in poverty. At the age of 79 he received a licence from James I to beg.

READING

Roy Porter, *London: A Social History*.
Michael J. Power, "John Stow and his London."

M. P.

[FROM] THE SURVEY of LONDON

SPORTS AND PASTIMES OF OLD TIME USED IN THIS CITY

"Let us now," saith Fitzstephen, "come to the sports and pastimes, seeing it is fit that a city should not only be commodious and serious, but also merry and sportful; whereupon in the seals of the popes, until the time of Pope Leo, on the one side was St. Peter fishing, with a key over him, reached as it were by the hand of God out of heaven, and about it this verse:

> 'Tu pro me navem liquisti, suscipe clavem.'[1]

And on the other side was a city, and this inscription on it: '*Aurea Roma*.'[2] Likewise to the praise of Augustus Cæsar and the city, in respect of the shows and sports, was written:

> 'Nocte pluit tota, redeunt spectacula mane,' etc.

> 'All night it raines, and shews at morrow tide returne again,
> And Cæsar with almighty Jove hath matcht an equal raign.'

"But London, for the shows upon theatres, and comical pastimes, hath holy plays, representations of miracles, which holy confessors have wrought, or representations of torments wherein the constancy of martyrs appeared. Every year also at Shrove Tuesday, that we may begin with children's sports, seeing we all have been children, the school-boys do bring cocks of the game to their master, and all the forenoon they delight themselves in cock-fighting: after dinner, all the youths go into the fields to play at the ball.

"The scholars of every school have their ball, or baston, in their hands; the ancient and wealthy men of the city come forth on horseback to see the sport of the young men, and to take part of the pleasure in beholding their agility. Every Friday in Lent a fresh company of young men comes into the field on horseback, and the best horseman conducteth the rest. Then march forth the citizens' sons, and other young men, with disarmed lances and shields, and there they practice feats of war.

[FROM] THE SURVEY of LONDON
1   "You left the boat for me, take up the key."

2   Golden Rome.

Many courtiers likewise, when the king lieth near, and attendants of noblemen, do repair to these exercises; and while the hope of victory doth inflame their minds, do show good proof how serviceable they would be in martial affairs.

"In Easter holidays they fight battles on the water; a shield is hung upon a pole, fixed in the midst of the stream, a boat is prepared without oars, to be carried by violence of the water, and in the fore part thereof standeth a young man, ready to give charge upon the shield with his lance; if so be he breaketh his lance against the shield, and doth not fall, he is thought to have performed a worthy deed; if so be, without breaking his lance, he runneth strongly against the shield, down he falleth into the water, for the boat is violently forced with the tide; but on each side of the shield ride two boats, furnished with young men, which recover him that falleth as soon as they may. Upon the bridge, wharfs, and houses, by the river's side, stand great numbers to see and laugh thereat.

"In the holidays all the summer the youths are exercised in leaping, dancing, shooting, wrestling, casting the stone, and practising their shields; the maidens trip in their timbrels, and dance as long as they can well see. In winter, every holiday before dinner, the boars prepared for brawn are set to fight, or else bulls and bears are baited.

"When the great fen, or moor, which watereth the walls of the city on the north side, is frozen, many young men play upon the ice; some, striding as wide as they may, do slide swiftly; others make themselves seats of ice, as great as millstones; one sits down, many hand in hand do draw him, and one slipping on a sudden, all fall together; some tie bones to their feet and under their heels; and shoving themselves by a little picked staff, do slide as swiftly as a bird flieth in the air, or an arrow out of a cross-bow. Sometime two run together with poles, and hitting one the other, either one or both do fall, not without hurt; some break their arms, some their legs, but youth desirous of glory in this sort exerciseth itself against the time of war. Many of the citizens do delight themselves in hawks and hounds; for they have liberty of hunting in Middlesex, Hartfordshire, all Chiltron, and in Kent to the water of Cray." Thus far Fitzstephen of sports.

These, or the like exercises, have been continued till our time, namely, in stage plays, whereof ye may read in anno 1391, a play by the parish clerks of London at the Skinner's well besides Smithfield, which continued three days together, the king, queen, and nobles of the realm being present. And of another, in the year 1409, which lasted eight days, and was of matter from the creation of the world, whereat was present most part of the nobility and gentry of England. Of late time, in place of those stage plays, hath been used comedies, tragedies, interludes, and histories, both true and feigned; for the acting whereof certain public places – have been erected. Also cocks of the game are yet cherished by divers men for their pleasures, much money being laid on their heads, when they fight in pits, whereof some be costly made for that purpose. The ball is used by noblemen and gentlemen in tennis courts, and by people of meaner sort in the open fields and streets.

The marching forth of citizens' sons, and other young men on horseback, with disarmed lances and shields, there to practise feats of war, man against man, hath long since been left off, but in their stead they have used on horseback to run at a dead mark, called a quinten; for note whereof I read,[3] that in the year of Christ 1253, the 38th of Henry III., the youthful citizens, for an exercise of their activity, set forth a game to run at the quinten; and whoever did best should have a peacock, which they had prepared as a prize. Certain of the king's servants, because the court lay then at Westminster came, as it were, in spite of the citizens, to that game, and giving reproachful names to the Londoners, which for the dignity of the city, and ancient privilege which they ought to have enjoyed, were called barons, the said Londoners, not able to bear so to be misused, fell upon the king's servants, and beat them shrewdly, so that upon complaint to the king he fined the citizens to pay a thousand marks. This exercise of running at the quinten was practised by the youthful citizens as well in summer as in winter, namely, in the feast of Christmas, I have seen a quinten set upon Cornehill, by the Leaden hall, where the attendants on the lords of merry disports have run, and made great pastime; for he that hit not the broad end of the quinten was of

3   From Matthew Paris.

all men laughed to scorn, and he that hit it full, if he rid not the faster, had a sound blow in his neck with a bag full of sand hung on the other end. I have also in the summer season seen some upon the river of Thames rowed in wherries, with staves in their hands, flat at the fore end, running one against another; and for the most part, one or both overthrown, and well ducked.

On the holy days in summer the youths of this city have in the field exercised themselves in leaping, dancing, shooting, wrestling, casting of the stone or ball, etc.

And for defence and use of the weapon, there is a special profession of men that teach it. Ye may read in mine *Annals* how that in the year 1222 the citizens kept games of defence, and wrestlings, near unto the hospital of St. Giles in the field, where they challenged, and had the mastery of the men in the suburbs, and other commoners, etc. Also, in the year 1453, of a tumult made against the mayor at the wrestling besides Clearke's well, etc. Which is sufficient to prove that of old time the exercising of wrestling, and such like, hath been much more used than of later years. The youths of this city also have used on holy days after evening prayer, at their masters' doors, to exercise their wasters and bucklers; and the maidens, one of them playing on a timbrel, in sight of their masters and dames, to dance for garlands hung athwart the streets; which open pastimes in my youth being now suppressed, worse practices within doors are to be feared. As for the baiting of bulls and bears, they are to this day much frequented, namely, in Bear gardens, on the Bank's side, wherein be prepared scaffolds for beholders to stand upon. Sliding upon the ice is now but children's play; but in hawking and hunting many grave citizens at this present have great delight, and do rather want leisure than goodwill to follow it.

Of triumphant shows made by the citizens of London, ye may read, in the year 1236, the 20th of Henry III., Andrew Bockwell then being mayor, how Helianor, daughter to Reymond, Earl of Provance, riding through the city towards Westminster, there to be crowned queen of England, the city was adorned with silks, and in the night with lamps, cressets, and other lights without number, besides many pageants and strange devices there presented; the citizens also rode to meet the king and queen, clothed in long garments embroidered about with gold, and silks of divers colours, their horses gallantly trapped to the number of three hundred and sixty, every man bearing a cup of gold or silver in his hand, and the king's trumpeters sounding before them. These citizens did minister wine, as botelers, which is their service, at their coronation. More, in the year 1293, for victory obtained by Edward I. against the Scots, every citizen, according to their several trade, made their several show, but especially the fishmongers, which in a solemn procession passed through the city, having, amongst other pageants and shows, four sturgeons gilt, carried on four horses; then four salmons of silver on four horses; and after them six and forty armed knights riding on horses, made like luces of the sea; and then one representing St. Magnus, because it was upon St. Magnus' day, with a thousand horsemen, etc.

One other show, in the year 1377, made by the citizens for disport of the young prince, Richard, son to the Black Prince, in the feast of Christmas, in this manner: – On the Sunday before Candlemas, in the night, one hundred and thirty citizens, disguised, and well horsed, in a mummery, with sound of trumpets, sackbuts, cornets, shalmes, and other minstrels, and innumerable torch lights of wax, rode from Newgate, through Cheape, over the bridge, through Southwarke, and so to Kennington beside Lambhith, where the young prince remained with his mother and the Duke of Lancaster his uncle, the Earls of Cambridge, Hertford, Warwicke, and Suffolke, with divers other lords. In the first rank did ride forty-eight in the likeness and habit of esquires, two and two together, clothed in red coats and gowns of say or sandal, with comely visors on their faces; after them came riding forty-eight knights in the same livery of colour and stuff; then followed one richly arrayed like an emperor; and after him some distance, one stately attired like a pope, whom followed twenty-four cardinals, and after them eight or ten with black visors, not amiable, as if they had been legates from some foreign princes. These maskers, after they had entered Kennington, alighted from their horses, and entered the hall on foot; which done, the prince, his mother, and the lords, came out of the chamber into the hall, whom the said mummers did salute, showing by a pair of dice upon the table their desire to play with the prince, which they so handled that the prince did always win when he cast them. Then the mummers set to the prince three jewels, one after another, which were a bowl of gold, a cup of gold, and a ring of gold, which the prince won at three casts. Then they set to the prince's mother, the duke, the earls, and other lords, to every one a ring of gold, which they did also win. After which they were feasted, and the music sounded, the prince and lords danced on the one part with the mummers, which did also dance; which jollity being ended, they were again made to drink, and then departed in order as they came.

The like was in Henry IV., in the 2nd of his reign, he then keeping his Christmas at Eltham, twelve aldermen of London and their sons rode in a mumming, and had great thanks.

Thus much for sportful shows in triumphs may suffice. Now for sports and pastimes yearly used.

First, in the feast of Christmas, there was in the king's house, wheresoever he was lodged, a lord of misrule, or master of merry disports, and the like had ye in the house of every nobleman of honour or good worship, were he spiritual or temporal. Amongst the which the mayor of London, and either of the sheriffs, had their several lords of misrule, ever contending, without quarrel or offence, who should make the rarest pastimes to delight the beholders. These lords beginning their rule on Alhollon eve, continued the same till the morrow after the Feast of the Purification, commonly called Candlemas day. In all which space there were fine and subtle disguisings, masks, and mummeries, with playing at cards for counters, nails, and points, in every house, more for pastime than for gain.

Against the feast of Christmas every man's house, as also the parish churches, were decked with holm, ivy, bays, and whatsoever the season of the year afforded to be green. The conduits and standards in the streets were likewise garnished; amongst the which I read, in the year 1444, that by tempest of thunder and lightning, on the 1st of February, at night, Powle's steeple was fired, but with great labour quenched; and towards the morning of Candlemas day, at the Leaden hall in Cornhill, a standard of tree being set up in midst of the pavement, fast in the ground, nailed full of holm and ivy, for disport of Christmas to the people, was torn up, and cast down by the malignant spirit (as was thought), and the stones of the pavement all about were cast in the streets, and into divers houses, so that the people were sore aghast of the great tempests.

In the week before Easter had ye great shows made for the fetching in of a twisted tree, or with, as they termed it, out of the woods into the king's house; and the like into every man's house of honour or worship.

In the month of May, namely, on May-day in the morning, every man, except impediment, would walk into the sweet meadows and green woods, there to rejoice their spirits with the beauty and savour of sweet flowers, and with the harmony of birds, praising God in their kind; and for example hereof, Edward Hall hath noted, that King Henry VIII., as in the 3rd of his reign, and divers other years, so namely, in the 7th of his reign, on May-day in the morning, with Queen Katherine his wife, accompanied with many lords and ladies, rode a-maying from Greenwitch to the high ground of Shooter's hill, where, as they passed by the way, they espied a company of tall yeomen, clothed all in green, with green hoods, and bows and arrows, to the number of two hundred; one being their chieftain, was called Robin Hoode, who required the king and his company to stay and see his men shoot; whereunto the king granting, Robin Hoode whistled, and all the two hundred archers shot off, loosing all at once; and when he whistled again they likewise shot again; their arrows whistled by craft of the head, so that the noise was strange and loud, which greatly delighted the king, queen, and their company. Moreover, this Robin Hoode desired the king and queen, with their retinue, to enter the green wood, where, in harbours made of boughs, and decked with flowers, they were set and served plentifully with venison and wine by Robin Hoode and his men, to their great contentment, and had other pageants and pastimes, as ye may read in my said author.

I find also, that in the month of May, the citizens of London of all estates, lightly in every parish, or sometimes two or three parishes joining together, had their several mayings, and did fetch in May-poles, with divers warlike shows, with good archers, morris dancers, and other devices, for pastime all the day long; and toward the evening they had stage plays, and bonfires in the streets. Of these mayings we read, in the reign of Henry VI., that the aldermen and sheriffs of London, being on May-day at the Bishop of London's wood, in the parish of Stebunheath,[4] and having there

---

4 Stepney.

a worshipful dinner for themselves and other commoners, Lydgate the poet, that was a monk of Bury, sent to them, by a pursuivant, a joyful commendation of that season, containing sixteen staves of metre royal, beginning thus:–

"Mightie Flora! goddess of fresh flowers, –
   Which clothed hath the soyle in lustie greene,
Made buds spring, with her sweete showers,
   By the influence of the sunne shine.
To doe pleasance of intent full cleane,
   Unto the States which now sit here,
Hath Vere downe sent her owne daughter deare.

Making the vertue, that dared in the roote,
   Called of clarkes the vertue vegitable,
For to transcend, most holsome and most soote,
   Into the crop, this season so agreeable,
The bawmy liquor is so commendable,
   That it rejoyceth with his fresh moysture,
Man, beast, and fowle, and every creature," etc.

These great Mayings and May-games, made by the governors and masters of this city, with the triumphant setting up of the great shaft (a principal May-pole in Cornehill, before the parish church of St. Andrew), therefore called Undershaft, by means of an insurrection of youths against aliens on May-day, 1517, the 9th of Henry VIII., have not been so freely used as afore, and therefore I leave them, and will somewhat touch of watches, as also of shows in the night.

Richard Mulcaster (1530?–1611)

A celebrated schoolmaster and author, Mulcaster received his MA in 1556 from Christ Church, Oxford, where he studied Hebrew and oriental languages as well as the classics. By 1559 he was teaching in London, and in 1561 was appointed headmaster of the newly formed Merchant Taylors' School. He continued in that capacity until 1586, during which time Spenser was one of his pupils. Although his teaching and administration greatly benefited the school, he resigned under apparently bitter circumstances in conflict with the governors. At the age of 66 he was elected High Master of St. Paul's School, a position he held for twelve years. Queen Elizabeth, who appears to have had a consistent interest in his welfare, presented him with the rectory of Stanford Rivers in Essex, where he and his wife of 50 years were eventually buried. As a teacher and theorist, Mulcaster was unusually progressive. He taught music and drama to the boys in his school, and directed them in the performance of plays, masques, and interludes at court.

Although he capitulated to the custom of denying girls access to public grammar schools, just as he repeatedly bowed to the class structure of Elizabethan society, Mulcaster, nonetheless, asserts their right and need to receive as good a mental education as boys. His *Positions Concerning the Training up of Children* (1581) was dedicated to Queen Elizabeth, to whom his comments on the education of maidens seems partly to be addressed. Although it is often correctly claimed that Elizabeth did little overtly to combat the patriarchal practices of her age, the example of her intellect and achievement nevertheless had a profound influence on thinkers such as Mulcaster.

READING

H. B. Wilson, *History of the Merchant Taylors' School.*

M. P.

[FROM] POSITIONS CONCERNING THE TRAINING UP OF CHILDREN

How much {a Woman Ought to Learn}

The next pointe *how much*, is a question of more enquirie, and therefore requireth advised handling. To appoint besides these thinges, which are already spoken of, how much further any *maide* maye proceede in matter of learning and train[ing], is a matter of some moment, and concerneth no mean ones. And yet some petie lowlinges, do sometimes seeke to resemble, where they have small reason, and will needes seeme like, where their petieship cannot light, using shew for a shadow, where they have no fitter shift. And therfore in so doing, they passe beyond the boundes both of their birth, and their best beseeming. Which then discovereth a verie meere follie, when a meane parent traineth up his daughter hie in those properties, which I shall streight waye speake of, and she matcheth lowe, but within her owne compasse. For in such a case those overraught qualities for the toyous-nesse thereof being misplaced in her, do cause the young woman rather to be toyed withall, as by them giving signe of some idle conceit otherwise, then to be thought verie well of, as one wisely brought up. There is a comlynesse in eche kinde, and a decentnesse in degree, which is best observed, when eche one provides according to his power, without overreaching. If some odde pro-perty do worke preferrement beyond proportion, it commonly stayes there, and who so shootes at the like, in hope to hit, may sooner misse: bycause the wayes to misse be so many, and to his is but one, and wounders which be but onse seene, be no examples to resemble. Every *maide* maye not hope to speede, as she would wishe, bycause some one hath sped better then she could wishe.

Where the question is *how much* a woman ought to learne, the answere may be, so much as shall be needefull. If that also come in doubt, the returne may be, either so much as her parentes con-ceive of her in hope, if her parentage be meane, or provide for her in state, if her birth beare a saile. For if the parentes be of calling, and in great account, and the daughters capable of some singular qualities, many commendable effects may be wrought therby, and the young maidens being well trained are verie soone commended to right honorable matches, whom they may well beseeme, and aunswere much better, their qualities in state having good correspondence, with their matches of state, and their wisedoms also putting to helping hand, for the procuring of their common good. Not here to note, what frute the common weale may reape, by such witts so worthily advaunced, besides their owne private. If the parentes be meane, and the *maidens* in their training shew forth at the verie first some singular rareness like to ensue, if they florish but their naturall, there hope maye grow great, that some great matche may as well like of a young maiden excellently quali-fied, as most do delite in brute or brutish thinges for some strannge qualitie, either in nature to embrase, or in art to marvell. And yet this hope may faile. For neither have great personages alwaye that judgement, nor young *maidens* alway that fortune, though the *maidens* remaine the gainers, for they have the qualities to comfort their mediocrity, and those great ones want judgement to set forth their nobilitie.

This *how much* consisteth either in perfiting of those forenamed foure, *reading* well, *writing* faire, *singing* sweete, *playing* fine, beyond all cry and above all comparison, that pure excelencie in things but ordinarie may cause extraordinairie liking: or else in skill of languages annexed to these foure, that moe good giftes may worke more wonder. For meane is a maime where excellencie is the marvell. To hope for hie mariages, is good meat, but not for mowers, to have leasure to take delite in these gentlewomanly qualities, is no worke for who will: Nay to be a paragon among princes, to use such singularities, for the singular good of the general state, and the wonder of her person, were a wish in dispaire, were not true proofe the just warrant, that such a thing may be wished, bycause in our time we have found it, even then, when we did wish it most, and in the end more marvellous, then at first we durst have wished. The eventes in these wymen which we see in our dayes, to have bene brought up in learning, do rule this conclusion. That such personages as be borne to be princes, or matches to great peeres, or to furnish out such traines, for some peculiar ornamentes to their place and calling, are to receive this kinde of education in the highest degree, that is convenient for their kinde. But princely *maidens* above all; by cause occasion of their height standes in neede of such giftes, both to honour themselves, and to discharge the duetie, which the countries committed to their hands, do daily call for, and besides what match is more honorable, then when desert for rare qualities, doth joine it selfe, with highenesse in degree?

[. . .] And is not a young gentlewoman, thinke you, thoroughly furnished, which can reade plainly and distinctly, write faire and swiftly, sing cleare & sweetely, play wel & finely, understand & speake the learned languages, and those toungues also which the time most embraseth, with some *Logicall* helpe to chop, and some *Rhetoricke* to brave. Besides the matter which is gathered, while these toungues be either learned, or lookt on, as wordes must have seates, no less then rayment bodies. Were it any argument of an unfurnished maiden, besides these qualities to draw cleane in good proportion, and with good symmetrie? Now if she be an honest woman, and a good house-wife to, were she not worth the wishing, and worthy the shryning? and yet such there be, and such we know. Or is it likely that her children shalbe eare a whit the worse brought up, if she be a *Lælia*, an *Hortensia*, or a *Cornelia*, which were so endued and noted for so doing? It is writen of *Eurydice* the *Epirote*, that after she began to have children, she sought to have learning, to bring them up skilfully, whom she brought forth naturally. Which thing she perfourmed in deede, a most care-full mother, and a most skilfull mistresse. For which her well doing, she hath wonne the reward, to be enrowled among the most rare matrones.[1]

Queen Elizabeth I (1533–1603)

Elizabeth was the daughter of Henry VIII and Anne Boleyn, his second wife. His first wife, Catherine of Aragon, was the mother of Queen Mary; and his third wife, Jane Seymour, was the mother of King Edward VI. Elizabeth was preceded on the throne by both Mary and Edward. When she at last became queen in 1558, she began a reign that proved to be the greatest in the history of England. Elizabeth's temperament and her Lutheran upbringing (according to her biographer J. E. Neale) enabled her to sustain a policy in religious politics that avoided the extremes of Mary (a Roman Catholic) and Edward (a radical Protestant). Against all male advice, she never married, although she had many amorous relationships, both real and theatrical, typically with the most brilliant of her courtiers. Her particular genius seems to have been in controlling the mythology that developed around her own person. She was constantly the subject of poetic invention. Cynthia, the moon goddess, to Raleigh; and the Faerie Queene to Spenser. A subtler mythology, especially in her many portraits, identified her with Astraea, the goddess of justice. However contrived and hyperbolic the praise of her was, she did in fact preside over one of the most productive artistic periods in English history. As both patron and participant, she was actively present in the theater, visual arts, music, and pageantry of her era.

Elizabeth, surprisingly, submitted to the traditional expectations of a woman writer. A true student of Roger Ascham, she was an accomplished translator, and she also wrote devotional literature. Although her speeches often survive not in her own words but in those of her auditors, she obviously had a great command of the art of rhetoric. That, too, is displayed in her letters and poems, which can easily be misread as confessional when they are more likely artful and manipulative. Although a brilliant woman herself, she seems to have been more comfortable in the company of talented, adoring men than in the company of women. Though her literary remains are few, they display her wit and subtle command of language. Most of her surviving poems are reprinted below, along with samples of each of her prose genres (speeches, letters, and prayers). The range of her literary production is only now being fully assessed.

Reading

Elizabeth I: Collected Works, ed. Leah S. Marcus, Janet Mueller, and Mary Beth Rose.
Christopher Hibbert, The Virgin Queen: The Personal History of Elizabeth I.
J. E. Neale, Queen Elizabeth I: A Biography.
Frances Yates, Astraea.

M. P.

Written on a Window Frame at Woodstock

O Fortune, thy wresting, wavering state
Hath fraught with cares my troubled wit,
Whose witness this present prison late

[FROM] POSITIONS CONCERNING THE TRAINING UP OF CHILDREN
1   As a source for these examples of learned maidens, Mulcaster cites Plutarch in his marginal notation.

Could bear, where once was joy flown quite.
Thou causedst the guilty to be loosed

From lands where innocents were enclosed,
And caused the guiltless to be reserved,
And freed those that death had well deserved.
But all herein can be naught wrought,
So God grant to my foes as they have thought.
    Finis. Elisabetha a prisoner, 1555

WRITTEN WITH A DIAMOND

*In her imprisonment at Woodstock, these verses she wrote with
her diamond in a glass window:*

Much suspected by me,
Nothing proved can be.
    Quod Elizabeth the prisoner   *said*

'TWAS CHRIST THE WORD

Hoc est corpus meum[1]
'Twas Christ the Word that spake it.
The same took bread and brake it,
And as the Word did make it,
So I believe arid take it.
    Queen Elizabeth

NO CROOKED LEG

No crooked leg, no blearèd eye,
No part deformèd out of kind,
Nor yet so ugly half can be
As is the inward, suspicious mind.

Your loving mistress, *Elizabeth R*

THE DOUBT OF FUTURE FOES

Verses made by the queen's majesty

The doubt of future foes
Exiles my present joy
And wit me warns to shun such snares
As threatens mine annoy.

For falsehood now doth flow
And subjects' faith doth ebb,
Which should not be if reason ruled
Or wisdom weaved the web.

'TWAS CHRIST THE WORD
1   "This is my body."

10

But clouds of joys untried
Do cloak aspiring minds
Which turns to rage of late repent
By changèd course of winds.

The top of hope supposed
The root of rue shall be
And fruitless all their grafted guile,
As shortly you shall see.

Their dazzled eyes with pride,
Which great ambition blinds,
Shall be unsealed by worthy wights

20

Whose foresight falsehood finds.

The daughter of debate
That discord aye doth sow
Shall reap no gain where former rule
Still peace hath taught to know.

No foreign banished wight
Shall anchor in this port:
Our realm brooks no seditious sects—
Let them elsewhere resort.

My rusty sword through rest

30

Shall first his edge employ
To pull their tops who seek such change
Or gape for future joy.
                    Vivat Regina[1]

ON MONSIEUR'S[1] DEPARTURE

I grieve and dare not show my discontent;
I love, and yet am forced to seem to hate;
I do, yet dare not say I ever meant;
I seem stark mute, but inwardly do prate.
I am, and not; I freeze and yet am burned,
Since from myself another self I turned.

My care is like my shadow in the sun—
Follows me flying, flies when I pursue it,
Stands, and lies by me, doth what I have done;

10

His too familiar care doth make me rue it.
    No means I find to rid him from my breast,
    Till by the end of things it be suppressed.

Some gentler passion slide into my mind,
For I am soft, and made of melting snow;
Or be more cruel, Love, and so be kind.
Let me or float or sink, be high or low;
    Or let me live with some more sweet content,
    Or die, and so forget what love e'er meant.
                    Elizabetha Regina.

THE DOUBT OF FUTURE FOES
1 "Long live the Queen."

ON MONSIEUR'S DEPARTURE
1 Monsieur is the Duke of Anjou, one of her suitors.

WHEN I WAS FAIR AND YOUNG

When I was fair and young, and favor graced me,
Of many was I sought unto, their mistress for to be.
But I did scorn them all, and said to them therefore,
"Go, go, go seek some otherwhere; importune me no more."

But there fair Venus' son, that brave, victorious boy,
Said, "What, thou scornful dame, sith that thou art so coy,
I will so wound thy heart, that thou shalt learn therefore."
"Go, go, go seek some otherwhere; importune me no more."

But then I felt straightway a change within my breast:
10   The day unquiet was; the night I could not rest,
For I did sore repent that I had said before,
"Go, go, go seek some otherwhere; importune me no more."

NOW LEAVE AND LET ME REST

1. Now leave and let me rest. Dame Pleasure, be content—
Go choose among the best; my doting days be spent.
By sundry signs I see thy proffers are but vain,
And wisdom warneth me that pleasure asketh pain;
And Nature that doth know how time her steps doth try,
Gives place to painful woe, and bids me learn to die.

2. Since all fair earthly things, soon ripe, will soon be rot
And all that pleasant springs, soon withered, soon forgot,
And youth that yields men joys that wanton lust desires
10   In age repents the toys that reckless youth requires.
All which delights I leave to such as folly trains
By pleasures to deceive, till they do feel the pains.

3. And from vain pleasures past I fly, and fain would know
The happy life at last whereto I hope to go.
For words or wise reports ne yet examples gone
'Gan bridle youthful sports, till age came stealing on.
The pleasant courtly games that I do pleasure in,
My elder years now shames such folly to begin.

4. And all the fancies strange that fond delight brought forth
20   I do intend to change, and count them nothing worth.
For I by proffers vain am taught to know the skill
What might have been forborne in my young reckless will;
By which good proof I fleet from will to wit again,
In hope to set my feet in surety to remain.

VERSE EXCHANGE BETWEEN QUEEN ELIZABETH AND
SIR WALTER RALEIGH

[RALEIGH TO ELIZABETH]

Fortune hath taken away my love,
My life's joy and my soul's heaven above.

Fortune hath taken thee away, my princess,
My world's joy and my true fantasy's mistress.

Fortune hath taken thee away from me;
Fortune hath taken all by taking thee.
Dead to all joys, I only live to woe:
So is Fortune become my fantasy's foe.

In vain, my eyes, in vain ye waste your tears;
10 In vain, my sights, the smoke of my despairs,
In vain you search the earth and heaven above.
In vain you search, for Fortune keeps my love.

Then will I leave my love in Fortune's hand;
Then will I leave my love in worldlings' band,
And only love the sorrows due to me—
Sorrow, henceforth, that shall my princess be—

And only joy that Fortune conquers kings.
Fortune, that rules the earth and earthly things,
Hath taken my love in spite of virtue's might:
20 So blind a goddess did never virtue right.

With wisdom's eyes had but blind Fortune seen,
Then had my love, my love forever been.
But love, farewell—though Fortune conquer thee,
No fortune base nor frail shall alter me.

[ELIZABETH TO RALEIGH]

Ah, silly Pug,[1] wert thou so sore afraid?
Mourn not, my Wat, nor be thou so dismayed.
It passeth fickle Fortune's power and skill
To force my heart to think thee any ill.
No Fortune base, thou sayest, shall alter thee?
And may so blind a witch so conquer me?
No, no, my Pug, though Fortune were not blind,
Assure thyself she could not rule my mind.
Fortune, I know, sometimes doth conquer kings,
10 And rules and reigns on earth and earthly things,
But never think Fortune can bear the sway
If virtue watch, and will her not obey.
Ne chose I thee by fickle Fortune's rede,   *decree*
Ne she shall force me alter with such speed
But if to try this mistress' jest with thee.
Pull up thy heart, suppress thy brackish tears,
Torment thee not, but put away thy fears.
Dead to all joys and living unto woe,
Slain quite by her that ne'er gave wise men blow,
20 Revive again and live without all dread,
The less afraid, the better thou shalt speed.

VERSE EXCHANGE BETWEEN QUEEN ELIZABETH AND
SIR WALTER RALEIGH
1   One of her terms of endearment for Raleigh, whom she also calls by
his nickname, Wat.

SONG ON THE ARMADA VICTORY, DECEMBER 1588

*A song made by her majesty and sung before her at her
coming from Whitehall to Paul's through Fleet Street in Anno Domini 1588.*   St. Paul's

*Sung in December after the scattering of the Spanish
navy.*

Look and bow down Thine ear, O Lord.
From Thy bright sphere behold and see
Thy handmaid and Thy handiwork,
Amongst Thy priests, offering to Thee
Zeal for incense, reaching the skies;
Myself and scepter, sacrifice.

My soul, ascend His holy place.
Ascribe Him strength and sing Him praise,
For He refraineth princes' sprites
And hath done wonders in my days.
He made the winds and waters rise
To scatter all mine enemies—

This Joseph's Lord and Israel's God,
The fiery Pillar and day's Cloud,
That saved his saints from wicked men
And drenched the honor of the proud;
And hath preserved in tender love
The spirit of his turtle dove.
Finis.

LETTER FROM PRINCESS ELIZABETH TO QUEEN MARY, AUGUST 2, 1556

To the queen's most excellent majesty

When I revolve in mind (most noble queen) the old love of paynims[1] to their prince and the reverent fear of Romans to their Senate, I can but muse for my part and blush for theirs, to see the rebellious hearts and devilish intents of Christians in names, but Jews in deed,[2] toward their oincted[3] king. Which, methinks, if they had feared God though they could not have loved the state, they should for dread of their own plague have refrained that wickedness which their bounden duty to your majesty hath not restrained. But when I call to remembrance that the devil *tanquam leo rugiens circumit querens quem devorare potest*[4] I do the less marvel though he have gotten such novices into his professed house, as vessels (without God's grace) more apt to serve his palace than meet to inhabit English land. I am the bolder to call them his imps for that Saint Paul sayeth, *Seditiosi filii sunt diaboli*,[5] and since I have so good a buckler I fear the less to enter into their judgment. Of this I assure your majesty, though it be my part above the rest to bewail such things though my name had not been in them, yet it vexeth me too much than[6] the devil owen[7] me such a hate as to put me in any part of his mischievous instigations. Whom, as I profess him my foe that is all

LETTER FROM PRINCESS ELIZABETH TO QUEEN MARY,
AUGUST 2, 1556

1 *pagans.*
2 In that Jews had been accused by Christians of killing their king, Jesus.
3 *anointed.*

4 1 Peter 5: 8: "As a roaring lion goes about, seeking whom he may devour."
5 "The seditious are children of the devil" (cf. Ephesians 2: 2).
6 *that.*
7 *owes.*

Christians' enemy, so wish I he had some other way invented to spite me. But since it hath pleased God thus to bewray[8] their malice afore they finish their purpose, I most humbly thank Him both that He hath ever thus preserved your majesty through His aid (much like a lamb from the horns of these Bashan bulls),[9] and also stirs up the hearts of your loving subjects to resist them and deliver you, to His honor and their shame.

The intelligence of which, proceeding from your majesty, deserveth more humble thanks than with my pen I can render, which, as infinite, I will leave to number. And among earthly things I chiefly wish this one: that there were as good surgeons for making anatomies of hearts that might show my thoughts to your majesty as there are expert physicians of the bodies, able to express the inward griefs of their maladies to their patient. For then I doubt not but know well that whatsoever other should suggest by malice, yet your majesty should be sure by knowledge, so that the more such misty clouds obfuscates the clear light of my truth, the more my tried thoughts should glister to the dimming of their hidden malice. But since wishes are vain and desires oft fails, I must crave that my deeds may supply that my thoughts cannot declare, and they be not misdeemed there as the facts have been so well tried. And like as I have been your faithful subject from the beginning of your reign, so shall no wicked persons cause me to change to the end of my life. And thus I commit your majesty to God's tuition, whom I beseech long time to preserve, ending with the new remembrance of my old suit, more for that it should not be forgotten than for that I think it not remembered. From Hatfield this present Sunday, the second day of August.

Your majesty's obedient subject and humble sister, *Elizabeth*

QUEEN ELIZABETH'S FIRST SPEECH, HATFIELD, NOVEMBER 20, 1558

Queen Elizabeth's speech to her secretary and other her lords before her coronation.

Words spoken by her majesty to Mr. Cecil:[1]

I give you this charge, that you shall be of my Privy Council and content yourself to take pains for me and my realm. This judgment I have of you: that you will not be corrupted with any manner of gift, and that you will be faithful to the state, and that without respect of my private will, you will give me that counsel that you think best, and if you shall know anything necessary to be declared to me of secrecy, you shall show it to myself only. And assure yourself I will not fail to keep taciturnity therein, and therefore herewith I charge you.

Words spoken by the queen to the lords:

My lords, the law of nature moveth me to sorrow for my sister; the burden that is fallen upon me maketh me amazed; and yet, considering I am God's creature, ordained to obey His appointment, I will thereto yield, desiring from the bottom of my heart that I may have assistance of His grace to be the minister of his heavenly will in this office now committed to me. And as I am but one body naturally considered, though by His permission a body politic to govern,[2] so I shall desire you all, my lords (chiefly you of the nobility, everyone in his degree and power), to be assistant to me, that I with my ruling and you with your service may make a good account to almighty God and leave some comfort to our posterity in earth. I mean to direct all my actions by good advice and counsel. And therefore, considering that divers of you be of the ancient nobility,[3] having your beginnings and estates of my progenitors, kings of this realm, and thereby ought in honor to have

---

8 *expose.*
9 A reference to Psalm 22: 12.

QUEEN ELIZABETH'S FIRST SPEECH, HATFIELD, NOVEMBER 20, 1558
1 Sir William Cecil (1520–98) served as Princess Elizabeth's surveyor from 1550 until his death.

2 On the concept of the two bodies of the monarch, see Ernest Kantorowicz, *The King's Two Bodies.*
3 The landed nobility had a permanent place on her Council because of their rank.

the more natural care for maintaining of my estate and this commonwealth; some others have been of long experience in governance and enabled by my father of noble memory, my brother, and my late sister to bear office; the rest of you being upon special trust lately called to her service only and trust, for your service considered and rewarded; my meaning is to require of you all nothing more but faithful hearts in such service as from time to time shall be in your powers towards the preservation of me and this commonwealth. And for counsel and advice I shall accept you of my nobility, and such others of you the rest as in consultation I shall think meet and shortly appoint, to the which also, with their advice, I will join to their aid, and for ease of their burden, others meet for my service. And they which I shall not appoint, let them not think the same for any disability in them, but for that I do consider a multitude doth make rather discord and confusion than good counsel. And of my goodwill you shall not doubt, using yourselves as appertaineth to good and loving subjects.

A COPY OF "THE GOLDEN SPEECH" FROM THE PAPERS OF
SIR THOMAS EGERTON, PRIVY COUNCILLOR

Queen Elizabeth's speech[1]

Mr. Speaker, we perceive your coming is to present thanks unto me; know it I accept with no less joy than your loves can desire to offer such a present, and more esteem it than any treasure or riches (for that we know to prize), but loyalty, love, and thanks I count invaluable. And though God hath raised me high, yet this I count the glory of my crown—that I have reigned with your loves. This makes I do not so much rejoice that God hath made me to be a queen, as to be a queen over so thankful a people, and to be the mean under God to conserve you in safety and preserve you from danger—yea, to be the instrument to set the Last Judgment Day before mine eyes and so to rule as I shall be judged, and to answer before a higher Judge, to whose judgment seat I do appeal that never thought was cherished in my heart that tended not to my people's good. And if my kingly bounty have been abused and my grants turned to the hurt of my people, contrary to my will and meaning; or if any in authority under me have neglected or perverted what I have committed to them, I hope God will not lay their culps unto my charge.

To be a king and wear a crown is a thing more glorious to them that see it than it is pleasant to them that bear it. For myself, I was never so much enticed with the glorious name of a king or royal authority of a queen as delighted that God had made me His instrument to maintain His truth and glory, and to defend this kingdom from dishonor, damage, tyranny, and oppression. But should I ascribe anything of this to myself, or my sexly weakness, I were not worthy to live, and of all, most unworthy of the mercies I have had from God. But to God only and wholly, all is to be given and ascribed. The cares and troubles of a crown I cannot resemble more fitly than to the confections of a learned physician, perfumed with some aromatical savor, or to bitter pills gilded over, by which it is made acceptable or less offensive which indeed is bitter and unpleasant to take. And for my part, were it not for conscience' sake to discharge the duty which God hath laid upon me, and to maintain His glory and keep you in safety, in mine own disposition, I should willingly resign the place I hold to any other, and glad to be free of the glory with the labors. For it is not my desire to be or reign longer than my life and reign shall be for your good. And though you have had and may have many mightier and wiser princes sitting in this seat, yet you never had nor shall have any that will love you better. Thus, Mr. Speaker, I commend me to your loyal love, and you to my best care and your further counsels. And I pray you, Mr. Comptroller and you of my Councils, that before these gentlemen depart into their countries, you bring them all to kiss my hand.

A COPY OF "THE GOLDEN SPEECH" FROM THE PAPERS OF
SIR THOMAS EGERTON, PRIVY COUNCILLOR
1   A report of this most celebrated of the Queen's parliamentary
addresses. Preserved in the papers of Sir Thomas Egerton (1540?–1607).

PRAYER ON THE DEFEAT OF THE SPANISH ARMADA, SEPTEMBER 1588

A godly prayer and thanksgiving, worthy the Christian Deborah and Theodosia[1] of our days.

Everlasting and omnipotent Creator, Redeemer, and Conserver, when it seemed most fit time to Thy worthy providence to bestow the workmanship of this world or globe, with Thy rare judgment Thou didst divide into four singular parts the form of all this mold, which aftertime hath termed elements, they all serving to continue in orderly government the whole of all the mass; which all, when of Thy most singular bounty and never-earst-seen[2] care Thou hast this year made serve for instruments both to daunt our foes and to confound their malice,[3] I most humbly, with bowed heart and bended knees, do render my humblest acknowledgments and lowliest thanks; and not the least for that the weakest sex hath been so fortified by Thy strongest help that neither my people might find lack by my weakness nor foreigners triumph at my ruin. Such hath been Thy unwonted grace in my days, although Satan hath never made holiday[4] in busy practices both for my life and state, yet that Thy mighty hand hath overspread both with shade of Thy blessed wings so that both neither hath been overthrown nor received shame but obtained victory to Thy most great glory and their greatest ignomy;[5] for which, Lord, of Thy mere goodness grant us grace to be hourly thankful and ever mindful. And if it may please Thee to pardon my request, give us the continuance in my days of like goodness, that mine eyes never see change of such grace to me, but specially to this my kingdom, which, Lord, grant to flourish many ages after my end, amen.

George Gascoigne (c. 1534–1577)

Gascoigne belongs to the generation of writers before the canonical greats like Sidney and Shakespeare, and he has been read much less widely. Like many literary pioneers, he has often been treated as someone whose work in drama, lyric poetry, and metrical theory made the way straight for the titans who came later. His translations of a modern comedy (Ariosto's *Supposes*) and a tragedy by Euripides (*Jocasta*) are among the earliest English examples of both forms, but they predate the professional stage. Likewise, his *Certayne Notes of Instruction* is the earliest surviving attempt to wrestle with the problems of writing English poetry in classicizing humanist forms, but it was swept from view by the later efforts of Philip Sidney, George Puttenham, and others.

Like John Lyly, he was writing at a time when writers were unsure how to apply the new humanist canons of literary form and taste in English. And like Lyly, his response was to try to demonstrate his versatility. Lyly did this by writing one text (*Euphues*) which includes many different prose forms. Gascoigne went one step further and published a volume entitled *A Hundreth Sundrie Flowres* (1573) which contained plays, lyric verse, a prose treatise, and a lengthy prose fiction (*The Adventures of Master F.J.*). It was deemed libelous and recalled. Two years later, a sanitized version appeared entitled *The Posies of George Gascoigne*, but it too attracted the attention of government censors. The two poems in this selection can be read as commentaries on this performative desire to be many things to many people – "Gascoigne's Woodmanship" appears to follow the author's life and failed attempts to win fame and patronage, and "Gascoigne's Goodnight" is a *memento mori* commenting on the futility of all worldly ambition. Like all early modern poems on these thoroughly conventional themes, we must beware of taking them as the literal view of their author.

READING

George Gascoigne, *A Hundreth Sundrie Flowres*, ed. G. W. Pigman.
Felicity A. Hughes, "Gascoigne's Poses".

J. H.

PRAYER ON THE DEFEAT OF THE SPANISH ARMADA,
SEPTEMBER 1588
1   Deborah was a leader of Israel (see Judges 4–5); Theodosia was a medieval saint known for her protection of religion.
2   *never before seen.*

3   The idea that the four elements joined forces to destroy the Spanish fleet.
4   *rested.*
5   *ignominy.*

[FROM] *A HUNDRETH SUNDRIE FLOWRES* (1573)

Gascoigne's Woodmanship[1]

Gascoigne's woodmanship written to the Lord Grey of Wilton upon this occasion, the said Lord Grey delighting (amongst many other good qualities) in choosing of his winter deer, and killing the same with his bow, did furnish Master Gascoigne with a cross bow *cum pertinenciis,*[2] and vouchsafed to use his company in the said exercise, calling him one of his woodmen. Now Master Gascoigne shooting very often, could never hit any deer, yea and oftentimes he let the herd pass by as though he had not seen them. Whereat when this noble Lord took some pastime, and had often put him in remembrance of his good skill in choosing, and readiness in killing of a winter deer, he thought good thus to excuse it in verse.

	My worthy Lord, I pray you wonder not	
	To see your woodman shoot so oft awry,	
	Nor that he stands amazed like a sot,	*fool*
	And lets the harmless deer (unhurt) go by.	
	Or if he strike a doe which is but carrion,[3]	
	Laugh not good Lord, but favour such a fault,	
	Take well in worth, he would fain hit the barren,	
	But though his heart be good, his hap is not:	*luck*
	And therefore now I crave your Lordship's leave,	
10	To tell you plain what is the cause of this:	
	First if it please your honour to perceive,	
	What makes your woodman shoot so oft amiss,	
	Believe me L.[4] the case is nothing strange,	
	He shoots awry almost at every mark,	
	His eyes have been so used for to range,	*wander*
	That now God knows they be both dim and dark.	
	For proof he bears the note of folly now,	
	Who shot sometimes to hit Philosophy,	
	And ask you why? forsooth I make avow,	*will explain*
20	Because his wanton wits went all awry.	*undisciplined*
	Next that, he shot to be a man of law,	*aimed*
	And spent sometime with learned Littleton,[5]	
	Yet in the end, he proved but a daw,	*fool*
	For law was dark and he had quickly done.	
	Then could he wish Fitzherbert[6] such a brain,	
	As *Tully*[7] had, to write the law by art,	
	So that with pleasure, or with little pain,	
	He might perhaps, have caught a truant's part.	*attain*
	But all too late, he most misliked the thing,	
30	Which most might help to guide his arrow straight,	
	He winked wrong, and so let slip the string,	*aimed*
	Which cast him wide, for all his quaint conceit.	*shot*
	From thence he shot to catch a courtly grace,	
	And thought even there to wield the world at will,	
	But out alas he much mistook the place,	
	And shot awry at every rover still.	*target*

[FROM] *A HUNDRETH SUNDRIE FLOWRES* (1573)

1 Many of the experiences that Gascoigne narrates here reflect his own life. He was a law student, did spend himself into debt trying to become a presence at court, and did serve as a soldier in the Netherlands.

2 "with all the relevant accessories."

3 "Carrion" means inedible, in this case because the doe is pregnant.

This is made clear two lines later when the speaker wishes he could shoot the "barren" ones.

4 A short form for "Lord."

5 Littleton's *Tenures* was the first law book printed in England. It concerned property rights, and was a standard text for law students.

6 Sir Antony Fitzherbert was the author of another legal text.

7 See the gazetteer under Cicero.

The blazing baits which draw the gazing eye,   *bright-coloured*
Unfeathered there his first affection,
No wonder then although he shot awry,
40   Wanting the feathers of discretion.
Yet more than them, the marks of dignity,
He much mistook and shot the wronger way,
Thinking the purse of prodigality,
Had been best mean to purchase such a prey.
He thought the flattering face which fleareth still,   *mocks*
Had been full fraught with all fidelity,
And that such words as courtiers use at will,
Could not have varied from the verity.
But when his bonnet buttoned with gold,
50   His comely cape beguarded all with gay,   *ornamentation*
His bombast hose, with linings manifold,   *padded*
His knit silk stocks and all his quaint array,
Had picked his purse of all the Peter Pence,   *i.e. coins*
Which might have paid for his promotion,
Then (all too late) he found that light expense,   *frivolous*
Had quite quenched out the court's devotion.
So that since then the taste of misery,
Hath been always full bitter in his bit,
And why? forsooth because he shot awry,
60   Mistaking still the marks which others hit.
But now behold what mark the man doth find,
He shoots to be a soldier in his age,
Mistrusting all the virtues of the mind,
He trusts the power of his personage.
As though long limbs led by a lusty heart,
Might yet suffice to make him rich again,
But Flushing[8] frays have taught him such a part,
That now he thinks the wars yield no such gain.
And sure I fear, unless your lordship deign,
70   To train him yet into some better trade,
It will be long before he hit the vein,
Whereby he may a richer man be made.
He cannot climb as other catchers can,   *hunters*
To lead a charge before himself be led.[9]
He cannot spoil the simple sakeless man,   *plunder/innocent*
Which is content to feed him with his bread.
He cannot pinch the painful soldier's pay,   *careful*
And shear him out his share in ragged sheets,
He cannot stop to take a greedy prey
80   Upon his fellows grovelling in the streets.
He cannot pull the spoil from such as pill,   *pillage*
And seem full angry at such foul offence,
Although the gain content his greedy will,
Under the cloak of contrary pretence:
And nowadays, the man that shoots not so,
May shoot amiss, even as your woodman doth:
But then you marvel why I let them go,
And never shoot, but say farewell forsooth:
Alas my Lord, while I do muse hereon,

---

8   A town in the Netherlands where English armies fought against the
Spanish during the 1570s.
9   i.e. To take command before he has been properly trained. The next
ten lines all revolve around common vices of military officers – robbing
the dead, misappropriating their soldiers' wages, robbing the local
population, and seizing the lion's share of the pillage.

90   And call to mind my youthful years misspent,
      They give me such a bone to gnaw upon,
      That all my senses are in silence pent.
      My mind is rapt in contemplation,
      Wherein my dazzling eyes only behold,
      The black hour of my constellation,[10]
      Which framed me so luckless on the mould:
      Yet therewithal I cannot but confess,
      That vain presumption makes my heart to swell,
      For thus I think, not all the world (I guess,)
100   Shoots bet than I, nay some shoots not so well.
      In *Aristotle* somewhat did I learn,
      To guide my manners all by comeliness,
      And *Tully* taught me somewhat to discern,
      Between sweet speech and barbarous rudeness.
      Old *Parkins, Rastell,* and *Dan Bracton's* books,[11]
      Did lend me somewhat of the lawless law,
      The crafty courtiers with their lawless looks,
      Must needs put some experience in my maw:
      Yet cannot these with many mast'ries more,   *accomplishments*
110   Make me shoot straight at any gainful prick,   *bull's eye*
      Where some that never handled such a bow,
      Can hit the white, or touch it near the quick,   *centre*
      Who can nor speak, nor write in pleasant wise,
      Nor lead their life by *Aristotle's* rule,
      Nor argue well on questions that arise,
      Nor plead a case more than my Lord Mayor's mule,
      Yet can they hit the marks that I do miss,
      And win the mean which may the man maintain.   *wealth*
      Now when my mind doth mumble upon this,
120   No wonder then although I pine for pain:
      And whiles mine eye behold this mirror thus,
      The herd goeth by, and farewell gentle does:
      So that your lordship quickly may discuss
      What blinds mine eyes so oft (as I suppose).
      But since my Muse can to my Lord rehearse
      What makes me miss, and why I do not shoot,
      Let me imagine in this worthless verse:
      If right before me, at my standing's foot
      There stood a doe, and I should strike her dead,
130   And then she prove a carrion carcass too,
      What figure might I find within my head,
      To 'scuse the rage which ruled me so to do?
      Some might interpret by plain paraphrase,
      That lack of skill or fortune led the chance,
      But I must otherwise expound the case,
      I say *Jehovah* did this doe advance,
      And made her bold to stand before me so,
      Till I had thrust mine arrow to her heart,
      That by the sudden of her overthrow,
140   I might endeavour to amend my part,
      And turn mine eyes that they no more behold,
      Such guileful marks as seem more than they be:
      And though they glister outwardly like gold,

---

10   i.e. the unfortunate disposition of the heavens at the hour of his   11   All authors of law books.
birth.

Are inwardly like brass, as men may see:
And when I see the milk hang in her teat,
Methinks it saith, old babe now learn to suck,
Who in thy youth couldst never learn the feat
To hit the whites which live with all good luck.
Thus have I told my Lord, (God grant in season)
150   A tedious tale in rhyme, but little reason.

Gascoigne's Goodnight

When thou hast spent the lingering day in pleasure and delight,
Or after toil and weary way, dost seek to rest at night:
Unto thy pains or pleasures past, add this one labour yet,
Ere sleep close up thine eye too fast, do not thy God forget,
But search within thy secret thoughts what deeds did thee befall:
And if thou find amiss in aught, to God for mercy call:
Yea though thou find nothing amiss, which thou canst call to mind
Yet evermore remember this, there is the more behind:
And think how well soever it is, that thou hast spent the day,
10   It comes of God, and not of thee, so to direct thy way.
Thus if thou try thy daily deeds, and pleasure in this pain,   *evaluate*
Thy life shall cleanse thy corn from weeds, & thine shall be the gain:
But if thy sinful sluggish eye, will venture for to wink,   *sleep*
Before thy wading will may try, how far thy soul may sink,
Beware and wake, for else thy bed, which soft and smooth is made,
May heap more harm upon thy head, than blows of enemy's blade.
Thus if this pain procure thine ease, in bed as thou dost lie,
Perhaps it shall not God displease, to sing thus soberly:
I see that sleep is lent me here, to ease my weary bones,
20   As death at last shall eke appear, to ease my grievous groans.   *also*
My daily sports, my paunch full fed, have caused my drowsy eye,
As careless life in quiet led, might cause my soul to die:
The stretching arms, the yawning breath, which I to bedward use,
Are patterns of the pangs of death, when life will me refuse:
And of my bed in sundry part in shadows doth resemble   *images*
The sundry shapes of death, whose dart shall make my flesh to tremble,
My bed itself is like the grave, my sheets the winding sheet,[12]
My clothes the mould which I must have to cover me most meet: *earth*
The hungry fleas which frisk so fresh, to worms I can compare
30   Which greedily shall gnaw my flesh, and leave the bones full bare:
The waking cock that early crows to wear the night away,
Puts in my mind the trump that blows before the latter day.[13]
And as I rise up lustily, when sluggish sleep is past,
So hope I to rise joyfully, to judgement at the last.
Thus will I wake, thus will I sleep, thus will I hope to rise,
Thus will I neither wail nor weep, but sing in godly wise.
My bones shall in this bed remain, my soul in God shall trust,
By whom I hope to rise again from death and earthly dust.

---

12   A winding sheet was the cloth wrapping placed around a corpse.   13   i.e. the trumpets that will sound before the Last Judgment.

Certain Sermons or Homilies (1547, 1563)

The Book of Homilies, as it is commonly known, was one of the most important instruments in the establishment of a Protestant Church of England. Henry VIII's decision to break with the papacy and establish an independent Church of England in 1534 had not been accompanied by any serious alterations of the old Catholic liturgy, largely because of the king's lack of interest. In fact, Henry's Act of Six Articles (1539) was expressly designed to rein in Protestant reform of church doctrine. With the accession of his nine-year-old son Edward VI in 1547, however, Archbishop Cranmer and his political allies began an organized program of Calvinist reformation in England. Two of the most serious problems they faced were promulgating their new doctrines to ordinary lay citizens (most of whom were illiterate) and controlling what individual ministers were saying from their pulpits about these doctrines. Levels of ability, dedication, education, and commitment to the new order varied widely in the clergy, and Edward's ministers were under no illusions about how difficult it was for the central government to regulate the enforcement of its policies on a local level.

In response to this situation, the first *Book of Homilies* (1547) provided 12 sermons on a variety of themes that were to be read aloud in every parish church in the country. That same year, an injunction was issued to all Church of England ministers requiring them to read one of the homilies each Sunday; the preface of the text added the further requirement that the homilies be read in the order in which they are printed, and to repeat the process until they received further instructions from the Privy Council. In 1548, all licences to preach in England were revoked unless they were signed by the king, the Duke of Somerset, or Cranmer. The Church of England was now an active ideological arm of the state. After Mary's reign (and the return to Roman Catholicism which came with it), Queen Elizabeth reissued the first collection (with a few changes to make it simpler to understand) and in 1563 issued a second volume to supplement it. In 1570, the *Homily against Disobedience and Wilful Rebellion* (occasioned by the Northern Rebellion of the previous year) was added. Elizabeth's motives were the same as Cranmer's had been: a desire to restrict the content of sermons to a controlled set of safe, orthodox views. The Puritans and some of the bishops were in favour of ministers writing their own sermons, but the queen was unyielding. Even James I, who spoke in favor of a preaching ministry at the Hampton Court Conference (1604), stressed that any sermon that discussed the power of monarchs or matters of state should restrict itself to the terms and views of the homily on obedience.

If only because of this uniformity and omnipresence, it is difficult to overstate the importance of the *Book of Homilies* as a representative text of Early Modern English culture. A copy of it was in every church in the land, and it was the most direct, frequently articulated vision of church, state, and nation that ordinary people heard from 1547 until the 1590s, after which point their influence began to decline. When other Renaissance English texts repeat commonplace views on religious and social order, it is usually the views of the *Book of Homilies* to which they refer. Authorship for the individual homilies has proved difficult to determine. The original 1547 homilies are commonly ascribed to Cranmer, Bishop Nicholas Ridley of London, and Hugh Latimer, but other writers have claims as well. The second volume has contributions from Bishop John Jewel and Archbishop Matthew Parker, among others. Parker wrote the homily on the Northern Rebellion in 1569. The selections below show the Elizabethan state Church discussing issues of obedience, biblical interpretation, and gender roles within marriage.

READING

Ronald B. Bond (ed. and introd.), *Certain Sermons or Homilies and A Homily against Disobedience and Wilful Rebellion.*
Ian Lancashire, "Elizabethan Homilies 1623: Editor's Introduction."

J. H.

A FRUITFUL EXHORTATION TO THE READING AND KNOWLEDGE OF HOLY SCRIPTURE (1547)

Unto a Christian man there can be nothing either more necessary or profitable than the knowledge of holy Scripture; forasmuch as in it is contained God's true word, setting forth his glory and also man's duty. And there is no truth nor doctrine necessary for our justification and everlasting salvation, but that is or may be drawn out of that fountain and well of truth. Therefore as many as be desirous to enter into the right and perfect way unto God must apply their minds to know holy Scripture; without the which they can neither sufficiently know God and his will, neither their office and duty. And, as drink is pleasant to them that be dry, and meat to them that be hungry, so is the reading, hearing, searching, and studying of holy Scripture, to them that be desirous to know God or themselves, and to do his will. And their stomachs only do loathe and abhor the heavenly knowledge and food of God's word, that be so drowned in worldly vanities, that they neither favour God, nor any godliness: for that is the cause why they desire such vanities rather than the true knowledge of God. As they that are sick of an ague,[1] whatsoever they eat and drink, though it be never so pleasant, yet it is as bitter to them as wormwood, not for the bitterness of the meat, but for the corrupt and bitter humour that is in their own tongue and mouth; even so is the sweetness of God's word bitter, not of itself, but only unto them that have their minds corrupted with long custom of sin and love of this world.

Therefore, forsaking the corrupt judgement of fleshly men, which care not but for their carcass, let us reverently hear and read holy Scriptures, which is the food of the soul. Let us diligently search for the well of life in the books of the New and Old Testament, and not run to the stinking puddles of men's traditions, devised by men's imagination, for our justification and salvation. For in holy Scripture is fully contained what we ought to do and what to eschew, what to believe, what to love, and what to look for at God's hands at length. In these books we shall find the Father, from whom, the Son, by whom, and the Holy Ghost, in whom, all things have their being and keeping up; and these three Persons to be but one God and one substance. In these books we may learn to know ourselves, how vile and miserable we be; and also to know God, how good he is of himself, and how he maketh us and all creatures partakers of his goodness. We may learn also in these books to know God's will and pleasure, as much as for this present time is convenient for us to know. And, as the great Clerk and godly Preacher St. John Chrysostom[2] saith, "whatsoever is required to the salvation of man is fully contained in the Scripture of God. He that is ignorant may there learn and have knowledge. He that is hardhearted and an obstinate sinner shall there find everlasting torments prepared of God's justice, to make him afraid, and to mollify (or soften) him. He that is oppressed with misery in this world shall there find relief in the promises of everlasting life, to his great consolation and comfort. He that is wounded by the devil unto death shall find there medicine, whereby he may be restored again unto health."[3] "If it shall require to teach any truth or reprove false doctrine, to rebuke any vice, to commend any virtue, to give good counsel, to comfort, or to exhort, or to do any other thing requisite for our salvation; all those things," saith St. Chrysostom, "we may learn plentifully of the Scripture."[4] "There is," saith Fulgentius,[5] "abundantly enough both for men to eat and children to suck. There is whatsoever is meet[6] for all ages and for all degrees[7] and sorts of men."[8]

These books therefore ought to be much in our hands, in our eyes, in our ears, in our mouths, but most of all in our hearts. For the Scripture of God is the heavenly meat of our souls: "the hearing and keeping of it" maketh us "blessed, sanctifieth" us, and maketh us holy: "it turneth our souls: it is a light lantern to our feet: it is a sure, steadfast, and everlasting" instrument of salvation: "it giveth wisdom to the humble and lowly hearted; it" comforteth, "maketh glad," cheereth, and cherisheth "our consciences: it is a more excellent" jewel or treasure "than any gold or precious stone: it is more sweet than honey or honeycomb": it is called "the best part," which Mary "did

1   acute fever.
2   John Chrysostom (c.354–407) was a bishop of Constantinople and one of the Fathers of the Christian Church. He was removed from office and exiled after offending Empress Eudoxia. He earned his nickname, which means "golden mouth," for his skill at preaching sermons, many of which were collected and published.

3   Pseudo-Chrysostom, *In Evangelium Matheai*, Hom. 41. As Ronald Bond has shown, this passage and the two subsequent ones can be found in Thomas Cranmer's commonplace book.
4   Chrystostom, *In Epistolam 2 ad Timotheum* 4.9.
5   Fulgentius (468–533), Bishop of Ruspe, was an early Church Father noted for his immense theological learning, his command of Greek literature, and his saintly life.
6   appropriate.
7   social classes.
8   from Fulgentius, *Sermo I: 'De dispensatoribus Domini'*.

choose"; for it hath in it everlasting comfort.[9] The words of holy Scripture be called "words of ever-lasting life";[10] for they be God's instrument, ordained for the same purpose. They have power to turn through God's promise, and they be effectual through God's assistance; and, being received in a faithful heart, they have ever an heavenly spiritual working in them.[11] They are "lively, quick, and mighty in operation and sharper than any two-edged sword, and enter through even unto the dividing asunder of the soul and the spirit, of the joints and the marrow."[12] Christ calleth him a wise builder that buildeth upon his word, upon his sure and substantial foundation.[13] By this word of God we shall be judged; for "the word that I speak," saith Christ, "is it that shall judge in the last day."[14] He that keepeth the word of Christ is promised the love and favour of God, and that he shall be the dwelling-place or temple of the blessed Trinity.[15] This word whosoever is diligent to read, and in his heart to print that he readeth, the great affection to the transitory things of this world shall be minished[16] in him, and the great desire of heavenly things, that be therein promised of God, shall increase in him. And there is nothing that so much strengtheneth our faith and trust in God, that so much keepeth up innocency and pureness of the heart, and also of outward godly life and conversation, as continual reading and recording of God's word, For that thing which, by continual use of reading of holy Scripture and diligent searching[17] of the same, is deeply printed and graven in the heart, at length turneth almost into nature. And moreover, the effect and virtue of God's word is to illuminate the ignorant, and to give more light unto them that faithfully and diligently read it; to comfort their hearts, and to encourage them to perform that, which of God is commanded. It teacheth patience in all adversity, in prosperity, humbleness; what honour is due unto God, what mercy and charity to our neighbour.[18] It giveth good counsel in all doubtful things. It showeth of whom we shall look for aid and help in all perils, and that God is the only giver of victory in all battles and temptations of our enemies, bodily and ghostly.[19] And in reading of God's word he most profiteth not always that is most ready in turning of the book, or in saying of it without the book;[20] but he that is most turned into it, that is most inspired with the Holy Ghost, most in his heart and life altered and changed into that thing which he readeth; he that is daily less and less proud, less wrathful, less covetous, and less desirous of worldly and vain pleasures; he that daily, forsaking his old vicious life, increaseth in virtue more and more. And, to be short, there is nothing that more maintaineth godliness of the mind, and driveth away ungodliness, than doth the continual reading or hearing of God's word, if it be joined with a godly mind and a good affection to know and follow God's will. For without a single eye, pure intent, and good mind, nothing is allowed for good before God. And, on the other side, nothing more darkeneth Christ and the glory of God, nor bringeth in more blindness and all kinds of vices, than doth the ignorance of God's word."[21]

The Second Part of the Sermon of the Knowledge of Holy Scripture

In the first part of this Sermon, which exhorteth to the knowledge of holy Scripture, was declared wherefore the knowledge of the same is necessary and profitable to all men, and that by the true knowledge and understanding of Scripture the most necessary points of our duty towards God and our neighbours are also known. Now as concerning the same matter you shall hear what followeth.

If we profess Christ, why be we not ashamed to be ignorant in his doctrine, seeing that every man is ashamed to be ignorant in that learning which he professeth? That man is ashamed to

9   This sentence conflates several scriptural passages including Matthew 4:4, Luke 11:28, John 17:17, Psalms 19:7–10, 199:105, 130, Luke 10:42.

10   John 6:68.

11   Colossians 1:6, 29.

12   Hebrews 4:12.

13   Matthew 7:24–27.

14   John 12:48.

15   John 14:23.

16   *lessened.*

17   *exploring.*

18   1 Samuel 14:4–23; 2 Chronicles 20:7, 17, 29; 1 Corinthians 15:57, 1 John 5:4.

19   *spiritual.*

20   i.e. by heart.

21   Isaiah 5:13, 24; Matthew 22:29; 1 Corinthians 14.

be called a philosopher which readeth not the books of philosophy; and to be called a lawyer, an astronomer, or a physician, that is ignorant in the books of law, astronomy, and physic.[22] How can any man then say that he professeth Christ and his religion, if he will not apply himself, as far forth as he can or may conveniently, to read and hear, and so to know, the books of Christ's Gospel and doctrine? Although other sciences be good and to be learned, yet no man can deny but this is the chief, and passeth all other incomparably. What excuse shall we therefore make at the last day[23] before Christ, that delight to read or hear men's fantasies and inventions more than his most holy Gospel; and will find no time to do that which chiefly, above all things, we should do; and will rather read other things than that for the which we ought rather to leave reading of all other things? Let us therefore apply ourselves, as far forth as we can have time and leisure, to know God's word, by diligent hearing[24] and reading thereof, as many as profess God, and have faith and trust in him.

But they that have no good affection to God's word, to colour this their fault, allege commonly two vain and feigned excuses. Some go about to excuse them by their own frailness and fearfulness, saying that they dare not read holy Scripture, lest through their ignorance they should fall into any error. Other pretend that the difficulty to understand it, and the hardness thereof, is so great, that it is meet to be read only of clerks and learned men.

As touching the first, ignorance of God's word is the cause of all error, as Christ himself affirmed to the Saducees,[25] saying, that "they erred, because they knew not the Scripture."[26] How should they then eschew error that will be still ignorant? And how should they come out of ignorance that will not read nor hear that thing which should give them knowledge? He that now hath most knowledge was at the first ignorant: yet he forbare not to read, for fear he should fall into error; but he diligently read, lest he should remain in ignorance, and through ignorance in error. And, if you will not know the truth of God (a thing most necessary for you), lest you fall into error, by the same reason you may then lie still, and never go, lest, if you go, you fall in the mire; nor eat any good meat, lest you take a surfeit;[27] nor sow your corn, nor labour in your occupation, nor use your merchandise, for fear you lose your seed, your labour, your stock: and so, by that reason, it should be best for you to live idly, and never to take in hand to do any manner of good thing, lest peradventure some evil thing may chance thereof. And, if you be afraid to fall into error by reading of holy Scripture, I shall show you how you may read it without danger of error. Read it humbly with a meek and lowly heart, to the intent you may glorify God, and not yourself with the knowledge of it, and read it not without daily praying to God, that he would direct your reading to good effect; and take upon you to expound it no further than you can plainly understand it. For, as St. Augustine[28] saith, the knowledge of holy Scripture is a great, large, and a high palace, but the door is very low; so that the high and arrogant man cannot run in, but he must stoop low and humble himself that shall enter into it. Presumption and arrogancy is the mother of all error: and humility needeth to fear no error. For humility will only search to know the truth: it will search and will bring together one place with another; and where it cannot find out the meaning, it will pray, it will ask of other that know, and will not presumptuously and rashly define any thing which it knoweth not. Therefore the humble man may search any truth boldly in the Scripture without any danger of error. And, if he be ignorant, he ought the more to read and to search holy Scripture, to bring him out of ignorance. I say not nay, but a man may prosper with only hearing; but he may much more profit with both hearing and reading.

This have I said as touching the fear to read through ignorance of the person. And concerning the hardness of Scripture, he that is so weak that he is not able to brook strong meat, yet he may suck the sweet and tender milk, and defer the rest until he wax stronger and come to more knowledge.[29] For God receiveth the learned and unlearned, and casteth away none, but is

---

22   i.e. medicine.
23   i.e. the Last Judgment.
24   One of the many moments in the homilies in which we are reminded that these were sermons delivered to a largely illiterate audience. It was incumbent on this text to recognize the value of listening to Scripture as well as reading it.

25   One of the three main groups into which Jews were divided at the time of Christ (the others being the Pharisees and the Essenes).
26   Matthew 22:29.
27   i.e. become sick as a result of eating too much.
28   See the gazetteer. The quoted passage comes from *Confessions* 3.5.
29   1 Corinthians 3:2; Hebrews 5:12–14.

indifferent[30] unto all. And the Scripture is full, as well of low valleys, plain ways, and easy for every man to use and to walk in, as also of high hills and mountains, which few men can climb unto. And "whosoever giveth his mind to holy Scriptures with diligent study and burning desire, it cannot be," saith St. John Chrysostom, "that he should be left without help. For either God Almighty will send him some godly doctor to teach him, as he did to instruct Eunuchus, a noble-man of Ethiopia, and treasurer unto Queen Candace;[31] who having a great affection to read the Scripture, although he understood it not, yet, for the desire that he had unto God's word, God sent his Apostle Philip to declare unto him the true sense of the Scripture that he read; or else, if we lack a learned man to instruct and teach us, yet God himself from above will give light unto our minds, and teach us those things which are necessary for us, and wherein we be ignorant." And in another place Chrysostom saith, that "man's human and worldly wisdom or science needeth not to the understanding of Scripture, but the revelation of the Holy Ghost, who inspireth the true meaning unto them that with humility and diligence do search therefore."[32] "He that asketh, shall have, and he that seeketh shall find, and he that knocketh, shall have the door open."[33] If we read once, twice, or thrice, and understand not, let us not cease so, but still continue reading, praying, asking of other; and so, by still knocking, at the last the door shall be opened as St. Augustine saith.[34] Although many things in the Scripture be spoken in obscure mysteries, yet there is nothing spoken under dark mysteries in one place but the self-same thing in other places is spoken more familiarly and plainly to the capacity both of learned and unlearned.[35] And those things in the Scripture that be plain to understand and necessary for salvation, every man's duty is to learn them, to print them in memory, and effectually to exercise them; and, as for the dark mysteries, to be contented to be ignorant in them until such time as it shall please God to open those things unto him. In the mean season,[36] if he lack either aptness or opportunity, God will not impute it to his folly: but yet it behooveth not[37] that such as be apt should set aside reading, because some other be unapt to read. Nevertheless, for the hardness of such places the reading of the whole ought not to be set apart. And briefly to conclude: as St. Augustine saith, by the Scripture all men be amended, weak men be strengthened, and strong men be comforted. So that surely none be enemies to the reading of God's word but such as either be so ignorant that they know not how wholesome a thing it is, or else be so sick that they hate the most comfortable medicine that should heal them,[38] or so ungodly, that they would wish the people still to continue in blindness and ignorance of God.

Thus we have briefly touched some part of the commodities of God's holy word, which is one of God's chief and principal benefits given and declared to mankind here in earth. Let us thank God heartily for this his great and special gift, beneficial favour, and fatherly providence. Let us be glad to "revive this" precious "gift" of our heavenly Father.[39] Let us hear, read, and know these holy rules, injunctions, and statutes of our Christian religion, and upon that we have made profession to God at our baptism. Let us with fear and reverence lay up in the chest of our hearts these nec-essary and fruitful lessons. Let us "night and day" muse, and "have meditation" and contemplation "in them."[40] Let us ruminate and as it were chew the cud, that we may have the sweet juice, spiri-tual effect, marrow, honey, kernel, taste, comfort and consolation of them; let us stay, quiet, and certify[41] our consciences, with the most infallible certainty, truth, and perpetual assurance of them. Let us pray to God, the only Author of these heavenly studies, that we may speak, think, believe, live, and depart hence, according to the wholesome doctrine and verities of them. And by that means in this world we shall have God's defence, favour, and grace, with the unspeakable solace of

---

30   *just.*
31   See Acts 8:27 ff.
32   John Chrysostom, *Homilies on Genesis* 21.
33   Matthew 7:7–8.
34   See *Sermo 270: 'In die Pentecostes'* 1 and *Enarratio in Psalmos* 33 1.
35   See Augustine, *De doctrina Christiana* ("On Christian Doctrine") 2.6. The Augustinian principles of reading the Bible found in this homily are more fully expounded in this treatise.

36   i.e. the mean time.
37   i.e. It is not proper that.
38   Augustine, *Letters* 137.5.18.
39   2 Timothy 1:6.
40   Psalms 1:2.
41   *inform with certainty.*

peace and quietness of conscience, and after this miserable life we shall enjoy the endless bliss and glory of heaven. Which he grant us all that died for us all, Jesus Christ: to whom with the Father and the Holy Ghost be all honour and glory both now and everlastingly.

An Exhortation Concerning Good Order, and Obedience to Rulers and Magistrates (1547)[42]

Almighty God hath created and appointed all things, in heaven, earth, and waters, in a most excellent and perfect order. In heaven he hath appointed distinct (or several) orders and states of archangels and angels. In earth he hath assigned and appointed kings and princes, with other governors under them, in all good and necessary order. The water above is kept, and raineth down in due time and season. The sun, moon, stars, rainbow, thunder, lightning, clouds, and all birds of the air, do keep their order. The earth, trees, seeds, plants, herbs, corn, grass, and all manner of beasts, keep themselves in their order. All the parts of the whole year, as winter, summer, months, nights, and days, continue in their order. All kinds of fishes in the sea, rivers, and waters, with all fountains, and springs, yea, the seas themselves, keep their comely course and order. And man himself also hath all his parts both within and without, as soul, heart, mind, memory, understanding, reason, speech, with all and singular corporal members of his body, in a profitable, necessary, and pleasant order. Every degree of people, in their vocation, calling, and office, hath appointed to them their duty and order. Some are in high degree, some in low; some kings and princes, some inferiors and subjects; priests and laymen, masters and servants, fathers and children, husbands and wives, rich and poor; and every one hath need of other. So that in all things is to be lauded and praised the goodly order of God: without the which no house, no city, no commonwealth can continue and endure (or last); for where there is no right order, there reigneth all abuse, carnal liberty,[43] enormity, sin, and Babylonical[44] confusion. Take away kings, princes, rulers, magistrates, judges, and such estates of God's order, no man shall ride or go by the highway unrobbed; no man shall sleep in his own house or bed unkilled; no man shall keep his wife, children, and possessions in quietness; all things shall be common; and there must needs follow all mischief and utter destruction both of souls, bodies, goods, and commonwealths.[45]

But blessed be God that we in this realm of England feel not the horrible calamities, miseries, and wretchedness which all they undoubtedly feel and suffer that lack this godly order. And praised be God that we know the great excellent benefit of God showed towards us in this behalf. God hath sent us his high gift, our most dear Sovereign Lady Queen Elizabeth,[46] with godly, wise, and honourable counsel, with other superiors and inferiors, in a beautiful order, and goodly. Wherefore let us subjects do our bounden duties, giving hearty thanks to God, and praying for the preservation of this godly order. Let us all obey, even from the bottom of our hearts, all their godly proceedings, laws, statutes, proclamations, and injunctions, with all other their godly orders. Let us consider the Scriptures of the Holy Ghost, which persuade and command us all obediently to be

---

42 Almost all constitutional arrangements in the Christian world claimed some kind of divine authorization for their power, but the English monarch's new position as supreme head of the Church of England made church and state effectively one and the same. This homily is concerned to justify this new claim of authority, to question the legitimacy of the papal authority that Henry VIII had rejected, and to make it clear that the king's rejection of papal authority in no way licences his subjects to do the same. Regional rebellions against royal authority were a persistent problem for the Tudor monarchs.

43 i.e. a worldly, unregenerate freedom, rather than the spiritual freedom promised to true Christians. The distinction between "liberty" (the justified freedom of citizens under the law), and "licence" (an unjustly claimed freedom from legal or moral restriction) was strenuously and repeatedly debated in Early Modern political and religious debates.

44 Originally, this word meant "tumultuous" or "confused," but in the sectarian discourse of sixteenth-century religious debates, it was also used as a synonym for "popish."

45 As many previous commentators have noticed, this passage reflects a widespread theme in Early Modern culture. The most famous of its many analogues is Ulysses' speech on hierarchy in Shakespeare's *Troilus and Cressida* I.iii.75 ff.

46 Elizabeth I (1558–1603) appears here because this text is drawn from the edition of the homilies that was produced during her reign. The 1547 edition would have named Edward VI (1547–53) in this passage. Edward took the throne as a boy of nine upon Henry VIII's death and died of consumption just seven years later. The Council of Regency that was to govern the nation until his majority was dominated, until 1552, by the Duke of Somerset, who used his position to advance a program of genuine Protestant reform.

subject, first and chiefly to the Queen's majesty, Supreme Governor over all, and next to her honourable counsel, and to all other noblemen, magistrates, and officers, which by God's goodness be placed and ordered.

For Almighty God is the only author and provider for this forenamed state and order; as it is written of God in the Book of the Proverbs: "Through me kings do reign; through me counsellors make just laws: through me do princes bear rule, and all judges of the earth execute judgement: I am loving to them that love me."[47] Here let us mark well and remember, that the high power and authority of kings, with their making of laws, judgements, and offices, are the ordinances, not of man, but of God; and therefore is this word, "Through me," so many times repeated. Here is also well to be considered and remembered, that this good order is appointed by God's wisdom, favour, and love specially for them that love God; and therefore he saith, "I love them that love me."

Also in the Book of Wisdom we may evidently learn that a king's power, authority, and strength, is a great benefit of God, given of his great mercy to the comfort of our great misery. For thus we read there spoken to kings: "Hear, O ye kings, and understand; learn ye that be judges of the ends of the earth; give ear ye that rule the multitudes: for the power is given you of the Lord, and the strength, from the Highest."[48] Let us learn also here by the infallible and undeceivable Word of God, that kings, and other supreme and higher officers are ordained of God, who is Most Highest: and therefore they are here taught diligently to apply and give themselves to knowledge and wisdom, necessary for the ordering of God's people to their governance committed (or whom to govern they are charged of God). And they be here also taught by Almighty God, that they should acknowledge themselves to have all their power and strength, not from Rome,[49] but immediately of God Most Highest.

We read in the Book of Deuteronomy that all punishment pertaineth to God, by this sentence: "Vengeance is mine, and I will reward."[50] But this sentence we must understand to pertain also unto the magistrates, which do exercise God's room[51] in judgement and punishing by good and godly laws here in earth.[52] And the places of Scripture which seem to remove from among all Christian men judgement, punishment, or killing, ought to be understand, that no man of his own private authority may be judge over others, may punish, or may kill, but we must refer all judgement to God, to kings and rulers, and judges under them, which be God's officers to execute justice, and by plain words of Scripture have their authority and use of the sword granted from God; as we are taught by St. Paul, the dear and chosen Apostle of our Saviour Christ, whom we ought diligently to obey, even as we would obey our Saviour Christ if he were present. Thus St. Paul writeth to the Romans: "Let every soul submit himself unto the authority of the higher powers. For there is no power but of God: the powers that be be ordained of God. Whosoever therefore withstandeth the power withstandeth the ordinance of God: but they that resist" or are against "shall receive to themselves damnation. For rulers are not fearful to them that do good, but to them that do evil. Wilt thou be without fear of that power? Do well then, and so shalt thou be praised of the same: for he is the minister of God for thy wealth. But and if thou do that which is evil, then fear; for he beareth not the sword for nought, for he is the minister of God, to take vengeance on him that doth evil. Wherefore ye must needs obey, not only for fear of vengeance, but also because of conscience. And even for this cause pay ye tribute: for they are God's ministers, serving for the same purpose."[53] Here let us learn of St. Paul, the "chosen vessel"[54] of God, that all persons having souls, (he excepteth none, nor exempteth none, neither priest, apostle, nor prophet, saith St. Chrysostom,)[55] do owe, of bounden duty and even in conscience, obedience, submission, and subjection to the high powers which be set in authority by God; for as much as they be God's

47 Proverbs 8:15–17.
48 Wisdom of Solomon 6:1–3.
49 At the zenith of its influence in the Early Modern period, the papacy claimed that all Christian monarchs held their crowns at the discretion of the Pope (as Christ's vicar on earth). This claim of papal authority was resisted by even Catholic monarchs and is, naturally, opposed by the homily writers at every opportunity.
50 Deuteronomy 32:35.

51 *office.*
52 This interpretation flies in the face of most readings of this well-known passage (which stress the extent to which only God can truly judge anyone). It is a fine example of how the writer of this homily tries to close off any potential justification for resisting royal authority.
53 Romans 13:1–6.
54 Acts 9:15.
55 *Homilies on the Letter to the Romans* 23.1.

lieutenants, God's presidents, God's officers, God's Commissioners, God's Judges, ordained of God himself, of whom only they have all their power and all their authority. And the same St. Paul threateneth no less pain than everlasting damnation to all disobedient persons, to all resisters against this general and common authority; forasmuch as they resist not man, but God; not man's device and invention, but God's wisdom, God's order, power, and authority.

The second part of the Sermon of Obedience

For as much as God hath created and disposed all things in a comely order, we have been taught, in the first part of this Sermon concerning good Order and Obedience, that we ought also in all commonweals to observe and keep a due order, and to be obedient to the powers, their ordinances and laws; and that all rulers are appointed of God, for a godly order to be kept in the world; and also how the magistrates ought to learn how to rule and govern according to God's laws; and that all subjects are bound to obey them as God's ministers, yea, although they be evil, not only for fear, but also for conscience's sake.

And here, good people, let us all mark diligently, that it is not lawful for inferiors and subjects in any case, to resist (or stand against) the superior powers: for St. Paul's words be plain, that "whosoever withstandeth shall get to themselves damnation"; for "whosoever withstandeth withstandeth the ordinance of God."[56] Our Saviour Christ himself and his Apostles received many and divers injuries of the unfaithful and wicked men in authority: yet we never read that they, or any of them, caused any sedition or rebellion against authority. We read oft that they patiently suffered all troubles, vexations, slanders, pangs, and pains, and death itself obediently, without tumult or resistance. They "committed their cause to him that judgeth righteously,"[57] and prayed for their enemies heartily and earnestly. They knew that the authority of the powers was God's ordinance; and therefore, both in their words and deeds, they taught ever obedience to it, and never taught nor did the contrary. The wicked judge Pilate said to Christ, "Knowest thou not, that I have power to crucify thee, and have power also to loose[58] thee? Jesus answered, Thou couldest have no power at all against me, except it were given thee from above."[59] Whereby Christ taught us plainly that even the wicked rulers have their power and authority from God. And therefore it is not lawful for their subjects by force to withstand them, although they abuse their power: much less then it is lawful for subjects to withstand their godly and Christian princes, which do not abuse their authority, but use the same to God's glory and to the profit and commodity of God's people.

The holy Apostle Peter commandeth "servants to be obedient to their masters, not only if they be good and gentle, but also if they be" evil and "froward,"[60] affirming, that the vocation and calling of God's people is to be patient and of the suffering side. And there he bringeth in the patience of our Saviour Christ, to persuade obedience to governors, yea, although they be wicked and wrong-doers. But let us now hear St. Peter himself speak, for his words certify best our conscience. Thus he uttereth them in his first Epistle: "Servants, obey your masters with fear, not only if they be good and gentle, but also if they be froward.[61] For it is thankworthy, if a man for conscience toward God endureth grief, and suffer wrong undeserved. For what praise is it, when ye be beaten for your faults, if ye take it patiently? But when ye do well, if you then suffer wrong, and take it patiently, then is there cause to have thank of God. For hereunto verily were ye called: for so did Christ suffer for us, leaving us an example, that we should follow his steps."[62] All these be the very words of St. Peter.

St. David also teacheth us a good lesson in this behalf: who was many times most cruelly and wrongfully persecuted of King Saul, and many times also put in jeopardy and danger of his life by King Saul and his people; yet he neither withstood, neither used any force or violence against King Saul, his mortal (or deadly) enemy, but did ever to his liege lord and master King Saul most true,

---

56 Romans 12:2.
57 1 Peter 2:23.
58 *release.*
59 John 19:10–11.

60 1 Peter 2:18–21.
61 *unreasonable.*
62 1 Peter 2:18 ff.

most diligent, and most faithful service. Insomuch that, when the Lord God had given King Saul into David's hands in his own cave, he would not hurt him, when he might, without all bodily peril, easily have slain him;[63] no, he would not suffer any of his servants once to lay their hand upon King Saul, but prayed to God in this wise: "Lord, keep me from doing that thing unto my master, the Lord's anointed; keep me that I lay not my hand upon him, seeing he is the anointed of the Lord. For as truly as the Lord liveth, except the Lord smite him, or except his day come, or that he go down to war, and in battle perish, the Lord be merciful unto me, that I lay not my hand upon the Lord's anointed." And that David might have killed his enemy King Saul it is evidently proved in the first Book of the Kings,[64] both by the cutting off the lap of Saul's garment, and also by plain confession of King Saul. Also another time, as is mentioned in the same book, when the most unmerciful and most unkind King Saul did persecute poor David, God did again give King Saul into David's hands by casting of King Saul and his whole army into a dead sleep; so that David and one Abisai with him came in the night into Saul's host, where "Saul lay sleeping, and his spear stuck in the ground at his head. Then said Abisai unto David, God hath delivered thine enemy into thy hands at this time: now therefore let me smite him once with my spear to the earth, and I will not smite him again the second time"; meaning thereby to have killed him with one stroke, and to have made him sure for ever. "And David" answered and "said to Abisai, Destroy him not: for who can lay his hands on the Lord's anointed, and be guiltless? And David said furthermore, As sure as the Lord liveth, the Lord shall smite him, or his day shall come to die, or he shall descend" (or go down) "into battle, and there perish. The Lord keep me from laying my hands upon the Lord's anointed: but take thou now the spear that is at his head, and the cruse[65] of water, and let us go":[66] and so he did. Here is evidently proved that we may not withstand nor in any wise hurt an anointed king; which is God's lieutenant, vice-regent, and highest minister in that country where he is king.

But peradventure some here would say, that David in his own defence might have killed King Saul lawfully and with a safe conscience. But holy David did know that he might in no wise withstand, hurt, or kill his sovereign lord and king: he did know that he was but King Saul's subject, though he were in great favour with God, and his enemy King Saul out of God's favour. Therefore, though he were never so much provoked, yet he refused utterly to hurt the Lord's anointed. He durst not, for offending God and his own conscience, (although he had occasion and opportunity,) once lay his hands upon God's high officer the king, whom he did know to be a person reserved and kept for his office sake only to God's punishment and judgement. Therefore he prayeth so oft and so earnestly, that he lay not his hands upon the Lord's anointed. And by these two examples St. David, being named in Scripture "a man after God's own heart,"[67] giveth a general rule and lesson to all subjects in the world not to withstand their liege lord and king, not to take a sword by their private authority against their king, God's anointed; who only beareth the sword by God's authority, for the maintenance of the good and for the punishment of the evil; who only by God's law hath the use of the sword at his commandment, and also hath all power, jurisdiction, regiment, coercion, and punishment, as supreme governor of all his realms and dominions, and that even by the authority of God, and by God's ordinances.

Yet another notable story and doctrine is in the Second Book of the Kings, that maketh also for this purpose.[68] When an Amalechite, by King Saul's own consent and commandment, had killed King Saul, he went to David, supposing to have had great thank for his message that he had killed David's deadly enemy; and therefore he made great haste to tell to David the chance,[69] bringing with him King Saul's crown that was upon his head, and his bracelet that was upon his arm, to persuade his tidings to be true. But godly David was so far from rejoicing at this news, that immediately and forthwith he rent his clothes off his back, he mourned and wept, and said to the messenger, "How is it that thou wast not afraid to lay thy hands on the Lord's anointed to destroy

63   1 Samuel 24.

64   The author is here referring to all of the books in the Hebrew Bible which refer to the kings of Israel, not just the two books named "Kings." As will be seen below, the references here are from the books of Samuel.

65   *storage or drinking vessel.*

66   1 Samuel 26:7–12.

67   Psalms 139:3, 20–26; 1 Samuel 13:14; Acts 13:22.

68   2 Samuel 1:1–16.

69   *outcome.*

him?" And by and by David made one of his servants to kill the messenger, saying, "Thy blood be on thine own head, for thine own mouth hath testified and witnessed against thee, granting that thou hast slain the Lord's anointed."

These examples being so manifest and evident, it is an intolerable ignorance, madness, and wickedness for subjects to make any murmuring, rebellion, resistance (or withstanding), commotion, or insurrection against their most dear and most dread Sovereign Lord and King, ordained and appointed of God's goodness for their commodity, peace, and quietness.

Yet let us believe undoubtedly, good Christian people, that we may not obey kings, magistrates, or any other, though they be our own fathers, if they would command us to do anything contrary to God's commandments. In such a case we ought to say with the Apostle, "We must rather obey God than man."[70] But nevertheless in that case we may not in any wise withstand violently or rebel against rulers, or make any insurrection, sedition, or tumults, either by force of arms or otherwise, against the anointed of the Lord or any of his appointed officers; but we must in such case patiently suffer all wrongs, and injuries, referring the judgement of our cause only to God. Let us fear the terrible punishment of Almighty God against traitors and rebellious persons by the example of Korah, Dathan, and Abiram,[71] which repugned and grudged against God's magistrates and officers, and therefore the earth opened and swallowed them up alive. Others, for their wicked murmuring and rebellion, were by a sudden fire, sent of God, utterly consumed.[72] Other, for their froward behaviour to their rulers and governors, God's ministers, were suddenly stricken with a foul leprosy.[73] Other were stinged to death with wonderful[74] strange fiery serpents.[75] Others were sore plagued, so that there was killed in one day the number of fourteen thousand and seven hundred, for rebellion against them whom God had appointed to be in authority. Absalom also, rebelling against his father King David, was punished with a strange and notable death.[76]

The third part of the Sermon of Obedience

Ye have heard before, in this Sermon of good Order and Obedience, manifestly proved both by Scriptures and examples, that all subjects are bounden to obey their magistrates, and for no cause to resist (or withstand), rebel, or make any sedition against them, yea, although they be wicked men. And let no man think that he can escape unpunished that committeth treason, conspiracy, or rebellion against his Sovereign Lord the King, though he commit the same never so secretly, either in thought, word, or deed, never so privily in his privy chamber by himself, or openly communicating and consulting with other. For treason will not be hid; treason will out at the length. God will have that most detestable vice both opened and punished; for that it is so directly against his ordinance and against his high principal judge and anointed in earth. The violence and injury that is committed against authority is committed against God, the commonweal, and the whole realm; which God will have known, and condignly[77] (or worthily) punished one way or other. For it is notably written of the Wise Man in Scripture, in the Book called Ecclesiastes: "Wish the king no evil in thy thought, nor speak no hurt of him in thy privy chamber: for the bird of the air shall betray thy voice, and with her feathers shall betray thy words."[78]

These lessons and examples are written for our learning. Let us all therefore fear the most detestable vice of rebellion, ever knowing and remembering that he that resisteth (or withstandeth) common authority resisteth (or withstandeth) God and his ordinance; as it may be proved by many other more places of holy Scripture.

---

70   Acts 5:29.
71   Numbers 16:1–33.
72   Numbers 11:1.
73   Numbers 12:1–10.
74   In Early Modern English, this word meant "remarkable" or "unprecedented." Unlike in modern English, it has no necessary positive connotation.

75   Numbers 21:5–6.
76   2 Samuel 18:9–15.
77   *suitably*.
78   Ecclesiastes 10:20.

And here let us take heed that we understand not these or such other like places, which so straitly command obedience to superiors, and so straitly punished rebellion, and disobedience to the same, to be meant in any condition of the pretenced or coloured power of the Bishop of Rome.[79] For truly the Scripture of God alloweth no such usurped power, full of enormities, abusions,[80] and blasphemies: but the true meaning of these and such places be to extol and set forth God's true ordinance, and the authority of God's anointed kings, and of their officers appointed under them. And concerning the usurped power of the Bishop of Rome, which he most wrongfully challengeth as the successor of Christ and Peter; we may easily perceive how false, feigned, and forged it is, not only in that it hath no sufficient ground in holy Scripture, but also by the fruits and doctrine thereof. For our Saviour Christ and St. Peter teach, most earnestly and agreeably, obedience to kings, as to the chief and supreme rulers in this world next under God; but the Bishop of Rome teacheth, that they that are under him are free from all burdens and charges of the commonwealth and obedience toward their prince, most clearly against Christ's doctrine and St. Peter's. He ought therefore rather to be called Antichrist and the successor of the Scribes and Pharisees, than Christ's vicar or St. Peter's successor; seeing that not only in this point, but also in other weighty matters of Christian religion, in matters of remission and forgiveness of sins and of salvation, he teacheth so directly against both St. Peter and against our Saviour Christ: who not only taught obedience to kings, but also practised obedience in their conversation and living: for we read that they both paid tribute to the king.[81] And also we read that the holy Virgin Mary, mother to our Saviour Christ, and Joseph, who was taken for his father, at the Emperor's commandment went to the city of David, named Bethlehem, to be taxed among others,[82] and to declare their obedience to the magistrates for God's ordinances' sake. And here let us not forget the blessed Virgin Mary's obedience: for although she was highly in God's favour, and Christ's natural mother, and was also great with child at the same time, and so nigh her travail,[83] that she was delivered in her journey, yet she gladly without any excuse or grudging, for conscience's sake did take that cold and foul winter journey; being in the mean season so poor that she lay in the stable, and there she was delivered of Christ.

And according to the same lo how St. Peter agreeth, writing by express words in his first Epistle: "Submit yourselves" (or be subject), saith he, "unto kings, as unto the chief heads, and unto rulers, as unto them that are sent of him for the punishment of evil doers, and for the praise of them that do well; for so is the will of God."[84] I need not to expound these words, they be so plain of themselves. St. Peter doth not say, "Submit yourselves unto" me as supreme head of the Church: neither he saith, "Submit yourselves" from time to time to my successors in Rome: but he saith, "Submit yourselves unto your king, your supreme head," and unto those that he appointeth in authority under him; "for" that you shall so show your obedience, "it is the will of God"; God wills that you be in subjection to your head and king. This is God's ordinance, God's commandment, and God's holy will, that the whole body of every realm, and all the members and parts of the same, shall be subject to their head, their king; and that, as St. Peter writeth, "for the Lord's sake," and, as St. Paul writeth, "for conscience's sake," and not for fear only.[85]

Thus we learn by the word of God to yield to our king that is due to our king,[86] that is, honour, obedience, payments of due taxes, customs, tributes, subsidies, love, and fear.[87]

Thus we know partly our bounden duties to common authority: now let us learn to accomplish the same. And let us most instantly and heartily pray to God, the only author of all authority, for all them that be in authority; according as St. Paul willeth, writing thus to Timothy in his first Epistle: "I exhort therefore that, above all things, prayers, supplications, intercessions, and giving of thanks be done for all men, for kings, and for all that be in authority, that we may live a quiet and a peaceable life with all godliness and honesty: for that is good and accepted" (or allowable)

79 The English Reformation began as a contest between the royal power of Henry VIII and the power of the papacy, the homilists take care to impugn the sources of the pope's authority whenever possible. The independence of monarchs under God that this homily asserts requires that this be made explicit.

80 *perversions.*

81 Matthew 17:24–27.

82 Luke 2:4–7.

83 *labor.*

84 1 Peter 2:13–15.

85 1 Peter 2:13; Romans 13:5.

86 Matthew 22:21.

87 Romans 13:1–7.

"in the sight of God our Saviour."[88] Here St. Paul maketh an earnest and an especial exhortation concerning giving of thanks and prayer for kings and rulers, saying, "Above all things," as he might say, in any wise principally and chiefly, "let prayer be made for kings." Let us heartily thank God for his great and excellent benefit and providence concerning the state of kings. Let us pray for them that they may have God's favour and God's protection. Let us pray that they may ever in all things have God before their eyes. Let us pray that they may have wisdom, strength, justice, clemency, and zeal to God's glory, to God's verity, to Christian souls, and to the commonwealth. Let us pray that they may rightly use their sword and authority for the maintenance and defence of the catholic[89] faith contained in holy Scripture and of their good and honest subjects, for the fear and punishment of the evil and vicious people. Let us pray that they may most faithfully follow the kings and captains in the Bible, David, Ezekias,[90] Josias, and Moses, with such other. And let us pray for ourselves that we may live godly in holy and Christian conversation: so shall we have God of our side; and then let us not fear what man can do against us: so we shall live in true obedience, both to our most merciful King in Heaven, and to our most Christian Queen in earth: so shall we please God, and have the exceeding benefit, peace of conscience, rest, and quietness, here in this world; and after this life we shall enjoy a better life, rest, peace, and the everlasting bliss of heaven. Which he grant us all that was "obedient" for us all, "even to the death of the cross,"[91] Jesus Christ: to whom with the Father and the Holy Ghost be all honour and glory both now and ever. Amen.

AN INFORMATION FOR THEM WHICH TAKE OFFENCE AT CERTAIN PLACES OF THE HOLY SCRIPTURE (1563)

The first part

The great utility and profit that Christian men and women may take, if they will, by hearing and reading the holy Scriptures, dearly beloved, no heart can sufficiently conceive, much less is any tongue able with words to express. Wherefore Satan, our old enemy, seeing the Scriptures to be the very mean[92] and right way to bring the people to the true knowledge of God, and that Christian religion is greatly furthered by diligent hearing and reading of them, he also, perceiving what an hindrance and let they be to him and his kingdom, doeth what he can to drive the reading of them out of God's Church. And for that end he hath always stirred up, in one place or other, cruel tyrants, sharp persecutors, and extreme enemies unto God and his infallible truth, to pull with violence the holy Bibles out of the people's hands, and have most spitefully destroyed and consumed the same to ashes in the fire, pretending, most untruly, that the much hearing and reading of God's word is an occasion of heresy and carnal liberty,[93] and the overthrow of all good order in all well-ordered commonwealths.

If to know God aright be an occasion of evil, then we must needs grant, that the hearing and reading of the holy Scriptures is the cause of heresy, carnal liberty, and the subversion of all good orders. But the knowledge of God and of ourselves is so far off from being an occasion of evil, that it is the readiest, yea, the only mean to bridle carnal liberty, and to kill all our fleshly affections. And the ordinary way to attain this knowledge is with diligence to hear and read the holy Scriptures. For "the whole Scriptures" saith St. Paul, "were given by the inspiration of God:"[94] and shall we Christian men think to learn the knowledge of God and of ourselves in any earthly man's work of writing sooner or better than in the holy Scriptures written by the inspiration of the Holy Ghost? "The Scriptures were not brought unto us by the will of man; but holy men of God," as

---

88   1 Timothy 2: 1–3.

89   In this context, the adjective "catholic" refers to the whole body of Christians (of all denominations); the word originally meant "universal."

90   An obsolete spelling of Hezekiah. He and Josias were both virtuous kings of Judah (see 2 Kings). The latter was noted for repairing the

temple and reforming the worship of God in his kingdom, and is thus a useful model for a Protestant sermon.

91   Philippians 2:8.

92   *commonly held*.

93   See note 43 above.

94   2 Timothy 3:16.

witnesseth St. Peter, "spake as they were moved by the holy spirit of God."[95] The Holy Ghost is the Schoolmaster of truth, which leadeth his scholars, as our Saviour Christ saith of him, "into all truth."[96] And whoso is not led and taught by this schoolmaster cannot but fall into deep error, how godly soever his pretence is, what knowledge and learning soever he hath of all other works and writings, or how fair soever a show or face of truth he hath in the estimation and judgement of the world.

If some man will say, I would have a true pattern and a perfect description of an upright life approved in the sight of God, can we find, think ye, any better, or any such again, as Christ Jesus is, and his doctrine? Whose virtuous conversation and godly life the Scripture so lively painteth and setteth forth before our eyes, that we, beholding that pattern, might shape and frame our lives, as nigh as may be, agreeable to the perfection of the same. "Follow you me," saith St. Paul, "as I follow Christ."[97] And St. John in his Epistle saith, "Whoso abideth in Christ must walk even so as he hath walked before him."[98] And where shall we learn the order of Christ's life but in the Scripture?

Another would have a medicine to heal all diseases and maladies of the mind. Can this be found or gotten otherwhere than out of God's own book, his sacred Scriptures? Christ taught so much, when he said to the obstinate Jews, "Search the Scriptures, for in them ye think to have eternal life."[99] If the Scriptures contain in them everlasting life, it must needs follow, that they have also present remedy against all that is an hindrance and let unto eternal life.

If we desire the knowledge of heavenly wisdom, why had we rather learn the same of man than of God himself, who, as St. James saith, is the giver of wisdom?[100] Yea, why will we not learn it at Christ's own mouth, who, promising to be present with his Church till the world's end,[101] doth perform his promise in that he is not only with us by his grace and tender pity, but also in this, that he speaketh presently unto us in the holy Scriptures, to the great and endless comfort of all them that have any feeling of God at all in them? Yea, he speaketh now in the Scriptures more profitably to us, than he did by the word of mouth to the carnal Jews, when he lived with them here upon earth. For they, I mean the Jews, could neither hear nor see those things which we may now both hear and see, if we will bring with us those ears and eyes that Christ is heard and seen with, that is, diligence to hear and read his holy Scriptures, and true faith to believe his most comfortable promises.

If one could show but the print of Christ's foot, a great number, I think, would fall down and worship it: but to the holy Scriptures, where we may see daily, if we will, I will not say the print of his feet only, but the whole shape and lively image of him, alas, we give little reverence, or none at all. If any could let us see Christ's coat, a sort of us would make hard shift[102] except we might come nigh to gaze upon it, yea, and kiss it too: and yet all the clothes that ever he did wear can nothing so truly nor so lively express him unto us, as do the Scriptures. Christ's images made in wood, stone, or metal, some men, for the love they bear to Christ, do garnish and beautify the same with pearl, gold, and precious stone: and should we not, good brethren, much rather embrace and reverence God's holy books, the sacred Bible, which do represent Christ unto us more truly than can any image? The image can but express the form or shape of his body, if it can do so much: but the Scriptures do in such sort set forth Christ, that we may see both God and man; we may see him, I say, speaking unto us, healing our infirmities, dying for our sins, rising from death for our justification. And, to be short, we may in the Scriptures so perfectly see whole Christ with the eye of faith.[103] As we, lacking faith, could not with these bodily eyes see him, though he stood now present here before us.

Let every man, woman, and child therefore, with all their heart thirst and desire God's holy Scriptures, love them, embrace them, have their delight and pleasure in hearing and reading them;

95   2 Peter 1:21.
96   John 16:13.
97   1 Corinthians 11:1.
98   1 John 2:6.
99   John 5:39.

100   James 1:5.
101   Matthew 28:20.
102   *extraordinary measures.*
103   See Luke 11:34.

so as at length we may be transformed and changed into them. For the holy Scriptures are God's treasure house, wherein are found all things needful for us to see, to hear, to learn, and to believe, necessary for the attaining of eternal life.

Thus much is spoken, only to give you a taste of some of the commodities which ye may take by hearing and reading the holy Scriptures; for, as I said in the beginning, no tongue is able to declare and utter all. And, although it is more clear than the noon day that to be ignorant of the Scriptures is the cause of error, as Christ saith to the Saducees, "Ye err, not knowing the Scriptures;"[104] and that error doth hold back and pluck men away from the knowledge of God; and, as St. Jerome saith, "not to know the Scriptures, is to be ignorant of Christ":[105] yet, this notwithstanding, some there be that think it not meet for all sorts of men to read the Scriptures, because they are, as they think, in sundry places stumbling blocks to the unlearned; first, for that the phrase of the Scriptures is sometime so homely, gross, and plain, that it offendeth the fine and delicate wits of some courtiers; furthermore, for that the Scripture also reporteth, even of them that have their commendation to be the children of God, that they did divers acts, whereof some are contrary to the law of nature, some repugnant to the law written, and other some seem to fight manifestly against public honesty; all which things, say they, are unto the simple an occasion of great offence, and cause many to think evil of the Scriptures, and to discredit their authority. Some are offended at the hearing and reading of the diversity of the rites and ceremonies of the sacrifices and oblations of the Law. And some worldly witted men, think it a great decay to the quiet and prudent governing of their commonwealths to give ear to the simple and plain rules and precepts of our Saviour Christ in his Gospel; as being offended that a man should be ready to turn his right ear to him that strake him on the left, and to him which would take away his coat, to offer him also his cloak,[106] with such other sayings of perfection in Christ's meaning; for carnal reason,[107] being always an enemy to God, and not perceiving the things of God's Spirit, doth abhor such precepts;[108] which yet rightly understood infringeth no judicial policies, nor Christian men's governments. And some there be, which hearing the Scriptures to bid us to live without carefulness,[109] without study or forecasting, do deride the simplicity of them. Therefore, to remove and put away occasions of offence, so much as may be, I will answer orderly to these objections.

First, I shall rehearse some of those places that men are offended at for the homeliness and grossness of speech, and will show the meaning of them.

In the Book of Deuteronomy it is written, that Almighty God made a law, if a man died without issue, his brother or next kinsman should marry his widow, and the child that was first borne between them should be called his child that was dead, that the dead man's name might not be put out in Israel; and if the brother or next kinsman would not marry the widow, then she before the magistrates of the city should pull off his shoe and spit in his face, saying, "So be it done to that man that will not build his brother's house."[110] Here, dearly beloved, the pulling off his shoe and spitting in his face were ceremonies, to signify unto all the people of that city, that the woman was not now in fault that God's law in that point was broken, but the whole shame and blame thereof did now redound to that man, which openly before the magistrates refused to marry her: and it was not a reproach to him alone, but to all his posterity also; for they were called ever after, "The house of him whose shoe is pulled off."

Another place out of the Psalms. "I will break," saith David, "the horns of the ungodly, and the horns of the righteous shall be exalted."[111] By "an horn" in the Scripture is understood power, might, strength, and sometime rule and government. The Prophet then saying, "I will break the horns of the ungodly," meaneth, that all the power, strength, and might of God's enemies shall not only be weakened and made feeble, but shall at length also be clean broken and destroyed; though for a time, for the better trial of his people, God suffereth the enemies to prevail and have the upper

---

104 Matthew 22:29.
105 From the *Commentary on the Prophet Isaiah* 1.1.
106 Matthew 5:39–40.
107 i.e. worldly or unregenerate reason. See note 43 above.
108 Romans 8:7; 1 Corinthians 2:14.
109 i.e. care for the future. See Matthew 6:25–34.
110 Deuteronomy 25:5–9.
111 Psalms 75:10.

hand. In the hundred and thirty-second Psalm it is said, "I will make David's horn to flourish."[112] Here "David's horn" signifieth his kingdom. Almighty God therefore by this manner of speaking promiseth to give David victory over all his enemies, and to stablish him in his kingdom spite[113] of all his enemies.

And in the threescore Psalm it is written, "Moab is my washpot, and over Edom will I cast my shoe," etc.[114] In that place the Prophet showeth how graciously God hath dealt with his people, the children of Israel, giving them great victories upon their enemies on every side. For, the Moabites and Idumeans being two great nations, proud people, stout and mighty, God brought them under and made them servants to the Israelites; servants, I say, to stoop down, to pull off their shoes and wash their feet. Then, "Moab is my washpot, and over Edom will I cast out my shoe," is as if he had said, The Moabites and the Idumeans, for all their stoutness against us in the wilderness, are now made our subjects, our servants, yea, underlings to pull off our shoes and wash our feet. Now, I pray you, what uncomely manner of speech is this, so used in common phrase among the Hebrews? It is a shame that Christian men should be so light headed, to toy as ruffians do of such manner speeches, uttered in good grave signification by the Holy Ghost. More reasonable it were for vain man to learn to reverence the form of God's words, than to gaud at them[115] to their damnation.

Some again are offended to hear that the godly fathers had many wives and concubines, although after the phrase of the Scripture a concubine is an honest name;[116] for every concubine is a lawful wife, but every wife is not a concubine. And, that ye may the better understand this to be true, ye shall note that it was permitted to the fathers of the Old Testament to have at one time more wives than one: for what purpose ye shall afterward hear. Of which wives, some were free women born, some were bond-women and servants. She that was free born had a prerogative above those that were servants and bond-women. The free-born woman was by marriage made the ruler of the house under her husband, and is called the mother of the household, the mistress or the dame of the house after our manner of speaking, and had by her marriage an interest, a right, and an ownership of his goods unto whom she was married. Other servants and bond-women were given by the owners of them, as the manner was then, I will not say always, but for the most part, unto their daughters at that day of their marriage, to be handmaidens unto them. After such a sort did Pharaoh King of Egypt give unto Sarah, Abraham's wife, Hagar the Egyptian to be her maid. So did Laban give unto his daughter Leah, at the day of her marriage, Zilpah, to be her handmaid; and to his other daughter Rachel, he gave another handmaid, named Bilhah.[117] And the wives, that were the owners of their handmaid, gave them in marriage to their husbands upon divers occasions. Sarah gave her maid Hagar in marriage to Abraham.[118] Leah gave in like manner her maid Zilpah to her husband Jacob. So did Rachel, his other wife, give him Bilhah, her maid, saying unto him, "Go in unto her, and she shall bear upon my knees":[119] which is as if she had said, Take her to wife, and the children that she shall bear will I take upon my lap, and make of them as if they were mine own. These handmaidens or bondwomen, although by marriage they were made wives, yet they had not this prerogative, to rule in the house, but were still underlings, and in subjection to their mistress, and were never called mothers of the household, mistresses, or dames of the house, but are called sometimes wives, sometime concubines. The plurality of wives was by a special prerogative suffered to the fathers of the Old Testament, not for satisfying their carnal and fleshly lust, but to have many children; because every one of them hoped, and begged oft times of God in their prayers, that that blessed seed, which God promised should come into the world to break the serpent's head[120] might come and be born of his stock and kindred.

---

112   Psalms 132:17.
113   i.e. in spite.
114   Psalms 60:8.
115   i.e. make sport of them.
116   Concubines were legally recognized by the laws of the ancient Hebrews; they were, in effect, "secondary wives."

117   Genesis 29:24, 29.
118   Genesis 16:3.
119   Genesis 30:3.
120   See Genesis 3:15.

Now of those which take occasion of carnality and evil life by hearing and reading in God's book what God had suffered, even in those men whose commendation is praised in the Scripture. As that Noah, whom St. Peter calleth the eighth "preacher of righteousness,"[121] was so drunk with wine, that in his sleep he uncovered his own privities.[122] The just man Lot was in like manner drunken, and in his drunkenness lay with his own daughters, contrary to the law of nature.[123] Abraham, whose faith was so great, that for the same he deserved to be called of God's own mouth, "a father of many nations, the father of all believers,"[124] besides with Sarah his wife, had also carnal company with Hagar, Sarah's handmaid. The patriarch Jacob had to his wives two sisters at one time.[125] The Prophet David, and king Solomon his son, had many wives and concubines etc.[126] Which things we see plainly to be forbidden us by the law of God, and are now repugnant to all public honesty. These and such like in God's book, good people, are not written that we should or may do the like, following their examples, or that we ought to think that God did allow every of these things in those men: but we ought rather to believe and to judge, that Noah in his drunkenness offended God highly. Lot lying with his daughters committed horrible incest. We ought then to learn by them this profitable lesson, that, if so godly men as they were, which otherwise felt inwardly God's Holy Spirit inflaming in their hearts with the fear and love of God, could not by their own strength keep themselves from committing horrible sin, but did so grievously fall that without God's great mercy they had perished everlastingly, how much more ought we then, miserable wretches, which have no feeling of God within us at all, continually to fear, not only that we may fall as they did, but also be overcome and drowned in sin, which they were not; and so by considering their fall, take the better occasion to acknowledge our own infirmity and weakness, and therefore more earnestly to call unto Almighty God with hearty prayer incessantly for his grace to strengthen us, and to defend us from all evil. And, though through infirmity we chance at any time to fall, yet we may, by hearty repentance and true faith, speedily rise again, and not sleep and continue in sin, as the wicked doth.

Thus, good people, should we understand such matters expressed in the divine Scriptures, that this holy "table" of God's word be not turned to us to be "a snare, a trap, and a stumbling-stone,"[127] to take hurt by the abuse of our understanding: but let us esteem them in such a reverent humility, that we may find our necessary food therein, to strengthen us, to comfort us, to instruct us, as God of his great mercy hath appointed them, in all necessary works; so that we may be perfect before him in the whole course of our life. Which he grant us who hath redeemed us, our Lord and Saviour Jesus Christ: to whom with the Father and the Holy Ghost be all honour and glory for evermore. Amen.

The second part of the information for them which take offence at certain places of the holy Scripture

Ye have heard, good people, in the Homily last read unto you, the great commodity of holy Scriptures: ye have heard how ignorant men, void of godly understanding, seek quarrels to discredit them: some of their reasons have ye heard answered. Now we will proceed, and speak of such politic wise men which be offended, for that Christ's precepts should seem to destroy all order in governance, as they do allege for example such as these be: "If any man strike thee on the right cheek, turn the other unto him also.[128] If any man will contend to take thy coat from thee, let him have cloak and all.[129] Let not thy left hand know what thy right hand doth. If thine eye, thine hand, or thy foot offend thee, pull out thine eye, cut off thine hand, thy foot, and cast it from thee.[130] If thine enemy," saith St. Paul, "be anhungered, give him meat, if he be thirsty, give him drink: so

---

121 2 Peter 2:5.
122 Genesis 9:21.
123 Genesis 19:30–36.
124 Genesis 17:4–6; Romans 4:11–18.
125 Genesis 29:23–30.

126 2 Samuel 3:2–5; 5:13; 1 Kings 11:1–3.
127 Psalms 69:22.
128 Matthew 5:39–40.
129 Matthew 5:40.
130 Matthew 18:8–9.

doing, thou shalt heap hot burning coals upon his head."[131] These sentences, good people, unto a natural[132] man seem mere absurdities, contrary to all reason. "For a natural man, as St. Paul saith, "understandeth not the things that belong to God, neither can he" so long as old Adam dwelleth in him.[133] Christ therefore meaneth, that he would have his faithful servants so far from vengeance and resisting wrong, that he would rather have him ready to suffer another wrong, than by resisting to break charity, and to be out of patience. He would have our good deeds so far from all carnal respects, that he would not have our nighest friends know of our well doing, to win vain glory. And though our friends and kinsfolk be as dear as our right eyes and our right hands, yet, if they would pluck us from God, we ought to renounce them and forsake them.

Thus, if ye will be profitable hearers and readers of the holy Scriptures, ye must first deny yourselves, and keep under your carnal senses, taken by the outward words, and search the inward meaning; reason must give place to God's Holy Spirit; you must submit your worldly wisdom and judgement unto his divine wisdom and judgement. Consider that the Scripture, in what strange form soever it be pronounced, is the word of the living God. Let that always come to your remembrance, which is so oft repeated of the prophet Esaias:[134] "The mouth of the Lord," saith he, "hath spoken it." The almighty and everlasting "God, who" with his only word "created heaven and earth," hath decreed it. "The Lord of Hosts, whose ways are in the seas, whose paths are in the deep waters,"[135] that Lord and God by whose word all things in heaven and in earth are created, governed, and preserved, hath so provided it. "The God of gods, and Lord of all lords," yea, God that is "God alone,"[136] incomprehensible, almighty, and everlasting, he hath spoken it: it is his word. It cannot therefore be but truth, which proceedeth from the God of all truth; it cannot be but wisely and prudently commanded, what Almighty God hath devised; how vainly soever, through want of grace, we miserable wretches do imagine and judge of his most holy word.

The Prophet David, describing an happy man, saith: "Blessed is the man that doth not walk after the counsel of the ungodly, nor stand in the way of sinners, nor sit in the seat of the scornful."[137] There are three sorts of people, whose company the prophet would have him to flee and avoid which shall be an happy man and partaker of God's blessing. First, he may not "walk after the counsel of the ungodly." Secondly, he may not "stand in the way of sinners." Thirdly, he must not "sit in the seat of the scornful." By these three sorts of people, "ungodly men," "sinners," and "scorners," all impiety is signified and fully expressed. By the "ungodly" he understandeth those which have no regard of Almighty God, being void of all faith, whose hearts and minds are so set upon the world, that they study only how to accomplish their worldly practices, their carnal imaginations, their filthy lust and desire, without any fear of God. The second sort he calleth "sinners": not such as do fall through ignorance or of frailness; for then who should be found free? What man ever lived upon earth, Christ only excepted, but he hath sinned? "The just man falleth seven times, and riseth again."[138] Though the godly do fall, yet they walk not on purposely in sin; they stand not still to continue and tarry in sin; they sit not down like careless men, without all fear of God's just punishment for sin; but defying sin, through God's great grace and infinite mercy, they rise again, and fight against sin. The prophet then calleth them "sinners" whose hearts are clean turned from God, and whose whole conversation of life is nothing but sin: they delight so much in the same, that they choose continually to abide and dwell in sin. The third sort he calleth "scorners," that is, a sort of men whose hearts are so stuffed with malice, that they are not contented to dwell in sin, and to lead their lives in all kind of wickedness, but also they do contemn and scorn in other all godliness, true religion, all honesty and virtue.

Of the two first sorts of men, I will not say but they may take repentance, and be converted unto God. Of the third sort, I think I may, without danger of God's judgement, pronounce, that never any yet converted unto God by repentance, but continued still in their abominable wicked-

---

131   Romans 12:20.
132   i.e. in an unregenerate state of nature; unenlightened.
133   1 Corinthians 2:14.
134   A variant of "Isaiah."

135   Psalms 77:19; Isaiah 43:16; 51:15; 54:5; 2 Peter 3:5, 7.
136   Deuteronomy 10:17; Psalms 86:10.
137   Psalms 1:1.
138   Proverbs 24:16.

ness, heaping up to themselves damnation, against the day of God's inevitable judgement. Examples of such scorners we read of in the second book of Chronicles.[139] When the good king Hezekiah in the beginning of his reign had destroyed idolatry, purged the temple, and reformed religion in his realm, he sent messengers into every city, to gather the people unto Jerusalem, to solemnise the feast of Easter in such sort as God had appointed. "The posts went from city to city, through the land of Ephraim and Manasses even unto Zabulon."[140] And what did the people, think ye? Did they laud and praise the name of the Lord, which had given them so good a king, so zealous a prince to abolish idolatry, and to restore again God's true religion? No, no. The Scripture saith, "The people laughed them to scorn, and mocked the king's messengers." And in the last chapter of the same book it is written, that Almighty "God, having compassion upon his people, sent his messengers, the prophets, unto them," to call them from their abominable idolatry and wicked kind of living. "But they mocked his messengers, they despised his words, and misused his prophets, until the wrath of the Lord arose against his people, and till there was no remedy":[141] for he gave them up into the hands of their enemies, even unto Nebuchadnezzar king of Babylon, who spoiled them of their goods, burnt their city, and led them, their wives, and their children, captives unto Babylon. The wicked people that were in the days of Noah made but a mock at the word of God, when Noah told them that God would take vengeance upon them for their sins. The flood therefore came suddenly upon them, and drowned them, with the whole world. Lot preached to the Sodomites, that, except they repented, both they and their city should be destroyed. They thought his sayings impossible to be true, they scorned and mocked his admonition, and reputed him as an old doting fool. But, when God by his holy angels had taken Lot, his wife, and two daughters from among them, he rained down fire and brimstone from heaven, and burnt up those scorners and mockers of his holy word. And what estimation had Christ's doctrine among the Scribes and Pharisees? What reward had he among them? The Gospel reporteth thus: "The Pharisees, which were covetous, did scorn him in his doctrine."[142] O then ye see that worldly rich men scorn the doctrine of their salvation. The worldly wise men scorn the doctrine of Christ, as foolishness to their understanding. These scorners have ever been, and ever shall be to the world's end. For St. Peter prophesied, that such scorners should be in the world before the latter day.[143] Take heed therefore, my brethren, take heed. Be ye not scorners of God's most holy word. Provoke him not to pour out his wrath now upon you, as he did then upon those gibers and mockers. Be not wilful murderers of your own souls. Turn unto God while there is yet time of mercy: ye shall else repent it in the world to come, when it shall be too late; for there shall be "judgement without mercy."[144]

This might suffice to admonish us, and cause us henceforth to reverence God's holy Scriptures: but "all men have not faith."[145] This therefore shall not satisfy and content all men's minds; but, as some are carnal, so they will still continue, and abuse the Scriptures carnally to their greater damnation. "The unlearned and unstable," saith St. Peter, "pervert the holy Scriptures to their own destruction."[146] Jesus Christ, as St. Paul saith, "is to the Jews an offence, to the Gentiles foolishness; but to God's children, as well of the Jews as of the Gentiles, he is the power and wisdom of God."[147] The holy man Simeon saith, "that he is set forth for the fall and rising again of many in Israel."[148] As Christ Jesus is a fall to the reprobate, which yet perish through their own default, so is his word, yea, the whole book of God, a cause of damnation unto them through their incredulity. And, as he is a rising up to none other than those which are God's children by adoption, so is his word, yea, the whole Scripture, "the power of God to salvation to them" only "that do believe it."[149] Christ himself, the Prophets before him, the Apostles after him, all the true Ministers of

139 2 Chronicles 30:1–10.
140 Usually spelled "Zebulon" today.
141 2 Chronicles 36:15–20.
142 Luke 16:14.
143 2 Peter 3:3–4.
144 James 2:13.

145 2 Thessalonians 3:2.
146 2 Peter 3:16.
147 1 Corinthians 1:23–24.
148 Luke 2:34.
149 Romans 1:16.

God's holy word, yea, every word in God's book, is unto the reprobate "the savour of death unto death."[150] Christ Jesus, the Prophets, the Apostles, and all the true ministers of his word, yea, every jot and tittle in the holy Scripture, have been, is, and shall be for evermore "the savour of life unto" eternal "life" unto all those whose hearts God hath purified by true faith. Let us earnestly take heed that we make no jesting stock of the books of holy Scriptures. The more obscure and dark the sayings be to our understanding, the further let us think ourselves to be from God and his Holy Spirit, who was the Author of them. Let us with more reverence endeavour ourselves to search out the wisdom hidden in the outward bark of the Scripture. If we can not understand the sense and the reason of the saying, yet let us not be scorners, jesters, and deriders; for that is the uttermost token and show of a reprobate, of a plain enemy to God and his wisdom. They be not idle fables to jest at, which God doth seriously pronounce; and for serious matters let us esteem them.

And though in sundry places of the Scriptures be set out divers rites and ceremonies, oblations[151] and sacrifices, let us not think strange of them, but refer them to the times and people for whom they served; although yet to learned men they be not unprofitable to be considered, but to be expounded as figures and shadows[152] of things and persons afterward openly revealed in the New Testament. Though the rehearsal of the genealogies and pedigrees of the fathers be not to much edification of the plain ignorant people, yet is there nothing so impertinently uttered in all the whole book of the Bible, but may serve to spiritual purpose in some respect to all such as will bestow their labours to search out the meanings. These may not be condemned because they serve not to our understanding, nor make to our edification. But let us turn our labour to understand, and to carry away, such sentences and stories as be more fit for our capacity and instruction.

And, whereas we read in divers Psalms how David did wish to the adversaries of God sometimes shame, rebuke, and confusion, sometime the decay of their offspring and issue, sometime that they might perish and come suddenly to destruction,[153] (as he did wish to the Captains of the Philistines, "Cast forth," saith he, "thy lightning, and tear them; shoot out thine arrows and consume them;")[154] with such other manner of imprecations; yet ought we not to be offended at such prayers of David, being a Prophet as he was, singularly beloved of God, and rapt in spirit, with an ardent zeal to God's glory. He spake them not as of a private hatred and in a stomach[155] against their persons, but wished spiritually the destruction of such corrupt errors and vices, which reigned in all devilish persons set against God. He was of like mind as St. Paul was, when he did deliver Hymeneus and Alexander with the notorious fornicator to Satan to their temporal confusion, "that their spirit might be saved against the day of the Lord."[156] And, when David did profess in some places that he hated the wicked, yet in other places of his Psalms he professeth that he hated them "with a perfect hate," not with a malicious hate to the hurt of the soul. Which perfection of spirit, because it cannot be performed in us, so corrupted in affections as we be, we ought not to use in our private causes the like words in form, for that we cannot fulfil the like words in sense. Let us not therefore be offended, but search out the reason of such words before we be offended; that we may the more reverently judge of such sayings, though strange to our carnal understandings, yet, to them that be spiritually minded, judged to be zealously and godly pronounced.

God therefore, for his mercy's sake, vouchsafe to purify our minds through faith in his Son Jesus Christ, and to instill the heavenly drops of his grace into our hard stony hearts, to supple the same; that we be not contemners and deriders of his infallible word, but that with all humbleness of mind and Christian reverence we may endeavour ourselves to hear and to read his sacred Scriptures, and inwardly so to digest them, as shall be to the comfort of our souls and sanctification of his holy Name. To whom with the Son and the Holy Ghost, three persons and one living God, be all laud, honour, and praise for ever and ever. Amen.

---

150   2 Corinthians 2:16.
151   i.e. presentations to God.
152   *reflected images.*
153   Psalms 35:4, 8, 26; 68:30; 109:13.

154   Psalms 144:6.
155   i.e. in a rage.
156   1 Timothy 1:20; 1 Corinthians 5:5.

AN HOMILY OF THE STATE OF MATRIMONY (1563)[157]

The word of Almighty God doth testify and declare whence the original beginning of matrimony cometh, and why it is ordained. It is instituted of God, to the intent that man and woman should live lawfully in a perpetual friendly fellowship, to bring forth fruit, and to avoid fornication: by which means a good conscience might be preserved on both parties in bridling the corrupt inclinations of the flesh within the limits of honesty; for God hath straitly forbidden all whoredom and uncleanness, and hath from time to time taken grievous punishment of this inordinate lust, as all stories and ages have declared. Furthermore, it is also ordained, that the Church of God and his kingdom might by this kind of life be conserved and enlarged, not only in that God giveth children by his blessing, but also in that they be brought up by the parents godly in the knowledge of God's word; that thus the knowledge of God and true religion might be delivered by succession from one to another, that finally many might enjoy that everlasting immortality.

Wherefore, forasmuch as matrimony serveth us as well to avoid sin and offence as to increase the kingdom of God, you, as all other which enter the state, must acknowledge this benefit of God with pure and thankful minds, for that he hath so ruled your hearts that ye follow not the example of the wicked world, who set their delight in filthiness of sin, but both of you stand in the fear of God, and abhor all filthiness. For that is surely the singular gift of God, where the common example of the world declareth how the devil hath their hearts bound and entangled in divers[158] snares, so that they in their wifeless state run into open abominations without any grudge of their conscience. Which sort of men that live so desperately and filthily, what damnation tarieth for them Saint Paul describeth it to them, saying, "Neither whoremongers neither adulterers shall inherit the kingdom of God."[159] This horrible judgement of God ye be escaped through his mercy, if so be that ye live inseparately according to God's ordinance.

But yet I would not have you careless, without watching. For the devil will assay to attempt all things to interrupt and hinder your hearts and godly purpose, if ye will give him any entry. For he will either labour to break this godly knot once begun betwixt you, or else at the least he will labour to encumber it with divers griefs and displeasures. And this is the principal craft, to work dissension of hearts of the one from the other; that whereas now there is pleasant and sweet love betwixt you, he will in the stead thereof bring in most bitter and unpleasant discord. And surely that same adversary of ours doth, as it were from above, assault man's nature and condition. For this folly is ever from our tender age grown up with us, to have a desire to rule, to think highly by ourself, so that none thinketh it meet to give place to another. That wicked vice of stubborn will and self love is more meet to break and to dissever the love of heart, than to preserve concord. Wherefore married persons must apply their minds in most earnest wise to concord, and must crave continually of God the help of his holy Spirit, so to rule their hearts, and to knit their minds together, that they be not dissevered by any division of discord.

This necessity of prayer must be oft in the occupying and using of married persons, that oft times the one should pray for the other, lest hate and debate do arise betwixt them. And because few do consider this thing, but more few do perform it, (I say, to pray diligently), we see how wonderfully the devil deludeth and scorneth this state, how few Matrimonies there be without chidings, brawlings, tauntings, repentings, bitter cursings, and fightings. Which things whosoever doth commit, they do not consider that it is the instigation of the ghostly enemy, who taketh great delight therein: for else they would with all earnest endeavour strive against these mischiefs, not only with prayer, but also with all possible diligence; yea they would not give place to the provocation of wrath, which stirreth them either to such rough and sharp words or stripes,[160] which is

---

157 This is one of the clearest articulations of conventional gender roles in Early Modern England. It is especially notable for the overt way in which a husband's authority over his wife is analogized to a monarch's rule over the state. While hardly unique in this, it makes clear how seriously gender conformity was taken and the extent to which any derogation from this norm was seen as a political threat to the stability of the culture as a whole.

158 *various*.

159 1 Corinthians 6:9.

160 i.e. blows from a whip or other weapon.

surely compassed by the devil: whose temptation, if it be followed, must needs begin and weave the web of all miseries and sorrows. For this is most certainly true, that of such beginnings must needs ensue the breach of true concord in heart, whereby all love must needs shortly be banished. Then can it not be but a miserable thing to behold, that yet they are of necessity compelled to live together, which yet cannot be in quiet together. And this is most customably[161] everywhere to be seen. But what is the cause thereof? Forsooth, because they will not consider the crafty trains of the devil, and therefore give not themselves to pray to God that he would vouchsafe to repress his power. Moreover, they do not consider how they promote the purpose of the devil, in that they follow the wrath of their hearts, while they threat one another, while they in their folly turn all upside down, while they will never give over their right, as they esteem it, yea, while many times they will not give over the wrong part indeed. Learn thou therefore, if thou desirest to be void of all these miseries, if thou desirest to live peaceably and comfortably in wedlock, how to make thy earnest prayer to God, that he would govern both your hearts by his holy Spirit, to restrain the devil's power, whereby your concord may remain perpetually.

But to this prayer must be joined a singular diligence, whereof Saint Peter giveth his precept, saying, "You husbands, deal with your wives according to knowledge, giving honour unto the wife, as unto the weaker vessel, and as unto them that are heirs also of the grace of life, that your prayers be not hindered."[162] This precept doth particularly pertain to the husband: for he ought to be the leader and author of love in cherishing and increasing concord; which then shall take place, if he will use measureableness[163] and not tyranny, and if he yield some things to the woman. For the woman is a weak creature, not endued[164] with like strength and constancy of mind: therefore they be the sooner disquieted, and they be the more prone to all weak affections and dispositions of mind, more than men be; and lighter they be and more vain in their fantasies[165] and opinions. These things must be considered of the man, that he be not too stiff; so that he ought to wink at some things, and must gently expound all things, and to forbear.

Howbeit the common sort of men doth judge that such moderation should not become a man: For they say that it is a token of womanish cowardice, and therefore they think that it is a man's part to fume in anger, to fight with fist and staff. Howbeit, howsoever they imagine, undoubtedly Saint Peter doth better judge what should be seeming to a man, and what he should most reasonably perform. For he saith reasoning should be used, and not fighting. Yea, he saith more, that the woman ought to have a certain "honour" attributed to her; that is to say, she must be spared and borne with, the rather for that she is "the weaker vessel," of a frail heart, inconstant, and with a word soon stirred to wrath. And therefore, considering these her frailties, she is to be the rather spared. By this means thou shalt not only nourish concord, but shalt have her heart in thy power and will; for honest natures will sooner be retained to do their duties rather by gentle words, than by stripes. But he which will do all things with extremity and severity, and doth use always rigor in words and stripes, what will that avail in the conclusion? Verily nothing but that he thereby setteth forward the devil's work; he banisheth away concord, charity, and sweet amity, and bringeth in dissension, hatred, and irksomeness, the greatest griefs that can be in the mutual love and fellowship of man's life. Beyond all this, it bringeth another evil therewith; for it is the destruction and interruption of prayer. For in the time that the mind is occupied with dissension and discord there can be no true prayer used. For the Lord's prayer hath not only a respect to particular persons, but to the whole universal; in the which we openly pronounce that we will forgive them which have offended against us, even as we ask forgiveness of our sins of God. Which thing how can it be done rightly, when their hearts be at dissension? How can they pray each for other, when they be at hate betwixt themselves? Now, if the aid of prayer be taken away, by what means can they sustain themselves in any comfort? For they cannot otherwise either resist the devil, or yet have their hearts stayed in stable comfort in all perils and necessities, but by prayer. Thus all discommodities,[166] as well worldly as ghostly, follow this froward testiness and cumbrous fierceness in

161   *habitually.*
162   1 Peter 3:7.
163   *moderation.*

164   *endowed.*
165   *whimsies.*
166   *disadvantages.*

manners; which be more meet for brute beasts than for reasonable creatures. Saint Peter doth not allow these things, but the devil desireth them gladly. Wherefore take the more heed. And yet a man may be a man, although he doth not use such extremity, yea, though he should dissemble some things in his wife's manners. And this is the part of a Christian man, which both pleaseth God, and serveth also in good use to the comfort of their marriage state.

Now as concerning the wife's duty. What shall become her? Shall she abuse the gentleness and humanity of her husband and, at her pleasure turn all things upside down? No surely; for that is far repugnant against God's commandment, For thus doth Saint Peter preach to them, "Ye wives, be ye in subjection to obey your own husbands."[167] To obey is another thing than to control or command; which yet they may do to their children and to their family; but as for their husbands, them must they obey, and cease from commanding, and perform subjection. For this surely doth nourish concord very much, when the wife is ready at hand at her husband's commandment, when she will apply herself to his will, when she endevoureth herself to seek his contentation and to do him pleasure, when she will eschew all things that might offend him. For thus will most truly be verified the saying of the Poet, "A good wife by obeying her husband, shall bear the rule": so that he shall have a delight and a gladness the sooner at all times to return home to her. But on the contrary part, when the wives be stubborn, froward, and malapert,[168] their husbands are compelled thereby to abhor and flee from their own houses, even as they should have battle with their enemies.

Howbeit, it can scantly be but that some offences shall sometime chance betwixt them: for no man doth live without fault; specially for that the woman is the more frail part. Therefore let them beware that they stand not in their faults and wilfulness; but rather let them acknowledge their follies, and say, My husband, so it is, that by my anger I was compelled to do this or that: forgive it me, and hereafter I will take better heed. Thus ought the woman more readily to do, the more they be ready to offend. And they shall not do this only to avoid strife and debate, but rather in the respect of the commandment of God, as Saint Paul expresseth it in this form of words: "Let women be subject to their husbands, as to the Lord: for the husband is the head of the woman, as Christ is the head of the Church."[169] Here you understand that God hath commanded that ye should acknowledge the authority of the husband, and refer to him the honour of obedience. And Saint Peter saith in that place before rehearsed, that "holy matrons did in former time deck themselves," not with gold and silver, but in "putting their whole hope in God," and in "obeying their husbands, as Sara obeyed Abraham, calling him lord, whose daughters ye be," saith he, if ye follow her example.[170] This sentence is very meet for women to print in their remembrance. Truth it is, that they must specially feel the grief and pains of their matrimony, in that they relinquish the liberty of their own rule, in the pain of their travailing, in the bringing up of their children; in which offices they be in great perils, and be grieved with great afflictions, which they might be without if they lived out of matrimony. But Saint Peter saith that this is the chief ornament of "holy matrons," in that they "set their hope" and trust "in God"; that is to say, in that they refused not from marriage for the business thereof, for the gifts and perils thereof, but committed all such adventures[171] to God, in most sure trust of help, after that they have called upon his aid. O woman, do thou the like, and so shalt thou be most excellently beautified before God and all his angels and saints. And thou needest not to seek further for doing any better works. For, obey thy husband, take regard of his requests, and give heed unto him to perceive what he requireth of thee; and so shalt thou honour God, and live peaceably in thy house. And, beyond this, God shall follow thee with his benediction, that all things shall well prosper both to thee and to thy husband, as the Psalm saith: "Blessed is the man which feareth God, and walketh in his ways. Thou shalt have the fruit of thine own hands; happy shalt thou be, and well it shall go with thee. Thy wife shall be as a vine plentifully spreading about thy house. Thy children shall be as the young springs of the olives about thy table. Lo, thus shall that man be blessed," saith David, "that feareth the Lord."[172]

---

167   1 Peter 3:1.
168   *impudent.*
169   Ephesians 5:22–23.

170   1 Peter 3:3–6.
171   *outcomes.*
172   Psalm 128:1–4.

This let the wife have ever in mind, the rather admonished thereto by the apparel of her head, whereby is signified that she is under covert and obedience of her husband. And, as that apparel is of nature so appointed, to declare her subjection, so biddeth St. Paul that all other of her raiment should express both "shamefastness and sobriety."[173] For if it be not lawful for the woman to have her head bare, but to bear thereon the sign of her power, wheresoever she goeth, more is it required that she declare the thing that is meant thereby. And therefore these ancient women of the old world called their husbands lords, and showed them reverence in obeying them.

But peradventure she will say that those men loved their wives indeed. I know that well enough, and bear it well in mind. But when I do admonish you of your duties, then call not to consideration what their duties be. For, when we ourselves do teach our children to obey us as their parents, or when we reform our servants, and tell them that they should obey their masters, not only at the eye, but as the Lord: if they should tell us again our duties, we should not think it well done. For, when we be admonished of our duties and faults, we ought not then to seek what other men's duties be. For, though a man had a companion in his fault, yet should he not thereby be without his fault. But this must be only looked on, by what means thou mayest make thyself without blame. For Adam did lay the blame upon the woman, and she turned it unto the serpent; but yet neither of them was thus excused.[174] And therefore bring not such excuses to me at this time, but apply all thy diligence to hear thine obedience to thy husband. For, when I take in hand to admonish thy husband to love thee and to cherish thee, yet will I not cease to set out the law that is appointed for the woman, as well as I would require of the man what is written for his law. Go thou therefore about such things as becometh thee only, and show thyself tractable to thy husband. Or rather, if thou wilt obey thy husband for God's precept, then allege such things as be in his duty to do, but perform thou diligently those things which the lawmaker hath charged thee to do: for thus is it most reasonable to obey God, if thou wilt not suffer thyself to transgress his law. He that loveth his friend seemeth to do no great thing; but he that honoureth him that is hurtful and hateful to him, this man is worthy most commendation: Even so think thou, if thou canst suffer an extreme husband, thou shalt have a great reward therefore; but if thou lovest him only because he is gentle and courteous, what reward will God give thee therefore? Yet I speak not these things, that I would wish the husbands to be sharp towards their wives; but I exhort the women, that they would patiently bear the sharpness of their husbands. For, when either parts do their best to perform their duties the one to the other, then followeth thereon great profit to their neighbours for their example's sake. For when the woman is ready to suffer a sharp husband, and the man will not extremely intreat his stubborn and troublesome wife, then be all things in quiet, as in a most sure haven.

Even thus was it done in old time, that every one did their own duty and office, and was not busy to require the duty of their neighbours. Consider, I pray thee, that Abraham took to him his brother's son:[175] his wife did not blame him therefore. He commanded him to go with him a long journey: she did not gainsay it, but obeyed his precept. Again, after all those great miseries, labours and pains of that journey, when Abraham was made as lord over all, yet did he give place to Lot of his superiority.[176] Which matter Sarah took so little to grief, that she never once suffered her tongue to speak such words as the common manner of women is wont to do in these days: when they see their husbands in such rooms to be made underlings, and to be put under their youngers, then they upbraid them with cumbrous talk, and call them fools, dastards,[177] and cowards for so doing. But Sarah was so far from speaking any such thing, that it came never into her mind and thought so to say, but allowed the wisdom and will of her husband. Yea, besides all this, after the said Lot had thus his will, and left to his uncle the less portion of land, he chanced to fall into extreme peril: which chance when it came to the knowledge of this said Patriarch, he incontinently[178] put all his men in harness, and prepared himself with all his family and friends against the host of the Persians. In which case Sarah did not counsel him to the contrary, nor did say, as

173   1 Timothy 2:9.
174   Genesis 3:12–19.
175   Genesis 12:4–5.

176   Genesis 13:8–11.
177   *cowards* (usually used in chivalric or military contexts).
178   *immediately.*

then might have been said, My husband, whither goest thou so unadvisedly? Why runnest thou thus on head? Why dost thou offer thyself to so great perils, and art thus ready to jeopardize thine own life, and to peril the lives of all thine, for such a man as hath done thee such wrong? At the least way, if thou regardest not thyself, yet have compassion on me, which for thy love have forsaken my kindred and my country, and have the want both of my friends and kinsfolk, and am thus come into so far countries with thee. Have pity on me, and make me not here a widow, to cast me into such cares and troubles. Thus might she have said: but Sarah neither said nor thought such words, but she kept herself in silence in all things. Furthermore, all that time when she was barren, and took no pain, as other women did, by bringing forth fruit in his house, what did he? He complained not to his wife, but to Almighty God.[179] And consider how either of them did their duties as became them; for neither did he despise Sarah because she was barren, nor never did cast it in her teeth. Consider again how Abraham expelled the handmaid out of his house, when she required it:[180] so that by this I may truly prove that the one was pleased and contented with the other in all things. But yet set not your eyes only on this matter, but look further what was done before this, that Hagar used her mistress despitefully, and that Abraham himself was somewhat provoked against her; which must needs be an intolerable matter and a painful to a free-hearted woman and a chaste. Let not therefore the woman be too busy to call for the duty of her husband, where she should be ready to perform her own; for that is not worthy any great commendation. And even so again let not the man only consider what belongeth to the woman, and to stand too earnestly gazing thereon; for that is not his part or duty. But, as I have said, let either parts be ready and willing to perform that which belongeth especially to themself. For, if we be bound to hold out our left cheek to strangers which will smite us on the right cheek, how much more ought we to suffer an extreme and unkind husband!

But yet I mean not that a man should beat his wife. God forbid that; for that is the greatest shame that can be, not so much to her that is beaten, as to him that doth the deed. But, if by such fortune thou chancest upon such an husband, take it not too heavily; but suppose thou that thereby is laid up no small reward hereafter, and in this life time no small commendation to thee, if thou canst be quiet. But yet to you that be men thus I speak: let there be none so grievous fault to compel you to beat your wives. But what say I your wives? No, it is not to be borne with that an honest man should lay hands on his maid servant to beat her. Wherefore, if it be a great shame for a man to beat his bondservant, much more rebuke it is to lay violent hands upon his freewoman. And this thing may be well understood by the laws which the paynims[181] have made, which doth discharge her any longer to dwell with such an husband, as unworthy to have any further company with her, that doth smite her. For it is an extreme point thus so vilely to entreat her like a slave, that is fellow to thee of thy life, and so joined unto thee before time in the necessary matters of thy living. And therefore a man may well liken such a man, if he may be called a man rather than a wild beast, to a killer of his father or his mother. And whereas we be commanded to forsake our father and mother for our wives' sake,[182] and yet thereby do work them none injury, but do fulfil the law of God, how can it not appear then to be a point of extreme madness to intreat her despitefully for whose sake God hath commanded thee to leave parents? Yea, who can suffer such despite? Who can worthily express the inconvenience that is, to see what weepings and wailings be made in the open streets, when neighbours run together to the house of so unruly an husband, as to a Bedlam[183] man who goeth about to overturn all that he hath at home? Who would not think that it were better for such a man to wish the ground to open and swallow him in, than once ever after to be seen in the market?

But peradventure thou wilt object that the woman provoketh thee to this point. But consider thou again that the woman is a frail vessel, and thou art therefore made the ruler and head over her, to bear the weakness of her in this her subjection. And therefore study thou to declare the

179   Genesis 15:2–3; 16:1–2.
180   Genesis 21:9–14.
181   An archaic term for non-Christians usually applied to Muslims.
182   Genesis 2:24; Matthew 19:5.

183   i.e. a madman. The term comes from the Hospital of St. Mary of Bethlehem, a hospital for those suffering from mental illnesses in Early Modern London.

honest commendation of thine authority; which thou canst no ways better do than to forbear to urge her in her weakness and subjection. For, even as the King appeareth so much the more noble, the more excellent and noble he maketh his officers and lieutenants, whom if he should dishonour, and despise the authority of their dignity, he should deprive himself of a great part of his own honour; even so, if thou dost despise her that is set in the next room beside thee, thou dost much derogate[184] and decay the excellency and virtue of thine own authority. Recount all these things in thy mind, and be gentle and quiet. Understand that God hath given thee children with her, and art made a father, and by such reason appease thyself. Dost thou not see the husbandmen,[185] what diligence they use to till that ground which once they have taken to farm, though it be never so full of faults? As for an example, though it be dry, though it bringeth forth weeds, though the soil cannot bear too much wet, yet he tilleth it, and so winneth fruit thereof: Even in like manner, if thou wouldst use like diligence to instruct and order the mind of thy spouse, if thou wouldst diligently apply thyself to weed out by little and little the noisome weeds of uncomely manners out of her mind, with wholesome precepts, it could not be, but in time thou shouldst feel the pleasant fruit thereof to both your comforts. Therefore, that this thing chance not so, perform this thing that I do here counsel thee. Whensoever any displeasant matter riseth at home, if thy wife hath done ought amiss, comfort her, and increase not the heaviness.[186] For, though thou shouldst be grieved with never so many things, yet shalt thou find nothing more grievous than to want the benevolence of thy wife at home; what offence soever thou canst name, yet shalt thou find none more intolerable than to be at debate with thy wife. And for this cause most of all oughtest thou to have this love in reverence. And, if reason moveth thee to bear any burden at any other man's hands, much more at thy wife's. For, if she be poor, upbraid her not; if she be simple, taunt her not, but be the more courteous; for she is thy body, and made "one flesh" with thee.[187]

But thou peradventure wilt say, that she is a wrathful woman, a drunkard, a beastly, without wit and reason. For this cause bewail her the more. Chafe not in anger, but pray unto Almighty God. Let her be admonished and helped with good counsel, and do thou thy best endeavour that she may be delivered of all these affections.[188] But, if thou shouldst beat her, thou shalt increase her evil affections; for frowardness and sharpness is not amended with frowardness, but with softness and gentleness. Furthermore, consider what reward thou shalt have at God's hand: for, where thou mightest beat her, and yet for the respect of the fear of God thou wilt abstain and bear patiently her great offences, the rather in respect of that Law which forbiddeth that a man should cast out his wife what fault soever she be made the cumbered with, thou shalt have a very great reward. And before the receipt of that reward thou shalt feel many commodities; for by this means she shall be more obedient, and thou for her sake shalt be made the more meek. It is written in a story of a certain strange[189] philosopher, which had a cursed wife, a froward, and a drunkard; when he was asked for what consideration he did so bear her evil manners, he made answer, "By this means," said he, "I have at home a schoolmaster, and an example how I should behave myself abroad: for I shall" saith he, "be the more quiet with others, being thus daily exercised and taught in the forbearing of her."[190] Surely it is a shame that paynims should be wiser than we; we, I say, that be commanded to resemble angels, or rather God himself through meekness. And for the love of virtue this said philosopher Socrates would not expel his wife out of his house; yea, some say that he did therefore marry his wife, to learn this virtue by that occasion. Wherefore, seeing many men be far behind the wisdom of this man, my counsel is, that first and before all things, that man do his best endeavour to get him a good wife, endued with all honesty and virtue; but, if it so chance that he is deceived, that he hath chosen such a wife as is neither good nor tolerable, then let the husband follow this philosopher, and let him instruct his wife in every condition, and never lay these matters to sight. For the merchant man, except he first be at composition[191] with his factor to use his inter-

---

184   *lessen.*
185   *farmers.*
186   *anger.*
187   Genesis 2:24; Ephesians 5:28, 31.
188   *maladies.*

189   *foreign.*
190   The philosopher in question is Socrates whose wife, Xanthippe, was reputed by many ancient writers to be a very abrasive personality. This quotation is derived from Xenophon, *Symposium* 2.10.
191   i.e. in agreement with.

affairs[192] quietly, he will neither stir his ship to sail, nor yet will lay hands upon his merchandise. Even so let us do all things that we may have the fellowship of our wives, which is the factor of all our doings at home, in great quiet and rest. And by these means all things shall prosper quietly, and so shall we pass through the dangers of the troublous sea of this world. For this state of life will be more honourable and comfortable than our houses, than servants, than money, than lands and possessions, than all things that can be told. As all these with sedition and discord, can never work us any comfort; so shall all things turn to our commodity and pleasure, if we draw this yoke in one concord of heart and mind.

Whereupon do your best endeavour that after this sort ye use your matrimony, and so shall ye be armed on every side. Ye have escaped the snares of the devil and the unlawful lusts of the flesh, ye have the quietness of conscience, by this institution of matrimony ordained by God: therefore use of prayer to him, that he would be present by you, that he would continue concord and charity betwixt you. Do the best ye can of your parts to custom yourselves to softness and meekness, and bear well in worth such oversights as chance; and thus shall your conversation be most pleasant and comfortable. And although (which can no otherwise be) some adversities shall follow, and otherwhiles now one discommodity, now another shall appear, yet in this common trouble and adversity lift up both your hands unto heaven; call upon the help and assistance of God, the Author of your marriage; and surely the promise of relief is at hand. For Christ affirmeth in his Gospel, "Where two or three be gathered together in my name, and be agreed, what matter soever they pray for, it shall be granted them of my heavenly Father."[193] Why therefore shouldst thou be afraid of the danger, where thou hast so ready a promise and so nigh an help? Furthermore, you must understand how necessary it is for Christian folk to bear Christ's cross; for else we shall never feel how comfortable God's help is unto us.

Therefore give thanks to God for his great benefit, in that ye have taken upon you this state of wedlock; and pray you instantly[194] that Almighty God may luckily defend and maintain you therein, that neither ye be overcome with any temptation nor with any adversity. But before all things, take good heed that ye give no occasion to the devil to let[195] and hinder your prayers by discord and dissension. For there is no stronger defence and stay[196] in all our life than is prayer: in the which we may call for the help of God and obtain it; whereby we may win his blessing, his grace, his defence, and protection, so to continue therein to a better life to come. Which grant us he that died for us all: to whom be all honour and praise forever and ever, Amen.

The Book of Common Prayer (1548)

The Book of Common Prayer, which established the official order of worship for the Church of England, was the product of efforts to reform medieval worship practices in England. These efforts began slowly (*c*.1534) during the reign of Henry VIII, who resisted the Lutheran inspiration of Thomas Cranmer, Archbishop of Canterbury. However, the year after the accession of Edward VI, which took place in 1547 upon the death of Henry VIII, this reformist movement reached its fruition when Parliament passed a Uniformity Act (December 1548), to which *The Book of Common Prayer* was appended. The prayer book contained all that

was necessary for every form of worship throughout the Church year, except the musical settings for the sung portions of the service. This moderate version was replaced in 1552 by the ill-fated *Second Book of Common Prayer* which was in use less than a year. When King Edward VI died in 1553, his half-sister Mary, who succeeded him, reinstated the medieval Latin liturgy. After her death and the accession of Elizabeth I in 1558 a third prayer book was prepared. Although reformist in spirit, also, this 1559 version was consistent with Elizabeth's opposition to both Roman Catholic and Puritan fanaticism. Book V of

---

192   i.e. business between two people.
193   Matthew 18:19–20.
194   *persistently.*

195   *obstruct.*
196   *support.*

Richard Hooker's *Of the Laws of Ecclesiastical Polity* (1557) includes a theological commentary on the Elizabethan version of *The Book of Common Prayer*. The wide cultural impact of the prayer book has been succinctly described by A. L. Rowse: "It is impossible to over-estimate the influence of the church's routine of prayer and good works upon [Elizabethan] society: the effect on imagination and conduct of the liturgy with its piercing and affecting phrases, repeated Sunday by Sunday" (p. 433). The prayer book has, however, been subject to periodic revision since Elizabeth's time.

READING

John E. Booty, *The Godly Kingdom of Tudor England: Great Books of the English Reformation.*
Edward Cardwell, *A History of Conferences and Other Proceedings Connected with the Revision of the Book of Common Prayer from the Year 1558 to the Year 1690.*
Edward C. Ratcliff, *The Book of Common Prayer of the Church of England: Its Making and Revisions.*
A. L. Rowse, *The England of Elizabeth.*

M. P.

[FROM] THE BOOKE OF THE COMMON PRAYER

[OR, THE FIRST PRAYER BOOK OF KING EDWARD VI]

An Ordre for Mattyns dayly through the yere.

The priest beeyng in the quier[1] shall begynne with a loude voyce the Lordes prayer, called the *Pater noster.*

Oure father whiche arte in heauen, hallowed be thy name. Thy kyngdom come. Thy wyll be done in earth as it is in heauen. Geue vs this daye oure dayly bread. And forgeue vs oure trespasses, as we forgeue them that trespasse agaynst vs. And leade vs not into temptacion. But deliuer vs from euell. Amen.

Then lykewyse he shall saye.

O Lorde, open thou my lyppes.

Aunswere.

And my mouthe shall shewe forth thy prayse.

Priest.

Glory be to the father, and to the sonne, and to the holye ghost. As it was in the begynning, is now, and euer shalbe world without ende. Amen.

Prayse ye the Lorde.

And from Easter to Trinitie Sondaye.

Alleluya.

Then shalbe saied or song without any Inuitatori this Psalme, *Venite exultemus, etc.*[2] in Englishe, as foloweth.

O come, lette vs syng vnto the Lorde: lette vs hartely reioyce in the strengthe of oure saluacion.

Let vs come before his presence with thankesgeuing: and shewe oure selfe glad in hym with Psalmes.

For the Lord is a great God: and a great kyng aboue all goddes.

In his hande are all the corners of the yearth: and the strength of the hylles is his also.

The sea is his, and he made it: and his handes prepared the drye lande.

O come, let vs worship and fall downe: and kneele before the Lorde oure maker.

[FROM] THE BOOKE OF THE COMMON PRAYER
[OR, THE FIRST PRAYER BOOK OF KING EDWARD VI]

2   Psalm 95.

1   *choir.*

For he is (the Lord) oure God: and we are the people of his pasture, and the shepe of his handes.

To daye, yf ye wyll heare his voyce, harden not your hartes: as in the prouocacion, and as in the daie of temptacion in the wildernes.

When your fathers tempted me: proued me, and sawe my workes.

Fourtye yeares long was I greued with this generacion, and sayed: it is a people that do erre in their hartes: For they haue not knowen my wayes.

Unto whom I sware in my wrath: that they should not entre into my rest.

Glory be to the father, and to the sonne: and to the holy ghost. As it was in the beginnyng, is nowe, and euer shalbe: worlde without end. Amen.

> ¶ Then shal folow certaine Psalmes in ordre as they been appointed in a table made for y purpose, except there be propre Psalmes appointed for that day. And at the end of euery Psalme thoughout the yeare, and lykewyse in the ende of *Benedictus, Benedicite, Magnificat,* and *Nunc dimittis,* shalbe repeated.

Glory be to the father and to the sonne. etc.

> ¶ Then shalbe read. ii. lessons distinctely with a loude voice, that the people maye heare. The fyrst of the olde testament, the second of the newe. Like as they be appoynted by the Kalender,[3] excepte there be propre lessons assigned for that daye: The ministre that readeth the lesson standing and turnyng hym so as he maye beste be hearde of all suche as be present. And before euery lesson, the minister shal saye thus.
>
> The fyrste, seconde. iii. or. iiii. Chapter of *Genesis*, or *Exodus*, Matthewe, Marke, or other lyke as is appoynted in the Kalender. And in the ende of every Chapter he shall saye.

Here endeth suche a Chapter of suche a booke.

> ¶ And (to thende the people may the better heare) in such places where they doe syng, there shall the lessons be songe in a playne tune after the maner of distincte readying: and lykewyse the Epistle and Gospell.

> ¶ After the fyrste lesson shall folowe *Te deum laudamus* in Englyshe, dayly throughout the yeare, excepte in Lente, all the whiche tyme in the place of *Te deum* shalbe vsed *Benedicite omnia opera Domini Domino*, in Englyshe as foloweth.

TE DEUM LAUDAMUS

We praise the, O God, we knowlage[4] thee to be the Lorde.

All the earth doeth wurship thee, the father euerlastyng.

To thee al Angels cry aloud, the heauens and all the powers therin.

To thee Cherubin, and Seraphin continually doe crye.

Holy, holy, holy, Lorde Gode of Sabaoth.

Heauen and earth are replenyshed with the maiestie of thy glory.

The gloryous coupany of the Apostles, praise thee.

The goodly felowshyp of the Prophetes, praise thee.

The noble armie of Martyrs, praise thee.

The holy churche throughout all the worlde doeth knowlage thee.

The father of an infinite maiestie.

Thy honourable, true, and onely sonne.

The holy gost also beeyng the coumforter.

Thou art the kyng of glory, O Christe.

Thou art the euerlastyng sonne of the father.

3   "A Table and Kalendar for Psalmes and Lessons, with necessary rules   4   *acknowledge.*
perteinyng to the same" is the first section of the Book of Common
Prayer after the Preface.

Whan thou tookest vpon thee to delyuer manne, thou dyddest not abhorre the virgins wombe.

Whan thou haddest ouercomed the sharpenesse of death, thou diddest open the kyngdome of heauen to all beleuers.

Thou sittest on the ryghthande of God in the glory of the father.

We beleue that thou shalt come to be our iudge.

We therfore praye thee, helpe thy seruantes whom thou haste redemed with thy precious bloud.

Make them to be noumbred with they sainctes, in glory euerlastyng.

O Lorde saue thy people: and blesse thyne heritage.

Gouerne them, and lift them vp for euer.

Day by day we magnifie thee.

And we wurship thy name euer world without ende.

Uouchsafe, O Lorde, to kepe vs this daye without synne.

O Lorde, haue mercy upon vs: haue mercy upon vs.

O Lorde, let thy mercy lighten vpon vs: as our trust is in thee.

O Lorde, in thee haue I trusted: let me neuer be confounded.

BENEDICITE OMNIA OPERA DOMINI DOMINO

O all ye workes of the Lorde: speake good of the Lorde: prayse hym, and set hym vp for euer.

O ye Angels of the Lorde, speake good of the Lorde: prayse hym, and set hym vp for euer.

O ye heauens, speake good of the Lord: prayse hym and set hym vp for euer.

O ye Sunne and Moone, speake good of the Lorde: prayse hym and set hym vp for euer.

O ye sterres of heauen, speake good of the lorde: prayse him and set him vp for euer.

O ye showers and dewe, speake good of the lord: praise him, and set him vp for euer.

O ye windes of God, speake good of the Lord: praise him, and set him vp for euer.

O ye fier and heate, prayse ye the Lorde: praise him, and set him vp for euer.

O ye winter and summer, speake good of the Lorde: praise him, and set him VP for euer.

O ye dewes and frostes, speake good of the Lord: praise him, and set him vp for euer.

O ye frost and colde, speake good of the Lorde: praise him, and set him vp for euer.

O ye yse[5] and snowe speake good of the Lorde: praise him, and set him vp for euer.

O ye nyghtes and dayes, speake good of the Lorde: praise him, and set him vp for euer.

O ye light and darkenes, speake good of the Lorde: praise him, and set him vp for euer.

O ye lighteninges and cloudes, speake good of the Lorde: praise him, and set him vp for euer.

O let the yearthe speake good of the Lord: yea, let it prayse him, and set him vp for euer.

O ye mountaynes and hilles, speake good of the Lord: prayse him, and set him vp for euer.

O al ye greene thynges vpon the earth, speake good of the Lorde: praise him and set him vp for euer.

O ye welles, speake good of the Lord: praise him, and set him vp for euer.

O ye seas and floudes, speake good of the Lorde: praise him, and set him vp for euer.

O ye whales, and all that moue in the waters, speake good of the Lorde: praise him, and set him vp for euer.

O all ye foules of the ayre, speake good of the lorde: prayse him and set him vp for euer.

O all ye beastes and catell, speake ye good of the Lord: praise him, and set him vp for euer.

O ye children of men, speake good of the lorde: praise him, and set him vp for euer.

O ye seruauntes of the Lord, speake good of the Lord: praise him, and set him vp for euer.

O ye spirites and soules of the righteous; speake good of the Lorde: praise him, and set him vp for euer.

O ye holy and humble men of heart, speak ye good of the Lorde: prayse ye him, and set him vp for euer.

O Ananias, Asarias, and Misael,[6] speake ye good of the Lorde: prayse ye him and set him vp for euer.

---

5   *ice.*

6   Hananiah, Azariah, and Mishael are, like Daniel, children without blemish and endowed with wisdom (Daniel 1:4–7).

Glory be to the father, and the sonne: and to the holy gost.

As it was in the beginning, is now, and euer shalbe: worlde without ende. Amen.

¶And after the second lesson, throughout the whole yere, shalbe vsed *Benedictus dominus deus Israel etc.* in Englishe as foloweth.

Blessed be the lorde God of Israel: for he hath visited and redemed his people.

And hath lyfted vp an horne of saluacyon to vs: in the house of his seruaunt Dauid.

As he spake by the mouth of his holy Prophetes: which hath bene syns the world began.

That we shoulde be saued from our enemies: and from the handes of all that hate vs.

To perfourme the mercy promised to our fathers: and to remember his holy couenaunt.

To perfourme the othe[7] whiche he sware to our father Abraham: that he woulde geue vs.

That we being deliuered out of the handes of our enemies: might serue him without feare.

In holynesse and ryghteousnes before him all the dayes of our lyfe.

And thou childe, shalte bee called the prophete of the highest: for thou shalte goe before the face of the Lord, to prepare his wayes.

To geue knowledge of saluacion vnto his people: for the remission of their sinnes.

Through the tender mercie of our god: whereby the daye spryng from on hygh hath visited vs.

To geue lighte to them that sitte in darkenes, and in the shadowe of death: and to guide our fete into the way of peace.

Glory be to the father. etc.

Then shalbe said dailye through the yere, the praiers folowyng, as well at euensong as at Matins, all deuoutely kneelyng.

Lorde haue mercie vpon vs. Criste haue mercie vpon vs. Lorde haue mercie vpon vs.

Then the minister shal say the *Crede* and the Lordes praier in englishe, with a loude voice. etc.

Answere.

But deliuer vs from euill. Amen.

Prieste.

O Lorde shewe thy mercie vpon vs.

Answere.

And graunte vs thy saluacion.

Prieste.

O Lorde saue the kyng.

Answere.

And mercifully heare vs, when we cal vpon thee.

Prieste.

7   *oath, promise.*

Indue thy ministers with righteousnes.

    Answere.

And make thy chosen people ioyfull.

    Prieste.

O lorde saue thy people.

    Answere.

And blesse thyne inheritaunce.

    Prieste.

Geue peace in oure time, O Lorde.

    Answere.

Because there is none other that fyghteth for vs, but only thou, O God.

    Prieste.

O God, make cleane our hartes within vs.

    Answere.

And take not thyne holy spirite from vs.

    Prieste.

The lorde be with you.

    Answere.

And with thy spirite.

> Then shal dayly folowe three Collectes. The firste of the day, which shalbe the same that is appointed at the Communion. The seconde for peace. The thirde for grace to lyue wel. And the two laste Collectes shall neuer alter, but dailye bee saide at Matins throughout al the yere, as foloweth. The priest standyying vp and saiyng.

Let vs praye.

    ¶Then the Collect of the daie.

THE SECOND COLLECT: FOR PEACE

O God, which art author of peace, and louer of concorde, in knowledge of whome standeth oure eternall life, whose seruice is perfect fredome: defende vs thy humble seruauntes, in al assaultes of our enemies: that wee surely trustying in thy defence, maye not feare the power of any aduersaries: through the myght of Jesu Christ our lorde. Amen.

THE THYRDE COLLECTE: FOR GRACE

O Lorde oure heauenly father, almightye and euerliuying God, whiche haste[8] safelye brought vs to the beginning of this day: Defend vs in the same with thy mighty power, and graunt that the

---

8 *hast.*

daye wee fall into no synne, neyther runne into any kinde of daunger, but that al our doinges may be ordred by thy gouernaunce, to do alwaies that is righteous in thy sight: through Jesus Christe our lorde. Amen.

* * *

The Order of the Purificacion of Woemen[9]

The woman shall come into the churche, and there shal kneele downe in some conueniente place, nygh vnto the quire doore: and the prieste standying by her, shall saye these woordes or suche lyke, as the case shall require.

For asmuche as it hath pleased almightie god of hys goodnes to geue you safe deliueraunce: and your childe baptisme, and hath preserued you in the greate daunger of childebirth: ye shal therefore geue hartie thankes vnto god, and pray.

Then shall the prieste say this psalme.

I have lifted vp mine iyes vnto the hilles, for whence commeth my helpe?[10]
My help cummeth euen from the lord, which hath made heauen and earth.
He will not suffer thy foote to be moued, and he that kepeth thee wil not slepe.
Beholde he that kepeth Israel, shal neither slumber nor slepe.
The lorde himselfe is thy keper, the lorde is thy defence vpon thy right hande.
So that the sonne shall not burne thee by daye, neyther the moone by nyght.
The lord shal preserue thee from al euil, yea it is euen he that shal kepe thy soule.
The lord shal preserue thy going out, and thy cumming in, from this tyme furth for euermore.
Glorye to the father, etc.
As it was in the beginning, etc.
    Lord haue mercie vpon vs.
    Christ haue mercie vpon vs.
    Lorde haue mercie vpon vs.
¶Our father whiche art in heauen, etc.
And leade vs not into temptacion.

Aunswere.

But deliuer vs from euil. Amen.

Priest.

O lord saue this woman thy seruaunt.

Aunswere.

Whiche putteth her trust in thee.

Priest.

Bee thou to her a strong tower.

Aunswere.

9   This service is both a symbolic rite of purification after childbirth   10   Psalm 121.
and, given the high maternal and infant mortality rate, a celebration of
the mother's survival of the pains and risk of labor.

From the face of her enemie.

Priest.

The lorde heare our prayer.

Aunswere.

And let our crye come to thee.

Priest.

¶Let vs pray.

O almightie God, which hast deliuered this woman thy seruant from the great payne and peril of childbirth: Graunt we beseche thee (most mercifull father) that she through thy helpe may both faithfully lyue, and walke in her vocacyon accordynge to thy will in thys lyfe presente: and also may be partaker of euerlastyng glorye in the lyfe to come: through Jesus Christ our lorde. Amen.

The woman that is purifyed, must offer her Crysome, and other accustomed offeringes. And if there be a communion, it is conuenient that she receiue the holy communion.

Anonymous Carols (1550–?)

Although the term "carol" has come to be used quite loosely, as in *The Oxford Book of Carols*, to refer to songs with a religious impulse, until about 1550 its meaning was more precise. Before the reign of Elizabeth I a carol was "a song on any subject, composed of uniform stanzas and provided with a burden" (Greene, pp. xxxii–iii). The presence of a burden is thus the distinguishing formal feature of the carol. Unlike a refrain, which is a repeated element within a stanza, a burden is a repeated element that is independent of any stanza. The burden is sung before the first stanza and after each succeeding stanza in the song (Greene, p. clx). Carols dealing with the Christmas story are obviously the most famous examples of this genre, but there are also many carols on other seasons of the Church year and on such secular subjects as sexual love, women, and marriage. Like hymns and ballads, carols provide an important glimpse of Renaissance popular culture.

READING

Percy Dearmer, R. Vaughan Williams, and Martin Shaw (eds.), *The Oxford Book of Carols.*
Richard Leighton Greene (ed.), *The Early English Carols.*

M. P.

[ALL THIS TYME]

All this tyme this songe is best:
"Verbum caro factum est."[1]

[1]

This nyght ther is a child born
That sprange owt of Jessis thorn,[2]
We must synge and say therforn,
"Verbum caro factum est."

ALL THIS TYME
1   "The Word is made flesh."

2   Out of Jesse's tree.

[2]
Jhesus is the childes name,
And Mary myld is his dame;
All owr sorow shall torn to game:
    Verbum caro factum est.

10

[3]
Hit fell vpon high mydnyght:
The sterres shon both fayre and bright;
The angelles song with all ther mytht,
    "Verbum caro factum est."

[4]
Now knele we down on owr kne,
And pray we to the Trynyte
Owr helpe, owr socowr for to be;   *succour*
    Verbum caro factum est.

[TYDYNGES, TYDYNGES]

Tydynges, tydynges that be trwe:
Sorowe ys paste, and joye dothe renwe.

[1]
Qwhereas Adam cawsed be synne
    Owre nature thus to be mortall,
A mayden Son dothe nowe begyn
    For to repayse vs from that fall,
        And that ys trwe:
    The name of hym ys Cryste Jhesu.

[2]
Sum of oure kynde hathe hadd suche grase
10   That syn hys byrthe they dyd hym se,
Bothe Sonne and mother fase to fase
    In the chefe cyte calde Jure.[1]
        And that ys trwe:
    Bothe kynges and schepardes they yt knwe.

[3]
The prophettes therof ware nothyng dysmayde,
    Of that tydynges before that they hadde tolde,
For nowe yt ys fall ryghthe as they sayde:
A clen mayde hathe born a kyng.
    And that ys trwe,
20
For he ys born to ware the purpull hwe.

[NOW LET VS SYNG]

Now let vs syng, both more and lesse,
Of Cristes commyng, "Deo gracias."[1]

TYDYNGES, TYDYNGES
1   Chief city called Jerusalem.

NOW LET VS SYNG
1   "Thanks be to God."

[1]

A virgyn pure,
This is full sure
        Gabriell dide her grete,
And all her cure,
I am full sure,
Euer dyde endure.
        Deo gracias.

[2]

A babe was born
Erly by the morn
        And layd betwen the ox and the asse;
The child they knew
That was born new;
On hym thei blew.
        Deo gracias.

[3]

An angell full sone
Sang fro abone,   *from above*
        "Gloria in excelsis."
That lady alon
Myght mak no mone
For love of on.
        Deo gracias.

[4]

This babe vs bowght
Whan we were browght
        Into gret thowght and dredfull case;
Therefor we syng,
Both old and yonge,
Of Cristes commynge,
        "Deo gracias."

[SYNG WE WITH MYRTH]

Syng we with myrth, joye, and solas
In honowr of this Cristemas,

[1]

Glorius God had gret pyte
How longe mans sowle in payn shuld be;
He sent his Son to mak vs free,
        Which for manus sake
Off a maydyn pure
Agaynst nature
        Owr flesshe dide take.

[2]

In Bedlem owr Saviowr   *Bethlehem*
Withowt fode in a manjowre   *manger*
Was born (hit was his plesure)
        Bestes amonge.

Angelles hevynly
Made armonye   *harmony*
    And joyfull songe.

[3]

The eighth day he was circonsisid,
Leste Moyses lawe shuld be dispised;
A name to hym they haue devised:
    "Call hym Jhesus."
20 For Gabryell
His moder dide tell
    That it should be thus.

[4]

A newe-made sterre, more large and clere
Than other sterres, than dide appere;
Fro Caldey the felosafers in fere[1]
    Into Bedlem yt browght;
Ther it dide stond
Still till that they fonde
30   Hym that they sowght.

[5]

The kynges browght ther offrynge,
Gold that betokneth a worthy kynge,
Insens presthode, myr buryinge
    For his manhode.
The angell com,
Bade them go home
    Not by Herode.

[6]

Trust in God, man, and in non other;
Mistrust hym not; he is thy brother;
40 Thow hast a mediatrix of his moder;
    Syke for thy synne;
Crye marcy;
He will not denye,
    Thy sowle to wynne.

[SYNGE WE ALL]

Synge we all, for tyme it is:
Mary hath born the flowre-de-lice.[1]

[1]

For his love that bought vs all dere,
Lystyn, lordyinges that ben here,
And I will tell you in fere
    Wherof com the flowr-de-lyce.

[2]

On Cristmas nyght whan it was cold,
Owr Lady lay amonge bestes bolde,

SYNG WE WITH MYRTH
1 From the Chaldees the philosophers [Wise Men] in company.

SYNGE WE ALL
1 Fleur-de-lis, a symbol of the Trinity.

And ther she bare Jhesu, Josepff tolde,
10   And therof com the flowr-de-lice.

[3]

Off that berth witnesse Seynt Johan
That it was of myche renown;
Baptized he was in flom Jordan,   *river*
          And therof cam the flowr-de-lice.

[4]

On Good Fryday that child was slayn,
Betyn with skorges, and for to-flayn;
That day he suffred myche payn,
          And therof com the flowr-de-lice.

[BY REASON OF TWO]

By reason of two and poore of one[1]
This tyme God and man was set at one.

[1]

God against nature thre wonders haith wrought:
          First of the vile earthe mad man without man,
Then woman without woman of man maid of nought,
          And so man without man in woman than.
          Thus, lo, God and man together begane,
                    As two for to joine together in one,
                    As at this good tyme to be sett at one;
10   Thus God bagane
                    This world for to forme and to encrease man.

[2]

Angell in heaven for offence was damned,
          And man also for beinge variable;
Whether shuld be saved was examyned,
          Man or yet angell; then God was greable   *agreeable*
          To answer for man, for man was not able,
                    And said man had mocyon and angell had none,
                    Wherefore God and man shuld be seit at one
                    Thanke we him than
20   That thus did leaue angell and saved man.

[3]

The devill clamed man by bargan as this:
          For an appell, he said, man was bought and solde;
God aunswered and said the bargan was his:
          "Withe myne to be thyne how durst thoue be so bolde?
          Man myne, syne thyne; wherfore thoue art now told
                    Thoue bought nought; then taike nought; thi bargan is don;
                    Wherfore God and man shal be set att one."
                    Nowe blessed be he,
                    For we that are bownde, loe, nowe are maid[2] free.

BY REASON OF TWO   2   Possibly a pun on made/maid.
1   The two are man and God, and the one missing is woman.

[4]

30   Betwene God and man ther was great distaunce,
        For man said that God shuld haue kept him vpryght,
    And God said man maid all the variaunce,
        For th'apple to sett his commaundement so light;
        Wherfore, of his mercye sparinge the ryght,
            He thought God and man shuld be set at one.
            Seing that God and man was set at one,
                What kindnes was this;
    To agree with man and the fault not his!

[5]

    Withe man and woman ther was great traverse:
40   Man said to the woman, "Woe myght thou be!"
    "Nay," quod the woman, "Why dost thoue reverse?
        For womans entisinge woe be to the!   *enticing*
        For God made man the heade and ruler of me."
            Thus God sawe man and woman were not at one;
            He thought in a woman to sett theime at one
                To our solace;
    His mercye he graunted for our trespace.

[6]

    The ritche and the pore ther title did reherse:
        The pore clamed heauen throughe his pacient havour;
50   He saide, "Beati pauperes,"[3] and further the verse;
        The riche man by ritches thought hym in favour,
        For who was so ritche as was our Saviour?
            And againe who so pure as he was one
            In hey when he ley to set vs at one?
                Who graunt vs peace
    And at the last ende the great joyes endles.

[SHALL I, MODER, SHALL I?]

    "Shall I, moder, shall I,
        Shall I do soo?
    Shall I dye for mannys sake,
        And I never synned thereto?

[1]

    "I was borun in a stall
        Betwen bestes two,
    To this world browght in thrall,
        To leve in care and woo.   *woe*

[2]

    "Whan I was viii days elde,
        The lawe fulfilled I thoo,
10   Circumsised as a childe;
        Than began all my woo.

[3]

    "Thowgh my Fader be a Kyng,
        Myselff I went hym froo

---

3   "Blessed are the poor [in spirit]" (Matthew 5:3).

Into this world to suffre many a thyng—
    See, man, what thow haste do.

[4]

"Man, I am thy frend ay:
    Thyself art thy foo;
To my Fader lok thow pray,
20   And leve thy synnes that thou hast do.

[5]

"The Jeves were so fell   *Jews*
    That to Judas could they goo;
They kyssed me, as I you tell;
    'Hayle, Kyng!' said they tho.

[6]

"They bond me to a pyler anon,
    Honde and fote both twoo;
They skorged me with skorges son;
    The blode ran my body froo.

[7]

"They clothed me in a mantell rede
30   From the toppe to the too,
With a crown of thorn on my hede;
    With staves they bett it therto.

[8]

"They browght me into Cayfas¹ hall,
    Ther he was bisshop thoo;
Fals witnes on me they gan call;
    Moder, what shall I doo?

[9]

"I toke the cros on my bak full still;
    To Caluary than muste I goo;
I sett it down vpon an hill
40   With other crossis moo.

[10]

"They hangid me vp that tide,
    Hondes and fette they naylid also,
And a theff on euery side
    To lykyn my body too.

[11]

"With a spere both sharpe and kene
    They clave my hart in two;
Water and blode ther owt ran—
    See, man, what thou haste do!

[12]

"With a spere both sharpe and hend
50   They clave my harte in iii;

SHALL I, MODER, SHALL I?
1   Caiaphas, the High Priest (Matthew 26:57).

Than yeldyd I vp the gost and dyed,
That here all men may see."

[13]
God, that dyed on the rode
And spred his armes in the este
Send vs all his blessyng
And send vs all good reste.

[GAWDE, FOR THY JOYES FIVE]

Gawde, for thy joyes five,
Mary, moder, maydyn, and wyff.

[1]
Gaude, to whom Gabryell was sent,
From Nazareth to Galalie,
And said that God Omnipotent
Wold haue his Son be born of the.

[2]
Gaude: thow bare hym withowt payn,
And with payn thow saweste hym dy on tre,
But gaude whan he rose agayn,
For he appered firste to the.

[3]
Gaude: thow saweste hym assende
By his own strenth above the skye;
An hoste of angelles down he sent
And assumpte thy sowle with thy bodye.

[4]
Gaude: thy dignyte ys gret,
For next vnto the Trynyte
Above all seyntes is thy sete,
And all joye is in the sight of the.

[5]
Gaude, moder and maydyn pure,
For thy joyes shall never cesse
(Thereof thow art siker and sure)
But ever florisshe and encrese.

[OF ALL CREATURES WOMEN BE BEST]

Of all creatures women be best,
Cuius contrarium verum est.[1]

[1]
In euery place ye may well see
That women be trewe as tirtyll on tree,

OF ALL CREATURES WOMEN BE BEST
1   "Whose contrary is true."

Not lyberall in langage, but euer in secrete,
And gret joye amonge them ys for to be.

[2]
The stedfastnes of women will neuer be don,
So jentyll, so curtes they be euerychon,
Meke as a lambe, still as a stone;
Croked nor crabbed fynd ye none.

[3]
Men be more cumbers a thowsand fold,
And I mervayll how they dare be so bold
Agaynst women for to hold,
Seyng them so pascyent, softe, and cold.

[4]
For, tell a woman all your cownsayle,
And she can kepe it wonderly well;
She had lever go quyk to hell
Than to her neyghbowr she wold it tell.

[5]
For by women men be reconsiled;
For by women was neuer man begiled;
For they be of the condicion of curtes Gryzell;[2]
For they be so meke and mylde.

[6]
Now say well by women, or elles be still,
For they neuer displesed man by ther will;
To be angry or wroth they can no skill,
For I dare say they thynk non yll.

[7]
Trow ye that women list to smater
Or agaynst ther husbondes for to clater?
Nay, they had leuer fast, bred and water,
Then for to dele in suche a mater.

[8]
Thowgh all the paciens in the world were drownd,
And non were lefte here on the grownd,
Agayn in a woman it myght be fownd,
Suche vertu in them dothe abownd.

[9]
To the tavern they will not goo,
Nor to the ale-hows neuer the moo,
For, God, wot, ther hartes wold be woo
To spende ther husbondes money soo.

[10]
Yff here were a woman or a mayd
That lyst for to go fresshely arayed,
Of with fyne kyrchers to go displayed,
Ye wold say, "They be prowde"; it is yll said.

10

20

30

40

---

2   Griselda, a medieval heroine known for her patience.

[GRENE GROWITH THE HOLY]

Grene growith the holy,
So doth the iue,
Thow wynter blastys blow neuer so hye,
Grene growth the holy.

[1]

As the holy grouth grene
And neuer chaungyth hew,
So I am euer hath bene,
Vnto my lady trew.

[2]

As the holy grouth grene
10   With iue all alone
When flowerys cannot be sene,
And grenewode leuys¹ be gone.

[3]

Now vnto my lady
Promyse to her I make,
Frome all other only
To her I me betake.

[4]

Adew, myne owne lady,
Adew my specyall,
Who hath my hart trewly,
20   Be suere, and euer shall.

Edmund Spenser (1552–1599)

Spenser is one of the most important poets to have written in English, and his influence extends through Milton to Wordsworth, Keats, and Tennyson. Spenser's poetry is both sensuously delightful and politically incorrect on all fronts. His most ambitious poem, *The Faerie Queene*, was written as the first English epic (*Beowulf* then being unknown.) This massive poem is written in a fictional Elizabethan version of Middle English as though in order to create a world that is both romantically of the past and realistically in the present. In *The Faerie Queene* Spenser set out to build on the tradition of Virgil's *Aeneid*, to exceed the accomplishments of the Italian poets Ariosto and Tasso, and to fuse the Arthurian romance with Renaissance epic in order to fashion (as Virgil had done for Rome) a unifying myth of Elizabethan culture. He was also a master of those other popular forms of Elizabethan poetry: lyric, pastoral, and satire.

Although Spenser was born in London and was educated there under Richard Mulcaster at the Merchant

Taylors' School and later at Cambridge, most of his poetry was written in Ireland during an 18-year period, beginning in 1580. During those years, Spenser helped to administer brutal Elizabethan policy in that country. His celebration of English culture, which *The Faerie Queene* did much to mythologize, was thus produced in exile, and his art is one of the best illustrations of Walter Benjamin's thesis that "there is no document of civilization which is not at the same time a document of barbarism" (1968: 258). The "barbaric" side of Spenser, which fictionally erupts in such acts of self-righteous violence as Guyon's destruction of the Bower of Bliss, is revealed more fully and systematically in his *View of the State of Ireland* (1598), which advocates the extermination of Irishmen who remain unreconciled to English rule. This may have been Spenser's last work. (Given its contents, it has an understandably troubled history of transmission, which makes Sir James Ware's 1633 version the most revealing.) Ireland and its mythic

GRENE GROWITH THE HOLY
1 *Greenwood leaves.*

history are important elements also in the final "Mutability Cantos" of *The Faerie Queene*, which rely heavily on iconoclasm and definitions of alien otherness for its glorification of Elizabethan culture (see Greenblatt 1980).

Before the publication of the first three books of *The Faerie Queene* in 1590, Spenser's most important work was *The Shepheard's Calendar* (1579), a brilliant sequence of 12 pastoral eclogues, one for each of the months of the year. *The Shepheard's Calendar* perfectly illustrates the characteristic irony of the pastoral mode, which lies in the discrepancy between the sophistication of the pastoral poet's perspective and the rustic simplicity of his subject matter. Spenser's text includes an introduction and commentary, signed "E. K.," which inaugurates the tradition of the ironic footnote, later developed by T. S. Eliot in *The Waste Land* and by Virginia Woolf in *Three Guineas*. That Spenser, like Virgil, thought pastoral an essential preparation for the writing of epic poetry is implied in the opening lines of *The Faerie Queene*, which announce that he has exchanged his "oaten reeds" for "trumpets stern." Spenser's characteristic sensuousness – which is also a distinguishing feature of Sir Guyon, the hero of *The Faerie Queene*, Book II – is already evident in his pastoral poetry.

Spenser worked systematically through several well established poetic genres – pastoral, satire, epic, sonnet – transforming them as he went. One of the most radical of these transformations was his basing the *Amoretti* sonnets on the courtship of his second wife, Elizabeth Boyle, whom he married just before its publication in 1594. By ending his sequence with the "Epithalamion" (or marriage song), he departed sharply from the Italian tradition of the ideal but inaccessible lady. Apparently by way of the influence of the French poet Clément Marot, however, Spenser returned to the Italian form of linked quatrains and five-rhymed stanzas (abab bcbc cdcd ee). Like *The Shepheard's Calendar*, his sonnet sequence is arranged according to the cycle of the calendar. Another distinguishing feature of the *Amoretti* is its tone of assured, mature love that is implied by the title, which is best translated, "intimate little tokens of love."

Although Spenser does not mention Sidney by name, his dedicatory letter to his friend Sir Walter Raleigh makes clear how close *The Faerie Queene* comes to embodying the conception of poetry Sidney proposes in his *Apology for Poetry*. Spenser's epic poem is about the fashioning of the self, in the ethical and political sense; it yokes together the impulses of history's particularity and philosophy's abstraction, as Sidney describes them; and it generates, in effect, a world of its own, analogous to but separate from that of Elizabethan England. The letter to Raleigh also indicates the incompleteness of the poem as Spenser left it. Instead of 12 books, one for each of the Aristotelian virtues, Spenser completed six and a portion of a seventh book. The poem can, however, be read with great satisfaction in various ways: one book at a time, the first three books as they were originally published, or the six completed books and "The Mutability Cantos."

The second book of the poem continues and expands on the first in that Guyon (or Temperance) is what Red Cross Knight becomes. Thus, Book I is more about becoming, and Book II is more about the dynamics of experience. Or, in Sidney's terms, Book I is principally concerned with thinking well, and Book II with doing well. In order to choose the good, Guyon must come to terms with the essential components of experience, which include his own passions and the situations presented to him by the world. Coming to terms with both makes thoughtful action possible. Temptation comes from these two components of experience also: it may arise from the passions that dominate a person's character, or it may arise from a particular situation. Pyrocles and Cymocles (Canto V) are perhaps the clearest examples of the first sort of temptation, the temptation that arises from within. The Cave or Mammon and the Bower of Bliss are examples of the second sort, temptation that arises from a given situation (Cantos VII and XII). Whatever the source of temptation, however, Spenser is primarily interested in its effect. Ultimately the poem affirms the whole range of experience – including temptations of all sorts – both because they are real and because to know temptation is necessary for doing good. It is in this sense that Spenser sides with Aristotle's model of virtue over Plato's: in Plato's *Phaedrus* the passions are set against each other – fear and pain against the appetites – whereas in Aristotle's *Ethics* and *Poetics* the passions are brought to consciousness under the reign of reason. Indeed, a major part of Book II is devoted to providing a psychological foundation for morality. From his encounter with Amavia in Canto I, Guyon knows abstractly what constitutes virtue. It remains for him to fill out that understanding with experience.

The Faerie Queene ends (or stops) with "The Mutability Cantos" in which both the theme and the form of the poem deal with the impossible human need to contain change. James Nohrnberg, in one of the most comprehensive studies of Spenser ever published, recommends the following aphorism to readers of Spenser: "He who cannot attract Pan approaches Proteus in vain." The relevance of this quip is that the poem insists upon two emphases: Proteus is Spenser's "everlasting store" from which the world recreates itself, while Pan is the source of universal form. Spenser joins the comprehension of Pan to the variegation of Proteus. No wonder, then, that the poem reaches no final end.

READING

Northrop Frye, *Anatomy of Criticism*.
Jonathan Goldberg, *Endlesse Worke: Spenser and the Structures of Discourse*.
Stephen Greenblatt, *Renaissance Self-Fashioning*.
A. C. Hamilton, ed., *A Spenser Encyclopedia*.
Frank Kermode, *Shakespeare, Spenser, Donne: Renaissance Essays*.
Willy Maley, *Salvaging Spenser: Colonialism, Culture and Identity*.
James Nohrnberg, *The Analogy of "The Faerie Queene."*

M. P.

[FROM] THE SHEPHEARDES CALENDER

Aprill.[1]

Ægloga Quarta.   *Fourth Eclogue*

ARGVMENT.

This Æglogue is purposely intended to the honor and prayse of our most gracious souereigne, Queene Elizabeth. The speakers herein be Hobbinoll and Thenott, two shepheardes: the which Hobbinoll being before mentioned, greatly to haue loued Colin, is here set forth more largely, complayning him of that boyes great misaduenture in Love, whereby his mynd was alienate and with drawen not onely from him, who moste loued him, but also from all former delightes and studies, aswell in pleasaunt pyping, as conning[2] ryming and singing, and other his laudable exercises. Whereby he taketh occasion, for proofe of his more excellencie and skill in poetrie, to recorde a songe, which the sayd Colin sometime made in honor of her Maiestie, whom abruptely he termeth Elysa.

Thenot.   Hobbinoll.

Tell me good Hobbinoll, what garres thee greete?
What? hath some Wolfe thy tender Lambes ytorne?
Or is thy Bagpype broke, that soundes so sweete?
Or art thou of thy loued lasse forlorne?

Or bene thine eyes attempred to the yeare,   *are*
Quenching the gasping furrowes thirst with rayne?
Like April shoure, so stremes the trickling teares
Adowne thy cheeke, to quenche thy thristye payne.

<hr>

THE SHEPHEARDES CALENDER

1   "The Shepheardes Calender" is divided into 12 books, which in turn fall into three groups: plaintive, recreative, and moral eclogues. "Aprill" is part of the second group. The eclogue, a classical poetic form that was refined by Virgil, is usually a dialogue between shepherds about the simple, rustic life. Like all forms of pastoral, however, there is also the sense of the simple life being artfully observed from a sophisticated perspective or contrasted with the life of the court. In addition to the poetic voices of Thenot and Hobbinoll and Colin Clout, Spenser's poetic persona, there is also the voice of a commentator, "E. K.," who provides the glosses and presumably the argument. Part of the fiction of the poem, then, is that it is being mediated by the scholarly E. K. The illustration shows Colin piping for Queen Elizabeth and the ladies of her court, who accompany his song on various instruments. Thenot and Nobbinoll are behind him. Taurus, the bull in the clouds above, is the astrological sign for April.

2   Learning.

Hobbinoll.

Nor thys, nor that, so muche doeth make me mourne,
But for the ladde, whome long I lovd so deare,
Nowe loues a lasse, that all his loue doth scorne:
He plongd in payne, his tressed locks dooth teare.

Shepheards delights he dooth them all forsweare,
Hys pleasaunt Pipe, whych made vs meriment,
He wylfully hath broke, and doth forbeare
His wonted songs, wherein he all outwent.

Thenot.

What is he for a Ladde, you so lament?
Ys loue such pinching payne to them, that proue?
And hath he skill to make so excellent,
Yet hath so little skill to brydle loue?

Hobbinoll.

Colin thou kenst, the Southerne shepheardes boye: *knowest*
Him Loue hath wounded with a deadly darte.
Whilome on him was all my care and ioye,   *once*
Forcing with gyfts to winne his wanton heart.   *trying*

But now from me hys madding mynd is starte,[3]
And woes the Widdowes daughter of the glenne: *woos*
So nowe fayre *Rosalind* hath bredde hys smart,
So now his frend is chaunged for a frenne.   *stranger*

Thenot.

But if hys ditties bene so trimly dight,
I pray thee *Hobbinoll*, recorde some one:
The whiles our flockes doe graze about in sight,
And we close shrowded in thys shade alone.

Hobbinol.

Contented I: then will I singe his laye
Of fayre *Elisa*, Queene of shepheardes all:
Which once he made, as by a spring he laye,
And tuned it vnto the Waters fall.

Ye dayntye Nymphs, that in this blessed Brooke
   doe bathe your brest,
For sake your watry bowres, and hether looke,
    at my request:
And eke you Virgins, that on *Parnasse* dwell,
Whence floweth *Helicon* the learned well,
  Helpe me to blaze
  Her worthy praise,
Which in her sexe doth all excell.

Of fayre *Elisa* be your siluer song,
   that blessed wight:
The flowre of Virgins, may shee florish long,
   In princely plight.
For shee is *Syrinx* daughter without spotte,
Which *Pan* the shepheards God of her begot:

---

3   Now his foolish mind has rebelled against me.

So sprong her grace
Of heauenly race,
No mortall blemishe may her blotte.

See, where she sits vpon the grassie greene,
   (O seemely sight)
Yclad in Scarlot like a mayden Queene,
   And Ermines white.
Vpon her head a Cremosin coronet,   *crimson*
60   With Damaske roses and Daffadillies set:
   Bayleaues betweene,
   And Primroses greene
Embellish the sweete Violet.

Tell me, haue ye seene her angelick face,
   Like *Phœbe* fayre?
Her heauenly haueour, her princely grace
   can you well compare?
The Redde rose medled with the White yfere,[4]
In either cheeke depeincten liuely chere.   *depicts*
70   Her modest eye,
   Her Maiestie,
Where haue you seene the like, but there?

I sawe *Phœbus* thrust out his golden hedde,
   vpon her to gaze:
But when he sawe, how broade her beames did spredde,
   it did him amaze.
He blusht to see another Sunne belowe,
Ne durst againe his fyrye face out showe:
   Let him, if he dare,
80   His brightnesse compare
With hers, to haue the ouerthrowe.

Shewe thy selfe *Cynthia* with thy siluer rayes,
   and be not abasht:
When shee the beames of her beauty displayes,
   O how art thou dasht?
But I will not match her with *Latonaes* seede,
Such follie great sorow to *Niobe* did breede.
   Now she is a stone,
   And makes dayly mone,
90   Warning all other to take heede.

Pan may be proud, that euer he begot
   such a Bellibone,
And *Syrinx* reioyse, that euer was her lot
   to beare such an one.
Soone as my younglings cryen for the dam,
To her will I offer a milkwhite Lamb:
   Shee is my goddesse plaine,
   And I her shepherds swayne,
Albee forswonck and forswatt I am.

4   The house of Tudor (Elizabeth's family) descends from the houses of
Lancaster and York, which were respectively symbolized by the red and
the white rose. The Tudor rose blends these colors.

100 I see *Calliope* speede her to the place,
        where my Goddesse shines:
     And after her the other Muses trace,
        with their Violines.
     Bene they not Bay braunches, which they doe beare,   *are*
     All for *Elisa* in her hand to weare?
        So sweetely they play,
        And sing all the way,
     That it a heauen is to heare.

     Lo how finely the graces can it foote
110   to the Instrument:
     They dauncen deffly, and singen soote,   *deftly/sweet*
        in their meriment.
     Wants not a fourth grace, to make the daunce euen?
     Let that rowme to my Lady be yeuen:
        She shalbe a grace,
        To fyll the fourth place,
     And reigne with the rest in heauen.

     And whither rennes this beuie of Ladies bright,
        raunged in a rowe?
120 They bene all Ladyes of the lake behight,
        that vnto her goe.
     Chloris, that is the chiefest Nymph of al,
     Of Oliue braunches beares a Coronall: *crown*
        Oliues bene for peace,
        When wars doe surcease:
     Such for a Princesse bene principall.   *princely*

     Ye shepheards daughters, that dwell on the greene,
        hye you there apace:
     Let none come there, but that Virgins bene,
130   to adorne her grace.
     And when you come, whereas shee is in place,
     See, that your rudenesse doe not you disgrace:
        Binde your fillets faste,   *head-bands*
        And gird in your waste,
     For more finesse, with a tawdrie lace.

     Bring hether the Pincke and purple Cullambine,
        With Gelliflowres:
     Bring Coronations, and Sops in wine,   *carnations/pinks*
        worne of Paramoures.
140 Strowe me the ground with Daffadowndillies,
     And Cowslips, and Kingcups, and loued Lillies:
        The pretie Pawnce,   *pansy*
        And the Cheuisaunce,
     Shall match with the fayre flowre Delice.   *fleur-de-lis*

     Now ryse vp *Elisa*, decked as thou art,
        in royall aray:
     And now ye daintie Damsells may depart
        echeone her way.
     I feare, I haue troubled your troupes to longe:
150 Let dame *Eliza* thanke you for her song.
        And if you come hether,
        When Damsines I gether,   *plums*
     I will part them all you among.

Thenot.

And was thilk same song of *Colins* owne making?   *this*
Ah foolish boy, that is with loue yblent: *blinded*
Great pittie is, he be in such taking,
For naught caren, that bene so lewdly bent.

Hobbinol.

Sicker I hold him, for a greater fon,[5]
That loues the thing, he cannot purchase.
160   But let vs homeward: for night draweth on,
And twincling starres the daylight hence chase.

Thenots Embleme.

O quam te memorem virgo?

Hobbinols Embleme.

O dea certe.[6]

GLOSSE.

1   Gars thee greete) causeth thee weepe and complain.
4   Forlorne) left and forsaken.
5   Attempred to the yeare) agreeable to the season of the yeare, that is Aprill, which moneth
       is most bent to shoures and seasonable rayne: to quench, that is, to delaye the drought,
       caused through drynesse of March wyndes.
10   The Ladde) Colin Clout.   *11* The Lasse) Rosalinda.
12   Tressed locks) wrethed and curled.
17   Is he for a ladde) A straunge manner of speaking .s. what maner of Ladde is he?
19   To make) to rime and versifye. For in this word making, our olde Englishe Poetes were wont
       to comprehend all the skil of Poetrye, according to the Greeke woorde ποιεῖν, to make,
       whence commeth the name of Poets.
21   Colin thou kenst) knowest. Seemeth hereby that Colin perteyneth to some Southern noble
       man, and perhaps in Surrye or Kent, the rather bicause he so often nameth the Kentish
       downes, and before, As lythe as lasse of Kent.
26   The Widowes) He calleth Rosalind the Widowes daughter of the glenne, that is, of a country
       Hamlet or borough, which I thinke is rather sayde to coloure and concele the person, then
       simply spoken. For it is well knowen, euen in spighte of Colin and Hobbinoll, that shee
       is a Gentle woman of no meane house, nor endewed with anye vulgare and common gifts
       both of nature and manners: but suche indeede, as neede nether Colin be ashamed to haue
       her made knowne by his verses, nor Hobbinol be greued, that so she should be commended
       to immortalitie for her rare and singular Vertues: Specially deseruing it no lesse, then
       eyther Myrto the most excellent Poete Theocritus his dearling, or Lauretta the diuine
       Petrarches Goddesse, or Himera the worthye Poete Stesichorus hys Idole: Vpon whom he
       is sayd so much to haue doted, that in regard of her excellencie, he scorned and wrote
       against the beauty of Helena. For which his præsumptuous and vnheedie hardinesse, he
       is sayde by vengeaunce of the Gods, thereat being offended, to haue lost both his eyes.
28   Frenne) a straunger. The word I thinke was first poetically put, and afterwarde vsed in
       commen custome of speach for forenne.
29   Dight) adorned.   *33* Laye) a songe. as Roundelayes and Virelayes. In all this songe is not
       to be respected, what the worthinesse of her Maiestie deserueth, nor what to the highnes

---

5   Surely I take him for a greater fool.

6   The emblems are from *Aeneid* 1.327–8, where Aeneas sees Venus
    disguised as one of Diana's attendants and says, "By what name should
    I call thee, O maiden? . . . O goddess certainly."

of a Prince is agreeable, but what is moste comely for the meanesse of a shepheards witte, or to conceiue, or to vtter. And therefore he calleth her Elysa, as through rudenesse tripping in her name: and a shepheards daughter, it being very vnfit, that a shepheards boy brought vp in the shepefold, should know, or euer seme to haue heard of a Queenes roialty.

37   Ye daintie) is, as it were an Exordium ad preparandos animos.

41   Virgins) the nine Muses, daughters of Apollo and Memorie, whose abode the Poets faine to be on Parnassus, a hill in Grece, for that in that countrye specially florished the honor of all excellent studies.

42   Helicon) is both the name of a fountaine at the foote of Parnassus, and also of a mounteine in Bæotia, out of which floweth the famous Spring Castalius, dedicate also to the Muses: of which spring it is sayd, that when Pegasus the winged horse of Perseus (whereby is meant fame and flying renowme) strooke the grownde with his hoofe, sodenly thereout sprange a wel of moste cleare and pleasaunte water, which fro thence forth was consecrate to the Muses and Ladies of learning.

46   Your siluer song) seemeth to imitate the lyke in Hesiodus ἀργύρεον μέλος.

50   Syrinx) is the name of a Nymphe of Arcadie, whom when Pan being in loue pursued, she flying from him, of the Gods was turned into a reede. So that Pan catching at the Reedes in stede of the Damosell, and puffing hard (for he was almost out of wind) with hys breath made the Reedes to pype: which he seeing, tooke of them, and in remembraunce of his lost loue, made him a pype thereof. But here by Pan and Syrinx is not to bee thoughte, that the shephearde simplye meante those Poetical Gods: but rather supposing (as seemeth) her graces progenie to be diuine and immortall (so as the Paynims were wont to iudge of all Kinges and Princes, according to Homeres saying.

Θνμὸς δὴ μέγας ἐστὶ διοτρεφέως βασιλήως,
τιμή δ' ἐκ διός ἐστι φιλεῖ δε ὁ μητίετα Ζεύς.)

could deuise no parents in his iudgement so worthy for her, as Pan the shepeheards God, and his best beloued Syrinx. So that by Pan is here meant the most famous and victorious King, her highnesse Father, late of worthy memorye K. Henry the eyght. And by that name, oftymes (as hereafter appeareth) be noted kings and mighty Potentates: And in some place Christ himself, who is the verye Pan and god of Shepheardes.

59   Cremosin coronet) he deuiseth her crowne to be of the finest and most delicate flowers, instede of perles and precious stones, wherewith Princes Diademes vse to bee adorned and embost.   63 Embellish) beautifye and set out.

65   Phebe) the Moone, whom the Poets faine to be sister vnto Phæbus, that is the Sunne.   68 Medled) mingled.

68   Yfere) together. By the mingling of the Redde rose and the White, is meant the vniting of the two principall houses of Lancaster and of Yorke: by whose longe discord and deadly debate, this realm many yeares was sore traueiled, and almost cleane decayed. Til the famous Henry the seuenth, of the line of Lancaster, taking to wife the most vertuous Princesse Elisabeth, daughter to the fourth Edward of the house of Yorke, begat the most royal Henry the eyght aforesayde, in whom was the firste vnion of the Whyte Rose and the Redde.

73   I saw Phæbus) the sunne. A sensible Narration, and present view of the thing mentioned, which they call παρουσία.

82   Cynthia) the Moone so called of Cynthus a hyll, where she was honoured.

86–7   Latonaes seede) Was Apollo and Diana. Whom when as Niobe the wife of Amphion scorned, in respect of the noble fruict of her wombe, namely her seuen sonnes, and so many daughters, Latona being therewith displeased, commaunded her sonne Phœbus to slea al the sonnes, and Diana all the daughters: whereat the vnfortunate Niobe being sore dismayed, and lamenting out of measure, was feigned of the Poetes, to be turned into a stone vpon the sepulchre of her children, for which cause the shepheard sayth, he will not compare her to them, for feare of like mysfortune.

92   A Bellibone) or a Bonibell. homely spoken for a fayre mayde or Bonilasse.

99   Forswonck and forswatt) ouerlaboured and sunneburnt.

100   Calliope) one of the nine Muses: to whome they assigne the honor of all Poetical Inuention,
and the firste glorye of the Heroicall verse. other say, that shee is the Goddesse of
Rhetorick: but by Virgile it is manifeste, that they mystake the thyng. For there in hys
Epigrams, that arte semeth to be attributed to Polymnia, saying:

Signat cuncta manu, loquiturque Polymnia gestu.

which seemeth specially to be meant of Action and elocution, both special partes of
Rhetorick: besyde that her name, which (as some construe it) importeth great remembraunce, conteineth another part. but I holde rather with them, which call her Polymnia
or Polyhymnia of her good singing.

104   Bay branches) be the signe of honor and victory, and therfore of myghty Conquerors worn
in theyr triumphes, and eke of famous Poets, as saith Petrarch in hys Sonets.

Arbor vittoriosa triomphale,
Honor d' Imperadori & di Poëti, &c.

109   The Graces) be three sisters, the daughters of Iupiter, (whose names are Aglaia, Thalia,
Euphrosyne, and Homer onely addeth a fourth .s. Pasithea) otherwise called Charites, that
is thanks. whom the Poetes feyned to be the Goddesses of al bountie and comelines, which
therefore (as sayth Theodontius) they make three, to wete, that men first ought to be
gracious and bountiful to other freely, then to receiue benefits at other mens hands
curteously, and thirdly to requite them thankfully: which are three sundry Actions in
liberalitye. And Boccace saith, that they be painted naked, (as they were indeede on the
tombe of C. Iulius Cæsar) the one hauing her backe toward vs, and her face fromwarde,
as proceeding from vs: the other two toward vs, noting double thanke to be due to vs for
the benefit, we haue done.

111   Deaffly) Finelye and nimbly.   111   Soote) Sweete.   112   Meriment) Mirth.

118   Beuie) A beauie of Ladyes, is spoken figuratiuely for a company or troupe. the terme is taken
of Larkes. For they say a Beuie of Larkes, euen as a Couey of Partridge, or an eye of
Pheasaunts.

120   Ladyes of the lake) be Nymphes. For it was an olde opinion amongste the Auncient Heathen,
that of euery spring and fountaine was a goddesse the Soueraigne. Whiche opinion
stucke in the myndes of men not manye yeares sithence, by meanes of certain fine
fablers and lowd lyers, such as were the Authors of King Arthure the great and such
like, who tell many an vnlawfull leasing of the Ladyes of the Lake, that is, the Nymphes.
For the word Nymphe in Greeke signifieth Well water, or otherwise a Spouse or
Bryde.

120   Behight) called or named.

122   Chloris) the name of a Nymph, and signifieth greenesse, of whome is sayd, that
Zephyrus the Westerne wind being in loue with her, and coueting her to wyfe, gaue her
for a dowrie, the chiefedome and soueraigntye of al flowres and greene herbes, growing
on earth.

124   Oliues bene) The Oliue was wont to be the ensigne of Peace and quietnesse, eyther for that
it cannot be planted and pruned, and so carefully looked to, as it ought, but in time of
peace: or els for that the Oliue tree, they say, will not growe neare the Firre tree, which
is dedicate to Mars the God of battaile, and vsed most for speares and other instruments
of warre. Whereupon is finely feigned, that when Neptune and Minerua stroue for the
naming of the citie of Athens, Neptune striking the ground with his mace, caused a horse
to come forth, that importeth warre, but at Mineruaes stroke sprong out an Oliue, to note
that it should be a nurse of learning, and such peaceable studies.

133   Binde your) Spoken rudely, and according to shepheardes simplicitye.

136   Bring) all these be names of flowers. Sops in wine a flowre in colour much like to a Coronation, but differing in smel and quantitye. Flowre delice, that which they vse to misterme, Flowre de luce, being in Latine called Flos delitiarum.

145   Now rise) is the conclusion. For hauing so decked her with prayses and comparisons, he returneth all the thanck of hys laboure to the excellencie of her Maiestie.

152   When Damsins) A base reward of a clownish giuer.

155   Yblent) Y, is a poeticall addition. blent blinded.

Embleme.

This Poesye is taken out of Virgile, and there of him vsed in the person of Æneas to his mother Venus, appearing to him in likenesse of one of Dianaes damosells: being there most diuinely set forth. To which similitude of diuinitie Hobbinoll comparing the excelency of Elisa, and being through the worthynes of Colins song, as it were, ouercome with the hugenesse of his imagination, brusteth out in great admiration, (O quam te memorem virgo?) being otherwise vnhable, then by soddein silence, to expresse the worthinesse of his conceipt. Whom Thenot answereth with another part of the like verse, as confirming by his graunt and approuaunce, that Elisa is nowhit inferiour to the Maiestie of her, of whome that Poete so boldly pronounced, O dea certe.

AMORETTI.

SONNET. I.

Happy ye leaues when as those lilly hands,
  which hold my life in their dead doing might
shall handle you and hold in loues soft bands,
  lyke captiues trembling at the victors sight.
And happy lines, on which with starry light,
  those lamping eyes will deigne sometimes to look   *flashing*
  and reade the sorrowes of my dying spright,   *spirit*
  written with teares in harts close bleeding book.
And happy rymes bath'd in the sacred brooke,
10   of *Helicon*[1] whence she deriued is,
  when ye behold that Angels blessed looke,
  my soules long lacked foode, my heauens blis.
Leaues, lines, and rymes, seeke her to please alone,
  whom if ye please, I care for other none.

SONNET. II.

Vnquiet thought, whom at the first I bred,
  Of th'inward bale of my loue pined hart:
and sithens haue with sighes and sorrowes fed,
  till greater then my wombe thou woxen[2] art.
Breake forth at length out of the inner part,
  in which thou lurkest lyke to vipers brood:
and seeke some succour both to ease my smart
  and also to sustayne thy selfe with food.
But if in presence of that fayrest proud

AMORETTI   2   Past participle of "to wax."
1   The Hippocrene flowed from Helicon, a mountain in Boeotia that
was sacred to the Muses.

10
thou chance to come, fall lowly at her feet:
    and with meeke humblesse and afflicted mood,
    pardon for thee, and grace for me intreat.
Which if she graunt, then liue and my loue cherish,
    if not, die soone, and I with thee will perish.

SONNET. III.

The souerayne beauty which I doo admyre,
    witnesse the world how worthy to be prayzed:
    the light wherof hath kindled heauenly fyre,
    in my fraile spirit by her from basenesse raysed.
That being now with her huge brightnesse dazed,
    base thing I can no more endure to view:
    but looking still on her I stand amazed,
    at wondrous sight of so celestiall hew.
So when my toung would speak her praises dew,
10
    it stopped is with thoughts astonishment:
    and when my pen would write her titles true,
    it rauisht is with fancies wonderment:
Yet in my hart I then both speake and write
    the wonder that my wit cannot endite.

SONNET. IV.

New yeare forth looking out of Ianus[3] gate,
    Doth seeme to promise hope of new delight:
    and bidding th'old Adieu, his passed date
    bids all old thoughts to die in dumpish spright.
And calling forth out of sad Winters night,
    fresh loue, that long hath slept in cheerlesse bower:
    wils him awake, and soone about him dight
    his wanton wings and darts of deadly power.
For lusty spring now in his timely howre,
10
    is ready to come forth him to receiue:
    and warnes the Earth with diuers colord flowre,
    to decke hir selfe, and her faire mantle weaue.
Then you faire flowre, in whom fresh youth doth raine,
    prepare your selfe new loue to entertaine.

SONNET. V.

Rvdely thou wrongest my deare harts desire,
    In finding fault with her too portly pride: *stately*
    the thing which I doo most in her admire,
    is of the world vnworthy most enuide.   *envied*
For in those lofty lookes is close implide,
    scorn of base things, and sdeigne of foule dishonor:
    thretning rash eies which gaze on her so wide,
    that loosely they ne dare to looke vpon her.

3   Janus, ancient Roman god of doors and gates, had two faces, on the
back and front of his head, looking forward and backward.

Such pride is praise, such portlinesse is honor,
10   that boldned innocence beares in hir eies:
and her faire countenance like a goodly banner,
spreds in defiaunce of all enemies.
Was neuer in this world ought worthy tride,
    without some spark of such self-pleasing pride.

SONNET. VI.

Be nought dismayd that her vnmoued mind
    doth still persist in her rebellious pride:
such loue not lyke to lusts of baser kynd,
the harder wonne, the firmer will abide.
The durefull Oake, whose sap is not yet dride,   *durable*
is long ere it conceiue the kindling fyre:
but when it once doth burne, it doth diuide
great heat, and makes his flames to heauen aspire.
So hard it is to kindle new desire,
10   in gentle brest that shall endure for euer:
deepe is the wound, that dints the parts entire
with chast affects, that naught but death can seuer.
Then thinke not long in taking litle paine,
    to knit the knot, that euer shall remaine.

SONNET. VII.

Fayre eyes, the myrrour of my mazed hart,
    what wondrous vertue is contaynd in you
the which both lyfe and death forth from you dart
into the obiect of your mighty view?
For when ye mildly looke with louely hew,
then is my soule with life and loue inspired:
but when ye lowre, or looke on me askew,
then doe I die, as one with lightning fyred.
But since that lyfe is more then death desyred,
10   looke euer louely, as becomes you best,
that your bright beams of my weak eies admyred,
may kindle liuing fire within my brest.
Such life should be the honor of your light,
    such death the sad ensample of your might.

SONNET. VIII.

More then most faire, full of the liuing fire,
    Kindled aboue vnto the maker neere:
no eies but ioyes, in which al powers conspire,
that to the world naught else be counted deare.
Thrugh your bright beams doth not the blinded guest
shoot out his darts to base affections wound?[4]
but Angels come to lead fraile mindes to rest
in chast desires on heauenly beauty bound.

---

4   An ancient theory of vision held that the eye's beams illuminate the
thing it looks upon.

You frame my thoughts and fashion me within,
10   you stop my toung, and teach my hart to speake,
    you calme the storme that passion did begin,
    strong thrugh your cause, but by your vertue weak.
Dark is the world, where your light shined neuer;
    well is he borne, that may behold you euer.

SONNET. IX.

Long-while I sought to what I might compare
    those powrefull eies, which lighten my dark spright,
    yet find I nought on earth to which I dare
    resemble th'ymage of their goodly light.
Not to the Sun: for they doo shine by night;
    nor to the Moone: for they are changed neuer;
    nor to the Starres: for they haue purer sight;
    nor to the fire: for they consume not euer;
Nor to the lightning: for they still perseuer;
10   nor to the Diamond: for they are more tender;
    nor vnto Christall: for nought may them seuer;
    nor vnto glasse: such basenesse mought offend her;
Then to the Maker selfe they likest be,
    whose light doth lighten all that here we see.

SONNET. X.

Vnrighteous Lord of loue what law is this,
    That me thou makest thus tormented be?
    the whiles she lordeth in licentious blisse
    of her freewill, scorning both thee and me.
See how the Tyrannesse doth ioy to see
    the huge massacres which her eyes do make:
    and humbled harts brings captiues vnto thee,
    that thou of them mayst mightie vengeance take.
But her proud hart doe thou a little shake
10   and that high look, with which she doth comptroll
    all this worlds pride bow to a baser make,
    and al her faults in thy black booke enroll.
That I may laugh at her in equall sort,
    as she doth laugh at me and makes my pain her sport.

SONNET. XI.

Dayly when I do seeke and sew for peace,   *sue*
    And hostages doe offer for my truth:
    she cruell warriour doth her selfe addresse
    to battell, and the weary war renew'th.
Ne wilbe moou'd with reason or with rewth,
    to graunt small respit to my restlesse toile:
    but greedily her fell intent poursewth,
    Of my poore life to make vnpittied spoile.

Yet my poore life, all sorrowes to assoyle,   *assail*
10   I would her yield, her wrath to pacify:
        but then she seekes with torment and turmoyle,
        to force me liue and will not let me dy.
        All paine hath end and euery war hath peace,
        but mine no price nor prayer may surcease.

SONNET. XII.

One day I sought with her hart-thrilling eies,
    to make a truce and termes to entertaine:
    all fearelesse then of so false enimies,
    which sought me to entrap in treasons traine.
So as I then disarmed did remaine,
    a wicked ambush which lay hidden long
    in the close couert of her guilefull eyen,
    thence breaking forth did thick about me throng.
Too feeble I t'abide the brunt so strong,
10   was forst to yeeld my selfe into their hands:
    who me captiuing streight with rigorous wrong,
    haue euer since me kept in cruell bands.
So Ladie now to you I doo complaine,
    against your eies that iustice I may gaine.

SONNET. XIII.

In that proud port, which her so goodly graceth,   *stature*
    whiles her faire face she reares vp to the skie:
    and to the ground her eie lids low embaseth,
    most goodly temperature ye may descry,
Myld humblesse mixt with awfull maiesty.
    for looking on the earth whence she was borne,
    her minde remembreth her mortalitie,
    what so is fayrest shall to earth returne.
But that same lofty countenance seemes to scorne
10   base thing, and thinke how she to heauen may clime:
    treading downe earth as lothsome and forlorne,
    that hinders heauenly thoughts with drossy slime.
Yet lowly still vouchsafe to looke on me,
    such lowlinesse shall make you lofty be.

SONNET. XIV.

Retourne agayne my forces late dismayd,
    Vnto the siege[5] by you abandon'd quite,
    great shame it is to leaue like one afrayd,
    so fayre a peece for one repulse so light.
Gaynst such strong castles needeth greater might,
    then those small forts which ye were wont belay;
    such haughty mynds enur'd to hardy fight,
    disdayne to yield vnto the first assay.

5   The extended image here is that of courtship as laying siege to a
castle.

Bring therefore all the forces that ye may,
10   and lay incessant battery to her heart,
playnts, prayers, vowes, ruth, sorrow, and dismay,
those engins can the proudest loue conuert.
And if those fayle fall downe and dy before her,
so dying liue, and liuing do adore her.

SONNET. XV.

Ye tradefull Merchants that with weary toyle,
do seeke most pretious things to make your gain:
and both the Indias of their treasures spoile,
what needeth you to seeke so farre in vaine?
For loe my loue doth in her selfe containe
all this worlds riches that may farre be found,
if Saphyres, loe her eies be Saphyres plaine,
if Rubies, loe hir lips be Rubies sound:
If Pearles, hir teeth be pearles both pure and round;
10   if Yuorie, her forhead yuory weene;
if Gold, her locks are finest gold on ground;
if siluer, her faire hands are siluer sheene:
But that which fairest is, but few behold,
her mind adornd with vertues manifold.

SONNET. XVI.

One day as I vnwarily did gaze
on those fayre eyes my loues immortall light:
the whiles my stonisht hart stood in amaze,
through sweet illusion of her lookes delight;
I mote perceiue how in her glauncing sight,
legions of loues with little wings did fly:
darting their deadly arrowes fyry bright,
at euery rash beholder passing by.
One of those archers closely I did spy,
10   ayming his arrow at my very hart:
when suddenly with twincle of her eye,
the Damzell broke his misintended dart.
Had she not so doon, sure I had bene slayne,   *done*
yet as it was, I hardly scap't with paine.

SONNET. XVII.

The glorious pourtraict of that Angels face,   *portrait*
Made to amaze weake mens confused skil:
and this worlds worthlesse glory to embase,
what pen, what pencill can expresse her fill?
For though he colours could deuize at will,
and eke his learned hand at pleasure guide,
least trembling it his workmanship should spill,
yet many wondrous things there are beside.

The sweet eye-glaunces, that like arrowes glide,
10   the charming smiles, that rob sence from the hart:
       the louely pleasance and the lofty pride,
       cannot expressed be by any art.
A greater craftesmans hand thereto doth neede,
       that can expresse the life of things indeed.

SONNET. XVIII.

The rolling wheele that runneth often round,
       The hardest steele in tract of time doth teare:
       and drizling drops that often doe redound,
       the firmest flint doth in continuance weare.
Yet cannot I with many a dropping teare,
       and long intreaty soften her hard hart:
       that she will once vouchsafe my plaint to heare,
       or looke with pitty on my payneful smart.
But when I pleade, she bids me play my part,
10   and when I weep, she sayes teares are but water:
       and when I sigh, she sayes I know the art,
       and when I waile, she turnes hir selfe to laughter.
So doe I weepe, and wayle, and pleade in vaine,
       whiles she as steele and flint doth still remayne.

SONNET. XIX.

The merry Cuckow, messenger of Spring,
       His trompet shrill hath thrise already sounded:
       that warnes al louers wayt vpon their king,
       who now is comming forth with girland crouned.
With noyse whereof the quyre of Byrds resounded
       their anthemes sweet devized of loues prayse,
       that all the woods theyr ecchoes back rebounded,
       as if they knew the meaning of their layes.
But mongst them all, which did Loues honor rayse
10   no word was heard of her that most it ought,
       but she his precept proudly disobayes,
       and doth his ydle message set at nought.
Therefore O loue, vnlesse she turne to thee
       ere Cuckow end, let her a rebell be.

SONNET. XX.

In vaine I seeke and sew to her for grace,
       and doe myne humbled hart before her poure:
       the whiles her foot she in my necke doth place,
       and tread my life downe in the lowly floure.
And yet the Lyon that is Lord of power,
       and reigneth ouer euery beast in field:
       in his most pride disdeigneth to deuoure
       the silly lambe that to his might doth yield.

But she more cruell and more saluage wylde,   *savage*
10   then either Lyon or the Lyonesse:
    shames not to be with guiltlesse bloud defylde,
    but taketh glory in her cruelnesse.
Fayrer then fayrest let none euer say,
    that ye were blooded in a yeelded pray.

SONNET. XXI.

Was it the worke of nature or of Art,
    which tempred so the feature of her face,
    that pride and meeknesse mixt by equall part,
    doe both appeare t'adorne her beauties grace?
For with mild pleasance, which doth pride displace,
    she to her loue doth lookers eyes allure:
    and with sterne countenance back again doth chace
    their looser lookes that stir vp lustes impure.
With such strange termes her eyes she doth inure,
10   that with one looke she doth my life dismay:
    and with another doth it streight recure,
    her smile me drawes, her frowne me driues away.
Thus doth she traine and teach me with her lookes,
    such art of eyes I neuer read in bookes.

SONNET. XXII.

This holy season fit to fast and pray,[6]
    Men to deuotion ought to be inclynd:
    therefore, I lykewise on so holy day,
    for my sweet Saynt some seruice fit will find.
Her temple fayre is built within my mind,
    in which her glorious ymage placed is,
    on which my thoughts doo day and night attend
    lyke sacred priests that neuer thinke amisse.
There I to her as th'author of my blisse,
10   will builde an altar to appease her yre:
    and on the same my hart will sacrifise,
    burning in flames of pure and chast desyre:
The which vouchsafe O goddesse to accept,
    amongst thy deerest relicks to be kept.

SONNET. XXIII.

Penelope for her *Vlisses* sake,
    Deuiz'd a Web her wooers to deceaue:[7]
    in which the worke that she all day did make
    the same at night she did againe vnreaue:
Such subtile craft my Damzell doth conceaue,
    th'importune suit of my desire to shonne:
    for all that I in many dayes doo weaue,
    in one short houre I find by her vndonne.

---

6 Lent, perhaps.

7 Penelope (in Homer's *Odyssey*) put off her suitors by unweaving at night the tapestry she wove by day; see gazetteer.

So when I thinke to end that I begonne,
10   I must begin and neuer bring to end:
for with one looke she spils that long I sponne,
and with one word my whole years work doth rend.
Such labour like the Spyders web I fynd,
whose fruitlesse worke is broken with least wynd.

SONNET. XXIV.

When I behold that beauties wonderment,
And rare perfection of each goodly part:
of natures skill the onely complement,
I honor and admire the makers art.
But when I feele the bitter balefull smart,
which her fayre eyes vnwares doe worke in mee:
that death out of theyr shiny beames doe dart,
I thinke that I a new *Pandora*[8] see;
Whom all the Gods in councell did agree,
10   into this sinfull world from heauen to send:
that she to wicked men a scourge should bee,
for all their faults with which they did offend.
But since ye are my scourge I will intreat,
that for my faults ye will me gently beat.

SONNET. XXV.

How long shall this lyke dying lyfe endure,
And know no end of her owne mysery:
but wast and weare away in termes vnsure,
twixt feare and hope depending doubtfully?
Yet better were attonce to let me die,
and shew the last ensample of your pride:
then to torment me thus with cruelty,
to proue your powre, which I too wel haue tride.
But yet if in your hardned brest ye hide
10   a close intent at last to shew me grace:
then all the woes and wrecks which I abide,
as meanes of blisse I gladly wil embrace;
And wish that more and greater they might be,
that greater meede at last may turne to mee.

SONNET. XXVI.

Sweet is the Rose, but growes vpon a brere;
Sweet is the Iunipere, but sharpe his bough;
sweet is the Eglantine; but pricketh nere;
sweet is the firbloome, but his braunches rough.
Sweet is the Cypresse, but his rynd is tough,
sweet is the nut, but bitter is his pill;
sweet is the broome-flowre, but yet sowre enough;
and sweet is Moly,[9] but his root is ill.

8 According to Hesiod, Pandora released all desires from her box, cre-   9 A fabulous plant thought to have magical powers.
ating chaos in the world; but she shut the box before hope was released.

So euery sweet with soure is tempred still,
   that maketh it be coueted the more:
   for easie things that may be got at will,
   most sorts of men doe set but little store.
Why then should I accoumpt of little paine,
   that endlesse pleasure shall vnto me gaine?

SONNET. XXVII.

Faire proud now tell me why should faire be proud,
   Sith all worlds glorie is but drosse vncleane:
   and in the shade of death it selfe shall shroud,
   how euer now thereof ye little weene.
That goodly Idoll now so gay beseene,
   shall doffe her fleshes borowd fayre attyre:
   and be forgot as it had neuer beene,
   that many now much worship and admire.
Ne any then shall after it inquire,
   ne any mention shall thereof remaine:
   but what this verse, that neuer shall expyre,
   shall to you purchas with her thankles paine.
Faire be no lenger proud of that shall perish,
   but that which shal you make immortall, cherish.

SONNET. XXVIII.

The laurell leafe,[10] which you this day doe weare,
   giues me great hope of your relenting mynd:
   for since it is the badg which I doe beare,
   ye bearing it doe seeme to me inclind:
The powre thereof, which ofte in me I find,
   let it lykewise your gentle brest inspire
   with sweet infusion, and put you in mind
   of that proud mayd, whom now those leaues attyre:
Proud *Daphne* scorning Phæbus louely fyre,
   on the Thessalian shore from him did flee:
   for which the gods in theyr reuengefull yre
   did her transforme into a laurell tree.
Then fly no more fayre loue from Phebus chace,
   but in your brest his leafe and loue embrace.

SONNET. XXIX.

See how the stubborne damzell doth depraue
   my simple meaning with disdaynfull scorne:
   and by the bay which I vnto her gaue,
   accoumpts my selfe her captiue quite forlorne.

---

10 The (bay) laurel is the emblem of poets as well as
victorious soldiers, according to Ovid, because Cupid made Apollo
(Phoebus) love Daphne, while making her scorn him. In flight from
Apollo, she was transformed into a laurel tree.

The bay (quoth she) is of the victours borne,
   yielded them by the vanquisht as theyr meeds,
   and they therewith doe poetes heads adorne,
   to sing the glory of their famous deedes.
But sith she will the conquest challeng needs,
   let her accept me as her faithfull thrall,
   that her great triumph which my skill exceeds,
   I may in trump of fame blaze ouer all.
Then would I decke her head with glorious bayes,
   and fill the world with her victorious prayse.

10

SONNET. XXX.

My loue is lyke to yse, and I to fyre;
   how comes it then that this her cold so great
   is not dissolu'd through my so hot desyre,
   but harder growes the more I her intreat?
Or how comes it that my exceeding heat
   is not delayd by her hart frosen cold:
   but that I burne much more in boyling sweat,
   and feele my flames augmented manifold?
What more miraculous thing may be told
   that fire which all thing melts, should harden yse:
   and yse which is congeald with sencelesse cold,
   should kindle fyre by wonderfull deuyse?
Such is the powre of loue in gentle mind,
   that it can alter all the course of kynd.

ice

10

SONNET. XXXI.

Ah why hath nature to so hard a hart,
   giuen so goodly giftes of beauties grace?
   whose pryde depraues each other better part,
   and all those pretious ornaments deface.
Sith to all other beastes of bloody race,
   a dreadfull countenaunce she giuen hath:
   that with theyr terrour al the rest may chace,
   and warne to shun the daunger of theyr wrath.
But my proud one doth worke the greater scath,
   through sweet allurement of her louely hew:
   that she the better may in bloody bath
   of such poore thralls her cruell hands embrew.
But did she know how ill these two accord,
   such cruelty she would haue soone abhord.

10

SONNET. XXXII.

The paynefull smith with force of feruent heat,
   the hardest yron soone doth mollify:
   that with his heauy sledge he can it beat,
   and fashion to what he it list apply.

Yet cannot all these flames in which I fry,
    her hart more harde then yron soft awhit:
    ne all the playnts and prayers with which I
    doe beat on th'anduyle of her stubberne wit: *anvil*
But still the more she feruent sees my fit,
10   the more she frieseth in her wilfull pryde:
    and harder growes the harder she is smit,
    with all the playnts which to her be applyde.
What then remaines but I to ashes burne,
    and she to stones at length all frosen turne?

SONNET. XXXIII.

Great wrong I doe, I can it not deny,
    to that most sacred Empresse my dear dred,
    not finishing her Queene of faery,
    that mote enlarge her liuing prayses dead:[11]
But lodwick, this of grace to me aread:
    doe ye not thinck th'accomplishment of it,
    sufficient worke for one mans simple head,
    all were it as the rest but rudely writ.
How then should I without another wit,
10   thinck euer to endure so tædious toyle?
    sins that this one is tost with troublous fit,
    of a proud loue, that doth my spirite spoyle.
Ceasse then, till she vouchsafe to grawnt me rest,
    or lend you me another liuing brest.

SONNET. XXXIV.

Lyke as a ship that through the Ocean wyde,
    by conduct of some star doth make her way,
    whenas a storme hath dimd her trusty guyde,
    out of her course doth wander far astray.
So I whose star, that wont with her bright ray
    me to direct, with cloudes is ouercast,
    doe wander now in darknesse and dismay,
    through hidden perils round about me plast.
Yet hope I well, that when this storme is past
10   my *Helice*[12] the lodestar of my lyfe
    will shine again, and looke on me at last,
    with louely light to cleare my cloudy grief.
Till then I wander carefull comfortlesse,
    in secret sorow and sad pensiuenesse.

SONNET. XXXV.

My hungry eyes through greedy couetize,
    still to behold the obiect of their paine:
    with no contentment can themselues suffize,
    but hauing pine and hauing not complaine.

11 Spenser is here addressing his friend Lodowick Bryskett about his anxiety over not having finished *The Faerie Queene*.   12 The constellation of the Lesser Bear, which contains the pole star.

For lacking it they cannot lyfe sustayne,
   and hauing it they gaze on it the more:
   in their amazement lyke *Narcissus* vaine
   whose eyes him staru'd: so plenty makes me poore.
Yet are mine eyes so filled with the store
10   of that faire sight, that nothing else they brooke,
   but lothe the things which they did like before,
   and can no more endure on them to looke.
All this worlds glory seemeth vayne to me,
   and all their showes but shadowes sauing she.

SONNET. XXXVI.

Tell me when shall these wearie woes haue end,
   Or shall their ruthlesse torment neuer cease:
   but al my dayes in pining languor spend,
   without hope of aswagement or release?
Is there no meanes for me to purchace peace,
   or make agreement with her thrilling eyes:
   but that their cruelty doth still increace,
   and dayly more augment my miseryes?
But when ye haue shewed all extremityes,
10   then thinke how litle glory ye haue gayned,
   by slaying him, whose lyfe though ye despyse,
   mote haue your life in honour long maintayned.
But by his death which some perhaps will mone,   *moan*
   ye shall condemned be of many a one.

SONNET. XXXVII.

What guyle is this, that those her golden tresses,
   She doth attyre vnder a net of gold:
   and with sly skill so cunningly them dresses,
   that which is gold or heare, may scarse be told?
Is it that mens frayle eyes, which gaze too bold,
   she may entangle in that golden snare:
   and being caught may craftily enfold
   theyr weaker harts, which are not wel aware?
Take heed therefore, myne eyes, how ye doe stare
10   henceforth too rashly on that guilefull net,
   in which if euer ye entrapped are,
   out of her bands ye by no meanes shall get.
Fondnesse it were for any being free,
   to couet fetters, though they golden bee.

SONNET. XXXVIII.

Arion,[13] when through tempests cruel wracke,
   He forth was thrown into the greedy seas:
   through the sweet musick which his harp did make
   allur'd a Dolphin him from death to ease.

13 Mythical poet who was saved from drowning by a dolphin that was
charmed by his song.

But my rude musick, which was wont to please
  some dainty eares, cannot with any skill,
  the dreadfull tempest of her wrath appease,
  nor moue the Dolphin from her stubborne will,
But in her pride she dooth perseuer still,
10 all carelesse how my life for her decayse:
  yet with one word she can it saue or spill,
  to spill were pitty, but to saue were prayse.
Chose rather to be praysd for dooing good,
  then to be blam'd for spilling guiltlesse blood,

SONNET. XXXIX.

Sweet smile, the daughter of the Queene of loue,
  Expressing all thy mothers powrefull art:
  with which she wonts to temper angry Ioue,
  when all the gods he threats with thundring dart.
Sweet is thy vertue as thy selfe sweet art,
  for when on me thou shinedst late in sadnesse,
  a melting pleasance ran through euery part,
  and me reuiued with hart robbing gladnesse.
Whylest rapt with ioy resembling heauenly madnes,
10 my soule was rauisht quite as in a traunce:
  and feeling thence no more her sorowes sadnesse,
  fed on the fulnesse of that chearefull glaunce.
More sweet than Nectar or Ambrosiall meat,
  seemd euery bit, which thenceforth I did eat.

SONNET. XL.

Mark when she smiles with amiable cheare,
  And tell me whereto can ye lyken it:
  when on each eyelid sweetly doe appeare
  an hundred Graces as in shade to sit.
Lykest it seemeth in my simple wit
  vnto the fayre sunshine in somers day:
  that when a dreadfull storme away is flit,
  thrugh the broad world doth spred his goodly ray:
At sight whereof each bird that sits on spray,
10 and euery beast that to his den was fled,
  comes forth afresh out of their late dismay,
  and to the light lift vp theyr drouping hed.
So my storme beaten hart likewise is cheared,
  with that sunshine when cloudy looks are cleared.

SONNET. XLI.

Is it her nature or is it her will,
  to be so cruell to an humbled foe?
  if nature, then she may it mend with skill,
  if will, then she at will may will forgoe.

But if her nature and her wil be so,
 that she will plague the man that loues her most:
 and take delight t'encrease a wretches woe,
 then all her natures goodly guifts are lost.
And that same glorious beauties ydle boast,
10 is but a bayt such wretches to beguile,
 as being long in her loues tempest tost,
 she meanes at last to make her piteous spoyle.
O fayrest fayre let neuer it be named,
 that so fayre beauty was so fowly shamed.

SONNET. XLII.

The loue which me so cruelly tormenteth,
 So pleasing is in my extreamest paine:
 that all the more my sorrow it augmenteth,
 the more I loue and doe embrace my bane.
Ne doe I wish (for wishing were but vaine)
 to be acquit fro my continuall smart:
 but ioy her thrall for euer to remayne,
 and yield for pledge my poore captyued hart;
The which that it from her may neuer start,
10 let her, yf please her, bynd with adamant chayne:
 and from all wandring loues which mote peruart
 his safe assurance, strongly it restrayne.
Onely let her abstaine from cruelty,
 and doe me not before my time to dy.

SONNET. XLIII.

Shall I then silent be or shall I speake?
 And if I speake, her wrath renew I shall:
 and if I silent be, my hart will breake,
 or choked be with ouerflowing gall.
What tyranny is this both my hart to thrall,
 and eke my toung with proud restraint to tie?
 that nether I may speake nor thinke at all,
 but like a stupid stock in silence die.
Yet I my hart with silence secretly
10 will teach to speak, and my iust cause to plead:
 and eke mine eies with meeke humility,
 loue learned letters to her eyes to read.
Which her deep wit, that true harts thought can spel,
 wil soone conceiue, and learne to construe well.

SONNET. XLIV.

When those renoumed noble Peres of Greece,   *peers*
 thrugh stubborn pride amongst themselues did iar
 forgetfull of the famous golden fleece,
 then Orpheus with his harp theyr strife did bar.

But this continuall cruell ciuill warre,
  the which my selfe against my selfe doe make:
  whilest my weak powres of passions warreid arre,
  no skill can stint nor reason can aslake.
But when in hand my tunelesse harp I take,
  then doe I more augment my foes despight:
  and griefe renew, and passions doe awake
  to battaile fresh against my selfe to fight.
Mongst whome the more I seeke to settle peace,
  the more I fynd their malice to increace.

SONNET. XLV.

Leaue lady in your glasse of christall clene,
  Your goodly selfe for euermore to vew:
  and in my selfe, my inward selfe I meane,
  most liuely lyke behold your semblant trew.
Within my hart, though hardly it can shew
  thing so diuine to vew of earthly eye:
  the fayre Idea[14] of your celestiall hew,
  and euery part remaines immortally:
And were it not that through your cruelty,
  with sorrow dimmed and deformd it were:
  the goodly ymage of your visnomy,
  clearer then christall would therein appere.
But if your selfe in me ye playne will see,
  remoue the cause by which your fayre beames darkned be.

SONNET. XLVI.

When my abodes prefixed time is spent,
  My cruell fayre streight bids me wend my way:
  but then from heauen most hideous stormes are sent
  as willing me against her will to stay.
Whom then shall I or heauen or her obay?
  the heauens know best what is the best for me:
  but as she will, whose will my life doth sway,
  my lower heauen, so it perforce must bee.
But ye high heuens, that all this sorowe see,
  sith all your tempests cannot hold me backe:
  aswage your stormes, or else both you and she
  will both together me too sorely wrack.
Enough it is for one man to sustaine
  the stormes, which she alone on me doth raine.

SONNET. XLVII.

Trust not the treason of those smyling lookes,
  vntill ye haue theyr guylefull traynes well tryde:
  for they are lyke but vnto golden hookes,
  that from the foolish fish theyr bayts doe hyde:

---

14   Perhaps refers to the Platonic idea of ideal or eternal beauty.

So she with flattring smyles weake harts doth guyde
   vnto her loue, and tempte to theyr decay,
   whome being caught she kills with cruell pryde,
   and feeds at pleasure on the wretched pray:
Yet euen whylst her bloody hands them slay,
   her eyes looke louely and vpon them smyle:
   that they take pleasure in her cruell play,
   and dying doe them selues of payne beguyle.
O mighty charm which makes men loue theyr bane,
   and thinck they dy with pleasure, liue with payne.

10

SONNET. XLVIII.

Innocent paper whom too cruell hand
   Did make the matter to auenge her yre:
   and ere she could thy cause wel vnderstand,
   did sacrifize vnto the greedy fyre.
Well worthy thou to haue found better hyre,
   then so bad end for hereticks ordayned:
   yet heresy nor treason didst conspire,
   but plead thy maisters cause vniustly payned.
Whom she all carelesse of his griefe constrayned
   to vtter forth the anguish of his hart:
   and would not heare, when he to her complayned
   the piteous passion of his dying smart.
Yet liue for euer, though against her will,
   and speake her good, though she require it ill.

10

SONNET. XLIX.

Fayre cruell, why are ye so fierce and cruell?
   Is it because your eyes haue powre to kill?
   then know, that mercy is the mighties iewell,
   and greater glory thinke to saue, then spill.
But if it be your pleasure and proud will,
   to shew the powre of your imperious eyes:
   then not on him that neuer thought you ill,
   but bend your force against your enemyes.
Let them feele th'utmost of your crueltyes,
   and kill with looks, as Cockatrices[15] doo:
   but him that at your footstoole humbled lies,
   with mercifull regard, giue mercy too.
Such mercy shal you make admyred to be,
   so shall you liue by giuing life to me.

10

SONNET. L.

Long languishing in double malady,
   of my harts wound and of my bodies griefe:
   there came to me a leach that would apply
   fit medicines for my bodies best reliefe.

15   A fabulous reptile that was thought to kill its prey with its breath
or a look.

Vayne man (quod I) that hast but little priefe,
   in deep discouery of the mynds disease,
   is not the hart of all the body chiefe?
   and rules the members as it selfe doth please?
Then with some cordialls seeke first to appease
10   the inward languour of my wounded hart,
   and then my body shall haue shortly ease:
   but such sweet cordialls passe Physitions art.
Then my lyfes Leach doe you your skill reueale,
   and with one salue both hart and body heale.

SONNET. LI.

Doe I not see that fayrest ymages
   Of hardest Marble are of purpose made?
   for that they should endure through many ages,
   ne let theyr famous moniments to fade.
Why then doe I, vntrainde in louers trade,
   her hardnes blame which I should more commend?
   sith neuer ought was excellent assayde,
   which was not hard t'atchiue and bring to end.
Ne ought so hard, but he that would attend,
10   mote soften it and to his will allure:
   so doe I hope her stubborne hart to bend,
   and that it then more stedfast will endure.
Onely my paines wil be the more to get her,
   but hauing her, my ioy wil be the greater.

SONNET. LII.

So oft as homeward I from her depart,
   I goe lyke one that hauing lost the field,
   is prisoner led away with heauy hart,
   despoyld of warlike armes and knowen shield,
So doe I now my selfe a prisoner yeeld,
   to sorrow and to solitary paine:
   from presence of my dearest deare exylde,
   longwhile alone in languor to remaine,
There let no thought of ioy or pleasure vaine,
10   dare to approch, that may my solace breed:
   but sudden dumps and drery sad disdayne
   of all worlds gladnesse more my torment feed.
So I her absens will my penaunce make,
   that of her presens I my meed may take.

SONNET. LIII.

The Panther knowing that his spotted hyde
   Doth please all beasts but that his looks them fray:
   within a bush his dreadfull head doth hide,
   to let them gaze whylest he on them may pray.

Right so my cruell fayre with me doth play:
    for with the goodly semblant of her hew,
    she doth allure me to mine owne decay,
    and then no mercy will vnto me shew.
Great shame it is, thing so diuine in view,
    made for to be the worlds most ornament:
    to make the bayte her gazers to embrew,
    good shames to be to ill an instrument.
But mercy doth with beautie best agree,
    as in theyr maker ye them best may see.

SONNET. LIV.

Of this worlds Theatre in which we stay,
    My loue lyke the Spectator ydly sits
    beholding me that all the pageants play,
    disguysing diuersly my troubled wits.
Sometimes I joy when glad occasion fits,
    and mask in myrth lyke to a Comedy:
    soone after when my ioy to sorrow flits,
    I waile and make my woes a Tragedy.
Yet she beholding me with constant eye,
    delights not in my merth nor rues my smart:
    but when I laugh she mocks, and when I cry
    she laughes, and hardens euermore her hart.
What then can moue her? if nor merth nor mone,
    she is no woman, but a sencelesse stone.

SONNET. LV.

So oft as I her beauty doe behold,
    And therewith doe her cruelty compare:
    I maruaile of what substance was the mould
    the which her made attonce so cruell faire.
Not earth; for her high thoghts more heauenly are,
    not water; for her loue doth burne like fyre:
    not ayre; for she is not so light or rare,
    not fyre; for she doth friese with faint desire.
Then needs another Element inquire
    whereof she mote be made; that is the skye.
    for to the heauen her haughty lookes aspire:
    and eke her mind is pure immortall hye.
Then sith to heauen ye lykened are the best,
    be lyke in mercy as in all the rest.

SONNET. LVI.

Fayre ye be sure, but cruell and vnkind,
    As is a Tygre that with greedinesse
    hunts after bloud, when he by chance doth find
    a feeble beast, doth felly him oppresse.

Fayre be ye sure, but proud and pittilesse,
    as is a storme, that all things doth prostrate:
    finding a tree alone all comfortlesse,
    beats on it strongly it to ruinate.
Fayre be ye sure, but hard and obstinate,
    as is a rocke amidst the raging floods:
    gaynst which a ship of succour desolate,
    doth suffer wreck both of her selfe and goods.
That ship, that tree, and that same beast am I,
    whom ye doe wreck, doe ruine, and destroy.

10

SONNET. LVII.

Sweet warriour when shall I haue peace with you?
    High time it is, this warre now ended were:
    which I no lenger can endure to sue,
    ne your incessant battry more to beare:
So weake my powres, so sore my wounds appeare,
    that wonder is how I should liue a iot,
    seeing my hart through launched euery where
    with thousand arrowes, which your eies have shot:
Yet shoot ye sharpely still, and spare me not,
    but glory thinke to make these cruel stoures.
    ye cruell one, what glory can be got,
    in slaying him that would liue gladly yours?
Make peace therefore, and graunt me timely grace,
    that al my wounds wil heale in little space.

10

SONNET. LVIII.

By her that is most assured to her selfe.

Weake is th'assurance that weake flesh reposeth
    In her owne powre, and scorneth others ayde:
    that soonest fals when as she most supposeth
    her selfe assurd, and is of nought affrayd.
All flesh is frayle, and all her strength vnstayd,
    like a vaine bubble blowen vp with ayre:
    deuouring tyme and changeful chance haue prayd
    her glories pride that none may it repayre.
Ne none so rich or wise, so strong or fayre,
    but fayleth trusting on his owne assurance:
    and he that standeth on the hyghest stayre
    fals lowest: for on earth nought hath enduraunce.
Why then doe ye proud fayre, misdeeme so farre,
    that to your selfe ye most assured arre?

10

SONNET. LIX.

Thrise happie she, that is so well assured
    Vnto her selfe and setled so in hart:
    that nether will for better be allured,
    ne feard with worse to any chaunce to start,

But like a steddy ship doth strongly part
   the raging waues and keepes her course aright:
   ne ought for tempest doth from it depart,
   ne ought for fayrer weathers false delight.
Such selfe assurance need not feare the spight
10   of grudging foes, ne fauour seek of friends:
   but in the stay of her owne stedfast might,
   nether to one her selfe nor other bends.
Most happy she that most assured doth rest,
   but he most happy who such one lones best.

SONNET. LX.

They that in course of heauenly spheares are skild,
   To euery planet point his sundry yeare:[16]   *appoint*
   in which her circles voyage is fulfild,
   as Mars in three score yeares doth run his spheare.
So since the winged God his planet cleare,
   began in me to moue, one yeare is spent:
   the which doth longer vnto me appeare,
   then al those fourty which my life outwent.[17]
Then by that count, which louers books inuent,
10   the spheare of Cupid fourty yeares containes:[18]
   which I haue wasted in long languishment,
   that seemd the longer for my greater paines.
But let my loues fayre Planet short her wayes
   this yeare ensuing, or else short my dayes.

SONNET. LXI.

The glorious image of the makers beautie,
   My souerayne saynt, the Idoll of my thought,
   dare not henceforth aboue the bounds of dewtie,
   t'accuse of pride, or rashly blame for ought.
For being as she is diuinely wrought,
   and of the brood of Angels heuenly borne:
   and with the crew of blessed Saynts vpbrought,
   each of which did her with theyr guifts adorne;
The bud of ioy, the blossome of the morne,
10   the beame of light, whom mortal eyes admyre:
   what reason is it then but she should scorne
   base things that to her loue too bold aspire?
Such heauenly formes ought rather worshipt be,
   then dare be lou'd by men of meane degree.

SONNET. LXII.

The weary yeare his race now hauing run,
   The new begins his compast course anew:

16 Each planet's movement in relation to the sun and stars determines its own distinct year.

17 Spenser was 40 or 41, apparently, when this sonnet was written, which may have been in 1593, his marriage occurring a year later. From this, his birthdate would be calculated as 1552.

18 A year of unsatisfied love seems like 40, which is in keeping with the relative time schemes of the rest of the sonnet.

with shew of morning mylde he hath begun,
 betokening peace and plenty to ensew.
So let vs, which this chaunge of weather vew,
 chaunge eeke our mynds and former liues amend,
 the old yeares sinnes forepast let vs eschew,
 and fly the faults with which we did offend.
Then shall the new yeares ioy forth freshly send,
10 into the glooming world his gladsome ray:
 and all these stormes which now his beauty blend,
 shall turne to caulmes and tymely cleare away.
So likewise loue cheare you your heauy spright,
 and chaunge old yeares annoy to new delight.

SONNET. LXIII.

After long stormes and tempests sad assay,   *struggle*
 Which hardly I endured heretofore:
 in dread of death and daungerous dismay,
 with which my silly barke was tossed sore: *simple*
I doe at length descry the happy shore,
 in which I hope ere long for to arryue:
 fayre soyle it seemes from far and fraught with store   *loaded*
 of all that deare and daynty is alyue.
Most happy he that can at last atchyue   *achieve*
10 the ioyous safety of so sweet a rest:
 whose least delight sufficeth to depriue
 remembrance of all paines which him opprest.
All paines are nothing in respect of this,
 all sorrowes short that gaine eternall blisse.

SONNET. LXIV.

Comming to kisse her lyps, (such grace I found)
 Me seemd I smelt a gardin of sweet flowres:
 that dainty odours from them threw around
 for damzels fit to decke their louers bowres.
Her lips did smell lyke vnto Gillyflowers,   *carnations*
 her ruddy cheekes lyke vnto Roses red:
 her snowy browes lyke budded Bellamoures,
 her louely eyes lyke Pincks but newly spred,
Her goodly bosome lyke a Strawberry bed,
10 her neck lyke to a bounch of Cullambynes: *columbines*
 her brest lyke lillyes, ere theyr leaues be shed,
 her nipples lyke yong blossomd Iessemynes: *jasmines*
Such fragrant flowres doe giue most odorous smell,
 but her sweet odour did them all excell.

SONNET. LXV.

The doubt which ye misdeeme, fayre loue, is vaine,
 That fondly feare to loose your liberty,
 when loosing one, two liberties ye gayne,
 and make him bond that bondage earst dyd fly.

Sweet be the bands, the which true loue doth tye,
    without constraynt or dread of any ill:
    the gentle birde feeles no captiuity
    within her cage, but singes and feeds her fill.
There pride dare not approch, nor discord spill
    the league twixt them, that loyal loue hath bound:
    but simple truth and mutuall good will,
    seekes with sweet peace to salue each others wound:
There fayth doth fearlesse dwell in brasen towre,
    and spotlesse pleasure builds her sacred bowre.

10

SONNET. LXVI.

To all those happy blessings which ye haue,
    with plenteous hand by heauen vpon you thrown,
    this one disparagement they to you gaue,
    that ye your loue lent to so meane a one.
Yee whose high worths surpassing paragon,
    could not on earth haue found one fit for mate,
    ne but in heauen matchable to none,
    why did ye stoup vnto so lowly state?
But ye thereby much greater glory gate,
    then had ye sorted with a princes pere: *peer*
    for now your light doth more it selfe dilate,
    and in my darknesse greater doth appeare.
Yet since your light hath once enlumind me,
    with my reflex yours shall encreased be.

10

SONNET. LXVII.

Lyke as a huntsman after weary chace,
    Seeing the game from him escapt away,
    sits downe to rest him in some shady place,
    with panting hounds beguiled of their pray:
So after long pursuit and vaine assay,
    when I all weary had the chace forsooke,
    the gentle deare returnd the selfe-same way,
    thinking to quench her thirst at the next brooke.
There she beholding me with mylder looke,
    sought not to fly, but fearelesse still did bide:
    till I in hand her yet halfe trembling tooke,
    and with her owne goodwill hir fyrmely tyde.
Strange thing me seemd to see a beast so wyld,
    so goodly wonne with her owne will beguyld.

10

SONNET. LXVIII.

Most glorious Lord of lyfe that on this day,
    Didst make thy triumph ouer death and sin:
    and hauing harrowd hell didst bring away
    captiuity thence captiue vs to win:

This ioyous day, deare Lord, with ioy begin,
   and grant that we for whom thou diddest dye
   being with thy deare blood clene washt from sin,
   may liue for euer in felicity.
And that thy loue we weighing worthily,
10   may likewise loue thee for the same againe:
   and for thy sake that all lyke deare didst buy,
   with loue may one another entertayne.
So let vs loue, deare loue, lyke as we ought,
   loue is the lesson which the Lord vs taught.

SONNET. LXIX.

The famous warriors of the anticke world,
   Vsed Trophees to erect in stately wize:
   in which they would the records haue enrold,
   of theyr great deeds and valarous emprize.
What trophee then shall I most fit deuize,
   in which I may record the memory
   of my loues conquest, peerelesse beauties prise,
   adorn'd with honour, loue, and chastity.
Euen this verse vowd to eternity,
10   shall be thereof immortall moniment:
   and tell her prayse to all posterity,
   that may admire such worlds rare wonderment.
The happy purchase of my glorious spoile,
   gotten at last with labour and long toyle.

SONNET. LXX.

Fresh spring the herald of loues mighty king,
   In whose cote armour richly are displayd
   all sorts of flowers the which on earth do spring
   in goodly colours gloriously arrayd:
Goe to my loue, where she is carelesse layd,
   yet in her winters bowre not well awake:
   tell her the ioyous time wil not be staid
   vnlesse she doe him by the forelock take.
Bid her therefore her selfe soone ready make,
10   to wayt on loue amongst his louely crew:
   where euery one that misseth then her make,
   shall be by him amearst with penance dew.
Make hast therefore sweet loue, whilest it is prime,
   for none can call againe the passed time.

SONNET. LXXI.

I ioy to see how in your drawen work,
   Your selfe vnto the Bee ye doe compare;
   and me vnto the Spyder that doth lurke,
   in close awayt to catch her vnaware.   *ambush*

Right so your selfe were caught in cunning snare
  of a deare foe, and thralled to his loue:
  in whose streight bands ye now captiued are
  so firmely, that ye neuer may remoue.
But as your worke is wouen all aboue,
10 with woodbynd flowers and fragrant Eglantine:
  so sweet your prison you in time shall proue,   *discover*
  with many deare delights bedecked fyne.
And all thensforth eternall peace shall see,
  betweene the Spyder and the gentle Bee.

SONNET. LXXII.

Oft when my spirit doth spred her bolder winges,
  In mind to mount vp to the purest sky:
  it down is weighd with thoght of earthly things
  and clogd with burden of mortality,
Where when that souerayne beauty it doth spy,
  resembling heauens glory in her light:
  drawne with sweet pleasures bayt, it back doth fly,
  and vnto heauen forgets her former flight.
There my fraile fancy fed with full delight,
10 doth bath in blisse and mantleth most at ease:
  ne thinks of other heauen, but how it might
  her harts desire with most contentment please.
Hart need not wish none other happinesse,
  but here on earth to haue such heuens blisse.

SONNET. LXXIII.

Being my selfe captyued here in care,
  My hart, whom none with seruile bands can tye,
  but the fayre tresses of your golden hayre,   *hair*
  breaking his prison forth to you doth fly.
Lyke as a byrd that in ones hand doth spy
  desired food, to it doth make his flight:
  euen so my hart, that wont on your fayre eye
  to feed his fill, flyes backe vnto your sight.
Doe you him take, and in your bosome bright,
10 gently encage, that he may be your thrall:
  perhaps he there may learne with rare delight,
  to sing your name and prayses ouer all.
That it hereafter may you not repent,
  him lodging in your bosome to haue lent.

SONNET. LXXIV.

Most happy letters fram'd by skilfull trade,
  with which that happy name was first desynd:
  the which three times thrise happy hath me made,
  with guifts of body, fortune and of mind.

The first my being to me gaue by kind,
    from mothers womb deriu'd by dew descent,
    the second is my souereigne Queene most kind,
    that honour and large richesse to me lent.
The third my loue, my liues last ornament,
10   by whom my spirit out of dust was raysed:
    to speake her prayse and glory excellent,
    of all aliue most worthy to be praysed.
Ye three Elizabeths[19] for euer liue,
    that three such graces did vnto me giue.

SONNET. LXXV.

One day I wrote her name vpon the strand,
    but came the waues and washed it away:
    agayne I wrote it with a second hand,
    but came the tyde, and made my paynes his pray.
Vayne man, sayd she, that doest in vaine assay,
    a mortall thing so to immortalize,
    for I my selue shall lyke to this decay,
    and eek my name bee wyped out lykewize.
Not so, (quod I) let baser things deuize
10   to dy in dust, but you shall liue by fame:
    my verse your vertues rare shall eternize,
    and in the heuens wryte your glorious name.
Where whenas death shall all the world subdew,
    our loue shall liue, and later life renew.

SONNET. LXXVI.

Fayre bosome fraught with vertues richest tresure,
    The neast of loue, the lodging of delight:
    the bowre of blisse, the paradice of pleasure,
    the sacred harbour of that heuenly spright:
How was I rauisht with your louely sight,
    and my frayle thoughts too rashly led astray?
    whiles diuing deepe through amorous insight,
    on the sweet spoyle of beautie they did pray.
And twixt her paps like early fruit in May,   *breasts*
10   whose haruest seemd to hasten now apace:
    they loosely did theyr wanton winges display,
    and there to rest themselues did boldly place.
Sweet thoughts I enuy your so happy rest,
    which oft I wisht, yet neuer was so blest.

SONNET. LXXVII.

Was it a dreame, or did I see it playne,
    a goodly table of pure yvory:
    all spred with iuncats, fit to entertayne
    the greatest Prince with pompous roialty?

19 i.e., his mother, Elizabeth Boyle (his bride-to-be), and Queen
Elizabeth.

Mongst which there in a siluer dish did ly
   twoo golden apples of vnualewd price: *invaluable*
   far passing those which Hercules came by,[20]
   or those which Atalanta did entice.[21]
Exceeding sweet, yet voyd of sinfull vice,
10   That many sought yet none could euer taste,
   sweet fruit of pleasure brought from paradice
   by Loue himselfe and in his garden plaste.
Her brest that table was so richly spredd,
   my thoughts the guests, which would thereon haue fedd.

SONNET. LXXVIII.

Lackyng my loue I go from place to place,
   lyke a young fawne that late hath lost the hynd:
   and seeke each where, where last I sawe her face,
   whose ymage yet I carry fresh in mynd.
I seeke the fields with her late footing synd,
   I seeke her bowre with her late presence deckt,
   yet nor in field nor bowre I her can fynd:
   yet field and bowre are full of her aspect.
But when myne eyes I thereunto direct,
10   they ydly back returne to me agayne,
   and when I hope to see theyr trew obiect,
   I fynd my selfe but fed with fancies vayne.
Ceasse then myne eyes, to seeke her selfe to see,
   and let my thoughts behold her selfe in mee.

SONNET. LXXIX.

Men call you fayre, and you doe credit it,   *believe*
   For that your selfe ye dayly such doe see:
   but the trew fayre, that is the gentle wit,   *beauty*
   and vertuous mind, is much more praysd of me.
For all the rest, how euer fayre it be,
   shall turne to nought and loose that glorious hew:
   but onely that is permanent and free
   from frayle corruption, that doth flesh ensew.   *immediately follow*
That is true beautie: that doth argue you
10   to be diuine and borne of heauenly seed:
   deriu'd from that fayre Spirit, from whom al true
   and perfect beauty did at first proceed.
He onely fayre, and what he fayre hath made,
   all other fayre lyke flowres vntymely fade.

SONNET. LXXX.

After so long a race as I haue run
   Through Faery land, which those six books compile,[22]

20   The eleventh labor of Hercules was to get possession of the apples of the Hesperides.

21   Atalanta refused to marry any man who could not defeat her in a footrace. Following Aphrodite's advice, Hippomenes dropped three apples in succession, which Atalanta could not resist collecting. By this means he won the race and her.

22   The six-book edition of *The Faerie Queene* was published in 1596.

giue leaue to rest me being halfe fordonne,
    and gather to my selfe new breath awhile.
Then as a steed refreshed after toyle,
    out of my prison I will breake anew:
    and stoutly will that second worke assoyle,   *assail*
    with strong endeuour and attention dew.
Till then giue leaue to me in pleasant mew,
10   to sport my muse and sing my loues sweet praise:[23]
    the contemplation of whose heauenly hew,
    my spirit to an higher pitch will rayse.
But let her prayses yet be low and meane,
    fit for the handmayd of the Faery Queene.

SONNET. LXXXI.

Fayre is my loue, when her fayre golden heares,
    with the loose wynd ye wauing chance to marke:
    fayre when the rose in her red cheekes appeares,
    or in her eyes the fyre of loue does sparke.
Fayre when her brest lyke a rich laden barke,
    with pretious merchandize she forth doth lay:
    fayre when that cloud of pryde, which oft doth dark
    her goodly light with smiles she driues away.
But fayrest she, when so she doth display
10   the gate with pearles and rubyes richly dight:
    throgh which her words so wise do make their way
    to beare the message of her gentle spright.
The rest be works of natures wonderment,
    but this the worke of harts astonishment.

SONNET. LXXXII.

Ioy my life, full oft for louing you
    I blesse my lot, that was so lucky placed:
    but then the more your owne mishap I rew,
    that are so much by so meane loue embased.
For had the equall heuens so much you graced
    in this as in the rest, ye mote inuent
    som heuenly wit, whose verse could haue enchased
    your glorious name in golden moniment.
But since ye deignd so goodly to relent
10   to me your thrall, in whom is little worth,
    that little that I am, shall all be spent,
    in setting your immortall prayses forth.
Whose lofty argument vplifting me,
    shall lift you vp vnto an high degree.

SONNET. LXXXIII.

My hungry eyes, through greedy couetize,
    Still to behold the obiect of theyr payne:
    with no contentment can themselues suffize,
    but hauing pine, and hauing not complayne.

23 *Amoretti* and *Epithalamion* were published in 1595.

For lacking it, they cannot lyfe sustayne,
   and seeing it, they gaze on it the more:
   in theyr amazement lyke Narcissus vayne
   whose eyes him staru'd: so plenty makes me pore.
Yet are myne eyes so filled with the store
10   of that fayre sight, that nothing else they brooke:
   but loath the things which they did like before,
   and can no more endure on them to looke.
All this worlds glory seemeth vayne to me,
   and all theyr shewes but shadowes sauing she.

SONNET. LXXXIV.

Let not one sparke of filthy lustfull fyre
   breake out, that may her sacred peace molest:
   ne one light glance of sensuall desyre
   Attempt to work her gentle mindes vnrest.
But pure affections bred in spotlesse brest,
   and modest thoughts breathd from wel tempred sprites,
   goe visit her in her chast bowre of rest,
   accompanyde with angelick delightes.
There fill your selfe with those most ioyous sights,
10   the which my selfe could neuer yet attayne:
   but speake no word to her of these sad plights,
   which her too constant stiffenesse doth constrayn.
Onely behold her rare perfection,
   and blesse your fortunes fayre election.[24]

SONNET. LXXXV.

The world that cannot deeme of worthy things,
   when I doe praise her, say I doe but flatter:
   so does the Cuckow, when the Mauis sings,   *thrush*
   begin his witlesse note apace to clatter.
But they that skill not of so heauenly matter,
   all that they know not, enuy or admyre,
   rather then enuy let them wonder at her,
   but not to deeme of her desert aspyre.
Deepe in the closet of my parts entyre,
10   her worth is written with a golden quill:
   that me with heauenly fury doth inspire,
   and my glad mouth with her sweet prayses fill.
Which when as fame in her shrill trump shal thunder,
   let the world chose to enuy or to wonder.

SONNET. LXXXVI.

Venemous toung tipt with vile adders sting,[25]
   Of that selfe kynd with which the Furies fell
   theyr snaky heads doe combe, from which a spring
   of poysoned words and spitefull speeches well.

---

24 As in the sense of God's selection of a soul for salvation.

25 Spenser writes here and elsewhere with particular bitterness about liars and defamers. See also his *Muiopotomos* and *FQ*, VI.

Let all the plagues and horrid paines of hell,
    vpon thee fall for thine accursed hyre:
    that with false forged lyes, which thou didst tel,
    in my true loue did stirre vp coles of yre,
The sparkes whereof let kindle thine own fyre,
    and catching hold on thine owne wicked hed
    consume thee quite, that didst with guile conspire
    in my sweet peace such breaches to haue bred.
Shame be thy meed, and mischiefe thy reward,
    dew to thy selfe that it for me prepard.

10

SONNET. LXXXVII.

Since I did leaue the presence of my loue,
    Many long weary dayes I haue outworne:
    and many nights, that slowly seemd to moue
    theyr sad protract from euening vntill morne.
For when as day the heauen doth adorne,
    I wish that night the noyous day would end:
    and when as night hath vs of light forlorne,
    I wish that day would shortly reascend.
Thus I the time with expectation spend,
    and faine my griefe with chaunges to beguile,
    that further seemes his terme still to extend,
    and maketh euery minute seeme a myle.
So sorrow still doth seeme too long to last,
    but ioyous houres doo fly away too fast.

10

SONNET. LXXXVIII.

Since I haue lackt the comfort of that light,
    The which was wont to lead my thoughts astray:
    I wander as in darknesse of the night,
    affrayd of euery dangers least dismay.
Ne ought I see, though in the clearest day,
    when others gaze vpon theyr shadowes vayne:
    but th'onely image of that heauenly ray,
    whereof some glance doth in mine eie remayne.
Of which beholding the Idæa playne,
    through contemplation of my purest part:
    with light thereof I doe my selfe sustayne,
    and thereon feed my loue-affamisht hart.
But with such brightnesse whylest I fill my mind,
    I starue my body and mine eyes doe blynd.

10

SONNET. LXXXIX.

Lyke as the Culuer on the bared bough,   *dove*
    Sits mourning for the absence of her mate:
    and in her songs sends many a wishfull vow,
    for his returne that seemes to linger late.

So I alone now left disconsolate,
   mourne to my selfe the absence of my loue:
   and wandring here and there all desolate,
    seek with my playnts to match that mournful doue:
Ne ioy of ought that vnder heauen doth houe,
     10   can comfort me, but her owne ioyous sight:
   whose sweet aspect both God and man can moue,
    in her vnspotted pleasauns to delight.
Dark is my day, whyles her fayre light I mis,
    and dead my life that wants such liuely blis.

EPITHALAMION.[1]

Ye learned sisters[2] which haue oftentimes
Beene to me ayding, others to adorne:
Whom ye thought worthy of your gracefull rymes,
That euen the greatest did not greatly scorne
To heare theyr names sung in your simple layes,
But ioyed in theyr prayse.
And when ye list your owne mishaps to mourne,
Which death, or loue, or fortunes wreck did rayse,
Your string could soone to sadder tenor turne,
10   And teach the woods and waters to lament
Your dolefull dreriment.   *sadness*
Now lay those sorrowfull complaints aside,
And hauing all your heads with girland crownd,   *garland*
Helpe me mine owne loues prayses to resound,
Ne let the same of any be enuide:
So Orpheus did for his owne bride,[3]
So I vnto my selfe alone will sing,
The woods shall to me answer and my Eccho ring.

Early before the worlds light giuing lampe,
20   His golden beame vpon the hils doth spred,
Hauing disperst the nights vnchearefull dampe,
Doe ye awake and with fresh lusty hed,
Go to the bowre of my beloued loue,
My truest turtle doue,[4]
Bid her awake; for Hymen[5] is awake,
And long since ready forth his maske to moue,
With his bright Tead that flames with many a flake,   *torch*
And many a bachelor to waite on him,
In theyr fresh garments trim.
30   Bid her awake therefore and soone her dight,   *dress*
For lo the wished day is come at last,
That shall for al the paynes and sorrowes past,
Pay to her vsury of long delight:

EPITHALAMION.

1   A wedding song, or more literally, "on the marriage bed." The Roman poet Catullus' *Epithalamium 61* is an important classical reference point, as is the biblical Song of Songs. The form of Spenser's poem is that of the Italian *canzone*, in which longer stanzas of the same length are followed by a *tornata*, which turns back and reflects on the previous stanzas. This poem is intricately structured on figures of time, which include 365 long lines for the year, 24 stanzas for the hours of the wedding day, and divisions of those stanzas for the seasons (e.g., 1–12

and 13–24 for the equinoxes or spring and fall); see A. Kent Hieatt's *Short Time's Endless Monument* for more details.
2   The nine muses.
3   Orpheus, a legendary pre-Homeric poet, according to Ovid called Hymen, the god of marriage, to sing at his wedding.
4   The turtledove as an image of faithful love appears in Ovid and in the Song of Songs.
5   The god of marriage.

And whylest she doth her dight,
Doe ye to her of ioy and solace sing,
That all the woods may answer and your eccho ring.

Bring with you all the Nymphes that you can heare
Both of the riuers and the forrests greene:
And of the sea that neighbours to her neare,
40 Al with gay girlands goodly wel beseene.
And let them also with them bring in hand
Another gay girland
For my fayre loue of lillyes and of roses,
Bound trueloue wize with a blew silke riband.
And let them make great store of bridale poses,   *bouquets*
And let them eeke bring store of other flowers
To deck the bridale bowers.
And let the ground whereas her foot shall tread,
For feare the stones her tender foot should wrong
50 Be strewed with fragrant flowers all along,
And diapred lyke the discolored mead.[6]
Which done, doe at her chamber dore awayt,
For she will waken strayt,
The whiles doe ye this song vnto her sing,
The woods shall to you answer and your Eccho ring.

Ye Nymphes of Mulla[7] which with carefull heed,
The siluer scaly trouts doe tend full well,
And greedy pikes which vse therein to feed,
(Those trouts and pikes all others doo excell)
60 And ye likewise which keepe the rushy lake,
Where none doo fishes take,
Bynd vp the locks the which hang scatterd light,
And in his waters which your mirror make,
Behold your faces as the christall bright,
That when you come whereas my loue doth lie,
No blemish she may spie.
And eke ye lightfoot mayds which keepe the deere,
That on the hoary mountayne vse to towre,
And the wylde wolues which seeke them to deuoure,
70 With your steele darts doo chace from comming neer,
Be also present heere,
To helpe to decke her and to help to sing,
That all the woods may answer and your eccho ring.

Wake, now my loue, awake; for it is time,[8]
The Rosy Morne long since left Tithones[9] bed,
All ready to her siluer coche to clyme,
And Phœbus gins to shew his glorious hed.
Hark how the cheerefull birds do chaunt theyr laies
And carroll of loues praise.
80 The merry Larke hir mattins sings aloft,
The thrush replyes, the Mauis descant playes,   *mavis*
The Ouzell shrills, the Ruddock warbles soft,   *blackbird/robin*
So goodly all agree with sweet consent,

---

6   Variegated, like a multicolored meadow.

7   Irish girls. Mulla is what Spenser called Awbeg, a river that bordered his Irish estate, Kilcolman, where he married Elizabeth Boyle in
1594.

8   Cf. Song of Songs 2:10.

9   In Greek mythology Tithonus was loved by Eos, the dawn
goddess.

To this dayes merriment.
Ah my deere loue why doe ye sleepe thus long,
When meeter were that ye should now awake,
T'awayt the comming of your ioyous make,   *mate*
And hearken to the birds louelearned song,
The deawy leaues among.
90   For they of ioy and pleasance to you sing,
That all the woods them answer and theyr eccho ring.

My loue is now awake out of her dreames,
And her fayre eyes like stars that dimmed were
With darksome cloud, now shew theyr goodly beames
More bright then Hesperus[10] his head doth rere.
Come now ye damzels, daughters of delight,
Helpe quickly her to dight,
But first come ye fayre houres[11] which were begot
In Ioues sweet paradice, of Day and Night,   *Jove's*
100   Which doe the seasons of the yeare allot,
And al that euer in this world is fayre
Doe make and still repayre.
And ye three handmayds[12] of the Cyprian Queene,   *Venus*
The which doe still adorne her beauties pride,
Helpe to addorne my beautifullest bride:
And as ye her array, still throw betweene
Some graces to be seene,
And as ye vse to Venus, to her sing,
The whiles the woods shal answer and your eccho ring.

110   Now is my loue all ready forth to come,
Let all the virgins therefore well awayt,
And ye fresh boyes that tend vpon her groome
Prepare your selues; for he is comming strayt.
Set all your things in seemely good aray   *order*
Fit for so ioyfull day,
The ioyfulst day that euer sunne did see.
Faire Sun, shew forth thy fauourable ray,
And let thy lifull heat not feruent be
For feare of burning her sunshyny face,
120   Her beauty to disgrace.
O fayrest Phœbus, father of the Muse,
If euer I did honour thee aright,
Or sing the thing, that mote thy mind delight,   *could*
Doe not thy seruants simple boone refuse,
But let this day let this one day be myne,
Let all the rest be thine.
Then I thy souerayne prayses loud wil sing,
That all the woods shal answer and theyr eccho ring.

Harke how the Minstrels gin to shrill aloud
130   Their merry Musick that resounds from far,
The pipe, the tabor, and the trembling Croud,   *fiddle*

10   This reference to Hesperus, the evening star, anticipates the marriage night to come.
11   The sidereal hours. During Spenser's time it was commonly thought that the earth was the fixed center of the universe, that between the earth and the stars were the spheres of the sun and the planets, and that beyond these was the outer sphere of the fixed stars. It was also thought that in 24 hours the sphere of the fixed stars rotated around the earth, while the sun and the planets took slightly longer. Thus, while the stars complete 360 degrees, the sun completes only 359 degrees. This partly explains why the 359th line is an important structural divide in the poem.
12   The three graces, attendants to Venus.

That well agree withouten breach or iar.
But most of all the Damzels doe delite,
When they their tymbrels smyte,
And thereunto doe daunce and carrol sweet,
That all the sences they doe rauish quite,
The whyles the boyes run vp and downe the street,
Crying aloud with strong confused noyce,
As if it were one voyce.
140   Hymen io Hymen, Hymen they do shout,
That euen to the heauens theyr shouting shrill
Doth reach, and all the firmament doth fill,
To which the people standing all about,
As in approuance doe thereto applaud
And loud aduaunce her laud,
And euermore they Hymen Hymen sing,
That al the woods them answer and theyr eccho ring.

Loe where she comes along with portly pace,
Lyke Phœbe from her chamber of the East,[13]   *the moon*
150   Arysing forth to run her mighty race,
Clad all in white, that seemes a virgin best.   *suits*
So well it her beseemes that ye would weene   *think*
Some angell she had beene.
Her long loose yellow locks lyke golden wyre,
Sprinckled with perle, and perling flowres a tweene,
Doe lyke a golden mantle her attyre,
And being crowned with a girland greene,
Seeme lyke some mayden Queene.
Her modest eyes abashed to behold
160   So many gazers, as on her do stare,
Vpon the lowly ground affixed are.
Ne dare lift vp her countenance too bold,
But blush to heare her prayses sung so loud,
So farre from being proud.
Nathlesse doe ye still loud her prayses sing,
That all the woods may answer and your eccho ring.

Tell me ye merchants daughters did ye see
So fayre a creature in your towne before?
So sweet, so louely, and so mild as she,
170   Adornd with beautyes grace and vertues store,
Her goodly eyes lyke Saphyres shining bright,
Her forehead yuory white,
Her cheekes lyke apples which the sun hath rudded,
Her lips lyke cherryes charming men to byte,
Her brest like to a bowle of creame vncrudded,   *uncurdled*
Her paps lyke lyllies budded,
Her snowie necke lyke to a marble towre,
And all her body like a pallace fayre,
Ascending vppe with many a stately stayre,
180   To honors seat and chastities sweet bowre.
Why stand ye still ye virgins in amaze,
Vpon her so to gaze,
Whiles ye forget your former lay to sing,
To which the woods did answer and your eccho ring?

13 See Psalm 19:4–5.

Bvt if ye saw that which no eyes can see,
The inward beauty of her liuely spright,
Garnisht with heauenly guifts of high degree,
Much more then would ye wonder at that sight,
And stand astonisht lyke to those which red
190   Medusaes[14] mazeful hed.
There dwels sweet loue and constant chastity,
Vnspotted fayth and comely womanhed,
Regard of honour and mild modesty,
There Vertue raynes as Queene in royal throne,
And giueth lawes alone.
The which the base affections doe obay,
And yeeld theyr seruices vnto her will,
Ne thought of thing vncomely euer may
Thereto approch to tempt her mind to ill.
200   Had ye once seene these her celestial threasures,
And vnreuealed pleasures,
Then would ye wonder and her prayses sing,
That al the woods should answer and your echo ring.

Open the temple gates vnto my loue,
Open them wide that she may enter in,
And all the postes adorne as doth behoue,
And all the pillours deck with girlands trim,
For to recyue this Saynt with honour dew,
That commeth in to you.
210   With trembling steps and humble reuerence,
She commeth in, before th'almighties vew:
Of her ye virgins learne obedience,
When so ye come into those holy places,
To humble your proud faces;
Bring her vp to th'high altar that she may,
The sacred ceremonies there partake,
The which do endlesse matrimony make,
And let the roring Organs loudly play
The praises of the Lord in liuely notes,
220   The whiles with hollow throates
The Choristers the ioyous Antheme sing,
That al the woods may answere and their eccho ring.

Behold whiles she before the altar stands
Hearing the holy priest that to her speakes
And blesseth her with his two happy hands,
How the red roses flush vp in her cheekes,
And the pure snow with goodly vermill stayne,
Like crimsin dyde in grayne,
That euen th'Angels which continually,
230   About the sacred Altare doe remaine,
Forget their seruice and about her fly,
Ofte peeping in her face that seemes more fayre,
The more they on it stare.
But her sad eyes still fastened on the ground,
Are gouerned with goodly modesty,
That suffers not one looke to glaunce awry,
Which may let in a little thought vnsownd.

14   According to Ovid, Medusa's head had the power to turn men to
stone.

Why blush ye loue to giue to me your hand,
The pledge of all our band?   *marriage*
240   Sing ye sweet Angels, Alleluya sing,
That all the woods may answere and your eccho ring.

Now al is done; bring home the bride againe,
Bring home the triumph of our victory,
Bring home with you the glory of her gaine,
With ioyance bring her and with iollity.   *rejoicing*
Neuer had man more ioyfull day then this,
Whom heauen would heape with blis.
Make feast therefore now all this liue long day,
This day for euer to me holy is,
250   Poure out the wine without restraint or stay,
Poure not by cups, but by the belly full,
Poure out to all that wull,   *want it*
And sprinkle all the postes and wals with wine,
That they may sweat, and drunken be withall.
Crowne ye God Bacchus with a coronall,
And Hymen also crowne with wreathes of vine,
And let the Graces daunce vnto the rest;
For they can doo it best:
The whiles the maydens doe theyr carroll sing,
260   To which the woods shal answer and theyr eccho ring.

Ring ye the bels, ye yong men of the towne,
And leaue your wonted labors for this day:
This day is holy; doe ye write it downe,
That ye for euer it remember may.
This day the sunne is in his chiefest hight,
With Barnaby the bright,[15]
From whence declining daily by degrees,
He somewhat loseth of his heat and light,
When once the Crab behind his back he sees.
270   But for this time it ill ordained was,
To chose the longest day in all the yeare,
And shortest night, when longest fitter weare:
Yet neuer day so long, but late would passe.
Ring ye the bels, to make it weare away,
And bonefiers make all day,
And daunce about them, and about them sing:
That all the woods may answer, and your eccho ring.

Ah when will this long weary day haue end,
And lende me leaue to come vnto my loue?
280   How slowly do the houres theyr numbers spend?
How slowly does sad Time his feathers moue?
Hast thee O fayrest Planet to thy home
Within the Westerne fome:
Thy tyred steedes long since haue need of rest.
Long though it be, at last I see it gloome,
And the bright euening star with golden creast
Appeare out of the East.
Fayre childe of beauty, glorious lampe of loue
That all the host of heauen in rankes doost lead,

15   The wedding occurred on St. Barnabas' Day (June 11), when the
sun was in the house of the Crab.

290 And guydest louers through the nights dread,
How chearefully thou lookest from aboue,
And seemst to laugh atweene thy twinkling light
As ioying in the sight
Of these glad many which for ioy doe sing,
That all the woods them answer and their echo ring.

Now ceasse ye damsels your delights forepast;   *past*
Enough is it, that all the day was youres:
Now day is doen, and night is nighing fast:
Now bring the Bryde into the brydall boures.
300 Now night is come, now soone her disaray,
And in her bed her lay;
Lay her in lillies and in violets,
And silken courteins ouer her display,
And odourd sheetes, and Arras couerlets.
Behold how goodly my faire loue does ly
In proud humility;
Like vnto Maia, when as Ioue her tooke,[16]
In Tempe, lying on the flowry gras,
Twixt sleepe and wake, after she weary was,
310 With bathing in the Acidalian brooke.
Now it is night, ye damsels may be gon,
And leaue my loue alone,
And leaue likewise your former lay to sing:
The woods no more shal answere, nor your echo ring.

Now welcome night, thou night so long expected,
That long daies labour doest at last defray,
And all my cares, which cruell loue collected,
Hast sumd in one, and cancelled for aye: *forever*
Spread thy broad wing ouer my loue and me,
320 That no man may vs see,
And in thy sable mantle vs enwrap,
From feare of perrill and foule horror free.
Let no false treason seeke vs to entrap,
Nor any dread disquiet once annoy
The safety of our ioy:
But let the night be calme and quietsome,
Without tempestuous storms or sad afray:
Lyke as when Ioue with fayre Alcmena lay,
When he begot the great Tirynthian groome:[17]
330 Or lyke as when he with thy selfe did lie,
And begot Maiesty.
And let the mayds and yongmen cease to sing:
Ne let the woods them answer, nor theyr eccho ring.

Let no lamenting cryes, nor dolefull teares,
Be heard all night within nor yet without:
Ne let false whispers breeding hidden feares,
Breake gentle sleepe with misconceiued dout.
Let no deluding dreames, nor dreadful sights
Make sudden sad affrights;
340 Ne let housefyres, nor lightnings helpelesse harmes,
Ne let the Pouke, nor other euill sprights,

16 According to Hesiod, Jove loved Maia when she was half asleep.   17 Alcmena, the wife of a Theban general, was seduced by Jove and
gave birth to Hercules (the "Tirynthian groom").

Ne let mischiuous witches with theyr charmes,
Ne let hob Goblins, names whose sence we see not,
Fray vs with things that be not.
Let not the shriech Oule, nor the Storke be heard:
Nor the night Rauen that still deadly yels,
Nor damned ghosts cald vp with mighty spels,
Nor griesly vultures make vs once affeard:
Ne let th'unpleasant Quyre of Frogs still croking
350   Make vs to wish theyr choking.
Let none of these theyr drery accents sing;
Ne let the woods them answer, nor theyr eccho ring.

Bvt let stil Silence trew night watches keepe,
That sacred peace may in assurance rayne,
And tymely sleep, when it is tyme to sleepe,
May poure his limbs forth on your pleasant playne,
The whiles an hundred little winged loues,
Like diuers fethered doues,
Shall fly and flutter round about your bed,
360   And in the secret darke, that none reproues,
Their prety stealthes shal worke, and snares shal spread
To filch away sweet snatches of delight,
Conceald through couert night.
Ye sonnes of Venus, play your sports at will,
For greedy pleasure, carelesse of your toyes,
Thinks more vpon her paradise of ioyes,
Then what ye do, albe it good or ill.
All night therefore attend your merry play,
For it will soone be day:
370   Now none doth hinder you, that say or sing,
Ne will the woods now answer, nor your Eccho ring.

Who is the same, which at my window peepes?
Or whose is that faire face, that shines so bright?
Is it not Cinthia, she that neuer sleepes,   *moon goddess*
But walkes about high heauen al the night?
O fayrest goddesse, do thou not enuy
My loue with me to spy:
For thou likewise didst loue, though now vnthought,
And for a fleece of woll, which priuily,
380   The Latmian shephard once vnto thee brought,   *Endymion*
His pleasures with thee wrought.
Therefore to vs be fauorable now;
And sith of wemens labours thou hast charge,
And generation goodly dost enlarge,
Encline thy will t'effect our wishfull vow,
And the chast wombe informe with timely seed,
That may our comfort breed:
Till which we cease our hopefull hap to sing,
Ne let the woods vs answere, nor our Eccho ring.

390   And thou great Iuno, which with awful might
The lawes of wedlock still dost patronize,
And the religion of the faith first plight
With sacred rites hast taught to solemnize:
And eeke for comfort often called art

Of women in their smart,
Eternally bind thou this louely band,
And all thy blessings vnto vs impart.
And thou glad Genius, in whose gentle hand,
The bridale bowre and geniall bed remaine,
400   Without blemish or staine,
And the sweet pleasures of theyr loues delight
With secret ayde doest succour and supply,
Till they bring forth the fruitfull progeny,
Send vs the timely fruit of this same night.
And thou fayre Hebe, and thou Hymen free,
Grant that it may so be.
Til which we cease your further prayse to sing,
Ne any woods shal answer, nor your Eccho ring.

And ye high heauens, the temple of the gods,
410   In which a thousand torches flaming bright
Doe burne, that to vs wretched earthly clods,
In dreadful darknesse lend desired light;
And all ye powers which in the same remayne,
More then we men can fayne,
Poure out your blessing on vs plentiously,
And happy influence vpon vs raine,
That we may raise a large posterity,
Which from the earth, which they may long possesse,
With lasting happinesse,
420   Vp to your haughty pallaces may mount,
And for the guerdon of theyr glorious merit   *reward*
May heauenly tabernacles there inherit,
Of blessed Saints for to increase the count.
So let vs rest, sweet loue, in hope of this,
And cease till then our tymely ioyes to sing,
The woods no more vs answer, nor our eccho ring.

Song made in lieu of many ornaments,
With which my loue should duly haue bene dect,
Which cutting off through hasty accidents,
430   Ye would not stay your dew time to expect,
But promist both to recompens,
Be vnto her a goodly ornament,
And for short time an endlesse moniment.

FINIS.

[From] The Faerie Queene

A Letter of the Authors expounding his
whole intention in the course of this worke: which
for that it giueth great light to the Reader, for
the better vnderstanding is hereunto
annexed.

To the Right noble, and Valorous, Sir Walter Raleigh knight, Lo. Wardein of the Stanneryes, and her
Maiesties liefetenaunt of the County of Cornewayll.

Sir knowing how doubtfully all Allegories may be construed, and this booke of mine, which I haue entituled the Faery Queene, being a continued Allegory, or darke conceit, I haue thought good aswell for auoyding of gealous opinions and misconstructions, as also for your better light in reading thereof, (being so by you commanded,) to discouer vnto you the general intention and meaning, which in the whole course therof I haue fashioned, without expressing of any particular purposes or by-accidents therein occasioned. The generall end therefore of all the booke is to fashion a gentleman or noble person in vertuous and gentle discipline:[1] Which for that I conceiued shoulde be most plausible and pleasing, being coloured with an historicall fiction, the which the most part of men delight to read, rather for variety of matter, then for profite of the ensample: I chose the historye of king Arthure, as most fitte for the excellency of his person, being made famous by many mens former workes, and also furthest from the daunger of enuy, and suspition of present time. In which I haue followed all the antique Poets historicall, first Homere, who in the Persons of Agamemnon and Vlysses hath ensampled a good gouernour and a vertuous man, the one in his Ilias, the other in his Odysseis: then Virgil, whose like intention was to doe in the person of Aeneas: after him Ariosto comprised them both in his Orlando: and lately Tasso disseuered them againe, and formed both parts in two persons, namely that part which they in Philosophy call Ethice, or vertues of a priuate man, coloured in his Rinaldo: The other named Politice in his Godfredo.[2] By ensample of which excellente Poets, I labour to pourtraict in Arthure, before he was king, the image of a braue knight, perfected in the twelue priuate morall vertues, as Aristotle hath deuised,[3] the which is the purpose of these first twelue bookes: which if I finde to be well accepted, I may be perhaps encoraged, to frame the other part of polliticke vertues in his person, after that hee came to be king. To some I know this Methode will seeme displeasaunt, which had rather haue good discipline deliuered plainly in way of precepts, or sermoned at large, as they vse, then thus clowdily enwrapped in Allegoricall deuises. But such, me seeme, should be satisfide with the vse of these dayes, seeing all things accounted by their showes, and nothing esteemed of, that is not delightfull and pleasing to commune sence. For this cause is Xenophon preferred before Plato, for that the one in the exquisite depth of his iudgement, formed a Commune welth such as it should be, but the other in the person of Cyrus and the Persians fashioned a gouernement such as might best be: So much more profitable and gratious is doctrine by ensample, then by rule. So haue I laboured to doe in the person of Arthure: whome I conceiue after his long education by Timon, to whom he was by Merlin deliuered to be brought vp, so soone as he was borne of the Lady Igrayne, to haue seene in a dream or vision the Faery Queen, with whose excellent beauty rauished, he awaking resolued to seeke her out, and so being by Merlin armed, and by Timon throughly instructed, he went to seeke her forth in Faerye land. In that Faery Queene I meane glory in my generall intention, but in my particular I conceiue the most excellent and glorious person of our soueraine the Queene, and her kingdome in Faery land. And yet in some places els, I doe otherwise shadow her. For considering she beareth two persons, the one of a most royall Queene or Empresse, the other of a most vertuous and beautifull Lady, this latter part in some places I doe express in Belphœbe, fashioning her name according to your owne excellent conceipt of Cynthia, (Phœbe and Cynthia being both names of Diana.)[4] So in the person of Prince Arthure I sette forth magnificence in particular, which vertue for that (according to Aristotle and the rest) it is the perfection of all the rest, and conteineth in it them all, therefore in the whole course I mention the deedes of Arthure applyable to that vertue, which I write of in that booke. But of the xii. other vertues, I make xii. other knights the patrones, for the more variety of the history: Of which these three bookes contayn three. The first of the knight of the Redcrosse, in whome I expresse Holynes: The seconde of Sir Guyon, in whome I sette forth Temperaunce: The third of Britomartis a Lady knight, in whome I picture Chastity. But because the beginning of the whole worke seemeth abrupte and as depending vpon other antecedents, it needs that ye know the occasion of these three knights seuerall aduentures. For the Methode of a Poet historicall is not such, as of an Historiographer. For an Historiographer discourseth of affayres orderly as they were donne, accounting as well the times as the actions, but a Poet thrusteth into the middest, euen where it most concerneth him,

[FROM] THE FAERIE QUEENE

1 Spenser's purpose echoes Sir Philip Sidney's theory of poetry in *An Apology for Poetry*.

2 Here Spenser names two 16th-century poets who influenced his conception of epic: Ariosto (1474–1533) is the author of *Orlando Furioso*, and Tasso (1544–1595) is the author of *Rinaldo* and *Jerusalem Delivered*.

3 Medieval commentators, rather than Aristotle himself, had enumerated twelve virtues.

4 Raleigh had used these names for Queen Elizabeth in his poem *Cynthia*. "Conceit" here means imaginative depiction.

and there recoursing to the thinges forepaste, and diuining of thinges to come, maketh a pleasing Analysis of all. The beginning therefore of my history, if it were to be told by an Historiographer, should be the twelfth booke, which is the last, where I deuise that the Faery Queene kept her Annuall feaste xii. dayes, vppon which xii. seuerall dayes, the occasions of the xii. seuerall aduentures hapned, which being vndertaken by xii. seuerall knights, are in these xii books seuerally handled and discoursed. The first was this. In the beginning of the feast, there presented him selfe a tall clownishe younge man,[5] who falling before the Queen of Faries desired a boone (as the manner then was) which during that feast she might not refuse: which was that hee might haue the atchieuement of any aduenture, which during that feaste should happen, that being graunted, he rested him on the floore, vnfitte through his rusticity for a better place. Soone after entred a faire Ladye in mourning weedes, riding on a white Asse, with a dwarfe behind her leading a warlike steed, that bore the Armes of a knight, and his speare in the dwarfes hand. Shee falling before the Queene of Faeries, complayned that her father and mother an ancient King and Queene, had bene by an huge dragon many years shut vp in a brasen Castle, who thence suffred them not to yssew: and therefore besought the Faery Queene to assygne her some one of her knights to take on him that exployt. Presently that clownish person vpstarting, desired that aduenture: whereat the Queene much wondering, and the Lady much gainesaying, yet he earnestly importuned his desire. In the end the Lady told him that vnlesse that armour which she brought, would serue him (that is the armour of a Christian man specified by Saint Paul v. Ephes.) that he could not succeed in that enterprise, which being forthwith put vpon him with dewe furnitures thereunto, he seemed the goodliest man in al that company, and was well liked of the Lady. And eftesoones taking on him knighthood, and mounting on that straunge Courser, he went forth with her on that aduenture: where beginneth the first booke, vz.

A gentle knight was pricking on the playne. &c.

The second day ther came in a Palmer bearing an Infant with bloody hands, whose Parents he complained to haue bene slayn by an Enchaunteresse called Acrasia: and therfore craued of the Faery Queene, to appoint him some knight, to performe that aduenture, which being assigned to Sir Guyon, he presently went forth with that same Palmer: which is the beginning of the second booke and the whole subiect thereof. The third day there came in, a Groome who complained before the Faery Queene, that a vile Enchaunter called Busirane had in hand a most faire Lady called Amoretta, whom he kept in most grieuous torment, because she would not yield him the pleasure of her body. Whereupon Sir Scudamour the louer of that Lady presently tooke on him that aduenture. But being vnable to performe it by reason of the hard Enchauntments, after long sorrow, in the end met with Britomartis, who succoured him, and reskewed his loue.

But by occasion hereof, many other aduentures are intermedled, but rather as Accidents, then intendments. As the loue of Britomart, the ouerthrow of Marinell, the misery of Florimell, the vertuousnes of Belphœbe, the lasciuiousnes of Hellenora, and many the like.

Thus much Sir, I haue briefly ouerronne to direct your vnderstanding to the wel-head of the History, that from thence gathering the whole intention of the conceit, ye may as in a handfull gripe al the discourse, which otherwise may happily seeme tedious and confused. So humbly crauing the continuance of your honorable fauour towards me, and th' eternall establishment of your happines, I humbly take leaue.

23. Ianuary. 1589.

Yours most humbly affectionate.

Ed. Spenser.

---

5 St. George, who becomes the patron saint of England and who is
the hero of Book I, begins his quest as an unpromising hero.

The Second Booke of the Faerie Qveene.
Contayning, the Legend of Sir Gvyon.
Or Of Temperaunce.

i

Right well I wote most mighty Soueraine,   *know*
  That all this famous antique history,
  Of some th'aboundance of an idle braine
  Will iudged be, and painted forgery,
  Rather then matter of iust memory,
  Sith none, that breatheth liuing aire, does know,
  Where is that happy land of Faery,
  Which I so much do vaunt, yet no where show,
But vouch antiquities, which no body can know.

ii

But let that man with better sence aduize,
  That of the world least part to vs is red:
  And dayly how through hardy enterprize,
  Many great Regions are discouered,
  Which to late age were neuer mentioned.
  Who euer heard of th'Indian *Peru*?
  Or who in venturous vessell measured
  The *Amazons* huge riuer now found trew?
Or fruitfullest *Virginia* who did euer vew?[1]

iii

Yet all these were, when no man did them know;
  Yet haue from wisest ages hidden beene:
  And later times things more vnknowne shall show.
  Why then should witlesse man so much misweene   *misunderstand*
  That nothing is, but that which he hath seene?
  What if within the Moones faire shining spheare?[2]
  What if in euery other starre vnseene
  Of other worldes he happily should heare?
He wonder would much more: yet such to some appeare.

iv

Of Faerie lond yet if he more inquire,
  By certaine signes here set in sundry place
  He may it find; ne let him then admire,
  But yield his sence to be too blunt and bace,
  That no'te without an hound fine footing trace.
  And thou, O fairest Princesse vnder sky,[3]
  In this faire mirrhour maist behold thy face,
  And thine owne realmes in lond of Faery,
And in this antique Image thy great auncestry.

10

20

30

The Second Booke of the Faerie Qveene.
Contayning, the Legend of Sir Gvyon.
Or Of Temperaunce
1 It was a Renaissance commonplace to think of newly discovered lands in America as like Paradise.

2 Life on the moon was thought possible by such Renaissance thinkers as Nicholas of Cusa and Giordano Bruno.
3 i.e. Queen Elizabeth, who is both the ostensible audience for the poem and its central character, the Faerie Queene.

v

The which O pardon me thus to enfold
  In couert vele,[4] and wrap in shadowes light,
  That feeble eyes your glory may behold,
40 Which else could not endure those beames bright,
  But would be dazled with exceeding light.
  O pardon, and vouchsafe with patient eare
  The braue aduentures of this Faery knight
  The good Sir *Guyon* gratiously to heare,
In whom great rule of Temp'raunce goodly doth appeare.

Cant. I.

  Guyon by Archimage abusd,   *deceived*
    The Redcrosse knight awaytes,
  Findes Mordant and Amauia slaine
    With pleasures poisoned baytes.

i

That cunning Architect of cancred guile,   *Archimago*
  Whom Princes late displeasure left in bands,
  For falsed letters and suborned wile,
  Soone as the *Redcrosse* knight he vnderstands
  To beene departed out of *Eden* lands,
  To serue againe his soueraine Elfin Queene,
  His artes he moues, and out of caytiues hands
  Himselfe he frees by secret meanes vnseene;
His shackles emptie left, him selfe escaped cleene.

ii

10 And forth he fares full of malicious mind,
  To worken mischiefe and auenging woe,
  Where euer he that godly knight may find,
  His onely hart sore, and his onely foe,
  Sith *Vna* now he algates must forgoe,   *completely*
  Whom his victorious hands did earst restore
  To natiue crowne and kingdome late ygoe:
  Where she enioyes sure peace for euermore,
As weather-beaten ship arriu'd on happie shore.

iii

Him therefore now the obiect of his spight
20 And deadly food he makes: him to offend
  By forged treason, or by open fight
  He seekes, of all his drift the aymed end:
  Thereto his subtile engins he does bend,
  His practick wit, and his faire filed tong,
  With thousand other sleights: for well he kend,   *knew*
  His credit now in doubtfull ballaunce hong;
For hardly could be hurt, who was already stong.

iv

Still as he went, he craftie stales did lay,   *baits*
  With cunning traines him to entrap vnwares,   *snares*
30 And priuie spials plast in all his way,   *spies*

---

4 i.e. in the poem's allegory; see the Letter to Raleigh for Spenser's
theory of allegory.

To weete what course he takes, and how he fares;
To ketch him at a vantage in his snares.
But now so wise and warie was the knight
By triall of his former harmes and cares,
That he describe, and shonned still his slight:
The fish that once was caught, new bait will hardly bite.

v

Nath'lesse th'Enchaunter would not spare his paine,
  In hope to win occasion to his will;
  Which when he long awaited had in vaine,
40   He chaungd his minde from one to other ill:
  For to all good he enimy was still.
  Vpon the way him fortuned to meet,
  Faire marching vnderneath a shady hill,
  A goodly knight, all armd in harnesse meete,
That from his head no place appeared to his feete.

vi

His carriage was full comely and vpright,
  His countenaunce demure and temperate,
  But yet so sterne and terrible in sight,
  That cheard his friends, and did his foes amate:
50   He was an Elfin borne of noble state,
  And mickle worship in his natiue land;   *honor*
  Well could he tourney and in lists debate,
  And knighthood tooke of good Sir *Huons* hand,
When with king *Oberon* he came to Faerie land.

vii

Him als accompanyd vpon the way
  A comely Palmer, clad in blacke attire,
  Of ripest yeares, and haires all hoarie gray,
  That with a staffe his feeble steps did stire,   *steer*
  Least his long way his aged limbes should tire:
60   And if by lookes one may the mind aread,
  He seemd to be a sage and sober sire,
  And euer with slow pace the knight did lead,
Who taught his trampling steed with equall steps to tread.

viii

Such whenas *Archimago* them did view,
  He weened well to worke some vncouth wile,
  Eftsoones vntwisting his deceiptfull clew,
  He gan to weaue a web of wicked guile,
  And with faire countenance and flattring stile,
  To them approching, thus the knight bespake:
70   Faire sonne of *Mars*, that seeke with warlike spoile,
  And great atchieu'ments great your selfe to make,
Vouchsafe to stay your steed for humble misers sake.

ix

He stayd his steed for humble misers sake,
  And bad tell on the tenor of his plaint;
  Who feigning then in euery limbe to quake,
  Through inward feare, and seeming pale and faint
  With piteous mone his percing speach gan paint;
  Deare Lady how shall I declare thy cace,

Whom late I left in langourous constraint?

80   Would God thy selfe now present were in place,
To tell this ruefull tale; thy sight could win thee grace.

x

Or rather would, O would it so had chaunst,
    That you, most noble Sir, had present beene,
    When that lewd ribauld with vile lust aduaunst
    Layd first his filthy hands on virgin cleene,
    To spoile her daintie corse so faire and sheene,   *body*
    As on the earth, great mother of vs all,
    With liuing eye more faire was neuer seene,
    Of chastitie and honour virginall:
90 Witnesse ye heauens, whom she in vaine to helpe did call.

xi

How may it be, (said then the knight halfe wroth,)
    That knight should knighthood euer so haue shent?   *disgraced*
    None but that saw (quoth he) would weene for troth,   *think*
    How shamefully that Maid he did torment.
    Her looser golden lockes he rudely rent,
    And drew her on the ground, and his sharpe sword
    Against her snowy brest he fiercely bent,
    And threatned death with many a bloudie word;
Toung hates to tell the rest, that eye to see abhord.

xii

100 Therewith amoued from his sober mood,
    And liues he yet (said he) that wrought this act,
    And doen the heauens afford him vitall food?
    He liues, (quoth he) and boasteth of the fact,
    Ne yet hath any knight his courage crackt.
    Where may that treachour then (said he) be found,
    Or by what meanes may I his footing tract?
    That shall I shew (said he) as sure, as hound
The stricken Deare doth chalenge by the bleeding wound.

xiii

He staid not lenger talke, but with fierce ire
110   And zealous hast away is quickly gone
    To seeke that knight, where him that craftie Squire
    Supposd to be. They do arriue anone,
    Where sate a gentle Lady all alone,
    With garments rent, and haire discheueled,
    Wringing her hands, and making piteous mone;
    Her swollen eyes were much disfigured,
And her faire face with teares was fowly blubbered.

xiv

The knight approching nigh, thus to her said,
    Faire Ladie, through foule sorrow ill bedight,
120   Great pittie is to see you thus dismaid,
    And marre the blossome of your beautie bright:
    For thy appease your griefe and heauie plight,
    And tell the cause of your conceiued paine.
    For if he liue, that hath you doen despight,
    He shall you doe due recompence againe,
Or else his wrong with greater puissance maintaine.

xv

Which when she heard, as in despightfull wise,
  She wilfully her sorrow did augment,
  And offred hope of comfort did despise:
130   Her golden lockes most cruelly she rent,
  And scratcht her face with ghastly dreriment,
  Ne would she speake, ne see, ne yet be seene,
  But hid her visage, and her head downe bent,
  Either for grieuous shame, or for great teene,   *sorrow*
As if her hart with sorrow had transfixed beene.

xvi

Till her that Squire bespake, Madame my liefe,
  For Gods deare loue be not so wilfull bent,
  But doe vouchsafe now to receiue reliefe,
  The which good fortune doth to you present.
140   For what bootes it to weepe and to wayment,   *lament*
  When ill is chaunst, but doth the ill increase,
  And the weake mind with double woe torment?
  When she her Squire heard speake, she gan appease
Her voluntarie paine, and feele some secret ease.

xvii

Eftsoone she said, Ah gentle trustie Squire,
  What comfort can I wofull wretch conceaue,
  Or why should euer I henceforth desire
  To see faire heauens face, and life not leaue,
  Sith that false Traytour did my honour reaue?
150   False traytour certes (said the Faerie knight)
  I read the man, that euer would deceaue
  A gentle Ladie, or her wrong through might:
Death were too little paine for such a foule despight.

xviii

But now, faire Ladie, comfort to you make,
  And read, who hath ye wrought this shamefull plight;
  That short reuenge the man may ouertake,
  Where so he be, and soone vpon him light.
  Certes (saide she) I wote not how he hight,   *I don't know what his name is*
  But vnder him a gray steede did he wield,
160   Whose sides with dapled circles weren dight;
  Vpright he rode, and in his siluer shield
He bore a bloudie Crosse, that quartred all the field.

xix

Now by my head (said *Guyon*) much I muse,
  How that same knight should do so foule amis,
  Or euer gentle Damzell so abuse:
  For may I boldly say, he surely is
  A right good knight, and true of word ywis: *surely*
  I present was, and can it witnesse well,
170   When armes he swore, and streight did enterpris
  Th'aduenture of the *Errant damozell*,   *Una*
In which he hath great glorie wonne, as I heare tell.

xx

Nathlesse he shortly shall againe be tryde,
  And fairely quite him of th'imputed blame,

Else be ye sure he dearely shall abyde,
Or make you good amendment for the same:
All wrongs haue mends, but no amends of shame.
Now therefore Ladie, rise out of your paine,
And see the saluing of your blotted name.
180   Full loth she seemd thereto, but yet did faine;
For she was inly glad her purpose so to gaine.

xxi

Her purpose was not such, as she did faine,
Ne yet her person such, as it was seene,
But vnder simple shew and semblant plaine
Lurckt false *Duessa* secretly vnseene,
As a chast Virgin, that had wronged beene:
So had false *Archimago* her disguisd,
To cloke her guile with sorrow and sad teene;
And eke himselfe had craftily deuisd
190   To be her Squire, and do her seruice well aguisd.

xxii

Her late forlorne and naked he had found,
Where she did wander in waste wildernesse,
Lurking in rockes and caues farre vnder ground,
And with greene mosse cou ring her nakednesse,
To hide her shame and loathly filthinesse;
Sith her Prince *Arthur* of proud ornaments
And borrow'd beautie spoyld. Her nathelesse
Th'enchaunter finding fit for his intents,
Did thus reuest, and deckt with due habiliments.

xxiii

200   For all he did, was to deceiue good knights,
And draw them from pursuit of praise and fame,
To slug in slouth and sensuall delights,
And end their daies with irrenowmed shame.
And now exceeding griefe him ouercame,
To see the *Redcrosse* thus aduaunced hye;
Therefore this craftie engine he did frame,   *scheme*
Against his praise to stirre vp enmitye
Of such, as vertues like mote vnto him allye.[5]

xxiv

So now he *Guyon* guides an vncouth way   *strange*
210   Through woods and mountaines, till they came at last
Into a pleasant dale, that lowly lay
Betwixt two hils, whose high heads ouerplast,
The valley did with coole shade ouercast,
Through midst thereof a little riuer rold,
By which there sate a knight with helme vnlast,
Himselfe refreshing with the liquid cold,
After his trauell long, and labours manifold.

xxv

Loe yonder he, cryde *Archimage* alowd,
That wrought the shamefull fact, which I did shew;

5   To stir up enmity between those whose virtues might otherwise
incline them to an alliance with Redcrosse is a key feature of
Archimago's plan.

220

And now he doth himselfe in secret shrowd,
   To flie the vengeance for his outrage dew;
   But vaine: for ye shall dearely do him rew,
   So God ye speed, and send you good successe;
   Which we farre off will here abide to vew.
   So they him left, inflam'd with wrathfulnesse,
That streight against that knight his speare he did addresse.

xxvi

Who seeing him from farre so fierce to pricke,
   His warlike armes about him gan embrace,
   And in the rest his readie speare did sticke;
230
   Tho when as still he saw him towards pace,
   He gan rencounter him in equall race.
   They bene ymet, both readie to affrap,   *strike*
   When suddenly that warriour gan abace
   His threatned speare, as if some new mishap
Had him betidde, or hidden daunger did entrap.[6]

xxvii

And cryde, Mercie Sir knight, and mercie Lord,
   For mine offence and heedlesse hardiment,
   That had almost committed crime abhord,
   And with reprochfull shame mine honour shent,
240
   Whiles cursed steele against that badge I bent,
   The sacred badge of my Redeemers death,
   Which on your shield is set for ornament:
   But his fierce foe his steede could stay vneath,
Who prickt with courage kene, did cruell battell breath.[7]

xxviiii

But when he heard him speake, streight way he knew
   His error, and himselfe inclyning sayd;
   Ah deare Sir *Guyon*, well becommeth you,
   But me behoueth rather to vpbrayd,
250
   Whose hastie hand so farre from reason strayd,
   That almost it did haynous violence
   On that faire image of that heauenly Mayd,
   That decks and armes your shield with faire defence:
Your court'sie takes on you anothers due offence.

xxix

So bene they both attone, and doen vpreare
   Their beuers bright, each other for to greete;
   Goodly comportance each to other beare,
   And entertaine themselues with court'sies meet.
   Then said the *Redcrosse* knight, Now mote I weet,   *might I know*
260
   Sir *Guyon*, why with so fierce saliaunce,
   And fell intent ye did at earst me meet;
   For sith I know your goodly gouernaunce,
Great cause, I weene, you guided, or some vncouth chaunce.

xxx

Certes (said he) well mote I shame to tell
   The fond encheason, that me hither led.   *foolish reason*
   A false infamous faitour late befell

---

6   At the last moment Guyon regains control of himself.   7   See Plato's metaphor of the unruly horse as one aspect of the soul in
                                                                Phaedrus, 253d–255.

Me for to meet, that seemed ill bested,
And playnd of grieuous outrage, which he red
A knight had wrought against a Ladie gent;
270   Which to auenge, he to this place me led,
Where you he made the marke of his intent,
And now is fled; foule shame him follow, where he went.

xxxi

So can he turne his earnest vnto game,
Through goodly handling and wise temperance.
By this his aged guide in presence came;
Who soone as on that knight his eye did glance,
Eft soones of him had perfect cognizance,
Sith him in Faerie court he late auizd;
And said, Faire sonne, God giue you happie chance,
280   And that deare Crosse vpon your shield deuizd,
Wherewith aboue all knights ye goodly seeme aguizd.[8]

xxxii

Ioy may you haue, and euerlasting fame,
Of late most hard atchieu'ment by you donne,
For which enrolled is your glorious name
In heauenly Registers aboue the Sunne,
Where you a Saint with Saints your seat haue wonne:
But wretched we, where ye haue left your marke,
Must now anew begin, like race to runne;
God guide thee, *Guyon,* well to end thy warke,
290   And to the wished hauen bring thy weary barke.

xxxiii

Palmer, (him answered the *Redcrosse* knight)
His be the praise, that this atchieu'ment wrought,
Who made my hand the organ of his might;
More then goodwill to me attribute nought:
For all I did, I did but as I ought.[9]
But you, faire Sir, whose pageant next ensewes,
Well mote yee thee, as well can wish your thought,
That home ye may report thrise happie newes;
For well ye worthie bene for worth and gentle thewes.   *manners*

xxxiv

300   So courteous conge both did giue and take,   *farewell*
With right hands plighted, pledges of good will.
Then *Guyon* forward gan his voyage make,[10]
With his blacke Palmer, that him guided still.
Still he him guided ouer dale and hill,
And with his steedie staffe did point his way:
His race with reason, and with words his will,
From foule intemperance he oft did stay,
And suffred not in wrath his hastie steps to stray.

---

8   Here in brief is Spenser's anatomy of the moral part of the soul: Temperance (Guyon) through the exercise of reason (the Palmer) comes to recognize holiness (Redcrosse).

9   Redcrosse here recalls his recognition of grace (his spiritually productive lack of self-sufficiency), which was his principal achievement in Book I.

10   Like Redcrosse at the beginning of Book I, Guyon here is not yet the embodiment of his virtue; rather he will achieve temperance as a consequence of becoming himself.

XXXV

In this faire wize they traueild long yfere,   *together*
  Through many hard assayes, which did betide;
310   Of which he honour still away did beare,
  And spred his glorie through all countries wide.
  At last as chaunst them by a forest side
  To passe, for succour from the scorching ray,
  They heard a ruefull voice, that dearnly cride   *dismally*
  With percing shriekes, and many a dolefull lay;[11]
Which to attend, a while their forward steps they stay.

xxxvi

But if that carelesse heauens (quoth she) despise
  The doome of iust reuenge, and take delight
320   To see sad pageants of mens miseries,
  As bound by them to liue in liues despight,
  Yet can they not warne death from wretched wight.
  Come then, come soone, come sweetest death to mee,
  And take away this long lent loathed light:
  Sharpe be thy wounds, but sweet the medicines bee,
That long captiued soules from wearie thraldome free.

xxxvii

But thou, sweet Babe, whom frowning froward fate
  Hath made sad witnesse of thy fathers fall,
  Sith heauen thee deignes to hold in liuing state,
330   Long maist thou liue, and better thriue withall,
  Then to thy lucklesse parents did befall:
  Liue thou, and to thy mother dead attest,
  That cleare she dide from blemish criminall;
  Thy litle hands embrewd in bleeding brest
Loe I for pledges leaue. So giue me leaue to rest.

xxxviii

With that a deadly shrieke she forth did throw,
  That through the wood reecchoed againe,
  And after gaue a grone so deepe and low,[12]
  That seemd her tender heart was rent in twaine,
340   Or thrild with point of thorough piercing paine;
  As gentle Hynd, whose sides with cruell steele
  Through launched, forth her bleeding life does raine,
  Whiles the sad pang approching she does feele,
Brayes out her latest breath, and vp her eyes doth seele.

xxxix

Which when that warriour heard, dismounting straict
  From his tall steed, he rusht into the thicke,
  And soone arriued, where that sad pourtraict
  Of death and dolour lay, halfe dead, halfe quicke,
  In whose white alabaster brest did sticke
350   A cruell knife, that made a griesly wound,
  From which forth gusht a streme of gorebloud thick,
  That all her goodly garments staind around,
And into a deepe sanguine dide the grassie ground.

---

11 Amavia's story, which follows, is that of one whose nature (as her name declares) is to love life.

12 Here, as so often at key moments in *FQ*, sound precedes sight.

xl

Pittifull spectacle of deadly smart,
  Beside a bubbling fountaine low she lay,
  Which she increased with her bleeding hart,
  And the cleane waues with purple gore did ray;
  Als in her lap a louely babe did play
  His cruell sport, in stead of sorrow dew;
360 For in her streaming blood he did embay
  His litle hands, and tender ioynts embrew;
Pitifull spectacle, as euer eye did view.

xli

Besides them both, vpon the soiled gras
  The dead corse of an armed knight was spred,
  Whose armour all with bloud besprinckled was;
  His ruddie lips did smile, and rosy red
  Did paint his chearefull cheekes, yet being ded:
  Seemd to haue beene a goodly personage,
  Now in his freshest flowre of lustie hed,
370 Fit to inflame faire Lady with loues rage,
But that fiers fate did crop the blossome of his age.

xlii

Whom when the good Sir *Guyon* did behold,
  His hart gan wexe as starke, as marble stone,
  And his fresh bloud did frieze with fearefull cold,
  That all his senses seemd bereft attone:
  At last his mightie ghost gan deepe to grone,   *spirit*
  As Lyon grudging in his great disdaine,
  Mournes inwardly, and makes to himselfe mone;
  Till ruth and fraile affection did constraine
380 His stout courage to stoupe, and shew his inward paine.

xliii

Out of her gored wound the cruell steele
  He lightly snatcht, and did the floudgate stop
  With his faire garment: then gan softly feele
  Her feeble pulse, to proue if any drop
  Of liuing bloud yet in her veynes did hop;   *pulse*
  Which when he felt to moue, he hoped faire
  To call backe life to her forsaken shop;   *form*
  So well he did her deadly wounds repaire,
  That at the last she gan to breath out liuing aire.

xliv

390 Which he perceiuing greatly gan reioice,
  And goodly counsell, that for wounded hart
  Is meetest med'cine, tempred with sweet voice;
  Ay me, deare Lady, which the image art
  Of ruefull pitie, and impatient smart,
  What direfull chance, armd with reuenging fate,
  Or cursed hand hath plaid this cruell part,
  Thus fowle to hasten your vntimely date;
Speak; O deare Lady speake: help neuer comes too late.

xlv

Therewith her dim eie-lids she vp gan reare,
400 On which the drery death did sit, as sad
  As lump of lead, and made darke clouds appeare;

But when as him all in bright armour clad
Before her standing she espied had,
As one out of a deadly dreame affright,
She weakely started, yet she nothing drad:
Streight downe againe her selfe in great despight
She groueling threw to ground, as hating life and light.

xlvi

The gentle knight her soone with carefull paine
Vplifted light, and softly did vphold:
Thrise he her reard, and thrise she sunke againe,
Till he his armes about her sides gan fold,
And to her said; Yet if the stony cold
Haue not all seized on your frozen hart,
Let one word fall that may your griefe vnfold,
And tell the secret of your mortall smart;
He oft finds present helpe, who does his griefe impart.

410

xlvii

Then casting vp a deadly looke, full low
Shee sight from bottome of her wounded brest,
And after, many bitter throbs did throw
With lips full pale and foltring tongue opprest,
These words she breathed forth from riuen chest;
Leaue, ah leaue off, what euer wight thou bee,
To let a wearie wretch from her dew rest,
And trouble dying soules tranquilitee.
Take not away now got, which none would giue to me.

420

xlviii

Ah farre be it (said he) Deare dame fro mee,
To hinder soule from her desired rest,
Or hold sad life in long captiuitee:
For all I seeke, is but to haue redrest
The bitter pangs, that doth your heart infest.
Tell then, O Lady tell, what fatall priefe   *experience*
Hath with so huge misfortune you opprest?
That I may cast to compasse your reliefe,   *plan to accomplish*
Or die with you in sorrow, and partake your griefe.

430

xlix

With feeble hands then stretched forth on hye,
As heauen accusing guiltie of her death,
And with dry drops congealed in her eye,
In these sad words she spent her vtmost breath:
Heare then, O man, the sorrowes that vneath
My tongue can tell, so farre all sense they pas:
Loe this dead corpse, that lies here vnderneath,
The gentlest knight, that euer on greene gras
Gay steed with spurs did pricke, the good Sir *Mordant* was.   *i.e., death-giving*

440

l

Was, (ay the while, that he is not so now)
My Lord my loue; my deare Lord, my deare loue,
So long as heauens iust with equall brow
Vouchsafed to behold vs from aboue,
One day when him high courage did emmoue,
As wont ye knights to seeke aduentures wilde,

450
He pricked forth, his puissant force to proue,
Me then he left enwombed of this child,   *Ruddymane (bloody-handed)*
This lucklesse child, whom thus ye see with bloud defild.

li
Him fortuned (hard fortune ye may ghesse)
To come, where vile *Acrasia*[13] does wonne,
Acrasia a false enchaunteresse,
That many errant knights hath foule fordonne: *destroyed*
Within a wandring Island, that doth ronne
And stray in perilous gulfe, her dwelling is;
Faire Sir, if euer there ye trauell, shonne
460
The cursed land where many wend amis,
And know it by the name; it hight the *Bowre of blis*.

lii
Her blisse is all in pleasure and delight,
Wherewith she makes her louers drunken mad,
And then with words and weedes of wondrous might,
On them she workes her will to vses bad:
My lifest Lord she thus beguiled had;   *dearest*
For he was flesh: (all flesh doth frailtie breed.)
Whom when I heard to beene so ill bestad,
Weake wretch I wrapt my selfe in Palmers weed,
470
And cast to seeke him forth through daunger and great dreed.

liii
Now had faire *Cynthia* by euen tournes   *the moon*
Full measured three quarters of her yeare,
And thrise three times had fild her crooked hornes,
Whenas my wombe her burdein would forbeare,
And bad me call *Lucina* to me neare.   *goddess of childbirth*
Lucina came: a manchild forth I brought:
The woods, the Nymphes, my bowres, my midwiues weare,
Hard helpe at need. So deare thee babe I bought,
Yet nought too deare I deemd, while so my dear I sought.

liv
Him so I sought, and so at last I found,
480
Where him that witch had thralled to her will,
In chaines of lust and lewd desires ybound,
And so transformed from his former skill,   *intelligence*
That me he knew not, neither his owne ill;
Till through wise handling and faire gouernance,
I him recured to a better will,
Purged from drugs of foule intemperance:
Then meanes I gan deuise for his deliuerance.

lv
Which when the vile Enchaunteresse perceiu'd,
490
How that my Lord from her I would repriue,
With cup thus charmd, him parting she deceiu'd;
Sad verse, giue death to him that death does giue,
And losse of loue, to her that loues to liue,
So soone as Bacchus with the Nymphe does lincke:

13   Acrasia's name is drawn from the Greek *akrastos*, meaning the lack
of the power to control oneself.

So parted we and on our iourney driue,
Till comming to this well, he stoupt to drincke:
The charme fulfild, dead suddenly he downe did sincke,

lvi

Which when I wretch, Not one word more she sayd
   But breaking off the end for want of breath,
500   And slyding soft, as downe to sleepe her layd,
   And ended all her woe in quiet death.
   That seeing good Sir *Guyon*, could vneath
   From teares abstaine, for griefe his hart did grate,
   And from so heauie sight his head did wreath,
   Accusing fortune, and too cruell fate,
Which plunged had faire Ladie in so wretched state.

lvii

Then turning to his Palmer said, Old syre
   Behold the image of mortalitie,[14]
   And feeble nature cloth'd with fleshly tyre,
510   When raging passion with fierce tyrannie
   Robs reason of her due regalitie,
   And makes it seruant to her basest part:
   The strong it weakens with infirmitie,
   And with bold furie armes the weakest hart;
The strong through pleasure soonest falles, the weake through smart.

lviii

But temperance (said he) with golden squire
   Betwixt them both can measure out a meane,[15]
   Neither to melt in pleasures whot desire,
   Nor fry in hartlesse griefe and dolefull teene.
520   Thrise happie man, who fares them both atweene:
   But sith this wretched woman ouercome
   Of anguish, rather then of crime hath beene,
   Reserue her cause to her eternall doome,
And in the meane vouchsafe her honorable toombe.

lix

Palmer (quoth he) death is an equall doome
   To good and bad, the common Inne of rest;
   But after death the tryall is to come,
   When best shall be to them, that liued best:
   But both alike, when death hath both supprest,
530   Religious reuerence doth buriall teene,
   Which who so wants, wants so much of his rest: *lacks*
   For all so great shame after death I weene,
As selfe to dyen bad, vnburied bad to beene.

lx

So both agree their bodies to engraue;
   The great earthes wombe they open to the sky,
   And with sad Cypresse seemely it embraue,
   Then couering with a clod their closed eye,
   They lay therein those corses tenderly,
   And bid them sleepe in euerlasting peace.

---

14   Like Redcrosse earlier, Guyon begins his journey with an abstract
idea of his virtue that he eventually grounds on experience.

15   Temperance as the golden mean: cf. Aristotle's *Nicomachaean Ethics*,
2, 1107a.

540

But ere they did their vtmost obsequy,
Sir *Guyon* more affection to increace,
Bynempt a sacred vow, which none should aye releace.   *made*

lxi

The dead knights sword out of his sheath he drew,
    With which he cut a locke of all their heare,
    Which medling with their bloud and earth, he threw
    Into the graue, and gan deuoutly sweare;
    Such and such euill God on *Guyon* reare,
    And worse and worse young Orphane be thy paine,
    If I or thou dew vengeance doe forbeare,

550
        Till guiltie bloud her guerdon doe obtaine:[16]
So shedding many teares, they closd the earth againe.

Cant. II.

Babes bloudie hands may not be clensd:
    the face of golden Meane.
Her sisters two Extremities
    striue her to banish cleane.

i

Thus when Sir *Guyon* with his faithfull guide
    Had with due rites and dolorous lament
    The end of their sad Tragedie vptyde,
    The litle babe vp in his armes he hent;   *took*
    Who with sweet pleasance and bold blandishment
    Gan smyle on them, that rather ought to weepe,
    As carelesse of his woe, or innocent
    Of that was doen, that ruth emperced deepe
In that knights heart, and wordes with bitter teares did steepe.

ii

10

Ah lucklesse babe, borne vnder cruell starre,
    And in dead parents balefull ashes bred,[1]
    Full litle weenest thou, what sorrowes are
    Left thee for portion of thy liuelihed,
    Poore Orphane in the wide world scattered,
    As budding braunch rent from the natiue tree,
    And throwen forth, till it be withered:
    Such is the state of men: thus enter wee
Into this life with woe, and end with miseree.

iii

Then soft himselfe inclyning on his knee
20
        Downe to that well, did in the water weene
    (So loue does loath disdainfull nicitee)
    His guiltie hands from bloudie gore to cleene.
    He washt them oft and oft, yet nought they beene
    For all his washing cleaner. Still he stroue,

---

16   Unlike Redcrosse, Guyon sets his own course, emphasizing the self-direction of temperance, but also the danger of forgetting Redcrosse's principle of grace.

CANT. II.

1   This allusion to the phoenix, the bird that is reborn out of its own ashes, not only contradicts Amavia's account of Ruddymane's birth but also calls into question Guyon's readiness to universalize the human condition. Here he seems under the morbid spell of Amavia's story, as the Palmer observes in stanza v.

Yet still the litle hands were bloudie seene;
The which him into great amaz'ment droue,
And into diuerse doubt his wauering wonder cloue.

iv

He wist not whether blot of foule offence
  Might not be purgd with water nor with bath;
  Or that high God, in lieu of innocence,
  Imprinted had that token of his wrath,
  To shew how sore bloudguiltinesse he hat'th;
  Or that the charme and venim, which they druncke,
  Their bloud with secret filth infected hath,
  Being diffused through the senselesse truncke,
That through the great contagion direfull deadly stunck,

v

Whom thus at gaze, the Palmer gan to bord
  With goodly reason, and thus faire bespake;
  Ye bene right hard amated, gratious Lord,
  And of your ignorance great maruell make,
  Whiles cause not well conceiued ye mistake.
  But know, that secret vertues are infusd
  In euery fountaine, and in euery lake,
  Which who hath skill them rightly to haue chusd,
To proofe of passing wonders hath full often vsd.

vi

Of those some were so from their sourse indewd
  By great Dame Nature,[2] from whose fruitfull pap
  Their welheads spring, and are with moisture deawd;
  Which feedes each liuing plant with liquid sap,
  And filles with flowres faire *Floraes* painted lap:[3]
  But other some by gift of later grace,
  Or by good prayers, or by other hap,
  Had vertue pourd into their waters bace,
And thenceforth were renowmd, and sought from place to place.

vii

Such is this well, wrought by occasion straunge,
  Which to her Nymph befell. Vpon a day,
  As she the woods with bow and shafts did raunge,
  The hartlesse Hind and Robucke to dismay,   *timid*
  Dan Faunus chaunst to meet her by the way,
  And kindling fire at her faire burning eye,
  Inflamed was to follow beauties chace,
  And chaced her, that fast from him did fly;
As Hind from her, so she fled from her enimy.[4]

viii

At last when fayling breath began to faint,
  And saw no meanes to scape, of shame affrayd,
  She set her downe to weepe for sore constraint,[5]

30

40

50

60

2 The Palmer's ability to read the occult virtues in nature implies
powers in the natural world that Spenser later explores in "The
Mutability Cantos." See also Alanus de Insulis, *De Planctu Naturae*.
3 See Botticelli's magnificent visual representation of Flora in his
Primavera.

4 The story of the nymph illustrates the complex relationships
between the concupiscent and irascible passions; the first, overly
desirous or eager, and the second, too easily angered.
5 Combines a sense of repression, constraint, and distress.

And to *Diana* calling lowd for ayde,
Her deare besought, to let her dye a mayd.
The goddesse heard, and suddeine where she sate,
70   Welling out streames of teares, and quite dismayd
With stony feare of that rude rustick mate,
Transformd her to a stone from stedfast virgins state.

ix

Lo now she is that stone, from whose two heads,
As from two weeping eyes, fresh streames do flow,
Yet cold through feare, and old conceiued dreads;
And yet the stone her semblance seemes to show,
Shapt like a maid, that such ye may her know;
And yet her vertues in her water byde:
For it is chast and pure, as purest snow,
80   Ne lets her waues with any filth be dyde,
But euer like her selfe vnstained hath beene tryde.

x

From thence it comes, that this babes bloudy hand
May not be clensd with water of this well:
Ne certes Sir striue you it to withstand,
But let them still be bloudy, as befell,
That they his mothers innocence may tell,
As she bequeathd in her last testament;
That as a sacred Symbole it may dwell
In her sonnes flesh, to minde reuengement,
90   And be for all chast Dames an endlesse moniment.[6]

xi

He hearkned to his reason, and the childe
Vptaking, to the Palmer gaue to beare;
But his sad fathers armes with bloud defilde,
An hcauie load himselfe did lightly reare,   *earlier*
And turning to that place, in which whyleare   *saddle*
He left his loftie steed with golden sell,   *armor*
And goodly gorgeous barbes, him found not theare.
By other accident that earst befell,
He is conuaide, but how or where, here fits not tell.

xii

100   Which when Sir *Guyon* saw, all were he wroth,
Yet algates mote he soft himselfe appease,
And fairely fare on foot, how euer loth;
His double burden did him sore disease.   *discomfort*
So long they traueiled with litle ease,
Till that at last they to a Castle came,
Built on a rocke adioyning to the seas;
It was an auncient worke of antique fame,
And wondrous strong by nature, and by skilfull frame.

xiii

Therein three sisters dwelt of sundry sort,
110   The children of one sire by mothers three;[7]

---

6   The Palmer's explications are less reductive than Guyon's.

7   Possibly the three parts of the Platonic soul: reason, appetite, and spirit, which manifest justice when they are in harmony (see *Republic*, 9, 580–1).

Who dying whylome did diuide this fort
    To them by equall shares in equall fee:
    But strifull minde, and diuerse qualitee
    Drew them in parts, and each made others foe:
    Still did they striue, and dayly disagree;
    The eldest did against the youngest goe,
And both against the middest meant to worken woe.

xiv

Where when the knight arriu'd, he was right well
    Receiu'd, as knight of so much worth became,
120   Of second sister, who did far excell
    The other two; *Medina* was her name,[8]
    A sober sad, and comely curteous Dame;
    Who rich arayd, and yet in modest guize,
    In goodly garments, that her well became,
    Faire marching forth in honorable wize,
Him at the threshold met, and well did enterprize.   *entertain*

xv

She led him vp into a goodly bowre,
    And comely courted with meet modestie,
    Ne in her speach, ne in her hauiour,
130   Was lightnesse seene, or looser vanitie,
    But gratious womanhood, and grauitie,
    Aboue the reason of her youthly yeares:
    Her golden lockes she roundly did vptye
    In breaded tramels, that no looser heares
Did out of order stray about her daintie eares.

xvi

Whilest she her selfe thus busily did frame,
    Seemely to entertaine her new-come guest,
    Newes hereof to her other sisters came,
    Who all this while were at their wanton rest,
140   Accourting each her friend with lauish fest:
    They were two knights of perelesse puissance,
    And famous far abroad for warlike gest,   *deed*
    Which to these Ladies loue did countenaunce,
And to his mistresse each himselfe stroue to aduaunce.

xvii

He that made loue vnto the eldest Dame,
    Was hight Sir *Huddibras*, an hardy man;
    Yet not so good of deedes, as great of name,
    Which he by many rash aduentures wan,
    Since errant armes to sew he first began;   *pursue*
150   More huge in strength, then wise in workes he was,
    And reason with foole-hardize ouer ran;
    Sterne melancholy did his courage pas,   *surpass*
And was for terrour more, all armd in shyning bras.

xviii

But he that lou'd the youngest, was *Sans-loy*,[9]
    He that faire *Vna* late fowle outraged,

8   Medina is the mean between her defective and excessive sisters, who   9   Literally, "without law"; he is the same Saracen who, in Book I,
are either all abstinence (Elissa) or all pleasure (Perissa); see Aristotle's   attacked Una when she was separated from the Red Cross knight.
Ethics, 2, 1107a.

The most vnruly, and the boldest boy,
That euer warlike weapons menaged,
And to all lawlesse lust encouraged,
Through strong opinion of his matchlesse might:
Ne ought he car'd, whom he endamaged
By tortious wrong, or whom bereau'd of right.
He now this Ladies champion chose for loue to fight.

160

xix

These two gay knights, vowd to so diuerse loues,
Each other does enuie with deadly hate,
And dayly warre against his foeman moues,
In hope to win more fauour with his mate,
And th'others pleasing seruice to abate,
To magnifie his owne. But when they heard,
How in that place straunge knight arriued late,
Both knights and Ladies forth right angry far'd,
And fiercely vnto battell sterne themselues prepar'd.

170

xx

But ere they could proceede vnto the place,
Where he abode, themselues at discord fell,
And cruell combat ioynd in middle space:
With horrible assault, and furie fell,
They heapt huge strokes, the scorned life to quell,
That all on vprore from her settled seat
The house was raysd, and all that in did dwell;
Seemd that lowde thunder with amazement great
Did rend the ratling skyes with flames of fouldring heat.   *thundering*

180

xxi

The noyse thereof cald forth that straunger knight,
To weet, what dreadfull thing was there in hand;
Where when as two braue knights in bloudy fight
With deadly rancour he enraunged fond,
His sunbroad shield about his wrest he bond,
And shyning blade vnsheathd, with which he ran
Vnto that stead, their strife to vnderstond;
And at his first arriuall, them began
With goodly meanes to pacifie, well as he can.

xxii

But they him spying, both with greedy forse
Attonce vpon him ran, and him beset
With strokes of mortall steele without remorse,
And on his shield like yron sledges bet: *beat*
As when a Beare and Tygre being met
In cruell fight on lybicke Ocean[10] wide,
Espye a traueiler with feet surbet,   *bruised*
Whom they in equall pray hope to deuide,
They stint their strife, and him assaile on euery side.

190

xxiii

But he, not like a wearie traueilere,
Their sharpe assault right boldly did rebut,
And suffred not their blowes to byte him nere,

200

10   The moving sand dunes in the Libyan desert.

But with redoubled buffes them backe did put:
Whose grieued mindes, which choler did englut,
Against themselues turning their wrathfull spight,
Gan with new rage their shields to hew and cut;
But still when *Guyon* came to part their fight,
With heauie load on him they freshly gan to smight.

xxiv

As a tall ship tossed in troublous seas,
  Whom raging windes threatning to make the pray
  Of the rough rockes, do diuersly disease,
  Meetes two contrary billowes by the way,
  That her on either side do sore assay,
  And boast to swallow her in greedy graue;
  She scorning both their spights, does make wide way,
  And with her brest breaking the fomy waue,
Does ride on both their backs, and faire her selfe doth saue.

xxv

So boldly he him beares, and rusheth forth
  Betweene them both, by conduct of his blade.
  Wondrous great prowesse and heroick worth
  He shewd that day, and rare ensample made,
  When two so mighty warriours he dismade:
  Attonce he wards and strikes, he takes and payes,
  Now forst to yield, now forcing to inuade,
  Before, behind, and round about him layes:
So double was his paines, so double be his prayse.

xxvi

Straunge sort of fight, three valiaunt knights to see
  Three combats ioyne in one, and to darraine   *engage*
  A triple warre with triple enmitee,
  All for their Ladies froward loue to gaine,
  Which gotten was but hate. So loue does raine
  In stoutest minds, and maketh monstrous warre;
  He maketh warre, he maketh peace againe,
  And yet his peace is but continuall iarre:
O miserable men, that to him subiect arre.

xxvii

Whilst thus they mingled were in furious armes,
  The faire *Medina* with her tresses torne,
  And naked brest, in pitty of their harmes,
  Emongst them ran, and falling them beforne,
  Besought them by the womb, which them had borne,
  And by the loues, which were to them most deare,
  And by the knighthood, which they sure had sworne,
  Their deadly cruell discord to forbeare,
And to her iust conditions of faire peace to heare.

xxviii

But her two other sisters standing by,
  Her lowd gainsaid, and both their champions bad
  Pursew the end of their strong enmity,
  As euer of their loues they would be glad.
  Yet she with pitthy words and counsell sad,   *serious*
  Still stroue their stubborne rages to reuoke,

210

220

230

240

250
>That at the last suppressing fury mad,
>They gan abstaine from dint of direfull stroke,
>And hearken to the sober speaches, which she spoke.

xxix

>Ah puissaunt Lords, what cursed euill Spright,
>   Or fell *Erinnys*,[11] in your noble harts
>   Her hellish brond hath kindled with despight,
>   And stird you vp to worke your wilfull smarts?
>   Is this the ioy of armes? be these the parts
>   Of glorious knighthood, after bloud to thrust,
>   And not regard dew right and iust desarts?
260
>   Vaine is the vaunt, and victory vniust,
>That more to mighty hands, then rightfull cause doth trust.

xxx

>And were there rightfull cause of difference,
>   Yet were not better, faire it to accord,
>   Then with bloud guiltinesse to heape offence,
>   And mortall vengeaunce ioyne to crime abhord?
>   O fly from wrath, fly, O my liefest Lord:
>   Sad be the sights, and bitter fruits of warre,
>   And thousand furies wait on wrathfull sword;
>   Ne ought the prayse of prowesse more doth marre,
270
>Then fowle reuenging rage, and base contentious iarre.

xxxi

>But louely concord, and most sacred peace
>   Doth nourish vertue, and fast friendship breeds;
>   Weake she makes strong, and strong thing does increace,
>   Till it the pitch of highest prayse exceeds:
>   Braue be her warres, and honorable deeds,
>   By which she triumphes ouer ire and pride,
>   And winnes an Oliue girlond for her meeds:
>   Be therefore, O my deare Lords, pacifide,
>And this misseeming discord meekely lay aside.

xxxii

280
>Her gracious wordes their rancour did appall,
>   And suncke so deepe into their boyling brests,
>   That downe they let their cruell weapons fall,
>   And lowly did abase their loftie crests
>   To her faire presence, and discrete behests.
>   Then she began a treatie to procure,
>   And stablish termes betwixt both their requests,
>   That as a law for euer should endure;
>Which to obserue in word of knights they did assure.

xxxiii

>Which to confirme, and fast to bind their league,
290
>   After their wearie sweat and bloudy toile,
>   She them besought, during their quiet treague,   *truce*
>   Into her lodging to repaire a while,
>   To rest themselues, and grace to reconcile.

11   Variously named the Erinyes, the Furies, or the Eumenides, they
are spirits of fury and retribution in man that become eventually tamed
by law in Aeschylus' *The Eumenides*.

They soone consent: so forth with her they fare,
  Where they are well receiu'd, and made to spoile
  Themselues of soiled armes, and to prepare
Their minds to pleasure, and their mouthes to dainty fare.

xxxiv

And those two froward sisters, their faire loues
  Came with them eke, all were they wondrous loth,
  And fained cheare, as for the time behoues,
  But could not colour yet so well the troth,
  But that their natures bad appeard in both:
  For both did at their second sister grutch,   *complain*
  And inly grieue, as doth an hidden moth
  The inner garment fret, not th'vtter touch;
One thought their cheare too litle, th'other thought too mutch.

xxxv

Elissa (so the eldest hight) did deeme
  Such entertainment base, ne ought would eat,
  Ne ought would speake, but euermore did seeme
  As discontent for want of merth or meat;
  No solace could her Paramour intreat
  Her once to show, ne court, nor dalliance,
  But with bent lowring browes, as she would threat,
  She scould, and frownd with froward countenaunce,
Vnworthy of faire Ladies comely gouernaunce.

xxxvi

But young *Perissa* was of other mind,
  Full of disport, still laughing, loosely light,
  And quite contrary to her sisters kind;
  No measure in her mood, no rule of right,
  But poured out in pleasure and delight;
  In wine and meats she flowd aboue the bancke,
  And in excesse exceeded her owne might;
  In sumptuous tire she ioyd her selfe to prancke,
But of her loue too lauish (litle haue she thancke.)

xxxvii

Fast by her side did sit the bold *Sans-loy*,
  Fit mate for such a mincing mineon,
  Who in her loosenesse tooke exceeding ioy;
  Might not be found a franker franion,
  Of her lewd parts to make companion;
  But *Huddibras*, more like a Malecontent,
  Did see and grieue at his bold fashion;
  Hardly could he endure his hardiment,
Yet still he sat, and inly did him selfe torment.

xxxviii

Betwixt them both the faire *Medina* sate
  With sober grace, and goodly carriage:
  With equall measure she did moderate
  The strong extremities of their outrage;
  That forward paire she euer would asswage,
  When they would striue dew reason to exceed;
  But that same froward twaine would accourage,
  And of her plenty adde vnto their need:
So kept she them in order, and her selfe in heed.   *authority*

xxxix

Thus fairely she attempered her feast,
　And pleasd them all with meete satietie,
　At last when lust of meat and drinke was ceast,
　She *Guyon* deare besought of curtesie,
　To tell from whence he came through ieopardie,
　And whither now on new aduenture bound.
　Who with bold grace, and comely grauitie,
350　　Drawing to him the eyes of all around,
From lofty siege began these words aloud to sound.[12]

xl

This thy demaund, O Lady, doth reuiue
　Fresh memory in me of that great Queene,
　Great and most glorious virgin Queene aliue,
　That with her soueraigne powre, and scepter shene
　All Faery lond does peaceably sustene.
　In widest Ocean she her throne does reare,
　That ouer all the earth it may be seene;
　As morning Sunne her beames dispredden cleare,
360　And in her face faire peace, and mercy doth appeare.

xli

In her the richesse of all heauenly grace
　In chiefe degree are heaped vp on hye:
　And all that else this worlds enclosure bace
　Hath great or glorious in mortall eye,
　Adornes the person of her Maiestie;
　That men beholding so great excellence,
　And rare perfection in mortalitie,
　Do her adore with sacred reuerence,
As th'Idole of her makers great magnificence.

xlii

370　To her I homage and my seruice owe,
　In number of the noblest knights on ground,
　Mongst whom on me she deigned to bestowe
　Order of *Maydenhead*, the most renownd,[13]
　That may this day in all the world be found:
　An yearely solemne feast she wontes to make
　The day that first doth lead the yeare around;
　To which all knights of worth and courage bold
Resort, to heare of straunge aduentures to be told.

xliii

There this old Palmer shewed himselfe that day,
380　　And to that mighty Princesse did complaine
　Of grieuous mischiefes, which a wicked Fay
　Had wrought, and many whelmd in deadly paine,
　Whereof he crau'd redresse. My Soueraine,
　Whose glory is in gracious deeds, and ioyes
　Throughout the world her mercy to maintaine,
　Eftsoones deuisd redresse for such annoyes;
Me all vnfit for so great purpose she employes.

12　Guyon's account of his adventures parallels Odysseus' (in Homer's *Odyssey*, 9–12) and Aeneas' (in Virgil's *Aeneid*, 2–3).

13　Perhaps an allusion to the Order of the Garter, which was instituted by Edward III (*c.* 1346).

xliv

Now hath faire *Phœbe* with her siluer face[14]
   Thrise seene the shadowes of the neather world,
390   Sith last I left that honorable place,
   In which her royall presence is introld;
   Ne euer shall I rest in house nor hold,
   Till I that false *Acrasia* haue wonne;
   Of whose fowle deedes, too hideous to be told,
   I witnesse am, and this their wretched sonne,
Whose wofull parents she hath wickedly fordonne.

xlv

Tell on, faire Sir, said she, that dolefull tale,
   From which sad ruth does seeme you to restraine,
   That we may pitty such vnhappy bale,
400   And learne from pleasures poyson to abstaine:
   Ill by ensample good doth often gayne.
   Then forward he his purpose gan pursew,
   And told the storie of the mortall payne,
   Which *Mordant* and *Amauia* did rew;
As with lamenting eyes him selfe did lately vew.

xlvi

Night was far spent, and now in *Ocean* deepe
   Orion, flying fast from hissing snake,[15]
   His flaming head did hasten for to steepe,
   When of his pitteous tale he end did make;
410   Whilest with delight of that he wisely spake,
   Those guestes beguiled, did beguile their eyes
   Of kindly sleepe, that did them ouertake.
   At last when they had markt the chaunged skyes,
They wist their houre was spent; then each to rest him hyes.   *knew*

Cant. III.

Vaine Braggadocchio getting Guyons
horse is made the scorne
Of knighthood trew, and is of fayre
Belphœbe fowle forlorne.   *defeated*

i

Soone as the morrow faire with purple beames
   Disperst the shadowes of the mistie night,
   And *Titan* playing on the eastern streames,
   Gan cleare the deawy ayre with springing light,
   Sir *Guyon* mindfull of his vow yplight,
   Vprose from drowsie couch, and him addrest
   Vnto the iourney which he had behight:
   His puissaunt armes about his noble brest,
And many-folded shield he bound about his wrest.

ii

10   Then taking *Congé* of that virgin pure,   *farewell*
   The bloudy-handed babe vnto her truth
   Did earnestly commit, and her coniure,

---

14 It is now the beginning of summer, since Phoebe (Diana or the   15 Orion sets as Scorpio rises.
moon) has completed her three cycles.

In vertuous lore to traine his tender youth,
   And all that gentle noriture ensu'th: *training*
   And that so soone as ryper yeares he raught,
   He might for memorie of that dayes ruth,
   Be called *Ruddymane*, and thereby taught,
T'auenge his Parents death on them, that had it wrought.

iii

So forth he far'd, as now befell, on foot,
20   Sith his good steed is lately from him gone;
   Patience perforce; helpelesse what may it boot
   To fret for anger, or for griefe to mone?
   His Palmer now shall foot no more alone:
   So fortune wrought, as vnder greene woods syde
   He lately heard that dying Lady grone,
   He left his steed without, and speare besyde,
And rushed in on foot to ayd her, ere she dyde.

iv

The whiles a losell wandring by the way,[1]   *scoundrel*
   One that to bountie neuer cast his mind,
30   Ne thought of honour euer did assay
   His baser brest, but in his kestrell kind
   A pleasing vaine of glory vaine did find,
   To which his flowing toung, and troublous spright
   Gaue him great ayd, and made him more inclind:
   He that braue steed there finding ready dight,
Purloynd both steed and speare, and ran away full light.   *fast*

v

Now gan his hart all swell in iollitie,
   And of him selfe great hope and helpe conceiu'd,
   That puffed vp with smoke of vanitie,
40   And with selfe-loued personage deceiu'd,
   He gan to hope, of men to be receiu'd
   For such, as he him thought, or faine would bee:
   But for in court gay portaunce he perceiu'd,
   And gallant shew to be in greatest gree,
Eftsoones to court he cast t'auaunce his first degree.

vi

And by the way he chaunced to espy
   One sitting idle on a sunny bancke,
   To whom auaunting in great brauery,   *bravado*
   As Peacocke, that his painted plumes doth prancke,
50   He smote his courser in the trembling flancke,
   And to him threatned his hart-thrilling speare:
   The seely man seeing him ryde so rancke,
   And ayme at him, fell flat to ground for feare,
And crying Mercy lowd, his pitious hands gan reare.

CANT. III.
1   The braggart solider is a type that is common in Western literature
at least since Roman times. His extravagant talk is a sure sign of his
cowardice.

vii

Thereat the Scarcrow wexed wondrous prowd,
    Through fortune of his first aduenture faire,
    And with big thundring voyce reuyld him lowd;
    Vile Caytiue, vassall of dread and despaire,
    Vnworthie of the commune breathed aire,
60   Why liuest thou, dead dog, a lenger day,
    And doest not vnto death thy selfe prepaire.
    Dye, or thy selfe my captiue yield for ay;
Great fauour I thee graunt, for aunswere thus to stay.

viii

Hold, O deare Lord, hold your dead-doing hand,
    Then loud he cryde, I am your humble thrall.
    Ah wretch (quoth he) thy destinies withstand
    My wrathfull will, and do for mercy call.
    I giue thee life: therefore prostrated fall,
    And kisse my stirrup; that thy homage bee.
70   The Miser threw him selfe, as an Offall,
    Streight at his foot in base humilitee,
And cleeped him his liege, to hold of him in fee.   *called*

ix

So happy peace they made and faire accord:
    Eftsoones this liege-man gan to wexe more bold,
    And when he felt the folly of his Lord,
    In his owne kind he gan him selfe vnfold:
    For he was wylie witted, and growne old
    In cunning sleights and practick knauery.
    From that day forth he cast for to vphold
80   His idle humour with fine flattery,
And blow the bellowes to his swelling vanity.

x

Trompart fit man for *Braggadocchio*,
    To serue at court in view of vaunting eye;
    Vaine-glorious man, when fluttring wind does blow
    In his light wings, is lifted vp to skye:
    The scorne of knighthood and trew cheualrye,
    To thinke without desert of gentle deed,
    And noble worth to be aduaunced hye:
    Such prayse is shame; but honour vertues meed
90 Doth beare the fairest flowre in honorable seed.

xi

So forth they pas, a well consorted paire,
    Till that at length with *Archimage* they meet:
    Who seeing one that shone in armour faire,
    On goodly courser thundring with his feet,
    Eftsoones supposed him a person meet,
    Of his reuenge to make the instrument:
    For since the *Redcrosse* knight he earst did weet,
    To beene with *Guyon* knit in one consent,
The ill, which earst to him, he now to *Guyon* ment.

xii

100 And comming close to *Trompart* gan inquere
    Of him, what mighty warriour that mote bee,   *might*
    That rode in golden sell with single spere,

But wanted sword to wreake his enmitee.
He is a great aduenturer, (said he)
That hath his sword through hard assay forgone,
And now hath vowd, till he auenged bee,
Of that despight, neuer to wearen none;
That speare is him enough to doen a thousand grone.

xiii

Th'enchaunter greatly ioyed in the vaunt,
And weened well ere long his will to win,
And both his foen with equall foyle to daunt.   *foes*
Tho to him louting lowly, did begin
To plaine of wrongs, which had committed bin
By *Guyon*, and by that false *Redcrosse* knight,
Which two through treason and deceiptfull gin,
Had slaine Sir *Mordant*, and his Lady bright:
That mote him honour win, to wreake so foule despight.

xiv

Therewith all suddeinly he seemd enraged,
And threatned death with dreadfull countenaunce,
As if their liues had in his hand beene gaged;
And with stiffe force shaking his mortall launce,
To let him weet his doughtie valiaunce,
Thus said; Old man, great sure shalbe thy meed,
If where those knights for feare of dew vengeaunce
Do lurke, thou certainly to me areed,
That I may wreake on them their hainous hatefull deed.

xv

Certes, my Lord, (said he) that shall I soone,
And giue you eke good helpe to their decay,
But mote I wisely you aduise to doon;
Giue no ods to your foes, but do puruay
Your selfe of sword before that bloudy day:
For they be two the prowest knights on ground,
And oft approu'd in many hard assay,
And eke of surest steele, that may be found,
Do arme your selfe against that day, them to confound.

xvi

Dotard (said he) let be thy deepe aduise;
Seemes that through many yeares thy wits thee faile.
And that weake eld hath left thee nothing wise,   *old age*
Else neuer should thy iudgement be so fraile,
To measure manhood by the sword or maile.
Is not enough foure quarters of a man,
Withouten sword or shield, an host to quaile?
Thou little wotest, what this right hand can:
Speake they, which haue beheld the battailes, which it wan.

xvii

The man was much abashed at his boast;
Yet well he wist, that who so would contend
With either of those knights on euen coast,
Should need of all his armes, him to defend;
Yet feared least his boldnesse should offend,
When *Braggadocchio* said, Once I did sweare,

110

120

130

140

150

When with one sword seuen knights I brought to end,
   Thence forth in battell neuer sword to beare,
But it were that, which noblest knight on earth doth weare.

xviii

Perdie Sir knight, said then th'enchaunter bliue,   *abruptly*
   That shall I shortly purchase to your hond:
   For now the best and noblest knight aliue
   Prince *Arthur* is, that wonnes in Faerie lond;   *lives*
   He hath a sword, that flames like burning brond.
   The same by my deuice I vndertake
160   Shall by to morrow by thy side be fond.
   At which bold word that boaster gan to quake,
And wondred in his mind, what mote that monster make.

xix

He stayd not for more bidding, but away
   Was suddein vanished out of his sight:
   The Northerne wind his wings did broad display
   At his commaund, and reared him vp light
   From off the earth to take his aerie flight.
   They lookt about, but no where could espie
   Tract of his foot: then dead through great affright
170   They both nigh were, and each bad other flie:
Both fled attonce, ne euer backe returned eie.

xx

Till that they come vnto a forrest greene,
   In which they shrowd themselues from causelesse feare;
   Yet feare them followes still, where so they beene,
   Each trembling leafe, and whistling wind they heare,
   As ghastly bug their haire on end does reare: *goblin*
   Yet both doe striue their fearfulnesse to faine.
   At last they heard a horne, that shrilled cleare
   Throughout the wood, that ecchoed againe,
180   And made the forrest ring, as it would riue in twaine.

xxi

Eft through the thicke they heard one rudely rush;
   With noyse whereof he from his loftie steed
   Downe fell to ground, and crept into a bush,
   To hide his coward head from dying dreed.
   But *Trompart* stoutly stayd to taken heed
   Of what might hap. Eftsoone there stepped forth
   A goodly Ladie clad in hunters weed,[2]
   That seemd to be a woman of great worth,
And by her stately portance, borne of heauenly birth.

xxii

190   Her face so faire as flesh it seemed not,
   But heauenly pourtraict of bright Angels hew,
   Cleare as the skie, withouten blame or blot,
   Through goodly mixture of complexions dew;
   And in her cheekes the vermeill red did shew

---

2 Belphoebe represents Queen Elizabeth, according to Spenser in his Letter to Raleigh. There is a subtle mixture here of Elizabeth's image of virgin chastity and sexual allure, which she uniquely managed to sustain as an essential part of the ideology of her reign. Here and throughout the rest of this canto there are numerous allusions to Virgil's *Aeneid*, especially Book 1.

Like roses in a bed of lillies shed,
The which ambrosiall odours from them threw,
And gazers sense with double pleasure fed,
Hable to heale the sicke, and to reuiue the ded.

xxiii

In her faire eyes two liuing lamps did flame,
    Kindled aboue at th'heauenly makers light,
    And darted fyrie beames out of the same,
    So passing persant, and so wondrous bright,   *piercing*
    That quite bereau'd the rash beholders sight:
    In them the blinded god his lustfull fire
    To kindle oft assayd, but had no might;
    For with dredd Maiestie, and awfull ire,
She broke his wanton darts, and quenched base desire.

xxiv

Her iuorie forhead, full of bountie braue,
    Like a broad table did it selfe dispred,
    For Loue his loftie triumphes to engraue,
    And write the battels of his great godhed:
    All good and honour might therein be red:
    For there their dwelling was. And when she spake,
    Sweet words, like dropping honny she did shed,
    And twixt the perles and rubins softly brake
A siluer sound, that heauenly musicke seemd to make,

xxv

Vpon her eyelids many Graces sate,
    Vnder the shadow of her euen browes,
    Working belgards, and amorous retrate,   *lovely glances*
    And euery one her with a grace endowes:
    And euery one with meekenesse to her bowes.
    So glorious mirrhour of celestiall grace,
    And soueraine moniment of mortall vowes,
    How shall fraile pen descriue her heauenly face,
For feare through want of skill her beautie to disgrace?

xxvi

So faire, and thousand thousand times more faire
    She seemd, when she presented was to sight,
    And was yclad, for heat of scorching aire,
    All in a silken Camus lylly whight,   *chemise*
    Purfled vpon with many a folded plight,   *decorated*
    Which all aboue besprinckled was throughout
    With golden aygulets, that glistred bright,   *sequins*
    Like twinckling starres, and all the skirt about
Was hemd with golden fringe.

xxvii

Below her ham her weed did somewhat traine,   *thigh, dress*
    And her streight legs most brauely were embayld
    In gilden buskins of costly Cordwaine,
    All bard with golden bendes, which were entayld
    With curious antickes, and full faire aumayld: *designs*
    Before they fastned were vnder her knee
    In a rich Iewell, and therein entrayld
    The ends of all their knots, that none might see,
How they within their fouldings close enwrapped bee.

200

210

220

230

240

xxviii

Like two faire marble pillours they were seene,
  Which doe the temple of the Gods support,
  Whom all the people decke with girlands greene,
  And honour in their festiuall resort;
  Those same with stately grace, and princely port
  She taught to tread, when she her selfe would grace,
250   But with the wooddie Nymphes when she did play,
  Or when the flying Libbard she did chace,   *leopard*
She could them nimbly moue, and after fly apace.

xxix

And in her hand a sharpe bore-speare she held,
  And at her backe a bow and quiuer gay,
  Stuft with steele-headed darts, wherewith she queld
  The saluage beastes in her victorious play,
  Knit with a golden bauldricke, which forelay
  Athwart her snowy brest, and did diuide
  Her daintie paps; which like young fruit in May
260   Now little gan to swell, and being tide,
Through her thin weed their places only signifide.

xxx

Her yellow lockes crisped, like golden wyre,
  About her shoulders weren loosely shed,
  And when the winde emongst them did inspyre,
  They waued like a penon wide dispred,
  And low behinde her backe were scattered:
  And whether art it were, or heedlesse hap,
  As through the flouring forrest rash she fled,
  In her rude haires sweet flowres themselues did lap,   *loose*
270 And flourishing fresh leaues and blossomes did enwrap.

xxxi

Such as *Diana* by the sandie shore
  Of swift *Eurotas*, or on *Cynthus* greene,
  Where all the Nymphes haue her vnwares forlore,
  Wandreth alone with bow and arrowes keene,
  To seeke her game: Or as that famous Queene
  Of *Amazons*, whom *Pyrrhus* did destroy,
  The day that first of *Priame* she was seene,
  Did shew her selfe in great triumphant ioy,
To succour the weake state of sad afflicted *Troy*.

xxxii

280 Such when as hartlesse *Trompart* her did vew,
  He was dismayed in his coward mind,
  And doubted, whether he himselfe should shew,
  Or fly away, or bide alone behind:
  Both feare and hope he in her face did find,
  When she at last him spying thus bespake;
  Hayle Groome; didst not thou see a bleeding Hind,
  Whose right haunch earst my stedfast arrow strake?
If thou didst, tell me, that I may her ouertake.

xxxiii

Wherewith reviu'd, this answere forth he threw;
290 O Goddesse, (for such I thee take to bee)
  For neither doth thy face terrestriall shew,

Nor voyce sound mortall; I auow to thee,
Such wounded beast, as that, I did not see,
Sith earst into this forrest wild I came.
But mote thy goodlyhed forgiue it mee,
To weet, which of the Gods I shall thee name,
That vnto thee due worship I may rightly frame.

xxxiv

To whom she thus; but ere her words ensewed,
  Vnto the bush her eye did suddein glaunce,
  In which vaine *Braggadocchio* was mewed,   *concealed*
  And saw it stirre: she left her percing launce,
  And towards gan a deadly shaft aduaunce,
  In mind to marke the beast. At which sad stowre,
  Trompart forth stept, to stay the mortall chaunce,
  Out crying, O what euer heauenly powre,
Or earthly wight thou be, withhold this deadly howre.

xxxv

O stay thy hand, for yonder is no game
  For thy fierce arrowes, them to exercize,
  But loe my Lord, my liege, whose warlike name
  Is farre renowmd through many bold emprize;
  And now in shade he shrowded yonder lies,
  She staid: with that he crauld out of his nest,
  Forth creeping on his caitiue hands and thies,
  And standing stoutly vp, his loftie crest
Did fiercely shake, and rowze, as comming late from rest.

xxxvi

As fearefull fowle, that long in secret caue
  For dread of soaring hauke her selfe hath hid,
  Not caring how, her silly life to saue,
  She her gay painted plumes disorderid,
  Seeing at last her selfe from daunger rid,
  Peepes foorth, and soone renewes her natiue pride;
  She gins her feathers foule disfigured
  Proudly to prune, and set on euery side,
So shakes off shame, ne thinks how erst she did her hide.

xxxvii

So when her goodly visage he beheld,
  He gan himselfe to vaunt: but when he vewed
  Those deadly tooles, which in her hand she held,
  Soone into other fits he was transmewed,
  Till she to him her gratious speach renewed;
  All haile, Sir knight, and well may thee befall,
  As all the like, which honour haue pursewed
  Through deedes of armes and prowesse martiall;
All vertue merits praise, but such the most of all.

xxxviii

To whom he thus; O fairest vnder skie,
  True be thy words, and worthy of thy praise,
  That warlike feats doest highest glorifie.
  Therein haue I spent all my youthly daies,
  And many battailes fought, and many fraies
  Throughout the world, wher so they might be found,

340   Endeuouring my dreadded name to raise
      Aboue the Moone, that fame may it resound
      In her eternall trompe, with laurell girland cround.

                    xxxix
      But what art thou, O Ladie, which doest raunge
         In this wilde forrest, where no pleasure is,
         And doest not it for ioyous court exchaunge,
         Emongst thine equall peres, where happie blis
         And all delight does raigne, much more then this?
         There thou maist loue, and dearely loued bee,
         And swim in pleasure, which thou here doest mis;
350   There maist thou best be seene, and best maist see:
      The wood is fit for beasts, the court is fit for thee.

                     xl
      Who so in pompe of proud estate (quoth she)
         Does swim, and bathes himselfe in courtly blis,
         Does waste his dayes in darke obscuritee,
         And in obliuion euer buried is:
         Where ease abounds, yt's eath to doe amis;   *easy*
         But who his limbs with labours, and his mind
         Behaues with cares, cannot so easie mis.
         Abroad in armes, at home in studious kind
360   Who seekes with painfull toile, shall honor soonest find.

                     xli
      In woods, in waues, in warres she wonts to dwell,
         And will be found with perill and with paine;
         Ne can the man, that moulds in idle cell,
         Vnto her happie mansion attaine:
         Before her gate high God did Sweat ordaine,
         And wakefull watches euer to abide:
         But easie is the way, and passage plaine
         To pleasures pallace; it may soone be spide,
      And day and night her dores to all stand open wide.

                     xlii
370   In Princes court, The rest she would haue said,
         But that the foolish man, fild with delight
         Of her sweet words, that all his sence dismaid,
         And with her wondrous beautie rauisht quight,
         Gan burne in filthy lust, and leaping light,
         Thought in his bastard armes her to embrace.
         With that she swaruing backe, her Iauelin bright
         Against him bent, and fiercely did menace:
      So turned her about, and fled away apace.

                     xliii
      Which when the Peasant saw, amazd he stood,
380   And grieued at her flight; yet durst he not
         Pursew her steps, through wild vnknowen wood;
         Besides he feard her wrath, and threatned shot
         Whiles in the bush he lay, not yet forgot:
         Ne car'd he greatly for her presence vaine,
         But turning said to *Trompart*, What foule blot
         Is this to knight, that Ladie should againe
      Depart to woods vntoucht, and leaue so proud disdaine?

xliv

Perdie (said *Trompart*) let her passe at will,
   Least by her presence daunger mote befall.
390   For who can tell (and sure I feare it ill)
   But that she is some powre celestiall?
   For whiles she spake, her great words did apall
   My feeble courage, and my hart oppresse,
   That yet I quake and tremble ouer all.
And I (said *Braggadocchio*) thought no lesse,
When first I heard her horne sound with such ghastlinesse.

xlv

For from my mothers wombe this grace I haue
   Me giuen by eternall destinie,
   That earthly thing may not my courage braue
400   Dismay with feare, or cause one foot to flie,
   But either hellish feends, or powres on hie:
   Which was the cause, when earst that horne I heard,
   Weening it had beene thunder in the skie,
   I hid my selfe from it, as one affeard;
But when I other knew, my selfe I boldly reard.

xlvi

But now for feare of worse, that may betide,
   Let vs soone hence depart. They soone agree;
   So to his steed he got, and gan to ride,
   As one vnfit therefore, that all might see
410   He had not trayned bene in cheualree.
   Which well that valiant courser did discerne;
   For he despysd to tread in dew degree,
   But chaufd and fom'd, with courage fierce and sterne,
And to be easd of that base burden still did erne.

Cant. IV.

Guyon does Furor bind in chaines,
and stops Occasion:
Deliuers Phedon, and therefore
by Strife is rayld upon.

i

In braue pursuit of honorable deed,
   There is I know not what great difference
   Betweene the vulgar and the noble seed,
   Which vnto things of valorous pretence
   Seemes to be borne by natiue influence;
   As feates of armes, and loue to entertaine,
   But chiefly skill to ride, seemes a science
   Proper to gentle bloud; some others faine
To menage steeds, as did this vaunter; but in vaine.

ii

10 But he the rightfull owner of that steed,
   Who well could menage and subdew his pride,
   The whiles on foot was forced for to yeed,
   With that blacke Palmer, his most trusty guide;
   Who suffred not his wandring feet to slide.
   But when strong passion, or weake fleshlinesse

Would from the right way seeke to draw him wide,
He would through temperance and stedfastnesse,
Teach him the weake to strengthen, and the strong suppresse.

iii

It fortuned forth faring on his way,
   He saw from farre, or seemed for to see
   Some troublous vprore or contentious fray,
   Whereto he drew in haste it to agree.
   A mad man, or that feigned mad to bee,
   Drew by the haire along vpon the ground,
   A handsome stripling with great crueltee,
   Whom sore he bett, and gor'd with many a wound,
That cheekes with teares, and sides with bloud did all abound.

iv

And him behind, a wicked Hag did stalke,
   In ragged robes, and filthy disaray,
   Her other leg was lame, that she no'te walke,   *couldn't*
   But on a staffe her feeble steps did stay;
   Her lockes, that loathly were and hoarie gray,
   Grew all afore, and loosely hong vnrold,
   But all behind was bald, and worne away,
   That none thereof could euer taken hold,
And eke her face ill fauourd, full of wrinckles old.

v

And euer as she went, her tongue did walke
   In foule reproch, and termes of vile despight,
   Prouoking him by her outrageous talke,
   To heape more vengeance on that wretched wight;
   Sometimes she raught him stones, wherwith to smite,   *gave*
   Sometimes her staffe, though it her one leg were,
   Withouten which she could not go vpright;
   Ne any euill meanes she did forbeare,
That might him moue to wrath, and indignation reare.

vi

The noble *Guyon* mou'd with great remorse,
   Approching, first the Hag did thrust away,
   And after adding more impetuous forse,
   His mightie hands did on the madman lay,
   And pluckt him backe; who all on fire streight way,
   Against him turning all his fell intent,
   With beastly brutish rage gan him assay,
   And smot, and bit, and kickt, and scratcht, and rent,
And did he wist not what in his auengement.

vii

And sure he was a man of mickle might,   *great*
   Had he had gouernance, it well to guide:
   But when the franticke fit inflamd his spright,
   His force was vaine, and strooke more often wide,
   Then at the aymed marke, which he had eide:
   And oft himselfe he chaunst to hurt vnwares,
   Whilst reason blent through passion, nought descride,   *saw*
   But as a blindfold Bull at randon fares,
And where he hits, nought knowes, and whom he hurts, nought cares.

viii

His rude assault and rugged handeling
 Straunge seemed to the knight, that aye with foe
 In faire defence and goodly menaging
 Of armes was wont to fight, yet nathemoe
 Was he abashed now not fighting so,
 But more enfierced through his currish play,
70 Him sternely grypt, and haling to and fro
 To ouerthrow him strongly did assay,
But ouerthrew himselfe vnwares, and lower lay.

ix

And being downe the villein sore did beat,
 And bruze with clownish fistes his manly face:
 And eke the Hag with many a bitter threat,
 Still cald vpon to kill him in the place.
 With whose reproch and odious menace
 The knight emboyling in his haughtie hart,
 Knit all his forces, and gan soone vnbrace
80 His grasping hold: so lightly did vpstart,
And drew his deadly weapon, to maintaine his part.

x

Which when the Palmer saw, he loudly cryde,
 Not so, O *Guyon*, neuer thinke that so
 That Monster can be maistred or destroyd:
 He is not, ah, he is not such a foe,
 As steele can wound, or strength can ouerthroe.
 That same is *Furor*, cursed cruell wight,
 That vnto knighthood workes much shame and woe;
 And that same Hag, his aged mother, hight
90 *Occasion*, the root of all wrath and despight.

xi

With her, who so will raging *Furor* tame,
 Must first begin, and well her amenage: *tame*
 First her restraine from her reprochfull blame,
 And euill meanes, with which she doth enrage
 Her franticke sonne, and kindles his courage,
 Then when she is withdrawen, or strong withstood,
 It's eath his idle furie to asswage,   *easy*
 And calme the tempest of his passion wood;
The bankes are ouerflowen, when stopped is the flood.

xii

100 Therewith Sir *Guyon* left his first emprise,
 And turning to that woman, fast her hent
 By the hoare lockes, that hong before her eyes,
 And to the ground her threw: yet n'ould she stent
 Her bitter rayling and foule reuilement,
 But still prouokt her sonne to wreake her wrong;
 But nathelesse he did her still torment,
 And catching hold of her vngratious tong,
Thereon an yron lock did fasten firme and strong.

xiii

Then when as vse of speach was from her reft,
110 With her two crooked handes she signes did make,
 And beckned him, the last helpe she had left:

But he that last left helpe away did take,
   And both her hands fast bound vnto a stake,
   That she note stirre. Then gan her sonne to flie
   Full fast away, and did her quite forsake;
   But *Guyon* after him in haste did hie,
And soone him ouertooke in sad perplexitie.

xiv

In his strong armes he stiffely him embraste,
   Who him gainstriuing, nought at all preuaild:
   For all his power was vtterly defaste,
120   And furious fits at earst quite weren quaild:
   Oft he re'nforst, and oft his forces fayld,
   Yet yield he would not, nor his rancour slacke.
   Then him to ground he cast, and rudely hayld,
   And both his hands fast bound behind his backe,
And both his feet in fetters to an yron racke.

xv

With hundred yron chaines he did him bind,
   And hundred knots that did him sore constraine:
   Yet his great yron teeth he still did grind,
130   And grimly gnash, threatning reuenge in vaine;
   His burning eyen, whom bloudie strakes did staine,
   Stared full wide, and threw forth sparkes of fire,
   And more for ranck despight, then for great paine,
   Shakt his long lockes, colourd like copper-wire,
And bit his tawny beard to shew his raging ire.

xvi

Thus when as *Guyon Furor* had captiu'd,
   Turning about he saw that wretched Squire,
   Whom that mad man of life nigh late depriu'd,
   Lying on ground, all soild with bloud and mire:
140   Whom when as he perceiued to respire,
   He gan to comfort, and his wounds to dresse.
   Being at last recured, he gan inquire,   *recovered*
   What hard mishap him brought to such distresse,
And made that caitiues thral, the thral of wretchednesse.

xvii

With hart then throbbing, and with watry eyes,
   Faire Sir (quoth he) what man can shun the hap,
   That hidden lyes vnwares him to surpryse?
   Misfortune waites aduantage to entrap
150   The man most warie in her whelming lap.
   So me weake wretch, of many weakest one,
   Vnweeting, and vnware of such mishap,
   She brought to mischiefe through occasion,
Where this same wicked villein did me light vpon.

xviii

It was a faithlesse Squire, that was the sourse
   Of all my sorrow, and of these sad teares,
   With whom from tender dug of commune nourse,   *breast*
   Attonce I was vpbrought, and eft when yeares
   More rype vs reason lent to chose our Peares,
160   Our selues in league of vowed loue we knit:

In which we long time without gealous feares,
  Or faultie thoughts continewd, as was fit;
And for my part I vow, dissembled not a whit.

xix

It was my fortune commune to that age,
  To loue a Ladie faire of great degree,
  The which was borne of noble parentage,
  And set in highest seat of dignitee,
  Yet seemd no lesse to loue, then loued to bee:
  Long I her seru'd, and found her faithfull still,
170   Ne euer thing could cause vs disagree:
Loue that two harts makes one, makes eke one will:
Each stroue to please, and others pleasure to fulfill.

xx

My friend, hight *Philemon*, I did partake
  Of all my loue and all my privitie;
  Who greatly ioyous seemed for my sake,
  And gratious to that Ladie, as to mee,
  Ne euer wight, that mote so welcome bee,
  As he to her, withouten blot or blame,
  Ne euer thing, that she could thinke or see,
180   But vnto him she would impart the same:
O wretched man, that would abuse so gentle Dame.

xxi

At last such grace I found, and meanes I wrought,
  That I that Ladie to my spouse had wonne;
  Accord of friends, consent of parents sought,
  Affiance made, my happinesse begonne,
  There wanted nought but few rites to be donne,
  Which mariage make; that day too farre did seeme:
  Most ioyous man, on whom the shining Sunne
  Did shew his face, my selfe I did esteeme,
190 And that my falser friend did no lesse ioyous deeme.

xxii

But ere that wished day his beame disclosd,
  He either enuying my toward good,
  Or of himselfe to treason ill disposd,
  One day vnto me came in friendly mood,
  And told for secret how he vnderstood
  That Ladie whom I had to me assynd,
  Had both distaind her honorable blood;
  And eke the faith, which she to me did bynd;
And therfore wisht me stay, till I more truth should fynd.

xxiii

200 The gnawing anguish and sharpe gelosy,
  Which his sad speech infixed in my brest,
  Ranckled so sore, and festred inwardly,
  That my engreeued mind could find no rest,
  Till that the truth thereof I did outwrest,
  And him besought by that same sacred band
  Betwixt vs both, to counsell me the best.
  He then with solemne oath and plighted hand
Assur'd, ere long the truth to let me vnderstand.

xxiv

Ere long with like againe he boorded mee,
   Saying, he now had boulted all the floure,   *sifted*
   And that it was a groome of base degree,
   Which of my loue was partner Paramoure:
   Who vsed in a darkesome inner bowre
   Her oft to meet: which better to approue,
   He promised to bring me at that howre,
   When I should see, that would me nearer moue,
And driue me to withdraw my blind abused loue.

xxv

This gracelesse man for furtherance of his guile,
   Did court the handmayd of my Lady deare,
   Who glad t'embosome his affection vile,
   Did all she might, more pleasing to appeare.
   One day to worke her to his will more neare,
   He woo'd her thus: *Pryene* (so she hight)
   What great despight doth fortune to thee beare,
   Thus lowly to abase thy beautie bright,
That it should not deface all others lesser light?

xxvi

But if she had her least helpe to thee lent,
   T'adorne thy forme according thy desart,
   Their blazing pride thou wouldest soone haue blent,
   And staynd their prayses with thy least good part;
   Ne should faire *Claribell* with all her art,
   Though she thy Lady be, approch thee neare:
   For proofe thereof, this euening, as thou art,
   Aray thy selfe in her most gorgeous geare,
That I may more delight in thy embracement deare.

xxvii

The Maiden proud through prayse, and mad through loue
   Him hearkned to, and soone her selfe arayd,
   The whiles to me the treachour did remoue
   His craftie engin, and as he had sayd,
   Me leading, in a secret corner layd,
   The sad spectatour of my Tragedie;
   Where left, he went, and his owne false part playd,
   Disguised like that groome of base degree,
Whom he had feignd th'abuser of my loue to bee.

xxviii

Eftsoones he came vnto th'appointed place,
   And with him brought *Pryene*, rich arayd,
   In *Claribellaes* clothes. Her proper face
   I not descerned in that darkesome shade,
   But weend it was my loue, with whom he playd.
   Ah God, what horrour and tormenting griefe
   My hart, my hands, mine eyes, and all assayd?
   Me liefer were ten thousand deathes priefe,
Then wound of gealous worme, and shame of such repriefe.   *reproof*

xxix

I home returning, fraught with fowle despight,
   And chawing vengeance all the way I went,
   Soone as my loathed loue appeard in sight,

With wrathfull hand I slew her innocent;
 That after soone I dearely did lament:
 For when the cause of that outrageous deede
260 Demaunded, I made plaine and euident,
 Her faultie Handmayd, which that bale did breede,
Confest, how *Philemon* her wrought to chaunge her weede.

xxx

Which when I heard, with horrible affright
 And hellish fury all enragd, I sought
 Vpon my selfe that vengeable despight
 To punish: yet it better first I thought,
 To wreake my wrath on him, that first it wrought.
 To *Philemon*, false faytour *Philemon*   *villain*
 I cast to pay, that I so dearely bought;
270 Of deadly drugs I gaue him drinke anon,
And washt away his guilt with guiltie potion.

xxxi

Thus heaping crime on crime, and griefe on griefe,
 To losse of loue adioyning losse of frend,
 I meant to purge both with a third mischiefe,
 And in my woes beginner it to end:
 That was *Pryene*, she did first offend,
 She last should smart: with which cruell intent,
 When I at her my murdrous blade did bend,
 She fled away with ghastly dreriment,
280 And I pursewing my fell purpose, after went.

xxxii

Feare gaue her wings, and rage enforst my flight;
 Through woods and plaines so long I did her chace,
 Till this mad man, whom your victorious might
 Hath now fast bound, me met in middle space,
 As I her, so he me pursewd apace,
 And shortly ouertooke: I, breathing yre,
 Sore chauffed at my stay in such a cace,
 And with my heat kindled his cruell fyre;
Which kindled once, his mother did more rage inspyre.

xxxiii

290 Betwixt them both, they haue me doen to dye,
 Through wounds, and strokes, and stubborne handeling,
 That death were better, then such agony,
 As griefe and furie vnto me did bring;
 Of which in me yet stickes the mortall sting,
 That during life will neuer be appeasd.
 When he thus ended had his sorrowing,
 Said *Guyon*, Squire, sore haue ye beene diseasd;
But all your hurts may soone through temperance be easd.

xxxiv

Then gan the Palmer thus, Most wretched man,
300 That to affections does the bridle lend;
 In their beginning they are weake and wan,
 But soone through suff'rance grow to fearefull end;
 Whiles they are weake betimes with them contend:
 For when they once to perfect strength do grow,

Strong warres they make, and cruell battry bend
Gainst fort of Reason, it to ouerthrow:
Wrath, gelosie, griefe, loue this Squire haue layd thus low.

XXXV

Wrath, gealosie, griefe, loue do thus expell:
  Wrath is a fire, and gealosie a weede,
  Griefe is a flood, and loue a monster fell;
  The fire of sparkes, the weede of little seede,
  The flood of drops, the Monster filth did breede:
  But sparks, seed, drops, and filth do thus delay;
  The sparks soone quench, the springing seed outweed,
  The drops dry vp, and filth wipe cleane away:
So shall wrath, gealosie, griefe, loue dye and decay.

XXXVI

Vnlucky Squire (said *Guyon*) sith thou hast
  Falne into mischiefe through intemperaunce,
  Henceforth take heede of that thou now hast past,
  And guide thy wayes with warie gouernaunce,
  Least worse betide thee by some later chaunce.
  But read how art thou nam'd, and of what kin.
  Phedon I hight (quoth he) and do aduaunce
  Mine auncestry from famous *Coradin*,
Who first to rayse our house to honour did begin.

XXXVII

Thus as he spake, lo far away they spyde
  A varlet running towards hastily,
  Whose flying feet so fast their way applyde,
  That round about a cloud of dust did fly,
  Which mingled all with sweate, did dim his eye.
  He soone approched, panting, breathlesse, whot,
  And all so soyld, that none could him descry;
  His countenaunce was bold, and bashed not
For *Guyons* lookes, but scornefull eyglaunce at him shot.

XXXVIII

Behind his backe he bore a brasen shield,
  On which was drawen faire, in colours fit,
  A flaming fire in midst of bloudy field,
  And round about the wreath this word was writ,
  Burnt I do burne. Right well beseemed it,
  To be the shield of some redoubted knight;
  And in his hand two darts exceeding flit,   *swift*
  And deadly sharpe he held, whose heads were dight
In poyson and in bloud, of malice and despight.

XXXIX

When he in presence came, to *Guyon* first
  He boldly spake, Sir knight, if knight thou bee,
  Abandon this forestalled place at erst,
  For feare of further harme, I counsell thee,
  Or bide the chaunce at thine owne ieoperdie.
  The knight at his great boldnesse wondered,
  And though he scornd his idle vanitie,
  Yet mildly him to purpose answered;
For not to grow of nought he it coniectured.

xl

Varlet, this place most dew to me I deeme,
  Yielded by him, that held it forcibly.
  But whence should come that harme, which thou doest seeme
  To threat to him, that minds his chaunce t'abye?   *to take*
  Perdy (said he) here comes, and is hard by
  A knight of wondrous powre, and great assay,
  That neuer yet encountred enemy,
360   But did him deadly daunt, or fowle dismay;
Ne thou for better hope, if thou his presence stay.

xli

How hight he then (said *Guyon*) and from whence?
  Pyrochles is his name,[1] renowmed farre
  For his bold feats and hardy confidence,
  Full oft approu'd in many a cruell warre,
  The brother of *Cymochles*, both which arre
  The sonnes of old *Acrates* and *Despight*,
  Acrates sonne of *Phlegeton* and *Iarre*;
370   But *Phlegeton* is sonne of *Herebus* and *Night*;
But *Herebus* sonne of *Aeternitie* is hight.

xlii

So from immortall race he does proceede,
  That mortall hands may not withstand his might,
  Drad for his derring do, and bloudy deed;
  For all in bloud and spoile is his delight.
  His am I *Atin*, his in wrong and right,
  That matter make for him to worke vpon,
  And stirre him vp to strife and cruell fight.
  Fly therefore, fly this fearefull stead anon,
Least thy foolhardize worke thy sad confusion.

xliii

380 His be that care, whom most it doth concerne,
  (Said he) but whither with such hasty flight
  Art thou now bound? for well mote I discerne
  Great cause, that carries thee so swift and light.
  My Lord (quoth he) me sent, and streight behight
  To seeke *Occasion*, where so she bee:
  For he is all disposd to bloudy fight,
  And breathes out wrath and hainous crueltie;
Hard is his hap, that first fals in his ieopardie.

xliv

Madman (said then the Palmer) that does seeke
390 *Occasion* to wrath, and cause of strife;
  She comes vnsought, and shonned followes eke.
  Happy, who can abstaine, when Rancour rife
  Kindles Reuenge, and threats his rusty knife;
  Woe neuer wants, where euery cause is caught,
  And rash *Occasion* makes vnquiet life.
  Then loe, where bound she sits, whom thou hast sought,
(Said *Guyon*,) let that message to thy Lord be brought.

CANT. IV.
1 The etymology of these names helps to sustain the allegory: Pyrochles: moved by fire (or anger); Cymochles; moved by waves (of uncontrollable passion); Acrates: ungovernable; Despite: malice; Phlegeton: a god of fire (see also Phlegethon, the Burning River of Hell in *Aeneid*, 6); Jar: discord; Erebus: Virgil's name for the regions of Hell.

xlv

That when the varlet heard and saw, streight way
  He wexed wondrous wroth, and said, Vile knight,
400   That knights and knighthood doest with shame vpbray,
  And shewst th'ensample of thy childish might,
  With silly weake old woman thus to fight.
  Great glory and gay spoile sure hast thou got,
  And stoutly prou'd thy puissaunce here in sight;
  That shall *Pyrochles* well requite, I wot,
And with thy bloud abolish so reprochfull blot.

xlvi

With that one of his thrillant darts he threw,   *piercing*
  Headed with ire and vengeable despight;
  The quiuering steele his aymed end well knew,
410   And to his brest it selfe intended right:
  But he was warie, and ere it empight   *hit*
  In the meant marke, adaunst his shield atweene,
  On which it seizing, no way enter might,
  But backe rebounding, left the forckhead keene;
Eftsoones he fled away, and might no where be seene.

Cant. V.

Pyrochles does with Guyon fight,
And Furors chayne vnbinds:
Of whom sore hurt, for his renenge
Atin Cymochles finds.

i

Who euer doth to temperaunce apply
  His stedfast life, and all his actions frame,
  Trust me, shall find no greater enimy,
  Then stubborne perturbation, to the same;
  To which right well the wise do giue that name,
  For it the goodly peace of stayed mindes
  Does ouerthrow, and troublous warre proclame:
  His owne woes authour, who so bound it findes,
As did *Pyrochles*, and it wilfully vnbindes.

ii

10 After that varlets flight, it was not long,
  Ere on the plaine fast pricking *Guyon* spide
  One in bright armes embatteiled full strong,
  That as the Sunny beames do glaunce and glide
  Vpon the trembling waue, so shined bright,
  And round about him threw forth sparkling fire,
  That seemd him to enflame on euery side:
  His steed was bloudy red, and fomed ire,
When with the maistring spur he did him roughly stire.   *incite*

iii

Approching nigh, he neuer stayd to greete
20   Ne chaffar words, prowd courage to prouoke,   *exchange*
  But prickt so fiers, that vnderneath his feete
  The smouldring dust did round about him smoke,
  Both horse and man nigh able for to choke;

And fairly couching his steele-headed speare,
Him first saluted with a sturdy stroke;
It booted nought Sir *Guyon* comming neare
To thinke, such hideous puissaunce on foot to beare.

iv

But lightly shunned it, and passing by,
  With his bright blade did smite at him so fell,
  That the sharpe steele arriuing forcibly
  On his broad shield, bit not, but glauncing fell
  On his horse necke before the quilted sell,   *saddle*
  And from the head the body sundred quight.
  So him dismounted low, he did compell
  On foot with him to matchen equall fight;
The truncked beast fast bleeding, did him fowly dight.

v

Sore bruzed with the fall, he slow vprose,
  And all enraged, thus him loudly shent;
  Disleall knight, whose coward courage chose   *disloyal*
  To wreake it selfe on beast all innocent,[1]
  And shund the marke, at which it should be ment,
  Thereby thine armes seeme strong, but manhood fraile;
  So hast thou oft with guile thine honour blent;   *tarnished*
  But litle may such guile thee now auaile,
If wonted force and fortune do not much me faile.

vi

With that he drew his flaming sword, and strooke
  At him so fiercely, that the vpper marge
  Of his seuenfolded shield away it tooke,
  And glauncing on his helmet, made a large
  And open gash therein: were not his targe,
  That broke the violence of his intent,
  The weary soule from thence it would discharge;
  Nathelesse so sore a buff to him it lent,
That made him reele, and to his brest his beuer bent.

vii

Exceeding wroth was *Guyon* at that blow,
  And much ashamd, that stroke of liuing arme
  Should him dismay, and make him stoup so low,
  Though otherwise it did him litle harme:
  Tho hurling high his yron braced arme,
  He smote so manly on his shoulder plate,
  That all his left side it did quite disarme;
  Yet there the steele stayd not, but inly bate
Deepe in his flesh, and opened wide a red floodgate.

viii

Deadly dismayd, with horrour of that dint
  Pyrochles was, and grieued eke entyre;
  Yet nathemore did it his fury stint,
  But added flame vnto his former fire,

CANT. V.

1   By injuring the horse, Guyon has violated the chivalric codes,
making him vulnerable to Pyrochles' accusation of cowardice.

That welnigh molt his hart in raging yre,
Ne thenceforth his approued skill, to ward,   *parry*
70   Or strike, or hurtle round in warlike gyre,
Remembred he, ne car'd for his saufgard,
But rudely rag'd, and like a cruell Tygre far'd.

ix
He hewd, and lasht, and foynd, and thundred blowes,   *thrust*
And euery way did seeke into his life,
Ne plate, ne male could ward so mighty throwes,
But yielded passage to his cruell knife.
But *Guyon*, in the heat of all his strife,
Was warie wise, and closely did awayt
Auauntage, whilest his foe did rage most rife;
80   Sometimes a thwart, sometimes he strooke him strayt,
And falsed oft his blowes, t'illude him with such bayt.   *to deceive*

x
Like as a Lyon, whose imperiall powre
A prowd rebellious Vnicorne defies,
T'auoide the rash assault and wrathfull stowre   *combat*
Of his fiers foe, him to a tree applies,
And when him running in full course he spies,
He slips aside; the whiles that furious beast
His precious horne, sought of his enimies,
Strikes in the stocke, ne thence can be releast,
90   But to the mighty victour yields a bounteous feast.

xi
With such faire slight him *Guyon* often faild,
Till at the last all breathlesse, wearie, faint
Him spying, with fresh onset he assaild,
And kindling new his courage seeming queint,
Strooke him so hugely, that through great constraint
He made him stoup perforce vnto his knee,
And do vnwilling worship to the Saint,
That on his shield depainted he did see;
Such homage till that instant neuer learned hee.

xii
100   Whom *Guyon* seeing stoup, pursewed fast
The present offer of faire victory,
And soone his dreadfull blade about he cast,
Wherewith he smote his haughty crest so hye,
That streight on ground made him full low to lye;
Then on his brest his victour foote he thrust,
With that he cryde, Mercy, do me not dye,
Ne deeme thy force by fortunes doome vniust,
That hath (maugre her spight) thus low me laid in dust.   *damn*

xiii
Eftsoones his cruell hand Sir *Guyon* stayd,
110   Tempring the passion with aduizement slow,
And maistring might on enimy dismayd:
For th'equall dye of warre he well did know;
Then to him said, Liue and allegaunce owe,
To him that giues thee life and libertie,

And henceforth by this dayes ensample trow,
That hasty wroth, and heedlesse hazardrie
Do breede repentaunce late, and lasting infamie.

xiv

So vp he let him rise, who with grim looke
  And count'naunce sterne vpstanding, gan to grind
120 His grated teeth for great disdeigne, and shooke
  His sandy lockes, long hanging downe behind,
  Knotted in bloud and dust, for griefe of mind,
  That he in ods of armes was conquered;
  Yet in himselfe some comfort he did find,
  That him so noble knight had maistered,
Whose bounty more then might, yet both he wondered.

xv

Which *Guyon* marking said, Be nought agrieu'd,
  Sir knight, that thus ye now subdewed arre:
  Was neuer man, who most conquestes atchieu'd,
130 But sometimes had the worse, and lost by warre,
  Yet shortly gaynd, that losse exceeded farre:
  Losse is no shame, nor to be lesse then foe,
  But to be lesser, then himselfe, doth marre
  Both loosers lot, and victours prayse alsoe.
Vaine others ouerthrowes, who selfe doth ouerthrowe.

xvi

Fly, O *Pyrochles*, fly the dreadfull warre,
  That in thy selfe thy lesser parts do moue,
  Outrageous anger, and woe-working iarre,
  Direfull impatience, and hart murdring loue;
140 Those, those thy foes, those warriours far remoue,
  Which thee to endlesse bale captiued lead.
  But sith in might thou didst my mercy proue,
  Of curtesie to me the cause aread,
That thee against me drew with so impetuous dread.

xvii

Dreadlesse (said he) that shall I soone declare:
  It was complaind, that thou hadst done great tort   *wrong*
  Vnto an aged woman, poore and bare,
  And thralled her in chaines with strong effort,
  Voide of all succour and needfull comfort:
150 That ill beseemes thee, such as I thee see,
  To worke such shame. Therefore I thee exhort,
  To chaunge thy will, and set *Occasion* free,
And to her captiue sonne yield his first libertee.

xviii

Thereat Sir *Guyon* smilde, And is that all
  (Said he) that thee so sore displeased hath?
  Great mercy sure, for to enlarge a thrall,
  Whose freedome shall thee turne to greatest scath.
  Nath'lesse now quench thy whot emboyling wrath:
  Loe there they be; to thee I yield them free.
160 Thereat he wondrous glad, out of the path
  Did lightly leape, where he them bound did see,
And gan to breake the bands of their captiuitee.

xix

Soone as *Occasion* felt her selfe vntyde,
  Before her sonne could well assoyled bee,   *released*
  She to her vse returnd, and streight defyde
  Both *Guyon* and *Pyrochles*: th'one (said shee)
  Bycause he wonne; the other because hee
  Was wonne: So matter did she make of nought,
  To stirre vp strife, and do them disagree:
  But soone as *Furor* was enlargd, she sought
To kindle his quencht fire, and thousand causes wrought.

xx

It was not long, ere she inflam'd him so,
  That he would algates with *Pyrochles* fight,
  And his redeemer chalengd for his foe,
  Because he had not well mainteind his right,
  But yielded had to that same straunger knight:
  Now gan *Pyrochles* wex as wood, as hee,
  And him affronted with impatient might:
  So both together fiers engrasped bee,
Whiles *Guyon* standing by, their vncouth strife does see.

xxi

Him all that while *Occasion* did prouoke
  Against *Pyrochles*, and new matter framed
  Vpon the old, him stirring to be wroke
  Of his late wrongs, in which she oft him blamed
  For suffering such abuse, as knighthood shamed,
  And him dishabled quite. But he was wise
  Ne would with vaine occasions be inflamed;
  Yet others she more vrgent did deuise:
Yet nothing could him to impatience entise.

xxii

Their fell contention still increased more,
  And more thereby increased *Furors* might,
  That he his foe has hurt, and wounded sore,
  And him in bloud and durt deformed quight.
  His mother eke, more to augment his spight,
  Now brought to him a flaming fire brond,
  Which she in *Stygian* lake, ay burning bright,
  Had kindled: that she gaue into his hond,
That armd with fire, more hardly he mote him withstond.

xxiii

Tho gan that villein wex so fiers and strong,
  That nothing might sustaine his furious forse;
  He cast him downe to ground, and all along
  Drew him through durt and myre without remorse,
  And fowly battered his comely corse,
  That *Cuyon* much disdeignd so loathly sight.
  At last he was compeld to cry perforse,
  Helpe, O Sir *Guyon*, helpe most noble knight,
To rid a wretched man from hands of hellish wight.

xxiv

The knight was greatly moued at his plaint,
  And gan him dight to succour his distresse,
  Till that the Palmer, by his graue restraint,

Him stayd from yielding pitifull redresse;
And said, Deare sonne, thy causelesse ruth represse,
Ne let thy stout hart melt in pitty vayne:
He that his sorrow sought through wilfulnesse,
And his foe fettred would release agayne,
Deserues to tast his follies fruit, repented payne.

xxv

Guyon obayd; So him away he drew
From needlesse trouble of renewing fight
Already fought, his voyage to pursew.
But rash *Pyrochles* varlet, *Atin* hight,
When late he saw his Lord in heauy plight,
Vnder Sir *Guyons* puissaunt stroke to fall,
Him deeming dead, as then he seemd in sight,
Fled fast away, to tell his funerall
Vnto his brother, whom *Cymochles* men did call.

220

xxvi

He was a man of rare redoubted might,
Famous throughout the world for warlike prayse,
And glorious spoiles, purchast in perilous fight:
Full many doughtie knights he in his dayes
Had doen to death, subdewde in equall frayes,
Whose carkases, for terrour of his name,
Of fowles and beastes he made the piteous prayes,
And hong their conquered armes for more defame
On gallow trees, in honour of his dearest Dame.

230

xxvii

His dearest Dame is that Enchaunteresse,
The vile *Acrasia*, that with vaine delightes,
And idle pleasures in her *Bowre* of *Blisse*,[2]
Does charme her louers, and the feeble sprightes
Can call out of the bodies of fraile wightes:
Whom then she does transforme to monstrous hewes,
And horribly misshapes with vgly sightes,
Captiu'd eternally in yron mewes,   *cages*
And darksom dens, where *Titan* his face neuer shewes.

240

xxviii

There *Atin* found *Cymochles* soiourning,
To serue his Lemans loue: for he, by kind,
Was giuen all to lust and loose liuing,
When euer his fiers hands he free mote find:
And now he has pourd out his idle mind
In daintie delices, and lauish ioyes,
Hauing his warlike weapons cast behind,
And flowes in pleasures, and vaine pleasing toyes,
Mingled emongst loose Ladies and lasciuious boyes.

250

xxix

And ouer him, art striuing to compaire
With nature, did an Arber greene dispred,
Framed of wanton Yuie, flouring faire,

2   Tasso's *Jerusalem Delivered*, 15–16, is an important source for the
descriptions of the Bower of Bliss here and in Canto XII.

Through which the fragrant Eglantine did spred
His pricking armes, entrayld with roses red,
Which daintie odours round about them threw,
And all within with flowres was garnished,
260   That when myld *Zephyrus* emongst them blew,
Did breath out bounteous smels, and painted colors shew.

xxx
And fast beside, there trickled softly downe
A gentle streame, whose murmuring waue did play
Emongst the pumy stones, and made a sowne,
To lull him soft a sleepe, that by it lay;
The wearie Traueiler, wandring that way,
Therein did often quench his thristy heat,
And then by it his wearie limbes display,
Whiles creeping slomber made him to forget
270   His former paine, and wypt away his toylsom sweat.

xxxi
And on the other side a pleasaunt groue
Was shot vp high, full of the stately tree,
That dedicated is t'*Olympicke Ioue*,
And to his sonne *Alcides*, whenas hee   *Hercules*
Gaynd in *Nemea* goodly victoree;
Therein the mery birds of euery sort
Chaunted alowd their chearefull harmonie:
And made emongst them selues a sweet consort,
That quickned the dull spright with musicall comfort.

xxxii
280   There he him found all carelesly displayd,
In secret shadow from the sunny ray,
On a sweet bed of lillies softly layd,
Amidst a flocke of Damzels fresh and gay,
That round about him dissolute did play
Their wanton follies, and light meriment;
Euery of which did loosely disaray
Her vpper parts of meet habiliments,
And shewd them naked, deckt with many ornaments.

xxxiii
And euery of them stroue, with most delights,
290   Him to aggrate, and greatest pleasures shew;   *please*
Some framd faire lookes, glancing like euening lights,
Others sweet words, dropping like honny dew;
Some bathed kisses, and did soft embrew
The sugred licour through his melting lips:
One boastes her beautie, and does yeeld to vew
Her daintie limbes aboue her tender hips;
Another her out boastes, and all for tryall strips.

xxxiv
He, like an Adder, lurking in the weeds,
His wandring thought in deepe desire does steepe,
300   And his fraile eye with spoyle of beautie feedes;
Sometimes he falsely faines himselfe to sleepe,

Whiles through their lids his wanton eies do peepe,
To steale a snatch of amorous conceipt,
Whereby close fire into his heart does creepe:
So, them deceiues, deceiu'd in his deceipt,
Made drunke with drugs of deare voluptuous receipt.

image

XXXV

Atin arriuing there, when him he spide,
Thus in still waues of deepe delight to wade,
Fiercely approching, to him lowdly cride,
310 *Cymochles*; oh no, but *Cymochles* shade,
In which that manly person late did fade,
What is become of great *Acrates* sonne?
Or where hath he hong vp his mortall blade,
That hath so many haughtie conquests wonne?
Is all his force forlorne, and all his glory donne?

XXXVI

Then pricking him with his sharpe-pointed dart,
He said; Vp, vp, thou womanish weake knight,
That here in Ladies lap entombed art,
Vnmindfull of thy praise and prowest might,
320 And weetlesse eke of lately wrought despight,
Whiles sad *Pyrochles* lies on senselesse ground,
And groneth out his vtmost grudging spright,
Through many a stroke, and many a streaming wound,
Calling thy helpe in vaine, that here in ioyes art dround.

XXXVII

Suddeinly out of his delightfull dreame
The man awoke, and would haue questiond more;
But he would not endure that wofull theame
For to dilate at large, but vrged sore
With percing words, and pittifull implore,
330 Him hastie to arise. As one affright
With hellish feends, or *Furies* mad vprore,
He then vprose, inflam'd with fell despight,
And called for his armes; for he would algates fight.

XXXVIII

They bene ybrought; he quickly does him dight,
And lightly mounted, passeth on his way,
Ne Ladies loues, ne sweete entreaties might
Appease his heat, or hastie passage stay;
For he has vowd, to beene aueng'd that day,
(That day it selfe him seemed all too long:)
340 On him, that did *Pyrochles* deare dismay:
So proudly pricketh on his courser strong,
And *Atin* aie him pricks with spurs of shame and wrong.

Cant. VI.

Guyon is of immodest Merth
led into loose desire,
Fights with Cymochles, whiles his bro-
ther burnes in furious fire.

i

A harder lesson, to learne Continence[1]
   In ioyous pleasure, then in grieuous paine:
   For sweetnesse doth allure the weaker sence
   So strongly, that vneathes it can refraine
   From that, which feeble nature couets faine;
   But griefe and wrath, that be her enemies,
   And foes of life, she better can restraine;
   Yet vertue vauntes in both their victories,
And *Guyon* in them all shewes goodly maisteries.

ii

Whom bold *Cymochles* trauelling to find,
   With cruell purpose bent to wreake on him
   The wrath, which *Atin* kindled in his mind,
   Came to a riuer, by whose vtmost brim
   Wayting to passe, he saw whereas did swim
   A long the shore, as swift as glaunce of eye,
   A litle Gondelay, bedecked trim
   With boughes and arbours wouen cunningly,
That like a litle forrest seemed outwardly.

iii

And therein sate a Ladie fresh and faire,[2]
   Making sweet solace to her selfe alone;
   Sometimes she sung, as loud as larke in aire;
   Sometimes she laught, that nigh her breth was gone,
   Yet was there not with her else any one,
   That might to her moue cause of meriment:
   Matter of merth enough, though there were none,
   She could deuise, and thousand waies inuent,
To feede her foolish humour, and vaine iolliment.

iv

Which when farre off *Cymochles* heard, and saw,
   He loudly cald to such, as were a bord,
   The little barke vnto the shore to draw,
   And him to ferrie ouer that deepe ford:
   The merry marriner vnto his word
   Soone hearkned, and her painted bote streightway
   Turnd to the shore, where that same warlike Lord
   She in receiu'd; but *Atin* by no way
She would admit, albe the knight her much did pray.

v

Eftsoones her shallow ship away did slide,
   More swift, then swallow sheres the liquid skie,
   Withouten oare or Pilot it to guide,
   Or winged canuas with the wind to flie,
   Only she turn'd a pin, and by and by
   It cut away vpon the yielding waue,
   Ne cared she her course for to apply:
   For it was taught the way, which she would haue,
And both from rocks and flats it selfe could wisely saue.

CANT. VI.
1 Cf. Aristotle's *Nicomachaean Ethics*, 2. 3.

2 Phaedria's name is derived from the Greek word for "glittering."

vi

And all the way, the wanton Damzell found
  New merth, her passenger to entertaine:
  For she in pleasant purpose did abound,
  And greatly ioyed merry tales to faine,
50   Of which a store-house did with her remaine,
  Yet seemed, nothing well they her became;
  For all her words she drownd with laughter vaine,
And wanted grace in vtt'ring of the same,
That turned all her pleasance to a scoffing game.

vii

And other whiles vaine toyes she would deuize
  As her fantasticke wit did most delight,
  Sometimes her head she fondly would aguize   *deck*
  With gaudie girlonds, or fresh flowrets dight
  About her necke, or rings of rushes plight;
60   Sometimes to doe him laugh, she would assay
  To laugh at shaking of the leaues light,
  Or to behold the water worke, and play
About her litle frigot, therein making way.

viii

Her light behauiour, and loose dalliaunce
  Gaue wondrous great contentment to the knight,
  That of his way he had no souenaunce,   *recollection*
  Nor care of vow'd reuenge, and cruell fight,
  But to weake wench did yeeld his martiall might.
  So easie was to quench his flamed mind
70   With one sweet drop of sensuall delight,
  So easie is, t'appease the stormie wind
Of malice in the calme of pleasant womankind.

ix

Diuerse discourses in their way they spent,
  Mongst which *Cymochles* of her questioned,
  Both what she was, and what that vsage ment,
  Which in her cot she daily practised.   *boat*
  Vaine man (said she) that wouldest be reckoned
  A straunger in thy home, and ignoraunt
  Of *Phædria* (for so my name is red)
80   Of *Phædria*, thine owne fellow seruaunt;
For thou to serue *Acrasia* thy selfe doest vaunt.

x

In this wide Inland sea, that hight by name
  The *Idle lake*, my wandring ship I row,
  That knowes her port, and thither sailes by ayme,
  Ne care, ne feare I, how the wind do blow,
  Or whether swift I wend, or whether slow:
  Both slow and swift a like do serue my tourne,
  Ne swelling *Neptune*, ne loud thundring *Ioue*
  Can chaunge my cheare, or make me euer mourne;
90 My litle boat can safely passe this perilous bourne.

xi

Whiles thus she talked, and whiles thus she toyd,
  They were farre past the passage, which he spake,
  And come vnto an Island, waste and voyd,

That floted in the midst of that great lake,
There her small Gondelay her port did make,
And that gay paire issuing on the shore
Disburdned her. Their way they forward take
Into the land, that lay them faire before,
Whose pleasaunce she him shew'd, and plentifull great store.

xii

100   It was a chosen plot of fertile land,
Emongst wide waues set, like a litle nest,
As if it had by Natures cunning hand
Bene choisely picked out from all the rest,
And laid forth for ensample of the best:
No daintie flowre or herbe, that growes on ground,
No arboret with painted blossomes drest,   *shrub*
And smelling sweet, but there it might be found
To bud out faire, and her sweet smels throw all around.

xiii

110   No tree, whose braunches did not brauely spring;
No braunch, whereon a fine bird did not sit:
No bird, but did her shrill notes sweetly sing;
No song but did containe a louely dit:
Trees, braunches, birds, and songs were framed fit,
For to allure fraile mind to carelesse ease.
Carelesse the man soone woxe, and his weake wit
Was ouercome of thing, that did him please;
So pleased, did his wrathfull purpose faire appease.

xiv

Thus when he had his eyes and senses fed
With false delights, and fild with pleasures vaine,
120   Into a shadie dale she soft him led,
And laid him downe vpon a grassie plaine;
And her sweet selfe without dread, or disdaine,
She set beside, laying his head disarm'd
In her loose lap, it softly to sustaine,
Where soone he slumbred, fearing not be harm'd,
The whiles with a loud lay she thus him sweetly charm'd.

xv

Behold, O man, that toilesome paines doest take,
The flowres, the fields, and all that pleasant growes,
How they themselues doe thine ensample make,
130   Whiles nothing enuious nature them forth throwes
Out of her fruitfull lap; how, no man knowes,
They spring, they bud, they blossome fresh and faire,
And deck the world with their rich pompous showes;
Yet no man for them taketh paines or care,
Yet no man to them can his carefull paines compare.

xvi

The lilly, Ladie of the flowring field,
The Flowre-deluce, her louely Paramoure,[3]
Bid thee to them thy fruitlesse labours yield,

3   In Phaedria's blasphemous appropriation of Jesus' Sermon on the
Mount (Matthew 6:25–34), the lily becomes a seductive whore.

And soone leaue off this toylesome wearie stoure;
140   Loe loe how braue she decks her bounteous boure,
With silken curtens and gold couerlets,
Therein to shrowd her sumptuous Belamoure,
Yet neither spinnes nor cardes, ne cares nor frets,
But to her mother Nature all her care she lets.

xvii

Why then dost thou, O man, that of them all
Art Lord, and eke of nature Soueraine,
Wilfully make thy selfe a wretched thrall,
And wast thy ioyous houres in needlesse paine,
Seeking for daunger and aduentures vaine?
150   What bootes it all to haue, and nothing vse?
Who shall him rew, that swimming in the maine,
Will die for thirst, and water doth refuse?
Refuse such fruitlesse toile, and present pleasures chuse.

xviii

By this she had him lulled fast a sleepe,
That of no worldly thing he care did take;
Then she with liquors strong his eyes did steepe,
That nothing should him hastily awake:
So she him left, and did her selfe betake
Vnto her boat againe, with which she cleft
160   The slouthfull waue of that great griesly lake;
Soone she that Island farre behind her left,
And now is come to that same place, where first she weft.

xix

By this time was the worthy *Guyon* brought
Vnto the other side of that wide strond,
Where she was rowing, and for passage sought:
Him needed not long call, she soone to hond
Her ferry brought, where him she byding fond,
With his sad guide; himselfe she tooke a boord,
But the *Blacke Palmer* suffred still to stond,
170   Ne would for price, or prayers once affoord,
To ferry that old man ouer the perlous foord.

xx

Guyon was loath to leaue his guide behind,
Yet being entred, might not backe retyre;
For the flit barke, obaying to her mind,
Forth launched quickly, as she did desire,
Ne gaue him leaue to bid that aged sire
Adieu, but nimbly ran her wonted course
Through the dull billowes thicke as troubled mire,
Whom neither wind out of their seat could forse,
180   Nor timely tides did driue out of their sluggish sourse.

xxi

And by the way, as was her wonted guize,
Her merry fit she freshly gan to reare,
And did of ioy and iollitie deuize,
Her selfe to cherish, and her guest to cheare:
The knight was courteous, and did not forbeare
Her honest merth and pleasaunce to partake;

But when he saw her toy, and gibe, and geare;
    And passe the bonds of modest merimake,
Her dalliance he despisd, and follies did forsake.

xxii

190 Yet she still followed her former stile,
    And said, and did all that mote him delight,
    Till they arriued in that pleasant Ile,
    Where sleeping late she left her other knight.
    But when as *Guyon* of that land had sight,
    He wist himselfe amisse, and angry said;
    Ah Dame, perdie ye haue not doen me right,
    Thus to mislead me, whiles I you obaid:
Me litle needed from my right way to haue straid.

xxiii

Faire Sir (quoth she) be not displeasd at all;
200   Who fares on sea, may not commaund his way,
    Ne wind and weather at his pleasure call:
    The sea is wide, and easie for to stray;
    The wind vnstable, and doth neuer stay.
    But here a while ye may in safety rest,
    Till season serue new passage to assay;
    Better safe port, then be in seas distrest.
Therewith she laught and did her earnest end in iest.

xxiv

But he halfe discontent, mote nathelesse
    Himselfe appease, and issewd forth on shore:
210   The ioyes whereof, and happie fruitfulnesse,
    Such as he saw, she gan him lay before,
    And all though pleasant, yet she made much more:
    The fields did laugh, the flowres did freshly spring,
    The trees did bud, and earely blossomes bore,
    And all the quire of birds did sweetly sing,
And told that gardins pleasures in their caroling.

xxv

And she more sweet, then any bird on bough,
    Would oftentimes emongst them beare a part,
    And striue to passe (as she could well enough)
220   Their natiue musicke by her skilfull art:
    So did she all, that might his constant hart
    Withdraw from thought of warlike enterprize,
    And drowne in dissolute delights apart,
    Where noyse of armes, or vew of martiall guize
Might not reuiue desire of knightly exercize.

xxvi

But he was wise, and warie of her will,
    And euer held his hand vpon his hart:
    Yet would not seeme so rude, and thewed ill,
    As to despise so courteous seeming part,
230   That gentle Ladie did to him impart,
    But fairely tempring fond desire subdewd,
    And euer her desired to depart.
    She list not heare, but her disports poursewd,
And euer bad him stay, till time the tide renewd.

xxvii

And now by this, *Cymochles* howre was spent,
   That he awoke out of his idle dreme,
   And shaking off his drowzie dreriment,
   Gan him auize, how ill did him beseeme,
   In slouthfull sleepe his molten hart to steme,
240   And quench the brond of his conceiued ire.
   Tho vp he started, stird with shame extreme,
   Ne staied for his Damzell to inquire,
But marched to the strond, there passage to require.

xxviii

And in the way he with Sir *Guyon* met,
   Accompanyde with *Phædria* the faire,
   Eftsoones he gan to rage, and inly fret,
   Crying, Let be that Ladie debonaire,
   Thou recreant knight, and soone thy selfe prepaire
   To battell, if thou meane her loue to gaine:
250   Loe, loe alreadie, how the fowles in aire
   Doe flocke, awaiting shortly to obtaine
Thy carcasse for their pray, the guerdon of thy paine.

xxix

And therewithall he fiercely at him flew,
   And with importune outrage him assayld;
   Who soone prepard to field, his sword forth drew,
   And him with equall value counteruayld:
   Their mightie strokes their haberieons dismayld,   *mail*
   And naked made each others manly spalles;
   The mortall steele despiteously entayld
260   Deepe in their flesh, quite through the yron walles,
That a large purple streme adown their giambeux falles.   *leg armor*

xxx

Cymochles, that had neuer met before
   So puissant foe, with enuious despight
   His proud presumed force increased more,
   Disdeigning to be held so long in fight;
   Sir *Guyon* grudging not so much his might,
   As those vnknightly raylings, which he spoke,
   With wrathfull fire his courage kindled bright,
   Thereof decuising shortly to be wroke,   *avenged*
270 And doubling all his powres, redoubled euery stroke.

xxxi

Both of them high attonce their hands enhaunst,
   And both attonce their huge blowes downe did sway;
   Cymochles sword on *Guyons* shield yglaunst,
   And thereof nigh one quarter sheard away;
   Bug *Guyons* angry blade so fierce did play
   On th'others helmet, which as *Titan* shone,   *the sun*
   That quite it cloue his plumed crest in tway,
   And bared all his head vnto the bone;
Wherewith astonisht, still he stood, as senselesse stone.

xxxii

280 Still as he stood, faire *Phædria*, that beheld
   That deadly daunger, soone atweene them ran;
   And at their feet her selfe most humbly feld,

Crying with pitteous voice, and count'nance wan;
Ah well away, most noble Lords, how can
Your cruell eyes endure so pitteous sight,
To shed your liues on ground? wo worth the man,
That first did teach the cursed steele to bight
In his owne flesh, and make way to the liuing spright.

xxxiii

If euer loue of Ladie did empierce
 Your yron brestes, or pittie could find place,
 Withhold your bloudie hands from battell fierce,
 And sith for me ye fight, to me this grace
 Both yeeld, to stay your deadly strife a space.
 They stayd a while: and forth she gan proceed:
 Most wretched woman, and of wicked race,
 That am the author of this hainous deed,
And cause of death betweene two doughtie knights doe breed.

xxxiv

But if for me ye fight, or me will serue,
 Not this rude kind of battell, nor these armes
 Are meet, the which doe men in bale to sterue,
 And dolefull sorrow heape with deadly harmes:
 Such cruell game my scarmoges disarmes:
 Another warre, and other weapons I
 Doe loue, where loue does giue his sweet alarmes,
 Without bloudshed, and where the enemy
Does yeeld vnto his foe a pleasant victory.

xxxv

Debatefull strife, and cruell enmitie
 The famous name of knighthood fowly shend;
 But louely peace, and gentle amitie,
 And in Amours the passing houres to spend,
 The mightie martiall hands doe most commend;
 Of loue they euer greater glory bore,
 Then of their armes: *Mars* is *Cupidoes* frend,
 And is for *Venus* loues renowmed more,
Then all his wars and spoiles, the which he did of yore.

xxxvi

Therewith she sweetly smyld. They though full bent
 To proue extremities of bloudie fight,
 Yet at her speach their rages gan relent,
 And calme the sea of their tempestuous spight,
 Such powre haue pleasing words: such is the might
 Of courteous clemencie in gentle hart.
 Now after all was ceast, the Faery knight
 Besought that Damzell suffer him depart,
And yield him readie passage to that other part.

xxxvii

She no lesse glad, then he desirous was
 Of his departure thence; for of her ioy
 And vaine delight she saw he light did pas,
 A foe of folly and immodest toy,
 Still solemne sad, or still disdainfull coy,
 Delighting all in armes and cruell warre,

That her sweet peace and pleasures did annoy,
　Troubled with terrour and vnquiet iarre,
That she well pleased was thence to amoue him farre.

xxxviii

Tho him she brought abord, and her swift bote
　Forthwith directed to that further strand;
　The which on the dull waues did lightly flote
　And soone arriued on the shallow sand,
　Where gladsome *Guyon* salied forth to land,
　And to that Damzell thankes gaue for reward.
340　Vpon that shore he spied *Atin* stand,
　There by his maister left, when late he far'd
In *Phædrias* flit barke ouer that perlous shard.   *obstacle*

xxxix

Well could he him remember, sith of late
　He with *Pyrochles* sharp debatement made;
　Streight gan he him reuile, and bitter rate,
　As sbepheards curre, that in darke euenings shade
　Hath tracted forth some saluage beastes trade;
　Vile Miscreant (said he) whither doest thou flie
　The shame and death, which will thee soone inuade?
350　What coward hand shall doe thee next to die,
That art thus foully fled from famous enemie?

xl

With that he stiffely shooke his steelehead dart:
　But sober *Guyon*, hearing him so raile,
　Though somewhat moued in his mightie hart,
　Yet with strong reason maistred passion fraile,
　And passed fairely forth.　He turning taile,
　Backe to the strond retyrd, and there still stayd,
　Awaiting passage, which him late did faile;
　The whiles *Cymochles* with that wanton mayd
360　The hastie heat of his auowd reuenge delayd.

xli

Whylest there the varlet stood, he saw from farre
　An armed knight, that towards him fast ran,
　He ran on foot, as if in lucklesse warre
　His forlorne steed from him the victour wan;
　He seemed breathlesse, hartlesse, faint, and wan,
　And all his armour sprinckled was with bloud,
　And soyld with durtie gore, that no man can
　Discerne the hew thereof.　He neuer stood,
But bent his hastie course towards the idle flood.

xlii

370　The varlet saw, when to the flood he came,
　How without stop or stay he fiercely lept,
　And deepe him selfe beducked in the same,
　That in the lake his loftie crest was steept,
　Ne of his safetie seemed care he kept,
　But with his raging armes he rudely flasht
　The waues about, and all his armour swept,
　That all the bloud and filth away was washt,
Yet still he bet the water, and the billowes dasht.

xliii

Atin drew nigh, to weet what it mote bee;
    For much he wondred at that vncouth sight;
    Whom should he, but his owne deare Lord, there see,
    His owne deare Lord *Pyrochles*, in sad plight,
    Readie to drowne himselfe for fell despight.
    Harrow now out, and well away, he cryde,
    What dismall day hath lent this cursed light,
    To see my Lord so deadly damnifyde?
Pyrochles, O *Pyrochles*, what is thee betyde?

xliv

I burne, I burne, I burne, then loud he cryde,
    O how I burne with implacable fire,
    Yet nought can quench mine inly flaming syde,
    Nor sea of licour cold, nor lake of mire,
    Nothing but death can doe me to respire.
    Ah be it (said he) from *Pyrochles* farre
    After pursewing death once to require,
    Or think, that ought those puissant hands may marre:
Death is for wretches borne vnder vnhappie starre.

xlv

Perdie, then is it fit for me (said he)
    That am, I weene, most wretched man aliue,
    Burning in flames, yet no flames can I see,
    And dying daily, daily yet reuiue:
    O *Atin*, helpe to me last death to giue.
    The varlet at his plaint was grieued so sore,
    That his deepe wounded hart in two did riue,
    And his owne health remembring now no more,
Did follow that ensample, which he blam'd afore.

xlvi

Into the lake he lept, his Lord to ayd,
    (So Loue the dread of daunger doth despise)
    And of him catching hold him strongly stayd
    From drowning.   But more happie he, then wise
    Of that seas nature did him not auise.
    The waues thereof so slow and sluggish were,
    Engrost with mud, which did them foule agrise,   *horrify*
    That euery weightie thing they did vpbeare,
Ne ought mote euer sinke downe to the bottome there.

xlvii

Whiles thus they strugled in that idle waue,
    And stroue in vaine, the one himselfe to drowne,
    The other both from drowning for to saue,
    Lo, to that shore one in an auncient gowne,
    Whose hoarie locks great grauitie did crowne,
    Holding in hand a goodly arming sword,
    By fortune came, led with the troublous sowne:
    Where drenched deepe he found in that dull ford
The carefull seruant, striuing with his raging Lord.

xlviii

Him *Atin* spying, knew right well of yore,
    And loudly cald, Helpe helpe, O *Archimage*;
    To saue my Lord, in wretched plight forlore;

Helpe with thy hand, or with thy counsell sage:
  Weake hands, but counsell is most strong in age.
  Him when the old man saw, he wondred sore,
430   To see *Pyrochles* there so rudely rage:
  Yet sithens helpe, he saw, he needed more
Then pittie, he in hast approched to the shore.

xlix

And cald, *Pyrochles*, what is this, I see?
  What hellish furie hath at earst thee hent?
  Furious euer I thee knew to bee,
  Yet neuer in this straunge astonishment.
  These flames, these flames (he cryde) do me torment.
  What flames (quoth he) when I thee present see,
  In daunger rather to be drent, then brent?
440   Harrow, the flames, which me consume (said hee)
Ne can be quencht, within my secret bowels bee.

l

That cursed man, that cruell feend of hell,
  Furor, oh *Furor* hath me thus bedight:
  His deadly wounds within my liuers swell,
  And his whot fire burnes in mine entrails bright,
  Kindled through his infernall brond of spight,
  Sith late with him I batteil vaine would boste;
  That now I weene *Ioues* dreaded thunder light
450   Does scorch not halfe so sore, nor damned ghoste
In flaming *Phlegeton* does not so felly roste.

li

Which when as *Archimago* heard, his griefe
  He knew right well, and him attonce disarmd:
  Then searcht his secret wounds, and made a priefe   *examination*
  Of euery place, that was with brusing harmd,
  Or with the hidden fire too inly warmd.
  Which done, he balmes and herbes thereto applyde,
  And euermore with mighty spels them charmd,
  That in short space he has them qualifyde,
And him restor'd to health, that would haue algates dyde.

Cant. VII.

Guyon findes Mammon in a delue,   *ravine*
Sunning bis threasure hore: *ancient*
Is by him tempted, and led downe,
To see bis secret store.

i

As Pilot well expert in perilous waue,
  That to a stedfast starre his course hath bent,
  When foggy mistes, or cloudy tempests haue
  The faithfull light of that faire lampe yblent,   *blinded*
  And couer'd heauen with hideous dreriment,
  Vpon his card and compas firmes his eye,
  The maisters of his long experiment,
  And to them does the steddy helme apply,
Bidding his winged vessell fairely forward fly:

ii

10 So *Guyon* hauing lost his trusty guide,
　Late left beyond that *ydle lake*, proceedes
　Yet on his way, of none accompanide;
　And euermore himselfe with comfort feedes,
　Of his owne vertues, and prayse-worthy deedes.[1]
　So long he yode, yet no aduenture found,
　Which fame of her shrill trompet worthy reedes:
　For still he traueild through wide wastfull ground,
That nought but desert wildernesse shew'd all around.

iii

At last he came vnto a gloomy glade,
20 　Couer'd with boughes and shrubs from heauens light,
　Whereas he sitting found in secret shade
　An vncouth, saluage, and vnciuile wight,
　Of griesly hew, and fowle ill fauour'd sight;
　His face with smoke was tand, and eyes were bleard,
　His head and beard with sout were ill bedight,
　His cole-blacke hands did seeme to haue beene seard
In smithes fire-spitting forge, and nayles like clawes appeard.

iv

His yron coate all ouergrowne with rust,[2]
　Was vnderneath enueloped with gold,
30 　Whose glistring glosse darkned with filthy dust,
　Well yet appeared, to haue beene of old
　A worke of rich entayle, and curious mould,
　Wouen with antickes and wild Imagery:
　And in his lap a masse of coyne he told,
　And turned vpsidowne, to feede his eye
And couetous desire with his huge threasury.

v

And round about him lay on euery side
　Great heapes of gold, that neuer could be spent:
　Of which some were rude owre, not purifide
40 　Of *Mulcibers* deuouring element;
　Some others were new driuen, and distent
　Into great Ingoes, and to wedges square;
　Some in round plates withouten moniment;
　But most were stampt, and in their metall bare
The antique shapes of kings and kesars straunge and rare.

vi

Soone as he *Guyon* saw, in great affright
　And hast he rose, for to remoue aside
　Those pretious hils from straungers enuious sight,
　And downe them poured through an hole full wide,
50 　Into the hollow earth, them there to hide.
　But *Guyon* lightly to him leaping, stayd
　His hand, that trembled, as one terrifyde;
　And though him selfe were at the sight dismayd,
Yet him perforce restraynd, and to him doubtfull sayd.

CANT. VII.
1 See Aquinas, *Summa Theologica*, 2. 132. 1: "Now it is not a sin to know and approve one's own good."

2 Here and following there are continued allusions to the Sermon on the Mount, esp. Matthew 6:19.

vii

What art thou man, (if man at all thou art)
　　That here in desert hast thine habitaunce,
　　And these rich heapes of wealth doest hide apart
　　From the worldes eye, and from her right vsaunce?
　　Thereat with staring eyes fixed askaunce,
60　　In great disdaine, he answerd; Hardy Elfe,
　　That darest vew my direfull countenaunce,
　　I read thee rash, and heedlesse of thy selfe,
To trouble my still seate, and heapes of pretious pelfe.

viii

God of the world and worldlings I me call,
　　Great *Mammon*, greatest god below the skye,
　　That of my plenty poure out vnto all,
　　And vnto none my graces do enuye:
　　Riches, renowme, and principality,
　　Honour, estate, and all this worldes good,
70　　For which men swinck and sweat incessantly,　　　　*labor*
　　Fro me do flow into an ample flood,
And in the hollow earth haue their eternall brood.

ix

Wherefore if me thou deigne to serue and sew,
　　At thy commaund lo all these mountaines bee;
　　Or if to thy great mind, or greedy vew
　　All these may not suffise, there shall to thee
　　Ten times so much be numbred francke and free.
　　Mammon[3] (said he) thy godheades vaunt is vaine,
　　And idle offers of thy golden fee;
80　　To them, that couet such eye-glutting gaine,
Proffer thy giftes, and fitter seruaunts entertaine.

x

Me ill besits, that in der-doing armes,　　　　*courageous*
　　And honours suit my vowed dayes do spend,
　　Vnto thy bounteous baytes, and pleasing charmes,
　　With which weake men thou witchest, to attend:
　　Regard of worldly mucke doth fowly blend,
　　And low abase the high heroicke spright,
　　That ioyes for crownes and kingdomes to contend;
　　Faire shields, gay steedes, bright armes be my delight:
90 Those be the riches fit for an aduent'rous knight.

xi

Vaine glorious Elfe (said he) doest not thou weet,
　　That money can thy wantes at will supply?
　　Sheilds, steeds, and armes, and all things for thee meet
　　It can puruay in twinckling of an eye;
　　And crownes and kingdomes to thee multiply.
　　Do not I kings create, and throw the crowne
　　Sometimes to him, that low in dust doth ly?
　　And him that raignd, into his rowme thrust downe,
And whom I lust, do heape with glory and renowne?

3　A Syriac word meaning "wealth." See also Matthew 6:24.

xii

¹⁰⁰

All otherwise (said he) I riches read,
  And deeme them roote of all disquietnesse;
  First got with guile, and then preseru'd with dread,
  And after spent with pride and lauishnesse,
  Leauing behind them griefe and heauinesse.
  Infinite mischiefes of them do arize,
  Strife, and debate, bloudshed, and bitternesse,
  Outrageous wrong, and hellish couetize,
That noble heart as great dishonour doth despize.

xiii

¹¹⁰

Ne thine be kingdomes, ne the scepters thine;
  But realmes and rulers thou doest both confound,
  And loyall truth to treason doest incline;
  Witnesse the guiltlesse bloud pourd oft on ground,
  The crowned often slaine, the slayer cround,
  The sacred Diademe in peeces rent,
  And purple robe gored with many a wound;
  Castles surprizd, great cities sackt and brent:
So mak'st thou kings, and gaynest wrongfull gouernement.

xiv

¹²⁰

Long were to tell the troublous stormes, that tosse
  The priuate state, and make the life vnsweet:
  Who swelling sayles in Caspian sea doth crosse,
  And in frayle wood on *Adrian* gulfe doth fleet,
  Doth not, I weene, so many euils meet.
  Then *Mammon* wexing wroth, And why then, said,
  Are mortall men so fond and vndiscreet,
  So euill thing to seeke vnto their ayd,
And hauing not complaine, and hauing it vpbraid?

xv

¹³⁰

Indeede (quoth he) through fowle intemperaunce,
  Frayle men are oft captiu'd to couetise:
  But would they thinke, with how small allowaunce
  Vntroubled Nature doth her selfe suffise,[4]
  Such superfluities they would despise,
  Which with sad cares empeach our natiue ioyes:
  At the well head the purest streames arise:
  But mucky filth his braunching armes annoyes,
And with vncomely weedes the gentle waue accloyes.

xvi

¹⁴⁰

The antique world, in his first flowring youth,
  Found no defect in his Creatours grace,
  But with glad thankes, and vnreproued truth,
  The gifts soueraigne bountie did embrace:
  Like Angels life was then mens happy cace;
  But later ages pride, like corn-fed steed,
  Abusd her plenty, and fat swolne encreace
  To all licentious lust, and gan exceed
The measure of her meane, and naturall first need.

---

4 Cf. Boethius, *The Consolation of Philosophy*, II.5, and Aristotle's
Politics, I. 8–9.

xvii

Then gan a cursed hand the quiet wombe
  Of his great Grandmother with steele to wound,
  And the hid treasures in her sacred tombe,
  With Sacriledge to dig.   Therein he found
  Fountaines of gold and siluer to abound,
150   Of which the matter of his huge desire
  And pompous pride eftsoones he did compound;
  Then auarice gan through his veines inspire
His greedy flames, and kindled life-deuouring fire.

xvliii

Sonne (said he then) let be thy bitter scorne,
  And leaue the rudenesse of that antique age
  To them, that liu'd therein in state forlorne;
  Thou that doest liue in later times, must wage
  Thy workes for wealth, and life for gold engage.
160   If then thee list my offred grace to vse,
  Take what thou please of all this surplusage;
  If thee list not, leaue haue thou to refuse:
But thing refused, do not afterward accuse.

xix

Me list not (said the Elfin knight) receaue[5]
  Thing offred, till I know it well be got,
  Ne wote I, but thou didst these goods bereaue
  From rightfull owner by vnrighteous lot,
  Or that bloud guiltinesse or guile them blot.
  Perdy (quoth he) yet neuer eye did vew,
  Ne toung did tell, ne hand these handled not,
170   But safe I haue them kept in secret mew,
From heauens sight, and powre of all which them pursew.

xx

What secret place (quoth he) can safely hold
  So huge a masse, and hide from heauens eye?
  Or where hast thou thy wonne, that so much gold   *home*
  Thou canst preserue from wrong and robbery?
  Come thou (quoth he) and see. So by and by
  Through that thicke couert he him led, and found
  A darkesome way, which no man could descry,
  That deepe descended through the hollow ground,
180 And was with dread and horrour compassed around.

xxi

At length they came into a larger space,
  That stretcht it selfe into an ample plaine,
  Through which a beaten broad high way did trace,
  That streight did lead to *Plutoes* griesly raine:
  By that wayes side, there sate infernall Payne,[6]
  And fast beside him sat tumultuous Strife:
  The one in hand an yron whip did straine,
  The other brandished a bloudy knife,
And both did gnash their teeth, and both did threaten life.

---

5 See Aristotle, *Nicomachaean Ethics*, 4.

6 ThIs account recalls *Aeneid*, 6, a continual source for Spenser's
emphasis on the teleological development of his hero.

xxii

190   On thother side in one consort there sate,
      Cruell Reuenge, and rancorous Despight,
      Disloyall Treason, and hart-burning Hate,
      But gnawing Gealosie out of their sight
      Sitting alone, his bitter lips did bight,
      And trembling Feare still to and fro did fly,
      And found no place, where safe he shroud him might,
      Lamenting Sorrow did in darknesse lye,
And Shame his vgly face did hide from liuing eye.

xxiii

And ouer them sad Horrour with grim hew,
200   Did alwayes sore, beating his yron wings;
      And after him Owles and Night-rauens flew,
      The hatefull messengers of heauy things,
      Of death and dolour telling sad tidings;
      Whiles sad *Celeno*, sitting on a clift,[7]
      A song of bale and bitter sorrow sings,
      That hart of flint a sunder could haue rift:
Which hauing ended, after him she flyeth swift.

xxiv

All these before the gates of *Pluto* lay,
      By whom they passing, spake vnto them nought.
210   But th'Elfin knight with wonder all the way
      Did feed his eyes, and fild his inner thought.
      At last him to a litle dore he brought,
      That to the gate of Hell, which gaped wide,
      Was next adioyning, ne them parted ought:
      Betwixt them both was but a litle stride,
That did the house of Richesse from hell-mouth diuide.

xxv

Before the dore sat selfe-consuming Care,
      Day and night keeping wary watch and ward,
      For feare least Force or Fraud should vnaware
220   Breake in, and spoile the treasure there in gard:
      Ne would he suffer Sleepe once thither-ward
      Approch, albe his drowsie den were next;
      For next to death is Sleepe to be compard:
      Therefore his house is vnto his annext;
Here Sleep, there Richesse, and Hel-gate them both betwext.

xxvi

So soone as *Mammon* there arriu'd, the dore
      To him did open, and affoorded way;
      Him followed eke Sir *Guyon* euermore,
      Ne darkenesse him, ne daunger might dismay.
230   Soone as he entred was, the dore streight way
      Did shut, and from behind it forth there lept
      An vgly feend, more fowle then dismall day,[8]
      The which with monstrous stalke behind him stept,
And euer as he went, dew watch vpon him kept.

---

7   Like the Sphinx, she has the face and breasts of a woman and the
body of a beast of prey (see *Aeneid*, 3. 245).

8   Possibly derived from Pausanius' Eurynomous (*Description of Greece*,
10. 28. 7).

xxvii

Well hoped he, ere long that hardy guest,
  If euer couetous hand, or lustfull eye,
  Or lips he layd on thing, that likt him best,
  Or euer sleepe his eye-strings did vntye,
  Should be his pray. And therefore still on hye
240   He ouer him did hold his cruell clawes,
  Threatning with greedy gripe to do him dye
  And rend in peeces with his rauenous pawes,
If euer he transgrest the fatall *Stygian* lawes.

xxviii

That houses forme within was rude and strong,
  Like an huge caue, hewne out of rocky clift,
  From whose rough vaut the ragged breaches hong,
  Embost with massy gold of glorious gift,
  And with rich metall loaded euery rift,
  That heauy ruine they did seeme to threat;
250   And ouer them *Arachne* high did lift
  Her cunning web, and spred her subtile net,
Enwrapped in fowle smoke and clouds more blacke then let.

xxix

Both roofe, and floore, and wals were all of gold,
  But ouergrowne with dust and old decay,
  And hid in darkenesse, that none could behold
  The hew thereof: for vew of chearefull day
  Did neuer in that house it selfe display,
  But a faint shadow of vncertain light;
  Such as a lamp, whose life does fade away:
260   Or as the Moone cloathed with clowdy night,
Does shew to him, that walkes in feare and sad affright.

xxx

In all that rowme was nothing to be seene,
  But huge great yron chests and coffers strong,
  All bard with double bends, that none could weene
  Them to efforce by violence or wrong;
  On euery side they placed were along.
  But all the ground with sculs was scattered,
  And dead mens bones, which round about were flong,
  Whose liues, it seemed, whilome there were shed,
270   And their vile carcases now left vnburied.

xxxi

They forward passe, ne *Guyon* yet spoke word,
  Till that they came vnto an yron dore,
  Which to them opened of his owne accord,
  And shewd of richesse such exceeding store,
  As eye of man did neuer see before;
  Ne euer could within one place be found,
  Though all the wealth, which is, or was of yore,
  Could gathered be through all the world around,
And that aboue were added to that vnder ground.

xxxii

280   The charge thereof vnto a couetous Spright
  Commaunded was, who thereby did attend,
  And warily awaited day and night,

From other couetous feends it to defend,
Who it to rob and ransacke did intend.
Then *Mammon* turning to that warriour, said;
Loe here the worldes blis, loe here the end,
To which all men do ayme, rich to be made:
Such grace now to be happy, is before thee laid.

xxxiii

Certes (said he) I n'ill thine offred grace,   *don't want*
   Ne to be made so happy do intend:
   Another blis before mine eyes I place,
   Another happinesse, another end.
   To them, that list, these base regardes I lend:
   But I in armes, and in atchieuements braue,
   Do rather choose my flitting houres to spend,
   And to be Lord of those, that riches haue,
Then them to haue my selfe, and be their seruile sclaue.

290

xxxiv

Thereat the feend his gnashing teeth did grate,
   And grieu'd, so long to lacke his greedy pray;
   For well he weened, that so glorious bayte
   Would tempt his guest, to take thereof assay:
   Had he so doen, he had him snatcht away,
   More light then Culuer in the Faulcons fist.
   Eternall God thee saue from such decay.
   But whenas *Mammon* saw his purpose mist,
Him to entrap vnwares another way he wist.

300

xxxv

Thence forward he him led, and shortly brought
   Vnto another rowme, whose dore forthright,
   To him did open, as it had beene taught:
   Therein an hundred raunges weren pight,[9]   *placed*
   And hundred fornaces all burning bright;
   By euery fornace many feends did bide,
   Deformed creatures, horrible in sight,
   And euery feend his busie paines applide,
To melt the golden metall, ready to be tride.

310

xxxvi

One with great bellowes gathered filling aire,
   And with forst wind the fewell did inflame;
   Another did the dying bronds repaire
   With yron toungs, and sprinckled oft the same
   With liquid waues, fiers *Vulcans* rage to tame,
   Who maistring them, renewd his former heat;
   Some scumd the drosse, that from the metall came;
   Some stird the molten owre with ladles great;
And euery one did swincke, and euery one did sweat.   *work*

320

xxxvii

But when as earthly wight they present saw,
   Glistring in armes and battailous aray,
   From their whot worke they did themselues withdraw

9   This recalls Vulcan's forge in *Aeneid*, 8. 418, and anticipates Blake's
printing house in hell in *The Marriage of Heaven and Hell*.

To wonder at the sight: for till that day,
They neuer creature saw, that came that way.
330   Their staring eyes sparckling with feruent fire,
And vgly shapes did nigh the man dismay,
That were it not for shame, he would retire,
Till that him thus bespake their soueraigne Lord and sire

xxxviii

Behold, thou Faeries sonne, with mortall eye,
That liuing eye before did neuer see:
The thing, that thou didst craue so earnestly,
To weet, whence all the wealth late shewd by mee,
Proceeded, lo now is reueald to thee.
Here is the fountaine of the worldes good:
340   Now therefore, if thou wilt enriched bee,
Auise thee well, and chaunge thy wilfull mood,
Least thou perhaps hereafter wish, and be withstood.

xxxix

Suffise it then, thou Money God (quoth hee)
That all thine idle offers I refuse.
All that I need I haue; what needeth mee
To couet more, then I haue cause to vse?
With such vaine shewes thy worldlings vile abuse:
But giue me leaue to follow mine emprise.
Mammon was much displeasd, yet no'te he chuse,
350   But beare the rigour of his bold mesprise,
And thence him forward led, him further to entise.

xl

He brought him through a darksome narrow strait,
To a broad gate, all built of beaten gold:
The gate was open, but therein did wait
A sturdy villein, striding stiffe and bold,
As if that highest God defie he would:
In his right hand an yron club he held,
But he himselfe was all of golden mould,
Yet had both life and sence, and well could weld
360   That cursed weapon, when his cruell foes he queld.

xli

Disdayne he called was, and did disdaine[10]
To be so cald, and who so did him call:
Sterne was his looke, and full of stomacke vaine,
His portaunce terrible, and stature tall,
Far passing th'hight of men terrestriall;
Like an huge Gyant of the *Titans* race,
That made him scorne all creatures great and small,
And with his pride all others powre deface:
More fit amongst blacke fiendes, then men to haue his place.

xlii

370   Soone as those glitterand armes he did espye,
That with their brightnesse made that darknesse light,
His harmefull club he gan to hurtle hye,
And threaten batteill to the Faery knight;

10   Disdain is the arrogance of the rich and powerful. See Aristotle's
Nicomachaean Ethics, 4. 3.

Who likewise gan himselfe to batteill dight,
Till *Mammon* did his hasty hand withhold,
And counseld him abstaine from perilous fight:
For nothing might abash the villein bold,
Ne mortall steele emperce his miscreated mould.

xliii

So hauing him with reason pacifide,
And the fiers Carle comnaunding to forbeare,   *villain*
He brought him in. The rowme was large and wide,
As it some Gyeld or solemne Temple weare:
Many great golden pillours did vpbeare
The massy roofe, and riches huge sustayne,
And euery pillour decked was full deare
With crownes and Diademes, and titles vaine,
Which mortall Princes wore, whiles they on earth did rayne.

380

xliv

A route of people there assembled were,
Of euery sort and nation vnder skye,
Which with great vprore preaced to draw nere
To th'vpper part, where was aduaunced hye
A stately siege of soueraigne maiestye;   *throne*
And thereon sat a woman gorgeous gay,
And richly clad in robes of royaltye,
That neuer earthly Prince in such aray
His glory did enhaunce, and pompous pride display.

390

xlv

Her face right wondrous faire did seeme to bee,
That her broad beauties beam great brightnes threw
Through the dim shade, that all men might it see:
Yet was not that same her owne natiue hew,
But wrought by art and counterfetted shew,
Thereby more louers vnto her to call;
Nath'lesse most heauenly faire in deed and vew
She by creation was, till she did fall;
Thenceforth she sought for helps, to cloke her crime withall.

400

xlvi

There, as in glistring glory she did sit,
She held a great gold chaine ylincked well,[11]
Whose vpper end to highest heauen was knit,
And lower part did reach to lowest Hell;
And all that preace did round about her swell,
To catchen hold of that long chaine, thereby
To clime aloft, and others to excell:
That was *Ambition*, rash desire to sty,   *rise*
And euery lincke thereof a step of dignity.

410

xlvii

Some thought to raise themselues to high degree,
By riches and vnrighteous reward,
Some by close shouldring, some by flatteree;   *intrigue*
Others through friends, others for base regard;
And all by wrong wayes for themselues prepard.

11 Her chain of ambition is a parody of the golden chain of being in
the *Iliad*, 8. 19–22.

420
Those that were vp themselues, kept others low,
Those that were low themselues, held others hard,
Ne suffred them to rise or greater grow,
But euery one did striue his fellow downe to throw.

xlviii

Which whenas *Guyon* saw, he gan inquire,
What meant that preace about that Ladies throne,
And what she was that did so high aspire.
Him *Mammon* answered; That goodly one,
Whom all that folke with such contention,
Do flocke about, my deare, my daughter is;
430
Honour and dignitie from her alone
Deniued are, and all this worldes blis
For which ye men do striue: few get, but many mis.

xlix

And faire *Philotime* she rightly hight,
The fairest wight that wonneth vnder skye,
But that this darksome neather world her light
Doth dim with horrour and deformitie,
Worthy of heauen and hye felicitie,
From whence the gods haue her for enuy thrust:
But sith thou hast found fauour in mine eye,
440
Thy spouse I will her make, if that thou lust,
That she may thee aduance for workes and merites iust.

l

Gramercy *Mammon* (said the gentle knight)
For so great grace and offred high estate;
But I, that am fraile flesh and earthly wight,
Vnworthy match for such immortall mate
My selfe well wote, and mine vnequall fate;
And were I not, yet is my trouth yplight,
And loue auowd to other Lady late,
That to remoue the same I haue no might:
450
To chaunge loue causelesse is reproch to warlike knight.

li

Mammon emmoued was with inward wrath;
Yet forcing it to faine, him forth thence led
Through griesly shadowes by a beaten path,
Into a gardin goodly garnished
With hearbs and fruits, whose kinds mote not be red:
Not such, as earth out of her fruitfull woomb
Throwes forth to men, sweet and well sauoured,
But direfull deadly blacke both leafe and bloom,
Fit to adorne the dead, and decke the drery toombe.

lii

460
There mournfull *Cypress* grew in greatest store,[12]
And trees of bitter *Gall*, and *Heben* sad,

12 The plants in Persephone's garden are poisonous and symbols of death and mourning (see John Gerard, *The General Historie of Plants* {1597}.) Her golden apple tree fuses classical and Christian mythology: the apple tree of Persephone (in Claudian's *Rape of Proserpine*, 2) with Adam and Eve's forbidden fruit (Genesis 2 and 3). Hercules' eleventh labor was to get golden apples from the garden of the Hesperides. Like the descent into the underworld in the *Odyssey* and the *Aeneid*, this episode is a visit to a storehouse of mythology. However, here as in much Renaissance appropriation of classical myth, the survival of the pagan gods occurs as a typological allegory of Christian thought (see Jean Seznec, *The Survival of the Pagan Gods*).

Dead sleeping *Poppy*, and blacke *Hellebore*,
　Cold *Coloquintida*, and *Tetra* mad,
　Mortall *Samnitis*, and *Cicuta* bad,
　With which th'vniust *Atheniens* made to dy
　Wise *Socrates*, who thereof quaffing glad
　Pourd out his life, and last Philosophy
To the faire *Critias*[13] his dearest Belamy.   *friend*

liii

470

The *Gardin* of *Proserpina* this hight;   *was called*
　And in the midst thereof a siluer seat,
　With a thicke Arber goodly ouer dight,
　In which she often vsd from open heat
　Her selfe to shroud, and pleasures to entreat.
　Next thereunto did grow a goodly tree,
　With braunches broad dispred and body great,
　Clothed with leaues, that none the wood mote see
And loaden all with fruit as thicke as it might bee.

liv

480

Their fruit were golden apples glistring bright,
　That goodly was their glory to behold,
　On earth like neuer grew, ne liuing wight
　Like euer saw, but they from hence were sold;
　For those, which *Hercules* with conquest bold
　Got from great *Atlas* daughters, hence began,[14]
　And planted there, did bring forth fruit of gold:
　And those with which th'*Eubœan* young man wan
Swift *Atalanta*, when through craft he her out ran.

lv

490

Here also sprong that goodly golden fruit,
　With which *Acontius* got his louer trew,
　Whom he had long time sought with fruitlesse suit:
　Here eke that famous golden Apple grew,
　The which emongst the gods false *Ate* threw;[15]
　For which th'*Idœan* Ladies disagreed,
　Till partiall *Paris* dempt it *Venus* dew,
　And had of her, faire *Helen* for his meed,
That many noble *Greekes* and *Troians* made to bleed.

lvi

500

The warlike Elfe much wondred at this tree,
　So faire and great, that shadowed all the ground,
　And his broad braunches, laden with rich fee,
　Did stretch themselues without the vtmost bound
　Of this great gardin, compast with a mound,
　Which ouer-hanging, they themselues did steepe,
　In a blacke flood which flow'd about it round;
　That is the riuer of *Cocytus*[16] deepe,
In which full many soules do endlesse waile and weepe.

13　The story of Socrates' death is actually told in Plato's *Phaedo*.
Perhaps Spenser is remembering Critias' understanding of temperance
in *Charmides*.

14　The stories of Atalanta and Hippomenes (Ovid, *Metamorphoses*, 10.
560) and of Acontius and Cydippe (Ovid, *Heroides*, 20 and 21) are about
a girl's being tricked and seduced with a piece of fruit.
15　Ate's apple of discord led to the Trojan War.
16　A river in Hades.

lvii

Which to behold, he clomb vp to the banke,
   And looking downe, saw many damned wights,
   In those sad waues, which direfull deadly stanke,
   Plonged continually of cruell Sprights,
   That with their pitteous cryes, and yelling shrights,
510   They made the further shore resounden wide:
   Emongst the rest of those same ruefull sights,
   One cursed creature he by chaunce espide,
That drenched lay full deepe, vnder the Garden side.[17]

lviii

Deepe was he drenched to the vpmost chin,
   Yet gaped still, as coueting to drinke
   Of the cold liquor, which he waded in,
   And stretching forth his hand, did often thinke
   To reach the fruit, which grew vpon the brincke:
   But both the fruit from hand, and floud from mouth
520   Did flie abacke, and made him vainely swinke:
   The whiles he steru'd with hunger and with drouth
He daily dyde, yet neuer throughly dyen couth.

lix

The knight him seeing labour so in vaine,
   Askt who he was, and what he ment thereby:
   Who groning deepe, thus answerd him againe;
   Most cursed of all creatures vnder skye,
   Lo *Tantalus*, I here tormented lye:
   Of whom high *Ioue* wont whylome feasted bee,
   Lo here I now for want of food doe dye:
530   But if that thou be such, as I thee see,
Of grace I pray thee, giue to eat and drinke to mee.

lx

Nay, nay, thou greedie *Tantalus* (quoth he)
   Abide the fortune of thy present fate,
   And vnto all that liue in high degree,
   Ensample be of mind intemperate,
   To teach them how to vse their present state.
   Then gan the cursed wretch aloud to cry,
   Accusing highest *Ioue* and gods ingrate,
   And eke blaspheming heauen bitterly,
540   As authour of vniustice, there to let him dye.

lxi

He lookt a little further, and espyde
   Another wretch, whose carkasse deepe was drent   *submerged*
   Within the riuer, which the same did hyde:
   But both his hands most filthy feculent,   *soiled*
   Aboue the water were on high extent,
   And faynd to wash themselues incessantly;
   Yet nothing cleaner were for such intent,
   But rather fowler seemed to the eye;
So lost his labour vaine and idle industry.

17   The story of Tantalus is derived from the *Odyssey* 11, and from
Pindar's *Olympia* 1.

lxii

550
The knight him calling, asked who he was,
　　Who lifting vp his head, him answerd thus:
　　I *Pilate* am the falsest Iudge, alas,
　　And most vniust, that by vnrighteous
　　And wicked doome, to Iewes despiteous
　　Deliuered vp the Lord of life to die,
　　And did acquite a murdrer felonous;
　　The whiles my hands I washt in puritie,
The whiles my soule was soyld with foule iniquitie.

lxiii

Infinite moe, tormented in like paine
560
　　He there beheld, too long here to be told:
　　Ne *Mammon* would there let him long remaine,
　　For terrour of the tortures manifold,
　　In which the damned soules he did behold,
　　But roughly him bespake. Thou fearefull foole;
　　Why takest not of that same fruit of gold,
　　Ne sittest downe on that same siluer stoole,
To rest thy wearie person, in the shadow coole.

lxiv

All which he did, to doe him deadly fall
　　In frayle intemperance through sinfull bayt;
570
　　To which if he inclined had at all,
　　That dreadfull feend, which did behind him wayt,
　　Would him haue rent in thousand peeces strayt:
　　But he was warie wise in all his way,
　　And well perceiued his deceiptfull sleight,
　　Ne suffred lust his safetie to betray;
So goodly did beguile the Guyler of the pray.

lxv

And now he has so long remained there,
　　That vitall powres gan wexe both weake and wan,
　　For want of food, and sleepe, which two vpbeare,
580
　　Like mightie pillours, this fraile life of man,
　　That none without the same enduren can.
　　For now three dayes of men were full outwrought,
　　Since he this hardie enterprize began;
　　For thy great *Mammon* fairely he besought,
Into the world to guide him backe, as he him brought.

lxvi

The God, though loth, yet was constraind t'obay,
　　For lenger time, then that, no liuing wight
　　Below the earth, might suffred be to stay:
　　So backe againe, him brought to liuing light.
590
　　But all so soone as his enfeebled spright
　　Gan sucke this vitall aire into his brest,
　　As ouercome with too exceeding might,
　　The life did flit away out of her nest,
And all his senses were with deadly fit opprest.

Cant. VIII.

Sir Guyon laid in swowne is by
Acrates sonnes despoyld,
Whom Arthur soone hath reskewed   infidel
And paynim brethren foyld.

i

And is there care in heauen? and is there loue
  In heauenly spirits to these creatures bace,
  That may compassion of their euils moue?
  There is: else much more wretched were the cace
  Of men, then beasts. But O th'exceeding grace¹
  Of highest God, that loues his creatures so,
  And all his workes with mercy doth embrace,
  That blessed Angels, he sends to and fro,
To serue to wicked man, to serue his wicked foe.

ii

10   How oft do they, their siluer bowers leaue,
  To come to succour vs, that succour want?
  How oft do they with golden pineons, cleaue
  The flitting skyes, like flying Pursuiuant,   messenger
  Against foule feends to aide vs millitant?
  They for vs fight, they watch and dewly ward,
  And their bright Squadrons round about vs plant,
  And all for loue, and nothing for reward:
O why should heauenly God to men haue such regard?

iii

During the while, that *Guyon* did abide
20   In *Mammons* house, the Palmer, whom whyleare   before
  That wanton Mayd of passage had denide,
  By further search had passage found elsewhere,
  And being on his way, approched neare,
  Where *Guyon* lay in traunce, when suddenly
  He heard a voice, that called loud and cleare,
  Come hither, come hither, O come hastily;
That all the fields resounded with the ruefull cry.

iv

The Palmer lent his eare vnto the noyce,
  To weet, who called so importunely:
30   Againe he heard a more efforced voyce,   powerful
  That bad him come in haste. He by and by
  His feeble feet directed to the cry;
  Which to that shadie delue him brought at last,
  Where *Mammon* earst did sunne his threasury:
  There the good *Guyon* he found slumbring fast
In senselesse dreame; which sight at first him sore aghast.

v

Beside his head there sate a faire young man,²
  Of wondrous beautie, and of freshest yeares,

CANT. VIII.

1   In the Protestant tradition especially, angels were thought to be
agents of God's grace (see, for example, Hebrews 1:14).

2   On the appropriation of Cupid to Christian tradition, see Erwin
Panofsky, "Blind Cupid" in *Studies in Iconology*, pp. 95–169.

Whose tender bud to blossome new began,
And flourish faire aboue his equall peares;
His snowy front curled with golden heares,
Like *Phœbus* face adornd with sunny rayes,
Diuinely shone, and two sharpe winged sheares,
Decked with diuerse plumes, like painted layes,
Were fixed at his backe, to cut his ayerie wayes.

vi

Like as *Cupido* on *Idæan* hill,
When hauing laid his cruell bow away,
And mortall arrowes, wherewith he doth fill
The world with murdrous spoiles and bloudie pray,
With his faire mother he him dights to play,
And with his goodly sisters, *Graces* three;
The Goddesse pleased with his wanton play,
Suffers her selfe through sleepe beguild to bee,
The whiles the other Ladies mind their merry glee.

vii

Whom when the Palmer saw, abasht he was
Through fear and wonder, that he nought could say,
Till him the child bespoke, Long lackt, alas,
Hath bene thy faithfull aide in hard assay,
Whiles deadly fit thy pupill doth dismay;
Behold this heauie sight, thou reuerend Sire,
But dread of death and dolour doe away;
For life ere long shall to her home retire,
And he that breathlesse seemes, shal corage bold respire.

viii

The charge, which God doth vnto me arret,   *assign*
Of his deare safetie, I to thee commend;
Yet will I not forgoe, ne yet forget
The care thereof my selfe vnto the end,
But euermore him succour, and defend
Against his foe and mine: watch thou I pray;
For euill is at hand him to offend.[3]
So hauing said, eftsoones he gan display
His painted nimble wings, and vanisht quite away.

ix

The Palmer seeing his left empty place,
And his slow eyes beguiled of their sight,
Woxe sore affraid, and standing still a space,   *became*
Gaz'd after him, as fowle escapt by flight;
At last him turning to his charge behight,
With trembling hand his troubled pulse gan try;
Where finding life not yet dislodged quight,
He much reioyst, and courd it tenderly,
As chicken newly hatcht, from dreaded destiny.

3   The achievement of temperance is possible only with the assistance of divine grace, which is the essential argument of Paul's Epistle to the Romans. This is also the most important Christian supplement to Aristotelian ethics. Cymochles and Pyrochles are enemies of this basic tenet of Christian theology and ethics.

x

At last he spide, where towards him did pace
   Two Paynim knights,[4] all armd as bright as skie,
   And them beside an aged Sire did trace,
   And farre before a light-foot Page did flie,
   That breathed strife and troublous enmitie;
   Those were the two sonnes of *Acrates* old,
   Who meeting earst with *Archimago* slie,
   Foreby that idle strond, of him were told,
90   That he, which earst them combatted, was *Guyon* bold.

xi

Which to auenge on him they dearely vowd,
   Where euer that on ground they mote him fynd;
   False *Archimage* prouokt their courage prowd,
   And stryfull *Atin* in their stubborne mynd
   Coles of contention and whot vengeance tynd.   *kindled*
   Now bene they come, whereas the Palmer sate,
   Keeping that slombred corse to him assynd;
   Well knew they both his person, sith of late
With him in bloudie armes they rashly did debate.

xii

100   Whom when *Pyrochles* saw, inflam'd with rage,
   That sire he foule bespake, Thou dotard vile,
   That with thy brutenesse shendst thy comely age,   *shames*
   Abandone soone, I read, the caitiue spoile
   Of that same outcast carkasse, that erewhile
   Made it selfe famous through false trechery,
   And crownd his coward crest with knightly stile;   *title*
   Loe where he now inglorious doth lye,
To proue he liued ill, that did thus foully dye.

xiii

To whom the Palmer fearelesse answered;
110   Certes, Sir knight, ye bene too much to blame,
   Thus for to blot the honour of the dead,
   And with foule cowardize his carkasse shame,
   Whose liuing hands immortalizd his name.
   Vile is the vengeance on the ashes cold,
   And enuie base, to barke at sleeping fame:
   Was neuer wight, that treason of him told;
Your selfe his prowesse prou'd and found him fiers and bold.

xiv

Then said *Cymochles*; Palmer, thou doest dote,
   Ne canst of prowesse, ne of knighthood deeme,
120   Saue as thou seest or hearst. But well I wote,
   That of his puissance tryall made extreeme;
   Yet gold all is not, that doth golden seeme;
   Ne all good knights, that shake well speare and shield:

---

4   By designating them "paynim knights," Spenser makes them part of his fraternity of Muslim infidels, which includes Sansloy, Sansjoy, and Sansfoy. Like most Renaissance Christians, Spenser stands opposed to reconciling the differences among Judaism, Islam, and Christianity on behalf of a poetic theology. In this respect he remains, despite his Neoplatonism, in opposition to Pico della Mirandola's eloquent eclecticism in *Oration on the Dignity of Man* (c. 1486). (On this and related matters, see Edgar Wind, *Pagan Mysteries in the Renaissance* [esp. pp. 17–25] and Frances Yates, *The Occult Philosophy in the Elizabethan Age*, Chs. 1 and 2.)

The worth of all men by their end esteeme,
　　And then due praise, or due reproch them yield;
Bad therefore I him deeme, that thus lies dead on field.

xv

Good or bad (gan his brother fierce reply)
　　What doe I recke, sith that he dyde entire?
　　Or what doth his bad death now satisfy
130　　The greedy hunger of reuenging ire,
　　Sith wrathfull hand wrought not her owne desire?
　　Yet since no way is left to wreake my spight,
　　I will him reaue of armes, the victors hire,　　　　　　　　*strip/prize*
　　And of that shield, more worthy of good knight;
For why should a dead dog be deckt in armour bright?

xvi

Faire Sir, said then the Palmer suppliaunt,
　　For knighthoods loue, do not so foule a deed,
　　Ne blame your honour with so shamefull vaunt
　　Of vile reuenge. To spoile the dead of weed　　　　　　*clothes*
140　　Is sacrilege, and doth all sinnes exceed;
　　But leaue these relicks of his liuing might,
　　To decke his herce, and trap his tomb-blacke steed.
　　What herce or steed (said he) should he haue dight,
But be entombed in the rauen or the kight?

xvii

With that, rude hand vpon his shield he laid,
　　And th'other brother gan his helme vnlace,
　　Both fiercely bent to haue him disaraid;
　　Till that they spide, where towards them did pace
　　An armed knight, of bold and bounteous grace,⁵
150　　Whose squire bore after him an heben launce,
　　Amd couerd shield. Well kend him so farre space
　　Th'enchaunter by his armes and amenaunce,　　　　　　*bearing*
When vnder him he saw his Lybian steed to praunce.

xviii

And to those brethren said, Rise rise by liue,
　　And vnto battell doe your selues addresse;
　　For yonder comes the prowest knight aliue,
　　Prince *Arthur*, flowre of grace and nobilesse,
　　That hath to Paynim knights wrought great distresse,
　　And thousand Sar'zins foully donne to dye.
160　　That word so deepe did in their harts impresse,
　　That both eftsoones vpstarted furiously,
And gan themselues prepare to battell greedily.

xix

But fierce *Pyrochles*, lacking his owne sword,
　　The want thereof now greatly gan to plaine,
　　And *Archimage* besought, him that afford,
　　Which he had brought for *Braggadocchio* vaine.

---

5 Arthur appears in each book of *The Faerie Queene* as a perfect embodiment of the virtue being celebrated. In this respect he is analogous to Christ on the level of the poem's polysemous allegory. Accordingly, here his covered shield has often been interpreted as an emblem of incarnate human faith rather than of miraculous divinity. In Book I. viii, on the other hand, Arthur fights the giant Orgoglio with his dazzling shield uncovered.

So would I (said th'enchaunter) glad and faine
Beteeme to you this sword, you to defend,
Or ought that else your honour might maintaine,
170   But that this weapons powre I well haue kend,
To be contrarie to the worke, which ye intend.

xx

For that same knights owne sword this is of yore,
Which *Merlin* made by his almightie art
For that his noursling, when he knighthood swore,
Therewith to doen his foes eternall smart.
The metall first he mixt with *Medæwart*,
That no enchauntment from his dint might saue;
Then it in flames of *Aetna* wrought apart,
And seuen times dipped in the bitter waue
180   Of hellish *Styx*, which hidden vertue to it gaue.

xxi

The vertue is, that neither steele, not stone
The stroke thereof from entrance may defend;
Ne euer may be vsed by his fone,   *foes*
Ne forst his rightfull owner to offend,
Ne euer will it breake, ne euer bend.
Wherefore *Morddure* it rightfully is hight.
In vaine therefore, *Pyrochles*, should I lend
The same to thee, against his lord to fight,
For sure it would deceiue thy labour, and thy might.

xxii

190   Foolish old man, said then the Pagan wroth,
That weenest words or charmes may force withstond:
Soone shalt thou see, and then beleeue for troth,
That I can carue with this inchaunted brond[6]   *sword*
His Lords owne flesh. Therewith out of his hond
That vertuous steele he rudely snatcht away,
And *Guyons* shield about his wrest he bond;
So readie dight, fierce battaile to assay,
And match his brother proud in battailous array.

xxiii

By this that straunger knight in presence came,
200   And goodly salued them; who nought againe
Him answered, as courtesie became,
But with sterne lookes, and stomachous disdaine,
Gaue signes of grudge and discontentment vaine:
Then turning to the Palmer, he gan spy
Where at his feete, with sorrowfull demaine
And deadly hew, an armed corse did lye,
In whose dead face he red great magnanimity.

xxiv

Said he then to the Palmer, Reuerend syre,
What great misfortune hath betidd this knight?
210   Or did his life her fatall date expyre,
Or did he fall by treason, or by fight?

6   An echo of the description of the sword of Turnus in the *Aeneid*, 12.
90–1.

How euer, sure I rew his pitteous plight.
Not one, nor other, (said the Palmer graue)
Hath him befalne, but cloudes of deadly night
A while his heauie eylids couer'd haue,
And all his senses drowned in deepe senselesse waue.

xxv

Which, those his cruell foes, that stand hereby,
    Making aduantage, to reuenge their spight,
    Would him disarme, and treaten shamefully,
    Vnworthy vsage of redoubted knight.
    But you, faire Sir, whose honorable sight
    Doth promise hope of helpe, and timely grace,
    Mote I beseech to succour his sad plight,
    And by your powre protect his feeble cace.
First praise of knighthood is, foule outrage to deface.

xxvi

Palmer, (said he) no knight so rude, I weene,
    As to doen outrage to a sleeping ghost:
    Ne was there euer noble courage seene,
    That in aduauntage would his puissance bost:
    Honour is least, where oddes appeareth most.
    May be, that better reason will asswage
    The rash reuengers heat. Words well dispost
    Haue secret powre, t'appease inflamed rage:
If not, leaue vnto me thy knights last patronage.

xxvii

Tho turning to those brethren, thus bespoke,
    Ye warlike payre, whose valorous great might
    It seemes, just wrongs to vengeance doe prouoke,
    To wreake your wrath on this dead seeming knight,
    Mote ought allay the storme of your despight,
    And settle patience in so furious heat?
    Not to debate the chalenge of your right,
    But for this carkasse pardon I entreat,
Whom fortune hath alreadie laid in lowest seat.

xxviii

To whom *Cymochles* said; For what art thou,
    That mak'st thy selfe his dayes-man,[7] to prolong
    The vengeance prest? Or who shall let me now,
    On this vile bodie from to wreake my wrong,
    And make his carkasse as the outcast dong?
    Why should not that dead carrion satisfie
    The guilt, which if he liued had thus long,
    His life for due reuenge should deare abie?   *pay*
The trespasse still doth liue, albe the person die.

xxix

Indeed (then said the Prince) the euill donne
    Dyes not, when breath the bodie first doth leaue,
    But from the grandsyre to the Nephewes sonne,
    And all his seed the curse doth often cleaue,

7   Job longs for a daysman to stand between him and God in order to
right their imbalance of power (Job 9:33.) In this sense a daysman is
more than a witness or legal advocate.

Till vengeance vtterly the guilt bereaue:
So streightly God doth iudge. But gentle knight,
That doth against the dead his hand vpreare,
250   His honour staines with rancour and despight,
And great disparagment makes to his former might.

xxx

Pyrochles gan reply the second time,
And to him said, Now felon sure I read,
How that thou art partaker of his crime:
Therefore by Termagaunt[8] thou shalt be dead.
With that his hand, more sad then lomp of lead,
Vphifting high, he weened with Morddure,
His owne good sword Morddure, to cleaue his head.
The faithfull steele such treason no'uld endure,   *wouldn't*
260   But swaruing from the marke, his Lords life did assure.

xxxi

Yet was the force so furious and so fell,
That horse and man it made to reele aside;
Nath'lesse the Prince would not forsake his sell: *saddle*
For well of yore he learned had to ride,
But full of anger fiercely to him cride;
False traitour miscreant, thou broken hast
The law of armes, to strike foe vndefide.
But thou thy treasons fruit, I hope, shalt taste
Right sowre, and feele the law, the which thou hast defast.

xxxii

270   With that his balefull speare he fiercely bent
Against the Pagans brest, and therewith thought
His cursed life out of her lodge haue rent:
But ere the point arriued, where it ought,
That seuen-fold shield, which he from Guyon brought
He cast betwene to ward the bitter stound: *blow*
Through all those foldes the steelehead passage wrought
And through his shoulder pierst; wherwith to ground
He groueling fell, all gored, in his gushing wound.

xxxiii

Which when his brother saw, fraught with great griefe
280   And wrath, he to him leaped furiously,
And fowly said, By Mahoune, cursed thiefe,   *Mohammed*
That direfull stroke thou dearely shalt aby.
Then hurling vp his harmefull blade on hye,
Smote him so hugely on his haughtie crest,
That from his saddle forced him to fly:
Else mote it needes downe to his manly brest
Haue cleft his head in twaine, and life thence dispossest.

xxxiv

Now was the Prince in daungerous distresse,
Wanting his sword, when he on foot should fight:
290   His single speare could doe him small redresse,

---

8   A violent warrior god that medieval Christians erroneously thought   tained ideological investment in creating an imaginary Orient (see his
was worshipped by Muslims. Though in some ways a small detail, this   *Orientalism*, esp. ch. 1.).
is a telling example of Edward Said's thesis that the West has had a sus-

Against two foes of so exceeding might,
The least of which was match for any knight.
And now the other, whom he earst did daunt,
Had reard himselfe againe to cruell fight,
Three times more furious, and more puissaunt,
Vnmindfull of his wound, of his fate ignoraunt.

xxxv

So both attonce him charge on either side,
With hideous strokes, and importable powre,
That forced him his ground to trauerse wide,
And wisely watch to ward that deadly stowre: *peril*
For in his shield, as thicke as stormie showre,
Their strokes did raine, yet did he neuer quaile,
Ne backward shrinke, but as a stedfast towre,
Whom foe with double battry doth assaile,
Them on her bulwarke beares, and bids them nought auaile.

xxxvi

So stoutly he withstood their strong assay,   *attack*
Till that at last, when he aduantage spyde,
His poinant speare he thrust with puissant sway   *force*
At proud *Cymochles*, whiles his shield was wyde,
That through his thigh the mortall steele did gryde: *pierce*
He swaruing with the force, within his flesh
Did breake the launce, and let the head abyde:
Out of the wound the red bloud flowed fresh,
That vnderneath his feet soone made a purple plesh.   *pool*

xxxvii

Horribly then he gan to rage, and rayle,
Cursing his Gods, and himselfe damning deepe:
Als when his brother saw the red bloud rayle   *also*
Adowne so fast, and all his armour steepe,
For very felnesse lowd he gan to weepe,
And said, Caytiue, cursse on thy cruell hond,
That twise hath sped; yet shall it not thee keepe
From the third brunt of this my fatall brond:
Loe where the dreadfull Death behind thy backe doth stond.

xxxviii

With that he strooke, and th'other strooke withall,
That nothing seem'd mote beare so monstrous might:
The one vpon his couered shield did fall,
And glauncing downe would not his owner byte:
But th'other did vpon his troncheon smyte,
Which hewing quite a sunder, further way
It made, and on his hacqueton did lyte,   *underjacket*
The which diuiding with importune sway,
It seizd in his right side, and there the dint did stay.

xxxix

Wyde was the wound, and a large lukewarme flood,
Red as the Rose, thence gushed grieuously;
That when the Paynim spyde the streaming blood,
Gaue him great hart, and hope of victory.
On th'other side, in huge perplexity,
The Prince now stood, hauing his weapon broke;

Nought could he hurt, but still at ward did ly: *guard*
340   Yet with his troncheon he so rudely stroke
Cymochles twise, that twise him forst his foot reuoke.

xl

Whom when the Palmer saw in such distresse,
    Sir *Guyons* sword he lightly to him raught,
    And said; Faire Son, great God thy right hand blesse,
    To vse that sword so wisely as it ought.
    Glad was the knight, and with fresh courage fraught,
    When as againe he armed felt his hond;
    Then like a Lion, which hath long time saught
    His robbed whelpes, and at the last them fond
350 Emongst the shepheard swaynes, then wexeth wood and yond.   *furious*

xli

So fierce he laid about him, and dealt blowes
    On either side, that neither mayle could hold,
    Ne shield defend the thunder of his throwes:
    Now to *Pyrochles* many strokes he told;
    Eft to *Cymochles* twise so many fold:
    Then backe againe turning his busie hond,
    Them both attonce compeld with courage bold,
    To yield wide way to his hart-thrilling brond;
And though they both stood stiffe, yet could not both withstond.

xlii

360 As saluage Bull, whom two fierce mastiues bayt,
    When rancour doth with rage him once engore,
    Forgets with warie ward them to awayt,
    But with his dreadfull hornes them driues afore,
    Or flings aloft, or treads downe in the flore,
    Breathing out wrath, and bellowing disdaine,
    That all the forrest quakes to heare him rore:
    So rag'd Prince *Arthur* twixt his foemen twaine,
That neither could his mightie puissance sustaine.

xliii

But euer at *Pyrochles* when he smit,
370   Who *Guyons* shield cast euer him before,
    Whereon the Faery Queenes pourtract was writ,
    His hand relented, and the stroke forbore,
    And his deare hart the picture gan adore,
    Which oft the Paynim sau'd from deadly stowre.   *blow*
    But him henceforth the same can saue no more;
    For now arriued is his fatall howre,
That no'te auoyded be by earthly skill or powre.

xliv

For when *Cymochles* saw the fowle reproch,
    Which them appeached, prickt with guilty shame,
380   And inward griefe, he fiercely gan approch,
    Resolu'd to put away that loathly blame,   *blemish*
    Or dye with honour and desert of fame;
    And on the hauberk stroke the Prince so sore,
    That quite disparted all the linked frame,
    And pierced to the skin, but bit no more,
Yet made him twise to reele, that neuer moou'd afore.

xlv

Whereat renfierst with wrath and sharpe regret,
  He stroke so hugely with his borrowed blade,
  That it empierst the Pagans burganet,
390 And cleauing the hard steele, did deepe inuade
  Into his head, and cruell passage made
  Quite through his braine. He tombling downe on ground,
  Breathd out his ghost, which to th'infernall shade
  Fast flying, there eternall torment found,
For all the sinnes, wherewith his lewd life did abound.

xlvi

Which when his german saw, the stony feare   *brother*
  Ran to his hart, and all his sence dismayd,
  Ne thenceforth life ne courage did appeare,
  But as a man, whom hellish feends haue frayd,
400 Long trembling still he stood: at last thus sayd;
  Traytour what hast thou doen? how euer may
  Thy cursed hand so cruelly haue swayd
  Against that knight: Harrow and well away,
After so wicked deed why liu'st thou lenger day?

xlvii

With that all desperate as loathing light,
  And with reuenge desiring soone to dye,
  Assembling all his force and vtmost might,
  With his owne sword he fierce at him did flye,
  And strooke, and foynd, and lasht outrageously,   *thrust*
410 Withouten reason or regard. Well knew
  The Prince, with patience and sufferaunce sly
  So hasty heat soone cooled to subdew:
Tho when this breathless woxe, that batteil gan renew.

xlviii

As when a windy tempest bloweth hye,
  That nothing may withstand his stormy stowre,
  The cloudes, as things affrayd, before him flye;
  But all so soone as his outrageous powre
  Is layd, they fiercely then begin to shoure,
  And as in scorne of his spent stormy spight,
420 Now all attonce their malice forth do poure;
  So did Prince *Arthur* beare himselfe in fight,
And suffred rash *Pyrochles* wast his idle might.

xlix

At last when as the Sarazin perceiu'd,
  How that straunge sword refusd, to serue his need,
  But when he stroke most strong, the dint deceiu'd,
  He flong it from him, and deuoyd of dreed,
  Vpon him lightly leaping without heed,
  Twixt his two mighty armes engrasped fast,
  Thinking to ouerthrow and downe him tred:
430 But him in strength and skill the Prince surpast,
And through his nimble sleight did vnder him down cast.

l

Nought booted it the Paynim then to striue;
  For as a Bittur in the Eagles claw,   *bittern*
  That may not hope by flight to scape aliue,

Still waites for death with dread and trembling aw;
So he now subiect to the victours law,
Did not once moue, nor vpward cast his eye,
For vile disdaine and rancour, which did gnaw
His hart in twaine with sad melancholy,
440   As one that loathed life, and yet despisd to dye.

li

But full of Princely bounty and great mind,
The Conquerour nought cared him to slay,
But casting wrongs and all reuenge behind,
More glory thought to giue life, then decay,
And said, Paynim, this is thy dismall day;
Yet if thou wilt renounce thy miscreaunce,   *infidelity*
And my trew liegeman yield thy selfe for ay,
Life will I graunt thee for thy valiaunce,
And all thy wrongs will wipe out of my souenaunce.

lii

450   Foole (said the Pagan) I thy gift defye,
But vse thy fortune, as it doth befall,
And say, that I not ouercome do dye,
But in despight of life, for death do call.
Wroth was the Prince, atd sory yet withall,
That he so wilfully refused grace;[9]
Yet sith his fate so cruelly did fall,
His shining Helmet he gan soone vnlace,
And left his headlesse body bleeding all the place.

liii

By this Sir *Guyon* from his traunce awakt,
460   Life hauing maistered her sencelesse foe;
And looking vp, when as his shield he lakt,
And sword saw not, he wexed wondrous woe:
But when the Palmer, whom he long ygoe
Had lost, he by him spide, right glad he grew,
And said, Deare sir, whom wandring to and fro
I long haue lackt, I ioy thy face to vew;
Firme is thy faith, whom daunger neuer fro me drew.

liv

But read what wicked hand hath robbed mee
Of my good sword and shield? The Palmer glad,
470   With so fresh hew vprising him to see,
Him answered; Faire sonne, be no whit sad
For want of weapons, they shall soone be had.
So gan he to discourse the whole debate,
Which that straunge knight for him sustained had,
And those two Sarazins confounded late,
Whose carcases on ground were horribly prostrate.

lv

Which when he heard, and saw the tokens trew,
His hart with great affection was embayd,
And to the Prince bowing with reuerence dew,
480   As to the Patrone of his life, thus sayd;

---

9   Beyond redemption, Pyrochles refuses Arthur's gift of grace.

My Lord, my liege, by whose most gratious ayd
I liue this day, and see my foes subdewd,
What may suffise, to be for meede repayd
Of so great graces, as ye haue me shewd,
But to be euer bound

lvi

To whom the Infant thus, Faire Sir, what need
Good turnes be counted, as a seruile bond,
To bind their doers, to receiue their meede?
Are not all knights by oath bound, to withstond
Oppressours powre by armes and puissant hond?
Suffise, that I haue done my dew in place.
So goodly purpose they together fond,   *found*
Of kindnesse and of curteous aggrace;   *goodwill*
The whiles false *Archimage* and *Atin* fled apace.

Cant. IX.

*The bouse of Temperance, in which
doth sober Alma dwell,
Besiegd of many foes, whom straunger
knightes to flight compell.*

i

Of all Gods workes, which do this world adorne,
There is no one more faire and excellent,
Then is mans body both for powre and forme,[1]
Whiles it is kept in sober gouernment;
But none then it, more fowle and indecent,
Distempred through misrule and passions bace:
It growes a Monster, and incontinent
Doth loose his dignitie and natiue grace.
Behold, who list, both one and other in this place.

ii

After the Paynim brethren conquer'd were,
The *Briton* Prince recou'ring his stolne sword,
And *Guyon* his lost shield, they both yfere   *together*
Forth passed on their way in faire accord,
Till him the Prince with gentle court did bord;   *address*
Sir knight, mote I of you this curt'sie read,
To weet why on your shield so goodly scord   *know*
Beare ye the picture of that Ladies head?[2]
Full liuely is the semblaunt, though the substance dead.   *image*

CANT. IX.

1   The analogy between bodily and architectural form as mediated by geometry has been a source of continual fascination. For example, Vitruvius' *The Ten Books on Architecture*: "Without symmetry and proportion there can be no principles in the design of any temple; that is, if there is no precise relation between its members, as in the case of those of a well-shaped man" (3.1.1).

2   An important issue throughout this canto is the representation of the body. This consists of at least three stages: (1) the effort to imagine the complete shape of one's own or another's body, especially when it is only possible to have fragmentary images of any body (as here, just the head of the Faerie Queene); (2) the effort to "fashion" (Spenser's word in his Letter to Raleigh) the sense of a whole person out of the frag-

ments available (e.g., Guyon's quest for a life of temperance in the face of his animating passions); and (3) the artistic representation of those images in a painting or poem (whether Guyon's shield or Spenser's poem). For a recent discussion of these problems in the medium of photography, see William A. Ewing, *The Body: Photographs of the Human Form*. Spenser captures here the simultaneous desire and anxiety about seeing the body whole, about developing a sense of the self that will include the reality of one's body, and about the challenges and consequences of representing the body in art, with all the risks that the representation will become a seductive object. Not the least of Spenser's difficulties is St. Paul's determination to champion in life and in language the spirit over the flesh (or the letter).

iii

Faire Sir (said he) if in that picture dead
    Such life ye read, and vertue in vaine shew,
    What mote ye weene, if the trew liuely-head
    Of that most glorious visage ye did vew?
    But if the beautie of her mind ye knew,
    That is her bountie, and imperiall powre,
    Thousand times fairer then her mortall hew,
    O how great wonder would your thoughts deuoure,
And infinite desire into your spirite poure!

iv

She is the mighty Queene of *Faerie*,
    Whose faire retrait I in my shield do beare;   *portrait*
    She is the flowre of grace and chastitie,
    Throughout the world renowmed far and neare,
    My liefe, my liege, my Soueraigne, my deare,
    Whose glory shineth as the morning starre,
    And with her light the earth enlumines cleare;
    Far reach her mercies, and her prayses farre,
As well in state of peace, as puissaunce in warre.

v

Thrise happy man, (said then the *Briton* knight)
    Whom gracious lot, and thy great valiaunce
    Haue made thee souldier of that Princesse bright,
    Which with her bounty and glad countenance
    Doth blesse her seruaunts, and them high aduaunce.
    How may straunge knight hope euer to aspire,
    By faithfull seruice, and meet amenance,   *good conduct*
    Vnto such blisse? sufficient were that hire
For losse of thousand liues, to dye at her desire.

vi

Said *Guyon*, Noble Lord, what meed so great,   *reward*
    Or grace of earthly Prince so soueraine,
    But by your wondrous worth and warlike feat
    Ye well may hope, and easely attaine?
    But were your will, her sold to entertaine,   *prize, receive*
    And numbred be mongst knights of *Maydenhed*,
    Great guerdon, well I wote, should you remaine,
    And in her fauour high be reckoned,
As *Arthegall*, and *Sophy* now beene honored.[3]

vii

Certes (then said the Prince) I God auow,
    That sith I armes and knighthood first did plight,
    My whole desire hath beene, and yet is now,
    To serue that Queene with all my powre and might.
    Now hath the Sunne with his lamp-burning light,
    Walkt round about the world, and I no lesse,
    Sith of that Goddesse I haue sought the sight,
    Yet no where can her find: such happinesse
Heauen doth to me enuy, and fortune fauourlesse.

---

3 Arthegall is the hero of *The Faerie Queene*, V; Sophy is derived from
the Greek word for "wisdom." There may be implicit here a plan for
later portions of the poem that were never written.

viii

Fortune, the foe of famous cheuisaunce   *accomplishment*
  Seldome (said *Guyon*) yields to vertue aide,
  But in her way throwes mischiefe and mischaunce,
  Whereby her course is stopt, and passage staid.
  But you, faire Sir, be not herewith dismaid,
  But constant keepe the way, in which ye stand;
  Which were it not, that I am else delaid
  With hard aduenture, which I haue in hand,
I labour would to guide you through all Faery land.

70

ix

Gramercy Sir (said he) but mote I weete,
  What straunge aduenture do ye now pursew?
  Perhaps my succour, or aduizement meete
  Mote stead you much your purpose to subdew.
  Then gan Sir *Guyon* all the story shew
  Of false *Acrasia*, and her wicked wiles,
  Which to auenge, the Palmer him forth drew
  From Faery court.   So talked they, the whiles
They wasted had much way, and measurd many miles.

80

x

And now faire *Phœbus* gan decline in hast
  His weary wagon to the Westerne vale,
  Whenas they spide a goodly castle, plast
  Foreby a riuer in a pleasaunt dale,
  Which choosing for that euenings hospitale,
  They thither marcht: but when they came in sight,
  And from their sweaty Coursers did auale,   *dismount*
  They found the gates fast barred long ere night,
And euery loup fast lockt, as fearing foes despight.

90

xi

Which when they saw, they weened fowle reproch
  Was to them doen, their entrance to forstall,
  Till that the Squire gan nigher to approch;
  And wind his horne vnder the castle wall,
  That with the noise it shooke, as it would fall:
  Eftsoones forth looked from the highest spire
  The watch, and lowd vnto the knights did call,
  To weete, what they so rudely did require.
Who gently answered, They entrance did desire.

xii

Fly fly, good knights, (said he) fly fast away
  If that your liues ye loue, as meete ye should;
  Fly fast, and saue your selues from neare decay,
  Here may ye not haue entraunce, though we would:
  We would and would againe, if that we could;
  But thousand enemies about vs raue,
  And with long siege vs in this castle hould:
  Seuen yeares this wize they vs besieged haue,
And many good knights slaine, that haue vs sought to saue.

100

xiii

Thus as he spoke, loe with outragious cry
110   A thousand villeins round about them swarmd[4]
    Out of the rockes and caues adioyning nye,
    Vile caytiue wretches, ragged, rude, deformd,
    All threatning death, all in straunge manner armd,
    Some with vnweldy clubs, some with long speares,
    Some rusty kniues, some staues in fire warmd.
    Sterne was their looke, like wild amazed steares,
Staring with hollow eyes, and stiffe vpstanding heares.

xiv

Fiersly at first those knights they did assaile,
    And droue them to recoile: but when againe
    They gaue fresh charge, their forces gan to faile,
120   Vnhable their encounter to sustaine;
    For with such puissaunce and impetuous maine
    Those Champions broke on them, that forst them fly,
    Like scattered Sheepe, whenas the Shepheards swaine
    A Lyon and a Tigre doth espye,
With greedy pace forth rushing from the forest nye.

xv

A while they fled, but soone returnd againe
    With greater fury, then before was found;
    And euermore their cruell Capitaine
130   Sought with his raskall routs t'enclose them round,
    And ouerrun to tread them to the ground.
    But soone the knights with their bright-burning blades
    Broke their rude troupes, and orders did confound,
    Hewing and slashing at their idle shades;
For though they bodies seeme, yet substance from them fades.

xvi

As when a swarme of Gnats at euentide
    Out of the fennes of Allan[5] do arise,
    Their murmuring small trompets sounden wide,
    Whiles in the aire their clustring army flies,
140   That as a cloud doth seeme to dim the skies;
    Ne man nor beast may rest, or take repast,
    For their sharpe wounds, and noyous iniuries,
    Till the fierce Northerne wind with blustring blast
Doth blow them quite away, and in the *Ocean* cast.

xvii

Thus when they had that troublous rout disperst,
    Vnto the castle gate they come againe,
    And entraunce crau'd, which was denied erst.
    Now when report of that their perilous paine,
    And combrous conflict, which they did sustaine,
150   Came to the Ladies eare, which there did dwell,

4   Spenser's later description of Irish rebels may be anticipated here in this depiction of Maleger's disordered troops. (See the passage below from *View of the Present State of Ireland*.) His association of the Irish with the pagan otherness of Muslims – both manifestations of intemperate disorder – develops through the rest of the poem until its culmination in the "Mutability Cantos."

5   Fens of Allan: in central Ireland. Mapping the geography of Ireland as a subtle form of the shaping of English culture is the subject of Bernhard Klein's "'And quickly make that, which was nothing at all': English national identity and the mapping of Ireland." See also Andrew Hadfield's comprehensive study, *Spenser's Irish Experience*.

She forth issewed with a goodly traine
Of Squires and Ladies equipaged well,
And entertained them right fairely, as befell.

xviii

Alma she called was, a virgin bright;
That had not yet felt *Cupides* wanton rage,[6]
Yet was she woo'd of many a gentle knight,
And many a Lord of noble parentage,
That sought with her to lincke in marriage:
For she was faire, as faire mote euer bee,
160   And in the flowre now of her freshest age;
Yet full of grace and goodly modestee,
That euen heauen reioyced her sweete face to see.

xix

In robe of lilly white she was arayd,
That from her shoulder to her heele downe raught,   *reached*
The traine whereof loose far behind her strayd,
Braunched with gold and pearle, most richly wrought,
And borne of two faire Damsels, which were taught
That seruice well.   Her yellow golden heare
Was trimly wouen, and in tresses wrought,
170   Ne other tyre she on her head did weare,
But crowned with a garland of sweete Rosiere.

xx

Goodly she entertaind those noble knights,
And brought them vp into her castle hall;
Where gentle court and gracious delight
She to them made, with mildnesse virginall,
Shewing her selfe both wise and liberall:
There when they rested had a season dew,
They her besought of fauour speciall,
Of that faire Castle to affoord them vew;
180   She graunted, and them leading forth, the same did shew.

xxi

First she them led vp to the Castle wall,
That was so high, as foe might not it clime,
And all so faire, and fensible withall,   *fortified*
Not built of bricke, ne yet of stone and lime,
But of thing like to that *Ægyptian* slime,
Whereof king *Nine* whilome built *Babell* towre;[7]
But O great pitty, that no lenger time
So goodly workemanship should not endure:
Soone it must turne to earth; no earthly thing is sure.

---

6   In the Aristotelian context of the poem Alma is the rational part of the soul that is able to choose temperance, but she is also associated with Venus (as her garland suggests). Although he is in one sense her offspring, Cupid (in his carnal aspect) is someone she has not yet known. Earlier, however, Cupid was appropriated to Christian allegory.

7   The multiple cultural allusions are thick here. Ninus and Semiramis are the legendary founders of Babylon. According to Genesis 11:3, the Tower of Babel's bricks were secured with slime. But there is also an allusion to God's making the body of man from dirt (Genesis 2: 7) from which the word "humanity" might be derived. There is here, however, a sense of both the nobility and the loathsomeness of the body, both captured in the surrealism of the body as a castle under siege.

xxii

190   The frame thereof seemd partly circulare,[8]
And part triangulare, O worke diuine;
Those two the first and last proportions are,
The one imperfect, mortall, fœminine;
Th'other immortall, perfect, masculine,
And twixt them both a quadrate was the base,
Proportioned equally by seuen and nine;
Nine was the circle set in heauens place,
All which compacted made a goodly diapase.

xxiii

200   Therein two gates were placed seemly well:
The one before, by which all in did pas,
Did th'other far in workmanship excell;
For not of wood, nor of enduring bras,
But of more worthy substance fram'd it was;
Doubly disparted, it did locke and close,
That when it locked, none might thorough pas,
And when it opened, no man might it close,
Still open to their friends, and closed to their foes.

xxiv

210   Of hewen stone the porch was fairely wrought,
Stone more of valew, and more smooth and fine,
Then Iet or Marble far from Ireland brought;
Ouer the which was cast a wandring vine,
Enchaced with a wanton yuie twine.
And ouer it a faire Portcullis hong,
Which to the gate directly did incline,
With comely compasse, and compacture strong,
Neither vnseemely short, nor yet exceeding long.

xxv

Within the Barbican a Porter sate,
Day and night duely keeping watch and ward,
Nor wight, nor word mote passe out of the gate,
220   But in good order, and with dew regard;
Vtterers of secrets he from thence debard,
Bablers of folly, and blazers of crime.
His larumbell might lowd and wide be hard,
When cause requird, but neuer out of time;
Early and late it rong, at euening and at prime.

---

8   The effort to reconcile the perfect proportions of the body with geometrical forms and ratios, a project derived from Vitruvius, is the inspiration behind Leonardo's famous drawing of "Human Proportions." The relevant written text in Leonardo's *Notebooks*, includes this passage: "The architect Vitruvius states in his work on architecture that the measurements of a man are arranged by Nature thus: . . . If you set your legs so far apart as to take a fourteenth part from your height, and you open and raise your arms until you touch the line of the crown of the head with your middle fingers, you must know that the centre of the circle formed by the extremities of the outstretched limbs will be the navel, and the space between the legs will form an equilateral triangle" (p. 213). Efforts to reconcile the circle with the square and the triangle and to determine the numerical proportions of the body are parts of the complex history of the nude in Western art. (See Kenneth Clark, *The Nude*, which has much to say about assumptions of geometric proportion.) There follows here in Spenser's text a catalogue of the parts of the body: mouth, anus, chin, beard, moustache, nose, tongue, oral cavity, teeth, stomach. Galen's *On the Natural Faculties* was a key classical source on anatomy for Spenser, as it was for most medieval and Renaissance writers. But the freedom with which he experiments with received ideas suggests the possible influence of London science and medicine, which was independent of the control of the major universities (see Christopher Hill, *Intellectual Origins of the English Revolution*, Ch. 2).

xxvi

And round about the porch on euery side
  Twise sixteen warders sat, all armed bright
  In glistring steele, and strongly fortifide:
  Tall yeomen seemed they, and of great might,
230 And were enraunged ready, still for fight.
  By them as *Alma* passed with her guestes,
  They did obeysaunce, as beseemed right,
  And then againe returned to their restes:
The Porter eke to her did lout with humble gestes.

xxvii

Thence she them brought into a stately Hall,
  Wherein were many tables faire dispred,
  And ready dight with drapets festiuall,
  Against the viaundes should be ministred.
  At th'upper end there sate, yclad in red
240 Downe to the ground, a comely personage,
  That in his hand a white rod menaged,
  He Steward was hight *Diet*; rype of age,
And in demeanure sober, and in counsell sage.

xxviii

And through the Hall there walked to and fro
  A iolly yeoman, Marshall of the same,
  Whose name was *Appetite*; he did bestow
  Both guestes and meate, when euer in they came,
  And knew them how to order without blame,
  As him the Steward bad.   They both attone
250 Did dewty to their Lady, as became;
  Who passing by, forth led her guestes anone
Into the kitchin rowme, ne spard for nicenesse none.

xxix

It was a vaut ybuilt for great dispence,
  With many raunges reard along the wall;
  And one great chimney, whose long tonnell thence
  The smoke forth threw.   And in the midst of all
  There placed was a caudron wide and tall,
  Vpon a mighty furnace, burning whot,
  More whot, then *Aetn'*, or flaming *Mongiball*:
260 For day and night it brent, ne ceased not,
So long as any thing it in the caudron got.

xxx

But to delay the heat, least by mischaunce
  It might breake out, and set the whole on fire,
  There added was by goodly ordinaunce,
  An huge great paire of bellowes, which did styre   *move*
  Continually, and cooling breath inspyre.
  About the Caudron many Cookes accoyld,
  With hookes and ladles, as need did require;
  The whiles the viandes in the vessell boyld
270 They did about their businesse sweat, and sorely toyld.

xxxi

The maister Cooke was cald *Concoction*,
  A carefull man, and full of comely guise:
  The kitchin Clerke, that hight *Digestion*,

Did order all th'Achates in seemely wise,   *provisious*
  And set them forth, as well he could deuise.
  The rest had seuerall offices assind,
  Some to remoue the scum, as it did rise;
  Others to beare the same away did mind;
And others it to vse according to his kind.

xxxii

280   But all the liquour, which was fowle and wast,
  Not good nor seruiceable else for ought,
  They in another great round vessell plast,
  Till by a conduit pipe it thence were brought:
  And all the rest, that noyous was, and nought,   *noxious*
  By secret wayes, that none might it espy,
  Was close conuaid, and to the back-gate brought,
  That cleped was *Port Esquiline*,[9] whereby
It was auoided quite, and throwne out priuily.

xxxiii

Which goodly order, and great workmans skill
290   Whenas those knights beheld, with rare delight,
  And gazing wonder they their minds did fill;
  For neuer had they seene so straunge a sight.
  Thence backe againe faire *Alma* led them right,
  And soone into a goodly Parlour brought,
  That was with royall arras richly dight,
  In which was nothing pourtrahed, nor wrought,   *portrayed*
Not wrought, nor pourtrahed, but easie to be thought.[10]

xxxiv

And in the midst thereof vpon the floure,
  A louely beuy of faire Ladies sate,
300   Courted of many a iolly Paramoure,
  The which them did in modest wise amate,
  And eachone sought his Lady to aggrate: *please*
  And eke emongst them litle *Cupid* playd
  His wanton sports, being returned late
From his fierce warres, and hauing from him layd
His cruell bow, wherewith he thousands hath dismayd.

xxxv

Diuerse delights they found them selues to please;
  Some song in sweet consort, some laught for ioy,
  Some plaid with strawes, some idly sat at ease;
310   But other some could not abide to toy,
  All pleasaunce was to them griefe and annoy:
  This frownd, that faund, the third for shame did blush,
  Another seemed enuious, or coy,
  Another in her teeth did gnaw a rush:
But at these straungers presence euery one did hush.

xxxvi

Soone as the gracious *Alma* came in place,
  They all attonce out of their seates arose,
  And to her homage made, with humble grace:

---

9 The Esquiline gate in ancient Rome was the dump.

10 This suggests the art of memory tradition, a system of education that taught how to transform verbal texts into a series of mental images that could be easily remembered as a means of recalling the verbal material (see Frances Yates, *The Art of Memory*).

Whom when the knights beheld, they gan dispose
320   Themselues to court, and each a Damsell chose:
    The Prince by chaunce did on a Lady light,
    That was right faire and fresh as morning rose,
    But somwhat sad, and solemne eke in sight,
As if some pensiue thought constraind her gentle spright.

xxxvii

In a long purple pall, whose skirt with gold
    Was fretted all about, she was arayd;
    And in her hand a Poplar braunch did hold:
    To whom the Prince in curteous manner said;
    Gentle Madame, why beene ye thus dismaid,
330   And your faire beautie do with sadnesse spill?
    Liues any, that you hath thus ill apaid?
    Or doen you loue, or doen you lacke your will?
What euer be the cause, it sure beseemes you ill.

xxxviii

Faire Sir, (said she halfe in disdainefull wise,)
    How is it, that this mood in me ye blame,
    And in your selfe do not the same aduise?
    Him ill beseemes, anothers fault to name,
    That may vnwares be blotted with the same:
    Pensiue I yeeld I am, and sad in mind,[11]
340   Through great desire of glory and of fame;
    Ne ought I weene are ye therein behind,
That baue twelue moneths sought one, yet no where can her find.

xxxix

The Prince was inly moued at her speach,
    Well weeting trew, what she had rashly told;
    Yet with faire semblaunt sought to hide the breach,
    Which chaunge of colour did perforce vnfold,
    Now seeming flaming whot, now stony cold.
    Tho turning soft aside, he did inquire,
    What wight she was, that Poplar braunch did hold:
350   It answered was, her name was *Prays-desire*,[12]
That by well doing sought to honour to aspire.

xl

The whiles, the *Faerie* knight did entertaine
    Another Damsell of that gentle crew,
    That was right faire, and modest of demaine,
    But that too oft she chaung'd her natiue hew:
    Straunge was her tyre, and all her garment blew,
    Close round about her tuckt with many a plight: *pleat*
    Vpon her fist the bird, which shonneth vew,
    And keepes in couerts close from liuing wight,
360   Did sit, as yet ashamd, how rude *Pan* did her dight.

xli

So long as *Guyon* with her commoned,   *accompanied*
    Vnto the ground she cast her modest eye,
    And euer and anone with rosie red

---

11   This suggests the creative kind of melancholy that Dürer captures in his engraving *Melancholia I.*

12   She is the emanation of Arthur's desire for the highest form of glory, which is symbolized by the poplar, the tree sacred to Hercules.

The bashfull bloud her snowy cheekes did dye,
That her became, as polisht yuory,
Which cunning Craftesmans hand hath ouerlayd
With faire vermilion or pure Castory.   *red dye*
Great wonder had the knight, to see the mayd
So straungely passioned, and to her gently sayd,

xlii

370   Faire Damzell, seemeth, by your troubled cheare,
That either me too bold ye weene, this wise
You to molest, or other ill to feare
That in the secret of your hart close lyes,
From whence it doth, as cloud from sea arise.
If it be I, of pardon I you pray;
But if ought else that I mote not deuise,
I will, if please you it discure, assay,
To ease you of that ill, so wisely as I may.

xliii

She answerd nought, but more abasht for shame,
380   Held downe her head, the whiles her louely face
The flashing bloud with blushing did inflame,
And the strong passion mard her modest grace,
That *Guyon* meruayld at her vncouth cace:
Till *Alma* him bespake, Why wonder yee
Faire Sir at that, which ye so much embrace?
She is the fountaine of your modestee;
You shamefast are, but *Shamefastnesse* it selfe is shee.

xliv

Thereat the Elfe did blush in priuitee,
And turnd his face away; but she the same
390   Dissembled faire, and faynd to ouersee.
Thus they awhile with court and goodly game,
Themselues did solace each one with his Dame,
Till that great Ladie thence away them sought,
To vew her castles other wondrous frame.
Vp to a stately Turret she them brought,
Ascending by ten steps of Alablaster wrought.

xlv

That Turrets frame most admirable was,
Like highest heauen compassed around,
And lifted high aboue this earthly masse,
400   Which it suruew'd, as hils doen lower ground;
But not on ground mote like to this be found,
Not that, which antique *Cadmus* whylome built
In *Thebes*, which *Alexander* did confound;[13]
Nor that proud towre of *Troy*, though richly guilt,
From which young *Hectors* bloud by cruell *Greekes* was spilt.

xlvi

The roofe hereof was arched ouer head,
And deckt with flowers and herbars daintily;
Two goodly Beacons, set in watches stead,
Therein gaue light, and flam'd continually:

13   The story is told in Ovid, *Metamorphoses*, 3. 1–137.

410

For they of liuing fire most subtilly
    Were made, and set in siluer sockets bright,
    Couer'd with lids deuiz'd of substance sly,
    That readily they shut and open might.
O who can tell the prayses of that makers might!

xlvii

Ne can I tell, ne can I stay to tell
    This parts great workmanship, and wondrous powre,
    That all this other worlds worke doth excell,
    And likest is vnto that heauenly towre,
    That God hath built for his owne blessed bowre.
420   Therein were diuerse roomes, and diuerse stages,
    But three the chiefest, and of greatest powre,
    In which there dwelt three honorable sages,
The wisest men, I weene, that liued in their ages.[14]

xlviii

Not he, whom *Greece*, the Nourse of all good arts,
    By *Phœbus* doome, the wisest thought aliue,
    Might be compar'd to these by many parts:
    Nor that sage *Pylian* syre,[15] which did suruiue
    Three ages, such as mortall men contriue,
    By whose aduise old *Priams* cittie fell,
430   With these in praise of pollicies mote striue.
    These three in these three roomes did sundry dwell,
And counselled faire *Alma*, how to gouerne well.

xlix

The first of them could things to come foresee:
    The next could of things present best aduize;
    The third things past could keepe in memoree,
    So that no time, nor reason could arize,
    But that the same could one of these comprize.
    For thy the first did in the forepart sit,
    That nought mote hinder his quicke preiudize:
440   He had a sharpe foresight, and working wit,
That neuer idle was, ne once could rest a whit.

l

His chamber was dispainted all within,
    With sundry colours, in the which were writ
    Infinite shapes of things dispersed thin;
    Some such as in the world were neuer yit,
    Ne can deuized be of mortall wit;
    Some daily seene, and knowen by their names,
    Such as in idle fantasies doe flit:
    Infernall Hags, *Centaurs*, feendes, *Hippodames*,
450   Apes, Lions, Ægles, Owles, fooles, louers, children, Dames.

li

And all the chamber filled was with flyes,
    Which buzzed all about, and made such sound,
    That they encombred all mens eares and eyes,
    Like many swarmes of Bees assembled round,

14   Judgment mediates here between imagination and memory, each   15   Nestor of Pylos (*Iliad*, 1. 248).
representing one of the three stages of life.

After their hiues with honny do abound:
All those were idle thoughts and fantasies,
Deuices, dreames, opinions vnsound,
Shewes, visions, sooth-sayes, and prophesies;
And all that fained is, as leasings, tales, and lies.

lii

460
Emongst them all sate he, which wonned there,
That hight *Phantastes* by his nature trew;
A man of yeares yet fresh, as mote appere,
Of swarth complexion, and of crabbed hew,
That him full of melancholy did shew;[16]
Bent hollow beetle browes, sharpe staring eyes,
That mad or foolish seemd: one by his vew
Mote deeme him borne with ill disposed skyes,
When oblique *Saturne* sate in the house of agonyes.

liii

470
Whom *Alma* hauing shewed to her guestes,
Thence brought them to the second roome, whose wals
Were painted faire with memorable gestes,
Of famous Wisards, and with picturals
Of Magistrates, of courts, of tribunals,
Of commen wealthes, of states, of pollicy,
Of lawes, of iudgements, and of decretals;
All artes, all science, all Philosophy,
And all that in the world was aye thought wittily.

liv

480
Of those that roome was full, and them among
There sate a man of ripe and perfect age,
Who did them meditate all his life long,
That through continuall practise and vsage,
He now was growne right wise, and wondrous sage.
Great pleasure had those stranger knights, to see
His goodly reason, and graue personage,
That his disciples both desir'd to bee;
But *Alma* thence them led to th'hindmost roome of three.

lv

490
That chamber seemed ruinous and old,
And therefore was remoued farre behind,
Yet were the wals, that did the same vphold,
Right firme and strong, though somewhat they declind;
And therein sate an old oldman, halfe blind,
And all decrepit in his feeble corse,
Yet liuely vigour rested in his mind,
And recompenst him with a better scorse:
Weake body well is chang'd for minds redoubled forse.

lvi

This man of infinite remembrance was,
And things foregone through many ages held,
Which he recorded still, as they did pas,

---

16   Phantastes' melancholy seems to turn toward despair, unlike
Praise-desire's (see E. Panofsky and F. Saxl's *Melancholia*).

500

Ne suffred them to perish through long eld,
As all things else, the which this world doth weld,
But laid them vp in his immortall scrine,   *scroll*
Where they for euer incorrupted dweld:
The warres he well remembred of king *Nine*,
Of old *Assaracus*, and *Inachus* diuine.[17]

lvii

The yeares of *Nestor* nothing were to his,
Ne yet *Mathusalem*, though longest liu'd;
For he remembred both their infancies:
Ne wonder then, if that he were depriu'd
Of natiue strength now, that he them suruiu'd.
510   His chamber all was hangd about with rolles,
And old records from auncient times deriu'd,
Some made in books, some in long parchment scrolles,
That were all worme-eaten, and full of canker holes.

lviii

Amidst them all he in a chaire was set,
Tossing and turning them withouten end;
But for he was vnhable them to fet,
A litle boy did on him still attend,
To reach, when euer he for ought did send;
And oft when things were lost, or laid amis,
520   That boy them sought, and vnto him did lend.
Therefore he *Anamnestes* cleped is,
And that old man *Eumnestes*, by their propertis.

lix

The knights there entring, did him reuerence dew
And wondred at his endlesse exercise,
Then as they gan his Librarie to vew,
And antique Registers for to auise,
There chaunced to the Princes hand to rize,
An auncient booke, hight *Briton moniments*,
That of this lands first conquest did deuize,
530   And old diuision into Regiments,
Till it reduced was to one mans gouernments.

lx

Sir *Guyon* chaunst eke on another booke,
That hight *Antiquitie* of *Faerie* lond,
In which when as he greedily did looke,
Th'off-spring of Elues and Faries there he fond,
As it deliuered was from hond to hond:
Whereat they burning both with feruent fire,
Their countries auncestry to vnderstond,
Crau'd leaue of *Alma*, ard that aged sire,
540   To read those bookes; who gladly graunted their desire.

17   The point of these names is their antiquity: Ninus of Babylon,
Assaracus of Troy. Inachus was a river god and father of Io, who was
raped by Zeus.

Cant. X.

A chronicle of Briton kings,
from Brute to Vthers rayne.[1]
And rolles of Elfin Emperours,
till time of Gloriane.

i

Who now shall giue vnto me words and sound,
    Equall vnto this haughtie enterprise?
Or who shall lend me wings, with which from ground
    My lowly verse may loftily arise,
    And lift it selfe vnto the highest skies?
    More ample spirit, then hitherto was wount,
    Here needes me, whiles the famous auncestries
    Of my most dreaded Soueraigne I recount,
By which all earthly Princes she doth farre surmount.

ii

10   Ne vnder Sunne, that shines so wide and faire,
    Whence all that liues, does borrow life and light,
    Liues ought, that to her linage may compaire,
    Which though from earth it be deriued right,
    Yet doth it selfe stretch forth to heauens hight,
    And all the world with wonder ouerspred;
    A labour huge, exceeding farre my might:
    How shall fraile pen, with feare disparaged,
Conceiue such soueraine glory, and great bountihed?   *virtue*

iii

Argument worthy of *Mæonian* quill,[2]
20   Or rather worthy of great *Phœbus* rote,   *harp*
    Whereon the ruines of great *Ossa* hill,[3]
    And triumphes of *Phlegræan Ioue*[4] he wrote,   *Jove*
    That all the Gods admird his loftie note.
    But if some relish of that heauenly lay
    His learned daughters[5] would to me report,
    To decke my song withall, I would assay,
Thy name, O soueraine Queene, to blazon farre away.

iv

Thy name O soueraine Queene, thy realme and race,
    From this renowmed Prince[6] deriued arre,
30   Who mightily vpheld that royall mace,
    Which now thou bear'st, to thee descended farre
    From mightie kings and conquerours in warre,
    Thy fathers and great Grandfathers of old,
    Whose noble deedes aboue the Northerne starre
    Immortall fame for euer hath enrold;
As in that old mans booke they were in order told.

CANT. X.

1   Brute was the legendary founder of Britain, and Uther was Arthur's father. Spenser's source for this mythological chronicle is a mixture of Geoffrey of Monmouth's *Historia Regum Britanniae*, *The Mirror for Magistrates*, Raphael Holinshed's *Chronicles*, and John Stow's *Chronicles of England*. Guyon's reading of the *Antiquity of Fairyland* is more important than the accuracy of its narrative or that of Spenser's sources. The emergence of law and civilization out of chaos and barbarism, made possible by the leadership of a national hero, is the key lesson Guyon learns here.

2   Possibly the plectrum that Homer used in playing his lyre.

3   The mountain used by the giants in their effort to reach Mt. Olympus.

4   "Phlegraean" recalls Jove's triumph over the giants at Phlegra.

5   The muses.

6   Arthur.

v

The land, which warlike Britons now possesse,
  And therein haue their mightie empire raysd,
  In antique times was saluage wildernesse,
  Vnpeopled, vnmanurd, vnprou'd, vnpraysd,
  Ne was it Island then, ne was it paysd   *poised*
  Amid the *Ocean* waues, ne was it sought
  Of marchants farre, for profits therein praysd,
  But was all desolate, and of some thought
By sea to haue bene from the *Celticke* mayn-land brought.

vi

Ne did it then deserue a name to haue,
  Till that the venturous Mariner that way
  Learning his ship from those white rocks to saue,
  Which all along the Southerne sea-coast lay,
  Threatning vnheedie wrecke and rash decay,
  For safeties sake that same his sea-marke made,
  And namd it *Albion.* But later day
  Finding in it fit ports for fishers trade,
Gan more the same frequent, and further to inuade.

vii

But farre in land a saluage nation dwelt,
  Of hideous Giants, and halfe beastly men,
  That neuer tasted grace, nor goodnesse felt,
  But like wild beasts lurking in loathsome den,
  And flying fast as Roebucke through the fen,
  All naked without shame, or care of cold,
  By hunting and by spoiling liued then;
  Of stature huge, and eke of courage bold,
That sonnes of men amazd their sternnesse to behold,

viii

But whence they sprong, or how they were begot,
  Vneath is to assure; vneath to wene   *impossible*
  That monstrous error, which doth some assot,
  That *Dioclesians* fiftie daughters[7] shene   *beautiful*
  Into this land by chaunce haue driuen bene,
  Where companing with feends and filthy Sprights,
  Through vaine illusion of their lust vnclene,
  They brought forth Giants and such dreadfull wights,
As farre exceeded men in their immeasurd mights.

ix

They held this land, and with their filthinesse
  Polluted this same gentle soyle long time:
  That their owne mother loathd their beastlinesse,
  And gan abhorre her broods vnkindly crime,
  All were they borne of her owne natiue slime,
  Vntill that *Brutus* anciently deriu'd
  From royall stocke of old *Assaracs*[8] line,

40

50

60

70

7 Dioclesian, king of Syria, had 33 daughters who, by conflation with the Greek Danaides, were thought to be the mothers of the legendary giants of Britain. Throughout this mythic history, Spenser is appropriating classical materials to enhance the ancient history of Britain.

8 Assaracus, the founder of the Trojan dynasty and great-grandfather of Aeneas.

80
 Driuen by fatall error, here arriu'd,
 And them of their vniust possession depriu'd.

x

But ere he had established his throne,
 And spred his empire to the vtmost shore,
 He fought great battels with his saluage fone;   *foes*
 In which he them defeated euermore,
 And many Giants left on groning flore;
 That well can witnesse yet vnto this day
 The westerne Hogh,[9] besprincled with the gore   *Hoe*
 Of mightie *Goëmot*, whom in stout fray
90 *Corineus* conquered, and cruelly did slay.

xi

And eke that ample Pit, yet farre renownd,
 For the large leape, which *Debon*[10] did compell
 Coulin to make, being eight lugs of grownd;   *rods*
 Into the which returning backe, he fell,
 But those three monstrous stones doe most excell
 Which that huge sonne of hideous *Albion*,
 Whose father *Hercules* in Fraunce did quell,
 Great *Godmer* threw, in fierce contention,
At bold *Canutus*; but of him was slaine anon.

xii

100
In meed of these great conquests by them got,
 Corineus had that Prouince vtmost west,
 To him assigned for his worthy lot,
 Which of his name and memorable gest   *deeds*
 He called *Cornewaile*, yet so called best:
 And *Debons* shayre was, that is *Deuonshyre*:
 But *Canute* had his portion from the rest,
 The which he cald *Canutium*, for his hyre;   *reward*
Now *Cantium*, which Kent we commenly inquire.

xiii

110
Thus *Brute* this Realme vnto his rule subdewd,
 And raigned long in great felicitie,
 Lou'd of his friends, and of his foes eschewd,
 He left three sonnes, his famous progeny,
 Borne of faire *Inogene* of *Italy*;
 Mongst whom he parted his imperiall state,
 And *Locrine* left chiefe Lord of *Britany*.[11]
 At last ripe age bad him surrender late
His life, and long good fortune vnto finall fate.

xiv

Locrine was left the soueraine Lord of all;
 But *Albanact* had all the Northrene part,
120 Which of himselfe *Albania* he did call;
 And *Camber* did possesse the Westerne quart,
 Which *Seuerne* now from *Logris* doth depart:
 And each his portion peaceably enioyd,

---

9 The hill at Plymouth where, according to legend, Corineus slew the giant Gogmagog.

10 Spenser's sources for Debon, Coulin, Cantus, and Godmer are yet to be found.

11 Based on Geoffrey's account (2. 1–6).

Ne was there outward breach, nor grudge in hart,
That once their quiet gouernment annoyd,
But each his paines to others profit still employd.

xv

Vntill a nation straung,[12] with visage swart,
  And courage fierce, that all men did affray,
  Which through the world then swarmd in euery part,
130 And ouerflow'd all countries farre away,
  Like *Noyes* great flood, with their importune sway,
  This land inuaded with like violence,
  And did themselues through all the North display:
  Vntill that *Locrine* for his Realmes defence,
Did head against them make, and strong munifience.   *fortification*

xvi

He them encountred, a confused rout,
  Foreby the Riuer, that whylome was hight
  The auncient *Abus*, where with courage stout
  He them defeated in victorious fight,
140 And chaste so fiercely after fearfull flight,
  That forst their Chieftaine, for his safeties sake,
  (Their Chieftaine *Humber* named was aright)
  Vnto the mightie streame him to betake,
Where he an end of battell, and of life did make.

xvii

The king returned proud of victorie,
  And insolent wox through vnwonted ease,   *became*
  That shortly he forgot the ieopardie,
  Which in his land he lately did appease,
  And fell to vaine voluptuous disease:
150 He lou'd faire Ladie *Estrild*, lewdly lou'd,
  Whose wanton pleasures him too much did please,
  That quite his hart from *Guendolene* remou'd,
From *Guendolene* his wife, though alwaies faithfull prou'd.

xviii

The noble daughter of *Corineus*
  Would not endure to be so vile disdaind,
  But gathering force, and courage valorous,
  Encountred him in battell well ordaind,
  In which him vanquisht she to fly constraind:
  But she so fast pursewd, that him she tooke,
160 And threw in bands, where he till death remaind;
  Als his faire Leman, flying through a brooke,
She ouerhent, nought moued with her piteous looke.   *overtook*

xix

But both her selfe, and eke her daughter deare,
  Begotten by her kingly Paramoure,
  The faire *Sabrina* almost dead with feare,
  She there attached, farre from all succoure;
  The one she slew in that impatient stoure,   *battle*
  But the sad virgin innocent of all,

12 Huns.

Adowne the rolling riuer she did poure,
Which of her name now *Seuerne* men do call:
Such was the end, that to disloyall loue did fall.

xx

Then for her sonne, which she to *Locrin* bore,
Madan was young, vnmeet the rule to sway,
In her owne hand the crowne she kept in store,
Till ryper yeares he raught, and stronger stay: reached
During which time her powre she did display
Through all this realme, the glorie of her sex,[13]
And first taught men a woman to obay:
But when her sonne to mans estate did wex,   grow
She it surrendred, ne her selfe would lenger vex.

xxi

Tho *Madan* raignd, vnworthie of his race: then
For with all shame that sacred throne he fild:
Next *Memprise*, as vnworthy of that place,
In which being consorted with *Manild*,
For thirst of single kingdome him he kild.
But *Ebranck* salued both their infamies[14]
With noble deedes, and warreyd on *Brunchild*
In *Henault*, where yet of his victories
Braue moniments remaine, which yet that land enuies.

xxii

An happie man in his first dayes he was,
And happie father of faire progeny:
For all so many weekes as the yeare has,
So many children he did multiply;
Of which were twentie sonnes, which did apply
Their minds to praise, and cheualrous desire:
Those germans did subdew all Germany,   brothers
Of whom it hight; but in the end their Sire
With foule repulse from Fraunce was forced to retire.

xxiii

Which blot his sonne succeeding in his seat,
The second *Brute*, the second both in name,
And eke in semblance of his puissance great,
Right well recur'd, and did away that blame
With recompence of euerlasting fame.
He with his victour sword first opened
The bowels of wide *Fraunce*, a forlorne Dame,
And taught her first how to be conquered;
Since which, with sundrie spoiles she hath beene ransacked.

xxiv

Let *Scaldis* tell, and let tell *Hania*,[15]
And let the marsh of *Estham bruges* tell,
What colour were their waters that same day,
And all the moore twixt *Eluersham* and *Dell*,
With bloud of *Henalois*, which therein fell.
How oft that day did sad *Brunchildis* see

13 As such, Gwendolen is a type of Elizabeth.
14 Based on Stow's *Chronicles*.

15 The locations here are based on Stow.

The greene shield dyde in dolorous vermell?
That not *Scuith guiridh* it mote seeme to bee,   *green shield*
But rather *y Scuith gogh*, signe of sad crueltee.   *red shield*

xxv

His sonne king *Leill* by fathers labour long,
  Enioyd an heritage of lasting peace,
And built *Cairleill*, and built *Cairleon* strong.   *Carlisle, Chester*
220   Next *Huddibras* his realme did not encrease,[16]
  But taught the land from wearie warres to cease,
  Whose footsteps *Bladud* following, in arts
  Exceld at *Athens* all the learned preace,
    From whence he brought them to these saluage parts,
And with sweet science mollifide their stubborne harts.

xxvi

Ensample of his wondrous faculty,
  Behold the boyling Bathes at *Cairbadon*,
  Which seeth with secret fire eternally,
  And in their entrails, full of quicke Brimston,
230   Nourish the flames, which they are warm'd vpon,
  That to their people wealth they forth do well,
  And health to euery forreine nation:
    Yet he at last contending to excell
The reach of men, through flight into fond mischief fell.

xxvii

Next him king *Leyr* in happie peace long raind,[17]
  But had no issue male him to succeed,
  But three faire daughters, which were well vptraind,
  In all that seemed fit for kingly seed:
  Mongst whom his realme he equally decreed
240   To haue diuided. Tho when feeble age
  Nigh to his vtmost date he saw proceed,
    He cald his daughters; and with speeches sage
Inquyrd, which of them most did loue her parentage.

xxviii

The eldest *Gonorill* gan to protest,
  That she much more then her owne life him lou'd:
  And *Regan* greater loue to him profest,
  Then all the world, when euer it were proou'd;
  But *Cordeill* said she lou'd him, as behoou'd:
  Whose simple answere, wanting colours faire
250   To paint it forth, him to displeasance moou'd,
    That in his crowne he counted her no haire,
But twixt the other twaine his kingdome whole did shaire.

xxix

So wedded th'one to *Maglan* king of Scots,
  And th'other to the king of *Cambria*,   *Wales*
  And twixt them shayrd his realme by equall lots:
  But without dowre the wise *Cordelia*
  Was sent to *Aganip* of *Celtica*.   *France*
  Their aged Syre, thus eased of his crowne,

16 Based on Geoffrey.   17 Based on Geoffrey, 2. 11–14; this is one of the sources for
Shakespeare's *King Lear*.

A priuate life led in *Albania*,   *Scotland*
260   With *Gonorill*, long had in great renowne,
That nought him grieu'd to bene from rule deposed downe.

xxx

But true it is, that when the oyle is spent,
    The light goes out, and weeke is throwne away;
So when he had resigned his regiment,
His daughter gan despise his drouping day,
And wearie waxe of his continuall stay.
Tho to his daughter *Regan* he repayrd,
Who him at first well vsed euery way;
But when of his departure she despayrd,
270   Her bountie she abated, and his cheare empayrd.

xxxi

The wretched man gan then auise too late,   *perceive*
    That loue is not, where most it is profest,
Too truely tryde in his extreamest state;
At last resolu'd likewise to proue the rest,
He to *Cordelia* him selfe addrest,
Who with entire affection him receau'd,
As for her Syre and king her seemed best;
And after all an army strong she leau'd,
To war on those, which him had of his realme bereau'd.   *stolen*

xxxii

280   So to his crowne she him restor'd againe,
    In which he dyde, made ripe for death by eld,
    And after wild, it should to her remaine:
    Who peaceably the same long time did weld: *govern*
    And all mens harts in dew obedience held:
    Till that her sisters children, woxen strong
    Through proud ambition, against her rebeld,
    And ouercommen kept in prison long,
Till wearie of that wretched life, her selfe she hong.

xxxiii

Then gan the bloudie brethren both to raine:
290   But fierce *Cundah* gan shortly to enuie
    His brother *Morgan*, prickt with proud disdaine,
    To haue a pere in part of soueraintie,
    And kindling coles of cruell enmitie,
    Raisd warre, and him in battell ouerthrew:
    Whence as he to those woodie hils did flie,
    Which hight of him *Glamorgan*, there him slew:
Then did he raigne alone, when he none equall knew.

xxxiv

His sonne *Riuallo* his dead roome did supply,[18]
    In whose sad time bloud did from heauen raine:
300   Next great *Gurgustus*, then faire *Cæcily*
    In constant peace their kingdomes did containe,
    After whom *Lago*, and *Kinmarke* did raine,
    And *Gorbogud*, till farre in yeares he grew:

18   The following two stanzas are based on Geoffrey.

Then his ambitious sonnes vnto them twaine
  Arraught the rule, and from their father drew,
Stout *Ferrex* and sterne *Porrex* him in prison threw.

xxxv

But O, the greedy thirst of royall crowne,
  That knowes no kinred, nor regardes no right,
  Stird *Porrex* vp to put his brother downe;
  Who vnto him assembling forreine might,
  Made warre on him, and fell him selfe in fight:
  Whose death t'auenge, his mother mercilesse,
  Most mercilesse of women, *Wyden* hight,
  Her other sonne fast sleeping did oppresse,
And with most cruell hand him murdred pittilesse.

xxxvi

Here ended *Brutus* sacred progenie,
  Which had seuen hundred yeares this scepter borne,
  With high renowme, and great felicitie;
  The noble braunch from th'antique stocke was torne
  Through discord, and the royall throne forlorne:
  Thenceforth this Realme was into factions rent,
  Whilest each of *Brutus* boasted to be borne,
  That in the end was left no moniment
Of *Brutus*, nor of Britons glory auncient.

xxxvii

Then vp arose a man of matchlesse might,[19]
  And wondrous wit to menage high affaires,
  Who stird with pitty of the stressed plight
  Of this sad Realme, cut into sundry shaires
  By such, as claymd themselues *Brutes* rightfull haires,
  Gathered the Princes of the people loose,
  To taken counsell of their common cares;
  Who with his wisedom won, him streight did choose
Their king, and swore him fealty to win or loose.

xxxviii

Then made he head against his enimies,
  And *Ymner* slew, of *Logris* miscreate;   *England*
  Then *Ruddoc* and proud *Stater*, both allyes,
  This of *Albanie* newly nominate,   *Scotland*
  And that of *Cambry* king confirmed late,   *Wales*
  He ouerthrew through his owne valiaunce;
  Whose countreis he redus'd to quiet state,
  And shortly brought to ciuill gouernaunce,
Now one, which earst were many, made through variaunce.

xxxix

Then made he sacred lawes, which some men say
  Were vnto him reueald in vision,
  By which he freed the Traueilers high way,
  The Churches part, and Ploughmans portion,
  Restraining stealth, and strong extortion;

19   The age of Dunwallo, the lawgiver, introduces a period of civilized
order. The messianic sense here is partly derived from Virgil's *Aeneid*, 1.
276–306.

The gracious *Numa* of great *Britanie*:[20]
For till his dayes, the chiefe dominion
By strength was wielded without pollicie;
Therefore he first wore crowne of gold for dignitie.

350

xl

Donwallo dyde (for what may liue for ay?)
And left two sonnes, of pearelesse prowesse both;
That sacked *Rome* too dearely did assay,
The recompence of their periured oth,
And ransackt *Greece* well tryde, when they were wroth;
Besides subiected *Fraunce*, and *Germany*,
Which yet their prayses speake, all be they loth,
And inly tremble at the memory
Of *Brennus* and *Bellinus*, kings of Britany.

360

xli

Next them did *Gurgunt*, great *Bellinus* sonne
In rule succeede, and eke in fathers prayse;
He Easterland subdewd, and Danmarke wonne,   *Austria (?)*
And of them both did foy and tribute raise,   *allegiance*
The which was dew in his dead fathers dayes:
He also gaue to fugitiues of *Spayne*,
Whom he at sea found wandring from their wayes,
A seate in *Ireland* safely to remayne,
Which they should hold of him, as subiect to *Britayne*.

xlii

After him raigned *Guitheline* his hayre,
The iustest man and trewest in his dayes,
Who had to wife Dame *Mertia* the fayre,
A woman worthy of immortall prayse,
Which for this Realme found many goodly layes,   *laws*
And wholesome Statutes to her husband brought;
Her many deemd to haue beene of the *Fayes*,
As was *Aegerie*, that *Numa* tought;
Those yet of her be *Mertian* lawes both nam'd and thought.

370

xliii

Her sonne *Sisillus* after her did rayne,
And then *Kimarus*, and then *Danius*;
Next whom *Morindus* did the crowne sustaine,
Who, had he not with wrath outrageous,
And cruell rancour dim'd his valorous
And mightie deeds, should matched haue the best:
As well in that same field victorious
Against the forreine *Morands* he exprest;
Yet liues his memorie, though carcas sleepe in rest.

380

xliv

Fiue sonnes he left begotten of one wife,
All which successiuely by turnes did raine;
First *Gorboman* a man of vertuous life;
Next *Archigald*, who for his proud disdaine,
Deposed was from Princedome soueraine,

390

<hr>

20 Numa Pompilus, Romulus' successor, established the foundation
for Roman legal and religious institutions, according to Livy.

And pitteous *Elidure* put in his sted;
  Who shortly it to him restord againe,
  Till by his death he it recouered;
But *Peridure* and *Vigent* him disthronized.

xlv

In wretched prison long he did remaine,
  Till they outraigned had their vtmost date,
  And then therein reseized was againe,
  And ruled long with honorable state,
  Till he surrendred Realme and life to fate.
  Then all the sonnes of these fiue brethren raynd
  By dew successe, and all their Nephewes late,
  Euen thrise eleuen descents the crowne retaynd,
Till aged *Hely* by dew heritage it gaynd.

xlvi

He had two sonnes, whose eldest called *Lud*
  Left of his life most famous memory,
  And endlesse moniments of his great good:
  The ruin'd wals he did reædifye
  Of *Troynouant*, gainst force of enimy,   *London*
  And built that gate, which of his name is hight,
  By which he lyes entombed solemnly.
  He left two sonnes, too young to rule aright,
Androgeus and *Tenantius*, pictures of his might.

xlvii

Whilst they were young, *Cassibalane* their Eme   *Uncle*
  Was by the people chosen in their sted,
  Who on him tooke the royall Diademe,
  And goodly well long time it gouerned,
  Till the prowd *Romanes* him disquieted,
  And warlike *Cæsar*, tempted with the name
  Of this sweet Island, neuer conquered,
  And enuying the Britons blazed fame,
(O hideous hunger of dominion) hither came.

xlviii

Yet twise they were repulsed backe againe,
  And twise renforst, backe to their ships to fly,
  The whiles with bloud they all the shore did staine,
  And the gray *Ocean* into purple dy:
  Ne had they footing found at last perdie,   *in fact*
  Had not *Androgeus*, false to natiue soyle,
  And enuious of Vncles soueraintie,
  Betrayd his contrey vnto forreine spoyle:
Nought else, but treason, from the first this land did foyle.

xlix

So by him *Cæsar* got the victory,
  Through great bloudshed, and many a sad assay,
  In which him selfe was charged heauily
  Of hardy *Nennius*, whom he yet did slay,
  But lost his sword, yet to be seene this day.
  Thenceforth this land was tributarie made
  T'ambitious *Rome*, and did their rule obay,
  Till *Arthur* all that reckoning defrayd;
Yet oft the Briton kings against them strongly swayd.

400

410

420

430

440

l

Next him *Tenantius* raigned, then *Kimbeline*,
 What time th'eternall Lord in fleshly slime
 Enwombed was, from wretched *Adams* line
 To purge away the guilt of sinfull crime:
 O ioyous memorie of happy time,
 That heauenly grace so plenteously displayd;
 (O too high ditty for my simple rime.)
 Soone after this the *Romanes* him warrayd;
450 For that their tribute he refusd to let be payd.

li

Good *Claudius*, that next was Emperour,
 An army brought, and with him battell fought,
 In which the king was by a Treachetour   *traitor*
 Disguised slaine, ere any thereof thought:
 Yet ceased not the bloudy fight for ought;
 For *Aruirage* his brothers place supplide,
 Both in his armes, and crowne, and by that draught
 Did driue the *Romanes* to the weaker side,
That they to peace agreed.   So all was pacifide.

lii

460 Was neuer king more highly magnifide,
 Nor dred of *Romanes*, then was *Aruirage*,
 For which the Emperour to him allide
 His daughter *Genuiss'* in marriage:
 Yet shortly he renounst the vassalage
 Of *Rome* againe, who hither hastly sent
 Vespasian, that with great spoile and rage
 Forwasted all, till *Genuissa* gent   *noble*
Perswaded him to ceasse, and her Lord to relent.

liii

He dyde; and him succeeded *Marius*,
470 Who ioyd his dayes in great tranquillity,
 Then *Coyll*, and after him good *Lucius*,
 That first receiued Christianitie,
 The sacred pledge of Christes Euangely;   *gospel*
 Yet true it is, that long before that day
 Hither came *Ioseph* of *Arimathy*,[21]   *Arimathea*
 Who brought with him the holy grayle, (they say)
And preacht the truth, but since it greatly did decay.

liv

This good king shortly without issew dide,
 Whereof great trouble in the kingdome grew,
480 That did her selfe in sundry parts diuide,
 And with her powre her owne selfe ouerthrew,
 Whilest *Romanes* dayly did the weake subdew:
 Which seeing stout *Bunduca*, vp arose,[22]   *Boadicea*
 And taking armes, the *Britons* to her drew;
 With whom she marched streight against her foes,
And them vnwares besides the *Seuerne* did enclose.

---

21   Joseph of Arimathea is associated with the Holy Grail in legend but not in the chronicles.

22   As a powerful female warrior and ruler, famous in both history and in legend, Boadicea is a type of Elizabeth. Boadicea's story appears in Tacitus' *Agricola*, 16, not in Geoffrey.

lv

There she with them a cruell battell tride,
　　Not with so good successe, as she deseru'd;
　　By reason that the Captaines on her side,
490　　Corrupted by *Paulinus*, from her sweru'd:[23]
　　Yet such, as were through former flight preseru'd,
　　Gathering againe, her Host she did renew,
　　And with fresh courage on the victour seru'd:
　　But being all defeated, saue a few,
Rather then fly, or be captiu'd her selfe she slew.

lvi

O famous morniment of womens prayse,[24]
　　Matchable either to *Semiramis*,
　　Whom antique history so high doth raise,
　　Or to *Hypsiphil'* or to *Thomiris*:
500　　Her Host two hundred thousand numbred is;
　　Who whiles good fortune fauoured her might,
　　Triumphed oft against her enimis;
　　And yet though ouercome in haplesse fight,
She triumphed on death, in enemies despight.

lvii

Her reliques *Fulgent* hauing gathered,
　　Fought with *Seuerus*, and him ouerthrew;
　　Yet in the chace was slaine of them, that fled:
　　So made them victours, whom he did subdew.
　　Then gan *Carausius* tirannize anew,
510　　And gainst the *Romanes* bent their proper powre,
　　But him *Allectus* treacherously slew,
　　And took on him the robe of Emperoure:
Nath'lesse the same enjoyed but short happy howre:

lviii

For *Asclepiodate* him ouercame,
　　And left inglorious on the vanquisht playne,
　　Without or robe, or rag, to hide his shame.
　　Then afterwards he in his stead did rayne;
　　But shortly was by *Coyll* in battell slaine:
　　Who after long debate, since *Lucies* time,
520　　Was of the *Britons* first crownd Soueraine:
　　Then gan this Realme renewe her passed prime:
He of his name *Coylchester* built of stone and lime.

lix

Which when the *Romanes* heard, they hither sent
　　Constantius, a man of mickle might,
　　With whom king *Coyll* made an agreement,
　　And to him gaue for wife his daughter bright,
　　Faire *Helena*, the fairest liuing wight;
　　Who in all godly thewes, and goodly prayse　　　　　　　　*qualities*
　　Did far excell, but was most famous hight
530　　For skill in Musicke of all in her dayes,
Aswell in curious instruments, as cunning layes.

23　See Tacitus, *Agricola*, 16.
24　There is a distinct instability of reference here to powerful women of the past: Semiramis, legendary queen of Babylon, was celebrated for her sexual power as much as for her military might; Hysipyle and Tomyris are female rulers who rose to power through treachery. Perhaps the epithet "stout Bunduca" (54.6) implies that a woman cannot be both beautiful and powerful – at least not until Elizabeth.

lx

Of whom he did great *Constantine*[25] beget,
　Who afterward was Emperour of *Rome*;
　To which whiles absent he his mind did set,
　Octauius here lept into his roome,
　And it vsurped by vnrighteous doome:
　But he his title iustifide by might,
　Slaying *Traherne*, and hauing ouercome
　The *Romane* legion in dreadfull fight:
540　So settled he his kingdome, and confirmd his right.

lxi

But wanting issew male, his daughter deare
　He gaue in wedlocke to *Maximian*,
　And him with her made of his kingdome heyre,
　Who soone by meanes thereof the Empire wan,
　Till murdred by the friends of *Gratian*;
　Then gan the Hunnes and Picts inuade this land,
　During the raigne of *Maximinian*;
　Who dying left none heire them to withstand,
But that they ouerran all parts with easie hand.

lxii

550　The weary *Britons*, whose war-hable youth
　Was by *Maximian* lately led away,
　With wretched miseries, and woefull ruth,
　Were to those Pagans made an open pray,
　And dayly spectacle of sad decay:
　Whom *Romane* warres, which now foure hundred yeares,
　And more had wasted, could no whit dismay;
　Till by consent of Commons and of Peares,
They crownd the second *Constantine* with ioyous teares,

lxiii

Who hauing oft in battell vanquished
560　Those spoilefull Picts, and swarming Easterlings,
　Long time in peace his Realme established,
　Yet oft annoyd with sundry bordragings　　　　　　　　　*raids*
　Of neighbour Scots, and forrein Scatterlings,
　With which the world did in those dayes abound:
　Which to outbarre, with painefull pyonings　　　　　　　*digging*
　From sea to sea he heapt a mightie mound,
Which from *Alcluid* to *Panwelt* did that border bound.

lxiv

Three sonnes he dying left, all vnder age;
　By meanes whereof, their vncle *Vortigere*
570　Vsurpt the crowne, during their pupillage;
　Which th'Infants tutors gathering to feare,
　Them closely into *Armorick* did beare:　　　　　　　　　*Brittany*
　For dread of whom, and for those Picts annoyes,
　He sent to *Germanie*, straunge aid to reare,
　From whence eftsoones arriued here three hoyes　　　　　*ships*
Of *Saxons*, whom he for his safetie imployes.

25　As joint ruler of Rome and Britain, Constantine united the two
civilizations (see Geoffrey, 5. 7–8).

lxv

Two brethren were their Capitains, which hight
Hengist and *Horsus*, well approu'd in warre,
And both of them men of renowmed might;
580   Who making vantage of their ciuill iarre,
And of those forreiners, which came from farre,
Grew great, and got large portions of land,
That in the Realme ere long they stronger arre,
Then they which sought at first their helping hand,
And *Vortiger* enforst the kingdome to aband.

lxvi

But by the helpe of *Vortimere* his sonne,
He is againe vnto his rule restord,
And *Hengist* seeming sad, for that was donne,
Receiued is to grace and new accord,
590   Through his faire daughters face, and flattring word;
Soone after which, three hundred Lordes he slew
Of British bloud, all sitting at his bord;
Whose dolefull moniments who list to rew,
Th'eternall markes of treason may at *Stonheng* vew.

lxvii

By this the sonnes of *Constantine*, which fled,
Ambrose and *Vther* did ripe years attaine,
And here arriuing, strongly challenged
The crowne, which *Vortiger* did long detaine:
Who flying from his guilt, by them was slaine,
600   And *Hengist* eke soone brought to shamefull death.
Thenceforth *Aurelius* peaceably did rayne,
Till that through poyson stopped was his breath;
So now entombed lyes at Stoneheng by the heath.

lxviii

After him *Vther*, which *Pendragon* hight,
Succeding There abruptly it did end,
Without full point, or other Cesure right,
As if the rest some wicked hand did rend,
Or th'Authour selfe could not at least attend
To finish it: that so vntimely breach
610   The Prince him selfe halfe seemeth to offend,
Yet secret pleasure did offence empeach,
And wonder of antiquitie long stopt his speach.

lxix

At last quite rauisht with delight, to heare
The royall Ofspring of his natiue land,
Cryde out, Deare countrey, O how dearely deare
Ought thy remembraunce, and perpetuall band
Be to thy foster Childe, that from thy hand
Did commun breath and nouriture receaue?   *nurture*
How brutish is it not to vnderstand,
620   How much to her we owe, that all vs gaue,
That gaue vnto vs all, what euer good we haue.

lxx

But *Guyon* all this while his booke did read,
Ne yet has ended: for it was a great
And ample volume, that doth far excead

My leasure, so long leaues here to repeat:
It told, how first *Prometheus* did create
A man, of many partes from beasts deriued,[26]
And then stole fire from heauen, to animate
His worke, for which he was by *Ioue* depriued

630   Of life him selfe, and hart-strings of an Ægle riued.   *torn*

lxxi

That man so made, he called *Elfe*, to weet   *to wit*
    Quick, the first authour of all Elfin kind:
    Who wandring through the world with wearie feet,
    Did in the gardins of *Adonis* find
    A goodly creature, whom he deemd in mind
    To be no earthly wight, but either Spright,
    Or Angell, th'authour of all woman kind;
    Therefore a *Fay* he her according hight,
Of whom all *Faeryes* spring, and fetch their lignage right.

lxxii

640   Of these a mightie people shortly grew,
    And puissaunt kings, which all the world warrayd,
    And to them selues all Nations did subdew:
    The first and eldest, which that scepter swayd,
    Was *Elfin*; him all *India* obayd,
    And all that now *America* men call:
    Next him was noble *Elfinan*, who layd
    Cleopolis foundation first of all: *London's*
But *Elfiline* enclosd it with a golden wall.

lxxiii

His sonne was *Elfinell*, who ouercame
650   The wicked *Gobbelines* in bloudy field:
    But *Elfant* was of most renowmed fame,
    Who all of Christall did *Panthea* build:
    Then *Elfar*, who two brethren gyants kild,
    The one of which had two heads, th'other three:
    Then *Elfinor*, who was in Magick skild;
    He built by art vpon the glassy See
A bridge of bras, whose sound heauens thunder seem'd to bee.

lxxiv

He left three sonnes, the which in order raynd,
    And all their Ofspring, in their dew descents,
660   Euen seuen hundred Princes, which maintaynd
    With mightie deedes their sundry gouernments;
    That were too long their infinite contents
    Here to record, ne much materiall:
    Yet should they be most famous moniments,
    And braue ensample, both of martiall,
And ciuill rule to kings and states imperiall.

lxxv

After all these *Elficleos* did rayne,[27]
    The wise *Elficleos* in great Maiestie,
    Who mightily that scepter did sustayne,

26 According to Natalis Comes, Prometheus was the creator of man
out of the parts of various beasts (*Mythologiae*, 4. 6).

27 Elficleos are the Tudor monarchs: Henry VII (Elficleos), his son
Prince Arthur (Elferon), Henry VIII (Oberon), Elizabeth I (Tanaquill).
The Puritan and Catholic extremes of Edward VI and Mary are absent
here.

670 And with rich spoiles and famous victorie,
Did high aduaunce the crowne of *Faery*:
He left two sonnes, of which faire *Elferon*
The eldest brother did vntimely dy;
Whose emptie place the mightie *Oberon*
Doubly supplide, in spousall, and dominion.

lxxvi

Great was his power and glorie ouer all,
Which him before, that sacred seate did fill,
That yet remaines his wide memoriall:
He dying left the fairest *Tanaquill*,
680 Him to succeede therein, by his last will:
Fairer and nobler liueth none this howre,
Ne like in grace, ne like in learned skill;
Therefore they *Glorian* call that glorious flowre,
Long mayst thou *Glorian* liue, in glory and great powre.

lxxvii

Beguild thus with delight of nouelties,
And naturall desire of countreys state,
So long they red in those antiquities,
That how the time was fled, they quite forgate, *forgot*
Till gentle *Alma* seeing it so late,
690 Perforce their studies broke, and them besought
To thinke, how supper did them long awaite.
So halfe vnwilling from their bookes them brought,
And fairely feasted, as so noble knights she ought.

Cant. XI.

The enimies of Temperaunce
besiege her dwelling place:
Prince Artbur them repelles, and fowle
Maleger doth deface.

i

What warre so cruell, or what siege so sore,
As that, which strong affections do apply
Against the fort of reason euermore
To bring the soule into captiuitie:
Their force is fiercer through infirmitie
Of the fraile flesh, relenting to their rage,
And exercise most bitter tyranny
Vpon the parts, brought into their bondage:
No wretchednesse is like to sinfull vellenage. *slavery*

ii

10 But in a body, which doth freely yeeld
His partes to reasons rule obedient,
And letteth her that ought the scepter weeld,
All happy peace and goodly gouernment
Is setled there in sure establishment;
There *Alma* like a virgin Queene most bright,
Doth florish in all beautie excellent:
And to her guestes doth bounteous banket dight,
Attempred goodly well for health and for delight. *seasoned*

iii

20
Early before the Morne with cremosin ray,
The windowes of bright heauen opened had,
Through which into the world the dawning day
Might looke, that maketh euery creature glad,
Vprose Sir *Guyon,* in bright armour clad,
And to his purposd iourney him prepar'd:
With him the Palmer eke in habit sad,   *serious*
Him selfe addrest to that aduenture hard:
So to the riuers side they both together far'd.

iv

30
Where them awaited ready at the ford
The *Ferriman,* as *Alma* had behight,   *commanded*
With his well rigged boate: They go abord,
And he eftsoones gan launch his barke forthright.
Ere long they rowed were quite out of sight,
And fast the land behind them fled away.
But let them pas, whiles wind and weather right
Do serue their turnes: here I a while must stay,
To see a cruell fight doen by the Prince this day.

v

40
For all so soone, as *Guyon* thence was gon
Vpon his voyage with his trustie guide,
That wicked band of villeins fresh begon
That castle to assaile on euery side,[1]
And lay strong siege about it far and wide.
So huge and infinite their numbers were,
That all the land they vnder them did hide;
So fowle and vgly, that exceeding feare
Their visages imprest, when they approched neare.

vi

50
Them in twelue troupes their Captain did dispart   *divide*
And round about in fittest steades did place,
Where each might best offend his proper part,
And his contrary obiect most deface,
As euery one seem'd meetest in that cace.
Seuen of the same against the Castle gate,[2]
In strong entrenchments he did closely place,
Which with incessaunt force and endlesse hate,
They battred day and night, and entraunce did awate.

vii

60
The other fiue, fiue sundry wayes he set,[3]
Against the fiue great Bulwarkes of that pile,
And vnto each a Bulwarke did arret,   *assign*
T'assayle with open force or hidden guile,
In hope thereof to win victorious spoile.
They all that charge did feruently apply,

CANT. XI.

1 Laying siege to the Castle of Alma, which has in the previous canto
been allegorized as the body, is sin's attack on the soul through the
senses. Medieval versions of this formula include *Ancrene Riwle, Piers
Plowman,* and *The Castle of Perseverance.*

2 The seven deadly sins: pride, envy, anger, avarice, sloth, gluttony,
and lechery (see Morton W. Bloomfield, *The Seven Deadly Sins*).
3 The five senses: seeing, hearing, tasting, smelling, and feeling.

With greedie malice and importune toyle,
And planted there their huge artillery,
With which they dayly made most dreadfull battery.

viii

The first troupe was a monstrous rablement
Of fowle misshapen wights, of which some were
Headed like Owles, with beckes vncomely bent,
Others like Dogs, others like Gryphons dreare,
And some had wings, and some had clawes to teare,
And euery one of them had Lynces eyes,
And euery one did bow and arrowes beare:
All those were lawlesse lustes, corrupt enuies,
And couetous aspectes, all cruell enimies.

ix

Those same against the bulwarke of the *Sight*
Did lay strong siege, and battailous assault,
Ne once did yield it respit day nor night,
But soone as *Titan* gan his head exault,
And soone againe as he his light with hault,   — *withheld*
Their wicked engins they against it bent:
That is each thing, by which the eyes may fault,
But two then all more huge and violent,
Beautie, and money, they that Bulwarke sorely rent.

x

The second Bulwarke was the *Hearing* sence,
Gainst which the second troupe dessignment makes;
Deformed creatures, in straunge difference,
Some hauing heads like Harts, some like to Snakes,
Some like wild Bores late rouzd out of the brakes;   *thickets*
Slaunderous reproches, and fowle infamies,
Leasings, backbytings, and vaine-glorious crakes,   *lies/boasts*
Bad counsels, prayses, and false flatteries.
All those against that fort did bend their batteries.

xi

Likewise that same third Fort, that is the *Smell*
Of that third troupe was cruelly assayd:
Whose hideous shapes were like to feends of hell,
Some like to hounds, some like to Apes, dismayd,
Some like to Puttockes, all in plumes arayd: *kites*
All shap't according their conditions,
For by those vgly formes weren pourtrayd,
Foolish delights and fond abusions,
Which do that sence besiege with light illusions.

xii

And that fourth band, which cruell battry bent,
Against the fourth Bulwarke, that is the *Tast*,
Was as the rest, a grysie rablement,
Some mouth'd like greedy Oystriges, some fast
Like loathly Toades, some fashioned in the wast
Like swine; for so deformd is luxury,
Surfeat, misdiet, and vnthriftie wast,
Vaine feasts, and idle superfluity:
All those this sences Fort assayle incessantly.

xiii

But the fift troupe most horrible of hew,
   And fierce of force, was dreadfull to report:
   For some like Snailes, some did like spyders shew,
   And some like vgly Vrchins thicke and short: *hedgehogs*
   Cruelly they assayled that fift Fort,
   Armed with darts of sensuall delight,
   With stings of carnall lust, and strong effort
   Of feeling pleasures, with which day and night
Against that same fift bulwarke they continued fight.

xiv

Thus these twelue troupes with dreadfull puissance
   Against that Castle restlesse siege did lay,
   And euermore their hideous Ordinance
   Vpon the Bulwarkes cruelly did play,
   That now it gan to threaten neare decay:
   And euermore their wicked Capitaine
   Prouoked them the breaches to assay,
   Somtimes with threats, somtimes with hope of gaine,
Which by the ransack of that peece they should attaine.

xv

On th'other side, th'assieged Castles ward
   Their stedfast stonds did mightily maintaine,
   And many bold repulse, and many hard
   Atchieuement wrought with perill and with paine,
   That goodly frame from ruine to sustaine:
   And those two brethren Giants did defend
   The walles so stoutly with their sturdie maine,
   That neuer entrance any durst pretend,
But they to direfull death their groning ghosts did send.

xvi

The noble virgin, Ladie of the place,
   Was much dismayed with that dreadfull sight:
   For neuer was she in so euill cace,
   Till that the Prince seeing her wofull plight,
   Gan her recomfort from so sad affright,
   Offring his seruice, and his dearest life
   For her defence, against that Carle to fight,   *boor*
   Which was their chiefe and th'author of that strife:
She him remercied as the Patrone of her life.

xvii

Eftsoones himselfe in glitterand armes he dight,
   And his well proued weapons to him hent;   *took*
   So taking courteous conge he behight,   *farewell*
   Those gates to be vnbar'd, and forth he went.
   Faire mote he thee, the prowest and most gent,   *prosper*
   That euer brandished bright steele on hye:
   Whom soone as that vnruly rablement,
   With his gay Squire issuing did espy,
They reard a most outrageous dreadfull yelling cry.

xviii

And therewith all attonce at him let fly
   Their fluttring arrowes, thicke as flakes of snow,
   And round about him flocke impetuously,

Like a great water flood, that tombling low
From the high mountaines, threats to ouerflow
With suddein fury all the fertile plaine,
160   And the sad husbandmans long hope doth throw
A downe the streame, and all his vowes make vaine,
Nor bounds nor banks his headlong ruine may sustaine.

                              xix
Vpon his shield their heaped hayle he bore,
And with his sword disperst the raskall flockes,
Which fled a sunder, and him fell before,
As withered leaues drop from their dried stockes,
When the wroth Western wind does reaue their locks;
And vnder neath him his courageous steed,
The fierce *Spumador* trode them downe like docks,   *weeds*
170   The fierce *Spumador* borne of heauenly seed:
Such as *Laomedon* of *Phœbus* race did breed.

                              xx
Which suddeine horrour and confused cry,
When as their Captaine heard, in haste he yode,   *went*
The cause to weet, and fault to remedy;
Vpon a Tygre swift and fierce he rode,
That as the winde ran vnderneath his lode,
Whiles his long legs nigh raught vnto the ground;
Full large he was of limbe, and shoulders brode,
But of such subtile substance and vnsound,
180   That like a ghost he seem'd, whose graue-clothes were vnbound.[4]

                              xxi
And in his hand a bended bow was seene,
And many arrowes vnder his right side,
All deadly daungerous, all cruell keene,
Headed with flint, and feathers bloudie dide,
Such as the *Indians* in their quiuers hide;
Those could he well direct and streight as line,
And bid them strike the marke, which he had eyde,
Ne was their salue, ne was their medicine,
That mote recure their wountds: so inly they did tine.   *injure*

                              xxii
190   As pale and wan as ashes was his looke,
His bodie leane and meagre as a rake,
And skin all withered like a dryed rooke,
Thereto as cold and drery as a Snake,
That seem'd to tremble euermore, and quake:
All in a canuas thin he was bedight,
And girded with a belt of twisted brake,   *brush*
Vpon his head he wore an Helmet light,
Made of a dead mans skull, that seem'd a ghastly sight.

                              xxiii
Maleger was his name, and after him,
200   There follow'd fast at hand two wicked Hags,
With hoarie lockes all loose, and visage grim;

4   Maleger, whose name means "desperately diseased," is a composite
of Satan, sin, and death.

Their feet vnshod, their bodies wrapt in rags,
And both as swift on foot, as chased Stags;
And yet the one her other legge had lame,
Which with a staffe, all full of litle snags
She did support, and *Impotence* her name:
But th'other was *Impatience*, arm'd with raging flame.

xxiv

Soone as the Carle from farre the Prince espyde,
  Glistring in armes and warlike ornament,
210   His Beast he felly prickt on either syde,   *fiercely*
  And his mischieuous bow full readie bent,
  With which at him a cruell shaft he sent:
  But he was warie, and it warded well
  Vpon his shield, that it no further went,
  But to the ground the idle quarrell fell:
Then he another and another did expell.

xxv

Which to preuent, the Prince his mortall speare
  Soone to him raught, and fierce at him did ride,
  To be auenged of that shot whyleare: *immediately*
220   But he was not so hardie to abide
  That bitter stownd, but turning quicke aside
  His light-foot beast, fled fast away for feare:
  Whom to pursue, the Infant after hide,
  So fast as his good Courser could him beare,
But labour lost it was, to weene approch him neare.

xxvi

For as the winged wind his Tigre fled,
  That vew of eye could scarse him ouertake,
  Ne scarse his feet on ground were seene to tred;
  Through hils and dales he speedie way did make,
230   Ne hedge ne ditch his readie passage brake,
  And in his flight the villein turn'd his face,
  (As wonts the *Tartar* by the *Caspian* lake,
  When as the *Russian* him in fight does chace)
Vnto his Tygres taile, and shot at him apace.

xxvii

Apace he shot, and yet he fled apace,
  Still as the greedy knight nigh to him drew,
  And oftentimes he would relent his pace,
  That him his foe more fiercely should pursew:
  Who when his vncouth manner he did vew,
240   He gan auize to follow him no more,
  But keepe his standing, and his shaftes eschew,
  Vntill he quite had spent his perlous store,
And then assayle him fresh, ere he could shift for more.

xxviii

But that lame Hag, still as abroad he strew
  His wicked arrowes, gathered them againe,
  And to him brought, fresh battell to renew:
  Which he espying, cast her to restraine
  From yielding succour to that cursed Swaine,
  And her attaching, thought her hands to tye;

250

But soone as him dismounted on the plaine,
  That other Hag did farre away espy
Binding her sister, she to him ran hastily.

xxix

And catching hold of him, as downe he lent,
  Him backward ouerthrew, and downe him stayd
  With their rude hands and griesly graplement,
  Till that the villein comming to their ayd,
  Vpon him fell, and lode vpon him layd;
  Full litle wanted, but he had him slaine,
  And of the battell balefull end had made,

260
  Had not his gentle Squire beheld his paine,
And commen to his reskew, ere his bitter bane.   *death*

xxx

So greatest and most glorious thing on ground
  May often need the helpe of weaker hand;
  So feeble is mans state, and life vnsound,
  That in assurance it may neuer stand,
  Till it dissolued be from earthly band.
  Proofe be thou Prince, the prowest man aliue,
  And noblest borne of all in *Britayne* land;
  Yet thee fierce Fortune did so nearely driue,

270
That had not grace thee blest, thou shouldest not suruiue.

xxxi

The Squire arriuing, fiercely in his armes
  Snatcht first the one, and then the other Iade,
  His chiefest lets and authors of his harmes,   *obstacles*
  And them perforce withheld with threatned blade,
  Least that his Lord they should behind inuade;
  The whiles the Prince prickt with reprochfull shame,
  As one awakt out of long slombring shade,
  Reuiuing thought of glorie and of fame,
Vnited all his powres to purge himselfe from blame.

xxxii

280
Like as a fire, the which in hollow caue
  Hath long bene vnderkept, and downe supprest,
  With murmurous disdaine doth inly raue,
  And grudge, in so streight prison to be prest,
  At last breakes forth with furious vnrest,
  And striues to mount vnto his natiue seat;
  All that did earst it hinder and molest,
  It now deuoures with flames and scorching heat,
And carries into smoake with rage and horror great.

xxxiii

So mightily the *Briton* Prince him rouzd
290
  Out of his hold, and broke his caitiue bands,
  And as a Beare whom angry curres haue touzd,   *worried*
  Hauing off-shakt them, and escapt their hands,
  Becomes more fell, and all that him withstands
  Treads downe and ouerthrowes. Now had the Carle
  Alighted from his Tigre, and his hands
  Discharged of his bow and deadly quar'le,
To seize vpon his foe flat lying on the marle.

xxxiv

Which now him turnd to disauantage deare;
   For neither can he fly, nor other harme,
   But trust vnto his strength and manhood meare,
   Sith now he is farre from his monstrous swarme,
   And of his weapons did himselfe disarme.
   The knight yet wrothfull for his late disgrace,
   Fiercely aduaunst his valorous right arme,[5]
   And him so sore smote with his yron mace,
That groueling to the ground he fell, and fild his place.

xxxv

Well weened he, that field was then his owne,
   And all his labour brought to happie end,
   When suddein vp the villein ouerthrowne,
   Out of his swowne arose, fresh to contend,
   And gan himselfe to second battell bend,
   As hurt he had not bene. Thereby there lay
   An huge great stone, which stood vpon one end,
   And had not bene remoued many a day;
Some land-marke seem'd to be, or signe of sundry way.

xxxvi

The same he snatcht, and with exceeding sway
   Threw at his foe, who was right well aware
   To shunne the engin of his meant decay;
   It booted not to thinke that throw to beare,
   But ground he gaue, and lightly leapt areare:
   Eft fierce returning, as a Faulcon faire
   That once hath failed of her souse full neare,   *swoop*
   Remounts againe into the open aire,
And vnto better fortune doth her selfe prepaire.

xxxvii

So braue returning, with his brandisht blade,
   He to the Carle himselfe againe addrest,
   And strooke at him so sternely, that he made
   An open passage through his riuen brest,
   That halfe the steele behind his back did rest;
   Which drawing backe, he looked euermore
   When the hart bloud should gush out of his chest,
   Or his dead corse should fall vpon the flore;
But his dead corse vpon the flore fell nathemore.

xxxviii

Ne drop of bloud appeared shed to bee,
   All were the wounde so wide and wonderous,
   That through his carkasse one might plainely see:
   Halfe in a maze with horror hideous,
   And halfe in rage, to be deluded thus,
   Againe through both the sides he strooke him quight,
   That made his spright to grone full piteous:
   Yet nathemore forth fled his groning spright,
But freshly as at first, prepard himselfe to fight.

300

310

320

330

340

5   Arthur's battle with Maleger is a type for Christ's battle against
Satan, sin, and death.

xxxix

Thereat he smitten was with great affright,
  And trembling terror did his hart apall,
  Ne wist he, what to thinke of that same sight,
  Ne what to say, ne what to doe at all;
  He doubted, least it were some magicall
  Illusion, that did beguile his sense,
  Or wandring ghost, that wanted funerall,
350   Or aerie spirit vnder false pretence,
Or hellish feend raysd vp through diuelish science.

xl

His wonder farre exceeded reasons reach,
  That he began to doubt his dazeled sight,
  And oft of error did himselfe appeach: *accuse*
  Flesh without bloud, a person without spright,
  Wounds without hurt, a bodie without might,
  That could doe harme, yet could not harmed bee,
  That could not die, yet seem'd a mortall wight,
  That was most strong in most infirmitee;
360 Like did he neuer heare, like did he neuer see.

xli

A while he stood in this astonishment,
  Yet would he not for all his great dismay
  Giue ouer to effect his first intent,
  And th'vtmost meanes of victorie assay,
  Or th'vtmost issew of his owne decay.
  His owne good sword *Morddure*, that neuer fayld
  At need, till now, he lightly threw away,
  And his bright shield, that nought him now auayld,
And with his naked hands him forcibly assayld.

xlii

370 Twixt his two mightie armes him vp he snatcht,
  And crusht his carkasse so against his brest,
  That the disdainfull soule he thence dispatcht,
  And th'idle breath all vtterly exprest:
  Tho when he felt him dead, a downe he kest
  The lumpish corse vnto the senselesse grownd;
  Adowne he kest it with so puissant wrest,
  That backe againe it did aloft rebownd,
And gaue against his mother earth a gronefull sownd.

xliii

As when *Ioues* harnesse-bearing Bird from hie
380 Stoupes at a flying heron with proud disdaine,
  The stone-dead quarrey fals so forciblie,
  That it rebounds against the lowly plaine,
  A second fall redoubling backe againe.
  Then thought the Prince all perill sure was past,
  And that he victor onley did remaine;
  No sooner thought, then that the Carle as fast
Gan heap huge strokes on him, as ere he downe was cast.

xliv

Nigh his wits end then woxe th'amazed knight,
  And thought his labour lost and trauell vaine,
390 Against this lifelesse shadow so to fight:

Yet life he saw, and felt his mightie maine,
That whiles he marueild still, did still him paine:
For thy he gan some other wayes aduize,
How to take life from that dead-liuing swaine,
Whom still he marked freshly to arize
From th'earth, and from her wombe new spirits to reprize.

xlv

He then remembred well, that had bene sayd,
How th'Earth his mother was, and first him bore;
She eke so often, as his life decayd,
400   Did life with vsury to him restore,
And raysd him vp much stronger then before,
So soone as he vnto her wombe did fall;
Therefore to ground he would him cast no more,
Ne him commit to graue terrestriall,
But beare him farre from hope of succour vsuall.

xlvi

Tho vp he caught him twixt his puissant hands,
And hauing scruzd out of his carrion corse
The lothfull life, now loosd from sinfull bands,   *bondage*
Vpon his shoulders carried him perforse
410   Aboue three furlongs, taking his full course,
Vntill he came vnto a standing lake;
Him thereinto he threw without remorse,
Ne stird, till hope of life did him forsake;
So end of that Carles dayes, and his owne paines did make.

xlvii

Which when those wicked Hags from farre did spy,
Like two mad dogs they ran about the lands,
And th'one of them with dreadfull yelling cry,
Throwing away her broken chaines and bands,
And hauing quencht her burning fier brands,
420   Hedlong her selfe did cast into that lake;
But *Impotence* with her owne wilfull hands,
One of *Malegers* cursed darts did take,
So riu'd her trembling hart, and wicked end did make.

xlviii

Thus now alone he conquerour remaines;
Tho comming to his Squire, that kept his steed,
Thought to haue mounted, but his feeble vaines
Him faild thereto, and serued not his need,
Through losse of blood, which from his wounds did bleed,[6]
That he began to faint, and life decay:
430   But his good Squire him helping vp with speed,
With stedfast hand vpon his horse did stay,
And led him to the Castle by the beaten way.

xlix

Where many Groomes and Squiers readie were,
To take him from his steed full tenderly,
And eke the fairest *Alma* met him there
With balme and wine and costly spicery,

---

6 Analogous to Christ's crucifixion.

To comfort him in his infirmity;
Eftsoones she causd him vp to be conuayd,
And of his armes despoyled easily,
440   In sumptuous bed she made him to be layd,
And all the while his wounds were dressing, by him stayd.

Cant. XII.

Cuyon, by Palmers gouernance,
passing through perils great,
Doth ouerthrow the Bowre of blisse,
and Acrasie defeat.

i

Now gins this goodly frame of Temperance
    Fairely to rise, and her adorned hed
    To pricke of highest praise forth to aduance,
    Formerly grounded, and fast setteled
    On firme foundation of true bountihed;
    And this braue knight, that for that vettue fights,
    Now comes to point of that same perilous sted,
    Where Pleasure dwelles in sensuall delights,
Mongst thousand dangers, and ten thousand magick mights.

ii

10   Two dayes now in that sea he sayled has,[1]
    Ne euer land beheld, ne liuing wight,
    Ne ought saue perill, still as he did pas:
    Tho when appeared the third *Morrow* bright,
    Vpon the waues to spred her trembling light,
    An hideous roaring farre away they heard,
    That all their senses filled with affright,
    And streight they saw the raging surges reard
Vp to the skyes, that them of drowning made affeard.

iii

Said then the Boteman, Palmer stere aright,
20   And keepe an euen course; for yonder way
    We needes must passe (God do vs well acquight,)   *deliver*
    That is the *Gulfe of Greedinesse*,[2] they say,
    That deepe engorgeth all this worldes pray:
    Which hauing swallowd vp excessiuely,
    He soone in vomit vp againe doth lay,
    And belcheth forth his superfluity,
That all the seas for feare do seeme away to fly.

iv

On th'other side an hideous Rocke[3] is pight,
    Of mightie *Magnes* stone, whose craggie clift   *lodestone*
30   Depending from on high, dreadfull to sight,
    Ouer the waues his rugged armes doth lift,
    And threatneth downe to throw his ragged rift
    On who so commeth nigh; yet nigh it drawes

CANT. XII.
1   The principal sources for Guyon's voyage to the Bower of Bliss are
the heroes' journeys in Homer's *Odyssey* and Virgil's *Aeneid*.

2   Equivalent to Charybdis in Homer and Virgil.
3   Equivalent to Homer's Scylla.

All passengers, that none from it can shift:
For whiles they fly that Gulfes deuouring iawes,
They on this rock are rent, and sunck in helplesse wawes.   *waves*

v

Forward they passe, and strongly he them rowes,
Vntill they nigh vnto that Gulfe arriue,
Where streame more violent and greedy growes:
40   Then he with all his puissance doth striue
To strike his oares, and mightily doth driue
The hollow vessell through the threatfull waue,
Which gaping wide, to swallow them aliue,
In th'huge abysse of his engulfing graue,
Doth rore at them in vaine, and with great terror raue.

vi

They passing by, that griesly mouth did see,
Sucking the seas into his entralles deepe,
That seem'd more horrible then hell to bee,
Or that darke dreadfull hole of *Tartare* steepe,[4]
50   Through which the damned ghosts doen often creepe
Backe to the world, bad liuers to torment: *sinners*
But nought that falles into this direfull deepe,
Ne that approcheth nigh the wide descent,
May backe returne, but is condemned to be drent.

vii

On th'other side, they saw that perilous Rocke,
Threatning it selfe on them to ruinate,
On whose sharpe clifts the ribs of vessels broke,
And shiuered ships, which had bene wrecked late,
Yet stuck, with carkasses exanimate   *dead*
60   Of such, as hauing all their substance spent
In wanton ioyes, and lustes intemperate,
Did afterwards make shipwracke violent,
Both of their life, and fame for euer fowly blent.

viii

For thy, this hight *The Rocke of* vile *Reproch*,
A daungerous and detestable place,
To which nor fish nor fowle did once approch,
But yelling Meawes, with Seagulles hoarse and bace,
And Cormoyrants, with birds of rauenous race,
Which still sate waiting on that wastfull clift,
70   For spoyle of wretches, whose vnhappie cace,
After lost credite and consumed thrift,
At last them driuen hath to this despairefull drift.

ix

The Palmer seeing them in safetie past,
Thus said; Behold th'ensamples in our sights,
Of lustfull luxurie and thriftlesse wast:
What now is left of miserable wights,
Which spent their looser daies in lewd delights,
But shame and sad reproch, here to be red,

---

4   Tartarus was the place of damnation in Hades.

By these rent reliques, speaking their ill plights?
80   Let all that liue, hereby be counselled,
To shunne *Rocke of Reproch*, and it as death to dred.

x

So forth they rowed, and that *Ferryman*
    With his stiffe oares did brush the sea so strong,
    That the hoare waters from his frigot ran,
    And the light bubbles daunced all along,
    Whiles the salt brine out of the billowes sprong.
    At last farre off they many Islands spy,
    On euery side floting the floods emong:
    Then said the knight, Loe I the land descry,
90 Therefore old Syre thy course do thereunto apply.

xi

That may not be, said then the *Ferryman*
    Least we vnweeting hap to be fordonne:
    For those same Islands, seeming now and than,
    Are not firme lande, nor any certein wonne,
    But straggling plots, which to and fro do ronne
    In the wide waters: therefore are they hight
    The *wandring Islands*. Therefore doe them shonne;
    For they haue oft drawne many a wandring wight
Into most deadly daunger and distressed plight.

xii

100 Yet well they seeme to him, that farre doth vew,
    Both faire and fruitfull, and the ground dispred
    With grassie greene of delectable hew,
    And the tall trees with leaues apparelled,
    Are deckt with blossomes dyde in white and red,
    That mote the passengers thereto allure;
    But whosoeuer once hath fastened
    His foot thereon, may neuer it recure,
But wandreth euer more vncertein and vnsure.

xiii

As th'Isle of *Delos* whylome men report
110   Amid th' *Aegæan* sea long time did stray,
    Ne made for shipping any certaine port,
    Till that *Latona*[5] traueiling that way,
    Flying from *Iunoes* wrath and hard assay,
    Of her faire twins was there deliuered,
    Which afterwards did rule the night and day;
    Thenceforth it firmely was established,
And for *Apolloes* honor highly herried.   *praised*

xiv

They to him hearken, as beseemeth meete,
    And passe on forward: so their way does ly,
120   That one of those same Islands, which doe fleet
    In the wide sea, they needes must passen by,
    Which seemd so sweet and pleasant to the eye,
    That it would tempt a man to touchen there:

---

5 Leto, mother of Apollo and Diana.

Vpon the banck they sitting did espy
A daintie damzell, dressing of her heare,
By whom a litle skippet floting did appeare.

xv

She them espying, loud to them can call,
  Bidding them nigher draw vnto the shore;
  For she had cause to busie them withall;
130   And therewith loudly laught: But nathemore
  Would they once turne, but kept on as afore:
  Which when she saw, she left her lockes vndight,
  And running to her boat withouten ore
  From the departing land it launched light,
And after them did driue with all her power and night.

xvi

Whom ouertaking, she in merry sort
  Them gan to bord, and purpose diuersly,
  Now faining dalliance and wanton sport,
  Now throwing forth lewd words immodestly;
140   Till that the Palmer gan full bitterly
  Her to rebuke, for being loose and light:
  Which not abiding, but more scornefully
  Scoffing at him, that did her iustly wite,   *rebuke*
She turnd her bote about, and from them rowed quite.

xvii

That was the wanton *Phœdria*, which late
  Did ferry him ouer the *Idle lake*:
  Whom nought regarding, they kept on their gate,
  And all her vaine allurements did forsake,
  When them the wary Boateman thus bespake;
150   Here now behoueth vs well to auyse,
  And of our safetie good heede to take;
  For here before a perlous passage lyes,
Where many Mermayds haunt, making false melodies.

xviii

But by the way, there is a great Quicksand,
  And a whirlepoole of hidden ieopardy,
  Therefore, Sir Palmer, keepe an euen hand;
  For twixt them both the narrow way doth ly.
  Scarse had he said, when hard at hand they spy
160   That quicksand nigh with water couered;
  But by the checked waue they did descry
  It plaine, and by the sea discoloured:
It called was the quicksand of *Vnthriftyhed*.

xix

They passing by, a goodly Ship did see,
  Laden from far with precious merchandize,
  And brauely furnished, as ship might bee,
  Which through great disauenture, or mesprize,
  Her selfe had runne into that hazardize;
  Whose mariners and merchants with much toyle,
  Labour'd in vaine, to haue recur'd their prize,
170   And the rich wares to saue from pitteous spoyle,
But neither toyle nor trauell might her backe recoyle.

xx

On th'other side they see that perilous Poole,
  That called was the *Whirlepoole of decay,*
  In which full many had with haplesse doole   *grief*
  Beene suncke, of whom no memorie did stay:
  Whose circled waters rapt with whirling sway,
  Like to a restlesse wheele, still running round,
  Did couet, as they passed by that way,
  To draw their boate within the vtmost bound
180 Of his wide *Labyrinth,* and then to haue them dround.

xxi

But th'heedfull Boateman strongly forth did stretch
  His brawnie armes, and all his body straine,
  That th'vtmost sandy breach they shortly fetch,
  Whiles the dred daunger does behind remaine.
  Suddeine they see from midst of all the Maine,
  The surging waters like a mountaine rise,
  And the great sea puft vp with proud disdaine,
  To swell aboue the measure of his guise,
As threatning to deuoure all, that his powre despise.

xxii

190 The waues come rolling, and the billowes rore
  Outragiously, as they enraged were,
  Or wrathfull *Neptune* did them driue before
  His whirling charet, for exceeding feare:
  For not one puffe of wind there did appeare,
  That all the three thereat woxe much afrayd,
  Vnweeting, what such horrour straunge did reare.
  Eftsoones they saw an hideous hoast arrayd,
Of huge Sea monsters, such as liuing sence dismayd.

xxiii

Most vgly shapes, and horrible aspects,[6]
200 Such as Dame Nature selfe mote feare to see,
  Or shame, that euer should so fowle defects
  From her most cunning hand escaped bee;
  All dreadfull pourtraicts of deformitee:
  Spring-headed *Hydraes,* and sea-shouldring Whales,
  Great whirlpooles, which all fishes make to flee,
  Bright Scolopendraes, arm'd with siluer scales,
Mighty *Monoceroses,* with immeasured tayles.

xxiv

The dreadfull Fish, that hath deseru'd the name
  Of Death, and like him lookes in dreadfull hew,
210 The griesly Wasserman, that makes his game
  The flying ships with swiftnesse to pursew,
  The horrible Sea-satyre, that doth shew
  His fearefull face in time of greatest storme,
  Huge *Ziffius,* whom Mariners eschew
  No lesse, then rockes, (as trauellers informe,)
And greedy *Rosmarines* with visages deforme.

---

6 A mix of natural and fabulous sea creatures.

xxv

All these, and thousand thousands many more,
  And more deformed Monsters thousand fold,
  With dreadfull noise, and hollow rombling rore,
220 Came rushing in the fomy waues enrold,
  Which seem'd to fly for feare, them to behold:
  Ne wonder, if these did the knight appall;
  For all that here on earth we dreadfull hold,
  Be but as bugs to fearen babes withall,
Compared to the creatures in the seas entrall.

xxvi

Feare nought, (then said the Palmer well auiz'd;)
  For these same Monsters are not these in deed,
  But are into these fearefull shapes disguiz'd
  By that same wicked witch, to worke vs dreed,
230 And draw from on this iourney to proceede.
  Tho lifting vp his vertuous staffe on hye,
  He smote the sea, which calmed was with speed,
  And all that dreadfull Armie fast gan flye
Into great *Tethys*[7] bosome, where they hidden lye.

xxvii

Quit from that daunger, forth their course they kept,
  And as they went, they heard a ruefull cry
  Of one, that wayld and pittifully wept,
  That through the sea the resounding plaints did fly:
  At last they in an Island did espy
240 A seemely Maiden, sitting by the shore,
  That with great sorrow and sad agony,
  Seemed some great misfortune to deplore,
And lowd to them for succour called euermore.

xxviii

Which *Guyon* hearing, streight his Palmer bad,
  To stere the boate towards that dolefull Mayd,
  That he might know, and ease her sorrow sad:
  Who him auizing better, to him sayd;
  Faire Sir, be not displeasd, if disobayd:
  For ill it were to hearken to her cry;
250 For she is inly nothing ill apayd,
  But onely womanish fine forgery,
Your stubborne hart t'affect with fraile infirmity.

xxix

To which when she your courage hath inclind
  Through foolish pitty, then her guilefull bayt
  She will embosome deeper in your mind,
  And for your ruine at the last awayt.
  The knight was ruled, and the Boateman strayt
  Held on his course with stayed stedfastnesse,
  Ne euer shruncke, ne euer sought to bayt
260 His tyred armes for toylesome wearinesse,
But with his oares did sweepe the watry wildernesse.

---

7 Wife of the Titan Oceanus.

xxx

And now they nigh approched to the sted,
  Where as those Mermayds dwelt: it was a still
  And calmy bay, on th'one side sheltered
  With the brode shadow of an hoarie hill,
  On th'other side an high rocke toured still,
  That twixt them both a pleasaunt port they made,
  And did like an halfe Theatre fulfill:
  There those fiue sisters had continuall trade,
And vsd to bath themselues in that deceiptfull shade.

270

xxxi

They were faire Ladies, till they fondly striu'd
  With th'*Heliconian* maides for maistery;
  Of whom they ouer-comen, were depriu'd
  Of their proud beautie, and th'one moyity
  Transform'd to fish, for their bold surquedry,   *presumption*
  But th'vpper halfe their hew retained still,
  And their sweet skill in wonted melody;
  Which euer after they abusd to ill,
T'allure weake trauellers, whom gotten they did kill.

xxxii

280

So now to *Guyon*, as he passed by,
  Their pleasaunt tunes they sweetly thus applide;
  O thou faire sonne of gentle Faery,
  That art in mighty armes most magnifide
  Aboue all knights, that euer battell tride,
  O turne thy rudder hither-ward a while:
  Here may thy storme-bet vessell safely ride;
  This is the Port of rest from troublous toyle,
The worlds sweet In, from paine and wearisome turmoyle.

xxxiii

With that the rolling sea resounding soft,
290
  In his big base them fitly answered,
  And on the rocke the waues breaking aloft,
  A solemne Meane vnto them measured,
  The whiles sweet *Zephirus*[8] lowd whisteled
  His treble, a straunge kinde of harmony;
  Which *Guyons* senses softly tickeled,
  That he the boateman bad row easily,
And let him heare some part of their rare melody.

xxxiv

But him the Palmer from that vanity,
  With temperate aduice discounselled,
300
  That they it past, and shortly gan descry
  The land, to which their course they leueled;
  When suddeinly a grosse fog ouer spred
  With his dull vapour all that desert has,
  And heauens chearefull face enueloped,
  That all things one, and one as nothing was,
And this great Vniuerse seemd one confused mas.

8 The west wind, which stimulates sexual desire.

XXXV

Thereat they greatly were dismayd, ne wist
　　How to direct their way in darkenesse wide,
　　But feard to wander in that wastfull mist,
310　　For tombling into mischiefe vnespide.
　　Worse is the daunger hidden, then descride.
　　Suddeinly an innumerable flight
　　Of harmefull fowles about them fluttering, cride,
　　And with their wicked wings them oft did smight,
And sore annoyed, groping in that griesly night.

XXXVI

Euen all the nation of vnfortunate
　　And fatall birds about them flocked were,
　　Such as by nature men abhorre and hate,
　　The ill-faste Owle, deaths dreadfull messengere,
320　　The hoars Night-rauen, trump of dolefull drere,
　　The lether-winged Bat, dayes enimy,
　　The ruefull Strich, still waiting on the bere,　　　　　　*screech owl*
　　The Whistler shrill, that who so heares, doth dy,　　　　*plover*
The hellish Harpies, prophets of sad destiny.

XXXVII

All those, and all that else does horrour breed,
　　About them flew, and fild their sayles with feare:
　　Yet stayd they not, but forward did proceed,
　　Whiles th'one did row, and th'other stifly steare;
　　Till that at last the weather gan to cleare,
330　　And the faire land it selfe did plainly show.
　　Said then the Palmer, Lo where does appeare
　　The sacred soile, where all our perils grow;
Therefore, Sir knight, your ready armes about you throw.

XXXVIII

He hearkned, and his armes about him tooke;
　　The whiles the nimble boate so well her sped,
　　That with her crooked keele the land she strooke,
　　Then forth the noble *Guyon* sallied,
　　And his sage Palmer, that him gouerned;
　　But th'other by his boate behind did stay.
340　　They marched fairly forth, of nought ydred,
　　Both firmely armd for euery hard assay,
With constancy and care, gainst daunger and dismay.

XXXIX

Ere long they heard an hideous bellowing
　　Of many beasts, that roard outrageously,
　　As if that hungers point, or *Venus* sting
　　Had them enraged with fell surquedry;　　　　　　　　*arrogance*
　　Yet nought they feard, but past on hardily,
　　Vntill they came in vew of those wild beasts:[9]
　　Who all attonce, gaping full greedily,
350　　And rearing fiercely their vpstarting crests,
Ran towards, to deuoure those vnexpected guests.

9　Formerly men but now transformed by Acrasia.

xl

But soone as they approcht with deadly threat,
  The Palmer ouer them his staffe vpheld,
  His mighty staffe, that could all charmes defeat:
  Eftsoones their stubborne courages were queld,
  And high aduaunced crests downe meekely feld,
  In stead of fraying, they them selues did feare,
  And trembled, as them passing they beheld:
  Such wondrous powre did in that staffe appeare,
360 All monsters to subdew to him, that did it beare.

xli

Of that same wood it fram'd was cunningly,
  Of which *Caduceus* whilome was made,
  Caduceus the rod of *Mercury*,
  With which he wonts the *Stygian* realmes inuade,
  Through ghastly horrour, and eternall shade;
  Th' infernall feends with it he can asswage,
  And *Orcus* tame, whom nothing can perswade,   *Pluto*
  And rule the *Furyes*, when they most do rage:
Such vertue in his staffe had eke this Palmer sage.

xlii

370 Thence passing forth, they shortly do arriue,
  Whereas the Bowre of *Blisse* was situate;
  A place pickt out by choice of best aliue,
  That natures worke by art can imitate:
  In which what euer in this worldly state
  Is sweet, and pleasing vnto liuing sense,
  Or that may dayntiest fantasie aggrate,
  Was poured forth with plentifull dispence,
And made there to abound with lauish affluence.

xliii

Goodly it was enclosed round about,
380   Aswell their entred guestes to keepe within,
  As those vnruly beasts ro hold without;
  Yet was the fence thereof but weake and thin;
  Nought feard their force, that fortilage to win,
  But wisedomes powre, and temperaunces might,
  By which the mightiest things efforced bin:
  And eke the gate was wrought of substaunce light,
Rather for pleasure, then for battery or fight.

xliv

Yt framed was of precious yuory,
  That seemd a worke of admirable wit;
390   And therein all the famous history
  Of *Iason* and *Medæa* was ywrit;[10]
  Her mighty charmes, het furious louing fit,
  His goodly conquest of the golden fleece,
  His falsed faith, and loue too lightly flit,
  The wondred *Argo*, which in venturous peece
First through the *Euxine* seas bore all the flowr of *Greece*.

10 See *The Voyage of the Argo* by Apollonius of Rhodes.

xlv

Ye might haue seene the frothy billowes fry
  Vnder the ship, as thorough them she went,
  That seemd the waues were into yuory,
400   Or yuory into the waues were sent;
  And other where the snowy substaunce sprent   *sprinkled*
  With vermell, like the boyes bloud therein shed,
  A piteous spectacle did represent,
  And otherwhiles with gold besprinkeled;
Yt seemd th'enchaunted flame, which did *Creüsa* wed.

xlvi

All this, and more might in that goodly gate
  Be red; that euer open stood to all,
  Which thither came: but in the Porch there sate
  A comely personage of stature tall,
410   And semblaunce pleasing, more then naturall,
  That trauellers to him seemd to entize;
  His looser garment to the ground did fall,
  And flew about his heeles in wanton wize,
Not fit for speedy pace, or manly exercize.

xlvii

They in that place him *Genius* did call:[11]
  Not that celestiall powre, to whom the care
  Of life, and generation of all
  That liues, pertaines in charge particulare,
420   Who wondrous things concerning our welfare,
  And straunge phantomes doth let vs oft forsee,
  And oft of secret ill bids vs beware:
  That is our Selfe, whom though we do not see,
Yet each doth in him selfe it well perceiue to bee.

xlviii

Therefore a God him sage Antiquity
  Did wisely make, and good *Agdistes* call:
  But this same was to that quite contrary,
  The foe of life, that good enuyes to all,
  That secretly doth vs procure to fall,
  Through guilefull semblaunts, which he makes vs see.
430   He of this Gardin had the gouernall,
  And Pleasures porter was deuizd to bee,
Holding a staffe in hand for more formalitee.

xlix

With diuerse flowres he daintily was deckt,
  And strowed round about, and by his side
  A mighty Mazer bowle of wine was set,   *wooden*
  As if it had to him bene sacrifide;
  Wherewith all new-come guests he gratifide:
  So did he eke Sir *Guyon* passing by:
  But he his idle curtesie defide,
440   And ouerthrew his bowle disdainfully;
And broke his staffe, with which he charmed semblants sly.

11 Spenser adapts the common medieval and Renaissance distinction
between two kinds of Genius: the principle of universal generative
power and the local or personal genius (see C. S. Lewis, *The Allegory of
Love*, pp. 361–3).

l

Thus being entred, they behold around
    A large and spacious plaine, on euery side
    Strowed with pleasauns, whose faire grassy ground
    Mantled with greene, and goodly beautifide
    With all the ornaments of *Floraes* pride,
    Wherewith her mother Art, as halfe in scorne
    Of niggard Nature, like a pompous bride
    Did decke her, and too lauishly adorne,
When forth from virgin bowre she comes in th'early morne.

450

li

Thereto the Heauens alwayes Iouiall,
    Lookt on them louely, still in stedfast state,
    Ne suffred storme nor frost on them to fall,
    Their tender buds or leaues to violate,
    Nor scorching heat, nor cold intemperate
    T'afflict the creatures, which therein did dwell,
    But the milde aire with season moderate
    Gently attempred, and disposd so well,
That still it breathed forth sweet spirit and holesome smell.

lii

More sweet and holesome, then the pleasaunt hill
    Of *Rhodope*,[12] on which the Nimphe, that bore
    A gyaunt babe, her selfe for griefe did kill;
    Or the Thessalian *Tempe*,[13] where of yore
    Faire *Daphne Phœbus* hart with loue did gore;
    Or *Ida*, where the Gods lou'd to repaire,
    When euer they their heauenly bowres forlore;
    Or sweet *Parnasse*, the haunt of Muses faire;
Or *Eden* selfe, if ought with *Eden* mote compaire.

460

liii

Much wondred *Guyon* at the faire aspect
    Of that sweet place, yet suffred no delight
    To sincke into his sence, nor mind affect,
    But passed forth, and lookt still forward right,
    Bridling his will, and maistering his might:
    Till that he came vnto another gate;
    No gate, but like one, being goodly dight
    With boughes and braunches, which did broad dilate
Their clasping armes, in wanton wreathings intricate.

470

liv

So fashioned a Porch with rare deuice,
    Archt ouer head with an embracing vine,
    Whose bounches hanging downe, seemed to entice
    All passers by, to tast their lushious wine,
    And did themselues into their hands incline,
    As freely offering to be gathered:
    Some deepe empurpled as the *Hyacint*,
    Some as the Rubine, laughing sweetly red,
Some like faire Emeraudes, not yet well ripened.

480

12 Named for a nymph who was transformed into a mountain; here   13 Daphne was here transformed into a laurel in order to escape
also a mountain in Thrace.   Phoebus.

lv

And them amongst, some were of burnisht gold,
  So made by art, to beautifie the rest,
  Which did themselues emongst the leaues enfold,
490   As lurking from the vew of couetous guest,
  That the weake bowes, with so rich load opprest,
  Did bow adowne, as ouer-burdened.
  Vnder that Porch a comely dame did rest,
  Clad in faire weedes, but fowle disordered,
And garments loose, that seemd vnmeet for womanhed.

lvi

In her left hand a Cup of gold she held,
  And with her right the riper fruit did reach,
  Whose sappy liquor, that with fulnesse sweld,
  Into her cup she scruzd, with daintie breach   *squeezed*
500   Of her fine fingers, without fowle empeach,
  That so faire wine-presse made the wine more sweet:
  Thereof she vsd to giue to drinke to each,
  Whom passing by she happened to meet:
It was her guise, all Straungers goodly so to greet.

lvii

So she to *Guyon* offred it to tast;
  Who taking it out of her tender hond,
  The cup to ground did violently cast,
  That all in peeces it was broken fond,
  And with the liquor stained all the lond:
510   Whereat *Excesse* exceedingly was wroth,
  Yet no'te the same amend, ne yet withstond,
  But suffered him to passe, all were she loth;
Who nought regarding her displeasure forward goth.

lviii

There the most daintie Paradise on ground,
  It selfe doth offer to his sober eye,
  In which all pleasures plenteously abound,
  And none does others happinesse enuye:
  The painted flowres, the trees vpshooting hye,
  The dales for shade, the hilles for breathing space,
520   The trembling groues, the Christall running by;
  And that, which all faire workes doth most aggrace,
The art, which all that wrought, appeared in no place.

lix

One would haue thought, (so cunningly, the rude,
  And scorned parts were mingled with the fine,)
  That nature had for wantonesse ensude
  Art, and that Art at nature did repine;
  So striuing each th'other to vndermine,
  Each did the others worke more beautifie;
  So differing both in willes, agreed in fine:
530   So all agreed through sweete diuersitie,
This Gardin to adorne with all varietie.

lx

And in the midst of all, a fountaine stood,
  Of richest substaunce, that on earth might bee,
  So pure and shiny, that the siluer flood

Through euery channell running one might see;
Most goodly it with curious imageree
Was ouer-wrought, and shapes of naked boyes,
Of which some seemd with liuely iollitee,
To fly about, playing their wanton toyes,
540 Whilest others did them selues embay in liquid ioyes.   *bathe*

lxi

And ouer all, of purest gold was spred,
A trayle of yuie in his natiue hew:
For the rich mettall was so coloured,
That wight, who did not well auis'd it vew,
Would surely deeme it to be yuie trew:
Low his lasciuious armes adown did creepe,
That themselues dipping in the siluer dew,
Their fleecy flowres they tenderly did steepe,
Which drops of Christall seemd for wantones to weepe.

lxii

550 Infinit streames continually did well
Out of this fountaine, sweet and faire to see,
The which into an ample lauer fell,
And shortly grew to so great quantitie,
That like a little lake it seemd to bee;
Whose depth exceeded not three cubits hight,
That through the waues one might the bottom see,
All pau'd beneath with Iaspar shining bright,
That seemd the fountaine in that sea did sayle vpright.

lxiii

And all the margent round about was set,
560 With shady Laurell trees, thence to defend
The sunny beames, which on the billowes bet,
And those which therein bathed, mote offend.
As *Guyon* hapned by the same to wend,
Two naked Damzelles he therein espyde,
Which therein bathing, seemed to contend,
And wrestle wantonly, ne car'd to hyde,
Their dainty parts from vew of any, which them eyde.

lxiv

Sometimes the one would lift the other quight
Aboue the waters, and then downe againe
570 Her plong, as ouer maistered by might,
Where both awhile would couered remaine,
And each the other from to rise restraine;
The whiles their snowy limbes, as through a vele,
So through the Christall waues appeared plaine:
Then suddeinly both would themselues vnhele,
And th'amarous sweet spoiles to greedy eyes reuele.

lxv

As that faire Starre, the messenger of morne,   *Venus*
His deawy face out of the sea doth reare:
Or as the *Cyprian* goddesse, newly borne
580 Of th'Oceans fruitfull froth, did first appeare:
Such seemed they, and so their yellow heare
Christalline humour dropped downe apace.

Whom such when *Guyon* saw, he drew him neare,
And somewhat gan relent his earnest pace,
His stubborne brest gan secret pleasaunce to embrace.

lxvi

The wanton Maidens him espying, stood
  Gazing a while at his vnwonted guise;
  Then th'one her selfe low ducked in the flood,
  Abasht, that her a straunger did a vise:
590   But th'other rather higher did arise,
  And her two lilly paps aloft displayd,
  And all, that might his melting hart entise
  To her delights, she vnto him bewrayd: *displayed*
The rest hid vnderneath, him more desirous made.

lxvii

With that, the other likewise vp arose,
  And her faire lockes, which formerly were bownd
  Vp in one knot, she low adowne did lose:
  Which flowing long and thick, her cloth'd arownd,
  And th'yuorie in golden mantle gownd:
600   So that faire spectacle from him was reft,
  Yet that, which reft it, no lesse faire was fownd:
  So hid in lockes and waues from lookers theft,
Nought but her louely face she for his looking left.

lxviii

Withall she laughed, and she blusht withall,
  That blushing to her laughter gaue more grace,
  And laughter to her blushing, as did fall:
  Now when they spide the knight to slacke his pace,
  Them to behold, and in his sparkling face
  The secret signes of kindled lust appeare,
610   Their wanton meriments they did encreace,
  And to him beckned, to approch more neare,
And shewd him many sights, that courage cold could reare.

lxix

On which when gazing him the Palmer saw,
  He much rebukt those wandring eyes of his,
  And counseld well, him forward thence did draw.
  Now are they come nigh to the *Bowre of blis*
  Of her fond fauorites so nam'd amis:
  When thus the Palmer; Now Sir, well auise;
  For here the end of all our trauell is:
620   Here wonnes *Acrasia*, whom we must surprise,
Else she will slip away, and all our drift despise.

lxx

Eftsoones they heard a most melodious sound,
  Of all that mote delight a daintie eare,
  Such as attonce might not on liuing ground,
  Saue in this Paradise, be heard elswhere:
  Right hard it was, for wight, which did it heare,
  To read, what manner musicke that mote bee:
  For all that pleasing is to liuing eare,
  Was there consorted in one harmonee,
630   Birdes, voyces, instruments, windes, waters, all agree.

lxxi

The ioyous birdes shrouded in chearefull shade,
   Their notes vnto the voyce attempred sweet;
   Th'Angelicall soft trembling voyces made
   To th'instruments diuine respondence meet:
   The siluer sounding instruments did meet
   With the base murmure of the waters fall:
   The waters fall with difference discreet,
   Now soft, now loud, vnto the wind did call:
The gentle warbling wind low answered to all.

lxxii

640   There, whence that Musick seemed heard to bee,
   Was the faire Witch her selfe now solacing,
   With a new Louer, whom through sorceree
   And witchcraft, she from farre did thither bring:
   There she had him now layd a slombering,
   In secret shade, after long wanton ioyes:
   Whilst round about them pleasauntly did sing
   Many faire Ladies, and lasciuious boyes,
That euer mixt their song with light licentious toyes.

lxxiii

And all that while, right ouer him she hong,
650   With her false eyes fast fixed in his sight,
   As seeking medicine, whence she was stong,
   Or greedily depasturing delight: *devouring*
   And oft inclining downe with kisses light,
   For feare of waking him, his lips bedewd,
   And through his humid eyes did sucke his spright,
   Quite molten into lust and pleasure lewd;
Wherewith she sighed soft, as if his case she rewd.

lxxiv

The whiles some one did chaunt this louely lay;[14]
   Ah see, who so faire thing doest faine to see,
660   In springing flowre the image of thy day;
   Ah see the Virgin Rose, how sweetly shee
   Doth first peepe forth with bashfull modestee,
   That fairer seemes, the lesse ye see her may;
   Lo see soone after, how more bold and free
   Her bared bosome she doth broad display;
Loe see soone after, how she fades, and falles away.

lxxv

So passeth, in the passing of a day,
   Of mortall life the leafe, the bud, the flowre,
   Ne more doth flourish after first decay,
670   That earst was sought to decke both bed and bowre,
   Of many a Ladie, and many a Paramowre:
   Gather therefore the Rose, whilest yet is prime,
   For soone comes age, that will her pride deflowre:
   Gather the Rose of loue, whilest yet is time,
Whilest louing thou mayst loued be with equall crime.

14 A classic instance of *carpe diem*.

lxxvi

He ceast, and then gan all the quire of birdes
   Their diuerse notes t'attune vnto his lay,
   As in approuance of his pleasing words.
   The constant paire heard all, that he did say,
680   Yet swarued not, but kept their forward way,
   Through many couert groues, and thickets close,
   In which they creeping did at last display
   That wanton Ladie, with her louer lose,
Whose sleepie head she in her lap did soft dispose.

lxxvii

Vpon a bed of Roses she was layd,
   As faint through heat, or dight to pleasant sin,
   And was arayd, or rather disarayd,
   All in a vele of silke and siluer thin,
   That hid no whit her alablaster skin,
690   But rather shewd more white, if more might bee:
   More subtile web *Arachne* cannot spin,
   Nor the fine nets, which oft we wouen see
Of scorched deaw, do not in th'aire more lightly flee.

lxxviii

Her snowy brest was bare to readie spoyle
   Of hungry eies, which n'ote therewith be fild,
   And yet through languour of her late sweet toyle,
   Few drops, more cleare then Nectar, forth distild,
   That like pure Orient perles adowne it trild,
   And her faire eyes sweet smyling in delight,
700   Moystened their fierie beames, with which she thrild
   Fraile harts, yet quenched not; like starry light
Which sparckling on the silent waues, does seeme more bright.

lxxix

The young man sleeping by her, seemd to bee
   Some goodly swayne of honorable place,
   That certes it great pittie was to see
   Him his nobilitie so foule deface;
   A sweet regard, and amiable grace,
   Mixed with manly sternnesse did appeare
710   Yet sleeping, in his well proportiond face,
   And on his tender lips the downy heare
Did now but freshly spring, and silken blossomes beare.

lxxx

His warlike armes, the idle instruments
   Of sleeping praise, were hong vpon a tree,
   And his braue shield, full of old moniments,
   Was fowly ra'st, that none the signes night see;
   Ne for them, ne for honour cared hee,
   Ne ought, that did to his aduauncement tend,
   But in lewd loues, and wastfull luxuree,
   His dayes, his goods, his bodie he did spend:
720   O horrible enchantment, that him so did blend.

lxxxi

The noble Elfe, and carefull Palmer drew
   So nigh them, minding nought, but lustfull game,
   That suddein forth they on them rusht, and threw

A subtile net, which onely for the same
The skilfull Palmer formally did frame.
So held them vnder fast, the whiles the rest
Fled all away for feare of fowler shame.
The faire Enchauntresse, so vnwares opprest,
Tryde all her arts, and all her sleights, thence out to wrest.

lxxxii

730
And eke her louer stroue: but all in vaine;
For that same net so cunningly was wound,
That neither guile, nor force might it distraine.
They tooke them both, and both them strongly bound
In captiue bandes, which there they readie found:
But her in chaines of adamant he tyde;
For nothing else might keepe her safe and sound;
But *Verdant* (so he hight) he soone vntyde,
And counsell sage in steed thereof to him applyde.

lxxxiii

But all those pleasant bowres and Pallace braue,
740
Guyon broke downe, with rigour pittilesse;
Ne ought their goodly workmanship might saue
Them from the tempest of his wrathfulnesse,
But that their blisse he turn'd to balefulnesse:
Their groues he feld, their gardins did deface,
Their arbers spoyle, their Cabinets suppresse,   *summer/houses*
Their banket houses burne, their buildings race,
And of the fairest late, now made the fowlest place.

lxxxiv

Then led they her away, and eke that knight
They with them led, both sorrowfull and sad:
750
The way they came, the same retourn'd they right,
Till they arriued, where they lately had
Charm'd those wild-beasts, that rag'd with furie mad.
Which now awaking, fierce at them gan fly,
As in their mistresse reskew, whom they lad;
But them the Palmer soone did pacify.
Then *Guyon* askt, what meant those beastes, which there did ly.

lxxxv

Said he, These seeming beasts are men indeed,
Whom this Enchauntresse hath transformed thus,
Whylome her louers, which her lusts did feed,
760
Now turned into figures hideous,
According to their mindes like monstruous.[15]
Sad end (quoth he) of life intemperate,
And mournefull meed of ioyes delicious:
But Palmer, if it mote thee so aggrate,
Let them returned be vnto their former state.

lxxxvi

Streight way he with his vertuous staffe them strooke,
And streight of beasts they comely men became;
Yet being men they did vnmanly looke,
And stared ghastly, some for inward shame,

---

15 The physical transformation matches the psychological state.

770   And some for wrath, to see their captiue Dame:
       But one aboue the rest in speciall,
       That had an hog beene late, hight *Grille* by name,[16]
       Repined greatly, and did him miscall,
That had from hoggish forme him brought to naturall.

lxxxvii

Said *Guyon*, See the mind of beastly man,
       That hath so soone forgot the excellence
       Of his creation, when he life began,
       That now he chooseth, with vile difference,
       To be a beast, and lacke intelligence.
780   To whom the Palmer thus, The donghill kind
       Delights in filth and foule incontinence:
       Let *Grill* be *Grill*, and haue his hoggish mind,
But let vs hence depart, whilest wether serues and wind.

TWO CANTOS OF MVTABILITIE: WHICH, BOTH FOR FORME AND MATTER, APPEARE TO BE PARCELL OF SOME FOLLOWING BOOKE OF THE FAERIE QUEENE, VNDER THE LEGEND OF *CONSTANCIE*

Canto VI.

Proud Change (*not pleasd, in mortall things,*
    beneath the Moone, to raigne)
Pretends, as well of Gods, as Men,
    to be the Soueraine.

i

What man that sees the euer-whirling wheele
       Of *Change*, the which all mortall things doth sway,   rule
       But that therby doth find, and plainly feele,
       How *MVTABILITY* in them doth play
       Her cruell sports, to many mens decay?[1]
       Which that to all may better yet appeare,
       I will rehearse that whylome I heard say,
       How she at first her selfe began to reare,
Gainst all the Gods, and th'empire sought from them to beare.

ii

10   But first, here falleth fittest to vnfold
       Her antique race and linage ancient,
       As I haue found it registred of old,
       In *Faery* Land mongst records permanent:
       She was, to weet, a daughter by descent
       Of those old *Titans*, that did whylome striue
       With *Saturnes* sonne for heauens regiment,   Jove
       Whom, though high *Ioue* of kingdome did depriue,
Yet many of their stemme long after did suruiue.

16   Based on Plutarch's *Whether the Beasts Have the Use of Reason.*

TWO CANTOS OF MVTABILITIE: WHICH, BOTH FOR FORME AND
MATTER, APPEARE TO BE PARCELL OF SOME FOLLOWING BOOKE
OF THE FAERIE QUEENE, VNDER THE LEGEND OF CONSTANCIE
1   Change would appear to be the impersonal abstract principle, while
mutability is its allegorical personification. One purpose of the poem is
to bring about a shift in the awareness of change as an abstraction
outside the self to the acknowledgment of mutability as a process
working within each person. Cf. Ecclesiastes 2:15: "As it happeneth to
the fool, so it happeneth even to me."

iii

And many of them,[2] afterwards obtain'd
   Great power of Ioue, and high authority;
   As *Hecaté*,[3] in whose almighty hand,
   He plac't all rule and principality,
   To be by her disposed diuersly,
   To Gods, and men, as she them list diuide:
   And drad *Bellona*,[4] that doth sound on hie   *dreaded*
   Warres and allarums vnto Nations wide,
That makes both heauen and earth to tremble at her pride.

iv

So likewise did this *Titanesse* aspire,
   Rule and dominion to her selfe to gaine;
   That as a Goddesse, men might her admire,
   And heauenly honours yield, as to them twaine.
   At first, on earth she sought it to obtaine;
   Where she such proofe and sad examples shewed
   Of her great power, to many ones great paine.
   That not men onely (whom she soone subdewed)
But eke all other creatures, her bad doings rewed.   *rued*

v

For, she the face of earthly things so changed,
   That all which Nature had establisht first
   In good estate, and in meet order ranged,
   She did peruert, and all their statutes burst:
   And all the worlds faire frame (which none yet burst
   Of Gods or men to alter or misguide)
   She alter'd quite, and made them all accurst
   That God had blest; and did at first prouide
In that still happy state for euer to abide.

vi

Ne shee the lawes of Nature onely brake,
   But eke of Iustice, and of Policie;
   And wrong of right, and bad of good did make,
   And death for life exchanged foolishlie:
   Since which, all liuing wights haue learn'd to die,
   And all this world is woxen daily worse.[5]   *grown*
   O pittious worke of *MVTABILITIE*!
   By which, we all are subiect to that curse,
And death in stead of life haue sucked from our Nurse.

vii

And now, when all the earth she thus had brought
   To Her behest, and thralled to her might,
   She gan to cast in her ambitious thought,
   T'attempt th'empire of the heauens hight,
   And *Ioue* himselfe to shoulder from his right.
   And first, she past the region of the ayre,[6]

---

2 Children of earth and sky, the Titans (according to Hesiod) revolted against their father in favor of Saturn, who in turn was overthrown by his son Jove (or Zeus.) It is Jove who initiates the Olympian order of twelve gods and establishes justice.

3 Hecate is the presiding deity of witches and the underworld.

4 Bellona is variously depicted as the daughter, sister, or wife of Mars, the god of war.

5 Although the mythological context here is ostensibly pagan, these effects in Christian thought are the consequence of Adam's sin.

6 She travels through the Ptolemaic circles and invades the circle of Cynthia, the moon goddess, who is allegorically identified throughout the poem with Queen Elizabeth. The image of her throne being drawn by horses alludes to Plato's allegory of the soul in the *Phaedrus*. This subtly equates Elizabeth (Cynthia) with the essence of the soul.

And of the fire, whose substance thin and slight,
Made no resistance, ne could her contraire,   *oppose*
But ready passage to her pleasure did prepaire.

viii

Thence, to the Circle of the Moone she clambe,
  Where *Cynthia* raignes in euerlasting glory,
  To whose bright shining palace straight she came,
  All fairely deckt with heauens goodly story;
  Whose siluer gates (by which there sate an hory
  Old aged Sire, with hower-glasse in hand,
70   Hight *Tyme*) she entred, were he liefe or sory: *called*
  Ne staide till she the highest stage had scand,
Where *Cynthia* did sit, that neuer still did stand.

ix

Her sitting on an Iuory throne shee found,
  Drawne of two steeds, th'one black, the other white,
  Environd with tenne thousand starres around,
  That duly her attended day and night;
  And by her side, there ran her Page, that hight
  Vesper, whom we the Euening-starre intend:
  That with his Torche, still twinkling like twylight,
80   Her lightened all the way where she should wend,   *go*
And joy to weary wandring trauailers did lend:

x

That when the hardy *Titanesse* beheld
  The goodly building of her Palace bright,
  Made of the heauens substance, and vp-held
  With thousand Crystall pillors of huge hight,
  Shee gan to burne in her ambitious spright,
  And t'envie her that in such glorie raigned.
  Eftsoones she cast by force and tortious might,   *evil*
  Her to displace; and to her selfe to haue gained
90 The kingdome of the Night, and waters by her wained.

xi

Boldly she bid the Goddesse downe descend,
  And let her selfe into that Ivory throne;
  For, shee her selfe more worthy thereof wend,   *considered*
  And better able it to guide alone:
  Whether to men, whose fall she did bemone,
  Or vnto Gods, whose state she did maligne,
  Or to th'infernall Powers, her need giue lone
  Of her faire light, and bounty most benigne,
Her selfe of all that rule shee deemed most condigne.

xii

100   But shee that had to her that soueraigne seat
  By highest *Ioue* assign'd, therein to beare
  Nights burning lamp, regarded not her threat,
  Ne yielded ought for fauour or for feare;
  But with sterne countenaunce and disdainfull cheare,   *mood*
  Bending her horned browes, did put her back:
  And boldly blaming her for comming there,
  Bade her attonce from heauens coast to pack,
Or at her perill bide the wrathfull Thunders wrack.

xiii

Yet nathemore the *Giantesse* forbare:

110   But boldly preacing-on, raught forth her hand   *reached*
           To pluck her downe perforce from off her chaire;
           And there-with lifting vp her golden wand,
           Threatned to strike her if she did with-stand.
           Where-at the starres, which round about her blazed,
           And eke the Moones bright wagon, still did stand,
           All beeing with so bold attempt amazed,
And on her vncouth habit and sterne looke still gazed.

xiv

Meane-while, the lower World, which nothing knew
           Of all that chaunced here, was darkned quite;
120   And eke the heauens, and all the heauenly crew
           Of happy wights, now vnpurvaide of light,
           Were much afraid, and wondred at that sight;
           Fearing least *Chaos* broken had his chaine,
           And brought againe on them eternall night:
           But chiefely *Mercury*, that next doth raigne,
Ran forth in haste, vnto the king of Gods to plaine.   *complain*

xv

All ran together with a great out-cry,
           To *Ioues* faire Palace, fixt in heauens hight;[7]
           And beating at his gates full earnestly,
130   Gan call to him aloud with all their might,
           To know what meant that suddaine lack of light.
           The father of the Gods when this he heard,
           Was troubled much at their so strange affright,
           Doubting least *Typhon*[8] were againe vprear'd,
Or other his old foes, that once him sorely fear'd.

xvi

Eftsoones the sonne of *Maia*[9] forth he sent
           Downe to the Circle of the Moone, to knowe
           The cause of this so strange astonishment,
           And why shee did her wonted course forslowe;
140   And if that any were on earth belowe
           That did with charmes or Magick her molest,
           Him to attache, and downe to hell to throwe:
           But, if from heauen it were, then to arrest
The Author, and him bring before his presence prest.

xvii

The wingd-foot God, so fast his plumes did beat,
           That soone he came where-as the *Titanesse*
           Was striuing with faire *Cynthia* for her seat:
           At whose strange sight, and haughty hardinesse,
           He wondred much, and feared her no lesse.
150   Yet laying feare aside to doe his charge,
           At last, he bade her (with bold stedfastnesse)
           Ceasse to molest the Moone to walke at large,
Or come before high *Ioue*, her dooings to discharge.

7   The three worlds of the poem – Earth, Cynthia's palace, and Jove's   8   Typhon is a monstrous creature, offspring of Earth and Tartarus, who
palace – seem to encircle each other in three increasingly large circles.   is the source of the volcanic eruptions of Mount Etna.
                                                                                9   Mercury.

xviii

And there-with-all, he on her shoulder laid
  His snaky-wreathed Mace, whose awfull power   *caduceus*
  Doth make both Gods and hellish fiends affraid:
  Where-at the *Titanesse* did sternely lower,
  And stoutly answer'd, that in euill hower
  He from his *Ioue* such message to her brought,
160 To bid her leaue faire *Cynthias* siluer bower;
  Sith shee his *Ioue* and him esteemed nought,
No more then *Cynthia's* selfe; but all their kingdoms sought.

xix

The Heauens Herald staid not to reply,
  But past away, his doings to relate
  Vnto his Lord; who now in th'highest sky,
  Was placed in his principall Estate,
  With all the Gods about him congregate:
  To whom when *Hermes* had his message told,
  It did them all exceedingly amate,
170 Saue *Ioue*; who, changing nought his count'nance bold,
Did vnto them at length these speeches wise vnfold;

xx

Harken to mee awhile yee heauenly Powers;
  Ye may remember since th'Earths cursed seed[10]
  Sought to assaile the heauens eternall towers,
  And to vs all exceeding feare did breed:
  But how we then defeated all their deed,
  Yee all doe knowe, and them destroied quite;
  Yet not so quite, but that there did succeed
  An off-spring of their bloud,[11] which did alite
180 Vpon the fruitfull earth, which doth vs yet despite.

xxi

Of that bad seed is this bold woman bred,
  That now with bold presumption doth aspire
  To thrust faire *Phœbe* from her siluer bed,
  And eke our selues from heauens high Empire,
  If that her might were match to her desire:
  Wherefore, it now behoues vs to advise
  What way is best to driue her to retire;
  Whether by open force, or counsell wise,
Areed ye sonnes of God, as best ye can deuise.

xxii

190 So hauing said, he ceast; and with his brow
  (His black eye-brow, whose doomefull dreaded beck
  Is wont to wield the world vnto his vow,
  And euen the highest Powers of heauen to check)
  Made signe to them in their degrees to speake:
  Who straight gan cast their counsell graue and wise.
  Meane-while, th'Earths daughter, thogh she nought did reck
  Of *Hermes* message; yet gan now advise,
What course were best to take in this hot bold emprize.

---

10 i.e. the Titans.

11 For the story of the origin of men from the blood of the giants, see Ovid's *Metamorphoses*, 1. 151–62.

xxiii

Eftsoones she thus resolv'd; that whil'st the Gods
   (After returne of *Hermes* Embassie)
   Were troubled, and amongst themselues at ods,
   Before they could new counsels re-allie,   *reform*
   To set vpon them in that extasie;
   And take what fortune time and place would lend:
   So, forth she rose, and through the purest sky
   To *Ioues* high Palace straight cast to ascend,
To prosecute her plot: Good on-set boads good end.

xxiv

Shee there arriuing, boldly in did pass;
   Where all the Gods she found in counsell close,   *secret*
   All quite vnarm'd, as then their manner was.
   At sight of her they suddaine all arose,
   In great amaze, ne wist what way to chose.
   But *Ioue*, all fearelesse, forc't them to aby;
   And in his soueraine throne, gan straight dispose
   Himselfe more full of grace and Maiestie,
That mote encheare his friends, and foes mote terrifie.

xxv

That, when the haughty *Titanesse* beheld,
   All were she fraught with pride and impudence,
   Yet with the sight thereof was almost queld;
   And inly quaking, seem'd as reft of sense,
   And voyd of speech in that drad audience;   *dread*
   Vntill that *Ioue* himselfe, her selfe bespake:
   Speake thou fraile woman, speake with confidence,
   Whence art thou, and what doost thou here now make?
What idle errand hast thou, earths mansion to forsake?

xxvi

Shee, halfe confused with his great commaund,
   Yet gathering spirit of her natures pride,
   Him boldly answer'd thus to his demaund:
   I am a daughter, by the mothers side,
   Of her that is Grand-mother magnifide
   Of all the Gods, great *Earth*, great *Chaos* child:
   But by the fathers (be it not envide)
   I greater am in bloud (whereon I build)
Then all the Gods, though wrongfully from heauen exil'd.

xxvii

For, *Titan* (as ye all acknowledge must)
   Was *Saturnes* elder brother by birth-right;
   Both sonnes of *Vranus*: but by vniust
   And guilefull meanes, through *Corybantes*[12] slight,   *trick*
   The younger thrust the elder from his right:
   Since which, thou *Ioue*, iniuriously hast held
   The Heauens rule from *Titans* sonnes by might;
   And them to hellish dungeons downe hast feld:
Witnesse ye Heauens the truth of all that I haue teld.

---

12 Attendants to Rhea, who deceives Saturn by giving him a stone instead of her newborn son Jove.

xxviii

Whil'st she thus spake, the Gods that gaue good eare
    To her bold words, and marked well her grace,
    Beeing of stature tall as any there
    Of all the Gods, and beautifull of face,
    As any of the Goddesses in place,
    Stood all astonied, like a sort of Steeres;
250   Mongst whom, some beast of strange and forraine race,
    Vnwares is chaunc't, far straying from his peeres:
So did their ghastly gaze bewray their hidden feares.

xxix

Till hauing pauz'd awhile, *Ioue* thus bespake;
    Will neuer mortall thoughts ceasse to aspire,
    In this bold sort, to Heauen claime to make,
    And touch celestiall seates with earthly mire?
    I would haue thought, that bold *Procrustes* hire,   *punishment*
    Or *Typhons* fall, or proud *Ixions* paine,
    Or great *Prometheus*, tasting of our ire,[13]
260   Would haue suffiz'd, the rest for to restraine;
And warn'd all men by their example to refraine:

xxx

But now, this off-scum of that cursed fry,[14]
    Dare to renew the like bold enterprize,
    And chalenge th'heritage of this our skie;
    Whom what should hinder, but that we likewise
    Should handle as the rest of her allies,
    And thunder-driue to hell? With that, he shooke
    His Nectar-deawed locks, with which the skyes
    And all the world beneath for terror quooke,   *quaked*
270   And eft his burning levin-brond in hand he tooke.   *lightning*

xxxi

But, when he looked on her louely face,
    In which, faire beames of beauty did appeare,
    That could the greatest wrath soone turne to grace
    (Such sway doth beauty euen in Heauen beare)
    He staide his hand: and hauing chang'd his cheare,
    He thus againe in milder wise began;
    But ah! if Gods should striue with flesh yfere,
    Then shortly should the progeny of Man
Be rooted out, if *Ioue* should doe still what he can:

xxxii

280   But thee faire *Titans* child, I rather weene,   *think*
    Through some vaine errour or inducement light,
    To see that mortall eyes haue neuer seene;
    Or through ensample of thy sisters might,
    Bellona; whose great glory thou doost spight,
    Since thou hast seene her dreadfull power belowe,
    Mongst wretched men (dismaide with her affright)
    To bandie Crownes, and Kingdomes to bestowe:
And sure thy worth, no lesse then hers doth seem to showe.

13   These three mythic figures were violently punished for angering   14   That is, mankind as the offspring of the Titans and giants.
the gods.

xxxiii

But wote thou this, thou hardy *Titanesse*,   *know*
 That not the worth of any liuing wight
 May challenge ought in Heauens interesse;
 Much lesse the Title of old *Titans* Right:
 For, we by Conquest of our soueraine might,
 And by eternall doome of Fates decree,
 Haue wonne the Empire of the Heauens bright;
 Which to our selues we hold, and to whom wee
Shall worthy deeme partakers of our blisse to bee.

290

xxxiv

Then ceasse thy idle claime thou foolish gerle,
 And seeke by grace and goodnesse to obtaine
 That place from which by folly *Titan* fell;
 There-to thou maist perhaps, if so thou faine
 Haue *Ioue* thy gratious Lord and Soueraigne.
 So, hauing said, she thus to him replide;
 Ceasse *Saturnes* sonne, to seeke by proffers vaine
 Of idle hopes t'allure mee to thy side,
For to betray my Right, before I haue it tride.

300

xxxv

But thee, O *Ioue*, no equall Iudge I deeme
 Of my desert, or of my dewfull Right;
 That in thine owne behalfe maist partiall seeme:
 But to the highest him, that is behight
 Father of Gods and men by equall might;
 To weet, the God of Nature, I appeale.
 There-at *Ioue* wexed wroth, and in his spright
 Did inly grudge, yet did it well conceale;
And bade *Dan Phœbus*[15] Scribe her Appellation seale.

310

xxxvi

Eftsoones the time and place appointed were,
 Where all, both heauenly Powers, and earthly wights,
 Before great Natures presence should appeare,
 For triall of their Titles and best Rights:
 That was, to weet, vpon the highest hights
 Of *Arlo-hill* (Who knowes not *Arlo-hill?*)[16]   *peak*
 That is the highest head (in all mens sights)
 Of my old father *Mole*,[17] whom Shepheards quill
Renowmed hath with hymnes fit for a rurall skill.

320

xxxvii

And, were it not ill fitting for this file,
 To sing of hilles and woods, mongst warres and Knights,
 I would abate the sternenesse of my stile,
 Mongst these sterne stounds to mingle soft delights;
 And tell how *Arlo* through *Dianaes* spights
 (Beeing of old the best and fairest Hill
 That was in all this holy-Islands hights)
 Was made the most vnpleasant, and most ill.
Meane while, O *Clio*, lend *Calliope*[18] thy quill.

330

---

15 Apollo.
16 Arlo Hill is Spenser's name for Galtymore, a mountain in County Limerick, Ireland, which was the location of important events in Irish legend.

17 Mole is Spenser's name for a range of mountains in County Cork where Colin Clout sits in his poem *Colin Clout's Come Home Again*.
18 The epic muse (Calliope) here takes up the pen of history's muse (Clio).

xxxviii

Whylome, when *IRELAND* florished in fame
    Of wealths and goodnesse, far aboue the rest[19]
    Of all that beare the *British* Islands name,
    The Gods then vs'd (for pleasure and for rest)
    Oft to resort there-to, when seem'd them best:
    But none of all there-in more pleasure found,
340   Then *Cynthia*; that is soueraine Queene profest
    Of woods and forrests, which therein abound,
Sprinkled with wholsom waters, more then most on ground.[20]

xxxix

But mongst them all, as fittest for her game,
    Either for chace of beasts with hound or boawe,
    Or for to shroude in shade from *Phœbus* flame,
    Or bathe in fountaines that doe freshly flowe,
    Or from high hilles, or from the dales belowe,
    She chose this *Arlo*; where shee did resort
    With all her Nymphes enranged on a rowe,
350   With whom the woody Gods did oft consort:
For, with the Nymphes, the Satyres loue to play and sport.

xl

Amongst the which, there was a Nymph that hight
    Molanna; daughter of old father *Mole*,
    And sister vnto *Mulla*, faire and bright:
    Vnto whose bed false *Bregog* whylome stole,
    That Shepheard *Colin* dearely did condole,
    And made her lucklesse loues well knowne to be.
    But this *Molanna*, were she not so shole,   *shallow*
    Were no lesse faire and beautifull then shee:
360   Yet as she is, a fairer flood may no man see.

xli

For, first, she springs out of two marble Rocks,
    On which, a groue of Oakes high mounted growes,
    That as a girlond seemes to deck the locks
    Of som faire Bride, brought forth with pompous showes
    Out of her bowre, that many flowers strowes:
    So, through the flowry Dales she tumbling downe,
    Through many woods, and shady coverts flowes
    (That on each side her siluer channell crowne)
Till to the Plaine she come, whose Valleyes shee doth drowne.

xlii

370   In her sweet streames, *Diana* vsed oft
    (After her sweatie chace and toilesome play)
    To bathe her selfe; and after, on the soft
    And downy grasse, her dainty limbes to lay
    In couert shade, where none behold her may:
    For, much she hated sight of liuing eye.

19   The allusion here is to Ireland's high state of civilization from the 6th to the 9th century.

20   Especially when compared to Guyon's destruction of the Bower of Bliss and Spenser's defense of Elizabethan policy in Ireland, this professed love of Ireland suggests an extraordinarily complex – perhaps ambivalent – reaction on Spenser's part. The purpose of these river narratives is to illustrate mutability in nature – how the Irish landscape has changed – and in man – how the wolf and the thief have assumed power. Molanna is the river Behanna; Mulla is the river Awbeg; Fanchin is the river Funsheon.

Foolish God *Faunus*,[21] though full many a day
   He saw her clad, yet longed foolishly
To see her naked mongst her Nymphes in priuity.

xliii

No way he found to compasse his desire,
   But to corrupt *Molanna*, this her maid,
   Her to discouer for some secret hire:
   So, her with flattering words he first assaid;
   And after, pleasing gifts for her purvaid,
   Queene-apples, and red Cherries from the tree,   *quinces*
   With which he her allured and betraid,
   To tell what time he might her Lady see
When she her selfe did bathe, that he might secret bee.

380

xliv

There-to hee promist, if shee would him pleasure
   With this small boone, to quit her with a better;
   To weet, that where-as shee had out of measure
   Long lov'd the *Fanchin*, who by nought did set her,
   That he would vndertake, for this to get her
   To be his Loue, and of him liked well:
   Besides all which, he vow'd to be her debter
   For many moe good turnes then he would tell;
The least of which, this little pleasure should excell.

390

xlv

The simple maid did yield to him anone;
   And eft him placed where he close might view
   That neuer any saw, saue onely one;[22]
   Who, for his hire to so foole-hardy dew,
   Was of his hounds devour'd in Hunters hew.
   Tho, as her manner was on sunny day,
   Diana, with her Nymphes about her, drew
   To this sweet spring; where, doffing her array,
She bath'd her louely limbes, for *Ioue* a likely pray.

400

xlvi

There *Faunus* saw that pleased much his eye,
   And made his hart to tickle in his brest,
   That for great ioy of some-what he did spy,
   He could him not containe in silent rest;
   But breaking forth in laughter, loud profest
   His foolish thought. A foolish *Faune* indeed,
   That couldst not hold thy selfe so hidden blest,
   But wouldest needs thine owne conceit areed.   *thought*
Babblers vnworthy been of so diuine a meed.   *reward*

410

xlvii

The Goddesse, all abashed with that noise,
   In haste forth started from the guilty brooke;
   And running straight where-as she heard his voice,
   Enclos'd the bush about, and there him tooke,
   Like darred Larke; not daring vp to looke
   On her whose sight before so much he sought.

420

---

21   The Roman god of nature.   22   Actaeon. For the myth of Diana and Actaeon, see Ovid's *Metamor-*
phoses, 3. 173–252.

Thence, forth they drew him by the hornes, and shooke
Nigh all to peeces, that they left him nought;
And then into the open light they forth him brought.

xlviii

Like as an huswife, that with busie care
Thinks of her Dairie to make wondrous gaine,
Finding where-as some wicked beast vnware
That breakes into her Dayr'house, there doth draine
Her creaming pannes, and frustrate all her paine;
Hath in some snare or gin set close behind,   *trap*
Entrapped him, and caught into her traine,
Then thinkes what punishment were best assign'd,
And thousand deathes deuiseth in her vengefull mind:

430

xlix

So did *Diana* and her maydens all
Vse silly *Faunus*, now within their baile:
They mocke and scorne him, and him foule miscall;
Some by the nose him pluckt, some by the taile,
And by his goatish beard some did him haile:
Yet he (poore soule) with patience all did beare;
For, nought against their wils might countervaile:
Ne ought he said what euer he did heare;
But hanging downe his head, did like a Mome appeare.   *fool*

440

l

At length, when they had flouted him their fill,
They gan to cast what penaunce him to giue.
Some would haue gelt him, but that same would spill   *destroy*
The Wood-gods breed, which must for euer liue:
Others would through the riuer him haue driue,
And ducked deepe: but that seem'd penaunce light;
But most agreed and did this sentence giue,
Him in Deares skin to clad; and in that plight,
To hunt him with their hounds, him selfe saue how hee might.

450

li

But *Cynthia's* selfe, more angry then the rest,
Thought not enough, to punish him in sport,
And of her shame to make a gamesome iest;
But gan examine him in straighter sort,
Which of her Nymphes, or other close consort,
Him thither brought, and her to him betraid?
He, much affeard, to her confessed short,
That 'twas *Molanna* which her so bewraid.
Then all attonce their hands vpon *Molanna* laid.

lii

460

But him (according as they had decreed)
With a Deeres-skin they couered, and then chast
With all their hounds that after him did speed;
But he more speedy, from them fled more fast
Then any Deere: so sore him dread aghast.
They after follow'd all with shrill out-cry,
Shouting as they the heauens would haue brast:
That all the woods and dales where he did flie,
Did ring againe, and loud reeccho to the skie.

liii

So they him follow'd till they weary were;
　　When, back returning to *Molann'* againe,
470　　They, by commaund'ment of *Diana*, there
　　Her whelm'd with stones. Yet *Faunus* (for her paine)
　　Of her beloued *Fanchin* did obtaine,
　　That her he would receiue vnto his bed.
　　So now her waues passe through a pleasant Plaine,
　　Till with the *Fanchin* she her selfe doe wed,
And (both combin'd) themselues in one faire riuer spred.

liv

Nath' lesse, *Diana*, full of indignation,
　　Thence-forth abandond her delicious brooke;
480　　In whose sweet streame, before that bad occasion,
　　So much delight to bathe her limbes she tooke:
　　Ne onely her, but also quite forsooke
　　All those faire forrests about *Arlo* hid,
　　And all that Mountaine, which doth over-looke
　　The richest champian that may else be rid,　　*field*
And the faire *Shure*, in which are thousand Salmons bred.

lv

Them all, and all that she so deare did way,
　　Thence-forth she left; and parting from the place,
　　There-on an heauy haplesse curse did lay,
490　　To weet, that Wolues, where she was wont to space,
　　Should harbour'd be, and all those Woods deface,
　　And Thieues should rob and spoile that Coast around.
　　Since which, those Woods, and all that goodly Chase,
　　Doth to this day with Wolues and Thieues abound:
Which too-too true that lands in-dwellers since haue found.

Canto VII.

Pealing, from Ioue, *to* Natur's *Bar,*　　*appealing/court*
　　bold Alteration *pleades*
Large Euidence: but Nature *soone*
　　her righteous Doome areads.

i

Ah! whither doost thou now thou greater Muse[1]
　　Me from these woods and pleasing forrests bring?
　　And my fraile spirit (that dooth oft refuse
　　This too high flight, vnfit for her weake wing)
　　Lift vp aloft, to tell of heauens King
　　(Thy soueraine Sire) his fortunate successe,
　　And victory, in bigger noates to sing,　　*louder notes*
　　Which he obtain'd against that *Titanesse*,
That him of heauens Empire sought to dispossesse.

CANTO VII.
1　Like the narrator of Milton's *Paradise Lost*, Book 3, Spenser's persona is unequal to the task of rising to the realm of God without the aid of his muse. The muse is Urania, the figure for heavenly wisdom. There is also an implicit allusion here to the Christian principle of grace.

ii

10
Yet sith I needs must follow thy behest,   *since*
   Doe thou my weaker wit with skill inspire,
   Fit for this turne; and in my feeble brest
   Kindle fresh sparks of that immortall fire,
   Which learned minds inflameth with desire
   Of heauenly things: for, who but thou alone,
   That art yborne of heauen and heauenly Sire,
   Can tell things doen in heauen so long ygone;   *ago*
So farre past memory of man that may be knowne.

iii

Now, at the time that was before agreed,
20
   The Gods assembled all on *Arlo* hill;
   As well those that are sprung of heauenly seed,
   As those that all the other world doe fill,
   And rule both sea and land vnto their will:
   Onely th'infernall Powers might not appeare;
   Aswell for horror of their count'naunce ill,
   As for th'vnruly fiends which they did feare;
Yet *Pluto* and *Proserpina*² were present there.

iv

And thither also came all other creatures,
   What-euer life or motion doe retaine,
30
   According to their sundry kinds of features;
   That *Arlo* scarsly could them all containe;
   So full they filled euery hill and Plaine:
   And had not *Natures* Sergeant (that is *Order*)
   Them well disposed by his busie paine,
   And raunged farre abroad in euery border,
They would haue caused much confusion and disorder.

v

Then forth issewed (great goddesse) great dame *Nature*,
   With goodly port and gracious Maiesty;
   Being far greater and more tall of stature
40
   Then any of the gods or Powers on hie:
   Yet certes by her face and physnomy,
   Whether she man or woman inly were,
   That could not any creature well descry:³
   For, with a veile that wimpled euery where,
Her head and face was hid, that mote to none appeare.

vi

That some doe say was so by skill deuized,
   To hide the terror of her vncouth hew,
   From mortall eyes that should be sore agrized;   *horrified*
   For that her face did like a Lion shew,
50
   That eye of wight could not indure to view:
   But others tell that it so beautious was,
   And round about such beames of splendor threw,
   That it the Sunne a thousand times did pass,
Ne could be seene, but like an image in a glass.

---

2 Divine rulers of the underworld, whose marriage is associated with natural fertility in Claudian's *De Raptu Proserpina*.

3 As the embodiment of all the things that are, Nature is both andro-gynous and indefinable.

vii

That well may seemen true: for, well I weene
  That this same day, when she on *Arlo* sat,
  Her garment was so bright and wondrous sheene,
  That my fraile wit cannot deuize to what
  It to compare, nor finde like stuffe to that,
60 As those three sacred *Saints*, though else most wise,
  Yet on mount *Thabor* quite their wits forgat,
  When they their glorious Lord in strange disguise
Transfigur'd sawe; his garments so did daze their eyes.

viii

In a fayre Plaine vpon an equall Hill,
  She placed was in pauilion;
  Not such as Craftes-men by their idle skill
  Are wont for Princes states to fashion:
  But th'earth her self of her owne motion,
  Out of her fruitfull bosome made to growe
70 Most dainty trees; that, shooting vp anon,
  Did seeme to bow their bloosming heads full lowe,
For homage vnto her, and like a throne did shew.

ix

So hard it is for any liuing wight,
  All her array and vestiments to tell,
  That old *Dan Geffrey* (in whose gentle spright
  The pure well head of Poesie did dwell)
  In his *Foules parley* durst not with it mel,
  But it transferd to *Alane*, who he thought
  Had in his *Plaint of kindes* describ'd it well:
80 Which who will read set forth so as it ought,
Go seek he out that *Alane* where he may be sought.[4]

x

And all the earth far vnderneath her feete
  Was dight with flowres, that voluntary grew
  Out of the ground, and sent forth odours sweet,
  Tenne thousand mores of sundry sent and hew,
  That might delight the smell, or please the view:
  The which, the Nymphes, from all the brooks thereby
  Had gathered, which they at her foot-stoole threw;
  That richer seem'd then any tapestry,
90 That Princes bowres adorne with painted imagery.[5]

xi

And *Mole* himselfe, to honour her the more,
  Did deck himself in freshest faire attire,
  And his high head, that seemeth alwaies hore
  With hardned frosts of former winters ire,
  He with an Oaken girlond now did tire,   *attire*
  As if the loue of some new Nymph late seene,
  Had in him kindled youthfull fresh desire,
  And made him change his gray attire to greene;
Ah gentle *Mole*! such ioyance hath thee well beseene.   *adorned*

---

4 See Chaucer ("Dan Geffrey"), *Parliament of Fowls*, 302–18.

5 Renaissance tapestries were decorated with intricate patterns of plants and animals.

xii

100 Was neuer so great ioyance since the day,
That all the gods whylome assembled were,
On *Hæmus* hill in their diuine array,
To celebrate the solemne bridall cheare,
Twixt *Peleus*, and dame *Thetis* pointed there;
Where *Phœbus* self, that god of Poets hight,
They say did sing the spousall hymne full cleere,
That all the gods were rauisht with delight
Of his celestiall song, and Musicks wondrous might.

xiii

This great Grandmother of all creatures bred
110 Great *Nature*, euer young yet full of eld,
Still moouing, yet vnmoued from her sted;
Vnseene of any, yet of all beheld;
Thus sitting in her throne as I haue teld,
Before her came dame *Mutabilitie*;
And being lowe before her presence feld,
With meek obaysance and humilitie,
Thus gan her plaintif Plea, with words to amplifie;

xiv

To thee O greatest goddesse, onely great,[6]
An humble suppliant loe, I lowely fly
120 Seeking for Right, which I of thee entreat;
Who Right to all dost deale indifferently,   *fairly*
Damning all Wrong and tortious Iniurie,   *evil*
Which any of thy creatures doe to other
(Oppressing them with power, vnequally)
Sith of them all thou art the equall mother,
And knittest each to each, as brother vnto brother.

xv

To thee therefore of this same *Ioue* I plaine,   *complain*
And of his fellow gods that faine to be,
That challenge to themselues the whole worlds raign;
130 Of which, the greatest part is due to me,
And heauen it selfe by heritage in Fee:
For, heauen and earth I both alike do deeme,
Sith heauen and earth are both alike to thee;
And, gods no more then men thou doest esteeme:
For, euen the gods to thee, as men to gods do seeme.

xvi

Then weigh, O soueraigne goddesse, by what right
These gods do claime the worlds whole souerainty;
And that is onely dew vnto thy might
Arrogate to themselues ambitiously:
140 As for the gods owne principality,
Which *Ioue* vsurpes vniustly; that to be

---

6   The power of Mutability's appeal to Nature is derived from several elements: (1) the narrator's insistence on his inadequacy, humility, and piety before the court of Nature; (2) Mutability's bold challenge to the rights of all the gods to be superior to men and to Nature (this challenge involves the idea that in the light of nature there is no hierarchy either among men or among the gods, that the principle of change levels all living things, and that − if this is true − the gods may be an empty concept; (3) the beauty and nostalgia of the scene, which provides a defense against the threatening theological and philosophical issues raised here.

My heritage, *Ioue's* self cannot deny,
From my great Grandsire *Titan*, vnto mee,
Deriu'd by dew descent; as is well knowen to thee.

xvii

Yet mauger *Ioue*, and all his gods beside,   *despite*
I doe possesse the worlds most regiment;   *strongest rule*
As, if ye please it into parts diuide,
And euery parts inholders to conuent,
Shall to your eyes appeare incontinent.
150   And first, the Earth (great mother of vs all)[7]
That only seems vnmov'd and permanent,
And vnto *Mutability* not thrall;
Yet is she chang'd in part, and eeke in generall.

xviii

For, all that from her springs, and is ybredde,
How-euer fayre it flourish for a time,
Yet see we soone decay; and, being dead,
To turne again vnto their earthly slime:
Yet, out of their decay and mortall crime,
We daily see new creatures to arize;
160   And of their Winter spring another Prime,
Vnlike in forme, and chang'd by strange disguise:
So turne they still about, and change in restlesse wise.

xix

As for her tenants; that is, man and beasts,
The beasts we daily see massacred dy,
As thralls and vassalls vnto mens beheasts:
And men themselues doe change continually,
From youth to eld, from wealth to pouerty,
From good to bad, from bad to worst of all.
Ne doe their bodies only flit and fly:
170   But eeke their minds (which they immortall call)
Still change and vary thoughts, as new occasions fall.

xx

Ne is the water in more constant case;
Whether those same on high, or these belowe.
For, th'Ocean moueth stil, from place to place;
And euery Riuer still doth ebbe and flowe:
Ne any Lake, that seems most still and slowe,
Ne Poole so small, that can his smoothnesse holde,
When any winde doth vnder heauen blowe;
With which, the clouds are also tost and roll'd;
180   Now like great Hills; and, streight, like sluces, them vnfold.

xxi

So likewise are all watry liuing wights
Still tost, and turned, with continuall change,
Neuer abyding in their stedfast plights.
The fish, still floting, doe at randon range,
And neuer rest; but euermore exchange
Their dwelling places, as the streames them carrie:

---

7   For the next several stanzas the influence of Lucretius' *The Nature of Things* is an important source.

Ne haue the watry foules a certaine grange,
        Wherein to rest, ne in one stead do tarry;
But flitting still doe flie, and still their places vary.

xxii

190   Next is the Ayre: which who feeles not by sense
        (For, of all sense it is the middle meane)
        To flit still? and, with subtill influence
        Of his thin spirit, all creatures to maintaine,
        In state of life? O weake life! that does leane
        On thing so tickle as th'vnsteady ayre;
        Which euery howre is chang'd, and altred cleane
        With euery blast that bloweth fowle or faire:
The faire doth it prolong; the fowle doth it impaire.

xxiii

Therein the changes infinite beholde,
200   Which to her creatures euery minute chaunce;
        Now, boyling hot: streight, friezing deadly cold:
        Now, faire sun-shine, that makes all skip and daunce:
        Streight, bitter storms and balefull countenance,
        That makes them all to shiuer and to shake:
        Rayne, hayle, and snowe do pay them sad penance,
        And dreadfull thunder-claps (that make them quake)
With flames and flashing lights that thousand changes make.

xxiv

Last is the fire: which, though it liue for euer,
        Ne can be quenched quite; yet, euery day,
210   Wee see his parts, so soone as they do seuer,
        To lose their heat, and shortly to decay;
        So, makes himself his owne consuming pray.
        Ne any liuing creatures doth he breed:
        But all, that are of others bredd, doth slay;
        And, with their death, his cruell life dooth feed;
Nought leauing, but their barren ashes, without seede.

xxv

Thus, all these fower (the which the ground-work bee
        Of all the world, and of all liuing wights)
        To thousand sorts of *Change* we subiect see:
220   Yet are they chang'd (by other wondrous slights)
        Into themselues, and lose their natiue mights;
        The Fire to Aire, and th'Ayre to Water sheere,
        And Water into Earth: yet Water fights
        With Fire, and Aire with Earth approaching neere:
Yet all are in one body, and as one appeare.

xxvi

So, in them all raignes *Mutabilitie*;
        How-euer these, that Gods themselues do call,
        Of them doe claime the rule and souerainty:
        As, *Vesta*, of the fire æthereall;
230   *Vulcan*, of this, with vs so vsuall;
        Ops, of the earth; and *Iuno* of the Ayre;
        Neptune, of Seas; and Nymphes, of Riuers all.
        For, all those Riuers to me subiect are:
And all the rest, which they vsurp, be all my share.

xxvii

Which to approuen true, as I haue told,
　Vouchsafe, O goddesse, to thy presence call
　The result which doe the world in being hold:
　As, times and seasons of the yeare that fall:
　Of all the which, demand in generall,
240　Or iudge thy selfe, by verdit of thine eye,
　Whether to me they are not subiect all.
　　Nature did yeeld thereto; and by-and-by,
Bade *Order* call them all, before her Maiesty.

xxviii

So, forth issew'd the Seasons of the yeare;
　First, lusty *Spring*, all dight in leaues of flowres[8]
　That freshly budded and new bloosmes did beare
　(In which a thousand birds had built their bowres
　That sweetly sung, to call forth Paramours):
　And in his hand a iauelin he did beare,
250　And on his head (as fit for warlike stoures)　　　*conflicts*
　A guilt engrauen morion he did weare;　　　*helmet*
That as some did him loue, so others did him feare.

xxix

Then came the iolly *Sommer*, being dight
　In a thin silken cassock coloured greene,
　That was vnlyned all, to be more light:
　And on his head a girlond well beseene
　He wore, from which as he had chauffed been
　The sweat did drop; and in his hand he bore
　A boawe and shaftes, as he in forrest greene
260　Had hunted late the Libbard or the Bore,　　　*leopard*
And now would bathe his limbes, with labor heated sore.

xxx

Then came the *Autumne* all in yellow clad,
　As though he ioyed in his plentious store,
　Laden with fruits that made him laugh, full glad
　That he had banisht hunger, which to-fore
　Had by the belly oft him pinched sore.
　Vpon his head a wreath that was enrold
　With eares of corne, of euery sort he bore:
　And in his hand a sickle he did holde,
270　To reape the ripened fruits the which the earth had yold.　　　*yielded*

xxxi

Lastly, came *Winter* cloathed all in frize,
　Chattering his teeth for cold that did him chill,
　Whil'st on his hoary beard his breath did freese;
　And the dull drops that from his purpled bill
　As from a limbeck did adown distill.　　　*alembic*
　In his right hand a tipped staffe he held,
　With which his feeble steps he stayed still:
　For, he was faint with cold, and weak with eld;
That scarse his loosed limbes he hable was to weld.　　　*control*

8　There may be an allusion here to the visual depiction of the seasons
and months in the famous illuminations to *The Très Riches Heures of Jean,
Duke of Berry* (1409–16).

xxxii

280 These, marching softly, thus in order went,
    And after them, the Monthes all riding came;
    First,[9] sturdy *March* with brows full sternly bent,
    And armed strongly, rode vpon a Ram,   *Aries*
    The same which ouer *Hellespontus* swam:
    Yet in his hand a spade he also hent,
    And in a bag all sorts of seeds ysame,   *together*
    Which on the earth he strowed as he went,
And fild her womb with fruitfull hope of nourishment.

xxxiii

Next came fresh *Aprill* full of lustyhed,
290   And wanton as a Kid whose horne new buds:
    Vpon a Bull he rode, the same which led   *Taurus*
    Europa floting through th'*Argolick* fluds:[10]   *Greek*
    His hornes were gilden all with golden studs
    And garnished with garlonds goodly dight
    Of all the fairest flowres and freshest buds
    Which th'earth brings forth, and wet he seem'd in sight
With waues, through which he waded for his loues delight.

xxxiv

Then came faire *May*, the fayrest mayd on ground,
    Deckt all with dainties of her seasons pryde,
300   And throwing flowres out of her lap around:
    Vpon two brethrens shoulders she did ride,
    The twinnes of *Leda*;[11] which on eyther side
    Supported her like to their soueraine Queene.
    Lord! how all creatures laught, when her they spide,
    And leapt and daunc't as they had rauisht beene!
And *Cupid* selfe about her fluttred' all in greene.

xxxv

And after her, came iolly *Iune*, arrayd
    All in greene leaues, as he a Player were;
    Yet in his time, he wrought as well as playd,
310   That by his plough-yrons mote right well appeare: *plow-share*
    Vpon a Crab he rode, that him did beare   *Cancer*
    With crooked crawling steps an vncouth pase,
    And backward yode, as Bargemen wont to fare   *went*
    Bending their force contrary to their face,
Like that vngracious crew which faines demurest grace.

xxxvi

Then came hot *Iuly* boyling like to fire,
    That all his garments he had cast away:
    Vpon a Lyon raging yet with ire   *Leo*
    He boldly rode and made him to obay:
320   It was the beast that whylome did forray
    The Nemæan forrest, till th'*Amphytrionide*
    Him slew, and with his hide did him array;
    Behinde his back a sithe, and by his side
Vnder his belt he bore a sickle circling wide.

---

9   Until the middle of the 18th century, the year was usually calculated as beginning in March. However, the Elizabethans worked with
several calendar systems at once, including the ecclesiastical, agricultural, and folk calendars.

10   Zeus in the form of the bull abducted Europa, according to Ovid.
11   The Gemini, Castor and Pollux.

xxxvii

The sixt was *August*, being rich arrayd
  In garment all of gold downe to the ground:
  Yet rode he not, but led a louely Mayd
  Forth by the lilly hand, the which was cround
  With eares of corne, and full her hand was found;
330   That was the righteous Virgin,[12] which of old   *Virgo*
  Liv'd here on earth, and plenty made abound;
  But, after Wrong was lov'd and Iustice solde,
She left th'vnrighteous world and was to heauen extold.

xxxviii

Next him, *September* marched eeke on foote;
  Yet was he heauy laden with the spoyle
  Of haruests riches, which he made his boot,
  And him enricht with bounty of the soyle:
  In his one hand, as fit for haruests toyle,
  He held a knife-hook; and in th'other hand   *Libra*
340   A paire of waights, with which he did assoyle   *determine*
  Both more and lesse, where it in doubt did stand,
And equall gaue to each as Iustice duly scann'd.

xxxix

Then came *October* full of merry glee:
  For, yet his noule was totty of the must,
  Which he was treading in the wine-fats see,
  And of the ioyous oyle, whose gentle gust
  Made him so frollick and so full of lust:
  Vpon a dreadfull Scorpion he did ride,   *Scorpio*
  The same which by *Dianaes* doom vniust
350   Slew great *Orion*: and eeke by his side
He had his ploughing share, and coulter ready tyde.

xl

Next was *Nouember*, he full grosse and fat,
  As fed with lard, and that right well might seeme;
  For, he had been a fatting hogs of late,
  That yet his browes with sweat, did reek and steem,
  And yet the season was full sharp and breem;   *cold*
  In planting eeke he took no small delight:
  Whereon he rode, not easie was to deeme;
  For it a dreadfull *Centaure* was in sight,   *Sagittarius*
360   The seed of *Saturne*, and faire *Nais*, *Chiron* hight.

xli

And after him, came next the chill *December*:
  Yet he through merry feasting which he made,
  And great bonfires, did not the cold remember;
  His Sauiours birth his mind so much did glad:
  Vpon a shaggy-bearded Goat he rade,   *Capricorn*
  The same wherewith *Dan Ioue* in tender yeares,[13]
  They say, was nourisht by th'*Idæan* mayd;
  And in his hand a broad deepe boawle he beares;
Of which, he freely drinks an health to all his peeres.

12 Also identified with Astraea, the Roman goddess of justice and allegorical symbol of Elizabeth (see Frances Yates's *Astraea*.)

13 While being hidden from Saturn, Zeus was nourished by a goat, perhaps by Amalthea, "the Idaean maid."

xlii

370   Then came old *Ianuary*, wrapped well
   In many weeds to keep the cold away;
   Yet did he quake and quiuer like to quell,
   And blowe his nayles to warme them if he may:
   For, they were numbd with holding all the day
   An hatchet keene, with which he felled wood,
   And from the trees did lop the needlesse spray:
   Vpon an huge great Earth-pot steane he stood;   *urn*
From whose wide mouth, there flowed forth the Romane floud.[14]   *Aquarius*

xliii

And lastly, came cold *February*, sitting
380   In an old wagon, for he could not ride;
   Drawne of two fishes for the season fitting,   *Pisces*
   Which through the flood before did softly slyde
   And swim away: yet had he by his side
   His plough and harnesse fit to till the ground,
   And tooles to prune the trees, before the pride
   Of hasting Prime did make them burgein round: *spring*
So past the twelue Months forth, and their dew places found.

xliv

And after these, there came the *Day*, and *Night*,
   Riding together both with equall pase,
390   Th'one on a Palfrey blacke, the other white;
   But *Night* had couered her vncomely face
   With a blacke veile, and held in hand a mace,
   On top whereof the moon and stars were pight,   *put*
   And sleep and darknesse round about did trace:
   But *Day* did beare, vpon his scepters hight,
The goodly Sun, encompast all with beames bright.

xlv

Then came the *Howres*, faire daughters of high *Ioue*,[15]
   And timely *Night*, the which were all endewed
   With wondrous beauty fit to kindle loue;
400   But they were Virgins all, and loue eschewed,
   That might forslack the charge to them fore-shewed   *neglect*
   By mighty *Ioue*; who did them Porters make
   Of heauens gate (whence all the gods issued)
   Which they did dayly watch, and nightly wake
By euen turnes, ne euer did their charge forsake.

xlvi

And after all came *Life*, and lastly *Death*;
   Death with most grim and griesly visage seene,
   Yet is he nought but parting of the breath;
   Ne ought to see, but like a shade to weene,   *understand*
410   Vnbodied, vnsoul'd, vnheard, vnseene.
   But *Life* was like a faire young lusty boy,
   Such as they faine *Dan Cupid* to haue beene,
   Full of delightfull health and liuely ioy,
Deckt all with flowres, and wings of gold fit to employ.

---

14   Aquarius is the water-bearer.   15   According to Homer, the Gates of Heaven are kept by the Hours.

xlvii

When these were past, thus gan the *Titanesse*;
  Lo, mighty mother, now be iudge and say,
  Whether in all thy creatures more or lesse
  CHANGE doth not raign and beare the greatest sway:
  For, who sees not, that *Time* on all doth pray?
420   But *Times* do change and moue continually.
  So nothing here long standeth in one stay:
  Wherefore, this lower world who can deny
But to be subiect still to *Mutabilitie*?

xlviii

Then thus gan *Ioue*; Right true it is, that these
  And all things else that vnder heauen dwell
  Are chaung'd of *Time*, who doth them all disseise   *deprive*
  Of being: But, who is it (to me tell)
  That *Time* himselfe doth moue and still compell
  To keepe his course? Is not that namely wee
430   Which poure that vertue from our heauenly cell,   *planet*
  That moues them all, and makes them changed be?
So them we gods doe rule, and in them also thee.

xlix

To whom, thus *Mutability*: The things
  Which we see not how they are mov'd and swayd,
  Ye may attribute to your selues as Kings,
  And say they by your secret powre are made:
  But what we see not, who shall vs perswade?
  But were they so, as ye them faine to be,
  Mov'd by your might, and ordred by your ayde;
440   Yet what if I can proue, that euen yee
Your selues are likewise chang'd, and subiect vnto mee?

l

And first, concerning her that is the first,
  Euen you faire *Cynthia*, whom so much ye make
  Ioues dearest darling, she was bred and nurst
  On *Cynthus* hill,[16] whence she her name did take:
  Then is she mortall borne, how-so ye crake;   *brag*
  Besides, her face and countenance euery day
  We changed see, and sundry forms partake,
  Now hornd, now round, now bright, now brown and gray:
450   So that *as changefull as the Moone* men vse to say.

li

Next, *Mercury*, who though he lesse appeare
  To change his hew,[17] and alwayes seeme as one;
  Yet, he his course doth altar euery yeare,
  And is of late far out of order gone:
  So *Venus* eeke, that goodly Paragone,
  Though faire all night, yet is she darke all day;
  And *Phœbus* self, who lightsome is alone,   *radiant*
  Yet is he oft eclipsed by the way,
And fills the darkned world with terror and dismay.

---

16 Birthplace of Apollo and Diana on the island of Delos.

17 Because it was thought the planets' orbits were circular, their courses were thought to be irregular until Kepler's law of elliptical orbits (1609).

lii

460
Now *Mars* that valiant man is changed most:
　For, he some times so far runs out of square,
　That he his way doth seem quite to haue lost,
　And cleane without his vsuall sphere to fare;
　That euen these Star-gazers stonisht are
　At sight thereof, and damne their lying bookes:
　So likewise, grim Sir *Saturne* oft doth spare
　His sterne aspect, and calme his crabbed lookes:
So many turning cranks these haue, so many crookes.　　　　　*windings/bendings*

liii

But you *Dan Ioue*, that only constant are,
470
　And King of all the rest, as ye do clame,
　Are you not subiect eeke to this misfare?
　Then let me aske you this withouten blame,
　Where were ye borne? some *say* in *Crete* by name,
　Others in *Thebes*, and others other-where;
　But wheresoeuer they comment the same,
　They all consent that ye begotten were,
And borne here in this world, ne other can appeare.

liv

Then are ye mortall borne, and thrall to me,
　Vnlesse the kingdome of the sky yee make
480
　Immortall, and vnchangeable to be;
　Besides, that power and vertue[18] which ye spake,
　That ye here worke, doth many changes take,
　And your owne natures change: for, each of you
　That vertue haue, or this, or that to make,
　Is checkt and changed from his nature trew,
By others opposition or obliquid view.

lv

Besides, the sundry motions of your Spheares,
　So sundry waies and fashions as clerkes faine,
　Some in short space, and some in longer yeares;
490
　What is the same but alteration plaine?
　Onely the starrie skie doth still remaine:
　Yet do the Starres and Signes therein still moue,
　And euen it self is mov'd, as wizards saine.
　But all that moueth, doth mutation loue:
Therefore both you and them to me I subject proue.

lvi

Then since within this wide great *Vniuerse*
　Nothing doth firme and permanent appeare,
　But all things tost and turned by transuerse:
　What then should let, but I aloft should reare
500
　My Trophee, and from all, the triumph beare?
　Now iudge then (O thou greatest goddesse trew!)
　According as thy selfe doest see and heare,
　And vnto me addoom that is my dew;
That is the rule of all, all being rul'd by you.

18　The "virtue" is the astrological influence of a planet.

lvii

So hauing ended, silence long ensewed,
   Ne *Nature* to or fro spake for a space,
   But with firme eyes affixt, the ground still viewed.
   Meane while, all creatures, looking in her face,
   Expecting th'end of this so doubtfull case,
510   Did hang in long suspence what would ensew,
   To whether side should fall the soueraigne place:
   At length, she looking vp with chearefull view,
The silence brake, and gaue her doome in speeches few.

lviii

I well consider all that ye haue sayd,
   And find that all things stedfastnes doe hate
   And changed be: yet being rightly wayd
   They are not changed from their first estate;
   But by their change their being doe dilate:[19]
520   And turning to themselues at length againe,
   Doe worke their owne perfection so by fate:
   Then ouer them Change doth not rule and raigne;
But they raigne ouer change, and doe their states maintaine.

lix

Cease therefore daughter further to aspire,
   And thee content thus to be rul'd by me:
   For thy decay thou seekst by thy desire;
   But time shall come that all shall changed bee,[20]
   And from thenceforth, none no more change shall see.
   So was the *Titaness* put downe and whist,   *silenced*
   And *Ioue* confirm'd in his imperiall see.   *throne*
530   Then was that whole assembly quite dismist,
   And *Natur's* selfe did vanish, whither no man wist.   *knew*

The VIII. Canto, vnperfite.

i

When I bethinke me on that speech whyleare,[1]   *just heard*
   Of *Mutability*, and well it way:
   Me seemes, that though she all vnworthy were
   Of the Heav'ns Rule; yet very sooth to say,
   In all things else she beares the greatest sway.
   Which makes me loath this state of life so tickle,   *unstable*
   And loue of things so vaine to cast away;
   Whose flowring pride, so fading and so fickle,
Short *Time* shall soon cut down with his consuming sickle.

ii

10   Then gin I thinke on that which Nature sayd,
   Of that same time when no more *Change* shall be,
   But stedfast rest of all things firmely stayd
   Vpon the pillours of Eternity,

---

19   Nature's answer – that being is constant and is "dilated" by change
– combines the thought of many ancient authorities, from Plato and
Aristotle to Boethius.
20   Cf. 1 Corinthians 15:52; "For the trumpet shall sound, and the
dead shall be raised incorruptible, and we shall be changed."

THE VIII. CANTO, VNPERFITE.
1   These two stanzas respectively respond to Mutability's speech and
Nature's answer, the first with a tragic vision and the second with a
divinely comic vision.

That is contrayr to *Mutabilitie*:
For, all that moueth, doth in *Change* delight:
But thence-forth all shall rest eternally
With Him that is the God of Sabbaoth hight: *called*
O! that great Sabbaoth God, grant me that Sabaoths sight.[2]

FINIS.

[FROM] A VIEW OF THE STATE OF IRELAND, WRITTEN DIALOGUE-WISE BETWEENE EUDOXUS AND IRENÆUS[1]

Eudox.   Doe you then thinke the winter time fittest for the services of Ireland? how falls it then
that our most imployments bee in summer, and the armies then led commonly forth?

Iren.   It is surely misconceived; for it is not with Ireland as it is with other countryes, where the
warres flame most in summer, and the helmets glister brightest in the fairest sunshine: But in
Ireland the winter yeeldeth best services, for then the trees are bare and naked, which use both
to cloath and house the kerne; the ground is cold and wet, which useth to be his bedding; the
aire is sharpe and bitter, to blowe thorough his naked sides and legges; the kyne are barren and
without milke, which useth to be his onely foode, neither if he kill them, will they yeeld him
flesh, nor if he keepe them, will they give him food, besides being all with calfe (for the most
part) they will, thorough much chasing and driving, cast all their calves, and lose their milke,
which should releive him the next summer.

Eudox.   I doe well understand your reason; but by your leave, I have heard it otherwise said, of
some that were outlawes: That in summer they kept themselves quiet, but in winter they would
play their parts, and when the nights were longest, then burne and spoyle most, so that they
might safely returne before day.

Iren.   I have likewise heard, and also seene proofe thereof true: But that was of such outlawes as
were either abiding in well inhabited countryes, as in Mounster, or bordering on the English
pale, as Feagh Mac Hugh, the Cavanaghes, the Moors, the Dempsies, or such like:[2] For, for them
the winter indeede is the fittest time for spoyling and robbing, because the nights are then (as
you said) longest and darkest, and also the countryes round about are then most full of corne,
and good provision to be gotten every where by them, but it is farre otherwise with a strong
peopled enemy, that possesse a whole countrey; for the other being but a few, and indeede privily
lodged, and kept in out villages, and corners nigh to the woodes and mountaines, by some of
their privy friends, to whom they bring their spoyles and stealthes, and of whom they continually receive secret releife; but the open enemy having all his countrey wasted, what by himselfe,
and what by the souldiours, findeth them succour in no place: Townes there are none, of which
he may get spoyle, they are all burnt: bread he hath none, he ploweth not in summer: Flesh he

2   "Sabbath" literally means "a time of rest," and "Sabaoth" (as in the
phrase "Yahweh Sabaoth") the "Lord of Hosts." The poem ends – or
stops – with this sense of God as eternal rest and absolute power. Spenser
leaves his reader also with a sense of the efforts of his own art (1) to
contain not only all of existence but also the principles of change and
nothingness; (2) to conceive of all of the structures that order existence
– hierarchy, power, precedent (in the courts of Cynthia and Jove); time,
change, androgynous sexuality (in the realm of Nature) – (3) to affirm
the necessary double vision of art (tragic and comic, order and change,
philosophically abstract and historically and imaginatively concrete, the
longing for an end and finality and the necessity of continuity); (4) to
recognize the power and limits of an individual poet's ability to encom-
pass the whole vision of art and life.

[FROM] A VIEW OF THE STATE OF IRELAND, WRITTEN
DIALOGUE-WISE BETWEENE EUDOXUS AND IRENÆUS
1   The names of the speakers seem to mean "man of good reputation" and "man from Ireland." There are several indications in the
dialogue that Irenæus is Spenser's persona. He speaks as someone
who has just returned to England from Ireland. England is clearly
the setting of the conversation. Although *A View* was entered into
the Stationers' Register in 1598, it was not published until 1633
(long after Spenser's death) in *Ancient Irish Chronicles*, edited by Sir
James Ware, a Dublin antiquarian. This is the version of Spenser's
text that has been most commonly read and the one that makes the
case most brutally for the use of violence in subduing the Irish. It is
a major document in the discourse of English colonialism.
2   There is a useful map of Ireland as it was in Spenser's time in
Andrew Hadfield and Willy Maley's edition of *A View*.

hath, but if he kill it in winter, he shall want milke in summer, and shortly want life. Therefore if they bee well followed but one winter, you shall have little worke with them the next summer.

Eudox. I doe now well perceive the difference, and doe verily thinke that the winter time is there fittest for service; withall I conceive the manner of your handling of the service, by drawing suddaine draughts upon the enemy, when he looketh not for you, and to watch advantages upon him, as hee doth upon you. By which straight keeping of them in, and not suffering them at any time long to rest, I must needes thinke that they will soone be brought lowe, and driven to great extreamities. All which when you have: performed, and brought them to the very last cast, suppose that they will offer, either to come to you and submit themselves, or that some of them will seeke to withdraw themselves, what is your advice to doe? will you have them received?

Iren. No, but at the beginning of those warres, and when the garrisons are well planted, and fortified, I would wish a proclamation were made generally, to come to their knowledge: That what persons soever would within twenty dayes absolutely submit themselves, (excepting onely the very principalls and ringleaders,) should finde grace: I doubt not, but upon the settling of these garrisons, such a terrour and neere consideration of their perillous state, would be strucken into most of them, that they will covet to drawe away from their leaders. And againe I well know that the rebells themselves (as I saw by proofe in Desmonds warre)[3] will turne away all their rascall people, whom they thinke unserviceable, as old men, women, children, and hyndes, (which they call churles,) which would onely waste their victualls, and yeeld them no ayde; but their cattle they will surely keepe away: These therefore, though policy would turne them backe againe, that they might the rather consume and afflict the other rebells, yet in a pittyfull commisseration I would wish them to be received; the rather for that this sort of base people doth not for the most part rebell of themselves, having no heart thereunto, but are by force drawne by the grand rebells into their action, and carryed away with the violence of the streame, else they should be sure to loose all that they have, and perhaps their lives too: The which they now carry unto them, in hope to enjoy them there, but they are there by the strong rebells themselves, soone turned out of all, so that the constraint hereof may in them deserve pardon. Likewise if any of their able men or gentlemen shall then offer to come away, and to bring their cattle with them, as some no doubt may steale them away privily, I wish them also to be received, for the disabling of the enemy, but withall, that good assurance may be taken for their true behaviour and absolute submission, and that then they be not suffered to remaine any longer in those parts, no nor about the garrisons, but sent away into the inner parts of the realme, and dispersed in such sort as they may not come together, nor easily returne if they would: For if they might bee suffered to remaine about the garrisons, and there inhabite, as they will offer to till the ground, and yeeld a great part of the profit thereof, and of their cattle, to the Coronell, wherewith they have heretofore tempted many, they would (as I have by experience knowne) bee ever after such a gaule and inconvenience to them, as that their profit shall not recompence their hurt; for they will privily releive their friends that are forth; they will send the enemy secret advertizements of all their purposes and journeyes, which they meane to make upon them; they will not also sticke to drawe the enemy privily upon them, yea and to betray the forte it selfe, by discovery of all her defects and disadvantages (if any be) to the cutting of all their throates. For avoiding whereof and many other inconveniencies, I wish that they should be carried farre from hence into some other parts, so that (as I say) they come in and submit themselves, upon the first summons: But afterwards I would have none received, but left to their fortune and miserable end: my reason is, for that those which will afterwards remaine without, are stout and obstinate rebells, such as will never be made dutiful and obedient, nor brought to labour or civill conversation, having once tasted that licentious life, and being acquainted with spoyle and outrages, will ever after be ready for the like occasions, so as there is no hope of their amendment or recovery, and therefore needefull to be cut off.

---

3 Here is one of several places where Spenser identifies himself as Irenæus.

Eudox.   Surely of such desperate persons, as will follow the course of their owne folly, there is no compassion to bee had, and for others you have proposed a mercifull meanes, much more then they have deserved, but what then shall be the conclusion of this warre? for you have prefixed a short time of its continuance.

Iren.   The end will (I assure me) bee very short and much sooner then can be in so great a trouble, as it seemeth hoped for, although there should none of them fall by the sword, nor bee slaine by the souldiour, yet thus being kept from manurance, and their cattle from running abroad, by this hard restraint they would quickly consume themselves, and devoure one another. The proofe whereof, I saw sufficiently exampled in these late warres of Mounster; for not withstanding that the same was a most rich and plentifull countrey, full of corne and cattle, that you would have thought they should have beene able to stand long, yet ere one yeare and a halfe they were brought to such wretchednesse, as that any stony heart would have rued the same.[4] Out of every corner of the woods and glynnes they came creeping forth upon their hands, for their legges could not beare them; they looked like anatomies of death, they spake like ghosts crying out of their graves; they did eate the dead carrions, happy where they could finde them, yea, and one another soone after, insomuch as the very carcasses they spared not to scrape out of their graves; and, if they found a plot of water-cresses or shamrocks, there they flocked as to a feast for the time, yet not able long to continue therewithall; that in short space there were none almost left, and a most populous and plentifull countrey suddainely left voyde of man and beast; yet sure in all that warre, there perished not many by the sword, but all by the extremitie of famine, which they themselves had wrought.

Eudox.   It is a wonder that you tell, and more to bee wondred how it should so shortly come to passe.

Iren.   It is most true, and the reason also very ready; for you must conceive that the strength of all that nation, is the Kerne, Galloglasse, Stocah, Horseman, and Horseboy, the which having beene never used to have any thing of their owne, and now being upon spoyle of others, make no spare of any thing, but havocke and confusion of all they meet with, whether it bee their owne friends goods, or their foes. And if they happen to get never so great spoyle at any time, the same they waste and consume in a tryce, as naturally delighting in spoyle, though it doe themselves no good. On the other side, whatsoever they leave unspent, the souldier when hee commeth there, spoyleth and havocketh likewise, so that betweene both nothing is very shortly left. And yet this is very necessary to bee done for the soone finishing of the warre, and not only this in this wise, but also those subiects which doe border upon those parts, are either to bee removed and drawne away, or likewise to bee spoyled, that the enemy may find no succour thereby. For what the souldier spares, the rebell will surely spoyle.

Eudox.   I doe now well understand you. But now when all things are brought to this passe, and all filled with these ruefull spectacles of so many wretched carcases starving, goodly countreys wasted, so huge desolation and confusion, that even I that doe but heare it from you, and do picture it in my minde, doe greatly pittie and commisserate it. If it shall happen, that the state of this miserie and lamentable image of things shall bee tolde, and feelingly presented to her Sacred Maiestie, being by nature full of mercy and clemency, who is most inclinable to such pittifull complaints, and will not endure to heare such tragedies made of her poore people and subiects, as some about her may insinuate; then she perhappes, for very compassion of such calamities, will not onely stoppe the streame of such violences, and returne to her wonted mildnesse, but also conne them little thankes which have beene the authours and counsellours of such bloodie platformes. So I remember that in the late govevernment of that good Lord Grey, when

---

4   Greenblatt comments, "Spenser's own account presses in upon us the fact that he was involved intimately, on an almost daily basis, throughout the island, in the destruction of Hiberno-Norman civilization, the exercise of a brutal force that had few if any of the romantic trappings with which Elizabeth contrived to soften it at home. Here, on the periphery, Spenser was an agent of and an apologist for massacre, the burning of mean hovels and of crops with the deliberate intention of starving the inhabitants, forced relocation of peoples, the manipulation of treason charges so as to facilitate the seizure of lands, the endless repetition of acts of military 'justice' calculated to intimidate and break the spirit" (1980: 186).

after long travell, and many perillous assayes, he had brought things almost to this passe that you speake of, that it was even made ready for reformation, and might have beene brought to what her Maiestie would, like complaint was made against him, that he was a bloodie man, and regarded not the life of her subiects no more than dogges, but had wasted and consumed all, so as now she had nothing almost left, but to raigne in their ashes; eare was soon lent therunto, and all suddenly turned topside-turvy; the noble Lord eft-soones was blamed; the wretched people pittied; and new counsells plotted, in which it was concluded that a general pardon should be sent over to all that would accept of it, upon which all former purposes were blancked, the Governour at a bay, and not only all that great and long charge which shee had before beene at quite lost and cancelled, but also that hope of good which was even at the doore put back, and cleane frustrated. All which, whether it be true, or no, your selfe can well tell.

Iren.   Too true, Eudoxus, the more the pitty, for I may not forget so memorable a thing: neither can I bee ignorant of that perillous device, and of the whole meanes by which it was compassed, and very cunningly contrived by sowing first dissention betweene him, and an other Noble Personage; wherein they both at length found how notably they had beene abused, and how thereby under hand this universall alteration of things was brought about, but then too late to stay the same; for in the meane time all that was formerly done with long labor, and great toyle, was (as you say) in a moment undone, and that good Lord blotted with the name of a bloody man, whom, who that well knew, knew to be most gentle, affable, loving, and temperate; but that the necessitie of that present state of things inforced him to that violence, and almost changed his naturall disposition.

Richard Hakluyt (1553?–1616)

Although he never went to sea, Richard Hakluyt was a dedicated compiler of the accounts of others' adventures. His greatest work was *The Principal Navigations, Voyages, Traffiques, and Discoveries of the English Nation, made by Sea or ouerland, to the remote and farthest distant quarters of the Earth, at any time within the compass of these 1600 yeres*, which first appeared in 1589 and then in a greatly expanded three-volume edition in 1598–1600. By profession a preacher, Hakluyt was educated at Westminster School in London and at Christ Church, Oxford. His fascination with geography began, according to his own account, with a visit to the Middle Temple chambers of a cousin, who showed him a map of the world and directed him to read from Psalm 107 that they who go down to the sea in ships see the works of the Lord. Essentially a feat of collecting, translating, and editing, *The Principal Navigations*, along with Foxe's compilation, *The Book of Martyrs*, was one of the most popular books of its time. Hakluyt was sustained in his endeavor by a combination of patriotism and the desire to tell the complete story of English achievements at sea. His translation of Emanuel van Meteren's narrative of the victory of the English fleet over the Spanish Armada is a prime example of the ideological dilemma Hakluyt faced. On the one hand he is committed to the celebration of English national achievement, but on the other hand his Pauline theology requires him to attribute such victories to God. Hakluyt's work continued to be added to after his death by Samuel Purchas and others. The Hakluyt Society of London issues modern editions of his works and those of other chroniclers of nautical adventure.

READING

Richard Hakluyt, *The Principal Navigations, Voyages, Traffiques, and Discoveries of the English Nation*.
Richard Helgerson, *Forms of Nationhood: The Elizabethan Writing of England*, ch. 4.
Garrett Mattingly, *The Armada*.
Boise Penrose, *Tudor and Early Stuart Voyaging*.
D. B. Quinn (ed.), *The Hakluyt Handbook*.

M. P.

[FROM] THE PRINCIPAL NAVIGATIONS, VOYAGES, TRAFFIQUES, AND DISCOVERIES OF THE ENGLISH NATION

The miraculous victory atchieved by the English Fleete, under the discreet and happy conduct of the right honourable, right prudent, and valiant lord, the L. Charles Howard, L. high Admirall of

England, &c. Upon the Spanish huge Armada sent in the yeere 1588. for the invasion of England, together with the wofull and miserable successe of the said Armada afterward, upon the coasts of Norway, of the Scottish Westerne Isles, of Ireland, of Spaine, of France, and of England, &c. Recorded in Latine by Emanuel van Meteran in the 15. booke of his history of the low Countreys.[1]

Having in part declared the strange and wonderfull events of the yeere eightie eight, which hath bene so long time foretold by ancient prophesies; we will now make relation of the most notable and great enterprise of all others which were in the foresaid yeere atchieved, in order as it was done. Which exploit (although in very deed it was not performed in any part of the low Countreys) was intended for their ruine and destruction. And it was the expedition which the Spanish king,[2] having a long time determined the same in his minde, and having consulted thereabout with the Pope,[3] set foorth and undertooke against England and the low Countreys. To the end that he might subdue the Realme of England, and reduce it unto his catholique Religion, and by that meanes might be sufficiently revenged for the disgrace, contempt and dishonour, which hee (having 34. yeeres before enforced them to the Popes obedience) had endured of the English nation, and for divers other injuries which had taken deepe impression in his thoughts. And also for that hee deemed this to bee the most readie and direct course, whereby hee might recover his heredetarie possession of the lowe Countreys, having restrained the inhabitants from sayling upon the coast of England. Which verily, upon most weighty arguments and evident reasons, was thought would undoubtly have come to passe, considering the great aboundance and store of all things necessary wherewith those men were furnished, which had the managing of that action committed unto them. But now let us describe the matter more particularly.

The Spanish King having with small fruite and commoditie, for above twentie yeeres together, waged warre against the Netherlanders, after deliberation with his counsellers thereabout, thought it most convenient to assault them once againe by Sea, which had bene attempted sundry times heretofore, but not with forces sufficient. Unto the which expedition it stoode him nowe in hand to joyne great puissance, as having the English people his professed enemies; whose Island is so situate, that it may either greatly helpe or hinder all such as saile into those parts. For which cause hee thought good first of all to invade England, being perswaded by his Secretary Escovedo, and by divers other well experienced Spaniards and Dutchmen, and by many English fugitives, that the conquest of that Iland was lesse difficult then the conquest of Holland and Zeland. Moreover the Spaniards were of opinion, that it would bee farre more behoveful for their King to conquere England and the lowe Countreys all at once, then to be constrained continually to maintaine a warlike Navie to defend his East and West Indie Fleetes, from the English Drake,[4] and from such like valiant enemies.

And for the same purpose the king Catholique had given commandement long before in Italy and Spaine, that a great quantitie of timber should be felled for the building of shippes; and had besides made great preparation of things and furniture requisite for such an expedition; as namely in founding of brasen Ordinance, in storing up of corne and victuals, in trayning of men to use warlike weapons, in leavying and mustering of souldiers: insomuch that about the beginning of the yeere 1588. he had finished such a mightie Navie, and brought it into Lisbon haven, as never the like had before that time sailed upon the Ocean sea.

A very large and particular description of this Navie was put in print and published by the Spaniards; wherein were set downe the number, names, and burthens of the shippes, the number of Mariners and souldiers throughout the whole Fleete; likewise the quantitie of their Ordinance, of their armour, of bullets, of match, of gun-poulder, of victuals, and of all their Navall furniture was in the saide description particularized. Unto all these were added the names of the Governours,

[FROM] THE PRINCIPAL NAVIGATIONS, VOYAGES, TRAFFIQUES, AND DISCOVERIES OF THE ENGLISH NATION

1 Emmanuel van Meteren's *Belgische ofte Nederlantsche Historien van Onser Tijden* was published in 1605. It sets out to demonstrate the Netherlanders' defense of their cultural integrity against all forces of oppression that they have experienced. The Protestant battle against

Spain in the Netherlands is also a major part of the legacy and mythology of Sir Philip Sidney.

2 Philip II, who had been Queen Mary's husband.

3 Sixtus V.

4 Sir Francis Drake.

Captaines, Noblemen and gentlemen voluntaries, of whom there was so great a multitude, that scarce was there any family of accompt, or any one principall man throughout all Spaine, that had not a brother, sonne or kinseman in that Fleete: who all of them were in good hope to purchase unto themselves in that Navie (as they termed it) invincible, endlesse glory and renowne, and to possesse themselves of great Seigniories and riches in England, and in the lowe Countreys. But because the said description was translated and published out of Spanish into divers other languages, we will here onely make an abridgement or briefe rehearsall thereof.

> Portugal furnished and set foorth under the conduct of the duke of Medina Sidonia generall of the Fleete, ten Galeons,[5] two Zabraes, 1300. Mariners, 3300. souldiers, 300. great pieces, with all requisite furniture.
>
> Biscay, under the conduct of John Martines de Ricalde Admiral of the whole Fleete, set forth tenne Galeons, 4. Pataches, 700. mariners, 2000. souldiers, 250. great pieces, &c.
>
> Guipusco, under the conduct of Michael de Oquendo, tenne Galeons, 4. Pataches, 700. mariners, 2000. souldiers, 310. great pieces.
>
> Italy with the Levant Islands, under Martine de Vertendona, 10. Galeons, 800. mariners, 2000. souldiers, 310. great pieces, &c.
>
> Castile, under Diego Flores de Valdez, 14. Galeons, two Pataches, 1700. mariners, 2400. souldiers, and 380. great pieces, &c.
>
> Andaluzia, under the conduct of Petro de Valdez, 10. Galeons, one Patache, 800. mariners, 2400. souldiers, 280. great pieces, &c.
>
> Item, under the conduct of John Lopez de Medina, 23. great Flemish hulkes, with 700. mariners, 3200. souldiers, and 400. great pieces.
>
> Item, under Hugo de Moncada, foure Galliasses containing 1200. gally-slaves, 460. mariners, 870. souldiers, 200. great pieces, &c.
>
> Item, under Diego de Mandrana, foure Gallies of Portugall, with 888. gally-slaves, 360. mariners, 20. great pieces, and other requisite furniture.
>
> Item, under Anthonie de Mendoza, 22. Pataches and Zabraes, with 574. mariners, 488. souldiers, and 193. great pieces.

Besides the ships aforementioned there were 20. caravels rowed with oares, being appointed to performe necessary services unto the greater ships: insomuch that all the ships appertayning to this Navie amounted unto the summe of 150. eche one being sufficiently provided of furniture and victuals.

The number of Mariners in the saide Fleete were above 8000. of slaves 2088. of souldiers 20000. (besides noblemen and gentlemen voluntaries) of great cast pieces 2650. The foresaid ships were of an huge and incredible capacitie and receipt. For the whole Fleete was large ynough to containe the burthen of 60. thousand tunnes.

The Galeons were 64. in number, being of an huge bignesse, and very stately built, being of marveilous force also, and so high, that they resembled great castles, most fit to defend themselves and to withstand any assault, but in giving any other ships the encounter farre inferiour unto the English and Dutch ships, which can with great dexteritie weild and turne themselves at all assayes. The upperworke of the said Galeons was of thicknesse and strength sufficient to beare off musket-shot. The lower worke and the timbers thereof were out of measure strong, being framed of planckes and ribs foure or five foote in thicknesse, insomuch that no bullets could pierce them, but such as were discharged hard at hand: which afterward prooved true, for a great number of bullets were founde to sticke fast within the massie substance of those thicke planckes. Great and well pitched Cables were twined about the masts of their shippes, to strengthen them against the battery of shot.

The Galliasses were of such bignesse, that they contained within them chambers, chapels, turrets, pulpits, and other commodities of great houses. The Galliasses were rowed with great oares,

---

5   For descriptions and illustrations of these different ships and other nautical terminology, see William Falconer, *A New Universal Dictionary of the Marine Microform: being, a copious explanation of the technical terms and phrases usually employed in the construction, equipment, machinery, movements,* *and military, as well as naval operations of ships: with such parts of astronomy and navigation, as will be found useful to practical navigators / Illustrated with a variety of modern designs . . .* (1815). There is a brief discussion (but no lexicon) of Hakluyt's nautical terminology in *The Hakluyt Handbook.*

there being in eche one of them 300. slaves for the same purpose, and were able to do great service with the force of their Ordinance. All these together with the residue aforenamed were furnished and beautified with trumpets, streamers, banners, warlike ensignes, and other such like ornaments.

Their pieces of brasen ordinance were 1600. and of yron a 1000.

The bullets thereto belonging were 120. thousand.

Item of gun-poulder 5600. quintals.[6] Of matche 1200. quintals.

Of muskets and kaleivers 7000. Of haleberts and partisans 10000.

Moreover they had great store of canons, double-canons, culverings and field-pieces for land services.

Likewise they were provided of all instruments necessary on land to conveigh and transport their furniture from place to place; as namely of carts, wheeles, wagons, &c. Also they had spades, mattocks and baskets to set pioners on worke. They had in like sort great store of mules and horses, and whatsoever else was requisite for a land-armie. They were so well stored of biscuit, that for the space of halfe a yeere, they might allow eche person in the whole Fleete halfe a quintall every moneth; whereof the whole summe amounteth unto an hundreth thousand quintals.

Likewise of wine they had 147. thousand pipes, sufficient also for halfe a yeeres expedition. Of bacon 6500. quintals. Of cheese three thousand quintals. Besides fish, rise, beanes, pease, oile, vineger, &c.

Moreover they had 12000. pipes of fresh-water, and all other necessary provision, as namely candles, lanternes, lampes, sailes, hempe, oxe-hides and lead to stop holes that should be made with the battery of gunshot. To be short, they brought all things expedient either for a Fleete by sea, or for an armie by land.

This Navie (as Diego Pimentelli afterward confessed) was esteemed by the King himselfe to containe 32000. persons, and to cost him every day 30. thousand ducates.

There were in the said Navie five terzaes of Spaniards, (which terzaes the Frenchmen call Regiments) under the commaund of five governours termed by the Spaniards, Masters of the field, and amongst the rest there were many olde and expert souldiers chosen out of the garisons of Sicilie, Naples, and Terçera. Their Captaines or Colonels were Diego Pimentelli, Don Francisco de Toledo, Don Alonço de Luçon, Don Nicolas de Isla, Don Augustin de Mexia; who had eche of them 32. companies under their conduct. Besides the which companies there were many bands also of Castilians and Portugals, every one of which had their peculiar governours, captaines, officers, colours and weapons.

It was not lawfull for any man, under grievous penaltie, to cary any women or harlots in the Fleete: for which cause the women hired certaine shippes, wherein they sailed after the Navie: some of the which being driven by tempest arrived upon the coast of France.

The generall of this mightie Navie, was Don Alonso Perez de Guzman duke of Medina Sidonia, Lord of S. Lucar, and knight of the golden Fleece: by reason that the Marques of santa Cruz appointed for the same dignitie, deceased before the time.

John Martines de Ricalde was Admirall of the Fleete.

Francis Bovadilla was chiefe Marshall: who all of them had their officers fit and requisite for the guiding and managing of such a multitude. Likewise Martin Alorcon was appointed Vicar generall of the Inquisition, being accompanied with more then a hundreth Monkes, to wit, Jesuites, Capuchines, and friers mendicant. Besides whom also there were Phisitians, Chirurgians,[7] Apothecaries, and whatsoever else perteined unto the hospitall.

Over and besides the forenamed governours and officers being men of chiefe note, there were 124. very noble and worthy Gentlemen, which went voluntarily of their owne costs and charges, to the ende they might see fashions, learne experience, and attaine unto glory. Amongst whom was the prince of Ascoli, Alonzo de Leiva, the marques de Pennafiel, the marques de Ganes, the marques de Barlango, count de Paredes, count de Yelvas, and divers other marqueses and earles of the honourable families of Mendoza, of Toledo, of Pachieco, of Cordova, of Guzman, of Manricques, and a great number of others.

---

6   A quintal is a unit of approximately 100 pounds.   7   i.e. physicians and surgeons.

While the Spaniards were furnishing this their Navie, the duke of Parma,[8] at the direction of king Philip, made great preparation in the low Countreys, to give ayd & assistance unto the Spaniards; building ships for the same purpose, and sending for Pilots and ship-wrights out of Italy.

In Flanders hee caused certaine deepe chanels to be made, and among the rest the chanell of Yper commonly called Yper-lee, employing some thousands of workemen about that service: to the end that by the said chanel he might transport ships from Antwerp and Ghendt to Bruges, where hee had assembled above a hundreth small ships called hoyes being well stored with victuals, which hoyes hee was determined to have brought into the sea by the way of Sluys, or else to have conveyed them by the saide Yper-lee being now of greater depth, into any port of Flanders whatsoever.

In the river of Waten he caused 70. ships with flat bottomes to be built, every one of which should serve to cary 30. horses, having eche of them bridges likewise for the horses to come on boord, or to goe foorth on land. Of the same fashion he had provided 200. other vessels at Neiuport, but not so great. And at Dunkerk hee procured 28. ships of warre, such as were there to be had, and caused a sufficient number of Mariners to be levied at Hamburgh, Breme, Emden, and at other places. Hee put in the ballast of the said ships, great store of beames of thicke plankes, being hollow and beset with yron pikes beneath, but on eche side full of claspes and hookes, to joyne them together.

Hee had likewise at Greveling provided 20. thousand of caske, which in a short space might be compact and joyned together with nailes and cords, and reduced into the forme of a bridge. To be short, whatsoever things were requisite for the making of bridges, and for the barring and stopping up of havens mouthes with stakes, posts, and other meanes, he commanded to be made ready. Moreover not farre from Neiuport haven, he had caused a great pile of wooden fagots to be layd, and other furniture to be brought for the rearing up of a mount. The most part of his ships conteined two ovens a piece to bake bread in, with a great number of sadles, bridles, and such other like apparell for horses. They had horses likewise, which after their landing should serve to convey, and draw engines, field-pieces, and other warlike provisions.

Neere unto Neiuport he had assembled an armie, over the which he had ordained Camillo de Monte to be Campmaster. This army consisted of 30. bands or ensignes of Italians, of tenne bands of Wallons, eight of Scots, and eight of Burgundians, all which together amount unto 56. bands, every band containing a hundreth persons. Neare unto Dixmud there were mustered 80. bands of Dutch men, sixtie of Spaniards, sixe of high Germans, and seven bands of English fugitives, under the conduct of sir William Stanlie an English knight.

In the suburbes of Cortreight there were 4000. horsemen together with their horses in a readinesse; and at Waten 900. horses, with the troupe of the Marques del Gwasto Captaine generall of the horsemen.

Unto this famous expedition and presupposed victorie, many potentates, princes, and honourable personages hied themselves: out of Spaine the prince of Melito called the duke of Pastrana and taken to be the sonne of one Ruygomes de Silva, but in very deed accompted among the number of king Philips base sonnes. Also the Marques of Burgrave, one of the sonnes of Archiduke Ferdinand and Philippa Welsera. Vespasian Gonsaga of the family of Mantua, being for chivalry a man of great renowne, and heretofore Vice-roy in Spaine. Item John Medices base sonne unto the duke of Florence. And Amadas of Savoy, the duke of Savoy his base sonne, with many others of inferiour degrees.

Likewise Pope Sixtus quintus for the setting forth of the foresaid expedition, as they use to do against Turkes & infidels, published a Cruzado, with most ample indulgences which were printed in great numbers. These vaine buls the English and Dutchmen deriding, sayd that the devill at all passages lay in ambush like a thiefe, no whit regarding such letters of safe conduct. Some there be which affirme that the Pope had bestowed the realme of England with the title of Defensor fidei,[9] upon the king of Spaine, giving him charge to invade it upon this condition, that hee should enjoy

---

8 One of the objects of the Armada was to convey troops under Parma's command to seize the English throne for Philip.

9 "Defender of the Faith" was a title also bestowed on Henry VIII by Pope Leo X.

the conquered realm, as a vassal and tributarie, in that regard, unto the sea of Rome. To this purpose the said Pope proffered a million of gold, the one halfe thereof to be paied in readie money, and the other halfe when the realme of England or any famous port thereof were subdued. And for the greater furtherance of the whole businesse, he dispatched one D. Allen an English man (whom hee had made Cardinall for the same ende and purpose) into the Low countries, unto whom he committed the administration of all matters ecclesiasticall throughout England. This Allen being enraged against his owne native countrey, caused the Popes bull to be translated into English, meaning upon the arrival of the Spanish fleete, to have it so published in England. By which Bull the excommunications of the two former Popes were confirmed, and the Queenes most sacred Majestie was by them most unjustly deprived of all princely titles and dignities, her subjects being enjoined to perform obedience unto the duke of Parma, and unto the Popes Legate.[10]

But that all matters might be performed with greater secrecie, and that the whole expedition might seeme rather to be intended against the Low countries, then against England, and that the English people might be perswaded that all was but bare words & threatnings, and that nought would come to effect, there was a solemne meeting appointed at Borborch in Flanders for a treatie of peace betweene her majestie and the Spanish king.

Against which treatie the united provinces making open protestation, used all meanes possible to hinder it, alleaging that it was more requisite to consult how the enemie now pressing upon them might be repelled from off their frontiers. Howbeit some there were in England that greatly urged and prosecuted this league, saying, that it would be very commodious unto the state of the realme, as well in regard of traffique and navigation, as for the avoiding of great expenses to maintaine the warres, affirming also, that at the same time peace might easily and upon reasonable conditions be obtained of the Spaniard. Others thought by this meanes to divert some other way, or to keepe backe the navy now comming upon them, and so to escape the danger of that tempest. Howsoever it was, the duke of Parma by these wiles enchanted and dazeled the eyes of many English & Dutch men that were desirous of peace: whereupon it came to passe, that England and the united provinces prepared in deed some defence to withstand that dreadfull expedition and huge Armada, but nothing in comparison of the great danger which was to be feared, albeit the constant report of the whole expedition had continued rife among them for a long time before. Howbeit they gave eare unto the relation of certaine that sayd, that this navie was provided to conduct and waft over the Indian Fleets: which seemed the more probable because the Spaniards were deemed not to be men of so small discretion as to adventure those huge and monstrous ships upon the shallow and dangerous chanel of England.

At length when as the French king about the end of May signified unto her Majestie in plaine termes that she should stand upon her guard, because he was now most certainly enformed, that there was so dangerous an invasion imminent upon her realme, that he feared much least all her land and sea-forces would be sufficient to withstand it, &c. then began the Queens Majestie more carefully to gather her forces together, & to furnish her own ships of warre, & the principall ships of her subjects with souldiers, weapons, and other necessary provision. The greatest and strongest ships of the whole navy she sent unto Plimmouth under the conduct of the right honorable Lord Charles Howard, lord high Admirall of England, &c. Under whom the renoumed Knight Sir Francis Drake was appointed Vice-admiral. The number of these ships was about an hundreth. The lesser ships being 30. or 40. in number, and under the conduct of the lord Henry Seimer were commanded to lie between Dover and Caleis.

On land likewise throughout the whole realme, souldiers were mustered and trained in all places, and were committed unto the most resolute and faithfull captaines. And whereas it was commonly given out that the Spaniard having once united himselfe unto the duke of Parma, ment to invade by the river of Thames, there was at Tilburie in Essex over-against Gravesend, a mightie army encamped, and on both sides of the river fortifications were erected, according to the prescription

10   A bull of excommunication from the Roman Catholic Church was issued by Rome against Queen Elizabeth in 1570, which became an incentive to disobedience and violence against her (see J. E. Neale, *Queen Elizabeth I: a biography*, ch. XII.)

of Frederike Genebelli an Italian enginier. Likewise there were certaine ships brought to make a bridge, though it were very late first. Unto the sayd army came in proper person the Queens most roiall Majestie, representing Tomyris that Scythian warlike princesse, or rather divine Pallas her selfe. Also there were other such armies levied in England.

The principall catholique Recusants (least they should stirre up any tumult in the time of the Spanish invasion) were sent to remaine at certaine convenient places, as namely in the Isle of Ely and at Wisbich. And some of them were sent unto other places, to wit, unto sundry bishops and noblemen, where they were kept from endangering the state of the common wealth, and of her sacred Majestie, who of her most gracious clemencie gave expresse commandement, that they should be intreated with all humanitie and friendship.

The provinces of Holland and Zeland, &c. giving credite unto their intelligence out of Spain, made preparation to defend themselves: but because the Spanish ships were described unto them to be so huge, they relied partly upon the shallow and dangerous seas all along their coasts. Wherfore they stood most in doubt of the duke of Parma his small and flat-bottomed ships. Howbeit they had all their ships of warre to the number of 90. and above, in a readinesse for all assayes: the greater part whereof were of a small burthen, as being more meete to saile upon their rivers and shallow seas: and with these ships they besieged all the havens in Flanders, beginning at the mouth of Scheld, or from the towne of Lillo, and holding on to Greveling and almost unto Caleis, & fortified all their sea-townes with strong garrisons.

Against the Spanish fleets arrivall, they had provided 25. or 30. good ships, committing the government of them unto Admirall Lonck, whom they commanded to joine himselfe unto the lord Henry Seymer, lying betweene Dover and Cales. And when as the foresaid ships, (whereof the greater part besieged the haven of Dunkerke) were driven by tempest into Zeland. Justin of Nassau the Admiral of Zeland supplied that squadron with 35. ships being of no great burthen, but excellently furnished with gunnes, mariners and souldiers in great abundance, and especially with 1200. brave Musquetiers, having bene accustomed unto sea-fights, and being chosen out of all their companies for the same purpose: and so the said Justin of Nassau kept such diligent ward in that Station that the duke of Parma could not issue foorth with his navy into the sea out of any part of Flanders.

In the meane while the Spanish Armada set saile out of the haven of Lisbon upon the 19. of May, An. Dom. 1588. under the conduct of the duke of Medina Sidonia, directing their course for the Baie of Corunna, aliâs the Groine of Gallicia, where they tooke in souldiers and warlike provision, this port being in Spaine the neerest unto England. As they were sailing along, there arose such a mightie tempest, that the whole Fleete was dispersed, so that when the duke was returned unto his company, he could not escry above 80. ships in all, whereunto the residue by litle and litle joyned themselves, except eight which had their mastes blowen over-board. One of the foure gallies of Portingal escaped very hardly, retiring her selfe into the haven. The other three were upon the coast of Baion in France, by the assistance and courage of one David Gwin an English captive (whom the French and Turkish slaves aided in the same enterprise) utterly disabled and vanquished: one of the three being first overcome, which conquered the two other, with the slaughter of their governours and souldiers, and among the rest of Don Diego de Mandrana with sundry others: and so those slaves arriving in France with the three Gallies, set themselves at libertie.

The navy having refreshed themselves at the Groine, & receiving daily commandement from the king to hasten their journey, hoised up sailes the 11. day of July, and so holding on their course till the 19. of the same moneth, they came then unto the mouth of the narow seas or English chanel. From whence (striking their sailes in the meane season) they dispatched certaine of their smal ships unto the duke of Parma. At the same time the Spanish Fleete was escried by an English pinasse, captaine whereof was M. Thomas Fleming, after they had bene advertised of the Spaniards expedition by their scoutes and espials, which having ranged along the coast of Spaine, were lately returned home into Plimmouth for a new supply of victuals and other necessaries, who considering the foresayd tempest were of opinion that the navy being of late dispersed and tossed up and downe the maine Ocean, was by no means able to performe their intended voiage.

Moreover, the L. Charles Howard L. high admiral of England had received letters from the court, signifying unto him that her Majestie was advertised that the Spanish Fleete would not come foorth, nor was to be any longer expected for, and therefore, that upon her Majesties commandement he must send backe foure of her tallest and strongest ships unto Chattam.

The lord high Admiral of England being thus on the sudden, namely upon the 19. of July about foure of the clocke in the afternoone, enformed by the pinasse of captaine Fleming aforesaid, of the Spaniards approch, with all speed and diligence possible he warped his ships, and caused his mariners and souldiers (the greater part of whom was absent for the cause aforesayd) to come on boord, and that with great trouble and difficultie, insomuch that the lord Admiral himselfe was faine to lie without in the road with six ships onely all that night, after the which many others came foorth of the haven. The very next day being the 20. of July about high noone, was the Spanish Fleete escried by the English, which with a Southwest wind came sailing along, and passed by Plimmouth: in which regard (according to the judgement of many skilful navigators) they greatly overshot themselves, whereas it had bene more commodious for them to have staied themselves there, considering that the Englishmen being as yet unprovided, greatly relied upon their owne forces, and knew not the estate of the Spanish navy. Moreover, this was the most convenient port of all others, where they might with greater securitie have bene advertised of the English forces, and how the commons of the land stood affected, and might have stirred up some mutinie, so that hither they should have bent all their puissance, and from hence the duke of Parma might more easily have conveied his ships.

But this they were prohibited to doe by the king and his counsell, and were expressely commanded to unite themselves unto the souldiers and ships of the said duke of Parma, and so to bring their purpose to effect. Which was thought to be the most easie and direct course, for that they imagined that the English and Dutch men would be utterly daunted and dismaied thereat, and would each man of them retire unto his owne Province and Porte for the defence thereof, and transporting the armie of the duke under the protection of their huge navy, they might invade England.

It is reported that the chiefe commanders in the navy, and those which were more skilfull in navigation, to wit, John Martines de Ricalde, Diego Flores de Valdez, and divers others found fault that they were bound unto so strict directions and instructions, because that in such a case many particular accidents ought to concurre and to be respected at one and the same instant, that is to say, the opportunitie of the wind, weather, time, tide, and ebbe, wherein they might saile from Flanders to England. Oftentimes also the darkenesse and light, the situation of places, the depths and shoulds were to be considered; all which especially depended upon the conveniencie of the windes, and were by so much the more dangerous.

But it seemeth that they were enjoined by their commission to ancre neere unto, or about Caleis, whither the duke of Parma with his ships and all his warrelike provision was to resort, and while the English and Spanish great ships were in the midst of their conflict, to passe by, and to land his souldiers upon the Downes.

The Spanish captives reported that they were determined first to have entred the river of Thames, and thereupon to have passed with small ships up to London, supposing that they might easily winne that rich and flourishing Citie being but meanely fortified and inhabited with Citizens not accustomed to the warres, who durst not withstand their first encounter, hoping moreover to finde many rebels against her Majestie and popish catholiques, or some favourers of the Scottish queene (which was not long before most justly beheaded) who might be instruments of sedition.

Thus often advertising the duke of Parma of their approch, the 20. of July they passed by Plimmouth, which the English ships pursuing and getting the wind of them, gave them the chase and the encounter, and so both Fleets frankly exchanged their bullets.

The day following which was the 21. of July, the English ships approched within musquet shot of the Spanish: at what time the lorde Charles Howard most hotly and valiantly discharged his Ordinance upon the Spanish Vice-admirall. The Spaniards then well perceiving the nimblenesse of the English ships in discharging upon the enimie on all sides, gathered themselves close into the forme of an halfe moone, and slackened their sailes, least they should outgoe any of their companie. And while they were proceeding on in this maner, one of their great Galliasses was so furiously battered with shot, that the whole navy was faine to come up rounder together for the safegard thereof; whereby it came to passe that the principall Galleon of Sivill (wherein Don Pedro de Valdez, Vasques de Silva, Alonzo de Sayas, and other noble men were embarqued) falling foule of another shippe, had her fore-mast broken, and by that meanes was not able to keepe way with the Spanish Fleete, neither would the sayde Fleete stay to succour it, but left the distressed Galeon behind. The lord Admirall of England when he saw this ship of Valdez, & thought she had bene voyd of Mariners and Souldiers, taking with him as many shippes as he could, passed by it, that he might not loose sight of the Spanish Fleet that night. For sir Francis Drake (who was notwithstanding appointed to beare out his lanterne that night) was giving of chase unto five great Hulkes which had separated themselves from the Spanish Fleete: but finding them to be Easterlings, he dismissed them. The lord Admirall all that night following the Spanish lanterne in stead of the English, found himselfe in the morning to be in the midst of his enimies Fleete, but when he perceived it, hee cleanly conveyed himselfe out of that great danger.

The day folowing, which was the two and twentie of July, Sir Francis Drake espied Valdez his shippe, whereunto hee sent foorth his pinnasse, and being advertised that Valdez himselfe was there, and 450. persons with him, he sent him word that he should yeeld himselfe. Valdez for his honors sake caused certaine conditions to be propounded unto Drake; who answered Valdez that he was not now at laisure to make any long parle, but if he would yeeld himselfe, he should find him friendly and tractable: howbeit if he had resolved to die in fight, he should proove Drake to be no dastard.

Upon which answere Valdez and his company understanding that they were fallen into the hands of fortunate Drake, being mooved with the renoume and celebritie of his name, with one consent yeelded themselves, and found him very favourable unto them. Then Valdez with 40. or 50. noblemen and gentlemen pertaining unto him, came on boord sir Francis Drakes ship. The residue of his company were caried unto Plimmouth, where they were detained a yere & an halfe for their ransome.

Valdez comming unto Drake and humbly kissing his hand protested unto him, that he and his had resolved to die in battell, had they not by good fortune fallen into his power, whom they knew to be right curteous and gentle, and whom they had heard by generall report to bee most favourable unto his vanquished foe; insomuch that he sayd it was to bee doubted whether his enimies had more cause to admire and love him for his great, valiant, and prosperous exploites, or to dread him for his singular felicitie and wisedom, which ever attended upon him in the warres, and by the which hee had attained unto so great honour. With that Drake embraced him and gave him very honourable entertainement, feeding him at his owne table, and lodging him in his cabbin.

Here Valdez began to recount unto Drake the forces of all the Spanish Fleet, and how foure mightie Gallies were separated by tempest from them: and also how they were determined first to have put into Plimmouth haven, not expecting to bee repelled thence by the English ships which they thought could by no meanes withstand their impregnable forces, perswading themselves that by means of their huge Fleete, they were become lords and commaunders of the maine Ocean. For which cause they marveled much how the English men in their small ships durst approch within musket shot of the Spaniards mightie woodden castles, gathering the wind of them with many other such like attempts.

Immediately after, Valdez and his company, being a man of principal authoritie in the Spanish Fleete, and being descended of one and the same familie with that Valdez, which in the yeere 1574. besieged Leiden in Holland, were sent captives into England. There were in the sayd ship 55. thousand ducates in ready money of the Spanish kings gold, which the souldiers merily shared among themselves.

The same day was set on fire one of their greatest shippes, being Admirall of the squadron of Guipusco, and being the shippe of Michael de Oquendo Vice-admirall of the whole Fleete, which contained great store of gunnepowder and other warrelike provision. The upper part onely of this shippe was burnt, and all the persons therein contained (except a very few) were consumed with fire. And thereupon it was taken by the English, and brought into England with a number of miserable burnt and skorched Spaniards. Howbeit the gunpowder (to the great admiration of all men) remained whole and unconsumed.

In the meane season the lord Admirall of England in his ship called the Arke-royall, all that night pursued the Spaniards so neere, that in the morning hee was almost left alone in the enimies Fleete, and it was foure of the clocke at afternoone before the residue of the English Fleet could overtake him.

At the same time Hugo de Moncada governour of the foure Galliasses, made humble sute unto the Duke of Medina that he might be licenced to encounter the Admirall of England: which libertie the duke thought not good to permit unto him, because hee was loth to exceed the limites of his commision and charge.

Upon Tuesday which was the three and twentie of July, the navie being come over against Portland, the wind began to turne Northerly, insomuch that the Spaniards had a fortunate and fit gale to invade the English. But the Englishmen having lesser and nimbler Ships, recovered againe the vantage of the winde from the Spaniards, whereat the Spaniards seemed to bee more incensed to fight then before. But when the English Fleete had continually and without intermission from morning to night, beaten and battered them with all their shot both great and small: the Spaniardes uniting themselves, gathered their whole Fleete close together into a roundell, so that it was apparant that they ment not as yet to invade others, but onely to defend themselves and to make hast unto the place prescribed unto them, which was neere unto Dunkerk, that they might joine forces with the duke of Parma, who was determined to have proceeded secretly with his small shippes under the shadow and protection of the great ones, and so had intended circumspectly to performe the whole expedition.

This was the most furious and bloodie skirmish of all, in which the lord Admirall of England continued fighting amidst his enimies Fleete, and seeing one of his Captaines afarre off, hee spake unto him in these wordes: Oh George what doest thou? Wilt thou nowe frustrate my hope and opinion conceived of thee? Wilt thou forsake mee nowe? With which wordes hee being enflamed, approched foorthwith, encountered the enemie, and did the part of a most valiant Captaine. His name was George Fenner, a man that had bene conversant in many Sea-fights.

In this conflict there was a certaine great Venetian ship with other small ships surprised and taken by the English.

The English navie in the meane while increased, whereunto out of all Havens of the Realme resorted ships and men: for they all with one accord came flocking thither as unto a set field, where immortall fame and glory was to be attained, and faithfull service to bee performed unto their prince and countrey.

In which number there were many great and honourable personages, as namely, the Erles of Oxford, of Northumberland, of Cumberland, &c. with many Knights and Gentlemen: to wit, Sir Thomas Cecill, Sir Robert Cecill, Sir Walter Raleigh, Sir William Hatton, Sir Horatio Palavicini, Sir Henry Brooke, Sir Robert Carew, Sir Charles Blunt, Master Ambrose Willoughbie, Master Henry Nowell, Master Thomas Gerard, Master Henry Dudley, Master Edward Darcie, Master Arthur Gorge, Master Thomas Woodhouse, Master William Harvie, &c. And so it came to passe that the number of the English shippes amounted unto an hundreth: which when they were come before Dover, were increased to an hundred and thirtie, being notwithstanding of no proportionable bignesse to encounter with the Spaniards, except two or three and twentie of the Queenes greater shippes, which onely, by reason of their presence, bred an opinion in the Spaniardes mindes concerning the power of the English Fleet: the mariners and souldiers whereof were esteemed to be twelve thousand.

The foure and twentie of July when as the sea was calme, and no winde stirring, the fight was onely betweene the foure great Galleasses and the English shippes, which being rowed with Oares, had great vauntage of the sayde English shippes, which notwithstanding for all that would not bee forced to yeeld, but discharged their chaine-shot to cut asunder their Cables and Cordage of the Galleasses, with many other such Stratagemes. They were nowe constrained to send their men on land for a newe supplie of Gunne-powder, whereof they were in great skarcitie, by reason they had so frankely spent the greater part in the former conflicts.

The same day, a Counsell being assembled, it was decreed that the English Fleete should bee devided into foure squadrons: the principall whereof was committed unto the lord Admirall: the second, to Sir Francis Drake: the third, to Captaine Hawkins: the fourth, to Captaine Frobisher.

The Spaniards in their sailing observed very diligent and good order, sayling three and foure, and sometimes more ships in a ranke, and folowing close up one after another, and the stronger and greater ships protecting the lesser.

The five and twentie of July when the Spaniardes were come over-against the Isle of Wight, the lord Admirall of England being accompanied with his best ships (namely the Lion, Captaine whereof was the lord Thomas Howard: The Elizabeth Jonas under the commandement of Sir Robert Southwel sonne in lawe unto the lord Admirall: the Beare under the lord Sheffield nephew unto the lord Admirall: the Victorie under Captaine Barker: and the Galeon Leicester under the fore-named Captaine George Fenner) with great valour and dreadfull thundering of shot, encountered the Spanish Admiral being in the very midst of all his Fleet. Which when the Spaniard perceived, being assisted with his strongest ships, he came forth and entered a terrible combate with the English: for they bestowed each on other the broad sides, and mutually discharged all their Ordinance, being within one hundred, or an hundred and twentie yards one of another.

At length the Spaniardes hoised up their sayles, and againe gathered themselves up close into the forme of a roundel. In the meane while Captaine Frobisher had engaged himselfe into a most dangerous conflict. Whereupon the lord Admirall comming to succour him, found that hee had valiantly and discreetly behaved himselfe, and that hee had wisely and in good time given over the fight, because that after so great a batterie he had sustained no damage.

For which cause the day following, being the sixe and twentie of July, the lord Admirall rewarded him with the order of knighthood, together with the lord Thomas Howard, the lord Sheffield, M. John Hawkins and others.

The same day the lord Admirall received intelligence from Newhaven in France, by certaine of his Pinnasses, that all things were quiet in France, and that there was no preparation of sending aide unto the Spaniards, which was greatly feared from the Guisian faction, and from the Leaguers: but there was a false rumour spread all about, that the Spaniards had conquered England.

The seven and twentie of July, the Spaniards about the sunne-setting were come over-against Dover, and rode at ancre within the sight of Caleis, intending to hold on for Dunkerk, expecting there to joyne with the duke of Parma his forces, without which they were able to doe litle or nothing.

Likewise the English Fleete following up hard upon them, ancred just by them within culvering-shot. And here the lord Henry Seymer united himselfe unto the lord Admiral with his fleete of 30. ships which road before the mouth of Thames.

As the Spanish navie therefore lay at ancre, the duke of Medina sent certaine messengers unto the duke of Parma, with whom upon that occasion many Noblemen and Gentlemen went to refresh themselves on land: and amongst the rest the prince of Ascoli, being accounted the kings base sonne, and a very proper and towardly yong gentleman, to his great good, went on shore, who was by so much the more fortunate, in that hee had not opportunitie to returne on boord the same ship, out of which he was departed, because that in returning home it was cast away upon the Irish coast, with all the persons contained therein.

The duke of Parma being advertised of the Spanish Fleetes arrivall upon the coast of England, made all the haste hee could to bee present himselfe in this expedition for the performance of his charge: vainely perswading himselfe that nowe by the meanes of Cardinall Allen, hee should be crowned king of England, and for that cause hee had resigned the governement of the Lowe countries unto Count Mansfeld the elder. And having made his vowes unto S. Mary of Hall in Henault (whom he went to visite for his blind devotions sake) hee returned toward Bruges the 28. of July.

The next day travelling to Dunkerk hee heard the thundering Ordinance of either Fleet: and the same evening being come to Dixmud, hee was given to understand the hard successe of the Spanish Fleete.

Upon Tuesday which was the thirtieth of July, about high noone, hee came to Dunkerk, when as al the Spanish Fleete was now passed by: neither durst any of his ships in the meane space come foorth to assist the sayd Spanish Fleete for feare of five and thirtie warrelike ships of Holland and Zeland, which there kept watch and warde under the conduct of the Admirall Justin of Nassau.

The foresayd five and thirtie shippes were furnished with most cunning mariners and olde expert souldiers, amongst the which were twelve hundred Musketiers, whom the States had chosen out of all their garisons, and whom they knew to have bene heretofore experienced in sea-fights.

This navie was given especially in charge not to suffer any shippe to come out of the Haven, nor to permit any Zabraes, Pataches or other small vessels of the Spanish Fleete (which were more likely to aide the Dunkerkers) to enter thereinto, for the greater ships were not to be feared by reason of the shallow sea in that place. Howbeit the prince of Parma his forces being as yet unreadie, were not come on boord his shippes, onely the English Fugitives being seven hundred in number under the conduct of Sir William Stanley, came in fit time to have bene embarked, because they hoped to give the first assault against England. The residue shewed themselves unwilling and loath to depart, because they sawe but a few mariners, who were by constraint drawne into this expedition, and also because they had very bare provision of bread, drinke, and other necessary victuals.

Moreover, the shippes of Holland and Zeland stood continually in their sight, threatening shot and powder, and many inconveniences unto them: for feare of which shippes, the Mariners and Seamen secretly withdrew themselves both day and night, least that the duke of Parma his souldiers should compell them by maine force to goe on boord, and to breake through the Hollanders Fleete, which all of them judged to bee impossible by reason of the straightnesse of the Haven.

But it seemeth that the Duke of Parma and the Spaniards grounded upon a vaine and presumptuous expectation, that all the ships of England and of the Low countreys would at the first sight of the Spanish and Dunkerk Navie have betaken themselves to flight, yeelding them sea roome, and endevouring onely to defend themselves, their havens, and sea coasts from invasion. Wherefore their intent and purpose was, that the Duke of Parma in his small and flat-bottomed shippes, should as it were under the shadow and wings of the Spanish fleet, convey over all his troupes, armour, and warlike provision, and with their forces so united, should invade England: or while the English fleete were busied in fight against the Spanish, should enter upon any part of the coast, which he thought to be most convenient. Which invasion (as the captives afterward confessed) the Duke of Parma thought first to have attempted by the river of Thames; upon the bankes whereof having at his first arrivall landed twenty or thirty thousand of his principall souldiers, he supposed that he might easily have woonne the Citie of London; both because his small shippes should have followed and assisted his land-forces, and also for that the Citie it-selfe was but meanely fortified and easie to overcome, by reason of the Citizens delicacie and discontinuance from the warres, who with continuall and constant labour might be vanquished, if they yeelded not at the first assault. They were in good hope also to have mette with some rebels against her Majestie, and such as were discontented with the present state, as Papists, and others. Likewise they looked for ayde from the favourers of the Scottish Queene, who was not long before put to death; all which they thought would have stirred up seditions and factions.

Whenas therefore the Spanish fleet rode at anker before Caleis, to the end they might consult with the Duke of Parma what was best to be done according to the Kings commandement, and the present estate of their affaires, and had now (as we will afterward declare) purposed upon the second of August being Friday, with one power and consent to have put their intended businesse in practise; the L. Admirall of England being admonished by her Majesties letters from the Court, thought it most expedient either to drive the Spanish fleet from that place, or at leastwise to give them the encounter: and for that cause (according to her Majesties prescription) he tooke forthwith eight of his woorst & basest ships which came next to hand, & disburthening them of all things which seemed to be of any value, filled them with gun-powder, pitch, brimstone, and with other combustible and firy matter; and charging all their oridnance with powder, bullets, and stones, he sent the sayd ships upon the 28 of July being Sunday, about two of the clocke after midnight, with the winde and tide against the Spanish fleet: which when they had proceeded a good space, being forsaken of the Pilots, and set on fire, were directly carried upon the King of Spaines Navie: which fire in the dead of the night put the Spaniards into such a perplexity and horrour (for they feared lest they were like unto those terrible ships, which Frederic Jenebelli three yeeres before, at the siege of Antwerpe, had furnished with gun-powder, stones, and dreadfull engines, for the dissolution of the Duke of Parma his bridge, built upon the river of Scheld) that cutting their cables whereon their ankers were fastened, and hoising up their sailes, they betooke themselves very confusedly unto the maine sea.

In this sudden confusion, the principall and greatest of the foure galliasses falling fowle of another ship, lost her rudder: for which cause when she could not be guided any longer, she was by the force of the tide cast into a certaine showld upon the shore of Caleis, where she was immediatly assaulted by divers English pinasses, hoyes, and drumblers.

And as they lay battering of her with their ordinance, and durst not boord her, the L. Admirall sent thither his long boat with an hundreth choise souldiers under the command of Captaine Amias Preston. Upon whose approach their fellowes being more emboldened, did offer to boord the galliasse: against whom the governour thereof and Captaine of all the foure galliasses, Hugo de Moncada, stoutly opposed himselfe, fighting by so much the more valiantly, in that he hoped presently to be succoured by the Duke of Parma. In the meane season, Moncada, after he had endured the conflict a good while, being hitte on the head with a bullet, fell downe starke dead, and a great number of Spaniards also were slaine in his company. The greater part of the residue leaping over-boord into the sea, to save themselves by swimming, were most of them drowned. Howbeit there escaped among others Don Anthonio de Manriques, a principall officer in the Spanish fleet (called by them their Veador generall) together with a few Spaniards besides: which Anthonio was the first man that carried certaine newes of the successe of the fleet into Spaine.

This huge and monstrous galliasse, wherein were contained three hundred slaves to lug at the oares, and foure hundred souldiers, was in the space of three houres rifled in the same place; and there were found amongst divers other commodities 50000 ducats of the Spanish kings treasure. At length when the slaves were released out of their fetters, the English men would have set the sayd ship on fire, which Monsieur Gourdon the governor of Caleis, for feare of the damage which might thereupon ensue to the Towne and Haven, would not permit them to do, but drave them from thence with his great ordinance.

Upon the 29 of July in the morning, the Spanish Fleet after the foresayd tumult, having arranged themselves againe into order, were, within sight of Greveling, most bravely and furiously encountered by the English; where they once againe got the winde of the Spaniards: who suffered themselves to be deprived of the commodity of the place in Caleis rode, and of the advantage of the winde neere unto Dunkerk, rather then they would change their array or separate their forces now conjoyned and united together, standing onely upon their defence.

And albeit there were many excellent and warlike ships in the English fleet, yet scarse were there 22 or 23 among them all which matched 90 of the Spanish ships in bignesse, or could conveniently assault them. Wherefore the English shippes using their prerogative of nimble stirrage, whereby they could turne and wield themselves with the winde which way they listed, came often times very neere upon the Spaniards, and charged them so sore, that now and then they were but a pikes length asunder: & so continually giving them one broad side after another, they discharged all their shot both great and small upon them, spending one whole day from morning till night in that violent kinde of conflict, untill such time as powder and bullets failed them. In regard of which want they thought it convenient not to pursue the Spaniards any longer, because they had many great vantages of the English, namely for the extraordinary bignesse of their ships, and also for that they were so neerely conjoyned, and kept together in so good array, that they could by no meanes be fought withall one to one. The English thought therefore, that they had right well acquited themselves, in chasing the Spaniards first from Caleis, and then from Dunkerk, and by that meanes to have hindered them from joyning with the Duke of Parma his forces, and getting the winde of them, to have driven them from their owne coasts.

The Spaniards that day sustained great losse and damage having many of their shippes shot thorow and thorow, and they discharged likewise great store of ordinance against the English; who indeed sustained some hinderance, but not comparable to the Spaniards losse: for they lost not any one shippe or person of account. For very diligent inquisition being made, the English men all that time wherein the Spanish Navy sayled upon their seas, are not found to have wanted above one hundreth of their people: albeit Sir Francis Drakes shippe was pierced with shot above forty times, and his very cabben was twise shot thorow, and about the conclusion of the fight, the bedde of a certaine gentleman lying weary thereupon, was taken quite from under him with the force of a bullet. Likewise, as the Earle of Northumberland and Sir Charles Blunt were at dinner upon a time, the bullet of a demi-culvering brake thorow the middest of their cabbin, touched their feet, and strooke downe two of the standers by, with many such accidents befalling the English shippes, which it were tedious to rehearse. Whereupon it is most apparant, that God miraculously preserved the English nation. For the L. Admirall wrote unto her Majestie that in all humane reason, and according to the judgement of all men (every circumstance being duly considered) the English men were not of any such force, whereby they might, without a miracle, dare once to approch within sight of the Spanish Fleet: insomuch that they freely ascribed all the honour of their victory unto God, who had confounded the enemy, and had brought his counsels to none effect.

The same day the Spanish ships were so battered with English shot, that that very night and the day following, two or three of them suncke right downe: and among the rest a certaine great ship of Biscay, which Captaine Crosse assaulted, which perished even in the time of the conflict, so that very few therin escaped drowning; who reported that the governours of the same shippe slew one another upon the occasion following: one of them which would have yeelded the shippe was suddenly slaine; the brother of the slaine party in revenge of his death slew the murtherer, and in the meane while the ship suncke.

The same night two Portugall galeons of the burthen of seven or eight hundreth tunnes a piece, to wit the Saint Philip and the Saint Matthew, were forsaken of the Spanish Fleet, for they were so torne with shotte, that the water entered into them on all sides. In the galeon of Saint Philip was Francis de Toledo, brother unto the Count de Orgas, being Colonell over two and thirty bands: besides other gentlemen; who seeing their mast broken with shotte, they shaped their course, as well as they could, for the coast of Flanders: whither when they could not attaine, the principall men in the ship committing themselves to their skiffe, arrived at the next towne, which was Ostend; and the ship it selfe being left behinde with the residue of their company, was taken by the Ulishingers.

In the other galeon, called the S. Matthew, was embarked Don Diego Pimentelli another campmaster and colonell of 32 bands, being brother unto the marques of Tamnares, with many other gentlemen and captaines. Their ship was not very great, but exceeding strong, for of a great number of bullets which had batterd her, there were scarse 20 wherewith she was pierced or hurt: her upper worke was of force sufficient to beare off a musket shot: this shippe was shot thorow and pierced in the fight before Greveling; insomuch that the leakage of the water could not be stopped: whereupon the duke of Medina sent his great skiffe unto the governour thereof, that he might save himselfe and the principal persons that were in his ship: which he, upon a hault courage, refused to do: wherefore the Duke charged him to saile next unto himselfe: which the night following he could not performe, by reason of the great abundance of water which entered his ship on all sides; for the avoiding wherof, and to save his ship from sincking, he caused 50 men continually to labor at the pumpe, though it were to small purpose. And seeing himselfe thus forsaken & separated from his admirall, he endevored what he could to attaine unto the coast of Flanders: where, being espied by 4 or 5 men of warre, which had their station assigned them upon the same coast, he was admonished to yeeld himselfe unto them. Which he refusing to do, was strongly assaulted by them altogether, and his ship being pierced with many bullets, was brought into farre worse case then before, and 40 of his souldiers were slaine. By which extremity he was enforced at length to yeeld himselfe unto Peter Banderduess & other captaines, which brought him and his ship into Zeland; and that other ship also last before mentioned: which both of them, immediatly after the greater and better part of their goods were unladen, suncke right downe.

For the memory of this exploit, the foresayd captaine Banderduess caused the banner of one of these shippes to be set up in the great Church of Leiden in Holland, which is of so great a length, that being fastened to the very roofe, it reached downe to the ground.

About the same time another small ship being by necessity driven upon the coast of Flanders, about Blankenberg, was cast away upon the sands, the people therein being saved. Thus almighty God would have the Spaniards huge ships to be presented, not onely to the view of the English, but also of the Zelanders; that at the sight of them they might acknowledge of what small ability they had beene to resist such impregnable forces, had not God endued them with courage, providence, and fortitude, yea, and fought for them in many places with his owne arme.

The 29 of July the Spanish fleet being encountered by the English (as is aforesayd) and lying close together under their fighting sailes, with a Southwest winde sailed past Dunkerk, the English ships stil following the chase. Of whom the day following when the Spaniards had got sea roome, they cut their maine sailes; whereby they sufficiently declared that they meant no longer to fight but to flie. For which cause the L. Admirall of England dispatched the L. Henrie Seymer with his squadron of small ships unto the coast of Flanders, where, with the helpe of the Dutch ships, he might stop the prince of Parma his passage, if perhaps he should attempt to issue forth with his army. And he himselfe in the meane space pursued the Spanish fleet untill the second of August, because he thought they had set saile for Scotland. And albeit he followed them very neere, yet did he not assault them any more, for want of powder and bullets. But upon the fourth of August, the winde arising, when as the Spaniards had spread all their sailes, betaking themselves wholly to flight, and leaving Scotland on the left hand, trended toward Norway (whereby they sufficiently declared that their whole intent was to save themselves by flight, attempting for that purpose, with their battered and crazed ships, the most dangerous navigation of the Northren seas) the English seeing that they were now proceeded unto the latitude of 57 degrees, and being unwilling to participate that danger whereinto the Spaniards plunged themselves, and because they wanted things necessary, and especially powder & shot, returned backe for England; leaving behinde them certaine pinasses onely, which they enjoyned to follow the Spaniards aloofe, and to observe their course. And so it came to passe that the fourth of August, with great danger and industry, the English arrived at Harwich: for they had bene tossed up and downe with a mighty tempest for the space of two or three dayes together, which it is likely did great hurt unto the Spanish fleet, being (as I sayd before) so maimed and battered. The English now going on shore, provided themselves foorthwith of victuals, gunne-powder, and other things expedient, that they might be ready at all assayes to entertaine the Spanish fleet, if it chanced any more to returne. But being afterward more certainely informed of the Spaniards course, they thought it best to leave them unto those boisterous and uncouth Northren seas, and not there to hunt after them.

The Spaniards seeing now that they wanted foure or five thousand of their people and having divers maimed and sicke persons, and likewise having lost 10 or 12 of their principall ships, they consulted among themselves, what they were best to doe, being now escaped out of the hands of the English, because their victuals failed them in like sort, and they began also to want cables, cordage, ankers, masts, sailes, and other naval furniture, and utterly despaired of the Duke of Parma his assistance (who verily hoping and undoubtedly expecting the returne of the Spanish Fleet, was continually occupied about his great preparation, commanding abundance of ankers to be made, & other necessary furniture for a Navy to be provided) they thought it good at length, so soone as the winde should serve them, to fetch a compasse about Scotland and Ireland, and so to returne for Spaine.

For they well understood, that commandement was given thorowout all Scotland, that they should not have any succour or assistance there. Neither yet could they in Norway supply their wants. Wherefore, having taken certaine Scotish and other fisherboats, they brought the men on boord their owne ships, to the end they might be their guides and Pilots. Fearing also least their fresh water should faile them, they cast all their horses and mules overboord: and so touching no where upon the coast of Scotland, but being carried with a fresh gale betweene the Orcades and

Faar-Isles, they proceeded farre North, even unto 61 degrees of latitude, being distant from any land at the least 40 leagues. Heere the Duke of Medina generall of the Fleet commanded all his followers to shape their course for Biscay: and he himselfe with twenty or five and twenty of his ships which were best provided of fresh water and other necessaries, holding on his course over the maine Ocean, returned safely home. The residue of his ships being about forty in number, and committed unto his Vice-admirall, fell neerer with the coast of Ireland, intending their course for Cape Clare, because they hoped there to get fresh water, and to refresh themselves on land. But after they were driven with many contrary windes, at length, upon the second of September, they were cast by a tempest arising from the Southwest upon divers parts of Ireland, where may of their ships perished. And amongst others, the shippe of Michael de Oquendo, which was one of the great Galliasses: and two great ships of Venice also, namely, la Ratta and Belanzara, with other 36 or 38 ships more, which perished in sundry tempests, together with most of the persons contained in them.

Likewise some of the Spanish ships were the second time carried with a strong West winde into the chanell of England, whereof some were taken by the English upon their coast, and others by the men of Rochel upon the coast of France.

Moreover, there arrived at Newhaven in Normandy, being by tempest inforced so to doe, one of the foure great Galliasses, where they found the ships with the Spanish women which followed the Fleet at their setting forth. Two ships also were cast away upon the coast of Norway, one of them being of a great burthen; howbeit all the persons in the sayd great ship were saved: insomuch that of 134 ships, which set saile out of Portugall, there returned home 53 onely small and great: namely of the foure galliasses but one, and but one of the foure gallies. Of the 91 great galleons and hulks there were missing 58, and 33 returned: of the pataches and zabraes 17 were missing, and 18 returned home. In briefe, there were missing 81 ships, in which number were galliasses, gallies, galeons, and other vessels both great and small. And amongst the 53 ships remaining, those also are reckoned which returned home before they came into the English chanell. Two galeons of those which were returned, were by misfortune burnt as they rode in the haven; and such like mishaps did many others undergo. Of 30000 persons which went in this expedition, there perished (according to the number and proportion of the ships) the greater and better part; and many of them which came home, by reason of the toiles and inconveniences which they sustained in this voyage, died not long after their arrivall. The Duke of Medina immediatly upon his returne was deposed from his authority, commanded to his private house, and forbidden to repaire unto the Court; where he could hardly satisfie or yeeld a reason unto his malicious enemies and back-biters. Many honourable personages and men of great renowme deceased soone after their returne; as namely John Martines de Ricalde, with divers others. A great part also of the Spanish Nobility and Gentry employed in this expedition perished either by fight, diseases, or drowning, before their arrival; & among the rest Thomas Perenot of Granduell a Dutchman, being earle of Cantebroi, and sonne unto Cardinall Granduell his brother.

Upon the coast of Zeland Don Diego de Pimentell, brother unto the Marques de Tamnares, and kinseman unto the earle of Beneventum & Calva, and Colonell over 32 bands with many other in the same ship was taken and detained as prisoner in Zeland.

Into England (as we sayd before) Don Pedro de Valdez, a man of singular experience, and greatly honoured in his countrey, was led captive, being accompanied with Don Vasquez de Silva, Don Alonzo de Sayas, and others.

Likewise upon the Scotish Westerne Isles of Lewis, and Ila, and about Cape Cantyre upon the maine land, there were cast away certaine Spanish shippes, out of which were saved divers Captaines and Gentlemen, and almost foure hundred souldiers, who for the most part, after their shipwracke, were brought unto Edenborough in Scotland, and being miserably needy and naked, were there clothed at the liberality of the King and the Marchants, and afterward were secretly shipped for Spaine; but the Scotish fleet wherein they passed touching at Yarmouth on the coast of Norfolke, were there stayed for a time untill the Councels pleasure was knowen; who in regard of their manifolde miseries, though they were enemies, wincked at their passage.

Upon the Irish coast many of their Noblemen and Gentlemen were drowned; and divers slaine by the barbarous and wilde Irish. Howbeit there was brought prisoner out of Ireland, Don Alonzo de Luçon, Colonell of two and thirtie bandes, commonly called a terza of Naples; together with Rodorigo de Lasso, and two others of the family of Cordova, who were committed unto the custodie of Sir Horatio Palavicini, that Monsieur de Teligny the sonne of Monsieur de la Noüe (who being taken in fight neere Antwerpe, was detained prisoner in the Castle of Turney) might be raunsomed for them by way of exchange. To conclude, there was no famous nor woorthy family in all Spaine, which in this expedition lost not a sonne, a brother, or a kinseman.

For the perpetuall memorie of this matter, the Zelanders caused newe coine of Silver and brasse to be stamped: which on the one side contained the armes of Zeland, with this inscription: GLORY TO GOD ONELY: and on the other side, the pictures of certeine great ships, with these words: THE SPANISH FLEET: and in the circumference about the ships: IT CAME, WENT, AND WAS. Anno 1588. That is to say, the Spanish fleet came, went, and was vanquished this yere; for which, glory be given to God onely.

Likewise they coined another kinde of money; upon the one side whereof was represented a ship fleeing, and a ship sincking: on the other side foure men making prayers and giving thanks unto God upon their knees; with this sentence: Man purposeth; God disposeth: 1588. Also, for the lasting memory of the same matter, they have stamped in Holland divers such like coines, according to the custome of the ancient Romans.

While this wooderfull and puissant Navie was sayling along the English coastes, and all men did now plainely see and heare that which before they would not be perswaded of, all people thorowout England prostrated themselves with humble prayers and supplications unto God: but especially the outlandish Churches (who had greatest cause to feare, and against whom by name, the Spaniards had threatened most grievous torments) enjoyned to their people continuall fastings and supplications, that they might turne away Gods wrath and fury now imminent upon them for their sinnes: knowing right well, that prayer was the onely refuge against all enemies, calamities, and necessities, and that it was the onely solace and reliefe for mankinde, being visited with affliction and misery. Likewise such solemne dayes of supplication were observed thorowout the united Provinces.

Also a while after the Spanish Fleet was departed, there was in England, by the commandement of her Majestie, and in the united Provinces, by the direction of the States, a solemne festivall day publikely appointed, wherein all persons were enjoyned to resort unto the Church, and there to render thanks and praises unto God: and the Preachers were commanded to exhort the people thereunto. The foresayd solemnity was observed upon the 29 of November; which day was wholly spent in fasting, prayer, and giving of thanks.

Likewise, the Queenes Majestie herselfe, imitating the ancient Romans, rode into London in triumph, in regard of her owne and her subjects glorious deliverance. For being attended upon very solemnely by all the principall estates and officers of her Realme, she was carried thorow her sayd City of London in a tryumphant chariot, and in robes of triumph, from her Palace unto the Cathedrall Church of Saint Paul, out of the which the ensignes and colours of the vanquished Spaniards hung displayed. And all the Citizens of London in their Liveries stood on either side the street, by their severall Companies, with their ensignes and banners: and the streets were hanged on both sides with Blew cloth, which, together with the foresayd banners, yeelded a very stately and gallant prospect. Her Majestie being entered into the Church, together with her Clergie and Nobles gave thanks unto God, and caused a publike Sermon to be preached before her at Pauls crosse: wherein none other argument was handled, but that praise, honour, and glory might be rendered unto God, and that Gods name might be extolled by thanksgiving. And with her owne princely voice she most Christianly exhorted the people to doe the same: whereupon the people with a loud acclamation wished her a most long and happy life, to the confusion of her foes.

John Lyly (1553?–1606)

John Lyly's writing career provides us with a fascinating sixteenth-century example of the rise and fall of a literary fad. His first published work, the prose fiction *Euphues: The Anatomy of Wit* (1578), appeared when he was in his mid-twenties and was a huge success, begetting an equally popular sequel (*Euphues and his England* in 1580) and many imitators. Robert Greene's *Menaphon* (1589) and Thomas Lodge's *Rosalynde* (1590), both of which contain direct references to Euphues in their subtitles, are two of the more notable examples of the many attempts to cash in on Lyly's success. "Euphuism," the name given to Lyly's prose style, used common rhetorical tropes of balance, parallelism, and antithesis (both in sound and sense), but in relentless profusion matched by an equally profuse use of arcane classical literary allusions. It is mannered and artificial even by Early Modern standards, but its contemporary success makes it all the more fascinating to examine from a modern perspective. Like most fads, it became an object of mockery once its popularity began to wane, and writers as diverse as Sidney, Shakespeare, and Michael Drayton criticized its excessive ornamentation. Lyly went on to write plays and sue unsuccessfully for the office of Master of the Revels. In later life, he abandoned literature and became a Member of Parliament.

His prose works thus embody one of the most difficult challenges for any reader of literature from a different historical era: how can we learn to enjoy texts that were considered pleasurable in their own day, but seem anything but in the present day? As immensely popular and influential as they were in the late sixteenth century, Lyly's fiction has been studied in the twentieth century more out of a sense of duty than pleasure. Modern criticism has focused on its stylistic characteristics and heavy-handed moralizing in an attempt to either explain (or deplore) the appeal of rhetorical excess and didactic writing. Beginning with Richard Helgerson, however, more and more critics have come to realize that the rhetorical excess is gleeful and that the mor-

alizing is too inconsistent and at odds with the action to be taken seriously. What has often been considered as a ponderous collection of humanist moral exempla is in fact an exposé of the limits of all didactic writing. The characters' heads are stuffed with sage moral precepts on all subjects, but they can deploy them only in ways that make themselves and those around them miserable. This is, of course, the familiar procedure of many comic send-ups of intellectual pretensions, and the humor with which Lyly suffused his texts has long been ignored. Modern anthologies have tended to add to these difficulties by only including the opening courtly love narrative from *The Anatomy of Wit*. This has prevented readers from appreciating the text as the heterogeneous generic mixture that it is: the courtly romance is followed by a redaction of Ovid's cures for love (see gazetteer), an address on female conduct, a treatise on education, a debate with an atheist, and some moral letters. The only common threads are Euphues himself and his unchanging habits of mind, and it is essential to consider how Lyly shows off his ability to adapt his writing to a whole range of humanistic prose genres. Our sample of these other genres in the present text is offered in the hope that it inspires readers to explore the whole and to see how, despite his many changes in character, Euphues never truly *learns* anything. The pleasure of the text comes in seeing Lyly gently mocking the humanist intellectual pretensions which he so skillfully deploys.

READING

Richard Helgerson, *The Elizabethan Prodigals*.
Joan Pong Linton, "The Humanist in the Market: Gendering Exchange and Authorship in Lyly's Euphues Romances," in Relihan (ed.) *Framing Elizabethan Fiction: Contemporary Approaches to Elizabethan Narrative Prose*.

J. H.

[FROM] EUPHUES: THE ANATOMY OF WIT

Very pleasant for all Gentlemen to read, and most necessary to remember: wherein are contained the delights that Wit followeth in his youth by the pleasantness of love, and the happiness he reapeth in age, by the perfectness of wisdom.

THE EPISTLE DEDICATORY

TO THE RIGHT HONOURABLE MY VERY GOOD LORD AND MASTER, SIR WILLIAM WEST, KNIGHT, LORD DELAWARE, JOHN LYLY WISHETH LONG LIFE WITH INCREASE OF HONOUR

Parrhasius[1] drawing the counterfeit of Helen, Right Honourable, made the attire of her head loose; who being demanded why he did so he answered she was loose. Vulcan was painted curiously,[2] yet with a polt-foot;[3] Venus cunningly, yet with her mole. Alexander having a scar in his cheek held his finger upon it that Apelles[4] might not paint it. Apelles painted him with his finger cleaving to his face. "Why," quoth Alexander, "I laid my finger on my scar because I would not have thee see it." "Yea," said Apelles, "and I drew it there because none else should perceive it; for if thy finger had been away either thy scar would have been seen or my art misliked." Whereby I gather that in all perfect works as well the fault as the face is to be shown. The fairest leopard is set down with his spots, the sweetest rose with his prickles, the finest velvet with his brack.[5] Seeing then that in every counterfeit as well the blemish as the beauty is coloured[6] I hope I shall not incur the displeasure of the wise in that in the discourse of Euphues I have as well touched the vanities of his love as the virtues of his life. The Persians, who above all their kings most honoured Cyrus, caused him to be engraven as well with his hooked nose as his high forehead. He that loved Homer best concealed not his flattering; and he that praised Alexander most bewrayed his quaffing.[7] Demonides must have a crooked shoe for his wry foot, Damocles a smooth glove for his straight hand.[8] For as every painter that shadoweth a man in all parts giveth every piece his just proportion, so he that deciphereth the qualities of the mind ought as well to show every humour[9] in his kind as the other doth every part in his colour. The surgeon that maketh the anatomy showeth as well the muscles in the heel as the veins of the heart.

If then the first sight of Euphues shall seem too light to be read of the wise or too foolish to be regarded of the learned, they ought not to impute it to the iniquity of the author but to the necessity of the history. Euphues beginneth with love as allured by wit, but endeth not with lust as bereft of wisdom. He wooeth women provoked by youth, but weddeth not himself to wantonness as pricked by pleasure. I have set down the follies of his wit without breach of modesty and the sparks of his wisdom without suspicion of dishonesty. And, certes,[10] I think there be more speeches which for gravity will mislike the foolish than unseemly terms which for vanity may offend the wise.

Which discourse, Right Honourable, I hope you will the rather pardon for the rudeness in that it is the first, and protect it the more willingly if it offend in that it shall be the last. It may be that fine wits will descant upon him that, having no wit, goeth about to make the Anatomy of Wit; and certainly their jesting in my mind is tolerable. For if the butcher should take upon him to cut the anatomy of a man because he hath skill in opening an ox, he would prove himself a calf;[11] or if the horse-leech[12] would adventure to minister a potion to a sick patient in that he hath knowledge to give a drench[13] to a diseased horse, he would make himself an ass. The shoemaker must not go above his latchet, nor the hedger meddle with anything but his bill. It is unseemly for the painter to feather a shaft, or the fletcher[14] to handle the pencil. All which things make most against me in that a fool hath intruded himself to discourse of wit. But as I was willing to commit the

---

EUPHUES: THE ANATOMY OF WIT

1 Greek painter of the 5th century BCE. The "Helen" he is painting here is, of course, Helen of Troy (see gazetteer).

2 *skillfully.*

3 *club-foot.*

4 See gazetteer.

5 *flaw.*

6 *depicted.*

7 "Quaffing" here refers to his high alcohol consumption; the writer referred to is probably Plutarch.

8 Demonides is a character in Plutarch; the Damocles reference has never been satisfactorily explained.

9 disposition. See the gazetteer under *Humours.*

10 *certainly.*

11 *dolt.*

12 *veterinarian.*

13 *medicinal drink.*

14 *arrow-maker.*

fault, so am I content to make amends. Howsoever the case standeth I look for no praise for my labour, but pardon for my good will; it is the greatest reward that I dare ask, and the least that they can offer. I desire no more, I deserve no less. Though the style nothing delight the dainty ear of the curious sifter,[15] yet will the matter recreate the mind of the courteous reader. The variety of the one will abate the harshness of the other. Things of greatest profit are set forth with least price. When the wine is neat there needeth no ivy bush.[16] The right coral needeth no colouring. Where the matter itself bringeth credit, the man with his gloss winneth small commendation. It is therefore, methinketh, a greater show of a pregnant wit than perfect wisdom in a thing of sufficient excellency to use superfluous eloquence. We commonly see that a black ground doth best beseem a white counterfeit. And Venus, according to the judgement of Mars, was then most amiable[17] when she sat close by Vulcan. If these things be true which experience trieth that a naked tale doth most truly set forth the naked truth, that where the countenance is fair there need no colours, that painting is meeter for ragged walls than fine marble, that verity then shineth most bright when she is in least bravery[18] – shall satisfy mine own mind, though I cannot feed their humours which greatly seek after those that sift the finest meal and bear the whitest mouths.[19] It is a world to see how Englishmen desire to hear finer speech than the language will allow, to eat finer bread than is made of wheat, to wear finer cloth than is wrought of wool. But I let pass their fineness, which can no way excuse my folly. If your Lordship shall accept my good will, which I always desired, I will patiently bear the ill will of the malicious, which I never deserved.

Thus committing this simple pamphlet to your Lordship's patronage and your honour to the Almighty's protection, for the preservation of the which, as most bounden, I will pray continually, I end.

Your Lordship's servant to command,

J. LYLY.

TO THE GENTLEMEN READERS

I was driven into a quandary, Gentlemen, whether I might send this my pamphlet to the printer or to the pedlar. I thought it too bad for the press and too good for the pack.[20] But seeing my folly in writing to be as great as others', I was willing my fortune should be as ill as any man's. We commonly see the book that at Christmas lieth bound on the stationer's stall at Easter to be broken in the haberdasher's shop;[21] which sith it is the order of proceeding, I am content this winter to have my doings read for a toy that in summer they may be ready for trash. It is not strange whenas the greatest wonder lasteth but nine days,[22] that a new work should not endure but three months. Gentlemen use books as gentlewomen handle their flowers, who in the morning stick them in their heads and at night strew them at their heels. Cherries be fulsome when they be through ripe because they be plenty, and books be stale when they be printed in that they be common. In my mind printers and tailors are bound chiefly to pray for gentlemen: the one hath so many fantasies to print, the other such divers fashions to make, that the pressing-iron of the one is never out of the fire nor the printing-press of the other any time lieth still. But a fashion is but a day's wearing and a book but an hour's reading; which seeing it is so, I am of a shoemaker's mind, who careth not so the shoe hold the plucking on, nor so my labours last the running over. He that cometh in print because he would be known is like the fool that cometh into the market because he would be seen. I am not he that seeketh praise for his labour, but pardon for his offence; neither do I set this forth for any devotion in print, but for duty which I owe to my patron. If one write never so well he cannot

---

15   i.e. the overly fastidious reader.

16   The ivy bush was the traditional Early Modern sign of a tavern. Lyly's proverb implies that any tavern that does not water down its drinks will not need to advertise.

17   *lovely.*

18   i.e. The truth is clearest when it is expressed simply.

19   i.e. are the most fastidious.

20   i.e. A peddler's pack. Long popular poems, usually ballads, were commonly sold by street vendors and itinerant peddlers. The best-known literary representation of this practice is Autolycus in Shakespeare's *Winter's Tale* IV.iv.255ff.

21   Paper was so expensive in Early Modern Europe that unsold books were broken up to provide wrapping paper, lids for jars, and so forth. Many writers joke about this very public indicator of bad sales.

22   A "nine-days wonder" is a colloquial expression for a fleeting fad.

please all, and write he never so ill he shall please some. Fine heads will pick a quarrel with me if all be not curious, and flatterers a thank if anything be current. But this is my mind, let him that findeth fault amend it and him that liketh it use it. Envy braggeth but draweth no blood, the malicious have more mind to grip than might to cut. I submit myself to the judgement of the wise and I little esteem the censure of fools. The one will be satisfied with reason, the other are to be answered with silence. I know gentlemen will find no fault without cause, and bear with those that deserve blame; as for others I care not for their jests, for I never meant to make them my judges.

Farewell.

EUPHUES

There dwelt in Athens a young gentleman of great patrimony[23] and of so comely a personage that it was doubted whether he were more bound to Nature for the lineaments of his person or to Fortune for the increase of his possessions. But Nature, impatient of comparisons, and as it were disdaining a companion or co-partner in her working, added to this comeliness of his body such a sharp capacity of mind that not only she proved Fortune counterfeit but was half of that opinion that she herself was only current. This young gallant, of more wit than wrath, and yet of more wrath than wisdom, seeing himself inferior to none in pleasant conceits[24] thought himself superior to all in honest conditions, insomuch that he deemed himself so apt to all things that he gave himself almost to nothing but practising of those things commonly which are incident to these sharp wits – fine phrases, smooth quipping, merry taunting, using jesting without mean, and abusing mirth without measure. As therefore the sweetest rose hath his prickle, the finest velvet his brack, the fairest flour his bran, so the sharpest wit hath his wanton will and the holiest head his wicked way. And true it is that some men write, and most men believe, that in all perfect shapes a blemish bringeth rather a liking every way to the eyes than a loathing any way to the mind. Venus had her mole in her cheek which made her more amiable; Helen her scar on her chin which Paris called *cos amoris*, the whetstone of love; Aristippus his wart, Lycurgus his wen.[25] So likewise in the disposition of the mind, either virtue is overshadowed with some vice or vice overcast with some virtue: Alexander valiant in war, yet given to wine; Tully eloquent in his glozes,[26] yet vainglorious; Solomon wise, yet too too wanton; David holy, but yet an homicide; none more witty than Euphues, yet at the first none more wicked.[27]

The freshest colours soonest fade, the keenest razor soonest turneth his edge, the finest cloth is soonest eaten with moths, and the cambric sooner stained than the coarse canvas. Which appeareth well in this Euphues, whose wit being like wax apt to receive any impression, and having the bridle in his own hands either to use the rein or the spur, disdaining counsel, leaving his country, loathing his old acquaintance, thought either by wit to obtain some conquest or by shame to abide some conflict and, leaving the rule of reason, rashly ran into destruction; who, preferring fancy before friends and his present humour before honour to come, laid reason in water, being too salt for his taste, and followed unbridled affection most pleasant for his tooth.

When parents have more care how to leave their children wealthy than wise and are more desirous to have them maintain the name than the nature of a gentleman, when they put gold into the hands of youth where they should put a rod under their girdle, when instead of awe they make them past grace and leave them rich executors of goods and poor executors of godliness, then it is no marvel that the son, being left rich by his father's will, become reckless by his own will.

But it hath been an old saw and not of less truth than antiquity that wit is the better if it be the dearer bought; as in the sequel of this history shall most manifestly appear. It happened this young imp to arrive at Naples (a place of more pleasure than profit and yet of more profit than

23 *inherited wealth.*
24 *witty notions.*
25 For Paris and Helen of Troy, see the gazetteer; Aristippus was an ancient Greek philosopher; Lycurgus was a 4th-century BC Athenian politician. A "wen" is a wart or boil.

26 *commentaries.*
27 For Tully and Alexander the Great, see the gazetteer. Solomon and David were the two wisest kings of Israel in the Hebrew Bible and remained by-words for wisdom through the Early Modern period; both, however, fell from grace with God because of their sins.

piety); the very walls and windows whereof showed it rather to be the Tabernacle of Venus than the Temple of Vesta.[28] There was all things necessary and in readiness that might either allure the mind to lust or entice the heart to folly: a court more meet for an atheist than for one of Athens, for Ovid than for Aristotle, for a graceless lover than for a goodly liver; more fitter for Paris than Hector, and meeter for Flora than Diana.[29] Here my youth (whether for weariness he could not or for wantonness would not go any further) determined to make his abode; whereby it is evidently seen that the fleetest fish swalloweth the delicatest bait, that the highest soaring hawk traineth to the lure, and that the wittiest sconce[30] is inveigled with the sudden view of alluring vanities.

Here he wanted no companions, which courted him continually with sundry kinds of devices whereby they might either soak his purse to reap commodity or soothe his person to win credit; for he had guests and companions of all sorts. There frequented to his lodging and mansion house as well the spider to suck poison of his fine wit as the bee to gather honey, as well the drone as the dove, the fox as the lamb, as well Damocles to betray him as Damon to be true to him.[31] Yet he behaved himself so warily that he singled his game[32] wisely, he could easily discern Apollo's music from Pan his pipe; and Venus's beauty from Juno's bravery, and the faith of Laelius from the flattery of Aristippus.[33] He welcomed all but trusted none; he was merry, but yet so wary that neither the flatterer could take advantage to entrap him in his talk nor the wisest any assurance of his friendship. Who being demanded of one what countryman he was, he answered, 'What countryman am I not? If I be in Crete I can lie, if in Greece I can shift, if in Italy I can court it. If thou ask whose son I am also, I ask thee whose son I am not. I can carouse with Alexander, abstain with Romulus, eat with the Epicure, fast with the Stoic, sleep with Endymion, watch with Chrysippus"[34] – using these speeches and other like.

An old gentleman in Naples seeing his pregnant wit, his eloquent tongue somewhat taunting yet with delight, his mirth without measure yet not without wit, his sayings vainglorious yet pithy, began to bewail his nurture and to muse at his nature, being incensed against the one as most pernicious and inflamed with the other as most precious. For he well knew that so rare a wit would in time either breed an intolerable trouble or bring an incomparable treasure to the common weal; at the one he greatly pitied, at the other he rejoiced. Having therefore gotten opportunity to communicate with him his mind, with watery eyes, as one lamenting his wantonness, and smiling face, as one loving his wittiness, encountered him on this manner:–

"Young gentleman, although my acquaintance be small to entreat you and my authority less to command you, yet my good will in giving you good counsel should induce you to believe me and my hoary hairs (ambassadors of experience) enforce you to follow me; for by how much the more I am a stranger to you, by so much the more you are beholding[35] to me. Having therefore opportunity to utter my mind, I mean to be importunate with you to follow my meaning. As thy birth doth show the express and lively image of gentle blood, so thy bringing up seemeth to me to be a great blot to the lineage of so noble a brute; so that I am enforced to think that either thou didst want one to give thee good instructions or that thy parents made thee a wanton with too much cockering,[36] either they were too foolish in using no discipline or thou too froward[37] in rejecting

28   i.e. It was a city more given to sexual pleasure than domestic virtue. Naples in this text was usually read as a thinly disguised version of contemporary London; Athens was taken to refer to Oxford.
29   See the gazetteer for all these figures, who expand upon the contrast between virtue and vice represented by the two goddesses.
30   *head.*
31   Croll and Clemons cite a flatterer named Damocles mentioned in Cicero's *Tusculan Disputations*; Damon was an ancient Greek exemplar of true friendship who almost lost his life for his friend Phintias (usually corrupted to Pythias).
32   i.e. He could distinguish his friends from his enemies.
33   Comparisons of the genuine and the false; Laelius was a Roman politician for whom Cicero (see gazetteer) wrote his essay on friendship. Aristippus was well known for his excessive and luxurious lifestyle.

34   Euphues plays on national stereotypes of Cretans as liars, Greeks as deceivers, and so forth. Alexander the Great had a reputation for getting drunk and losing control. Romulus was one of the mythic founders of Rome. Epicureanism and Stoicism were ancient schools of philosophy, with the former having an undeserved reputation for promoting hedonism. Endymion was a mortal lover of the moon goddess Selene who slept eternally in a cave. Chrysippus was a 3rd century BCE Stoic philosopher.
35   *obliged.*
36   *indulgence.*
37   *stubborn.*

their doctrine, either they willing to have thee idle or thou wilful to be ill employed. Did they not remember that which no man ought to forget, that the tender youth of a child is like the tempering of new wax apt to receive any form? He that will carry a bull with Milo[38] must use to carry him a calf also, he that coveteth to have a straight tree must not bow him being a twig. The potter fashioneth his clay when it is soft, and the sparrow is taught to come when he is young. As therefore the iron being hot receiveth any form with the stroke of the hammer and keepeth it, being cold, for ever, so the tender wit of a child, if with diligence it be instructed in youth, will with industry use those qualities in his age.

"They might also have taken example of the wise husbandmen who in their fattest and most fertile ground sow hemp before wheat, a grain that drieth up the superfluous moisture and maketh the soil more apt for corn; or of good gardeners who in their curious knots mix hyssop with thyme as aiders the one to the growth of the other, the one being dry, the other moist; or of cunning painters who for the whitest work cast the blackest ground, to make the picture more amiable. If therefore thy father had been as wise an husbandman as he was a fortunate husband or thy mother as good a housewife as she was a happy wife, if they had been both as good gardeners to keep their knot as they were grafters to bring forth such fruit, or as cunning painters as they were happy parents, no doubt they had sowed hemp before wheat, that is discipline before affection, they had set hyssop with thyme, that is manners with wit, the one to aid the other; and to make thy dexterity more, they had cast a black ground for their white work, that is they had mixed threats with fair looks.

"But things past are past calling again, it is too late to shut the stable door when the steed is stolen. The Trojans repented too late when their town was spoiled. Yet the remembrance of thy former follies might breed in thee a remorse of conscience and be a remedy against further concupiscence. But now to thy present time. The Lacedaemonians[39] were wont to show their children drunken men and other wicked men, that by seeing their filth they might shun the like fault and avoid such vices when they were at the like state. The Persians to make their youth abhor gluttony would paint an Epicure[40] sleeping with meat in his mouth and most horribly overladen with wine, that by the view of such monstrous sights they might eschew the means of the like excess. The Parthians, to cause their youth to loathe the alluring trains of women's wiles and deceitful enticements, had most curiously carved in their houses a young man blind; besides whom was adjoined a woman, so exquisite that in some men's judgement Pygmalion's[41] image was not half so excellent, having one hand in his pocket as noting their theft, and holding a knife in the other hand to cut his throat.

"If the sight of such ugly shapes caused a loathing of the like sins, then, my good Euphues, consider their plight and beware of thine own peril. Thou art here in Naples a young sojourner, I an old senior, thou a stranger, I a citizen, thou secure doubting no mishap, I sorrowful dreading thy misfortune. Here mayest thou see that which I sigh to see, drunken sots wallowing in every house, in every chamber, yea, in every channel;[42] here mayest thou behold that which I cannot without blushing behold nor without blubbering utter, those whose bellies be their gods, who offer their goods as sacrifice to their guts, who sleep with meat in their mouths, with sin in their hearts, and with shame in their houses. Here, yea here, Euphues, mayest thou see, not the carved visard[43] of a lewd woman, but the incarnate visage of a lascivious wanton, not the shadow of love but the substance of lust. My heart melteth in drops of blood to see a harlot with the one hand rob so many coffers and with the other to rip so many corses.[44] Thou art here amidst the pikes between Scylla and Charybdis,[45] ready if thou shun Syrtis to sink into Symplegades.[46] Let the Lacedaemonian, the

38   Milon of Croton was an Olympic wrestler from the 6th century BC. His immense strength became proverbial in ancient and Early Modern times.

39   The ancient Greek name for the Spartans.

40   See note 34 above.

41   See gazetteer.

42   *gutter.*

43   *mask.*

44   *bodies.*

45   See gazetteer. To be "between Scylla and Charybdis" was a common metaphor for being caught in an unpleasant dilemma.

46   Syrtis was a sand bar in the Mediterranean; the Symplegades, or "Clashing Rocks," were floating islands that would smash against each other from time to time, crushing ships that were trying to navigate the passage.

Persian, the Parthian, yea, the Neapolitan cause thee rather to detest such villainy at the sight and view of their vanity.

"Is it not far better to abhor sins by the remembrance of others' faults than by repentance of thine own follies? Is not he accounted most wise whom other men's harms do make most wary? But thou wilt haply[47] say that although there be many things in Naples to be justly condemned, yet there are some things of necessity to be commended, and as thy will doth lean unto the one so thy wit would also embrace the other.

"Alas, Euphues, by how much the more I love the high climbing of thy capacity, by so much the more I fear thy fall. The fine crystal is sooner crazed[48] than the hard marble; the greenest beech burneth faster than the driest oak; the fairest silk is soonest soiled; and the sweetest wine turneth to the sharpest vinegar. The pestilence doth most rifest infect the clearest complexion, and the caterpillar cleaveth unto the ripest fruit; the most delicate wit is allured with small enticement unto vice and most subject to yield unto vanity. If therefore thou do but hearken unto the Sirens[49] thou wilt be enamoured, if thou haunt their houses and places thou shalt be enchanted. One drop of poison infecteth the whole tun[50] of wine, one leaf of Coloquintida[51] marreth and spoileth the whole pot of porridge, one iron-mole[52] defaceth the whole piece of lawn. Descend into thine own conscience and consider with thyself the great difference between staring and stark-blind, wit and wisdom, love and lust. Be merry but with modesty, be sober but not too sullen, be valiant but not too venturous. Let thy attire be comely but not costly, thy diet wholesome but not excessive, use pastime as the word importeth to pass the time in honest recreation. Mistrust no man without cause, neither be thou credulous without proof, be not light to follow every man's opinion, nor obstinate to stand in thine own conceit. Serve God, love God, fear God, and God will so bless thee as either thy heart can wish or thy friends desire. And so I end my counsel, beseeching thee to begin to follow it."

This old gentleman having finished his discourse, Euphues began to shape him an answer in this sort: "Father and friend (your age showeth the one, your honesty the other), I am neither so suspicious to mistrust your good will nor so sottish to mislike your good counsel; as I am therefore to thank you for the first, so it stands me upon to think better on the latter. I mean not to cavil with you as one loving sophistry,[53] neither to control you as one having superiority; the one would bring my talk into the suspicion of fraud, the other convince me of folly.

"Whereas you argue, I know not upon what probabilities but sure I am upon no proof, that my bringing-up should be a blemish to my birth. I answer, and swear too, that you were not therein a little overshot; either you gave too much credit to the report of others or too much liberty to your own judgement. You convince[54] my parents of peevishness[55] in making me a wanton, and me of lewdness in rejecting correction. But so many men so many minds; that may seem in your eye odious, which in an other's eye may be gracious. Aristippus a philosopher, yet who more courtly? Diogenes[56] a philosopher, yet who more carterly? Who more popular than Plato, retaining always good company? Who more envious than Timon,[57] denouncing all human society? Who so severe as the Stoics, which like stocks[58] were moved with no melody? Who so secure as the Epicures, which wallowed in all kind of licentiousness? Though all men be made of one metal yet they be not cast all in one mould. There is framed of the self-same clay as well the tile to keep out water as the pot to contain liquor, the sun doth harden the dirt and melt the wax, fire maketh the gold to shine and the straw to smother, perfumes doth refresh the dove and kill the beetle, and the nature of the man disposeth that consent of the manners.

---

47 *perhaps.*
48 *cracked.*
49 See gazetteer.
50 *barrel.*
51 *colocynth,* or *bitter apple.*
52 *mold stain:* "lawn" is a form of linen.
53 *pointless arguing.*
54 *convict.*
55 *folly.*
56 Diogenes the Cynic was a 4th-century BC Greek philosopher who attacked all forms of social rank and convention. "Carterly" means "rude" or "ill-bred."
57 A famous misanthrope in ancient Athens, and the subject of Shakespeare's *Timon of Athens.*
58 *tree stumps* or *blocks of wood.*

"Now whereas you seem to love my nature and loathe my nurture, you bewray your own weakness in thinking that nature may anyways be altered by education; and as you have examples to confirm your pretence, so I have most evident and infallible arguments to serve for my purpose. It is natural for the vine to spread; the more you seek by art to alter it, the more in the end you shall augment it. It is proper for the palm-tree to mount; the heavier you load it the higher it sprouteth. Though iron be made soft with fire it returneth to his hardness; though the falcon be reclaimed to the fist she retireth to her haggardness;[59] the whelp of a mastiff will never be taught to retrieve the partridge; education can have no show where the excellency of nature doth bear sway. The silly mouse will by no manner of means be tamed; the subtle fox may well be beaten, but never broken from stealing his prey; if you pound spices they smell the sweeter; season the wood never so well, the wine will taste of the cask; plant and translate the crab-tree where and whensoever it please you and it will never bear sweet apple – unless you graft by art, which nothing toucheth nature. Infinite and innumerable were the examples I could allege and declare to confirm the force of nature and confute these your vain and false forgeries, were not the repetition of them needless, having showed sufficient, or bootless, seeing those alleged will not persuade you. And can you be so unnatural, whom Dame Nature hath nourished and brought up so many years, to repine[60] as it were against Nature?

"The similitude you rehearse of the wax argueth your waxing and melting brain, and your example of the hot and hard iron showeth in you but cold and weak disposition. Do you not know that which all men do affirm and know, that black will take no other colour? That the stone Asbestos being once made hot will never be made cold? That fire cannot be forced downward? That Nature will have course after kind? Can the Ethiope change or alter his skin?[61] Or the leopard his hue? Is it possible to gather grapes of thorns or figs of thistles? Or to cause anything to strive against Nature?

"But why go I about to praise Nature, the which as yet was never any imp so wicked and barbarous, any Turk so vile and brutish, any beast so dull and senseless, that could, or would, or durst dispraise or contemn? Doth not Cicero conclude and allow that if we follow and obey Nature we shall never err? Doth not Aristotle allege and confirm that Nature frameth or maketh nothing in any point rude, vain, and imperfect? Nature was had in such estimation and admiration among the heathen people that she was reputed for the only goddess in heaven. If Nature, then, have largely and bountifully endued[62] me with her gifts, why deem you me so untoward[63] and graceless? If she have dealt hardly with me, why extol you so much my birth? If Nature bear no sway, why use you this adulation? If Nature work the effect, what booteth any education? If Nature be of strength or force, what availeth discipline or nurture? If of none, what helpeth Nature? But let these sayings pass as known evidently and granted to be true, which none can or may deny unless he be false or that he be an enemy to humanity.

"As touching my residence and abiding here in Naples, my youthly and lusty affections, my sports and pleasures, my pastimes, my common dalliance, my delights, my resort and company, and companions which daily use to visit me – although to you they breed more sorrow and care than solace and comfort because of your crabbed age, yet to me they bring more comfort and joy than care and grief, more bliss than bale,[64] more happiness than heaviness, because of my youthful gentleness. Either you would have all men old as you are or else you have quite forgotten that you yourself were young or even knew young days; either in your youth you were a very vicious and ungodly man, or now being aged very superstitious and devout above measure.

"Put you no difference between the young flourishing bay tree and the old withered beech? No kind of distinction between the waxing and the waning of the moon? And between the rising and the setting of the sun? Do you measure the hot assaults of youth by the cold skirmishes of age, whose years are subject to more infirmities than our youth? We merry, you melancholy; we zealous

---

59   *untamed nature.*
60   *complain.*
61   The blackness of Ethiopians was proverbial in Early Modern Europe.

62   *endowed.*
63   *perverse.*
64   *evil.*

in affection, you jealous in all your doings; you testy without cause, we hasty for no quarrel; you careful, we careless; we bold, you fearful; we in all points contrary unto you, and ye in all points unlike unto us.

"Seeing therefore we be repugnant each to the other in nature, would you have us alike in qualities? Would you have one potion ministered to the burning fever and to the cold palsy; one plaster[65] to an old issue and a fresh wound; one salve for all sores; one sauce for all meats? No, no, Eubulus![66] But I will yield to more than either I am bound to grant, either thou able to prove: suppose that, which I never will believe, that Naples is a cankered storehouse of all strife, a common stews for all strumpets, the sink of shame, and the very nurse of all sin. Shall it therefore follow of necessity that all that are wooed of love should be wedded to lust; will you conclude, as it were *ex consequenti*,[67] that whosoever arriveth here shall be enticed to folly and, being enticed, of force shall be entangled? No, no, it is the disposition of the thought that altereth the nature of the thing. The sun shineth upon the dunghill and is not corrupted, the diamond lieth in the fire and is not consumed, the crystal toucheth the toad and is not poisoned, the bird Trochilus liveth by the mouth of the crocodile and is not spoiled,[68] a perfect wit is never bewitched with lewdness neither enticed with lasciviousness.

Is it not common that the holm-tree springeth amidst the beech? That the ivy spreadeth upon the hard stones? That the soft feather-bed breaketh the hard blade? If experience have not taught you this you have lived long and learned little, or if your moist brain have forgot it you have learned much and profited nothing. But it may be that you measure my affections by your own fancies, and knowing yourself either too simple to raise the siege by policy or too weak to resist the assault by prowess, you deem me of as little wit as yourself or of less force; either of small capacity or of no courage. In my judgement, Eubulus, you shall as soon catch a hare with a tabor[69] as you shall persuade youth with your aged and overworn eloquence to such severity of life, which as yet there was never Stoic so strict nor Jesuit so superstitious, neither Votary[70] so devout but would rather allow it in words than follow it in works, rather talk of it than try it. Neither were you such a saint in your youth that, abandoning all pleasures, all pastimes, and delights, you would choose rather to sacrifice the first fruits of your life to vain holiness than to youthful affections. But as to the stomach quatted[71] with dainties all delicates seem queasy, and as he that surfeited with wine useth afterward to allay with water, so these old huddles[72] having overcharged their gorges with fancy account all honest recreation mere folly, and having taken a surfeit of delight seem now to savour it with despite.

"Seeing therefore it is labour lost for me to persuade you and wind vainly wasted for you to exhort me, here I found you and here I leave you, having neither bought nor sold with you but changed ware for ware. If you have taken little pleasure in my reply, sure I am that by your counsel I have reaped less profit. They that use to steal honey burn hemlock to smoke the bees from their hives; and it may be that to get some advantage of me you have used these smoky arguments, thinking thereby to smother me with the conceit of strong imagination. But as the chameleon though he have most guts draweth least breath or as the elder tree though he be fullest of pith is farthest from strength, so though your reasons seem inwardly to yourself somewhat substantial and your persuasions pithy in your own conceit, yet being well weighed without they be shadows without substance and weak without force. The bird Taurus hath a great voice but a small body; the thunder a great clap yet but a little stone; the empty vessel giveth a greater sound than the full barrel. I mean not to apply it, but look into yourself and you shall certainly find it; and thus I leave you seeking it – but were it not that my company stay my coming I would surely help you to look[73] it, but I am called hence by my acquaintance.

Euphues having thus ended his talk departed, leaving this old gentleman in a great quandary; who, perceiving that he was more inclined to wantonness than to wisdom, with a deep sigh, the tears

---

65 *bandage.*
66 The name means "good counsel" in Greek.
67 "by consequence."
68 *destroyed.*
69 *drum.*

70 One who is bound to a certain religious practice, usually by a vow.
71 *glutted.*
72 *misers.*
73 *look for.*

trickling down his cheeks, said: "Seeing thou wilt not buy counsel at the first hand good cheap, thou shalt buy repentance at the second hand at such an unreasonable rate that thou wilt curse thy hard pennyworth and ban[74] thy hard heart. Ah Euphues, little dost thou know that if thy wealth waste thy wit will give but small warmth, and if thy wit incline to wilfulness that thy wealth will do thee no great good. If the one had been employed to thrift, the other to learning, it had been hard to conjecture whether thou shouldest have been more fortunate by riches or happy by wisdom, whether more esteemed in the commonweal for wealth to maintain war or for counsel to conclude peace. But alas, why do I pity that in thee which thou seemest to praise in thyself?" And so saying he immediately went to his own house, heavily bewailing the young man's unhappiness.

Here ye may behold, gentlemen, how lewdly[75] wit standeth in his own light, how he deemeth no penny good silver but his own, preferring the blossom before the fruit, the bud before the flower, the green blade before the ripe ear of corn, his own wit before all men's wisdom. Neither is that geason[76] seeing for the most part it is proper to all those of sharp capacity to esteem of themselves as most proper. If one be hard in conceiving they pronounce him a dolt, if given to study they proclaim him a dunce, if merry a jester, if sad a saint, if full of words a sot, if without speech a cipher, if one argue with them boldly then is he impudent, if coldly an innocent, if there be reasoning of divinity they cry *Quae supra nos nihil ad nos*,[77] if of humanity *Sententias loquitur carnifex*.[78] Hereof cometh such great familiarity between the ripest wits when they shall see the disposition the one of the other, the *sympathia*[79] of affections, and as it were but a pair of shears to go between their natures;[80] one flattereth an other in his own folly and layeth cushions under the elbow of his fellow when he seeth him take a nap with fancy; and as their wit wresteth them to vice, so it forgeth them some feat[81] excuse to cloak their vanity.

Too much study doth intoxicate their brains. "For," say they, "although iron the more it is used the brighter it is, yet silver with much wearing doth waste to nothing; though the cammock[82] the more it is bowed the better it serveth, yet the bow the more it is bent and occupied the weaker it waxeth; though the camomile the more it is trodden and pressed down the more it spreadeth, yet the violet the oftener it is handled and touched the sooner it withereth and decayeth. Besides this, a fine wit, a sharp sense, a quick understanding, is able to attain to more in a moment or a very little space than a dull and blockish head in a month. The scythe cutteth far better and smoother than the saw, the wax yieldeth better and sooner to the seal than the steel to the stamp or hammer, the smooth and plain beech is easier to be carved and occupied than the knotty box. For neither is there anything but that hath his contraries."

Such is the nature of these novices that think to have learning without labour and treasure without travail, either not understanding, or else not remembering, that the finest edge is made with the blunt whetstone and the fairest jewel fashioned with the hard hammer. I go not about, gentlemen, to inveigh against wit, for then I were witless, but frankly to confess mine own little wit. I have ever thought so superstitiously of wit that I fear I have committed idolatry against wisdom; and if Nature had dealt so beneficially with me to have given me any wit, I should have been readier in the defence of it to have made an apology, than any way to turn to apostasy. But this I note, that for the most part they stand so on their pantofles[83] that they be secure of perils, obstinate in their own opinions, impatient of labour, apt to conceive wrong, credulous to believe the worst, ready to shake off their old acquaintance without cause, and to condemn them without colour.[84] All which humours are by so much the more easier to be purged, by how much the less they have festered the sinews. But return we again to Euphues.

Euphues having sojourned by the space of two months in Naples, whether he were moved by the courtesy of a young gentleman named Philautus[85] or enforced by destiny, whether his pregnant wit

74   *curse.*
75   *ignorantly.*
76   *amazing.*
77   "Things beyond us are no concern of ours."
78   "The executioner is pronouncing the sentence."
79   *sympathy.*

80   i.e. They are cut from the same cloth.
81   *apt.*
82   *crooked staff.*
83   Literally, "shoes." The expression means to stand on one's dignity.
84   *an excuse.*
85   The name means "selfish man."

or his pleasant conceits wrought the greater liking in the mind of Euphues, I know not for certainty; but Euphues showed such entire love towards him that he seemed to make small account of any others, determining to enter into such an inviolable league of friendship with him as neither time by piecemeal should impair, neither fancy utterly dissolve, nor any suspicion infringe. "I have read," saith he, "and well I believe it, that a friend is in prosperity a pleasure, a solace in adversity, in grief a comfort, in joy a merry companion, at all times another I, in all places the express image of mine own person; inasmuch that I cannot tell whether the immortal gods have bestowed any gift upon mortal men either more noble or more necessary than friendship. Is there anything in the world to be reputed (I will not say compared) to friendship? Can any treasure in this transitory pilgrimage be of more value than a friend – in whose bosom thou mayest sleep secure without fear, whom thou mayest make partner of all thy secrets without suspicion of fraud and partaker of all thy misfortune without mistrust of fleeting,[86] who will account thy bale his bane, thy mishap his misery, the pricking of thy finger the piercing of his heart? But whither am I carried? Have I not also learned that one should eat a bushel of salt with him whom he meaneth to make his friend? That trial maketh trust? That there is falsehood in fellowship? And what then? Doth not the sympathy of manners make the conjunction of minds? Is it not a byword, like will to like? Not so common as commendable it is to see young gentlemen choose them such friends with whom they may seem, being absent, to be present, being asunder, to be conversant, being dead, to be alive. I will therefore have Philautus for my fere,[87] and by so much the more I make myself sure to have Philautus, by how much the more I view in him the lively image of Euphues."

Although there be none so ignorant that doth not know, neither any so impudent that will not confess friendship to be the jewel of human joy; yet whosoever shall see this amity grounded upon a little affection will soon conjecture that it shall be dissolved upon a light occasion; as in the sequel of Euphues and Philautus you shall see, whose hot love waxed soon cold. For as the best wine doth make the sharpest vinegar, so the deepest love turneth to the deadliest hate. Who deserved the most blame in my opinion it is doubtful, and so difficult, I dare not presume to give verdict. For love being the cause for which so many mischiefs have been attempted, I am not yet persuaded whether of them was most to be blamed, but certainly neither of them was blameless. I appeal to your judgement, gentlemen, not that I think any of you of the like disposition able to decide the question, but being of deeper discretion than I am are more fit to debate the quarrel. Though the discourse of their friendship and falling out be somewhat long, yet, being somewhat strange, I hope the delightfulness of the one will attenuate the tediousness of the other.

Euphues had continual access to the place of Philautus and no little familiarity with him, and finding him at convenient leisure, in these short terms unfolded his mind unto him.

"Gentleman and friend, the trial I have had of thy manners cutteth off divers terms which to another I would have used in the like manner. And since a long discourse argueth folly, and delicate words incur the suspicion of flattery, I am determined to use neither of them knowing either of them to breed offence. Weighing with myself the force of friendship by the effects, I studied ever since my first coming to Naples to enter league with such a one as might direct my steps, being a stranger, and resemble my manners, being a scholar; the which two qualities as I find in you able to satisfy my desire, so I hope I shall find a heart in you willing to accomplish my request. Which if I may obtain, assure yourself that Damon to his Pythias, Pylades to his Orestes, Titus to his Gysippus, Theseus to his Pirithoüs, Scipio to his Laelius, was never found more faithful than Euphues will be to his Philautus."[88]

Philautus by how much the less he looked for this discourse, by so much the more he liked it, for he saw all qualities both of body and mind in Euphues; unto whom he replied as followeth:–

"Friend Euphues (for so your talk warranteth me to term you), I dare neither use a long process, neither loving speech, lest unwittingly I should cause you to convince me of those things which

---

86   *inconstancy.*
87   *companion.*

88   All of these are classical examples of strong male friendship except for Titus and Gysippus, who are discussed in Boccaccio's *Decameron.*

you have already condemned. And verily I am bold to presume upon your courtesy since you yourself have used so little curiosity,[89] persuading myself that my short answer will work as great an effect in you as your few words did in me. And seeing we resemble (as you say) each other in qualities, it cannot be that the one should differ from the other in courtesy; seeing the sincere affection of the mind cannot be expressed by the mouth and that no art can unfold the entire love of the heart, I am earnestly to beseech you not to measure the firmness of my faith by the fewness of my words, but rather think that the overflowing waves of goodwill leave no passage for many words. Trial shall prove trust. Here is my hand, my heart, my lands, and my life at thy commandment. Thou mayest well perceive that I did believe thee that[90] so soon I did love thee, and I hope that thou wilt the rather love me in that I did believe thee." Either Euphues and Philautus stood in need of friendship or were ordained to be friends; upon so short warning to make so soon a conclusion might seem in mine opinion, if it continued, miraculous, if shaken off, ridiculous. But after many embracings and protestations one to another, they walked to dinner, where they wanted neither meat, neither music, neither any other pastime; and having banqueted, to digest their sweet confections, they danced all that afternoon. They used not only one board,[91] but one bed,[92] one book (if so be it they thought not one too many). Their friendship augmented every day, inasmuch that the one could not refrain the company of the other one minute. All things went in common between them; which all men accounted commendable.

Philautus being a town-born child, both for his own continuance and the great countenance[93] which his father had while he lived, crept into credit with Don Ferardo, one of the chief governors of the city. Who, although he had a courtly crew of gentlewomen sojourning in his palace, yet his daughter, heir to his whole revenues, stained the beauty of them all; whose modest bashfulness caused the other to look wan for envy, whose lily cheeks dyed with a vermilion red made the rest to blush at her beauty. For as the finest ruby staineth the colour of the rest that be in place, or as the sun dimmeth the moon that she cannot be discerned, so this gallant[94] girl, more fair than fortunate, and yet more fortunate than faithful, eclipsed the beauty of them all and changed their colours. Unto her had Philautus access, who won her by right of love and should have worn her by right of law, had not Euphues by strange destiny broken the bonds of marriage and forbidden the banns of matrimony.

It happened that Don Ferardo had occasion to go to Venice about certain his own affairs, leaving his daughter the only steward of his household; who spared not to feast Philautus her friend with all kinds of delights and delicates, reserving only her honesty as the chief stay[95] of her honour. Her father being gone, she sent for her friend to supper; who came not, as he was accustomed, solitarily alone but accompanied with his friend, Euphues. The gentlewoman, whether it were for niceness or for niggardness[96] of courtesy, gave him such a cold welcome that he repented that he was come.

Euphues though he knew himself worthy every way to have a good countenance, yet could he not perceive her willing any way to lend him a friendly look. Yet, lest he should seem to want gestures[97] or to be dashed out of conceit with her coy[98] countenance, he addressed him to a gentlewoman called Livia, unto whom he uttered this speech:–

"Fair lady, if it be the guise of Italy to welcome strangers with strangeness, I must needs say the custom is strange and the country barbarous; if the manner of ladies to salute gentlemen with coyness, then I am enforced to think the women without courtesy to use such welcome, and the men past shame that will come. But hereafter I will either bring a stool on mine arm for an unbidden guest, or a visard on my face for a shameless gossip."

Livia replied: "Sir, our country is civil and our gentlewomen are courteous; but in Naples it is counted a jest at every word to say, 'In faith you are welcome.'"

---

89 *elaborateness.*
90 *in that.*
91 *table.*
92 Friends and siblings of the same sex frequently shared beds in Early
Modern Europe, even in the upper classes.
93 *favor.*

94 *handsome.*
95 *support.*
96 *miserliness.*
97 *manners.*
98 *disdainful.*

As she was yet talking, supper was set on the board. Then Philautus spake thus unto Lucilla: "Yet, gentlewoman, I was the bolder to bring my shadow with me (meaning Euphues), knowing that he should be the better welcome for my sake."

Unto whom the gentlewoman replied: "Sir, as I never when I saw you thought that you came without your shadow, so now I cannot a little marvel to see you so overshot in bringing a new shadow with you."

Euphues, though he perceived her coy nip, seemed not to care for it, but taking her by the hand said: "Fair lady, seeing the shade doth often shield your beauty from the parching sun, I hope you will the better esteem of the shadow; and by so much the less it ought to be offensive by how much the less it is able to offend you, and by so much the more you ought to like it by how much the more you use to lie in it."

"Well, gentleman," answered Lucilla, "in arguing of the shadow we forgo the substance. Pleaseth it you, therefore, to sit down to supper?" And so they all sat down; but Euphues fed of one dish which ever stood before him, the beauty of Lucilla. Here Euphues at the first sight was so kindled with desire that almost he was like to burn to coals.

Supper being ended, the order was in Naples that the gentlewomen would desire to hear some discourse, either concerning love or learning. And although Philautus was requested, yet he posted it over to Euphues, whom he knew most fit for that purpose. Euphues, being thus tied to the stake[99] by their importunate entreaty, began as followeth:–

"He that worst may is always enforced to hold the candle, the weakest must still to the wall, where none will the devil himself must bear the cross. But were it not, gentlewomen, that your list[100] stands for law, I would borrow so much leave as to resign mine office to one of you, whose experience in love hath made you learned and whose learning hath made you so lovely; for me to entreat of the one, being a novice, or to discourse of the other, being a truant, I may well make you weary but never the wiser, and give you occasion rather to laugh at my rashness than to like my reasons. Yet I care the less to excuse my boldness to you who were the cause of my blindness. And since I am at mine own choice either to talk of love or of learning, I had rather for this time be deemed an unthrift in rejecting profit than a Stoic in renouncing pleasure.

"It hath been a question often disputed, but never determined, whether the qualities of the mind or the composition of the man cause women most to like, or whether beauty or wit move men most to love. Certes by how much the more the mind is to be preferred before the body, by so much the more the graces of the one are to be preferred before the gifts of the other; which if it be so that the contemplation of the inward quality ought to be respected more than the view of the outward beauty, then doubtless women either do or should love those best whose virtue is best, not measuring the deformed man with the reformed mind. The foul toad hath a fair stone in his head,[101] the fine gold is found in the filthy earth, the sweet kernel lieth in the hard shell. Virtue is harboured in the heart of him that most men esteem misshapen. Contrariwise if we respect more the outward shape than the inward habit – good God, into how many mischiefs do we fall! Into what blindness are we led! Do we not commonly see that in painted pots is hidden the deadliest poison, that in the greenest grass is the greatest serpent, in the clearest water the ugliest toad? Doth not experience teach us that in the most curious sepulchre are enclosed rotten bones? That the cypress tree beareth a fair leaf but no fruit? That the estridge[102] carrieth fair feathers but rank flesh? How frantic are those lovers which are carried away with the gay glistering[103] of the fine face? The beauty whereof is parched with the summer's blaze and chipped with the winter's blast, which is of so short continuance that it fadeth before one perceive it flourish, of so small profit that it poisoneth those that possess it, of so little value with the wise that they account it a delicate bait with a deadly hook, a sweet panther with a devouring paunch, a sour poison in a silver pot.

---

99   i.e. put on the spot.
100 *desire.*
101 A common Early Modern folk belief.

102 *ostrich.*
103 *radiance.*

"Here I could enter into discourse of such fine dames as being in love with their own looks make such coarse account of their passionate lovers; for commonly if they be adorned with beauty they be so strait-laced and made so high in the instep[104] that they disdain them most that most desire them. It is a world to see the doting of their lovers and their dealing with them, the revealing of whose subtle trains[105] would cause me to shed tears and you, gentlewomen, to shut your modest ears. Pardon me, gentlewomen, if I unfold every wile and show every wrinkle of women's disposition. Two things do they cause their servants to vow unto them, secrecy and sovereignty: the one to conceal their enticing sleights, by the other to assure themselves of their only service. Again – but ho there! If I should have waded any further and sounded the depth of their deceit, I should either have procured your displeasure or incurred the suspicion of fraud, either armed you to practise the like subtlety or accused myself of perjury. But I mean not to offend your chaste minds with the rehearsal of their unchaste manners, whose ears I perceive to glow and hearts to be grieved at that which I have already uttered; not that amongst you there be any such, but that in your sex there should be any such.

"Let not gentlewomen, therefore, make too much of their painted sheath, let them not be so curious in their own conceit or so currish to their loyal lovers. When the black crow's foot shall appear in their eye or the black ox tread on their foot,[106] when their beauty shall be like the blasted rose, their wealth wasted, their bodies worn, their faces wrinkled, their fingers crooked, who will like of them in their age who loved none in their youth? If you will be cherished when you be old, be courteous while you be young; if you look for comfort in your hoary hairs, be not coy when you have your golden locks; if you would be embraced in the waning of your bravery, be not squeamish in the waxing of your beauty; if you desire to be kept like the roses when they have lost their colour, smell sweet as the rose doth in the bud; if you would be tasted for old wine, be in the mouth a pleasant grape – so shall you be cherished for your courtesy, comforted for your honesty, embraced for your amity, so shall you be preserved with the sweet rose and drunk with the pleasant wine.

"Thus far I am bold, gentlewomen, to counsel those that be coy, that they weave not the web of their own woe nor spin the thread of their own thraldom by their own overthwartness.[107] And seeing we are even in the bowels[108] of love, it shall not be amiss to examine whether man or woman be soonest allured, whether be most constant the male or the female. And in this point I mean not to be mine own carver, lest I should seem either to pick a thank[109] with men or a quarrel with women. If therefore it might stand with your pleasure, Mistress Lucilla, to give your censure, I would take the contrary; for sure I am though your judgement be sound, yet affection[110] will shadow it."

Lucilla, seeing his pretence, thought to take advantage of his large proffer, unto whom she said: "Gentleman, in mine opinion women are to be won with every wind, in whose sex there is neither force to withstand the assaults of love, neither constancy to remain faithful. And because your discourse hath hitherto bred delight, I am loath to hinder you in the sequel of your devices."

Euphues, perceiving himself to be taken napping, answered as followeth: "Mistress Lucilla, if you speak as you think, these gentlewomen present have little cause to thank you: if you cause me to commend women, my tale will be accounted a mere trifle and your words the plain truth. Yet knowing promise to be debt, I will pay it with performance. And I would the gentlemen here present were as ready to credit my proof as the gentlewomen are willing to hear their own praises; or I as able to overcome as Mistress Lucilla would be content to be overthrown. Howsoever the matter shall fall out, I am of the surer side: for if my reasons be weak, then is our sex strong; if forcible, then your judgement feeble; if I find truth on my side, I hope I shall, for my wages, win the good will of women; if I want proof, then, gentlewomen, of necessity you must yield to men. But to the matter.

---

104 i.e. proud.
105 *tricks.*
106 i.e. when old age comes.
107 *contrariness.*

108 *heart.*
109 *ingratiate himself.*
110 *partiality.*

"Touching the yielding to love, albeit their hearts seem tender, yet they harden them like the stone of Sicilia, the which the more it is beaten the harder it is; for being framed as it were of the perfection of men, they be free from all such cogitations as may any way provoke them to uncleanness, inasmuch as they abhor the light love of youth which is grounded upon lust and dissolved upon every light occasion. When they see the folly of men turn to fury, their delight to doting, their affection to frenzy; when they see them as it were pine in pleasure and to wax pale through their own peevishness; their suits, their service, their letters, their labours, their loves, their lives seem to them so odious that they harden their hearts against such concupiscence[111] to the end they might convert them from rashness to reason, from such lewd disposition to honest discretion. Hereof it cometh that men accuse women of cruelty because they themselves want civility, they account them full of wiles in not yielding to their wickedness, faithless for resisting their filthiness. But I had almost forgot myself – you shall pardon me, Mistress Lucilla, for this time, if thus abruptly I finish my discourse. It is neither for want of good will or lack of proof, but that I feel in myself such alteration that I can scarcely utter one word. Ah Euphues, Euphues!"

The gentlewomen were struck into such a quandary with this sudden change that they all changed colour. But Euphues, taking Philautus by the hand and giving the gentlewomen thanks for their patience and his repast, bade them all farewell and went immediately to his chamber.

But Lucilla, who now began to fry in the flames of love, all the company being departed to their lodgings, entered into these terms and contrarieties:–

"Ah, wretched wench Lucilla, how art thou perplexed! What a doubtful fight dost thou feel betwixt faith and fancy, hope and fear, conscience and concupiscence! O my Euphues, little dost thou know the sudden sorrow that I sustain for thy sweet sake, whose wit hath bewitched me, whose rare qualities have deprived me of mine old quality, whose courteous behaviour without curiosity, whose comely feature without fault, whose filed[112] speech without fraud hath wrapped me in this misfortune. And canst thou, Lucilla, be so light of love in forsaking Philautus to fly to Euphues? Canst thou prefer a stranger before thy countryman; a starter[113] before thy companion? Why Euphues doth perhaps desire my love, but Philautus hath deserved it. Why Euphues' feature is worthy as good as I, but Philautus his faith is worthy a better. Aye, but the latter love is most fervent; aye, but the first ought to be most faithful. Aye, but Euphues hath greater perfection; aye, but Philautus hath deeper affection.

"Ah fond wench, dost thou think Euphues will deem thee constant to him, when thou hast been inconstant to his friend? Weenest thou that he will have no mistrust of thy faithfulness, when he hath had trial of thy fickleness? Will he have no doubt of thine honour, when thou thyself callest thine honesty in question? Yes, yes, Lucilla, well doth he know that the glass once crazed will with the least clap be cracked, that the cloth which staineth with milk will soon lose his colour with vinegar, that the eagle's wing will waste the feather as well of the phoenix as of the pheasant, that she that hath been faithless to one will never be faithful to any.

"But can Euphues convince me of fleeting, seeing for his sake I break my fidelity? Can he condemn me of disloyalty, when he is the only cause of my disliking? May he justly condemn me of treachery, who hath this testimony as trial of my good will? Doth he not remember that the broken bone once set together is stronger than ever it was? That the greatest blot is taken off with the pumice? That though the spider poison the fly, she cannot infect the bee? That although I have been light to Philautus, yet I may be lovely to Euphues? It is not my desire but his deserts that moveth my mind to this choice, neither the want of the like good will in Philautus but the lack of the like good qualities that removeth my fancy from the one to the other.

"For as the bee that gathereth honey out of the weed when she espieth the fair flower flieth to the sweetest; or as the kind[114] spaniel though he hunt after birds yet forsakes them to retrieve the partridge; or as we commonly feed on beef hungrily at the first, yet seeing the quail more dainty change our diet; so I although I loved Philautus for his good properties, yet seeing Euphues to excel him I ought by nature to like him better. By so much the more, therefore, my change is to

---

111 *strong sexual desire.*
112 *polished.*

113 *newcomer.*
114 *instinct-following.*

be excused, by how much the more my choice is excellent; and by so much the less I am to be condemned, by how much the more Euphues is to be commended. Is not the diamond of more value than the ruby because he is of more virtue? Is not the emerald preferred before the sapphire for his wonderful property? Is not Euphues more praiseworthy than Philautus being more witty?

"But fie, Lucilla, why dost thou flatter thyself in thine own folly! Canst thou feign Euphues thy friend, whom by thine own words thou hast made thy foe? Didst not thou accuse women of inconstancy? Didst not thou account them easy to be won? Didst not thou condemn them of weakness? What sounder argument can he have against thee than thine own answer; what better proof than thine own speech; what greater trial than thine own talk? If thou hast belied women, he will judge thee unkind; if thou have revealed the troth, he must needs think thee inconstant; if he perceive thee to be won with a nut, he will imagine that thou wilt be lost with an apple;[115] if he find thee wanton before thou be wooed, he will guess thou wilt be wavering when thou art wedded.

"But suppose that Euphues love thee, that Philautus leave thee, will thy father, thinkest thou, give thee liberty to live after thine own lust? Will he esteem him worthy to inherit his possessions whom he accounteth unworthy to enjoy thy person? Is it like that he will match thee in marriage with a stranger, with a Grecian, with a mean man? Aye, but what knoweth my father whether he be wealthy, whether his revenues be able to countervail[116] my father's lands, whether his birth be noble, yea or no? Can any one make doubt of his gentle blood that seeth his gentle conditions? Can his honour he called into question whose honesty is so great? Is he to be thought thriftless who in all qualities of the mind is peerless? No, no, the tree is known by his fruit, the gold by his touch,[117] the son by the sire. And as the soft wax receiveth whatsoever print be in the seal and showeth no other impression, so the tender babe, being sealed with his father's gifts, representeth his image most lively.

"But were I once certain of Euphues' good will I would not so superstitiously account of my father's ill will. Time hath weaned me from my mother's teat, and age rid me from my father's correction. When children are in their swathing-clouts, then are they subject to the whip and ought to be careful of the rigour of their parents. As for me, seeing I am not fed with their pap, I am not to be led by their persuasions. Let my father use what speeches he list, I will follow mine own lust. Lust, Lucilla? What saith thou? No, no, mine own love I should have said; for I am as far from lust as I am from reason, and as near to love as I am to folly. Then stick to thy determination and show thyself what love can do, what love dares do, what love hath done. Albeit I can no way quench the coals of desire with forgetfulness, yet will I rake them up in the ashes of modesty; seeing I dare not discover my love for maidenly shamefastness, I will dissemble it till time[118] I have opportunity. And I hope so to behave myself, as Euphues shall think me his own and Philautus persuade himself I am none but his. But I would to God Euphues would repair hither, that the sight of him might mitigate some part of my martyrdom."

She, having thus discoursed with herself her own miseries, cast herself on the bed. And there let her lie. And return we to Euphues, who was so caught in the gin[119] of folly that he neither could comfort himself nor durst ask counsel of his friend, suspecting that which indeed was true, that Philautus was corrival with him and cockmate[120] with Lucilla. Amidst, therefore, these his extremities between hope and fear, he uttered these or the like speeches:–

"What is he, Euphues, that, knowing thy wit and seeing thy folly, but will rather punish thy lewdness than pity thy heaviness? Was there ever any so fickle so soon to be allured? Any ever so faithless to deceive his friend? Ever any so foolish to bathe himself in his own misfortune? Too true it is that as the sea-crab swimmeth always against the stream, so wit always striveth against wisdom; and as the bee is oftentimes hurt with her own honey, so is wit not seldom plagued with his own conceit.

"O ye gods, have ye ordained for every malady a medicine, for every sore a salve, for every pain a plaster, leaving only love remediless? Did ye deem no man so mad to be entangled with desire?

115   A 16th-century proverb of inconstancy in England.
116   *equal*.
117   *touchstone*.

118   i.e. till the time when.
119   *snare*.
120   *intimate*.

Or thought ye them worthy to be tormented that were so misled? Have ye dealt more favourably with brute beasts than with reasonable creatures? The filthy sow when she is sick eateth the sea-crab and is immediately recured; the tortoise having tasted the viper sucketh *Origanum* and is quickly revived; the bear ready to pine licketh up the ants and is recovered; the dog having surfeited to procure his vomit eateth grass and findeth remedy; the hart being pierced with the dart runneth out of hand to the herb *Dictanum* and is healed. And can men by no herb, by no art, by no way procure a remedy for the impatient disease of love? Ah well I perceive that love is not unlike the fig-tree, whose fruit is sweet, whose root is more bitter than the claw of a bitter;[121] or like the apple in Persia, whose blossom savoureth like honey, whose bud is more sour than gall.

"But O impiety! O broad blasphemy against the heavens! Wilt thou be so impudent, Euphues, to accuse the gods of iniquity? No, fond fool, no! Neither is it forbidden us by the gods to love, by whose divine providence we are permitted to live, neither do we want remedies to recure our maladies, but reason to use the means. But why go I about to hinder the course of love with the discourse of law? Hast thou not read, Euphues, that he that loppeth the vine causeth it to spread fairer? That he that stoppeth the stream forceth it to swell higher? That he that casteth water on the fire in the smith's forge maketh it to flame fiercer? Even so he that seeketh by counsel to moderate his overlashing[122] affections increaseth his own misfortune.

"Ah my Lucilla, would thou wert either less fair or I more fortunate, either I wiser or thou milder; either I would I were out of this mad mood, either I would we were both of one mind. But how should she be persuaded of my loyalty that yet had never one simple proof of my love? Will she not rather imagine me to be entangled with her beauty than with her virtue; that my fancy being so lewdly chained at the first will be as lightly changed at the last; that there is nothing which is permanent that is violent? Yes, yes, she must needs conjecture so – although it be nothing so – for by how much the more my affection cometh on the sudden, by so much the less will she think it certain. The rattling thunderbolt hath but his clap, the lightning but his flash; and as they both come in a moment, so do they both end in a minute.

"Aye but, Euphues, hath she not heard also that the dry touchwood is kindled with lime; that the greatest mushroom groweth in one night; that the fire quickly burneth the flax; that love easily entereth into the sharp wit without resistance and is harboured there without repentance? If, therefore, the gods have endowed her with as much bounty as beauty, if she have no less wit than she hath comeliness, certes she will neither conceive sinisterly of my sudden suit, neither be coy to receive me into her service, neither suspect me of lightness in yielding so lightly, neither reject me disdainfully for loving so hastily.

"Shall I not then hazard my life to obtain my love? And deceive Philautus to receive Lucilla? Yes, Euphues, where love beareth sway, friendship can have no show. As Philautus brought me for his shadow the last supper, so will I use him for my shadow till I have gained his saint. And canst thou, wretch, be false to him that is faithful to thee? Shall his courtesy be cause of thy cruelty? Wilt thou violate the league of faith to inherit the laud of folly? Shall affection be of more force than friendship, love than law, hurt than loyalty? Knowest thou not that he that loseth his honesty hath nothing else to lose?

"Tush, the case is light where reason taketh place; to love and to live well is not granted to Jupiter. Whoso is blinded with the caul of beauty discerneth no colour of honesty. Did not Gyges cut Candaules a coat by his own measure?[123] Did not Paris, though he were a welcome guest to Menelaus, serve his host a slippery prank?[124] If Philautus had loved Lucilla he would never have suffered Euphues to have seen her. Is it not the prey that enticeth the thief to rifle? Is it not the pleasant bait that causeth the fleetest fish to bite? Is it not a byword amongst us that gold maketh an honest man an ill man? Did Philautus account Euphues too simple to decipher beauty or super-

---

121　*bitter drink.*
122　*exaggerated.*
123　Herodotus (see gazetteer) tells the story of King Candaules making his subject Gyges hide himself in the king's bedchamber in

order to see the beauty of the queen. Gyges was inflamed with lust for her, and subsequently killed Candaules to marry her.
124　See gazetteer under Paris.

stitious not to desire it? Did he deem him a saint in rejecting fancy, or a sot in not discerning? Thought he him a Stoic that he would not be moved, or a stock that he could not?

"Well, well, seeing the wound that bleedeth inward is most dangerous, that the fire kept close burneth most furious, that the oven dammed up baketh soonest, that sores having no vent fester inwardly, it is high time to unfold my secret love to my secret friend. Let Philautus behave himself never so craftily he shall know that it must be a wily mouse that shall breed in the cat's ear, and because I resemble him in wit I mean a little to dissemble with him in wiles.

"But, O my Lucilla, if thy heart be made of that stone which may be mollified only with blood, would I had sipped of that river in Caria which turneth those that drink of it to stones. If thine ears be anointed with the oil of Syria that bereaveth hearing, would mine eyes had been rubbed with the syrup of the cedar tree which taketh away sight. If Lucilla be so proud to disdain poor Euphues, would Euphues were so happy to deny Lucilla; or if Lucilla be so mortified to live without love, would Euphues were so fortunate to live in hate. Aye, but my cold welcome foretelleth my cold suit; aye, but her privy glances signify some good fortune. Fie, fond fool Euphues, why goest thou about to allege those things to cut off thy hope which she perhaps would never have found, or to comfort thyself with those reasons which she never meaneth to propose?

"Tush, it were no love if it were certain, and a small conquest it is to overthrow those that never resisted. In battles there ought to be a doubtful fight and a desperate end, in pleading a difficult entrance and a diffused[125] determination, in love a life without hope and a death without fear. Fire cometh out of the hardest flint with the steel, oil out of the driest jet[126] by the fire, love out of the stoniest heart by faith, by trust, by time. Had Tarquinius used his love with colours of continuance,[127] Lucretia would either with some pity have answered his desire or with some persuasion have stayed her death.[128] It was the heat of his lust that made her haste to end her life; wherefore love in neither respect is to be condemned, but he of rashness, to attempt a lady furiously, and she of rigour, to punish his folly in her own flesh; a fact (in mine opinion) more worthy the name of cruelty than chastity, and fitter for a monster in the deserts than a matron of Rome. Penelope, no less constant than she yet more wise, would be weary to unweave that in the night she spun in the day, if Ulysses had not come home the sooner.[129] There is no woman, Euphues, but she will yield in time; be not therefore dismayed either with high looks or froward words."

Euphues having thus talked with himself, Philautus entered the chamber; and finding him so worn and wasted with continual mourning, neither joying in his meat nor rejoicing in his friend, with watery eyes uttered this speech:—

"Friend and fellow, as I am not ignorant of thy present weakness, so I am not privy of the cause; and although I suspect many things, yet can I assure myself of no one thing. Therefore, my good Euphues, for these doubts and dumps of mine either remove the cause or reveal it. Thou hast hitherto found me a cheerful companion in thy mirth, and now shalt thou find me as careful with thee in thy moan. If altogether thou mayest not be cured, yet mayest thou be comforted. If there be any thing that either by my friends may be procured or by my life attained, that may either heal thee in part or help thee in all, I protest to thee by the name of a friend that it shall rather be gotten with the loss of my body, than lost by getting a kingdom. Thou hast tried me, therefore trust me; thou hast trusted me in many things, therefore try me in this one thing. I never yet failed, and now I will not faint. Be bold to speak and blush not; thy sore is not so angry[130] but I can salve it, thy wound is not so deep but I can search it, thy grief is not so great but I can ease it. If it be ripe it shall be lanced, if it be broken it shall be tainted,[131] be it never so desperate it shall be cured. Rise therefore, Euphues, and take heart at grace; younger thou shalt never be, pluck up thy stomach, if love itself have stung thee it shall not stifle thee. Though thou be enamoured of some lady thou shalt not be enchanted. They that begin to pine of a consumption without delay preserve them-

---

125 *verbose.*
126 A glossy black mineral.
127 i.e. the appearance of persistence.
128 For the story of Tarquinius and Lucretia, see Lucretia in the gazetteer.

129 See gazetter under Penelope.
130 *painful.*
131 *treated with ointment.*

selves with cullises;[132] he that feeleth his stomach enflamed with heat cooleth it eftsoons[133] with conserves; delays breed dangers, nothing so perilous as procrastination."

Euphues, hearing this comfort and friendly counsel, dissembled his sorrowing heart with a smiling face, answering him forthwith as followeth: "True it is, Philautus, that he which toucheth the nettle tenderly is soonest stung, that the fly which playeth with the fire is singed in the flame, that he that dallieth with women is drawn to his woe. And as the adamant[134] draweth the heavy iron, the harp the fleet dolphin, so beauty allureth the chaste mind to love and the wisest wit to lust. The example whereof I would it were no less profitable than the experience to me is like to be perilous. The vine watered with wine is soon withered, the blossom in the fattest ground is quickly blasted, the goat the fatter she is the less fertile she is; yea, man the more witty he is the less happy he is. So it is, Philautus, (for why should I conceal it from thee of whom I am to take counsel?) that since my last and first being with thee at the house of Ferardo, I have felt such a furious battle in mine own body as, if it be not speedily repressed by policy, it will carry my mind (the grand captain in this fight) into endless captivity. Ah Livia, Livia, thy courtly grace without coyness, thy blazing beauty without blemish, thy courteous demeanour without curiosity, thy sweet speech savoured with wit, thy comely mirth tempered with modesty, thy chaste looks yet lovely, thy sharp taunts yet pleasant have given me such a check that sure I am at the next view of thy virtues I shall take the mate. And taking it not of a pawn but of a prince[135] the loss is to be accounted the less. And though they be commonly in a great choler that receive the mate, yet would I willingly take every minute ten mates to enjoy Livia for my loving mate.

"Doubtless if ever she herself have been scorched with the flames of desire she will be ready to quench the coals with courtesy in another, if ever she have been attached[136] of love she will rescue him that is drenched in desire, if ever she have been taken with the fever of fancy she will help his ague who by a quotidian fit is converted into frenzy.[137] Neither can there be under so delicate a hue lodged deceit, neither in so beautiful a mould a malicious mind. True it is that the disposition of the mind followeth the composition of the body; how then can she be in mind any way imperfect who in body is perfect every way?

"I know my success will be good, but I know not how to have access to my goddess; neither do I want courage to discover my love to my friend, but some colour to cloak my coming to the house of Ferardo. For if they be in Naples as jealous as they be in the other parts of Italy, then it behoveth me to walk circumspectly and to forge some cause for my often coming. If therefore, Philautus, thou canst set but this feather to mine arrow thou shalt see me shoot so near that thou wilt account me for a cunning archer. And verily if I had not loved thee well, I would have swallowed mine own sorrow in silence, knowing that in love nothing is so dangerous as to participate[138] the means thereof to another, and that two may keep counsel if one be away. I am, therefore, enforced perforce to challenge that courtesy at thy hands which erst thou didst promise with thy heart, the performance whereof shall bind me to Philautus and prove thee faithful to Euphues. Now if thy cunning be answerable to thy good will, practise some pleasant conceit upon thy poor patient: one dram of Ovid's art, some of Tibullus's drugs, one of Propertius's pills,[139] which may cause me either to purge my new disease or recover my hoped desire: But I fear me where so strange a sickness is to be recured of so unskilful a physician, that either thou wilt be too bold to practise or my body too weak to purge. But seeing a desperate disease is to be committed to a desperate doctor, I will follow thy counsel and become thy cure,[140] desiring thee to be as wise in ministering the physic as I have been willing to put my life into thy hands."

Philautus, thinking all to be gold that glistered and all to be gospel that Euphues uttered, answered his forged gloze with this friendly close: "In that thou hast made me privy to thy purpose, I will not conceal my practice; in that thou cravest my aid, assure thyself I will be the finger next the thumb; inasmuch as thou shalt never repent thee of the one or the other. For persuade thyself

---

132   *broth.*

133   *presently.*

134   *magnet.*

135   The chess piece we now call a bishop.

136   *under the command.*

137   *madness.*

138   *share.*

139   Ovid (see gazetteer), Tibullus, and Propertius were all Roman love poets. Euphues is suggesting that he will adapt some of the seduction techniques described in their poems to his current situation.

140   *charge* (i.e. patient).

that thou shalt find Philautus during life ready to comfort thee in thy misfortunes and succour thee in thy necessity. Concerning Livia, though she be fair yet is she not so amiable as my Lucilla, whose servant I have been the term of three years – but lest comparisons should seem odious, chiefly where both the parties be without comparison, I will omit that. And seeing that we had both rather be talking with them than tattling of them, we will immediately go to them. And truly, Euphues, I am not a little glad that I shall have thee not only a comfort in my life, but also a companion in my love. As thou hast been wise in thy choice, so I hope thou shalt be fortunate in thy chance. Livia is a wench of more wit than beauty, Lucilla of more beauty than wit, both of more honesty than honour,[141] and yet both of such honour as in all Naples there is not one in birth to be compared with either of them. How much, therefore, have we to rejoice in our choice?

"Touching our access, be thou secure. I will flap Ferardo in the mouth with some conceit and fill his old head so full of new fables that thou shalt rather be earnestly entreated to repair to his house, than evil entreated to leave it. As old men are very suspicious to mistrust every thing, so are they very credulous to believe any thing; the blind man doth eat many a fly."

"Yea, but," said Euphues, "take heed, my Philautus, that thou thyself swallow not a gudgeon,"[142] which word Philautus did not mark until he had almost digested it.

"But," said Philautus, "let us go devoutly to the shrine of our saints, there to offer our devotion; for my books teach me that such a wound must be healed where it was first hurt, and for this disease we will use a common remedy, but yet comfortable. The eye that blinded thee shall make thee see, the scorpion that stung thee shall heal thee, a sharp sore hath a short cure – let us go." To the which Euphues consented willingly, smiling to himself to see how he had brought Philautus into a fool's paradise.

Here you may see, gentlemen, the falsehood in fellowship, the fraud in friendship, the painted sheath with the leaden dagger,[143] the fair words that make fools fain. But I will not trouble you with superfluous addition, unto whom I fear me I have been tedious with the bare discourse of this rude history.

Philautus and Euphues repaired to the house of Ferardo, where they found Mistress Lucilla and Livia, accompanied with other gentlewomen, neither being idle nor well employed, but playing at cards. But when Lucilla beheld Euphues she could scarcely contain herself from embracing him, had not womanly shamefastness, and Philautus his presence, stayed her wisdom. Euphues, on the other side, was fallen into such a trance that he had not the power either to succour himself or salute the gentlewomen. At the last Lucilla began, as one that best might be bold, on this manner:–

"Gentlemen, although your long absence gave me occasion to think that you disliked your late entertainment, yet your coming at the last hath cut off my former suspicion. And by so much the more you are welcome, by how much the more you were wished for. But you, gentleman" (taking Euphues by the hand), "were the rather wished for, for that your discourse being left imperfect caused us all to long (as women are wont for things that like them) to have an end thereof."

Unto whom Philautus replied as followeth: "Mistress Lucilla, though your courtesy made us nothing to doubt of our welcome, yet modesty caused us to pinch courtesy who should come first. As for my friend, I think he was never wished for here so earnestly of any as of himself, whether it might be to renew his talk or recant his sayings I cannot tell."

Euphues taking the tale out of Philautus's mouth answered: Mistress Lucilla, to recant verities were heresy, and renew the praises of women flattery. The only cause I wished myself here was to give thanks for so good entertainment, the which I could no ways deserve, and to breed a greater acquaintance if it might be to make amends."

Lucilla, inflamed with his presence, said: "Nay, Euphues, you shall not escape so; for if my courtesy, as you say, were the cause of your coming, let it also be the occasion of the ending your former discourse. Otherwise I shall think your proof naked and you shall find my reward nothing."

141   *social position.*
142   A small fish used for bait.

143   i.e. Something that is superficially sound, but fundamentally false.

Euphues, now as willing to obey as she to command, addressed himself to a farther conclusion; who, seeing all the gentlewomen ready to give him the hearing, proceeded as followeth:–

"I have not yet forgotten that my last talk with these gentlewomen tended to their praises, and therefore the end must tie up the just proof; otherwise I should set down Venus' shadow without the lively substance.

"As there is no one thing which can be reckoned either concerning love or loyalty wherein women do not excel men, yet in fervency above all others they so far exceed that men are liker to marvel at them than to imitate them, and readier to laugh at their virtues than emulate them. For as they be hard to be won without trial of great faith, so are they hard to be lost without great cause of fickleness. It is long before the cold water seethe,[144] yet being once hot it is long before it be cooled; it is long before salt come to his saltness, but being once seasoned it never loseth his savour.

"I, for mine own part, am brought into a Paradise by the only imagination of woman's virtues; and were I persuaded that all the devils in hell were women, I would never live devoutly to inherit heaven, or that they were all saints in heaven, I would live more strictly for fear of hell. What could Adam have done in his Paradise before his fall without a woman, or how would he have risen again after his fall without a woman? Artificers are wont in their last works to excel themselves. Yea, God, when He made all things, at the last made man as most perfect, thinking nothing could be framed more excellent; yet after him He created a woman, the express image of Eternity, the lively picture of Nature, the only steel glass[145] for man to behold his infirmities by comparing them with women's perfections. Are they not more gentle, more witty, more beautiful than men? Are not men so bewitched with their qualities that they become mad for love, and women so wise that they detest lust?

"I am entered into so large a field that I shall sooner want time than proof, and so cloy you with variety of praises that I fear me I am like to infect women with pride, which yet they have not, and men with spite, which yet I would not. For as the horse if he knew his own strength were no ways to be bridled, or the unicorn his own virtue were never to be caught, so women, if they knew what excellency were in them, I fear me men should never win them to their wills or wean them from their mind."

Lucilla began to smile, saying, "In faith, Euphues, I would have you stay there. For as the sun when he is at the highest beginneth to go down, so when the praises of women are at the best, if you leave not, they will begin to fail."

But Euphues (being rapt with the sight of his saint) answered, "No, no, Lucilla –"

But whilst he was yet speaking Ferardo entered, whom they all dutifully welcomed home. Who, rounding Philautus in the ear, desired him to accompany him immediately without farther pausing, protesting it should be as well for his preferment as for his own profit.

Philautus consenting, Ferardo said to his daughter: "Lucilla, the urgent affairs I have in hand will scarce suffer me to tarry with you one hour. Yet my return, I hope, will be so short that my absence shall not breed thy sorrow. In the mean season I commit all things into thy custody, wishing thee to use thy accustomable courtesy. And seeing I must take Philautus with me, I will be so bold to crave you, gentleman (his friend), to supply his room,[146] desiring you to take this hasty warning for a hearty welcome and so to spend this time of mine absence in honest mirth. And thus I leave you."

Philautus knew well the cause of this sudden departure, which was to redeem certain lands that were mortgaged in his father's time to the use of Ferardo; who on that condition had beforetime promised him his daughter in marriage. But return we to Euphues.

Euphues was surprised with such incredible joy at this strange event that he had almost swooned; for seeing his corrival to be departed and Ferardo to give him so friendly entertainment, doubted not in time to get the good will of Lucilla. Whom finding in place convenient without company, with a bold courage and comely gesture he began to assay her in this sort:–

144 *boil.*
145 *mirror.*

146 i.e. take his place.

"Gentlewoman, my acquaintance being so little I am afraid my credit will be less, for that they commonly are soonest believed that are best beloved, and they liked best whom we have known longest. Nevertheless the noble mind suspecteth no guile without cause, neither condemneth any wight[147] without proof. Having, therefore, notice of your heroical heart, I am the better persuaded of my good hap.

"So it is, Lucilla, that coming to Naples but to fetch fire, as the byword is, not to make my place of abode,[148] I have found such flames that I can neither quench them with the water of free will, neither cool them with wisdom. For as the hop, the pole being never so high, groweth to the end, or as the dry beech kindled at the root never leaveth until it come to the top, or as one drop of poison disperseth itself into every vein, so affection having caught hold of my heart and the sparkles of love kindled my liver[149] will suddenly, though secretly, flame up into my head and spread itself into every sinew. It is your beauty (pardon my abrupt boldness), lady, that hath taken every part of me prisoner and brought me to this deep distress. But seeing women, when one praiseth them for their deserts, deem that he flattereth them to obtain his desire, I am here present to yield myself to such trial as your courtesy in this behalf shall require.

"Yet will you commonly object this to such as serve you and starve to win your good will: that hot love is soon cold, that the bavin[150] though it burn bright is but a blaze, that scalding water if it stand a while turneth almost to ice, that pepper though it be hot in the mouth is cold in the maw, that the faith of men though it fry in their words it freezeth in their works. Which things, Lucilla, albeit they be sufficient to reprove the lightness of some one, yet can they not convince[151] every one of lewdness; neither ought the constancy of all to be brought in question through the subtlety of a few. For although the worm entereth almost into every wood, yet he eateth not the cedar tree; though the stone *Cylindrus* at every thunderclap roll from the hill, yet the pure sleek-stone mounteth at the noise;[152] though the rust fret the hardest steel, yet doth it not eat into the emerald; though Polypus change his hue, yet the *Salamander* keepeth his colour; though Proteus transform himself into every shape, yet Pygmalion retaineth his old form; though Aeneas were too fickle to Dido, yet Troilus was too faithful to Cressida;[153] though others seem counterfeit in their deeds, yet, Lucilla, persuade yourself that Euphues will be always current in his dealings.

"But as the true gold is tried by the touch, the pure flint by the stroke of the iron, so the loyal heart of the faithful lover is known by the trial of his lady. Of the which trial, Lucilla, if you shall account Euphues worthy, assure yourself he will be as ready to offer himself a sacrifice for your sweet sake as yourself shall be willing to employ him in your service. Neither doth he desire to be trusted any way until he shall be tried every way, neither doth he crave credit at the first, but a good countenance till time his desire shall be made manifest by his deserts. Thus not blinded by light affection, but dazzled with your rare perfection and boldened by your exceeding courtesy, I have unfolded mine entire love; desiring you, having so good leisure, to give so friendly an answer as I may receive comfort and you commendation."

Lucilla although she were contented to hear this desired discourse, yet did she seem to be somewhat displeased. And truly I know not whether it be peculiar to that sex to dissemble with those whom they most desire, or whether by craft they have learned outwardly to loathe that which inwardly they most love. Yet wisely did she cast this in her head, that if she should yield at the first assault he would think her a light huswife, if she should reject him scornfully a very haggard;[154] minding therefore that he should neither take hold of her promise, neither unkindness of her preciseness,[155] she fed him indifferently with hope and despair, reason and affection, life and death. Yet in the end, arguing wittily upon certain questions, they fell to such agreement as poor

---

147   *living being.*
148   i.e. Not to stay for a long time.
149   The liver was thought to be the physiological seat of love in Early Modern Europe.
150   *bundle of brushwood.*
151   *convict.*
152   This reference has never been satisfactorily explained.

153   "Polypus" is an archaic name for an octopus. For Proteus, Pygmalion, Aeneas and Dido, see the gazetteer. Troilus and Cressida were a pair of Trojan lovers during the Trojan War. When Cressida was sent to the Greek camp to accompany her father, they swore eternal love, but she betrayed him.
154   *wild, untamed woman.*
155   *moral strictness.*

Philautus would not have agreed unto if he had been present, yet always keeping the body unde-filed. And thus she replied:—

"Gentleman, as you may suspect me of idleness in giving ear to your talk, so may you convince me of lightness in answering such toys. Certes as you have made mine ears glow at the rehearsal of your love, so have you galled my heart with the remembrance of your folly. Though you came to Naples as a stranger yet were you welcome to my father's house as a friend. And can you then so much transgress the bounds of honour (I will not say of honesty) as to solicit a suit more sharp to me than death? I have hitherto, God be thanked, lived without suspicion of lewdness. And shall I now incur the danger of sensual liberty? What hope can you have to obtain my love, seeing yet I could never afford you a good look? Do you, therefore, think me easily enticed to the bent of your bow because I was easily entreated to listen to your late discourse? Or seeing me (as finely you gloze) to excel all other in beauty, did you deem that I would exceed all other in beastliness?

"But yet I am not angry, Euphues, but in an agony; for who is she that will not fret or fume with one that loveth her, – if this love to delude me be not dissembled? It is that which causeth me most to fear; not that my beauty is unknown to myself, but that commonly we poor wenches arc deluded through light belief, and ye men are naturally inclined craftily to lead your life. When the fox preacheth the geese perish. The crocodile shroudeth greatest treason under most pitiful tears; in a kissing mouth there lieth a galling mind. You have made so large proffer of your service and so fair promises of fidelity, that were I not over chary of mine honesty you would inveigle me to shake hands with chastity. But certes, I will either lead a virgin's life in earth (though I lead apes in hell),[156] or else follow thee rather than thy gifts; yet am I neither so precise to refuse thy proffer, neither so peevish to disdain thy good-will. So excellent always are the gifts which are made acceptable by the virtue of the giver.

"I did at the first entrance discern thy love, but yet dissemble it. Thy wanton glances, thy scald-ing sighs, thy loving signs caused me to blush for shame and to look wan for fear, lest they should be perceived of any. These subtle shifts, these painted practices (if I were to be won) would soon wean me from the teat of Vesta to the toys of Venus. Besides this, thy comely grace, thy rare qualities, thy exquisite perfection were able to move a mind half mortified to transgress the bonds of maidenly modesty. But God shield, Lucilla, that thou shouldest be so careless of thine honour as to commit the state thereof to a stranger. Learn thou by me, Euphues, to despise things that be amiable, to forgo delightful practices; believe me it is piety to abstain from pleasure.

"Thou art not the first that hath solicited this suit, but the first that goeth about to seduce me; neither discernest thou more than other, but darest more than any; neither hast thou more art to discover thy meaning, but more heart to open thy mind. But thou preferrest me before thy lands, thy livings, thy life, thou offerest thyself a sacrifice for my security, thou profferest me the whole and only sovereignty of thy service; truly I were very cruel and hard-hearted if I should not love thee. Hard-hearted albeit I am not, but truly love thee I cannot, whom I doubt to be my lover. Moreover I have not been used to the court of Cupid, wherein there be more sleights than there be hares in Athos, than bees in Hybla, than stars in heaven.

"Besides this, the common people here in Naples are not only both very suspicious of other men's matters and manners, but also very jealous over other men's children and maidens. Either, therefore, dissemble thy fancy or desist from thy folly. But why shouldest thou desist from the one, seeing thou canst cunningly dissemble the other? My father is now gone to Venice, and as I am uncertain of his return so am I not privy to the cause of his travel. But yet is he so from hence that he seeth me in his absence. Knowest thou not, Euphues, that kings have long arms and rulers large reaches? Neither let this comfort thee, that at his departure he deputed thee in Philautus's place. Although my face cause him to mistrust my loyalty, yet my faith enforceth him to give me this liberty; though he be suspicious of my fair hue, yet is he secure of my firm honesty.

"But alas, Euphues, what truth can there be found in a traveller, what stay in a stranger; whose words and bodies both watch but for a wind, whose feet are ever fleeting, whose faith plighted on

---

156 A common Early Modern proverb had this as the fate of women who die virgins.

the shore is turned to perjury when they hoist sail? Who more traitorous to Phyllis than Demophon?[157] Yet he a traveller. Who more perjured to Dido than Aeneas? And he a stranger. Both these queens, both they caitiffs. Who more false to Ariadne than Theseus?[158] Yet he a sailor. Who more fickle to Medea than Jason? Yet he a starter.[159] Both these daughters to great princes, both they unfaithful of promises. Is it then likely that Euphues will be faithful to Lucilla being in Naples but a sojourner?

"I have not yet forgotten the invective (I can no otherwise term it) which thou madest against beauty, saying it was a deceitful bait with a deadly hook and a sweet poison in a painted pot. Canst thou then he so unwise to swallow the bait which will breed thy bane?[160] To swill the drink that will expire[161] thy date? To desire the wight that will work thy death? But it may be that with the scorpion thou canst feed on the earth, or with the quail and roebuck be fat with poison, or with beauty live in all bravery.

"I fear me thou hast the stone *Continens* about thee, which is named of the contrary; that though thou pretend faith in thy words, thou devisest fraud in thy heart, that though thou seem to prefer love, thou art inflamed with lust. And what for that? Though thou have eaten the seeds of rocket[162] which breed incontinency, yet have I chewed the leaf cress which maintaineth modesty. Though thou bear in thy bosom the herb Araxa, most noisome to virginity, yet have I the stone that groweth in the mount Tmolus, the upholder of chastity.[163]

'You may, gentleman, account me for a cold prophet, thus hastily to divine of your disposition. Pardon me, Euphues, if in love I cast beyond the moon,[164] which bringeth us women to endless moan. Although I myself were never burnt, whereby I should dread the fire, yet the scorching of others in the flames of fancy warneth me to beware; though I as yet never tried any faithless, whereby I should be fearful, yet have I read of many that have been perjured, which causeth me to be careful; though I am able to convince none by proof, yet am I enforced to suspect one upon probabilities. Alas, we silly souls, which have neither wit to decipher the wiles of men nor wisdom to dissemble our affections, neither craft to train in young lovers, neither courage to withstand their encounters, neither discretion to discern their doubling, neither hard hearts to reject their complaints – we, I say, are soon enticed, being by nature simple, and easily entangled, being apt to receive the impression of love. But alas, it is both common and lamentable to behold simplicity entrapped by subtlety, and those that have most might to be infected with most malice. The spider weaveth a fine web to hang the fly, the wolf weareth a fair face to devour the lamb, the merlin[165] striketh at the partridge, the eagle often snappeth at the fly, men are always laying baits for women which are the weaker vessels. But as yet I could never hear man by such snares to entrap man. For true it is, that men themselves have by use observed, that it must be a hard winter when one wolf eateth another. I have read that the bull being tied to the fig-tree loseth his strength, that the whole herd of deer stand at the gaze if they smell a sweet apple, that the dolphin by the sound of music is brought to the shore. And then no marvel it is that if the fierce bull be tamed with the fig tree that women, being as weak as sheep, be overcome with a fig, if the wild deer be caught with an apple that the tame damsel is won with a blossom, if the fleet dolphin be allured with harmony that women be entangled with the melody of men's speech, fair promises, and solemn protestations.

"But folly it were for me to mark their mischiefs. Sith I am neither able, neither they willing, to amend their manners, it becometh me rather to show what our sex should do than to open what yours doth. And seeing I cannot by reason restrain your importunate suit, I will by rigour done on myself cause you to refrain the means. I would to God Ferardo were in this point like to Lysander,[166]

---

157 Demophon was the son of the Athenian hero Theseus. Sent out of the city by his father for safety, he became the lover of a Thracian woman named Phyllis.

158 See the gazetteer under Theseus.

159 In Euripides' tragedy *Medea*, the Greek hero Jason abandons the barbarian princess Medea, who sacrificed her family's interests for him, for the daughter of the King of Corinth. In revenge, she kills his new bride, her father, and the two children whom she had by Jason. A "starter" is someone who is fickle or inconstant.

160 *death.*

161 *bring to an end.*

162 *arugula.*

163 For the sources of these arcane pieces of knowledge, see Croll and Clemons' edition.

164 i.e. speculate idly.

165 *falcon.*

166 A Spartan general of the 5th century BC.

which would not suffer his daughters to wear gorgeous apparel, saying it would rather make them common than comely. I would it were in Naples a law, which was a custom in Egypt that women should always go barefoot, to the intent they might keep themselves always at home; that they should be ever like to that snail which hath ever his house on his head. I mean so to mortify myself that instead of silks I will wear sackcloth, for ouches[167] and bracelets lear and caddis,[168] for the lute use the distaff, for the pen the needle, for lovers' sonnets David's psalms.

"But yet I am not so senseless altogether to reject your service; which if I were certainly assured to proceed of a simple mind it should not receive so simple a reward. And what greater trial can I have of thy simplicity and truth than thine own request which desireth a trial. Aye, but in the coldest flint there is hot fire, the bee that hath honey in her mouth hath a sting in her tail, the tree that beareth the sweetest fruit hath a sour sap, yea the words of men though they seem smooth as oil yet their hearts are as crooked as the stalk of ivy. I would not, Euphues, that thou shouldest condemn me of rigour in that I seek to assuage thy folly by reason; but take this by the way that although as yet I am disposed to like of none, yet whensoever I shall love any I will not forget thee. In the mean season account me thy friend, for thy foe I will never be."

Euphues was brought into a great quandary and as it were cold shivering to hear this new kind of kindness, such sweet meat, such sour sauce, such fair words, such faint promises, such hot love, such cold desire, such certain hope, such sudden change; and stood like one that had looked on Medusa's head and so had been turned into a stone.[169]

"Lucilla, seeing him in this pitiful plight and fearing he would take stand[170] if the lure were not cast out, took him by the hand and, wringing him softly, with a smiling countenance began thus to comfort him; "Methinks, Euphues, changing so your colour upon the sudden, you will soon change your copy.[171] Is your mind on your meat? A penny for your thought."

"Mistress," quoth he, "if you would buy all my thoughts at that price, I should never be weary of thinking; but seeing it is too dear, read it and take it for nothing."

"It seems to me," said she, "that you are in some brown study what colours you might best wear for your lady."

"Indeed, Lucilla, you level shrewdly at my thought by the aim of your own imagination. For you have given unto me a true-love's knot wrought of changeable silk, and you deem me that I am devising how I might have my colours changeable also that they might agree. But let this with such toys and devices pass. If it please you to command me any service, I am here ready to attend your leisure."

"No service, Euphues, but that you keep silence until I have uttered my mind; and secrecy when I have unfolded my meaning."

"If I should offend in the one I were too bold, if in the other too beastly."

"Well then, Euphues," said she, "so it is that for the hope that I conceive of thy loyalty and the happy success that is like to ensue of this our love, I am content to yield thee the place in my heart which thou desirest and deservest above all other; which consent in me, if it may any ways breed thy contentation, sure I am that it will every way work my comfort. But as either thou tenderest mine honour or thine own safety, use such secrecy in this matter that my father have no inkling hereof before I have framed his mind fit for our purpose. And though women have small force to overcome men by reason, yet have they good fortune to undermine them by policy. The soft drops of rain pierce the hard marble, many strokes overthrow the tallest oak, a silly woman in time may make such a breach into a man's heart as her tears may enter without resistance; then doubt not but I will so undermine mine old father as quickly I will enjoy my new friend. Tush, Philautus was liked for fashion sake, but never loved for fancy sake; and this I vow by the faith of a virgin and by the love I bear thee (for greater bands to confirm my vow I have not) that my father shall

167   brooches.
168   cloth tape and worsted ribbon, respectively.
169   In Greek mythology, Medusa was one of the three monstrous Gorgons, all of whom could turn anyone who looked at them to stone. She was slain by the hero Perseus.
170   A term from falconry for a bird that is not returning to its master.
171   i.e. change your course of action.

sooner martyr me in the fire than marry me to Philautus. No, no, Euphues, thou only hast won me by love and shalt only wear me by law; I force[172] not Philautus his fury so I may have Euphues his friendship, neither will I prefer his possessions before thy person, neither esteem better of his lands than of thy love. Ferardo shall sooner disherit me of my patrimony than dishonour me in breaking my promise. It is not his great manors but thy good manners that shall make my marriage. In token of which my sincere affection, I give thee my hand in pawn and thy heart for ever to be thy Lucilla."

Unto whom Euphues answered in this manner: "If my tongue were able to utter the joys that my heart hath conceived, I fear me though I be well beloved yet I should hardly he believed. Ah my Lucilla, how much am I bound to thee which preferrest mine unworthiness before thy father's wrath, my happiness before thine own misfortune, my love before thine own life! How might I excel thee in courtesy, whom no mortal creature can exceed in constancy! I find it now for a settled truth, which erst I accounted for a vain talk, that the purple dye will never stain, that the pure civet[173] will never lose his savour, that the green laurel will never change his colour, that beauty can never be blotted with discourtesy. As touching secrecy in this behalf, assure thyself that I will not so much as tell it to myself. Command Euphues to run, to ride, to undertake any exploit be it never so dangerous, to hazard himself in any enterprise be it never so desperate."

As they were thus pleasantly conferring the one with the other, Livia (whom Euphues made his stale)[174] entered into the parlour. Unto whom Lucilla spake in these terms, "Dost thou not laugh, Livia, to see my ghostly father keep me here so long at shrift?"

"Truly," answered Livia, "methinks that you smile at some pleasant shift. Either he is slow in inquiring of your faults or you slack in answering of his questions."

And thus being supper time they all sat down, Lucilla well pleased, no man better content than Euphues. Who after his repast, having no opportunity to confer with his lover, had small lust to continue with the gentlewomen any longer; seeing therefore he could frame no means to work his delight, he coined an excuse to hasten his departure, promising the next morning to trouble them again as a guest more bold than welcome, although indeed he thought himself to be the better welcome in saying that he would come.

But as Ferardo went in post, so he returned in haste, having concluded with Philautus that the marriage should immediately be consummated. Which wrought such a content in Philautus that he was almost in an ecstasy through the extremity of his passions; such is the fullness and force of pleasure that there is nothing so dangerous as the fruition. Yet knowing that delays bring dangers, although he nothing doubted of Lucilla whom he loved, yet feared he the fickleness of old men, which is always to be mistrusted. He urged therefore Ferardo to break[175] with his daughter. Who, being willing to have the match made, was content incontinently to procure the means; finding, therefore, his daughter at leisure, and having knowledge of her former love, spake to her as followeth:–

"Dear Daughter, as thou hast long time lived a maiden, so now thou must learn to be a mother; and as I have been careful to bring thee up a virgin, so am now desirous to make thee a wife. Neither ought I in this matter to use any persuasions, for that maidens commonly nowadays are no sooner born but they begin to bride it; neither to offer any great portions, for that thou knowest thou shalt inherit all my possessions. Mine only care hath been hitherto to match thee with such an one as should be of good wealth able to maintain thee, of great worship able to compare with thee in birth, of honest conditions to deserve thy love, and an Italian-born to enjoy my lands. At the last I have found one answerable to my desire, a gentleman of great revenues, of a noble progeny, of honest behaviour, of comely personage, born and brought up in Naples – Philautus, thy friend as I guess, thy husband, Lucilla, if thou like it; neither canst thou dislike him who wanteth nothing that should cause thy liking, neither hath anything that should breed thy loathing. And surely I rejoice the more that thou shalt be linked to him in marriage whom thou hast loved as I hear being

172   *constrain.*
173   A perfume base obtained from the civet-cat.
174   *decoy.*
175   *make things known.*

a maiden, neither can there any jars[176] kindle between them where the minds be so united, neither any jealousy arise where love hath so long been settled.

"Therefore, Lucilla, to the end the desire of either of you may now be accomplished to the delight of you both, I am here come to finish the contract by giving hands, which you have already begun between yourselves by joining of hearts; that as God doth witness the one in your consciences, so the world may testify the other by your conversations. And therefore, Lucilla, make such answer to my request as may like me and satisfy thy friend."

Lucilla, abashed with this sudden speech of her father yet boldened by the love of her friend, with a comely bashfulness answered him in this manner:–

"Reverend sir, the sweetness that I have found in the undefiled estate of virginity causeth me to loathe the sour sauce which is mixed with matrimony, and the quiet life which I have tried being a maiden maketh me to shun the cares that are always incident to a mother; neither am I so wedded to the world that I should be moved with great possessions, neither so bewitched with wantonness that I should be enticed with any man's proportion, neither, if I were so disposed, would I be so proud to desire one of noble progeny or so precise to choose one only in mine own country, for that commonly these things happen always to the contrary. Do we not see the noble to match with the base, the rich with the poor, the Italian oftentimes with the Portugal? As love knoweth no laws, so it regardeth no conditions, as the lover maketh no pause where he liketh, so he maketh no conscience of these idle ceremonies.

"In that Philautus is the man that threateneth such kindness at my hands and such courtesy at yours that he should account me his wife before he woo me, certainly he is like, for me, to make his reckoning twice, because he reckoneth without his hostess. And in this Philautus would either show himself of great wisdom to persuade, or me of great lightness to be allowed; although the loadstone draw iron yet it cannot move gold, though the jet gather up the light straw yet can it not take up the pure steel. Although Philautus think himself of virtue sufficient to win his lover, yet shall he not obtain Lucilla. I cannot but smile to hear that a marriage should be solemnised where never was any mention of assuring,[177] and that the wooing should be a day after the wedding. Certes, if when I looked merrily on Philautus he deemed it in the way of marriage; or if, seeing me disposed to jest, he took me in good earnest, then sure he might gather some presumption of my love, but no promise. But methinks it is good reason that I should be at mine own bridal, and not given in the church before I know the bridegroom.

"Therefore dear father, in mine opinion as there can be no bargain where both be not agreed, neither any indentures sealed where the one will not consent, so can there be no contract where both be not content, no banns asked lawfully where one of the parties forbiddeth them, no marriage made where no match was meant. But I will hereafter frame myself to be coy, seeing I am claimed for a wife because I have been courteous, and give myself to melancholy, seeing I am accounted won in that I have been merry. And if every gentleman be made of the metal that Philautus is, then I fear I shall be challenged of as many as I have used to company with, and be a common wife to all those that have commonly resorted hither.

"My duty therefore ever reserved, I here on my knees forswear Philautus for my husband, although I accept him for my friend. And seeing I shall hardly be induced ever to match with any, I beseech you, if by your fatherly love I shall be compelled, that I may match with such a one as both I may love and you may like."

Ferardo, being a grave and wise gentleman, although he were throughly angry, yet he dissembled his fury to the end he might by craft discover her fancy. And whispering Philautus in the ear (who stood as though he had a flea in his ear),[178] desired him to keep silence until he had undermined her by subtlety. Which Philautus having granted, Ferardo began to sift his daughter with this device:–

"Lucilla, thy colour showeth thee to be in a great choler, and thy hot words bewray thy heavy wrath; but be patient, seeing all my talk was only to try thee. I am neither so unnatural to wrest

---

176   *disputes.*
177   *a betrothal.*

178   i.e. like one who has been rejected.

thee against thine own will, neither so malicious to wed thee to any against thine own liking. For well I know what jars, what jealousy, what strife, what storms ensue, where the match is made rather by the compulsion of the parents than by consent of the parties. Neither do I like thee the less in that thou likest Philautus so little, neither can Philautus love thee the worse in that thou lovest thyself so well, wishing rather to stand to thy chance than to the choice of any other.

"But this grieveth me most, that thou art almost vowed to the vain order of the vestal virgins, despising, or at the least not desiring, the sacred bands of Juno[179] her bed. If thy mother had been of that mind when she was a maiden, thou hadst not now been born to be of this mind to be a virgin. Weigh with thyself what slender profit they bring to the commonwealth, what slight plea-sure to themselves, what great grief to their parents, which joy most in their offspring and desire most to enjoy the noble and blessed name of a grandfather. Thou knowest that the tallest ash is cut down for fuel because it beareth no good fruit, that the cow that gives no milk is brought to the slaughter, that the drone that gathereth no honey is contemned, that the woman that maketh herself barren by not marrying is accounted among the Grecian ladies worse than a carrion, as Homer reporteth. Therefore, Lucilla, if thou have any care to be a comfort to my hoary hairs or a commodity to thy commonweal, frame thyself to that honourable estate of matrimony which was sanctified in Paradise, allowed of the Patriarchs, hallowed of the old Prophets, and commended of all persons.

"If thou like any be not ashamed to tell it me, which only am to exhort thee, yea, and, as much as in me lieth, to command thee to love one. If he be base, thy blood will make him noble, if beggarly, thy goods shall make him wealthy, if a stranger, thy freedom may enfranchise him; if he be young he is the more fitter to he thy fere, if he be old the liker to thine aged father. For I had rather thou shouldest lead a life to thine own liking in earth, than to thy great torments lead apes in Hell. Be bold therefore to make me partner of thy desire which will be partaker of thy disease, yea, and a furtherer of thy delights as far as either my friends, or my lands, or my life will stretch."

Lucilla, perceiving the drift of the old fox her father, weighed with herself what was best to be done. At the last, not weighing her father's ill-will but encouraged by love, shaped him an answer which pleased Ferardo but a little and pinched Philautus on the parson's side[180] on this manner:–

"Dear father Ferardo, although I see the bait you lay to catch me, yet I am content to swallow the hook; neither are you more desirous to take me napping, than I willing to confess my meaning. So it is that love hath as well inveigled me as others which make it as strange[181] as I. Neither do I love him so meanly that I should be ashamed of his name, neither is his personage so mean that I should love him shamefully. It is Euphues that lately arrived here at Naples that hath battered the bulwark of my breast and shall shortly enter as conqueror into my bosom. What his wealth is I neither know it nor weigh it; what his wit is all Naples doth know it and wonder at it; neither have I been curious to inquire of his progenitors, for that I know so noble a mind could take no original but from a noble man: for as no bird can look against the sun but those that be bred of the eagle, neither any hawk soar so high as the brood of the hobby,[182] so no wight can have such excellent qualities except he descend of a noble race, neither be of so high capacity unless he issue of a high progeny. And I hope Philautus will not be my foe, seeing I have chosen his dear friend, neither you, father, be displeased in that Philautus is displaced. You need not muse that I should so suddenly be entangled, love gives no reason of choice, neither will it suffer any repulse. Myrrha was enamoured of her natural father, Biblis of her brother, Phaedra of her son-in-law.[183] If nature can no way resist the fury of affection, how should it be stayed by wisdom?"

Ferardo, interrupting her in the middle of her discourse, although he were moved with inward grudge yet he wisely repressed his anger, knowing that sharp words would but sharpen her froward will; and thus answered her briefly:–

179 Juno was the goddess of marriage.
180 i.e. which showed Philautus how diminished his stock was with her.
181 i.e. others who pretend not to know about love.

182 A species of falcon.
183 All these examples of unnatural love come from Greek mythology.

"Lucilla, as I am not presently to grant my good will, so mean I not to reprehend thy choice. Yet wisdom willeth me to pause until I have called what may happen to my remembrance, and warneth thee to be circumspect lest thy rash conceit bring a sharp repentance. As for you, Philautus, I would not have you despair, seeing a woman doth oftentimes change her desire."

Unto whom Philautus in few words made answer: "Certainly Ferardo I take the less grief in that I see her so greedy after Euphues; and by so much the more I am content to leave my suit, by how much the more she seemeth to disdain my service. But as for hope, because I would not by any means taste one dram thereof, I will abjure all places of her abode and loathe her company, whose countenance I have so much loved. As for Euphues —" And there staying his speech, he flung out of the doors; and repairing to his lodging, uttered these words:—

"Ah most dissembling wretch Euphues! O counterfeit companion! Couldst thou under the show of a steadfast friend cloak the malice of a mortal foe? Under the colour of simplicity shroud the image of deceit? Is thy Livia turned to my Lucilla, thy love to my lover, thy devotion to my saint? Is this the courtesy of Athens, the cavilling of scholars, the craft of Grecians? Couldst thou not remember, Philautus, that Greece is never without some wily Ulysses, never void of some Sinon,[184] never to seek of some deceitful shifter? Is it not commonly said of Grecians that craft cometh to them by kind, that they learn to deceive in their cradle? Why then did his pretended courtesy bewitch thee with such credulity? Shall my good will be the cause of his ill will? Because I was content to be his friend, thought he me meet to be made his fool? I see now that as the fish Scolopidus in the flood Araris at the waxing of the moon is as white as the driven snow and at the waning as black as the burnt coal, so Euphues which at the first increasing of our familiarity was very zealous is now at the last cast become most faithless.

"But why rather exclaim I not against Lucilla, whose wanton looks caused Euphues to violate his plighted faith? Ah wretched wench! Canst thou be so light of love as to change with every wind? So inconstant as to prefer a new lover before thine old friend? Ah, well I wot[185] that a new broom sweepeth clean, and a new garment maketh thee leave off the old though it be fitter, and new wine causeth thee to forsake the old though it be better; much like to the men in the island Scyrum which pull up the old tree when they see the young begin to spring, and not unlike unto the widow of Lesbos which changed all her old gold for new glass. Have I served thee three years faithfully and am I served so unkindly? Shall the fruit of my desire be turned to disdain?

"But unless Euphues had inveigled thee thou hadst yet been constant; yea, but if Euphues had not seen thee willing to be won he would never have wooed thee. But had not Euphues enticed thee with fair words thou wouldst never have loved him; but hadst thou not given him fair looks he would never have liked thee. Aye, but Euphues gave the onset; aye, but Lucilla gave the occasion. Aye, but Euphues first brake[186] his mind; aye, but Lucilla first bewrayed her meaning. Tush, why go I about to excuse any of them, seeing I have just cause to accuse them both? Neither ought I to dispute which of them hath proffered me the greatest villainy sith that either of them hath committed perjury. Yet although they have found me dull in perceiving their falsehood, they shall not find me slack in revenging their folly. As for Lucilla, seeing I mean altogether to forget her, I mean also to forgive her, lest in seeking means to be revenged mine old desire be renewed."

Philautus, having thus discoursed with himself, began to write to Euphues as followeth:—

"Although hitherto, Euphues, I have shrined thee in my heart for a trusty friend, I will shun thee hereafter as a trothless foe; and although I cannot see in thee less wit than I was wont, yet do I find less honesty. I perceive at the last (although, being deceived, it be too late) that musk, although it be sweet in the smell, is sour in the smack; that the leaf of the cedar tree, though it be fair to be seen, yet the syrup depriveth sight; that friendship, though it be plighted by shaking the hand, yet it is shaken off by fraud of the heart.

"But thou hast not much to boast of, for as thou hast won a fickle lady so hast thou lost a faithful friend. How canst thou be secure of her constancy, when thou hast had such trial of her

184   For Ulysses and Sinon, see the gazetteer.   186   *made known.*
185   *know.*

lightness? How canst thou assure thyself that she will be faithful to thee, which hath been faithless to me?

"Ah Euphues, let not my credulity be an occasion hereafter for thee to practise the like cruelty. Remember this, that yet there hath never been any faithless to his friend that hath not also been fruitless to his God. But I weigh this treachery the less in that it cometh from a Grecian in whom is no troth. Thought I be too weak to wrestle for a revenge, yet God, who permitteth no guile to be guiltless, will shortly requite this injury; though Philautus have no policy to undermine thee, yet thine own practices will be sufficient to overthrow thee.

"Couldst thou, Euphues, for the love of a fruitless pleasure violate the league of faithful friendship? Didst thou weigh more the enticing looks of a lewd wench than the entire love of a loyal friend? If thou didst determine with thyself at the first to be false why didst thou swear to be true? If to be true, why art thou false? If thou wast minded both falsely and forgedly to deceive me, why didst thou flatter and dissemble with me at the first? If to love me, why dost thou flinch at the last? If the sacred bands of amity did delight thee, why didst thou break them? If dislike thee, why didst thou praise them? Dost thou not know that a perfect friend should be like the glaze-worm which shineth most bright in the dark; or like the pure frankincense which smelleth most sweet when it is in the fire; or, at the least, not unlike to the damask rose which is sweeter in the still[187] than on the stalk? But thou, Euphues, dost rather resemble the swallow which in the summer creepeth under the eaves of every house and in the winter leaveth nothing but dirt behind her; or the bumble-bee which having sucked honey out of the fair flower doth leave it and loathe it; or the spider which in the finest web doth hang the fairest fly.

"Dost thou think, Euphues, that thy craft in betraying me shall any whit cool my courage in revenging thy villainy? Or that a gentleman of Naples will put up such an injury at the hands of a scholar? And if I do, it is not for want of strength to maintain my just quarrel, but of will which thinketh scorn to get so vain a conquest. I know that Menelaus for his ten years' war endured ten years' woe, that after all his strife he won but a strumpet, that for all his travels he reduced (I cannot say reclaimed) but a straggler;[188] which was as much, in my judgement, as to strive for a broken glass which is good for nothing. I wish thee rather Menelaus' care than myself his conquest; that thou, being deluded by Lucilla, mayest rather know what it is to he deceived, than I, having conquered thee, should prove what it were to bring back a dissembler. Seeing, therefore, there can no greater revenge light upon thee than that, as thou hast reaped where another hath sown, so another may thresh that which thou hast reaped, I will pray that thou mayest be measured unto with the like measure that thou hast meten unto others; that as thou hast thought it no conscience to betray me, so others may deem it no dishonesty to deceive thee; that as Lucilla made it a light matter to forswear her old friend Philautus, so she may make it a mock to forsake her new fere Euphues. Which if it come to pass, as it is like by my compass,[189] then shalt thou see the troubles and feel the torments which thou hast already thrown into the hearts and eyes of others.

"Thus hoping shortly to see thee as hopeless as myself is hapless, I wish my wish were as effectually ended as it is heartily looked for. And so I leave thee.

Thine once,

Philautus."

Philautus dispatching a messenger with this letter speedily to Euphues, went into the fields to walk there, either to digest his choler or chew upon his melancholy. But Euphues having read the contents was well content, setting his talk at naught and answering his taunts in these gibing terms:—

"I remember Philautus how valiantly Ajax boasted in the feats of arms, yet Ulysses bare away the armour;[190] and it may be that though thou crack of thine own courage, thou mayest easily lose

---

187   i.e. when made into perfume.

188   See Menelaus and Helen of Troy in the gazetteer.

189   i.e. in my judgment.

190   A reference to the debate between Ajax and Ulysses for the arms of the dead hero Achilles in *Metamorphoses* 13. Ulysses convinced the audience to award the arms to him, and the incident is usually read as a demonstration of the superiority of rhetoric and guile to military prowess in political situations.

the conquest. Dost thou think Euphues such a dastard that he is not able to withstand thy courage or such a dullard that he cannot descry thy craft. Alas, good soul! It fareth with thee as with the hen which when the puttock[191] hath caught her chicken beginneth to cackle; and thou having lost thy lover beginnest to prattle.

"Tush, Philautus, I am in this point of Euripides his mind,[192] who thinks it lawful for the desire of a kingdom to transgress the bounds of honesty and for the love of a lady to violate and break the bands of amity. The friendship between man and man as it is common so is it of course, between man and woman as it is seldom so is it sincere; the one proceedeth of the similitude of manners the other of the sincerity of the heart. If thou hadst learned the first point of hawking, thou wouldst have learned to have held fast; or the first note of descant,[193] thou wouldst have kept *sol fa* to thyself.

"But thou canst blame me no more of folly in leaving thee to love Lucilla than thou mayest reprove him of foolishness that having a sparrow in his hand letteth her go to catch the pheasant, or him of unskilfullness that seeing the heron leaveth to level his shot at the stock-dove, or that woman of coyness that having a dead rose in her bosom throweth it away to gather the fresh violet. Love knoweth no laws. Did not Jupiter transform himself into the shape of Amphitryon to embrace Alcmene; into the form of a swan to enjoy Leda; into a bull to beguile Io; into a shower of gold to win Danae? Did not Neptune change himself into a heifer, a ram, a flood, a dolphin, only for the love of those he lusted after? Did not Apollo convert himself into a shepherd, into a bird, into a lion, for the desire he had to heal his disease?[194] If the gods thought no scorn to become beasts to obtain their best beloved, shall Euphues be so nice in changing his copy to gain his lady? No, no; he that cannot dissemble in love is not worth to live. I am of this mind that both might and malice, deceit and treachery, all perjury, any impiety may lawfully be committed in love, which is lawless.

"In that thou arguest Lucilla of lightness thy will hangs in the light of thy wit. Dost thou not know that the weak stomach, if it be cloyed with one diet, doth soon surfeit? That the clown's garlic cannot ease the courtier's disease so well as the pure treacle?[195] That far fet and dear bought is good for ladies? That Euphues being a more dainty morsel than Philautus ought better to be accepted?

"Tush, Philautus, set thy heart at rest, for thy hap willeth thee to give over all hope both of my friendship and her love. As for revenge, thou art not so able to lend a blow as I to ward it, neither more venturous to challenge the combat than I valiant to answer the quarrel. As Lucilla was caught by fraud so shall she be kept by force, and as thou wast too simple to espy my craft so I think thou wilt be too weak to withstand my courage; if thy revenge stand only upon thy wish, thou shalt never live to see my woe or to have thy will. And so farewell.

Euphues."

This letter being dispatched Euphues sent it and Philautus read it; who disdaining those proud terms disdained also to answer them, being ready to ride with Ferardo.

Euphues, having for a space absented himself from the house of Ferardo, because he was at home, longed sore to see Lucilla; which now opportunity offered unto him, Ferardo being gone again to Venice with Philautus. But in his absence one Curio,[196] a gentleman of Naples of little wealth and less wit, haunted Lucilla her company, and so enchanted her that Euphues was also cast off with Philautus. Which thing being unknown to Euphues caused him the sooner to make his repair to the presence of his lady: Whom he finding in her muses began pleasantly to salute in this manner:–

"Mistress Lucilla, although my long absence might breed your just anger (for that lovers desire nothing so much as often meeting), yet I hope my presence will dissolve your choler (for that lovers are soon pleased when of their wishes they be fully possessed). My absence is the rather to be excused

---

191   A bird of prey.
192   The source of this reference has never been found, and it may well be one of the many misremembered citations in this text. Like many Early Modern authors, Lyly does not always check his facts carefully.
193   *musical composition.*

194   As earlier editors have pointed out, all of these divine transformations for erotic purposes are listed in Ovid's *Metamorphoses* 6.103–24.
195   i.e. Home remedies do not work on sophisticated people, only a pure medicinal compound.
196   In this context, the name means "plaything" or "trinket."

in that your father hath been always at home, whose frowns seemed to threaten my ill fortune; and my presence at this present the better to be accepted in that I have made such speedy repair to your presence."

Unto whom Lucilla answered with this gleek:[197] Truly, Euphues, you have missed the cushion:[198] for I was neither angry with your long absence, neither am I well pleased at your presence. The one gave me rather a good hope hereafter never to see you, the other giveth me a greater occasion to abhor you."

Euphues, being nipped on the head, with a pale countenance, as though his soul had forsaken his body, replied as followeth: "If this sudden change, Lucilla, proceed of any desert of mine, I am here not only to answer the fact but also to make amends for my fault; if of any new motion or mind to forsake your new friend, I am rather to lament your inconstancy than revenge it. But I hope that such hot love cannot be so soon cold, neither such sure faith be rewarded with so sudden forgetfulness."

Lucilla, not ashamed to confess her folly, answered him with this frump: "Sir, whether your deserts or my desire have wrought this change it will boot you little to know. Neither do I crave amends, neither fear revenge. As for fervent love you know there is no fire so hot but it is quenched with water, neither affection so strong but is weakened with reason. Let this suffice thee that thou know I care not for thee."

"Indeed," said Euphues, "to know the cause of your alteration would boot me little, seeing the effect taketh such force. I have heard that women either love entirely or hate deadly, and seeing you have put me out of doubt of the one, I must needs persuade myself of the other. This change will cause Philautus to laugh me to scorn and double thy lightness in turning so often. Such was the hope that I conceived of thy constancy that I spared not in all places to blaze thy loyalty, but now my rash conceit will prove me a liar and thee a light huswife."

"Nay," said Lucilla, "now shalt not though laugh Philautus to scorn, seeing you have both drunk of one cup. In misery, Euphues, it is a great comfort to have a companion. I doubt not but that you will both conspire against me to work some mischief, although I nothing fear your malice. Whosoever accounteth you a liar for praising me may also deem you a lecher for being enamoured of me; and whosoever judgeth me light in forsaking of you may think thee as lewd in loving of me. For thou that thoughtest it lawful to deceive thy friend must take no scorn to be deceived of thy foe."

"Then I perceive, Lucilla," said he, "that I was made thy stale and Philautus thy laughing-stock; whose friendship (I must confess indeed) I have refused, to obtain thy favour. And since another hath won that we both have lost, I am content for my part; neither ought I to be grieved, seeing thou art fickle."

"Certes, Euphues," said Lucilla, "you spend your wind in waste; for your welcome is but small and your cheer is like to be less. Fancy giveth no reason of his change neither will be controlled for any choice. This is, therefore, to warn you that from henceforth you neither solicit this suit, neither offer any way your service. I have chosen one (I must needs confess neither to be compared to Philautus in wealth, nor to thee in wit, neither in birth to the worst of you both). I think God gave it me for a just plague for renouncing Philautus and choosing thee; and since I am an example to all women of lightness, I am like also to be a mirror to them all of unhappiness. Which ill luck I must take by so much the more patiently, by how much the more I acknowledge myself to have deserved it worthily."[199]

"Well, Lucilla," answered Euphues, "this case breedeth my sorrow the more in that it is so sudden, and by so much the more I lament it by how much the less I looked for it. In that my welcome is so cold and my cheer so simple, it nothing toucheth me — seeing your fury is so hot and my misfortune so great — that I am neither willing to receive it nor you to bestow it. If tract of time or want of trial had caused this metamorphosis, my grief had been more tolerable and your

197 gibe.
198 i.e. missed the target.

199 This paragraph is perhaps the clearest example of the complete artificiality of all the emotions and personal transformations in this text.

fleeting more excusable. But coming in a moment undeserved, unlooked for, unthought of it increaseth my sorrow and thy shame."

"Euphues," quoth she, "you make a long harvest for a little corn and angle for the fish that is already caught. Curio, yea Curio, is he that hath my love at his pleasure and shall also have my life at his commandment; and although you deem him unworthy to enjoy that which erst you accounted no wight worthy to embrace, yet seeing I esteem him more worth than any he is to be reputed as chief. The wolf chooseth him for her mate that hath or doth endure most travail for her sake. Venus was content to take the blacksmith with his polt-foot. Cornelia[200] here in Naples disdained not to love a rude miller. As for changing did not Helen the pearl of Greece, thy countrywoman, first take Menelaus, then Theseus, and last of all Paris?[201] If brute beasts give us examples that those are most to be liked of whom we are best beloved, or if the princess of beauty, Venus; and her heirs, Helen and Cornelia, show that our affection standeth on our free will, then am I rather to he excused than accused. Therefore, good Euphues, be as merry as you may be, for time may so turn that once again you may be."

"Nay, Lucilla," said he, "my harvest shall cease seeing others have reaped my corn; as for angling for the fish that is already caught, that were but mere folly. But in my mind, if you be a fish, you are either an eel which as soon as one hath hold of her tail will slip out of his hand, or else a minnow which will be nibbling at every bait but never biting. But what fish soever you be, you have made both me and Philautus to swallow a gudgeon.

"If Curio be the person, I would neither wish thee a greater plague nor him a deadlier poison. I, for my part, think him worthy of thee and thou unworthy of him: for although he be in body deformed, in mind foolish, an innocent born, a beggar by misfortune, yet doth he deserve a better than thyself, whose corrupt manners have stained thy heavenly hue, whose light behaviour hath dimmed the lights of thy beauty, whose inconstant mind hath betrayed the innocency of so many a gentleman.

"And in that you bring in the example of a beast to confirm your folly you show therein your beastly disposition, which is ready to follow such beastliness. But Venus played false. And what for that? Seeing her lightness serveth for an example, I would wish thou mightest try her punishment for a reward: that being openly taken in an iron net all the world might judge whether thou be fish or flesh;[202] and certes, in my mind no angle will hold thee, it must be a net. Cornelia loved a miller and thou a miser; can her folly excuse thy fault? Helen of Greece, my countrywoman born but thine by profession, changed and rechanged at her pleasure, I grant. Shall the lewdness of others animate thee in thy lightness? Why then dost thou not haunt the stews because Lais[203] frequented them? Why dost thou not love a bull seeing Pasiphaë loved one?[204] Why art thou not enamoured of thy father knowing that Myrrha[205] was so incensed? These are set down that we, viewing their incontinency, should fly the like impudency, not follow the like excess; neither can they excuse thee of any inconstancy.

"Merry I will be as I may; but if I may hereafter as thou meanest, I will not. And therefore farewell Lucilla, the most inconstant that ever was nursed in Naples; farewell Naples, the most cursed town in all Italy; and women all, farewell."

Euphues, having thus given her his last farewell, yet, being solitary, began afresh to recount his sorrow on this manner:–

"Ah Euphues, into what a quandary art thou brought! In what sudden misfortune art thou wrapped! It is like to fare with thee as with the eagle which dieth neither for age nor with sickness, but with famine: for although thy stomach hunger yet thy heart will not suffer thee to eat.

200 An unknown literary figure.
201 Lyly has the chronology wrong: Theseus is said to have abducted Helen of Troy (see gazetteer) as a girl, before she married Menelaus.
202 A reference to the story of Aphrodite (Venus) and Ares (Mars). See the gazetteer under Hephaestus.
203 A famous ancient prostitute.

204 The wife of the legendary King Minos of Crete. After Minos angered the god Poseidon, he caused her to fall in love with a bull. After consummating her passion (in some versions, with a machine made for her by the craftsman Daedalus), she gave birth to the Minotaur, a monster with the head of a bull and the body of a man.
205 A woman from Greek mythology who fell in love with her father. See the gazetteer under Adonis.

And why shouldst thou torment thyself for one in whom is neither faith nor fervency? Oh the counterfeit love of women! Oh inconstant sex! I have lost Philautus, I have lost Lucilla, I have lost that which I shall hardly find again, a faithful friend.

"Ah foolish Euphues, why didst thou leave Athens, the nurse of wisdom, to inhabit Naples, the nourisher of wantonness? Had it not been better for thee to have eaten salt with the philosophers in Greece than sugar with the courtiers of Italy? But behold the course of youth which always inclineth to pleasure. I forsook mine old companions to search for new friends, I rejected the grave and fatherly counsel of Eubulus to follow the brainsick humour of mine own will. I addicted myself wholly to the service of women to spend my life in the laps of ladies, my lands in maintenance of bravery, my wit in the vanities of idle sonnets. I had thought that women had been as we men, that is, true, faithful, zealous, constant; but I perceive they be rather woe unto men by their falsehood, jealousy, inconstancy. I was half persuaded that they were made of the perfection of man and would be comforters, but now I see they have tasted of the infection of the serpent and will be corrosives. The physician saith it is dangerous to minister physic unto the patient that hath a cold stomach and a hot liver, lest in giving warmth to the one he inflame the other; so verily it is hard to deal with a woman whose words seem fervent, whose heart is congealed into hard ice, lest trusting their outward talk he be betrayed with their inward treachery.

"I will to Athens there to toss[206] my books, no more in Naples to live with fair looks. I will so frame myself as all youth hereafter shall rather rejoice to see mine amendment, than be animated to follow my former life. Philosophy, Physic, Divinity shall be my study. Oh the hidden secrets of nature, the express image of moral virtues, the equal balance of justice, the medicines to heal all diseases, how they begin to delight me! The axioms of Aristotle, the Maxims of Justinian, the Aphorisms of Galen[207] have suddenly made such a breach into my mind that I seem only to desire them, which did only erst detest them.

"If wit be employed in the honest study of learning, what thing so precious as wit? If in the idle trade of love, what thing more pestilent than wit? The proof of late hath been verified in me, whom nature hath endued with a little wit which I have abused with an obstinate will. Most true it is that the thing the better it is the greater is the abuse: and that there is nothing but through the malice of man may he abused. Doth not the fire (an element so necessary that without it man cannot live) as well burn the house as burn in the house, if it be abused? Doth not treacle as well poison as help if it be taken out of time? Doth not wine if it be immoderately taken kill the stomach, enflame the liver, murder the drunken? Doth not physic destroy if it be not well tempered? Doth not law accuse if it be not rightly interpreted? Doth not divinity condemn if it be not faithfully construed? Is not poison taken out of the honeysuckle by the spider, venom out of the rose by the canker, dung out of the maple tree by the scorpion? Even so the greatest wickedness is drawn out of the greatest wit if it be abused by will or entangled with the world or inveigled with women.

"But seeing I see mine own impiety, I will endeavour myself to amend all that is past and to be a mirror of godliness hereafter. The rose though a little it be eaten with the canker yet being distilled yieldeth sweet water, the iron though fretted with the rust yet being burnt in the fire shineth brighter; and wit, although it hath been eaten with the canker of his own conceit and fretted with the rust of vain love, yet being purified in the still of wisdom and tried in the fire of zeal will shine bright and smell sweet in the nostrils of all young novices.

"As therefore I gave a farewell to Lucilla, a farewell to Naples, a farewell to women, so now do I give a farewell to the world; meaning rather to macerate[208] myself with melancholy than pine in folly, rather choosing to die in my study amidst my books than to court it in Italy in the company of ladies."

Euphues, having thus debated with himself, went to his bed, there either with sleep to deceive his fancy, or with musing to renew his ill fortune or recant his old follies.

But it happened immediately Ferardo to return home. Who hearing this strange event was not a little amazed; and was now more ready to exhort Lucilla from the love of Curio, than before to

206   i.e. to continually turn the leaves of.
207   See the gazetteer for all three of these fundamental classical authors.

208   *waste away.*

the liking of Philautus. Therefore in all haste, with watery eyes and a woeful heart, began on this manner to reason with his daughter:—

"Lucilla (daughter I am ashamed to call thee, seeing thou hast neither care of thy father's tender affection nor of thine own credit), what sprite hath enchanted thy spirit that every minute thou alterest thy mind? I had thought that my hoary hairs should have found comfort by thy golden locks and my rotten age great ease by thy ripe years. But alas, I see in thee neither wit to order thy doings, neither will to frame thyself to discretion, neither the nature of a child, neither the nurture of a maiden, neither (I cannot without tears speak it) any regard of thine honour, neither any care of thine honesty. I am now enforced to remember thy mother's death, who I think was a prophetess in her life; for oftentimes she would say that thou hadst more beauty than was convenient for one that should be honest, and more cockering than was meet for one that should be a matron.

"Would I had never lived to be so old or thou to be so obstinate; either would I had died in my youth in the court or thou in thy cradle; I would to God that either I had never been born or thou never bred. Is this the comfort that the parent reapeth for all his care? Is obstinacy paid for obedience, stubbornness rendered for duty, malicious desperateness for filial fear? I perceive now that the wise painter saw more than the foolish parent can, who painted love going downward, saying it might well descend but ascend it could never. Danaus,[209] whom they report to be the father of fifty children, had among them all but one that disobeyed him in a thing most dishonest; but I that am father to one more than I would be, although one be all, have that one most disobedient to me in a request lawful and reasonable. If Danaus seeing but one of his daughters without awe became himself without mercy, what shall Ferardo do in this case who hath one and all most unnatural to him in a most just cause?

"Shall Curio enjoy the fruit of my travails, possess the benefit of my labours, inherit the patrimony of mine ancestors, who hath neither wisdom to increase them nor wit to keep them? Wilt thou, Lucilla, bestow thyself on such an one as hath neither comeliness in his body nor knowledge in his mind nor credit in his country? Oh I would thou hadst either been ever faithful to Philautus or never faithless to Euphues, or would thou wouldst be more fickle to Curio. As thy beauty hath made thee the blaze of Italy, so will thy lightness make thee the byword of the world. O Lucilla, Lucilla, would thou wert less fair or more fortunate, either of less honour or greater honesty, either better minded or soon buried!

"Shall thine old father live to see thee match with a young fool? Shall my kind heart be rewarded with such unkind hate? Ah Lucilla, thou knowest not the care of a father nor the duty of a child, and as far art thou from piety, as I from cruelty. Nature will not permit me to disherit my daughter, and yet it will suffer thee to dishonour thy father. Affection causeth me to wish thy life; and shall it entice thee to procure my death? It is mine only comfort to see thee flourish in thy youth; and is it thine to see me fade in mine age? To conclude, I desire to live to see thee prosper – and thou to see me perish.

"But why cast I the effect of this unnaturalness in thy teeth, seeing I myself was the cause? I made thee a wanton and thou hast made me a fool, I brought thee up like a cockney[210] and thou hast handled me like a coxcomb[211] (I speak it to mine own shame), I made more of thee than became a father and thou less of me than beseemed a child. And shall my loving care be cause of thy wicked cruelty? Yea, yea, I am not the first that hath been too careful nor the last that shall be handled so unkindly; it is common to see fathers too fond and children too froward.

"Well, Lucilla, the tears which thou seest trickle down my cheeks and the drops of blood (which thou canst not see) that fall from my heart enforce me to make an end of my talk. And if thou have any duty of a child or care of a friend or courtesy of a stranger or feeling of a Christian or humanity of a reasonable creature, then release thy father of grief and acquit thyself of ungratefulness. Otherwise thou shalt but hasten my death, and increase thine own defame; which if thou do the gain is mine and the loss thine, and both infinite."

---

209 A mythical father of fifty daughters who ordered them to kill   210 *indulged child.*
their husbands on their wedding night. All obeyed except one.   211 *fool.*

Lucilla, either so bewitched that she could not relent or so wicked that she would not yield to her father's request, answered him on this manner:–

"Dear father, as you would have me to show the duty of a child so ought you to show the care of a parent; and as the one standeth in obedience so the other is grounded upon reason. You would have me as I owe duty to you to leave Curio, and I desire you as you owe me any love that you suffer me to enjoy him. If you accuse me of unnaturalness in that I yield not to your request, I am also to condemn you of unkindness in that you grant not my petition. You object I know not what to Curio; but it is the eye of the master that fatteth the horse, and the love of the woman that maketh the man. To give reason for fancy were to weigh the fire and measure the wind. If, therefore, my delight be the cause of your death, I think my sorrow would be an occasion of your solace. And if you be angry because I am pleased, certes I deem you would be content if I were deceased; which if it be so that my pleasure breed your pain and mine annoy your joy, I may well say that you are an unkind father and I an unfortunate child. But, good father, either content yourself with my choice, or let me stand to the main chance;[212] otherwise the grief will be mine and the fault yours, and both intolerable."

Ferardo, seeing his daughter to have neither regard of her own honour nor his request, conceived such an inward grief that in short space he died, leaving Lucilla the only heir of his lands and Curio to possess them. But what end came of her, seeing it is nothing incident to the history of Euphues, it were superfluous to insert it, and so incredible that all women would rather wonder at it than believe it. Which event being so strange, I had rather leave them in a muse what it should be than in a maze[213] in telling what it was.

Philautus, having intelligence of Euphues his success and the falsehood of Lucilla, although he began to rejoice at the misery of his fellow, yet seeing her fickleness could not but lament her folly and pity his friend's misfortune, thinking that the lightness of Lucilla enticed Euphues to so great liking. Euphues and Philautus having conference between themselves, casting discourtesy in the teeth each of the other, but chiefly noting disloyalty in the demeanour of Lucilla, after much talk renewed their old friendship, both abandoning Lucilla as most abominable. Philautus was earnest to have Euphues tarry in Naples and Euphues desirous to have Philautus to Athens; but the one was so addicted to the court, the other so wedded to the university, that each refused the offer of the other. Yet this they agreed between themselves that though their bodies were by distance of place severed, yet the conjunction of their minds should neither be separated by the length of time nor alienated by change of soil. "I for my part," said Euphues, "to confirm this league give thee my hand and my heart." And so likewise did Philautus; and so shaking hands they bid each other farewell.

Euphues to the intent he might bridle the overlashing affections of Philautus, conveyed into his study a certain pamphlet which he termed "A cooling card for Philautus" – yet generally to be applied to all lovers – which I have inserted as followeth.

A COOLING CARD[214] FOR PHILAUTUS AND ALL FOND LOVERS

Musing with myself, being idle, how I might be well employed, friend Philautus, I could find nothing either more fit to continue our friendship or of greater force to dissolve our folly than to write a remedy for that which many judge past cure, for love, Philautus, with the which I have been so tormented that I have lost my time, thou so troubled that thou hast forgot reason, both so mangled with repulse, inveigled by deceit, and almost murdered by disdain, that I can neither remember our miseries without grief nor redress our mishaps without groans. How wantonly, yea, and how willingly have we abused our golden time and misspent our gotten treasure. How curious[215] were we to please our lady, how careless to displease our Lord. How devote in serving

---

212 i.e. take my own chances.
213 i.e. amazed.

214 An Early Modern term for something that dampens the enthusiasm of the person who receives it.
215 *excessively careful.*

our goddess, how desperate in forgetting our God. Ah my Philautus, if the wasting of our money might not dehort[216] us, yet the wounding of our minds should deter us; if reason might nothing persuade us to wisdom, yet shame should provoke us to wit.

If Lucilla read this trifle she will straight proclaim Euphues for a traitor, and seeing me turn my tippet,[217] will either shut me out for a wrangler[218] or cast me off for a wiredrawer;[219] either convince me of malice in bewraying their sleights or condemn me of mischief in arming young men against fleeting minions.[220] And what then? Though Curio be as hot as a toast, yet Euphues is as cold as a clock; though he be a cock of the game, yet Euphues is content to be craven and cry creak;[221] though Curio be old huddle and twang "*Ipse*, he,"[222] yet Euphues had rather shrink in the wetting than waste in the wearing. I know Curio to be steel to the back,[223] standard-bearer in Venus's camp, sworn to the crew, true to the crown, knight marshal to Cupid, and heir apparent to his kingdom.[224] But by that time that he hath eaten but one bushel of salt with Lucilla he shall taste ten quarters[225] of sorrow in his love. Then shall he find for every pint of honey a gallon of gall, for every dram of pleasure an ounce of pain, for every inch of mirth an ell[226] of moan.

And yet, Philautus, if there be any man in despair to obtain his purpose or so obstinate in his opinion that, having lost his freedom by folly, would also lose his life for love, let him repair hither and he shall reap such profit as will either quench his flames or assuage his fury, either cause him to renounce his lady as most pernicious or redeem his liberty as most precious. Come therefore to me all ye lovers that have been deceived by fancy, the glass of pestilence, or deluded by women, the gate to perdition; be as earnest to seek a medicine as you were eager to run into a mischief. The earth bringeth forth as well endive to delight the people as hemlock to endanger the patient, as well the rose to distil as the nettle to sting, as well the bee to give honey as the spider to yield poison. If my lewd life, gentlemen, have given you offence, let my good counsel make amends; if by my folly any be allured to lust, let them by my repentance be drawn to continency. Achilles' spear could as well heal as hurt,[227] the scorpion though he sting yet he stints the pain, though the herb Nerius poison the sheep yet is it a remedy to man against poison, though I have infected some by example yet I hope I shall comfort many by repentance.

Whatsoever I speak to men, the same also I speak to women. I mean not to run with the hare and hold with the hound, to carry fire in the one hand and water in the other, neither to flatter men as altogether faultless, neither to fall out with women as altogether guilty. For as I am not minded to pick a thank with the one, so am I not determined to pick a quarrel with the other. If women be not perverse they shall reap profit by remedy of pleasure. If Phyllis were now to take counsel she would not be so foolish to hang herself, neither Dido so fond to die for Aeneas, neither Pasiphaë so monstrous to love a bull, nor Phaedra so unnatural to be enamoured of her son.[228]

This is, therefore, to admonish all young imps and novices in love not to blow the coals of fancy with desire but to quench them with disdain. When love tickleth thee decline it lest it stifle thee; rather fast than surfeit, rather starve than strive to exceed. Though the beginning of love bring delight, the end bringeth destruction. For as the first draught of wine doth comfort the stomach, the second inflame the liver, the third fume into the head, so the first sip of love is pleasant, the second perilous, the third pestilent. If thou perceive thyself to be enticed with their wanton glances or allured with their wicked guiles, either enchanted with their beauty or enamoured with their bravery,[229] enter with thyself into this meditation: –

216   *dissuade.*
217   i.e. turn coat (become a traitor).
218   *disputatious person.*
219   Someone who spins out an argument to extreme length.
220   A contemptuous term for a mistress or paramour.
221   To "cry creak" is to confess oneself beaten.
222   *Ipse* is a Latin term meaning "he himself."
223   i.e. a staunch fellow.
224   The references to Venus and Cupid mixed with military language are allusions to Ovid's description of male lovers as soldiers in the

army of Venus in his *Amores* and *Ars amatoria* (see Ovid in the gazetteer).
225   An obsolete dry measure equal to eight bushels.
226   A obsolete unit of length equal to 45 inches.
227   Achilles wounded the hero Telephus with his spear, and then subsequently cured the wound by laying his spear on it again. The best-known citation of this story is in Ovid's *Remedies of Love*, lines 47–8.
228   See Dido and Theseus in the gazetteer and notes 183 and 204 above.
229   *fine clothes.*

"What shall I gain if I obtain my purpose? Nay rather, what shall I lose in winning my pleasure? If my lady yield to be my lover is it not likely she will be another's leman?[230] And if she be a modest matron my labour is lost. This therefore remaineth, that either I must pine in cares or perish with curses. If she be chaste then is she coy, if light then is she impudent. If a grave matron who can woo her; if a lewd minion who would wed her? If one of the vestal virgins they have vowed virginity, if one of Venus's court they have vowed dishonesty. If I love one that is fair it will kindle jealousy, if one that is foul it will convert me into frenzy; if fertile to bear children my care is increased, if barren my curse is augmented; if honest I shall fear her death, if immodest I shall be weary of her life. To what end then shall I live in love, seeing always it is a life more to be feared than death? For all my time wasted in sighs and worn in sobs, for all my treasure spent on jewels and spilt in jollity, what recompense shall I reap besides repentance, what other reward shall I have than reproach, what other solace than endless shame?"

But haply thou wilt say, "If I refuse their courtesy I shall be accounted a meacock,[231] a milksop, taunted and retaunted with check and checkmate, flouted and reflouted with intolerable glee." Alas, fond fool, art thou so pinned to their sleeves that thou regardest more their babble than thine own bliss, more their frumps[232] than thine own welfare? Wilt thou resemble the kind spaniel which the more he is beaten the fonder he is, or the foolish eyas[233] which will never away? Dost thou not know that women deem none valiant unless he be too venturous? That they account one a dastard[234] if he be not desperate, a pinchpenny if he be not prodigal, if silent a sot, if full of words a fool? Perversely do they always think of their lovers and talk of them scornfully, judging all to be clowns[235] which be no courtiers and all to be pinglers[236] that be not coursers.[237]

Seeing, therefore, the very blossom of love is sour, the bud cannot be sweet. In time prevent danger, lest untimely thou run into a thousand perils. Search the wound while it is green; too late cometh the salve when the sore festereth, and the medicine bringeth double care when the malady is past cure. Beware of delays. What less than the grain of mustard-seed; in time almost what thing is greater than the stalk thereof? The slender twig groweth to a stately tree, and that which with the hand might easily have been pulled up will hardly with the axe be hewn down. The least spark if it be not quenched will burst into a flame, the least moth in time eateth the thickest cloth; and I have read that in a short space there was a town in Spain undermined with conies,[238] in Thessaly with moles, with frogs in France, in Africa with flies. If these silly worms[239] in tract of time overthrow so stately towns, how much more will love which creepeth secretly into the mind (as the rust doth into the iron and is not perceived) consume the body, yea, and confound the soul. Defer not from hour to day, from day to month, from month to year, and always remain in misery. He that today is not willing will tomorrow be more wilful.

But alas, it is no less common than lamentable to behold the tottering estate of lovers who think by delays to prevent dangers, with oil to quench fire, with smoke to clear the eyesight. They flatter themselves with a fainting farewell, deferring ever until tomorrow; whenas their morrow doth always increase their sorrow. Let neither their amiable countenances, neither their painted protestations, neither their deceitful promises allure thee to delays. Think this with thyself, that the sweet songs of Calypso[240] were subtle snares to entice Ulysses, that the crab then catcheth the oyster when the sun shineth, that Hyena when she speaketh like a man deviseth most mischief, that women when they be most pleasant pretend most treachery. Follow Alexander, which hearing the commendation and singular comeliness of the wife of Darius, so courageously withstood the assaults of fancy that he would not so much as take a view of her beauty. Imitate Cyrus,[241] a king endued with such continency that he loathed to look on the heavenly hue of Panthea, and when Araspus told

---

230 sweetheart.
231 weakling.
232 jeers.
233 young, untrained hawk.
234 coward.
235 i.e. rustic.
236 dabblers.
237 ardent pursuers.

238 rabbits.
239 In this context, a word applied to any objectionable animal.
240 A sea nymph who rescued Odysseus from drowning in Homer's *Odyssey* (see gazetteer). She tried for seven years to persuade him to stay with her and live as an immortal, but he never abandoned his determination to go home to Ithaca and his wife.
241 See gazetteer.

him that she excelled all mortal wights in amiable show, "By so much the more," said Cyrus, "I ought to abstain from her sight: for if I follow thy counsel in going to her, it may be I shall desire to continue with her and by my light affection neglect my serious affairs." Learn of Romulus to refrain from wine be it never so delicate, of Agesilaus to despise costly apparel be it never so curious, of Diogenes to detest women be they never so comely.[242] He that toucheth pitch shall be defiled, the sore eye infecteth the sound, the society with women breedeth security in the soul and maketh all the senses senseless.

Moreover take this counsel as an article of the creed, which I mean to follow as the chief argument of my faith: that idleness is the only nurse and nourisher of sensual appetite, the sole maintenance of youthful affection, the first shaft that Cupid shooteth into the hot liver of a heedless lover. I would to God I were not able to find this for a truth by mine own trial; and I would the example of others' idleness had caused me rather to avoid that fault than experience of mine own folly. How dissolute have I been in striving against good counsel, how resolute in standing in mine own conceit; how forward to wickedness, how froward to wisdom; how wanton with too much cockering, how wayward in hearing correction. Neither was I much unlike these abbey-lubbers[243] in my life (though far unlike them in belief), which laboured till they were cold, eat till they sweat, and lay in bed till their bones ached. Hereof cometh it, gentlemen, that love creepeth into the mind by privy craft and keepeth his hold by main courage.

The man being idle, the mind is apt to all uncleanness; the mind being void of exercise, the man is void of honesty. Doth not the rust fret the hardest iron if it be not used? Doth not the moth eat the finest garment if it be not worn? Doth not moss grow on the smoothest stone if it be not stirred? Doth not impiety infect the wisest wit if it be given to idleness? Is not the standing water sooner frozen than the running stream? Is not he that sitteth more subject to sleep than he that walketh? Doth not common experience make this common unto us that the fattest ground bringeth forth nothing but weeds if it be not well tilled? That the sharpest wit inclineth only to wickedness if it be not exercised? Is it not true which Seneca[244] reporteth, that as too much bending breaketh the bow so too much remission spoileth the mind? Besides this, immoderate sleep, immodest play, insatiable swilling of wine doth so weaken the senses and bewitch the soul that before we feel the motion of love we are resolved into lust. Eschew idleness, my Philautus: so shalt thou easily unbend the bow and quench the brands of Cupid. Love gives place to labour, labour and thou shalt never love. Cupid is a crafty child, following those at an inch that study pleasure and flying those swiftly that take pains.

Bend thy mind to the law, whereby thou mayest have understanding of old and ancient customs, defend thy clients, enrich thy coffers, and carry credit in thy country. If law seem loathsome unto thee, search the secrets of physic, whereby thou mayest know the hidden natures of herbs, whereby thou mayest gather profit to thy purse and pleasure to thy mind. What can be more exquisite in human affairs than for every fever be it never so hot, for every palsy be it never so cold, for every infection be it never so strange, to give a remedy? The old verse standeth as yet in his old virtue, "That Galen giveth goods, Justinian honours."

If thou be so nice[245] that thou canst no way brook the practice of physic or so unwise that thou wilt not beat thy brains about the institutes of the law, confer all thy study, all thy time, all thy treasure to the attaining of the sacred and sincere knowledge of divinity; by this mayest thou bridle thine incontinency, rein thine affections, restrain thy lust. Here shalt thou behold as it were in a glass that all the glory of man is as the grass, that all things under heaven are but vain, that our life is but a shadow, a warfare, a pilgrimage, a vapour, a bubble, a blast; of such shortness that David saith it is but a span long, of such sharpness that Job noteth it replenished with all miseries, of such uncertainty that we are no sooner born but we are subject to death, the one foot no sooner on the ground but the other ready to slip into the grave. Here shalt thou find ease for thy

---

242 Romulus was the mythical founder of the city of Rome. Agesilaus was a 4th-century BC king of Sparta. For Diogenes, see note 56 above.

243 i.e. dissolute monks (a typically sectarian term of abuse in Protestant England).

244 See gazetteer.

245 *fastidious.*

burden of sin, comfort for the conscience pined[246] with vanity, mercy for thine offences by the martyrdom of thy sweet Saviour. By this thou shalt be able to instruct those that be weak, to confute those that be obstinate, to confound those that be erroneous, to confirm the faithful, to comfort the desperate, to cut off the presumptuous, to save thine own soul by thy sure faith, and edify the hearts of many by thy sound doctrine.

If this seem too strait a diet for thy straining disease or too holy a profession for so hollow a person, then employ thyself to martial feats, to jousts, to tourneys, yea, to all torments rather than to loiter in love and spend thy life in the laps of ladies. What more monstrous can there be than to see a young man abuse those gifts to his own shame which God hath given him for his own preferment? What greater infamy than to confer the sharp wit to the making of lewd sonnets, to the idolatrous worshipping of their ladies, to the vain delights of fancy, to all kinds of vice as it were against kind and course of nature? Is it not folly to show wit to women which are neither able nor willing to receive fruit thereof? Dost thou not know that the tree Silvacenda beareth no fruit in Pharos? That the Persian trees in Rhodes do only wax green but never bring forth apple? That Amomus and Nardus[247] will only grow in India, Balsamum only in Syria, that in Rhodes no eagle will build her nest, no owl live in Crete, no wit spring in the will of women? Mortify therefore thy affections and force not Nature against Nature to strive in vain.

Go into the country. Look to thy grounds, yoke thine oxen, follow thy plough, graft thy trees, behold thy cattle, and devise with thyself how the increase of them may increase thy profit. In autumn pull thine apples, in summer ply thy harvest, in the spring trim thy gardens, in the winter thy woods; and thus beginning to delight to be a good husband thou shalt begin to detest to be in love with an idle huswife. When profit shall begin to fill thy purse with gold then pleasure shall have no force to defile thy mind with love. For honest recreation after thy toil use hunting or hawking, either rouse the deer or unperch the pheasant; so shalt thou root out the remembrance of thy former love and repent thee of thy foolish lust. And although thy sweetheart bind thee by oath always to hold a candle at her shrine and to offer thy devotion to thine own destruction, yet go, run, fly into the country; neither water thou thy plants,[248] in that thou departest from thy pigsney,[249] neither stand in a mammering[250] whether it be best to depart or not; but by how much the more thou art unwilling to go by so much the more hasten thy steps, neither feign for thyself any sleeveless[251] excuse whereby thou mayest tarry. Neither let rain nor thunder, neither lightning nor tempest, stay thy journey; and reckon not with thyself how many miles thou hast gone – that showeth weariness – but how many thou hast to go – that proveth manliness.

But foolish and frantic lovers will deem my precepts hard and esteem my persuasions haggard. I must of force confess that it is a corrosive to the stomach of a lover but a comfort to a godly liver to run through a thousand pikes, to escape ten thousand perils. Sour potions bring sound health, sharp purgations make short diseases, and the medicine the more bitter it is the more better it is in working. To heal the body we try physic, search cunning, prove sorcery, venture through fire and water, leaving nothing unsought that may be gotten for money, be it never so much, or procured by any means, be they never so unlawful. How much more ought we to hazard all things for the safeguard of mind and quiet of conscience!

And, certes, easier will the remedy be when the reason is espied. Do you not know the nature of women, which is grounded only upon extremities? Do they think any man to delight in them unless he dote on them? Any to be zealous except they be jealous? Any to be fervent in case he be not furious? If he be cleanly then term they him proud, if mean in apparel a sloven, if tall a lungis,[252] if short a dwarf, if bold blunt, if shamefast a coward; inasmuch as they have neither mean in their frumps nor measure in their folly.

But at the first the ox wieldeth not the yoke, nor the colt the snaffle, nor the lover good counsel; yet time causeth the one to bend his neck, the other to open his mouth, and should enforce the

---

246 *afflicted.*
247 Both amomus and nardus are aromatic plants.
248 i.e do not cry.
249 *sweetheart.*

250 *state of hesitation.*
251 *futile.*
252 *tall, ungainly man.*

third to yield his right to reason. Lay before thine eyes the slights and deceits of thy lady, her snatching in jest and keeping in earnest, her perjury, her impiety, the countenance she showeth to thee of course,[253] the love she beareth to others of zeal, her open malice, her dissembled mischief. O, I would in repeating their vices thou couldest be as eloquent as in remembering them thou oughtest to be penitent. Be she never so comely, call her counterfeit; be she never so straight, think her crooked; and wrest all parts of her body to the worst, be she never so worthy. If she be well set then call her a boss,[254] if slender a hazel twig, if nut-brown as black as a coal, if well coloured a painted wall; if she be pleasant then is she a wanton, if sullen a clown, if honest then is she coy, if impudent a harlot. Search every vein and sinew of their disposition; if she have no sight I in descant[255] desire her to chant it, if no cunning to dance request her to trip it, if no skill in music proffer her the lute, if an ill gait then walk with her, if rude in speech talk with her; if she be gag-toothed[256] tell her some merry jest to make her laugh, if pink-eyed some doleful history to cause her weep: in the one her grinning will show her deformed, in the other her whining like a pig half roasted.

It is a world to see how commonly we are blinded with the collusions of women, and more enticed by their ornaments being artificial than their proportion being natural. I loathe almost to think on their ointments and apothecary drugs, the sleeking of their faces, and all their slibber-sauces[257] which bring queasiness to the stomach and disquiet to the mind. Take from them their periwigs, their paintings, their jewels, their rolls, their bolsterings,[258] and thou shalt soon perceive that a woman is the least part of herself. When they be once robbed of their robes then will they appear so odious, so ugly, so monstrous that thou wilt rather think them serpents than saints, and so like hags that thou wilt fear rather to be enchanted than enamoured. Look in their closets and there shalt thou find an apothecary's shop of sweet confections, a surgeon's box of sundry salves, a pedlar's pack of new fangles. Besides all this, their shadows,[259] their spots,[260] their lawns, their lyfkies,[261] their ruffs, their rings show them rather Cardinals' courtesans than modest matrons, and more carnally affected than moved in conscience. If every one of these things severally be not of force to move thee yet all of them jointly should mortify thee.

Moreover, to make thee the more stronger to strive against these sirens and more subtle to deceive these tame serpents, my counsel is that thou have more strings to thy bow than one. It is safe riding at two anchors, a fire divided in twain burneth slower, a fountain running into many rivers is of less force, the mind enamoured on two women is less affected with desire and less infected with despair, one love expelleth another and the remembrance of the latter quencheth the concupiscence of the first.

Yet if thou be so weak, being bewitched with their wiles, that thou hast neither will to eschew nor wit to avoid their company, if thou be either so wicked that thou wilt not or so wedded that thou canst not abstain from their glances, yet at the least dissemble thy grief. If thou be as hot as the mount Aetna, feign thyself as cold as the hill Caucasus; carry two faces in one hood, cover thy flaming fancy with feigned ashes, show thyself sound when thou art rotten, let thy hue be merry when thy heart is melancholy, bear a pleasant countenance with a pined conscience, a painted sheath with a leaden dagger. Thus dissembling thy grief thou mayest recure thy disease. Love creepeth in by stealth and by stealth slideth away.

If she break promise with thee in the night or absent herself in the day, seem thou careless, and then will she be careful; if thou languish, then will she be lavish of her honour, yea, and of the other strange beast, her honesty. Stand thou on thy pantofles and she will vail bonnet.[262] Lie thou aloof and she will seize on the lure. If thou pass by her door and be called back, either seem deaf and not to hear or desperate and not to care. Fly the places, the parlours, the portals wherein thou hast been conversant with thy lady; yea, Philautus, shun the street where Lucilla doth dwell, lest the sight of her window renew the sum of thy sorrow.

---

253   i.e. for form's sake.
254   i.e. if she is stocky, say that she's fat.
255   i.e. if she cannot sing in harmony.
256   i.e. if she has protruding teeth.
257   A term for all unpleasant-smelling cosmetics.

258   *padding.*
259   *veils* (to keep off the sun).
260   *beauty spots.*
261   *bodices.*
262   i.e. show deference.

Yet, although I would have thee precise in keeping these precepts, yet would I have thee to avoid solitariness, that breeds melancholy, melancholy madness, madness mischief and utter desolation. Have ever some faithful fere with whom thou mayest communicate thy counsels, some Pylades to encourage Orestes, some Damon to release Pythias, some Scipio to recure Laelius.[263] Phyllis in wandering the woods hanged herself:[264] Asiarchus forsaking company spoiled himself with his own bodkin; Biarus a Roman, more wise than fortunate, being alone destroyed himself with a potsherd.[265] Beware solitariness. But although I would have thee use company for thy recreation, yet would I have thee always to leave the company of those that accompany thy lady; yea, if she have any jewel of thine in her custody, rather lose it than go for it, lest in seeking to recover a trifle thou renew thine old trouble.

Be not curious to curl thy hair, nor careful to be neat in thine apparel; be not prodigal of thy gold, nor precise in thy going; be not like the Englishman, which preferreth every strange fashion before the use of his country; be thou dissolute[266] lest thy lady think thee foolish in framing thyself to every fashion for her sake. Believe not their oaths and solemn protestations, their exorcisms and conjurations, their tears which they have at commandment, their alluring looks, their treading on the toe, their unsavoury toys. Let every one loathe his lady, and be ashamed to be her servant. It is riches and ease that nourisheth affection, it is play, wine, and wantonness that feedeth a lover as fat as a fool; refrain from all such meats as shall provoke thine appetite to lust, and all such means as may allure thy mind to folly. Take clear water for strong wine, brown bread for fine manchet,[267] beef and brewis[268] for quails and partridge, for ease labour, for pleasure pain, for surfeiting hunger, for sleep watching, for the fellowship of ladies the company of philosophers.

If thou say to me, "Physician, heal thyself," I answer that I am meetly well purged of that disease; and yet was I never more willing to cure myself than to comfort my friend. And seeing the cause that made in me so cold a devotion should make in thee also as frozen a desire, I hope thou wilt be as ready to provide a slave as thou wast hasty in seeking a sore.

And yet, Philautus, I would not that all women should take pepper in the nose[269] in that I have disclosed the legerdemains[270] of a few; for well I know none will wince except she be galled, neither any be offended unless she be guilty. Therefore I earnestly desire thee that thou show this "cooling card" to none except thou show also this my defence to them all. For although I weigh nothing the ill-will of light huswives, yet would I be loath to lose the good will of honest matrons.

Thus, being ready to go to Athens, and ready there to entertain thee whensoever thou shalt repair thither, I bid thee farewell and fly women.

Thine ever,
Euphues.

TO THE GRAVE MATRONS, AND HONEST MAIDENS OF ITALY

Gentlewomen, because I would neither be mistaken of purpose, neither misconstrued of malice, lest either the simple should suspect me of folly or the subtle condemn me of blasphemy against the noble sex of women, I thought good that this my faith should be set down to find favour with the one and confute the cavils of the other. Believe me, gentlewomen, although I have been bold to inveigh against many, yet am I not so brutish to envy them all; though I seem not so gamesome as Aristippus to play with Lais,[271] yet am I not so dogged as Diogenes[272] to abhor all ladies, neither would I you should think me so foolish (although of late I have been very fantastical) that for the

---

263 The same classical examples of strong male friendship found in note 88 above.

264 See note 157 above.

265 The stories of Asiarchus and Biarus have never been discovered, and at least one of Lyly's editors (Bond) thinks that he made them up.

266 negligent.

267 A superior kind of wheaten bread.

268 broth.

269 i.e. take offense.

270 tricks.

271 The philosopher Aristippus was said to have had a liaison with Lais, perhaps the most famous prostitute of antiquity.

272 See note 56 above; Diogenes was also reputed to be a misogynist.

light behaviour of a few I should call in question the demeanour of all. I know that as there hath been an unchaste Helen in Greece, so there hath been also a chaste Penelope; as there hath been a prodigious Pasiphaë, so there hath been a godly Theocrita;[273] though many have desired to be beloved as Jupiter loved Alcmene,[274] yet some have wished to be embraced as Phrigius embraced Pieria;[275] as there hath reigned a wicked Jezebel, so hath there ruled a devout Deborah;[276] though many have been as fickle as Lucilla, yet hath there many been as faithful as Lucretia. Whatsoever therefore I have spoken of the spleen against the slights and subtleties of women I hope there is none will mislike it if she be honest, neither care I if any do if she be an harlot. The sour crab hath the show of an apple as well as the sweet pippin, the black raven the shape of a bird as well as the white swan, the lewd wight the name of a woman as well as the honest matron. There is great difference between the standing puddle and the running stream, yet both water; great odds between the adamant and the pumice, yet both stones; a great distinction to be put between vitrum[277] and the crystal, yet both glass; great contrariety between Lais and Lucretia, yet both women. Seeing, therefore, one may love the clear conduit-water though he loathe the muddy ditch and wear the precious diamond though he despise the ragged brick, I think one may also with safe conscience reverence the modest sex of honest matrons though he forswear the lewd sort of unchaste minions. Ulysses though he detested Calypso with her sugared voice, yet he embraced Penelope with her rude distaff. Though Euphues abhor the beauty of Lucilla, yet will he not abstain from the company of a grave maiden. Though the tears of the hart be salt, yet the tears of the boar be sweet; though the tears of some women be counterfeit to deceive, yet the tears of many be current to try their love. I, for my part, will honour those always that be honest and worship them in my life whom I shall know to be worthy in their living, neither can I promise such preciseness that I shall never be caught again with the bait of beauty; for although the falsehood of Lucilla have caused me to forsake my wonted dotage, yet the faith of some lady may cause me once again to fall into mine old disease. For as the fire-stone in Liguria though it be quenched with milk yet again it is kindled with water, or as the roots of Anchusa though it be hardened with water yet it is again made soft with oil, so the heart of Euphues enflamed erst with love although it be cooled with the deceits of Lucilla yet will it again flame with the loyalty of some honest lady, and though it be hardened with the water of wiliness yet will it be mollified with the oil of wisdom. I presume, therefore, so much upon the discretion of you gentlewomen that you will not think the worse of me in that I have thought so ill of some women, or love me the worse in that I loathe some so much. For this is my faith, that some one rose will be blasted in the bud, some other never fall from the stalk; that the oak will soon be eaten with the worm, the walnut tree never; that some women will easily be enticed to folly, some other never allured to vanity. You ought, therefore, no more to be aggrieved with that which I have said than the mintmaster to see the coiner hanged, or the true subject the false traitor arraigned, or the honest man the thief condemned.

And so farewell.

You have heard, Gentlemen, how soon the hot desire of Euphues was turned into a cold devotion; not that fancy caused him to change, but that the fickleness of Lucilla enforced him to alter his mind. Having therefore determined with himself never again to be entangled with such fond delights, according to the appointment made with Philautus, he immediately repaired to Athens, there to follow his own private study. And calling to mind his former looseness and how in his youth he had misspent his time, he thought to give a caveat to all parents how they might bring their children up in virtue, and a commandment to all youth how they should frame themselves to their fathers' instructions; in the which is plainly to be seen what wit can and will do if it be well employed. Which discourse following, although it bring less pleasure to your youthful minds

---

273 Another of Lyly's mistaken or imagined references.
274 The product of this union was the demi-god Hercules.
275 In contrast to the primarily sexual liaison between Jupiter and Alcmene, Phrigius and Pieria represented a classical example of chaste, spiritual love between men and women.

276 Jezebel is the biblical type of the harlot; Deborah was the judge of Israel in Judges 4:4.
277 *ordinary glass.*

than his first course, yet will it bring more profit; in the one being contained the race[278] of a lover, in the other the reasons of a philosopher.[279]

{From "Euphues and his Ephebus"}

Euphues, having ended his discourse and finished those precepts which he thought necessary for the instructing of youth, gave his mind to the continual study of philosophy, inasmuch as he became Public Reader in the university, with such commendation as never any before him. In the which he continued for the space of ten years, only searching out the secrets of nature and the hidden mysteries of philosophy. And having collected into three volumes his lectures, thought for the profit of young scholars to set them forth in print; which if he had done, I would also in this his Anatomy have inserted. But he, altering his determination, fell into this discourse with himself:—

"Why, Euphues, art thou so addicted to the study of the heathen that thou hast forgotten thy God in heaven? Shall thy wit be rather employed to the attaining of human wisdom than divine knowledge? Is Aristotle more dear to thee with his books than Christ with his blood? What comfort canst thou find in philosophy for thy guilty conscience, what hope of the resurrection, what glad tidings of the Gospel?

"Consider with thyself that thou art a gentleman, yea, and a Gentile, and if thou neglect thy calling thou art worse than a Jew. Most miserable is the estate of those gentlemen which think it a blemish to their ancestors and a blot to their own gentry to read or practise divinity. They think it now sufficient for their felicity to ride well upon a great horse, to hawk, to hunt, to have a smack[280] in philosophy, neither thinking of the beginning of wisdom, neither the end, which is Christ; only they account divinity most contemptible, which is and ought to be most notable. Without this there is no lawyer be he never so eloquent, no physician be he never so excellent, no philosopher be he never so learned, no king, no kaiser, be he never so royal in birth, so politic in peace, so expert in war, so valiant in prowess, but he is to be detested and abhorred.

"Farewell, therefore, the fine and filed phrase of Cicero, the pleasant Elegies of Ovid, the depth and profound knowledge of Aristotle; farewell rhetoric, farewell philosophy, farewell all learning which is not sprung from the bowels of the holy Bible. In this learning shall we find milk for the weak and marrow for the strong, in this shall we see how the ignorant may be instructed, the obstinate confuted, the penitent comforted, the wicked punished, the godly preserved.

"Oh I would gentlemen would sometimes sequester themselves from their own delights and employ their wits in searching these heavenly and divine mysteries. It is common, yea, and lamentable, to see that if a young youth have the gifts of nature, as a sharp wit, or of fortune, as sufficient wealth to maintain him gallantly, he employeth the one in the vain inventions of love, the other in the vile bravery of pride, the one in the passions of his mind and praises of his lady, the other in furnishing of his body and furthering of his lust. Hereof it cometh that such vain ditties, such idle sonnets, such enticing songs are set forth to the gaze of the world and grief of the godly. I myself know none so ill as myself, who in times past have been so superstitiously addicted that I thought no heaven to the paradise of love, no angel to be compared to my lady. But as repentance hath caused me to leave and loathe such vain delights, so wisdom hath opened unto me the perfect gate to eternal life.

"Besides this, I myself have thought that in divinity there could be no eloquence which I might imitate, no pleasant invention which I might follow, no delicate phrase that might delight me; but now I see that in the sacred knowledge of God's will the only eloquence, the true and perfect phrase, the testimony of salvation doth abide. And seeing without this all learning is ignorance, all wisdom mere folly, all wit plain bluntness, all justice iniquity, all eloquence barbarism, all beauty deformity, I will spend all the remainder of my life in studying the Old Testament, wherein is prefig-

278 course.
279 What follows in the full-length text is "Euphues and his Ephebus," a translation and redaction of two well-known treatises on education: Plutarch's *De educatione puerorum* and Erasmus's *Colloquium*

puerpera. Included here is the conclusion, which shows Euphues abandoning learning with the same unmotivated and arbitrary abruptness with which he renounced love in favour of learning.
280 *a superficial knowledge.*

ured the coming of my Saviour, and the New Testament, wherein my Christ doth suffer for my sins and is crucified for my redemption; whose bitter agonies should cast every good Christian into a shivering ague to remember His anguish, whose sweating of water and blood should cause every devote and zealous Catholic to shed tears of repentance in remembrance of His torments."

Euphues, having discoursed this with himself, did immediately abandon all light company, all the disputations in schools, all philosophy, and gave himself to the touchstone of holiness in divinity, accounting all other things as most vile and contemptible.

EUPHUES TO THE GENTLEMEN SCHOLARS IN ATHENS[281]

The merchant that travelleth for gain, the husbandman that toileth for increase, the lawyer that pleadeth for gold, the craftsman that seeketh to live by his labour, all these after they have fatted themselves with sufficient either take their ease or less pain than they were accustomed. Hippomenes ceased to run when he had gotten the goal, Hercules to labour when he had obtained the victory, Mercury to pipe when he had cast Argus in a slumber.[282] Every action hath his end; and then we leave to sweat when we have found the sweet. The ant though she toil in summer, yet in winter she leaveth to travail. The bee though she delight to suck the fair flower, yet is she at last cloyed with honey. The spider that weaveth the finest thread ceaseth at the last, when she hath finished her web.

But in the action and study of the mind, gentlemen, it is far otherwise; for he that tasteth the sweet of learning endureth all the sour of labour. He that seeketh the depth of knowledge is as it were in a labyrinth in which the farther he goeth the farther he is from the end; or like the bird in the limebush, which the more she striveth to get out the faster she sticketh in. And certainly it may be said of learning as it was feigned of nectar, the drink of the gods, the which the more it was drunk the more it would overflow the brim of the cup; neither is it far unlike the stone that groweth in the river of Caria, the which the more it is cut the more it increaseth. And it fareth with him that followeth it as with him that hath the dropsy,[283] who the more he drinketh the more he thirsteth. Therefore in my mind the student is at less ease than the ox that draweth or the ass that carrieth his burden, who neither at the board when others eat is void of labour, neither in his bed when others sleep is without meditation.

But as in manuary crafts, though they be all good, yet that is accounted most noble that is most necessary, so in the actions and studies of the mind, although they be all worthy, yet that deserveth greatest praise which bringeth greatest profit. And so we commonly do make best account of that which doth us most good. We esteem better of the physician that ministereth the potion than of the apothecary that selleth the drugs. How much more ought we with all diligence, study, and industry to spend our short pilgrimage in the seeking out of our salvation. Vain is philosophy, vain is physic, vain is law, vain is all learning without the taste of divine knowledge.

I was determined to write notes of philosophy, which had been to feed you fat with folly; yet that I might seem neither idle, neither you evil employed, I have here set down a brief discourse which of late I have had with an heretic, which kept me from idleness and may, if you read it, deter you from heresy. It was with an Atheist, a man in opinion monstrous yet tractable to be persuaded. By this shall you see the absurd dotage of him that thinketh there is no God, or an insufficient God; yet here shall you find the sum of faith which justifieth only in Christ, the weakness of the law, the strength of the Gospel, and the knowledge of God's will. Here shall ye find hope if ye be in despair, comfort if ye be distressed, if ye thirst drink, meat if ye hunger. If ye fear Moses who saith, *Without you fulfil the law you shall perish*, behold Christ which saith, *I have overcome the law*. And that in these desperate days wherein so many sects are sown, and in the waning of the world

---

281   This section (and other references in the text) were read by Lyly's contemporaries as an attack on Oxford University. For this reason, all editions of the text after the first ended with a disclaimer written by Lyly to the Oxford faculty.

282   For Hippomenes and Hercules, see the gazetteer under Atalanta and Hercules. Argus was a herdsman with 100 eyes who was set to watch the nymph Io. Mercury (Hermes) put him to sleep with his pipe music and then killed him.

283   A disease characterized by a fluid build-up in the joints.

wherein so many false Christs are come, you might have a certainty of your salvation, I mean to set down the touchstone whereunto every one ought to trust and by the which every one should try himself; which if you follow. I doubt not but that as you have proved learned philosophers, you will also proceed excellent divines, which God grant.[284]

John Florio (1553?–1625)

John Florio was the son of Michael Angelo Florio, a Protestant refugee and preacher to the Italian population of London (*c.* 1550). The father published a biography of Lady Jane Grey and translated into Italian works that were then attributed to her. John Florio entered Magdalen College, Oxford, in 1581. He enjoyed the patronage of three great earls – Leicester, Southampton, and Pembroke – and was reader in Italian to Queen Anne in 1603, the year his translation of Montaigne's *Essais* appeared. His Italian–English dictionary of 1598 was also of major importance. Florio's translation of Montaigne – his greatest work – is still the most elegant translation of Montaigne in English.

As a medium for weighing or testing ideas, the essay is largely a creation of Montaigne's. Michel Eyquem de Montaigne (1533–95) is often thought of as the essence of the Renaissance gentleman-scholar. Urbane and supremely well educated in fields ranging from music and law to philosophy and languages, he is one of the original French skeptics and a major force in what John Donne called the "New Philosophy." A principal source for Shakespeare's Edmund in *King Lear*, Montaigne questioned the superiority of civilization over nature and wondered about his cat, whether she played with him or he with her. His *Essais* appeared in three editions (1582, 1587, and 1588). "Of Cannibals" is not so much an apology for the noble savage as it is, indirectly, a critique of the barbarism of Europeans.

The argument of the essay is still a hot topic among anthropologists who study cannibalism. There is a calm, stoical outrageousness in all that Montaigne wrote. Concerning his own detachment he declared:

> A man that is able may have wives, children, goods, and chiefly health, but not so tie himself unto them that his felicity depend on them. We should reserve a storehouse for ourselves, what need soever chance; altogether ours, and wholly free, wherein we may hoard up and establish our true liberty and principal retreat and solitariness, wherein we must go alone to ourselves, take our ordinary entertainment, and so privately that no acquaintance or communication of any strange thing may therein find place.

This voice is a precursor of Virginia Woolf's in *A Room of One's Own*.

READING

Frank Lestringant, *Cannibals: The Discovery and Representation of the Cannibal from Columbus to Jules Verne.*

M. A. Screech, *Montaigne and Melancholy: The Wisdom of the "Essays."*

Frances Yates, *John Florio: The Life of an Italian in Shakespeare's England.*

M. P.

[FROM] THE ESSAYES OF MICHAEL LORD OF MONTAIGNE
OF THE CANNIBALS

At what time King *Pyrrhus* came into *Italy*, after he had surveyed the marshaling of the Army which the Romans sent against him: *I wot not,* said he, *what barbarous men these are* (for so were the Grecians wont to call all strange nations), *but the disposition of this Army which I see is nothing barbarous.* So said the Grecians of that which *Flaminius* sent into their country. And *Philip*, viewing from a Tower the order and distribution of the Roman camp in his kingdom under *Publius Sulpitius Galba.*[1] Lo how a man ought to take heed lest he overweeningly follow vulgar opinions, which should be measured by the rule of reason and not by the common report.

---

284   In the full-length text, this is followed by "Euphues and Atheos," a debate in which Euphues persuades an atheist to embrace Christianity, and several moralizing letters from Euphues to various others.

[FROM] THE ESSAYES OF MICHAEL LORD OF MONTAIGNE
OF THE CANNIBALS
1   See Plutarch's *Life of Pyrrhus* and *Life of Flaminius.*

I have had long time dwelling with me a man who for the space of ten or twelve years had dwelled in that other world which in our age was lately discovered, in those parts where *Villegaignon* first landed, and surnamed *Antarctic France*.[2] This discovery of so infinite and vast a country seemeth worthy great consideration. I wot not whether I can warrant myself that some other be not discovered hereafter, since so many worthy men, and better learned than we are, have so many ages been deceived in this. I fear me our eyes be greater than our bellies, and that we have more curiosity than capacity. We embrace all, but we fasten nothing but wind. *Plato* maketh *Solon* to report (PLAT. *Timæ.*)[3] that he had learned of the Priests of the city of *Saïs* in *Egypt* that whilom and before the general Deluge, there was a great Island called *Atlantis* situated at the mouth of the strait of *Gibraltar*, which contained more firm land than *Africa* and *Asia* together. And that the Kings of that country, who did not only possess that Island but had so far entered into the mainland that of the breadth of *Africa* they held as far as *Egypt*, and of *Europe's* length, as far as *Tuscany*. And that they undertook to invade *Asia* and to subdue all the nations that compass the Mediterranean Sea, to the gulf of the Black Sea, and to that end they traversed all *Spain*, *France*, and *Italy*, so far as *Greece*, where the Athenians made head against them. But that a while after, both the Athenians themselves and that great Island, were swallowed up by the Deluge. It is very likely this extreme ruin of waters wrought strange alterations in the habitations of the earth, as some hold that the Sea hath divided *Sicily* from *Italy*,

> Men say sometimes this land by that forsaken,
> And that by this, were split, and ruin-shaken,
> Whereas till then both lands as one were taken.
> VIRG. *Æn.* iii. 414, 416.

Cyprus from *Syria*, the Island of *Negroponte* from the mainland of *Bœotia*, and in other places joined lands that were sundered by the Sea, filling with mud and sand the channels between them.

> The fen long barren, to be rowed in, now
> Both feeds the neighbor towns, and feels the plow.
> HOR. *Art. Poet.* 65.

But there is no great apparency the said Island should be the new world we have lately discovered, for it well-nigh touched *Spain*, and it were an incredible effect of inundation to have removed the same more than twelve hundred leagues, as we see it is. Besides, our modern Navigations have now almost discovered that it is not an Island but rather firm land and a continent, with the East *Indies* on one side and the countries lying under the two Poles on the other; from which if it be divided, it is with so narrow a strait and interval that in no way deserveth to be named an Island. For it seemeth there are certain motions in these vast bodies, some natural and othersome febricitant, as well as in ours. When I consider the impression my river of *Dordogne* worketh in my time toward the right shore of her descent, and how much it hath gained in twenty years, and how many foundations of diverse houses it hath overwhelmed and violently carried away, I confess it to be an extraordinary agitation. For should it always keep one course or had it ever kept the same; the figure of the world had ere this been overthrown. But they are subject to changes and alterations. Sometimes they overflow and spread themselves on one side, sometimes on another; and other times they contain themselves in their natural beds or channels. I speak not of sudden inundations, whereof we now treat the causes. In *Médoc*, alongst the Seacoast, my brother the Lord of *Arsac* may see a town of his buried under the sands which the Sea casteth up before it; the tops of some buildings are yet to be discerned. His Rents and Domains have been changed into barren pastures. The inhabitants thereabouts affirm that some years since, the Sea encroacheth so much upon them that they have lost four leagues of firm land. These sands are her forerunners. And we see great hillocks of gravel moving, which march half a league before it and usurp on the firm land.

---

2   Durand de Villegagnon landed in Brazil in 1557.   3   Plato, *Timaeus*, 24e.

The other testimony of antiquity, to which some will refer this discovery, is in *Aristotle* (if at least that little book *Of Unheard-of Wonders* be his), where he reporteth that certain Carthaginians having sailed athwart the *Atlantic* Sea without the strait of *Gibraltar*, after long time they at last discovered a great fertile Island, all replenished with goodly woods and watered with great and deep rivers, far distant from all land; and that both they and others, allured by the goodness and fertility of the soil, went thither with their wives, children, and household, and there began to inhabit and settle themselves. The Lords of *Carthage*, seeing their country by little and little to be dispeopled, made a law and express inhibition that upon pain of death no more men should go thither, and banished all that were gone thither to dwell, fearing (as they said) that in success of time they would so multiply as they might one day supplant them and overthrow their own estate. This narration of *Aristotle* hath no reference unto our new-found countries. This servant I had was a simple and rough-hewn fellow, a condition fit to yield a true testimony. For subtle people may indeed mark more curiously and observe things more exactly, but they amplify and gloss them, and the better to persuade and make their interpretations of more validity, they cannot choose but somewhat alter the story. They never represent things truly, but fashion and mask them according to the visage they saw them in; and to purchase credit to their judgment and draw you on to believe them, they commonly adorn, enlarge, yea, and Hyperbolize the matter. Wherein is required either a most sincere Reporter or a man so simple that he may have no invention to build upon and to give a true likelihood unto false devices, and be not wedded to his own will. Such a one was my man, who, besides his own report, hath many times showed me diverse Mariners and Merchants whom he had known in that voyage. So am I pleased with his information that I never inquire what Cosmographers say of it. We had need of Topographers to make us particular narrations of the places they have been in. For some of them, if they have the advantage of us that they have seen *Palestine*, will challenge a privilege to tell us news of all the world besides. I would have every man write what he knows and no more, not only in that but in all other subjects. For one may have particular knowledge of the nature of one river and experience of the quality of one fountain, that in other things knows no more than another man, who nevertheless, to publish this little scantling, will undertake to write of all the Physics. From which vice proceed diverse great inconveniences.

Now (to return to my purpose), I find (as far as I have been informed) there is nothing in that nation that is either barbarous or savage, unless men call that barbarism which is not common to them. As indeed we have no other aim of truth and reason than the example and *Idea* of the opinions and customs of the country we live in. There is ever perfect religion, perfect policy, perfect and complete use of all things. They are even savage, as we call those fruits wild which nature of herself and of her ordinary progress hath produced, whereas indeed they are those which ourselves have altered by our artificial devices and diverted from their common order, we should rather term savage. In those are the true and most profitable virtues and natural properties most lively and vigorous, which in these we have bastardized, applying them to the pleasure of our corrupted taste. And if, notwithstanding, in diverse fruits of those countries that were never tilled we shall find that in respect of ours they are most excellent and as delicate unto our taste, there is no reason art should gain the point of honor of our great and puissant mother Nature. We have so much by our inventions surcharged the beauties and riches of her works that we have altogether overchoked her. Yet, wherever her purity shineth she makes our vain and frivolous enterprises wonderfully ashamed.

> Ivies spring better of their own accord,
> Unhaunted plots much fairer trees afford.
> Birds by no art much sweeter notes record.
> PROP. i. *El.* ii. 10.

All our endeavor or wit cannot so much as reach to represent the nest of the least birdlet, its contexture, beauty, profit, and use, no nor the web of a silly spider. *All things*, saith *Plato, are produced either by nature, by fortune, or by art: the greatest and fairest by one or other of the two first, the least and imperfect by the last.*[4] Those nations seem, therefore, so barbarous unto me, because they have received very little fashion from human wit and are yet near their original naturality. The laws of nature do yet command them, which are but little bastardized by ours; and that with such purity as I am sometimes grieved the knowledge of it came no sooner to light, at what time there were men that better than we could have judged of it. I am sorry *Lycurgus* and *Plato* had it not, for meseemeth that what in those nations we see by experience doth not only exceed all the pictures wherewith licentious Poesy had proudly embellished the golden age, and all her quaint inventions to feign a happy condition of man, but also the conception and desire of Philosophy. They could not imagine a genuity so pure and simple as we see it by experience, nor ever believe our society might be maintained with so little art and human combination. It is a nation, would I answer *Plato*, that hath no kind of traffic, no knowledge of Letters, no intelligence of numbers, no name of magistrate nor of politic superiority; no use of service, of riches or of poverty; no contracts, no successions, no partitions, no occupation but idleness; no respect of kindred but common, no apparel but natural, no manuring of lands, no use of wine, corn, or metal. The very words that import lying, falsehood, treason, dissimulations, covetousness, envy, detraction, and pardon, were never heard of amongst them. How dissonant would he find his imaginary commonwealth from this perfection!

> Nature at first uprise,
> These manners did devise.
> [VIRG. *Georg.* i. 20.]

Furthermore, they live in a country of so exceeding pleasant and temperate situation that, as my testimonies have told me, it is very rare to see a sick body amongst them; and they have further assured me they never saw any man there either shaking with the palsy, toothless, with eyes dripping, or crooked and stooping through age. They are seated alongst the sea-coast, encompassed toward the land with huge and steep mountains, having between both a hundred leagues or thereabout of open and champaign ground. They have great abundance of fish and flesh that have no resemblance at all with ours, and eat them without any sauces or skill of Cookery, but plain boiled or broiled. The first man that brought a horse thither, although he had in many other voyages conversed with them, bred so great a horror in the land that before they could take notice of him they slew him with arrows.

Their buildings are very long, and able to contain two or three hundred souls, covered with barks of great trees, fastened in the ground at one end, interlaced and joined close together by the tops, after the manner of some of our Granges; the covering whereof hangs down to the ground and steadeth them as a flank. They have a kind of wood so hard that, riving and cleaving the same, they make blades, swords, and grid irons to broil their meat with. Their beds are of a kind of cotton cloth, fastened to the house roof, as our ship cabins. Every one hath his several couch, for the women lie from their husbands.

They rise with the Sun, and feed for all day as soon as they are up, and make no more meals after that. They drink not at meal, as *Suidas* reporteth[5] of some other people of the East which drank after meals, but drink many times a day and are much given to pledge carouses. Their drink is made of a certain root, and of the color of our Claret wines, which lasteth but two or three days. They drink it warm. It hath somewhat a sharp taste, wholesome for the stomach, nothing heady, but laxative for such as are not used unto it, yet very pleasing to such as are accustomed unto it. Instead of bread, they use a certain white composition, like unto Corianders confected. I have eaten some, the taste whereof is somewhat sweet and wallowish.

They spend the whole day in dancing. Their young men go ahunting after wild beasts with bows and arrows. Their women busy themselves therewhilst with warming of their drink, which is their chiefest office. Some of their old men, in the morning before they go to eating, preach in

---

4   Plato, *Laws*, 10, 888a–b.   5   Suidas, *Historica, caeteraque omnia quae ad cognitionem rerum spectant* (Basle, 1564).

common to all the household, walking from one end of the house to the other repeating one self-same sentence many times till he have ended his turn (for their buildings are a hundred paces in length). He commends but two things unto his auditory; *First, valor against their enemies; then lovingness unto their wives*. They never miss (for their restraint) to put men in mind of this duty that it is their wives which keep their drink lukewarm and well-seasoned. The form of their beds, cords, swords, blades, and wooden bracelets, wherewith they cover their hand wrists when they fight, and great Canes, open at one end, by the sound of which they keep time and cadence in their dancing, are in many places to be seen, and namely in mine own house. They are shaven all over, much more close and cleaner than we are, with no other Razors than of wood or stone. They believe their souls to be eternal, and those that have deserved well of their Gods to be placed in that part of heaven where the Sun riseth, and the cursed toward the West, in opposition. They have certain Prophets and Priests, which commonly abide in the mountains and very seldom show themselves unto the people. But when they come down, there is a great feast prepared and a solemn assembly of many townships together (each Grange as I have described maketh a village, and they are about a French league one from another). The Prophet speaks to the people in public, exhorting them to embrace virtue and follow their duty. All their moral discipline containeth but these two articles: first, an undismayed resolution to war; then an inviolable affection to their wives. He doth also Prognosticate of things to come, and what success they shall hope for in their enterprises. He either persuadeth or dissuadeth them from war; but if he chance to miss of his divination, and that it succeed otherwise than he foretold them, if he be taken, he is hewn in a thousand pieces and condemned for a false Prophet. And therefore he that hath once misreckoned himself is never seen again.

Divination is the gift of God, the abusing whereof should be a punishable imposture. When the Divines amongst the Scythians had foretold an untruth, they were couched along upon hurdles full of heath or brushwood, drawn by oxen, and so, manacled hand and foot, burned to death.[6] Those which manage matters subject to the conduct of man's sufficiency, are excusable, although they show the utmost of their skill. But those that gull and cony-catch us with the assurance of an extraordinary faculty and which is beyond our knowledge, ought to be double punished: first, because they perform not the effect of their promise; then for the rashness of their imposture and unadvisedness of their fraud.

They war against the nations that lie beyond their mountains, to which they go naked, having no other weapons than bows or wooden swords, sharp at one end as our broaches are. It is an admirable thing to see the constant resolution of their combats, which never end but by effusion of blood and murder, for they know not what fear or routs are. Every Victor brings home the head of the enemy he hath slain as a Trophy of his victory, and fasteneth the same at the entrance of his dwelling place. After they have long time used and treated their prisoners well and with all commodities they can devise, he that is the Master of them, summoning a great assembly of his acquaintance, tieth a cord to one of the prisoner's arms, by the end whereof he holds him fast, with some distance from him for fear he might offend him, and giveth the other arm, bound in like manner, to the dearest friend he hath, and both in the presence of all the assembly kill him with swords. Which done, they roast and then eat him in common, and send some slices of him to such of their friends as are absent. It is not, as some imagine, to nourish themselves with it (as anciently the Scythians were wont to do), but to represent an extreme and inexpiable revenge.

Which we prove thus: Some of them perceiving the Portuguese, who had confederated themselves with their adversaries, to use another kind of death when they took them prisoners – which was to bury them up to the middle, and against the upper part of the body to shoot arrows, and then being almost dead, to hang them up – they supposed that these people of the other world (as they who had sown the knowledge of many vices amongst their neighbors and were much more cunning in all kinds of evils and mischief than they) undertook not this manner of revenge without cause, and that consequently it was more smartful, and cruel than theirs, and thereupon began to leave their old fashion to follow this.

6 Herodotus, *History*, 4, 49.

I am not sorry we note the barbarous horror of such an action, but grieved that, prying so narrowly into their faults, we are so blinded in ours. I think there is more barbarism in eating men alive than to feed upon them being dead; to mangle by tortures and torments a body full of lively sense, to roast him in pieces, to make dogs and swine to gnaw and tear him in mammocks (as we have not only read but seen very lately, yea and in our own memory, not amongst ancient enemies but our neighbors and fellow-citizens; and which is worse, under pretense of piety and religion), than to roast and eat him after he is dead. *Chrysippus* and *Zeno*, archpillars of the Stoic sect, have supposed that it was no hurt at all, in time of need and to what end soever, to make use of our carrion bodies and to feed upon them, as did our forefathers, who being besieged by *Caesar* in the City of *Alexia*, resolved to sustain the famine of the siege with the bodies of old men, women, and other persons unserviceable and unfit to fight.

> *Gascons* (as fame reports)
> Lived with meats of such sorts.
> JUVEN. *Sat.* xv. 93.

And Physicians fear not, in all kinds of compositions of avail to our health, to make use of it, be it for outward or inward applications.[7] But there was never any opinion found so unnatural and immodest that would excuse treason, treachery, disloyalty, tyranny, cruelty, and suchlike, which are our ordinary faults. We may then well call them barbarous in regard of reason's rules, but not in respect of us that exceed them in all kind of barbarism. Their wars are noble and generous, and have as much excuse and beauty as this human infirmity may admit; they aim at nought so much, and have no other foundation amongst them, but the mere jealousy of virtue. They contend not for the gaining of new lands, for to this day they yet enjoy that natural uberty and fruitfulness which, without laboring toil, doth in such plenteous abundance furnish them with all necessary things that they need not enlarge their limits. They are yet in that happy estate as they desire no more than what their natural necessities direct them. Whatsoever is beyond it, is to them superfluous. Those that are much about one age do generally call one another brethren, and such as are younger they call children, and the aged are esteemed as fathers to all the rest. These leave this full possession of goods in common and without division to their heirs, without other claim or title but that which nature doth plainly impart unto all creatures, even as she brings them into the world. If their neighbors chance to come over the mountains to assail or invade them, and that they get the victory over them, the Victors' conquest is glory, and the advantage to be and remain superior in valor and virtue; else have they nothing to do with the goods and spoils of the vanquished, and so return into their country, where they neither want any necessary thing, nor lack this great portion, to know how to enjoy their condition happily, and are contented with what nature affordeth them. So do these when their turn cometh. They require no other ransom of their prisoners but an acknowledgment and confession that they are vanquished. And in a whole age, a man shall not find one that doth not rather embrace death than either by word or countenance remissly to yield one jot of an invincible courage. There is none seen that would not rather be slain and devoured than sue for life or show any fear. They use their prisoners with all liberty, that they may so much the more hold their lives dear and precious, and commonly entertain them with threats of future death, with the torments they shall endure, with the preparations intended for that purpose, with mangling and slicing of their members, and with the feast that shall be kept at their charge. All which is done to wrest some remiss, and exact some faint-yielding speech of submission from them, or to possess them with a desire to escape or run away; that so they may have the advantage to have daunted and made them afraid, and to have forced their constancy. For certainly true victory consisteth in that only point.

---

7   Mummies were used as an ingredient in medicine and in magic (thus Othello's reference to "juice of mummy").

No conquest such, as to suppress
Foes' hearts, the conquest to confess.
CLAUD. vi. *Cons. Hon. Pan.* 245.

The Hungarians, a most warlike nation, were whilom wont to pursue their prey no longer than they had forced their enemy to yield unto their mercy. For having wrested this confession from him, they set him at liberty without offense or ransom, except it were to make him swear never after to bear arms against them.[8] We get many advantages of our enemies that are but borrowed and not ours. It is the quality of porterly rascal and not of virtue, to have stronger arms and sturdier legs. Disposition is a dead and corporal quality. It is a trick of fortune to make our enemy stoop and to blear his eyes with the Sun's light. It is a prank of skill and knowledge to be cunning in the art of fencing, and which may happen unto a base and worthless man. The reputation and worth of a man consisteth in his heart and will; therein consists true honor. Constancy is valor, not of arms and legs, but of mind and courage; it consisteth not in the spirit and courage of our horse nor of our arms, but in ours. He that obstinately faileth in his courage, *If he slip or fall, he fights upon his knee.*[9] He that in danger of imminent death is no whit daunted in his assuredness, he that in yielding up his ghost beholding his enemy with a scornful and fierce look, he is vanquished, not by us, but by fortune; he is slain but not conquered. The most valiant are often the most unfortunate. So are there triumphant losses in envy of victories. Not those four sister victories, the fairest that ever the Sun beheld with his all-seeing eye, of *Salamis*, of *Platæa*, of *Mycale*, and of *Sicily*, durst ever dare to oppose all their glory together to the glory of the discomfiture of King *Leonidas* and his men at the passage of *Thermopylæ*. What man did ever run with so glorious an envy or more ambitious desire to the goal of a combat than Captain *Ischolas* to an evident loss and overthrow? Who so ingeniously or more politicly did ever assure himself of his welfare than he of his ruin?[10] He was appointed to defend a certain passage of *Peloponnesus* against the Arcadians, which finding himself altogether unable to perform, seeing the nature of the place and inequality of the forces, and resolving that whatsoever should present itself unto his enemy must necessarily be utterly defeated. On the other side, deeming it unworthy both his virtue and magnanimity and the Lacedemonian name, to fail or faint in his charge, between these two extremities he resolved upon a mean and indifferent course, which was this. The youngest and best-disposed of his troupe, he reserved for the service and defense of their country, to which he sent them back; and with those whose loss was least and who might best be spared, he determined to maintain that passage, and by their death to force the enemy to purchase the entrance of it as dear as possibly he could; as indeed it followed. For being suddenly environed round by the Arcadians, after a great slaughter made of them, both himself and all his were put to the sword. Is any Trophy assigned for conquerors that is not more duly due unto these conquered? A true conquest respecteth rather an undaunted resolution and honorable end, than a fair escape, and the honor of virtue doth more consist in combating than in beating.

But to return to our history, these prisoners, howsoever they are dealt withal, are so far from yielding that, contrariwise, during two or three months that they are kept, they ever carry a cheerful countenance and urge their keepers to hasten their trial; they outrageously defy, and injure them. They upbraid them with their cowardliness, and with the number of battles they have lost against theirs. I have a song made by a prisoner wherein is this clause, "Let them boldly come all together and flock in multitudes to feed on him, for with him they shall feed upon their fathers and grandfathers, that heretofore have served his body for food and nourishment. These muscles [saith he], this flesh, and these veins, are your own; fond men as you are, know you not that the substance of your forefathers' limbs is yet tied unto ours? Taste them well, for in them shall you find the relish of your own flesh." An invention that hath no show of barbarism. Those that paint them dying and

8   Nicolas Chalcocondylas, *De la décadence de l'empire grec*, 5, 9.

9   Seneca, *De constantia*, 2.

10   Diodorus Siculus, 15, 7.

that represent this action when they are put to execution, delineate the prisoners spitting in their executioners' faces and making mows at them. Verily, so long as breath is in their body, they never cease to brave and defy them, both in speech and countenance. Surely, in respect of us these are very savage men, for either they must be so in good sooth, or we must be so indeed. There is a wondrous distance between their form and ours.

Their men have many wives, and by how much more they are reputed valiant, so much the greater is their number. The manner and beauty in their marriages is wondrous strange and remarkable. For the same jealousy our wives have to keep us from the love and affection of other women, the same have theirs to procure it. Being more careful for their husbands' honor and content than of anything else, they endeavor and apply all their industry to have as many rivals as possibly they can, forasmuch as it is a testimony of their husbands' virtue. Our women would count it a wonder, but it is not so. It is virtue properly Matrimonial, but of the highest kind. And in the Bible, *Leah*, *Rachel, Sarah*, and *Jacob's* wives brought their fairest maidenservants unto their husbands' bed. And *Livia* seconded the lustful appetites of *Augustus*, to her great prejudice. And *Stratonica*, the wife of King *Dejotarus*, did not only bring a most beauteous chambermaid, that served her, to her husband's bed, but very carefully brought up the children he begot on her, and by all possible means aided and furthered them to succeed in their father's royalty.[11] And lest a man should think that all this is done by a simple, and servile, or awful duty unto their custom, and by the impression of their ancient custom's authority, without discourse or judgment and because they are so blockish and dull-spirited that they can take no other resolution, it is not amiss we allege some evidence of their sufficiency. Besides what I have said of one of their warlike songs, I have another amorous canzonet, which beginneth in this sense: *Adder, stay; stay, good adder, that my sister may by the pattern of thy party-colored coat draw the fashion and work of a rich lace for me to give unto my love; so may thy beauty, thy nimbleness or disposition be ever preferred before all other serpents.* The first couplet is the burden of the song. I am so conversant with Poesy that I may judge this invention hath no barbarism at all in it, but is altogether Anacreontic.[12] Their language is a kind of pleasant speech, and hath a pleasing sound and some affinity with the Greek terminations.

Three of that nation, ignorant how dear the knowledge of our corruptions will one day cost their repose, security, and happiness, and how their ruin shall proceed from this commerce, which I imagine is already well advanced (miserable as they are to have suffered themselves to be so cozened by a desire of new-fangled novelties, and to have quit the calmness of their climate to come and see ours), were at *Rouen* in the time of our late King *Charles* the Ninth, who talked with them a great while.[13] They were shown our fashions, our pomp, and the form of a fair City. Afterward some demanded their advice and would needs know of them what things of note and admirable they had observed amongst us. They answered three things, the last of which I have forgotten and am very sorry for it; the other two I yet remember. They said, *First, they found it very strange that so many tall men with long beards, strong and well-armed, as it were, about the King's person (it is very likely they meant the Switzers of his guard) would submit themselves to obey a beardless child, and that we did not rather choose one amongst them to command the rest. Secondly (they have a manner of phrase whereby they call men but a moiety one of another), they had perceived there were men amongst us full gorged with all sorts of commodities, and others which, hunger-starved and bare with need and poverty, begged at their gates; and found it strange, these moieties so needy could endure such an injustice, and that they took not the others by the throat or set fire on their houses.* I talked a good while with one of them, but I had so bad an interpreter, and who did so ill apprehend my meaning, and who through his foolishness was so troubled to conceive my imaginations, that I could draw no great matter from him. Touching that point wherein I demanded of him what good he received by the superiority he had amongst his countrymen (for he was a Captain and our Mariners called him King), he told me it was to march foremost in any charge of war. Further, I asked him, how many men did follow him. He showed me a distance of place, to signify they were as many as might be contained in so much ground, which I guessed to be about four or five thousand men. Moreover I demanded if, when wars were ended, all his authority expired;

---

11 On these examples of unjealous wives, see Tiraquellus, *De legibus connubialibus*, 13, 35.

12 Anacreon (*c.*540 BC), poet of Teos.

13 Rouen was taken by Royalists in 1562.

he answered that he had only this left him, which was that when he went on progress and visited the villages depending of him, the inhabitants prepared paths and highways athwart the hedges of their woods, for him to pass through at ease. All that is not very ill; but what of that? They wear no kind of breeches nor hose.

Sir Walter Raleigh (*c.*1552–1618)

Walter Raleigh lived and died as an ambitious courtier, knowing both the heights of royal favor under Elizabeth and the depths of its disfavor under her successor James I. His ambitions were never narrowly political, however: he organized two colonizing expeditions to Virginia, several military expeditions against the Spanish, and two voyages of exploration in search of "El Dorado," a legendary gold mine in South America. Even his literary productions tended to be ambitious, and during his long imprisonment in the Tower of London, he began a history of the world.

It was as a soldier that he first drew attention to himself. After a year at Oxford University, he spent his late teens and early twenties fighting with the Protestant forces in France. After the first of his expeditions against the Spanish, he went to Ireland in 1580 and was part of the military suppression of the rebels in Munster. His participation in the massacre of hundreds of Spanish prisoners at Smerwick is often excoriated, but it hardly stands out amidst the barbarities that the English routinely committed in Ireland. His success in Ireland obtained him an entrée to Elizabeth's court, and he rapidly became one of her favorites, gaining several lucrative positions, his knighthood, and the captaincy of the queen's guard. It was from this base that he launched his privateering and exploratory expeditions. In 1592, he was imprisoned in the Tower after Elizabeth learned of his marriage to one of her maids of honor, and it was during this time that he wrote the extant fragment of "Ocean to Cynthia." In 1595, he undertook his first voyage to Guiana and wrote an account of it in his *Discoverie of Guiana*. In the following year, he obtained his most significant military success by raiding the Spanish port of Cadiz. After the accession of James I, however, his fortunes unraveled quickly. James had been convinced by other English courtiers that Raleigh had opposed his succession, and soon had him charged with treason. He spent 13 years in the Tower, writing his history of the world and conducting experiments in chemistry. He was released in 1616 in order to lead another expedition to El Dorado; it was a disastrous failure, and he was executed upon his return.

The selection below is confined to his lyric poetry. The history of excerpting his prose works in anthologies has resulted in their reduction to a series of famous "sound bites," such as the passages on death at the end of the *History of the World*, which are more than usually distorting. We therefore urge the reader to obtain them complete elsewhere. Raleigh's poetry embodies all of the contradictory emotions of court life: on the one hand, an intense, ambivalent, and eroticized devotion to the queen ("Ocean to Cynthia") and courtly praise of her as a ruler ("Praised Be Diana's Fair and Harmless Light"). On the other hand, searing contempt for the posturing of public life and institutions ("The Lie"), contempt for earthly love ("Conceit Begotten by the Eyes"), and an affirmation of spiritual contemplation ("Like to an Hermit Poor"). It is not surprising that Raleigh was the subject of Stephen Greenblatt's first analysis of what he would later call "self-fashioning" as his work both exemplifies and denigrates self-creation with equal skill. "Ocean to Cynthia" is the most complex and interesting of these, and it stands as one of the best examples of how addressing a Renaissance monarch could only be done through the poetic vocabulary of myth. It must also be noted that the attribution of these poems is more troublesome than normal, and debates about what poems Raleigh wrote and when he wrote them have been an ongoing part of his critical reception.

READING

Anna Beer, *Sir Walter Ralegh and his Readers in the Seventeenth Century: Speaking to the People.*

Stephen Greenblatt, *Sir Walter Ralegh: the Renaissance Man and his Roles.*

Stephen Greenblatt (ed.), *New World Encounters.*

Michael Rudnick, *The Poems of Sir Walter Ralegh: A Historical Edition.*

J. H.

PRAISED BE DIANA'S FAIR AND HARMLESS LIGHT[1]

Praised be Diana's fair and harmless light,
Praised be the dews wherewith she moists the ground;
Praised be her beams, the glory of the night,
Praised be her power, by which all powers abound.

Praised be her nymphs, with whom she decks the woods,
Praised be her knights, in whom true honour lives,
Praised be that force by which she moves the floods,   *tides*
Let that Diana shine, which all these gives.

10   In Heaven Queen she is among the spheres,[2]
In aye she mistress-like makes all things pure;   *all times*
Eternity in her oft change she bears,
She beauty is; by her the fair endure.

Time wears her not, she doth his chariot guide;
Mortality below her orb[3] is placed;
By her the virtue of the stars down slide,
In her is virtue's perfect image cast.

A knowledge pure it is her worth to know;
With Circes[4] let them dwell that think not so.

LIKE TO A HERMIT POOR

Like to a hermit poor in place obscure
I mean to spend my days of endless doubt,
To wail such woes as time cannot recure,   *cure*
Where none but Love shall ever find me out.

My food shall be of care and sorrow made
My drink nought else but tears fallen from mine eyes,
And for my light in such obscured shade
The flames shall serve which from my heart arise.

A gown of grey my body shall attire,[5]
10   My staff of broken hope whereon I'll stay,   *rest*
Of late repentance linked with long desire
The couch is framed whereon my limbs I'll lay,

And at my gate despair shall linger still,
To let in death when Love and Fortune will.

PRAISED BE DIANA'S FAIR AND HARMLESS LIGHT
1   Diana, the virgin goddess of the moon, is being used as an indirect
vehicle for praising Elizabeth I.
2   Early Modern astronomers imagined that the moon and planets were
suspended in transparent, hollow spheres of crystal.

3   A term which means both sphere, in the astronomical sense, and
the orb that the British monarch holds as a symbol of authority.
4   The female magician of Homer's *Odyssey*. Here, a figure for witches
generally.
5   The speaker describes dressing himself as a pilgrim to a shrine.

CONCEIT, BEGOTTEN BY THE EYES[6]

Conceit, begotten by the eyes,
Is quickly born and quickly dies,
For while it seeks our hearts to have,
Meanwhile there Reason makes his grave:
For many things the eyes approve,
Which yet the heart doth seldom love.

For as the seeds in springtime sown
Die in the ground ere they be grown,
Such is conceit, whose rooting fails,
As child that in the cradle quails,
Or else within the mother's womb
Hath his beginning and his tomb.

Affection follows Fortune's wheels   *Passion*
And soon is shaken from her heels,
For following beauty or estate   *rank*
Her liking still is turned to hate:
For all affections have their change,
And fancy only loves to range.   *imagination*

Desire himself runs out of breath
And getting, doth but gain his death;
Desire nor reason hath nor rest,
And, blind, doth seldom choose the best:
Desire attained is not desire,
But as the cinders of the fire.

As ships in ports desired are drowned,
As fruit once ripe then falls to ground,
As flies that seek for flames are brought
To cinders by the flames they sought:
So fond desire, when it attains,
The life expires, the woe remains.

And yet some poets fain would prove
Affection to be perfect love,
And that desire is of that kind,
No less a passion of the mind,
As if wild beasts and men did seek
To like, to love, to choose alike.

AS YOU CAME FROM THE HOLY LAND[7]

As you came from the holy land
    Of Walsingham,[8]
Met you not with my true love
    By the way as you came?

---

6 This poem plays on the manifold meanings of the word "conceit" in Raleigh's day. In this context, it means "judgment," "understanding," and "whim."

7 The poem is structured as a dialogue between the lover and a pilgrim.

8 The site of a shrine to the Virgin Mary and an important pilgrimage destination in Early Modern England.

How shall I know your true love
   That have met many one,
As I went to the holy land
   That have come, that have gone?

10
She is neither white nor brown
   But as the heavens fair,
There is none hath a form so divine
   In the earth or the air.

Such a one did I meet, good sir,
   Such an angelic face,
Who like a queen, like a nymph, did appear
   By her gait, by her grace.   *bearing/appearance*

She hath left me here all alone,
   All alone as unknown,
Who sometimes did me lead with herself,
20
   And me loved as her own.

What's the cause that she leaves you alone
   And a new way doth take,
Who loved you once as her own
   And her joy did you make?

I have loved her all my youth.
   But now old, as you see;
Love likes not the falling fruit
   From the withered tree.

Know that love[9] is a careless child
40
   And forgets promise past,
He is blind, he is deaf when he list,   *wishes*
   And in faith never fast.   *secure*

His desire is a dureless content   *transient*
   And a trustless joy,
He is won with a world of despair
   And is lost with a toy.

Of womankind such indeed is the love,
   Or the word Love abused,
Under which many childish desires
30
   And conceits are excused.   *whims*

But true love is a durable fire,
   In the mind ever burning,
Never sick, never old, never dead,
   From itself never turning.

The Nymph's Reply to the Shepherd[10]

If all the world and love were young,
   And truth in every shepherd's tongue,

---

9 Here personified as Cupid.   10 This poem answers Christopher Marlowe's "Passionate Shepherd to his Love."

These pretty pleasures might me move,
To live with thee and be thy love.

Time drives the flocks from field to fold,
When rivers rage, and rocks grow cold,
And Philomel becometh dumb,   *nightingale*
The rest complains of cares to come.

The flowers do fade, and wanton fields,
10   To wayward winter reckoning yields;   *account*
A honey tongue, a heart of gall,
Is fancy's spring, but sorrow's fall.

Thy gowns, thy shoes, thy beds of roses,
Thy cap, thy kirtle, and thy posies,
Soon break, soon wither, soon forgotten,
In folly ripe, in reason rotten.

The belt of straw and ivy buds,
Thy coral clasps and amber studs,
All these in me no means can move,
20   To come to thee, and be thy love.

But could youth last, and love still breed,
Had joys no date, nor age no need,
Then these delights my mind might move,
To live with thee, and be thy love.

THE LIE[11]

Go, soul, the body's guest,
   Upon a thankless errand,
Fear not to touch the best,   i.e. most noble
   The truth shall be thy warrant:
Go, since I needs must die,
   And give the world the lie.

Say to the Court it glows
   And shines, like rotten wood;
Say to the Church it shows
10   What's good, and doth no good;
If Church and Court reply,
   Then give them both the lie.

Tell Potentates they live
   Acting but others' action,
Not loved unless they give,
   Not strong but by a faction;
If Potentates reply,
   Give potentates the lie.

Tell men of high condition,   *social position*
20   That manage the estate,   i.e. the nation

11   The phrase "to give the lie" meant to accuse someone of lying. In this poem, the speaker's soul tells unpleasant truths to the important institutions of Elizabethan England and calls their attempted justifications lies.

Their purpose is ambition,
    Their practice only hate;
And if they once reply,
    Then give them all the lie.

Tell them that brave it most,[12]
    They beg for more by spending,
Who in their greatest cost
    Like nothing but commending;   *approval*
And if they make reply,
30   Then give them all the lie.

Tell zeal it wants devotion,
    Tell love it is but lust,
Tell time it metes but motion,   *measures*
    Tell flesh it is but dust;
And wish them not reply,
    For thou must give the lie.

Tell age it daily wasteth,
    Tell honour how it alters,
Tell beauty how she blasteth,   *withers*
40   Tell favour how it falters;
And as they shall reply,
    Give every one the lie.

Tell wit how much it wrangles
    In tickle points of niceness,   i.e. in trivialities
Tell wisdom she entangles
    Herself in over-wiseness;
And when they do reply,
    Straight give them both the lie.

Tell Physic of her boldness,   *medicine*
50   Tell skill it is prevention,
Tell charity of coldness,
    Tell law it is contention;
And as they do reply
    So give them still the lie.

Tell fortune of her blindness,
    Tell nature of decay,
Tell friendship of unkindness,
    Tell justice of delay;
And if they will reply,
60   Then give them all the lie.

Tell Arts they have no soundness,
    But vary by esteeming;   *opinion*
Tell schools they want profoundness
    And stand too much on seeming;
If Arts and schools reply,
    Give Arts and schools the lie.

Tell faith it's fled the City,
    Tell how the country erreth,

Tell manhood shakes off pity,
    And virtue least preferreth;
And if they do reply,
    Spare not to give the lie.

So when thou hast, as I
    Commanded thee, done blabbing,
Although to give the lie
    Deserves no less than stabbing,
Stab at thee he that will,
    No stab thy soul can kill.

70 (line 70)

A FAREWELL TO FALSE LOVE

Farewell false Love, the oracle of lies,
A mortal foe and enemy to rest:
An envious boy, from whom all cares arise,
A bastard vile,[13] a beast with rage possessed,
A way of error, a temple full of treason,
In all effects contrary unto reason:

A poisoned serpent covered all with flowers,
Mother of sighs and murderer of repose,
A sea of sorrows whence are drawn such showers
As moisture lends to every grief that grows,
A school of guile, a net of deep deceit,
A gilded hook that holds a poisoned bait;

A fortress foiled, which reason did defend,
A Siren[14] song, a fever of the mind,
A maze wherein affection finds no end,   *passion*
A raging cloud that runs before the wind,
A substance like the shadow of the sun,
A goal of grief for which the wisest run;

A quenchless fire, a nurse of trembling fear,
A path that leads to peril and mishap,
A true retreat of sorrow and despair,
An idle boy that sleeps in pleasure's lap,
A deep mistrust of that which certain seems,
A hope of that which reason doubtful deems.

Sith, then, thy trains my younger years betrayed,   *Since*
And for my faith ingratitude I find,
And sith repentance hath my wrongs bewrayed,   *betrayed*
Whose course was ever contrary to kind,   *nature*
False Love, Desire, and Beauty frail, adieu –
Dead is the root whence all these fancies grew.

10 (line 10)   20 (line 20)   30 (line 30)

VERSES MADE THE NIGHT BEFORE HE DIED

Even such is Time, which takes in trust
Our youth, our joys, and all we have,

13 Cupid was the son of Venus by Mars and not by her husband   14 See gazetteer.
Vulcan.

And pays us but with age and dust;
  Who in the dark and silent grave,
When we have wandered all our ways,
  Shuts up the story of our days.
But from which earth and grave and dust
  The Lord will raise me up, I trust.

THE 21ST AND LAST BOOK OF THE OCEAN TO CYNTHIA[15]

Sufficeth it to you, my joys interred,[16]   *buried*
  In simple words that I my woes complain,
You that then died when first my fancy erred,   *love*
  Joys under dust that never live again.

If to the living were my Muse addressed,
  Or did my mind her own spirit still inhold,
Were not my living passion so repressed
  As to the dead the dead did these unfold,

Some sweeter words, some more becoming verse,   *suitable*
10   Should witness my mishap in higher kind;
But my love's wounds, my fancy in the hearse,
  The idea but resting of a wasted mind,   *remaining*

The blossoms fallen, the sap gone from the tree,
  The broken monuments of my great desires;
From these so lost what may th'affections be?   *emotions*
  What heat in cinders of extinguished fires?

Lost in the mud of those high-flowing streams,
  Which through more fairer fields their courses bend,
Slain with self-thoughts, amazed in fearful dreams,   *lost*
20   Woes without date, discomforts without end,

From fruitful trees I gather withered leaves,
  And glean the broken ears with miser's hand;
Who sometime did enjoy the weighty sheaves,
  I seek fair flowers amid the brinish sand.

All in the shade, even in the fair sun days,
  Under those healthless trees I sit alone,
Where joyful birds sing neither lovely lays,
  Nor Philomen recounts her direful moan.   *nightingale*

No feeding flocks, no shepherds' company,
30   That might renew my dolorous conceit,[17]
While happy then, while love and fantasy
  Confined my thoughts on that fair flock to wait;

15   This unfinished poem was written while Raleigh, once Elizabeth's favorite courtier, was imprisoned by the Queen for marrying without her consent. Balancing the reverence of a subject with the frustration of a jilted lover, he codes himself as the speaker Ocean (which plays on "Water," which is how his name was pronounced) and Queen Elizabeth as Cynthia (i.e. Diana, the virgin goddess of the moon). The poem is emblematic of how literary language is culturally determined: as a ruler, Elizabeth had to be reverenced. As a woman, however, she could only be addressed as a love object or an object of scorn. There were few other extant modes of address from men to women.
16   The speaker is addressing his woes directly.
17   i.e. that might revive my sad state of mind.

No pleasing streams fast to the ocean wending,
    The messengers sometimes of my great woe;
But all on earth, as from the cold storms bending,
    Shrink from my thoughts in high heavens and below.

O hopeful love, my object, and invention,
    O true desire, the spur of my conceit,
O worthiest spirit, my mind's impulsion,   *incitement*
    O eyes transpersant, my affection's bait;   *piercing*

O princely form, my fancy's adamant,   *lodestone*
    Divine conceit, my pain's acceptance,   *design*
O all in one oh, heaven on earth transparent,
    The seat of joys and love's abundance!

Out of that mass of miracles my Muse
    Gathered those flowers, to her pure senses pleasing;
Out of her eyes (the store of joys) did choose
    Equal delights, my sorrows counterpeising.   *balancing*

Her regal looks my rigorous sighs suppressed;
    Small drops of joys sweetened great worlds of woes;
One gladsome day a thousand cares redressed.
    Whom Love defends, what fortune overthrows?

When she did well, what did there else amiss?
    When she did ill, what empires could have pleased?
No other power effecting woe or bliss,
    She gave, she took, she wounded, she appeased.

The honour of her love, love still devising,
    Wounding my mind with contrary conceit,   *thoughts*
Transferred itself sometime to her aspiring,
    Sometime the trumpet of her thought's retreat.

To seek new worlds for gold, for praise, for glory,[18]
    To try desire, to try love severed far,   *test*
When I was gone, she sent her memory,
    More strong than were ten thousand ships of war,

To call me back, to leave great honour's thought,
    To leave my friends, my fortune, my attempt,
To leave the purpose I so long had sought,[19]
    And hold both cares and comforts in contempt.

Such heat in ice, such fire in frost remained,
    Such trust in doubt, such comfort in despair;
Much like the gentle lamb, though lately weaned,
    Plays with the dug, though finds no comfort there.   *teat*

But as a body, violently slain,
    Retaineth warmth although the spirit be gone,
And by a power in nature moves again,
    Till it be laid below the fatal stone;

40

50

60

70

18   Raleigh had served in several military and exploratory ventures for the Queen.

19   To find a ready source of gold for England in an unexplored part of the New World.

Or as the earth, even in cold winter days,
   Left for a time by her life-giving sun,
Doth by the power remaining of his rays
   Produce some green, though not as it hath done;

80

Or as a wheel, forced by the falling stream,
   Although the course be turned some other way,
Doth for a time go round upon the beam,
   Till, wanting strength to move, it stands at stay;

So my forsaken heart, my withered mind,
   Widow of all the joys it once possessed,
My hopes clean out of sight with forced wind,
   To kingdoms strange, to lands far-off, addressed,

Alone, forsaken, friendless, on the shore,
   With many wounds, with death's cold pangs embraced,
Writes in the dust, as one that could no more,
   Whom love, and time, and fortune, had defaced,

90

Of things so great, so long, so manifold,
   With means so weak, the soul even then departing,
The weal, the woe, the passages of old,
   And worlds of thoughts described by one last sighing;

As if, when after Phoebus is descended,   i.e. the Sun
   And leaves a light much like the past day's dawning,
And, every toil and labour wholly ended,
   Each living creature draweth to his resting,

100

We should begin by such a parting light
   To write the story of all ages past,
And end the same before th'approaching night.

Such is again the labour of my mind,
   Whose shroud, by sorrow woven now to end,
Hath seen that ever shining sun declined,
   So many years that so could not descend,

But that the eyes of my mind held her beams
   In every part transferred by love's swift thought;
Far off or near, in waking or in dreams,
   Imagination strong their lustre brought.

110

Such force her angel-like appearance had
   To master distance, time, or cruelty;
Such art to grieve, and after to make glad;
   Such fear in love, such love in majesty.

My weary limbs her memory embalmed;
   My darkest ways her eyes make clear as day.
What storms so great but Cynthia's beams appeased?
   What rage so fierce, that love could not allay?

120

Twelve years entire I wasted in this war,[20]
   Twelve years of my most happy younger days;

20 i.e. in Elizabeth's service.

But I in them, and they now wasted are,
   'Of all which past the sorrow only stays'.

So wrote I once, and my mishap foretold,
   My mind still feeling sorrowful success,
Even as before a storm the marble cold
   Doth by moist tears tempestuous times express.

So felt my heavy mind my harms at hand,
   Which my vain thought in vain sought to recure;
130   At middle day my sun seemed under land,
   When any little cloud did it obscure.

And as the icicles in a winter's day,
   Whenas the sun shines with unwonted warm,   *unusual*

So did my joys melt into secret tears,
   So did my heart dissolve in wasting drops;
And as the season of the year outwears,
   And heaps of snow from off the mountain tops

With sudden streams the valleys overflow,
   So did the time draw on my more despair;
140   Then floods of sorrow and whole seas of woe
   The banks of all my hope did overbear,

And drowned my mind in depths of misery.
   Sometime I died, sometime I was distract,   *insane*
My soul the stage of fancy's tragedy;
   Then furious madness, where true reason lacked,

Wrote what it would, and scourged mine own conceit.   *understanding*
   O heavy heart, who can thee witness bear?
What tongue, what pen, could thy tormenting treat,
   But thine own mourning thoughts which present were?

150   What stranger mind believe the meanest part?   *smallest*
   What altered sense conceive the weakest woe,
That tare, that rent, that pierced thy sad heart?
   And as a man distract, with treble might,

Bound in strong chains doth strive and rage in vain,
   Till, tired and breathless, he is forced to rest,
Finds by contention but increase of pain,
   And fiery heat inflamed in swollen breast;

So did my mind in change of passion
   From woe to wrath, from wrath return to woe,
160   Struggling in vain from love's subjection.

Therefore, all lifeless and all helpless bound,
   My fainting spirits sunk, and heart appaled,   *made weak*
My joys and hopes lay bleeding on the ground,
   That not long since the highest heaven scaled.

I hated life and cursed destiny;
   The thoughts of passed times, like flames of hell,
Kindled afresh within my memory
   The many dear achievements that befell

In those prime years and infancy of love,
170   Which to describe were but to die in writing;[21]
Ah, those I sought, but vainly, to remove,
          And vainly shall, by which I perish living.

And though strong reason hold before mine eyes
          The images and forms of worlds past,
Teaching the cause why all those flames that rise
          From forms external can no longer last,

Than that those seeming beauties hold in prime
          Love's ground, his essence, and his empery,   *dominion*
All slaves to age, and vassals unto time,
180   Of which repentance writes the tragedy.

But this my heart's desire could not conceive,
          Whose love outflew the fastest flying time,
A beauty that can easily deceive
          Th'arrest of years, and creeping age outclimb,

A spring of beauties which time ripeth not,
          Time that but works on frail mortality,
A sweetness which woe's wrongs outwipeth not,
          Whom love hath chose for his divinity,

A vestal fire that burns but never wasteth,   *chaste*
190   That loseth nought by giving light to all,
That endless shines each where, and endless lasteth,
          Blossoms of pride that can nor vade nor fall.

These were those marvellous perfections,
          The parents of my sorrow and my envy,
Most deathful and most violent infections;
          These be the tyrants that in fetters tie

Their wounded vassals, yet nor kill nor cure,
          But glory in their lasting misery,
That, as her beauties would, our woes should dure;   *last*
200   These be the effects of powerful empery.

Yet have these wonders want, which want compassion;   *lacks*
          Yet hath her mind some marks of human race;
Yet will she be a woman for a fashion,
          So doth she please her virtues to deface.

And like as that immortal power doth seat   *establish*
          An element of waters, to allay
The fiery sunbeams that on earth do beat,
          And temper by cold night the heat of day,

So hath perfection, which begat her mind,
210   Added thereto a change of fantasy,   *fancy*
And left her the affections of her kind,   *desires*
          Yet free from every evil but cruelty.

21   Raleigh is punning on a literal death, for writing openly about an
erotic attachment to the queen, and "dying" as climaxing sexually.

But leave her praise; speak thou of nought but woe;
 Write on the tale that Sorrow bids thee tell;
Strive to forget, and care no more to know
 Thy cares are known, by knowing those too well.

Describe her now as she appears to thee,
 Not as she did appear in days fordone;
In love, those things that were no more may be,
220 For fancy seldom ends where it begun.

And as a stream by strong hand bounded in
 From nature's course where it did sometime run,
By some small rent or loose part doth begin
 To find escape, till it a way hath won;

Doth then all unawares in sunder tear
 The forced bounds, and, raging, run at large
In th'ancient channels as they wonted were;
 Such is of women's love the careful charge,   *responsibility*

Held and maintained with multitude of woes;
230 Of long erections such the sudden fall.
One hour diverts, one instant overthrows,
 For which our life's, for which our fortune's, thrall.

So many years those joys have dearly bought,
 Of which when our fond hopes do most assure,
All is dissolved; our labours come to nought,
 Nor any mark thereof there doth endure;

No more than, when small drops of rain do fall
 Upon the parched ground by heat updried,
No cooling moisture is perceived at all,
240 Nor any show or sign of wet doth bide.

But as the fields, clothed with leaves and flowers,
 The banks of roses smelling precious sweet,
Have but their beauty's date and timely hours,   *duration*
 And then defaced by winter's cold and sleet,

So far as neither fruit nor form of flower
 Stays for a witness what such branches bare,
But as time gave, time did again devour,
 And change our rising joy to falling care;

So of affection which our youth presented.   *love*
250 When she that from the sun reaves power and light,   *steals*
Did but decline her beams as discontented,
 Converting sweetest days to saddest night,

All droops, all dies, all trodden under dust,
 The person, place, and passages forgotten,
The hardest steel eaten with softest rust,
 The firm and solid tree both rent and rotten.

Those thoughts, so full of pleasure and content,
 That in our absence were affection's food,
Are razed out and from the fancy rent,
260 In highest grace and heart's dear care that stood,

Are cast for prey to hatred and to scorn;
   Our dearest treasures and our heart's true joys,
The tokens hung on breast and kindly worn,
   Are now elsewhere disposed or held for toys,

And those which then our jealousy removed,
   And others for our sakes then valued dear,
The one forgot, the rest are dear beloved,
   When all of ours doth strange or vild appear.   *vile*

Those streams seem standing puddles, which before
270   We saw our beauties in, so were they clear;
Belphebe's course is now observed no more;[22]

That fair resemblance weareth out of date;
   Our ocean seas are but tempestuous waves,
And all things base, that blessed were of late.   *unworthy*

And as a field, wherein the stubble stands
   Of harvest past the ploughman's eye offends,
He tills again, or tears them up with hands,
   And throws to fire as foiled and fruitless ends,   *defeated*

And takes delight another seed to sow;
280   So doth the mind root up all wonted thought,   *habitual*
And scorns the care of our remaining woes;
   The sorrows, which themselves for us have wrought,

Are burnt to cinders by new kindled fires;
   The ashes are dispersed into the air;
The sighs, the groans of all our past desires
   Are clean outworn, as things that never were.

With youth is dead the hope of love's return,
   Who looks not back to hear our after cries;
Where he is not, he laughs at those that mourn;
290   Whence he is gone, he scorns the mind that dies;

When he is absent, he believes no words;
   When reason speaks, he careless stops his ears;
Whom he hath left, he never grace affords,
   But bathes his wings in our lamenting tears.

Unlasting passion, soon outworn conceit,   *vanity*
   Whereon I built, and on so dureless trust!   *transient*
My mind had wounds, I dare not say deceit,
   Where I resolved her promise was not just.

Sorrow was my revenge and woe my hate;
300   I powerless was to alter my desire;
My love is not of time or bound to date;
   My heart's internal heat and living fire

---

22   Belphebe is a character in Spenser's *Faerie Queene* who represents
Queen Elizabeth and the moon goddess Diana.

Would not, or could, be quenched with sudden showers;
　My bound respect was not confined to days,
My vowed faith not set to ended hours;
　I love the bearing and not bearing sprays

Which now to others do their sweetness send,
　Th'incarnate, snow-driven white, and purest azure,　*blue*
Who from high heaven doth on their fields descend,
　Filling their barns with grain, and towers with treasure.

310

Erring or never erring, such is Love
　As, while it lasteth, scorns th'accompt of those　*regard*
Seeking but self contentment to improve,
　And hides, if any be, his inward woes,

And will not know, while he knows his own passion,
　The often and unjust perseverance
In deeds of love and state, and every action
　From that first day and year of their joy's entrance.

But I, unblessed and ill born creature,
320　That did embrace the dust her body bearing,
That loved her both by fancy and by nature,
　That drew, even with the milk in my first sucking,

Affection from the parent's breast that bare me,
　Have found her as a stranger so severe,
Improving my mishap in each degree.　*increasing*
　But love was gone; so would I my life were!

A queen she was to me, no more Belphebe,
　A lion then, no more a milk-white dove;
A prisoner in her breast I could not be;
330　She did untie the gentle chains of love.

Love was no more the love of hiding

All trespass and mischance for her own glory.
　It had been such; it was still for the elect;　*chosen ones*
But I must be th'example in love's story;
　This was of all forepast the sad effect.

But thou, my weary soul and heavy thought,
　Made by her love a burden to my being,
Dost know my error never was forethought,
　Or ever could proceed from sense of loving.

340　Of other cause if then it had proceeding,
　I leave th'excuse, sith judgement hath been given;　*since*
The limbs divided, sundered, and a-bleeding,
　Cannot complain the sentence was uneven.

This did that nature's wonder, virtue's choice,
　The only paragon of time's begetting,
Divine in words, angelical in voice,
　That spring of joys, that flower of love's own setting,

The Idea[23] remaining of those golden ages,
    That beauty, braving heaven's and earth embalming,   *challenging*
350   Which after worthless worlds but play on stages;[24]
    Such didst thou her long since describe, yet sighing

That thy unable spirit could not find aught
    In heaven's beauties or in earth's delight,
For likeness fit to satisfy thy thought.
    But what hath it availed thee so to write?

She cares not for thy praise, who knows not theirs;
    It's now an idle labour, and a tale
Told out of time, that dulls the hearer's ears,
    A merchandise whereof there is no sale.

360   Leave them, or lay them up with thy despairs.
    She hath resolved, and judged thee long ago.
Thy lines are now a murmuring to her ears,
    Like to a falling stream, which, passing slow,

Is wont to nourish sleep and quietness.   *accustomed*
    So shall thy painful labours be perused,
And draw on rest, which sometime had regard;
    But those her cares thy errors have excused;

Thy days fordone have had their day's reward.
    So her hard heart, so her estranged mind,
370   In which above the heavens I once reposed;
    So to thy error have her ears inclined,

And have forgotten all thy past deserving,
    Holding in mind but only thine offence;
And only now affecteth thy depraving,   *defaming*
    And thinks all vain that pleadeth thy defence.

Yet greater fancy beauty never bred;
    A more desire the heart-blood never nourished;
Her sweetness an affection never fed,
    Which more in any age hath ever flourished.

380   The mind and virtue never have begotten
    A firmer love, since love on earth had power,
A love obscured, but cannot be forgotten,
    Too great and strong for time's jaws to devour,

Containing such a faith as ages wound not,
    Care, wakeful ever of her good estate,   *vigilant*
Fear, dreading loss, which sighs and joys not,
    A memory of the joys her grace begat,

A lasting gratefulness for those comforts past,
    Of which the cordial sweetness cannot die.
390   These thoughts, knit up by faith, shall ever last,
    These time assays, but never can untie,

---

23   The pattern or archetype in a Platonic sense. This timeless,   24   i.e. Which subsequent worthless worlds can only represent.
unchanging ideal state cannot exist in ordinary life, and Raleigh thus
locates it in past "golden ages" and makes it a subject for inadequate
representations ("play").

Whose life once lived in her pearl-like breast,
 Whose joys were drawn but from her happiness,
Whose heart's high pleasure, and whose mind's true rest,
 Proceeded from her fortune's blessedness;

Who was intentive, wakeful, and dismayed   *devoted*
 In fears, in dreams, in feverous jealousy;
Who long in silence served, and obeyed
 With secret heart and hidden loyalty,

400 Which never change to sad adversity,
 Which never age, or nature's overthrow,
Which never sickness or deformity,
 Which never wasting care or wearing woe,

If subject unto these she could have been

Which never words or wits malicious,
 Which never honour's bait, or world's fame,
Achieved by attempts adventurous,
 Or aught beneath the sun or heaven's frame,

Can so dissolve, dissever, or destroy,
410 The essential love of no frail parts compounded,
Though of the same now buried be the joy,
 The hope, the comfort, and the sweetness ended,

But that the thoughts and memories of these
 Work a relapse of passion, and remain
Of my sad heart the sorrow-sucking bees;[25]
 The wrongs received, the scorns, persuade in vain.

And though these medicines work desire to end,
 And are in others the true cure of liking,
The salves that heal love's wounds, and do amend
420 Consuming woe, and slake our hearty sighing,

They work not so in thy mind's long disease;
 External fancy time alone recureth,   *heals*
All whose effects do wear away with ease.
 Love of delight, while such delight endureth;

Stays by the pleasure, but no longer stays

But in my mind so is her love inclosed,
 And is thereof not only the best part
But into it the essence is disposed.   *deposited*
 O love (the more my woe), to it thou art

430 Even as the moisture in each plant that grows;
 Even as the sun unto the frozen ground;
Even as the sweetness to th'incarnate rose;   *crimson*
 Even as the centre in each perfect round;

As water to the fish, to men as air,
 As heat to fire, as light unto the sun;

---

25 i.e. His memories are drawing sorrow from his heart as a bee draws
nectar from a flower.

O love, it is but vain to say thou were;
    Ages and times cannot thy power outrun.

Thou art the soul of that unhappy mind
    Which, being by nature made an idle thought,
440   Begun even then to take immortal kind,
    When first her virtues in thy spirits wrought.

From thee therefore that mover cannot move,
    Because it is become thy cause of being;
Whatever error may obscure that love,
    Whatever frail effect of mortal living,

Whatever passion from distempered heart,
    What absence, time, or injuries effect,
What faithless friends or deep dissembled art
    Present to feed her most unkind suspect.

450   Yet as the air in deep caves underground
    Is strongly drawn when violent heat hath rent
Great clefts therein, till moisture do abound,
    And then the same, imprisoned and up-pent,   *pent up*

Breaks out in earthquakes tearing all asunder;
    So, in the centre of my cloven heart,
My heart, to whom her beauties were such wonder,
    Lies the sharp poisoned head of that love's dart,

Which, till all break and all dissolve to dust,
    Thence drawn it cannot be, or therein known.
460   There, mixed with my heart-blood, the fretting rust
    The better part hath eaten and outgrown.

But what of those or these, or what of aught
    Of that which was, or that which is, to treat?
What I possess is but the same I sought;
    My love was false, my labours were deceit.

Nor less than such they are esteemed to be;
    A fraud bought at the price of many woes;
A guile, whereof the profits unto me –
    Could it be thought premeditate for those?   *advocate*

470   Witness those withered leaves left on the tree,
    The sorrow-worn face, the pensive mind.
The external shows what may th'internal be;
    Cold care hath bitten both the root and rind.

But stay, my thoughts, make end, give fortune way.
    Harsh is the voice of woe and sorrow's sound;
Complaints cure not, and tears do but allay
    Griefs for a time, which after more abound.

To seek for moisture in th'Arabian sands
    Is but a loss of labour and of rest.
480   The links which time did break of hearty bands   *heart's chains*

Words cannot knit, or wailings make anew.
   Seek not the sun in clouds when it is set.
On highest mountains, where those cedars grew,
   Against whose banks the troubled ocean beat,

And were the marks to find thy hoped port,
   Into a soil far off themselves remove.
On Sestus' shore, Leander's late resort,[26]
   Hero hath left no lamp to guide her love.

Thou lookest for light in vain, and storms arise;
490   She sleeps thy death, that erst thy danger sighed,   *before*
Strive then no more; bow down thy weary eyes,
   Eyes which to all these woes thy heart have guided.

She is gone, she is lost, she is found, she is ever fair.
   Sorrow draws weakly, where love draws not too;
Woe's cries sound nothing, but only in love's ear;
   Do then by dying what life cannot do.

Unfold thy flocks and leave them to the fields,
   To feed on hills, or dales, where likes them best,
Of what the summer or the spring time yields,
500   For love and time hath given thee leave to rest.

Thy heart which was their fold, now in decay,
   By often storms and winter's many blasts,
All torn and rent becomes misfortune's prey;
   False hope, my shepherd's staff, now age hath brast.   *broken*

My pipe, which love's own hand gave my desire
   To sing her praises and my woe upon,
Despair hath often threatened to the fire,
   As vain to keep now all the rest are gone.

Thus home I draw, as death's long night draws on;
510   Yet, every foot, old thoughts turn back mine eyes.
Constraint me guides, as old age draws a stone
   Against the hill, which over-weighty lies

For feeble arms or wasted strength to move;
   My steps are backward, gazing on my loss,
My mind's affection and my soul's sole love,
   Not mixed with fancy's chaff or fortune's dross.

To God I leave it, who first gave it me,   *i.e. my soul*
   And I her gave, and she returned again,
As it was hers; so let his mercies be
520   Of my last comforts the essential mean.

But be it so or not, th'effects are past;
   Her love hath end; my woe must ever last.

---

26 The mythical lovers Hero and Leander lived on opposite sides of the Hellespont. Hero used to hang a lamp from her tower in order to guide Leander as he swam across. He drowned one stormy night when the light was extinguished. Christopher Marlowe wrote a well-known poem about this story.

Sir Philip Sidney (1554–1586)

When W. B. Yeats eulogized Robert Gregory as "our Sidney and our perfect man," he was making use of one of the most persistently mythologized figures from the Elizabethan age, itself perhaps the most persistently mythologized period in English history. Knighted in his lifetime, Philip Sidney was at various times a courtier, a diplomat, and a soldier who, in his periods away from the court, produced one of the most important and diverse bodies of literature from the sixteenth century. He wrote two versions of the *Arcadia*, a long prose romance which contains significant poetic elements as well; *Astrophil and Stella*, the best-known sonnet sequence in the English tradition; the *Defense of Poesy*, a significant early piece of English humanist literary criticism; and some verse settings of the Psalms. His literary versatility seemed to echo the diversity of his other activities and confirm his place as supreme English exemplar of the "Renaissance man." Dying young of wounds received in battle only helped to cement this image.

Ironically, it is only his literary accomplishment that survives close scrutiny; the rest is largely the result of posthumous myth-making by his family and his biographer Fulke Greville. Much of his writing seems to have been done at least partly to keep himself busy during periods of enforced absence from the court. He was frequently the dedicatee of contemporary books and poems, a sign of the hopes for his prospects and of recognition for his literary talent, but even Walter Raleigh's poetic epitaph, which celebrates his intellectual gifts and heroic death, recognizes that his potential was greater than his achievements. His life in the political and courtly worlds was never as prominent as he would have liked. His father was not a hereditary aristocrat, but a commoner who had been knighted as a reward for long service to the crown; Sidney was himself only knighted so that he could serve as a proxy for someone else to receive a much higher honor. He was employed upon two diplomatic embassies in Europe, but never received any significant commissions from the queen. He was nephew to the Earls of Leicester and Warwick, but he never achieved significant rank or wealth in his own right. With his uncles, he was part of the militant Protestant faction at court and believed that England's greatest enemy, Spain, had to be confronted aggressively, but the queen favoured policies more conducive to peace. When she did finally license military action against Spain, it was to be the campaign in which Sidney was killed.

His most widely read literary work, *Astrophil and Stella*, has encouraged the myth-making by hinting that the literary love it represents may have had an analogy in reality.

Sidney clearly connects Astrophil to himself and Stella to Penelope Rich, the wife of a prominent courtier, but it is unclear if this reflects an actual love affair. Such lightly coded allusions are common in Western love poetry: Petrarch, the originator of the sonnet sequence and the poet who established the terms for all Renaissance love poetry, celebrated his love for Laura, a much younger contemporary of his; the Roman poet Ovid (see gazetteer), from whom Petrarch draws heavily, celebrated a woman named Corinna in his *Amores*. Since the 1970s, however, scholars have come to see how all of these male poets use their loves, fictional or otherwise, to create a poetic persona for themselves that is openly and happily artificial. The historical "reality" behind their literary emotions is thus not only unknowable, but probably irrelevant. Fidelity to lived experience is a literary goal that only came into being with the modern novel, and we should remember how Sidney pities historians for being "captivated to the truth of a foolish world" in the *Defense of Poesy*. It is more productive to consider his sonnet sequence, like Shakespeare's, as an imaginative exploration of the possibilities of sexual desire and literary production, and it was this theme that provoked the Elizabethan vogue for sonnet sequences. This interest in exploring new possibilities is also manifest in both versions of his *Arcadia*, which is represented in this anthology only by some lyric poems. These long prose romances test the limits of nearly every convention of pastoral and chivalric literature at a historical moment when the European aristocracy was undergoing a profound identity crisis about its social role.

The *Defense of Poesy* brings into English literature the humanist debates about the function of literature that had been going on throughout the sixteenth century, especially in Italy. Combining classical ideas about literature from Aristotle and Horace with contemporary concerns to justify the value of vernacular literature, it explores literature's ability to encourage virtuous action and reflects on the contemporary literary scene. It also embodies a typically humanist disdain for the Middle Ages as a "misty time" which produced little of literary value and a strict Aristotelian notion of drama that would have precluded nearly all of Shakespeare's plays. The rhetorical flair with which Sidney wrote this text, along with its association with his poetry, has allowed it to eclipse other, less polished, critical works from his own day, an unfortunate piece of canonizing that has taken attention away from Puttenham's *Arte of English Poesie* and other interesting responses to the issues connected with vernacular literature. That said, the *Defense* remains an excellent place to begin when trying to understand how sixteenth-century writers viewed their work in both national and European contexts.

Edward Berry, *The Making of Sir Philip Sidney*.

Heather Dubrow, *Echoes of Desire: English Petrarchism and its Counterdiscourses*.

H. R. Woudhuysen, *Sir Philip Sidney and the Circulation of Manuscripts, 1558–1640*.

READING

Catherine Bates, "Astrophil and the Manic Wit of the Abject Male."

J. H.

THE DEFENCE OF POESY

When the right virtuous Edward Wotton and I were at the Emperor's Court together,[1] we gave ourselves to learn horsemanship of John Pietro Pugliano, one that with great commendation had the place of an esquire in his stable. And he according to the fertileness of the Italian wit, did not only afford us the demonstration of his practice, but sought to enrich our minds with the contemplations therein, which he thought most precious. But with none I remember mine ears were at that time more laden, than when (either angered with slow payment, or moved with our learner-like admiration) he exercised his speech in the praise of his faculty. He said soldiers were the noblest estate of mankind, and horsemen the noblest of soldiers. He said they were the masters of war and ornaments of peace, speedy goers and strong abiders, triumphers both in camps and courts. Nay, to so unbelieved a point he proceeded as that no earthly thing bred such wonder to a prince as to be a good horseman – skill of government was but a *pedanteria*[2] in comparison. Then would he add certain praises, by telling us what a peerless beast the horse was, the only serviceable courtier without flattery, the beast of most beauty, faithfulness, courage, and such more, that if I had not been a piece of a logician before I came to him, I think he would have persuaded me to have wished myself a horse. But thus much at least with his no few words he drave into me, that self-love is better than any gilding to make that seem gorgeous wherein ourselves be parties. Wherein, if Pugliano's strong affection and weak arguments will not satisfy you, I will give you a nearer example of myself, who (I know not by what mischance) in these my not old years and idlest times having slipped into the title of a poet, am provoked to say something unto you in the defence of that my unelected vocation, which if I handle with more good will than good reasons, bear with me, since the scholar is to be pardoned that followeth in the steps of his master. And yet I must say that, as I have more just cause to make a pitiful defence of poor poetry, which from almost the highest estimation of learning is fallen to be the laughing-stock of children, so have I need to bring some more available proofs: since the former is by no man barred of his deserved credit, the silly latter hath had even the names of philosophers used to the defacing of it, with great danger of civil war among the Muses.[3]

And first, truly, to all them that, professing learning, inveigh against poetry, may justly be objected, that they go very near to ungratefulness, to seek to deface that which, in the noblest nations and languages that are known, hath been the first lightgiver to ignorance, and first nurse, whose milk by little and little enabled them to feed afterwards of tougher knowledges. And will they now play the hedgehog that, being received into the den, drave out his host? Or rather the vipers, that with their birth kill their parents?

Let learned Greece in any of his manifold sciences be able to show me one book before Musaeus, Homer, and Hesiod, all three nothing else but poets.[4] Nay, let any history be brought that can say

---

THE DEFENCE OF POESY

1 Sidney and his friend Edward Wotton went on a diplomatic mission to the Emperor Maximilian II's court in Vienna in 1574–5.

2 "Pedantry," or a trivial piece of knowledge.

3 The nine ancient Greek goddesses who were thought to inspire intellectual and artistic endeavors. See gazetteer.

4 All of the poets named by Sidney in this paragraph are founders of their various poetic traditions, and he begins with the earliest known Greek poets: for Homer, who wrote the great epic poems known as the *Iliad* and the *Odyssey*, and Hesiod, see the gazetteer. Musaeus was associated with the mythical poet Orpheus, who is the subject of many myths; Early Modern writers often confused him with a much later poet of the same name.

any writers were there before them, if they were not men of the same skill, as Orpheus, Linus,[5] and some other are named, who, having been the first of that country that made pens deliverers of their knowledge to the posterity, may justly challenge to be called their fathers in learning: for not only in time they had this priority (although in itself antiquity be venerable) but went before them, as causes to draw with their charming sweetness the wild untamed wits to an admiration of knowledge. So, as Amphion was said to move stones with his poetry to build Thebes, and Orpheus to be listened to by beasts – indeed stony and beastly people – so among the Romans were Livius Andronicus and Ennius.[6] So in the Italian language the first that made it aspire to be a treasure-house of science were the poets Dante, Boccaccio, and Petrarch.[7] So in our English were Gower, and Chaucer,[8] after whom, encouraged and delighted with their excellent foregoing, others have followed, to beautify our mother tongue, as well in the same kind as other arts.

This did so notably show itself, that the philosophers of Greece durst not a long time appear to the world but under the mask of poets. So Thales, Empedocles, and Parmenides sang their natural philosophy in verses; so did Pythagoras and Phocylides their moral counsels; so did Tyrtaeus in war matters, and Solon in matters of policy: or rather they, being poets, did exercise their delightful vein in those points of highest knowledge, which before them lay hid to the world.[9] For that wise Solon was directly a poet it is manifest, having written in verse the notable fable of the Atlantic Island, which was continued by Plato.[10] And truly even Plato whosoever well considereth shall find that in the body of his work, though the inside and strength were Philosophy, the skin, as it were, and beauty depended most of poetry: for all standeth upon dialogues, wherein he feigns many honest burgesses of Athens speak of such matters, that, if they had been set on the rack, they would never have confessed them, besides his poetical describing the circumstances of their meetings, as the well ordering of a banquet, the delicacy of a walk, with interlacing mere tales, as Gyges' Ring and others, which who knoweth not to be flowers of poetry did never walk into Apollo's garden.[11]

And even historiographers (although their lips sound of things done, and verity be written in their foreheads) have been glad to borrow both fashion and, perchance, weight of the poets. So Herodotus entitled his History, by the name of the nine Muses;[12] and both he and all the rest that followed him, either stale or usurped of poetry, their passionate describing of passions, the many particularities of battles, which no man could affirm; or, if that be denied me, long orations put in the mouths of great kings and captains, which it is certain they never pronounced.[13]

So that truly philosopher nor historiographer could at the first have entered into the gates of popular judgements, if they had not taken a great passport of poetry, which in all nations at this day where learning flourisheth not, is plain to be seen; in all which they have some feeling of poetry.

---

5   Another poet associated with the earliest times in Greek mythic history.

6   Amphion was a mythical poet whose singing caused stones to move by themselves to form the walls of the city of Thebes. Livius Andronicus (c.284–240 BC) was the Greek who first translated Homer into Latin and is often referred to as the "father of Roman literature." Quintus Ennius (239–169 BCE) is another important early Roman poet.

7   Dante (1265–1321), Boccaccio (1313–75), and Petrarch (1304–74) were the three Renaissance Italian writers who established vernacular Italian as a literary language. See the gazetteer for more details.

8   John Gower (c.1330–1408), author of the Confessio Amantis, and Geoffrey Chaucer (c.1343–1400), author of The Canterbury Tales, were important writers in vernacular Middle English.

9   Sidney here lists some of the earliest known Greek philosophers: Thales (fl. c.600 BC) was an astronomer and geometer; Empedocles (c.495–c.435 BC) is named as the founder of rhetoric by Aristotle; Parmenides (c.515–c.450 BC) features in the Platonic debate that bears his name; Pythagoras (c.580–c.500 BC) was a mystic and mathematician; Phocylides (fl. mid-6th century BC) was a poet and moralist; Tyrtaeus was a 7th-century BC elegiac poet from Sparta; Solon (c.640–c.560 BCE) was a reforming Athenian politician and poet. The story of

the lost island of Atlantis is preserved in Plato's Timaeus (where Solon is acknowledged as the first to write about it). Solon's version of the tale (if it ever existed) has been lost.

10   Along with Aristotle, Plato was the most influential ancient philosopher on Early Modern thought (see gazetteer). He mounted a famous critique of poetry which Sidney addresses later in the Defense; for now, Sidney is content to point out how many literary techniques ("flowers of poetry") Plato uses in his philosophy.

11   Apollo was the Greek god of poetry, so those who have never walked in his garden are those cannot appreciate poetry. The story of Gyges' ring is told by Plato (in Republic 2) and Cicero (in De Officiis 2.9.38–9).

12   Herodotus (c.490–c.425 BC) was called by many ancient writers "the father of history" because his History of the Greek wars with Persia was written on a larger scale than any previous historical work. As Sidney remarks, his work was divided into nine books, each of them named for one of the Muses.

13   From ancient times until the late Renaissance, it was common for historians to put fictional speeches in the mouths of historical characters in their texts.

In Turkey, besides their law-giving divines, they have no other writers but poets. In our neigh-bour country Ireland, where truly learning goes very bare, yet are their poets held in a devout rev-erence. Even among the most barbarous and simple Indians[14] where no writing is, yet they have their poets who make and sing songs, which they call *areytos*, both of their ancestors' deeds, and praises of their gods: a sufficient probability that, if ever learning come among them, it must be by having their hard dull wits softened and sharpened with the sweet delights of poetry – for until they find a pleasure in the exercises of the mind, great promises of much knowledge will little per-suade them that know not the fruits of knowledge. In Wales, the true remnant of the ancient Britons, as there are good authorities to show the long time they had poets, which they called bards, so through all the conquests of Romans, Saxons, Danes, and Normans, some of whom did seek to ruin all memory of learning from among them, yet do their poets even to this day last; so as it is not more notable in the soon beginning than in long continuing.

But since the authors of most of our sciences were the Romans, and before them the Greeks, let us a little stand upon their authorities, but even so far as to see what names they have given unto this now scorned skill.

Among the Romans a poet was called *vates*, which is as much as a diviner, foreseer, or prophet, as by his conjoined words *vaticinium*[15] and *vaticinari*[16] is manifest: so heavenly a title did that excel-lent people bestow upon this heart-ravishing knowledge. And so far were they carried into the admiration thereof, that they thought in the chanceable hitting upon any such verses great foreto-kens of their following fortunes were placed. Whereupon grew the word of *Sortes Virgilianae*,[17] when by sudden opening Virgil's book they lighted upon any verse of his making, whereof the histories of the emperors' lives are full: as of Albinus, the governor of our island, who in his childhood met with this verse

Arma amens capio nec sat rationis in armis[18]

and in his age performed it. Which, although it were a very vain and godless superstition, as also it was, to think spirits were commanded by such verses – whereupon this word charms, derived of *carmina*, cometh – so yet serveth it to show the great reverence those wits were held in; and alto-gether not without ground, since both the oracles of Delphos and Sybilla's prophecies were wholly delivered in verses.[19] For that same exquisite observing of number and measure in the words, and that high flying liberty of conceit proper to the poet, did seem to have some divine force in it.

And may not I presume a little further, to show the reasonableness of this word *vates*, and say that the holy David's Psalms are a divine poem?[20] If I do, I shall not do it without the testimony of great learned men, both ancient and modern. But even the name of Psalms will speak for me, which being interpreted, is nothing but songs; then that it is fully written in metre, as all learned hebricians agree, although the rules be not yet fully found; lastly and principally, his handling his prophecy, which is merely poetical: for what else is the awaking his musical instruments, the often and free changing of persons, his notable *prosopopoeias*,[21] when he maketh you, as it were, see God coming in His majesty, his telling of the beasts' joyfulness and hills leaping, but a heavenly poesy, wherein almost he showeth himself a passionate lover of that unspeakable and everlasting beauty to be seen by the eyes of the mind, only cleared by faith? But truly now having named him, I fear I seem to profane that holy name, applying it to poetry, which is among us thrown down to so ridiculous an estimation. But they that with quiet judgements will look a little deeper into it, shall find the end and working of it such as, being rightly applied, deserveth not to be scourged out of the Church of God.

---

14 By "Indians," Sidney means the indigenous inhabitants of the modern West Indies.

15 *a prediction.*

16 *to prophesy.*

17 "Virgilian oracle," a practice in which Virgil's epic poem *The Aeneid* was opened at random and the verses found used to predict future events.

18 "I seize arms in a frenzy, but there is little reason in arming" (Virgil, *Aeneid* 2.314).

19 The god Apollo's oracle was at Delphi in Greece; "sibyl" is a name given to various female prophets and seers in the Greek and Roman world.

20 The Book of Psalms in the Hebrew Bible was, by tradition, written by King David himself.

21 A classical rhetorical trope in which an inanimate object or animal is endowed with human characteristics.

But now let us see how the Greeks have named it, and how they deemed of it. The Greeks called him a 'poet', which name hath, as the most excellent, gone through other languages. It cometh of this word *poiein*, which is, to make: wherein, I know not whether by luck or wisdom, we Englishmen have met with the Greeks in calling him a maker: which name, how high and incomparable a title it is, I had rather were known by marking the scope of other sciences than by any partial allegation.

There is no art delivered unto mankind that hath not the works of nature for his principal object, without which they could not consist, and on which they so depend, as they become actors and players, as it were, of what nature will have set forth. So doth the astronomer look upon the stars, and by that he seeth, set down what order nature hath taken therein. So doth the geometrician and arithmetician, in their diverse sorts of quantities. So doth the musicians in time tell you which by nature agree, which not. The natural philosopher thereon hath his name, and the moral philosopher standeth upon the natural virtues, vices, or passions of man; and follow nature (saith he) therein, and thou shalt not err. The lawyer saith what men have determined; the historian what men have done. The grammarian speaketh only of the rules of speech; and the rhetorician and logician, considering what in nature will soonest prove and persuade, thereon give artificial rules, which still are compassed within the circle of a question according to the proposed matter. The physician weigheth the nature of man's body, and the nature of things helpful, or hurtful unto it. And the metaphysic, though it be in the second and abstract notions, and therefore be counted supernatural, yet doth he indeed build upon the depth of nature. Only the poet, disdaining to be tied to any such subjection, lifted up with the vigour of his own invention, doth grow in effect another nature, in making things either better than nature bringeth forth, or, quite anew, forms such as never were in nature, as the Heroes, Demigods, Cyclops, Chimeras, Furies,[22] and such like: so as he goeth hand in hand with nature, not enclosed within the narrow warrant of her gifts, but freely ranging only within the zodiac of his own wit. Nature never set forth the earth in so rich tapestry as divers poets have done; neither with so pleasant rivers, fruitful trees, sweet-smelling flowers, nor whatsoever else may make the too much loved earth more lovely. Her world is brazen, the poets only deliver a golden.

But let those things alone, and go to man – for whom as the other things are, so it seemeth in him her uttermost cunning is employed – and know whether she have brought forth so true a lover as Theagenes, so constant a friend as Pylades, so valiant a man as Orlando, so right a prince as Xenophon's Cyrus, so excellent a man every way as Virgil's Aeneas.[23] Neither let this be jestingly conceived, because the works of the one be essential, the other in imitation or fiction; for any understanding knoweth the skill of each artificer standeth in that *idea* or fore-conceit of the work, and not in the work it self. And that the poet hath that *idea* is manifest, by delivering them forth in such excellency as he had imagined them. Which delivering forth also is not wholly imaginative, as we are wont to say by them that build castles in the air; but so far substantially it worketh, not only to make a Cyrus, which had been but a particular excellency as nature might have done, but to bestow a Cyrus upon the world to make many Cyruses, if they will learn aright, why and how that maker made him.

Neither let it be deemed too saucy a comparison to balance the highest point of man's wit with the efficacy of nature; but rather give right honour to the heavenly Maker of that maker, who having made man to His own likeness, set him beyond and over all the works of that second nature: which in nothing he showeth so much as in poetry, when with the force of a divine breath he bringeth things forth surpassing her doings – with no small arguments to the credulous of that first accursed

---

22   Cyclops are a race of one-eyed giants in Greek mythology; a chimera is a monster with the head of a lion, the body of a she-goat, and the tail of a snake; the Furies were the classical Greek spirits of revenge.

23   Theagenes is the literary type of the true lover, taken from Heliodorus' *Aethiopica* (4th century AD); Pylades typifies the devotion of a true friend in his friendship with Orestes, as represented in Aeschylus' *Oresteia*; Orlando represents a perfect knight and was the hero of Ariosto's Renaissance epic poem *Orlando Furioso*; Cyrus the Great was an emperor of ancient Persia whose idealized life story, told by the historian Xenophon (c.428–c.354 BCE), made him the type of a just ruler for Early Modern Europe; Virgil's Aeneas, after whom *The Aeneid* is named, is the mythical founder of Rome and exemplifies devotion to duty.

fall of Adam, since our erected wit maketh us know what perfection is, and yet our infected will[24] keepeth us from reaching unto it. But these arguments will by few be understood, and by fewer granted. Thus much (I hope) will be given me, that the Greeks with some probability of reason gave him the name above all names of learning.

Now let us go to a more ordinary opening of him, that the truth may be the more palpable: and so I hope, though we get not so unmatched a praise as the etymology of his names will grant, yet his very description, which no man will deny, shall not justly be barred from a principal commendation.

Poesy therefore is an art of imitation, for so Aristotle termeth it in the word *mimesis* – that is to say, a representing, counterfeiting, or figuring forth – to speak metaphorically, a speaking picture – with this end, to teach and delight.[25]

Of this have been three general kinds. The chief, both in antiquity and excellency, were they that did imitate the unconceivable excellencies of God. Such were David in his Psalms; Solomon in his Song of Songs, in his Ecclesiastes, and Proverbs; Moses and Deborah in their Hymns; and the writer of Job: which, beside other, the learned Emanuel Tremellius and Franciscus Junius[26] do entitle the poetical part of the Scripture. Against these none will speak that hath the Holy Ghost in due holy reverence. (In this kind, though in a full wrong divinity, were Orpheus, Amphion, Homer in his Hymns, and many other, both Greeks and Romans.) And this poesy must be used by whosoever will follow St. James's counsel in singing psalms when they are merry, and I know is used with the fruit of comfort by some, when, in sorrowful pangs of their death-bringing sins, they find the consolation of the never-leaving goodness.

The second kind is of them that deal with matters philosophical, either moral as Tyrtaeus, Phocylides, Cato, or natural, as Lucretius, and Virgil's *Georgics*; or astronomical, as Manilius and Pontanus; or historical, as Lucan: which who mislike, the fault is in their judgement quite out of taste, and not in the sweet food of sweetly uttered knowledge.[27]

But because this second sort is wrapped within the fold of the proposed subject, and takes not the free course of his own invention, whether they properly be poets or no let grammarians dispute, and go to the third, indeed right poets, of whom chiefly this question ariseth: betwixt whom and these second is such a kind of difference as betwixt the meaner sort of painters, who counterfeit only such faces as are set before them, and the more excellent, who having no law but wit, bestow that in colours upon you which is fittest for the eye to see: as the constant though lamenting look of Lucretia,[28] when she punished in herself another's fault, wherein he painteth not Lucretia whom he never saw, but painteth the outward beauty of such a virtue. For these third be they which most properly do imitate to teach and delight, and to imitate borrow nothing of what is, hath been, or shall be; but range, only reined with learned discretion, into the divine consideration of what may be and should be. These be they that, as the first and most noble sort may justly be termed *vates*, so these are waited on in the excellentest languages and best understandings with the fore described name of poets. For these indeed do merely make to imitate, and imitate both to delight and teach; and delight, to move men to take that goodness in hand, which without delight they would fly as from a stranger; and teach, to make them know that goodness whereunto they are moved – which being the noblest scope to which ever any learning was directed, yet want there not idle tongues to bark at them.

These be subdivided into sundry more special denominations. The most notable be the heroic, lyric, tragic, comic, satiric, iambic, elegiac, pastoral, and certain others, some of these being termed

24   "Wit" and "will" here stand for spiritual awareness and worldly desire respectively.

25   Aristotle, *Poetics* 1447aff.; the idea that poetry should both teach and delight was articulated by the Roman poet Horace.

26   Two sixteenth-century translators of the Bible into Latin.

27   For Tyrtaeus and Phocylides, see note 9 above. Marcus Cato "the Censor" (234–149 BC) was a politician who wrote a collection of moral maxims that has not survived to the present day; Lucretius (98–55 BC) wrote *De rerum natura* ("On Nature"), a didactic poem about the physical world; Virgil's *Georgics* (29 BC) is a didactic poem on agriculture; Marcus Manilius (fl. 1st century AD) and Giovanni Pontano (1426–1503) both wrote long poems on astronomy; Lucan (39–65 AD) wrote the *Pharsalia*, an epic poem on the Roman civil war.

28   In Roman legend, she was the chaste wife of a Roman general who is raped by the king's son, Sextus Tarquinius. After telling her husband, she commits suicide, and she became the literary model of the honorable wife. The story is narrated by Shakespeare in *The Rape of Lucrece* (1594).

according to the matter they deal with, some by the sorts of verses they liked best to write in;[29] for indeed the greatest part of poets have apparelled their poetical inventions in that numbrous[30] kind of writing which is called verse – indeed but apparelled, verse being but an ornament and no cause to poetry, since there have been many most excellent poets that never versified, and now swarm many versifiers that need never answer to the name of poets. For Xenophon, who did imitate so excellently as to give us *effigiem iusti imperii*, the portraiture of a just empire, under the name of Cyrus, (as Cicero saith of him) made therein an absolute heroical poem. So did Heliodorus in his sugared invention of that picture of love in Theagenes and Chariclea;[31] and yet both these wrote in prose: which I speak to show that it is not rhyming and versing that maketh a poet – no more than a long gown maketh an advocate, who though he pleaded in armour should be an advocate and no soldier. But it is that feigning notable images of virtues, vices, or what else, with that delightful teaching, which must be the right describing note to know a poet by; although indeed the senate of poets hath chosen verse as their fittest raiment, meaning, as in matter they passed all in all, so in manner to go beyond them: not speaking (table-talk fashion or like men in a dream) words as they chanceably fall from the mouth, but peising each syllable of each word by just pro-portion according to the dignity of the subject.

Now therefore it shall not be amiss first to weigh this latter sort of poetry by his works, and then by his parts; and if in neither of these anatomies he be condemnable, I hope we shall obtain a more favourable sentence.

This purifying of wit – this enriching of memory, enabling of judgement, and enlarging of conceit – which commonly we call learning, under what name so ever it come forth, or to what immediate end soever it be directed, the final end is to lead and draw us to as high a perfection as our degenerate souls, made worse by their clayey lodgings, can be capable of.

This, according to the inclination of man, bred many-formed impressions. For some that thought this felicity principally to be gotten by knowledge, and no knowledge to be so high or heavenly as acquaintance with the stars, gave themselves to astronomy; others, persuading themselves to be demigods if they knew the causes of things, became natural and supernatural philosophers; some an admirable delight drew to music; and some the certainty of demonstration to the mathematics. But all, one and other, having this scope: to know, and by knowledge to lift up the mind from the dungeon of the body to the enjoying his own divine essence.

But when by the balance of experience it was found that the astronomer, looking to the stars, might fall in a ditch, that the inquiring philosopher might be blind in himself, and the mathe-matician, might draw forth a straight line with a crooked heart, then lo, did proof, the overruler of opinions, make manifest that all these are but serving sciences, which, as they have each a private end in themselves, so yet are they all directed to the highest end of the mistress-knowledge, by the Greeks called *architectonike*, which stands (as I think) in the knowledge of a man's self, in the ethic and politic consideration, with the end of well doing and not of well knowing only – even as the saddler's next end is to make a good saddle, but his further end to serve a nobler faculty, which is horsemanship, so the horseman's to soldiery, and the soldier not only to have the skill, but to perform the practice of a soldier. So that, the ending end of all earthly learning being virtuous action, those skills that most serve to bring forth that have a most just title to be princes over all the rest.

Wherein, if we can, show we the poet's nobleness, by setting him before his other competitors. Among whom as principal challengers step forth the moral philosophers, whom, me thinketh, I see coming towards me with a sullen gravity, as though they could not abide vice by daylight, rudely clothed for to witness outwardly their contempt of outward things, with books in their hands against glory, whereto they set their names, sophistically speaking against subtlety, and angry

29   Sidney subdivides poetry into the forms recognized by the classi-cal authorities whom he is following here; "iambic" poetry here refers to a satiric form of verse as well as a metrical unit. For more on these verse forms, see the relevant entries in *The Oxford Companion to Classical Literature*.

30   Because of its metrical regularity, poetry (like music) was consid-ered a numeric ("numbrous") art form.

31   See note 23 above.

with any man in whom they see the foul fault of anger. These men casting largess as they go, of definitions, divisions and distinctions, with a scornful interrogative do soberly ask whether it be possible to find any path so ready to lead a man to virtue as that which teacheth what virtue is; and teach it not only by delivering forth his very being, his causes and effects, but also by making known his enemy, vice, which must be destroyed, and his cumbersome servant, passion, which must be mastered; by showing the generalities that containeth it, and the specialties that are derived from it; lastly, by plain setting down how it extendeth itself out of the limits of a man's own little world to the government of families and maintaining of public societies.

The historian scarcely giveth leisure to the moralist to say so much, but that he, laden with old mouse-eaten records, authorizing himself (for the most part) upon other histories, whose greatest authorities are built upon the notable foundation of hearsay; having much ado to accord differing writers and to pick truth out of their partiality; better acquainted with a thousand years ago than with the present age, and yet better knowing how this world goeth than how his own wit runneth; curious for antiquities and inquisitive of novelties; a wonder to young folks and a tyrant in table talk, denieth, in a great chafe, that any man for teaching of virtue and virtuous actions is comparable to him. 'I am *testis temporum, lux veritatis, vita memoriae, magistra vitae, nuncia vetustatis*.[32] The Philosopher' saith he, 'teacheth a disputative virtue, but I do an active. His virtue is excellent in the dangerless Academy of Plato, but mine showeth forth her honourable face in the battles of Marathon, Pharsalia, Poitiers, and Agincourt.[33] He teacheth virtue by certain abstract considerations, but I only bid you follow the footing of them that have gone before you. Old-aged experience goeth beyond the fine-witted philosopher, but I give the experience of many ages. Lastly, if he make the songbook, I put the learner's hand to the lute; and if he be the guide, I am the light.' Then would he allege you innumerable examples, confirming story by stories, how much the wisest senators and princes, have been directed by the credit of history, as Brutus, Alphonsus of Aragon, and who not, if need be?[34] At length, the long line of their disputation makes a point in this, that the one giveth the precept, and the other the example.

Now whom shall we find (since the question standeth for the highest form in the school of learning) to be moderator? Truly, as me seemeth, the poet; and if not a moderator, even the man that ought to carry the title from them both, and much more from all other serving sciences. Therefore compare we the poet with the historian and with the moral philosopher; and if he go beyond them both, no other human skill can match him. For as for the divine, with all reverence it is ever to be excepted, not only for having his scope as far beyond any of these as eternity exceedeth a moment, but even for passing each of these in themselves. And for the Lawyer, though *Ius*[35] be the daughter of Justice, and justice the chief of virtues, yet because he seeketh to make men good rather *formidine poenae*[36] than *virtutis amore*;[37] or, to say righter, doth not endeavour to make men good, but that their evil hurt not others; having no care, so he be a good citizen, how bad a man he be: therefore, as our wickedness maketh him necessary, and necessity maketh him honourable, so he is not in the deepest truth to stand in rank with these who all endeavour to take naughtiness away and plant goodness even in the secretest cabinet of our souls. And these four are all that any way deal in the consideration of men's manners, which being the supreme knowledge, they that best breed it deserve the best commendation.

The philosopher, therefore, and the historian are they which would win the goal, the one by precept, the other by example. But both, not having both, do both halt. For the philosopher, setting down with thorny arguments the bare rule, is so hard of utterance and so misty to be conceived, that one that hath no other guide but him shall wade in him till he be old before he shall find suf-

32   "I am the witness of time, the light of truth, the life of memory, the governess of life, the herald of antiquity" (Cicero, *De Oratore* 2.9.36). Cicero (106–43 BC) was a Roman orator and statesman whose rhetorical and philosophical works were enormously influential in Early Modern Europe.

33   Famous historical battles: Marathon saw the Greeks defeat the invading Persians in 490 BCE; Pharsalia (48 BC) ended the Roman civil wars as Caesar defeated Pompey, and is the subject of Lucan's epic poem

(see note 27 above); Poitiers (1356) and Agincourt (1415) were notable victories of the English over the French in the Hundred Years War.

34   Brutus (85–42 BC) was a Roman statesman who conspired to assassinate Julius Caesar in order to protect the Roman republic; Alphonsus was the King of Aragon from 1416 to 1458.

35   "Right."

36   "by the fear of punishment."

37   "by the love of virtue."

ficient cause to be honest. For his knowledge standeth so upon the abstract and general, that happy is that man who may understand him, and more happy that can apply what he doth understand. On the other side, the historian, wanting the precept, is so tied, not to what should be but to what is, to the particular truth of things and not to the general reason of things, that his example draweth no necessary consequence, and therefore a less fruitful doctrine.

Now doth the peerless poet perform both: for whatsoever the philosopher saith should be done, he gives a perfect picture of in someone by whom he presupposeth it was done, so as he coupleth the general notion with the particular example. A perfect picture I say, for he yieldeth to the powers of the mind an image of that whereof the philosopher bestoweth but a wordish description, which doth neither strike, pierce, nor possess the sight of the soul so much as that other doth. For as in outward things, to a man that had never seen an elephant, or a rhinoceros, who should tell him most exquisitely all their shapes, colour, bigness, and particular marks, or of a gorgeous palace, an *architector*,[38] with declaring the full beauties, might well make the hearer able to repeat, as it were by rote, all he had heard, yet should never satisfy his inward conceit with being witness to itself of a true lively knowledge; but the same man, as soon as he might see those beasts well painted, or the house well in model, should straightways grow, without need of any description, to a judicial comprehending of them: so no doubt the philosopher with his learned definitions – be it of virtues, vices, matters of public policy or private government – replenisheth the memory with many infallible grounds of wisdom, which, notwithstanding, lie dark before the imaginative and judging power, if they be not illuminated or figured forth by the speaking picture of poesy.

Tully[39] taketh much pains, and many times not without poetical helps, to make us know the force love of our country hath in us. Let us but hear old Anchises speaking in the midst of Troy's flames, or see Ulysses in the fulness of all Calypso's delights bewail his absence from barren and beggarly Ithaca.[40] Anger, the Stoics said, was a short madness: let but Sophocles bring you Ajax on a stage, killing or whipping sheep and oxen, thinking them the Army of Greeks, with their chieftains Agamemnon, and Menelaus, and tell me if you have not a more familiar insight into anger than finding in the schoolmen his *genus*[41] and difference.[42] See whether wisdom and temperance in Ulysses and Diomedes, valour in Achilles, friendship in Nisus and Euryalus, even to an ignorant man carry not an apparent shining;[43] and, contrarily, the remorse of conscience in Oedipus, the soon repenting pride in Agamemnon, the self-devouring cruelty in his father Atreus, the violence of ambition in the two Theban brothers, the sour-sweetness of revenge in Medea;[44] and, to fall lower, the Terentian Gnatho and our Chaucer's Pander so expressed that we now use their names to signify their trades:[45] and finally, all virtues, vices, and passions so in their own natural states, laid to the view, that we seem not to hear of them, but clearly to see through them.

But even in the most excellent determination of goodness, what philosopher's counsel can so readily direct a prince, as the feigned Cyrus in Xenophon; or a virtuous man in all fortunes, as Aeneas in Virgil; or a whole commonwealth, as the way of Sir Thomas More's *Utopia*?[46] I say the way, because where Sir Thomas More erred, it was the fault of the man and not of the poet, for that way of patterning a commonwealth was most absolute, though he perchance hath not so absolutely performed it. For the question is, whether the feigned image of poetry or the regular

---

38 "architect."

39 A common name used for the Roman politician and orator more commonly referred to as Cicero (see gazetteer). His full name was Marcus Tullius Cicero.

40 Anchises is the father of Aeneas in the *Aeneid*; "Ulysses" is the Latin form of "Odysseus," hero of *The Odyssey*, who lived with the nymph Calypso before returning home to the island of Ithaca.

41 "general term."

42 Sophocles (*c.*496–*c.*406 BC) was a Greek tragic dramatist who wrote a play about Ajax, who was one of the Greek heroes in the Trojan War. Agamemnon and Menelaus were the Kings of Argos and Sparta respectively and were the leaders of the Greek army.

43 Diomedes and Achilles are other Greek heroes from the Trojan War; Nisus and Euryalus are exemplars of friendship in *The Aeneid*.

44 Oedipus is the tragic protagonist of Sophocles' Theban plays; Atreus, King of Argos and the father of Agamemnon and Menelaus, served his uncle Thyestes the flesh of his own children in a banquet; the "Theban brothers" are Polynices and Eteocles, the sons of Oedipus who fight each other for the throne of Thebes after their father's death; Medea is the wife of Jason, hero of the Argonaut voyage, who kills their children after he deserts her.

45 Gnatho, a character in the Roman playwright Terence's *Eunuchus*, is the type of the parasite and hanger-on; Pandar, from Chaucer's *Troilus and Criseyde*, is the literary type of the pimp.

46 Thomas More (1478–1535) was an English statesman and humanist who was executed by Henry VIII; the title of his book about an imaginary commonwealth has become the name for the genre itself.

instruction of philosophy hath the more force in teaching: wherein if the philosophers have more rightly showed themselves philosophers than the poets have attained to the high top of their profession, as in truth

Mediocribus esse poetis,
non dii, non homines, non concessere columnae;[47]

it is, I say again, not the fault of the art, but that by few men that art can be accomplished.

Certainly, even our Saviour Christ could as well have given the moral commonplaces of uncharitableness and humbleness as the divine narration of Dives and Lazarus; or of disobedience and mercy, as that heavenly discourse of the lost child and the gracious father;[48] but that His through-searching wisdom knew the estate of Dives burning in hell, and Lazarus in Abraham's bosom, would more constantly (as it were) inhabit both the memory and judgement. Truly, for myself, meseems, I see before mine eyes the lost child's disdainful prodigality, turned to envy a swine's dinner: which by the learned divines are thought not historical acts, but instructing parables.

For conclusion, I say the philosopher teacheth, but he teacheth obscurely, so as the learned only can understand him, that is to say, he teacheth them that are already taught; but the poet is the food for the tenderest stomachs, the poet is indeed the right popular philosopher, whereof Aesop's tales give good proof: whose pretty allegories stealing under the formal tales of beasts, makes many, more beastly than beasts, begin to hear the sound of virtue from those dumb speakers.[49]

But now it may be alleged that if this imagining of matters be so fit for the imagination, then must the historian needs surpass, who bringeth you images of true matters, such as indeed were done, and not such as fantastically or falsely may be suggested to have been done. Truly, Aristotle himself, in his discourse of poesy, plainly determineth this question, saying that poetry is *philosophoteron* and *spuodaioteron*, that is to say, it is more philosophical and more studiously serious than history. His reason is, because poesy dealeth with *katholou*, that is to say, with the universal consideration, and the history with *kathekaston*, the particular: now, saith he, the universal weighs what is fit to be said or done, either in likelihood or necessity (which the poesy considereth in his imposed names), and the particular only marks whether Alcibiades[50] did, or suffered, this or that. Thus far Aristotle: which reason of his (as all his) is most full of reason. For indeed, if the question were whether it were better to have a particular act truly or falsely set down, there is no doubt which is to be chosen, no more than whether you had rather have Vespasian's picture right as he was, or, at the painter's pleasure, nothing resembling.[51] But if the question be for your own use and learning, whether it be better to have it set down as it should be, or as it was, then certainly is more doctrinable the Cyrus in Xenophon than the true Cyrus in Justin, and the feigned Aeneas in Virgil than the right Aeneas in Dares Phrygius:[52] as to a lady that desired to fashion her countenance to the best grace, a painter should more benefit her to portrait a most sweet face, writing Canidia upon it, than to paint Canidia as she was, who, Horace sweareth, was full ill favoured.[53]

If the poet do his part aright, he will show you in Tantalus,[54] Atreus, and such like, nothing that is not to be shunned; in Cyrus, Aeneas, Ulysses, each thing to be followed; where the historian, bound to tell things as things were, cannot be liberal (without he will be poetical) of a perfect pattern, but, as Alexander or Scipio himself,[55] show doings, some to be liked, some to be misliked.

---

47 "Neither gods, nor men, nor booksellers allow mediocrity in poets" (Horace, *Ars Poetica*, 372–3).

48 The story of Dives and Lazarus is in Luke 16:19–31; that of the Prodigal Son is in Luke 15:11–32.

49 Aesop is the reputed composer of a large number of ancient Greek beast fables that were widely known in Early Modern Europe.

50 Alcibiades (*c*.450–404 BCE) was an Athenian politician and military leader.

51 Emperor of Rome from 70 to 79 AD and famously ugly.

52 Justinus (fl. 2nd or 3rd century AD) wrote a historical epitome which contains a more restrained account of Cyrus's life than the version

in Xenophon. Dares Phrygius is a fictional character in Homer's *Iliad* whose name was attached to a late Roman history of the Trojan War.

53 Canidia was a courtesan who rejected the poet Horace's advances; in revenge, he described her as ugly in his poems.

54 Mythical king of Lydia and grandfather to Atreus; he is represented suffering a variety of torments in the Underworld for his offences against the gods.

55 Alexander the Great, King of Macedonia (356–323 BC), and Scipio Africanus, a Roman general (236–183 BC), were great classical military leaders.

And then how will you discern what to follow but by your own discretion, which you had without reading Quintus Curtius?[56] And whereas a man may say, though in universal consideration of doctrine the poet prevaileth, yet that the history, in his saying such a thing was done, doth warrant a man more in that he shall follow – the answer is manifest: that, if he stand upon that was (as if he should argue, because it rained yesterday, therefore it should rain today), then indeed hath it some advantage to a gross conceit; but if he know an example only informs a conjectured likelihood, and so go by reason, the poet doth so far exceed him as he is to frame his example to that which is most reasonable (be it in warlike, politic, or private matters), where the historian in his bare *Was* hath many times that which we call fortune to overrule the best wisdom. Many times he must tell events whereof he can yield no cause; or, if he do, it must be poetically.

For that a feigned example hath as much force to teach as a true example (for as for to move, it is clear, since the feigned may be tuned to the highest key of passion), let us take one example wherein an historian and a poet did concur. Herodotus and Justin do both testify that Zopyrus, King Darius' faithful servant, seeing his master long resisted by the rebellious Babylonians, feigned himself in extreme disgrace of his king: for verifying of which, he caused his own nose and ears to be cut off, and so flying to the Babylonians, was received, and for his known valour so sure credited, that he did find means to deliver them over to Darius.[57] Much like matter doth Livy record of Tarquinius and his son.[58] Xenophon excellently feigneth such another stratagem performed by Abradatas in Cyrus' behalf.[59] Now would I fain know, if occasion be presented unto you to serve your prince by such an honest dissimulation, why you do not as well learn it of Xenophon's fiction as of the other's verity; and truly so much the better, as you shall save your nose by the bargain: for Abradatas did not counterfeit so far. So then the best of the historian is subject to the poet; for whatsoever action, or faction, whatsoever counsel, policy, or war stratagem the historian is bound to recite, that may the poet (if he list) with his imitation make his own, beautifying it both for further teaching, and more delighting, as it please him: having all, from Dante's heaven to his hell, under the authority of his pen. Which if I be asked what poets have done so, as I might well name some, so yet say I, and say again, I speak of the art, and not of the artificer.

Now, to that which commonly is attributed to the praise of history, in respect of the notable learning is got by marking the success, as though therein a man should see virtue exalted and vice punished – truly that commendation is peculiar to poetry, and far off from history. For indeed poetry ever sets virtue so out in her best colours, making Fortune her well-waiting handmaid, that one must needs be enamoured of her. Well may you see Ulysses in a storm, and in other hard plights; but they are but exercises of patience and magnanimity, to make them shine the more in the near-following prosperity. And of the contrary part, if evil men come to the stage, they ever go out (as the tragedy writer answered to one that misliked the show of such persons) so manacled as they little animate folks to follow them. But the history, being captived to the truth of a foolish world, is many times a terror from well-doing, and an encouragement to unbridled wickedness. For see we not valiant Miltiades rot in his fetters?[60] The just Phocion and the accomplished Socrates put to death like traitors?[61] The cruel Severus live prosperously? The excellent Severus miserably murdered?[62] Sulla and Marius dying in their beds?[63] Pompey and Cicero slain then when they would have thought exile a happiness?[64] See we not virtuous Cato driven to kill himself, and rebel Caesar so advanced that his name yet, after 1600 years, lasteth in the highest honour?[65] And mark but

56   Roman historian (fl. 1st century AD) who wrote a history of Alexander the Great's life and conquests.

57   Darius was king of Persia from 521 to 486 BC; the story of Zopyrus is related in Herodotus' *History* (3.153–60) and Justinus's *Histories* (1.10).

58   The Roman historian Titus Livius (or "Livy," 59 BC–17 AD) records this in his *Histories* 1.3–4.

59   *Cyropaedia* 6.1.45–8.

60   Miltiades (*c.*550–489 BC) was the victor of the Battle of Marathon, but later died in prison.

61   Phocion (fl. 4th century BC) and Socrates (469–399 BC) were both Athenians of great personal integrity who were executed for treason.

62   Septimius Severus (ruled 193–211 CE) and Alexander Severus (ruled 222–35 AD) were both Roman emperors; the first was ruthless but successful, while the second was kindly but unsuccessful.

63   Rival Roman generals whose ambition caused a bloody civil war in the 1st century BC.

64   Roman general and statesman respectively who both unsuccessfully opposed Julius Caesar.

65   Cato Uticensis (95–46 BC) was a Roman politician who defended the republican system against Julius Caesar's tyrannical ambitions. Sidney's remark about Caesar shows how ambivalent his reputation was in Early Modern Europe: his prodigious talents and accomplishments were admired, but his ruthless personal ambition qualified this admiration.

even Caesar's own words of the aforenamed Sulla, (who in that only did honestly, to put down his dishonest tyranny), *litteras nescivet*,[66] as if want of learning caused him to do well. He meant it not by poetry, which, not content with earthly plagues, deviseth new punishments in hell for tyrants, nor yet by philosophy, which teacheth *occidentos esse*;[67] but no doubt by skill in history, for that indeed can afford you Cypselus, Periander, Phalaris, Dionysius, and I know not how many more of the same kennel, that speed well enough in their abominable injustice of usurpation.[68]

I conclude, therefore, that he excelleth history, not only in furnishing the mind with knowledge, but in setting it forward to that which deserveth to be called and accounted good: which setting forward, and moving to well doing, indeed setteth the laurel crown upon the poets as victorious, not only of the historian, but over the philosopher, howsoever in teaching it may be questionable.

For suppose it be granted (that which I suppose with great reason may be denied) that the philosopher, in respect of his methodical proceeding, doth teach more perfectly than the poet, yet do I think, that no man is so much *philophilosophos*[69] as to compare the philosopher in moving with the poet. And that moving is of a higher degree than teaching, it may by this appear, that it is well nigh both the cause and effect of teaching. For who will be taught, if he be not moved with desire to be taught? And what so much good doth that teaching bring forth (I speak still of moral doctrine) as that it moveth one to do that which it doth teach? For, as Aristotle saith, it is not *gnosis*[70] but *praxis*[71] must be the fruit. And how *praxis* can be, without being moved to practise, it is no hard matter to consider.

The philosopher showeth you the way, he informeth you of the particularities, as well of the tediousness of the way, as of the pleasant lodging you shall have when your journey is ended, as of the many by-turnings that may divert you from your way. But this is to no man but to him that will read him, and read him with attentive studious painfulness; which constant desire whosoever hath in him, hath already past half the hardness of the way, and therefore is beholding to the philosopher but for the other half. Nay truly, learned men have learnedly thought that where once reason hath so much overmastered passion as that the mind hath a free desire to do well, the inward light each mind hath in itself is as good as a philosopher's book; since in nature we know it is well to do well, and what is well, and what is evil, although not in the words of art which philosophers bestow upon us; for out of natural conceit the philosophers drew it. But to be moved to do that which we know, or to be moved with desire to know, *hoc opus, hic labor est*.[72]

Now therein of all Sciences (I speak still of human, and according to the human conceit) is our poet the monarch. For he doth not only show the way, but giveth so sweet a prospect into the way, as will entice any man to enter into it. Nay, he doth, as if your journey should lie through a fair vineyard, at the first give you a cluster of grapes, that full of that taste, you may long to pass further. He beginneth not with obscure definitions, which must blur the margin with interpretations, and load the memory with doubtfulness; but he cometh to you with words set in delightful proportion, either accompanied with, or prepared for, the well enchanting skill of music; and with a tale forsooth he cometh unto you, with a tale, which holdeth children from play, and old men from the chimney corner. And, pretending no more, doth intend the winning of the mind from wickedness to virtue – even as the child is often brought to take most wholesome things by hiding them in such other as have a pleasant taste, which, if one should begin to tell them the nature of *aloes* or *rhabarbarum*[73] they should receive, would sooner take their physic at their ears than at their mouth. So it is in men (most of which are childish in the best things, till they be cradled in their graves): glad they will be to hear the tales of Hercules, Achilles, Cyrus, Aeneas; and hearing them, must needs hear the right description of wisdom, value, and justice; which, if they had been barely, that is to say philosophically, set out, they would swear they be brought to school again.

---

66   "He did not know literature."

67   "They are to be killed."

68   Cypselus, Periander, Phalaris, and Dionysius were all autocratic rulers in ancient Greece.

69   "lover of philosophers."

70   "knowledge."

71   "action."

72   "This is the task, this is the work" (*Aeneid* 6.129).

73   Purgative medicines.

That imitation whereof poetry is, hath the most conveniency to nature of all other, insomuch that, as Aristotle saith, those things which in themselves are horrible, as cruel battles, unnatural monsters, are made in poetical imitation delightful. Truly, I have known men that even with reading *Amadis de Gaule*[74] (which God knoweth, wanteth much of a perfect poesy) have found their hearts moved to the exercise of courtesy, liberality, and especially courage. Who readeth Aeneas carrying old Anchises on his back, that wisheth not it were his fortune to perform so excellent an act?[75] Whom doth not those words of Turnus move, the tale of Turnus having planted his image in the imagination,

> *Fugientem haec terra videbit?*
> *Usque adeone mori miserum est?*[76]

Where the philosophers, as they think scorn to delight, so must they be content little to move – saving wrangling whether *virtus*[77] be the chief or the only good, whether the contemplative or the active life do excell – which Plato and Boethius[78] well knew, and therefore made mistress Philosophy very often borrow the masking raiment of poesy. For even those hard-hearted evil men who think virtue a school name, and know no other good but *indulgere genio*,[79] and therefore despise the austere admonitions of the philosopher, and feel not the inward reason they stand upon, yet will be content to be delighted – which is all the good-fellow poet seemeth to promise – and so steal to see the form of goodness (which seen they cannot but love) ere themselves be aware, as if they took a medicine of cherries.

Infinite proofs of the strange effects of this poetical invention might be alleged; only two shall serve, which are so often remembered as I think all men know them. The one of Menenius Agrippa,[80] who, when the whole people of Rome had resolutely divided themselves from the senate, with apparent show of utter ruin, though he were (for that time) an excellent orator, came not among them upon trust of figurative speeches or cunning insinuations, and much less with far-fet maxims of philosophy, which (especially if they were Platonic) they must have learned geometry before they could well have conceived; but forsooth he behaves himself like a homely and familiar poet. He telleth them a tale, that there was a time when all the parts of the body made a muti-nous conspiracy against the belly, which they thought devoured the fruits of each other's labour; they concluded they would let so unprofitable a spender starve. In the end, to be short (for the tale is notorious, and as notorious that it was a tale), with punishing the belly they plagued themselves. This applied by him wrought such effect in the people, as I never read that only words brought forth but then so sudden and so good an alteration; for upon reasonable conditions a perfect rec-oncilement ensued. The other is of Nathan the prophet,[81] who, when the holy David had so far for-saken God as to confirm adultery with murder, when he was to do the tenderest office of a friend in laying his own shame before his eyes, sent by God to call again so chosen a servant, how doth he it but by telling of a man whose beloved lamb was ungratefully taken from his bosom: the appli-cation most divinely true, but the discourse itself feigned; which made David (I speak of the second and instrumental cause) as in a glass see his own filthiness, as that heavenly psalm of mercy well testifieth.

By these, therefore, examples and reasons, I think it may be manifest that the poet, with that same hand of delight, doth draw the mind more effectually than any other art doth. And so a con-clusion not unfitly ensue: that, as virtue is the most excellent resting place for all worldly learning to make his end of, so poetry being the most familiar to teach it, and most princely to move towards it, in the most excellent work is the most excellent workman.

---

74 A popular Spanish chivalric romance that was translated into several other European languages.

75 *Aeneid* 2.700ff.; this image of Aeneas saving his father from the flames of Troy is one of the most famous in the poem.

76 "Shall this land see Turnus fleeing? Is death so terrible after all?" *Aeneid* 12.645–6. Turnus is the ruler whom Aeneas defeats and kills in order to establish his home in Italy.

77 "Virtue."

78 Roman philosopher (476–524 AD) whose most famous work, *The Consolation of Philosophy*, was widely read in Early Modern Europe.

79 "to indulge inclination."

80 A Roman consul. This story is also used by Shakespeare in *Coriolanus* I.i.

81 The biblical story is told in 2 Samuel 12.1–7.

But I am content not only to decipher him by his works (although works, in commendation or disparaise, must ever hold a high authority), but more narrowly will examine his parts; so that (as in a man) though altogether may carry a presence full of majesty and beauty, perchance in some one defectuous piece we may find blemish.

Now in his parts, kinds, or species (as you list to term them), it is to be noted that some poesies have coupled together two or three kinds, as the tragical and comical, whereupon is risen the tragi-comical. Some, in the manner, have mingled prose and verse, as Sannazzaro[82] and Boethius. Some have mingled matters heroical and pastoral. But that cometh all to one in this question, for, if severed they be good, the conjunction cannot be hurtful. Therefore, perchance forgetting some and leaving some as needless to be remembered, it shall not be amiss in a word to cite the special kinds, to see what faults may be found in the right use of them.

Is it then the Pastoral poem which is misliked? (For perchance where the hedge is lowest they will soonest leap over.) Is the poor pipe disdained, which sometimes out of Meliboeus' mouth can show the misery of people under hard lords or ravening soldiers, and again, by Tityrus, what blessed-ness is derived to them that lie lowest from the goodness of them that sit highest;[83] sometimes, under the pretty tales of wolves and sheep, can include the whole considerations of wrong-doing and patience; sometimes show that contentions for trifles can get but a trifling victory: where per-chance a man may see that even Alexander and Darius, when they strave who should be cock of this world's dunghill, the benefit they got was that the after-livers may say

> *Haec memini et victum frustra contendere Thirsin:*
> *Ex illo Corydon, Corydon est tempore nobis.*[84]

Or is it the lamenting Elegiac; which in a kind heart would move rather pity than blame; who bewails with the great philosopher Heraclitus, the weakness of mankind and the wretchedness of the world;[85] who surely is to be praised, either for compassionate accompanying just causes of lamen-tations, or for rightly painting out how weak be the passions of woefulness? Is it the bitter but wholesome Iambic, who rubs the galled mind, in making shame the trumpet of villainy, with bold and open crying out against naughtiness? Or the Satiric, who

> *Omne vafer vitrium ridenti tangit amico;*[86]

who sportingly never leaveth till he make a man laugh at folly, and at length ashamed, to laugh at himself, which he cannot avoid without avoiding the folly; who, while

> *circum praecordia ludit,*[87]

giveth us to feel how many headaches a passionate life bringeth us to; how, when all is done,

> *Est Ulubris animus si nos non deficit aequus?*[88]

No, perchance it is the Comic, whom naughty play-makers and stage-keepers have justly made odious. To the arguments of abuse I will answer after. Only this much now is to be said, that the

82   Jacopo Sannazaro (1458–1530) wrote a pastoral romance, *The Arcadia*, which is a direct source for Sidney's *Arcadia*. Both works mix passages of prose and verse.

83   Tityrus and Meliboeus are characters in Virgil's *Eclogues* (c.42–37 BC), which were the most important Latin models for pastoral poetry.

84   "I remember this, and how defeated Thyrsis struggled in vain. From then on, it is Corydon, Corydon for us" (*Eclogues* 7.69–70). The lines refer to a poetic competition between two shepherds, and Sidney is implying that Alexander and Darius' war for Asia was just as trivial.

85   Sidney is here discussing elegiac poetry as a form which focuses on loss and remembrance. Elegiac verses often treated erotic subjects as well, however. Heraclitus (c.540–c.480 BC) was a Pre-Socratic philoso-pher who believed that all matter in the universe was in a state of flux.

86   "The rogue skewers every one of his friend's faults while making him laugh" (Persius, *Satires* 1.116–17). The reference is to Horace's satiric technique.

87   "He frolics with the secrets of his heart" (Persius, *Satires* 1.117).

88   "If a balanced mind does not desert us, we can be happy at Ulubrae" (Horace, *Epistles* 1.11.30). Ulubrae was a proverbially dull small Roman town.

comedy is an imitation of the common errors of our life, which he representeth in the most ridiculous and scornful sort that may be, so as it is impossible that any beholder can be content to be such a one. Now, as in geometry the oblique must be known as well as the right, and in arithmetic the odd as well as the even, so in the actions of our life who seeth not the filthiness of evil wanteth a great foil to perceive the beauty of virtue. This doth the comedy handle so in our private and domestical matters as with hearing it we get as it were an experience what is to be looked for of a niggardly Demea, of a crafty Davus, of a flattering Gnatho, of a vainglorious Thraso;[89] and not only to know what effects are to be expected, but to know who be such, by the signifying badge given them by the comedian. And little reason hath any man to say that men learn the evil by seeing it so set out, since, as I said before, there is no man living but, by the force truth hath in nature, no sooner seeth these men play their parts, but wisheth them *in pistrinum*;[90] although perchance the sack of his own faults lie so hidden behind his back that he seeth not himself dance the same measure; whereto yet nothing can more open his eyes than to find his own actions contemptibly set forth.

So that the right use of comedy will (I think) by nobody be blamed; and much less of the high and excellent Tragedy, that openeth the greatest wounds, and showeth forth the ulcers that are covered with tissue; that maketh kings fear to be tyrants, and tyrants manifest their tyrannical humours; that, with stirring the affects of admiration and commiseration, teacheth the uncertainty of this world, and upon how weak foundations gilden roofs are builded; that maketh us know,

> *Qui sceptra saevus duro imperio regit,*
> *Timet timentes; metus in auctorem redit.*[91]

But how much it can move, Plutarch yieldeth a notable testimony of the abominable tyrant Alexander Pheraeus,[92] from whose eyes a tragedy, well made and represented, drew abundance of tears, who without all pity had murdered infinite numbers, and some of his own blood: so as he, that was not ashamed to make matters for tragedies, yet could not resist the sweet violence of a tragedy. And if it wrought no further good in him, it was that he, in despite of himself, withdrew himself from hearkening to that which might mollify his hardened heart. But it is not the tragedy they do mislike; for it were too absurd to cast out so excellent a representation of whatsoever is most worthy to be learned.

Is it the Lyric that most displeaseth, who with his tuned lyre and well accorded voice, giveth praise, the reward of virtue, to virtuous acts; who gives moral precepts, and natural problems; who sometimes raiseth up his voice to the height of the heavens, in singing the lauds of the immortal God? Certainly, I must confess my own barbarousness, I never heard the old Song of Percy and Douglas[93] that I found not my heart moved more than with a trumpet; and yet is it sung but by some blind crowder, with no rougher voice than rude style; which, being so evil apparelled in the dust and cobwebs of that uncivil age, what would it work, trimmed in the gorgeous eloquence of Pindar?[94] In Hungary, I have seen it the manner at all feasts, and other such like meetings, to have songs of their ancestors' valour, which that right soldierlike nation think one of the chiefest kindlers of brave courage. The incomparable Lacedemonians[95] did not only carry that kind of music ever with them to the field, but even at home, as such songs were made, so were they all content to be singers of them — when the lusty men were to tell what they did, the old men what they had done, and the young what they would do. And where a man may say that Pindar many times praiseth highly victories of small moment, matters rather of sport than virtue; as it may be answered, it was

89 Characters from Roman comedies by Terence, all of whom are dominated by the trait which Sidney ascribes to them.

90 "In the mill," a Roman punishment of hard labour for disobedient slaves.

91 "The cruel ruler who governs harshly fears those who fear him; terror returns to its author" (Seneca, *Oedipus* 3.705–6).

92 Plutarch (*c*.46–120 CE) was a Greek historian and philosopher; the story of Alexander of Pherae is in his *Life of Pelopidas* 29.

93 The "old song" is the 15th-century ballad *Chevy Chase*.

94 Ancient Greek lyric poet (518–*c*.446 BC) who wrote odes celebrating the winners of athletic contests.

95 Spartans, a famously warlike nation.

the fault of the poet, and not of the poetry, so indeed the chief fault was in the time and custom of the Greeks, who set those toys at so high a price that Philip of Macedon[96] reckoned a horserace won at Olympus among his three fearful felicities. But as the unimitable Pindar often did, so is that kind most capable and most fit to awake the thoughts from the sleep of idleness to embrace honourable enterprises.

There rests the Heroical – whose very name (I think) should daunt all backbiters: for by what conceit can a tongue be directed to speak evil of that which draweth with him no less champions than Achilles, Cyrus, Aeneas, Turnus, Tydeus, and Rinaldo?[97] – who doth not only teach and move to a truth, but teacheth and moveth to the most high and excellent truth; who maketh magnanimity and justice shine through all misty fearfulness and foggy desires; who, if the saying of Plato and Tully be true, that who could see virtue would be wonderfully ravished with the love of her beauty – this man sets her out to make her more lovely in her holiday apparel, to the eye of any that will deign not to disdain until they understand. But if anything be already said in the defence of sweet poetry, all concurreth to the maintaining the heroical, which is not only a kind, but the best and most accomplished kind of poetry. For as the image of each action stirreth and instructeth the mind, so the lofty image of such worthies most inflameth the mind with desire to be worthy, and informs with counsel how to be worthy. Only let Aeneas be worn in the tablet of your memory, how he governeth himself in the ruin of his country; in the preserving his old father, and carrying away his religious ceremonies; in obeying God's commandment, to leave Dido,[98] though not only all passionate kindness, but even the human consideration of virtuous gratefulness, would have craved other of him; how in storms, how in sports, how in war, how in peace, how a fugitive, how victorious, how besieged, how besieging, how to strangers, how to allies, how to enemies, how to his own; lastly, how in his inward self, and how in his outward government – and I think, in a mind not prejudiced with a prejudicating humour, he will be found in excellency fruitful, yea, even as Horace saith,

melius Chrysippo et Crantore.[99]

But truly I imagine it falleth out with these poet-whippers, as with some good women, who often are sick, but in faith they cannot tell where; so the name of poetry is odious to them, but neither his cause nor effects, neither the sum that contains him, nor the particularities descending from him, give any fast handle to their carping dispraise.

Since then poetry is of all human learning the most ancient and of most fatherly antiquity, as from whence other learning have taken their beginnings; since it is so universal that no learned nation doth despise it, nor barbarous nation is without it; since both Roman and Greek gave such divine names unto it, the one of prophesying, the other of making; and that indeed the name of making is fit for him, considering that where all other arts retain themselves within their subject, and receive, as it were, their being from it, the poet only bringeth his own stuff, and doth not learn a conceit out of a matter, but maketh matter for a conceit; since neither his description nor end containing any evil, the thing described cannot be evil; since his effects be so good as to teach goodness and delight the learners; since therein (namely in moral doctrine, the chief of all knowledges) he doth not only far pass the historian, but, for instructing, is well nigh comparable to the philosopher, for moving leaves him behind him; since the Holy Scripture (wherein there is no uncleanness) hath whole parts in it poetical, and that even our Saviour Christ vouchsafed to use the flowers of it; since all his kinds are not only in their united forms but in their severed dissections fully commendable; I think (and think I think rightly) the laurel crown appointed for triumphant captains doth worthily (of all other learnings) honour the poet's triumph.

---

96   King of Macedon (359–336 BC) and father of Alexander the Great.
97   All warrior heroes from epic poems. Tydeus was one of the "Seven Against Thebes" in Statius's *Thebaid* AD *c*.90; Rinaldo appears in Ariosto's *Orlando Furioso* and Tasso's *Jerusalem Delivered*.

98   Queen of Carthage in Virgil's *Aeneid*. She falls in love with Aeneas and kills herself when he leaves her to found Rome.
99   "Better than Chrysippus and Crantor" (Horace, *Epistles* 1.2.4). Horace is arguing that poets teach better than these two philosophers.

But because we have ears as well as tongues, and that the lightest reasons that may be will seem to weigh greatly, if nothing be put in the counterbalance, let us hear, and, as well as we can, ponder what objections be made against this art, which may be worthy either of yielding or answering.

First, truly I note not only in these *mysomousoi*, poet-haters, but in all that kind of people who seek a praise by dispraising others, that they do prodigally spend a great many wandering words in quips and scoffs, carping and taunting at each thing which, by stirring the spleen, may stay the brain from a through-beholding the worthiness of the subject. Those kind of objections, as they are full of a very idle easiness, since there is nothing of so sacred a majesty but that an itching tongue may rub it self upon it, so deserve they no other answer, but, instead of laughing at the jest, to laugh at the jester. We know a playing wit can praise the discretion of an ass, the comfortableness of being in debt, and the jolly commodities of being sick of the plague. So of the contrary side, if we will turn Ovid's verse

Ut lateat virtus, prox imitate mali,

that good lie hid in nearness of the evil, Agrippa will be as merry in showing the vanity of science as Erasmus was in the commending of folly.[100] Neither shall any man or matter escape some touch of these smiling railers. But for Erasmus and Agrippa, they had another foundation than the superficial part would promise. Marry, these other pleasant faultfinders, who will correct the verb before they understand the noun, and confute others' knowledge before they confirm their own – I would have them only remember that scoffing cometh not of wisdom. So as the best title in true English they get with their merriments is to be called good fools; for so have our grave forefathers ever termed that humorous kind of jesters.

But that which giveth greatest scope to their scorning humor is rhyming and versing. It is already said (and, as I think, truly said), it is not rhyming and versing that maketh poesy. One may be a poet without versing, and a versifier without poetry. But yet, presuppose it were inseparable (as indeed it seemeth Scaliger[101] judgeth), truly it were an inseparable commendation. For if *oratio* next to *ratio*, speech next to reason, be the greatest gift bestowed upon mortality, that cannot be praiseless which doth most polish that blessing of speech; which considers each word, not only (as a man may say) by his most forcible quality, but by his best measured quantity, carrying even in themselves a harmony – without, perchance, number, measure, order, proportion be in our time grown odious. But lay aside the just praise it hath, by being the only fit speech for music (music, I say, the most divine striker of the senses), thus much is undoubtedly true, that if reading be foolish without remembering, memory being the only treasure of knowledge, those words which are fittest for memory are likewise most convenient for knowledge. Now, that verse far exceedeth prose in the knitting up of the memory, the reason is manifest: the words (besides their delight, which hath a great affinity to memory) being so set as one cannot be lost but the whole work fails; which accusing itself, calleth the remembrance back to itself, and so most strongly confirmeth it. Besides, one word so, as it were, begetting another, as, be it in rhyme or measured verse, by the former a man shall have a near guess to the follower. Lastly, even they that have taught the art of memory have showed nothing so apt for it as a certain room divided into many places well and thoroughly known. Now, that hath the verse in effect perfectly, every word having his natural seat, which seat must needs make the word remembered. But what needeth more in a thing so known to all men? Who is it that ever was a scholar that doth not carry away some verses of Virgil, Horace, or Cato, which in his youth he learned, and even to his old age serve him for hourly lessons?[102] But the fitness it hath for memory is notably proved by all delivery of arts: wherein for the most part, from grammar, to logic, mathematics, physic, and the rest, the rules chiefly necessary to be borne away are compiled in verses. So that, verse being in itself sweet and orderly, and being best for memory, the only handle of knowledge, it must be in jest that any man can speak against it.

---

100   Two great humanist intellectuals: Cornelius Agrippa (c.1486–1535) wrote *The Uncertainty and Vanity of the Arts and Sciences*; Erasmus of Rotterdam (c.1466–1536) wrote *The Praise of Folly* as a satire of human weakness.

101   Julius Caesar Scaliger (1484–1558) was an Italian humanist who wrote a theoretical treatise on poetry.

102   The close study of short passages of poetry was an important technique for teaching Latin grammar in Early Modern Europe.

Now then go we to the most important imputations laid to the poor poets. For ought I can yet learn, they are these. First, that there being many other more fruitful knowledges, a man might better spend his time in them than in this. Secondly, that it is the mother of lies. Thirdly, that it is the nurse of abuse, infecting us with many pestilent desires; with a siren's sweetness drawing the mind to the serpent's tail of sinful fancies (and herein, especially, comedies give the largest field to ear, as Chaucer saith); how, both in other nations and in ours, before poets did soften us, we were full of courage, given to martial exercises, the pillars of manlike liberty, and not lulled asleep in shady idleness with poets' pastimes. And lastly, and chiefly, they cry out with open mouth as if they had shot Robin Hood, that Plato banished them out of his commonwealth. Truly, this is much, if there be much truth in it.

First, to the first. That a man might better spend his time, is a reason indeed; but it doth (as they say) but *petere principium*.[103] For if it be as I affirm, that no learning is so good as that which teacheth and moveth to virtue; and that none can both teach and move thereto so much as poetry: then is the conclusion manifest that ink and paper cannot be to a more profitable purpose employed. And certainly, though a man should grant their first assumption, it should follow (methinks) very unwillingly, that good is not good, because better is better. But I still and utterly deny that there is sprung out of the earth a more fruitful knowledge.

To the second, therefore, that they should be the principal liars, I will answer paradoxically, but truly, I think truly, that of all writers under the sun the poet is the least liar, and, though he would, as a poet can scarcely be a liar. The astronomer, with his cousin the geometrician, can hardly escape, when they take upon them to measure the height of the stars. How often, think you, do the physicians lie, when they aver things good for sicknesses, which afterwards send Charon[104] a great number of souls drowned in a potion, before they come to his ferry? And no less of the rest, which take upon them to affirm. Now, for the poet, he nothing affirms, and therefore never lieth. For, as I take it, to lie is to affirm that to be true which is false. So as the other artists, and especially the historian, affirming many things, can, in the cloudy knowledge of mankind, hardly escape from many lies. But the poet (as I said before) never affirmeth. The poet never maketh any circles about your imagination, to conjure you to believe for true what he writes. He citeth not authorities of other histories, even for his entry calleth the sweet Muses to inspire into him a good invention; in truth, not labouring to tell you what is or is not, but what should or should not be. And therefore, though he recount things not true, yet because he telleth them not for true, he lieth not – without we will say that Nathan lied in his speech before-alleged to David; which as a wicked man durst scarce say, so think I none so simple would say that Aesop lied in the tales of his beasts; for who thinks Aesop wrote it for actually true were well worthy to have his name chronicled among the beasts he writeth of. What child is there, that, coming to a play, and seeing *Thebes* written in great letters upon an old door, doth believe that it is Thebes? If then a man can arrive to the child's age to know that the poets' persons and doings are but pictures what should be, and not stories what have been, they will never give the lie to things not affirmatively but allegorically and figuratively written. And therefore, as in history, looking for truth, they may go away full fraught with falsehood, so in poesy, looking but for fiction, they shall use the narration but as an imaginative ground-plot of a profitable invention. But hereto is replied, that the poets give names to men they write of, which argueth a conceit of an actual truth, and so, not being true, proves a falsehood. And doth the lawyer lie, then, when under the names of *John-a-stiles* and *John-a-nokes*[105] he puts his case? But that is easily answered. Their naming of men is but to make their picture the more lively, and not to build any history: painting men, they cannot leave men nameless. We see we cannot play at chess but that we must give names to our chessmen; and yet, methinks, he were a very partial champion of truth that would say we lied for giving a piece of wood the reverend title of a bishop. The poet nameth Cyrus and Aeneas no other way than to show what men of their fames, fortunes, and estates should do.

---

103 "beg the question."
104 In Greek mythology, the boatman who ferried the souls of the dead over the River Styx to the Underworld.

105 Fictitious names used in legal examples.

Their third is, how much it abuseth men's wit, training it to wanton sinfulness and lustful love: for indeed that is the principal, if not only, abuse I can hear alleged. They say, the comedies rather teach than reprehend amorous conceits. They say the lyric is larded with passionate sonnets; the elegiac weeps the want of his mistress; and that even to the heroical, Cupid hath ambitiously climbed. Alas, Love, I would thou couldst as well defend thyself as thou canst offend others. I would those on whom thou dost attend could either put thee away, or yield good reason why they keep thee. But grant love of beauty to be a beastly fault (although it be very hard, since only man, and no beast, hath that gift to discern beauty); grant that lovely name of Love to deserve all hateful reproaches (although even some of my masters the philosophers spent a good deal of their lamp-oil in setting forth the excellency of it); grant, I say, whatsoever they will have granted, that not only love, but lust, but vanity, but (if they will list) scurrility, possesseth many leaves of the poets' books; yet think I, when this is granted, they will find their sentence may with good manners put the last words foremost, and not say that poetry abuseth man's wit, but that man's wit abuseth poetry.

For I will not deny but that man's wit may make poesy, which should be *eikastike* (which some learned have defined: figuring forth good things), to he *phantastike* (which doth, contrariwise, infect the fancy with unworthy objects),[106] as the painter, that should give to the eye either some excellent perspective, or some fine picture, fit for building or fortification, or containing in it some notable example (as Abraham sacrificing his son Isaac, Judith killing Holofernes, David fighting with Goliath),[107] may leave those, and please an ill-pleased eye with wanton shows of better hidden matters. But what, shall the abuse of a thing make the right use odious? Nay truly, though I yield that poesy may not only be abused, but that being abused, by the reason of his sweet charming force, it can do more hurt than any other army of words: yet shall it be so far from concluding that the abuse should give reproach to the abused, that, contrariwise, it is a good reason that whatsoever, being abused, doth most harm, being rightly used (and upon the right use each thing conceiveth his title), doth most good. Do we not see the skill of physic, the best rampire to our often-assaulted bodies, being abused, teach poison, the most violent destroyer? Doth not knowledge of law, whose end is to even and right all things, being abused, grow the crooked fosterer of horrible injuries? Doth not (to go to the highest) God's word abused breed heresy, and His name abused become blasphemy? Truly, a needle cannot do much hurt, and as truly (with leave of ladies be it spoken) it cannot do much good: with a sword thou mayst kill thy father, and with a sword thou mayst defend thy prince and country. So that, as in their calling poets fathers of lies they said nothing, so in this their argument of abuse they prove the commendation.

They allege herewith, that before poets began to be in price our nation had set their hearts' delight upon action, and not imagination: rather doing things worthy to be written, than writing things fit to be done. What that before-time was, I think scarcely Sphinx[108] can tell, since no memory is so ancient that hath not the precedent of poetry. And certain it is that, in our plainest homeliness, yet never was the Albion nation without poetry. Marry, this argument, though it be levelled against poetry, yet is it indeed a chain-shot against all learning, or bookishness as they commonly term it. Of such mind were certain Goths, of whom it is written that, having in the spoil of a famous city taken a fair library, one hangman (belike fit to execute the fruits of their wits) who had murdered a great number of bodies, would have set fire in it: no, said another very gravely,[109] take heed what you do, for while they are busy about these toys, we shall with more leisure conquer their countries. This indeed is the ordinary doctrine of ignorance, and many words sometimes I have heard spent in it. But because this reason is generally against all learning as well as poetry, or rather, all learning but poetry; because it were too large a digression to handle it, or at least too superfluous (since it is manifest that all government of action is to be gotten by knowl-

---

106   This distinction is analyzed by Plato in *Sophist* 235–6.
107   Biblical examples of heroic behavior found in Genesis 22, Judith 13 (from the Apocrypha), and 1 Samuel 17.

108   A mythical Greek monster with the body of a lion and the head of a woman; it plagued the city of Thebes until Oedipus solved its riddle.
109   *seriously.*

edge, and knowledge best by gathering many knowledges, which is reading), I only, with Horace, to him that is of that opinion

jubeo stultum esse libenter;[110]

for as for poetry itself, it is the freest from this objection.

For poetry is the companion of camps. I dare undertake, Orlando Furioso, or honest King Arthur, will never displease a soldier; but the quiddity of *ens* and *prima materia* will hardly agree with a corselet;[111] and therefore, as I said in the beginning, even Turks and Tartars are delighted with poets. Homer, a Greek, flourished before Greece flourished. And if to a slight conjecture a conjecture may be opposed, truly it may seem, that as by him their learned men took almost their first light of knowledge, so their active men, received their first motions of courage. Only Alexander's example may serve, who by Plutarch is accounted of such virtue, that Fortune was not his guide but his footstool; whose acts speak for him, though Plutarch did not: indeed the phoenix of warlike princes. This Alexander left his schoolmaster, living Aristotle, behind him, but took dead Homer with him. He put the philosopher Callisthenes[112] to death for his seeming philosophical, indeed mutinous, stubbornness, but the chief thing he was ever heard to wish for was, that Homer had been alive. He well found he received more bravery of mind by the pattern of Achilles than by hearing the definition of fortitude. And therefore, if Cato misliked Fulvius[113] for carrying Ennius with him to the field, it may be answered that, if Cato misliked it, the noble Fulvius liked it, or else he had not done it; for it was not the excellent Cato Uticensis[114] (whose authority I would much more have reverenced), but it was the former, in truth a bitter punisher of faults (but else a man that had never well sacrificed to the Graces: he misliked and cried out against all Greek learning, and yet, being eighty years old, began to learn it, belike fearing that Pluto understood not Latin). Indeed, the Roman laws allowed no person to be carried to the wars but he that was in the soldiers' roll; and therefore, though Cato misliked his unmustered person, he misliked not his work. And if he had, Scipio Nasica,[115] judged by common consent the best Roman, loved him. Both the other Scipio brothers, who had by their virtues no less surnames than of Asia and Afric, so loved him that they caused his body to be buried in their sepulture. So as Cato's authority, being but against his person, and that answered with so far greater than himself, is herein of no validity.

But now indeed my burden is great; that Plato's name is laid upon me, whom, I must confess, of all philosophers I have ever esteemed most worthy of reverence, and with good reason: since of all philosophers he is the most poetical.[116] Yet if he will defile the fountain out of which his flowing streams have proceeded, let us boldly examine with what reasons he did it. First, truly, a man might maliciously object that Plato, being a philosopher, was a natural enemy of poets. For indeed, after the philosophers had picked out of the sweet mysteries of poetry the right discerning true points of knowledge, they forthwith putting it in method, and making a school-art of that which the poets did only teach by a divine delightfulness, beginning to spurn at their guides, like ungrateful prentices, were not content to set up shop for themselves, but sought by all means to discredit their masters; which by the force of delight being barred them, the less they could overthrow them, the more they hated them. For indeed, they found for Homer seven cities strave who should have him for their citizen; where so many cities banished philosophers as not fit members to live among them. For only repeating certain of Euripides' verses, many Athenians had their lives saved of the Syracusans, where the Athenians themselves thought many philosophers unworthy to live.[117] Certain poets, as Simonides and Pindar, had so prevailed with Hiero the First, that of a tyrant they

110 "I readily order him to be a fool" (Horace, *Satires* 1.1.63).

111 Philosophical debates about essences ("quiddities"), being ("*ens*"), and the unformed matter of the universe ("*prima materia*"); a "corselet" in this context refers to a soldier's body armour.

112 Greek historian, and Aristotle's nephew (*c*.370–327 BCE). His history of Alexander is now lost.

113 The Roman consul Marcus Fulvius Nobilior took the poet Ennius to the siege of Ambracia.

114 For the Catos, see the gazetteer and note 65 above.

115 A conservative Roman consul of the 2nd century BC; the "other Scipios" were successful Roman generals.

116 In the *Republic* 3.392ff., Plato considers what role poetry should have in an ideal state and concludes that it should be banned. Plato's influence and authority were such that many Early Modern poetic theorists felt compelled to reply to his objections.

117 Both of these stories come from Plutarch's *Life of Nicias* 29.

made him a just king; where Plato could do so little with Dionysius, that he himself of a philosopher, was made a slave.[118] But who should do thus, I confess, should requite the objections made against poets with like cavillations against philosophers; as likewise one should do that should bid one read *Phaedrus* or *Symposium* in Plato, or the discourse of love in Plutarch, and see whether any poet do authorize abominable filthiness, as they do.[119] Again, a man might ask out of what commonwealth Plato doth banish them: in sooth, thence where himself alloweth community of women so as belike this banishment grew not for effeminate wantonness, since little should poetical sonnets be hurtful when a man might have what woman he listed. But I honour philosophical instructions, and bless the wits which bred them: so as they be not abused, which is likewise stretched to poetry.

St. Paul himself (who yet, for the credit of poets, twice citeth poets, and one of them by the name of 'their prophet') setteth a watch-word upon philosophy – indeed upon the abuse.[120] So doth Plato upon the abuse, not upon poetry. Plato found fault that the poets of his time filled the world with wrong opinions of the gods, making light tales of that unspotted essence, and therefore would not have the youth depraved with such opinions. Herein may much be said. Let this suffice: the poets did not induce such opinions, but did imitate those opinions already induced. For all the Greek stories can well testify that the very religion of that time stood upon many and many-fashioned gods, not taught so by the poets, but followed according to their nature of imitation. Who list[121] may read in Plutarch the discourses of Isis and Osiris, and of the cause why oracles ceased of the divine providence, and see whether the theology of that nation stood not upon such dreams which the poets indeed superstitiously observed – and truly (since they had not the light of Christ) did much better in it than the philosophers, who, shaking off superstition, brought in atheism. Plato therefore (whose authority I had much rather justly construe than unjustly resist) meant not in general of poets, in those words of which Julius Scaliger saith *Qua authoritate barbari quidam atque hispidi abuti velint ad poetas e republica exigendos;*[122] but only meant to drive out those wrong opinions of the Deity (whereof now, without further law, Christianity hath taken away all the hurtful belief) perchance (as he thought) nourished by then esteemed poets. And a man need go no further than to Plato himself to know his meaning: who in his dialogue called *Ion*, giveth high and rightly divine commendation unto poetry. So as, Plato, banishing the abuse, not the thing, not banishing it, but giving due honour to it, shall be our patron, and not our adversary. For indeed I had much rather (since truly I may do it) show their mistaking of Plato (under whose lion's skin they would make an ass-like braying against poesy) than go about to overthrow his authority; whom the wiser a man is, the more just cause he shall find to have in admiration; especially since he attributeth unto poesy more than myself do, namely, to be a very inspiring of a divine force, far above man's wit, as in the forenamed dialogue is apparent.

Of the other side, who would show the honours have been by the best sort of judgements granted them, a whole sea of examples would present themselves: Alexanders, Caesars, Scipios, all favourers of poets; Laelius, called the Roman Socrates, himself a poet, so as part of *Heautontimorumenos*[123] in Terence was supposed to be made by him; and even the Greek Socrates, whom Apollo confirmed to be the only wise man, is said to have spent part of his old time in putting Aesop's fables into verses. And therefore, full evil should it become his scholar Plato to put such words in his master's mouth against poets. But what need more? Aristotle writes the Art of Poesy; and why, if it should not be written? Plutarch teacheth the use to be gathered of them; and how, if they should not be read? And who reads Plutarch's either history or philosophy, shall find he trimmeth both their garments with guards of poesy. But I list not to defend poesy with the help of his underling historiography. Let it suffice to have showed it is a fit soil for praise to dwell upon; and what dispraise may set upon it, is either easily overcome, or transformed into just commendation.

118   Simonides of Ceos (556–468 BC) was a Greek lyric poet. Hiero the First was Tyrant of Syracuse from 478 to 467 BC; Plato visited his court, and there is a legend that Hiero sold him into slavery.

119   Like many Early Modern commentators, Sidney is uncomfortable with ancient Greek culture's tolerance and/or encouragement of male homosexuality.

120   See Acts 17.28 and Titus 1.12.

121   *wishes to.*

122   "Whose authority some uncultured and bestial men wish to abuse to expel poets from the state" (Scaliger, *Poetices* 1.2).

123   "The Self-Tormentor," a play by the Roman comic dramatist Terence (*c*.193–159 BC).

So that, since the excellencies of it may be so easily and so justly confirmed, and the low-creeping objections so soon trodden down: it not being an art of lies, but of true doctrine; not of effeminateness, but of notable stirring of courage; not of abusing man's wit but of strengthening man's wit; not banished, but honoured by Plato; let us rather plant more laurels for to engarland the poet's heads (which honour of being laureate, as besides them only triumphant captains were, is a sufficient authority to show the price they ought to be held in) than suffer the ill-favoured breath of such wrong-speakers once to blow upon the clear springs of poesy.

But since I have run so long a career in this matter, methinks, before I give my pen a full stop, it shall be but a little more lost time, to inquire why England, the mother of excellent minds, should be grown so hard a stepmother to poets, who certainly in wit ought to pass all other, since all only proceedeth from their wit, being indeed makers of themselves, not takers of others. How can I but exclaim

Musa, mihi causas memora, quo numine laeso?[124]

Sweet poesy, that hath anciently had kings, emperors, senators, great captains, such as, besides a thousand others, David, Adrian, Sophocles, Germanicus, not only to favour poets, but to be poets;[125] and of our nearer times can present for her patrons a Robert, king of Sicily, the great King Francis of France, King James of Scotland;[126] such cardinals as Bembus and Bibbiena;[127] such famous preachers and teachers as Beza and Melanchthon;[128] so learned philosophers as Fracastorius and Scaliger;[129] so great orators, as Pontanus and Muretus;[130] so piercing wits as George Buchanan;[131] so grave counsellors as, besides many, but before all, that Hospital of France,[132] than whom (I think) that realm never brought forth a more accomplished judgement, more firmly builded upon virtue: I say these, with numbers of others, not only to read others' poesies, but to poetize for others' reading – that poesy, thus embraced in all other places, should only find in our time a hard welcome in England, I think the very earth lamenteth it, and therefore decks our soil with fewer laurels than it was accustomed. For heretofore poets have in England also flourished, and, which is to be noted, even in those times when the trumpet of Mars did sound loudest. And now that an overfaint quietness should seem to strew the house for poets, they are almost in as good reputation as the mountebanks[133] at Venice. Truly even that, as of the one side it giveth great praise to poesy, which like Venus (but to better purpose) had rather be troubled in the net with Mars than enjoy the homely quiet of Vulcan:[134] so serves it for a piece of a reason why they are less grateful to idle England, which now can scarce endure the pain of a pen.

Upon this necessarily followeth, that base men with servile wits undertake it, who think it enough if they can be rewarded of the printer. And so as Epaminondas[135] is said with the honour of his virtue to have made an office, by his exercising it, which before was contemptible, to become highly respected; so these men, no more but setting their names to it, by their own disgracefulness disgrace the most graceful poesy. For now, as if all the Muses were got with child to bring forth bastard poets, without any commission they do post over the banks of the Helicon,[136] till they make the readers more weary than post-horses; while, in the mean time, they

---

124 "Remind me of the causes, O Muse, what deity was offended?" (*Aeneid* 1.8).

125 A list of biblical and classical poets who were also political figures: King David was a psalmist; Hadrian was Roman emperor (117–38 CE); Sophocles was a Greek tragic dramatist; Germanicus was a Roman general (15 BC–AD 19).

126 Robert of Anjou (1275–1343), Francis I (1494–1547), and James I (1566–1625) were all monarchs who patronized the arts.

127 Pietro Bembo (1470–1547) was an Italian poet, theorist, and churchman; he is also a character in Castiglione's *Courtier*. Cardinal Bibiena (1470–1520) wrote a comedy after Plautus.

128 Beza (1519–1605) and Melanchthon (1497–1560) were Protestant reformers and humanists.

129 Girolamo Frascatoro (c.1483–1533) and Scaliger were humanist scholars who wrote or theorized about poetry.

130 Giovanni Pontano (1426–1503) and Marc-Antoine Muret (1526–85) were humanist scholars and writers.

131 Scottish humanist (1506–85), political theorist, and tutor to King James VI and I.

132 Michel de L'Hôpital (c.1507–73), French politician and poet.

133 Quack doctors who sell "medicines" to the gullible.

134 Vulcan (Roman god of fire) trapped his wife Venus (the goddess of love) in bed with Mars (god of war) with a net, and then invited the other gods in to look.

135 4th-century BC Theban general.

136 The mountain on which the Muses live; Sidney is confusing it with the spring named Hippocrene, the waters of which give poetic inspiration.

Queis meliore luto finxit praecordia Titan[137]

are better content to suppress the outflowings of their wit, than, by publishing them, to be accounted knights of the same order. But I that, before ever I durst aspire unto the dignity, am admitted into the company of the paper-blurrers, do find the very true cause of our wanting estimation is want of desert – taking upon us to be poets in despite of Pallas.[138]

Now, wherein we want desert were a thankworthy labour to express; but if I knew, I should have mended myself. But I, as I never desired the title, so have I neglected the means to come by it. Only, overmastered by some thoughts, I yielded an inky tribute unto them. Marry, they that delight in poesy itself should seek to know what they do, and how they do; and especially look themselves in an unflattering glass of reason, if they be inclinable unto it. For poesy must not be drawn by the ears; it must be gently led, or rather it must lead – which was partly the cause that made the ancient-learned affirm it was a divine gift, and no human skill: since all other knowledges lie ready for any that hath strength of wit. A poet no industry can make, if his own genius be not carried into it; and therefore is an old proverb, *orator fit, poeta nascitur.*[139]

Yet confess I always that as the fertilest ground must be manured, so must the highest-flying wit have a Daedalus[140] to guide him. That Daedalus, they say, both in this and in other, hath three wings to bear itself up into the air of due commendation: that is art, imitation, and exercise. But these, neither artificial rules nor imitative patterns, we much cumber our selves withal. Exercise indeed we do, but that very fore-backwardly: for where we should exercise to know, we exercise as having known; and so is our brain delivered of much matter which never was begotten by knowledge. For there being two principal parts, matter to be expressed by words and words to express the matter, in neither we use art or imitation rightly. Our matter is *quodlibet*[141] indeed, though wrongly performing Ovid's Verse,

Quicquid conabor dicere, versus erit;[142]

never marshalling it into any assured rank, that almost the readers cannot tell where to find themselves.

Chaucer, undoubtedly, did excellently in his *Troilus and Criseyde*; of whom, truly, I know not whether to marvel more, either that he in that misty time could see so clearly, or that we in this clear age go so stumblingly after him. Yet had he great wants, fit to be forgiven in so reverent an antiquity. I account the *Mirror of Magistrates*[143] meetly furnished of beautiful parts, and in the Earl of Surrey's[144] lyrics, many things tasting of a noble birth, and worthy of a noble mind. The *Shepherd's Calendar* hath much poetry in his eclogues,[145] indeed worthy the reading, if I be not deceived. (That same framing of his style to an old rustic language I dare not allow, since neither Theocritus in Greek, Virgil in Latin, nor Sannazzaro in Italian did affect it.[146]) Besides these I do not remember to have seen but few (to speak boldly) printed that have poetical sinews in them; for proof whereof, let but most of the verses be put in prose, and then ask the meaning, and it will be found that one verse did but beget another, without ordering at the first what should be at the last; which becomes a confused mass of words, with a tingling sound of rhyme, barely accompanied with reason.

Our tragedies and comedies (not without cause cried out against), observing rules neither of honest civility nor skillful poetry – excepting *Gorboduc* (again, I say, of those that I have seen),

---

137   "Whose entrails Titan has moulded out of better clay" (Juvenal, *Satires* 14.35).
138   Another name for Athena, Greek goddess of wisdom.
139   "The orator is made, the poet is born."
140   Mythical Greek inventor and craftsman who made wings with which to escape from the island of Crete.
141   "What you please"; a technical term for the subject of a philosophical disputation.
142   "Whatever I try to say will become verse" (Ovid, *Tristia* 4.9.26).

143   A collection of tales relating the tragic fall of various rulers; a 1555 edition was suppressed, and it did not appear again until 1559.
144   Henry Howard, Earl of Surrey (*c.*1517–47) wrote Petrarchan love poetry in English and seems to have been the first English poet to use blank verse.
145   A pastoral poem by Edmund Spenser.
146   Greek, Roman, and Renaissance (respectively) authorities for pastoral poetry. Theocritus (3rd century BC) was the first pastoral poet.

which notwithstanding as it is full of stately speeches, and well-sounding phrases, climbing to the height of Seneca's style,[147] and as full of notable morality, which it doth most delightfully teach, and so obtain the very end of poesy, yet in truth it is very defectuous in the circumstances, which grieveth me, because it might not remain as an exact model of all tragedies. For it is faulty both in place and time, the two necessary companions of all corporal actions. For where the stage should always represent but one place, and the uttermost time presupposed in it should be, both by Aristotle's precept and common reason, but one day, there is both many days, and many places, inartificially imagined.[148]

But if it be so in *Gorboduc*, how much more in all the rest, where you shall have Asia of the one side, and Afric of the other, and so many other under-kingdoms, that the Player when he cometh in, must ever begin with telling where he is, or else the tale will not be conceived? Now you shall have three ladies walk to gather flowers: and then we must believe the stage to be a garden. By and by we hear news of shipwreck in the same place: then we are to blame if we accept it not for a rock. Upon the back of that comes out a hideous monster with fire and smoke: and then the miserable beholders are bound to take it for a cave. While in the mean time two armies fly in, represented with four swords and bucklers: and then what hard heart will not receive it for a pitched field?

Now, of time they are much more liberal: for ordinary it is that two young princes fall in love; after many traverses, she is got with child, delivered of a fair boy; he is lost, groweth a man, falleth in love, and is ready to get another child; and all this is in two hours' space: which, how absurd it is in sense, even sense may imagine, and art hath taught, and all ancient examples justified – and at this day, the ordinary players in Italy will not err in.[149] Yet will some bring in an example of *Eunuchus* in Terence, that containeth matter of two days, yet far short of twenty years. True it is, and so was it to be played in two days, and so fitted to the time it set forth. And though Plautus have in one place done amiss, let us hit it with him, and not miss with him.

But they will say: How then shall we set forth a story which contains both many places and many times? And do they not know that a tragedy is tied to the laws of poesy, and not of history; not bound to follow the story, but having liberty either to feign a quite new matter or to frame the history to the most tragical conveniency? Again, many things may be told which cannot be showed, if they know the difference betwixt reporting and representing. As, for example, I may speak (though I am here) of Peru, and in speech digress from that to the description of Calicut;[150] but in action I cannot represent it without Pacolet's horse;[151] and so was the manner the ancients took, by some *Nuntius*[152] to recount things done in former time or other place. Lastly, if they will represent an history, they must not (as Horace saith) begin *ab ovo*,[153] but they must come to the principal point of that one action which they will represent.

By example this will be best expressed.[154] I have a story of young Polydorus, delivered for safety's sake, with great riches, by his Father Priam to Polymnestor, king of Thrace, in the Trojan war time; he, after some years, hearing the overthrow of Priam, for to make the treasure his own, murdereth the child; the body of the child is taken up by Hecuba; she, the same day, findeth a sleight to be revenged most cruelly of the tyrant. Where now would one of our tragedy writers begin, but with the delivery of the child? Then should he sail over into Thrace, and so spend I know not how many years, and travel numbers of places. But where doth Euripides? Even with the finding of the body, the rest to be told by the spirit of Polydorus. This needs no further to be enlarged; the dullest wit may conceive it.

But besides these gross absurdities, how all their plays be neither right tragedies, nor right comedies, mingling kings and clowns, not because the matter so carrieth it, but thrust in the clown

---

147 *Gorboduc* (1561) was a tragedy written by Thomas Sackville and Edward Norton; Seneca "the Younger" (4 BCE–65 CE) was a Roman philosopher and dramatic poet whose tragedies were the models for Early Modern vernacular tragedy.

148 Aristotle does not, in fact, insist on unity of place, and is not as strict as Sidney on unity of time.

149 By these standards, of course, most of Shakespeare's plays would be deeply flawed.

150 A city in western India.

151 A magic horse which can transport one instantly to any destination; from the French romance *Valentine and Orson* (trans. *c*.1550).

152 "messenger".

153 "from the egg".

154 Sidney's example is the plot of Euripides' *Hecuba*.

by head and shoulders to play a part in majestical matters with neither decency nor discretion, so as neither the admiration and commiseration, nor the right sportfulness, is by their mongrel tragi-comedy obtained. I know Apuleius[155] did somewhat so, but that is a thing recounted with space of time, not represented in one moment; and I know the ancients have one or two examples of tragi-comedies, as Plautus hath *Amphitryo*;[156] but, if we mark them well, we shall find that they never, or very daintily, match hornpipes and funerals. So falleth it out that, having indeed no right comedy in that comical part of our tragedy, we have nothing but scurrility, unworthy of any chaste ears, or some extreme show of doltishness, indeed fit to lift up a loud laughter, and nothing else: where the whole tract of a comedy should be full of delight, as the tragedy should be still maintained in a well-raised admiration.

But our comedians think there is no delight without laughter; which is very wrong, for though laughter may come with delight, yet cometh it not of delight, as though delight should be the cause of laughter; but well may one thing breed both together. Nay, rather in themselves they have, as it were, a kind of contrariety: for delight we scarcely do but in things that have a conveniency to ourselves or to the general nature; laughter almost ever cometh of things most disproportioned to ourselves and nature. Delight hath a joy in it, either permanent or present. Laughter hath only a scornful tickling.

For example, we are ravished with delight to see a fair woman, and yet are far from being moved to laughter; we laugh at deformed creatures, wherein certainly we cannot delight. We delight in good chances, we laugh at mischances: we delight to hear the happiness of our friends, or country, at which he were worthy to be laughed at that would laugh; we shall, contrarily, laugh sometimes to find a matter quite mistaken and go down the hill against the bias in the mouth of some such men – as for the respect of them one shall be heartily sorry, he cannot choose but laugh, and so is rather pained than delighted with laughter.

Yet deny I not but that they may go well together. For as in Alexander's picture well set out, we delight without laughter and in twenty mad antics we laugh without delight; so in Hercules, painted with his great beard and furious countenance, in a woman's attire, spinning, at Omphale's commandment,[157] it breedeth both delight and laughter: for the representing of so strange a power in love procureth delight, and the scornfulness of the action stirreth laughter. But I speak to this purpose, that all the end of the comical part be not upon such scornful matters as stir laughter only, but, mixed with it, that delightful teaching which is the end of poesy. And the great fault even in that point of laughter, and forbidden plainly by Aristotle, is that they stir laughter in sinful things, which are rather execrable than ridiculous, or in miserable, which are rather to be pitied than scorned. For what is it to make folks gape at a wretched beggar and a beggarly clown; or, against law of hospitality, to jest at strangers, because they speak not English so well as we do? What do we learn, since it is certain

> *Nil habet infelix paupertas durius in se,*
> *Quam quod ridiculos homines facit?*[158]

But rather, a busy loving courtier, and a heartless threatening Thraso; a self-wise-seeming schoolmaster, an awry transformed traveller. These, if we saw walk in stage names, which we play naturally, therein were delightful laughter, and teaching delightfulness – as in the other, the tragedies of Buchanan do justly bring forth a divine admiration.

But I have lavished out too many words of this play matter. I do it because, as they are excelling parts of poesy, so is there none so much used in England, and none can be more pitifully abused; which, like an unmannerly daughter showing a bad education, causeth her mother Poesy's honesty to be called in question.

---

155 Apuleius (fl. 2nd century CE) was a Roman prose writer whose *Metamorphoses* (also known as *The Golden Ass*) is tonally and generically heterogeneous.
156 Tragicomedies became very popular in early 17th-century England.

157 In mythology, Omphale was a queen of Lydia whom Hercules served as a slave for a year; she made him dress as a woman and spin, while she adopted his lion skin and club.
158 "Unlucky poverty has nothing harder in it than that it makes men ridiculous" (Juvenal, *Satires* 3.152–3).

Other sort of poetry almost have we none, but that lyrical kind of songs and sonnets: which, Lord, if He gave us so good minds, how well it might be employed, and with how heavenly fruit, both private and public, in singing the praises of the immortal beauty: the immortal goodness of that God who giveth us hands to write, and wits to conceive; of which we might well want words, but never matter; of which we could turn our eyes to nothing, but we should ever have new-budding occasions. But truly many of such writings as come under the banner of unresistable love, if I were a mistress, would never persuade me they were in love: so coldly they apply fiery speeches, as men that had rather read lovers' writings – and so caught up certain swelling phrases which hang together like a man that once told me the wind was at northwest and by south, because he would be sure to name winds enough – than that in truth they feel those passions, which easily (as I think) may be bewrayed by that same forcibleness or *energia*[159] (as the Greeks call it) of the writer. But let this be a sufficient though short note, that we miss the right use of the material point of poesy.

Now, for the outside of it, which is words, or (as I may term it) diction, it is even well worse. So is that honey-flowing matron Eloquence apparelled, or rather disguised, in a courtesan-like painted affectation: one time, with so far-fet words that may seem monsters but must seem strangers to any poor Englishman; another time, with coursing of a letter, as if they were bound to follow the method of a dictionary; another time, with figures and flowers, extremely winter-starved. But I would this fault were only peculiar to versifiers, and had not as large possession among prose-printers; and (which is to be marvelled) among many scholars; and (which is to be pitied) among some preachers. Truly I could wish, if at least I might be so bold to wish in a thing beyond the reach of my capacity, the diligent imitators of Tully and Demosthenes[160] (most worthy to be imitated) did not so much keep Nizolian paper-books of their figures and phrases,[161] as by attentive translation (as it were) devour them whole, and make them wholly theirs: for now they cast sugar and spice upon every dish that is served to the table – like those Indians, not content to wear earrings at the fit and natural place of the ears, but they will thrust jewels through their nose and lips, because they will be sure to be fine. Tully, when he was to drive out Catiline, as it were with a thunderbolt of eloquence, often used the figure of repetition, as *Vivit. Vivit? Imo in senatum venit, &c.*[162] Indeed, inflamed with a well-grounded rage, he would have his words (as it were) double out of his mouth, and so do that artificially which we see men in choler do naturally. And we, having noted the grace of those words, hale them in sometimes to a familiar epistle, when it were too much choler to be choleric. How well store of *similiter cadences*[163] doth sound with the gravity of the pulpit, I would but invoke Demosthenes' soul to tell, who with a rare daintiness useth them. Truly they have made me think of the sophister that with too much subtlety would prove two eggs three, and though he might be counted a sophister, had none for his labour. So these men bringing in such a kind of eloquence, well may they obtain an opinion of a seeming finesse, but persuade few – which should be the end of their finesse. Now for similitudes, in certain printed discourses, I think all herbarists, all stories of beasts, fowls, and fishes are rifled up, that they may come in multitudes to wait upon any *of* our conceits; which certainly is as absurd a surfeit to the ears as is possible.[164] For the force of a similitude not being to prove anything to a contrary disputer, but only to explain to a willing hearer, when that is done, the rest is a most tedious prattling, rather over-swaying the memory from the purpose whereto they were applied, than any whit informing the judgement, already either satisfied, or by similitudes not to be satisfied. For my part, I do not doubt, when Antonius and Crassus,[165] the great forefathers of Cicero in eloquence, the one (as Cicero testifieth of them) pretended not to know art, the other not to set by it, because with a

---

159   "Energy," specifically a quality in language which makes its meaning clear.

160   Greek orator and politician (384–322 BC).

161   Sidney's critique of writers who slavishly imitate classical models; Marius Nizolius (c.1498–1566) published a lexical guide to Cicero's works that was widely used in the 16th century.

162   "He lives. He lives? He even comes into the Senate . . ." (Cicero, *In Catilinam* 1.1.2).

163   "similar cadences"; a rhetorical effect achieved by ending successive phrases with the same sound pattern.

164   An attack on John Lyly's *Euphues* (1578), which makes extensive use of such similitudes.

165   Classical Roman orators from the early 1st century BC.

plain sensibleness they might win credit of popular ears (which credit is the nearest step to persuasion, which persuasion is the chief mark of oratory), I do not doubt (I say) but that they used these knacks[166] very sparingly; which who doth generally use, any man may see doth dance to his own music, and so to be noted by the audience more careful to speak curiously than truly. Undoubtedly (at least to my opinion undoubtedly), I have found in divers smally learned courtiers a more sound style than in some professors of learning; of which I can guess no other cause, but that the courtier, following that which by practice he findeth fittest to nature, therein (though he know it not) doth according to art, though not by art: where the other, using art to show art, and not to hide art (as in these cases he should do) flieth from nature, and indeed abuseth art.

But what? Methinks I deserve to be pounded for straying from poetry to oratory. But both have such an affinity in the wordish consideration, that I think this digression will make my meaning receive the fuller understanding: which is not to take upon me to teach poets how they should do, but only, finding myself sick among the rest, to show some one or two spots of the common infection grown among the most part of writers, that, acknowledging ourselves somewhat awry, we may bend to the right use both of matter and manner: whereto our language giveth us great occasion, being indeed capable of any excellent exercising of it. I know some will say it is a mingled language. And why not so much the better, taking the best of both the other? Another will say it wanteth grammar. Nay truly, it hath that praise, that it wants not grammar: for grammar it might have, but it needs it not, being so easy in itself, and so void of those cumbersome differences of cases, genders, moods, and tenses, which I think was a piece of the Tower of Babylon's curse,[167] that a man should be put to school to learn his mother-tongue. But for the uttering sweetly and properly the conceits of the mind (which is the end of speech), that hath it equally with any other tongue in the world; and is particularly happy in compositions of two or three words together, near the Greek, far beyond the Latin, which is one of the greatest beauties can be in a language.[168]

Now of versifying there are two sorts, the one ancient, the other modern: the ancient marked the quantity of each syllable, and according to that framed his verse; the modern, observing only number (with some regard of the accent), the chief life of it standeth in that like sounding of the words, which we call rhyme. Whether of these be the more excellent, would bear many speeches: the ancient (no doubt) more fit for music, both words and time observing quantity, and more fit lively to express diverse passions by the low or lofty sound of the well-weighed syllable; the latter likewise, with his rhyme, striketh a certain music to the ear, and, in fine, since it doth delight, though by an other way, it obtains the same purpose: there being in either sweetness, and wanting in neither majesty. Truly the English, before any vulgar language I know, is fit for both sorts. For, for the ancient, the Italian is so full of vowels that it must ever be cumbered with elisions; the Dutch so, of the other side, with consonants, that they cannot yield the sweet sliding, fit for a verse; the French in his whole language hath not one word that hath his accent in the last syllable, saving two, called *antepenultima*;[169] and little more hath the Spanish, and therefore very gracelessly may they use dactyls.[170] The English is subject to none of these defects. Now for the rhyme, though we do not observe quantity, yet we observe the accent very precisely, which other languages either cannot do, or will not do so absolutely. That *caesura*,[171] or breathing place in the midst of the verse, neither Italian nor Spanish have, the French and we never almost fail of. Lastly, even the very rhyme itself, the Italian cannot put it in the last syllable, by the French named the masculine rhyme, but still in the next to the last, which the French call the female, or the next before that, which the Italians term *sdrucciola*.[172] The example of the former is *buono: suono*, of the *sdrucciola*, is *femina: semina*. The French, of the other side, hath both the male, as *bon: son*, and the female, as *plaise: taise*, but the *sdrucciola* he hath not: where the English hath all three, as *due: true, father: rather, motion:*

166　*trifles*.

167　Sidney is here conflating Babylon with the city of Babel (see Genesis 10:10).

168　The question of whether any modern language could produce literature equal to classical Greek and Latin was heavily debated in the 16th century.

169　"Third from the end".

170　A metrical unit consisting of one stressed and two unstressed syllables. Despite Sidney's claim, dactylic poetry is very difficult to write well in English.

171　"break".

172　"Three-syllable rhyme"; in prosody, a "masculine" rhyme occurs when the rhyming sound is a stressed syllable. Otherwise, it is "feminine."

potion – with much more which might he said, but that already I find the triflingness of this discourse is much too much enlarged.

So that since the ever-praiseworthy Poesy is full of virtue-breeding delightfulness, and void of no gift that ought to be in the noble name of learning; since the blames laid against it are either false or feeble; since the cause why it is not esteemed in England is the fault of poet-apes, not poets; since, lastly, our tongue is most fit to honour poesy, and to be honoured by poesy; I conjure you all that have had the evil luck to read this ink-wasting toy of mine, even in the name of the nine Muses, no more to scorn the sacred mysteries of poesy; no more to laugh at the name of poets, as though they were next inheritors to fools; no more to jest at the reverent title of a rhymer; but to believe, with Aristotle, that they were the ancient treasurers of the Grecians' divinity; to believe, with Bembus, that they were the first bringers-in of all civility; to believe, with Scaliger, that no philosopher's precepts can sooner make you an honest man than the reading of Virgil; to believe with Clauserus,[173] the translator of Cornutus, that it pleased the heavenly Deity, by Hesiod and Homer, under the veil of fables, to give us all knowledge, logic, rhetoric, philosophy, natural and moral, and *quid non?*;[174] to believe, with me, that there are many mysteries contained in poetry, which of purpose were written darkly, lest by profane wits it should be abused; to believe, with Landino,[175] that they are so beloved of the gods that whatsoever they write proceeds of a divine fury; lastly, to believe themselves when they tell you they will make you immortal by their verses. Thus doing, your name shall flourish in the printers' shops; thus doing, you shall be of kin to many a poetical preface; thus doing, you shall be most fair, most rich, most wise, most all, you shall dwell upon superlatives; thus doing, though you be *libertino patre natus*,[176] you shall suddenly grow *Herculea proles*,[177]

Si quid mea Carmina possunt;[178]

thus doing, your soul shall be placed with Dante's Beatrice,[179] or Virgil's Anchises. But if (fie of such a but) you be borne so near the dull-making cataract of Nilus[180] that you cannot hear the planet-like music of poetry; if you have so earth-creeping a mind that it cannot lift itself up to look to the sky of poetry, or rather, by a certain rustical disdain, will become such a mome, as to be a Momus of poetry;[181] then though I will not wish unto you the ass's ears of Midas,[182] nor to be driven by a poet's verses, as Bubonax[183] was, to hang himself, nor to be rhymed to death, as is said to be done in Ireland; yet thus much curse I must send you, in the behalf of all poets, that while you live, you live in love, and never get favour, for lacking skill of a sonnet; and when you die, your memory die from the earth for want of an epitaph.

ASTROPHIL AND STELLA

I

Loving in truth, and fain in verse my love to show,   *needing*
That the dear She might take some pleasure of my pain:
Pleasure might cause her read, reading might make her know,
Knowledge might pity win, and pity grace obtain,
I sought fit words to paint the blackest face of woe,
Studying inventions fine, her wits to entertain:

---

173 German humanist (*c.*1520–1611) who translated the Greek philosopher Cornutus.

174 "what not?"

175 15th-century humanist scholar who edited Dante's *Comedy.*

176 "son of a freed man."

177 "descendant of Hercules."

178 "If my songs can do anything" (Virgil, *Aeneid* 9.446).

179 Dante's spiritual muse, whom he meets in heaven in the *Paradiso.*

180 The Nile.

181 The mythical personification of mockery and abuse.

182 Apollo transformed Midas' ears after Midas judged Pan to be a better flute-player than the god.

183 In his edition of this text, Albert S. Cook shows that this is Sidney's mistake for "Bupalus," who was driven to suicide by the poems of Hipponax.

Oft turning others' leaves, to see if thence would flow   *pages*
Some fresh and fruitful showers upon my sun-burned brain.   *barren*
But words came halting forth, wanting Invention's stay,   *limping*
10   Invention, Nature's child, fled step-dame Study's blows,
And others' feet[1] still seemed but strangers in my way.
Thus great with child to speak, and helpless in my throes,   *pregnant*
Biting my truant pen, beating myself for spite,   *idle*
'Fool,' said my Muse to me, 'look in thy heart and write.'

2

Not at the first sight, nor with a dribbed shot   *wide*
Love gave the wound, which while I breathe will bleed:
But known worth did in mine[2] of time proceed,
Till by degrees it had full conquest got.
I saw and liked, I liked but loved not,
I loved, but straight did not what *Love* decreed:
At length to *Love's* decrees, I forc'd, agreed,
Yet with repining at so partial lot.   *complaining/destiny*
10   Now even that footstep of lost liberty   *trace*
Is gone, and now, like slave-born *Muscovite*,[3]
I call it praise to suffer Tyranny;
And now employ the remnant of my wit,
To make myself believe, that all is well,
While, with a feeling skill I paint my hell.

3

Let dainty wits cry on the Sisters nine,[4]
That bravely masked, their fancies may be told: *brightly dressed*
Or *Pindar's* Apes,[5] flaunt they in phrases fine,
Enam'lling with pied flowers their thoughts of gold: *multi-coloured*
Or else let them in statelier glory shine,
Ennobling new found Tropes[6] with problems old:
Or with strange similes enrich each line,
Of herbs or beasts, which *Ind* or *Africk* hold.[7]   *India/Africa*
For me in sooth, no Muse but one I know: *truth*
10   Phrases and Problems from my reach do grow,
And strange things cost too dear for my poor sprites.   *rare/spirits*
How then? even thus: in *Stella's* face I read,
What Love and Beauty be, then all my deed
But Copying is, what in her Nature writes.

4

Virtue alas, now let me take some rest,
Thou sett'st a bate between my will and wit,   *contention*
If vain love have my simple soul oppressed,   *futile*
Leave what thou lik'st not, deal thou not with it.
5   Thy sceptre use in some old *Cato's*[8] breast;

ASTROPHIL AND STELLA

1 A "foot" is a prosodic unit into which lines of poetry are divided (in the present case, iambic feet). In this sonnet, Astrophil is studying other poets to find a mode of poetry that will allow him to express his feelings for Stella.

2 A tunnel dug under the wall of a castle during a siege.

3 Muscovites were popularly believed to prefer life under tyranny to liberty.

4 The Muses (see gazetteer).

5 Greek poet (518–c.445 BC) who wrote victory odes in honor of the champions at the Olympics and other ancient games; his "Apes" are his imitators.

6 A trope is a rhetorical term for a figure of speech that changes the meaning of a word or words.

7 A slighting reference to the rhetorical excesses of Euphuism, a prose style popularized by John Lyly (c.1554–1606) and his wildly successful prose tale *Euphues: the Anatomy of Wit*. Euphuistic style was characterized, among other things, by a frequent use of similes drawn from obscure classical learning or folklore.

8 See gazetteer.

Churches or schools are for thy seat more fit:
I do confess, pardon a fault confessed,
My mouth too tender is for thy hard bit.   *bridle mouthpiece*
But if that needs thou wilt usurping be,
10   The little reason that is left in me,
And still th'effect of thy persuasions prove: *test*
I swear, my heart such one shall show to thee,
That shrines in flesh so true a Deity,   *enshrines*
That *Virtue*, thou thyself shalt be in love.

5

It is most true, that eyes are formed to serve
The inward light: and that the heavenly part   *reason/soul*
Ought to be king, from whose rules who do swerve,   *those who*
Rebels to Nature, strive for their own smart.   *punishment*
It is most true, what we call *Cupid's*[9] dart,
An image is, which for ourselves we carve;
And, fools, adore in temple of our heart,
Till that good God make Church and Churchmen starve.[10]
True, that true Beauty Virtue is indeed,
10   Whereof this Beauty can be but a shade,   *shadow*
Which elements with mortal mixture breed:
True, that on earth we are but pilgrims made,
And should in soul up to our country move: *i.e. heaven*
True, and yet true that I must *Stella* love.

6

Some Lovers speak when they their Muses entertain,
Of hopes begot by fear, of wot not what desires: *who knows what*
Of force of heav'nly beams,[11] infusing hellish pain:
Of living deaths, dear wounds, fair storms and freezing fires:[12]
Some one his song in *Jove*, and *Jove's* strange tales attires,   *Jupiter*
Bordered with bulls and swans, powdered with golden rain:[13]
Another humbler wit to shepherd's pipe retires,
Yet hiding royal blood full oft in rural vein.[14]
To some a sweetest plaint, a sweetest style affords,   *lamentation*
10   While tears pour out his ink, and sighs breathe out his words:
His paper, pale despair, and pain his pen doth move.
I can speak what I feel, and feel as much as they,
But think that all the Map of my state I display,   *epitome*
When trembling voice brings forth that I do *Stella* love.

7

When Nature made her chief work, *Stella's* eyes,
In colour black, why wrapped she beams so bright?
Would she in beamy black, like painter wise,   *radiant*
Frame daintiest lustre, mixed of shades and light?   *splendor*
Or did she else that sober hue devise,   *color*
In object best to knit and strength our sight,   *purpose/strengthen*

---

9   The Roman love god (son to Venus) whose arrows cause mortals
to fall in or out of love; see gazetteer.
10   i.e. Love makes both his devotees and his ministers suffer.
11   A reference to the glance of the women with whom these lovers
are in love. It was believed at this time that human eyesight worked by
sending out beams or rays to the objects it perceived, rather than acting
as a receiver for light from outside the self. The image of the eye's
"beams" is thus very important in love poetry of this period.

12   A list of common poetic descriptions of the pains of being in love.
13   A bull, a swan, and a shower of gold were all forms that Jupiter
assumed in order to have sex with mortal women (often against their
will).
14   Sidney is here referring to pastoral poetry, in which the speaker is
usually a poor shepherd, and which has historically been used as a poetic
vehicle for veiled social commentary and criticism.

Lest if no veil those brave gleams did disguise,
They sun-like should more dazzle than delight?
Or would she her miraculous power show,
That whereas black seems Beauty's contrary,
She even in black doth make all beauties flow?
Both so and thus, she minding Love should be
Placed ever there, gave him this mourning weed,
To honour all their deaths, who for her bleed.

8

Love born in Greece,[15] of late fled from his native place,
Forced by a tedious proof, that Turkish hard'ned heart,
Is no fit mark to pierce with his fine pointed dart:
And pleased with our soft peace, stayed here his flying race.
But finding these North climes do coldly him embrace,   *embraces*
Not used to frozen clips, he strave to find some part,
Where with most ease and warmth he might employ his art:
At length he perched himself in Stella's joyful face,
Whose fair skin, beamy eyes, like morning sun on snow,
Deceived the quaking boy, who thought from so pure light,   *shivering*
Effects of lively heat, must needs in nature grow.
But she most fair, most cold, made him thence take his flight
To my close heart, where, while some firebrands he did lay,   *captive*
He burnt un'wares his wings, and cannot fly away.

9

Queen Virtue's court, which some call Stella's face,
Prepared by Nature's choicest furniture,
Hath his front built of Alabaster pure;   *white stone*
Gold is the covering of that stately place.
The door by which sometimes comes forth her Grace,
Red Porphyr is, which lock of pearl makes sure: *decorative stone*
Whose porches rich (which name of cheeks endure)
Marble mixed red and white do interlace.
The windows now, through which this heav'nly guest
Looks o'er the world, and can find nothing such,
Which dare claim from those lights the name of best,
Of touch they are that without touch doth touch,[16]
Which Cupid's self from Beauty's mine did draw:
Of touch they are, and poor I am their straw.

10

Reason, in faith thou art well serv'd, that still
Wouldst brabbling be with sense and love in me: *quarreling*
I rather wished thee climb the Muses' hill,[17]
Or reach the fruit of Nature's choicest tree,
Or seek heav'n's course, or heav'n's inside to see:
Why shouldst thou toil our thorny soil to till?
Leave sense, and those which sense's objects be: *the senses*
Deal thou with powers of thoughts, leave love to will.
But thou wouldst needs fight both with love and sense,
With sword of wit, giving wounds of dispraise,   *reason*

15 A reference to Cupid's mother, the Greek goddess Aphrodite, whose seat was on Cyprus; Cyprus had been captured by the Turks in 1573.

16 A complex series of puns: the noun "touch" here refers to touchstone, a black quartz stone that was used in Early Modern Europe to test the purity of gold and silver; it also refers to jet, which can "attract" straw or paper when it is charged (or "touched") with static electricity.

17 The Muses lived on Mt. Helicon.

Till down-right blows did foil thy cunning **fence**:   *defense*
For soon as they strake thee with *Stella*'s **rays**,   *sight*
Reason thou kneeled'st, and offered'st straight to prove
By reason good, good reason her to love.

11

In truth, O Love, with what a boyish **kind**   *disposition*
Thou dost proceed in thy most serious ways:
That when the heav'n to thee his best displays,
Yet of that best thou leav'st the best behind.
For like a child that some fair book doth find,
With gilded leaves or coloured Vellum[18] **plays**,   *pages*
Or at the most on some fine picture stays,
But never heeds the fruit of writer's mind:
So when thou saw'st in Nature's cabinet

10   *Stella*, thou straight look'st babies in her **eyes**,   *i.e. seest thyself*
In her cheek's pit thou didst thy pitfold **set**,   *trap*
And in her breast bo-peep or couching **lies**,   *hiding*
Playing and shining in each outward part:
But, fool, seek'st not to get into her heart.

12

Cupid, because thou shin'st in *Stella*'s eyes,
That from her locks, thy day-**nets**, none 'scapes free,   *bird-catching nets*
That those lips swell, so full of thee they be,
That her sweet breath makes oft thy flames to rise,
That in her breast thy pap well sugared lies,
That her Grace gracious makes thy wrongs, that she
What words soe'er she speaks persuades for thee,
That her clear voice lifts thy fame to the skies.
Thou countest *Stella* thine, like those whose **powers**   *army*

10   Having got up a **breach** by fighting well,   *i.e. breach in a castle wall*
Cry 'Victory, this fair day all is ours.'
O no, her heart is such a Citadel,
So fortified with wit, stored with disdain,[19]
That to **win** it, is all the skill and pain.   *occupy*

13

Phoebus was Judge between *Jove*, *Mars*, and *Love*,[20]
Of those three gods, whose **arms** the fairest were: *coats of arms*
Jove's golden shield did Eagle **sables** bear,   *black*
Whose talons held young *Ganymede*[21] above:
But in **Vert** field *Mars* bare a golden spear,   *green*
Which through a bleeding heart his point did shove:
Each had his crest, *Mars* carried *Venus*' glove,
Jove on his helm the thunderbolt did rear.
Cupid then smiles, for on his crest there lies

10   *Stella*'s fair hair, her face he makes his shield,
Where roses **gules** are borne in silver field.   *red*
Phoebus drew wide the curtains of the skies
To **blaze** these last, and sware devoutly then,   *proclaim*
The first, thus matched, were scarcely gentlemen.[22]

---

18   A fine paper-like material made of calfskin.

19   The conceit of this sonnet is a competition between three gods over which of them has the fairest coat of arms; the archaic names for the various colors come from the language of heraldry.

20   See the gazetteer for references to all these gods and their attributes.

21   See gazetteer.

22   i.e. scarcely worthy of having a coat of arms at all.

14

Alas have I not pain enough my friend,
Upon whose breast a fiercer Gripe doth tire   *vulture/ear*
Than did on him who first stale down the fire,[23]
While *Love* on me doth all his quiver spend,
But with your Rhubarb words you must contend   *purgative*
To grieve me worse, in saying that Desire
Doth plunge my well-formed soul e'en in the mire   *swamp*
Of sinful thoughts, which do in ruin end?
If that be sin which doth the manners frame,
10 Well stayed with truth in word and faith of deed,   *supported*
Ready of wit and fearing naught but shame:
If that be sin which in fixed hearts doth breed
A loathing of all loose unchastity,
Then Love is sin, and let me sinful be.

15

You that do search for every purling spring,   *rippling*
Which from the ribs of old *Parnassus*[24] flows,
And every flower, not sweet perhaps, which grows
Near thereabout, into your Poesy wring;
You that do Dictionary's method bring
Into your rhymes, running in rattling rows:
You that poor *Petrarch's*[25] long deceased woes,
With new-born sighs and denizened wit do sing;   *newly accepted*
You take wrong ways, those far-fet helps be such,   *far-fetched*
10 As do bewray a want of inward touch: *betray*
And sure, at length stol'n goods do come to light,
But if (both for your love and skill) your name
You seek to nurse at fullest breasts of Fame,
Stella behold, and then begin to indite.   *write*

16

In nature apt to like when I did see   *i.e. By nature*
Beauties, which were of many Carats fine,
My boiling sprites did thither then incline,   *spirits*
And, Love, I thought that I was full of thee:
But finding not those restless flames in me,
Which others said did make their souls to pine:
I thought those babes of some pin's hurt did whine,
By my love judging what Love's pain might be.
But while I thus with this young lion played,
10 Mine eyes (shall I say cursed or blest) beheld
Stella; now she is named, need more be said?
In her sight I a lesson new have spelled,   *read*
I now have learned Love right, and learn'd even so,
As who that being poisoned doth poison know.   *i.e. those who*

17

His mother dear *Cupid* offended late,   *i.e. Venus*
Because that *Mars*, grown slacker in her love,
With pricking shot he did not throughly move,   *i.e. Cupid's arrows*
To keep the place of their first loving state.

---

23   A reference to the myth of Prometheus, who stole fire from the
gods and gave it to mortals; as punishment, he was chained to a rock
where a vulture came daily to gnaw out his liver (which grew back at
night).

24   See gazetteer.
25   See gazetteer.

The boy refused for fear of *Mars*'s hate,
Who threatened stripes, if he his wrath did prove: *blows/test*
But she in chafe him from her lap did shove,   *anger*
Brake bow, brake shafts, while *Cupid* weeping sate:
Till that his grandame *Nature* pitying it,
10 Of *Stella*'s brows made him two better bows,
And in her eyes of arrows infinite.
O how for joy he leaps, O how he crows,   *cries out*
And straight therewith, like wags new got to play,   *boys*
Falls to shrewd turns, and I was in his way.   *tricks*

18

With what sharp checks I in myself am shent,   *rebukes/disgraced*
When into Reason's audit I do go:
And by just counts my self a bankrupt know   *accounts*
Of all those goods, which heaven to me hath lent:
Unable quite to pay even Nature's rent,
Which unto it by birthright I do owe:
And which is worse, no good excuse can show,
But that my wealth I have most idly spent.
My youth doth waste, my knowledge brings forth toys,
10 My wit doth strive those passions to defend,
Which for reward spoil it with vain annoys.
I see my course to lose myself doth bend: *tend*
I see and yet no greater sorrow take,
Than that I lose no more for *Stella*'s sake.

19

On *Cupid*'s bow how are my heart-strings bent,
That see my wrack, and yet embrace the same?   *ruin*
When most I glory, then I feel most shame:
I willing run, yet while I run, repent.
My best wits still their own disgrace invent: *faculties*
My very ink turns straight to *Stella*'s name;
And yet my words, as them my pen doth frame,
Avise themselves that they are vainly spent.   *Advise*
For though she pass all things, yet what is all   *surpass*
10 That unto me, who fare like him that both
Looks to the skies, and in a ditch doth fall?[26]
O let me prop my mind, yet in his growth
And not in Nature for best fruits unfit:
'Scholar,' saith *Love*, 'bend hitherward your wit.'   *this way*

20

Fly, fly, my friends, I have my death wound; fly,
See there that boy, that murth'ring boy I say,   *i.e. Cupid*
Who like a thief, hid in dark bush doth lie,
Till bloody bullet get him wrongful prey.
So Tyrant he no fitter place could spy,   *i.e. like a tyrant*
Nor so fair level in so secret stay,   *aim*
As that sweet black which veils the heav'nly eye:
There himself with his shot he close doth lay.   *hidden*
Poor passenger, pass now thereby I did,   *passer-by*
10 And stayed pleased with the prospect of the place,
While that black hue from me the bad guest hid: *color*

26   The Greek philosopher Thales fell into a well while looking up at   the academic who is too concerned with abstract speculations to pay
the stars (Plato, *Theaetetus* 174a). For later writers, he was the type of   attention to everyday life.

But straight I saw the motions of lightning grace,
And then descried the glist'ring of his dart: *perceived/shining*
But ere I could fly thence, it pierced my heart.

21

Your words my friend, (right healthful caustics[27]) blame
My young mind marred, whom *Love* doth windlass so,   *ensnare*
That mine own writings like bad servants show
My wits, quick in vain thoughts, in virtue lame:
That *Plato* I read for naught, but if he tame
Such coltish gyres, that to my birth I owe   *revolutions*
Nobler desires, lest else that friendly foe,
Great expectation, wear a train of shame.   *garment*
For since mad March great promise made of me,
10   If now the May of my years much decline,
What can be hoped my harvest time will be?
Sure you say well, your wisdom's golden mine
Dig deep with learning's spade, now tell me this,
Hath this world aught so fair as *Stella* is?

22

In highest way of heav'n the Sun did ride,
Progressing then from fair twins' golden place: *Gemini's*
Having no scarf of clouds before his face,
But streaming forth of heat in his chief pride;   *splendor*
When some fair Ladies, by hard promise tied,
On horseback met him in his furious race,   *journey*
Yet each prepared, with fan's well-shading grace,
From that foe's wounds their tender skins to hide.
Stella alone with face unarmed marched,
10   Either to do like him, which open shone,
Or careless of the wealth because her own:
Yet were the hid and meaner beauties parched,
Her dainties bare went free; the cause was this,
The Sun which others burned, did her but kiss.

23

The curious wits, seeing dull pensiveness
Bewray itself in my long settled eyes,   *reveal*
Whence those same fumes of melancholy rise,
With idle pains, and missing aim, do guess.   *futile efforts*
Some that know how my spring I did address,
Deem that my Muse some fruit of knowledge plies: *applies*
Others, because the Prince my service tries,   *tests*
Think that I think state errors to redress.
But harder Judges judge ambition's rage,
10   Scourge of itself, still climbing slippery place,
Holds my young brain captived in golden cage.
O fools, or over-wise, alas the race
Of all my thoughts hath neither stop nor start,
But only *Stella*'s eyes and *Stella*'s heart.

24

Rich fools[28] there be, whose base and filthy heart
Lies hatching still the goods wherein they flow:

---

27   A caustic is a substance which destroys living tissue, used med-
ically to remove sores etc.

28   The first of a series of punning references to Lord Rich, who
married Penelope Devereux, the model for Stella.

And damning their own selves to *Tantal's*[29] smart,
Wealth breeding want, more blest, more wretched grow.   *desire*
Yet to those fools heav'n doth such wit impart,
As what their hands do hold, their heads do know,
And knowing, love, and loving, lay apart
As sacred things, far from all danger's show.
But that rich fool, who by blind Fortune's lot
10   The richest gem of Love and life enjoys,   i.e. Stella
And can with foul abuse such beauties blot;
Let him, deprived of sweet but unfelt joys,
(Exiled for ay from those high treasures, which   *ever*
He knows not) grow in only folly rich.

<h2 style="text-align:center">25</h2>

The wisest scholar of the wight most wise[30]
By *Phoebus'* doom, with sugared sentence says,   *judgement*
That Virtue, if it once met with our eyes,
Strange flames of *Love* it in our souls would raise;
But for that man with pain this truth descries,   *Because*
While he each thing in sense's balance weighs,
And so nor will, nor can behold those skies   *neither . . . nor . . .*
Which inward sun to *Heroic* mind displays,   *reason*
Virtue of late, with virtuous care to stir
10   Love of herself, takes *Stella's* shape, that she
To mortal eyes might sweetly shine in her.
It is most true, for since I her did see,
Virtue's great beauty in that face I prove,
And find th'effect, for I do burn in love.

<h2 style="text-align:center">26</h2>

Though dusty wits dare scorn Astrology,   *worthless*
And fools can think those Lamps of purest light,
Whose numbers, ways, greatness, eternity,
Promising wonders, wonder do invite,   *Foretelling*
To have for no cause birthright in the sky,
But for to spangle the black weeds of night: *garments*
Or for some brawl, which in that chamber high,   *dance*
They should still dance to please a gazer's sight.
For me, I do Nature unidle know,   *not idle*
10   And know great causes, great effects procure:
And know those Bodies high reign on the low.[31]
And if these rules did fail, proof makes me sure,
Who oft fore-judge my after-following race,
By only those two stars in *Stella's* face.

<h2 style="text-align:center">27</h2>

Because I oft in dark abstracted guise,
Seem most alone in greatest company,
With dearth of words, or answers quite awry,
To them that would make speech of speech arise,
They deem, and of their doom the rumour flies,   *judge/judgment*
That poison foul of bubbling pride doth lie

---

29 See gazetteer under Tantalus.
30 Plato was the student of Socrates, who was pronounced the wisest person of his time by the Delphic Oracle.

31 A reference to the hermetic concept of astrological influence on earthly events. It was widely believed that all events on earth corresponded to (and were directed by) movements in the heavenly bodies, and could thus be anticipated by interpreting the motions of the heavens.

So in my swelling breast that only I
Fawn on my self, and others do despise
Yet pride I think doth not my soul possess,
     10   Which looks too oft in his unflatt'ring glass:
But one worse fault, *Ambition*, I confess,
That makes me oft my best friends overpass,   *ignore*
Unseen, unheard, while thought to highest place
Bends all his powers, even unto *Stella's* grace.

28

You that with allegory's curious frame,   *ingenious*
Of other's children changelings use to make,[32]
With me those pains for God's sake, do not take:
I list not dig so deep for brazen fame.
When I say '*Stella*', I do mean the same
Princess of Beauty, for whose only sake
The reins of *Love* I love, though never slake,   *slacken*
And joy therein, though Nations count it shame.
I beg no subject to use eloquence,
     10   Nor in hid ways to guide Philosophy:
Look at my hands for no such quintessence;[33]
But know that I in pure simplicity,
Breathe out the flames which burn within my heart,
Love only reading unto me this art.

29

Like some weak Lords, neighboured by mighty kings,
To keep themselves and their chief cities free,
Do easily yield, that all their coasts may be
Ready to store their[34] camps of needful things:
So *Stella's* heart, finding what power *Love* brings,
To keep itself in life and liberty,
Doth willing grant, that in the frontiers he
Use all to help his other conquerings:
And thus her heart escapes, but thus her eyes
     10   Serve him with shot, her lips his heralds are:
Her breasts his tents, legs his triumphal car:
Her flesh his food, her skin his armour brave,   *splendid*
And I, but for because my prospect lies   *view*
Upon that coast, am giv'n up for a slave.

30[35]

Whether the Turkish new-moon minded be
To fill his horns this year on Christian coast;
How *Poles'* right king means, without leave of host,
To warm with ill-made fire cold *Muscovy*;
If French can yet three parts in one agree;

---

32 An allegory is an extended metaphor in which the elements of a narrative ("other's children") are used to signify something completely different (hence "changelings").

33 Originally an alchemical term referring to the "fifth essence" (the substance of which the heavenly bodies were composed) supposedly inherent in all matter. The term later came to mean the most essential part of any non-material thing.

34 "their" here refers to "mighty kings".

35 Sonnet 30 is made up of a series of questions concerning contemporary European events in 1582: the threat of a Turkish invasion, under the crescent moon banner of Islam; the Polish invasion of Russia ("Muscovy"); the civil strife in France between three factions (Catholics, Protestants, and *politiques*); the Diet (a kind of parliament) of the Holy Roman Emperor; the Spanish invasion of Holland, which was led by William of Orange; Sir Henry Sidney's taxation ("bit") of landowners in Ulster; and political unrest in the Scottish court. This last reference was modified to "no welt'ring" in the 1598 edition of the text in order to avoid giving offence to King James VI of Scotland (who was shortly to become King of England).

What now the Dutch in their full diets boast;
How *Holland* hearts, now so good towns be lost,
Trust in the shade of pleasant *Orange* tree;
How *Ulster* likes of that same golden bit,
10   Wherewith my father once made it half tame;
If in the Scottish Court be welt'ring yet;   *agitation*
These questions busy wits to me do frame;
I, cumbered with good manners, answer do,
But know not how; for still I think of you.

31

With how sad steps, O Moon, thou climb'st the skies,
How silently, and with how wan a face,
What, may it be that even in heav'nly place
That busy archer his sharp arrows tries?
Sure, if that long with *Love* acquainted eyes
Can judge of *Love*, thou feel'st a Lover's case;
I read it in thy looks, thy languished grace,
To me that feel the like, thy state descries.   *describes*
Then, e'en of fellowship, O Moon, tell me,
10   Is constant *Love* deemed there but want of wit?
Are beauties there as proud as here they be?
Do they above love to be loved, and yet
Those Lovers scorn whom that *Love* doth possess?
Do they call *Virtue* there ungratefulness?

32

Morpheus,[36] the lively son of deadly sleep,
Witness of life to them that living die:
A Prophet oft, and oft an history,
A Poet eke, as humours fly or creep,   *also/whimsies*
Since thou in me so sure a power dost keep,
That never I with closed-up sense do lie,
But by thy work my *Stella* I descry,
Teaching blind eyes both how to smile and weep,
Vouchsafe of all acquaintance this to tell,
10   Whence hast thou Ivory, Rubies, pearl and gold,
To show her skin, lips, teeth and head so well?
'Fool,' answers he, 'no *Ind*'s such treasures hold,   *India*
But from thy heart, while my sire charmeth thee,
Sweet *Stella*'s image I do steal to me.'

33

I might, unhappy word, O me, I might,
And then would not, or could not see my bliss:[37]
Till now, wrapped in a most infernal night,
I find how heav'nly day wretch I did miss.
Heart rend thyself thou dost thyself but right,
No lovely *Paris* made thy *Helen* his:[38]
No force, no fraud, robbed thee of thy delight,
Nor Fortune of thy fortune author is:
But to myself my self did give the blow,
10   While too much wit (forsooth) so troubled me,
That I respects for both our sakes must show: *consideration*

36   See gazetteer.
37   Sometimes taken as a reference to the abortive marriage plans
between Sidney and Penelope Devereux.
38   See the gazetteer under Paris and Helen of Troy.

And yet could not, by rising Morn foresee
How fair a day was near, O punished eyes,
That I had been more foolish, or more wise.

34

Come let me write, 'And to what end?' To ease
A burthen'd heart. 'How can words ease, which are   *burdened*
The glasses of thy daily vexing care?'   *mirrors*
Oft cruel fights well pictured forth do please.
'Art not ashamed to publish thy disease?'   *proclaim*
Nay, that may breed my fame, it is so rare:
'But will not wise men think thy words fond ware?'   *trivial matters*
Then be they close, and so none shall displease.   *silent*
'What idler thing then speak and not be heard?'

10   What harder thing than smart, and not to speak?   *ache*
Peace, foolish wit, with wit my wit is marred.
Thus write I while I doubt to write, and wreak
My harms on Ink's poor loss, perhaps some find
Stella's great pow'rs, that so confuse my mind.

35

What may words say, or what may words not say,
Where truth itself must speak like flattery?
Within what bounds can one his liking stay,
Where Nature doth with infinite agree?
What *Nestor's*[39] counsel can my flames allay,
Since Reason's self doth blow the coal in me?
And ah what hope, that hope should once see day,
Where *Cupid* is sworn page to Chastity?
Honour is honoured, that thou dost possess

10   Him as thy slave, and now long needy Fame
Doth even grow rich, naming my *Stella*'s name.[40]
Wit learns in thee perfection to express,
Not thou by praise, but praise in thee is raised:
It is a praise to praise, when thou art praised.

36[41]

Stella, whence doth this new assault arise,
A conquered, yelden, ransacked heart to win?   *defeated/yielded*
Whereto long since, through my long battered eyes,
Whole armies of thy beauties entered in.
And there long since, *Love* thy Lieutenant lies,
My forces razed, thy banners raised within: *wiped out*
Of conquest, do not these effects suffice,
But wilt new war upon thine own begin?
With so sweet voice, and by sweet Nature so,
In sweetest strength, so sweetly skilled withal,

10   In all sweet stratagems sweet Art can show,
That not my soul, which at thy foot did fall,
Long since forc'd by thy beams, but stone nor tree
By Sense's privilege,[42] can 'scape from thee.

39   See gazetteer.
40   Another pun on "Rich," which was Penelope Devereux's married name.

41   The organizing conceit of Sonnet 36 is that Astrophil is a conquered city, and Stella the conquering army; this is a reversal of the siege metaphor that was a commonplace image for male lovers seeking sexual favors from women.
42   i.e. by the immunity granted by their insensibility.

37[43]

My mouth doth water, and my breast doth swell,
My tongue doth itch, my thoughts in labour be:
Listen then Lordings with good ear to me,
For of my Life I must a riddle tell.
Toward *Aurora's* Court[44] a Nymph doth dwell,
Rich in all beauties which man's eye can see:
Beauties so far from reach of words, that we
Abase her praise, saying she doth excel:
Rich in the treasure of deserv'd renown,
Rich in the riches of a royal heart,
Rich in those gifts which give th'eternal crown;
Who though most rich in these and every part,
Which make the patents of true worldly bliss,   *proofs*
Hath no misfortune, but that Rich she is.

10 *(marginal, line 10)*

38

This night while sleep begins with heavy wings
To hatch mine eyes, and that unbitted thought   *cover/unbridled*
Doth fall to stray, and my chief powers are brought
To leave the sceptre of all subject things,   *governance*
The first that straight my fancy's error brings   *imagination's wandering*
Unto my mind, is *Stella's* image, wrought
By *Love's* own self, but with so curious draught,   *design*
That she, methinks, not only shines but sings.
I start, look, hark, but in what closed-up sense
Was held, in opened sense it flies away,
Leaving me naught but wailing eloquence:
I, seeing better sights in sight's decay,   *ruin*
Called it anew, and wooed sleep again:
But him her host that unkind guest had slain.

10 *(marginal, line 10)*

39

Come, sleep, O sleep, the certain knot of peace,
The baiting-place of wit, the balm of woe,   *resting place*
The poor man's wealth, the prisoner's release,
Th' indifferent Judge between the high and low;
With shield of proof shield me from out the prease *proven strength/crowd*
Of those fierce darts, despair at me doth throw:
O make in me those civil wars to cease;
I will good tribute pay if thou do so.
Take thou of me smooth pillows, sweetest bed,
A chamber deaf to noise, and blind to light:
A rosy garland,[45] and a weary head:
And if these things, as being thine by right,
Move not thy heavy grace, thou shalt in me,
Livelier than elsewhere, *Stella's* image see.

5 *(marginal, line 5)*
10 *(marginal, line 10)*

40

As good to write as for to lie and groan.
O *Stella* dear, how much thy power hath wrought,
That hast my mind, none of the basest, brought
My still-kept course, while others sleep, to moan.
Alas, if from the height of Virtue's throne,

---

43   Sonnet 37 is another series of puns on the name "Rich."
44   Aurora was the goddess of the dawn, so toward her court means
"east."

45   The rose is here being used as an emblem of silence.

Thou canst vouchsafe the influence of a thought
Upon a wretch, that long thy grace hath sought;
Weigh then how I by thee am overthrown:
And then, think thus, although thy beauty be
10   Made manifest by such a victory,
Yet noblest Conquerors do wrecks avoid.[46]
Since then thou hast so far subdued me,
That in my heart I offer still to thee,
O do not let thy Temple be destroyed.

41[47]

Having this day my horse, my hand, my lance
Guided so well, that I obtained the prize,
Both by the judgement of the English eyes,
And of some sent from that sweet enemy *France*;
Horsemen my skill in horsemanship advance;
Town-folks my strength; a daintier judge applies
His praise to sleight, which from good use doth rise;   *manual dexterity*
Some lucky wits impute it but to chance;
Others, because of both sides I do take
10   My blood from them, who did excel in this,
Think Nature me a man of arms did make.
How far they shot awry! The true cause is,
Stella look'd on, and from her heav'nly face
Sent forth the beams, which made so fair my race.   *course*

42

O eyes, which do the Spheres[48] of beauty move,
Whose beams be joys, whose joys all virtues be,
Who while they make *Love* conquer, conquer *Love*,
The schools where *Venus* hath learned chastity.
O eyes, where humble looks most glorious prove,
Only lov'd Tyrants, just in cruelty,
Do not, O do not from poor me remove,
Keep still my Zenith, ever shine on me.   *highest state*
For though I never see them, but straight ways
10   My life forgets to nourish languished sprites;
Yet still on me, O eyes, dart down your rays:
And if from Majesty of sacred lights,
Oppressing mortal sense, my death proceed,
Wracks Triumphs be, which *Love* (high set) doth breed.   *Wrecks*

43

Fair eyes, sweet lips, dear heart, that foolish I
Could hope, by *Cupid's* help, on you to prey;
Since to himself he doth your gifts apply,
As his main force, choice sport, and easeful stay.
For when he will see who dare him gainsay,
Then with those eyes he looks, lo by and by
Each soul doth at *Love's* feet his weapons lay,
Glad if for her he give them leave to die.
When he will play, then in her lips he is,

46   i.e. Noblest conquerors do not destroy the lands which they
conquer.
47   Sonnet 41's organizing conceit is that of a tournament, in which
Astrophil has won a prize for jousting.

48   A reference to the layers of transparent hollow globes which were
thought to enclose the earth by medieval and Renaissance astronomers.
The moon and planets were thought to be fixed in them and to move
as the spheres moved.

10 Where, blushing red, that *Love's* self them doth love,
    With either lip he doth the other kiss:
    But when he will, for quiet's sake remove
    From all the world, her heart is then his room,
    Where well he knows, no man to him can come.

44

My words I know do well set forth my mind,
My mind bemoans his sense of inward smart;   *hurt*
Such smart may pity claim of any heart,
Her heart, sweet heart, is of no Tiger's kind:
And yet she hears, yet I no pity find;
But more I cry, less grace she doth impart,
Alas, what cause is there so overthwart,   *perverse*
That Nobleness itself makes thus unkind?
I much do guess, yet find no truth save this,
10 That when the breath of my complaints doth touch
    Those dainty doors unto the Court of bliss,
    The heav'nly nature of that place is such,
    That once come there, the sobs of mine annoys
    Are metamorphosed straight to tunes of joys.

45

Stella oft sees the very face of woe
Painted in my beclouded stormy face:
But cannot skill to pity my disgrace,   *understand/misfortune*
Not though thereof the cause herself she know:
Yet hearing late a fable, which did show
Of Lovers never known, a grievous case,   *i.e. fictional lovers*
Pity thereof gat in her breast such place
That, from that sea deriv'd, tears' spring did flow.
Alas, if Fancy drawn by imaged things,   *Imagination*
10 Though false, yet with free scope more grace doth breed   *favor*
    Than servant's wrack, where new doubts honour brings;
    Then think my dear, that you in me do read
    Of Lover's ruin some sad Tragedy:
    I am not I, pity the tale of me.

46

I cursed thee oft, I pity now thy case,
Blind-hitting boy, since she that thee and me   *i.e. Cupid*
Rules with a beck, so tyrannizeth thee,   *whim*
That thou must want or food, or dwelling place.
For she protests to banish thee her face,
Her face? O *Love*, a Rogue thou then shouldst be,
If *Love* learn not alone to love and see,
Without desire to feed of further grace.
Alas poor wag, that now a scholar art   *boy/pupil*
10 To such a schoolmistress, whose lessons new
    Thou needs must miss, and so thou needs must smart.   *fail to learn/be punished*
    Yet Dear, let me this pardon get of you,
    So long (though he from book mitch to desire)   *is truant*
    Till without fuel you can make hot fire.

47

What, have I thus betrayed my liberty?
Can those black beams such burning marks engrave

In my free side?[49] Or am I born a slave,
Whose neck becomes such yoke of tyranny?
Or want I sense to feel my misery?
Or sprite, disdain of such disdain to have?
Who for long faith, tho' daily help I crave,
May get no alms but scorn of beggary.   charity
Virtue awake, Beauty but beauty is,
I may, I must, I can, I will, I do
Leave following that, which it is gain to miss.
Let her go. Soft, but here she comes. Go to,
Unkind, I love you not: O me, that eye
Doth make my heart to give my tongue the lie.

10

48

Soul's joy, bend not those morning stars from me,   i.e. Stella's eyes
Where Virtue is made strong by Beauty's might,
Where *Love* is chasteness, Pain doth learn delight,
And Humbleness grows one with Majesty.
Whatever may ensue, O let me be
Co-partner of the riches of that sight:
Let not mine eyes be hell-driv'n from that light:
O look, O shine, O let me die and see.
For though I oft myself of them bemoan,
That through my heart their beamy darts be gone,   radiant
Whose cureless wounds even now most freshly bleed:
Yet since my death-wound is already got,
Dear Killer, spare not thy sweet cruel shot:
A kind of grace it is to slay with speed.

10

49[50]

I on my horse, and *Love* on me, doth try
Our horsemanships, while by strange work I prove
A horseman to my horse, a horse to *Love*;
And now man's wrongs in me, poor beast, descry.   reveal
The reins wherewith my Rider doth me tie,
Are humbled thoughts, which bit of Reverence move,
Curb'd in with fear, but with gilt boss above   bridle cover
Of Hope, which makes it seem fair to the eye.
The Wand is Will, thou, Fancy, Saddle art,   riding crop
Girt fast by memory; and while I spur   Confined securely
My horse, he spurs with sharp desire my heart:
He sits me fast, however I do stir: securely
And now hath made me to his hand so right,
That in the Manage myself takes delight.   training

10

50

Stella, the fullness of my thoughts of thee
Cannot be stayed within my panting breast,   restrained
But they do swell and struggle forth of me,
Till that in words thy figure be expressed.
And yet as soon as they so formed be,
According to my Lord *Love's* own behest: command
With sad eyes I their weak proportion see,

49   i.e. Does Stella's glance brand me, like a free person who is branded
when sold into slavery?

50   Sonnet 49 is an extended metaphor in which the speaker rides his
horse and compares himself to a horse being ridden by Love. By the last
couplet, Love has become so skilled a rider that the speaker enjoys being
ridden.

To portrait that which in this world is best.
So that I cannot choose but write my mind,
10   And cannot choose but put out what I write,   *erase*
While these poor babes their death in birth do find:[51]
And now my pen these lines had dashed quite,
But that they stopped his fury from the same,
Because their forefront bare sweet *Stella*'s name.

51

Pardon mine ears, both I and they do pray,
So may your tongue still fluently proceed,
To them that do such entertainment need,
So may you still have somewhat new to say.
On silly me do not the burden lay,   *innocent*
Of all the grave conceits your brain doth breed;   *opinions*
But find some *Hercules* to bear, instead
Of *Atlas* tired,[52] your wisdom's heav'nly sway.
For me, while you discourse of courtly tides,[53]
10   Of cunningest fishers in most troubled streams,
Of straying ways, when valiant error guides:
Meanwhile my heart confers with *Stella*'s beams,
And is even irked that so sweet Comedy,
By such unsuited speech should hindered be.

52

A strife is grown between *Virtue* and *Love*,
While each pretends that *Stella* must be his:
Her eyes, her lips, her all, saith *Love*, do this,
Since they do wear his badge, most firmly prove.
But *Virtue* thus that title doth disprove,
That *Stella* (O dear name) that *Stella* is
That virtuous soul, sure heir of heav'nly bliss:
Not this fair outside, which our heart doth move.
And therefore, though her beauty and her grace
10   Be *Love's* indeed, in *Stella*'s self he may
By no pretence claim any manner place.
Well *Love*, since this demur our suit doth stay,   *delay/suit*
Let *Virtue* have that *Stella*'s self; yet thus,
That *Virtue* but that body grant to us.

53

In Martial sports I had my cunning tried,   i.e. jousting
And yet to break more staves did me address: *lances*
While with the people's shouts I must confess,
Youth, luck, and praise, even filled my veins with pride.
When *Cupid*, having me his slave descried
In *Mars's* livery, prancing in the press: *uniform/crowd*
'What now Sir Fool,' said he, 'I would no less,[54]
Look here, I say.' I look'd, and *Stella* spied,
Who hard by made a window send forth light.
10   My heart then quaked, then dazzled were mine eyes,

---

51 Astrophil is crossing out his lines of poetry about Stella as soon as they are written.
52 See Hercules and Atlas in the gazetteer.

53 This line, and the two after it, use metaphors of fishing and of wandering in order to represent the shifting situations ("tides") of court life in which the speaker professes to be completely uninterested.
54 Cupid wants Astrophil to be as strongly devoted to love as he presently is to military prowess.

One hand forgot to rule,[55] th'other to fight.
Nor trumpets' sound I heard, nor friendly cries;
My Foe came on, and beat the air for me,
Till that her blush taught me my shame to see.

54

Because I breathe not love to every one,
Nor do not use set colours for to wear,
Nor nourish special locks of vowed hair,
Nor give each speech a full point of a groan,   *period*
The courtly Nymphs, acquainted with the moan
Of them, who in their lips *Love's* standard bear;
'What, he?' say they of me, now I dare swear,
He cannot love: no, no, let him alone.'
And think so still, so *Stella* know my mind,
10   Profess in deed I do not *Cupids* art;
But you fair maids, at length this true shall find,
That his right badge is but worn in the heart:
Dumb Swans,[56] not chatt'ring Pies, do Lovers prove,   *magpies*
They love indeed, who quake to say they love.

55

Muses, I oft invoked your holy aid,
With choicest flowers[57] my speech to engarland so;
That it, despised in true but naked show,
Might win some grace in your sweet skill arrayed.
And oft whole troupes of saddest words I stayed,   *companies*
Striving abroad a foraging to go,
Until by your inspiring I might know,
How their black banner might be best displayed.
But now I mean no more your help to try,   *test*
10   Nor other sugaring of my speech to prove,   *test*
But on her name incessantly to cry:
For let me but name her whom I do love,
So sweet sounds straight mine ear and heart do hit,
That I well find no eloquence like it.

56

Fie, school of Patience, fie, your lesson is
Far far too long to learn it without book: *by heart*
What, a whole week without one piece of look,
And think I should not your large precepts miss?
When I might read those letters fair of bliss,
Which in her face teach virtue, I could brook   *endure*
Somewhat thy leaden counsels, which I took   *dull*
As of a friend that meant not much amiss:
But now that I, alas, do want her sight,   *lack*
10   What, dost thou think that I can ever take
In thy cold stuff a phlegmatic delight?   *sluggish*
No, Patience, if thou wilt my good, then make   *wish*
Her come, and hear with patience my desire,
And then with patience bid me bear my fire.

57

Woe, having made with many fights his own
Each sense of mine, each gift, each power of mind,

---

55 i.e. manage his horse.   57 Rhetorical flowers.
56 Swans do not sing.

Grown now his slaves, he forced them out to find
The thorough'st words, fit for woe's self to groan,
Hoping that when they might find *Stella* alone,
Before she could prepare to be unkind,
Her soul, armed but with such a dainty rind,   *outward form*
Should soon be pierced with sharpness of the moan.
She heard my plaints, and did not only hear,
10   But them (so sweet is she) most sweetly sing,[58]
With that fair breast making woe's darkness clear:
A pretty case! I hoped her to bring
To feel my griefs, and she with face and voice
So sweets my pains, that my pains me rejoice.

58

Doubt there hath been, when with his golden chain[59]
The Orator so far men's hearts doth bind,
That no pace else their guided steps can find,
But as he them more short or slack doth rein,
Whether with words this sovereignty he gain,
Cloth'd with fine tropes, with strongest reasons lin'd,
Or else pronouncing grace,[60] wherewith his mind
Prints his own lively form in rudest brain.
Now judge by this: in piercing phrases late,
10   Th' anatomy of all my woes I wrate,
Stella's sweet breath the same to me did read.
O voice, O face, maugre my speech's might,   *despite*
Which wooed woe, most ravishing delight
Even those sad words even in sad me did breed.

59

Dear, why make you more of a dog than me?
If he do love, I burn, I burn in love:
If he wait well, I never thence would move:
If he be fair, yet but a dog can be.
Little he is, so little worth is he;
He barks, my songs thine own voice oft doth prove: *try*
Bidden, perhaps he fetcheth thee a glove,
But I unbid, fetch even my soul to thee.
Yet while I languish, him that bosom clips,   *embraces*
10   That lap doth lap, nay lets, in spite of spite,
This sour-breath'd mate taste of those sugared lips.
Alas, if you grant only such delight
To witless things, then *Love* I hope (since wit
Becomes a clog) will soon ease me of it.   *relieve*

60

When my good Angel guides me to the place,
Where all my good I do in *Stella* see,
That heav'n of joys throws only down on me
Thundered disdains and lightnings of disgrace:
But when the rugged'st step of Fortune's race
Makes me fall from her sight, then sweetly she

---

58   i.e. Stella herself recites the poems that Astrophil has been writing
to convince her of how he suffers.

59   The goal of oratory is to sway the opinions of listeners in the direction which the speaker intends; here, a successful orator is described as
having his listeners' hearts on a chain which he controls.

60   Style, invention, and delivery are three of the parts of rhetoric
(arrangement and memory are the other two).

With words, wherein the Muses' treasures be,
Shows love and pity to my absent case.
Now I, wit-beaten long by hardest Fate,
10   So dull am, that I cannot look into   *sluggish*
The ground of this fierce *Love* and lovely hate: *reason for*
Then some good body tell me how I do,
Whose presence, absence, absence presence is;
Bless'd in my curse, and cursed in my bliss.

61

Oft with true sighs, oft with uncalled tears,
Now with slow words, now with dumb eloquence
I *Stella's* eyes assail, invade her ears;
But this, at last, is her sweet breath'd defence:
That who indeed in-felt, affection bears,   *inwardly felt*
So captives to his Saint both soul and sense,
That, wholly hers, all selfness he forbears,
Thence his desires he learns, his life's course thence.
Now since her chaste mind hates this love in me,
10   With chastened mind, I straight must show that she
Shall quickly me from what she hates remove.
O Doctor *Cupid*, thou for me reply,
Driv'n else to grant by Angel's Sophistry,   *specious reasoning*
That I love not, without I leave to love.   *cease*

62

Late tired with woe, even ready for to pine
With rage of *Love*, I called my Love unkind;
She in whose eyes *Love*, though unfelt, doth shine,
Sweet said that I true love in her should find.
I joyed, but straight thus watered was my wine,
That love she did, but loved a Love not blind,
Which would not let me, whom she loved, decline
From nobler course, fit for my birth and mind:
And therefore by her Love's authority,
10   Willed me these tempests of vain love to fly,
And anchor fast myself on *Virtue's* shore.
Alas, if this the only metal be
Of *Love*, new-coin'd to help my beggary,
Dear, love me not, that you may love me more.

63

O Grammar rules, O now your virtues show;
So children still read you with awful eyes,   *fearful*
As my young Dove may in your precepts wise
Her grant to me, by her own virtue know.   *gift*
For late with heart most high, with eyes most low,
I crav'd the thing which ever she denies:
She lightning *Love*, displaying *Venus'* skies,
Lest once should not be heard, twice said, No, no.
Sing then my Muse, now *Io Paean* sing,[61]
10   Heav'ns envy not at my high triumphing:
But Grammar's force with sweet success confirm,
For Grammar says, (O this, dear *Stella* weigh,)
For Grammar says, (to Grammar who says nay)
That in one speech two Negatives affirm.

---

61   A cry of triumph, originally in a hymn to a god.

First Song

Doubt you to whom my Muse these notes intendeth,
Which now my breast o'ercharged to Music lendeth?
To you, to you, all song of praise is due,
Only in you my song begins and endeth.

Who hath the eyes which marry state with pleasure,   *magnificence*
Who keeps the key of Nature's chiefest treasure?
To you, to you, all song of praise is due,
Only for you the heav'n forgat all measure.   *moderation*

Who hath the lips, where wit in fairness reigneth,
Who womankind at once both decks and staineth?
To you, to you, all song of praise is due,
Only by you *Cupid* his crown maintaineth.

Who hath the feet, whose step all sweetness planteth,
Who else, for whom Fame worthy trumpets wanteth?
To you, to you, all song of praise is due,
Only to you her Sceptre *Venus* granteth.

Who hath the breast, whose milk doth passions nourish,
Whose grace is such, that when it chides doth cherish?   *virtue*
To you, to you, all song of praise is due,
Only through you the tree of life doth flourish.

Who hath the hand which without stroke, subdueth,
Who long dead beauty with increase reneweth?
To you, to you, all song of praise is due,
Only at you all envy hopeless rueth.   *feels penitent*

Who hath the hair, which, loosest, fastest tieth,
Who makes a man live then glad when he dieth?
To you, to you, all song of praise is due:
Only of you the flatterer never lieth.

Who hath the voice, which soul from senses sunders,
Whose force but yours the bolts of beauty thunders?
To you, to you, all song of praise is due:
Only with you not miracles are wonders.

Doubt you to whom my Muse these notes intendeth,
Which now my breast o'ercharged to Music lendeth?
To you, to you, all song of praise is due:
Only in you my song begins and endeth.

64

No more, my dear, no more these counsels try,
O give my passions leave to run their race:
Let Fortune lay on me her worst disgrace,
Let folk o'ercharged with brain against me cry,   *intellect*
Let clouds bedim my face, break in mine eye,
Let me no steps but of lost labour trace,
Let all the earth with scorn recount my case,
But do not will me from my *Love* to fly.
I do not envy *Aristotle's* wit,

10
Nor do aspire to *Caesar's* bleeding fame,[62]
Nor ought do care though some above me sit,[63]
Nor hope, nor wish another course to frame,
But that which once may win thy cruel heart:
Thou art my Wit, and thou my Virtue art.

65

Love by sure proof I may call thee unkind,
That giv'st no better ear to my just cries:
Thou whom to me such good turns should bind,
As I may well recount, but none can prize:
For when, nak'd boy, thou couldst no harbour find
In this old world, grown now so too too wise:
I lodged thee in my heart, and being blind
By Nature born, I gave to thee mine eyes.
Mine eyes, my light, my heart, my life, alas,
10   If so great services may scorned be:
Yet let this thought thy Tig'rish courage pass: *penetrate*
That I perhaps am somewhat kin to thee;
Since in thine arms, if learn'd fame truth hath spread,
Thou bear'st the arrow, I the arrow-head.[64]

66

And do I see some cause a hope to feed,
Or doth the tedious burden of long woe
In weakened minds, quick apprehending breed,
Of every image, which may comfort show?
I cannot brag of word, much less of deed,
Fortune wheels still with me in one sort slow,   *always slow*
My wealth no more, and no whit less my need,
Desire still on stilts of fear doth go.   *crutches*
And yet amid all fears a hope there is
10   Stol'n to my heart, since last fair night, nay day,
Stella's eyes sent to me the beams of bliss,
Looking on me, while I looked other way:
But when mine eyes back to their heav'n did move,
They fled with blush, which guilty seemed of love.

67

Hope, art thou true, or dost thou flatter me?
Doth *Stella* now beam with piteous eye,
The ruins of her conquest to espy:
Will she take time, before all wracked be?
Her eye's speech is translated thus by thee:
But fail'st thou not in phrase so heav'nly high?
Look on again, the fair text better try:[65]
What blushing notes dost thou in margin see?
What sighs stol'n out, or killed before full born?
10   Hast thou found such and such like arguments?
Or art thou else to comfort me forsworn?
Well, how so thou interpret the contents,

---

62 See Aristotle and Julius Caesar in the gazetteer.
63 A reference to the speaker's lack of social ambitions. The seating
plan at Early Modern English banquets was determined by social status;
the higher one's rank, the closer to the head table ("higher") one sat.
64 The speaker is joking that he is like Cupid because he bears Cupid's
arrow-head in his breast (the one that caused him to love Stella).

65 The conceit of this poem lies in the speaker's request that Hope
"read" Stella's expression. The references to a "fair text," "margin," and
"arguments" all refer to this process of interpreting Stella's expression
as if it was a book.

I am resolved thy error to maintain,
Rather than by more truth to get more pain.

68

Stella, the only Planet of my light,
Light of my life, and life of my desire,
Chief good, whereto my hope doth only aspire,
World of my wealth, and heav'n of my delight.
Why dost thou spend the treasures of thy sprite,
With voice more fit to wed Amphion's lyre,[66]
Seeking to quench in me the noble fire,
Fed by thy worth, and kindled by thy sight?
And all in vain, for while thy breath most sweet,
With choicest words, thy words with reasons rare,
Thy reasons firmly set on Virtue's feet,
Labour to kill in me this killing care: *painful burden*
O think I then, what paradise of joy
It is, so fair a Virtue to enjoy.

69

O joy, too high for my low style to show:
O bliss, fit for a nobler seat than me: *residence*
Envy, put out thine eyes, lest thou do see
What Oceans of delight in me do flow.
My friend, that oft saw through all masks my woe,
Come, come, and let me pour myself on thee;
Gone is the winter of my misery,
My spring appears, O see what here doth grow.
For Stella hath with words where faith doth shine,
Of her high heart giv'n me the monarchy:
I, I, O I, may say, that she is mine.
And though she give but thus condition'lly
This realm of bliss, while virtuous course I take,
No kings be crowned, but they some covenants make. *promises*

70

My Muse may well grudge at my heav'nly joy,
If still I force her in sad rhymes to creep:
She oft hath drunk my tears, now hopes to enjoy
Nectar of Mirth, since I Jove's cup do keep[67]
Sonnets be not bound 'prentice to annoy: *apprentice*
Trebles sing high, as well as basses deep:
Grief but Love's winter livery is, the Boy
Hath cheeks to smile, as well as eyes to weep.
Come then my Muse, show thou height of delight
In well raised notes, my pen the best it may
Shall paint out joy, though but in black and white.
Cease eager Muse, peace pen, for my sake stay,
I give you here my hand for truth of this,
Wise silence is best music unto bliss.

71

Who will in fairest book of Nature know,
How Virtue may best lodged in beauty be,
Let him but learn of Love to read in thee,
Stella, those fair lines which true goodness show.

---

66   See gazetteer.   67   A reference to the myth of Ganymede (see gazetteer).

There shall he find all vices' overthrow,
Not by rude force, but sweetest sovereignty
Of reason, from whose light those night-birds fly;
That inward sun in thine eyes shineth so.
And not content to be Perfection's heir

10   Thyself, dost strive all minds that way to move,
Who mark in thee what is in thee most fair.
So while thy beauty draws the heart to love,
As fast thy Virtue bends that love to good: *firmly*
'But, ah,' Desire still cries, 'give me some food.'

72

Desire, though thou my old companion art,
And oft so clings to my pure Love, that I
One from the other scarcely can descry,
While each doth blow the fire of my heart;
Now from thy fellowship I needs must part,
Venus is taught with *Dian's* wings to fly:
I must no more in thy sweet passions lie;
Virtue's gold must now head my *Cupid's* dart.   *arrow*
Service and Honour, wonder with delight,

10   Fear to offend, will worthy to appear,
Care shining in mine eyes, faith in my sprite,
These things are left me by my only Dear;
But thou Desire, because thou wouldst have all,
Now banished art, but yet alas how shall?

Second Song

Have I caught my heav' nly jewel,
Teaching sleep most fair to be?
Now will I teach her that she,
When she wakes, is too too cruel.

Since sweet sleep her eyes hath charmed,
The two only darts of *Love*:
Now will I with that boy prove   *i.e. Cupid*
Some play, while he is disarmed.

Her tongue waking still refuseth,
10   Giving frankly niggard No: *ungenerous*
Now will I attempt to know,
What No her tongue sleeping, useth.

See the hand which waking guardeth,
Sleeping, grants a free resort:
Now will I invade the fort;[68]
Cowards *Love* with loss rewardeth.

But O fool, think of the danger,
Of her just and high disdain:
Now will I alas refrain,
20   *Love* fears nothing else but anger.

---

68   From classical times onward, one of the most common metaphors for a man attempting to "seduce" (forcibly or otherwise) a woman in Western poetry is that of an army besieging a castle. The last three stanzas of this poem reveal the speaker's rather sinister ambivalence about possessing Stella by force. In Sonnet 36, Sidney reverses the usual gender positions of this image.

Yet those lips so sweetly swelling,
Do invite a stealing kiss:
Now will I but venture this,
Who will read must first learn spelling.

Oh sweet kiss, but ah she is waking,
Louring beauty chastens me: *Frowning*
Now will I away hence flee:
Fool, more Fool, for no more taking.

73

Love still a boy, and oft a wanton is,   *brat*
Schooled only by his mother's tender eye:
What wonder then if he his lesson miss,
When for so soft a rod dear play he try?
And yet my Star, because a sugared kiss   *i.e. Stella*
In sport I sucked, while she asleep did lie,
Doth lour, nay, chide; nay, threat for only this:
Sweet, it was saucy *Love*, not humble I.
But no 'scuse serves, she makes her wrath appear
10   In Beauty's throne, see now who dares come near
Those scarlet judges,[69] threat'ning bloody pain?
O heav'nly fool, thy most kiss-worthy face,
Anger invests with such a lovely grace,
That Anger's self I needs must kiss again.

74

I never drank of *Aganippe*[70] well,
Nor ever did in shade of *Tempe*[71] sit:
And Muses scorn with vulgar brains to dwell,
Poor Layman I, for sacred rites unfit.
Some do I hear of Poets' fury tell,   *divine inspiration*
But (God wot) wot not what they mean by it: *know(s)*
And this I swear by blackest brook of hell,
I am no pick-purse of another's wit.[72]
How falls it then, that with so smooth an ease
10   My thoughts I speak; and what I speak doth flow
In verse, and that my verse best wits doth please?
Guess we the cause: 'What, is it thus?' Fie no:
'Or so?' Much less: 'How then?' Sure thus it is:
My lips are sweet, inspired with *Stella*'s kiss.

75[73]

Of all the Kings that ever here did reign,
Edward, named fourth, as first in praise I name,
Not for his fair outside, nor well lined brain,
Although less gifts imp[74] feathers oft on Fame,
Nor that he could, young-wise, wise-valiant, frame

---

69   The speaker is referring to Stella's red lips, but also evoking the red gowns that British judges wore then and now.

70   See gazetteer.

71   A mountain pass in Thessaly which linked Mt. Olympus to Mt. Ossa. It was there that the nymph Daphne was transformed into a laurel tree (see gazetteer). It is thus a place with strong associations for poetry.

72   i.e. I have not plagiarized my poetry from someone else.

73   This sonnet ostensibly sets out to praise Edward IV (reigned 1461–83), but Edward's status as a usurper of his throne from Henry VI and a man with a bad reputation for sexual overindulgence makes it clear that Sidney is being ironic. The "bloody Lion" refers to the red lion flag of Scotland, and "witty Lewis" is the French King Louis XI. Edward is the reigning king at the outset of Shakespeare's *Richard III*, in which one of his "loves" (Jane Shore) is discussed in much less elevated language than Sidney uses.

74   A term from falconry. To "imp" feathers onto a bird is to graft new ones on to replace feathers that have been lost.

His Sire's revenge, joined with a kingdom's gain:
And gained by *Mars*, could yet mad *Mars* so tame,
That Balance weighed what sword did late obtain,
Nor that he made the flour-de-luce so 'fraid,   *fleur-de-lis* (the French flag)

10   Though strongly hedged of bloody Lion's paws,
That witty *Lewis* to him a tribute paid.   *cunning*
Nor this, nor that, nor any such small cause,
But only for this worthy King durst prove
To lose his Crown, rather than fail his Love.

76[75]

She comes, and straight therewith her shining twins do move   i.e. Stella's eyes
Their rays to me, who in their tedious absence lay
Benighted in cold woe, but now appears my day,
The only light of joy, the only warmth of *Love*.
She comes with light and warmth, which like *Aurora* prove   *dawn*
Of gentle force, so that mine eyes dare gladly play
With such a rosy morn, whose beams most freshly gay
Scorch not, but only do dark chilling sprites remove.
But lo, while I do speak, it groweth noon with me,

10   Her flamy glist'ring lights increase with time and place,
My heart cries 'ah', it burns, mine eyes now dazzled be:
No wind, no shade can cool, what help then in my case,
But with short breath, long looks, stayed feet and walking head,
Pray that my sun go down with meeker beams to bed.

77

Those looks, whose beams be joy, whose motion is delight,
That face, whose lecture[76] shows what perfect beauty is:
That presence, which doth give dark hearts a living light:
That grace, which *Venus* weeps that she her self doth miss:
That hand, which without touch holds more then *Atlas*[77] might;
Those lips, which make death's pay a mean price for a kiss:
That skin, whose pass-praise hue scorns this poor term of white:
Those words, which do sublime the quintessence[78] of bliss: *extract*
That voice, which makes the soul plant himself in the ears:

10   That conversation sweet, where such high comforts be,
As constr'd in true speech, the name of heav'n it bears,   *construed*
Makes me in my best thoughts and quietest judgement see
That in no more but these I might be fully blest:
Yet ah, my Maiden Muse doth blush to tell the best.

78

O how the pleasant airs of true love be
Infected by those vapours, which arise
From out that noisome gulf, which gaping lies
Between the jaws of hellish Jealousy.
A monster, other's harm, self-misery,
Beauty's plague, Virtue's scourge, succour of lies:
Who his own joy to his own hurt applies,
And only cherish doth with injury.
Who since he hath, by Nature's special grace,

10   So piercing paws, as spoil when they embrace,
So nimble feet as stir still, though on thorns:

---

75   The next two sonnets are written in hexameters (lines of six feet),
rather than the usual pentameters.

76   i.e. That face, the reading of which shows what perfect beauty is.

77   See gazetteer.

78   See note 33 above.

So many eyes ay seeking their own woe,   *always*
So ample ears as never good news know:
Is it not evil that such a Devil wants horns?

79

Sweet kiss, thy sweets I fain would sweetly indite,   *proclaim*
Which even of sweetness sweetest sweet'ner art:
Pleasing'st consort,[79] where each sense holds a part,
Which, coupling Doves, guides *Venus'* chariot right.[80]
Best charge, and bravest retreat in *Cupid's* fight,
A double key, which opens to the heart,
Most rich, when most his riches it impart:
Nest of young joys, schoolmaster of delight,
Teaching the mean, at once to take and give   *moderation*
10 The friendly fray, where blows both wound and heal,
The pretty death,[81] while each in other live.
Poor hope's first wealth, hostage of promised weal,   *good*
Breakfast of *Love*, but lo, lo, where she is,
Cease we to praise, now pray we for a kiss.

80

Sweet swelling lip, well mayst thou swell in pride,
Since best wits think it wit thee to admire;
Nature's praise, Virtue's stall, *Cupid's* cold fire,   *throne*
Whence words, not words, but heav'nly graces slide.
The new *Parnassus*,[82] where the Muses bide,
Sweet'ner of music, wisdom's beautifier,
Breather of life, and fast'ner of desire,
Where Beauty's blush in Honour's grain is dyed.[83]   *crimson*
Thus much my heart compelled my mouth to say,
10 But now spite of my heart my mouth will stay,   *restrain*
Loathing all lies, doubting this Flattery is:
And no spur can his resty race renew,   *stubborn immobility*
Without how far this praise is short of you,
Sweet lip, you teach my mouth with one sweet kiss.

81

O kiss, which dost those ruddy gems impart,   *red*
Or gems, or fruits of new-found *Paradise*,   *either . . . or*
Breathing all bliss and sweet'ning to the heart,
Teaching dumb lips a nobler exercise.
O kiss, which souls, even souls together ties
By links of *Love*, and only Nature's art:
How fain would I paint thee to all men's eyes,
Or of thy gifts at least shade out some part.   *sketch*
But she forbids, with blushing words, she says,
10 She builds her fame on higher seated praise:
But my heart burns, I cannot silent be.
Then, since (dear life) you fain would have me peace,
And I, mad with delight, want wit to cease,
Stop you my mouth with still still kissing me.

---

79 "Consort" here refers to a musical harmony (in which each sense has a "part"), but also to any partnership or society.
80 See Aphrodite in the gazetteer.
81 The "pretty death" is the climax of the metaphor of love as a friendly combat, but it was also a euphemism for orgasm in Early Modern England.

82 See gazetteer.
83 Sidney is here punning on "grain" as an archaic term for the color scarlet and "dying in the grain," which means to dye something permanently (or "fast," which connects to the verb in the previous line).

82

Nymph of the garden, where all beauties be:
Beauties which do in excellency pass
His who till death looked in a wat'ry glass,
Or hers whom naked the *Trojan* boy did see.[84]
Sweet garden Nymph, which keeps the Cherry tree,
Whose fruit doth far th'*Hesperian* taste surpass.[85]
Most sweet-fair, most fair-sweet, do not alas,
From coming near those Cherries banish me:
For though full of desire, empty of wit,

10   Admitted late by your best-graced grace,
I caught at one of them a hungry bit;   *bite (i.e. kiss)*
Pardon that fault, once more grant me the place,
And I do swear even by the same delight,
I will but kiss, I never more will bite.

83

Good brother *Philip*,[86] I have borne you long,
I was content you should in favour creep,
While craftily you seemed your cut to keep,   *fortune*
As though that fair soft hand did you great wrong.
I bare (with Envy) yet I bare your song,
When in her neck you did *Love* ditties peep;
Nay, more fool I, oft suffered you to sleep
In Lilies' nest where *Love's* self lies along.   *i.e. Stella's breast*
What, doth high place ambitious thoughts augment?   *rank*

10   Is sauciness reward of courtesy?
Cannot such grace your silly self content,
But you must needs with those lips billing be?
And through those lips drink Nectar from that tongue;
Leave that Sir *Phip*, lest off your neck be wrung.

Third Song

If *Orpheus*'[87] voice had force to breathe such music's love
Through pores of senseless trees, as it could make them move:
If stones good measure danced, the *Theban* walls to build,
To cadence of the tunes, which *Amphion's* lyre did yield,[88]
More cause a like effect at leastwise bringeth:
O stones, O trees, learn hearing, *Stella* singeth.

If Love might sweeten so a boy of shepherd brood,[89]
To make a Lizard dull to taste Love's dainty food:
If Eagle fierce could so in *Grecian* Maid delight,

10   As his light was her eyes, her death his endless night:
Earth gave that Love, heav'n I trow Love refineth:
O birds, O beasts, look Love, lo, *Stella* shineth.

The birds, beasts, stones and trees feel this, and feeling, *Love*:
And if the trees, nor stones stir not the same to prove,
Nor beasts, nor birds do come unto this blessed gaze,
Know, that small Love is quick, and great Love doth amaze: *lively/bewilder*

---

84 References to Narcissus and Helen of Troy's abduction by Paris
respectively (see gazetteer).
85 A reference to the golden apples of the Hesperides (see gazetteer).
86 "Philip" is the conventional Early Modern name for a sparrow, here
used for one of Stella's pets. Sidney is also referring to himself, of course.
87 See gazetteer.

88 See gazetteer.
89 This line and the three after it contain references to stories from
the Roman historian Pliny's *Natural History*: the shepherd boy Thoas
was rescued from robbers by a dragon which he had helped once; an
eagle willingly died on the funeral pyre of the Greek girl who had tamed
and fed it.

They are amazed, but you with reason armed,
O eyes, O ears of men, how are you charmed!

84

Highway, since you my chief *Parnassus*[90] be,
And that my Muse to some ears not unsweet,
Tempers her words to trampling horses' feet
More oft than to a chamber melody;
Now, blessed you, bear onward blessed me
To her, where I my heart safeliest, shall meet.
My Muse and I must you of duty greet
With thanks and wishes, wishing thankfully.
Be you still fair, honoured by public heed,   *regard*
By no encroachment wronged, nor time forgot:
Nor blamed for blood, nor shamed for sinful deed.
And that you know, I envy you no lot   *destiny*
Of highest wish, I wish you so much bliss,
Hundreds of years you *Stella*'s feet may kiss.

85

I see the house, my heart thy self contain,
Beware full sails drown not thy tott'ring barge: *unstable*
Lest joy, by Nature apt sprites to enlarge,
Thee to thy wrack beyond thy limits strain.
Nor do like Lords, whose weak confused brain,
Not 'pointing to fit folks each undercharge,[91]
While every office themselves will discharge,
With doing all, leave nothing done but pain.
But give apt servants their due place, let eyes
See Beauty's total sum summed in her face:
Let ears hear speech, which wit to wonder ties,
Let breath suck up those sweets, let arms embrace
The globe of weal, lips *Love's* indentures make: *goodness/contracts*
Thou but of all the kingly Tribute take.

Fourth Song

Only joy, now here you are,
Fit to hear and ease my care:
Let my whispering voice obtain,
Sweet reward for sharpest pain:
Take me to thee, and thee to me.
'No. no, no, no, my Dear, let be.'

Night hath closed all in her cloak,
Twinkling stars Love-thoughts provoke:
Danger hence good care doth keep,
Jealousy itself doth sleep:
Take me to thee, and thee to me:
'No, no, no, no, my Dear, let be.'

Better place no wit can find,
Cupid's yoke to loose or bind:
These sweet flowers on fine bed too,
Us in their best language woo:

---

90   See gazetteer.

91   i.e. Not delegating minor tasks to the appropriate servants.

Take me to thee, and thee to me.
'No, no, no, no, my Dear, let be.'

This small light the Moon bestows,
20 Serves thy beams but to disclose,
So to raise my hap more high;   *fate*
Fear not else, none us can spy:
Take me to thee, and thee to me.
'No, no, no, no, my Dear, let be.'

That you heard was but a Mouse,
Dumb sleep holdeth all the house:
Yet asleep, methinks they say,
Young folks, take time while you may:
Take me to thee, and thee to me.
30 'No, no, no, no, my Dear, let be.'

Niggard Time threats, if we miss   *Miser*
This large offer of our bliss,
Long stay ere he grant the same:
Sweet then, while each thing doth frame:
Take me to thee, and thee to me.
'No, no, no, no, my Dear, let be.'

Your fair mother is abed,
Candles out, and curtains spread:
She thinks you do letters write:
40 Write, but first let me indite:
Take me to thee, and thee to me.
'No, no, no, no, my Dear, let be.'

Sweet alas, why strive you thus?   *struggle*
Concord better fitteth us:
Leave to *Mars* the force of hands,
Your power in your beauty stands:
Take me to thee, and thee to me.
'No, no, no, no, my Dear, let be.'

Woe to me, and do you swear
50 Me to hate? But I forbear,
Cursed be my dest'nies all,
That brought me so high to fall:
Soon with my death I will please thee.
'No, no, no, no, my Dear, let be.'

86

Alas, whence came this change of looks? If I
Have changed desert, let mine own conscience be
A still felt plague, to self condemning me:
Let woe gripe on my heart, shame load mine eye. *grip*
But if all faith, like spotless Ermine[92] lie
Safe in my soul, which only doth to thee
(As his sole object of felicity)   *happiness*
With wings of *Love* in air of wonder fly,
O ease your hand, treat not so hard your slave:

---

92 Ermine fur is pure white, and is often used as a symbol for purity
in poetry.

10   In justice pains come not till faults do call;
    Or if I needs (sweet Judge) must torments have,
    Use something else to chasten me withal,
    Then those blest eyes, where all my hopes do dwell,
    No doom should make one's heav'n become his hell.   *judgment*

Fifth Song

    While favour fed my hope, delight with hope was brought,
    Thought waited on delight, and speech did follow thought:
    Then grew my tongue and pen records unto thy glory:
    I thought all words were lost, that were not spent of thee:
    I thought each place was dark but where thy lights would be,
    And all ears worse than deaf, that heard not out thy story.

    I said, thou wert most fair, and so indeed thou art:
    I said, thou wert most sweet, sweet poison to my heart:
    I said, my soul was thine (O that I then had lied)
10   I said, thine eyes were stars, thy breast the milk'n way,
    Thy fingers *Cupid*'s shafts, thy voice the Angels' lay: *song*
    And all I said so well, as no man it denied.

    But now that hope is lost, unkindness kills delight,
    Yet thought and speech do live, though metamorphosed quite:
    For rage now rules the reins, which guided were by Pleasure.
    I think now of thy faults, who late thought of thy praise,
    That speech falls now to blame, which did thy honour raise,
    The same key op'n can, which can lock up a treasure.

    Thou then whom partial heavens conspir'd in one to frame,
20   The proof of Beauty's worth, th'inheritrix of fame,   *female inheritor*
    The mansion seat of bliss, and just excuse of Lovers;
    See now those feathers plucked, wherewith thou flew'st most high:
    See what clouds of reproach shall dark thy honour's sky,
    Whose own fault cast him down, hardly high state recovers.   *with difficulty*

    And, O my Muse, though oft you lulled her in your lap,
    And then, a heav'nly child, gave her Ambrosian pap: *i.e. food of the gods*
    And to that brain of hers your hid'nest gifts infused,
    Since she disdaining me, doth you in me disdain:
    Suffer not her to laugh, while both we suffer pain:
30   Princes in subjects wronged, must deem themselves abused.

    Your Client poor myself, shall *Stella* handle so?
    Revenge, revenge, my Muse, Defiance' trumpet blow:
    Threat'n what may be done, yet do more than you threat'n.
    Ah, my suit granted is, I feel my breast doth swell:
    Now child, a lesson new you shall begin to spell:
    Sweet babes must babies have, but shrewd girls must be beat'n.   *dolls/naughty*

    Think now no more to hear of warm fine odoured snow,[93]
    Nor blushing Lilies, nor pearls' ruby-hidden row,
    Nor of that golden sea, whose waves in curls are brok'n:
40   But of thy soul, so fraught with such ungratefulness,   *laden down*

93 This stanza outlines Astrophil's threat to stop praising Stella's
beauty and to write about her callous "ingratitude" for not succumbing
to his desires.

As where thou soon might'st help, most faith dost most oppress,
Ungrateful who is called, the worst of evils is spok'n,

Yet worse than worst, I say thou art a thief, a thief?
Now God forbid. A thief, and of worst thieves the chief:
Thieves steal for need, and steal but goods, which pain recovers,
But thou rich in all joys, dost rob my joys from me,
Which cannot be restored by time nor industry:
Of foes the spoil is evil, far worse of constant lovers.

Yet gentle English thieves do rob, but will not slay;
50   Thou English murd'ring thief, wilt have hearts for thy prey:
The name of murd'rer now on thy fair forehead sitteth:
And even while I do speak, my death wounds bleeding be:
Which (I protest) proceed from only Cruel thee,
Who may and will not save, murder in truth committeth.

But murder, private fault, seems but a toy to thee,
I lay then to thy charge unjustest Tyranny,
If Rule by force without all claim a Tyrant showeth,
For thou dost lord my heart, who am not born thy slave,
And which is worse, makes me most guiltless torments have,
60   A rightful Prince by unright deeds a Tyrant groweth.

Lo you grow proud with this, for tyrants make folk bow:
Of foul rebellion then I do appeach thee now;   *charge*
Rebel by Nature's law, Rebel by law of Reason,
Thou, sweetest subject, wert born in the realm of Love,
And yet against thy Prince thy force dost daily prove:
No virtue merits praise, once touched with blot of Treason.

But valiant Rebels oft in fools' mouths purchase fame:
I now then stain thy white with vagabonding shame,   *wandering* (i.e. inconstant)
Both Rebel to the Son, and Vagrant from the mother;
70   For wearing *Venus'* badge, in every part of thee,
Unto *Diana's* train thou runaway didst flee:[94]
Who faileth one, is false, though trusty to another.

What, is not this enough? nay far worse cometh here;
A witch I say, thou art, though thou so fair appear;
For I protest, my sight never thy face enjoyeth,
But I in me am changed, I am alive and dead:
My feet are turned to roots, my heart becometh lead,
No witchcraft is so evil, as which man's mind destroyeth.

Yet witches may repent, thou art far worse then they,
80   Alas, that I am forced such evil of thee to say,
I say thou art a Devil, though clothed in Angel's shining:
For thy face tempts my soul to leave the heav'n for thee,
And thy words of refuse, do power even hell on me:
Who tempt, and tempted plague, are Devils in true defining.

You then ungrateful thief, you murd'ring Tyrant you,
You Rebel runaway, to Lord and Lady untrue,

94 The speaker is asserting that, although Stella provokes amorous
love by her appearance, she behaves like a devotee of Diana (i.e. one
dedicated to virginity).

You witch, you Devil, (alas) you still of me beloved,
You see what I can say; mend yet your froward mind,   *intractable*
And such skill in my Muse you reconciled shall find,
90   That all these cruel words your praises shall be proved.

Sixth Song

O you that hear this voice,
O you that see this face,
Say whether of the choice   *which*
Deserves the former place:
Fear not to judge this bate,   *contention*
For it is void of hate.

This side doth beauty take,
For that doth Music speak,
Fit orators to make
10   The strongest judgements weak:
The bar to plead their right,
Is only true delight.

Thus doth the voice and face,
These gentle Lawyers wage,
Like loving brothers' case
For father's heritage,
That each, while each contends,
Itself to other lends.

For beauty beautifies,
20   With heav'nly hue and grace,
The heav'nly harmonies;
And in this faultless face,
The perfect beauties be
A perfect harmony.

Music more loft'ly swells
In speeches nobly placed:
Beauty as far excels,
In action aptly graced: *embellished*
A friend each party draws,
30   To countenance his cause:

Love more affected seems
To beauty's lovely light,
And wonder more esteems
Of Music's wondrous might:
But both to both so bent,
As both in both are spent.

Music doth witness call
The ear, his truth to try:
Beauty brings to the hall,
40   The judgement of the eye,
Both in their objects such,
As no exceptions touch.

The common sense, which might
Be Arbiter of this,

To be forsooth, upright,
To both sides partial is:
He lays on this chief praise,
Chief praise on that he lays.

50
Then reason, Princess high,
Whose throne is in the mind,
Which Music can in sky
And hidden beauties find,
Say whether thou wilt crown,
With limitless renown?

Seventh Song

Whose senses in so evil consort, their stepdame Nature lays,　　　　　*harmony*
That ravishing delight in them most sweet tunes do not raise;
Or if they do delight therein, yet are so cloyed with wit,
As with sententious lips to set a title vain on it:
O let them hear these sacred tunes, and learn in wonder's schools,
To be (in things past bounds of wit) fools, if they be not fools.

Who have so leaden eyes, as not to see sweet beauty's show,
Or seeing, have so wooden wits, as not that worth to know;
Or knowing, have so muddy minds, as not to be in love;
10　Or loving, have so frothy thoughts, as eas'ly thence to move:　　　　*trifling*
O let them see these heav'nly beams, and in fair letters read
A lesson fit, both sight and skill, love and firm love to breed.

Hear then, but then with wonder hear; see but adoring see,
No mortal gifts, no earthly fruits, now here descended be:
See, do you see this face? a face? nay image of the skies,
Of which the two life-giving lights are figured in her eyes:　　　　*i.e. sun and moon*
Hear you this soul-invading voice, and count it but a voice?
The very essence of their tunes, when Angels do rejoice.

Eighth Song

In a grove most rich of shade,
Where birds wanton music made,
May then young his pied weeds showing,　　　　*multi-colored clothes*
New-perfumed with flowers fresh growing,

Astrophil with *Stella* sweet,
Did for mutual comfort meet,
Both within themselves oppressed,
But each in the other blessed.

Him great harms had taught much care,
10　Her fair neck a foul yoke bare,
But her sight his cares did banish,
In his sight her yoke did vanish.

Wept they had, alas, the while,
But now tears themselves did smile,
While their eyes by love directed,
Interchangeably reflected.

Sigh they did, but now betwixt
Sighs of woe were glad sighs mixed,
With arms crossed,[95] yet testifying
20   Restless rest, and living dying.

Their ears hungry of each word,
Which the dear tongue would afford,
But their tongues restrained from walking,
Till their hearts had ended talking.

But when their tongues could not speak,
Love itself did silence break;
Love did set his lips asunder,
Thus to speak in love and wonder:

'*Stella* sovereign of my joy,
30   Fair triumpher of annoy,
Stella star of heavenly fire,
Stella lodestar of desire.

'*Stella*, in whose shining eyes,
Are the lights of *Cupid*'s skies,
Whose beams, where they once are darted,
Love therewith is straight imparted.

'*Stella*, whose voice when it speaks,
Senses all asunder breaks;
Stella, whose voice when it singeth,
40   Angels to acquaintance bringeth.

'*Stella*, in whose body is
Writ each character of bliss,
Whose face all, all beauty passeth,
Save thy mind which yet surpasseth.

'Grant, O grant, but speech alas,
Fails me fearing on to pass,
Grant, O me, what am I saying?
But no fault there is in praying.

'Grant, O dear, on knees I pray,
50   (Knees on ground he then did stay)
That not I, but since I love you,
Time and place for me may move you.

'Never season was more fit,
Never room more apt for it;
Smiling air allows my reason,
These birds sing: "Now use the season."

'This small wind which so sweet is,
See how it the leaves doth kiss,
Each tree in his best attiring,
60   Sense of love to love inspiring.

95 A conventional sign of melancholy in this period.

'Love makes earth the water drink,
Love to earth makes water sink;
And if dumb things be so witty,
Shall a heavenly grace want pity?'

There his hands in their speech, fain
Would have made tongue's language plain;
But her hands his hands repelling,
Gave repulse all grace expelling.

Then she spake; her speech was such,
70   As not ears but heart did touch:
While such wise she love denied,
And yet love she signified.

'Astrophil,' said she, 'my love
Cease in these effects to prove:[96]
Now be still, yet still believe me,
Thy grief more than death would grieve me.

'If that any thought in me,
Can taste comfort but of thee,
Let me, fed with hellish anguish,
80   Joyless, hopeless, endless languish.

'If those eyes you praised, be
Half so dear as you to me,
Let me home return, stark blinded
Of those eyes, and blinder minded.

'If to secret of my heart,
I do any wish impart,
Where thou art not foremost placed,
Be both wish and I defaced.

'If more may be said, I say,
90   All my bliss in thee I lay;
If thou love, my love content thee,
For all love, all faith is meant thee.

'Trust me while I thee deny,
In myself the smart I try,   *pain/prove*
Tyrant honour doth thus use thee,
Stella's self might not refuse thee.

'Therefore, Dear, this no more move,
Lest, though I leave not thy love,
Which too deep in me is framed,
100   I should blush when thou art named.'

Therewithal away she went,
Leaving him so passion rent,
With what she had done and spoken,
That therewith my song is broken.

96   The language of this stanza clearly echoes that of the first stanza
of Marlowe's "Passionate Shepherd to his Love," although it is impossible to tell which poem came first. Both poems were widely read and
hugely influential.

Ninth Song[97]

Go my flock, go get you hence,
Seek a better place of feeding,
Where you may have some defence
From the storms in my breast breeding,
And showers from mine eyes proceeding.

Leave a wretch, in whom all woe
Can abide to keep no measure,   *boundaries*
Merry flock, such one forego,
Unto whom mirth is displeasure,
10   Only rich in mischief's treasure.

Yet alas before you go,
Hear your woeful master's story,
Which to stones I else would show:
Sorrow only then hath glory,
When 'tis excellently sorry.

Stella fiercest shepherdess,
Fiercest but yet fairest ever;
Stella whom O heav'ns do bless,
Though against me she persever,
20   Though I bliss inherit never.

Stella hath refused me,
Stella who more love hath proved,
In this caitiff heart to be,   *miserable*
Then can in good ewes he moved
Toward *Lambkins* best beloved.

Stella hath refused me,
Astrophil that so well served,
In this pleasant spring must see
While in pride flowers be preserved,   *splendor*
30   Himself only winter-starved.

Why alas doth she then swear,
That she loveth me so dearly,
Seeing me so long to bear
Coals of love that burn so clearly;
And yet leave me helpless merely?   *absolutely*

Is that love? forsooth I trow,   *believe*
If I saw my good dog grieved,
And a help for him did know,
My love should not he believed,
40   But he were by me relieved.

No, she hates me, wellaway,   *alas*
Feigning love, somewhat to please me:

---

97   This song uses the conventions of pastoral poetry, so Astrophil is represented as a heart-broken shepherd complaining to his flock and Stella becomes the shepherdess who refuses to return his love. As he states in *The Defense of Poesy*, Sidney was very interested in the pastoral as a mode of writing in which dangerous or controversial ideas could be discussed in a seemingly innocent form (see the "Ister bank" eclogue in this volume).

For she knows, if she display
All her hate, death soon would seize me,
And of hideous torments ease me.

Then adieu, dear flock adieu:
But alas, if in your straying
Heavenly *Stella* meet with you,
Tell her in your piteous blaying,   *bleating*
50   Her poor slave's unjust decaying.

87

When I was forced from *Stella* ever dear,
Stella food of my thoughts, heart of my heart,
Stella whose eyes make all my tempests clear,
By iron laws of duty to depart:
Alas I found, that she with me did smart,   *suffer*
I saw that tears did in her eyes appear;
I saw that sighs her sweetest lips did part,
And her sad words my sadded sense did hear.   *saddened*
For me, I wept to see pearls scattered so,
10   I sighed her sighs, and wailed for her woe,
Yet swam in joy, such love in her was seen.
Thus while th'effect most bitter was to me,
And nothing than the cause more sweet could be,
I had been vexed, if vexed I had not been.

88

Out traitor absence, dar'st thou counsel me,
From my dear Captainess to run away?
Because in brave array here marcheth she,   *battle array*
That to win me, oft shows a present pay?   *offers/contentment*
Is faith so weak? Or is such force in thee?
When Sun is hid, can stars such beams display?
Cannot heav'n's food, once felt, keep stomachs free
From base desire on earthly cates to pray?   *food*
Tush absence, while thy mists eclipse that light,
10   My Orphan sense flies to the inward sight,   *i.e. the mind's eye*
Where memory sets forth the beams of love.
That, where before heart loved and eyes did see,
In heart both sight and love now coupled be;
United powers make each the stronger prove.

89

Now that of absence the most irksome night,
With darkest shade doth overcome my day;
Since *Stella*'s eyes, wont to give me my day,
Leaving my Hemisphere, leave me in night,
Each day seems long, and longs for long-stayed night,
The night as tedious, woos th'approach of day;
Tired with the dusty toils of busy day,   *labors*
Languished with horrors of the silent night,
Suff'ring the evils both of day and night,
10   While no night is more dark than is my day,
Nor no day hath less quiet than my night:
With such bad mixture of my night and day,
That living thus in blackest winter night,
I feel the flames of hottest summer day.

90

Stella think not that I by verse seek fame,
Who seek, who hope, who love, who live but thee;
Thine eyes my pride, thy lips my history:
If thou praise not, all other praise is shame.
Nor so ambitious am I, as to frame
A nest for my young praise in Laurel tree:[98]
In truth I swear, I wish not there should he
Graved in mine Epitaph a Poet's name: *Engraved*
Ne if I would, could I just title make,
10   That any laud thereof to me should grow,
Without my plumes from others' wings I take.[99]
For nothing from my wit or will doth flow,
Since all my words thy beauty doth indite,   *dictate*
And love doth hold my hand, and makes me write.

91

Stella, while now by honour's cruel might,
I am from you, light of my life, misled,
And that fair you my Sun, thus overspread
With absence' Veil, I live in Sorrow's night.
If this dark place yet show like candle light,
Some beauty's piece, as amber coloured head,
Milk hands, rose cheeks, or lips more sweet, more red,
Or seeing jets, black, but in blackness bright.   *eyes*
They please I do confess, they please mine eyes,
10   But why? because of you they models be,
Models such be wood-globes of glist'ring skies.   *glittering*
Dear, therefore be not jealous over me,
If you hear that they seem my heart to move,
Not them, O no, but you in them I love.

92

Be your words made (good Sir) of Indian ware,   *i.e. exotic materials*
That you allow me them by so small rate?   *cheap price*
Or do you cutted Spartans imitate?   *curt*
Or do you mean my tender ears to spare,
That to my questions you so total are?   *brief*
When I demand of *Phoenix Stella*'s state,
You say forsooth, you left her well of late.
O God, think you that satisfies my care?
I would know whether she did sit or walk,
10   How clothed, how waited on, sighed she or smiled
Whereof, with whom, how often did she talk,
With what pastime, time's journey she beguiled,
If her lips deigned to sweeten my poor name.
Say all, and all well said, still say the same.

Tenth Song

O dear life, when shall it be,
That mine eyes thine eyes may see?
And in them thy mind discover,
Whether absence have had force

---

98   A laurel wreath was a sign of Apollo (the god of poetry) and a mark
of poetic achievement; see Daphne in the gazetteer.

99   i.e. All of his poetic accomplishments have been borrowed from
someone else (Stella, who has inspired them).

Thy remembrance to divorce,
From the image of thy lover?

Or if I myself find not,
After parting aught forgot,   *anything*
Nor debarred from beauty's treasure,
10   Let not tongue aspire to tell,
In what high joys I shall dwell,
Only thought aims at the pleasure.

Thought therefore I will send thee,
To take up the place for me:
Long I will not after tarry,
There unseen thou mayst be bold,
Those fair wonders to behold,
Which in them my hopes do carry.

Thought see thou no place forbear,
20   Enter bravely everywhere,   *boldly*
Seize on all to her belonging;
But if thou wouldst guarded be,
Fearing her beams, take with thee
Strength of liking, rage of longing.

Think of that most grateful time,
When my leaping heart will climb,
In thy lips to have his biding,
There those roses for to kiss,
Which do breathe a sugared bliss,
30   Opening rubies, pearls dividing.

Think of my most Princely power,
When I blessed shall devour,
With my greedy lickerous senses,   *lustful*
Beauty, music, sweetness, love,
While she doth against me prove   *test*
Her strong darts, but weak defences.

Think, think of those dallyings,
When with Dovelike murmurings,
With glad moaning past anguish,
40   We change eyes, and heart for heart,
Each to other do impart,
Joying till joy make us languish.

O my thought my thoughts surcease,   *cease*
Thy delights my woes increase,
My life melts with too much thinking;¹⁰⁰
Think no more but die in me,
Till thou shalt revived be,
At her lips my Nectar drinking.

93

O fate, O fault, O curse, child of my bliss,
What sobs can give words grace my grief to show?

100 The climax of Astrophil's masturbatory fantasy about Stella
is both poetic and literal: he wants her to "die" (come to orgasm)
in his mind, while he "melts" as he thinks about her.

What ink is black enough to paint my woe?
Through me, wretch me, even *Stella* vexed is.
Yet truth (if Caitiff's breath may call thee) this
Witness with me, that my foul stumbling so,
From carelessness did in no manner grow,
But wit confused with too much care did miss.
And do I then myself this vain 'scuse give?
I have (live I and know this) harmed thee,
Though worlds 'quite me, shall I myself forgive?   *Requite* or *acquit*
Only with pains my pains thus eased be,
That all thy hurts in my heart's wrack I read;
I cry thy sighs; my dear, thy tears I bleed.

94

Grief find the words, for thou hast made my brain
So dark with misty vapours, which arise
From out thy heavy mould, that inbent eyes   *bodily matter/inward-looking*
Can scarce discern the shape of mine own pain.
Do thou then (for thou canst) do thou complain,
For my poor soul, which now that sickness tries,
Which even to sense, sense of itself denies,
Though harbingers of death lodge there his train.
Or if thy love of plaint yet mine forbears,
As of a caitiff worthy so to die,
Yet wail thyself, and wail with causeful tears,
That though in wretchedness thy life doth lie,
Yet growest more wretched than thy nature bears,
By being placed in such a wretch as I.

95

Yet sighs, dear sighs, indeed true friends you are,
That do not leave your least friend at the worst,
But, as you with my breast I oft have nursed,
So grateful now you wait upon my care.
Faint coward joy no longer tarry dare,   *linger*
Seeing hope yield when this woe strake him first:
Delight protests he is for th'accursed.
Though oft himself my mate-in-arms he sware.
Nay sorrow comes with such main rage, that he   *mighty*
Kills his own children, tears, finding that they
By love were made apt to consort with me.
Only true sighs, you do not go away,
Thank may you have for such a thankful part,
Thank-worthiest yet when you shall break my heart.

96

Thought with good cause thou lik'st so well the night,
Since kind or chance gives both one livery,   *nature/appearance*
Both sadly black, both blackly darkened be,
Night barred from Sun, thou from thy own sun's light;
Silence in both displays his sullen might,
Slow heaviness in both holds one degree,
That full of doubts, thou of perplexity;
Thy tears express night's native moisture right.
In both a mazeful solitariness: *bewildering*
In night of sprites the ghastly powers stir,
In thee or sprites or sprited ghastliness:
But, but (alas) night's side the odds hath far,

For that at length yet doth invite some rest,
Thou though still tired, yet still dost it detest.

97

Dian that fain would cheer her friend the Night,   Diana (i.e. the moon)
Shows her oft at the full her fairest face,
Bringing with her those starry Nymphs, whose chase
From heav'nly standing hits each mortal wight.   shooting position/creature
But ah poor Night, in love with Phoebus' light,
And endlessly despairing of his grace,
Herself (to show no other joy hath place)
Silent and sad in mourning weeds doth dight: dress
Even so (alas) a Lady Dian's peer,
With choice delights and rarest company,
Would fain drive clouds from out my heavy cheer.
But woe is me, though joy itself were she,
She could not show my blind brain ways of joy,
While I despair my Sun's sight to enjoy.

98

Ah bed, the field where joy's peace some do see,
The field where all my thoughts to war be trained,
How is thy grace by my strange fortune stained!
How thy lee shores by my sighs stormed be!   sheltered
With sweet soft shades thou oft invitest me
To steal some rest, but wretch I am constrained,
(Spurred with love's spur, though galled, and shortly reined   chafed
With care's hard hand) to turn and toss in thee.
While the black horrors of the silent night,
Paint woe's black face so lively to my sight,
That tedious leisure marks each wrinkled line:
But when Aurora leads out Phoebus' dance,   dawn
Mine eye then only wink, for spite perchance,   close
That worms should have their Sun, and I want mine.

99

When far spent night persuades each mortal eye,
To whom nor art nor nature granteth light,
To lay his then mark wanting shafts of sight,   target lacking
Closed with their quivers in sleep's armoury;
With windows ope then most my mind doth lie,
Viewing the shape of darkness and delight,
Takes in that sad hue, which with th'inward night
Of his mazed powers keeps perfect harmony: confused
But when birds charm, and that sweet air, which is   sing
Morn's messenger, with rose enamelled skies
Calls each wight to salute the flower of bliss;
In tomb of lids then buried are mine eyes,
Forced by their Lord, who is ashamed to find
Such light in sense, with such a darkened mind.

100

O tears, no tears, but rain from beauty's skies,
Making those Lilies and those Roses grow,
Which ay most fair, now more then most fair show,
While graceful pity beauty beautifies.
O honeyed sighs, which from that breast do rise,
Whose pants do make unspilling cream to flow,

Winged with whose breath, so pleasing *Zephyrs* blow,   *soft breezes*
As can refresh the hell where my soul fries.
O plaints conserved in such a sugared phrase,   *lamentations*
That eloquence itself envies your praise,
While sobbed out words a perfect Music give.
Such tears, sighs, plaints, no sorrow is, but joy:
Or if such heavenly signs must prove annoy,
All mirth farewell, let me in sorrow live.

101

Stella is sick, and in that sick-bed lies
Sweetness, which breathes and pants as oft as she:
And grace, sick too, such fine conclusion tries,
That sickness brags itself best graced to be.
Beauty is sick, but sick in so fair guise,
That in that paleness beauty's white we see;
And joy, which is inseparate from those eyes,
Stella now learns (strange case) to weep in thee.
Love moans thy pain, and like a faithful page,
As thy looks stir, runs up and down to make
All folks pressed at thy will thy pain to suage,   *enforced/assuage*
Nature with care sweats for her darling's sake,
Knowing worlds pass, ere she enough can find
Of such heav'n stuff, to clothe so heav'nly mind.

102

Where be those Roses gone, which sweetened so our eyes?
Where those red cheeks, which oft with fair increase did frame
The height of honour in the kindly badge of shame?
Who hath the crimson weeds stol'n from my morning skies?
How doth the colour vade of those vermilion dyes,   *fade*
Which Nature's self did make, and self engrained the same?   *dyed*
I would know by what right this paleness overcame
That hue, whose force my heart still unto thraldom ties?
Galen's[101] adoptive sons, who by a beaten way
Their judgements hackney on, the fault of sickness lay,   *ride*
But feeling proof makes me say they mistake it far:
It is but love, which makes this paper perfect white
To write therein more fresh the story of delight,
While beauty's reddest ink *Venus* for him doth stir.

103

O happy Thames, that didst my *Stella* bear,
I saw thyself with many a smiling line
Upon thy cheerful face, joy's livery wear:
While those fair planets on thy streams did shine.
The boat for joy could not to dance forbear,
While wanton winds with beauties so divine
Ravished, stayed not, till in her golden hair
They did themselves (O sweetest prison) twine.
And fain those *Aeol's*[102] youths there would their stay
Have made, but forced by Nature still to fly,
First did with puffing kiss those locks display:
She so dishevelled, blushed; from window I

---

101 See gazetteer.

102 In Homer's *Odyssey*, Aeolus is the ruler of the winds; hence, his "youths" are the breezes playing with Stella's hair.

With sight thereof cried out; O fair disgrace,
Let honour's self to thee grant highest place.

104

Envious wits what hath been mine offence,
That with such poisonous care my looks you mark,
That to each word, nay sigh of mine you hark,
As grudging me my sorrow's eloquence?
Ah, is it not enough, that I am thence,
Thence, so far thence, that scantly any spark
Of comfort dare come to this dungeon dark,
Where rig'rous exile locks up all my sense?
But if I by a happy window pass,
If I but stars upon mine armour bear,
Sick, thirsty, glad (though but of empty glass:)
Your moral notes straight my hid meaning tear
From out my ribs, and puffing prove that I   *scornfully*
Do *Stella* love. Fools, who doth it deny?

Eleventh Song

'Who is it that this dark night
Underneath my window plaineth?'   *laments*
It is one who from thy sight,
Being (ah) exiled, disdaineth
Every other vulgar light.

'Why alas, and are you he?
Be not yet those fancies changed?
Dear when you find change in me,
Though from me you be estranged,
Let my change to ruin be.

'Well in absence this will die,
Leave to see, and leave to wonder.'
Absence sure will help, if I
Can learn, how myself to sunder
From what in my heart doth lie.

'But time will these thoughts remove:
Time doth work what no man knoweth.'
Time doth as the subject prove,
With time still th'affection groweth
In the faithful Turtle dove.

'What if you new beauties see,
Will they not stir new affection?'
I will think they pictures be,
(Image like of Saints' perfection)[103]
Poorly counterfeiting thee.

'But your reason's purest light,
Bids you leave such minds to nourish.'
Dear, do reason no such spite,

103   The speaker is here comparing the real virtue of a saint with
people's superstitious faith in painted images of saints.

Never doth thy beauty flourish
30   More than in my reason's sight.

'But the wrongs love bears, will make
Love at length leave undertaking.'
No, the more fools it do shake,
In a ground of so firm making,
Deeper still they drive the stake.

'Peace, I think that some give ear:
Come no more, lest I get anger.'   *angry*
Bliss, I will my bliss forbear,
Fearing (sweet) you to endanger,
40   But my soul shall harbour there.

'Well, be gone, be gone, I say,
Lest that *Argus*[104] eyes perceive you.'
O unjustest fortune's sway,
Which can make me thus to leave you,
And from louts to run away.

105

Unhappy sight, and hath she vanished by
So near, in so good time, so free a place?
Dead glass, dost thou thy object so embrace,   *mirror*
As what my heart still sees thou canst not spy?
I swear by her I love and lack, that I
Was not in fault, who bent thy dazzling race   *path*
Only unto the heav'n of *Stella*'s face,
Counting but dust what in the way did lie.
But cease mine eyes, your tears do witness well
10   That you, guiltless thereof, your Nectar missed: *divine food*
Cursed be the page from whom the bad torch fell,   *page boy*
Cursed be the night which did your strife resist,
Cursed be the Coachman that did drive so fast,
With no less curse than absence makes me taste.

106

O absent presence *Stella* is not here;
False flatt'ring hope, that with so fair a face
Bare me in hand, that in this Orphan place,   i.e. Deceived me
Stella, I say my *Stella*, should appear.
What say'st thou now, where is that dainty cheer   *expression*
Thou told'st mine eyes should help their famished case?
But thou art gone, now that self felt disgrace
Doth make me most to wish thy comfort near.
But here I do store of fair Ladies meet,
10   Who may with charm of conversation sweet,
Make in my heavy mould new thoughts to grow: *body*
Sure they prevail as much with me, as he
That bade his friend, but then new maimed, to be
Merry with him, and not think of his woe.

104 Argus was a mythical herdsman with eyes all over his body. Hera
set him to guard the nymph Io (one of Zeus's mortal mistresses). Hermes
killed him, and his eyes were set in the tail of the peacock.

107

Stella, since thou so right a Princess art
Of all the powers which life bestows on me,
That ere by them ought undertaken be,
They first resort unto that sovereign part;
Sweet, for a while give respite to my heart,
Which pants as though it still should leap to thee:
And on my thoughts give thy Lieutenancy   *delegated authority*
To this great cause, which needs both use and art,   *experience*
And as a Queen, who from her presence sends
Whom she employs, dismiss from thee my wit,
10   Till it have wrought what thy own will attends.
On servants' shame oft Master's blame doth sit;
O let not fools in me thy works reprove,
And scorning say, 'See what it is to love.'

108

When sorrow (using mine own fire's might)
Melts down his lead into my boiling breast,
Through that dark furnace to my heart oppressed,
There shines a joy from thee my only light;
But soon as thought of thee breeds my delight,
And my young soul flutters to thee his nest,
Most rude despair my daily unbidden guest,
Clips straight my wings, straight wraps me in his night,
And makes me then bow down my head, and say,
10   Ah what doth *Phoebus'* gold that wretch avail,
Whom iron doors do keep from use of day?
So strangely (alas) thy works in me prevail,
That in my woes for thee thou art my joy,
And in my joys for thee my only annoy.   *vexation*

MISCELLANEOUS POETRY

POEMS FROM THE COUNTESS OF PEMBROKE'S ARCADIA[1]

1

Poor Painters oft with silly Poets join,   *ignorant*
To fill the world with strange but vain conceits: *conceptions*
One brings the stuff, the other stamps the coin,   *raw material*
Which breeds nought else but gloses of deceits.   *misrepresentations*
    Thus Painters *Cupid* paint, thus Poets do,
    A naked god, young, blind, with arrows two.[2]

Is he a God, that ever flies the light?
Or naked he, disguis'd in all untruth?
If he be blind, how hitteth he so right?   *shoots*
10   How is he young, that tam'd old *Phoebus'* youth?[3]   *Apollo's*
    But arrows two, and tipped with gold or lead:
    Some hurt accuse a third with horny head.[4]

MISCELLANEOUS POETRY
POEMS FROM THE COUNTESS OF PEMBROKE'S ARCADIA
1   Sidney wrote two versions of this long prose romance and both
contain lengthy poetic interludes and many occasional poems inserted
into passages of prose. The speakers are usually Arcadian shepherds (or
aristocratic heroes disguised as such).

2   See Cupid in the gazetteer.
3   A reference to the god Apollo's love for the nymph Daphne. As Ovid
relates in *Metamorphoses* 1, she was transformed into a laurel tree; the
god used the laurel as his symbol from that moment on.
4   A "horned head" was the metaphorical sign of a cuckold.

No, nothing so; an old false knave he is,
By *Argus* got on *Io*, then a cow:[5]
What time for her *Juno* her *Jove* did miss,
And charge of her to *Argus* did allow.
 Mercury kill'd his false sire for this act,
 His dam a beast was pardon'd beastly fact.   *mother*

 With father's death, and mother's guilty shame,
20 With *Jove's* disdain at such a rival's seed,
The wretch compell'd a runagate became,   *vagabond*
And learn'd what ill a miser state doth breed,   *wretched*
To lie, feign, gloze, to steal, pry, and accuse,   *flatter*
 Naught in himself each other to abuse.   *Wicked*

Yet bears he still his parents' stately gifts,
A horned head, cloven foot, and thousand eyes,
Some gazing still, some winking wily shifts,   *winking at/deceits*
With long large ears where never rumour dies.
 His horned head doth seem the heaven to spite:
30 His cloven foot doth never tread aright.

Thus half a man, with man he eas'ly haunts,
Cloth'd in the shape which soonest may deceive:
Thus half a beast, each beastly vice he plants,
In those weak hearts that his advice receive.
 He prowls each place still in new colours decked,   *guises*
 Sucking one's ill, another to infect.

To narrow breasts he comes all wrapped in gain: *miserly*
To swelling hearts he shines in honour's fire:
To open eyes all beauties he doth rain;
40 Creeping to each with flattering of desire.
 But for that Love's desire most rules the eyes,
 Therein his name, there his chief triumph lies.

Millions of years this old drivel *Cupid* lives;   *rogue*
While still more wretch, more wicked he doth prove:
Till now at length that *Jove* him office gives,
(At *Juno's* suit who much did *Argus* love)
In this our world a hangman[6] for to be,
Of all those fools that will have all they see.

2[7]

Geron. Up, up *Philisides*, let sorrows go,
 Who yields to woe, doth but increase his smart.   *pain*
 Do not thy heart, to plaintfull custom bring,   *mournful*
 But let us sing, sweet tunes do passions ease,
 An old man hear, who would thy fancies raise.

Philisides: Who minds to please the mind drowned in annoys *troubles*
 With outward joys, which inly cannot sink,   *inwardly*
 As well may think with oil to cool the fire:

5 Sidney's speaker is completely rewriting conventional mythology, in which Cupid is the son of Venus and Mars.

6 The "office" Cupid is given is that of a hangman, which in Early Modern England was regarded as the most detestable possible job.

7 The speakers in this poem are "Geron," whose name means "old man", and "Philisides," whose name is obviously meant to evoke the poet's own. The precise relationship between Philisides' thoughts and the author's is still ambiguous, and it is never wise to assume that Philisides is articulating Sidney's "true" thoughts.

10   Or with desire to make such foe a friend,
      Who doth his soul to endless malice bend.

      Geron. Yet sure an end, to each thing time doth give,
      Though woes now live, at length thy woes must die.
      Then virtue try, if she can work in thee
      That which we see in many time hath wrought,
      And weakest hearts to constant temper brought.   *temperament*

      Philisides. Who ever taught a skill-less man to teach,
      Or stop a breach,[8] that never Cannon saw?
      Sweet virtue's law bars not a causeful moan   *justifiable*
      Time shall in one my life and sorrows end,
20   And me perchance your constant temper lend.

      Geron. What can amend where physic is refused?   *medicine*
      The wits abus'd with will[9] no counsel take.
      Yet for my sake discover us thy grief.   *reveal to*
      Oft comes relief when most we seem in trap.
      The stars thy state, fortune may change thy hap.   *chance*

      Philisides. If fortune's lap became my dwelling place,
      And all the stars conspired to my good,
      Still were I one, this still should be my case,
      Ruin's relic, care's web, and sorrow's food: *garment*
30   Since she fair fierce to such a state me calls,
      Whose wit the stars, whose fortune fortune thralls.[10]

      Geron. Alas what falls are fal'n unto thy mind?
      That there where thou confessed thy mischief lies
      Thy wit dost use still still more harms to find.   *still yet*
      Whom wit makes vain, or blinded with his eyes,
      What counsel can prevail, or light give light?
      Since all his force against himself he tries.   *strength*
      Then each conceit that enters in by sight,
      Is made, forsooth, a Jurate of his woes,   *sworn witness*
40   Earth, sea, air, fire, heav'n, hell, and ghastly sprite.   *spirit*
      Then cries to senseless things, which neither knows
      What aileth thee, and if they knew thy mind
      Would scorn in man (their king) such feeble shows.
      Rebel, Rebel, in golden fetters bind
      This tyrant Love; or rather do suppress
      Those rebel thoughts which are thy slaves by kind.   *nature*
      Let not a glitt'ring name thy fancy dress   *imagination*
      In painted clothes, because they call it love.
      There is no hate that can thee more oppress.
50   Begin (and half the work is done) to prove   *demonstrate*
      By raising up, upon thyself to stand.
      And think she is a she, that doth thee move.
      He water ploughs, and soweth in the sand,
      And hopes the flick'ring wind with net to hold,
      Who hath his hopes laid up in woman's hand.
      What man is he that hath his freedom sold?
      Is he a manlike man, that doth not know man

---

8 i.e. in a castle wall.
9 Sidney discusses the contrast between wit and will in *The Defense of Poesy*, note 24.

10 i.e. Whose wit is controlled by the fates, and whose destiny is controlled by Fortune.

Hath power that Sex with bridle to withhold?
A fickle Sex, and true in trust to no man,
60   A servant Sex, soon proud if they be coi'de,   *coaxed*
And to conclude thy mistress is a woman.[11]

Histor. Those words did once the Loveliest shepherd use
That erst I knew, and with most plainfull muse;   *formerly/mournful*
Yet not of women Judging as he said,
But forced with rage, his rage on them upbraid.   *compelled by desire/reproved*

Philisides. O gods, how long this old fool hath annoy'd
My wearied ears! O gods yet grant me this,
That soon the world of his false tongue be void.
O noble age who place their only bliss
70   In being heard until the hearer die
Utt'ring a serpent's mind with serpent's hiss.
Then who will hear a well-authoriz'd lie,
(And patience hath) let him go learn of him
What swarms of virtues did in his youth fly
Such hearts of brass, wise heads, and garments trim
Were in his days: which heard, one nothing hears,
If from his words the falsehood he do skim.
And herein most their folly vain appears
That since they still allege, *When they were young*:
80   It shows they fetch their wit from youthful years
Like beast for sacrifice, where save the tongue
And belly nought is left, such sure is he,
This live-dead man in this old dungeon flung.
Old houses are thrown down for new we see:
The oldest Rams are culled from the flock:
No man doth wish his horse should aged be.
The ancient oak well makes a fired block: *dried*
Old men themselves, do love young wives to choose:
Only fond youth admires a rotten stock.   *foolish/dead tree*
90   Who once a white long beard, well handle does,
(As his beard him, not he his beard did bear)
Though cradle-witted, must not honour lose.   *childish*
Oh when will men leave off to judge by hair,
And think them old, that have the oldest mind,
With virtue fraught and full of holy fear!   *stored*

Geron. If that thy face were hid, or I were blind,
I yet should know a young man speaketh now,
Such wand'ring reasons in thy speech I find.   *inappropriate*
He is a beast, that beast's use will allow
100   For proof of man, who sprung of heav'nly fire
Hath strongest soul, when most his reins do bow.[12] *loins/submit*
But fondlings fond, know not your own desire   *simpletons*
Loathe to die young, and then you must be old,
Fondly blame that to which your selves aspire.
But this light choler that doth make you bold,   *foolish anger*
Rather to wrong than unto just defence,
Is past with me, my blood is waxen cold.

11   Geron's argument against love (like most such arguments from Ovid onward) is fundamentally an anti-feminist one, grounded on the supposed innate unworthiness of women. This is part of a well-established tradition in Early Modern literature.

12   i.e. Has strongest soul when he best controls his carnal urges.

Thy words, though full of malapert offence,   *insolent*
I weigh them not, but still will thee advise
110   How thou from foolish love mayest purge thy sense.
First think they err, that think them gaily wise,
Who well can set a passion out to show:
Such sight have they that see with goggling eyes.   *unsteady*
Passion bears high when puffing wit doth blow,
But is indeed a toy, if not a toy,
True cause of evils, and cause of causeless woe.
If once thou may'st that fancy gloss destroy   *deceptive appearance*
Within thyself, thou soon wilt be ashamed
To be a player of thine own annoy.
120   Then let thy mind with better books be tamed,
Seek to espy her faults as well as praise,
And let thine eyes to other sports be framed.
In hunting fearful beasts, do spend some days,
Or catch the birds with pitfalls, or with lime,[13]
Or train the fox that trains so crafty lays.   *track/decoys*
Lie but to sleep, and in the early prime   *early morning*
Seek skill of herbs in hills, haunt brooks near night,
And try with bait how fish will bite sometime.
Go graft again, and seek to graft them right,
130   Those pleasant plants, those sweet and fruitful trees,
Which both the palate, and the eyes delight.
Cherish the hives of wisely painful Bees: *diligent*
Let special care upon thy flock be staid,
Such active mind but seldom passion sees.

Philisides. Hath any man heard what this old man said?
Truly not I, who did my thoughts engage,
Where all my pains one look of hers hath paid.

Histor. Thus may you see, how youth esteemeth age
And never hath thereof arightly deemed
140   White hot desires do reign in fancy's rage   *madness*
Till age itself do make itself esteemed.

3[14]

Reason. Thou Rebel vile, come, to thy master yield.
Passion. No, Tyrant; no: mine, mine shall be the field.
R. Can *Reason* then a Tyrant counted be?
P. If *Reason* will, that *Passions* be not free.
R. But *Reason* will, that *Reason* govern most.
P. And *Passion* will, that *Passion* rule the rost.   *roost*
R. Your will is will; but *Reason* reason is.
P. Will hath his will, when *Reason's* will doth miss.
R. Whom *Passion* leans unto his death is bent.
10   *P.* And let him die, so that he die content.
R. By nature you to *Reason* faith have sworn.
P. Not so, but fellowlike together born.
R. Who *Passion* doth ensue, lives in annoy.   *vexation*
P. Who *Passion* doth forsake, Lives void of joy.
R. *Passion* is blind, and treads an unknown trace.
P. *Reason* hath eyes to see his own ill case;

13   Lime-covered sticks were a common means to trap birds in this   14   In Sidney's text, the two parts in this debate were spoken by teams
period, and this image is a common figure for entrapment in Early   of Arcadian shepherds.
Modern literature.

R. Dare *Passions* then abide in *Reason*'s light?
P. And is not *Reason* dimm'd with *Passion*'s might?
R. O foolish thing, which glory dost destroy.
20   P. O glorious title of a foolish toy.
R. Weakness you are, dare you with our strength fight?
P. Because our weakness weakeneth all your might.
R. O sacred *Reason,* help our virtuous toils.
P. O *Passion,* pass on feeble *Reason*'s spoils.
R. We with ourselves abide a daily strife.
P. We gladly use the sweetness of our life.
R. But yet our strife sure peace in end doth breed.
P. We now have peace, your peace we do not need.
R. We are too strong: but *Reason* seeks not blood.
30   P. Who be too weak, do feign they be too good.
R. Though we cannot o'ercome, our cause is just.
P. Let us o'ercome, and let us be unjust.
R. Yet *Passion,* yield at length to *Reason*'s stroke.
P. What shall we win by taking *Reason*'s yoke?
R. The joys you have shall be made permanent.
P. But so we shall with grief learn to repent.
R. Repent indeed, but that shall be your bliss.
P. How know we that, since present joys we miss?
R. You know it not: of *Reason* therefore know it.
40   P. No *Reason* yet had ever skill to show it.
R.?. Then let us both to heavenly rules give place,
    Which *Passions* kill, and *Reason* do deface.

<h2 style="text-align:center">4¹⁵</h2>

As I my little flock on *Ister* bank   *Danube*
(A little flock; but well my pipe they couth)   *knew*
Did piping lead, the Sun already sank
Beyond our world, and ere I gat my booth   *reached/shelter*
Each thing with mantle black the night doth soothe;
    Saving the glow worm, which would courteous be
    Of that small light oft watching shepherds see.

The welkin had full niggardly enclosed   *sky/miserly*
In coffer of dim clouds his silver groats,   *coins*
10   Ycleped stars; each thing to rest disposed: *Called*
The caves were full, the mountains void of goats:
The birds' eyes closed, closed their chirping notes.
    As for the Nightingale, wood music's King,
    It *August* was, he deigned not then to sing.

Amid my sheep, though I saw nought to fear,
Yet (for I nothing saw) I feared sore;   *greatly*
Then found I which thing is a charge to bear
For for my sheep I dreaded mickle more   *much*
Than ever for myself since I was bore: *born*
20   I sat me down: for see to go ne could,   *I could not*
    And sang unto my sheep lest stray they should.

15 The speaker in this much-discussed poem is Philisides, Sidney's own textual foil. The poem itself is a beast fable which embodies Sidney's observation (made in *The Defense of Poesy*) that pastoral poetry is often used to represent politically sensitive subject matter. Here, Sidney explores the necessity of a strong aristocracy as a balance against the potential for monarchal tyranny or mob rule by the commons. The specific implications of the poem are hard to determine, however, and many scholars have commented on the poem's deliberate ambiguity about what rights subjects have to rebel against their rulers. To deflect any possible direct application to the contemporary English setting, he sets the poem on the Danube and ascribes the story to Hubert Languet, a Protestant intellectual from Burgundy whom he got to know during his travels in Europe.

The song I sang old Languet had me taught,
Languet, the shepherd best swift *Ister* knew,
For clerkly rede, and hating what is naught, *learned counsel/evil*
For faithful heart, clean hands, and mouth as true:
With his sweet skill my skill-less youth he drew,
    To have a feeling taste of him that sits
    Beyond the heaven, far more beyond your wits.

      He said, the Music best thilke powers pleas'd *those*
30   Was jump concord between our wit and will:[16] *precise*
Where highest notes to godliness are raised,
And lowest sink not down to jot of ill:
With old true tales he wont mine ears to fill, *was accustomed*
    How shepherds did of yore, how now they thrive,
    Spoiling their flock, or while 'twixt them they strive. *among themselves*

He liked me, but pitied lustful youth:
His good strong staff my slipp'ry years upbore: *unreliable*
He still hop'd well, because I loved truth;
Till forced to part, with heart and eyes even sore,
40   To worthy Coredens[17] he gave me o'er.
    But thus in oak's true shade recounted he
    Which now in night's deep shade sheep heard of me.

Such manner time there was (what time I n'ot) *know not*
When all this Earth, this dam or mould of ours,
Was only won'd with such as beasts begot: *inhabited*
Unknown as then were they that builden towers:
The cattle wild, or tame, in nature's bowers
    Might freely roam, or rest, as seemed them:
    Man was not man their dwellings in to hem.

50   The beasts had sure some beastly policy: *form of government*
For nothing can endure where order n'is. *is not*
For once the Lion by the Lamb did lie;
The fearful Hind the Leopard did kiss: *female deer*
Hurtless was Tiger's paw and Serpent's hiss.
    This think I well, the beasts with courage clad
    Like Senators a harmless empire had.[18]

At which, whether the others did repine, *complain*
(For envy harb'reth most in feeblest hearts)
Or that they all to changing did incline,
60   (As even in beasts their dams leave changing parts) *mothers*
The multitude to *Jove* a suit emparts, *imparts*
    With neighing, blaying, braying, and barking, *bleating*
    Roaring, and howling for to have a King.

A King, in language theirs they said they would: *wanted*
(For then their language was a perfect speech)
The birds likewise with chirps, and pewing could, *crying*
Cackling, and chatt'ring, that of Jove beseech.

16 See Sidney's *Defense of Poesy*, note 24.
17 "Coredens" is a stock pastoral name for a shepherd. There may be an allusion here to another real person in Sidney's life, but it remains a mystery.
18 i.e. The more powerful animals ruled the weaker ones, but not oppressively.

Only the owl still warned them not to seech   *seek*
   So hastily that which they would repent:
70   But saw they would, and he to deserts went.

Jove wisely said (for wisdom wisely says)
'O beasts, take heed what you of me desire.
Rulers will think all things made them to please,
And soon forget the swink due to their hire.   *labor*
But since you will, part of my heav'nly fire
   I will you lend; the rest your selves must give,
   That it both seen and felt may with you live'.

Full glad they were and took the naked sprite,   *spirit*
Which straight the Earth yclothed in his clay: *flesh*
80 The Lion, heart; the Ounce gave active might;   *lynx*
The Horse, good shape; the Sparrow, lust to play;
Nightingale, voice, enticing songs to say.
   Elephant gave a perfect memory:
   And Parrot, ready tongue, that to apply.

The Fox gave craft; the Dog gave flattery;
Ass, patience; the Mole, a working thought;
Eagle, high look; Wolf secret cruelty:
Monkey, sweet breath; the Cow, her fair eyes brought;
The Ermine, whitest skin, spotted with nought;
90   The sheep, mild-seeming face; climbing, the Bear;
   The Stag did give the harm-eschewing fear.

The Hare, her sleights; the Cat, his melancholy;
Ant, industry; and Coney, skill to build;   *rabbit*
Cranes, order; Storks, to be appearing holy;
Chameleon, ease to change; Duck, ease to yield;
Crocodile, tears, which might be falsely spill'd:
   Ape great thing gave, though he did mowing stand,   *grimacing*
   The instrument of instruments, the hand.

Each other beast likewise his present brings:
100 And (but they drad their Prince they oft should want)[19]
They all consented were to give him wings:
And aye more awe towards him for to plant,   *ever/reverence*
To their own work this privilege they grant,
   That from thenceforth to all eternity,
   No beast should freely speak, but only he.

Thus Man was made; thus Man their Lord became:
Who at the first, wanting, or hiding pride,
He did to beasts' best use his cunning frame;   *knowledge apply*
With water drink, herbs meat, and naked hide,
110 And fellow-like let his dominion slide;   *take its course*
   Not in his sayings saying I, but we:
   As if he meant his lordship common be.

But when his seat so rooted he had found,   *throne*
That they now skill'd not, how from him to wend;   *knew/depart*
Then 'gan in guiltless earth full many a wound,   *began*

19 i.e. but for the fact that they feared their Prince would leave them.

Iron to seek, which 'gainst itself should bend,   *turn*
To tear the bowels, that good corn should send.[20]
   But yet the common Dam none did bemoan;   i.e. the Earth
   Because (though hurt) they never heard her groan.

120   Then 'gan he factions in the beasts to breed;
Where helping weaker sort, the nobler beasts,
(As Tigers, leopards, bears, and Lions' seed)
Disdained with this, in deserts sought their rests;
Where famine ravin taught their hungry chests,   *hunting prey*
   That craftily he forced them to do ill,
   Which being done he afterwards would kill.

For murder done, which never erst was seen,   *before*
By those great beasts, as for the weakers' good,
He chose themselves his guarders for to been,
130   'Gainst those of might, of whom in fear they stood,
As horse and dog, not great, but gentle blood:[21]
   Blithe were the commons, cattle of the field,
   Tho' when they saw their foen of greatness kill'd.   *Then/foes*
But they or spent, or made of slender might,   i.e. either exhausted or
Then quickly did the meaner cattle find,
The great beams gone, the house on shoulders light:[22]   *fall*
For by and by the horse fair bits did bind:
The dog was in a collar taught his kind.   nature (i.e. as a serving beast)
   As for the gentle birds, like case might rue
140   When falcon they, and goshawk saw in mew.   *cages*

Worst fell to smallest birds, and meanest heard,   *lowliest*
Who now his own, full like his own he used.
Yet first but wool, or feathers off he tear'd:
And when they were well us'd to be abused,
For hungry throat their flesh with teeth he bruised:
   At length for glutton taste he did them kill:
   At last for sport their silly lives did spill.   *defenseless*

But yet, O man, rage not beyond thy need:
Deem it no glory to swell in tyranny.
150   Thou art of blood; joy not to make things bleed:
Thou fearest death; think they are loath to die.
A plaint of guiltless hurt doth pierce the sky.   *cry*
   And you poor beasts, in patience bide your hell,
   Or know your strengths, and then you shall do well.

Thus did I sing, and pipe eight sullen hours   *slow-passing*
To sheep, whom love, not knowledge, made to hear,
Now fancy's fits, now fortune's baleful stours: *storms*
But then I homeward call'd my lambkins dear:
For to my dimmed eyes began t'appear
160   The night grown old, her black head waxen grey,
   Sure shepherd's sign, that morn would soon fetch day.

---

20 The image of farming and mining as rending of the earth's "flesh" is very common in classical writers. It is almost always associated with the end of mankind's innocence and the beginning of life in conflict with nature.

21 Sidney here and elsewhere in the poem imposes an Early Modern social structure onto the animals. Dogs and horses are "gentle" (that is, of gentle birth), but not "great" or noble, like the tigers, leopards, and so forth. The representation of the common people as cattle was very common in this period.

22 Earlier editors have usually read this line as a metaphor for the burdens of the state on the common people when there is no strong aristocracy.

5[23]

Strephon. Ye Goat-herd Gods, that love the grassy mountains,
    Ye Nymphs[24] which haunt the springs in pleasant valleys,
    Ye Satyrs[25] joyed with free and quiet forests,
    Vouchsafe your silent ears to plaining music,   *mournful*
    Which to my woes gives still an early morning:
    And draws the dolour on till weary evening.

Klaius. O *Mercury,* foregoer to the evening,
    O heavenly huntress of the savage mountains,
    O lovely star, entitled of the morning,[26]
10   While that my voice doth fill these woeful valleys,
    Vouchsafe your silent ears to plaining music,   *Condescend*
    Which oft hath Echo tir'd in secret forests.

Strephon. I that was once free-burgess of the forests,   *citizen*
    Where shade from Sun, and sport I sought in evening,
    I that was once esteem'd for pleasant music,
    Am banished now among the monstrous mountains
    Of huge despair, and foul affliction's valleys,
    Am grown a screech-owl[27] to myself each morning.

Klaius. I that was once delighted every morning,
20   Hunting the wild inhabiters of forests,
    I that was once the music of these valleys,
    So darkened am, that all my day is evening,
    Heart-broken so, that molehills seem high mountains,
    And fill the vales with cries in stead of music.

Strephon. Long since alas, my deadly Swannish music[28]
    Hath made itself a crier of the morning,
    And hath with wailing strength clim'd highest mountains:
    Long since my thoughts more desert be than forests:[29]
    Long since I see my joys come to their evening,
30   And state thrown down to over-trodden valleys.   *high rank*

Klaius. Long since the happy dwellers of these valleys,
    Have prayed me leave my strange exclaiming music,
    Which troubles their day's work, and joys of evening:
    Long since I hate the night, more hate the morning:
    Long since my thoughts chase me like beasts in forests,
    And make me wish myself laid under mountains.

Strephon. Meseems I see the high and stately mountains,
    Transform themselves to low dejected valleys:
    Me seems I hear in these ill-changed forests,
40   The Nightingales do learn of Owls their music:

---

23   The two speakers in this poem are shepherds who are both in love
with the same unattainable woman.
24   In mythology and pastoral poetry, the term "nymph" refers to a
diverse category of minor female divinities. They are usually represented
as attendants of a given place (i.e. a grove, cave, or river) and often
interact with mortals.
25   See gazetteer.
26   Klaius here invokes the planet Mercury, the moon (as Diana, the
huntress goddess), and the planet Venus, which is known as the morning
star.

27   In *Metamorphoses* 5, Ovid tells the story of Ascalaphus, who is
turned into a screech owl as punishment for being an informer. This
species of bird was associated with omens of disaster in literature ever
after.
28   In Early Modern England, swans were believed to sing only at
the point of their deaths (hence the expression "swan song" for a final
performance).
29   In this period, the word "desert" applied to any uninhabited
region, regardless of its climate or topography.

Me seems I feel the comfort of the morning
Turn'd to the mortal serene of an evening,   *noxious fog*

Klaius. Meseems I see a filthy cloudy evening;
As soon as Sun begins to climb the mountains:
Meseems I feel a noisome scent, the morning
When I do smell the flowers of these valleys:
Meseems I hear, when I do hear sweet music,
The dreadful cries of murdered men in forests.

Strephon. I wish to fire the trees of all these forests;
50   I give the Sun a last farewell each evening;
I curse the fiddling finders out of Music:
With envy I do hate the lofty mountains;
And with despite despise the humble valleys:
I do detest night, evening, day, and morning.

Klaius. Curse to myself my prayer is, the morning:
My fire is more, than can be made with forests;
My state more base, than are the basest valleys:
I wish no evenings more to see, each evening;
Shamed I hate myself in sight of mountains,
60   And stop mine ears, lest I grow mad with Music.

Strephon. For she, whose parts maintained a perfect music,[30]
Whose beauties shin'd more than the blushing morning,
Who much did pass in state the stately mountains,   *grandeur*
In straightness past the Cedars of the forests,
Hath cast me, wretch, into eternal evening,
By taking her two Suns from these dark valleys.

Klaius. For she, with whom compar'd, the Alps are valleys,
She, whose least word brings from the spheres their music,
At whose approach the Sun rase in the evening,   *rose*
70   Who, where she went, bare in her forehead morning,
Is gone, is gone from these our spoiled forests,
Turning to deserts our best pastur'd mountains.

Strephon. These mountains witness shall, so shall these valleys,
Klaius. These forests eke, made wretched by our music,
Both. Our morning hymn this is, and song at evening.

Sonnets

I

Thou blind man's mark, thou fool's self chosen snare,   *target*
Fond fancy's scum, and dregs of scattered thought,   *dross*
Band of all evils, cradle of causeless care,
Thou web of will, whose end is never wrought;

Desire, desire I have too dearly bought,
With price of mangled mind thy worthless ware,
Too long, too long asleep thou hast me brought,
Who should my mind to higher things prepare.

---

30   i.e. She, who is always perfectly in harmony with herself and her
surroundings.

But yet in vain thou hast my ruin sought,
In vain thou madest me to vain things aspire,
In vain thou kindlest all thy smoky fire;

For virtue hath this better lesson taught,
Within myself to seek my only hire: *reward*
Desiring nought but how to kill desire.

2

Leave me O Love, which reachest but to dust,
And thou my mind aspire to higher things:
Grow rich in that which never taketh rust:
What ever fades, but fading pleasure brings.

Draw in thy beams, and humble all thy might,
To that sweet yoke, where lasting freedoms be:[31]
Which breaks the clouds and opens forth the light,
That doth both shine and give us sight to see.

O take fast hold, let that light be thy guide,
In this small course which birth draws out to death,
And think how evil becometh him to slide,
Who seeketh heav'n, and comes of heav'nly breath.
   Then farewell world, thy uttermost I see,   *farthest limit*
   Eternal Love maintain thy life in me.

Splendidis longum valedico nugis.[32]

[FROM] THE PSALMS OF DAVID[33]

Psalm 22

Deus Deus meus

My God my God why hast Thou me forsaken?
   Woe me, from me why is Thy presence taken?
   So far from seeing mine unhealthful eyes,
   So far from hearing to my roaring cries.
O God my God I cry while day appeareth;
   But God Thy ear my crying never heareth.
   O God the night is privy to my plaint,
   Yet to my plaint Thou hast not audience lent.
But Thou art Holy and dost hold Thy dwelling
   Where Israel Thy lauds is ever telling;   *praises*
Our Fathers still in thee their trust did bear,   *ever*
   They trusted and by Thee deliver'd were.
They were set free when they upon Thee called,
   They hop'd on Thee, and they were not appalled.   *dismayed*

---

31 The "sweet yoke" in question is the discipline required to turn
from carnal love to the love of God.
32 "I bid a long farewell to glittering vanities."
33 Sidney's psalm settings were edited and extensively added to by
his sister, the Countess of Pembroke; for more of them, see her entry in
this anthology. For Psalms 22 and 30 below, the unindented lines indicate the beginnings of a verse in the scriptural original. In Psalm 23,
the first three tercets represent distinct verses; after that, each verse
occupies exactly two tercets. The range of verse forms Sidney employed
in his settings is also represented in the three very different forms
employed here.

But I a worm, not I of mankind am,
    Nay shame of men, the people's scorning game.
The lookers now at me poor wretch be mocking,
    With mows and nods they stand about me flocking.   *mocking gestures*
Let God help him (say they) whom he did trust;
20   Let God save him, in whom was all his lust.   *pleasure*
And yet ev'n from the womb thyself didst take me;
    At mother's breasts, thou didst good hope betake me.
No sooner my child eyes could look abroad,
    Than I was giv'n to Thee, Thou wert my God.
O be not far, since pain so nearly presseth,
    And since there is not One, who it redresseth.
I am enclosed with young Bulls' madded rout,   *herd*
    Nay Basan mighty Bulls[34] close me about.
With gaping mouths, these folks on me have charged,
30   Like lions fierce, with roaring jaws enlarged.
On me all this, who do like water slide;
    Whose loosed bones quite out of joint be wried;   *twisted*
    Whose heart with these huge flames, like wax o'er heated,
    Doth melt away though it be inmost seated.
My moistening strength is like a potsherd dried,
    My cleaving tongue close to my roof doth bide.
    And now am brought, alas, brought by Thy power
    Unto the dust of my death's running hour;
For bawling dogs have compassed me about,
40   Yea worse than dogs, a naughty wicked rout.
    My humble hands, my fainting feet they pierced;
They look, they gaze, my bones might be rehearsed;   *counted*
Of my poor weeds they do partition make
    And do cast lots, who should my vesture take.   *clothes*
But be not far O Lord, my strength, my comfort;
    Hasten to help me, in this deep discomfort.
Ah! from the sword yet save my vital sprite,   *spirit*
    My desolated life from dogged might.   *malicious*
From lion's mouth O help, and show to hear me
50   By aiding when fierce unicorns come near me.
To Brethren then I will declare Thy Fame,
    And with these Words, when they meet, praise Thy Name.
Who fear the lord all praise and glory bear him;
    You Israel's seed, you come of Jacob, fear him.
For he hath not abhorred nor yet disdain'd
    The silly wretch with foul affliction stain'd,   *helpless*
    Nor hid from him his face's fair appearing;
    But when he call'd this lord did give him hearing.
In congregation great I will praise Thee,
60   Who fear Thee shall my vows performed see.   *Those who*
Th' afflicted then shall eat, and be well pleased,
    And God shall be by those his seekers praised.
    Indeed O you, you that be such of mind,
    You shall the life that ever liveth find.
But what? I say from earth's remotest border
    Unto due thoughts mankind his thoughts shall order,
    And turn to God, and all the Nations be
    Made worshippers before Almighty Thee.

34   Basan (or "Bashan") refers to the country east of the River Jordan
in the Hebrew Bible. The fierce strength of its cattle is used proverbially several times in the scriptures.

And reason, since the Crown to God pertaineth,
　　And that by right upon all Realms he reigneth.
They that be made even fat, with earth's fat good,　　　　　　*rich/fertile*
　　Shall feed and laud the giver of their food.
To him shall kneel who to the dust be stricken,
　　Even he whose life no help of man can quicken.　　　　　　*enliven*
As they so theirs, Him shall their offspring serve,
　　And God shall them in his own court reserve.
They shall to children's children make notorious　　　　　　*widely known*
　　His righteousness, and this his doing glorious.

Psalm 23

Dominus regit me

The lord the lord my shepherd is,
　　And so can never I
　　　Taste misery.
He rests me in green pasture his.
　　By waters still and sweet
　　　He guides my feet.
He me revives, leads me the way
　　Which righteousness doth take,
　　　For his name's sake.
Yea tho' I should through valleys stray
　　Of death's dark shade I will
　　　No whit fear ill.
For thou Dear lord Thou me beset'st,　　　　　　*cover*
　　Thy rod and Thy staff be
　　　To comfort me.
Before me Thou a table set'st,
　　Ev'n when foe's envious eye
　　　Doth it espy.
With oil Thou dost anoint my head,
　　And so my cup dost fill
　　　That it doth spill.
Thus thus shall all my days be fed,
　　This mercy is so sure
　　　It shall endure,
And long yea long abide I shall,
　　There where the Lord of all
　　　Doth hold his hall.

Psalm 30

Exaltabo te Domine

O Lord Thou hast exalted me
　　And sav'd me from foes' laughing scorn;
I owe Thee praise, I will praise Thee.
For when my heart with woes was torn,
　　In Cries to Thee I showed my Cause
And was from evil by Thee upborn,

Yea from the grave's most hungry jaws;
   Thou would'st not set me on their score
   Whom Death to his cold bosom draws.
10   Praise, Praise this lord then evermore
   Ye saints of his, rememb'ring still
   With thanks his Holiness therefore;
For quickly ends his wrathful Will,
   But his dear favour where it lies
   From age to age life joys doth fill.
Well may the Evening clothe the eyes
   In clouds of tears, but soon as sun
   Doth rise again, new joys shall rise.
For proof, while I my race did run
20   Full of success, fond I did say   *foolish*
   That I should never be undone,
For then my Hill Good God did stay;[35]
   But, ah he strait his face did hide,
   And what was I but wretched clay?
Then thus to Thee I praying cried:
   What serves alas the blood of me
   When I within the pit do bide;
Shall ever dust give thanks to Thee,
   Or shall Thy Truth on mankind laid
30   In deadly dust declared be?
Lord hear, let mercy thine be staid   *fixed*
   On me, from me help this annoy.
   Thus much I said, this being said
Lo I that wailed, now dance for joy.
   Thou didst ungird my doleful sack[36]   *take off*
   And madest me gladsome weeds enjoy,   *clothes*
Therefore my tongue shall never lack
   Thy endless praise: O God my King
   I will thee thanks for ever sing.

Thomas Harriot (1560–1621) and John White (1540?–1590)

Thomas Harriot's *A briefe and true report of the new found land of Virginia* (1590), which includes magnificent drawings by John White, is one of the most important early records of European impressions of the New World. In 1578 Sir Walter Raleigh inherited from Sir Humphrey Gilbert, his half-brother, a patent authorizing him to exploit land in North America that is now Virginia and North Carolina. One of the first results of this arrangement was an expedition, conducted in 1584, in which it is possible that John White took part. The Island of Roanoke was established as the base of English exploration. Following the explorers' return to England later that year, a second expedition was organized. The plans for that 1585 expedition included roles for Thomas Harriot, as navigator and resident scientist, and John White, as cartographer and ethnographer. Sir Richard Grenville commanded a squadron of seven ships, which included a complement of 600 men. Although Raleigh supervised the organization of the expedition in England, he did not set sail with the fleet when it left from Plymouth on April 9th. In fact Raleigh never visited Virginia himself. In 1587 John White became the governor of the Roanoke colony. His drawings are a unique blend of his own eyewitness experience and the influence of drawings of American Indians by Jacques Le Moyne de Morgues,

---

35   The Authorized Version has "Lord, by thy favour thou hast made my mountain to stand strong."

36   i.e. sackcloth, the traditional garb of the penitent.

a French Huguenot artist. The drawings of Le Moyne and White were both published by Theodor de Bry. In 1588, while White was in England to appeal to Raleigh for more support for the colony, it was entirely destroyed and the colonists presumably killed. In a letter to Richard Hakluyt, written in 1593 from his house in Ireland, White referred to his last voyage to Virginia as "no less unfortunately ended then frowardly begun, and as lucklesse to many, as sinister to my selfe."

Only the briefest outline of Thomas Harriot's life is still traceable. His achievements are mainly known through his papers, which are in the British Library and Sion House. One of his publications in 1631 made important contributions to algebra. His observations with the tele-

scope occurred at the same time as Galileo's, including his discovery of sun spots (in 1607) and comets (in 1618). Although he and John White obviously superimposed their European ideas on the natural and cultural life of the New World, their delight and fascination with what they witnessed are also evident in their testimony.

READING

Paul Hulton (ed.), *America 1585: The Complete Drawings of John White*.
D. B. Quinn (ed.), *The Roanoke Voyages 1584–1590*.

M. P.

A BRIEFE AND TRUE REPORT OF THE NEW FOUND LAND OF VIRGINIA

The arriual of the Englifhemen in Virginia

The fea coafts of Virginia arre full of Ilāds, wehr by the entrance into the mayne lād is hard to finde. For although they bee feparated with diuers and fundrie large Diuifion, which feeme to yeeld conuenient entrance, yet to our great perill we proued that they wear fhallowe, and full of danger-ous flatts, and could neuer perce opp into the mayne lād, vntill wee made trialls in many places with or fmall pinnefl. At lengthe wee fownd an entrance vppon our mens diligent ferche therof. Afffter that wee had paffed opp, and fayled therin for afhort fpace we difcouered a migthye riuer fallnige downe in to the fownde ouer againft thofe Ilands, which neuerthelefs wee could not faile opp any thinge far by Reafon of the fhallewnes, the mouth ther of beinge annoyed with fands driuen in with the tyde therfore faylinge further, wee came vnto a Good bigg yland, the Inhabitante therof as foone as they faw vs began to make a great an horrible crye, as people which meuer befoer had feene men apparelled like vs, and camme a way makinge out crys like wild beafts or men out of their wyts. But beenge gentlye called backe, wee offred thē of our wares, as glaffes, kniues, babies, and other trifles, which wee thougt they deligted in. Soe they ftood ftill, and perceuinge our Good will and courtefie came fawninge vppon vs, and bade us welcome. Then they brougt vs to their village in the iland called, Roanoac, and vnto their Weroans or Prince, which entertained vs with Reafonable curtefie, althoug the wear amafed at the firft fight of vs. Suche was our arriuall into the parte of the world, which we call Virginia, the ftature of bodee of wich people, theyr attire, and maneer of lyuinge, their feafts, and banketts, I will particullerlye declare vnto yow.

A weroan or Great Lorde of Virginia

The Princes of Virginia are attyred in fuche manner as is exprefſed in this figure. They weare the haire of their heades long and bynde opp the ende of the fame in a knot vnder thier eares. Yet they cutt the topp of their heades from the forehead to the nape of the necke in manner of a cokfcombe, ftirkinge a faier loge pecher of fome berd att the Begininge of the crefte vppun their foreheads, and another fhort one on bothe feides about their eares. They hange at their eares ether thicke pearles, or fomwhat els, as the clawe of fome great birde, as cometh in to their fanfye. More-ouer They ether pownes, or paynt their forehead, cheeks, chynne, bodye, armes, and leggs, yet in another forte then the inhabitantz of Florida. They weare a chaine about their necks of pearles or beades of copper, wich they muche efteeme, and ther of wear they alfo brafelets ohn their armes. Vnder their brefts about their bellyes appeir certayne fpotts, whear they vfe to lett them felues bloode, when they are ficke. They hange before thē the fkinne of fome beafte verye feinelye dreffet in fuche forte, that the tayle hangeth downe behynde. They carye a quiuer made of fmall rufhes holding their bowe readie bent in on hand, and an arrowe in the other, radie to defend themfelues. In this manner they goe to warr, or tho their folemne feafts and banquetts. They take muche pleafure in huntinge of deer wher of ther is great ftore in the contrye, for yt is fruitfull, pleafant, and full of Goodly woods. Yt hathe alfo ftore of riuers full of diuers forts of fifhe. When they go to battel they paynt their bodyes in the moft terible manner that thei can deuife.

The woemẽ of Secotam are of Reaſonable good proportion. In their goinge they carrye their hãds danglinge downe, and air dadil in a deer skinne verye excellẽtlye wel dreſſed, hanginge downe frõ their nauell vnto the mydds of their thighes, which alſo couereth their hynder partz. The reſte of their bodies are all bare. The forr parte of their haire is cutt ſhorte, the reſt is not ouer Longe, thinne, and ſofte, and falling downe about their ſhoulders: They weare a Wrrath about their heads. Their foreheads, cheeks, chynne, armes and leggs are pownced. About their necks they wear a chaine, ether pricked or paynted. They haue ſmall eyes, plaine and flatt noſes, narrow foreheads, and broade mowths. For the moſt parte they hange at their eares chaynes of longe Pearles, and of ſome ſmootht bones. Yet their nayles are not longe, as the woemen of Florida. They are alſo deligtted with walkinge in to the fields, and beſides the riuers, to ſee the huntinge of deers and catchinge of fiſche.

The Priefts of the aforefaid Towne of Secota are well ftricken in yeers, and as yt feemeth of more experience then the common forte. They weare their heare cutt like a crefte, on the topps of thier heades as other doe, but the reft are cutt shorte, fauinge thofe which growe aboue their foreheads in manner of a perriwigge. They alfo haue fomwhat hanginge in their ears. They weare a shorte clocke made of fine hares skinnes quilted with the hayre outwarde. The reft of thier bodie is naked. They are notable enchaunters, and for their pleafure they frequent the riuers, to kill with their bowes, and catche wilde ducks, fwannes, and other fowles.

Virgins of good parentage are apparelled altogether like the woemen of Secota aboue men-
tionned, fauing that they weare hanginge abowt their necks in fteede of a chaine certaine thicke,
and rownde pearles, with little beades of copper, or polished bones betweene them. They pounce
their foreheads, cheeckes, armes and legs. Their haire is cutt with two ridges aboue their foreheads,
the reft is trufsed opp on a knott behinde, they haue broade mowthes, reafonable fair black eyes:
they lay their hands often vppon their Shoulders, and couer their brefts in token of maydenlike
modeftye. The reft of their bodyes are naked, as in the picture is to bee feene. They deligt alfo in
feeinge fishe taken in the riuers.

Sir Francis Bacon (1561–1626)

Bacon's life and writings testify to his desire to be both a statesman and an intellectual. Born the last son of Sir Nicholas Bacon, a courtier to both Henry VIII and Elizabeth I, he prepared to follow in his father's footsteps by attending Cambridge University and serving the English ambassador to France (where he continued to study). His father's early death left him without money or a secure position, however, so he was forced to take up the law, a profession at which he excelled. In a famous letter to his uncle Lord Burghley, he asks for his help in obtaining a position at court ("some middle place . . . to serve Her Majesty") and also declares that he has "taken all knowledge to be my province" in his philosophical projects. After damaging his chances of preferment under Elizabeth I by speaking against a tax subsidy in Parliament, he rose rapidly under James I. For the three-year period between 1618 and 1621, he was at the pinnacle of both the political and philosophical worlds, being Lord Chancellor to James I, a newly created peer (Baron Verulam), and the published author of *Instauratio Magna* (*Great Instauration*), i.e. renewal or restoration, an ambitious attempt to completely reform the practice of the natural sciences. His intellectual goals echo this worldly orientation, and his critiques of medieval and humanist intellectual methods consistently reject the acquisition of knowledge for its own sake. In *The Advancement of Learning* (1605), he explores the errors and prejudices that are hindering knowledge and asserts: "But this is that which will indeed dignify and exalt knowledge, if contemplation and action may be more nearly and straitly conjoined and united together." Knowledge was to be made useful to man, even as it was freed from the biases with which human desires had infected it. The political contacts that made him also caused his ruin in 1621, when he was found guilty of accepting bribes during his service as a judge. Although technically guilty of a few of the charges, he never deliberately perverted justice and his fall was really intended to embarrass James and his widely hated favorite, the Duke of Buckingham. Bacon spent his remaining years researching and writing at his country house.

His subsequent reputation has varied widely, with later commentators tending to overemphasize either the scientific or the political importance of his work; very few are comfortable with both. To some, he is a pioneer of the scientific method of induction and one of the first truly modern thinkers. To the great Victorian essayist Thomas Babington Macaulay, on the other hand, he was a Judas who turned on the Earl of Essex after the latter's strenuous attempts to promote him. Looking back from the twenty-first century, now that quantum mechanics, relativity, Heisenberg's Uncertainty Principle, and chaos theory have begun to upset science's claims to produce stable truth, it no longer seems so necessary to separate Bacon's quest for scientific certainty from the sometimes unpleasant contingencies of his political life. It is certainly true that his non-scientific writings have had a much wider readership and influence.

Bacon's writings are voluminous and wide-ranging. He brought the essay form into English (inspired by the *Essais* of the French skeptical thinker Montaigne) and produced three successively revised and expanded editions of his own *Essays* in his lifetime. *The Advancement of Learning* is a manifesto for the state-sponsored reform of all scientific endeavor and a superb dissection of the limits of science (or "natural philosophy") as it existed in Bacon's day. The themes of the *Advancement* are also treated in *New Atlantis*, a utopian fable which contained a model for a college devoted to scientific investigations. The *Instauratio Magna* confirms his critique of established science and offers an inductive method of proceeding from experimental observation (the *New Organon*) in its stead. He also wrote a history of King Henry VII, several legal works, *De sapientia veterum* (*Of the Wisdom of the Ancients*, an allegorical interpretation of some classical myths), several masques, a translation of the psalms, and many other works. It is impossible to summarize or condense this prodigious variety, and the selection below aims only to offer examples of his unsystematic thought (the *Essays*), his narrative works (the *New Atlantis*), and his scientific work (a selection from the *New Organon*).

Reading

Lisa Jardine and Andrew Stewart, *Hostage to Fortune: the Troubled Life of Francis Bacon*.

M. Peltonen (ed.), *The Cambridge Companion to Bacon*.

P. Urbach, *Francis Bacon's Philosophy of Science: an Account and a Reappraisal*.

P. Zagorin, *Francis Bacon*.

J. H.

[FROM] BOOK ONE OF THE NOVUM ORGANUM[1]

18. The discoveries which have hitherto been made in the sciences are such as lie close to vulgar[2] notions, scarcely beneath the surface. In order to penetrate into the inner and further recesses of nature, it is necessary that both notions and axioms be derived from things by a more sure and guarded way; and that a method of intellectual operation be introduced altogether better and more certain.

19. There are and can be only two ways of searching into and discovering truth. The one flies from the senses and particulars to the most general axioms,[3] and from these principles, the truth of which it takes for settled and immovable, proceeds to judgment and to the discovery of middle[4] axioms. And this way is now in fashion. The other derives axioms from the senses and particulars, rising by a gradual and unbroken ascent, so that it arrives at the most general axioms last of all. This is the true way, but as yet untried.

21. The understanding left to itself, in a sober, patient and grave mind, especially if it be not hindered by received doctrines, tries a little that other way, which is the right one, but with little progress; since the understanding, unless directed and assisted, is a thing unequal, and quite unfit to contend with the obscurity of things.[5]

31. It is idle to expect any great advancement in science from the superinducing[6] and engrafting of new things upon old. We must begin anew from the very foundations, unless we would revolve for ever in a circle with mean and contemptible progress.

32. The honour of the ancient authors,[7] and indeed of all, remains untouched; since the comparison I challenge is not of wits or faculties, but of ways and methods, and the part I take upon myself is not that of a judge, but of a guide.

33. This must be plainly avowed: no judgment can be rightly formed either of my method or of the discoveries to which it leads, by means of anticipations[8] (that is to say, of the reasoning which is now in use); since I cannot be called on to abide by the sentence of tribunal which is itself on its trial.

39. There are four classes of Idols[9] which beset men's minds. To these for distinction's sake I have assigned names, – calling the first class *Idols of the Tribe*; the second, *Idols of the Cave*; the third, *Idols of the Marketplace*; the fourth, *Idols of the Theatre*.

40. The formation of ideas and axioms by true induction[10] is no doubt the proper remedy to be applied for the keeping off and clearing away of idols. To point them out, however, is of great use; for the doctrine of Idols is to the Interpretation of Nature what the doctrine of the refutation of Sophisms[11] is to common Logic.

[FROM] BOOK ONE OF THE NOVUM ORGANUM

1 The title means "New Organon" and refers to Aristotle's term for a system of rules for scientific investigations.

2 *widely known.*

3 *empirical laws.*

4 *intermediate.*

5 Unlike many humanists, Bacon placed no great faith in the powers of the human mind to perceive or understand the world around it correctly.

6 *introducing.*

7 One of the most important themes of this text, and Bacon's work in general, is the danger of respecting ancient authorities (such as Aristotle) too much. The extent to which received authorities should be venerated or contravened was one of the crucial intellectual issues of the Early Modern period, and Bacon's position placed him (as he acknowledges) in the role of a reformer.

8 *preconceptions.*

9 *fallacies.*

10 i.e. the act of inferring general laws from observing specific instances.

11 i.e. specious or fallacious arguments.

41.   The Idols of the Tribe have their foundation in human nature itself, and in the tribe or race of men. For it is a false assertion that the sense of man is the measure of things.[12] On the contrary, all perceptions as well of the sense as of the mind are according to the measure of the individual and not according to the measure of the universe. And the human understanding is like a false mirror, which, receiving rays irregularly, distorts and discolours the nature of things by mingling its own nature with it.

42.   The Idols of the Cave[13] are the idols of the individual man. For every one (besides the errors common to human nature in general) has a cave or den of his own, which refracts and discolours the light of nature; owing either to his own proper and peculiar nature; or to his education and conversation with others; or to the reading of books, and the authority of those whom he esteems and admires; or to the differences of impressions, accordingly as they take place in a mind preoccupied and predisposed or in a mind indifferent[14] and settled; or the like. So that the spirit of man (according as it is meted out to different individuals) is in fact a thing variable and full of perturbation, and governed as it were by chance. Whence it was well observed by Heraclitus[15] that men look for sciences in their own lesser worlds, and not in the greater or common world.

43.   There are also Idols formed by the intercourse and association of men with each other, which I call Idols of the Marketplace, on account of the commerce and consort of men there. For it is by discourse that men associate; and words are imposed according to the apprehension of the vulgar. And therefore the ill and unfit choice of words wonderfully obstructs the understanding. Nor do the definitions or explanations wherewith in some things learned men are wont[16] to guard and defend themselves, by any means set the matter right. But words plainly force and overrule the understanding, and throw all into confusion, and lead men away into numberless empty controversies and idle fancies.[17]

44.   Lastly, there are Idols which have immigrated into men's minds from the various dogmas of philosophies, and also from wrong laws of demonstration. These I call Idols of the Theatre; because in my judgment all the received systems are but so many stage plays, representing worlds of their own creation after an unreal and scenic fashion. Nor is it only of the systems now in vogue, or only of the ancient sects and philosophies, that I speak; for many more plays of the same kind may yet be composed and in like artificial manner set forth; seeing that errors the most widely different have nevertheless causes for the most part alike. Neither again do I mean this only of entire systems, but also of many principles and axioms in science, which by tradition, credulity, and negligence have come to be received.

But of these several kinds of Idols I must speak more largely and exactly, that the understanding may be duly cautioned.

59.   But the Idols of the Market-place are the most troublesome of all: idols which have crept into the understanding through the alliances of words and names. For men believe that their reason governs words; but it is also true that words react on the understanding; and this it is that has rendered philosophy and the sciences sophistical[18] and inactive. Now words, being commonly framed and applied according to the capacity of the vulgar, follow those lines of division which are most obvious to the vulgar understanding. And whenever an understanding of greater acuteness or a

---

12   Bacon is here alluding to the famous assertion that "man is the measure of all things" that was attributed to Protagoras the Sophist (c.485–415 BCE) in Plato's *Theaetetus*.

13   Bacon here refers to the famous parable of the cave in Plato's *Republic* 7.514–17. In Plato's text, human beings are deluded by phantasms projected on a cave wall, preferring them to the real world outside the cave.

14   *impartial*.

15   Heraclitus of Ephesus (c.540–c.480 BCE) was a Greek philosopher who believed that it was impossible to obtain true knowledge based on observation of appearances.

16   *accustomed*.

17   *whims*.

18   i.e. self-regarding and uninterested in the truths of nature. Opponents of the ancient Greek sophists, a school of philosophers and teachers who taught students for payment, often derided them for being more interested in modes of argumentation than the quest for truth.

more diligent observation would alter those lines to suit the true divisions of nature, words stand in the way and resist the change. Whence it comes to pass that the high and formal discussions of learned men end oftentimes in disputes about words and names; with which (according to the use[19] and wisdom of the mathematicians) it would be more prudent to begin, and so by means of definitions, reduce them to order. Yet even definitions cannot cure this evil in dealing with natural and material things; since the definitions themselves consist of words, and those words beget others: so that it is necessary to recur to individual instances, and those in due series and order; as I shall say presently when I come to the method and scheme for the formation of notions and axioms.

78.   I now come to the *causes* of these errors, and of so long a continuance in them through so many ages; which are very many and very potent; – that all wonder how these considerations which I bring forward should have escaped men's notice till now, may cease; and the only wonder be, how now at last they should have entered into any man's head and become the subject of his thoughts; which truly I myself esteem as the result of some happy accident, rather than of any excellence of faculty in me; a birth of Time rather than a birth of Wit.[20] Now, in the first place, those so many ages, if you weigh the case truly, shrink into a very small compass. For out of the five and twenty centuries over which the memory and learning of men extends, you can hardly pick out six that were fertile in sciences or favourable to their development. In times no less than in regions there are wastes and deserts. For only three revolutions and periods of learning can properly be reckoned; one among the Greeks, the second among the Romans, and the last among us, that is to say, the nations of Western Europe; and to each of these hardly two centuries can justly be assigned. The intervening ages of the world, in respect of any rich or flourishing growth of the sciences, were unprosperous. For neither the Arabians nor the Schoolmen need be mentioned;[21] who in the intermediate times rather crushed the sciences with a multitude of treatises, than increased their weight. And therefore the first cause of so meagre a progress in the sciences is duly and orderly referred to the narrow limits of the time that has been favourable to them.

84.   Again, men have been kept back as by a kind of enchantment from progress in the sciences by reverence for antiquity, by the authority of men accounted great in philosophy, and then by general consent. Of the last I have spoken above.

As for antiquity, the opinion touching it which men entertain is quite a negligent one, and scarcely consonant with the word itself. For the old age of the world is to be accounted the true antiquity; and this is the attribute of our own times, not of that earlier age of the world in which the ancients lived; and which, though in respect of us it was the elder, yet in respect of the world it was the younger. And truly as we look for greater knowledge of human things and a riper judgment in the old man than in the young, because of his experience and of the number and variety of the things which he has seen and heard and thought of; so in like manner from our age, if it but knew its own strength and chose to essay[22] and exert it, much more might fairly be expected than from the ancient times, inasmuch as it is a more advanced age of the world, and stored and stocked with infinite experiments and observations.

Nor must it go for nothing that by the distant voyages and travels which have become frequent in our times, many things in nature have been laid open and discovered which may let in new light upon philosophy.[23] And surely it would be disgraceful if, while the regions of the material globe, – that is, of the earth, of the sea, and of the stars, – have been in our times laid widely open and

19 *practice.*
20 In keeping with his disparagement of individual "genius" as a means for advancing the sciences, Bacon was always careful to claim no special intellectual gifts for himself in his writings.
21 The "Arabs" here refer to the scientific, intellectual, and artistic achievements of the Muslim culture that dominated the southern Mediterranean world from the 8th century until Bacon's day; Bacon's judgment in this matter is prejudiced and grossly unfair. "Schoolmen" refer to the medieval Scholastic philosophers (especially Thomas

Aquinas and his teacher Albertus Magnus). The tendency to disparage medieval intellectual culture was very common in the Renaissance, despite the manifold continuities between the two epochs.
22 *try.*
23 "Philosophy" here refers to "natural philosophy" or what today would be called "the sciences." Bacon repeatedly analogizes the Early Modern European exploration of the globe to his projected quest for new scientific knowledge.

revealed, the intellectual globe should remain shut up within the narrow limits of old discoveries.

And with regard to authority,[24] it shows a feeble mind to grant so much to authors and yet deny time his rights, who is the author of authors, nay rather of all authority. For rightly is truth called the daughter of time, not of authority. It is no wonder therefore if those enchantments of antiquity and authority and consent have so bound up men's powers that they have been made impotent (like persons bewitched) to accompany with the nature of things.

85.   Nor is it only the admiration of antiquity, authority, and consent, that has forced the industry of man to rest satisfied with the discoveries already made; but also an admiration for the works themselves of which the human race has long been in possession. For when man looks at the variety and the beauty of the provision which the mechanical arts have brought together for men's use, he will certainly be more inclined to admire the wealth of man than to feel his wants: considering that the original observations and operations of nature (which are the life and moving principle of all that variety) are not many nor deeply fetched, and that the rest is but patience, and the subtle and ruled motion of the hand and instruments; – as the making of clocks (for instance) is certainly a subtle and exact work: their wheels seem to imitate the celestial orbs, and their alternating and orderly motion, the pulse of animals: and yet all this depends on one or two axioms of nature.

Again, if you observe the refinement of the liberal arts, or even that which relates to the mechanical preparation of natural substances; and take notice of such things as the discovery in astronomy of the motions of the heavens, of harmony in music, of the letters of the alphabet (to this day not in use among the Chinese) in grammar: or again in things mechanical, the discovery of the works of Bacchus[25] and Ceres – that is, of the arts of preparing wine and beer, and of making bread; the discovery once more of the delicacies of the table, of distillations and the like; and if you bear in mind the long periods which it has taken to bring these things to their present degree of perfection (for they are all ancient except distillation), and again (as has been said of clocks) how little they owe to observations and axioms of nature, and how easily and obviously and as it were by casual suggestion they may have been discovered; you will easily cease from wondering, and on the contrary will pity the condition of mankind, seeing that in a course of so many ages there has been so great a dearth and barrenness of arts and inventions. And yet these very discoveries which we have just mentioned, are older than philosophy and intellectual arts. So that, if the truth must be spoken, when the rational and dogmatical sciences began the discovery of useful works came to an end.

And again, if a man turn from the workshop to the library, and wonder at the immense variety of books he sees there, let him but examine and diligently inspect their matter and contents, and his wonder will assuredly be turned the other way; for after observing their endless repetitions, and how men are ever saying and doing what has been said and done before, he will pass from admiration of the variety to astonishment at the poverty and scantiness of the subjects which till now have occupied and possessed the minds of men.

And if again he descend to the consideration of those arts which are deemed curious[26] rather than safe, and look more closely into the works of the Alchemists[27] or the Magicians, he will be in doubt perhaps whether he ought rather to laugh over them or to weep. For the Alchemist nurses eternal hope, and when the thing fails, lays the blame upon some error of his own; fearing either that he has not sufficiently understood the words of his art or of his authors (whereupon he turns to tradition and auricular[28] whispers), or else that in his manipulations he has made some slip of a scruple[29] in weight or a moment in time (whereupon he repeats his trials to

24   i.e. the authority of classical writers who were thought to represent the apogee of Western intellectual endeavor.

25   For Bacchus and Ceres, see Dionysus and Demeter respectively in the gazetteer.

26   *overly inquisitive.*

27   Alchemists were Early Modern experimental chemists. Their chief goal was the transmutation of base metals into gold, and they were often associated with magicians because of their belief in the connectedness of all natural phenomena.

28   *hearsay.*

29   A very small unit of weight equal to 1.296 grams.

infinity); and when meanwhile among the chances of experiment he lights upon some conclusions either in aspect[30] new or for utility not contemptible, he takes these for earnest of what is to come, and feeds his mind upon them, and magnifies them to the most, and supplies the rest in hope. Not but that Alchemists have made a good many discoveries, and presented men with useful inventions. But their case may be well compared to the fable of the old man, who bequeathed to his sons gold buried in a vineyard, pretending not to know the exact spot; whereupon the sons applied themselves diligently to the digging of the vineyard, and though no gold was found there, yet the vintage by that digging was made more plentiful.

Again the students of natural magic,[31] who explain everything by Sympathies and Antipathies, have in their idle and most slothful conjectures ascribed to substances wonderful virtues and operations; and if ever they have produced works, they have been such as aim rather at admiration and novelty than at utility and fruit.

In superstitious[32] magic on the other hand (if of this also we must speak), it is especially to be observed that they are but subjects of a certain and definite kind wherein the curious and superstitious arts, in all nations and ages, and religions also, have worked or played. These therefore we may pass. Meanwhile it is nowise strange if opinion of plenty has been the cause of want.

98.   Now for grounds of experience – since to experience we must come – we have as yet had either none or very weak ones; no search has been made to collect a store of particular observations sufficient either in number, or in kind, or in certainty, to inform the understanding, or in any way adequate. On the contrary, men of learning, but easy withal and idle, have taken for the construction or for the confirmation of their philosophy[33] certain rumours and vague fames[34] or airs of experience, and allowed to these the weight of lawful evidence. And just as if some kingdom or state were to direct its counsels and affairs, not by letters and reports of ambassadors and trustworthy messengers, but by the gossip of the streets; such exactly is the system of management introduced into philosophy with relation to experience. Nothing duly investigated, nothing verified, nothing counted, weighed, or measured, is to be found in natural history: and what in observation is loose and vague, is in information deceptive and treacherous. And if any one thinks that this is a strange thing to say, and something like an unjust complaint, seeing that Aristotle,[35] himself so great a man, and supported by the wealth of so great a king, has composed so accurate a history of animals; and that others with greater diligence, though less pretence, have made many additions; while others, again, have compiled copious histories and descriptions of metals, plants, and fossils; it seems that he does not rightly apprehend what it is that we are now about. For a natural history which is composed for its own sake is not like one that is collected to supply the understanding with information for the building up of philosophy. They differ in many ways, but especially in this; that the former contains the variety of natural species only, and not experiments of the mechanical arts. For even as in the business of life a man's disposition and the secret workings of his mind and affections are better discovered when he is in trouble than at other times; so likewise the secrets of nature reveal themselves more readily under the vexations of art than when they go their own way. Good hopes may therefore be conceived of natural philosophy, when natural history, which is the basis and foundation of it, has been drawn up on a better plan; but not till then.

112.   Meantime, let no man be alarmed at the multitude of particulars, but let this rather encourage hope. For the particular phenomena of art and nature are but a handful to the inventions of the wit, when disjoined and separated from the evidence of things. Moreover this road has an issue

---

30   *appearance.*

31   Natural magic" was the supposed art of controlling phenomena by means of the natural affinities and relationships in nature (Bacon's "Sympathies and Antipathies"). It is separated from so-called "black" or, to use Bacon's term, "superstitious" magic in that it does not involve invoking spirits or divine forces. Although Bacon and many other scientific thinkers were profoundly skeptical about all magic, many people believed in its efficacy during Bacon's day.

32   See note 31 above.

33   Again, Bacon here refers to "natural philosophy" or what we would call "science."

34   *reports.*

35   See gazetteer. The "great king" who supported him was Alexander the Great.

in the open ground and not far off; the other has no issue at all, but endless entanglement. For men hitherto have made but short stay with experience, but passing her lightly by, have wasted an infinity of time on meditations and glosses[36] of the wit. But if some one were by that could answer our questions and tell us in each case what the fact in nature is, the discovery of all causes and sciences would be but the work of a few years.

122.   It may be thought also a strange and a harsh thing that we should at once and with one blow set aside all sciences and all authors; and that too without calling in any of the ancients to our aid and support, but relying on our own strength.

And I know that if I had chosen to deal less sincerely, I might easily have found authority for my suggestions by referring them either to the old times before the Greeks (when natural science was perhaps more flourishing, though it made less noise, not having yet passed into the pipes and trumpets of the Greeks), or even, in part at least, to some of the Greeks themselves; and so gained for them both support and honour; as men of no family devise for themselves by the good help of genealogies the nobility of a descent from some ancient stock. But for my part, relying on the evidence and truth of things, I reject all forms of fiction and imposture; nor do I think that it matters any more to the business in hand, whether the discoveries that shall now be made were long ago known to the ancients, and have their settings and their risings according to the vicissitude of things and course of ages, than it matters to mankind whether the New World be that island of Atlantis with which the ancients were acquainted,[37] or now discovered for the first time. For new discoveries must be sought from the light of nature, not fetched back out of the darkness of antiquity.

And as for the universality of the censure, certainly if the matter be truly considered, such a censure is not only more probable but more modest too, than a partial one would be. For if the errors had not been rooted in primary notions, there must have been some true discoveries to correct the false. But the errors being fundamental, and not so much of false judgment as of inattention and oversight, it is no wonder that men have not obtained what they have not tried for, nor reached a mark[38] which they never set up, nor finished a course which they never entered on or kept.

And as for the presumption implied in it; certainly if a man undertakes by steadiness of hand and power of eye to describe a straighter line or more perfect circle than any one else, he challenges a comparison of abilities; but if he only says that he with the help of a rule or a pair of compasses can draw a straighter line or a more perfect circle than any one else can by eye and hand alone, he makes no great boast. And this remark, be it observed, applies not merely to this first and inceptive[39] attempt of mine, but to all that shall take the work in hand hereafter. For my way of discovering sciences goes far to level men's wits, and leaves but little to individual excellence; because it performs everything by the surest rules and demonstrations. And therefore I attribute my part in all this, as I have often said rather to good luck than to ability, and account it a birth of time rather than of wit. For certainly chance has something to do with men's thoughts, as well as with their works and deeds.

129.   It remains for me to say a few words touching the excellency of the end in view. Had they been uttered earlier they might have seemed like idle wishes; now that hopes have been raised and unfair prejudices removed, they may perhaps have greater weight. Also if I had finished all myself, and had no occasion to call in others to help and take part in the work, I should even now have abstained from such language, lest it might be taken as a proclamation of my own deserts. But since I want to quicken[40] the industry and rouse and kindle the zeal of others, it is fitting that I put men in mind of some things.

---

36   i.e. dubious interpretations.

37   Plato describes the lost continent of Atlantis in the *Timaeus* and *Critias*, attributing his story to the Athenian law-giver Solon. It is highly unlikely to have been anything other than a fable. Bacon's larger point is that knowledge has its rises and falls along with human societies and that only nature, correctly interpreted, can lead us to stable truth.

38   *target.*

39   *initial.*

40   *energize.*

In the first place then, the introduction of famous discoveries appears to hold by far the first place among human actions; and this was the judgment of the former ages. For to the authors of inventions they awarded divine honours; while to those who did good service in the state (such as founders of cities and empires, legislators, saviours of their country from long endured evils, quellers of tyrannies, and the like) they decreed no higher honours than heroic. And certainly if a man rightly compare the two, he will find that this judgment of antiquity was just. For the benefits of discoveries may extend to the whole race of man, civil benefits only to particular places; the latter last not beyond a few ages, the former through all time. Moreover the reformation of a state in civil matters is seldom brought in without violence and confusion; but discoveries carry blessings with them, and confer benefits without causing harm or sorrow to any.

Again, discoveries are as it were new creations, and imitations of God's works; as well sang the poet:[41]

> To man's frail race great Athens long ago
> First gave the seed whence waving harvests grow,
> And *re-created* all our life below.

And it appears worthy of remark in Solomon, that though mighty in empire and in gold; in the magnificence of his works, his court, his household, and his fleet; in the lustre of his name and the worship of mankind; yet he took none of these to glory in, but pronounced that "The glory of God is to conceal a thing; the glory of the king to search it out."

Again, let a man only consider what a difference there is between the life of men in the most civilized province of Europe, and in the wildest and most barbarous districts of New India;[42] he will feel it be great enough to justify the saying that "man is a god to man" not only in regard of aid and benefit, but also by a comparison of condition. And this difference comes not from soil, not from climate, not from race, but from the arts.

Again, it is well to observe the force and virtue and consequences of discoveries; and these are to be seen nowhere more conspicuously than in those three which were unknown to the ancients, and of which the origin, though recent, is obscure and inglorious; namely, printing, gunpowder, and the magnet. For these three have changed the whole face and state of things throughout the world; the first in literature, the second in warfare, the third in navigation; whence have followed innumerable changes; insomuch that no empire, no sect, no star seems to have exerted greater power and influence in human affairs than these mechanical discoveries.

Further, it will not be amiss to distinguish the three kinds and as it were grades of ambition in mankind. The first is of those who desire to extend their own power in their native country; which kind is vulgar and degenerate. The second is of those who labour to extend the power of their country and its dominion among men. This certainly has more dignity, though not less covetousness. But if a man endeavour to establish and extend the power and dominion of the human race itself over the universe, his ambition (if ambition it can be called) is without doubt both a more wholesome thing, and a more noble than the other two. Now the empire of man over things depends on the arts and sciences. For we cannot command nature except by obeying her.

Again, if men have thought so much of some one particular discovery as to regard him as more than man who has been able by some benefit to make the whole human race his debtor, how much higher a thing to discover that by means of which all things else shall be discovered with ease! And yet (to speak the whole truth), as the uses of light are infinite, in enabling us to walk, to ply our arts, to read, to recognize one another; and nevertheless the very beholding of the light is itself a more excellent and a fairer thing than all the uses of it; – so assuredly the very contemplation of things, as they are, without superstition or imposture,[43] error or confusion, is in itself more worthy than all the fruit of inventions.

---

41 Lucretius, *On the Nature of Things* 6.1–3.
42 i.e. the New World.
43 *willful deception.*

Lastly, if the debasement of arts and sciences to purposes of wickedness, luxury, and the like, be made a ground of objection, let no one be moved thereby. For the same may be said of all earthly goods; of wit, courage, strength, beauty, wealth, light itself, and the rest. Only let the human race recover that right over nature which belongs to it by divine bequest, and let power be given it; the exercise thereof will be governed by sound reason and true religion.

[FROM] ESSAYS OR COUNSELS CIVIL AND MORAL (1625)

OF TRUTH

"What is truth?" said jesting Pilate;[1] and would not stay for an answer. Certainly there be that delight in giddiness,[2] and count it a bondage to fix a belief; affecting free-will in thinking, as well as in acting. And though the sects of philosophers[3] of that kind be gone, yet there remain certain discoursing wits which are of the same veins, though there be not so much blood in them as was in those of the ancients. But it is not only the difficulty and labour which men take in finding out of truth; nor again that when it is found it imposeth upon men's thoughts; that doth bring lies in favour; but a natural though corrupt love of the lie itself. One of the later school of the Grecians[4] examineth the matter, and is at a stand,[5] to think what should be in it, that men should love lies, where neither they make for pleasure, as with poets, nor for advantage, as with the merchant; but for the lie's sake. But I cannot tell: this same truth is a naked and open day-light, that doth not show the masks and mummeries and triumphs of the world, half so stately and daintily as candle-lights. Truth may perhaps come to the price of a pearl, that showeth best by day; but it will not rise to the price of a diamond or carbuncle,[6] that showeth best in varied lights. A mixture of a lie doth ever add pleasure. Doth any man doubt, that if there were taken out of men's minds vain opinions, flattering hopes, false valuations, imaginations as one would, and the like, but it would leave the minds of a number of men, poor shrunken things, full of melancholy and indisposition,[7] and unpleasing to themselves? One of the Fathers,[8] in great severity, called poesy *vinum daemonum* [devil's wine], because it filleth the imagination; and yet it is but with the shadow of a lie. But it is not the lie that passeth through the mind, but the lie that sinketh in and settleth in it, that doth the hurt; such as we spake of before. But howsoever these things are thus in men's depraved judgments and affections,[9] yet truth, which only doth judge itself, teacheth that the inquiry of truth, which is the love-making or wooing of it, the knowledge of truth, which is the presence of it, and the belief of truth, which is the enjoying of it, is the sovereign good of human nature. The first creature of God, in the works of the days,[10] was the light of the sense; the last was the light of reason; and his sabbath work ever since, is the illumination of his Spirit. First he breathed light upon the face of the matter or chaos; then be breathed light into the face of man; and still he breatheth and inspireth light into the face of his chosen. The poet[11] that beautified the sect that was otherwise inferior to the rest, saith yet excellently well: "It is a pleasure, to stand upon the shore, and to see ships tossed upon the sea; a pleasure, to stand in the window of a castle, and to see a battle and the adventures thereof below: but no pleasure is comparable to the standing upon the

---

THE ESSAYS (1625)

1   See John 18:38.

2   *fickleness.*

3   Bacon is referring to the Skeptics, an ancient philosophical tradition which held that certain knowledge about anything was impossible.

4   Lucian of Samosata (born *c.*120 CE), a rhetorician and prose writer in the late heyday of rhetoric in the Roman empire known as the Second Sophistic (Bacon's "later school"); the specific work referred to is a satire called *Lovers of Lies.*

5   i.e. is perplexed.

6   ruby; also applied to any red-colored gem stone.

7   *disorder.*

8   The "Fathers" refers to the Fathers of the Church (early Christian writers of the 1st through 5th centuries CE). Brian Vickers has shown that Bacon is conflating remarks by two Fathers (St. Augustine and St. Jerome) and that his probable source is an Early Modern text.

9   *passions or biases.*

10   i.e. the six days of creation in Genesis.

11   Lucretius (*c.*94–55 BCE), a Roman poet and Epicurean (Bacon's "sect"). The Epicureans were an ancient philosophical school that was wrongly accused of being blindly hedonistic in ancient and Early Modern times. The quote comes from Lucretius' poem *De rerum natura* ("On the Nature of Things") 2.1–10.

vantage ground of Truth" (a hill not to be commanded, and where the air is always clear and serene), "and to see the errors, and wanderings, and mists, and tempests, in the vale below"; so always that this prospect be with pity, and not with swelling or pride. Certainly, it is heaven upon earth, to have a man's mind move in charity, rest in providence, and turn upon the poles of truth.

To pass from theological and philosophical truth, to the truth of civil business;[12] it will be acknowledged, even by those that practise it not, that clear and round[13] dealing, is the honour of man's nature; and that mixture of falsehood is like alloy in coin of gold and silver, which may make the metal work the better, but it embaseth[14] it. For these winding and crooked courses are the goings of the serpent; which goeth basely upon the belly, and not upon the feet. There is no vice that doth so cover a man with shame as to be found false and perfidious. And therefore Montaigne[15] saith prettily, when he inquired the reason, why the word of the lie should be such a disgrace and such an odious charge? Saith he, "If it be well weighed, to say that a man lieth, is as much to say, as that he is brave towards God, and a coward towards men." For a lie faces[16] God, and shrinks from man. Surely the wickedness of falsehood and breach of faith cannot possibly be so highly expressed, as in that it shall be the last peal to call the judgments of God upon the generations of men; it being foretold, that when Christ cometh, "he shall not find faith upon the earth."[17]

OF DEATH

Men fear Death, as children fear to go in the dark; and as that natural fear in children is increased with tales, so is the other. Certainly, the contemplation of death, as the wages of sin and passage to another world, is holy and religious; but the fear of it, as a tribute due unto nature, is weak. Yet in religious meditations, there is sometimes mixture of vanity and of superstition. You shall read in some of the friars' books of mortification,[18] that a man should think with himself what the pain is if he have but his finger's end pressed or tortured, and thereby imagine what the pains of death are, when the whole body is corrupted, and dissolved; when many times death passeth with less pain than the torture of a limb; for the most vital parts are not the quickest[19] of sense. And by him[20] that spake only as a philosopher and natural[21] man, it was well said, *Pompa mortis magis terret, quam mors ipsa:* [it is the accompaniments of death that are frightful rather than death itself]. Groans, and convulsions, and a discoloured face, and friends weeping, and blacks, and obsequies, and the like, show death terrible. It is worthy the observing, that there is no passion in the mind of man so weak, but it mates and masters, the fear of death; and therefore death is no such terrible enemy when a man hath so many attendants about him that can win the combat of him. Revenge triumphs over death; love slights it; honour aspireth to it; grief flieth to it; fear preoccupateth[22] it; nay we read, after Otho the emperor had slain himself,[23] pity (which is the tenderest of affections) provoked many to die, out of mere compassion to their sovereign, and as the truest sort of followers. Nay, Seneca adds niceness and satiety: *Cogita quamdiu eadem feceris; mori velle, non tantum fortis aut miser, sed etiam fastidiosus potest.*[24] A man would die, though he were neither valiant nor miserable, only upon a weariness to do the same thing so oft over and over. It is no less worthy to observe, how little alteration in good spirits the approaches of death make; for they appear to be the same men till the last instant. Augustus Caesar[25] died in a compliment; *Livia, conjugii nostri*

---

12 secular political affairs.

13 honest.

14 depreciates.

15 Michel de Montaigne (1533–92) was a French aristocrat who pioneered the essay form in Early Modern Europe; like Bacon, Montaigne continually revised and expanded his collection of essays. The passage quoted is from the essay *Du démentir* ("On refuting lies").

16 i.e. a lie challenges God directly.

17 See Luke 18:8.

18 Catholic treatises which explored the idea that mortification (the infliction of pain on oneself) of the flesh was good for the *soul*.

19 keenest.

20 The reference is to the Roman philosopher Seneca (see gazetteer); the passage quoted is from his *Epistles* 24.14.

21 i.e. a man with a physical, and not spiritual, existence.

22 anticipates.

23 Otho was emperor for a brief while in AD 69, the "Year of the Four Emperors." He was an ambitious schemer, and it is very possible that there is a healthy dose of irony in Bacon's instancing of him.

24 Loosely quoted from Seneca, *Epistles* 77.6. The following sentence in the text is a translation of this passage.

25 Augustus Caesar, Tiberius, Vespasian, and Septimius Severus were all Roman emperors.

memor, vive et vale: [farewell, Livia; and forget not the days of our marriage]. Tiberius in dissimulation; as Tacitus[26] saith of him, *Jam Tiberium vires et corpus, non dissimulatio, deserebant*: [his powers of body were gone, but not his power of dissimulation]. Vespasian in a jest, sitting upon the stool, *Ut puto deus fio*: [I think I am becoming a god]. Galba with a sentence; *Feri, si ex re sit populi Romani*: [strike, if it be for the good of Rome]; holding forth his neck. Septimius Severus in despatch; *Adeste si quid mihi restat agendum*: [make haste, if there is anything more for me to do]. And the like. Certainly the Stoics[27] bestowed too much cost upon death, and by their great preparations made it appear more fearful. Better saith he, *qui finem vitae extremum inter munera ponat naturae*: [who accounts the close of life as one of the benefits of nature].[28] It is as natural to die as to be born; and to a little infant, perhaps, the one is as painful as the other. He that dies in an earnest pursuit, is like one that is wounded in hot blood; who, for the time, scarce feels the hurt; and therefore a mind fixed and bent upon somewhat that is good doth avert the dolours of death. But above all, believe it, the sweetest canticle[29] is, *Nunc dimittis*;[30] when a man hath obtained worthy ends and expectations. Death hath this also; that it openeth the gate to good fame, and extinguisheth envy. *Extinctus amabitur idem*: [the same man that was envied while he lived, shall be loved when he is gone].[31]

OF UNITY IN RELIGION

Religion being the chief band[32] of human society, it is a happy thing when itself is well contained within the true band of unity. The quarrels and divisions about religion were evils unknown to the heathen. The reason was, because the religion of the heathen, consisted rather in rites and ceremonies, than in any constant belief. For you may imagine what kind of faith theirs was, when the chief doctors and fathers of their church were the poets. But the true God hath this attribute, that he is a "jealous God";[33] and therefore, his worship and religion will endure no mixture, nor partner. We shall therefore speak a few words concerning the unity of the Church; what are the fruits thereof; what the bounds;[34] and what the means.

The fruits of unity (next unto the well pleasing of God, which is all in all) are two: the one towards those that are without[35] the church, the other towards those that are within. For the former; it is certain that heresies and schisms are of all others the greatest scandals; yea, more than corruption of manners. For as in the natural body a wound or solution of continuity[36] is worse than a corrupt humour;[37] so in the spiritual. So that nothing doth so much keep men out of the church, and drive men out of the church, as breach of unity. And therefore, whensoever it cometh to that pass, that one saith, *Ecce in deserto*, another saith, *Ecce in penetralibus*;[38] that is, when some men seek Christ in the conventicles[39] of heretics, and others in an outward face of a church, that voice had need continually to sound in men's ears, *Nolite exire*, – "Go not out." The doctor of the Gentiles[40] (the propriety of whose vocation, drew him to have a special care of those without) saith, "If an heathen come in, and hear you speak with several tongues,[41] will he not say that you are mad?"[42] And certainly it is little better, when atheists, and profane persons do bear of so many discordant

---

26   Tacitus (*c.*56–*c.*118) was a Roman historian. His major works, the *Histories* (covering Roman history from 69–96 CE) and the *Annals* (covering the period 14–66 CE) were widely read in Early Modern Europe.
27   An ancient philosophical movement with a strongly deterministic sense of how life unfolds according to the laws of fate. Seneca (see gazetteer) was strongly influenced by Stoic ideas.
28   "He" is the Roman satirical poet Juvenal; the passage is inaccurately remembered from *Satires* 10.358.
29   A hymn used as part of the liturgy of the Anglican Church.
30   A Latin short form for "Lord, now lettest thou thy servant depart in peace" (Luke 2:29). It is also the name of the canticle in the Anglican liturgy which marks the dismissal of the congregation, and (more broadly) the acceptance of death because of faith in Christ.
31   See the Roman poet Horace in *Epistles* 2.1.14.
32   *bond.*

33   See Exodus 20:5 and 34:14.
34   *limits.*
35   *outside.*
36   "The separation from each other of different parts of the body" (*OED*).
37   See Humors in the gazetteer.
38   "Behold, he is in the desert" and "Behold, he is in the secret chambers." Both phrases are taken from Christ's warning about false prophets in Matthew 24:26.
39   *illegal religious meetings.*
40   A common title given to St. Paul, whose apostolic missions were usually to Gentiles rather than Jews.
41   *languages.*
42   1 Corinthians 14:23.

and contrary opinions in religion; it doth avert them from the church, and maketh them "to sit down in the chair of the scorners."[43] It is but a light thing to be vouched[44] in so serious a matter, but yet it expresseth well the deformity. There is a master of scoffing,[45] that in his catalogue of books of a feigned library sets down this title of a book, *The Morris-Dance*[46] *of Heretics*. For indeed every sect of them hath a diverse posture or cringe by themselves, which cannot but move derision in worldlings, and depraved politics,[47] who are apt to contemn holy things.

As for the fruit towards those that are within; it is peace; which containeth infinite blessings. It establisheth faith. It kindleth charity. The outward peace of the church distilleth into peace of conscience. And it turneth the labours of writing and reading of controversies into treaties[48] of mortification and devotion.

Concerning the bounds of unity; the true placing of them importeth exceedingly. There appear to be two extremes. For to certain zelants[49] all speech of pacification is odious. "Is it peace, Jehu? What hast thou to do with peace? Turn thee behind me."[50] Peace is not the matter,[51] but following, and party.[52] Contrariwise, certain Laodiceans[53] and lukewarm persons think they may accommodate points of religion by middle ways, and taking part of both, and witty reconcilements; as if they would make an arbitrement[54] between God and man. Both these extremes are to be avoided; which will be done, if the league of Christians penned by our Saviour himself were in the two cross clauses thereof soundly and plainly expounded: "He that is not with us, is against us";[55] and again, "He that is not against us, is with us";[56] that is, if the points fundamental and of substance in religion were truly discerned and distinguished from points not merely of faith, but of opinion, order, or good intention. This is a thing may seem to many a matter trivial, and done already. But if it were done less partially,[57] it would be embraced more generally.

Of this I may give only this advice, according to my small model.[58] Men ought to take heed of rending God's Church by two kinds of controversies. The one is, when the matter of the point controverted is too small and light, not worth the heat and strife about it, kindled only by contradiction. For as it is noted by one of the fathers, "Christ's coat indeed had no seam, but the church's vesture was of divers colours";[59] whereupon he saith, *In veste varietas sit, scissura non sit*, [let there be variety in the garment, but let there be no division]:[60] they be two things, unity and uniformity. The other is, when the matter of the point controverted is great, but it is driven to an overgreat subtilty[61] and obscurity; so that it becometh a thing rather ingenious than substantial. A man that is of judgment and understanding shall sometimes hear ignorant men differ, and know well within himself that those which so differ mean one thing, and yet they themselves would never agree. And if it come so to pass in that distance of judgment which is between man and man, shall we not think that God above, that knows the heart, doth not discern that frail men in some of their contradictions intend the same thing; and accepteth of both? The nature of such controversies is excellently expressed by St. Paul in the warning and precept that he giveth concerning the same, *Devita profanas vocum novitates, et oppositiones falsi nominis scientiae*: [Avoid profane novelties of terms, and oppositions of science falsely so called].[62] Men create oppositions which are not: and put them into new terms so fixed, as whereas the meaning ought to govern the term, the term in effect governeth the meaning. There be also two false peaces or unities: the one, when the peace is grounded but upon an implicit ignorance; for all colours will agree in the dark: the other, when it

---

43 Psalms 1:1.
44 *used as evidence.*
45 A reference to the French humanist writer François Rabelais (*c.*1494–*c.*1553). The reference is to *Pantagruel* 2.7.
46 A costumed folk dance performed at holiday festivals.
47 *politicians.*
48 *treatises.*
49 *zealots.*
50 2 Kings 9:18–19.
51 *issue at stake.*
52 i.e. rigid party doctrine.
53 A reference to the people condemned for having "lukewarm" faith in Revelation 3:16.

54 *settlement of a dispute.*
55 Matthew 12:30 (misquoted).
56 Mark 9:40.
57 i.e. in a less biased manner.
58 *summary.*
59 John 19:23–4.
60 St. Augustine, *Commentary on Psalm 44*, 24. As several previous editors have pointed out, Bacon is misusing the original intent of Augustine's statement to support his point.
61 *subtlety.*
62 1 Timothy 6:20.

is pieced up[63] upon a direct admission of contraries in fundamental points. For truth and falsehood, in such things, are like the iron and clay in the toes of Nebuchadnezzar's image;[64] they may cleave, but they will not incorporate.

Concerning the means of procuring unity; men must beware, that in the procuring or muniting[65] of religious unity they do not dissolve and deface the laws of charity and of human society. There be two swords amongst Christians, the spiritual and temporal;[66] and both have their due office and place in the maintenance of religion. But we may not take up the third sword, which is Mahomet's[67] sword, or like unto it; that is, to propagate religion by wars or by sanguinary[68] persecutions to force consciences; except it be in cases of overt scandal, blasphemy, or intermixture of practice against the state; much less to nourish seditions; to authorize conspiracies and rebellions; to put the sword into the people's hands; and the like; tending to the subversion of all government, which is the ordinance of God. For this is but to dash the first table against the second,[69] and so to consider men as Christians, as we forget that they are men. Lucretius[70] the poet, when he beheld the act of Agamemnon, that could endure the sacrificing of his own daughter, exclaimed:

> tantum religio potuit suadere malorum:
> [to such ill actions Religion could persuade a man]

What would he have said, if he had known of the massacre in France, or the powder treason of England?[71] He would have been seven times more Epicure and atheist than he was. For as the temporal sword is to be drawn with great circumspection in cases of religion; so it is a thing monstrous to put it into the hands of the common people. Let that be left unto the Anabaptists,[72] and other furies. It was great blasphemy when the devil said, "I will ascend, and be like the highest";[73] but it is greater blasphemy to personate God, and bring him in saying, "I will descend, and be like the prince of darkness"; and what is it better, to make the cause of religion to descend to the cruel and execrable[74] actions of murthering princes, butchery of people, and subversion of states and governments? Surely this is to bring down the Holy Ghost, instead of the likeness of a dove,[75] in the shape of a vulture or raven; and set out on the bark[76] of a Christian church a flag of a bark of pirates, and assassins. Therefore it is most necessary that the church by doctrine and decree, princes by their sword, and all learnings, both Christian and moral,[77] as by their Mercury rod,[78] do damn and send to hell forever those facts and opinions tending to the support of the same; as hath been already in good part done. Surely in counsels concerning religion, that counsel of the apostle would be prefixed, *Ira hominis non implet justitiam Dei*: [The wrath of man worketh not the righteousness of God].[79] And it was a notable observation of a wise father,[80] and no less ingenuously confessed; "that those which held and persuaded pressure of consciences, were commonly interested[81] therein themselves for their own ends."

---

63 *patched together.*

64 A reference to the prophet Daniel's warning that Nebuchadnezzar's kingdom should be "partly strong, and partly broken" in Daniel 2:31–43.

65 *strengthening.*

66 "Sword" was a common metaphor for governmental authority in Early Modern England, both religious and secular ("temporal"). Luke 22:38 is its probable source. In Catholic countries, the Church still had a separate system of ecclesiastical courts, and all Europeans were used to their relationships with their churches being regulated by laws and punishments.

67 A common Early Modern spelling of Mohammed, the Prophet of Islam. Bacon is referring to the much misunderstood Islamic concept of a "holy war," although violent enforcement of official religious policies was the norm in all European nations in this period.

68 *bloody.*

69 A reference to the tables on which the Ten Commandments were written (Exodus 32:15–16). Bacon's point is that the laws concerning God (the first five commandments) should not be used to enforce the laws concerning human behavior (the second five commandments).

70 On Lucretius, see note 11 above. The passage is from *On the Nature of Things* 1.101.

71 A reference to the St. Bartholemew's Day Massacre (August 24, 1572), in which over 12,000 French Protestants were killed at the instigation of their Catholic opponents, and the Catholic conspiracy to blow up the Houses of Parliament on November 5, 1605.

72 A radical sect of 16th-century German Protestants who denied the legitimacy of any civil authority. Bacon's profound distrust of the capacity of ordinary people to participate in their own governance is clearly on view in this passage.

73 A reference to Isaiah 12:12–14 and to the fall of Lucifer in general.

74 *detestable.*

75 See Luke 3:22.

76 *boat.*

77 i.e. philosophical.

78 See Hermes in the gazetteer.

79 James 1:20.

80 This reference has never been traced.

81 *interested.*

OF SIMULATION AND DISSIMULATION[82]

Dissimulation is but a faint kind of policy or wisdom; for it asketh a strong wit and a strong heart to know when to tell truth, and to do it. Therefore it is the weaker sort of politics that are the great dissemblers.

Tacitus saith, "Livia sorted well with the arts of her husband and dissimulation of her son";[83] attributing arts or policy to Augustus, and dissimulation to Tiberius. And again, when Mucianus encourageth Vespasian, to take arms against Vitellius, he saith, "We rise not against the piercing judgment of Augustus, nor the extreme caution or closeness of Tiberius."[84] These properties, of arts or policy and dissimulation or closeness, are indeed habits and faculties several,[85] and to be distinguished. For if a man have that penetration of judgment as he can discern what things are to be laid open, and what to be secreted, and what to be showed at half lights, and to whom and when (which indeed are arts of state and arts of life, as Tacitus well calleth them)[86] to him, a habit of dissimulation is a hindrance and a poorness. But if a man cannot obtain to that judgment, then it is left to him generally to be close,[87] and a dissembler. For where a man cannot choose or vary in particulars,[88] there it is good to take the safest and wariest way in general; like the going softly, by one that cannot well see. Certainly the ablest men that ever were have had all an openness and frankness of dealing; and a name[89] of certainty and veracity; but then they were like horses well managed; for they could tell passing well when to stop or turn; and at such times when they thought the case indeed required dissimulation, if then they used it, it came to pass that the former opinion spread abroad of their good faith and clearness of dealing made them almost invisible.

There be three degrees of this hiding and veiling of a man's self. The first, closeness, reservation, and secrecy; when a man leaveth himself without observation,[90] or without hold to be taken, what he is. The second, dissimulation, in the negative; when a man lets fall signs and arguments, that he is not that he is. And the third, simulation, in the affirmative; when a man industriously and expressly feigns and pretends to be that he is not.

For the first of these, secrecy; it is indeed the virtue of a confessor. And assuredly the secret man heareth many confessions. For who will open himself to a blab or a babbler? But if a man be thought secret, it inviteth discovery; as the more close air sucketh in the more open;[91] and as in confession the revealing is not for worldly use, but for the ease of a man's heart, so secret men come to the knowledge of many things in that kind; while men rather discharge their minds than impart their minds. In few words, mysteries are due to secrecy. Besides (to say truth) nakedness is uncomely, as well in mind as body; and it addeth no small reverence to men's manners and actions, if they be not altogether open. As for talkers and futile[92] persons, they are commonly vain and credulous withal.[93] For he that talketh what he knoweth, will also talk what he knoweth not. Therefore set it down, that an habit of secrecy is both politic and moral. And in this part it is good that a man's face give his tongue leave to speak. For the discovery of a man's self by the tracts[94] of his countenance is a great weakness and betraying; by how much it is many times more marked and believed than a man's words.

For the second, which is dissimulation; it followeth many times upon secrecy by a necessity; so that he that will be secret must be a dissembler in some degree. For men are too cunning to suffer a man to keep an indifferent carriage[95] between both, and to be secret, without swaying the balance on either side. They will so beset a man with question, and draw him on, and pick it out of him, that, without an absurd silence, he must show an inclination one way; or if he do not, they will

---

82   As Bacon says in the third paragraph, simulation is pretending to be what one is not and dissimulation is concealing what one really is under some assumed guise. This essay treats both habits with regard to their usefulness in politics.

83   On Tacitus, see note 26 above. The passage is from *Annals* 5.1.

84   Tacitus, *Histories* 2.76.

85   *separate.*

86   See *Agricola* 39 and *Annals* 3.70.

87   *reticent.*

88   i.e. particular circumstances.

89   *reputation.*

90   i.e. beyond the power of observation.

91   i.e. as fresh air pours into a room which has been sealed.

92   *loquacious.*

93   i.e. as well.

94   *features.*

95   i.e. a disinterested manner.

gather as much by his silence as by his speech. As for equivocations, or oraculous[96] speeches, they cannot hold out long. So that no man can be secret, except he give himself a little scope of dissimulation; which is, as it were, but the skirts or train of secrecy.

But for the third degree, which is simulation and false profession; that I hold more culpable, and less politic;[97] except it be in great and rare matters.[98] And therefore a general custom of simulation (which is this last degree) is a vice, rising either of a natural falseness or fearfulness, or of a mind that hath some main[99] faults, which because a man must needs disguise, it maketh him practise simulation in other things, lest his hand should be out of ure.[100]

The great advantages of simulation and dissimulation are three. First, to lay asleep opposition, and to surprise. For where a man's intentions are published, it is an alarum to call up all that are against them. The second is, to reserve to a man's self a fair[101] retreat. For if a man engage himself by a manifest declaration, he must go through or take a fall. The third is, the better to discover the mind of another. For to him that opens himself men will hardly show themselves adverse; but will fair let him go on, and turn their freedom of speech to freedom of thought. And therefore it is a good shrewd proverb of the Spaniard, Tell a lie and find a troth. As if there were no way of discovery but by simulation. There be also three disadvantages, to set it even. The first, that simulation and dissimulation commonly carry with them a show of fearfulness, which in any business doth spoil the feathers of round flying up to the mark.[102] The second, that it puzzleth and perplexeth the conceits[103] of many, that perhaps would otherwise co-operate with him; and makes a man walk almost alone to his own ends. The third and greatest is, that it depriveth a man of one of the most principal instruments for action; which is trust and belief. The best composition[104] and temperature[105] is to have openness in fame[106] and opinion; secrecy in habit; dissimulation in seasonable use; and a power to feign, if there be no remedy.

Of Marriage and Single Life

He that hath wife and children hath given hostages to fortune; for they are impediments to great enterprises, either of virtue or mischief. Certainly the best works, and of greatest merit for the public, have proceeded from the unmarried or childless men; which both in affection and means have married and endowed the public. Yet it were great reason that those that have children should have greatest care of future times; unto which they know they must transmit their dearest pledges. Some there are, who though they lead a single life, yet their thoughts do end with themselves, and account future times impertinences.[107] Nay, there are some other that account wife and children but as bills of charges. Nay more, there are some foolish rich covetous men that take a pride in having no children, because they may be thought so much the richer. For perhaps they have heard some talk, Such an one is a great rich man, and another except to it, Yea, but he hath a great charge of children; as if it were an abatement[108] to his riches. But the most ordinary cause of a single life is liberty, especially in certain self-pleasing and humorous[109] minds, which are so sensible of every restraint, as they will go near to think their girdles and garters to be bonds and shackles. Unmarried men are best friends, best masters, best servants; but not always best subjects; for they are light to run away; and almost all fugitives are of that condition. A single life doth well with churchmen; for charity will hardly water the ground where it must first fill a pool. It is indifferent for judges and magistrates; for if they be facile and corrupt, you shall have a servant five times worse than a wife. For soldiers, I find the generals commonly in their hortatives[110] put men in mind of

96   ambiguous.
97   i.e. less a matter of expediency.
98   i.e. matters of state.
99   large.
100   use.
101   unobstructed.
102   i.e. prevents the arrow from flying straight to the target.
103   understandings.
104   mental constitution.
105   temperament.
106   reputation.
107   irrelevant matters.
108   decrease.
109   capricious.
110   encouraging speeches.

their wives and children; and I think the despising of marriage amongst the Turks maketh the vulgar[111] soldier more base. Certainly wife and children are a kind of discipline of humanity; and single men, though they may be many times more charitable, because their means are less exhaust, yet, on the other side, they are more cruel and hardhearted (good to make severe inquisitors), because their tenderness is not so oft called upon. Grave natures, led by custom, and therefore constant, are commonly loving husbands; as was said of Ulysses, *vetulam suam praetulit immortalitati.*[112] Chaste women are often proud and froward,[113] as presuming upon the merit of their chastity. It is one of the best bonds both of chastity and obedience in the wife, if she think her husband wise; which she will never do if she find him jealous. Wives are young men's mistresses; companions for middle age; and old men's nurses. So as a man may have a quarrel[114] to marry when he will. But yet he was reputed one of the wise men,[115] that made answer to the question, when a man should marry? – A young man not yet, an elder man not at all. It is often seen that bad husbands have very good wives; whether it be that it raiseth the price of their husband's kindness when it comes; or that the wives take a pride in their patience. But this never fails, if the bad husbands were of their own choosing, against their friends' consent; for then they will be sure to make good their own folly.

OF LOVE

The stage is more beholding to love, than the life of man. For as to the stage, love is ever matter of comedies, and now and then of tragedies; but in life it doth much mischief; sometimes like a siren, sometimes like a fury.[116] You may observe, that amongst all the great and worthy persons (whereof the memory remaineth, either ancient or recent) there is not one that hath been transported to the mad degree of love: which shows that great spirits and great business do keep out this weak passion. You must except nevertheless Marcus Antonius,[117] the half partner of the empire of Rome, and Appius Claudius,[118] the decemvir and lawgiver; whereof the former was indeed a voluptuous[119] man, and inordinate;[120] but the latter was an austere and wise man: and therefore it seems (though rarely) that love can find entrance not only into an open heart, but also into a heart well fortified, if watch be not well kept. It is a poor saying of Epicurus,[121] *Satis magnum alter alteri theatrum sumus* [Each is a sufficiently large theatre for the other]; as if man, made for the contemplation of heaven and all noble objects, should do nothing but kneel before a little idol and make himself a subject, though not of the mouth (as beasts are), yet of the eye; which was given him for higher purposes. It is a strange thing to note the excess of this passion, and how it braves the nature and value of things, by this; that the speaking in a perpetual hyperbole is comely in nothing but in love. Neither is it merely in the phrase; for whereas it hath been well said that the arch-flatterer, with whom all the petty flatterers have intelligence, is a man's self; certainly the lover is more. For there was never proud man thought so absurdly well of himself as the lover doth of the person loved; and therefore it was well said, "That it is impossible to love and to be wise."[122] Neither doth this weakness appear to others only, and not to the party loved; but to the loved most of all, except the love be reciproque.[123] For it is a true rule, that love is ever rewarded either with the reciproque

111 *common.*
112 The precise source of this passage is unknown. Ulysses' choice between immortality with the nymph Calypso and returning to his mortal wife was debated and referred to in many ancient texts. See Homer, *Odyssey*, 5.135 and 210–20.
113 *willful.*
114 *cause.*
115 Thales of Miletus, an ancient Greek mathematician and sage. One possible source for this example is Montaigne's *Essays* 2.8.
116 See Sirens and Furies in the gazetteer.
117 See gazetteer.
118 One of the decemvirs ("ten men") chosen to reform the laws of Rome in 451 BC. Roman historians record that he tried to seduce

and/or kidnap a young woman named Verginia, whose father killed her before allowing her to be dishonored. This in turn led to a rising by the plebeians and the overthrow of the decemvirs. Contemporary historians have cast doubts on the credibility of this story.
119 *sensual.*
120 *prone to excess.*
121 Quoted by Seneca in *Epistles* 7.11. Epicurus was a Greek philosopher whose professed hedonism was much misunderstood in antiquity and later (see note 11 above).
122 A common Early Modern cliché found in both Plutarch's *Lives* and Erasmus's *Adagia* (see gazetteer for both authors).
123 *reciprocal.*

or with an inward and secret contempt. By how much the more men ought to beware of this passion, which loseth not only other things, but itself! As for the other losses, the poet's relation doth well figure them: that he that preferred Helena,[124] quitted the gifts of Juno and Pallas. For whosoever esteemeth too much of amorous affection quitteth both riches and wisdom. This passion hath his floods in very times of weakness; which are great prosperity and great adversity; though this latter hath been less observed: both which times kindle love, and make it more fervent, and therefore show it to be the child of folly. They do best, who if they cannot but admit love, yet make it keep quarters;[125] and sever it wholly from their serious affairs and actions of life; for if it check once with business, it troubleth men's fortunes, and maketh men that they can no ways be true to their own ends. I know not how, but martial men are given to love: I think it is but as they are given to wine; for perils commonly ask to be paid in pleasures. There is in man's nature a secret inclination and motion towards love of others, which if it be not spent upon some one or a few, doth naturally spread itself towards many, and maketh men become humane and charitable; as it is seen sometime in friars. Nuptial love maketh mankind; friendly love perfecteth it; but wanton love corrupteth and embaseth[126] it.

OF NOBILITY

We will speak of nobility first as a portion of an estate,[127] then as a condition of particular persons. A monarchy where there is no nobility at all, is ever a pure and absolute tyranny; as that of the Turks. For nobility attempers[128] sovereignty, and draws the eyes of the people somewhat aside from the line royal. But for democracies, they need it not; and they are commonly more quiet and less subject to sedition, than where there are stirps[129] of nobles. For men's eyes are upon the business, and not upon the persons; or if upon the persons, it is for the business' sake, as fittest, and not for flags and pedigree. We see the Switzers[130] last well, notwithstanding their diversity of religion, and of cantons. For utility is their bond, and not respects.[131] The united provinces of the Low Countries[132] in their government excel; for where there is an equality, the consultations are more indifferent, and the payments and tributes more cheerful. A great and potent nobility addeth majesty to a monarch, but diminisheth power; and putteth life and spirit into the people, but presseth their fortune. It is well when nobles are not too great for sovereignty nor for justice; and yet maintained in that height, as the insolency of inferiors may be broken upon them before it come on too fast upon the majesty of kings. A numerous nobility causeth poverty and inconvenience in a state; for it is a surcharge of expense; and besides, it being of necessity that many of the nobility fall in time to be weak in fortune, it maketh a kind of disproportion between honour and means.[133]

As for nobility in particular persons; it is a reverend thing to see an ancient castle or building not in decay; or to see a fair timber tree sound and perfect. How much more to behold an ancient noble family, which has stood against the waves and weathers of time! For new nobility is but the act of power,[134] but ancient nobility is the act of time. Those that are first raised to nobility are commonly more virtuous, but less innocent, than their descendants; for there is rarely any rising but by a commixture of good and evil arts. But it is reason the memory of their virtues remain to their posterity, and their faults die with themselves. Nobility of birth commonly abateth[135] industry; and he that is not industrious, envieth him that is. Besides, noble persons cannot go much higher; and he that standeth at a stay[136] when others rise, can hardly avoid motions of envy.

124   See Paris, Juno, and Athena in the gazetteer.
125   i.e. in its appropriate place.
126   *degrades.*
127   *body politic.*
128   *moderates.*
129   *family groups.*
130   i.e. the Swiss. Early Modern Switzerland was a confederation of 13 cantons in a loose federal system which allowed for a great deal of local independence. As Bacon notes, it was a rare example of a European polity in which both Protestant and Catholic communities could coexist peacefully.
131   *deference to social rank.*
132   The part of Europe now occupied by the Netherlands, Belgium, and Luxembourg.
133   i.e. a disjunction between rank and income.
134   i.e. the creation of new nobles is an act of a monarch.
135   *discourages.*
136   *standstill.*

On the other side, nobility extinguisheth the passive envy from others towards them; because they are in possession of honour. Certainly, kings that have able men of their nobility shall find ease in employing them, and a better slide[137] into their business; for people naturally bend to them, as born in some sort to command.

OF TRAVEL

Travel, in the younger sort, is a part of education; in the elder, a part of experience. He that travelleth into a country before he hath some entrance into the language, goeth to school and not to travel. That young men travel under some tutor, or grave servant, I allow[138] well; so that he be such a one that hath the language, and hath been in the country before; whereby he may be able to tell them what things are worthy to be seen in the country where they go; what acquaintances they are to seek; what exercises or discipline[139] the place yieldeth. For else young men shall go hooded, and look abroad little. It is a strange thing, that in sea voyages, where there is nothing to be seen but sky and sea, men should make diaries; but in land-travel, wherein so much is to be observed, for the most part they omit it; as if chance were fitter to be registered than observation. Let diaries therefore be brought in use. The things to be seen and observed are: the courts of princes, especially when they give audience to ambassadors; the courts of justice, while they sit and hear causes; and so of consistories ecclesiastic;[140] the churches and monasteries, with the monuments which are therein extant; the walls and fortifications of cities and towns, and so the heavens and harbours; antiquities and ruins; libraries; colleges, disputations,[141] and lectures, where any are; shipping and navies; houses and gardens of state and pleasure, near great cities; armouries; arsenals; magazines;[142] exchanges; burses;[143] warehouses; exercises of horsemanship, fencing, training of soldiers, and the like; comedies, such whereunto the better sort of persons do resort; treasuries of jewels and robes; cabinets[144] and rarities; and, to conclude, whatsoever is memorable in the places where they go. After all which the tutors or servants ought to make diligent inquiry. As for triumphs, masks, feasts, weddings, funerals, capital executions, and such shows, men need not to be put in mind of them; yet are they not to be neglected. If you will have a young man to put his travel into a little room,[145] and in short time to gather much, this you must do. First, as was said, he must have some entrance into the language before he goeth. Then he must have such a servant or tutor as knoweth the country, as was likewise said. Let him carry with him also some card[146] or book describing the country where he travelleth; which will be a good key to his inquiry. Let him keep also a diary. Let him not stay long in one city or town; more or less as the place deserveth, but not long; nay, when he stayeth in one city or town, let him change his lodging from one end and part of the town to another; which is a great adamant[147] of acquaintance. Let him sequester himself from the company of his countrymen, and diet[148] in such places where there is good company of the nation where he travelleth. Let him upon his removes from one place to another, procure recommendation to some person of quality residing in the place whither he removeth; that he may use his favour in those things he desireth to see or know. Thus he may abridge his travel with much profit. As for the acquaintance which is to be sought in travel; that which is most of all profitable, is acquaintance with the secretaries and employed men of ambassadors: for so in travelling in one country he shall suck the experience of many. Let him also see and visit eminent persons in all kinds, which are of great name abroad; that he may be able to tell how the life agreeth with the fame. For quarrels, they are with care and discretion to be avoided. They are commonly for mis-

137   i.e. a smoother flow.
138   *approve.*
139   *education.*
140   i.e. ecclesiastical courts.
141   *formal academic debates.*
142   *warehouses.*

143   i.e. bourses; any place where merchants habitually meet to do business.
144   *museums.*
145   i.e. concentrate his travels in a short time.
146   *map.*
147   *magnet.*
148   *take meals.*

tresses, healths,[149] place,[150] and words.[151] And let a man beware how he keepeth company with choleric and quarrelsome persons; for they will engage him into their own quarrels. When a traveller returneth home, let him not leave the countries where he hath travelled altogether behind him; but maintain a correspondence by letters with those of his acquaintance, which are of most worth. And let his travel appear rather in his discourse than his apparel or gesture; and in his discourse let him be rather advised in his answers, than forward to tell stories; and let it appear that he doth not change his country manners[152] for those of foreign parts; but only prick[153] in some flowers of that he hath learned abroad into the customs of his own country.

Of Counsel

The greatest trust between man and man is the trust of giving counsel. For in other confidences men commit the parts of life; their lands, their goods, their children, their credit, some particular affair; but to such as they make their counsellors, they commit the whole: by how much the more they are obliged to all faith and integrity. The wisest princes need not think it any diminution to their greatness, or derogation to their sufficiency,[154] to rely upon counsel. God himself is not without but hath made it one of the great names of his blessed Son: The Counsellor.[155] Solomon hath pronounced that "in counsel is stability."[156] Things will have their first or second agitation: if they be not tossed upon the arguments of counsel, they will be tossed upon the waves of fortune; and be full of inconstancy, doing and undoing, like the reeling of a drunken man. Solomon's son found the force of counsel as his father saw the necessity of it.[157] For the beloved kingdom of God was first rent and broken by ill counsel;[158] upon which counsel there are set for our instruction the two marks[159] whereby bad counsel is for ever best discerned; that it was young counsel, for the person; and violent counsel, for the matter.

The ancient times do set forth in figure both the incorporation and inseparable conjunction of counsel with kings, and the wise and politic use of counsel by kings: the one, in that they say Jupiter did marry Metis,[160] which signifieth counsel; whereby they intend that Sovereignty is married to Counsel: the other in that which followeth, which was thus: They say, after Jupiter was married to Metis, she conceived by him and was with child, but Jupiter suffered her not to stay till she brought forth, but ate her up; whereby he became himself with child, and was delivered of Pallas[161] armed, out of his head. Which monstrous fable containeth a secret of empire; how kings are to make use of their counsel of state. That first they ought to refer matters unto them, which is the first begetting or impregnation; but when they are elaborate,[162] moulded, and shaped in the womb of their counsel, and grow ripe and ready to be brought forth, that then they suffer not their counsel to go through with the resolution and direction, as if it depended on them; but take the matter back into their own hands, and make it appear to the world that the decrees and final directions (which, because they come forth with prudence and power, are resembled to Pallas armed) proceeded from themselves; and not only from their authority, but (the more to add reputation to themselves) from their head and device.[163]

Let us now speak of the inconveniences of counsel, and of the remedies. The inconveniences that have been noted in calling and using counsel, are three. First, the revealing of affairs, whereby they become less secret. Secondly, the weakening of the authority of princes, as if they were less of themselves. Thirdly, the danger of being unfaithfully counselled, and more for the good of them that counsel than of him that is counselled. For which inconveniences, the doctrine of Italy, and

149   *drinking toasts.*
150   *issues of rank or social position.*
151   *verbal altercations.*
152   i.e. his own country's manners.
153   *plant.*
154   *competence.*
155   Isaiah 9:6.
156   Proverbs 20:18.

157   1 Kings 12:1–19.
158   i.e. the serpent's counsel to Eve in Genesis.
159   *distinguishing features.*
160   Bacon omits the detail that Zeus/Jupiter ate Metis because he was warned that her children would threaten his position as ruler of the gods.
161   See Athena in the gazetteer.
162   i.e. worked out in detail.
163   i.e. ingenuity.

practice of France, in some kings' times, hath introduced cabinet counsels; a remedy worse than the disease.[164]

As to secrecy; princes are not bound to communicate all matters with all counsellors; but may extract and select. Neither is it necessary that he that consulteth what he should do, should declare what he will do. But let princes beware that the unsecreting of their affairs comes not from themselves. And as for cabinet counsels, it may be their motto, *plenus rimarum sum* [I am full of cracks]:[165] one futile[166] person that maketh it his glory to tell, will do more hurt than many that know it their duty to conceal. It is true there be some affairs which require extreme secrecy, which will hardly go beyond one or two persons besides the king: neither are those counsels unprosperous; for besides the secrecy, they commonly go on constantly in one spirit of direction, without distraction. But then it must be a prudent king, such as is able to grind with a handmill;[167] and those inward counsellors had need also be wise men, and especially true and trusty to the king's ends; as it was with King Henry the Seventh of England, who in his great business imparted himself to none, except it were to Morton and Fox.[168]

For weakening of authority; the fable showeth the remedy. Nay, the majesty of kings is rather exalted than diminished when they are in the chair of counsel; neither was there ever prince bereaved of his dependences by his counsel; except where there hath been either an over-greatness in one counsellor or an over-strict combination in divers; which are things soon found and holpen.[169]

For the last inconvenience, that men will counsel with an eye to themselves; certainly, *non inveniet fidem super terram* [he shall not find faith on the earth][170] is meant of the nature of times, and not of all particular persons. There be that are in nature faithful, and sincere, and plain, and direct; not crafty and involved;[171] let princes, above all, draw to themselves such natures. Besides, counsellors are not commonly so united, but that one counsellor keepeth sentinel over another; so that if any do counsel out of faction or private ends, it commonly comes to the king's ear. But the best remedy is, if princes know their counsellors, as well as their counsellors know them:

> *Principis est virtus maxima nosse suos.*
> [It is a ruler's greatest merit to know his own people.][172]

And on the other side, counsellors should not be too speculative into their sovereign's person. The true composition of a counsellor is rather to be skilful in their master's business than in his nature; for then he is like to advise him, and not feed his humour.[173] It is of singular use to princes if they take the opinions of their counsel both separately and together. For private opinion is more free; but opinion before others is more reverent.[174] In private, men are more bold in their own humours; and in consort, men are more obnoxious to others' humours; therefore it is good to take both; and of the inferior[175] sort rather in private, to preserve freedom; of the greater rather in consort, to preserve respect. It is in vain for princes to take counsel concerning matters, if they take no counsel likewise concerning persons; for all matters are as dead images; and the life of the execution of affairs resteth in the good choice of persons. Neither is it enough to consult concerning persons *secundum genera* [according to types], as in an idea, or mathematical description, what the kind and character of the person should be; for the greatest errors are committed, and the most judgment is shown, in the choice of individuals. It was truly said, *optimi consiliarii mortui* [the best advisors are

---

164　An unpublished manuscript of this essay has Bacon elaborating on the dangers of informal groups of flatterers ("cabinet counsels") rather than constituted bodies like the Privy Council ("counsel of state"). His omission of this may well reflect his ongoing fear of offending James I or the Duke of Buckingham any further.

165　This Latin phrase is from the Roman playwright Terence's *Eunuchus*, and refers to people who let too much information out.

166　In this context, the word means "talkative."

167　i.e. work by himself.

168　Henry VII's chief counsellors were Archbishop John Morton, who was also Chancellor, and Richard Fox, who was the Bishop of Winchester.

169　helped

170　A reference to Luke 18:8.

171　*underhand.*

172　Martial, *Epigrams* 8.15.8.

173　i.e. mood or inclination.

174　*respectful.*

175　i.e. socially inferior (as opposed to the "greater" which refers to the aristocracy).

the dead]: books will speak plain when counsellors blanch. Therefore it is good to be conversant in them, specially the books of such as themselves have been actors upon the stage.[176]

The counsels at this day in most places are but familiar meetings, where matters are rather talked on than debated. And they run too swift to the order or act of counsel. It were better that in causes of weight, the matter were propounded one day and not spoken to till the next day; *in nocte consilium* [night is the season for counsel]. So was it done in the Commission of Union between England and Scotland;[177] which was a grave and orderly assembly. I commend set days for petitions; for both it gives the suitors more certainty for their attendance, and it frees the meetings for matters of estate, that they may *hoc agere* [do this].[178] In choice of committees; for ripening business for the counsel, it is better to choose indifferent[179] persons, than to make an indifferency by putting in those that are strong on both sides. I commend also standing commissions; as for trade, for treasure, for war, for suits,[180] for some provinces; for where there be divers particular counsels and but one counsel of estate (as it is in Spain), they are, in effect, no more than standing commissions: save that they have greater authority. Let such as are to inform counsels out of their particular professions (as lawyers, seamen, mintmen, and the like) be first heard before committees; and then, as occasion serves, before the counsel. And let them not come in multitudes, or in a tribunitious[181] manner; for that is to clamour counsels, not to inform them. A long table and a square table, or seats about the walls, seem things of form,[182] but are things of substance; for at a long table a few at the upper end, in effect, sway all the business; but in the other form there is more use of the counsellors' opinions that sit lower. A king, when he presides in counsel, let him beware how he opens his own inclination too much in that which he propoundeth; for else counsellors will but take the wind of him, and instead of giving free counsel, sing him a song of *placebo* [I shall please you].[183]

OF CUNNING

We take[184] cunning for a sinister or crooked wisdom. And certainly there is a great difference between a cunning man and a wise man; not only in point of honesty, but in point of ability. There be that can pack the cards,[185] and yet cannot play well; so there are some that are good in canvasses[186] and factions, that are otherwise weak men. Again, it is one thing to understand persons, and another thing to understand matters; for many are perfect in men's humours,[187] that are not greatly capable of the real part of business; which is the constitution of one that hath studied men more than books. Such men are fitter for practice than for counsel; and they are good but in their own alley:[188] turn them to new men, and they have lost their aim; so as the old rule to know a fool from a wise man, *Mitte ambos nudos ad ignotos, et videbis* [Send them both naked to those who do not know them and you will see],[189] doth scarce hold for them. And because these cunning men are like haberdashers[190] of small wares, it is not amiss to set forth their shop.

It is a point of cunning, to wait upon[191] him with whom you speak with your eye; as the Jesuits[192] give it in precept: for there be many wise men that have secret hearts and transparent countenances. Yet this would be done with a demure abasing of your eye sometimes, as the Jesuits also do use.

---

176   i.e. been involved in politics. The theatrical simile reveals a great deal about Bacon's view of the workings of power.

177   James I of England was also King James VI of Scotland, and he formed a committee to investigate joining the two kingdoms into one in 1604. The union did not take place until 1707.

178   The Latin source for this is Plutarch's *Caius Marcius Coriolanus* in the *Parallel Lives*.

179   *impartial.*

180   *supplications to the monarch.*

181   "factious or violent, after the manner attributed to the Roman tribunes" (*OED*).

182   *procedure.*

183   A reference to Psalms 116:4 and a common Early Modern joke about flattering one's superiors.

184   *understand.*

185   i.e. cheat by shuffling the cards into a prearranged order.

186   i.e. covert schemes.

187   i.e. know human nature well.

188   i.e. environment.

189   Ascribed to the Greek philosopher Aristippus.

190   Dealers in small articles for clothes; Bacon is implying that such men are peddling trifles.

191   *attend* (in this case, by looking closely).

192   The Society of Jesus is an order of priests founded in 1534 to combat the spread of Protestantism.

Another is, that when you have anything to obtain of present despatch,[193] you entertain and amuse the party with whom you deal with some other discourse; that he be not too much awake to make objections. I knew a counsellor and secretary, that never came to Queen Elizabeth of England with bills to sign, but he would always first put her into some discourse of estate,[194] that she mought[195] the less mind the bills.

The like surprise may be made by moving things when the party is in haste, and cannot stay to consider advisedly of that is moved.

If a man would cross a business that he doubts some other would handsomely and effectually move, let him pretend to wish it well, and move it himself in such sort as may foil it.

The breaking off in the midst of that one was about to say, as if he took himself up, breeds a greater appetite in him with whom you confer to know more.

And because it works better when anything seemeth to be gotten from you by question, than if you offer it of yourself, you may lay a bait for a question, by showing another visage and countenance than you are wont; to the end to give occasion for the party to ask what the matter is of the change? As Nehemias[196] did; "And I had not before that time been sad before the king."

In things that are tender[197] and unpleasing, it is good to break the ice by some whose words are of less weight, and to reserve the more weighty voice to come in as by chance, so that he may be asked the question upon the other's speech: as Narcissus did, relating to Claudius the marriage of Messalina and Silius.[198]

In things that a man would not be seen in himself, it is a point of cunning to borrow the name of the world; as to say, "The world says," or "There is a speech abroad."

I knew one that, when he wrote a letter, he would put that which was most material in the postscript, as if it had been a by-matter.

I knew another that, when he came to have speech, he would pass over that that he intended most; and go forth, and come back again, and speak of it as of a thing that he had almost forgot.

Some procure themselves to be surprised at such times as it is like the party that they work upon will suddenly come upon them; and to be found with a letter in their hand or doing somewhat which they are not accustomed; to the end they may be apposed of[199] those things which of themselves they are desirous to utter.

It is a point of cunning, to let fall those words in a man's own name, which he would have another man learn and use, and thereupon take advantage. I knew two[200] that were competitors for the secretary's place in Queen Elizabeth's time, and yet kept good quarter[201] between themselves; and would confer one with another upon the business; and the one of them said, That to be a secretary in the declination of a monarchy was a ticklish thing, and that he did not affect it: the other straight caught up those words, and discoursed with divers of his friends, that he had no reason to desire to be secretary in the declination of a monarchy. The first man took hold of it, and found means it was told the Queen; who hearing of a declination of a monarchy, took it so ill, as she would never after hear of the other's suit.

There is a cunning, which we in England call the turning of the cat[202] in the pan; which is, when that which a man says to another, he lays[203] it as if another had said it to him. And to say truth, it is not easy, when such a matter passed between two, to make it appear from which of them it first moved and began.

It is a way that some men have, to glance and dart at others by justifying themselves by negatives; as to say, "This I do not"; as Tigellinus did towards Burrhus,[204] *Se non diversas spes, sed*

---

193 i.e. urgent or pressing.

194 *the nation.*

195 *might.*

196 Nehemiah 2:1.

197 *sensitive.*

198 See the Roman historian Tacitus, *Annals* 11.29–30. Narcissus was an advisor to the Emperor Claudius and he used this tactic to inform the emperor that his wife had gone through a marriage ceremony with another man.

199 *questioned about.*

200 Previous editors have presumed that this refers to Sir Robert Cecil and Sir Thomas Bodley in 1596. Cecil was the successful candidate.

201 i.e. on good terms.

202 A corruption of the word "cate," meaning a food item.

203 *reports.*

204 Two of the Emperor Nero's courtiers.

incolumitatem imperatoris simpliciter spectare [He had no divergent goals, but looked only for the safety of the emperor].[205]

Some have in readiness so many tales and stories, as there is nothing they would insinuate, but they can wrap it into a tale; which serveth both to keep themselves more in guard,[206] and to make others carry it with more pleasure.

It is a good point of cunning, for a man to shape the answer he would have in his own words and propositions; for it makes the other party stick[207] the less.

It is strange how long some men will lie in wait to speak somewhat they desire to say; and how far about they will fetch; and how many other matters they will beat over, to come near it. It is a thing of great patience, but yet of much use.

A sudden, bold, and unexpected question doth many times surprise a man, and lay him open. Like to him that, having changed his name, and walking in Paul's,[208] another suddenly came behind him and called him by his true name whereat straightways he looked back.

But these small wares and petty points of cunning are infinite; and it were a good deed to make a list of them; for that nothing doth more hurt in a state than that cunning men pass for wise.

But certainly some there are that know the resorts and falls[209] of business, that cannot sink into the main of it; like a house that hath convenient stairs and entries, but never a fair room. Therefore you shall see them find out pretty looses[210] in the conclusion, but are no ways able to examine or debate matters. And yet commonly they take advantage of their inability, and would be thought wits of direction. Some build rather upon the abusing of others, and (as we now say) putting tricks upon them, than upon soundness of their own proceedings. But Solomon saith, *Prudens advertit ad gressus suos; stultus divertit ad dolos* [The wise man looks to his own way; the fool is diverted to deceits].[211]

OF INNOVATIONS[212]

As the births of living creatures at first are ill-shapen, so are all innovations, which are the births of time. Yet notwithstanding, as those that first bring honour into their family are commonly more worthy than most that succeed, so the first precedent (if it be good) is seldom attained by imitation. For ill,[213] to man's nature as it stands perverted, hath a natural motion, strongest in continuance; but good, as a forced[214] motion, strongest at first. Surely every medicine is an innovation; and he that will not apply new remedies must expect new evils; for time is the greatest innovator; and if time of course alter things to the worse, and wisdom and counsel shall not alter them to the better, what shall be the end? It is true, that what is settled by custom, though it be not good, yet at least it is fit; and those things which have long gone together are as it were confederate within themselves; whereas new things piece[215] not so well; but though they help by their utility, yet they trouble by their inconformity.[216] Besides, they are like strangers; more admired and less favoured. All this is true, if time stood still; which contrariwise moveth so round, that a froward[217] retention of custom is as turbulent a thing as an innovation; and they that reverence too much old times, are but a scorn to the new. It were good therefore that men in their innovations would follow the example of time itself; which indeed innovateth greatly, but quietly, by degrees scarce to he

205   Tacitus, *Annals* 14.57.
206   i.e. in safety.
207   *resist.*
208   St. Paul's Churchyard in London (a common meeting place in Early Modern times).
209   Usually glossed as "sources and outcomes," these terms also suggest "aids and downfalls."
210   i.e. make impressive statements. The verb "loose" here refers to the firing of an arrow from a bow.
211   See Proverbs 14:8.

212   i.e. changes to established orders (especially in a political context). To fully understand this essay, one must recall the suspicion with which supposedly fixed political systems (like monarchies) inevitably reacted to change. The word is most often used in this period as a slur impugning any change to an established orthodox view, although Bacon is clearly trying to overcome this prejudice.
213   *evil.*
214   *artificially induced* (and therefore finite).
215   *join.*
216   i.e. lack of conformity.
217   *stubborn.*

perceived. For otherwise, whatsoever is new is unlooked for; and ever it mends some, and pairs[218] others; and he that holpen[219] takes it for a fortune, and thanks the time; and he that is hurt, for a wrong, and imputeth it to the author. It is good also not to try experiments in states, except the necessity be urgent, or the utility evident; and well to beware that it be the reformation that draweth on the change, and not the desire of change that pretendeth the reformation.[220] And lastly, that the novelty, though it be not rejected, yet be held for a suspect; and, as the Scripture saith,[221] "hat we make a stand upon the ancient way, and then look about us, and discover what is the straight and right way, and so to walk in it."

OF DISCOURSE[222]

Some in their discourse desire rather commendation of wit, in being able to hold all arguments, than of judgment, in discerning what is true; as if it were a praise to know what might be said, and not what should be thought. Some have certain commonplaces[223] and themes wherein they are good, and want variety; which kind of poverty is for the most part tedious, and when it is once perceived, ridiculous. The honourablest part of talk is to give the occasion;[224] and again to moderate and pass to somewhat else; for then a man leads the dance. It is good, in discourse and speech of conversation, to vary and intermingle speech of the present occasion with arguments, tales with reasons, asking of questions with telling of opinions, and jest with earnest: for it is a dull thing to tire, and, as we say now, to jade, any thing too far. As for jest, there be certain things which ought to be privileged from it; namely, religion, matters of state, great persons, any man's present business of importance, and any case that deserveth pity. Yet there be some that think their wits have been asleep, except they dart out somewhat that is piquant, and to the quick.[225] That is a vein which would be bridled:

> Parce, puer, stimulis, et fortius utere loris.
> [Spare, child, the whip, and hold the reins tighter]

And generally, men ought to find the difference between saltness and bitterness. Certainly, he that hath a satirical vein, as he maketh others afraid of his wit, so he had need be afraid of others' memory. He that questioneth much, shall learn much, and content much; but especially if he apply his questions to the skill of the persons whom he asketh; for he shall give them occasion, to please themselves in speaking, and himself shall continually gather knowledge. But let his questions not be troublesome; for that is fit for a poser. And let him be sure to leave other men their turns to speak. Nay, if there be any that would reign and take up all the time, let him find means to take them off, and to bring others on; as musicians use to do with those that dance too long galliards.[226] If you dissemble sometimes your knowledge of that you are thought to know, you shall be thought another time to know that you know not. Speech of a man's self ought to be seldom, and well chosen. I knew one was wont to say in scorn, "He must needs be a wise man, he speaks so much of himself": and there is but one case wherein a man may commend himself with good grace; and that is in commending virtue in another; especially if it be such a virtue whereunto himself pretendeth. Speech of touch towards others[227] should be sparingly used; for discourse ought to be as a field,[228] without coming home to any man. I knew two noblemen, of the west part of England, whereof the one was given to scoff, but kept ever royal cheer[229] in his house; the other would ask of those that had been at the other's table, *Tell truly, was there never a flout*[230] *or dry blow*[231] *given?* To

---

218 *impairs.*
219 i.e. he that is helped.
220 i.e. uses reformation as a pretext.
221 Jeremiah 6:16.
222 i.e. conversation.
223 *standard topics.*
224 i.e. provide the subject.

225 i.e. hurtful.
226 A French dance.
227 i.e. Speech that refers directly to others.
228 *common land.*
229 i.e. food, drink, and entertainment.
230 *insult.*
231 *mocking remark.*

which the guest would answer, "Such and such a thing passed." The lord would say, "I thought he would mar a good dinner." Discretion of speech is more than eloquence; and to speak agreeably to him with whom we deal, is more than to speak in good words or in good order. A good continued speech, without a good speech of interlocution,[232] shows slowness: and a good reply or second speech, without a good settled speech, showeth shallowness and weakness. As we see in beasts, that those that are weakest in the course,[233] are yet nimblest in the turn; as it is betwixt the greyhound and the hare. To use too many circumstances[234] ere one come to the matter,[235] is wearisome; to use none at all, is blunt.

Of Plantations[236]

Plantations are amongst ancient, primitive, and heroical works. When the world was young it begat more children; but now it is old it begets fewer: for I may justly account new plantations to be the children of former kingdoms. I like a plantation in a pure[237] soil; that is, where people are not displanted[238] to the end to plant in others. For else it is rather an extirpation than a plantation. Planting of countries is like planting of woods; for you must make account to leese[239] almost twenty years' profit, and expect your recompense in the end. For the principal thing that hath been the destruction of most plantations, hath been the base and hasty drawing of profit in the first years. It is true, speedy profit is not to be neglected, as far as may stand with the good of the plantation, but no further. It is a shameful and unblessed thing to take the scum of people, and wicked condemned men, to be the people with whom you plant; and not only so, but it spoileth the plantation; for they will ever live like rogues, and not fall to work, but be lazy, and do mischief, and spend victuals,[240] and be quickly weary, and then certify[241] over to their country to the discredit of the plantation. The people wherewith you plant ought to be gardeners, ploughmen, labourers, smiths, carpenters, joiners, fishermen, fowlers,[242] with some few apothecaries,[243] surgeons, cooks, and bakers. In a country of plantation, first look about what kind of victual the country yields of itself to hand; as chestnuts, walnuts, pineapples, olives, dates, plums, cherries, wild honey, and the like; and make use of them. Then consider what victual or esculent[244] things there are, which grow speedily, and within the year; as parsnips, carrots, turnips, onions, radish, artichokes of Jerusalem, maize, and the like. For wheat, barley, and oats, they ask too much labour; but with pease and beans you may begin, both because they ask less labour, and because they serve for meat, as well as for bread. And of rice, likewise cometh a great increase, and it is a kind of meat. Above all, there ought to be brought store of biscuit, oat-meal, flour, meal,[245] and the like, in the beginning, till bread may be had. For beasts, or birds, take chiefly such as are least subject to diseases, and multiply fastest; as swine, goats, cocks, hens, turkeys, geese, house-doves, and the like. The victual in plantations ought to be expended almost as in a besieged town; that is, with certain allowance.[246] And let the main part of the ground employed to gardens or corn,[247] be to a common stock; and to be laid in, and stored up, and then delivered out in proportion; besides some spots of ground that any particular person will manure[248] for his own private. Consider likewise what commodities the soil where the plantation is doth naturally yield, that they may some way help to defray the charge of the plantation (so it be not, as was said, to the untimely prejudice of the main business), as it hath fared with tobacco in Virginia.[249] Wood commonly aboundeth but too much; and there-

---

232   i.e. speech from others.

233   i.e. running straight.

234   *details.*

235   *main point.*

236   The Colonies. England was engaged in numerous settlement ventures in North America during Bacon's lifetime, and the exploration of the "New World" is an important recurring image for scientific exploration in his works.

237   *unoccupied.*

238   *displaced.*

239   *lose.*

240   waste food

241   *testify.*

242   *bird hunters.*

243   *druggists*

244   *edible.*

245   *non-wheat flour.*

246   *ration.*

247   i.e. grain.

248   i.e. cultivate.

249   Tobacco grown in the early Virginia colonies was so profitable that little else was cultivated.

fore timber is fit to be one. If there be iron ore, and streams whereupon to set the mills, iron is a brave commodity where wood aboundeth. Making of bay-salt,[250] if the climate be proper for it, would be put in experience. Growing silk likewise, if any be, is a likely commodity. Pitch and tar,[251] where store of firs and pines are, will not fail. So drugs and sweet woods, where they are, cannot but yield great profit. Soap-ashes[252] likewise, and other things that may be thought of. But moil[253] not too much under ground; for the hope of mines is very uncertain, and useth to make the planters lazy in other things. For government, let it be in the hands of one, assisted with some counsel; and let them have commission to exercise martial laws, with some limitation. And above all, let men make that profit of being in the wilderness, as they have God always, and his service, before their eyes. Let not the government of the plantation depend upon too many counsellors and undertakers[254] in the country that planteth, but upon a temperate number; and let those be rather noblemen and gentlemen, than merchants; for they look ever to the present gain. Let there be freedoms from custom,[255] till the plantation be of strength; and not only freedom from custom, but freedom to carry their commodities where they may make their best of them, except there be some special cause of caution. Cram not in people, by sending too fast company after company; but rather hearken how they waste, and send supplies proportionably; but so as the number may live well in the plantation, and not by surcharge be in penury. It hath been a great endangering to the health of some plantations, that they have built along the sea and rivers, in marish[256] and unwholesome grounds. Therefore, though you begin there, to avoid carriage[257] and like discommodities, yet build still rather upwards from the streams, than along. It concerneth likewise the health of the plantation that they have good store of salt with them, that they may use it in their victuals, when it shall be necessary. If you plant where savages are, do not only entertain them with trifles and jingles; but use them justly and graciously, with sufficient guard nevertheless; and do not win their favour by helping them to invade their enemies, but for their defence it is not amiss; and send oft of them over to the country that plants, that they may see a better condition than their own, and commend it when they return.[258] When the plantation grows to strength, then it is time to plant with women as well as with men; that the plantation may spread into generations, and not be ever pieced from without. It is the sinfullest thing in the world to forsake or destitute a plantation once in forwardness;[259] for besides the dishonour, it is the guiltiness of blood of many commiserable[260] persons.

OF MASQUES[261] AND TRIUMPHS[262]

These things are but toys, to come amongst such serious observations. But yet, since princes will have such things, it is better they should be graced with elegancy than daubed[263] with cost. Dancing to song,[264] is a thing of great state[265] and pleasure. I understand it, that the song be in quire,[266] placed aloft,[267] and accompanied with some broken music; and the ditty fitted to the device. Acting in song, especially in dialogues, hath an extreme good grace; I say acting, not dancing (for that is a mean and vulgar thing); and the voices of the dialogue would be strong and manly (a bass and a tenor; no treble); and the ditty high[268] and tragical; not nice[269] or dainty. Several quires, placed

---

250 sea-salt.
251 Substances used for waterproofing in early modern Europe.
252 Used for making lye.
253 toil.
254 sponsors.
255 taxation.
256 marshy.
257 i.e. transport problems.
258 Like nearly all other Europeans of his day, Bacon takes the inferiority of indigenous peoples as a given.
259 i.e. once set in motion.
260 pitiable.

261 A popular form of entertainment in Early Modern English courts. They consisted of dumb-shows involving masked and costumed players who danced and acted out allegorical scenes or tableaus.
262 A public pageant; in Bacon's day, the term often referred to a tournament.
263 crudely decorated.
264 i.e. the masque.
265 splendor.
266 choir.
267 i.e. in a minstrels' gallery.
268 i.e. in the high style.
269 excessively intricate.

one over against another, and taking the voice by catches,[270] anthem-wise, give great pleasure. Turning dances into figure[271] is a childish curiosity. And generally let it be noted, that those things which I here set down are such as do naturally take the sense,[272] and not respect petty wonderments. It is true, the alterations of scenes,[273] so it be quietly and without noise, are things of great beauty and pleasure; for they feed and relieve the eye, before it be full of the same object. Let the scenes abound with light, specially coloured and varied; and let the masquers, or any other, that are to come down from the scene,[274] have some motions upon the scene itself before their coming down; for it draws the eye strangely,[275] and makes it with great pleasure to desire to see that it cannot perfectly discern. Let the songs be loud and cheerful, and not chirpings or pulings.[276] Let the music likewise be sharp and loud, and well placed. The colours that show best by candle-light are white, carnation, and a kind of sea-water-green; and oes, or spangs,[277] as they are of no great cost, so they are of most glory. As for rich embroidery, it is lost and not discerned. Let the suits of the masquers be graceful, and such as become the person when the vizards[278] are off; not after examples of known attires; Turks, soldiers, mariners, and the like. Let anti-masques[279] not be long; they have been commonly of fools, satyrs, baboons, wild-men, antics, beasts, sprites, witches, Ethiops,[280] pigmies, turquets,[281] nymphs, rustics, Cupids, statues moving, and the like. As for angels, it is not comical enough to put them in anti-masques; and anything that is hideous, as devils, giants, is on the other side as unfit. But chiefly, let the music of them be recreative,[282] and with some strange changes. Some sweet odours suddenly coming forth, without any drops falling, are, in such a company as there is steam and heat, things of great pleasure and refreshment. Double masques, one of men, another of ladies, addeth state and variety. But all is nothing except the room be kept clear and neat.

For jousts, and tourneys, and barriers;[283] the glories of them are chiefly in the chariots, wherein the challengers make their entry; especially if they be drawn with strange beasts: as lions, bears, camels, and the like; or in the devices[284] of their entrance; or in the bravery[285] of their liveries; or in the goodly furniture[286] of their horses and armour. But enough of these toys.

OF NATURE[287] IN MEN

Nature is often hidden; sometimes overcome; seldom extinguished. Force maketh nature more violent in the return; doctrine and discourse maketh nature less importune; but custom only doth alter and subdue nature. He that seeketh victory over his nature, let him not set himself too great nor too small tasks; for the first will make him dejected by often failings; and the second will make him a small proceeder, though by often prevailings. And at the first let him practise with helps, as swimmers do with bladders or rushes;[288] but after a time let him practise with disadvantages, as dancers do with thick shoes. For it breeds great perfection, if the practice be harder than the use.[289] Where nature is mighty, and therefore the victory hard, the degrees had need be, first to stay[290] and arrest nature in time; like to him that would say over the four and twenty letters when he was angry; then to go less in quantity; as if one should, in forbearing[291] wine, come from drinking

---

270 i.e. singing the song as a round.

271 i.e. arranging the dancers to form a shape or a name.

272 *grasp our attention.*

273 *changes of scenery.*

274 i.e. leave the stage to mix with the audience.

275 *extremely.*

276 *whining.*

277 i.e. small metal decorations sewed to costumes in order to catch the light.

278 *masks.*

279 Grotesque and/or comic interludes in the more solemn main masque.

280 A term which referred to any people of colour.

281 Bacon's own coinage: it means "little Turks," and may refer to costumed dwarfs.

282 *pleasurable.*

283 A martial exercise in which the combatants fought on foot in a fenced-off area.

284 The term refers to the heraldic design on the combatants' shields, and also to the way in which those designs combined with their clothes and horse trappings to suggest allegorical conceits.

285 *finery.*

286 *decorations and harness.*

287 i.e. natural inclination.

288 *hollow reeds.*

289 *normal performance.*

290 *stop.*

291 *giving up.*

healths,[292] to a draught at a meal; and lastly, to discontinue altogether. But if a man have the fortitude and resolution to enfranchise[293] himself at once, that is the best:

Optimus ille animi vindex laedentia pectus Vincula qui rupit, dedoluitque semel.
[The best liberator of the soul is he who has broken the chains which afflict his soul, and ceased to grieve][294]

Neither is the ancient rule amiss, to bend nature as a wand[295] to a contrary extreme, whereby to set it right; understanding it, where the contrary extreme is no vice. Let not a man force a habit upon himself with a perpetual continuance, but with some intermission. For both the pause rein-forceth the new onset;[296] and if a man that is not perfect be ever in practice, he shall as well, prac-tise his errors as his abilities, and induce one habit of both; and there is no means to help this but by seasonable intermissions. But let not a man trust his victory over his nature too far; for nature will lay buried a great time, and yet revive upon the occasion or temptation. Like as it was with Aesop's damsel, turned from a cat to a woman, who sat very demurely at the board's end, till a mouse ran before her.[297] Therefore let a man either avoid the occasion altogether; or put himself often to it, that he may be little moved with it. A man's nature is best perceived in privateness, for there is no affectation; in passion, for that putteth a man out of his precepts; and in a new case or experiment, for there custom[298] leaveth him. They are happy men whose natures sort with their vocations; otherwise they may say, *multum incola fuit anima mea* [My soul has long been a sojourner];[299] when they converse in those things they do not affect.[300] In studies, whatsoever a man commandeth upon himself, let him set hours for it; but whatsoever is agreeable to his nature, let him take no care for any set times; for his thoughts will fly to it of themselves; so as the spaces of other business or studies will suffice. A man's nature runs either to herbs or weeds; therefore let him seasonably water the one, and destroy the other.

OF CUSTOM AND EDUCATION

Men's thoughts are much according to their inclination;[301] their discourse and speeches according to their learning and infused opinions; but their deeds are after as they have been accustomed.[302] And therefore, as Machiavel[303] well noteth (though in an evil-favoured instance), there is no trust-ing to the force of nature nor to the bravery of words, except it be corroborate by custom. His instance is, that for the achieving of a desperate conspiracy, a man should not rest upon the fierce-ness of any man's nature, or his resolute undertakings; but take such an one as hath had his hands formerly in blood. But Machiavel knew not of a Friar Clement, nor a Ravillac, nor a Jaureguy, nor a Baltazar Gerard;[304] yet his rule holdeth still, that nature, nor the engagement of words, are not so forcible as custom. Only superstition is now so well advanced, that men of the first blood[305] are as firm as butchers by occupation; and votary resolution[306] is made equipollent[307] to custom even in matter of blood. In other things the predominancy of custom is everywhere visible; insomuch as a man would wonder to hear men profess, protest, engage, give great words, and then do just

292 *toasts.*

293 *liberate.*

294 From the Roman poet Ovid's *Remedia Amoris* (*Cures for Love*) 293–4.

295 *stick.*

296 *beginning.*

297 The mouse caused her true self to reappear. This fable was wrongly ascribed to Aesop (see gazetteer) in the Early Modern period.

298 *habit.*

299 The passage is from the Vulgate version of Psalms 120:6.

300 *enjoy.*

301 i.e. natural inclinations.

302 *habituated.*

303 A common English abbreviation for Niccolò Machiavelli (1469–1527), the Florentine statesman and political theorist. He is best known for his treatise on rulership called *Il Principe* (*The Prince*) and *The Discourses* (on the Roman historian Livy). Bacon's allusion is to *Discourses* 3.6.

304 Four men who attempted (in three cases successfully) to murder reigning monarchs.

305 i.e. men committing their first murder.

306 *vow.*

307 *equal in power.*

as they have done before; as if they were dead images,[308] and engines[309] moved only by the wheels of custom. We see also the reign or tyranny of custom, what it is. The Indians (I mean the sect of their wise men)[310] lay themselves quietly upon a stock of wood, and so sacrifice themselves by fire. Nay the wives strive to be burned with the corpses of their husbands. The lads of Sparta, of ancient time, were wont to be scourged[311] upon the altar of Diana, without so much as queching.[312] I remember, in the beginning of Queen Elizabeth's time of England, an Irish rebel condemned, put up a petition to the deputy that he might be hanged in a withe,[313] and not in an halter; because it had been so used with former rebels. There be monks in Russia, for penance, that will sit a whole night in a vessel of water, till they be engaged[314] with hard ice. Many examples may be put of the force of custom, both upon mind and body. Therefore, since custom is the principal magistrate of man's life, let men by all means endeavour to obtain good customs. Certainly custom is most perfect when it beginneth in young years: this we call education; which is, in effect, but an early custom. So we see, in languages the tongue is more pliant to all expressions and sounds, the joints are more supple to all feats of activity and motions, in youth than afterwards. For it is true that late learners cannot so well take the ply;[315] except it be in some minds that have not suffered themselves to fix, but have kept themselves open, and prepared to receive continual amendment, which is exceeding rare. But if the force of custom simple and separate be great, the force of custom copulate[316] and conjoined and collegiate is far greater. For there example teacheth, company comforteth, emulation quickeneth,[317] glory raiseth: so as in such places the force of custom is in his exaltation. Certainly the great multiplication[318] of virtues upon human nature resteth upon societies well ordained and disciplined. For commonwealths and good governments do nourish virtue grown, but do not much mend the seeds. But the misery is, that the most effectual means are now applied to the ends least to be desired.

Of Usury[319]

Many have made witty invectives against usury. They say that it is a pity the devil should have God's part, which is the tithe.[320] That the usurer is the greatest Sabbath-breaker, because his plough goeth every Sunday. That the usurer is the drone that Virgil speaketh of;

> *Ignavum fucos pecus a praesepibus arcent.*
> [They drive away the drones, a sluggish lot, from the hives][321]

That the usurer breaketh the first law that was made for mankind after the fall, which was, *in sudore vultus tui comedes panem tuum* [In the sweat of thy face shalt thou eat bread];[322] not, *in sudore vultus alieni* [In the sweat of another's face]. That usurers should have orange-tawny bonnets,[323] because they do judaize.[324] That it is against nature for money to beget money; and the like.[325] I say this

---

308 i.e. statues.
309 *machines.*
310 A reference to the Gymnosophists, an ancient school of Hindu philosophers. Self-immolation was *not* a typical part of their practice.
311 *whipped.*
312 *twitching with pain.*
313 A band made of branches twisted together.
314 *gripped.*
315 *change their habits.*
316 *united.*
317 *arouses.*
318 *proliferation.*
319 The practice of charging interest on loans. While loans at interest were widely used (and, indeed, economically essential) in Early

Modern Europe, this economic reality clashed with traditional Catholic teaching that it was sinful.
320 Literally, a tenth. It refers to the ten percent contribution of a community's wealth to support the ecclesiastical establishment (as established by the Mosaic law in Leviticus 27:32). Bacon is also referring to the maximum interest rate of ten percent established by King Henry VIII.
321 In *Georgics* 4.168.
322 Genesis 3:19. It is part of God's curse on mankind after the Fall.
323 Many Early Modern European cities required Jews to wear some distinguishing form of clothing.
324 *follow Jewish customs.* Bacon omits to point out that the vast majority of money-lenders were Christian and replicates a common anti-Semitic stereotype of his day.
325 Aristotle's argument against usury in *Politics* 1.10.

only, that usury is a *concessum propter duritiem cordis* [permitted because of the hardness of hearts];[326] for since there must be borrowing and lending, and men are so hard of heart as they will not lend freely, usury must be permitted. Some others have made suspicious and cunning propositions of banks, discovery of men's estates, and other inventions. But few have spoken of usury usefully. It is good to set before us the incommodities and commodities of usury, that the good may be either weighed out[327] or culled out; and warily to provide, that while we make forth[328] to that which is better, we meet not with that which is worse.

The discommodities of usury are, First, that it makes fewer merchants. For were it not for his lazy trade of usury, money would not lie still, but would in great part be employed upon merchandizing; which is the *vena porta*[329] of wealth in a state. The second, that it makes poor merchants. For as a farmer cannot husband[330] his ground so well if he sit at[331] a great rent; so the merchant cannot drive his trade so well, if he sit at great usury. The third is incident to the other two; and that is the decay of customs[332] of kings or states, which ebb or flow with merchandizing. The fourth, that it bringeth the treasure of a realm or state into a few hands. For the usurer being at certainties, and others at uncertainties at the end of the game most of the money will be in the box;[333] and ever a state flourisheth when wealth is more equally spread. The fifth, that it beats down the price of land; for the employment of money is chiefly either merchandizing or purchasing; and usury waylays both. The sixth, that it doth dull and damp all industries, improvements, and new inventions, wherein money would be stirring, if it were not for this slug.[334] The last, that it is the canker[335] and ruin of many men's estates; which in process of time breeds a public poverty.

On the other side, the commodities of usury are, first, that howsoever usury in some respect hindereth merchandizing, yet in some other it advanceth it; for it is certain that the greatest part of trade is driven by young merchants, upon borrowing at interest; so as if the usurer either call in or keep back his money, there will ensue presently a great stand of trade. The second is, that were it not for this easy borrowing upon interest, men's necessities would draw upon them a most sudden undoing;[336] in that they would be forced to sell their means (be it lands or goods) far under foot;[337] and so, whereas usury doth but gnaw upon them, bad markets would swallow them quite up. As for mortgaging or pawning, it will little mend the matter: for either men will not take pawns without use;[338] or if they do, they will look precisely[339] for the forfeiture. I remember a cruel moneyed man in the country, that would say, The devil take this usury, it keeps us from forfeitures[340] of mortgages and bonds. The third and last is, that it is a vanity to conceive that there would be ordinary borrowing without profit; and it is impossible to conceive the number of inconveniences that will ensue, if borrowing be cramped. Therefore to speak of the abolishing of usury is idle. All states have ever had it, in one kind or rate, or other. So as that opinion must be sent to Utopia.

To speak now of the reformation and reiglement[341] of usury; how the discommodities of it may be best avoided, and the commodities retained. It appears by the balance of commodities and discommodities of usury, two things are to be reconciled. The one, that the tooth of usury be grinded,[342] that it bite not too much; the other, that there be left open a means to invite moneyed men to lend to the merchants, for the continuing and quickening of trade. This cannot be done, except you introduce two several sorts of usury, a less and a greater. For if you reduce usury to one low rate, it will ease the common borrower, but the merchant will be to seek for money. And it is

---

326   See Matthew 19:8.
327   *measured.*
328   *go on.*
329   Literally, "gate-vein"; the main conduit or means of entrance.
330   *improve.*
331   *is liable for.*
332   *taxes.*
333   i.e. the usurer's strong box.
334   *impediment.*
335   *cause of corruption.*

336   Bacon himself died heavily in debt after spending the fortune of his wealthy wife and borrowing to support the lavish lifestyle of an Early Modern courtier.
337   i.e. below their real value.
338   *charging interest.*
339   *rigorously.*
340   *foreclosures.*
341   *regulation.*
342   i.e. blunted.

to be noted, that the trade of merchandize, being the most lucrative, may bear usury at a good rate; other contracts not so.

To serve both intentions, the way would be briefly thus. That there be two rates of usury: the one free, and general for all; the other under license only, to certain persons and in certain places of merchandizing. First therefore, let usury in general be reduced to five in the hundred;[343] and let that rate be proclaimed to be free and current; and let the state shut itself out to take any penalty for the same. This will preserve borrowing from any general stop or dryness. This will ease infinite borrowers in the country. This will, in good part, raise the price of land, because land purchased at sixteen years' purchase[344] will yield six in the hundred, and somewhat more; whereas this rate of interest yields but five. This by like reason will encourage and edge[345] industrious and profitable improvements; because many will rather venture in that kind than take five in the hundred, especially having been used to greater profit. Secondly, let there be certain persons licensed to lend to known merchants upon usury at a higher rate; and let it be with the cautions following. Let the rate be, even with the merchant himself, somewhat more easy than that he used formerly to pay; for by that means all borrowers shall have some ease by this reformation, be he merchant, or whosoever. Let it be no bank[346] or common stock, but every man be master of his own money. Not that I altogether mislike banks, but they will hardly be brooked,[347] in regard of certain suspicions. Let the state be answered some small matter[348] for the license, and the rest left to the lender; for if the abatement[349] be but small, it will no whit discourage the lender. For he, for example, that took before ten or nine in the hundred, will sooner descend to eight in the hundred, than give over his trade of usury, and go from certain gains, to gains of hazard.[350] Let these licensed lenders be in number indefinite, but restrained to certain principal cities and towns of merchandizing; for then they will be hardly able to colour other men's moneys[351] in the country: so as the license of nine will not suck away the current rate of five; for no man will send his moneys far off, nor put them into unknown hands.

If it be objected that this doth in a sort authorize usury, which before was in some places but permissive; the answer is, that it is better to mitigate usury by declaration[352] than to suffer it to rage by connivance.[353]

Of Beauty

Virtue is like a rich stone,[354] best plain set; and surely virtue is best in a body that is comely, though not of delicate[355] features; and that hath rather dignity of presence, than beauty of aspect. Neither is it almost[356] seen, that very beautiful persons are otherwise of great virtue; as if nature were rather busy not to err, than in labour to produce excellency. And therefore they prove accomplished,[357] but not of great spirit; and study rather behaviour[358] than virtue. But this holds not always:[359] for Augustus Caesar, Titus Vespasianus, Philip le Bel of France, Edward the Fourth of England, Alcibiades of Athens, Ismael the Sophy of Persia, were all high and great spirits;[360] and yet the most beautiful men of their times. In beauty, that of favour[361] is more than that of colour;[362] and that of decent and gracious motion[363] more than that of favour. That is the best part of

343   i.e. 5 percent.

344   A year's purchase is the revenue that the land would generate in one year.

345   *stimulate.*

346   Banks were common in continental Europe, but still regarded with suspicion in Britain.

347   *tolerated.*

348   i.e. given a small licensing fee.

349   i.e. the deduction for the government.

350   *chance* or *risk.*

351   i.e. pretend that money they have borrowed is in fact their own.

352   *openness.*

353   *implicit support.*

354   i.e. a gemstone.

355   *sensual.*

356   i.e. almost always.

357   *talented.*

358   i.e. how to interact with others.

359   Bacon's list of exceptions includes two Roman emperors (Augustus and Vespasian), two kings (Philip the Fair of France and Edward IV of England), an Athenian statesman (Alcibiades), and a king of Persia (Ismael).

360   i.e. people of great courage.

361   *feature.*

362   *complexion.*

363   *bodily movement.*

beauty, which a picture cannot express; no nor the first sight of the life. There is no excellent beauty that hath not some strangeness in the proportion. A man cannot tell whether Apelles[364] or Albert Durer[365] were the more trifler; whereof the one would make a personage by geometrical proportions; the other, by taking the best parts out of divers faces, to make one excellent. Such personages, I think, would please nobody but the painter that made them. Not but I think a painter may make a better face than ever was; but he must do it by a kind of felicity[366] (as a musician that maketh an excellent air in music), and not by rule. A man shall see faces, that if you examine them part by part, you shall find never a good; and yet altogether do well. If it be true that the principal part of beauty is in decent motion, certainly it is no marvel though persons in years seem many times more amiable; *pulchrorum autumnus pulcher* [the autumn of beautiful people is beautiful];[367] for no youth can be comely but by pardon,[368] and considering the youth as to make up the comeliness. Beauty is as summer fruits, which are easy to corrupt, and cannot last; and for the most part it makes a dissolute youth, and an age a little out of countenance; but yet certainly again, if it light well,[369] it maketh virtue shine, and vices blush.

Of Deformity[370]

Deformed persons are commonly even[371] with nature; for as nature hath done ill by them, so do they by nature; being for the most part (as the Scripture saith) "void of natural affection";[372] and so they have their revenge of nature. Certainly there is a consent between the body and the mind; and where nature erreth in the one, she ventureth[373] in the other. *Ubi peccat in uno, periclitatur in altero.*[374] But because there is in man an election[375] touching the frame of his mind, and a necessity in the frame of his body, the stars of natural inclination are sometimes obscured by the sun of discipline and virtue. Therefore it is good to consider of deformity, not as a sign, which is more deceivable;[376] but as a cause, which seldom faileth of the effect. Whosoever hath anything fixed in his person that doth induce contempt, hath also a perpetual spur in himself to rescue and deliver himself from scorn. Therefore all deformed persons are extreme bold. First, as in their own defence, as being exposed to scorn; but in process of time by a general habit. Also it stirreth in them industry, and especially of this kind, to watch and observe the weakness of others, that they may have somewhat to repay. Again, in their superiors, it quencheth jealousy towards them, as persons that they think they may at pleasure despise: and it layeth their competitors and emulators asleep; as never believing they should be in possibility of advancement, till they see them in possession.[377] So that upon the matter,[378] in a great wit, deformity is an advantage to rising. Kings in ancient times (and at this present in some countries) were wont to put great trust in eunuchs; because they that are envious towards all are more obnoxious[379] and officious towards one. But yet their trust towards them hath rather been as to good spials[380] and good whisperers, than good magistrates and officers. And much like is the reason of deformed persons. Still the ground is, they will, if they be of spirit,[381] seek to free themselves from scorn; which must be either by virtue or malice; and there-

---

364 Apelles (4th century BCE) was perhaps the most highly regarded painter in antiquity.

365 Albrecht Dürer (1471–1528) was a German painter who wrote a treatise on "correct" bodily proportions.

366 i.e. personal inspiration.

367 Plutarch, *Alcibiades* 1.3 (from the *Parallel Lives*). Plutarch attributes the saying to Euripides.

368 *allowance.*

369 i.e. lands on the right person.

370 There is a long-standing editorial tradition that this essay alludes to Robert Cecil, Earl of Salisbury (1563–1612), who was principal secretary to Elizabeth I and (apparently) a hunchback. It is certainly true that Cecil's condition did not inhibit his rise as a courtier.

371 *agreeable with.*

372 The relevant passages are Romans 1:31 and 2 Timothy 3:3. As is often the case, Bacon is distorting his evidence somewhat.

373 *risks failure.*

374 The Latin is a translation of the preceding sentence in English.

375 *freedom to choose.*

376 *deceitful.*

377 i.e. possession of favor or high office.

378 i.e. as a matter of fact.

379 *dependent.*

380 *spies.*

381 i.e. energetic and talented.

fore let it not be marvelled if sometimes they prove excellent persons;[382] as was Agesilaus, Zanger the son of Solyman, Aesop, Gasca, President of Peru; and Socrates may go likewise amongst them; with others.

OF STUDIES

Studies serve for delight, for ornament, and for ability. Their chief use for delight, is in privateness and retiring;[383] for ornament, is in discourse; and for ability, is in the judgment and disposition of business. For expert[384] men can execute, and perhaps judge of particulars, one by one; but the general counsels, and the plots and marshalling of affairs, come best from those that are learned.[385] To spend too much time in studies is sloth; to use them too much for ornament, is affectation; to make judgment wholly by their rules, is the humour of a scholar. They perfect nature, and are perfected by experience: for natural abilities are like natural plants, that need proyning[386] by study; and studies themselves do give forth directions too much at large,[387] except they be bounded in by experience. Crafty men contemn studies, simple men admire them, and wise men use them; for they teach not their own use; but that is a wisdom without[388] them, and above them, won by observation. Read not to contradict and confute; nor to believe and take for granted; nor to find talk and discourse; but to weigh and consider. Some books are to be tasted, others to be swallowed, and some few to be chewed and digested; that is, some books are to be read only in parts; others to be read, but not curiously;[389] and some few to be read wholly, and with diligence and attention. Some books also may be read by deputy, and extracts made of them by others; but that would be only in the less important arguments, and the meaner sort of books; else distilled books are like common distilled waters,[390] flashy[391] things. Reading maketh a full man; conference a ready man;[392] and writing an exact[393] man. And therefore, if a man write little, he had need have a great memory; if he confer little, he had need have a present wit: and if he read little, he had need have much cunning, to seem to know that he doth not. Histories make men wise; poets witty; the mathematics subtile;[394] natural philosophy deep; moral grave; logic and rhetoric able to contend. *Abeunt studia in mores* [Studies pass into character].[395] Nay there is no stond[396] or impediment in the wit, but may be wrought out by fit studies; like as diseases of the body may have appropriate exercises. Bowling is good for the stone[397] and reins;[398] shooting for the lungs and breast; gentle walking for the stomach; riding for the head; and the like. So if a man's wit be wandering, let him study the mathematics; for in demonstrations, if his wit be called away never so little, he must begin again. If his wit be not apt to distinguish or find differences, let him study the Schoolmen;[399] for they are *cymini sectores* [splitters of cumin seeds, or minute matters]. If he be not apt to beat over[400] matters, and to call up one thing to prove and illustrate another, let him study the lawyers' cases. So every defect of the mind may have a special receipt.[401]

382 Bacon's examples here are Agesilaus, king of Sparta; Zanger, who was the son of Sultan Suleiman the Magnificent; Pedro de la Gasca, a priest and lawyer who administered the Spanish colony in Peru; and Socrates (see gazetteer), who always describes himself as very ugly in Plato's dialogues.

383 private study, away from public business.

384 *experienced.*

385 The question of whether experience or education was a better basis for making decisions was frequently debated in Early Modern Europe.

386 *pruning.*

387 i.e. in a general or theoretical sense.

388 *beyond.* The notion that knowledge was only worth having for some extrinsic purpose, and not for its own sake, is an important recurring theme in Bacon's writing.

389 *very closely.*

390 i.e. distilled vegetable juices, taken for medicinal purposes.

391 *insipid.*

392 someone who can speak or write well at short notice.

393 *precise.*

394 *careful; discriminating.*

395 Ovid, *Heroides* 15.83.

396 *obstacle.*

397 kidney stones

398 *kidneys.*

399 A reference to the medieval Scholastic philosophers in general and (usually) Albertus Magnus (*c.*1206–80) and his pupil Thomas Aquinas (*c.*1225–74) in particular.

400 *debate.*

401 *remedy.*

OF VICISSITUDE[402] OF THINGS

Solomon saith, "There is no new thing upon the earth."[403] So that as Plato had an imagination, "That all knowledge was but remembrance";[404] so Solomon giveth his sentence, "That all novelty is but oblivion."[405] Whereby you may see that the river of Lethe[406] runneth as well above ground as below. There is an abstruse[407] astrologer that saith, "If it were not for two things that are constant (the one is, that the fixed stars ever stand a like distance one from another, and never come nearer together, nor go further asunder; the other, that the diurnal motion perpetually keepeth time), no individual would last one moment."[408] Certain it is, that the matter[409] is in a perpetual flux, and never at a stay. The great winding-sheets,[410] that bury all things in oblivion, are two; deluges[411] and earthquakes. As for conflagrations and great droughts, they do not merely[412] dispeople and destroy. Phaethon's[413] car went but a day. And the three years' drought in the time of Elias[414] was but particular, and left people alive. As for the great burnings by lightnings, which are often in the West Indies,[415] they are but narrow. But in the other two destructions, by deluge and earthquake, it is further to be noted, that the remnant of people which hap to be reserved,[416] are commonly ignorant and mountainous people, that can give no account of the time past; so that the oblivion is all one as if none had been left. If you consider well of the people of the West Indies, it is very probable that they are a newer or a younger people than the people of the Old World. And it is much more likely that the destruction that hath heretofore been there, was not by earthquakes (as the Egyptian priest told Solon concerning the island of Atlantis,[417] that it was swallowed by an earthquake), but rather that it was desolated by a particular deluge. For earthquakes are seldom in those parts. But on the other side, they have such pouring rivers, as the rivers of Asia and Africa and Europe, are but brooks to them. Their Andes likewise, or mountains, are far higher than those with us; whereby it seems that the remnants of generation of men were in such a particular deluge saved. As for the observation that Machiavel hath,[418] that the jealousy of sects[419] doth much extinguish the memory of things; traducing Gregory the Great,[420] that he did what in him lay to extinguish all heathen antiquities; I do not find that those zeals do any great effects, nor last long; as it appeared in the succession of Sabinian,[421] who did revive the former antiquities.

The vicissitude or mutations in the superior globe[422] are no fit matter for this present argument. It may be, Plato's great year,[423] if the world should last so long, would have some effect; not in renewing the state of like individuals (for that is the fume[424] of those that conceive the celestial bodies have more accurate influences upon these things below than indeed they have),[425] but in gross.[426] Comets, out of question, have likewise power and effect over the gross and mass of things; but they are rather gazed upon, and waited upon in their journey, than wisely observed in their effects; specially in their respective effects; that is, what kind of comet, for magnitude, colour, version of the beams, placing in the region of heaven, or lasting, produceth what kind of effects.

402 uncertain change or mutability.

403 See Ecclesiastes 1:9–10.

404 See *Phaedo* 72e and *Meno* 81cd.

405 See Ecclesiastes 1:9–11.

406 One of the rivers in the Underworld in Greek mythology. Its name means "forgetfulness," and the souls of the dead had to drink from it to forget their past lives on the surface world.

407 i.e. difficult to comprehend.

408 Previous editors have suggested the anti-Aristotelian philosopher Bernardino Telesio (1508–88) as the source of this quotation.

409 i.e. Matter in general.

410 The cloths that corpses were wrapped in before being interred.

411 *floods.*

412 *completely.*

413 See gazetteer.

414 See 1 Kings 17–18.

415 In Early Modern Europe, this terms referred to the New World as a whole, not just the Caribbean islands.

416 *spared.*

417 See Plato, *Timaeus* 25c–d.

418 See *Discourses* 2.5.

419 i.e. sectarian prejudices against those of a different religion.

420 Pope Gregory the Great (590–604).

421 The pontiff who succeeded Gregory and who reversed many of his predecessor's policies in this area.

422 *the heavens.*

423 See *Timaeus* 39d. The term refers to the length of time required for the stars to complete their revolutions and return to the places which they occupied when the world was created. The estimates for this time period vary widely, and are all in thousands of years.

424 *transient delusion.*

425 The belief that the movement of the celestial bodies influenced events on earth was still very common in Bacon's day.

426 *general.*

There is a toy which I have heard, and I would not have it given over,[427] but waited upon a little. They say it is observed in the Low Countries[428] (I know not in what part) that every five and thirty years the same kind and suit of years and weathers come about again; as great frosts, great wet, great droughts, warm winters, summers with little heat, and the like; and they call it the "Prime."[429] It is a thing I do the rather mention, because, computing backwards, I have found some concurrence.

But to leave these points of nature, and to come to men. The greatest vicissitude of things amongst men, is the vicissitude of sects and religions. For those orbs[430] rule in men's minds most. The true religion is "built upon the rock";[431] the rest are tossed upon the waves of time. To speak therefore of the causes of new sects; and to give some counsel concerning them, as far as the weakness of human judgment can give stay[432] to so great revolutions.

When the religion formerly received is rent by discords; and when the holiness of the professors of religion is decayed and full of scandal; and withal the times be stupid, ignorant, and barbarous; you may doubt[433] the springing up of a new sect; if then also there should arise any extravagant and strange spirit to make himself author thereof. All which points held when Mahomet[434] published his law. If a new sect have not two properties, fear it not; for it will not spread. The one is, the supplanting or the opposing of authority established; for nothing is more popular than that. The other is, the giving license to pleasures and a voluptuous life. For as for speculative heresies (such as were in ancient times the Arians,[435] and now the Arminians),[436] though they work mightily upon men's wits, yet they do not produce any great alterations in states; except it be by the help of civil occasions.[437] There be three manner of plantations of new sects. By the power of signs and miracles; by the eloquence and wisdom of speech and persuasion; and by the sword. For martyrdoms, I reckon them amongst miracles; because they seem to exceed the strength of human nature: and I may do the like of superlative and admirable holiness of life. Surely there is no better way to stop the rising of new sects and schisms, than to reform abuses; to compound[438] the smaller differences; to proceed mildly, and not with sanguinary[439] persecutions; and rather to take off[440] the principal authors by winning and advancing them, than to enrage them by violence and bitterness.

The changes and vicissitude in wars are many; but chiefly in three things; in the seats or stages of the war; in the weapons; and in the manner of the conduct. Wars, in ancient time, seemed more to move from east to west; for the Persians, Assyrians, Arabians, Tartars[441] (which were the invaders) were all eastern people. It is true, the Gauls were western; but we read but of two incursions of theirs: the one to Gallo-Graecia,[442] the other to Rome. But east and west have no certain points of heaven; and no more have the wars, either from the east or west, any certainty of observation. But north and south are fixed; and it hath seldom or never been seen that the far southern people have invaded the northern, but contrariwise. Whereby it is manifest that the northern tract of the world is in nature the more martial region: be it in respect of the stars of that hemisphere; or of the great continents that are upon the north, whereas the south part, for aught that is known, is almost all sea; or (which is most apparent) of the cold of the northern parts, which is that which, without aid of discipline, doth make the bodies hardest, and the courages warmest.

---

427   *forgotten.*

428   The land occupied by modern Belgium, the Netherlands, and Luxembourg.

429   i.e. the beginning of a new cycle of years.

430   *heavenly bodies* (i.e. influences).

431   See Matthew 16.18.

432   i.e. obstruct.

433   *dread.*

434   See note 67 above. "His law" refers to the Koran.

435   Followers of Arius (256–336), who believed that Christ was not fully divine. They were deemed heretics by the Church.

436   Followers of the Calvinist theologian Jacobus Arminius (1560–1609), who did not believe in Calvin's doctrine of predestination (i.e. that God has predestined some people for salvation and others for damnation). Despite Bacon's association of it with heresy, this has become an important strand of Protestant thought: John Wesley, founder of Methodism, held beliefs consistent with Arminianism.

437   i.e. political circumstances.

438   *settle.*

439   *bloody.*

440   *neutralize.*

441   The Early Modern term for the armies of Genghis Khan.

442   An obsolete term for Galatia, a region in modern central Turkey.

Upon the breaking and shivering of a great state and empire, you may be sure to have wars. For great empires, while they stand, do enervate and destroy the forces of the natives which they have subdued, resting upon their own protecting forces; and then when they fail also, all goes to ruin, and they become a prey. So was it in the decay of the Roman empire; and likewise in the empire of Almaigne,[443] after Charles the Great,[444] every bird taking a feather; and were not unlike to befall to Spain,[445] if it should break. The great accessions and unions of kingdoms do likewise stir up wars; for when a state grows to an over-power, it is like a great flood, that will be sure to overflow. As it hath been seen in the states of Rome, Turkey, Spain, and others. Look when the world hath fewest barbarous peoples, but such as commonly will not marry or generate, except they know means to live (as it is almost everywhere at this day, except Tartary), there is no danger of inundations of people; but when there be great shoals of people, which go on to populate, without foreseeing means of life and sustentation,[446] it is of necessity that once in an age or two they discharge a portion of their people upon other nations; which the ancient northern people were wont to do by lot; casting lots what part should stay at home, and what should seek their fortunes. When a warlike state grows soft and effeminate, they may be sure of a war. For commonly such states are grown rich in the time of their degenerating; and so the prey inviteth, and their decay in valour encourageth a war.

As for the weapons, it hardly falleth under rule and observation: yet we see even they have returns and vicissitudes. For certain it is, that ordnance[447] was known in the city of the Oxidrakes in India;[448] and was that which the Macedonians called thunder and lightning, and magic. And it is well known that the use of ordnance hath been in China above two thousand years. The conditions of weapons, and their improvement, are; First, the fetching[449] afar off; for that outruns the danger; as it is seen in ordnance and muskets. Secondly, the strength of the percussion; wherein likewise ordnance do exceed all arietations[450] and ancient inventions. The third is, the commodious use of them; as that they may serve in all weathers; that the carriage may be light and manageable; and the like.

For the conduct of the war: at the first, men rested[451] extremely upon number: they did put the wars likewise upon main force and valour; pointing[452] days for pitched fields, and so trying it out upon an even match and they were more ignorant in ranging and arraying their battles.[453] After they grew to rest upon number rather competent than vast; they grew to advantages of place, cunning diversions, and the like: and they grew more skilful in the ordering of their battles.

In the youth of a state, arms do flourish; in the middle age of a state, learning; and then both of them together for a time; in the declining age of a state, mechanical arts and merchandize. Learning hath his infancy, when it is but beginning and almost childish; then his youth, when it is luxuriant and juvenile; then his strength of years, when it is solid and reduced; and lastly, his old age, when it waxeth dry and exhaust. But it is not good to look too long upon these turning wheels of vicissitude, lest we become giddy. As for the philology[454] of them, that is but a circle of tales, and therefore not fit for this writing.

NEW ATLANTIS

We sailed from Peru, (where we had continued by the space of one whole year,) for China and Japan, by the South Sea; taking with us victuals for twelve months; and had good winds from the east,

---

443 *Germany.*
444 i.e. Charlemagne (c.742–814), the King of the Franks and the first Holy Roman Emperor.
445 In Bacon's day, Spain was the single most powerful nation in Europe; the wealth of its colonies in the New World was an important source of this power.
446 *maintenance.*
447 *artillery.*

448 See Philostratus, *Life of Apollonius Tyana* 2.33. In effect, Bacon is asserting (wrongly) that gunpowder was known in India in the 2nd century AD.
449 *striking.*
450 i.e. assaults with battering-rams (Latin *aries*).
451 *relied.*
452 *appointing.*
453 i.e. battalions, or troop formations.
454 *literary records.*

though soft and weak, for five months' space and more. But then the wind came about, and settled in the west for many days, so as we could make little or no way, and were sometimes in purpose to turn back. But then again there arose strong and great winds from the south, with a point east; which carried us up (for all that we could do) towards the north: by which time our victuals failed us, though we had made good spare[1] of them. So that finding ourselves in the midst of the greatest wilderness of waters in the world, without victual, we gave ourselves for lost men, and prepared for death. Yet we did lift up our hearts and voices to God above, who *showeth His wonders in the deep*;[2] beseeching Him of His mercy that as in the beginning He discovered the face of the deep, and brought forth dry land, so He would now discover land to us, that we might not perish.[3] And it came to pass that the next day about evening, we saw within a kenning[4] before us, towards the north, as it were thick clouds, which did put us in some hope of land; knowing how that part of the South Sea was utterly unknown; and might have islands or continents, that hitherto were not come to light. Wherefore we bent our course thither, where we saw the appearance of land, all that night; and in the dawning of next day, we might plainly discern that it was a land; flat to our sight, and full of boscage;[5] which made it show the more dark. And after an hour and a half's sailing, we entered into a good haven, being the port of a fair city; not great indeed, but well built, and that gave a pleasant view from the sea: and we thinking every minute long till we were on land, came close to the shore, and offered to land. But straightways we saw divers of the people, with batons in their hands, as it were forbidding us to land; yet without any cries or fierceness, but only as warning us off by signs that they made. Whereupon being not a little discomforted, we were advising with ourselves what we should do. During which time there made forth to us a small boat, with about eight persons in it; whereof one of them had in his hand a tipstaff[6] of a yellow cane, tipped at both ends with blue, who came aboard our ship, without any show of distrust at all. And when he saw one of our number present himself somewhat afore the rest, he drew forth a little scroll of parchment, (somewhat yellower than our parchment, and shining like the leaves of writing tables, but otherwise soft and flexible,) and delivered it to our foremost man. In which scroll were written in ancient Hebrew, and in ancient Greek, and in good Latin of the School,[7] and in Spanish, these words: "Land ye not, none of you; and provide to be gone from this coast within sixteen days, except you have further time given you. Meanwhile, if you want fresh water, or victual, or help for your sick, or that your ship needeth repair, write down your wants, and you shall have that which belongeth to mercy." This scroll was signed with a stamp of cherubim's wings, not spread but hanging downwards, and by them a cross. This being delivered, the officer returned, and left only a servant with us to receive our answer. Consulting hereupon among ourselves, we were much perplexed. The denial of landing and hasty warning us away troubled us much; on the other side, to find that the people had languages and were so full of humanity, did comfort us not a little. And above all, the sign of the cross to that instrument was to us a great rejoicing, and as it were a certain presage[8] of good. Our answer was in the Spanish tongue; "That for our ship, it was well; for we had rather met with calms and contrary winds than any tempests. For our sick, they were many, and in very ill case; so that if they were not permitted to land, they ran danger of their lives." Our other wants we set down in particular; adding, "that we had some little store of merchandise, which if it pleased them to deal for, it might supply our wants without being chargeable unto them." We offered some reward in pistolets[9] unto the servant, and a piece of crimson velvet to be presented to the officer; but the servant took them not, nor would scarce look upon them; and so left us, and went back in another little boat which was sent for him.

About three hours after we had despatched our answer, there came toward us a person (as it seemed) of place. He had on him a gown with wide sleeves, of a kind of water chamolet,[10] of an

---

NEW ATLANTIS

1   i.e. careful use of them.

2   Psalms 107:24.

3   Bacon is comparing the plight of the mariners to that of Noah and his family, waiting for a sign that the floodwaters had receded in Genesis 8.

4   *range of sight.*

5   *wooded areas.*

6   A staff with a metal tip, carried as a badge of office.

7   Academic Latin, as used in the universities.

8   *portent* or *omen.*

9   *gold coin.*

10   *costly fabric* (originally applied to camel-hair blends from Asia).

excellent azure colour, far more glossy than ours; his under-apparel was green; and so was his hat, being in the form of a turban, daintily made, and not so huge as the Turkish turbans; and the locks of his hair came down below the brims of it. A reverend man was he to behold. He came in a boat, gilt in some part of it, with four persons more only in that boat; and was followed by another boat, wherein were some twenty. When he was come within a flight-shot[11] of our ship, signs were made to us that we should send forth some to meet him upon the water; which we presently did in our ship-boat, sending the principal man amongst us save one, and four of our number with him. When we were come within six yards of their boat, they called to us to stay, and not to approach farther; which we did. And thereupon the man whom I before described stood up, and with a loud voice in Spanish, asked, "Are ye Christians?" We answered, "We were;" fearing the less, because of the cross we had seen in the subscription. At which answer the said person lifted up his right hand toward heaven, and drew it softly to his mouth, (which is the gesture they use when they thank God), and then said: "If ye will swear (all of you) by the merits of the Saviour that ye are no pirates, nor have shed blood lawfully or unlawfully within forty days past, you may have license to come on land." We said, "We were all ready to take that oath." Whereupon one of those that were with him, being (as it seemed) a notary, made an entry of this act. Which done, another of the attendants of the great person, which was with him in the same boat, after his lord had spoken a little to him, said aloud: "My lord would have you know, that it is not of pride or greatness that he cometh not aboard your ship; but for that in your answer you declare that you have many sick amongst you, he was warned by the Conservator of Health of the city that he should keep a distance." We bowed ourselves towards him, and answered, "We were his humble servants; and accounted for great honour and singular humanity toward us that which was already done; but hoped well that the nature of the sickness of our men was not infectious." So he returned; and a while after came the notary to us aboard our ship, holding in his hand a fruit of that country, like an orange, but of colour between orange-tawny and scarlet, which cast a most excellent odour. He used it (as it seemeth) for a preservative against infection. He gave us our oath; "By the name of Jesus and His merits": and after told us that the next day by six of the clock in the morning we should be sent to, and brought to the Strangers' House, (so he called it,) where we should he accommodated of things both for our whole and for our sick. So he left us; and when we offered him some pistolets, he smiling said, "He must not be twice paid for one labour": meaning (as I take it) that he had salary sufficient of the state for his service. For (as I after learned) they call an officer that taketh rewards, *twice paid*.[12]

The next morning early, there came to us the same officer that came to us at first with his cane, and told us, he came to conduct us to the Strangers' House; and that he had prevented[13] the hour, because we might have the whole day before us for our business. "For," said he," if you will follow my advice, there shall first go with me some few of you, and see the place, and how it may be made convenient for you; and then you may send for your sick, and the rest of your number which ye will bring on land." We thanked him and said that this care which he took of desolate strangers God would reward. And so six of us went on land with him: and when we were on land, he went before us and turned to us, and said he was but our servant and our guide. He led us through three fair streets; and all the way we went there were gathered some people on both sides standing in a row; but in so civil a fashion, as if it had been, not to wonder at us but to welcome us; and divers of them, as we passed by them, put their arms a little abroad; which is their gesture when they bid any welcome. The Strangers' House is a fair and spacious house, built of brick, of somewhat a bluer colour than our brick; and with handsome windows, some of glass, some of a kind of cambric[14] oiled. He brought us first into a fair parlour above stairs, and then asked us, "What number of persons we were? And how many sick?" We answered, "We were in all (sick and whole) one-and-fifty persons, whereof our sick were seventeen." He desired us have patience a little, and to stay till

---

11 A bow-shot, the maximum distance which a bow can fire an arrow.
12 Bacon's stress on the incorruptibility of Bensalem's government officials inevitably reminds us that taking bribes was the crime of which he was found guilty in 1621.

13 i.e. had come early in anticipation of the hour.
14 *fine white linen.*

he came back to us; which was about an hour after; and then he led us to see the chambers which were provided for us, being in number nineteen: they having cast it (as it seemeth) that four of those chambers, which were better than the rest, might receive four of the principal men of our company, and lodge them alone by themselves; and the other fifteen chambers were to lodge us two and two together. The chambers were handsome and cheerful chambers, and furnished civilly. Then he led us to a long gallery, like a dorture,[15] where he showed us all along the one side (for the other side was but wall and window) seventeen cells, very neat ones, having partitions of cedar wood. Which gallery and cells, being in all forty (many more than we needed) were instituted as an infirmary for sick persons. And he told us withal, that as any of our sick waxed well, he might be removed from his cell to a chamber; for which purpose there were set forth ten spare chambers, besides the number we spake of before. This done, he brought us back to the parlour, and lifting up his cane a little (as they do when they give any charge or command) said to us: "Ye are to know that the custom of the land requireth that after this day and tomorrow (which we give you for removing your people from your ship) you are to keep within doors for three days. But let it not trouble you, nor do not think yourselves restrained, but rather left to your rest and ease. You shall want nothing, and there are six of our people appointed to attend you, for any business you may have abroad." We gave him thanks with all affection and respect, and said, "God surely is manifested in this land." We offered him also twenty pistolets; but he smiled, and only said: "What? Twice paid!" And so he left us. Soon after our dinner was served in; which was right good viands, both for bread and meat: better than any collegiate[16] diet that I have known in Europe. We had also drink of three sorts, all wholesome and good: wine of the grape; a drink of grain, such as is with us our ale, but more clear; and a kind of cider made of a fruit of that country, a wonderful pleasing and refreshing drink. Besides, there were brought in to us great store of those scarlet oranges for our sick; which (they said) were an assured remedy for sickness taken at sea. There was given us also a box of small grey or whitish pills, which they wished our sick should take, one of the pills every night before sleep; which (they said) would hasten their recovery. The next day, after that our trouble of carriage and removing of our men and goods out of our ship was somewhat settled and quiet, I thought good to call our company together; and when they were assembled said unto them: "My dear friends, let us know ourselves, and how it standeth with us. We are men cast on land, as Jonah[17] was out of the whale's belly, when we were as buried in the deep: and now we are on land, we are but between death and life; for we are beyond both the Old World and the New;[18] and whether ever we shall see Europe, God only knoweth. It is a kind of miracle hath brought us hither: and it must be little less that shall bring us hence. Therefore in regard of our deliverance past, and our danger present and to come, let us look up to God, and every man reform his own ways. Besides, we are come here among a Christian people, full of piety and humanity: let us not bring that confusion of face upon ourselves, as to show our vices or unworthiness before them. Yet there is more. For they have by commandment (though in form of courtesy) cloistered us within these walls for three days: who knoweth whether it be not to take some taste of our manners and conditions? And if they find them bad, to banish us straightways; if good, to give us further time. For these men that they have given us for attendance may withal have an eye upon us. Therefore for God's love, and as we love the weal of our souls and bodies, let us so behave ourselves as we may be at peace with God, and may find grace in the eyes of this people." Our company with one voice thanked me for my good admonition, and promised me to live soberly and civilly, and without giving any the least occasion of offence. So we spent our three days joyfully and without care, in expectation what would be done with us when they were expired. During which time, we had every hour joy of the amendment of our sick; who thought themselves cast into some divine pool of healing, they mended so kindly and so fast.

15   *dormitory.*
16   *University.*
17   See Jonah 2:10.

18   Bensalem's location beyond both the Old World (Europe) and the New (the Americas) prepares the reader for their new ways of thinking about learning. Bacon can propagate his ideas for scientific reform in a hypothetical context.

The morrow after our three days were past, there came to us a new man that we had not seen before, clothed in blue as the former was, save that his turban was white, with a small red cross on top. He had also a tippet[19] of fine linen. At his coming in, he did bend to us a little, and put his arms abroad. We of our parts saluted him in a very lowly and submissive manner; as looking that from him we should receive sentence of life or death. He desired to speak with some few of us: whereupon six of us only stayed, and the rest voided the room. He said: "I am by office governor of this House of Strangers, and by vocation, I am a Christian priest; and therefore am come to you to offer you my service, both as strangers and chiefly as Christians. Some things I may tell you, which I think you will not be unwilling to hear. The state hath given you license to stay on land for the space of six weeks; and let it not trouble you if your occasions ask further time, for the law in this point is not precise; and I do not doubt but myself shall be able to obtain for you such further time as shall be convenient. Ye shall also understand, that the Strangers' House is at this time rich, and much aforehand;[20] for it hath laid up revenue these thirty-seven years, for so long it is since any stranger arrived in this part: and therefore take ye no care; the state will defray you all the time you stay; neither shall you stay one day the less for that. As for any merchandise ye have brought, ye shall be well used, and have your return either in merchandise or in gold and silver: for to us it is all one. And if you have any other request to make, hide it not. For ye shall find we will not make your countenance to fall by the answer ye shall receive. Only this I must tell you, that none of you must go above a *karan*" (that is with them a mile and a half) "from the walls of the city, without special leave." We answered, after we had looked awhile upon one another admiring this gracious and parent-like usage; "That we could not tell what to say: for we wanted words to express our thanks; and his noble free offers left us nothing to ask. It seemed to us that we had before us a picture of our salvation in heaven; for we that were awhile since in the jaws of death, were now brought into a place where we found nothing but consolations. For the commandment laid upon us, we would not fail to obey it, though it was impossible but our hearts should he inflamed to tread further upon this happy and holy ground." We added; "That our tongues should first cleave to the roofs of our mouths, ere we should forget either his reverend person or this whole nation in our prayers." We also most humbly besought him to accept of us as his true servants, by as just a right as ever men on earth were bounden; laying and presenting both our persons and all we had at his feet. He said; "He was a priest, and looked for a priest's reward: which was our brotherly love and the good of our souls and bodies." So he went from us, not without tears of tenderness in his eyes; and left us also confused with joy and kindness, saying among ourselves, "That we were come into a land of angels, which did appear to us daily and present us with comforts, which we thought not of, much less expected."

The next day, about ten of the clock, the governor came to us again, and after salutations said familiarly, "That he was come to visit us:" and called for a chair and sat him down; and we, being some ten of us (the rest were of the meaner[21] sort, or else gone abroad) sat down with him. And when we were set, he began thus: "We of this island of Bensalem,"[22] (for so they called it in their language) "have this; that by means of our solitary situation, and of the laws of secrecy which we have for our travellers, and our rare admission of strangers, we know well most part of the habitable world, and are ourselves unknown. Therefore because he that knoweth least is fittest to ask questions, it is more reason, for the entertainment of the time, that ye ask me questions, than that I ask you." We answered; "That we humbly thanked him that he would give us leave so to do. And that we conceived by the taste we had already, that there was no worldly thing on earth more worthy to be known than the state of that happy land. But above all," (we said) "since that we were met from the several ends of the world, and hoped assuredly that we should meet one day in the kingdom of heaven (for that we were both parts Christians), we desired to know (in respect that land was so remote, and so divided by vast and unknown seas from the land where our Saviour walked on earth) who was the apostle of that nation, and how it was converted to the faith?" It appeared in his face

---

19   A long thin piece of cloth that hangs down from a garment.
20   i.e. well prepared for the future.
21   In this context, an adjective meaning "lower class."

22   The name of the island is easily recognizable as a Hebrew compound meaning, roughly, "son of peace."

that he took great contentment in this our question; he said: "Ye knit my heart to you, by asking this question in the first place; for it showeth that you *first seek the kingdom of heaven*;[23] and I shall gladly, and briefly, satisfy your demand.

"About twenty years after the ascension of our Saviour, it came to pass that there was seen by the people of Renfusa (a city upon the eastern coast of our island) within night, (the night was cloudy and calm), as it might be some mile into the sea, a great pillar of light; not sharp, but in form of a column or cylinder, rising from the sea a great way up toward heaven; and on the top of it was seen a large cross of light, more bright and resplendent than the body of the pillar. Upon which so strange a spectacle, the people of the city gathered apace together upon the sands, to wonder; and so after put themselves into a number of small boats, to go nearer to this marvellous sight. But when the boats were come within about sixty yards of the pillar, they found themselves all bound, and could go no further; yet so as they might move to go about, but might not approach nearer; so as the boats stood all as in a theatre, beholding this light as a heavenly sign. It so fell out, that there was in one of the boats one of the wise men of the Society of Salomon's House; which house or college (my good brethren) is the very eye of this kingdom; who having awhile attentively and devoutly viewed and contemplated this pillar and cross, fell down upon his face; and then raised himself upon his knees, and lifting up his hands to heaven, made his prayers in this manner:

"'Lord God of heaven and earth, thou hast vouchsafed of thy grace to those of our order to know thy works of creation, and the secrets of them; and to discern (as far as appertaineth to the generations of men) between divine miracles, works of nature, works of art, and impostures and illusions of all sorts. I do here acknowledge and testify before this people, that the thing we now see before our eyes is thy Finger and a true Miracle. And forasmuch as we learn in our books that thou never workest miracles, but to a divine and excellent end (for the laws of nature are thine own laws, and thou exceedest them not but upon great cause) we most humbly beseech thee to prosper[24] this great sign, and to give us the interpretation and use of it in mercy; which thou dost in some part secretly promise by sending it unto us.

"When he had made his prayer, he presently found the boat he was in movable and unbound; whereas all the rest remained still fast; and taking that for an assurance of leave to approach, he caused the boat to be softly and with silence rowed toward the pillar. But ere he came near it, the pillar and cross of light broke up, and cast itself abroad, as it were, into a firmament of many stars, which also vanished soon after, and there was nothing left to be seen but a small ark or chest of cedar, dry, and not wet at all with water, though it swam. And in the fore end of it, which was towards him, grew a small green branch of palm; and when the wise man had taken it with all reverence into his boat, it opened of itself, and there were found in it a Book and a Letter; both written in fine parchment, and wrapped in sindons[25] of linen. The Book contained all the canonical books of the Old and New Testament, according as you have them (for we know well what the churches with you receive); and the Apocalypse itself, and some other books of the New Testament which were not at that time written, were nevertheless in the Book. And for the Letter, it was in these words:

"'I, Bartholomew,[26] a servant of the Highest, and apostle of Jesus Christ, was warned by an angel that appeared to me in a vision of glory, that I should commit this ark to the floods of the sea. Therefore I do testify and declare unto that people where God shall ordain this ark to come to land, that in the same day is come unto them salvation and peace and good-will from the Father, and from the Lord Jesus.

"There was also in both these writings, as well the Book as the Letter, wrought a great miracle, conform[27] to that of the Apostles in the original Gift of Tongues.[28] For there being at that time in

23   See Matthew 6:33.

24   i.e. to promote the success of.

25   *linen wrapper.*

26   In the Bible, St. Bartholomew is one of the twelve apostles. Later traditions represent him as evangelizing in many distant countries, which may be why Bacon chooses him in this context.

27   *conforming.*

28   A reference to Acts 2, in which Christ's apostles are given the gift of speaking foreign languages ("tongues") by the Holy Spirit.

this land Hebrews, Persians, and Indians, besides the natives, everyone read upon the Book and Letter, as if they had been written in his own language. And thus was this land saved from infidelity (as the remain of the old world was from water) by an ark, through the apostolical and miraculous evangelism of St. Bartholomew." And here he paused, and a messenger came, and called him from us. So this was all that passed in that conference.

The next day, the same governor came again to us immediately after dinner, and excused himself, saying, "That the day before he was called from us somewhat abruptly, but now he would make us amends, and spend time with us, if we held his company and conference agreeable." We answered, "That we held it so agreeable and pleasing to us, as we forgot both dangers past and fears to come, for the time we heard him speak; and that we thought an hour spent with him, was worth years of our former life." He bowed himself a little to us, and after we were set again, he said; "Well, the questions are on your part." One of our number said, after a little pause; "That there was a matter we were no less desirous to know than fearful to ask, lest we might presume too far. But encouraged by his rare humanity toward us (that could scarce think ourselves strangers, being his vowed and professed servants) we would take the hardiness to propound[29] it; humbly beseeching him, if he thought it not fit to be answered, that he would pardon it, though he rejected it." We said; "We well observed those his words, which he formerly spake, that this happy island where we now stood was known to few, and yet knew most of the nations of the world; which we found to be true, considering they had the languages of Europe, and knew much of our state and business; and yet we in Europe (notwithstanding all the remote discoveries and navigations of this last age) never heard any of the least inkling or glimpse of this island. This we found wonderful strange; for that all nations have inter-knowledge one of another either by voyage into foreign parts, or by strangers that come to them; and though the traveller into a foreign country doth commonly know more by the eye, than he that stayeth at home can by relation of the traveller; yet both ways suffice to make a mutual knowledge, in some degree, on both parts. But for this island, we never heard tell of any ship of theirs that had been seen to arrive upon any shore of Europe; no, nor of either the East or West Indies, nor yet of any ship of any other part of the world, that had made return for them. And yet the marvel rested not in this. For the situation of it (as his lordship said) in the secret conclave[30] of such a vast sea might cause it. But then that they should have knowledge of the languages, books, affairs, of those that lie such a distance from them, it was a thing we could not tell what to make of; for that it seemed to us a condition and propriety of divine powers and beings, to be hidden and unseen to others, and yet to have others open, and as in a light to them." At this speech the governor gave a gracious smile, and said; "That we did well to ask pardon for this question we now asked; for that it imported as if we thought this land a land of magicians, that sent forth spirits of the air into all parts, to bring them news and intelligence of other countries." It was answered by us all, in all possible humbleness, but yet with a countenance taking knowledge that we knew that he spake it but merrily. "That we were apt enough to think there was somewhat supernatural in this island, but yet rather as angelical than magical. But to let his lordship know truly what it was that made us tender and doubtful to ask this question, it was not any such conceit, but because we remembered he had given a touch[31] in his former speech, that this land had laws of secrecy touching strangers." To this he said, "You remember it aright; and therefore in that I shall say to you I must reserve some particulars, which it is not lawful for me to reveal; but there will be enough left to give you satisfaction.

"You shall understand (that which perhaps you will scarce think credible) that about three thousand years ago, or somewhat more, the navigation of the world (especially for remote voyages) was greater than at this day. Do not think with yourselves that I know not how much it is increased with you within these six-score years; I know it well, and yet I say, greater then than now; whether it was, that the example of the ark, that saved the remnant of men from the universal deluge, gave men confidence to venture upon the waters, or what it was; but such is the truth. The Phoenicians, and especially the Tyrians, had great fleets.[32] So had the Carthaginians[33] their colony, which is yet farther west. Toward the east, the shipping of Egypt and of Palestine was likewise great. China also, and the great Atlantis (that you call America), which have now but junks and canoes, abounded then in tall ships. This island (as appeareth by faithful registers of those times) had then fifteen hundred strong ships, of great content. Of all this there is with you sparing memory, or none; but we have large knowledge thereof.

"At that time, this land was known and frequented by the ships and vessels of all the nations before named. And (as it cometh to pass) they had many times men of other countries, that were no sailors, that came with them; as Persians, Chaldeans, Arabians, so as almost all nations of might and fame resorted hither; of whom we have some stirps[34] and little tribes with us at this day. And for our own ships, they went sundry voyages, as well to your Straits, which you call the Pillars of Hercules,[35] as to other parts in the Atlantic and Mediterranean seas; as to Paguin (which is the same with Cambaline)[36] and Quinzy,[37] upon the Oriental Seas, as far as to the borders of the East Tartary.

"At the same time, and an age after, or more, the inhabitants of the great Atlantis did flourish.[38] For though the narration and description which is made by a great man with you, that the descendants of Neptune planted there; and of the magnificent temple, palace, city, and hill; and the manifold streams of goodly navigable rivers (which as so many chains, environed the same site and temple); and the several degrees of ascent whereby men did climb up to the same, as if it had been a *scala coeli*;[39] be all poetical and fabulous; yet so much is true, that the said country of Atlantis, as well that of Peru, then called Coya, as that of Mexico, then named Tyrambel, were mighty and proud kingdoms, in arms, shipping, and riches; so mighty, as at one time (or at least within the space of ten years) they both made two great expeditions; they of Tyrambel through the Atlantic to the Mediterranean Sea; and they of Coya through the South Sea upon this our island. And for the former of these, which was into Europe, the same author amongst you (as it seemeth) had some relation from the Egyptian priest whom he citeth. For assuredly such a thing there was. But whether it were the ancient Athenians that had the glory of the repulse and resistance of those forces, I can say nothing; but certain it is, there never came back either ship or man from that voyage. Neither had the other voyage of those of Coya upon us had better fortune, if they had not met with enemies of greater clemency. For the King of this island (by name Altabin) a wise man and a great warrior, knowing well both his own strength and that of his enemies, handled the matter so, as he cut off their land forces from their ships, and entoiled[40] both their navy and their camp with a greater power than theirs, both by sea and land; and compelled them to render themselves without striking stroke; and after they were at his mercy, contenting himself only with their oath that they should no more bear arms against him, dismissed them all in safety. But the Divine Revenge overtook not long after those proud enterprises. For within less than the space of one hundred years, the Great Atlantis was utterly lost and destroyed; not by a great earthquake, as your man saith (for that whole tract is little subject to earthquakes) but by a particular deluge, or inundation; those countries having, at this day, far greater rivers, and far higher mountains to pour down waters, than any part of the old world. But it is true that the same inundation was not deep; not past forty foot,

32   Bacon here refers to several of the most active maritime cultures of the ancient Mediterranean. The Phoenicians lived in the land occupied by modern Syria and Lebanon and were trading in and around the whole Mediterranean by the 9th century BCE. Tyre was a principal port city of the Phoenicians.

33   Carthage, in modern Tunisia, was the centre of a thriving trading empire in the western Mediterranean from the 5th century BCE onward. It came into conflict with the burgeoning Roman empire and, after a series of wars, was utterly destroyed in 146 BCE.

34   Literally, "branches of a family." Bacon is proposing that all of these "lost" cultures have descendants in Bensalem.

35   The mythical hero Heracles (Latin "Hercules") is said to have erected two huge pillars, one on either side of the Straits of Gibraltar. For later writers, they marked the western boundary of the known world

and are often used as symbols of the limits of knowledge. For writers living after Columbus's voyage like Bacon, they became symbols of the old boundaries of knowledge that needed to be transcended.

36   *Beijing.*

37   The southern Chinese port city of Guangzhou ("Canton").

38   The myth of Atlantis is first recorded, as Bacon says here, by Plato in the *Timaeus*, where he ascribes the story to Egyptian priests, and the *Critias*. In this latter text, the island's constitution and the layout of its principal city are described. Speculation about a lost historical city upon which Plato's story was based has been rampant for millennia, but no credible evidence has been produced to verify any of it.

39   "a ladder to heaven."

40   *entrapped.*

in most places, from the ground, so that although it destroyed man and beast generally, yet some few wild inhabitants of the wood escaped. Birds also were saved by flying to the high trees and woods. For as for men, although they had buildings in many places higher than the depth of the water, yet that inundation, though it were shallow, had a long continuance; whereby they of the vale that were not drowned, perished for want of food, and other things necessary. So as marvel you not at the thin population of America, nor at the rudeness and ignorance of the people; for you must account your inhabitants of America as a young people, younger a thousand years at the least than the rest of the world; for that there was so much time between the universal flood and their particular inundation. For the poor remnant of human seed which remained in their mountains peopled the country again slowly, by little and little; and being simple and a savage people (not like Noah and his sons, which was the chief family of the earth)[41] they were not able to leave letters, arts, and civility to their posterity; and having likewise in their mountainous habitations been used (in respect of the extreme cold of those regions) to clothe themselves with the skins of tigers, bears, and great hairy goats, that they have in those parts; when after they came down into the valley, and found the intolerable heats which are there, and knew no means of lighter apparel, they were forced to begin the custom of going naked, which continueth at this day. Only they take great pride and delight in the feathers of birds, and this also they took from those their ancestors of the mountains, who were invited unto it by the infinite flight of birds that came up to the high grounds, while the waters stood below. So you see, by this main accident of time, we lost our traffic with the Americans, with whom of all others, in regard they lay nearest to us, we had most commerce. As for the other parts of the world, it is most manifest that in the ages following (whether it were in respect of wars, or by a natural revolution of time) navigation did everywhere greatly decay; and especially far voyages (the rather by the use of galleys, and such vessels as could hardly brook the ocean) were altogether left and omitted. So then, that part of intercourse which could be from other nations to sail to us, you see how it hath long since ceased; except it were by some rare accident, as this of yours. But now of the cessation of that other part of intercourse, which might be by our sailing to other nations, I must yield you some other cause. For I cannot say (if I shall say truly) but our shipping, for number, strength, mariners, pilots, and all things that appertain to navigation, is as great as ever; and therefore why we should sit at home, I shall now give you an account by itself; and it will draw nearer to give you satisfaction to your principal question.

"There reigned in this island, about nineteen hundred years ago, a King, whose memory of all others we most adore; not superstitiously, but as a divine instrument, though a mortal man: his name was Solamona; and we esteem him as the lawgiver of our nation. This King had a *large heart*,[42] inscrutable for good; and was wholly bent to make his kingdom and people happy. He therefore, taking into consideration how sufficient and substantive this land was to maintain itself without any aid at all of the foreigner; being five thousand six hundred miles in circuit, and of rare fertility of soil in the greatest part thereof; and finding also the shipping of this country might be plentifully set on work, both by fishing and by transportations from port to port, and likewise by sailing unto some small islands that are not far from us, and are under the crown and laws of this state; and recalling into his memory the happy and flourishing estate wherein this land then was, so as it might be a thousand ways altered to the worse, but scarce any one way to the better; thought nothing wanted to his noble and heroical intentions, but only (as far as human foresight might reach) to give perpetuity to that which was in his time so happily established. Therefore among his other fundamental laws of this kingdom, he did ordain the interdicts and prohibitions which we have touching entrance of strangers; which at that time (though it was after the calamity of America) was frequent; doubting novelties,[43] and commixture of manners. It is true, the like law against the admission of strangers without license is an ancient law in the Kingdom of China, and yet continues in use. But there it is a poor thing; and hath made them a curious, ignorant, fearful,

---

41 In Jewish and Christian tradition, of course, Noah and his family repopulated the entire earth. Bacon is here imagining that there were other survivors of the biblical flood who, not being God's chosen people, lived in a more debased state as a result.

42 1 Kings 4:29. The word "inscrutable" usually means "mysterious" or "unintelligible," but here refers to the depth and rarity of Solomon's goodness.

43 Literally, anything new or unfamiliar.

foolish nation. But our lawgiver made his law of another temper. For first, he hath preserved all points of humanity, in taking order and making provision for the relief of strangers distressed; whereof you have tasted." At which speech (as reason was) we all rose up and bowed ourselves. He went on: "That King also, still desiring to join humanity and policy[44] together; and thinking it against humanity to detain strangers here against their wills, and against policy that they should return and discover their knowledge of this estate, he took this course: he did ordain that of the strangers that should be permitted to land, as many (at all times) might depart as would; but as many as would stay should have very good conditions, and means to live from the state. Wherein he saw so far, that now in so many ages since the prohibition, we have memory not of one ship that ever returned; and but of thirteen persons only, at several times, that chose to return in our bottoms.[45] What those few that returned may have reported abroad I know not. But you must think, whatsoever they have said could be taken where they came but for a dream. Now for our travelling from hence into parts abroad, our Lawgiver thought fit altogether to restrain it. So is it not in China. For the Chinese sail where they will, or can; which showeth that their law of keeping out strangers is a law of pusillanimity[46] and fear. But this restraint of ours hath one only exception, which is admirable; preserving the good which cometh by communicating with strangers, and avoiding the hurt: and I will now open it to you. And here I shall seem a little to digress, but you will by and by find it pertinent. Ye shall understand, my dear friends, that among the excellent acts of that king, one above all hath the pre-eminence. It was the erection and institution of an order, or society, which we call *Salomon's House*, the noblest foundation (as we think) that ever was upon the earth, and the lantern of this kingdom. It is dedicated to the study of the works and creatures of God. Some think it beareth the founder's name a little corrupted, as if it should be Solamona's House. But the records write it as it is spoken. So as I take it to be denominate of the King of the Hebrews, which is famous with you, and no stranger to us. For we have some parts of his works which with you are lost; namely, that natural history which he wrote of all plants, from the *cedar of Libanus* to the *moss that groweth out of the wall*, and of all *things that have life and motion*.[47] This maketh me think that our king, finding himself to symbolize in many things with that king of the Hebrews (which lived many years before him) honoured him with the title of this foundation. And I am the rather induced to be of this opinion, for that I find in ancient records this order or society is sometimes called Solomon's House, and sometimes the College of the Six Days' Works; whereby I am satisfied that our excellent King had learned from the Hebrews that God had created the world and all that therein is within six days: and therefore he instituting that house for the finding out of the true nature of all things (whereby God might have the more glory in the workmanship of them, and men the more fruit in their use of them) did give it also that second name. But now to come to our present purpose. When the King had forbidden to all his people navigation into any part that was not under his crown, he made nevertheless this ordinance; that every twelve years there should be set forth out of this kingdom two ships, appointed to several voyages; that in either of these ships there should be a mission of three of the fellows or brethren of Salomon's House; whose errand was only to give us knowledge of the affairs and state of those countries to which they were designed, and especially of the sciences, arts, manufactures, and inventions of all the world; and withal to bring unto us books, instruments, and patterns in every kind; that the ships, after they had landed the brethren, should return; and that the brethren should stay abroad till the new mission. The ships are not otherwise fraught, than with store of victuals, and good quantity of treasure to remain with the brethren, for the buying of such things, and rewarding of such persons, as they should think fit. Now for me to tell you how the vulgar[48] sort of mariners are contained from being discovered at land; and how they that must be put on shore for any time, colour themselves under the names of other nations; and to what places these voyages have been designed; and what places of *rendezvous* are appointed for the new missions; and the like circum-

---

44 *political shrewdness.*
45 i.e. ships.
46 *cowardliness.*

47 1 Kings 4:33. Bacon is again reorienting conventional Western traditions: here, Solomon the wise lawgiver is being made into the model for a good scientist as well.
48 *lower-class.*

stances of the practice; I may not do it, neither is it much to your desire. But thus you see we maintain a trade, not for gold, silver, or jewels, nor for silks, nor for spices, nor any other commodity of matter; but only for God's first creature, which was *Light*; to have *light* (I say) of the growth of all parts of the world." And when he had said this, he was silent, and so were we all. For indeed we were all astonished to hear so strange things so probably told. And he, perceiving that we were willing to say somewhat, but had it not ready, in great courtesy took us off, and descended to ask us questions of our voyage and fortunes; and in the end concluded, that we might do well to think with ourselves what time of stay we would demand of the state, and bade us not to scant ourselves; for he would procure such time as we desired. Whereupon we all rose up, and presented ourselves to kiss the skirt of his tippet; but he would not suffer us, and so took his leave. But when it came once among our people that the state used to offer conditions to strangers that would stay, we had work enough to get any of our mem to look to our ship, and to keep them from going presently to the governor to crave conditions. But with much ado we refrained them, till we might agree what course to take.

We took ourselves now for free men, seeing there was no danger of our utter perdition, and lived most joyfully, going abroad and seeing what was to be seen in the city and places adjacent, within our tedder;[49] and obtaining acquaintance with many of the city, not of the meanest quality, at whose hands we found such humanity, and such a freedom and desire to take strangers as it were into their bosom, as was enough to make us forget all that was dear to us in our own countries; and continually we met with many things right worthy of observation and relation; as indeed, if there be a mirror in the world worthy to hold men's eyes, it is that country. One day there were two of our company bidden to a Feast of the Family, as they call it. A most natural, pious, and reverend custom it is, showing that nation to be compounded of all goodness. This is the manner of it. It is granted to any man that shall live to see thirty persons descended of his body alive together, and all above three years old, to make this feast, which is done at the cost of the state. The father of the family, whom they call the *Tirsan*, two days before the feast, taketh to him three of such friends as he liketh to choose, and is assisted also by the governor of the city or place where the feast is celebrated; and all the persons of the family, of both sexes, are summoned to attend him. These two days the Tirsan sitteth in consultation concerning the good estate of the family. There, if there be any discord or suits between any of the family, they are compounded and appeased. There, if any of the family be distressed or decayed, order is taken for their relief and competent means to live. There, if any be subject to vice, or take ill-courses, they are reproved and censured. So likewise direction is given touching marriages, and the courses of life which any of them should take, with divers other the like orders and advices. The governor assisteth, to the end to put in execution by his public authority the decrees and orders of the Tirsan, if they should be disobeyed, though that seldom needeth; such reverence and obedience they give to the order of nature. The Tirsan doth also then ever choose one man from among his sons, to live in house with him: who is called ever after the Son of the Vine. The reason will hereafter appear. On the feast day, the father or Tirsan cometh forth after divine service into a large room where the feast is celebrated; which room hath a half-pace[50] at the upper end. Against the wall, in the middle of the half-pace, is a chair placed for him, with a table and carpet before it. Over the chair is a state,[51] made round or oval, and it is of ivy; an ivy somewhat whiter than ours, like the leaf of a silver asp,[52] but more shining; for it is green all winter. And the state is curiously wrought with silver and silk of divers colours, broiding[53] or binding in the ivy; and is ever of the work of some of the daughters of the family, and veiled over at the top, with a fine net of silk and silver. But the substance of it is true ivy; whereof, after it is taken down, the friends of the family are desirous to have some leaf or sprig to keep. The Tirsan cometh forth with all his generation or lineage, the males before him, and the females following him; and if there be a mother from whose body the whole lineage is descended, there is a traverse placed in a loft above on the right hand of the chair, with a privy door, and a

---

49   *tether.*
50   *raised platform.*
51   *canopy.*

52   *aspen.*
53   *braiding.*

carved window of glass, leaded with gold and blue; where she sitteth, but is not seen. When the Tirsan is come forth, he sitteth down in the chair; and all the lineage place themselves against the wall, both at his back, and upon the return of the half-pace, in order of their years) without difference of sex, and stand upon their feet. When he is set, the room being always full of company, but well kept and without disorder, after some pause there cometh in from the lower end of the room a *Taratan* (which is as much as a herald) and on either side of him two young lads; whereof one carrieth a scroll of their shining yellow parchment, and the other a cluster of grapes of gold, with a long foot or stalk. The herald and children are clothed with mantles of sea-water green satin; but the herald's mantle is streamed with gold, and hath a train. Then the herald with three courtesies, or rather inclinations, cometh up as far as the half-pace, and there first taketh into his hand the scroll. This scroll is the King's Charter, containing gift of revenue, and many privileges, exemptions, and points of honour, granted to the Father of the Family; and it is ever styled and directed, "To such an one, our well-beloved friend and creditor," which is a title proper only to this case. For they say the King is debtor to no man, but for propagation of his subjects. The seal set to the King's charter is the King's image, embossed or moulded in gold; and though such charters be expedited of course, and as of right, yet they are varied by discretion, according to the number and dignity of the family. This charter the herald readeth aloud; and while it is read, the father or Tirsan standeth up, supported by two of his sons, such as he chooseth. Then the herald mounteth the half-pace, and delivereth the charter into his hand: and with that there is an acclamation by all that are present in their language, which is thus much: "Happy are the people of Bensalem." Then the herald taketh into his hand from the other child the cluster of grapes, which is of gold, both the stalk and the grapes. But the grapes are daintily enamelled: and if the males of the family be the greater number, the grapes are enamelled purple, with a little sun set on the top; if the females, then they are enamelled into a greenish yellow, with a crescent on the top. The grapes are in number as many as there are descendants of the family. This golden cluster the herald delivereth also to the Tirsan; who presently delivereth it over to that son that he had formerly chosen to be in house with him: who beareth it before his father as an ensign of honour when he goeth in public ever after; and is thereupon called the Son of the Vine. After this ceremony ended the father or Tirsan retireth; and after some time cometh forth again to dinner, where he sitteth alone under the state, as before; and none of his descendants sit with him, of what degree or dignity soever, except he hap to be of Salomon's House. He is served only by his own children, such as are male; who perform unto him all service of the table upon the knee; and the women only stand about him, leaning against the wall. The room below his half-pace hath tables on the sides for the guests that are bidden; who are served with great and comely order; and toward the end of dinner (which in the greatest feasts with them lasteth never above an hour and a half) there is an hymn sung, varied according to the invention of him that composeth it (for they have excellent poesy) but the subject of it is (always) the praises of Adam and Noah and Abraham; whereof the former two peopled the world, and the last was the Father of the Faithful: concluding ever with a thanksgiving for the nativity of our Saviour, in whose birth the births of all are only blessed. Dinner being done, the Tirsan retireth again; and having withdrawn himself alone into a place where he maketh some private prayers, he cometh forth the third time, to give the blessing; with all his descendants, who stand about him as at the first. Then he calleth them forth by one and by one, by name, as he pleaseth, though seldom the order of age be inverted. The person that is called (the table being before removed) kneeleth down before the chair, and the father layeth his hand upon his head, or her head, and giveth the blessing in these words: "Son of Bensalem (or daughter of Bensalem), thy father saith it; the man by whom thou hast breath and life speaketh the word; the blessing of the everlasting Father, the Prince of Peace, and the Holy Dove be upon thee, and make the days of thy pilgrimage good and many." This he saith to every of them; and that done, if there be any of his sons of eminent merit and virtue (so they be not above two) he calleth for them again, and saith, laying his arm over their shoulders, they standing: "Sons, it is well you are born, give God the praise, and persevere to the end." And withal delivereth to either of them a jewel, made in the figure of an ear of wheat, which they ever after wear in the front of their turban or hat. This done, they fall to music and dances, and other recreations, after their manner, for the rest of the day. This is the full order of that feast.

SIR FRANCIS BACON 639

By that time six or seven days were spent, I was fallen into straight[54] acquaintance with a merchant of that city, whose name was Joabin. He was a Jew and circumcised; for they have some few stirps of Jews yet remaining among them, whom they leave to their own religion. Which they may the better do, because they are of a far differing disposition from the Jews in other parts.[55] For whereas they hate the name of Christ, and have a secret inbred rancour against the people among whom they live; these (contrariwise) give unto our Saviour many high attributes, and love the nation of Bensalem extremely. Surely this man of whom I speak would ever acknowledge that Christ was born of a Virgin, and that he was more than a man; and he would tell how God made him ruler of the Seraphim which guard his throne; and they call him also the *Milken Way*, and the *Eliah*[56] of the *Messiah*, and many other high names; which though they be inferior to his divine majesty, yet they are far from the language of other Jews. And for the country of Bensalem, this man would make no end of commending it: being desirous, by tradition among the Jews there, to have it believed that the people thereof were of the generations of Abraham, by another son, whom they call Nachoran; and that Moses by a secret cabala ordained the laws of Bensalem which they now use; and that when the Messiah should come, and sit in his throne at Jerusalem, the king of Bensalem should sit at his feet, whereas other kings should keep a great distance. But yet setting aside these Jewish dreams, the man was a wise man, and learned, and of great policy, and excellently seen[57] in the laws and customs of that nation. Among other discourses, one day I told him I was much affected with the relation I had from some of the company of their custom in holding the Feast of the Family; for that (methought) I had never heard of a solemnity wherein nature did so much preside. And because propagation of families proceedeth from the nuptial copulation, I desired to know of him what laws and customs they had concerning marriage; and whether they kept marriage well, and whether they were tied to one wife? For that where population is so much affected, and such as with them it seemed to be, there is commonly permission of plurality of wives. To this he said: "You have reason for to commend that excellent institution of the Feast of the Family. And indeed we have experience, that those families that are partakers of the blessings of that feast do flourish and prosper ever after in an extraordinary manner. But hear me now, and I will tell you what I know. You shall understand that there is not under the heavens so chaste a nation as this of Bensalem, nor so free from all pollution or foulness. It is the virgin of the world. I remember I have read in one of your European books, of an holy hermit amongst you that desired to see the spirit of fornication;[58] and there appeared to him a little foul ugly Ethiope; but if he had desired to see the spirit of chastity of Bensalem, it would have appeared to him in the likeness of a fair beautiful Cherubim. For there is nothing among mortal men more fair and admirable, than the chaste minds of this people. Know, therefore, that with them there are no stews,[59] no dissolute houses, no courtesans, nor anything of that kind. Nay they wonder (with detestation) at you in Europe, which permit such things. They say ye have put marriage out of office; for marriage is ordained a remedy for unlawful concupiscence; and natural concupiscence seemeth as a spur to marriage. But when men have at hand a remedy more agreeable to their corrupt will, marriage is almost expulsed. And therefore there are with you seen infinite men that marry not, but choose rather a libertine and impure single life, than to be yoked in marriage; and many that do marry, marry late, when the prime and strength of their years are past. And when they do marry, what is marriage to them but a very bargain; wherein is sought alliance, or portion,[60] or reputation, with some desire (almost indifferent) of issue; and not the faithful nuptial union of man and wife, that was first instituted. Neither is it possible that those that have cast away so basely so much of their strength, should greatly esteem children (being of the same matter) as chaste men do. So likewise during

---

54 *honest.*

55 Bacon here rehearses some of the commonest anti-Semitic clichés of the Early Modern period. Their presence in a text about expanding scientific knowledge that was aimed at an educated audience shows how omnipresent such attitudes were in English culture.

56 In Christian typology, the coming of the prophet Elijah is the promised sign of the Saviour (see Malachi 4:5).

57 *well versed.*

58 Earlier editors have referenced a 19th-century version of this story in La Motte Fouqué's *Sintram*, but no precise Early Modern referent has ever been found.

59 *brothels.*

60 *dowry.* Bacon was himself a fine example of someone who married a rich heiress for her money alone. He spent it all and more, leaving behind vast debts when he died.

marriage is the case much amended, as it ought to be if those things were tolerated only for necessity? No, but they remain still as a very affront to marriage. The haunting of those dissolute places, or resort to courtesans, are no more punished in married men than in bachelors. And the depraved custom of change, and the delight in meretricious[61] embracements (where sin is turned into art), maketh marriage a dull thing, and a kind of imposition or tax. They hear you defend these things, as done to avoid greater evils; as advoutries,[62] deflowering of virgins, unnatural lust, and the like. But they say this is a preposterous wisdom; and they call it *Lot's offer*, who to save his guests from abusing, offered his daughters;[63] nay, they say further that there is little gained in this; for that the same vices and appetites do still remain and abound; unlawful lust being like a furnace, that if you stop the flames altogether, it will quench, but if you give it any vent it will rage. As for masculine love, they have no touch of it; and yet there are not so faithful and inviolate friendships in the world again as are there; and to speak generally (as I said before) I have not read of any such chastity in any people as theirs. And their usual saying is, *That whosoever is unchaste cannot reverence himself*; and they say *That the reverence of a man's self is, next religion, the chiefest bridle of all vices.*" And when he had said this, the good Jew paused a little; whereupon I, far more willing to hear him speak on than to speak myself; yet thinking it decent that upon his pause of speech I should not be altogether silent, said only this; "That I would say to him, as the widow of Sarepta said to Elias:[64] that he was come to bring to memory our sins; and that I confess the righteousness of Bensalem was greater than the righteousness of Europe." At which speech he bowed his head, and went on this manner: "They have also many wise and excellent laws, touching marriage. They allow no polygamy. They have ordained that none do intermarry or contract, until a month be past from their first interview. Marriage without consent of parents they do not make void, but they mulct[65] it in the inheritors; for the children of such marriages are not admitted to inherit above a third part of their parents' inheritance. I have read in a book of one of your men, of a feigned commonwealth, where the married couple are permitted, before they contract, to see one another naked.[66] This they dislike; for they think it a scorn to give a refusal after so familiar knowledge; but because of many hidden defects in men and women's bodies, they have a more civil way; for they have near every town a couple of pools (which they call Adam and Eve's pools) where it is permitted to one of the friends of the man and another of the friends of the woman, to see them severally bathe naked."

And as we were thus in conference, there came one that seemed to be a messenger, in a rich huke,[71] that spake with the Jew; whereupon he turned to me and said, "You will pardon me, for I am commanded away in haste." The next morning he came to me again, joyful as it seemed, and said: "There is word come to the governor of the city, that one of the Fathers of Salomon's House will be here this day seven-night; we have seen none of them this dozen years. His coming is in state; but the cause of this coming is secret. I will provide you and your fellows of a good standing to see his entry." I thanked him, and told him, "I was most glad of the news." The day being come, he made his entry. He was a man of middle stature and age, comely of person, and had an aspect as if he pitied men. He was clothed in a robe of fine black cloth, with wide sleeves and a cape: his under-garment was of excellent white linen down to the foot, girt with a girdle of the same; and a sindon or tippet of the same about his neck. He had gloves that were curious,[68] and set with stone; and shoes of peach-coloured velvet. His neck was bare to the shoulders. His hat was like a helmet, or Spanish montera; and his locks curled below it decently; they were of colour brown. His beard was cut round, and of the same colour with his hair, somewhat lighter. He was carried in a rich chariot without wheels, litter-wise, with two horses at either end, richly trapped in blue velvet embroidered; and two footmen on each side in the like attire. The chariot was all of cedar, gilt, and adorned with crystal; save that the fore end had panels of sapphires set in borders of gold, and the hinder end the like of emeralds of the Peru[69] colour. There was also a sun of gold, radiant,

---

61   i.e. pertaining to prostitutes.
62   *adulteries.*
63   Genesis 19:8.
64   1 Kings 17:8.
65   *punish.*

66   The reference is to Sir Thomas More's *Utopia* (see pp. 25–28 in this volume).
67   *hooded cloak.*
68   *finely made.*
69   *emerald green.*

upon the top, in the midst; and on the top before a small cherub of gold, with wings displayed. The chariot was covered with cloth-of-gold tissued upon blue. He had before him fifty attendants, young men all, in white satin loose coats to the mid-leg, and stockings of white silk; and shoes of blue velvet; and hats of blue velvet, with fine plumes of divers colours, set round like hat-bands. Next before the chariot went two men, bare-headed, in linen garments down to the foot, girt, and shoes of blue velvet, who carried the one a crosier,[70] the other a pastoral staff like a sheep-hook; neither of them of metal, but the crosier of balm-wood, the pastoral staff of cedar. Horsemen he had none, neither before nor behind his chariot; as it seemeth, to avoid all tumult and trouble. Behind his chariot went all the officers and principals of the companies of the city. He sat alone, upon cushions of a kind of excellent plush, blue; and under his foot curious carpets of silk of divers colours, like the Persian, but far finer. He held up his bare hand, as he went, as blessing the people, but in silence. The street was wonderfully well kept; so that there was never any army had their men stand in better battle-array, than the people stood. The windows likewise were not crowded, but everyone stood in them as if they had been placed. When the show was passed, the Jew said to me, "I shall not be able to attend you as I would, in regard of some charge the city hath laid upon me, for the entertaining of this great person." Three days after, the Jew came to me again, and said: "Ye are happy men; for the Father of Salomon's House taketh knowledge of your being here, and commanded me to tell you that he will admit all your company to his presence, and have private conference with one of you, that ye shall choose; and for this hath appointed the next day after tomorrow. And because he meaneth to give you his blessing, he hath appointed it in the forenoon." We came at our day and hour, and I was chosen by my fellows for the private access. We found him in a fair chamber, richly hanged, and carpeted under foot, without any degrees to the state.[71] He was set upon a low throne richly adorned, and a rich cloth of state over his head, of blue satin embroidered. He was alone, save that he had two pages of honour, on either hand one, finely attired in white. His undergarments were the like that we saw him wear in the chariot; but instead of his gown, he had on him a mantle with a cape, of the same fine black, fastened about him. When we came in, as we were taught, we bowed low at our first entrance; and when we were come near his chair, he stood up, holding forth his hand ungloved, and in posture of blessing; and we every one of us stooped down and kissed the hem of his tippet. That done, the rest departed, and I remained. Then he warned the pages forth of the room, and caused me to sit down beside him, and spake to me thus in the Spanish tongue:

"God bless thee, my son; I will give thee the greatest jewel I have. For I will impart unto thee, for the love of God and men, a relation of the true state of Salomon's House. Son, to make you know the true state of Salomon's House, I will keep this order. First, I will set forth unto you the end of our foundation. Secondly, the preparations and instruments we have for our works. Thirdly, the several employments and functions whereto our fellows are assigned. And fourthly, the ordinances[72] and rites which we observe.

"The end of our foundation is the knowledge of causes, and secret motions of things; and the enlarging of the bounds of human empire, to the effecting of all things possible.

"The preparations and instruments are these. We have large and deep caves of several depths; the deepest are sunk six hundred fathoms; and some of them are digged and made under great hills and mountains; so that if you reckon together the depth of the hill and the depth of the cave, they are (some of them) above three miles deep. For we find that the depth of a hill, and the depth of a cave from the flat, is the same thing; both remote alike from the sun and heaven's beams, and from the open air. These caves we call the Lower Region. And we use them for all coagulations, indurations,[73] refrigerations, and conservations of bodies. We use them likewise for the imitation of natural mines; and the producing also of new artificial metals, by compositions and materials which we use, and lay there for many years. We use them also sometimes (which may seem strange) for curing of some diseases, and for prolongation of life in some hermits that choose to live there,

70 In ordinary 17th-century use, a crosier was the episcopal staff of a bishop. Bacon's point seems to be that, in Bensalem, Salomon's House holds the respect and reverence that in Europe is paid to the Church.

71 i.e. without any steps up to the canopy.

72 *established rules.*

73 The process of becoming hard; solidifying.

well accommodated of all things necessary, and indeed live very long; by whom also we learn many things.

"We have burials in several earths, where we put divers cements, as the Chinese do their porcelain. But we have them in greater variety, and some of them more fine. We also have great variety of composts, and soils, for the making of the earth fruitful.

"We have high towers; the highest about half a mile in height, and some of them likewise set upon high mountains, so that the vantage of the hill with the tower is in the highest of them three miles at least. And these places we call the Upper Region; accounting the air between the high places and the low as a Middle Region. We use these towers, according to their several heights and situations, for insolation,[74] refrigeration, conservation; and for the view of divers meteors – as winds, rain, snow, hail, and some of the fiery meteors also. And upon them, in some places, are dwellings of hermits, whom we visit sometimes, and instruct what to observe.

"We have great lakes both salt and fresh, whereof we have use for the fish and fowl. We use them also for burials of some natural bodies, for we find a difference in things buried in earth or in air below the earth, and things buried in water. We have also pools, of which some do strain fresh water out of salt; and others by art do turn fresh water into salt. We have also some rocks in the midst of the sea, and some bays upon the shore, for some works wherein are required the air and vapour of the sea. We have likewise violent streams and cataracts, which serve us for many motions; and likewise engines for multiplying and enforcing of winds, to set also on going divers motions.

"We have also a number of artificial wells and fountains, made in imitation of the natural sources and baths; as tincted[75] upon vitriol, sulphur, steel, brass, lead, nitre,[76] and other minerals. And again we have little wells for infusions of many things, where the waters take the virtue quicker and better than in vessels or basins. And among them we have a water, which we call Water of Paradise, being, by that we do to it, made very sovereign for health, and prolongation of life.

"We have also great and spacious houses, where we imitate and demonstrate meteors; as snow, hail, rain, some artificial rains of bodies and not of water, thunders, lightnings; also generations of bodies in air; as frogs, flies, and divers others.[77]

"We have also certain chambers, which we call Chambers of Health, where we qualify the air as we think good and proper for the cure of divers diseases, and preservation of health.

"We have also fair and large baths, of several mixtures, for the cure of diseases, and the restoring of man's body from arefaction;[78] and others for the confirming of it in strength of sinews, vital parts, and the very juice and substance of the body.

"We have also large and various orchards and gardens, wherein we do not so much respect beauty, as variety of ground and soil, proper for divers trees and herbs; and some very spacious, where trees and berries are set whereof we make divers kinds of drinks, besides the vineyards. In these we practise likewise all conclusions[79] of grafting and inoculating, as well of wild trees as fruit trees, which produceth many effects. And we make (by art) in the same orchards and gardens, trees and flowers to come earlier or later than their seasons, and to come up and bear more speedily than by their natural course they do. We make them also by art greater much than their nature; and their fruit greater and sweeter and of differing taste, smell, colour, and figure, from their nature. And many of them we so order, as that they become of medicinal use.

"We have also means to make divers plants rise by mixtures of earths without seeds; and likewise to make divers new plants, differing from the vulgar; and to make one tree or plant turn into another.

"We have also parks and enclosures of all sorts of beasts and birds, which we use not only for view or rareness, but likewise for dissections and trials; that thereby may take light what may be wrought upon the body of man. Wherein we find many strange effects: as continuing life in them,

---

74   *exposure to the sun.*
75   *tinged.*
76   *saltpetre.*

77   Early Modern Europeans believed that these creatures reproduced asexually.
78   *drying.*
79   *experiments.*

though divers parts, which you account vital, be perished and taken forth; resuscitating of some that seem dead in appearance; and the like. We try also all poisons and other medicines upon them, as well of chirurgery as physic.[80] By art likewise, we make them greater or taller than their kind is; and contrariwise dwarf them and stay their growth; we make them more fruitful and bearing than their kind is; and contrariwise barren and not generative. Also we make them differ in colour, shape, activity, many ways. We find means to make commixtures and copulations of different kinds; which have produced many new kinds, and them not barren, as the general opinion is. We make a number of kinds of serpents, worms, flies, fishes, of putrefaction; whereof some are advanced (in effect) to be perfect creatures, like beasts or birds, and have sexes, and do propagate. Neither do we this by chance, but we know beforehand of what matter and commixture what kind of those creatures will arise.

"We have also particular pools, where we make trials upon fishes, as we have said before of beasts and birds.

"We have also places for breed and generation of those kinds of worms and flies which are of special use; such as are with you your silkworms and bees.

"I will not hold you long with recounting of our brew-houses, bake-houses, and kitchens, where are made divers drinks, breads, and meats, rare and of special effects. Wines we have of grapes, and drinks of other juice of fruits, of grains, and of roots; and of mixtures with honey, sugar, manna, and fruits dried and decocted.[81] Also of the tears or wounding of trees, and of the pulp of canes. And these drinks are of several ages, some to the age or last of forty years. We have drinks also brewed with several herbs, and roots, and spices; yea with several fleshes, and white meats; whereof some of the drinks are such, as they are in effect meat and drink both; so that divers, especially in age, do desire to live with them, with little or no meat or bread. And above all, we strive to have drinks of extreme thin parts,[82] to insinuate into the body, and yet without all biting, sharpness, or fretting; inasmuch as some of them put upon the back of your hand will, with a little stay, pass through to the palm, and yet taste mild to the mouth. We have also waters which we ripen in that fashion, as they become nourishing; so that they are indeed excellent drink, and many will use no other. Bread we have of several grains, roots, and kernels; yea and some of flesh and fish dried; with divers kinds of leavings and seasonings; so that some do extremely move appetites, some do nourish so, as divers do live of them, without any other meat, who live very long. So for meats, we have some of them so beaten and made tender and mortified, yet without all corrupting, as a weak heat of the stomach will turn them into good chylus,[83] as well as a strong heat would meat otherwise prepared. We have some meats also and bread and drinks, which taken by men enable them to fast long after; and some other, that used make the very flesh of men's bodies sensibly more hard and tough, and their strength far greater than otherwise it would be.

"We have dispensatories or shops of medicine. Wherein you may easily think, if we have such variety of plants and living creatures more than you have in Europe (for we know what you have), the simples, drugs, and ingredients of medicines, must likewise be in so much the greater variety. We have them likewise of divers ages, and long fermentations. And for their preparations, we have not only all manner of exquisite distillations and separations, and especially by gentle heats and percolations through divers strainers, yea, and substances; but also exact forms of composition, whereby they incorporate almost as they were natural simples.[84]

"We have also divers mechanical arts, which you have not; and stuffs made by them, as papers, linen, silks, tissues, dainty works of feathers of wonderful lustre, excellent dyes, and many others; and shops likewise, as well for such as are not brought into vulgar[85] use amongst us as for those that are. For you must know that of the things before recited, many of them are grown into use throughout the kingdom; but yet if they did flow from our invention, we have of them also for patterns and principals.

---

80 "Chirurgery" is an obsolete term for surgery; "physic" refers to treatment with medicines rather than surgery.

81 *concentrated.*

82 *fine constituent elements.*

83 *intestinal fluid to be absorbed in digestion.*

84 *pure, unmixed substance.*

85 *everyday.*

"We have also furnaces of great diversities, and that keep great diversity of heats; fierce and quick, strong and constant, soft and mild, blown, quiet, dry, moist, and the like. But above all, we have heats in imitation of the sun's and heavenly bodies' heats, that pass divers inequalities and (as it were) orbs, progresses, and returns, whereby we produce admirable effects. Besides, we have heats of dungs, and of bellies and maws of living creatures, and of their bloods and bodies, and of hays and herbs laid up moist, of lime[86] unquenched, and such like. Instruments also which generate heat only by motion. And farther, places for strong insulations; and again, places under the earth, which by nature or art yield heat. These divers heats we use as the nature of the operation which we intend requireth.

"We have also perspective houses, where we make demonstrations of all lights and radiations; and of all colours; and out of things uncoloured and transparent, we can represent unto you all several colours, not in rainbows, as it is in gems and prisms, but of themselves single. We represent also all multiplications of light, which we carry to great distance, and make so sharp as to discern small points and lines; also all colourations of light: all delusions and deceits of the sight, in figures, magnitudes, motions, colours; all demonstrations of shadows. We find also divers means, yet unknown to you, of producing of light originally from divers bodies. We procure means of seeing objects afar off, as in the heaven and remote places; and represent things near as afar off, and things afar off as near; making feigned distances. We have also helps for the sight, far above spectacles and glasses in use. We have also glasses and means to see small and minute bodies perfectly and distinctly; as the shapes and colours of small flies and worms, grains, and flaws in gems which cannot otherwise be seen; observations in urine and blood not otherwise to be seen. We make artificial rainbows, halos, and circles about light. We represent also all manner of reflections, refractions, and multiplications of visual beams of objects.

"We have also precious stones of all kinds, many of them of great beauty, and to you unknown, crystals likewise, and glasses of divers kind; and amongst them some of metals vitrificated,[87] and other materials besides those of which you make glass. Also a number of fossils, and imperfect minerals, which you have not. Likewise loadstones of prodigious virtue, and other rare stones, both natural and artificial.

"We have also sound-houses, where we practise and demonstrate all sounds and their generation. We have harmony which you have not, of quarter-sounds, and lesser slides of sounds. Divers instruments of music likewise to you unknown, some sweeter than any you have; together with bells and rings that are dainty and sweet. We represent small sounds as great and deep, likewise great sounds extenuate[88] and sharp; we make divers tremblings and warblings of sounds, which in their original are entire. We represent and imitate all articulate sounds and letters, and the voices and notes of beasts and birds. We have certain helps which set to the ear do further the hearing greatly. We have also divers strange and artificial echoes, reflecting the voice many times, and as it were tossing it; and some that give back the voice louder than it came, some shriller, and some deeper; yea, some rendering the voice differing in the letters or articulate sound from that they receive. We have all means to convey sounds in trunks[89] and pipes, in strange lines and distances.

"We have also perfume-houses, wherewith we join also practices of taste. We multiply smells, which may seem strange. We imitate smells, making all smells to breathe out of other mixtures than those that give them. We make divers imitations of taste likewise, so that they will deceive any man's taste. And in this house we contain also a confiture-house,[90] where we make all sweet-meats, dry and moist, and divers pleasant wines, milks, broths, and salads, far in greater variety than you have.

"We have also engine-houses, where are prepared engines and instruments for all sorts of motions. There we imitate and practise to make swifter motions than any you have, either out of your muskets or any engine that you have; and to make them and multiply them more easily and with small force, by wheels and other means; and to make them stronger and more violent than

---

86   *quicklime.*
87   *made into glass.*
88   *thin.*

89   *tubes.*
90   *confection-house.*

yours are, exceeding your greatest cannons and basilisks.[91] We represent also ordnance and instruments of war, and engines of all kinds; and likewise new mixtures and compositions of gunpowder, wild-fires burning in water and unquenchable. Also fire-works of all variety both for pleasure and use. We imitate also flights of birds; we have some degrees of flying in the air; we have ships and boats for going under water, and brooking[92] of seas; also swimming-girdles and supporters. We have divers curious clocks, and other like motions of return, and some perpetual motions. We imitate also motions of living creatures, by images of men, beasts, birds, fishes, and serpents. We have also a great number of other various motions, strange for equality, fineness, and subtlety.

"We have also a mathematical-house, where are represented all instruments, as well of geometry as astronomy, exquisitely made.

"We have also houses of deceits of the senses; where we represent all manner of feats of juggling, false apparitions, impostures and illusions, and their fallacies. And surely you will easily believe that we that have so many things truly natural which induce admiration, could in a world of particulars deceive the senses, if we would disguise those things and labour to make them more miraculous. But we do hate all impostures and lies, inasmuch as we have severely forbidden it to all our fellows, under pain of ignominy and fines, that they do not show any natural work or thing, adorned or swelling; but only pure as it is, and without all affectation of strangeness.

"These are (my son) the riches of Salomon's House.

"For the several employments and offices of our fellows, we have twelve that sail into foreign countries under the names of other nations (for our own we conceal) who bring us the books, and abstracts, and patterns of experiments of all other parts. These we call Merchants of Light.

"We have three that collect the experiments which are in all books. These we call Depredators.[93]

"We have three that collect the experiments of all mechanical arts, and also of liberal sciences, and also of practices which are not brought into arts. These we call Mystery-men.

"We have three that try new experiments, such as themselves think good. These we call Pioneers or Miners.

"We have three that draw the experiments of the former four into titles and tables, to give the better light for the drawing of observations and axioms out of them. These we call Compilers.

"We have three that bend themselves, looking into the experiments of their fellows, and cast about how to draw out of them things of use and practice for man's life and knowledge, as well for works as for plain demonstration of causes, means of natural divinations, and the easy and clear discovery of the virtues and parts of bodies. These we call Dowry-men or Benefactors.

"Then after divers meetings and consults of our whole number, to consider of the former labours and collections, we have three that take care, out of them, to direct new experiments, of a higher light, more penetrating into nature than the former. These we call Lamps.

"We have three others that do execute the experiments so directed, and report them. These we call Inoculators.

"Lastly, we have three that raise the former discoveries by experiments into greater observations, axioms, and aphorisms. These we call Interpreters of Nature.

"We have also, as you must think, novices and apprentices, that the succession of the former employed men do not fail; besides a great number of servants and attendants, men and women. And this we do also: we have consultations, which of the inventions and experiences which we have discovered shall be published, and which not; and take all an oath of secrecy, for the concealing of those which we think fit to keep secret; though some of those we do reveal sometime to the state, and some not.

"For our ordinances and rites, we have two very long and fair galleries; in one of these we place patterns and samples of all manner of the more rare and excellent inventions; in the other we place the statues of all principal inventors. There we have the statue of your Columbus, that discovered the West Indies, also the inventor of ships; your monk that was the inventor of ordnance and of

91   *large cannon.*
92   *endurance.*

93   Normally, this word means "plunderer." Bacon is here using it to refer to people who rifle old books to find what is useful in them.

gunpowder;[94] the inventor of music; the inventor of letters; the inventor of printing; the inventor of observations of astronomy; the inventor of works in metal; the inventor of glass; the inventor of silk of the worm; the inventor of wine; the inventor of corn and bread; the inventor of sugars; and all these by more certain tradition than you have. Then we have divers inventors of our own, of excellent works; which since you have not seen, it were too long to make descriptions of them; and besides, in the right understanding of those descriptions you might easily err. For upon every invention of value, we erect a statue to the inventor, and give him a liberal and honourable reward. These statues are some of brass, some of marble and touchstone, some of cedar and other special woods gilt and adorned, some of iron, some of silver, some of gold.

"We have certain hymns and services, which we say daily, of laud and thanks to God for His marvellous works; and forms of prayers, imploring His aid and blessing for the illumination of our labours; and the turning of them into good and holy uses.

"Lastly, we have circuits or visits of divers principal cities of the kingdom; where, as it cometh to pass, we do publish such new profitable inventions as we think good. And we do also declare natural divinations of diseases, plagues, swarms of hurtful creatures, scarcity, tempest, earthquakes, great inundations,[95] comets, temperature of the year, and divers other things; and we give counsel thereupon what the people shall do for the prevention and remedy of them."

And when he had said this he stood up, and I, as I had been taught, knelt down; and he laid his right hand upon my head, and said: "God bless thee, my son, and God bless this relation which I have made. I give thee leave to publish it for the good of other nations; for we here are in God's bosom, a land unknown." And so he left me; having assigned a value of about two thousand ducats[96] for a bounty to me and my fellows. For they give great largesses where they come upon all occasions.

[The rest was not perfected.]

Robert Southwell (1561–1595)

To say that Elizabethan England was a "Protestant" state is true at the level of official ideology, but misleading as a description of everyday religious practice. As hard as Elizabeth's ministers tried to reform the church's liturgy and traditions, pockets of Catholicism remained and were grudgingly tolerated (initially at least) by a monarch who was keen to avoid civil strife. Robert Southwell came from Norfolk, where the old faith was always strong, and he was sent to be educated in France at Douai, which was an important gathering place for English Catholic exiles. He became a Jesuit in 1578 and, after pleading with his superiors, was sent on a mission to England in 1586. The punishment for propagating the Catholic faith in England at that time was death, and Southwell knew that he was unlikely to ever return from his mission. He was betrayed and arrested in 1592, and executed three years later.

Despite his remarkable singleness of purpose and absolute devotion to Catholicism, his poetry includes both works that are markedly "Catholic" (like "Decease Release") and others that could easily be the work of a Protestant (like "Man's Civil War" and "Look Home"). This reminds us that the supposedly absolute divisions between Catholic and Protestant in official terms were often much less absolute in the minds of individual believers, and that humanist literary tropes cut across all such ideological lines. His faith was surely an enormous influence on his poetic productions, but it does not need to be seen as a limiting or determining influence. Evidence for this can be found in their popularity: Southwell's poems circulated quite widely in England despite the "criminal" identity of their author, and some, like "The Burning Babe," were greatly admired.

READING

Nancy Pollard Brown, "Paperchase: the Dissemination of Catholic Texts in Elizabethan England."
Ronald J. Carthell, "'The Secrecy of Man': Recusant Discourse and the Elizabethan Subject."

J. H.

---

94   Possibly an allusion to Roger Bacon, a 13th-century Franciscan monk who wrote about the composition and properties of gunpowder.

95   *floods*.

96   *gold coins*.

THE BURNING BABE

As I in hoary Winter's night
    Stood shivering in the snow,
Surprised I was with sudden heat,
    Which made my heart to glow;

And lifting up a fearful eye,
    To view what fire was near,
A pretty Babe all burning bright
    Did in the air appear;

Who scorched with excessive heat,
10   Such floods of tears did shed,
As though his floods should quench his flames,
    Which with his tears were fed:

Alas (quoth he) but newly born,
    In fiery heats I fry,[1]
Yet none approach to warm their hearts,
    Or feel my fire, but I;

My faultless breast the furnace is,
    The fuel wounding thorns:
Love is the fire, and sighs the smoke,
20   The ashes, shame and scorns;

The fuel Justice layeth on,
    And Mercy blows the coals,
The metal in this furnace wrought,
    Are men's defiled souls:

For which, as now on fire I am
    To work them to their good
So will I melt into a bath,
    To wash them in my blood.

With this he vanished out of sight,
30   And swiftly shrunk away,
And straight I called unto mind,
    That it was Christmas day.

DECEASE RELEASE[2]

Dum morior orior[3]

The pounded spice both taste and scent doth please,
In fading smoke the force doth incense show,

THE BURNING BABE

1 This word carries the sense of "burning with passion" as well as its literal meaning. As elsewhere in this poem, Southwell uses the poetic vocabulary of erotic love to describe Christ's love.

DECEASE RELEASE

2 This poem leaves the name in line 14 anonymous in some manuscripts, but it is usually associated with the Catholic Mary, Queen of Scots, who was executed by Elizabeth I.

3 "In dying, I rise"

The perished kernel springeth with increase,
The lopped tree doth best and soonest grow.

God's spice I was and pounding was my due,
In fading breath my incense savored best,
Death was the mean my kernel to renew,
By lopping shot I up to heavenly rest.

Some things more perfect are in their decay,
Like spark that going out gives clearest light,
Such was my hap whose doleful dying day   *fortune*
Began my joy and termed fortune's spite.   *finished*

Alive a Queen, now dead I am a Saint,
Once Mary called, my name now Martyr is,
From earthly reign debarred by restraint,
In lieu whereof I reign in heavenly bliss.

My life my grief, my death hath wrought my joy,
My friends my foil, my foes my weal procured,   *downfall/wellbeing*
My speedy death hath shortened long annoy,
And loss of life an endless life assured.

My scaffold was the bed where ease I found,
The block a pillow of Eternal rest,
My headman cast me in a blissful swounde,   *fainting fit*
His axe cut off my cares from cumbered breast.

Rue not my death, rejoice at my repose,
It was no death to me but to my woe,
The bud was opened to let out the rose,
The chains unloosed to let the captive go.

A prince by birth, a prisoner by mishap,
From Crown to cross, from throne to thrall I fell,
My right my ruth, my titles wrought my trap,   *ruin*
My weal my woe, my worldly heaven my hell.

By death from prisoner to a prince enhanced,
From cross to crown, from thrall to throne again,
My ruth my right, my trap my style advanced,[4]
From woe to weal, from hell to heavenly reign.

MAN'S CIVIL WAR

My hovering thoughts would fly to heaven
  And quiet nestle in the sky,
Fain would my ship in virtue's shore
  Without remove at anchor lie: i.e. removal

But mounting thoughts are hailed down   *showered*
  With heavy poise of mortal load,   *weight*

---

4 "Trap" has a double meaning of "snare" and "cloth covering the
harness of a horse." In the latter sense, "style" becomes the coat of arms
represented on the trap.

And blustering storms deny my ship
   In virtue's haven secure abode.

10   When inward eye to heavenly sights
   Doth draw my longing heart's desire,
The world with jesses⁵ of delights
   Would to her perch my thoughts retire,

Fond fancy trains to pleasure's lure,   *desire*
   Though reason stiffly do repine.   *complain*
Though wisdom woo me to the saint,
   Yet sense would win me to the shrine,   i.e. the senses

Where reason loathes, there fancy loves,
   And overrules the captive will,
Foes senses are to virtue's lore,
20   They draw the wit their wish to fill.   *lure*

Need craves consent of soul to sense,
   Yet diverse bents breed civil fray,   *different inclinations*
Hard hap where halves must disagree,   *fate*
   Or truce of halves the whole betray,

O cruel fight where fighting friend
   With love doth kill a favouring foe,
Where peace with sense is war with God,
   And self delight the seed of woe,

Dame pleasure's drugs are steeped in sin,
30   Their sugared taste doth breed annoy   *discomfort*
O fickle sense beware her gin,   *trap*
   Sell not thy soul for brittle joy.

LOOK HOME

Retired thoughts enjoy their own delights,
As beauty doth in self-beholding eye:
Man's mind a mirror is of heavenly sights,
A brief wherein all marvels summed lie.   *summary*
Of fairest forms, and sweetest shapes the store,
Most graceful all, yet thought may grace them more.

The mind a creature is, yet can create,
To nature's patterns adding higher skill:
Of finest works wit better could the state,⁶
10 If force of wit had equal power of will.
Device of man in working hath no end,
What thought can think another thought can mend.

Man's soul of endless beauty's image is,
Drawn by the work of endless skill and might:
This skillful might gave many sparks of bliss,
And to discern this bliss a native light.

MAN'S CIVIL WAR   LOOK HOME
5 The speaker compares his thoughts to a trained hawk; "jesses" refers   6 i.e. Human reason can improve the best of nature's works.
to the straps on a hawk's legs that were used to restrain them.

To frame God's image as his worths required: *merits*
His might, his skill, his word, and will conspired.

20   All that he had his image should present,
          All that it should present he could afford:
          To that he could afford his will was bent,
          His will was followed with performing word.
          Let this suffice, by this conceive the rest,
          He should, he could, he would, he did the best.

Mary Sidney Herbert,
Countess of Pembroke (1561–1621)

The Countess of Pembroke, sister of Sir Philip Sidney, was married to Henry Herbert, second Earl of Pembroke, when she was 15. From the year of her marriage until her husband's death in 1601 she lived at Wilton, near Salisbury, and occasionally at their London residence, Baynard's Castle. Wilton was a major center of literary activity during her years there; and it was from there that she acted as patron to several poets, including Samuel Daniel, Michael Drayton, and Edmund Spenser. After her husband's death her eldest son, William Herbert, third Earl of Pembroke, succeeded her as patron. The Countess also appears to have had a major influence on the literary development of her niece, Lady Mary Wroth. After a period of declining health in the years 1613–16, she died of smallpox in London at the age of 59.

The completion of her brother's work on the Psalms, which was left unfinished when he died in the Netherlands in 1585, was her most important literary achievement and, it appears, her obsession. That project included her editing of *The New Arcadia* and her execution of masterful metrical translations of the Psalms. Although Sidney had completed work on 43 of them before his death, the Countess not only finished the remaining 107 but also expertly revised her brother's work. She also wrote a superb dedicatory poem as a preface to the complete translation, "To the Angell spirit of the most excellent Sir Phillip Sidney," which is perhaps her finest independent piece of writing.

She had begun work on the Psalms by 1593 and completed the project before 1600. Although the collection was not published until 1823, it circulated in manuscript and had a profound influence on George Herbert and John Donne, who wrote a verse tribute to the translation.

For many poets – from Surrey to Milton – the Psalms in whatever version they were read served as a kind of primer to the writing of lyric poetry. The Countess's influence on the history of English poetry is, therefore, profound. Philip and Mary Sidney worked from the Latin text. It was not until after their deaths that it came to be generally understood that the original Hebrew Psalms were constructed on principles of varied parallelism instead of the patterns of rhythm and rhyme that were the basis of English versification.

Other translations by the Countess of Pembroke include Petrarch's *Triumph of Death*, Philip du Plessis-Mornay's *A Discourse of Life and Death*, and the pseudoclassical tragedy *Antonius*.

READING

Margaret P. Hannay, *Philip's Phoenix: Mary Sidney, Countess of Pembroke*.
J. C. A. Rathmell (ed.), *The Psalms of Sir Philip Sidney and the Countess of Pembroke*.

M. P.

TO THE ANGELL SPIRIT OF THE MOST EXCELLENT SIR PHILIP SIDNEY

To thee pure sprite, to thee alone's addres't
  this coupled worke, by double int'rest thine:
  First rais'de by thy blest hand, and what is mine
inspird by thee, thy secrett power imprest.
  So dar'd my Muse with thine it selfe combine,
  as mortall stuffe with that which is divine,
Thy lightning beames give lustre to the rest,

That heaven's King may daigne his owne transform'd
 in substance no, but superficiall tire
10 by thee put on; to praise, not to aspire
To, those high Tons, so in themselves adorn'd,
 which Angells sing in their cælestiall Quire,
 and all of tongues with soule and voice admire
Theise sacred Hymnes thy Kinglie Prophet form'd.

Oh, had that soule which honor brought to rest
 too soone not left and reft the world of all
 what man could showe, which wee perfection call
This half maim'd peece had sorted with the best.
 Deepe wounds enlarg'd, long festred in their gall
20 fresh bleeding smart; not eie but hart teares fall.
Ah memorie what needs this new arrest?

Yet here behold, (oh wert thou to behold!)
 this finish't now, thy matchlesse Muse begunne,
 the rest but peec't, as left by thee undone.
Pardon (oh blest soule) presumption too too bold:
 if love and zeale such error ill-become
 'tis zealous love, Love which hath never done,
Nor can enough in world of words unfold.

And sithe it hath no further scope to goe,
30 nor other purpose but to honor thee,
 Thee in thy workes where all the Graces bee,
As little streames with all their all doe flowe
 to their great sea, due tribute's gratefull fee:
 so press my thoughts my burthened thoughtes in mee,
To pay the debt of Infinits I owe

To thy great worth; exceeding Nature's store,
 wonder of men, sole borne perfection's kinde,
 Phœnix thou wert, so rare thy fairest minde
Heav'nly adorn'd, Earth justlye might adore,
40 where truthfull praise in highest glorie shin'de:
 For there alone was praise to truth confin'de;
And where but there, to live for evermore?

Oh! when to this Accompt, this cast upp Summe,
 this Reckoning made, this Audit of my woe,
 I call my thoughts, whence so strange passions flowe;
Howe workes my hart, my sences striken dumbe?
 that would thee more, then ever hart could showe,
 and all too short who knewe thee best doth knowe
There lives no witt that may thy praise become.

50 Truth I invoke (who scorne else where to move
 or here in ought my blood should partialize)
 Truth, sacred Truth, Thee sole to solemnize
Those precious rights well knowne best mindes approve:
 and who but doth, hath wisdome's open eies,
 not owly blinde the fairest light still flies
Confirme no lesse? At least 'tis seal'd above.

Where thou art fixt among thy fellow lights:
 my day put out, my life in darkenes cast,
 Thy Angell's soule with highest Angells plac't

60   There blessed sings enjoying heav'n-delights
    thy Maker's praise: as farr from earthy tast
    as here thy workes so worthilie embrac't
By all of worth, where never Envie bites.

As goodly buildings to some glorious ende
    cut of by fate, before the Graces hadde
    each wondrous part in all their beauties cladde,
Yet so much done, as Art could not amende;
    So thy rare workes to which no witt can adde,
    in all men's eies, which are not blindely madde,
70   Beyonde compare above all praise, extende.

Immortall Monuments of thy faire fame,
    though not compleat, nor in the reach of thought,
    howe on that passing peece time would have wrought
Had Heav'n so spar'd the life of life to frame
    the rest? But ah! such losse hath this world ought
    can equall it? or which like greevance brought?
Yet there will live thy ever praised name.

To which theise dearest offrings of my hart
    dissolv'd to Inke, while penn's impressions move
80   the bleeding veines of never dying love:
I render here: these wounding lynes of smart
    sadd Characters indeed of simple love
    not Art nor skill which abler wits doe prove,
Of my full soule receive the meanest part.

Receive theise Hymnes, theise obsequies receive;
    if any marke of thy sweet sprite appeare,
    well are they borne, no title else shall beare.
I can no more: Deare Soule I take my leave;
    Sorrowe still strives, would mount thy highest sphere
90   presuming so just cause might meet thee there,
Oh happie chaunge! could I so take my leave.

By the Sister of that
Incomparable Sidney

[FROM] THE PSALMS OF SIR PHILIP SIDNEY AND THE COUNTESS OF PEMBROKE

PSALM 44 *DEUS, AURIBUS*

Lorde, our fathers true relation   *account*
    Often made, hath made us knowe
How thy pow'r in each occasion,
    Thou of old for them didst showe;
    How thy hand the Pagan foe
Rooting hence, thie folke implanting,
    Leavelesse made that braunch to grow,
This to spring, noe verdure wanting.

Never could their sword procure them
10   Conquest of the promist land:

Never could their force assure them
    When theie did in danger stand.
    Noe, it was thie arme, thie hand,
Noe, it was thie favors treasure
    Spent uppon thie loved band,
Loved, whie? for thy wise pleasure.

Unto thee stand I subjected,
    I that did of Jacob spring:
Bidd then that I be protected,
    Thou that art my God, my king:
    By that succour thou didst bring,
Wee their pride that us assailed,
    Downe did tread, and back did fling,
In thy name confus'd and quailed.

For my trust was not reposed
    In my owne though strongest, bowe:
Nor my scabberd held enclosed
    That, whence should my saftie flowe
    Thou, O God, from every foe
Didst us shield, our haters shaming:
    Thence thy dailie praise wee showe,
Still thy name with honor naming.

But aloofe thou now dost hover,
    Grieving us with all disgrace:
Hast resign'd and given over
    In our Campe thy Captaines place.
    Back wee turne, that turned face,
Flieng them, that erst wee foiled:
    See our goods (O changed case,)
Spoil'd by them, that late we spoiled.

Right as sheepe to be devowred,
    Helplesse heere wee lie alone:
Scattringlie by thee out-powred,
    Slaves to dwell with lords unknown.
    Sold wee are, but silver none
Told for us: by thee so prised,
    As for nought to bee forgone,
Gracelesse, worthlesse, vile, despised.

By them all that dwell about us,
    Tos'd we flie as balls of scorne;
All our neighbours laugh and flout us,
    Men by thee in shame forlorne.
    Proverb-like our name is worne,
O how fast in foraine places!
    What hed-shakings are forborne!
Wordlesse taunts and dumbe disgraces!

Soe rebuke before mee goeth,
    As my self doe daily goe:
Soe Confusion on me groweth,
    That my face I blush to show.
    By reviling slaundring foe

Inly wounded thus I languish:
    Wreakfull spight with outward blow
Anguish adds to inward anguish.

All, this all on us hath lighted,
    Yet to thee our love doth last:
As wee were, wee are delighted
    Still to hold thie cov'nant fast.
    Unto none our hartes have past:
70   Unto none our feete have slidden:
    Though us downe to dragons cast
Thou in deadly shade hast hidden.

If our God wee had forsaken,
    Or forgott what hee assign'd:
If our selves we had betaken
    Godds to serve of other kind
    Should not hee our doubling find
Though conceal'd, and closlie lurking?
    Since his eye of deepest minde
80   Deeper sincks than deepest working?

Surelie Lord, this daily murther
    For thie sake we thus sustaine:
For thy sake esteem'd no further
    Than as sheepe, that must be slaine.
    Upp O Lord, up once againe:
Sleepe not ever, slack not ever:
    Why dost thou forgett our paine?
Why to hid thy face persever?

Heavie grief our soule abaseth,
90   Prostrate it on dust doth lie:
Earth our bodie fast embraceth,
    Nothing can the Claspe untie.
    Rise, and us with help supplie:
Lord, in mercie soe esteeme us,
    That we may thy mercie trie,
Mercie may from thrall redeeme us.

PSALM 59 *ERIPE ME DE INIMICIS*

Save me from such as me assaile:
    Let not my foes,
O God, against my life prevaile:
    Save me from those,
Who make a trade of cursed wrong
And, bredd in bloud, for bloud doe long.

Of these one sort doe seeke by slight
    My overthrow:
The stronger part with open might
10   Against me goe
And yet thou God, my wittness be
From all offence my soule is free.

But what if I from fault am free?
      Yet they are bent,
To band and stand against poore me,
      Poore innocent.
Rise God, and see how these things goe:
And rescue me from instant woe.

Rise, God of armies, mighty God
      Of Israell
Looke on them all who spredd abrode
      On earth doe dwell
And let thy hand no longer spare
Such as of malice wicked are.

When golden sunn in west doth sett,
      Retorn'd againe,
As houndes that howle their food to gett,
      They runn amaine
The cittie through from street to street,
With hungry maw some prey to meet.

Night elder growne, their fittest day,
      They babling prate,
How my lost life extinguish may
      Their deadly hate.
They prate and bable voide of feare,
For, tush, saie they, who now can heare?

Even thou canst heere, and heering scorne,
      All that they say;
For them (if not by thee upborne)
      What propps doe stay?
Then will I, as they wait for me
O God my fortresse, wait on thee.

Thou ever me with thy free grace
      Prevented hast:
With thee my praier shall take place
      Er from me past,
And I shall see who me doe hate
Beyond my wish in wofull state.

For feare my people it forgett
      Slay not outright
But scatter them and soe them sett
      In open sight
That by thy might they may be knowne,
Disgrac'd, debas'd, and overthrowne.

No witness of their wickednesse
      I neede produce
But their owne lipps, fitt to expresse
      Each vile abuse:
In cursing proud, proud when they ly
O let them deare such pride a-buy.

At length in rage consume them soe,
      That nought remayne:

Let them all beeing quite forgoe,
　　And make it playne,
That God who Jacobs rule upholds,
Rules all, all-bearing earth enfolds.

Now thus they fare: when sunn doth sett,
　　Retorn'd againe,
As hounds that howle their food to gett,
70　　　They runn amayne
The city through from street to street
With hungry mawes some prey to meet.

Abroad they range and hunt apace
　　Now that, now this,
As famine trailes a hungry trace;
　　And though they miss,
Yet will they not to kennell hye,
But all the night at bay do lye.

But I will of thy goodness sing
80　　And of thy might,
When early sunn againe shall bring
　　His cheerefull light;
For thou my refuge and my fort
In all distress dost mee support.

My strength doth of thy strength depend:
　　To thee I sing
Thou art my fort, me to defend.
　　My God, my king,
To thee I owe, and thy free grace,
90 That free I rest in fearless place.

PSALM 138 *CONFITEBOR TIBI*

Ev'n before kings by thee as gods commended,
And angells all, by whom thou art attended,
　　In harty tunes I will thy honor tell.
　　The pallace where thy holiness doth dwell
Shall be the place, where falling downe before thee,
With reverence meete I prostrate will adore thee.

There will I sing how thou thy mercy sendest,
And to thy promise due performance lendest,
　　Whereby thy name above all names doth fly.
10　　There will I sing, how when my carefull cry
Mounted to thee, my care was streight released,
My courage by thee mightily encreased.

Sure Lord, all Kings that understand the story
Of thy contract with me, nought but thy glory
　　And meanes shall sing whereby that glory grew;
　　Whose highly seated eye yet well doth view
With humbled look the soule that lowly lieth,
And, farr aloofe, aspiring things espieth.

On ev'ry side, though tribulation greive me,
20   Yet shalt thou aid, yet shalt thou still relieve me,
From angry foe thy succor shall me save.
Thou Lord shalt finish what in hand I have:
Thou Lord, I say, whose mercy lasteth ever,
Thy work begun, shall leave unended never.

PSALM 139 *DOMINE, PROBASTI*

O Lord in me there lieth nought,
    But to thy search revealed lies:
        For when I sitt
        Thou markest it:
    No lesse thou notest when I rise:
Yea closest closett of my thought
    Hath open windowes to thine eyes.

Thou walkest with me when I walk,
    When to my bed for rest I go,
10   I find thee there,
        And ev'ry where:
    Not yongest thought in me doth grow,
No not one word I cast to talk,
    But yet unutt'red thou dost know.

If forth I march, thou goest before,
    If back I torne, thou com'st behind:
        Soe foorth nor back
        Thy guard I lack,
    Nay on me too, thy hand I find.
20 Well I thy wisdom may adore,
    But never reach with earthy mind.

To shunn thy notice, leave thine ey,
    O whither might I take my way?
        To starry spheare?
        Thy throne is there.
    To dead mens undelightsome stay?
There is thy walk, and there to ly
    Unknown, in vain I should assay.   *try*

O Sun, whome light nor flight can match,
30   Suppose thy lightfull flightfull wings
        Thou lend to me,
        And I could flee
    As farr as thee the ev'ning brings:
Ev'n ledd to West he would me catch,
    Nor should I lurk with western things.

Doe thou thy best, O secret night,
    In sable vaile to cover me:
        Thy sable vaile
        Shall vainly faile:
40   With day unmask'd my night shall be,
For night is day, and darkness light,
    O father of all lights, to thee.

Each inmost peece in me is thine:
　While yet I in my mother dwelt,
　　All that me cladd
　　From thee I hadd.
　Thou in my frame hast strangly delt:
Needes in my praise thy workes must shine
　So inly them my thoughts have felt.

50　Thou, how my back was beam-wise laid,
　And raftring of my ribbs, dost know:
　　Know'st ev'ry point
　　Of bone and joynt,
　How to this whole these partes did grow,
In brave embrod'ry faire araid,
　Though wrought in shopp both dark and low.

Nay fashionless, ere forme I tooke,
　Thy all and more beholding ey
　　My shapelesse shape
60　　Could not escape:
　All these tyme fram'd successively
Ere one had beeing, in the booke
　Of thy foresight, enrol'd did ly.

My God, how I these studies prize,
　That doe thy hidden workings show!
　　Whose summ is such,
　　Noe suume soe much:
　Nay summ'd as sand they summlesse grow.
I lye to sleepe, from sleepe I rise,
70　　Yet still in thought with thee I goe,

My God if thou but one wouldst kill,
　Then straight would leave my further chase
　　This cursed brood
　　Inur'd to blood:
　Whose gracelesse tauntes at thy disgrace
Have aimed oft: and hating still
　Would with proud lies thy truth outface.

Hate not I them, who thee doe hate?
　Thyne, Lord, I will the censure be.
80　　Detest I not
　　The canckred knott,
　Whom I against thee banded see?
O Lord, thou know'st in highest rate
　I hate them all as foes to me.

Search me, my God, and prove my hart,
　Examyne me, and try my thought:
　　And mark in me
　　If ought there be
　That hath with cause their anger wrought.
90　If not (as not) my lives each part,
　Lord safely guide from danger brought.

PSALM 149 *CANTATE DOMINO*

In an earst unused song
To Jehova lift your voices:
Make his favourites among
    Sound his praise with cheerefull noises,
      Jacob, thou with joy relate
      Him that hath refram'd thy state:
Sonnes whom Sion entertaineth
Boast in him who on you raigneth.

Play on harp, on tabret play,
    Daunce Jehova publique daunces: 10
He their state that on him stay,
    Most afflicted, most advaunces.
      O how glad his saincts I see!
      Ev'n in bed how glad they be!
Heav'nly hymnes with throat unfolding,
Swordes in hand twice-edged holding.

Plague and chastise that they may
    Nations such as erst them pained,
Yea, their kings, in fetters lay;
    Lay their Nobles fast enchained,   20
      That the doom no stay may lett,
      By his sentence on them sett.
Lo! what honor all expecteth,
Whom the Lord with love affecteth!

PSALM 150 *LAUDATE DOMINUM*

O laud the Lord, the God of hosts commend,
    Exault his pow'r, advaunce his holynesse:
    With all your might lift his allmightinesse:
Your greatest praise upon his greatness spend.

Make Trumpetts noise in shrillest notes ascend:
    Make lute and lyre his loved fame expresse:
    Him lett the pipe, him lett the tabret blesse,
Him organs breath, that windes or waters lend.

Lett ringing Timbrells soe his honor sound,
    Lett sounding Cymballs soe his glory ring,   10
That in their tunes such mellody be found,
    As fitts the pompe of most Triumphant king.
Conclud: by all that aire, or life enfold,
Lett high Jehova highly be extold.

Robert Sidney (1563–1626)

Although Robert Sidney's life is well documented in surviving letters and related materials, as well as in his verse, there is still no full biography of him in his own right. Perhaps he is forever to be seen, as he lived, in the shadow of his older, much celebrated brother, Sir Philip Sidney.

Even their father advised Robert to "follow the direction of your most loving brother, who in loving you, is comparable with me, or exceedith me. Imitate his virtues, exercises, studies, and actions; he is a rare ornament of this age." But at age 22 Sir Robert attended his dying brother for three and a half weeks as he lay dying from the terrible wound he received at the battle at Zutphen. Against all probability, he was then suddenly catapulted into the position of head of his aristocratic family.

In 1575 Robert Sidney matriculated at Christ Church, Oxford. He married Barbara Gamage in 1584. Although they married only a few days after she became a rich heiress, who was much pursued, they appear to have had an affectionate marriage, despite his occasional interest in other women. They had 11 children, Mary (later Lady Mary Wroth) being the eldest daughter. Robert was knighted on October 7, 1586, at the camp near Zutphen in recognition of his conduct in battle. Nevertheless, that was a terrible year for him. His father (Sir Henry Sidney) died on May 5; his mother, Lady Sidney, on August 9; and his brother on October 17. Although he wrote about much else in his poetry, Robert Sidney kept what grief he knew to himself.

Both from his brother's correspondence with him and from the record of books dedicated to him – Robert Jones's *First Book of Songs and Ayres* and Robert Dowland's *Musicall Banquet* – it appears that Robert Sidney's talent as a musician at least equaled his ability as a poet. He lived to witness the deaths of his eldest son (Sir William), his son-in-law (Sir Robert Wroth), and his wife. His daughter's *The Countesse of Mountgomeries Urania* was published five years before his death. His own poems survive in an autograph notebook.

READING

P. J. Croft (ed.), *The Poems of Robert Sidney*.

M. P.

SONNET 15

You that have power to kill, have will to save:
O you, fair leader of the host of love,
From yielding hands disarmèd prayers approve
Which joys nor wealth, but life of captive crave,

No weak or foe or force me vanquished gave
That faint defence should scorn, not pity move:
Virtue, fortune, skill, to my aid I prove;
All by you broken, me forsaken have.

Your face, the field where beauty's orders shine,
10   What can resist? Your eyes, love's cannons strong,
The brave directions of your lips divine!

Wounded I try to 'scape: in guard along
Legions of worth and graces I descry.
What means then to withstand, what way to fly?

PASTORAL 7

Lysa, sweet nymph, did sit
Where an ungentle wind
To her fair face an open way did find:
As her the air did hit
Her smiling beams she threw
As if her eyes would warm the cold that blew.

Rosis, poor shepherd lad,
That thought a flowery field
He saw to rage of winter's blasts to yield,
10   Or else a garden, clad
In April's livery fair,
Have daintiest colours nipped with frosty air,

Sat where he thought he best
Might keep away the cold,
And with glad arms her body dear did fold;
Where, while into his breast
Thousand contentments sank
And with broad eyes he thousand beauties drank,

20

The flames of those fair eyes—
Which no cold e'er can slake—
In his close breast a hot fire soon did make;
Which when he felt to rise,
With looks where rage did swarm
And with hot sighs, he sought the nymph to warm:

But she complaining still
Of cold, the lad gan cry
'Alas, why do the fires in which I fry
The cold in her not kill?
Or else, why quencheth not

30

The cold in her my fires which burn so hot?'

SONNET 16

Most fair, when first with pleased but cursèd eyes
I did behold that piece of heaven in you,
O that I had, as to divinesse due,
Only of vows and prayers done sacrifice;

And blessèd so, in so contented wise,
From passions free enjoyèd pleasures true;
When you yourself (I would I said untrue)
Kindled the sparks whence love and rage did rise.

Yet on those hopes though false would I had stayed,

10

But I in searching out your truth did prove
My true mishaps in your betraying love.

Cruel, I love you still though thus betrayed,
Nor dare lay blame on you: but my fond mind
Do curse, which made such haste your faults to find.

SONNET 17

The endless alchemist, with blinded will,
That feeds his thoughts with hopes, his hopes on shows,
And more his work proves vain more eager grows
While dreams of gold his head with shadows fill,

Feels not more sure the scourge of flatt'ring skill,
When in false trust of wealth true need he knows,
Than I, on whom a storm of losses blows
And tides of errors run: yet sail on still

While my corrupted sense doth think it sees

10

The long sought land of rest, and while to bliss
I think there is a way, though yet I miss.

Thus shunning to have lost, I still do leese,
And hope and want: and strive and fail: and prove
Nor end with joys, nor end from cares in love.

PASTORAL 8

Nymph. Shepherd.

1

Nymph   Shepherd, why dost thou so look still on me,
From whence do these new humours grow in thee?
Shepherd Best Nymph, here saw I first, with comfort great,
The fairest day that e'er spread beams of gold:
Led hence astray, benighted since and cold,
I come to you (my sun) for light and heat.

2

Nymph   From them that led thee hence thy help must rise,
Mine eyes bestow their beams on better eyes.
Shepherd Nor can the moon though fair, the year renew,
Nor can the stars give day, though clear and bright:
Dead are all other flames, grown dim each light—
I must live cold and dark, or look on you.

3

Nymph   Thou wer'st as good to talk unto a stone:
Words not believed were better let alone.
Shepherd Soon as the spring cold winter doth remove,
From stocks which life none showed leaves in store rise.
The time that me restores moves in your eyes,
And I that from you freezed, here burn in love.

4

Nymph   What boots belief where no regard is born?
Thee and thy love, and vows and oaths I scorn.
Shepherd In earth, on naught the sun worth him doth shine,
Dressed in his beams yet she his glory shows.
In me, else little worth, your beauties knows
The temple where they are adored in shrine.

5

Nymph   Perhaps thou think'st desert will scorn abate,
But I hate thee, and in thee love do hate.
Shepherd To drown the fields the angry brooks do move
Their streams, yet even in that grows the field's pride.
On stone of wrongs, love's truth is perfect tried;
Loving all is in you, your hate I love.

6

Nymph   If scorn nor hate will serve, let this thee move—
That there is one that lives proud in my love.
Shepherd The humble shrub whose welfare heaven neglects
Looks yet to heaven as well as favoured pine.
Love whom you list: please your own choice, not mine.
My soul to love and look: naught else affects.

7

Nymph   What may I more to give thee answer say
         But that I now should bid thee go away?
Shepherd With his fair beams the sun would clear the air
40   Of clouds, yet are the clouds drawn by the same.
         I cannot part from that by which I am,
         Nor grow to be less fond, or you less fair.

8

Nymph   Then I will go:—shepherd, be here alone,
         Unlooked on love, unthought on make thy moan.
Shepherd Till in the heavens the moon her face shows new
         In their dead streams the seas her absence mourn.
         Live fairest still, best Nymph, soon to return:
         I cold and dark, will waste till I see you.

SONNET 18

Most fair: the field is yours—now stay your hands;
No power is left to strive, less to rebel.
I pleasure take that at your blows I fell,
And laurel wear in triumph of my bands.

Ah how your eyes, the joys of peace, seem brands
To waste what conquest hath assured so well;
How your lawgiving lips in proud red swell,
While my captivèd soul at mercy stands.

O best, O only fair: suffer these eyes
10   To live, which wait your will humble and true;
These knees, which from your feet do never rise,
These hands, which still held up swear faith to you,

O save: do not destroy what is your own.
Just prince to spoil himself was never known.

SONNET 19

When other creatures all, each in their kind,
Comfort of light, quiet from darkness fetch,
Of wretched monsters, I most monstrous wretch
Nor day from pains, nor night with rest can find;

But as the slave, whom storm or sun or wind
All day doth beat, in whose side bloody breach
The scourge doth leave, who on the oar doth stretch
His limbs all day, all night his wounds doth bind,

Chained to those beauties whence I cannot fly
10   I know no day so long, wherein each hour
Shows not new labours lost, and wherein I
Take not new wounds from their unsparing power:

Nor longest night is long enough for me
To tell my wounds, which restless bleeding be.

SONNET 20

Shine on fair stars, give comfort to these eyes
Which know no light but yours, no life but you;
Shine that their love, your worth, may have your due
While joys to them, glory to you doth rise.

But upon me amid your beams there lies
A blacker night than ever forest knew,
Who by your light discern the mourning true
Of widow sky, which husband-sun's loss tries.

10   Reign now alone, in you the night be blest,
My wants, another's store, grudge not to see;
But ere long will a sun rise from the East
In whose clear flames your sparks obscured will be:

Till then, in sprite those hid beams I adore
And know more stars I see, my night the more.

The Mirror for Magistrates (1563–1587)

The Mirror for Magistrates was a highly influential work of composite authorship that appeared in several editions between 1555 and 1610. The contributors to the first edition include William Baldwin, George Ferrers, Thomas Chaloner, and Thomas Phaer. The edition of 1563 includes the often commended "Induction" by Thomas Sackville (1536–1608), and the edition of 1587 adds two new tragedies by Thomas Churchyard (1520?–1604): "Shore's Wife" and "Cardinal Wolsey." Each of the poems in the collection is a didactic monologue spoken (usually from beyond the grave) by a famous person whose tragic life provides a cautionary tale. Shakespeare, especially in his history plays, was significantly influenced by the *Mirror* tradition.

READING

L. B. Campbell (ed.), *The Mirror for Magistrates.*

M. P.

THE MIRROR FOR MAGISTRATES

The Induction

The wrathfull winter prochinge on a pace,   *approaching*
With blustring blastes had al ybared the treen,   *trees*
And olde Saturnus with his frosty face
With chilling colde had pearst the tender green:
The mantels rent, wherein enwrapped been
The gladsom groves that nowe laye ouerthrowen,
The tapets torne, and euery blome downe blowen.   *branches*

The soyle that earst so seemely was to seen
Was all despoyled of her beauties hewe:
10   And soot freshe flowers (wherwith the sommers queen

Had clad the earth) now Boreas[1] blastes downe blewe.
And small fowles flocking, in theyr song did rewe
The winters wrath, wherwith eche thing defaste
In woful wise bewayld the sommer past.

   Hawthorne had lost his motley lyverye,
The naked twigges were shivering all for colde:
And dropping downe the teares abundantly,
Eche thing (me thought) with weping eye me tolde
The cruell season, bidding me withholde
My selfe within, for I was gotten out
Into the fieldes where as I walkte about.

   When loe the night with mistie mantels spred
Gan darke the daye, and dim the azure skyes,
And Venus in her message Hermes sped[2]
To bluddy Mars, to wyl him not to ryse,
While she her selfe approcht in speedy wise:
And Virgo hiding her disdaineful brest
With Thetis nowe had layd her downe to rest.

   Whiles Scorpio dreading Sagittarius dart,
Whose bowe prest bent in sight, the string had slypt,
Downe slyd into the Ocean flud aparte,
The Beare that in the Iryshe seas had dipt   *Irish*
His griesly feete, with spede from thence he whypt:
For Thetis hasting from the Virgines bed,
Pursued the Bear, that ear she came was fled.

   And Phaeton nowe neare reaching to his race
With glistering beames, gold streamynge where they bent,
Was prest to enter in his resting place.
Erythius that in the cart fyrste went
Had euen nowe attaynde his iourneyes stent.
And fast declining hid away his head,
while Titan couched him in his purple bed.

   And pale Cinthea with her borowed light
Beginning to supply her brothers place,
was past the Noonesteede syxe degrees in sight
when sparklyng starres amyd the heauens face
with twinkling light shoen on the earth apace,
That whyle they brought about the nightes chare,
The darke had dimmed the daye ear I was ware.

   And sorowing I to see the sommer flowers,
The liuely greene, the lusty leas forlorne,
The sturdy trees so shattered with the showers,
The fieldes so fade that floorisht so beforne,
It taught me wel all earthly thinges be borne
To dye the death, for nought long time may last.
The sommers beauty yeeldes to winters blast.

20

30

40

50

THE MIRROR FOR MAGISTRATES
1 The north wind.

2 Here and following are movements of the planets and other heavenly bodies as the season progresses. Sackville gives a sense of the relentless movement of the universe toward tragedy.

Then looking vpward to the heauens leames   *gleams*
with nightes starres thicke powdred euery where,
which erst so glistened with the golden streames
60   That chearefull Phebus spred downe from his sphere,
Beholding darke oppressing day so neare:
The sodayne sight reduced to my minde,
The sundry chaunges that in earth we fynde.

That musing on this worldly wealth in thought,
which comes and goes more faster than we see
The flyckering flame that with the fyer is wrought,
My busie minde presented vnto me
Such fall of pieres as in this realme had be:
That ofte I wisht some would their woes descryue.
70   To warne the rest whom fortune left aliue.

And strayt forth stalking with redoubled pace
For that I sawe the night drewe on so fast,
In blacke all clad there fell before my face
A piteous wight, whom woe had al forwaste,
Furth from her iyen the cristall teares outbrast,
And syghing sore her handes she wrong and folde,
Tare al her heare that ruth was to beholde.   *hair*

Her body small forwithered and forespent,
As is the stalke that sommers drought opprest,
80   Her wealked face with woful teares besprent,
Her colour pale, and (as it seemd her best)
In woe and playnt reposed was her rest.
And as the stone that droppes of water weares,
So dented were her cheekes with fall of teares.

Her iyes swollen with flowing streames aflote,
Wherewith her lookes throwen vp full piteouslye,
Her forceles handes together ofte she smote,
With dolefull shrikes, that eckoed in the skye:
Whose playnt such sighes dyd strayt accompany,
90   That in my doome was neuer man did see
A wight but halfe so woe begon as she.

I stoode agast beholding all her plight,
Tweene dread and dolour so distreynd in hart
That while my heares vpstarted with the sight,
The teares out streamde for sorowe of her smart:
But when I sawe no ende that could aparte
The deadly dewle, which she so sore dyd make,   *duel*
With dolefull voice then thus to her I spake.

Vnwrap thy woes what euer wight thou be
100   And stint betime to spill thy selfe wyth playnt,
Tell what thou art, and whence, for well I see
Thou canst not dure wyth sorowe thus attaynt.
And with that worde of sorowe all forfaynt
She looked vp, and prostrate as she laye
With piteous sound loe thus she gan to saye.

Alas, I wretche whom thus thou seest distreyned
With wasting woes that neuer shall aslake,

Sorrowe I am, in endeles tormentes payned,
Among the furies in the infernall lake:
110 Where Pluto god of Hel so griesly blacke
Doth holde his throne, and *Letheus* deadly taste[3]
Doth rieue remembraunce of eche thyng forepast.

    Whence come I am, the drery destinie
And luckeles lot for to bemone of those,
Whom Fortune in this maze of miserie
Of wretched chaunce most wofull myrrours chose
That when thou seest how lightly they did lose
Theyr pompe, theyr power, & that they thought most sure,
Thou mayest soone deeme no earthly ioye may dure.

120   Whose rufull voyce no sooner had out brayed
Those wofull wordes, wherewith she sorrowed so,
But out alas she shryght and never stayed,
Fell downe, and all to dasht her selfe for woe.
The colde pale dread my lyms gan overgo,   *limbs*
And I so sorrowed at her sorowes eft,
That what with griefe and feare my wittes were reft.

    I strecht my selfe, and strayt my hart reuiues,
That dread and dolour erst did so appale,
Lyke him that with the feruent feuer stryves
130 When sickenes seekes his castell health to skale:
With gathered spirites so forst I feare to auale.
And rearing her with anguishe all fordone,
My spirits returnd, and then I thus begonne.

    O Sorrowe, alas, sith Sorrowe is thy name,
And that to thee this drere doth well pertayne,
In vayne it were to seeke to ceas the same:
But as a man hym selfe with sorrowe slayne,
So I alas do comfort thee in payne,
That here in sorrowe art forsonke so depe
140 That at thy sight I can but sigh and wepe.

    I had no sooner spoken of a syke
But that the storme so rumbled in her brest,
As Eolus[4] could neuer roare the like,
And showers downe rayned from her iyen so fast,
That all bedreynt the place, till at the last
Well eased they the dolour of her minde,
As rage of rayne doth swage the stormy wynde.

    For furth she paced in her fearfull tale:
Cum, cum, (quod she) and see what I shall shewe,
150 Cum heare the playning, and the bytter bale
Of worthy men, by Fortune ouerthrowe.
Cum thou and see them rewing al in rowe.
They were but shades that erst in minde thou rolde.
Cum, cum with me, thine iyes shall them beholde.

---

3 The waters of Lethe in Hades were drunk by souls awaiting   4 In both the *Odyssey* and the *Aeneid* Aeolus imprisons the winds.
reincarnation.

What could these wordes but make me more agast?
To heare her tell whereon I musde while eare?
So was I mazed therewyth, tyll at the last,
Musing vpon her wurdes, and what they were,
All sodaynly well lessoned was my feare:
160   For to my minde returned howe she telde
Both what she was, and where her wun she helde.

Whereby I knewe that she a Goddesse was,
And therewithall resorted to my minde
My thought, that late presented me the glas
Of brittle state, of cares that here we finde,
Of thousand woes to silly men assynde:
And howe she nowe byd me come and beholde,
To see with iye that erst in thought I rolde.

Flat downe I fell, and with al reuerence
170   Adored her, perceyuing nowe that she
A Goddesse sent by godly prouidence,
In earthly shape thus showed her selfe to me,
To wayle and rue this worldes vncertayntye:
And while I honourd thus her godheds might,
With playning voyce these wurdes to me she shryght.

I shal the guyde first to the griesly lake,   *thee*
And thence vnto the blisfull place of rest.
Where thou shalt see and heare the playnt they make,
That whilom here bare swinge among the best.
180   This shalt thou see, but great is the vnrest
That thou must byde before thou canst attayne
Vnto the dreadfull place where these remayne.

And with these wurdes as I vpraysed stood,
And gan to folowe her that strayght furth paced,
Eare I was ware, into a desert wood
We nowe were cum: where hand in hand imbraced,
She led the way, and through the thicke so traced,
As but I had bene guyded by her might,
It was no waye for any mortall wight.

190   But loe, while thus amid the desert darke,
We passed on with steppes and pace vnmete:
A rumbling roar confusde with howle and barke
Of Dogs, shoke all the ground vnder our feete,
And stroke the din within our eares so deepe,
As halfe distraught vnto the ground I fell,
Besought retourne, and not to visite hell.

But she forthwith vplifting me apace
Remoued my dread, and with a stedfast minde
Bad me come on, for here was now the place,
200   The place where we our trauayle ende should finde.
Wherewith I arose, and to the place assynde
Astoynde I stalke, when strayt we approched nere
The dredfull place, that you wil dread to here.

An hydeous hole al vaste, withouten shape,
Of endles depth, orewhelmde with ragged stone,

Wyth ougly mouth, and grisly Iawes doth gape,
And to our sight confounds it selfe in one.
Here entred we, and yeding forth, anone
An horrible lothly lake we might discerne
210   As blacke as pitche, that cleped is Auerne.[5]

A deadly gulfe where nought but rubbishe growes,
With fowle blacke swelth in thickned lumpes that lyes,
Which vp in the ayer such stinking vapors throwes
That ouer there, may flye no fowle but dyes,
Choakt with the pestilent sauours that aryse.
Hither we cum, whence forth we still dyd pace,
In dreadful feare amid the dreadfull place.

And first within the portche and iawes of Hell
Sate diepe Remorse of conscience, al besprent
220   With teares: and to her selfe oft would she tell
Her wretchednes, and cursing neuer stent
To sob and sigh: but euer thus lament,
With thoughtful care, as she that all in vayne
Would weare and waste continually in payne.

Her iyes vnstedfast rolling here and there,
Whurld on eche place, as place that vengeaunce brought,
So was her minde continually in feare,
Tossed and tormented with the tedious thought
Of those detested crymes which she had wrought:
230   With dreadful cheare and lookes throwen to the skye,
Wyshyng for death, and yet she could not dye.

Next sawe we Dread al tremblyng how he shooke,
With foote vncertayne profered here and there:
Benumde of speache, and with a gastly looke
Searcht euery place al pale and dead for feare,
His cap borne vp with staring of his heare,
Stoynde and amazde at his owne shade for dreed,   *stunned*
And fearing greater daungers than was nede.

And next within the entry of this lake
240   Sate fell Reuenge gnashing her teeth for yre,
Deuising meanes howe she may vengeaunce take,
Neuer in rest tyll she haue her desire:
But frets within so farforth with the fyer
Of wreaking flames, that nowe determines she,
To dye by death, or vengde by death to be.

When fell Reuenge with bloudy foule pretence
Had showed her selfe as next in order set,
With trembling limmes we softly parted thence,
Tyll in our iyes another sight we met:
250   When fro my hart a sigh forthwith I fet
Rewing alas vpon the wofull plight
Of Miserie, that next appered in sight.

His face was leane, and sumdeale pyned away,
And eke his handes consumed to the bone,

5 Avernus, a lake near Cumae, was close to the cave where Aeneas
descended to the underworld.

But what his body was I can not say,
For on his carkas, rayment had he none
Saue cloutes & patches pieced one by one.
With staffe in hand, and skrip on shoulders cast,
His chiefe defence agaynst the winters blast.

260   His foode for most, was wylde fruytes of the tree,
Vnles sumtime sum crummes fell to his share:
Which in his wallet, long God wote kept he.
As on the which full dayntlye would he fare.
His drinke the running streame: his cup the bare
Of his palme closed, his bed the hard colde grounde.
To this poore life was Miserie ybound.

Whose wretched state when we had well behelde
With tender ruth on him and on his feres,
In thoughtful cares, furth then our pace we helde.
270   And by and by, an other shape apperes
Of Greedy care, stil brushing vp the breres,
His knuckles knobd, his fleshe deepe dented in,
With tawed handes, and hard ytanned skyn.

The morrowe graye no sooner hath begunne
To spreade his light euen peping in our iyes,
When he is vp and to his worke yrunne,
But let the nightes blacke mistye mantels rise,
And with fowle darke neuer so much disguyse
280   The fayre bright day, yet ceasseth he no whyle,
But hath his candels to prolong his toyle.

By him lay Heauy slepe the cosin of death
Flat on the ground, and stil as any stone,
A very corps, save yelding forth a breath.
Small kepe tooke he whom Fortune frowned on.
Or whom she lifted vp into the trone
Of high renowne, but as a liuing death,
So dead alyve, of lyef he drewe the breath.

290   The bodyes rest, the quyete of the hart,
The travayles ease, the still nightes feer was he.
And of our life in earth the better parte,
Reuer of sight, and yet in whom we see
Thinges oft that tide, and ofte that neuer bee.
Without respect esteming equally
Kyng Cresus pompe, and Irus pouertie.[6]

And next in order sad Olde age we found
His beard al hoare, his iyes hollow and blynde,
300   With drouping chere still poring on the ground,
As on the place where nature him assinde
To rest, when that the sisters had vntwynde
His vitall threde, and ended with theyr knyfe
The fleting course of fast declining life.

There heard we him with broken and hollow playnt
Rewe with him selfe his ende approching fast,

6 Croesus, the last king of Lydia; Irus, whom Odysseus fights in
Odyssey 18.

And all for nought his wretched minde torment.
With swete remembraunce of his pleasures past,
And freshe delites of lusty youth forwaste.
310 Recounting which, how would he sob & shrike?
And to be yong againe of Ioue beseke.

But and the cruell fates so fixed be
That time forepast can not retourne agayne,
This one request of Ioue yet prayed he:
That in such withered plight, and wretched paine,
As elde (accompanied with his lothsom trayne.)
Had brought on him, all were it woe and griefe.
He myght a while yet linger forth his lief,

And not so soone descend into the pit:
320 Where death, when he the mortall corps hath slayne,
With retcheles hande in grave doth couer it,
Thereafter neuer to enioye agayne
The gladsome light, but in the ground ylayne,
In depth of darkenes waste and weare to nought,
As he had neuer into the world been brought.

But who had seene him sobbing, howe he stoode
Vnto him selfe and howe he would bemone
His youth forepast, as though it wrought hym good
To talke of youth, al wer his youth foregone,
330 He would haue mused, & meruayld muche whereon   *marveled*
This wretched age should life desyre so fayne,
And knowes ful wel life doth but length his payne.

Crookebackt he was, toothshaken, and blere iyed,
Went on three feete, and sometime crept on fower,
With olde lame bones, that ratled by his syde,
His skalpe all pilde, & he with elde forlore:
His withered fist stil knocking at deathes dore,
Fumbling and driueling as he drawes his breth,
For briefe the shape and messenger of death.

340 And fast by him pale Maladie was plaste,
Sore sicke in bed, her colour al forgone,
Bereft of stomake, sauor, and of taste,
Ne could she brooke no meat but brothes alone.
Her breath corrupt, her kepers euery one
Abhorring her, her sickenes past recure,
Detesting phisicke, and all phisickes cure.   *medicine*

But oh the doleful sight that then we see,
We turnde our looke and on the other side
A griesly shape of Famine mought we see,
350 With greedy lookes, and gaping mouth that cryed,
And roard for meat as she should there haue dyed,
Her body thin and bare as any bone,
Wherto was left nought but the case alone.

And that alas was knawen on euery where,
All full of holes, that I ne mought refrayne
From teares, to se how she her armes could teare
And with her teeth gnashe on the bones in vayne:

When all for nought she fayne would so sustayne
Her starven corps, that rather seemde a shade,
360   Then any substaunce of a creature made.

Great was her force whom stonewall could not stay,
Her tearyng nayles snatching at all she sawe:
With gaping Iawes that by no meanes ymay
Be satisfyed from hunger of her mawe,
But eates her selfe as she that hath no lawe:
Gnawyng alas her carkas all in vayne,
Where you may count eche sinow, bone, and vayne.

On her while we thus firmely fixt our iyes,
That bled for ruth of such a drery sight,
370   Loe sodaynelye she shryght in so huge wyse,
As made hell gates to shyver with the myght.
Wherewith a darte we sawe howe it did lyght.
Ryght on her brest, and therewithal pale death
Enthryllyng it to reve her of her breath.

And by and by a dum dead corps we sawe,
Heauy and colde, the shape of death aryght,
That dauntes all earthly creatures to his lawe:
Agaynst whose force in vayne it is to fyght
Ne piers, ne princes, nor no mortall wyght,
380   No townes, ne realmes, cities, ne strongest tower,
But al perforce must yeeld vnto his power.

His Dart anon out of the corps he tooke,
And in his hand (a dreadfull sight to see)
With great tryumphe eftsones the same he shooke,
That most of all my feares affrayed me:
His bodie dight with nought but bones perdye
The naked shape of man there sawe I playne,
All save the fleshe, the synowe, and the vayne.   *sinew*

Lastly stoode Warre in glitteryng armes yclad.
390   With visage grym, sterne lookes, and blackely hewed
In his right hand a naked sworde he had,
That to the hiltes was al with blud embrewed:
And in his left (that kinges and kingdomes rewed)
Famine and fyer he held, and therewythall
He razed townes, and threwe downe towers and all.

Cities he sakt, and realmes that whilom flowred,
In honor, glory, and rule above the best,
He overwhelmde, and all theyr fame deuowred,
Consumed, destroyed, wasted, and neuer ceast,
400   Tyll he theyr wealth, theyr name, and all opprest.
His face forhewed with woundes, and by his side,
There hunge his targe with gashes depe and wyde.

In mids of which, depaynted there we founde
Deadly debate, al ful of snaky heare,
That with a blouddy fillet was ybound,
Outbrething nought but discord euery where.
And round about were portrayd here and there

The hugie hostes, Darius[7] and his power,
His kynges, prynces, his pieres, and all his flower.

410   Whom great Macedo vanquisht there in sight,
With diepe slaughter, dispoylyng all his pryde,
Pearst through his realmes, and daunted all his might.
Duke Hanniball beheld I there beside,
In Cannas field, victor howe he did ride,
And woful Romaynes that in vayne withstoode
And Consull Paulus covered all in blood.

Yet sawe I more the fight at Trasimene.
And Trebey field, and eke when Hanniball
And worthy Scipio last in armes were seene
420   Before Carthago gate, to trye for all
The worldes empyre, to whom it should befal.
There sawe I Pompeye, and Cesar clad in armes,
Theyr hostes alyed and al theyr civil harmes.

With conquerours hands forbathde in their owne blood,
And Cesar weping ouer Pompeyes head.
Yet sawe I Scilla and Marius where they stoode,
Theyr great crueltie, and the diepe bludshed
Of frendes: Cyrus I sawe and his host dead,
And howe the Queene with great despyte hath flonge
430   His head in bloud of them she overcome.

Xerxes the Percian kyng yet sawe I there
With his huge host that dranke the riuers drye,
Dismounted hilles, and made the vales vprere,
His hoste and all yet sawe I slayne perdye.
Thebes I sawe all razde howe it dyd lye
In heapes of stones, and Tyrus put to spoyle,
With walles and towers flat euened with the soyle.

But Troy alas (me thought) aboue them all,
It made myne iyes in very teares consume:
440   When I beheld the wofull werd befall,
That by the wrathfull wyl of Gods was come:
And Ioues vnmooved sentence and foredoome   *Jove's*
On Priam kyng, and on his towne so bent.
I could not lyn, but I must there lament.

And that the more sith destinie was so sterne
As force perforce, there might no force auayle,
But she must fall: and by her fall we learne,
That cities, towres, wealth, world, and al shall quayle.
No manhoode, might, nor nothing mought preuayle,
450   Al were there prest ful many a prynce and piere
And many a knight that solde his death full deere.

Not wurthy Hector[8] wurthyest of them all,
Her hope, her ioye, his force is nowe for nought.

---

7 Here follows a catalogue of the great warriors of antiquity: Darius   8 Hector, the eldest of King Priam's sons, was slain by Achilles.
II, Cyrus of Persia, Judas Maccabaeus, Hannibal, Scipio, Pompey, Julius
Caesar, Xerxes, and others.

O Troy, Troy, there is no boote but bale,
The hugie horse within thy walles is brought:
Thy turrets fall, thy knightes that whilom fought
In armes amyd the fyeld, are slayne in bed,
Thy Gods defylde, and all thy honour dead.

The flames vpspring, and cruelly they crepe
460   From wall to roofe, til all to cindres waste,
Some fyer the houses where the wretches slepe,
Sum rushe in here, sum run in there as fast.
In euery where or sworde or fyer they taste.
The walles are torne, the towers whurld to the ground,
There is no mischiefe but may there be found.

Cassandra[9] yet there sawe I howe they haled
From Pallas house, with spercled tresse vndone,   *shining hair*
Her wristes fast bound, and with Greeks rout empaled:
And Priam eke in vayne howe he did runne
470   To armes, whom Pyrrhus[10] with despite hath done
To cruel death, and bathed him in the bayne
Of his sonnes blud before the altare slayne.

But howe can I descryve the doleful sight,
That in the shylde so liuelike fayer did shyne?
Sith in this world I thinke was neuer wyght
Could haue set furth the halfe, not halfe so fyne.
I can no more but tell howe there is seene
Fayer Ilium fal in burning red gledes downe,
And from the soyle great Troy Neptunus towne.

480   Herefrom when scarce I could mine iyes withdrawe
That fylde with teares as doeth the spryngyng well,
We passed on so far furth tyl we sawe
Rude Acheron,[11] a lothsome lake to tell
That boyles and bubs vp swelth as blacke as hell.
Where grisly Charon at theyr fixed tide
Stil ferreies ghostes vnto the farder side,

The aged God no sooner sorowe spyed,
But hasting strayt vnto the banke apace
With hollow call vnto the rout he cryed,
490   To swarve apart, and geue the Goddesse place.
Strayt it was done, when to the shoar we pace,
Where hand in hand as we then linked fast,
Within the boate we are together plaste.

And furth we launch ful fraughted to the brinke,
Whan with the vnwonted weyght, the rustye keele
Began to cracke as if the same should sinke.
We hoyse vp mast and sayle, that in a whyle.
We set the shore, where scarcely we had while
For to arryve, but that we heard anone
500   A thre sound barke confounded al in one.

9   A prophetess and daughter of Priam and Hecuba.
10 The son of Achilles who slays Priam.

11 The "river of sorrows" in Hades, where Charon ferries the ghosts
of the dead to the side beyond the living.

We had not long furth past, but that we sawe,
Blacke Cerberus the hydeous hound of hell,
With bristles reard, and with a thre mouthed Iawe,
Foredinning the ayer with his horrible yel.
Out of the diepc darke cave where he did dwell,
The Goddesse strayt he knewe, and by and by
He peaste and couched, while that we passed by.

Thence cum we to the horrour and the hel,
The large great kyngdomes, and the dreadful raygne
510   Of Pluto[12] in his trone where he dyd dwell,
The wyde waste places, and the hugye playne:
The waylinges, shrykes, and sundry sortes of payne,
The syghes, the sobbes, the diepe and deadly groane,
Earth, ayer, and all resounding playnt and moane.

Here pewled the babes, and here the maydes vnwed
with folded handes theyr sory chaunce bewayled,
Here wept the gyltles slayne, and louers dead,
That slewe them selues when nothyng els auayled;
A thousand sortes of sorrowes here that wayled
520   with sighes and teares, sobs, shrykes, and all yfere,
That (oh alas) it was a hel to heare.

We stayed vs strayt, and wyth a rufull feare,
Beheld this heauy sight, while from mine eyes,
The vapored teares downstilled here and there,
And Sorowe eke in far more woful wyse.
Tooke on with playnt, vp heauing to the skyes
Her wretched handes, that with her crye the rout
Gan all in heapes to swarme vs round about.

Loe here (quoth Sorowe) Prynces of renowne,
530   That whilom sat on top of Fortunes wheele
Nowe layed ful lowe, like wretches whurled downe,
Euen with one frowne, that stayed but with a smyle,
And nowe behold the thing that thou erewhile,
Saw only in thought, and what thou now shalt heare
Recompt the same to Kesar, King, and Pier.

CARDINAL WOLSEY

HOW THOMAS WOLSEY[13]

did arise vnto great authority and gouernment,
his maner of life, pompe, and dignity, and
how hee fell downe into great disgrace,
and was arested of high treason.

Shall I looke on, when states step on the stage,
And play theyr parts, before the peoples face?
Some men liue now, scarce four score yeares of age,
Who in time past, did know the Cardnalls grace.

---

12   Ruler of the underworld.
13   Thomas Wolsey (1475?–1530), Cardinal (1515) and Lord Chancellor (1515–29) to Henry VIII. Because he opposed the King's divorce from Catherine of Aragon, he was stripped of his titles and accused of treason in 1530. A biography of Wolsey by George Cavendish was completed in 1558. It too is in the tradition of the "fall of princes."

A gamesom worlde, when Byshops run at bace,
Yea, get a fall, in striuing for the gole,
And body loase, and hazarde seely sole.

Ambitious minde, a world of wealth would haue,
So scrats and scrapes, for scorfe, and scoruy drosse:
And till the flesh, and bones, be layde in graue,
Wit neuer rests, to grope for mucke and mosse.
Fye on prowde pompe, and gilted bridels bosse:
O glorious golde, the gaping after thee,
So blindes mens eyes, they can no daunger see.

Now note my byrth, and marke how I began,
Beholde from whence, rose all this pryde of mine.
My father but, a playne poore honest man,
And I his son, of wit and iudgement fine,
Brought vp at schoole, and prou'd a good diuine:
For which great gifts, degree of schoole I had,
And Batchler was, and I a litle lad.

So, tasting some, of Fortunes sweete consayts,
I clapt the hoode, on shoulder, braue as Son,
And hopt at length, to bite at better bayts,
And fill my mouth, ere banket halfe were don.
Thus holding on, the course I thought to ron:
By many a feast, my belly grue so big,
That *Wolsey* streight, became a wanton twig.

Lo what it is, to feede on daynty meate,
And pamper vp, the gorge, with suger plate:
Nay, see how lads, in hope of higher seate
Rise early vp, and study learning late.
But hee thriues best, that hath a blessed fate,
And hee speeds worst, that worlde will nere aduaunce,
Nor neuer knowes, what meanes good lucke nor chaunce.

My chaunce was great, for from a poore mans son,
I rose aloft, and chopt and chaungde degree:
In *Oxford* first, my famous name begon,
Where many a day, the scholers honourd mee.
Then thought I how, I might a courtier bee:
So came to Court, and fethred there my wing,
With *Henry* th'eight, who was a worthy King.

Hee did with words, assay mee once or twice,
To see what wit, and ready sprite I had:
And-when hee saw, I was both graue and wice,
For some good cause, the King was wondrous glad.
Than downe I lookt, with sober countnaunce sad,
But heart was vp, as high as hope could go,
That suttell fox, might win some fauour so.

Wee worke with wiles, the mindes of men like wax,
The fawning whelp, gets many a peece of bred:
Wee follow Kings, with many coning knacks,
By searching out, how are theyr humours fed.
Hee haunts no Court, that hath a doltish hed:
For as in golde, the pretious stone is set,
So finest wits, in Court the credit get.

I quickely learnde, to kneele and kysse the hand,
To waite at heele, and turne like top about,
To stretch out necke, and lyke an Image stand,
60   To taunt, to skoffe, and face the matter out,
To preace in place, among the greatest rout:
Yet like a priest, my selfe did well behaue,
In fayre long gowne, and goodly garments graue.

Where *Wolsey* went, the world like Bees would swarme,
To heare my speach, and note my nature well.
I coulde with tongue, vse such a kinde of charme,
That voyce full cleare, should sounde like siluer bell.
When head deuisde, a long discours to tell,
With stories straunge, my speach should spised bee,
70   To make the worlde, to muse the more on mee.

Each tale was sweete, each worde a sentence wayde,
Each eare I pleasde, each eye gaue mee the vewe,
Each Iudgment markt, and paysed what I sayde,
Each minde I fed, with matter rare and newe,
Each day and howre, my grace and credit grewe:
So that the King, in hearing of this newes,
Deuysed howe, hee might my seruice vse.

Hee made mee then, his Chaplayne, to say masse
Before his grace, yea twise or thrise a weeke:
80   Now had I time, to trym my selfe by glasse,
Now founde I meane, some liuing for to seeke,
Now I became, both humble, mylde, and meeke,
Now I applyde, my wyts and sences throwe,
To reape some corne, if God would speede the plowe.

Whom most I sawe, in fauour with the King,
I followde fast, to get some hap thereby:
But I obserude, a nother fyner thing,
That was, to keepe, mee styll in Princes eye.
As vnder wyng, the hawke in winde doth lye,
90   So for a pray, I prowlled here and there,
And tryed frendes, and Fortune euery where.

The King at length, sent mee beyonde the seas,
Embastour then, with message good and greate:
And in that time, I did the King so pleas,
By short dispatch, and wrought so fine a feate,
That did aduaunce my selfe to higher seate,
The deanrie then, of *Lincolne* hee mee gaue:
And bownty shewde, before I gan to craue.

His Amner to, hee made mee all in haste,   *almoner*
100   And threefolde gyftes, hee threwe vpon mee still:
His counslour straight, listewise was *Wolsey* plaste,
Thus in shorte time, I had the world at will:
Which passed far, mans reason, wit, and skill.
O hap, thou haste, great secrets in thy might,
Which long lye hyd, from wily worldlyngs sight.

As shures of raine, fall quickly on the grasse,
That fading flowres, are soone refresht thereby:

Or as with Sun, the morning dewe doth passe,
And quiet calme, makes cleare a troubled skye:
110   So Princes powre, at twinkling of an eye
Sets vp a lofte, a favret on the wheele,
When giddy braynes, about the streetes doe reele.

They are but blinde, that wake where Fortune sleepes,
They worke in vayne, that striue with streame and tyde:
In double garde, they dwell, that destnye keepes,
In simple sorte, they liue that lacke a gyde:
They misse the marke, that shoote theyr arrowes wide,
They hit the pricke, that make theyr flight to glaunce
So nere the white, that shafte may light on chaunce.

120   Such was my lucke, I shot no shafte in vayne,
My bow stoode bent, and brased all the yeere:
I wayted harde, but neuer lost my payne:
Such wealth came in, to beare the charges cleere.
And in the end, I was the greatest peere
Among them all, for I so rulde the land,
By Kings consent, that all was in my hand.

Within on yeare, three Bishoprickes I had,
And in small space, a Cardnall I was made:
With long red robes, rich *Wolsey* then was clad,
130   I walkte in Sun, when others sate in shade:
I went abroade, with such a trayne and trade,
With crosses borne, before mee where I past,
That man was thought, to bee some God at last.

With sonnes of Earles, and Lordes I serued was,
An hundreth chaynes, at leaste were in my trayne:
I dayly dranke, in gold, but not in glas,
My bread was made, of fynest flowre and grayne:
My daynty mouth, did common meates disdayne,
I fed like Prince, on fowles most deare and straunge,
140   And bankets made, of fine conceites for chaunge.

My hall was full, of Knightes, and Squires of name,
And gentlemen, two hundreth tolde by powle:
Tale yeomen to, did howrely serue the same,
Whose names each weeke, I saw within checke rowle.
All went to church, when seruis bell did knowle,
All dinde and supte, and slepte at Cardnalls charge,
And all would wayte, when *Wolsey* tooke his barge.

My householde stuffe, my wealth and siluer plate,
Mighte well suffice, a Monarke at this day:
150   I neuer fed, but vnder cloth of state,
Nor walkt abroade, till Vshars clearde the way.   *ushers*
In house I had, musitions for to play,
In open streete, my trompets lowde did sownde,
Which pearst the skies, and seemde to shake the grownde.

My men most braue, martcht two and two in ranke,
Who helde in length, much more then half a mile:
Not one of these, but gaue his maister thanke,
For some good turne, or pleasure got some while.

I did not feede, my seruantes with a smile,
160   Or glosing wordes, that neuer bring forth frute,
But gaue them golde, or els preferde theyr sute.

In surety so, whiles God was pleasde, I stoode,
I knewe I must, leaue all my wealth behinde:
I sawe they lou'd, mee not for byrth or bloode,
But serude a space, to try my noble minde.
The more men gieue, the more in deede they finde
Of loue, and troth, and seruice, euery way:
The more they spare, the more doth loue decay.

I ioyde to see, my seruantes thriue so well,
170   And go so gay, with little that they gote:
For as I did, in honour still excell,
So would I oft, the wante of seruantes note:
Which made my men, on maister so to dote,
That when I sayde, let such a thing bee donne,
They woulde in deede, through fyre and water ronne.

I had in house, so many ofsars still,
Which were obayde, and honourde for their place,
That carelesse I, might sleepe or walke at will,
Saue that sometyme, I wayde a poore mans case,
180   And salude such sores, whose griefe might breede disgrace.
Thus men did wayte, and wicked world did gaze,
On mee and them, that brought vs all in maze.

For worlde was whist, and durst not speake a woorde
Of that they sawe, my credite curbde them so:
I waded far, and passed ore the foorde,
And mynded not, for to returne I troe.
The worlde was wise, yet scarce it selfe did knoe,
When wonder made, of men that rose by hap:
For Fortune rare, falls not in each mans lap.

190   I climde the clouds, by knowledge and good wit,
My men sought chaunce, by seruice or good lucke:
The worlde walkte lowe, when I aboue did sit,
Or downe did come, to trample on this mucke:
And I did swim, as dainty as a ducke,
When water serues, to keepe the body braue,
And to enioy, the gyftes that Fortune gaue.

And though my pompe, surpast all Prelates nowe,
And like a Prince, I liu'd and pleasure tooke:
That was not sure, so great a blur in browe,
200   If on my workes, indiffrent eyes doe looke.
I thought great scorne, such liuings heare to brooke,
Except I built, some howses for the poore,
And order tooke, to gieue great almes at doore.

A Colledge fayre, in *Oxford* I did make,
A sumptuous house, a stately worke in deede.
I gaue great lands, to that, for learning sake,
To bring vp youth, and succour scholers neede.
That charge of myne, full many a mouth did feede,
When I in Courte, was seeking some good turne,
210   To mend my torch, or make my candell burne.

More houses gay, I builte, then thowsands do
That haue enough, yet will no goodnes shoe:
And where I built, I did mayntayne it to,
With such great cost, as few bestowes I troe.
Of buildings large, I could reherse a roe,
That by mischaunce, this day haue lost my name,
Whereof I do, deserue the only fame.

And as for sutes, about the King was none
So apte as I, to speake and purchase grace.
220   Though long before, some say *Shores* wife[14] was one,
That oft kneelde downe, before the Princes face
For poore mens sutes, and holpe theire woefull case,
Yet shee had not, such credite as I gate,
Although a King, would heare the parret prate.

My wordes were graue, and bore an equall poyes,
In ballaunce just, for many a weighty cause:
Shee pleasde a Prince, with pretty merry toyes,
And had no sight, in state, nor course of lawes.
I coulde perswade, and make a Prince to pawes.
230   And take a breath, before hee drew the sworde,
And spy the time, to rule him with a worde.

I will not say, but fancy may do much,
Yet worlde will graunt, that wisdom may do more:
To wanton gyrls, affection is not such,
That Princes wise, will bee abusde therefore:
One sute of mine, was surely worth a score
Of hers indeede, for shee her time must watch,
And at all howres, I durst go draw the latch.

My voyce but heard, the dore was open streyght,
240   Shee might not come, till shee were calde or brought:
I rulde the King, by custom, arte, and sleight,
And knew full well, the secrets of his thought.
Without my minde, all that was done was nought,
In wars or peace, my counsayle swayed all,
For still the King, would for the Cardnall call.

I kept a court, my selfe, as great as his,
(I not compare, vnto my maister heere)
But looke my Lords, what liuely worlde was this,
That one poore man, became so great a peere?
250   Yet though this tale, be very straunge to heere,
Wit wins a worlde: and who hath hap and wit,
With triumph long, in Princely throne may sit.

What man like mee, bare rule in any age,
I shone like Sun, more cleare then morning star:
Was neuer parte, so playde in open stage
As mine, nor fame, of man flewe halfe so far.
I sate on bench, when thowsands at the bar

---

14   The subject of an earlier *Mirror* tragedy, Jane Shore left her
husband, a London merchant, to become the mistress of Edward IV in
1470. Condemned as a witch by Richard III after Edward's death, she
was forbidden to be given food or shelter, for which she begged until
she died.

Did pleade for right: for I in publique weale
Lorde Chaunclour was, and had the great broad seale,

260

Now haue I tolde, how I did rise aloft,
And sate with pride, and pomp, in golden hall,
And set my feete, on costly carpets soft,
And playde at goale, with goodly golden ball:
But after, Lord, I must rehearse my fall.
O trembling heart, thou canst not now for teares
Present that tale, vnto the hearers eares.

Best weepe it out, and sodayne silence keepe,
Till priuy pangs, make pinched heart complayne:
Or cast thy selfe, into some slumbring sleepe,

270

Till wakened wits, remembraunce bring agayne.
When heauy tears, do hollow cheekes distayne,
The world will thinke, thy sprits are growne so weake,
The feeble tongue, hath sure no powre to speake.

A tale by signes, with sighes and sobs set out,
Moues peoples mindes, to pity plaged men:
With howling voyce, do rather cry and showt,
And so by arte, shew forth thy sorrow then,
For if thou speake, some man will note with pen
What *Wolsey* sayde, and what thrue *Wolsey* downe,

280

And vnder foote, flings *Wolseys* great renowne.

What force of that, my fall must needs be herd,
Before I fell, I had a time to rise:
As fatall chaunce, and Fortune mee preferd,
So mischiefe came, and did my state despise.
Yf I might pleade, my case among the wise,
I could excuse, right much of mine offence:
But leaue a while, such matter in suspence.

The Pope, or pride, or peeuish parts of mine,
Made King to frowne, and take the seale from mee:

290

Now seru'd no words, nor plesaunt speeches fine,
Now *Wolsey*, lo, must needs disgraced bee.
Yet had I leaue (as dolefull prisner free)
To keepe a house (God wot) with heauy cheere,
Where that I founde, no wine, ne bread, nor beere.

My time was come, I coulde no longer liue,
What should I make, my sorrow further knowne?
Vpon some cause, that King that all did giue
Tooke all agayne, and so possest his owne.
My goods, my plate, and all was ouerthrowne,

300

And looke what I, had gathred many a day,
Within one howre, was cleanly swept away.

But harken now, how that my Fortune fell,
To *Yorke* I must, where I the Bishop was:
Where I by right, in grace a while did dwell,
And was in stawle, with honour great to pas.
The Priors then, and Abbots gan to smell,
Howe Cardnall must, bee honourd as hee ought,
And for that day, was great prouision brought.

At *Cawood*[15] then, where I great buildings made,
310   And did through cause, exspect my stawling day,
The King deuisde, a secrete vnder shade,
Howe Cardnall shoulde, bee reste and brought away.
One *Wealsh* a Knight, came downe in good aray,
And seasned sure, because from Courte hee cam,
On *Wolsey* wolfe, that spoyled many a lam.

Then was I led, toward Courte, like dog in string,
And brought as biefe, that Butcherrowe must see: *beef/butcher*
But still I hoapt, to come before the King,
And that repayre, was not denyde to mee.
320   But hee that kept, the Towre, my guide must bee.
Ah there I saw, what King thereby did meane,
And so I searcht, yf conscience now were cleane.

Some spots I founde, of pryde and popishe partes,
That might accuse, a better man then I:
Now *Oxford* came, to minde, with all theire artes,
And *Cambridge* to, but all not worth a flye:
For schoolemen can, no fowle defects supplye.
My sauce was sowre, though meate before was sweete,
Nowe *Wolsey* lackte, both conning, wit, and spreete.

330   A deepe conceyte, of that, possest my heade,
So fell I sicke, consumde as some did thinke.
So tooke in haste, my chamber and my bed,
On which deuise, perhaps the worlde might winke.
But in the heart, sharpe sorrow so did sinke,
That gladnes sweete, (forsooke my senses all)
In those extremes, did yeelde vnto my fall.

O let mee curse, the popish Cardnall hat,
Those myters big, beset with pearle and stones,
And all the rest, of trash I know not what,
340   The saints in shrine, theyr flesh and rotten bones,
The maske of Monkes, deuised for the nones,
And all the flocke, of Freers, what ere they are,
That brought mee vp, and left mee there so bare.

O cursed priestes, that prate for profits sake,
And follow floud, and tyde, where ere it floes:
O marchaunts fine, that do aduauntage take
Of euery grayne, how euer market goes.
O fie on wolues, that march in masking cloes,
For to deuoure, the lambs, when shepperd sleepes,
350   And woe to you, that promise neuer keepes.

You sayd I should, be reskude if I neede,
And you would curse, with candell, booke, and bell:
But when yee should, now serue my turne indeede,
Yee haue no house, I know not where yee dwell.
O Freers and Monkes, your harbour is in hell,
For in this world, yee haue no rightfull place,
Nor dare not once, in heauen shew your face.

15   Cawood Castle, near York.

Your fault not halfe, so great as was my pryde,
For which offence, fell *Lucifer* from skyes:
360   Although I would, that wilfull folly hyde,
The thing lyes playne, before the peoples eyes,
On which hye heart, a hatefull name doth ryes.
It hath beene sayde, of olde, and dayly will,
Pryde goes before, and shame comes after still.

Pryde is a thing, that God and man abores,
A swelling tode, that poysons euery place,
A stinking wounde, that breedeth many sores,
A priuy plague, found out in stately face,
A paynted byrd, that keepes a pecocks pace.
370   A lothsome lowt, that lookes like tinkers dog,
A hellish hownd, a swinish hatefull hog

That grunts and groanes, at euery thing it sees,
And holds vp snowt, like pig that coms from draffe.
Why should I make, of pride all these degrees,
That first tooke roote, from filthy drosse and chaffe,
And makes men stay, vpon a broken staffe?
No weakenes more, than thinke to stand vpright,
When stumbling blocke, makes men to fall downe right.

Hee needes must fall, that looks not where hee goes,
380   And on the starrs, walkes staring goezling like:
On sodayne oft, a blostring tempest bloes,   *blustering*
Than downe great trees, are tumbled in the dike.
Who knowes the time, and howre when God will strike?
Then looke about, and marke what steps yee take,
Before you pace, the pilgrimage yee make.

Run not on head, as all the worlde were youres,
Nor thrust them backe, that cannot bide a shocke:
Who striues for place, his owne decay procures:
Who alway brawles, is sure to catch a knocke:
390   Who beards a King, his head is neere the blocke:
But who doth stand, in feare, and worldly dreede,
Ere mischiefe coms, had neede to take good heede.

I hauing hap, did make account of none,
But such as fed, my humour good or bad.
To fawning doggs, sometimes I gaue a bone,
And flong some scrapps, to such as nothing had:
But in my hands, still kept the golden gad,
That seru'd my turne, and laught the rest to skorne,
As for himselfe, was Cardnall *Wolsey* borne.

400   No, no, good men, wee liue not for our selues,
Though each one catch, as mutch as hee may get:
Wee ought to looke, to those that diggs and delues,
That alwayes dwell, and liue in endles det.
Yf in such sort, wee would our compas set,
Wee should haue loue, where now but hate wee finde,
And hedstrong will, with cruell hollow minde.

I thought nothing, of duty, loue, or feare,
I snatcht vp all, and always sought to clime:

I punisht all, and would with no man beare,
410   I sought for all, and so could take the time.
I plide the Prince, whiles Fortune was in prime,
I fild the bags, and gold in hoorde I heapt,
Thought not on those, that thresht the corne I reapt.

So all I lost, and all I gat was nought,
And all by pride, and pompe lay in the dust:
I aske you all, what man aliue had thought,
That in this world, had beene so litle trust?
Why, all thinges heare, with time decline they must.
Than all is vaine, so all not worth a flye,
420   Yf all shall thinke, that all are borne to dye.

Yf all bee bace, and of so small a count,
Why doe wee all, in folly so abound?
Why doe the meane, and mighty seeke to mount,
Beyonde all hope, where is no surety found,
And where the wheele, is alwayes turning round?
The case is plaine, if all bee vnderstood,
Wee are so vaine, wee knowe not what is good.

Yet some will say, when they haue heapes of golde,
With flocks of friends, and seruaunts at theyr call,
430   They liue like Gods, in pleasure treble folde,
And haue no cause, to finde no fault at all.
O blinde conceite, these gloryes are but small,
And as for friends, they change their mindes so mych,
They stay not long, with neither poore nor rich.

With hope of friends, our selues wee do deceaue,
With feare of foes, we threatned are in sleepe:
But friends speake fayre, yet men alone they leaue
To sinke or swim, to mourne, to laugh, or weepe.
Yet whan foe smiles, the snake begins to creepe,
440   As world falles out, these dayes in compasse iust,
Wee knowe not howe, the friend or foe to trust.

Both can betray, the truest man aliue,
Both are to doubt, in matters of greate weight,
Both will somtime, for goodes and honour striue,
Both seemeth playne, yet both can shewe great sleight,
Both stoups full lowe, yet both can looke on height,
And best of both, not worth a cracked crowne:
Yet least of both, may loase a walled towne.

Talke not of frends, the name thereof is nought,
450   Then trust no foes, if frendes theire credit loes:
If foes and frendes, of on bare earth were wrought,
Blame nere of both, though both one nature shoes,
Grace passeth kinde, where grace and vertue floes,
But where grace wantes, make foes and frends alike,
The on drawes sworde, the other sure will strike.

I prou'd that true, by tryall twenty times,
When *Wolsey* stoode, on top of Fortunes wheele:
But such as to, the height of ladder climes,
Knowe not what led, lies hanging on theire heele,

460   Tell mee my mates, that heauy Fortune feele,
        Yf rising vp, breede not a gyddy brayne,
        And faling downe, bee not a greuous payne.

        I tolde you how, from *Cawood* I was led,
        And so fell sicke, when I arested was:
        What needeth nowe, more wordes heere in bee sed?
        I knewe full well, I must to pryson passe,
        And sawe my state, as brittell as a glasse:
        So gaue vp ghost, and bad the worlde farewell,
        Where in, God wot, I could no longer dwell.

470   Thus vnto dust, and ashes I returnde,
        When blase of life, and vitall breath went out,
        Like glowing cole, that is to sinders burnde:
        All fleshe and bloud, so ende, you neede not dout.
        But when the bruite, of this was blowne aboute,
        The worlde was glad, the Cardnall was in graue,
        This is of worlde, lo all the hope wee haue.

        Full many a yeare, the world lookt for my fall,
        And whan I fell, I made as great a cracke,
        As doth an oake, or mighty tottring wall,
480   That whirling winde, doth bring to ruin and wracke.
        Now babling world, wil talke behinde my backe
        A thousand things, to my reproache and shame:
        So will it to, of others do the same.

        But what of that? the best is wee are gone,
        And worst of all, when wee our tales haue tolde,
        Our open plagues, will warning bee to none,
        Men are by hap, and courage made so bolde:
        They thinke all is, theyr owne, they haue in holde.
        Well, let them say, and thinke what thing they please,
        This weltring world, both flowes and ebs like seas.

Christopher Marlowe (1564–1593)

The details we know of Christopher Marlowe's life paint a picture of many contradictions: he went to Cambridge University on a scholarship established for men intending to become ministers, yet he did not take holy orders and was accused of atheism later in life; he was in and out of legal trouble his entire adult life, and yet seems to have done some government service as a spy in France; he was a universally praised poet and playwright, and yet ended his life by being killed in a tavern brawl. At the time of his death, he was under summons to appear before the Privy Council. Since we lack definitive evidence, these contradictions can only be disentangled by using presumption and guesswork, and it is much safer to talk about his literary achievement. He was a hugely popular and influential playwright, and is rightly given the credit for making the dramatic blank verse line a vehicle for serious poetic expression. It is

conventional to say that he prepared the ground for Shakespeare's plays (which show many Marlovian influences, especially in the history plays), but this diminishes Marlowe's achievement. It is a better measure of his prodigious accomplishment to remember that if Shakespeare had died at the age of 29, he would be a minor footnote in literary history. Marlowe did die at the age of 29, and is still being read and performed all over the English-speaking world.

In this anthology, it is his lyric poetry and translations (rather than his plays) which are represented. The composition dates of all of them are speculative. *Hero and Leander* was published in two versions in 1598: one, published by Edward Blount, which presents Marlowe's text alone and the other, published by Paul Linley, which included Marlowe's text and the "completion" of the story by George

Chapman. Chapman's additions are much longer than Marlowe's original text, and they force the story into a conventional moral framework of sin and punishment that is absolutely antithetical to its spirit. It thus seems safer not to include them, especially since many Marlowe scholars now see his poem as complete in its own right and not as a fragment. The poem is the best example of the poetic fad known as "Ovidianism," which flourished in England during the 1590s and early 1600s. Taking their cue from the Roman poet Ovid (see gazetteer), this body of poetry was characterized by short epic poems on mythological and often erotic themes. Thomas Lodge's *Scillaes Metamorphosis* is the earliest example we have, and Shakespeare's *Venus and Adonis* and *Rape of Lucrece* also belong in this group. The short lyric poem "The Passionate Shepherd to his Love" was one of the most widely read and reproduced lyrics of its time, and two poetic replies to it (by Donne and Raleigh) are included in this volume. The suggested reasons for this poem's popularity have been many and various, but it seems clear that it is partly to do with the poem's indirect use of a tradition of love complaints that goes back to classical poetry; in particular, it arguably owes a great deal to the love song of the cyclops Polyphemus to the nymph Galatea in Ovid's *Metamorphoses* 13. Like that Ovidian poem, Marlowe's shepherd offers material wealth, rather than spir-

itual or emotional sincerity, as a lure to make the nymph love him; the last stanza even hints at social advancement and the pleasure of enjoying the tribute of inferiors. This mocking, materialist undertone combines with the sensuously beautiful language of the poem to create a poem that is much more complex than it looks at first. *All Ovid's Elegies*, published in 1595, is Marlowe's translations of Ovid's *Amores* which, together with that poet's *Art of Love* (*Ars amatoria*) and *Cures for Love* (*Remedia amoris*), form the basis for literary representations of sex and seduction to this day. Although occasionally inaccurate, Marlowe's version is valuable as poetry in its own right and as an insight into how Ovid was read in the sixteenth century. Not included here is his other great translation, that of the first book of the Roman poet Lucan's *Pharsalia* (published in 1600).

READING

Patrick Cheney, *Marlowe's Counterfeit Profession: Ovid, Spenser, Counter-Nationhood.*

Darryl Grantley and Peter Roberts (eds.), *Christopher Marlowe and English Renaissance Culture.*

Clark Hulse, *Metamorphic Verse: The Elizabethan Minor Epic.*

J. H.

HERO AND LEANDER

On *Hellespont*[1] guilty of True-love's blood,
In view and opposite two cities stood,
Seaborderers, disjoined by *Neptune's* might: *separated*
The one *Abydos*, the other *Sestos* hight.   *named*
At *Sestos*, *Hero* dwelt; *Hero* the fair,
Whom young *Apollo* courted for her hair,
And offered as a dower his burning throne,
Where she should sit for men to gaze upon.
The outside of her garments were of lawn,   *linen*
10   The lining, purple silk, with gilt stars drawn,
Her wide sleeves green, and bordered with a grove,
Where *Venus* in her naked glory strove,
To please the careless and disdainful eyes,
Of proud *Adonis* that before her lies.
Her kirtle blue, whereon was many a stain,   *gown*
Made with the blood of wretched Lovers slain.
Upon her head she ware a myrtle[2] wreath,
From whence her veil reached to the ground beneath.
Her veil was artificial flowers and leaves,
20   Whose workmanship both man and beast deceives.
Many would praise the sweet smell as she past,

HERO AND LEANDER
1   The Hellespont is the ancient name for the Dardanelles, the strait that connects the Aegean Sea to the Sea of Marmora. It is also, along with the Bosporus strait in modern Turkey, a symbolic boundary between Europe and Asia. The name means "Sea of Helle" and comes from the mythical princess of Thebes named Helle, who drowned there

while fleeing from her stepmother with her brother Phryxus. They were riding a winged ram with a golden fleece. Phryxus eventually arrived at Colchis (on the Black Sea) where he sacrificed the ram, but kept the fleece.
2   Myrtle was the sacred plant of the goddess Venus, whom Hero serves as priestess.

When 'twas the odour which her breath forth cast.
And there for honey, bees have sought in vain,
And beat from thence, have lighted there again.   *landed*
About her neck hung chains of pebble stone,
Which lightened by her neck, like Diamonds shone.   *illuminated*
She ware no gloves, for neither sun nor wind
Would burn or parch her hands, but to her mind,   *as she wished*
Or warm or cool them, for they took delight
30   To play upon those hands, they were so white.
Buskins of shells all silvered, used she,   *boots*
And branched with blushing coral to the knee;
Where sparrows perched, of hollow pearl and gold,
Such as the world would wonder to behold;
Those with sweet water oft her handmaid fills,
Which as she went would chirrup through the bills.
Some say, for her the fairest *Cupid* pined,
And looking in her face, was strooken blind.
But this is true, so like was one the other,
40   As he imagined *Hero* was his mother.
And oftentimes into her bosom flew,
About her naked neck his bare arms threw.
And laid his childish head upon her breast,
And with still panting rocked, there took his rest.
So lovely fair was *Hero, Venus'* Nun,[3]
As nature wept, thinking she was undone;
Because she took more from her than she left,
And of such wondrous beauty her bereft: *deprived*
Therefore in sign her treasure suffered wrack,
50   Since *Hero's* time, hath half the world been black.[4]
Amorous *Leander*, beautiful and young,
(Whose tragedy divine *Musaeus* sung)[5]
Dwelt at *Abydos*; since him, dwelt there none,
For whom succeeding times make greater moan.
His dangling tresses that were never shorn,   *hair*
Had they been cut, and unto *Colchos* borne,
Would have allured the vent'rous youth of Greece,
To hazard more, than for the golden Fleece.[6]
Fair *Cynthia*[7] wished, his arms might be her sphere,
60   Grief makes her pale, because she moves not there.
His body was as straight as *Circe's*[8] wand,
Jove might have sipped out *Nectar* from his hand.[9]
Even as delicious meat is to the taste,
So was his neck in touching, and surpassed

3   The description "Venus' Nun" would, for a 16th-century reader, have been associated with prostitutes. This is the first of the many places where the poem points out the paradoxical nature of Hero's vow of chastity to the goddess of sexual love.

4   This line has caused much comment. Conventionally, it is read as a mythopoeic explanation for the existence of dark-skinned races. This makes little sense in this context. Given Hero's control over the movements of the sun in the poem, it might well refer (somewhat hyperbolically) to the cycle of day and night, in which half the planet is in daylight and half in darkness at any one time. This would link Apollo's submission and offer of marriage to Hero at the beginning of the poem to what happens later. It also is consistent with Hero's unpredictable and dangerous effects on everyone with whom she comes into contact (see lines 103ff.)

5   Marlowe here conflates the mythical Musaeus, who was a companion of Orpheus (see gazetteer) with the historical poet of the same name (fl. *c.*5th century AD) who wrote the first poetic version of the Hero and Leander story. Marlowe (and many other poets in other European languages) used Musaeus' poem as a source, usually in its Latin translation.

6   See note 1. After Phryxus' death, the Greek hero Jason and his followers, the Argonauts, went on an expedition to Colchis to recover the Golden Fleece.

7   A nickname for Diana, goddess of the moon (see gazetteer).

8   In Homer's *Odyssey* 10, the sorceress Circe turns Odysseus' crew into swine with her magic wand.

9   Leander is here being compared to Ganymede, Jupiter's beautiful male cup-bearer (who features in Marlowe's play *Dido, Queen of Carthage* as well). This description sets up Leander's homoerotic encounter with Neptune in lines 650ff.

The white of *Pelops'* shoulder.[10] I could tell ye,
How smooth his breast was, and how white his belly,
And whose immortal fingers did imprint,
That heavenly path, with many a curious dint,   *indentation*
That runs along his back, but my rude pen,
70   Can hardly blazon forth the loves of men   *depict publicly*
Much less of powerful gods. Let it suffice,
That my slack muse, sings of *Leander*'s eyes,
Those orient cheeks and lips, exceeding his[11]   *lustrous*
That leapt into the water for a kiss
Of his own shadow, and despising many,
Died ere he could enjoy the love of any.
Had wild *Hippolytus*,[12] *Leander* seen,
Enamoured of his beauty had he been,
His presence made the rudest peasant melt,   *most uncultured*
80   That in the vast uplandish country dwelt,
The barbarous *Thracian*[13] soldier moved with nought,
Was moved with him, and for his favour sought.
Some swore he was a maid in man's attire,
For in his looks were all that men desire,
A pleasant smiling cheek, a speaking eye,
A brow for Love to banquet royally,
And such as knew he was a man would say,
Leander, thou art made for amorous play:
Why art thou not in love, and loved of all?
90   Though thou be fair, yet be not thine own thrall.   *slave*
    The men of wealthy *Sestos*, every year,
(For his sake whom their goddess held so dear,
Rose-cheeked *Adonis*) kept a solemn feast.
Thither resorted many a wand'ring guest,
To meet their loves; such as had none at all,
Came lovers home, from this great festival.
For every street like to a Firmament   *sky*
Glistered with breathing stars, who where they went,
Frighted the melancholy earth, which deemed,
100   Eternal heaven to burn, for so it seemed,
As if another *Phaeton*[14] had got
The guidance of the sun's rich chariot.
But far above the loveliest, *Hero* shined,
And stole away th'enchanted gazer's mind,
For like Sea-nymphs[15] inveigling harmony,
So was her beauty to the standers by.
Nor that night-wand'ring pale and watery star,[16]
(When yawning dragons draw her thirling car,
From *Latmos'* mount[17] up to the gloomy sky,
110   Where crowned with blazing light and majesty,
She proudly sits) more over-rules the flood,

---

10   According to Ovid in *Metamorphoses* 6, Pelops was killed by his father Tantalus and served to the gods in a banquet in order to test their divine powers. The goddess Demeter ate some of the flesh by mistake, and after the boy was brought back to life he was given an ivory prosthetic shoulder to replace what she had eaten.
11   A reference to the myth of Narcissus, who pined away after falling in love with his own reflection in a brook (*Metamorphoses* 3). Marlowe's suggestion that he drowned after falling into the brook is a common Early Modern variation on the story.
12   In Ovid's *Metamorphoses* 15, Hippolytus (the son of the hero Theseus) rejects the sexual advances of his stepmother Phaedra.

13   Thrace was the most northerly part of ancient Greece, situated between Macedonia and the Hellespont/Bosporus waterway. Its inhabitants were proverbially savage.
14   See gazetteer under Phaethon.
15   A reference to the Sirens, who were mythical nymphs living on an island near the coast of Sicily (see gazetteer).
16   The moon, which is the "watery star" because it controls the tides.
17   In Greek mythology, Mt. Latmus was where the youth Endymion lay in perpetual sleep. He was visited frequently there by Selene, the goddess of the moon.

Than she the hearts of those that near her stood.
Even as, when gaudy Nymphs pursue the chase,
Wretched *Ixion's* shaggy footed race,[18]
Incensed with savage heat, gallop amain,
From steep Pine-bearing mountains to the plain:
So ran the people forth to gaze upon her,
And all that viewed her, were enamoured on her.
And as in fury of a dreadful fight,

120   Their fellows being slain or put to flight,
Poor soldiers stand with fear of death dead strooken,   *stricken*
So at her presence all surprised and tooken,   *taken*
Await the sentence of her scornful eyes:
He whom she favours lives, the other dies.
There might you see one sigh, another rage,
And some (their violent passions to assuage)
Compile sharp satires, but alas too late,
For faithful love will never turn to hate.
And many seeing great princes were denied,

130   Pined as they went, and thinking on her died.
On this feast day, O cursed day and hour,
Went *Hero* thorough *Sestos*, from her tower
To *Venus* temple, where unhappily,
As after chanced, they did each other spy.
So fair a church as this, had *Venus* none,
The walls were of discoloured *Jasper* stone,   *multi-coloured*
Wherein was Proteus[19] carved, and o'erhead,
A lively vine of green sea agate spread;
Where by one hand, light headed *Bacchus* hung,

140   And with the other, wine from grapes out wrung.
Of Crystal shining fair, the pavement was,
The town of *Sestos*, called it *Venus'* glass.
There might you see the gods in sundry shapes,
Committing heady riots, incest, rapes: *impetuous*
For know, that underneath this radiant floor,
Was *Danae's* statue[20] in a brazen tower,
Jove, slyly stealing from his sister's bed,
To dally with *Idalian Ganymede*:
And for his love *Europa*, bellowing loud,

150   And tumbling with the Rainbow in a cloud,
Blood-quaffing *Mars*, heaving the iron net,
Which limping *Vulcan* and his *Cyclops* set:
Love kindling fire, to burn such towns as *Troy*,
Sylvanus weeping for the lovely boy
That now is turned into a *Cypress* tree,
Under whose shade the Wood-gods love to be.
And in the midst a silver altar stood,
There *Hero* sacrificing turtles' blood,   *turtle doves'*
Vailed to the ground, veiling her eye-lids close,   *bent down*

18   A reference to the centaurs, mythical creatures with the torso and head of a man and the body and legs of a horse. They were created when Ixion tried to seduce the goddess Hera. Zeus allowed him to have intercourse with a cloud shaped to look like Hera; the result of this coupling was Centaurus, who begot the proverbially wild and sexually predatory centaurs.

19   In *Odyssey* 4, a minor sea god who knows all things and has the power to assume any form he wishes (see gazetteer).

20   The next 11 lines all refer to examples of immoral behavior by the gods, particularly Jupiter. He changed himself into a shower of gold to penetrate the tower of the nymph Danae and impregnate her; his affection for Ganymede, his beautiful male cup-bearer, was frequently used by Marlowe and other Early Modern poets as an example of homoerotic attraction; he took the form of a bull to seduce Europa, the daughter of the king of Tyre; and he transformed into a rain cloud in order to consort with Iris, the messenger god who was often depicted as a rainbow. The war god Mars was trapped in bed with his lover Venus by her husband, the smith god Vulcan. Sylvanus was the Roman god of the woodlands and the "lovely boy" is Cyparissus who, in *Metamorphoses* 10, is transformed into a cypress tree.

160 And modestly they opened as she rose:
Thence flew Love's arrow with the golden head,[21]
And thus *Leander* was enamoured.
Stone still he stood, and evermore he gazed,
Till with the fire that from his count'nance blazed,   *face*
Relenting *Hero's* gentle heart was strook,
Such force and virtue hath an amorous look.
    It lies not in our power to love, or hate,
For will in us is over-ruled by fate.
When two are stripped,[22] long ere the course begin,
170 We wish that one should lose, the other win.
And one especially do we affect,
Of two gold Ingots like in each respect.
The reason no man knows, let it suffice,
What we behold is censured by our eyes.   *judged*
Where both deliberate, the love is slight,
Who ever loved, that loved not at first sight?
    He kneeled, but unto her devoutly prayed;
Chaste *Hero* to her self thus softly said:
Were I the saint he worships, I would hear him,
180 And as she spake those words, came somewhat near him.
He started up, she blushed as one ashamed;
Wherewith *Leander* much more was inflamed.
He touched her hand, in touching it she trembled,
Love deeply grounded, hardly is dissembled.   *disguised*
These lovers parleyed by the touch of hands,
True love is mute, and oft amazed stands.
Thus while dumb signs their yielding hearts entangled,
The air with sparks of living fire was spangled,
And night deep drenched in misty *Acheron*,[23]
190 Heaved up her head, and half the world upon,
Breathed darkness forth (dark night is *Cupid*'s day.)
And now begins *Leander* to display
Love's holy fire, with words, with sighs and tears,
Which like sweet music entered *Hero's* ears,
And yet at every word she turned aside,
And always cut him off as he replied.
At last, like to a bold sharp Sophister,[24]
With cheerful hope thus he accosted her.
    Fair creature, let me speak without offence,
200 I would my rude words had the influence,   *unlearned*
To lead thy thoughts, as thy fair looks do mine,
Then shouldst thou be his prisoner who is thine.
Be not unkind and fair, misshapen stuff
Are of behaviour boisterous and rough.
O shun me not, but hear me ere you go,
God knows I cannot force love, as you do.
My words shall be as spotless as my youth,
Full of simplicity and naked truth.
This sacrifice (whose sweet perfume descending,
210 From *Venus'* altar to your footsteps bending)

21 See the gazetteer under Cupid.
22 i.e. to prepare for a running race.
23 One of the four rivers in Hades; in Greek and Roman poetry, it is sometimes used as a name for the Underworld itself. In the first edition of Marlowe's poem, there was a marginal note describing this as "a periphrasis" (or, circumlocution) of night.

24 A name given to second- or third-year undergraduates at Cambridge University (where Marlowe had studied). The term also alludes to the Sophists, who were a group of ancient Greek teachers who taught rhetoric and other skills required to succeed in public life.

Doth testify that you exceed her far,
To whom you offer, and whose Nun you are,
Why should you worship her, her you surpass,
As much as sparkling Diamonds flaring glass.
A Diamond set in lead his worth retains,
A heavenly Nymph, beloved of human swains,   *youths,* or *servants*
Receives no blemish, but oft-times more grace,
Which makes me hope, although I am but base,
Base in respect of thee, divine and pure,
220   Dutiful service may thy love procure,
And I in duty will excel all other,
As thou in beauty dost exceed Love's mother.
Nor heaven, nor thou, were made to gaze upon,
As heaven preserves all things, so save thou one.
A stately builded ship, well rigged and tall,
The Ocean maketh more majestical:
Why vow'st thou then to live in *Sestos* here,
Who on Love's seas more glorious wouldst appear?
Like untuned golden strings[25] all women are,
230   Which long time lie untouched, will harshly jar.
Vessels of Brass oft handled, brightly shine,
What difference betwixt the richest mine   *mineral*
And basest mould, but use? for both not used,   *soil*
Are of like worth. Then treasure is abused,
When misers keep it; being put to loan,
In time it will return us two for one.
Rich robes, themselves and others do adorn,
Neither themselves nor others, if not worn.
Who builds a palace and rams up the gate,   *blocks*
240   Shall see it ruinous and desolate.
Ah simple *Hero,* learn thy self to cherish,
Lone women like to empty houses perish.
Less sins the poor rich man that starves himself,
In heaping up a mass of drossy pelf,   *riches*
Than such as you: his golden earth remains,
Which after his decease, some other gains.
But this fair gem,[26] sweet in the loss alone,
When you fleet hence, can be bequeathed to none.
Or if it could, down from th'enamelled sky,
250   All heaven would come to claim this legacy,
And with intestine broils the world destroy,
And quite confound nature's sweet harmony.
Well therefore by the gods decreed it is,
We human creatures should enjoy that bliss.
One is no number, maids are nothing then,
Without the sweet society of men.
Wilt thou live single still? one shalt thou be,
Though never-singling *Hymen* couple thee.
Wild savages, that drink of running springs,
260   Think water far excels all earthly things:
But they that daily taste neat wine, despise it.   *undiluted*
Virginity, albeit some highly prize it,
Compared with marriage, had you tried them both,
Differs as much, as wine and water doth.
Base bullion for the stamp's[27] sake we allow,

25 The strings of a harp or lyre.
26 The "gem" in question is Hero's virginity.

27 In this case, the stamp that places an image on a gold or silver coin.

Even so for men's impression do we you.
By which alone, our reverend fathers say,
Women receive perfection every way.
This idol which you term *Virginity*,
270   Is neither essence subject to the eye,
No, nor to any one exterior sense,
Nor hath it any place of residence,
Nor is't of earth or mould celestial,
Or capable of any form at all.
Of that which hath no being, do not boast,
Things that are not at all, are never lost.
Men foolishly do call it virtuous,
What virtue is it, that is born with us?
Much less can honour be ascribed thereto,
280   Honour is purchased by the deeds we do.
Believe me *Hero*, honour is not won,
Until some honourable deed be done.
Seek you for chastity, immortal fame,
And know that some have wronged *Diana's* name?[28]
Whose name is it, if she be false or not,
So she be fair, but some vile tongues will blot?
But you are fair (aye me) so wondrous fair,
So young, so gentle, and so debonair,   *affable*
As *Greece* will think, if thus you live alone,
290   Some one or other keeps you as his own.
Then *Hero* hate me not, nor from me fly,
To follow swiftly blasting infamy.
Perhaps, thy sacred Priesthood makes thee loath,   *unwilling*
Tell me, to whom mad'st thou that heedless oath?
      To *Venus*, answered she, and as she spake,
Forth from those two tralucent cisterns brake,   *translucent*
A stream of liquid pearl, which down her face
Made milk-white paths, whereon the gods might trace
To *Jove's* high court.[29] He thus replied: The rites
300   In which Love's beauteous Empress most delights,
Are banquets, Doric[30] music, midnight-revel,
Plays, masks, and all that stern age counteth evil.
Thee as a holy Idiot[31] doth she scorn,
For thou in vowing chastity, hast sworn
To rob her name and honour, and thereby
Commit'st a sin far worse than perjury.
Even sacrilege against her Deity,
Through regular and formal purity.   *outwardly conforming*
To expiate which sin, kiss and shake hands,
310   Such sacrifice as this, *Venus* demands.
      Thereat she smiled, and did deny him so,
As put thereby, yet might he hope for mo'.
Which makes him quickly reinforce his speech,
And her in humble manner thus beseech.
      Though neither gods nor men may thee deserve,
Yet for her sake whom you have vowed to serve,
Abandon fruitless cold Virginity,
The gentle queen of Love's sole enemy.

28   Diana was proverbially chaste (see gazetteer).
29   In classical mythology, the Milky Way led to Jupiter's court.

30   In ancient Greek history, a mode of music normally associated with courage and military affairs. Marlowe seems to have misremembered this.
31   "One who is unlearned in the mysteries of religion" (*OED*).

Then shall you most resemble *Venus'* Nun,[32]
320   When *Venus'* sweet rites are performed and done.
Flint-breasted *Pallas* joys in single life,
But *Pallas* and your mistress are at strife.
Love *Hero* then, and be not tyrannous,
But heal the heart, that thou hast wounded thus,
Nor stain thy youthful years with avarice,
Fair fools delight to be accounted nice.   *coy*, or *reserved*
The richest corn dies, if it be not reaped,
Beauty alone is lost, too warily kept.
These arguments he used, and many more,
330   Wherewith she yielded, that was won before.
Hero's looks yielded, but her words made war,
Women are won when they begin to jar.
Thus having swallowed *Cupid's* golden hook,
The more she strived, the deeper was she strook.
Yet evilly feigning anger, strove she still,
And would be thought to grant against her will.
So having paused a while, at last she said:
Who taught thee Rhetoric to deceive a maid?
Aye me, such words as these should I abhor,
340   And yet I like them for the Orator.
     With that *Leander* stooped, to have embraced her,
But from his spreading arms away she cast her,
And thus bespake him; Gentle youth forbear
To touch the sacred garments which I wear.
     Upon a rock, and underneath a hill,
Far from the town (where all is whist and still,   *quiet*
Save that the sea playing on yellow sand,
Sends forth a rattling murmur to the land,
Whose sound allures the golden *Morpheus*,
350   In silence of the night to visit us)
My turret stands, and there God knows I play
With *Venus'* swans and sparrows all the day.
A dwarfish beldame bears me company,   *old woman*, or *nurse*
That hops about the chamber where I lie,
And spends the night (that might be better spent)
In vain discourse, and apish merriment.
Come thither; As she spake this, her tongue tripped,
For unawares (*Come thither*) from her slipped,
And suddenly her former colour changed,
360   And here and there her eyes through anger ranged.
And like a planet, moving several ways,
At one self instant, she poor soul assays,   *tries*
Loving, not to love at all, and every part
Strove to resist the motions of her heart.
And hands so pure, so innocent, nay such,
As might have made heaven stoop to have a touch,
Did she uphold to *Venus* and again,
Vowed spotless chastity, but all in vain.
Cupid bears down her prayers with his wings,
370   Her vows above the empty air he flings:
All deep enraged, his sinewy bow he bent,
And shot a shaft that burning from him went,
Wherewith she strooken, looked so dolefully,
As made Love sigh, to see his tyranny.

32   See note 3 above.

And as she wept, her tears to pearl he turned,
And wound them on his arm, and for her mourned.
Then towards the palace of the Destinies,[33]
Laden with languishment and grief he flies.
And to those stern nymphs humbly made request,
380   Both might enjoy each other, and be blest.
But with a ghastly dreadful countenance,
Threatening a thousand deaths at every glance,
They answered Love, nor would vouchsafe so much
As one poor word, their hate to him was such.
Hearken a while, and I will tell you why:[34]
Heaven's winged herald, *Jove-born Mercury*,
The self-same day that he asleep had laid
Enchanted *Argus*,[35] spied a country maid,
Whose careless hair, in stead of pearl t'adorn it,
390   Glistered with dew, as one that seemed to scorn it;   *sparkled*
Her breath as fragrant as the morning rose,
Her mind pure, and her tongue untaught to glose.   *extenuate*
Yet proud she was, (for lofty pride that dwells
In towered courts, is oft in shepherds' cells.)
And too too well the fair vermilion knew,   *bright red*
And silver tincture of her cheeks, that drew
The love of every swain: On her, this god
Enamoured was, and with his snaky rod,[36]
Did charm her nimble feet, and made her stay
400   The while upon a hillock down he lay
And sweetly on his pipe began to play,
And with smooth speech, her fancy to assay,
Till in his twining arms he locked her fast,
And then he wooed with kisses, and at last,
As shepherds do, her on the ground he laid,
And tumbling in the grass, he often strayed
Beyond the bounds of shame, in being bold
To eye those parts, which no eye should behold.
And like an insolent commanding lover,
410   Boasting his parentage, would needs discover
The way to new *Elysium*:[37] but she,
Whose only dower was her chastity,
Having striven in vain, was now about to cry,
And crave the help of shepherds that were nigh.
Herewith he stayed his fury, and began
To give her leave to rise, away she ran,
After went *Mercury*, who used such cunning,
As she to hear his tale, left off her running.
Maids are not won by brutish force and might,
420   But speeches full of pleasure and delight.
And knowing *Hermes* courted her, was glad
That she such loveliness and beauty had
As could provoke his liking, yet was mute,

---

33   See the gazetteer under Fates.

34   The following inset story, which runs to line 484, originates with Marlowe and, except in its allusions to other myths, has no source in antiquity.

35   A mythical herdsman with eyes all over his body who was set by Juno to guard Io, a princess of Argos in whom Jupiter had become sexually interested. Mercury killed Argus and Juno sets his eyes in the tail of the peacock.

36   A reference to the caduceus, or herald's staff, that Mercury carried as Jupiter's messenger. It had two snakes entwined around it. In this context, it is an obvious phallic image as well.

37   Strictly speaking, Elysium refers to the Islands of the Blest, where the gods sent certain heroes for the afterlife instead of to Hades. Here, of course, it refers to Mercury's projected sexual conquest.

And neither would deny, nor grant his suit.
Still, vowed he love, she wanting no excuse
To feed him with delays, as women use:
Or thirsting after immortality,
All women are ambitious naturally,
Imposed upon her lover such a task,
As he ought not perform, nor yet she ask.
430   A draught of flowing *Nectar*,³⁸ she requested,
Wherewith the king of Gods and men is feasted.
He ready to accomplish what she willed,
Stole some from *Hebe*³⁹ (*Hebe*, *Jove*'s cup filled,)
And gave it to his simple rustic love,
Which being known (as what is hid from *Jove*?)
He inly stormed, and waxed more furious,
Than for the fire filched by *Prometheus*;
And thrusts him down from heaven: he wand'ring here,
440   In mournful terms, with sad and heavy cheer   *expression*
Complained to *Cupid*; *Cupid* for his sake,
To be revenged on *Jove* did undertake,
And those on whom heaven, earth and hell relies,
I mean the Adamantine Destinies,   *immovable*
He wounds with love, and forced them equally,
To dote upon deceitful *Mercury*.
They offered him the deadly fatal knife,
That shears the slender threads of human life,
At his fair feathered feet, the engines laid,   *tools*
450   Which th'earth from ugly *Chaos*' den upweighed:⁴⁰   *supported*
These he regarded not, but did entreat,   *plead for*
That *Jove*, usurper of his father's seat,
Might presently be banished into hell,
And aged *Saturn*⁴¹ in *Olympus* dwell.
They granted what he craved, and once again,
Saturn and *Ops*, began their golden reign.
Murder, rape, war, lust and treachery,
Were with *Jove* closed in *Stygian* Empery.⁴²
But long this blessed time continued not;
460   As soon as he his wished purpose got,
He reckless of his promise, did despise
The love of th'everlasting Destinies.
They seeing it, both *Love* and him abhorred,
And *Jupiter* unto his place restored.
And but that Learning, in despite of Fate,
Will mount aloft, and enter heaven gate,
And to the seat of *Jove* itself advance,
Hermes had slept in hell with Ignorance.
Yet as a punishment they added this,
470   That he and *Poverty* should always kiss.
And to this day is every scholar poor,
Gross gold, from them runs headlong to the boor.
Likewise the angry sisters thus deluded,

---

38   The mythical drink of the gods. If mortals consumed it, they immediately became immortal.
39   Hebe was Jupiter's daughter and the cup-bearer to the gods.
40   This confusing line refers to the fact that, in Greek mythology, the earth was formed out of Chaos; here, the Fates are being assigned the responsibility to maintain the earth's existence.

41   See the gazetteer entry on Saturn for the story of his relation to the Olympian gods. The "golden reign" refers to the first (Golden) age in Ovid's four ages of man (*Metamorphoses* 1) in which all of creation lived in harmony with no need for laws or restraints. This ended when Jupiter became ruler of the gods.
42   "Stygian" is the adjectival form of "Styx," the river which encircled the Underworld.

To venge themselves on *Hermes*, have concluded
That *Midas'* brood shall sit in Honour's chair,
To which the *Muses'* sons are only heir:
And fruitful wits that in aspiring are,
Shall discontent, run into regions far;
And few great lords in virtuous deeds shall joy,
480   But be surprised with every garish toy.
And still enrich the lofty servile clown,   *ignoramus*
Who with encroaching guile, keeps learning down.
Then muse not, *Cupid*'s suit no better sped,
Seeing in their loves, the Fates were injured.
    By this, sad *Hero*, with love unacquainted,
Viewing *Leander*'s face, fell down and fainted.
He kissed her, and breathed life into her lips,
Wherewith as one displeased, away she trips.
Yet as she went, full often looked behind,
490   And many poor excuses did she find,
To linger by the way, and once she stayed,
And would have turned again, but was afraid,
In offering parley, to be counted light.
So on she goes, and in her idle flight,
Her painted fan of curled plumes let fall,
Thinking to train *Leander* therewithal.
He being a novice, knew not what she meant,
But stayed, and after her a letter sent.
Which joyful *Hero* answered in such sort,
500   As he had hope to scale the beauteous fort,
Wherein the liberal Graces[43] locked their wealth,
And therefore to her tower he got by stealth.
Wide open stood the door, he need not clime,
And she herself before the 'pointed time,
Had spread the board, with roses strewed the room,
And oft looked out, and mused he did not come.
At last he came, O who can tell the greeting,
These greedy lovers had, at their first meeting.
He asked, she gave, and nothing was denied,
510   Both to each other quickly were affied.   *betrothed*
Look how their hands, so were their hearts united,
And what he did, she willingly requited.
(Sweet are the kisses, the embracements sweet,
When like desires and affections meet,
For from the earth to heaven, is *Cupid* raised,
Where fancy is in equal balance peised.)   *weighed*
Yet she this rashness suddenly repented,
And turned aside, and to herself lamented.
As if her name and honour had been wronged,
520   By being possessed of him for whom she longed;
Ay, and she wished, albeit not from her heart,
That he would leave her turret and depart.
The mirthful God of amorous pleasure smiled,
To see how he this captive Nymph beguiled.
For hitherto he did but fan the fire,
And kept it down that it might mount the higher.
Now waxed she jealous, lest his love abated,   *grew*
Fearing, her own thoughts made her to be hated.

---

43   Three minor Greek goddesses who represented the graceful and   Venus, Cupid, and/or the Muses. Here, of course, they are being invoked
beautiful aspects of human life. They are represented accompanying   metaphorically.

Therefore unto him hastily she goes,
530 And like light *Salmacis*,[44] her body throws
Upon his bosom, where with yielding eyes,
She offers up herself a sacrifice,
To slake his anger, if he were displeased,
O what god would not therewith be appeased?
Like *Aesop's* cock,[45] this jewel he enjoyed,
And as a brother with his sister toyed,
Supposing nothing else was to be done,
Now he her favour and good will had won.
But know you not that creatures wanting sense,
540 By nature have a mutual appetence,   *desire*
And wanting organs to advance a step,
Moved by Love's force, unto each other leap?
Much more in subjects having intellect,
Some hidden influence breeds like effect.
Albeit *Leander* rude in love, and raw,
Long dallying with *Hero*, nothing saw
That might delight him more, yet he suspected
Some amorous rites or other were neglected.
Therefore unto his body, hers he clung,
550 She, fearing on the rushes[46] to be flung,
Strived with redoubled strength: the more she strived,
The more a gentle pleasing heat revived,
Which taught him all that elder lovers know,
And now the same gan so to scorch and glow,
As in plain terms (yet cunningly) he craved it,
Love always makes those eloquent that have it.
She, with a kind of granting, put him by it,
And ever as he thought himself most nigh it,   *near*
Like to the tree of *Tantalus* she fled,
560 And seeming lavish, saved her maidenhead.
Ne'er king more sought to keep his diadem,   *crown*
Than *Hero* this inestimable gem.
Above our life we love a steadfast friend,
Yet when a token of great worth we send,
We often kiss it, often look thereon,
And stay the messenger that would be gone:
No marvel then, though *Hero* would not yield
So soon to part from that she dearly held.
Jewels being lost are found again, this never,
570 'Tis lost but once, and once lost, lost for ever.
    Now had the morn espied her lover's steeds,[47]
Whereat she starts, puts on her purple weeds,
And red for anger that he stayed so long,
All headlong throws her self the clouds among.
And now *Leander* fearing to be missed,
Embraced her suddenly, took leave, and kissed.
Long was he taking leave, and loath to go,
And kissed again, as lovers use to do.

44   Salmacis was a nymph who loved the beautiful youth Hermaph-
roditus. While embracing him, she prayed to the gods to make them
one, which they did; thereafter, he is represented with both male and
female physical attributes.
45   A reference to a story which is not, in fact, attributed to Aesop, in
which a rooster finds a jewel while scratching for corn in a barnyard.
Because he does not know its value, he ignores it.

46   It was still common in Early Modern Europe for the floors of large
banqueting rooms to be strewn with rushes, which would be changed
from time to time in order to keep the floor clean.
47   In classical mythology, Aurora, the goddess of the dawn, appeared
just before the horses pulling the chariot of the sun.

Sad *Hero* wrung him by the hand, and wept,
580   Saying, let your vows and promises be kept.
Then standing at the door, she turned about,
As loath to see *Leander* going out.
And now the sun that through th'orizon peeps,
As pitying these lovers, downward creeps.
So that in silence of the cloudy night,
Though it was morning, did he take his flight.
But what the secret trusty night concealed,
Leander's amorous habit soon revealed.
With *Cupid*'s myrtle was his bonnet crowned,
590   About his arms the purple riband wound,   *ribbon*
Wherewith she wreathed her largely spreading hair,
Nor could the youth abstain, but he must wear
The sacred ring wherewith she was endowed,
When first religious chastity she vowed:
Which made his love through *Sestos* to be known,
And thence unto *Abydos* sooner blown,
Than he could sail, for incorporeal Fame,
Whose weight consists in nothing but her name,
Is swifter than the wind, whose tardy plumes,
600   Are reeking water, and dull earthly fumes.   *steaming*
Home when he came he seemed not to be there,
But like exiled air thrust from his sphere,[48]
Set in a foreign place; and straight from thence,
Alcides like, by mighty violence,
He would have chased away the swelling main,
That him from her unjustly did detain.
Like as the sun in a Diameter,   *directly above*
Fires and inflames objects removed far,
And heateth kindly, shining laterally;
610   So beauty, sweetly quickens when 'tis nigh,   *stimulates*
But being separated and removed,
Burns where it cherished, murders where it loved.
Therefore even as an Index to a book,
So to his mind was young *Leander*'s look.
O none but gods have power their love to hide,
Affection by the count'nance is descried.
The light of hidden fire itself discovers,
And love that is concealed, betrays poor lovers.
His secret flame apparently was seen,
620   *Leander*'s Father knew where he had been,
And for the same mildly rebuked his son,
Thinking to quench the sparkles new begun.
But love resisted once, grows passionate,
And nothing more than counsel, lovers hate.
For as a hot proud horse highly disdains,
To have his head controlled, but breaks the reins,
Spits forth the ringled bit, and with his hooves,   *ringed*
Checks the submissive ground: so he that loves,
The more he is restrained, the worse he fares,
630   What is it now, but mad *Leander* dares?
O *Hero*, *Hero*, thus he cried full oft,
And then he got him to a rock aloft.

48   An arcane simile which seems to refer to the various spheres of
the Ptolemaic system of the universe. See Millar Maclure's edition of
Marlowe's poems for a detailed explanation.

Where having spied her tower, long stared he on't,
And prayed the narrow toiling *Hellespont*,
To part in twain, that he might come and go,
But still the rising billows answered no.   *waves*
With that he stripped him to the ivory skin,
And crying, Love I come, leaped lively in.
Whereat the sapphire visaged god[49] grew proud,
640   And made his capering *Triton* sound aloud,
Imagining, that *Ganymede* displeased,[50]
Had left the heavens, therefore on him he seiz'd.
Leander strived, the waves about him wound,
And pulled him to the bottom, where the ground
Was strewed with pearl, and in low coral groves,
Sweet singing Mermaids, sported with their loves
On heaps of heavy gold, and took great pleasure,
To spurn in careless sort, the shipwreck treasure.
For here the stately azure palace stood,
650   Where kingly *Neptune*, and his train abode.
The lusty god embraced him, called him love,
And swore he never should return to *Jove.*
But when he knew it was not *Ganymede*,
For under water he was almost dead,
He heaved him up, and looking on his face,
Beat down the bold waves with his triple mace,
Which mounted up, intending to have kissed him,
And fell in drops like tears, because they missed him.
Leander being up, began to swim,
660   And looking back, saw *Neptune* follow him.
Whereat aghast, the poor soul gan to cry,
O let me visit *Hero* ere I die.
The god put *Helle's*[51] bracelet on his arm,
And swore the sea should never do him harm.
He clapped his plump cheeks, with his tresses played,
And smiling wantonly, his love bewrayed.   *betrayed*
He watched his arms, and as they opened wide,
At every stroke, betwixt them would he slide,
And steal a kiss, and then run out and dance,
670   And as he turned, cast many a lustful glance,
And throw him gaudy toys to please his eye,
And dive into the water, and there pry
Upon his breast, his thighs, and every limb,
And up again, and close beside him swim,
And talk of love: *Leander* made reply,
You are deceived, I am no woman I.
Thereat smiled *Neptune*, and then told a tale,
How that a shepherd sitting in a vale,
Played with a boy so lovely fair and kind,
680   As for his love, both earth and heaven pined;
That of the cooling river durst not drink,
Lest water-nymphs should pull him from the brink.
And when he sported in the fragrant lawns,
Goat-footed Satyrs, and up-staring Fawns,
Would steal him thence. Ere half this tale was done,
Aye me, *Leander* cried, th'enamoured sun,

---

49   A reference to Neptune, god of the sea, and Triton, a merman who   50   See notes 9 and 20 above.
is frequently represented blowing on a conch-shell trumpet.   51   See note 1.

That now should shine on Thetis' glassy bower,[52]
Descends upon my radiant *Hero's* tower.
O that these tardy arms of mine were wings,
690   And as he spake, upon the waves he springs.
Neptune was angry that he gave no ear,
And in his heart revenging malice bare:
He flung at him his mace, but as it went,
He called it in, for love made him repent.
The mace returning back, his own hand hit,
As meaning to be venged for darting it.   *throwing*
When this fresh bleeding wound *Leander* viewed,
His colour went and came, as if he rued
The grief which *Neptune* felt. In gentle breasts,
700   Relenting thoughts, remorse and pity rests.
And who have hard hearts, and obdurate minds,
But vicious, harebrained, and illit'rate hinds?
The god seeing him with pity to be moved,
Thereon concluded that he was beloved.
(Love is too full of faith, too credulous,
With folly and false hope deluding us.)
Wherefore *Leander's* fancy to surprise,
To the rich *Ocean* for gifts he flies.
'Tis wisdom to give much, a gift prevails,
710   When deep persuading Oratory fails.
By this *Leander* being near the land,
Cast down his weary feet, and felt the sand.
Breathless albeit he were, he rested not,
Till to the solitary tower he got.
And knocked and called, at which celestial noise,
The longing heart of *Hero* much more joys
Than nymphs and shepherds, when the timbrel rings,   *tambourine*
Or crooked Dolphin when the sailor sings;
She stayed not for her robes, but straight arose,
720   And drunk with gladness, to the door she goes.
Where seeing a naked man, she screeched for fear,
Such sights as this, to tender maids are rare.
And ran into the dark herself to hide,
Rich jewels in the dark are soonest spied.
Unto her was he led, or rather drawn,
By those white limbs, which sparkled through the lawn.   *fine linen*
The nearer that he came, the more she fled,
And seeking refuge, slipped into her bed.
Whereon *Leander* sitting, thus began,
730   Through numbing cold, all feeble, faint and wan:
If not for love, yet love for pity sake,
Me in thy bed and maiden bosom take,
At least vouchsafe these arms some little room,
Who hoping to embrace thee, cheerly swum.   *cheerily*
This head was beat with many a churlish billow,
And therefore let it rest upon thy pillow.
Herewith affrighted *Hero* shrunk away,
And in her lukewarm place *Leander* lay.
Whose lively heat like fire from heaven fet,
740   Would animate gross clay,[53] and higher set

---

52   Thetis was a minor sea goddess, and her "glassy bower" is the sea
itself. She is best known in mythology as the mother of the hero
Achilles.

53   This couplet conflates two of the myths told about Prometheus:
that he fashioned mankind out of clay, and that he stole fire from heaven
(see the gazetteer).

The drooping thoughts of base declining souls,
Than dreary *Mars*, carousing *Nectar* bowls.   *bloody*
His hands he cast upon her like a snare,
She overcome with shame and sallow fear,
Like chaste *Diana*, when *Actaeon* spied her,
Being suddenly betrayed, dived down to hide her.
And as her silver body downward went,
With both her hands she made the bed a tent,
And in her own mind thought herself secure,
750   O'ercast with dim and darksome coverture.
And now she lets him whisper in her ear,
Flatter, entreat, promise, protest and swear;
Yet ever as he greedily assayed
To touch those dainties, she the *Harpy* played,[54]
And every limb did as a soldier stout,
Defend the fort, and keep the foe-man out.
For though the rising ivory mount he scaled,
Which is with azure circling lines empaled,   *fenced in*
Much like a globe, (a globe may I term this,
760   By which love sails to regions full of bliss,)
Yet there with *Sisyphus*[55] he toiled in vain,
Till gentle parley did the truce obtain.
Wherein Leander on her quivering breast,
Breathless spoke something, and sighed out the rest;
Which so prevailed, as he with small ado,
Enclosed her in his arms and kissed her too.
And every kiss to her was as a charm,
And to *Leander* as a fresh alarm.
So that the truce was broke, and she alas,
770   (Poor silly maiden) at his mercy was.
Love is not full of pity (as men say)
But deaf and cruel, where he means to prey.
Even as a bird, which in our hands we wring,
Forth plungeth, and oft flutters with her wing,
She trembling strove, this strife of hers (like that
Which made the world) another world begat,
Of unknown joy. Treason was in her thought,
And cunningly to yield her self she sought.
Seeming not won, yet won she was at length,
780   In such wars women use but half their strength.
Leander now like Theban *Hercules*,
Entered the orchard of th'*esperides*,[56]
Whose fruit none rightly can describe, but he
That pulls or shakes it from the golden tree;
And now she wished this night were never done,
And sighed to think upon th'approaching sun,
For much it grieved her that the bright day light,
Should know the pleasure of this blessed night,
And them like *Mars* and *Erycine* displayed,   *Venus*
790   Both in each other's arms chained as they laid.
Again she knew not how to frame her look,
Or speak to him who in a moment took,
That which so long so charily she kept,   *carefully*

54 In classical mythology, the Harpies were savage predatory birds   55 See gazetteer.
with the face of women; Aeneas encounters them in *Aeneid* 3. Metaphor-   56 See Hesperides in the gazetteer.
ically, the term is often used in Early Modern literature as a misogynist
insult for a stubborn or "troublesome" woman.

And fain by stealth away she would have crept,
And to some corner secretly have gone,
Leaving *Leander* in the bed alone.
But as her naked feet were whipping out,
He on the sudden clinged her so about,
That Mermaid-like unto the floor she slid,
800   One half appeared, the other half was hid.
Thus near the bed she blushing stood upright,
And from her countenance behold ye might,
A kind of twilight break, which through the hair,
As from an orient cloud, glimpse here and there.   *eastern*
And round about the chamber this false morn,
Brought forth the day before the day was born.
So *Hero's* ruddy cheek, *Hero* betrayed,
And her all naked to his sight displayed.
Whence his admiring eyes more pleasure took,
810   Than *Dis*,[57] on heaps of gold fixing his look.
By this *Apollo's* golden harp began,
To sound forth music to the *Ocean*,
Which watchful *Hesperus*[58] no sooner heard,
But he the day's bright-bearing Car prepared.
And ran before, as Harbinger of light,   *herald*
And with his flaring beams mocked ugly night,
Till she o'ercome with anguish, shame, and rage,
Danged down to hell her loathsome carriage.   *Dashed*

Desunt nonnulla[59]

[FROM] *ALL OVID'S ELEGIES*

Book One

ELEGIA I

We which were *Ovid's* five books now are three,
For these before the rest preferreth he.
If reading five thou plain'st of tediousness,   *complains*
Two ta'en away, thy labour will be less.
With Muse upreared I meant to sing of Arms,   *exalted*
Choosing a subject fit for fierce alarms,
Both verses were alike till love (men say)
Began to smile and took one foot away.[1]
Rash boy, who gave thee power to change a line?
10   We are the Muses' Prophets, none of thine.
What if thy mother take *Diana's* bow?[2]
Shall *Dian* fan, when love begins to glow?

57 See gazetteer.
58 In this context, Hesperus is the morning star; it can also be the first star of evening.
59 "Something is missing." This was printed in the first edition of the poem, though many modern scholars now believe that the poem is complete as it stands.

ELEGIA 1
1 A reference to classical Latin prosody: epic poetry was written in dactylic hexameters (lines of six feet). Elegy, the erotic mode in which

Ovid is writing, is written in alternating hexameter and pentameter lines (six and five feet respectively). Hence the speaker's complaint that Cupid stole a poetic "foot" and made him fall in love in order to prevent him from writing an epic.

2 The rhetorical questions in the six lines that follow represent the gods behaving in ways totally opposed to their normal character and interests: should Venus, the god of love, hunt like Diana? Should the virgin goddess Diana encourage sexual love? Should Ceres, the goddess of wheat, be worshipped in an uncultivated forest? For the portfolios of each god or goddess, see the gazetteer.

In woody groves is't meet that *Ceres* reign?
And quiver-bearing *Dian* till the plain?   *farm*
Who'll set the fair-tressed sun in battle 'ray   *array*
While *Mars* doth take the *Aonian* Harp to play?   i.e. the Muses' harp
Great are thy kingdoms, over strong and large,
Ambitious imp, why seek'st thou further charge?   *youth/responsibility*
Are all things thine? the Muses' *Tempe*³ thine?
20   Then scarce can *Phoebus* say, this Harp is mine.
When in this work's first verse I trod aloft,⁴
Love slacked my Muse, and made my numbers soft.   *made lax/verses*
I have no mistress, nor no favourite,
Being fittest matter for a wanton wit.   *amorous*
Thus I complained, but Love unlocked his quiver,
Took out the shaft ordained my hart to shiver: *shatter*
And bent his sinewy bow upon his knee,
Saying: "Poet here's a work beseeming thee."
Oh woe is me, he never shoots but hits,
30   I burn, love in my idle bosom sits.
Let my first verse be six, my last five feet,   *line*
Farewell stern war, for blunter Poets meet.   *suitable*
Elegian Muse, that warblest amorous lays,   i.e. the Muse of love poetry
Girt my shine brow with Sea-bank Myrtle praise.⁵

ELEGIA 4

Thy husband to a banquet goes with me,
Pray God it may his latest supper be,
Shall I sit gazing as a bashful guest,   *shy*
While others touch the damsel I love best?
Wilt lying under him his bosom clip;   *embrace*
About thy neck shall he at pleasure skip?
Marvel not, though the fair Bride⁶ did incite,
The drunken *Centaurs* to a sudden fight.
I am no half horse, nor in woods I dwell,
10   Yet scarce my hands from thee contain I well.   *can I withhold*
But how thou shouldst behave thy self now know;
Nor let the winds away my warnings blow.
Before thy husband come, though I not see,
What may be done, yet there before him be.
Lie with him gently, when his limbs he spread,
Upon the bed,⁷ but on my foot first tread.
View me, my becks, and speaking countenance   *gestures/expression*
Take, and receive each secret amorous glance.
Words without voice shall on my eyebrows sit,
20   Lines thou shalt read in wine by my hand writ.⁸
When our lascivious toys come in thy mind,   *activities*
Thy Rosy cheeks be to thy thumb inclined.
If ought of me thou speak'st in inward thought,   *anything*
Let thy soft finger to thy ear be brought.
When I (my light) do or say ought that please thee,
Turn round thy gold ring, as it were to ease thee.

3 See Muses in the gazetteer.
4 A reference to the common classical motif of the poet being borne
aloft into the sky by the power of his or her creativity.
5 Attributes of the goddess Venus (see gazetteer).
6 See the gazetteer under Lapiths and Centaurs.

7 As was normal for ancient Roman dinner parties, the guests at this
party are lying on couches rather than sitting at tables.
8 This famous image refers to wine spilled on the table, in which the
lover is writing messages with his finger.

Strike on the board like them that pray for evil,   *table*
When thou dost wish thy husband at the devil.
What wine he fills thee, wisely will him drink,
30   Ask thou the boy, what thou enough dost think.⁹
When thou hast tasted, I will take the cup,
And where thou drink'st, on that part I will sup.
If he gives thee what first himself did taste,
Even in his face his offered Gobbets cast.   *morsels*
Let not thy neck by his vile arms he pressed,
Nor lean thy soft head on his boist'rous breast.
Thy bosom's Roseate buds let him not finger,
Chiefly on thy lips let not his lips linger.
If thou givest kisses, I shall all disclose,
40   Say they are mine, and hands on thee impose.
Yet this I'll see, but if thy gown ought cover,   *covers anything*
Suspicious fear in all my veins will hover,
Mingle not thighs, nor to his leg join thine,
Nor thy soft foot with his hard foot combine.
I have been wanton, therefore am perplexed,   *lustful*
And with mistrust of the like measure vexed.
I and my wench oft under clothes did lurk,
When pleasure mov'd us to our sweetest work.
Do not thou so, but throw thy mantle hence.   *cloak*
50   Lest I should think thee guilty of offence.
Entreat thy husband drink, but do not kiss,
And while he drinks, to add more do not miss,
If he lies down with Wine and sleep oppressed,
The thing and place shall counsel us the rest.
When to go homewards we rise all along,
Have care to walk in middle of the throng.   *crowd*
There will I find thee, or be found by thee,
There touch what ever thou canst touch of me.
Aye me I warn what profits some few hours,¹⁰   *urge*
60   But we must part, when heav'n with black night lowers.   *looks threatening*
At night thy husband clips thee, I will weep
And to the door's sight of thy self will keep:
Then will he kiss thee, and not only kiss
But force thee give him my stol'n honey bliss.
Constrain'd against thy will give it the peasant
Forbear sweet words, and be your sport unpleasant.
To him I pray it no delight may bring
Or if it do to thee no joy thence spring:
But though this night thy fortune be to try it   *perform*
70   To me tomorrow constantly deny it.

ELEGIA 5

In summer's heat, and midtime of the day
To rest my limbs upon a bed I lay,
One window shut, the other open stood,
Which gave such light, as twinkles in a wood,
Like twilight glimpse at setting of the Sun
Or night being past, and yet not day begun.
Such light to shamefast maidens must be shown,

---

9   i.e. Get the slave serving the wine to get you what you want.   10   i.e. Alas, I am urging what will only benefit us for a few hours.

Where they may sport, and seem to be unknown.
Then came *Corinna* in a long loose gown,
Her white neck hid with tresses hanging down:
Resembling fair *Semiramis* going to bed,
Or *Layis* of a thousand lovers sped,[11]
I snatched her gown: being thin, the harm was small,
Yet strived she to be covered therewithal.
And striving thus as one that would be cast,   *thrown to the ground*
Betrayed her self, and yielded at the last.
Stark naked as she stood before mine eye,
Not one wen in her body could I spy.   *blemish*
What arms and shoulders did I touch and see,
How apt her breasts were to be pressed by me.
How smooth a belly under her waist saw I?
How large a leg, and what a lusty thigh?   *long*
To leave the rest all liked me passing well,
I clinged her naked body, down she fell,   *embraced*
Judge you the rest, being tired she bad me kiss;
Jove send me more such afternoons as this.

10

20

ELEGIA 7

Bind fast my hands, they have deserved chains,
While rage is absent, take some friend the pains.
For rage against my wench mov'd my rash arm,
My Mistress weeps whom my mad hand did harm.
I might have then my parents dear misus'd,
Or holy gods with cruel strokes abus'd.
Why? *Ajax*, master of the seven-fold shield,
Butchered the flocks he found in spacious field[12]
And he who on his mother veng'd his sire,
Against the destinies durst sharp darts require.[13]
Could I therefore her comely tresses tear?   *locks of hair*
Yet was she graced with her ruffled hair.
So fair she was, *Atalanta* she resembled,
Before whose bow th'*Arcadian* wild beasts trembled.[14]
Such *Ariadne* was, when she bewails
Her perjur'd *Theseus'* flying vows and sails,[15]
So chaste *Minerva* did *Cassandra* fall,[16]
Deflowr'd except, within thy Temple wall.
That I was mad, and barbarous all men cried,
She nothing said, pale fear her tongue had tied.
But secretly her looks with checks did trounce me,   *distress*
Her tears, she silent, guilty did pronounce me.
Would of mine arms, my shoulders had been scanted,   *deprived*
Better I could part of my self have wanted.   *lacked*
To mine own self have I had strength so furious?
And to my self could I be so injurious?
Slaughter and mischief's instruments, no better,

10

20

11 In Greek myth, Semiramis was a legendary queen of Nineveh, famous for her military conquests and power. Lais was a famous prostitute.

12 In some versions of the Trojan War story, Ajax and Odysseus competed for the arms of the dead Achilles. After the judgement of Agamemnon and Menelaus went in favour of Odysseus, Ajax went mad and slaughtered a flock of sheep, believing them to be his two commanders.

13 A reference to the story of Orestes (see gazetteer).

14 See gazetteer under Atalanta.

15 See gazetteer under Theseus.

16 See gazetteer.

Deserved chains these cursed hands shall fetter,
Punished I am, if I a *Roman* beat,[17]
30   Over my Mistress is my right more great?
Tydides left worst signs of villainy,[18]
He first a Goddess struck; another I.
Yet he harm'd less, whom I profess'd to love,
I harm'd: a foe did *Diomedes'* anger move.
Go now thou Conqueror glorious triumphs raise,
Pay vows to *Jove*, engirt thy hairs with bays,   *laurels*
And let the troops which shall thy Chariot follow,
"Io[19] a strong man conquered this Wench," hollow.   *cry out*
Let the sad captive foremost with locks spread
40   On her white neck but for hurt cheeks be led.
Meeter it were her lips were blue with kissing   *More suitable*
And on her neck a wanton's mark not missing.   *love bite*
But though I like a swelling flood was driven,
And as a prey unto blind anger given.
Was't not enough the fearful Wench to chide?   *berate*
Nor thunder in rough threatings haughty pride?   *threats*
Nor shamefully her coat pull o'er her crown,
Which to her waist her girdle still kept down.
But cruelly her tresses having rent   *hair*
50   My nails to scratch her lovely cheeks I bent.
Sighing she stood, her bloodless white looks showed
Like marble from the *Parian* Mountains hewed.[20]
Her half-dead joints, and trembling limbs I saw,
Like *Poplar* leaves blown with a stormy flaw,
Or slender ears, with gentle *Zephyr* shaken,   *west wind*
Or waters' tops with the warm south wind taken.
And down her cheeks, the trickling tears did flow,
Like water gushing from consuming snow.   *melting*
Then first I did perceive I had offended
60   My blood, the tears were that from her descended.
Before her feet thrice prostrate down I fell,
My feared hands thrice back she did repel.
But doubt thou not (revenge doth grief appease)   *satisfy*
With thy sharp nails upon my face to seize.
Bescratch mine eyes, spare not my locks to break,
(Anger will help thy hands though ne'er so weak.)
And lest the sad signs of my crime remain,
Put in their place thy keembed hairs again.   *combed*

ELEGIA 8

There is, who e'er will know a bawd aright
Give ear, there is an old trot *Dipsas* hight.[21]
Her name comes from the thing: she being wise,
Sees not the morn on rosy horses rise.

17   A Roman citizen; there were few, if any, enforceable laws against beating slaves.
18   "Tydides" means "Son of Tydeus" and refers to Diomedes, a Greek hero in the Trojan War. Encouraged by Athena, he fought with and wounded the goddess Aphrodite (Venus).
19   "Io" was a Greek shout of triumph that became a poetic convention in Latin and Early Modern English.
20   Paros is a Greek island that was famous in ancient times for the quality of its marble stone.
21   Ovid's character Dipsas became an emblematic female pimp or procurer for later literature. The explanation of her name in the following line refers to the Latin noun *dipsas*, which was a type of venomous serpent.

She magic arts and *Thessale*[22] charms doth know,
And makes large streams back to their fountains flow,
She knows with gras, with thrids on wrong wheels spun   *grass/threads*
And what with Mare's rank humour may be done.[23]
When she will, clouds the darkened heav'n obscure,
10   When she will, day shines everywhere most pure.
(If I have faith) I saw the stars drop blood,
The purple moon with sanguine visage stood.
Her I suspect among nights spirits to fly,
And her old body in bird's plumes to lie.
Fame saith as I suspect, and in her eyes   *Rumour*
Two eye-balls shine, and double light thence flies.   *Double pupils*
Great grand-sires from their ancient graves she chides   *rouses*
And with long charms the solid earth divides.
She draws chaste women to incontinence,
20   Nor doth her tongue want harmful eloquence.
By chance I heard her talk, these words she said
While closely hid betwixt two doors I laid.
Mistress thou knowest, thou hast a bless'd youth pleas'd,
He stayed, and on thy looks his gazes seized.
And why should'st not please? none thy face exceeds,
Aye me, thy body hath no worthy weeds.   *clothes*
As thou art fair, would thou wert fortunate,
Wert thou rich, poor should not be my state.
Th'opposed star of *Mars* hath done thee harm,
30   Now *Mars* is gone: *Venus* thy side doth warm.
And brings good fortune, a rich lover plants
His love on thee, and can supply thy wants.
Such is his form as may with thine compare,
Would he not buy thee, thou for him should'st care.[24]
She blushed: red shame becomes white cheeks, but this
If feigned, doth well; if true it doth amiss.
When on thy lap thine eyes thou dost deject,   *lower*
Each one according to his gifts respect.
Perhaps the *Sabines* rude, when *Tatius* reigned,[25]
40   To yield their love to more than one disdained.
Now *Mars* doth rage abroad without all pity,
And *Venus* rules in her *Aeneas'* City.[26]
Fair women play, she's chaste whom none will have,
Or, but for bashfulness herself would crave.
Shake off these wrinkles that thy front assault,   *frowns*
Wrinkles in beauty is a grievous fault.
Penelope in bows her youths' strength tried,[27]
Of horn the bow was that approv'd their side.   *strength*
Time flying slides hence closely, and deceives us,   *secretly*
50   And with swift horses the swift year soon leaves us.
Brass shines with use; good garments would be worn,

---

22   The Greek region of Thessaly was characterized as full of witches and magicians in ancient folklore.
23   i.e. The secretions from a mare in heat. This line and the preceding one refer to the materials Dipsas uses to cast magic spells.
24   i.e. He is sufficiently good-looking that if he did not try to win you over with gifts, he would be worth trying to seduce with gifts himself.
25   See gazetteer under Sabines.
26   A reference to the fact that Aeneas, hero of the *Aeneid* and Rome's mythical progenitor, was the son of the goddess Venus. More than this,

however, Ovid is here rewriting the official ideology of Augustan Rome: where Emperor Augustus tried to stress the "traditional" Roman values of marital fidelity, martial courage, and simple living, Ovid's elegies celebrate sexual infidelity, decadence, and luxury. See Ovid in the gazetteer.
27   A reference to *Odyssey* 21, in which Odysseus' wife Penelope has a contest among her suitors to string and fire her husband's bow. Unbeknown to her and the suitors, Odysseus is present and he wins the contest before killing all of the suitors.

Houses not dwelt in, are with filth forlorn.
Beauty not exercised with age is spent,
Nor one or two men are sufficient.
Many to rob is more sure, and less hateful,
From dog-kept flocks come preys to wolves most grateful.
Behold what gives the Poet but new verses?
And thereof many thousand he rehearses.
The Poet's God arrayed in robes of gold,   *i.e. Apollo*
60   Of his gilt Harp the well tun'd strings doth hold.
Let *Homer* yield to such as presents bring
(Trust me) to give, it is a witty thing.
Nor, so thou may'st obtain a wealthy prize,
The vain name of inferior slaves despise.²⁸
Nor let the arms of ancient lines beguile thee,   *lineage*
Poor lover with thy grandsires I exile thee.
Who seeks, for being fair, a night to have,
What he will give, with greater instance crave.   *urgency*
Make a small price, while thou thy nets dost lay,
70   Lest they should fly, being ta'en, the tyrant play.   *taken*
Dissemble so, as lov'd he may be thought,
And take heed lest he gets that love for nought.
Deny him oft, feign now thy head doth ache:
And *Isis*²⁹ now will show what 'scuse to make.
Receive him soon, lest patient use he gain,   *habit*
Or lest his love oft beaten back should wane.
To beggars shut, to bringers ope thy gate,
Let him within hear barred-out lovers prate.   *chatter*
And as first wrong'd the wronged sometimes banish,
80   Thy fault with his fault so repuls'd will vanish.
But never give a spacious time to ire,   *anger*
Anger delayed doth oft to hate retire.
And let thine eyes constrained learn to weep,   *i.e. learn to weep at will*
That this, or that man may thy cheeks moist keep.
Nor, if thou cozen'st one, dread to forswear,   *cheat/swear falsely*
"*Venus* to mocked men lends a senseless ear."
Servants fit for thy purpose thou must hire
To teach thy lover, what thy thoughts desire.
Let them ask somewhat, many asking little,
90   Within a while great heaps grow of a tittle.   *trifle*
And sister, Nurse, and mother spare him not,
By many hands great wealth is quickly got.
When causes fail thee to require a gift,
By keeping of thy birth make but a shift.   *ploy*
Beware lest he unrival'd loves secure,³⁰
Take strife away, love doth not well endure.
On all the bed men's tumbling let him view³¹
And thy neck with lascivious marks made blue.
Chiefly show him the gifts, which others send:
100   If he gives nothing, let him from thee wend.
When thou hast so much as he gives no more,
Pray him to lend what thou may'st ne'er restore.   *return*
Let thy tongue flatter, while thy mind harm works:

---

28   i.e. Do not despise him if he was once a slave (as long as he is rich).
29   An Egyptian moon goddess whose cult spread all over the Roman
empire. Her name is being used here as a euphemism for a woman's
menstrual period.

30   i.e. Beware lest he feel that he has no rivals for your love (or he
will get complacent).
31   i.e. Let him see signs that other men have been in your bed (to
provoke his jealousy and more presents).

Under sweet honey deadly poison lurks.
If this thou dost to me by long use known,
Nor let my words be with the winds hence blown,
Oft thou wilt say, live well, thou wilt pray oft,
That my dead bones may in their grave lie soft.
As thus she spake, my shadow me betrayed,
110   With much ado my hands I scarcely stayed.
But her bleare eyes, bald scalp's thin hoary fleeces   *dim*
And rivelled cheeks I would have pulled a pieces.   *wrinkled*
The gods send thee no house, a poor old age,
Perpetual thirst, and winter's lasting rage.

Book Two

ELEGIA 6

The parrot from east *India* to me sent,
Is dead, all fowls her exequies frequent.   *funeral rites*
Go goodly birds, striking your breasts bewail,
And with rough claws your tender cheeks assail.
For woeful hairs let piece-torn plumes abound,
For long-shrilled trumpets let your notes resound.
Why *Philomele* dost *Tereus'* lewdness mourn?[32]
All wasting years have that complaint outworn.
Thy tunes let this rare bird's sad funeral borrow,
10   *Itys* is great, but ancient cause of sorrow.
All you whose pinions in the clear air soar,   *wings*
But most thou friendly turtle-dove[33] deplore.
Full concord all your lives was you betwixt,
And to the end your constant faith stood fixed.
What *Pylades* did to *Orestes* prove,[34]
Such to the parrot was the turtle dove.
But what availed this faith? her rarest hue?
Or voice that how to change the wild notes knew?
What helps it thou wert given to please my wench,
20   Birds' hapless glory, death thy life doth quench.
Thou with thy quills might'st make green *Emeralds* dark
And pass our scarlet of red saffron's mark.
No such voice-feigning bird was on the ground,
Thou spokest thy words so well with stammering sound.
Envy hath rapt thee, no fierce wars thou movedst,   *abducted*
Vain bab'ling speech, and pleasant peace thou lovedst.
Behold how quails among their battles live,   *squabbles*
Which do perchance old age unto them give.
A little filled thee, and for love of talk,
30   Thy mouth to taste of many meats did balk.
Nuts were thy food, and Poppy caused thee sleep,
Pure water's moisture thirst away did keep.
The ravenous vulture lives, the Puttock hovers   *bird of prey*
Around the air, the Cadesse rain discovers,   *jackdaw*
And Crows survive arms-bearing *Pallas'* hate,[35]

---

32 For Philomele, Tereus, and Itys (line 10), see the gazetteer under Philomela.
33 Venus' bird and an emblem of true love.

34 Pylades was the loyal friend and cousin of Orestes and a common literary type for true friendship. For Orestes, see the gazetteer.
35 In *Metamorphoses* 2, the Crow describes how Minerva (Pallas Athena) punished him for revealing secrets.

Whose life nine ages scarce bring out of date.
Dead is that speaking image of man's voice,
The Parrot given me, the far world's best choice.
The greedy spirits take the best things first,
40   Supplying their void places with the worst.
Thersites did *Protesilaus* survive,
And *Hector* died his brothers yet alive.[36]
My wench's vows for thee what should I show,[37]
Which stormy South winds into sea did blow?
The seventh day came, none following mightst thou see
And the fates' distaff empty stood to thee,[38]
Yet words in thy benumbed palate rung,   *senseless*
Farewell *Corinna* cried thy dying tongue.
Elysium[39] hath a wood of home trees black,   *ilex*
50   Whose earth doth not perpetual green grass lack,
There good birds rest (if we believe things hidden)
Whence unclean fowls are said to be forbidden.
There harmless Swans feed all abroad the river,
There lives the *Phoenix* one alone bird ever,
There *Juno's* bird displays his gorgeous feather,   *peacock*
And loving Doves kiss eagerly together.
The Parrot into wood receiv'd with these,
Turns all the goodly birds to what she please.
A grave her bones hides, on her corpse' great grave,
60   The little stones these little verses have.
This tomb approves, I pleased my mistress well,   *demonstrates*
My mouth in speaking did all birds excel.

ELEGIA 9

O *Cupid* that dost never cease my smart,   *pain*
O boy that liest so slothful in my heart.
Why me that always was thy soldier found,
Dost harm, and in thy tents why dost me wound?   *in your own camp*
Why burns thy brand, why strikes thy bow thy friends?
More glory by thy vanquished foes ascends.
Did not *Pelides*[40] whom his Spear did grieve,
Being required, with speedy help relieve?
Hunters leave taken beasts, pursue the chase,
10   And than things found do ever further pace.[41]
We people wholly given thee, feel thine arms,   *to thee*
Thy dull hand stays thy striving enemies' harms.   *delays*
Dost joy to have thy hooked Arrows shaked,
In naked bones? love hath my bones left naked.
So many men and maidens without love,
Hence with great laud thou may'st a triumph move.   *From this/praise/prompt*

---

36   Thersites was a cowardly, spiteful Greek soldier in the Trojan War; Protesilaus, by contrast, was the first Greek soldier to set foot on Trojan soil and the first to be killed. Hector (see gazetteer) was the greatest Trojan hero in the war; he was killed by Achilles long before the siege of Troy ended.
37   i.e. Why should I call to mind the vows my beloved made for you?
38   A reference to one of the goddesses known collectively as the Fates (see gazetteer).
39   See gazetteer.
40   Another name for Achilles, who cured the wound his spear had caused to King Telephus of Mysia with rust from the same spear.
41   i.e. Hunters do not linger with animals they have already killed, but move on to seek more prey.

Rome if her strength the huge world had not filled,

With strawy cabins now her courts should build. *would*

The weary soldier hath the conquered fields,

His sword laid by, safe, though rude places yields.[42]

20

The Dock inharbours ships drawn from the floods, *seas*

Horses freed from service range abroad the woods.

And time it was for me to live in quiet,

That have so oft serv'd pretty wenches' diet.

Yet should I curse a God, if he but said,

Live without love, so sweet ill is a maid. *pretty poison*

For when my loathing it of heat deprives me,

I know not whither my mind's whirlwind drives me.

Even as a headstrong courser bears away, *horse*

30

His rider vainly striving him to stay,

Or as a sudden gale thrusts into sea,

The haven-touching bark now near the lea, *shore*

So wavering *Cupid* brings me back amain, *forcibly*

And purple Love resumes his darts again.

Strike boy, I offer thee my naked breast,

Here thou hast strength, here thy right hand doth rest.

Here of themselves thy shafts come, as if shot,

Better than I, their quiver knows them not.[43]

Hapless is he that all the night lies quiet *Unlucky*

40

And slumb'ring, thinks himself much blessed by it.

Fool, what is sleep but image of cold death,

Long shalt thou rest when Fates expire thy breath.

But me let crafty damsels' words deceive,[44]

Great joys by hope I inly shall conceive.

Now let her flatter me, now chide me hard, *berate*

Let me enjoy her oft, oft be debarred.

Cupid by thee, *Mars* in great doubt doth trample,[45]

And thy step-father fights by thy example. *i.e. Mars*

Light art thou, and more windy than thy wings,

50

Joys with uncertain faith thou tak'st and brings.

Yet love, if thou with thy fair mother hear,

Within my breast no desert empire bear. *barren*

Subdue the wand'ring wenches to thy reign, *fickle/rule*

So of both people shalt thou homage gain.

Book Three

ELEGIA 7

What man will now take liberal arts in hand,

Or think soft verse in any stead to stand. *support*

Wit was some-times more precious than gold,

Now poverty great barbarism we hold.

When our books did my mistress fair content,

I might not go, whither my papers went.

She prais'd me, yet the gate shut fast upon her,

I here and there go witty with dishonour.

42 Marlowe's source text was clearly flawed in this passage; the line
is meant to allude to the Roman practice of giving retired soldiers a plot
of land to farm in the conquered territories of the empire.

43 i.e. Cupid's arrows know my breast better than their own quiver.

44 i.e. Let me be deceived by women's words.

45 Marlowe's translation jumbles the Latin, which states that Mars is
now as unpredictable as Cupid has always been.

See a rich chuff whose wounds great wealth inferr'd,   *boor*

10   For bloodshed knighted, before me preferr'd.   *advanced*

Fool, canst thou him in thy white arms embrace?

Fool, canst thou lie in his enfolding space?

Know'st not this head a helm was wont to bear,   *helmet*

This side that serves thee, a sharp sword did wear.

His left hand whereon gold doth ill alight,   *descend*

A target bore: blood-sprinkled was his right.   *shield*

Canst touch that hand wherewith someone lies dead?

Ah whither is thy breast's soft nature fled?

Behold the signs of ancient fight, his scars,

20   What e'er he hath his body gained in wars.

Perhaps he'll tell how oft he slew a man,

Confessing this, why dost thou touch him then?

I the pure priest of *Phoebus* and the muses,

At thy deaf doors in verse sing my abuses,

Not what we slothful know, let wise men learn,

But follow trembling camps, and battles stern,   *fierce*

And for a good verse draw the first dart forth,   *instead of/spear*

Homer without this shall be nothing worth.

Jove being admonished gold had sovereign power,

30   To win the maid came in a golden shower.[46]

Till then, rough was her father, she severe,

The posts of brass, the walls of iron were.

But when in gifts the wise adulterer came,

She held her lap ope to receive the same.

Yet when old *Saturn* heaven's rule possessed,[47]

All gain in darkness the deep earth suppressed.

Gold, silver, iron's heavy weight, and brass,

In hell were harboured, here was found no mass.   *pieces of gold or silver*

But better things it gave, corn without ploughs,   *wheat*

40   Apples, and honey in oak's hollow boughs.

With strong ploughshares no man the earth did cleave,

The ditcher no marks on the ground did leave.   *ditch-digger*

Nor hanging oars the troubled seas did sweep,

Men kept the shore, and sailed not into deep.

Against thy self, man's nature, thou wert cunning,

And to thine own loss was thy wit swift running.

Why gird'st thy cities with a towered wall?   *encircle*

Why let'st discordant hands to armour fall?   *angry*

What dost with seas? With th'earth thou wert content,

50   Why seek'st not heav'n the third realm to frequent?   *the sky*

Heaven thou affects, with *Romulus*, temples brave   *favors*

Bacchus, *Alcides*, and now *Caesar* have.[48]

Gold from the earth instead of fruits we pluck,

Soldiers by blood to be enriched have luck.

Courts shut the poor out; wealth gives estimation,   *reputation*

Thence grows the Judge, and knight of reputation.

All, they possess: they govern fields, and laws,

They manage peace, and raw war's bloody jaws,

Only our loves let not such rich churls gain,   *rustic boors*

60   'Tis well, if some wench for the poor remain.

---

46   See Danae in the gazetteer.

47   This passage refers to the Golden Age of life on earth, before the reign of Jupiter and the Olympian gods; it is described by Ovid in *Metamorphoses* 1. See Cronus in the gazetteer.

48   These two lines list four mortals or demi-gods who have become divinities and acquired temples of their own: Romulus, the legendary founder of Rome, Bacchus (Dionysus), Hercules ("Alcides"), and Julius Caesar.

Now, *Sabine-like*, though chaste she seems to live,
One her commands, who many things can give.
For me, she doth keeper, and husband fear,
If I should give, both would the house forbear.
If of scorned lovers god be 'venger just,   *avenger*
O let him change goods so ill got to dust.

ELEGIA II

What day was that, which all sad haps to bring,   *bad omens*
White birds to lovers did not always sing.
Or is I think my wish against the stars?
Or shall I plain some God against me wars?   *complain*
Who mine was called, whom I lov'd more than any,
I fear with me is common now to many.
Err I? or by my books is she so known?
'Tis so: by my wit her abuse is grown.   *sin*
And justly: for her praise why did I tell?
10   The wench by my fault is set forth to sell.
The bawd I play, lovers to her I guide: *pimp*
Her gate by my hands is set open wide.
'Tis doubtful whether verse avail, or harm,
Against my good they were an envious charm.   *magic spell*
When *Thebes*, when *Troy*, when *Caesar* should be writ,
Alone *Corinna* moves my wanton wit.[49]
With Muse oppos'd would I my lines had done,
And *Phoebus* had forsook my work begun.
Nor, as use will not Poet's record hear,
20   Would I my words would any credit bear.   *would be believed*
Scylla by us her father's rich hair steals,[50]
And *Scylla's* womb mad raging dogs conceals.
We cause feet fly, we mingle hairs with snakes,
Victorious *Perseus* wing'd steeds back takes.
Our verse great *Tityus* a huge space out-spreads,
And gives the viper-curled Dog three heads.
We make *Enceladus* use a thousand arms,
And men enthralled by Mermaids' singing charms.
The East winds in *Ulysses'* bags we shut,

49   As at the beginning of the first elegy, the poet here complains that he should be writing epic poems about military themes like the ancient city of Thebes, the Trojan War, or Julius Caesar, but only feels inspired by his mistress.

50   From here until line 40, Ovid repeats a random collection of the most fantastic myths found in classical poetry. This begins as a demonstration of the absurdity of believing what poets say, but by the end of the poem (lines 41–4) Ovid cannot resist boasting and complaining simultaneously about the persuasive power of verse. The first Scylla was the daughter of the king of Megara, whose kingdom was safe as long as a purple hair on his head remained uncut. Scylla cut it off to win the love of King Minos, who was at war with her father. The other Scylla is the monster with barking dogs around her waist encountered by Odysseus in *Odyssey* 11. The god Mercury has winged feet, and the gorgon Medusa (whom Perseus killed) had snakes in place of hair; the winged horse Pegasus was created from drops of Medusa's blood. Tityus was a giant imprisoned in the Underworld, where also resides the three-headed dog Cerberus, who is chained at the gates to keep living souls out of the realm of the dead. Enceladus is another mythical giant, and "Mermaids" refers to the sirens whose singing lured sailors to their deaths in *Odyssey* 12. Also in the *Odyssey* is the story of Ulysses (Odysseus) being given a leather bag containing the power of all of the winds. For Tantalus and Niobe, see the gazetteer. Callisto was a mortal loved by Jupiter whom Juno changed into a bear; Jove in turn made her and her son Arcas into the constellations known as the Great and Little Bear. For Procne and Itys, see the gazetteer under Philomela. A swan, a shower of gold, and a bull are three of the forms which Jupiter assumed in order to consummate his lust for mortal women. For Proteus and Thebes, see the gazetteer. One of the tasks that Jason performed to gain the Golden Fleece was harnessing two fire-breathing bulls. The ships which "glister" in the sea refer to Aeneas' ships in *Aeneid* 9, which were transformed into sea-nymphs. For Atreus and Amphion, whose music could move stones, see the gazetteer.

30   And blabbing *Tantalus* in mid-waters put.
Niobe flint, *Callist'* we make a Bear,
Bird-changed *Procne* doth her *Itys* tear.
Jove turns himself into a Swan, or gold,
Or his Bull's horns *Europa's* hand doth hold.
Proteus what should I name? teeth, *Thebes'* first seed?
Oxen in whose mouths burning flames did breed?
Heav'n star *Electra* that bewailed her sisters?[51]
The ships, whose God-head in the sea now glisters?
The Sun turned back from *Atreus* cursed table?
40   And sweet-touched harp that to move stones was able?
Poets large power is boundless, and immense,
Nor have their words true history's pretence,
And my wench ought to have seem'd falsely praised,
Now your credulity harm to me hath raised.

THE PASSIONATE SHEPHERD TO HIS LOVE

Come live with me, and be my love,
And we will all the pleasures prove,   *test*
That Valleys, groves, hills and fields,
Woods, or steepy mountain yields.

And we will sit upon the Rocks,
Seeing the Shepherds feed their flocks,
By shallow Rivers, to whose falls,
Melodious birds sing Madrigals.   *songs*

And I will make thee beds of Roses,
10   And a thousand fragrant posies,[1]
A cap of flowers, and a kirtle,   *skirt*
Embroidered all with leaves of Myrtle.[2]

A gown made of the finest wool,
Which from our pretty Lambs we pull,
Fair lined slippers for the cold:
With buckles of the purest gold.

A belt of straw, and Ivy buds,
With Coral clasps and Amber studs,
And if these pleasures may thee move,
20   Come live with me, and be my love.

The Shepherds' Swains shall dance and sing,   *servants*
For thy delight each May morning.
If these delights thy mind may move;
Then live with me, and be my love.

---

51   Marlowe has mistranslated what is already a disputed line in Ovid.
It is now generally taken as a reference to the sisters of Phaethon (see
gazetteer), whose sisters wept for him until they were turned into trees;
their tears hardened into amber.

THE PASSIONATE SHEPHERD TO HIS LOVE
1   This word refers to both bunches of flowers and poetic verses or
mottoes.
2   Myrtle was the plant associated with the goddess of love, Venus.

William Shakespeare (1564–1616)

Shakespeare's titanic reputation as a dramatist tends to make students and general readers alike overlook his output of lyric poetry. During a period in which the theaters were closed because of the plague, he wrote two full-length works designed expressly for a reading (rather than a play-going) public. *The Rape of Lucrece* (published in 1593) and *Venus and Adonis* (published in 1594) are both Ovidian narrative poems or minor epics, and represent Shakespeare's contribution to a widespread contemporary literary fad for poems that formally or tonally reflected the works of the Roman poet Ovid (see gazetteer). This trend, which lasted from about 1590 until the early 1620s, produced such other notable works as Thomas Lodge's *Scillaes Metamorphosis* (1589) and Marlowe's *Hero and Leander* (1598). Sometimes called *epyllia* by modern scholars, these poems were usually retellings of classical or mythological erotic episodes and, following Ovid's example, are very prone to narrative digressions. In contrast to Petrarchan love poetry such as Sidney's *Astrophil and Stella*, Ovidian love poetry is usually about the consummation (rather than the frustration) of sexual desire, but also frequently subjects women who resist male advances to violent forms of punishment. As such, it can be read as the literary vehicle which enabled both the joyful and the sinister elements of seduction and sexuality to become major themes of lyric poetry. Shakespeare's two efforts in this vein comprise an interesting study in contrasts. *Venus and Adonis* takes the tragic story of a goddess's lost love and treats it in an often grotesquely comic fashion. *The Rape of Lucrece*, on the other hand, is as deadly serious as its subject implies, and is interesting for its choice of a story which connects a crime against an individual with a political revolution (the expulsion of the Tarquin kings from Rome). It is the psychological states of desire, revulsion, shame, and revenge that the rape brings to light that Shakespeare focuses on, rather than the crime itself, very much in the vein (albeit not the form) of Ovid's great collection of love complaints *The Heroides*.

Shakespeare also wrote the short philosophical lyric "The Phoenix and Turtle" (which appeared in an anthology in 1601), the pastoral "Lover's Complaint" (which was published in a volume with his sonnets), and at least some of the poems in the collection called *The Passionate Pilgrim* (1599). It is his sonnets, however, which have attracted the most critical and readerly interest of his non-dramatic poetry. Published in 1609, probably without the poet's permission, they were written and circulated in manuscript at the height of the English mania for sonnet sequences in the 1590s. The first major English sonnet sequence to be published was Philip Sidney's *Astrophil and Stella* (1591) and the next five years saw the appearance of other sequences by Edmund Spenser, Thomas Lodge, Samuel Daniel, Michael Drayton, and many others. The ultimate source for the sonnet sequence is the *Rime sparse* ("Scattered Rhymes") of the fourteenth-century Italian poet Petrarch, and this prototype set the thematic pattern for all of its successors to either imitate or work against. Sonnet sequences are exercises in the creation of a poetic self by a speaker who is in love with a disdainful or somehow unapproachable beloved. Usually it is a male speaker in love with a woman, but, in the case of Shakespeare's sonnets, the bulk of them revolve around a close (occasionally erotically charged) friendship between the speaker and a younger aristocratic male friend. Sonnets 127–52 introduce the famous unnamed "Dark Lady," with whom the speaker has an adulterous liaison of which he cannot approve but from which he cannot break free. For many years, much critical energy was devoted to trying to establish the biographical truth behind the tantalizing hints offered about the identity of these and other poetic "beloveds" in the sonnet sequences. More recently, however, scholarly attention has turned to the ways in which the artificiality of the poetic structure of the sequence is reflected by the artificiality of the emotions expressed. In other words, if there ever was a real man or woman behind the young man and the Dark Lady, it could not matter less to the reader's engagement with them: as poets have been doing since the days of the Roman elegists, personal experience is converted into the means for a poetic exploration of the self which does not need to be sincere to be effective.

READING

Ian Donaldson, *The Rapes of Lucretia: A Myth and Its Transformations*.

Joel Fineman, *Shakespeare's Perjured Eye: The Invention of Poetic Subjectivity in the Sonnets*.

Clark Hulse, *Metamorphic Verse: The Elizabethan Minor Epic*.

Arthur F. Marotti, "'Love Is Not Love': Elizabethan Sonnet Sequences and the Social Order."

Nancy Vickers, "'The Blazon of Sweet Beauty's Best': Shakespeare's Lucrece."

J. H.

THE RAPE OF LUCRECE

To the RIGHT HONORABLE HENRY WRIOTHESLY, Earl of Southampton, and Baron of Titchfield.[1]

The love I dedicate to your lordship is without end: whereof this pamphlet without beginning[2] is but a superfluous moiety. The warrant I have of your honourable disposition, not the worth of my untutored lines, makes it assured of acceptance. What I have done is yours; what I have to do is yours; being part in all I have, devoted yours. Were my worth greater, my duty would show greater; meantime, as it is, it is bound to your lordship, to whom I wish long life still lengthened with all happiness.

Your lordship's in all duty,
WILLIAM SHAKESPEARE.

The Argument

Lucius Tarquinius, for his excessive pride surnamed Superbus, after he had caused his own father-in-law Servius Tullius to be cruelly murdered, and, contrary to the Roman laws and customs, not requiring or staying for the people's suffrages, had possessed himself of the kingdom, went, accompanied with his sons and other noblemen of Rome, to besiege Ardea. During which siege the principal men of the army meeting one evening at the tent of Sextus Tarquinius, the king's son, in their discourses after supper every one commended the virtues of his own wife; among whom Collatinus extolled the incomparable chastity of his wife Lucretia. In that pleasant humour they all posted to Rome; and intending, by their secret and sudden arrival, to make trial of that which every one had before avouched, only Collatinus finds his wife, though it were late in the night, spinning amongst her maids: the other ladies were all found dancing and revelling, or in several disports. Whereupon the noblemen yielded Collatinus the victory, and his wife the fame. At that time Sextus Tarquinius being inflamed with Lucrece' beauty, yet smothering his passions for the present, departed with the rest back to the camp; from whence he shortly after privily withdrew himself, and was, according to his estate, royally entertained and lodged by Lucrece at Collatium. The same night he treacherously stealeth into her chamber, violently ravished her, and early in the morning speedeth away. Lucrece, in this lamentable plight, hastily dispatcheth messengers, one to Rome for her father, another to the camp for Collatine. They came, the one accompanied with Junius Brutus, the other with Publius Valerius; and finding Lucrece attired in mourning habit, demanded the cause of her sorrow. She, first taking an oath of them for her revenge, revealed the actor and whole manner of his dealing, and withal suddenly stabbed herself. Which done, with one consent they all vowed to root out the whole hated family of the Tarquins; and bearing the dead body to Rome, Brutus acquainted the people with the doer and manner of the vile deed, with a bitter invective against the tyranny of the king: wherewith the people were so moved, that with one consent and a general acclamation the Tarquins were all exiled, and the state government changed from kings to consuls.

From the besieged Ardea[3] all in post,	*in haste*
Borne by the trustless wings of false desire,	*treacherous*
Lust-breathed Tarquin leaves the Roman host,	
And to Collatium[4] bears the lightless fire	

THE RAPE OF LUCRECE
1   A 19-year-old aristocrat to whom Shakespeare also dedicated *Venus and Adonis*.
2   It was a classical convention for long narrative poems to begin in the middle of the story's action. In this case, Shakespeare begins with Tarquin's journey to Collatium, rather than with the beginning of the action summarized in the argument.
3   A city roughly 25 miles south of Rome.
4   Collatine and Lucrece's home city.

Which, in pale embers hid, lurks to aspire
  And girdle with embracing flames the waist
  Of Collatine's fair love, Lucrece the chaste.

Haply that name of chaste unhapp'ly set
This bateless edge on his keen appetite;   *sharp*
10   When Collatine unwisely did not let
To praise the clear unmatched red and white[5]
Which triumphed in that sky of his delight,
  Where mortal stars, as bright as heaven's beauties,
  With pure aspects did him peculiar duties.   *particular*

For he the night before, in Tarquin's tent,
Unlocked the treasure of his happy state;
What priceless wealth the heavens had him lent
In the possession of his beauteous mate;
Reck'ning his fortune at such high-proud rate
20   That kings might be espoused to more fame,
  But king nor peer to such a peerless dame.

O happiness enjoyed but of a few!
And, if possessed, as soon decayed and done
As is the morning silver-melting dew
Against the golden splendour of the sun!
An expired date, cancelled ere well begun: *contract*
  Honour and beauty, in the owner's arms,
  Are weakly fortressed from a world of harms.

Beauty itself doth of itself persuade
30   The eyes of men without an orator;
What needeth then apologies be made,   *vindications*
To set forth that which is so singular?
Or why is Collatine the publisher
  Of that rich jewel he should keep unknown
  From thievish ears, because it is his own?

Perchance his boast of Lucrece' sov'reignty
Suggested this proud issue of a king;   *offspring*
For by our ears our hearts oft tainted be.
Perchance that envy of so rich a thing,
40   Braving compare, disdainfully did sting   *daring*
  His high-pitched thoughts, that meaner men should vaunt
  That golden hap which their superiors want.   *fortune*

But some untimely thought did instigate
His all too timeless speed, if none of those.
His honour, his affairs, his friends, his state,
Neglected all, with swift intent he goes
To quench the coal which in his liver[6] glows.
  O rash-false heat, wrapped in repentant cold,
  Thy hasty spring still blasts, and ne'er grows old!   *is blasted*

---

5 In most Early Modern love poetry, especially after Petrarch, the   6 Early Modern Europeans thought the liver was the organ which
colours red and white connoted the red lips and cheeks and white   produced sexual desire.
skin of a conventionally beautiful woman. Here, Shakespeare adds a
metaphor comparing Lucrece's face to the sky and her eyes to stars.

50   When at Collatium this false lord arrived,
        Well was he welcomed by the Roman dame,
        Within whose face beauty and virtue strived
        Which of them both should underprop her fame: *support*
        When virtue bragged, beauty would blush for shame;
            When beauty boasted blushes, in despite
            Virtue would stain that o'er with silver white.[7]

        But beauty, in that white entituled,   *entitled*
        From Venus' doves doth challenge that fair field;[8]
        Then virtue claims from beauty beauty's red,
60   Which virtue gave the golden age to gild   *enrich*
        Their silver cheeks, and called it then their shield;
            Teaching them thus to use it in the fight,
            When shame assailed, the red should fence the white.

        This heraldry in Lucrece' face was seen,
        Argued by beauty's red and virtue's white;
        Of either's colour was the other queen,
        Proving from world's minority their right;
        Yet their ambition makes them still to fight,
            The sovereignty of either being so great
70   That oft they interchange each other's seat.

        Their silent war of lilies and of roses
        Which Tarquin view'd in her fair face's field,
        In their pure ranks his traitor eye encloses;[9]
        Where, lest between them both it should be killed,
        The coward captive vanquished doth yield
            To those two armies that would let him go
            Rather than triumph in so false a foe.

        Now thinks he that her husband's shallow tongue,
        The niggard prodigal that praised her so,   *miserly*
80   In that high task hath done her beauty wrong,
        Which far exceeds his barren skill to show;
        Therefore that praise which Collatine doth owe
            Enchanted Tarquin answers with surmise,   *pays out*
            In silent wonder of still-gazing eyes.

        This earthly saint, adored by this devil,
        Little suspecteth the false worshipper;
        For unstained thoughts do seldom dream on evil;
        Birds never limed[10] no secret bushes fear.
        So guiltless she securely gives good cheer
90   And reverend welcome to her princely guest,
            Whose inward ill no outward harm expressed;

        For that he coloured with his high estate,
        Hiding base sin in pleats of majesty;
        That nothing in him seemed inordinate,

---

7 The play of red and white is repeated here as the colour of modest
beauty (blushing red) and purity (white).

8 Shakespeare is punning here, conflating a battlefield with the field
upon which a heraldic device is painted. The pun is extended by the
rhyme word "shield," which is where a knight's coat of arms would be
painted.

9 The beauty and virtue manifest in Lucrece's face are metaphorically
capturing Tarquin's "traitor eye" as it looks at them.

10 A common means of catching birds in this period was to smear
lime on twigs; any birds landing on the twigs would be stuck to the
lime.

Save sometime too much wonder of his eye,
Which, having all, all could not satisfy;
But, poorly rich, so wanteth in his store   *lacks*
That cloyed with much he pineth still for more.   *sated*

But she, that never coped with stranger eyes,   *contended*
100   Could pick no meaning from their parling looks,   *speaking*
Nor read the subtle-shining secrecies
Writ in the glassy margents of such books.[11]   *clear margins*
She touched no unknown baits, nor feared no hooks;
Nor could she moralize his wanton sight,   *interpret morally/unchaste*
More than his eyes were opened to the light.

He stories to her ears her husband's fame,
Won in the fields of fruitful Italy;
And decks with praises Collatine's high name,
Made glorious by his manly chivalry
110   With bruised arms and wreaths of victory.   *battered*
Her joy with heaved-up hand she doth express,
And wordless so greets heaven for his success.

Far from the purpose of his coming hither,
He makes excuses for his being there.
No cloudy show of stormy blust'ring weather
Doth yet in his fair welkin once appear;   *sky*
Till sable Night, mother of dread and fear,   *black*
Upon the world dim darkness doth display,
And in her vaulty prison stows the day.

120   For then is Tarquin brought unto his bed,
Intending weariness with heavy sprite;   *Pretending/spirit*
For after supper long he questioned
With modest Lucrece, and wore out the night.
Now leaden slumber with life's strength doth fight;
And every one to rest himself betakes,
Save thieves and cares and troubled minds that wake.

As one of which doth Tarquin lie revolving   *pondering*
The sundry dangers of his will's obtaining;
Yet ever to obtain his will resolving,
130   Though weak-built hopes persuade him to abstaining;
Despair to gain doth traffic oft for gaining,
And when great treasure is the meed proposed,   *reward*
Though death be adjunct, there's no death supposed.   *connected*

Those that much covet are with gain so fond[12]   *infatuated*
That what[13] they have not, that which they possess,
They scatter and unloose it from their bond,   *grasp*
And so, by hoping more, they have but less;
Or, gaining more, the profit of excess
Is but to surfeit, and such griefs sustain
140   That they prove bankrupt in this poor-rich gain.

---

11 Early Modern books frequently had printed comments in the margin to explain the structure and meaning of what was written in the main text.

12 This stanza and the two after it comprise an elaborate exploration of how covetousness makes people unhappy with the riches they already have, and leads to misery whether it is gratified or not.

13 The first three lines of this stanza are syntactically ambiguous. Several solutions have been proposed, but perhaps the easiest is to read line 2 to imply "That *for* what . . ."

The aim of all is but to nurse the life
With honour, wealth and ease, in waning age;
And in this aim there is such thwarting strife
That one for all or all for one we gage: *pledge*
As life for honour in fell battle's rage;   *fierce*
   Honour for wealth; and oft that wealth doth cost
   The death of all, and all together lost.

So that in vent'ring ill we leave to be   *cease*
The things we are for that which we expect;
150   And this ambitious foul infirmity,
In having much, torments us with defect
Of that we have; so then we do neglect
   The thing we have, and, all for want of wit,   *reason*
   Make something nothing by augmenting it.

Such hazard now must doting Tarquin make,   *gamble*
Pawning his honour to obtain his lust;
And for himself himself he must forsake:[14]
Then where is truth, if there be no self-trust?
When shall he think to find a stranger just
160   When he himself himself confounds, betrays
   To sland'rous tongues and wretched hateful days?

Now stole upon the time the dead of night,
When heavy sleep had closed up mortal eyes;
No comfortable star did lend his light,   *reassuring*
No noise but owls' and wolves' death-boding cries;
Now serves the season that they may surprise
   The silly lambs. Pure thoughts are dead and still,   *helpless*
   While lust and murder wake to stain and kill.

And now this lustful lord, leaped from his bed,
170   Throwing his mantle rudely o'er his arm,
Is madly tossed between desire and dread;
Th'one sweetly flatters, th'other feareth harm;
But honest fear, bewitched with lust's foul charm,
   Doth too too oft betake him[15] to retire,
   Beaten away by brain-sick rude desire.

His falchion on a flint he softly smiteth,   *sword*
That from the cold stone sparks of fire do fly,
Whereat a waxen torch forthwith he lighteth,
Which must be lode-star to his lustful eye;   *pole star*
180   And to the flame thus speaks advisedly: *after reflection*
   'As from this cold flint I enforced this fire,
   So Lucrece must I force to my desire.'

Here pale with fear he doth premeditate
The dangers of his loathsome enterprise,
And in his inward mind he doth debate
What following sorrow may on this arise;
Then, looking scornfully, he doth despise

14   The two "selves" in this line refer to Tarquin's "honor" and "lust";   15   "him" refers to "honest fear" and not to Tarquin.
he must sacrifice the one to obtain the other.

His naked armour of still-slaughtered lust,[16]
And justly thus controls his thoughts unjust:

190 'Fair torch, burn out thy light, and lend it not
To darken her whose light excelleth thine;
And die, unhallowed thoughts, before you blot   *wicked*
With your uncleanness that which is divine;
Offer pure incense to so pure a shrine;
   Let fair humanity abhor the deed
   That spots and stains love's modest snow-white weed.   *garment*

'O shame to knighthood and to shining arms!
O foul dishonour to my household's grave!   *family tomb*
O impious act, including all foul harms!   *encompassing*
200 A martial man to be soft fancy's slave!   *infatuation's*
True valour still a true respect should have;
   Then my digression is so vile, so base,   *deviation from honor*
   That it will live engraven in my face.

'Yea though I die, the scandal will survive,
And be an eye-sore in my golden coat;   *coat of arms*
Some loathsome dash the herald will contrive,[17]
To cipher me how fondly I did dote;   *signify*
That my posterity, shamed with the note,   *descendants*
   Shall curse my bones, and hold it for no sin
210   To wish that I their father had not been.

'What win I, if I gain the thing I seek?
A dream, a breath, a froth of fleeting joy.
Who buys a minute's mirth to wail a week?
Or sells eternity to get a toy?
For one sweet grape who will the vine destroy?
   Or what fond beggar, but to touch the crown,   *foolish*
   Would with the sceptre straight be strucken down?

'If Collatinus dream of my intent,
Will he not wake, and in a desp'rate rage
220 Post hither, this vile purpose to prevent? –
This siege that hath engirt his marriage,   *surrounded*
This blur to youth, this sorrow to the sage,   *blemish*
   This dying virtue, this surviving shame,
   Whose crime will bear an ever-during blame.   *everlasting*

'O what excuse can my invention make,
When thou shalt charge me with so black a deed?
Will not my tongue be mute, my frail joints shake,
Mine eyes forgo their light, my false heart bleed?
The guilt being great, the fear doth still exceed;
230   And extreme fear can neither fight nor fly,
   But coward-like with trembling terror die.

'Had Collatinus killed my son or sire,   *father*
Or lain in ambush to betray my life,
Or were he not my dear friend, this desire

---

16 A difficult, paradoxical line: the safest gloss seems to be "His poor defense against his repeatedly sated lust," with the understanding that lust can never be completely "slaughtered."

17 In heraldry, a black bar in a coat of arms indicated that the family lineage had been corrupted somehow; usually it was a sign that there had been illegitimate births in the pedigree.

Might have excuse to work upon his wife,

As in revenge or quittal of such strife;   *payment*

But as he is my kinsman, my dear friend,

The shame and fault finds no excuse nor end.

'Shameful it is – ay, if the fact be known;   *act*

240   Hateful it is – there is no hate in loving;

I'll beg her love – but she is not her own;[18]

The worst is but denial and reproving.

My will is strong, past reason's weak removing. –

Who fears a sentence or an old man's saw[19]

Shall by a painted cloth be kept in awe.'

Thus graceless holds he disputation

'Tween frozen conscience and hot-burning will,

And with good thoughts makes dispensation,   *gives permission*

Urging the worsen sense for vantage still;

250   Which in a moment doth confound and kill

All pure effects, and doth so far proceed   *purposes*

That what is vile shows like a virtuous deed.

Quoth he, 'She took me kindly by the hand,

And gazed for tidings in my eager eyes,

Fearing some hard news from the warlike band,

Where her beloved Collatinus lies.

O how her fear did make her colour rise!

First red as roses that on lawn we lay,   *white linen*

Then white as lawn, the roses took away.

260   'And how her hand, in my hand being locked,

Forced it to tremble with her loyal fear!

Which struck her sad, and then it faster rocked

Until her husband's welfare she did hear;

Whereat she smiled with so sweet a cheer   *expression*

That had Narcissus[20] seen her as she stood

Self-love had never drowned him in the flood.

'Why hunt I then for colour or excuses?   *pretext*

All orators are dumb when beauty pleadeth;

Poor wretches have remorse in poor abuses;[21]

270   Love thrives not in the heart that shadows dreadeth;

Affection is my captain, and he leadeth;   *desire*

And when his gaudy banner is displayed,

The coward fights and will not be dismayed.

'Then, childish fear, avaunt! debating, die!   *begone!*

Respect and reason wait on wrinkled age!

My heart[22] shall never countermand mine eye;

Sad pause and deep regard beseem the sage;   *serious/are appropriate to*

My part is youth, and beats these from the stage:

Desire my pilot is, beauty my prize;

280   Then who fears sinking where such treasure lies?'

---

18   Being married, Lucrece is "not her own" because she is bound to Collatine.

19   A "sentence" in this context means a conventional moral cliché; a "saw" is a proverb or saying. The "painted cloth" of the following line refers to a common kind of wall hanging in Early Modern England.

Biblical or mythological scenes (often with a moral message) were painted on cloths and used as decorations.

20   See gazetteer.

21   i.e. it is low-born men who feel remorse for their petty sins (as opposed to princes like Tarquin).

22   "Heart" in this context meaning "compassion."

As corn o'ergrown by weeds, so heedful fear   *wheat*
Is almost choked by unresisted lust.
Away he steals with open list'ning ear,
Full of foul hope and full of fond mistrust;   *foolish*
Both which, as servitors to the unjust,
   So cross him with their opposite persuasion
   That now he vows a league, and now invasion.   *treaty*

Within his thought her heavenly image sits,
And in the selfsame seat sits Collatine.
290   That eye which looks on her confounds his wits;   *reason*
That eye which him beholds, as more divine,
Unto a view so false will not incline;
   But with a pure appeal seeks to the heart,
   Which once corrupted takes the worser part;

And therein heartens up his servile powers,[23]
Who, flatt'red by their leader's jocund show,   *lively*
Stuff up his lust, as minutes fill up hours;
And as their captain, so their pride doth grow,
Paying more slavish tribute than they owe.
300   By reprobate desire thus madly led,
   The Roman lord marcheth to Lucrece' bed.

The locks between her chamber and his will,
Each one by him enforced, retires his ward;   *withdraws its guard*
But, as they open, they all rate his ill,[24]
Which drives the creeping thief to some regard.
The threshold grates the door to have him heard;
   Night-wand'ring weasels shriek to see him there;
   They fright him, yet he still pursues his fear.

As each unwilling portal yields him way,   *door*
310   Through little vents and crannies of the place
The wind wars with his torch to make him stay,
And blows the smoke of it into his face,
Extinguishing his conduct in this case;   *guide*
   But his hot heart, which fond desire doth scorch,
   Puffs forth another wind that fires the torch;

And being lighted, by the light he spies
Lucretia's glove, wherein her needle sticks;
He takes it from the rushes[25] where it lies,
And griping it, the needle his finger pricks,   *grasping*
320   As who should say 'This glove to wanton tricks
   Is not inured. Return again in haste;   *immune*
   Thou see'st our mistress' ornaments are chaste.'

But all these poor forbiddings could not stay him;   *restrain*
He in the worst sense consters their denial: *construes*
The doors, the wind, the glove, that did delay him,
He takes for accidental things of trial;   *chance events*
Or as those bars which stop the hourly dial,[26]

---

23 "Powers" means "armies" or "troops"; the image is of the heart as the general of his desires.

24 i.e. The locks complain about his crime by squeaking as they open.

25 Rushes were commonly used to cover floors in Early Modern Europe.

26 A reference to the minute marks on the face of a clock.

Who with a ling'ring stay his course doth let,   *Which*
Till every minute pays the hour his debt.

'So, so,' quoth he, 'these lets attend the time,   *delays*
330   Like little frosts that sometime threat the spring,
To add a more rejoicing to the prime,   *spring*
And give the sneaped birds more cause to sing.   *thwarted*
Pain pays the income of each precious thing;   *entrance fee*
    Huge rocks, high winds, strong pirates, shelves and sands
    The merchant fears, ere rich at home he lands.'

Now is he come unto the chamber door
That shuts him from the heaven of his thought,
Which with a yielding latch, and with no more,
340   Hath barred him from the blessed thing be sought.
So from²⁷ himself impiety hath wrought,
    That for his prey to pray he doth begin,
    As if the heavens should countenance his sin.

But in the midst of his unfruitful prayer,
Having solicited th'eternal power
That his foul thoughts might compass his fair fair,²⁸
And they²⁹ would stand auspicious to the hour,
Even there he starts; quoth he 'I must deflower: *is startled*
    The powers to whom I pray abhor this fact;
350   How can they then assist me in the act?

'Then Love and Fortune be my gods, my guide!
My will is backed with resolution.
Thoughts are but dreams till their effects be tried;   *tested*
The blackest sin is clear'd with absolution;
Against love's fire fear's frost hath dissolution.
    The eye of heaven is out, and misty night
    Covers the shame that follows sweet delight.'

This said, his guilty hand plucked up the latch,
And with his knee the door he opens wide.
360   The dove sleeps fast that this night-owl will catch.
Thus treason works ere traitors be espied.
Who sees the lurking serpent steps aside;   *whoever*
    But she, sound sleeping, fearing no such thing,
    Lies at the mercy of his mortal sting.

Into the chamber wickedly he stalks
And gazeth on her yet unstained bed.
The curtains being close, about he walks,
Rolling his greedy eyeballs in his head.
By their high treason is his heart misled,
370   Which gives the watch-word to his hand full soon
    To draw the cloud that hides the silver moon.³⁰

Look as the fair and fiery-pointed sun,   *Just*
Rushing from forth a cloud, bereaves our sight;
Even so, the curtain drawn, his eyes begun
To wink, being blinded with a greater light;   *close*

---

27   i.e. So far from himself.   29   The divine powers.
28   Beautiful fair one.   30   i.e. To draw the curtain surrounding Lucrece's bed.

Whether it is that she reflects so bright
 That dazzleth them, or else some shame supposed,
 But blind they are, and keep themselves enclosed.

O, had they in that darksome prison died!
 Then had they seen the period of their ill;   *end*
Then Collatine again, by Lucrece' side,
In his clear bed might have reposed still;   *undefiled*
But they must ope, this blessed league to kill;   *open*
 And holy-thoughted Lucrece to their sight
 Must sell her joy, her life, her world's delight.

Her lily hand her rosy cheek lies under,
Coz'ning the pillow of a lawful kiss;   *Cheating*
Who, therefore angry, seems to part in sunder.
Swelling on either side to want his bliss;   *to seek after*
Between whose hills her head entombed is;
 Where, like a virtuous monument, she lies,
 To be admired of lewd unhallowed eyes.   *wicked*

Without the bed her other fair hand was,   *Outside*
On the green coverlet; whose perfect white
Showed like an April daisy on the grass,
With pearly sweat resembling dew of night.
Her eyes, like marigolds, had sheathed their light,
 And canopied in darkness sweetly lay,
 Till they might open to adorn the day.

Her hair, like golden threads, played with her breath –
O modest wantons! wanton modesty! –   *children/playful*
Showing life's triumph in the map of death,[31]
And death's dim look in life's mortality:
Each in her sleep themselves so beautify
 As if between them twain there were no strife,
 But that life lived in death and death in life.

Her breasts, like ivory globes circled with blue,[32]
A pair of maiden worlds unconquered,
Save of their lord no bearing yoke they knew,
And him by oath they truly honoured.
These worlds in Tarquin new ambition bred,
 Who like a foul usurper went about
 From this fair throne to heave the owner out.

What could he see but mightily he noted?
What did he note but strongly he desired?
What he beheld, on that he firmly doted,   *was infatuated*
And in his will his wilful eye he tired.   *sated*
With more than admiration he admired
 Her azure veins, her alabaster skin,
 Her coral lips, her snow-white dimpled chin.

As the grim lion fawneth o'er his prey,
Sharp hunger by the conquest satisfied,
So o'er this sleeping soul doth Tarquin stay,   *pause*

31 The "map" of death is its living counterfeit sleep; the subsequent 32 The blue of her veins.
line reverses the polarity of this comparison.

His rage of lust by gazing qualified;   *moderated*
Slacked, not suppressed; for standing by her side,
    His eye, which late this mutiny restrains,   *lately*
    Unto a greater uproar tempts his veins;

And they, like straggling slaves for pillage fighting,[33]
Obdurate vassals fell exploits effecting,   *fierce*
430   In bloody death and ravishment delighting,   *rape*
Nor children's tears nor mothers' groans respecting,
Swell in their pride, the onset still expecting.
    Anon his beating heart, alarum striking,
    Gives the hot charge, and bids them do their liking.

His drumming heart cheers up his burning eye,
His eye commends the leading to his hand;   *entrusts*
His hand, as proud of such a dignity,   *honor*
Smoking with pride, marched on to make his stand
On her bare breast, the heart of all her land;
440   Whose ranks of blue veins as his hand did scale,
        Left their round turrets destitute and pale.

They, must'ring to the quiet cabinet   *assembling/private office*
Where their dear governess and lady lies,
Do tell her she is dreadfully beset,   *surrounded*
And fright her with confusion of their cries.
She, much amazed, breaks ope her locked-up eyes,
    Who, peeping forth this tumult to behold,
    Are by his flaming torch dimmed and controlled.

Imagine her as one in dead of night
450   From forth dull sleep by dreadful fancy waking,
That thinks she hath beheld some ghastly sprite,   *spirit*
Whose grim aspect sets every joint a-shaking;
What terror 'tis! but she, in worser taking,   *capture*
    From sleep disturbed, heedfully doth view
    The sight which makes supposed terror true.   *imagined*

Wrapped and confounded in a thousand fears,   *confused*
Like to a new-killed bird she trembling lies;
She dares not look; yet, winking, there appears   *closing her eyes*
Quick-shifting antics, ugly in her eyes.   *grotesque figures*
460   "Such shadows are the weak brain's forgeries,[34]
        Who, angry that the eyes fly from their lights,[34]
        In darkness daunts them with more dreadful sights.

His hand that yet remains upon her breast –
Rude ram, to batter such an ivory wall! –
May feel her heart, poor citizen, distressed,
Wounding itself to death, rise up and fall,
Beating her bulk, that his hand shakes withal.   *body*
    This moves in him more rage and lesser pity,
    To make the breach and enter this sweet city.

33 This stanza and the one following comprise an extended metaphor   34 i.e. The brain, angry that it cannot see through her closed eyes,
in which parts of Tarquin are compared to elements of an army sacking   generates even more dreadful imaginary horrors than those which beset
a conquered city (Lucrece). His veins are "slaves" (i.e. ordinary soldiers)   her in reality.
fighting for pillage, his heart sounds the charge, etc.

470   First like a trumpet doth his tongue begin
       To sound a parley[35] to his heartless foe,
       Who o'er the white sheet peers her whiter chin,
       The reason of this rash alarm to know,
       Which he by dumb demeanour seeks to show;   *silent acting*
         But she with vehement prayers urgeth still
         Under what colour he commits this ill.   *pretence*

       Thus he replies: The colour in thy face,
       That even for anger makes the lily pale
       And the red rose blush at her own disgrace,
480   Shall plead for me and tell my loving tale.
       Under that colour am I come to scale   *banner*
         Thy never-conquered fort. The fault is thine,
         For those thine eyes betray thee unto mine.

       'Thus I forestall thee, if thou mean to chide: *prevent/rebuke*
       Thy beauty hath ensnared thee to this night,
       Where thou with patience must my will abide,
       My will that marks thee for my earth's delight,
       Which I to conquer sought with all my might;
         But as reproof and reason beat it dead,
490   By thy bright beauty was it newly bred.

       'I see what crosses my attempt will bring;   *annoyances*
       I know what thorns the growing rose defends;
       I think the honey guarded with a sting;
       All this beforehand counsel comprehends.
       But will is deaf and hears no heedful friends;   *watchful*
         Only he hath an eye to gaze on beauty,
         And dotes on what he looks, 'gainst law or duty.

       'I have debated, even in my soul,
       What wrong, what shame, what sorrow I shall breed;
500   But nothing can affection's course control,   *desire's*
       Or stop the headlong fury of his speed.
       I know repentant tears ensue the deed,   *follow*
         Reproach, disdain and deadly enmity;
         Yet strive I to embrace mine infamy.'

       This said, he shakes aloft his Roman blade,
       Which, like a falcon tow'ring in the skies,
       Coucheth the fowl below with his wings shade,   *Makes couch*
       Whose crooked beak threats if he mount he dies.   *flies off*
       So under his insulting falchion lies   *sword*
510   Harmless Lucretia, marking what he tells
         With trembling fear, as fowl hear falcons' bells.[36]

       'Lucrece,' quoth he, 'this night I must enjoy thee.
       If thou deny, then force must work my way,
       For in thy bed I purpose to destroy thee;
       That done, some worthless slave of thine I'll slay,
       To kill thine honour with thy life's decay;
         And in thy dead arms do I mean to place him,
         Swearing I slew him, seeing thee embrace him.

---

35 Continuing the military metaphor of this stanza, a "parley" is a   36 Trained hunting falcons usually had bells tied to their feet.
discussion between two rival armies during a temporary truce.

520

'So thy surviving husband shall remain
The scornful mark of every open eye;   *object*
Thy kinsmen hang their heads at this disdain,
Thy issue blurred with nameless bastardy;   *children*
And thou, the author of their obloquy,   *disgrace*
   Shalt have thy trespass cited up in rhymes
   And sung by children in succeeding times.

'But if thou yield, I rest thy secret friend: *stay*
The fault unknown is as a thought unacted;
"A little harm done to a great good end   *goal*
For lawful policy remains enacted.

530

"The poisonous simple sometime is compacted   *medicine/mixed*
   In a pure compound; being so applied,
   His venom in effect is purified.

'Then, for thy husband and thy children's sake,
Tender my suit; bequeath not to their lot
The shame that from them no device can take,
The blemish that will never be forgot;
Worse than a slavish wipe or birth-hour's blot;   *brand/birthmark*
   For marks descried in men's nativity   *revealed*
   Are nature's faults, not their own infamy.'

540

Here with a cockatrice' dead-killing eye
He rouseth up himself, and makes a pause;
While she, the picture of pure piety,
Like a white hind under the gripe's sharp claws,   *vulture*
Pleads in a wilderness where are no laws
   To the rough beast that knows no gentle right,
   Nor aught obeys but his foul appetite.   *anything*

But when a black-faced cloud the world doth threat,
In his dim mist th'aspiring mountains hiding,
From earth's dark womb some gentle gust doth get,   *is born*

550

Which blows these pitchy vapours from their biding,   *resting place*
Hind'ring their present fall by this dividing;   *rainfall*
   So his unhallowed haste her words delays,
   And moody Pluto winks while Orpheus plays.[37]

Yet, foul night-waking cat, he doth but dally,   *play*
While in his hold-fast foot the weak mouse panteth;
Her sad behaviour feeds his vulture folly,[38]   *serious*
A swallowing gulf that even in plenty wanteth;
His ear her prayers admits, but his heart granteth
   No penetrable entrance to her plaining.   *pleading*

560

   "Tears harden lust, though marble wear with raining.

Her pity-pleading eyes are sadly fixed
In the remorseless wrinkles of his face;   *frowns*
Her modest eloquence with sighs is mixed,
Which to her oratory adds more grace.
She puts the period often from his place,[39]

---

37   See the Orpheus entry in the gazetteer.
38   "Vulture folly" suggests something like "predatory madness"; the next line confirms this madness by stating that Tarquin's desire craves more even as it given what it wants.

39   This line and the two which follow describe Lucrece, in her distress, speaking in phrases and fragments rather than proper sentences.

And midst the sentence so her accent breaks
That twice she doth begin ere once she speaks.

She conjures him by high almighty Jove,
By knighthood, gentry, and sweet friendship's oath,
570   By her untimely tears, her husband's love,
By holy human law, and common troth,   *honesty*
By heaven and earth, and all the power of both,
   That to his borrowed bed he make retire,
   And stoop to honour, not to foul desire.   *submit*

Quoth she: 'Reward not hospitality
With such black payment as thou hast pretended;   *proposed*
Mud not the fountain that gave drink to thee;
Mar not the thing that cannot be amended;   *rectified*
End thy ill aim before thy shoot be ended.
580   He is no woodman that doth bend his bow
   To strike a poor unseasonable doe.   *out of season*

'My husband is thy friend – for his sake spare me;
Thyself art mighty – for thine own sake leave me;
Myself a weakling – do not then ensnare me;
Thou look'st not like deceit – do not deceive me.
My sighs like whirlwinds labour hence to heave thee.   *remove*
   If ever man were moved with woman's moans,
   Be moved with my tears, my sighs, my groans;

'All which together, like a troubled ocean,
590   Beat at thy rocky and wrack-threat'ning heart,   *destruction*
To soften it with their continual motion;
For stones dissolved to water do convert.
O, if no harder than a stone thou art,
   Melt at my tears, and be compassionate!
   Soft pity enters at an iron gate.

'In Tarquin's likeness I did entertain thee;
Hast thou[40] put on his shape to do him shame?
To all the host of heaven I complain me
Thou wrong'st his honour, wound'st his princely name.
600   Thou art not what thou seem'st; and if the same,
   Thou seem'st not what thou art, a god, a king;
   For kings like gods should govern everything.

'How will thy shame be seeded in thine age,   *ripened*
When thus thy vices bud before thy spring?
If in thy hope[41] thou dar'st do such outrage,
What dar'st thou not when once thou art a king?
O, be rememb'red, no outrageous thing
   From vassal actors can be wiped away;   *servant*
   Then kings' misdeeds cannot be hid in clay.   *death*

610   'This deed will make thee only loved for fear,
But happy monarchs still are feared for love;
With foul offenders thou perforce must bear,   *of necessity*
When they in thee the like offences prove.   *demonstrate*

---

40 Following from the previous line, Lucrece is implying that the real   41 The "hope" here is the kingdom that Tarquin stands to inherit.
Tarquin would never commit such a crime.

If but for fear of this, thy will remove;
 For princes are the glass, the school, the book,   *mirror*
 Where subjects' eyes do learn, do read, do look.

'And wilt thou be the school where Lust shall learn?
Must he in thee read lectures of such shame?
Wilt thou be glass wherein it shall discern
620 Authority for sin, warrant for blame,
To privilege dishonour in thy name?
 Thou back'st reproach against long-living laud,   *praise*
 And mak'st fair reputation but a bawd.   *pimp*

'Hast thou command? by him that gave it thee,
From a pure heart command thy rebel will;
Draw not thy sword to guard iniquity,
For it was lent thee all that brood to kill.   *i.e. criminals*
Thy princely office how canst thou fulfil,
630 When patterned by thy fault, foul sin may say
  He learned to sin, and thou didst teach the way?

'Think but how vile a spectacle it were
To view thy present trespass in another.
Men's faults do seldom to themselves appear;
Their own transgressions partially[42] they smother;
This guilt would seem death-worthy in thy brother.
 O, how are they wrapped in with infamies
 That from their own misdeeds askance their eyes!   *avert*

'To thee, to thee, my heaved-up hands appeal,
Not to seducing lust, thy rash relier;[43]
640 I sue for exiled majesty's repeal;
Let him return, and flatt'ring thoughts retire.
His true respect will prison false desire,
 And wipe the dim mist from thy doting eyne,   *eyes*
 That thou shalt see thy state and pity mine.'

'Have done,' quoth he, my uncontrolled tide
Turns not, but swells the higher by this let.   *delay*
Small lights are soon blown out, huge fires abide,
And with the wind in greater fury fret.   *destroy*
The petty streams[44] that pay a daily debt
650 To their salt sovereign, with their fresh falls' haste
  Add to his flow, but alter not his taste.'

'Thou art,' quoth she, 'a sea, a sovereign king;
And, lo, there falls into thy boundless flood
Black lust, dishonour, shame, misgoverning,
Who seek to stain the ocean of thy blood.
If all these petty ills shall change thy good,
 Thy sea within a puddle's womb is hearsed,   *entombed*
 And not the puddle in thy sea dispersed.

'So shall these slaves be king, and thou their slave;
660 Thou nobly base, they basely dignified;

42 Showing partiality to themselves.
43 i.e. On which you rashly rely. When Lucrece sues for "majesty's repeal" in the next line, it is to take its rightful in place of lust.

44 The image compares Lucrece's complaints to small streams that flow to the sea: their water may be fresh, but the sea is still salty. Her complaints will likewise have no effect.

Thou their fair life, and they thy fouler grave;
Thou loathed in their shame, they in thy pride.
The lesser thing should not the greater hide;
    The cedar stoops not to the base shrub's foot,
    But low shrubs wither at the cedar's root.

'So let thy thoughts, low vassals to thy state' –
No more,' quoth he; 'by heaven, I will not hear thee.
Yield to my love; if not, enforced hate,
Instead of love's coy touch, shall rudely tear thee;
670   That done, despitefully I mean to bear thee   *maliciously*
    Unto the base bed of some rascal groom,   *low-born*
    To be thy partner in this shameful doom.'

This said, he sets his foot upon the light,
For light and lust are deadly enemies;
Shame folded up in blind concealing night,
When most unseen, then most doth tyrannize.
The wolf hath seized his prey, the poor lamb cries,
    Till with her own white fleece her voice controlled   *linen/overpowered*
    Entombs her outcry in her lips' sweet fold;

680   For with the nightly linen that she wears
He pens her piteous clamours in her head,   *traps*
Cooling his hot face in the chastest tears
That ever modest eyes with sorrow shed.
O, that prone lust should stain so pure a bed!   *eager*
    The spots whereof could weeping purify,
    Her tears should drop on them perpetually.[45]

But she hath lost a dearer thing than life,
And he hath won what he would lose again.
This forced league doth force a further strife;
690   This momentary joy breeds months of pain;
This hot desire converts to cold disdain;
    Pure Chastity is rifled of her store,   *robbed*
    And Lust, the thief, far poorer than before.

Look as the full-fed hound or gorged hawk,   *Just*
Unapt for tender smell or speedy flight,   *weak scent*
Make slow pursuit, or altogether balk   *refuse*
The prey wherein by nature they delight,
So surfeit-taking Tarquin fares this night:
    His taste delicious, in digestion souring,
700   Devours his will, that lived by foul devouring.

O, deeper sin than bottomless conceit   *thought*
Can comprehend in still imagination!
Drunken Desire must vomit his receipt,[46]
Ere he can see his own abomination.   *Before*
While Lust is in his pride, no exclamation
    Can curb his heat or rein his rash desire,
    Till, like a jade, Self-will himself doth tire.   *worthless horse*

45 i.e. If tears could wash away the stigma of rape, Lucrece would cry   46 i.e. Uncontrolled desire will inevitably spurn what it wants when
perpetually.   it achieves it.

And then with lank and lean discoloured cheek,
With heavy eye, knit brow, and strengthless pace,
710   Feeble Desire, all recreant, poor and meek,   *cowardly*
Like to a bankrupt beggar wails his case:
The flesh being proud, Desire doth fight with Grace,
  For there it revels, and when that decays
  The guilty rebel for remission prays.   *forgiveness*

So fares it with this faultful lord of Rome,
Who this accomplishment so hotly chased;
For now against himself he sounds this doom,   *judgment*
That through the length of times he stands disgraced;
Besides, his soul's fair temple is defaced,
720   To whose weak ruins muster troops of cares,
  To ask the spotted princess how she fares.   *polluted*

She⁴⁷ says her subjects with foul insurrection   *rebellion*
Have battered down her consecrated wall,
And by their mortal fault brought in subjection
Her immortality, and made her thrall
To living death and pain perpetual;⁴⁸
  Which in her prescience she controlled still,   *foreknowledge*
  But her foresight could not forestall their will.

Ev'n in this thought through the dark night he stealeth,
730   A captive victor that hath lost in gain;
Bearing away the wound that nothing healeth,
The scar that will, despite of cure, remain;
Leaving his spoil perplex'd in greater pain,   *victim*
  She bears the load of lust he left behind,
  And he the burden of a guilty mind.

He like a thievish dog creeps sadly thence;
She like a wearied lamb lies panting there;
He scowls, and hates himself for his offence;
She, desperate, with her nails her flesh doth tear;
740   He faintly flies, sweating with guilty fear;
  She stays, exclaiming on the direful night;   *crying out*
  He runs, and chides his vanished, loathed delight.   *rebukes*

He thence departs a heavy convertite;   *sad penitent*
She there remains a hopeless castaway;
He in his speed looks for the morning light;
She prays she never may behold the day.
'For day,' quoth she, 'night's scapes doth open lay,   *transgressions*
  And my true eyes have never practised how
  To cloak offences with a cunning brow.   *false expression*

750   'They think not but that every eye can see
The same disgrace which they themselves behold;
And therefore would they still in darkness be,
To have their unseen sin remain untold;
For they their guilt with weeping will unfold,   *reveal*
  And grave, like water that doth eat in steel,   *engrave*
  Upon my cheeks what helpless shame I feel.'

47   Tarquin's soul.   48   The sins committed by Tarquin's passions have exposed his soul to
eternal damnation.

Here she exclaims against repose and rest,
And bids her eyes hereafter still be blind.   *forever*
She wakes her heart by beating on her breast,
760   And bids it leap from thence, where it may find
Some purer chest to close so pure a mind.
   Frantic with grief thus breathes she forth her spite
   Against the unseen secrecy of night:

'O comfort-killing Night, image of hell!
Dim register and notary of shame!   *keeper of records*
Black stage for tragedies and murders fell!
Vast sin-concealing chaos! nurse of blame!   *fault*
Blind muffled bawd! dark harbour for defame!   *disgrace*
   Grim cave of death! Whisp'ring conspirator
770   With close-tongued treason and the ravisher!

'O hateful, vaporous and foggy Night!
Since thou art guilty of my cureless crime,
Muster thy mists to meet the eastern light,
Make war against proportioned course of time;
Or if thou wilt permit the sun to climb
   His wonted height, yet ere he go to bed,   *accustomed*
   Knit poisonous clouds about his golden head.

'With rotten damps ravish the morning air;
Let their exhaled unwholesome breaths make sick
780   The life of purity, the supreme fair,[49]
Ere he arrive his weary noon-tide prick;
And let thy misty vapours march so thick
   That in their smoky ranks his smoth'red light
   May set at noon and make perpetual night.

'Were Tarquin Night, as he is but Night's child,
The silver-shining queen[50] he would distain;   *dim*
Her twinkling handmaids too, by him defiled,
Through Night's black bosom should not peep again;
So should I have, co-partners in my pain;
790   And fellowship in woe doth woe assuage,
   As palmers' chat makes short their pilgrimage.   *pilgrims'*

'Where now I have no one to blush with me,
To cross their arms and hang their heads with mine,[51]
To mask their brows and hide their infamy;
But I alone alone must sit and pine,
Seasoning the earth with show'rs of silver brine,
   Mingling my talk with tears, my grief with groans,
   Poor wasting monuments of lasting moans.

'O Night, thou furnace of foul-reeking smoke,
800   Let not the Jealous Day behold that face
Which underneath thy black all-hiding cloak
Immodestly lies martyred with disgrace!
Keep still possession of thy gloomy place,

49   The "supreme fair" is the sun, and the "noontide prick" in the fol-   50   The "queen" in this stanza is the moon, and her "handmaids" are
lowing line refers to the mark on a sundial which indicated twelve   the stars.
o'clock.   51   The bodily gestures of the next two lines are all signs of melan-
                                                                             choly and sadness.

That all the faults which in thy reign are made
May likewise be sepulchred in thy shade!

'Make me not object to the tell-tale Day.
The light will show, charactered in my brow,   *written*
The story of sweet chastity's decay,   *dissolution*
The impious breach of holy wedlock vow;
810   Yea, the illiterate, that know not how
To cipher what is writ in learned books,   *interpret*
Will quote my loathsome trespass in my looks.   *observe*

'The nurse, to still her child, will tell my story,
And fright her crying babe with Tarquin's name;
The orator, to deck his oratory,   *decorate*
Will couple my reproach to Tarquin's shame;
Feast-finding minstrels,[52] tuning my defame,
Will tie the hearers to attend each line,
How Tarquin wronged me, I Collatine.

820   'Let my good name, that senseless reputation,
For Collatine's dear love be kept unspotted;
If that be made a theme for disputation,   *academic debate*
The branches of another root[53] are rotted,
And undeserved reproach to him allotted
That is as clear from this attaint of mine   *imputation of dishonor*
As I ere this was pure to Collatine.

'O unseen shame! invisible disgrace!
O unfelt sore! crest-wounding,[54] private scar!
Reproach is stamped in Collatinus' face,
830   And Tarquin's eye may read the mot afar,   *motto*
"How he in peace is wounded, not in war.
"Alas, how many bear such shameful blows,
Which not themselves, but he that gives them knows!

'If, Collatine, thine honour lay in me,
From me by strong assault it is bereft.
My honey lost, and I, a drone-like bee,
Have no perfection[55] of my summer left,
But robbed and ransacked by injurious theft.
In thy weak hive a wand'ring wasp hath crept,
840   And sucked the honey which thy chaste bee kept.

'Yet am I guilty of thy honour's wrack;   *destruction*
Yet for thy honour did I entertain him;
Coming from thee, I could not put him back,
For it had been dishonour to disdain him;
Besides, of weariness he did complain him,
And talked of virtue: O unlooked-for evil,
When virtue is profaned in such a devil!

52 Minstrels were often hired to play at banquets in Early Modern
Europe.
53 i.e. Collatine.
54 In keeping with the heraldic motif that the poem uses, this adjective refers to the crest of a family's coat of arms and implies damage to
the reputation of a noble family.

55 "Perfection" in this case means "maturity" or "full growth" and
refers to the "honey" (Lucrece's honor) that she has conserved so
carefully until now.

'Why should the worm intrude the maiden bud?
Or hateful cuckoos hatch in sparrows' nests?
850   Or toads infect fair founts with venom mud?
Or tyrant folly lurk in gentle breasts?   *madness*
Or kings be breakers of their own behests?   *orders*
    "But no perfection is so absolute
    That some impurity doth not pollute.

'The aged man that coffers up his gold
Is plagued with cramps and gouts and painful fits,
And scarce hath eyes his treasure to behold,
But like still-pining Tantalus[56] he sits,
And useless barns the harvest of his wits,   *stores*
860   Having no other pleasure of his gain
    But torment that it cannot cure his pain.

'So then he hath it when he cannot use it,
And leaves it to be mast'red by his young;
Who in their pride do presently abuse it.   *immediately*
Their father was too weak, and they too strong,
To hold their cursed-blessed fortune long.
    "The sweets we wish for turn to loathed sours
    "Even in the moment that we call them ours.

'Unruly blasts wait on the tender spring;   *winds*
870   Unwholesome weeds take root with precious flowers:
The adder hisses where the sweet birds sing;
What virtue breeds, iniquity devours.
We have no good that we can say is ours
    But ill-annexed Opportunity   *evilly added*
    Or kills his life or else his quality.[57]

'O Opportunity, thy guilt is great!
'Tis thou that executest the traitor's treason;
Thou set'st the wolf where he the lamb may get;
Whoever plots the sin, thou point'st the season;   *appoints*
880   'Tis thou that spurn'st at right, at law, at reason;   *spurns*
    And in thy shady cell, where none may spy him,
    Sits Sin, to seize the souls that wander by him.

'Thou mak'st the vestal violate her oath;   *vestal virgin*
Thou blow'st the fire when temperance is thawed;   *moderation*
Thou smother'st honesty, thou murd'rest troth;
Thou foul abettor! thou notorious bawd!   *accomplice/pimp*
Thou plantest scandal and displacest laud.   *praise*
    Thou ravisher, thou traitor, thou false thief,
    Thy honey turns to gall, thy joy to grief!

890   'Thy secret pleasure turns to open shame,
Thy private feasting to a public fast,
Thy smoothing titles to a ragged name,   *imperfect*
Thy sugared tongue to bitter wormwood taste;
Thy violent vanities can never last.
    How comes it then, vile Opportunity,
    Being so bad, such numbers seek for thee?

---

56 See gazetteer.
57 "His life" here refers to the "good" from two lines before: Opportunity destroys either a good thing, or the quality in something that makes it good. The "or . . . or . . ." is a common Early Modern version of "Either . . . or . . ."

'When wilt thou be the humble suppliant's friend,
And bring him where his suit may be obtained?   *legal action*
When wilt thou sort an hour great strifes to end?
900   Or free that soul which wretchedness hath chained?
Give physic to the sick, ease to the pained?
　　The poor, lame, blind, halt, creep, cry out for thee;
　　But they ne'er meet with Opportunity.

'The patient dies while the physician sleeps;
The orphan pines while the oppressor feeds;   *goes hungry*
Justice is feasting while the widow weeps;
Advice is sporting while infection breeds;   *Doctor's advice*
Thou grant'st no time for charitable deeds;
　　Wrath, envy, treason, rape, and murder's rages,
910   　　Thy heinous hours wait on them as their pages.   *page-boys*

'When Truth and Virtue have to do with thee,
A thousand crosses keep them from thy aid;   *delays*
They buy thy help, but Sin ne'er gives a fee;
He gratis comes, and thou art well apaid   *contented*
As well to hear as grant what he hath said.
　　My Collatine would else have come to me
　　When Tarquin did, but he was stayed by thee.

'Guilty thou art of murder and of theft,
Guilty of perjury and subornation,   *i.e. encouraging crime in others*
920   Guilty of treason, forgery and shift,   *deceit*
Guilty of incest, that abomination;
An accessory by thine inclination
　　To all sins past and all that are to come,
　　From the creation to the general doom.   *Last Judgment*

'Misshapen Time, copesmate of ugly Night,   *companion*
Swift subtle post, carrier of grisly care,   *courier*
Eater of youth, false slave to false delight,
Base watch of woes, sin's pack-horse, virtue's snare;   *watchman*
Thou nursest all and murd'rest all that are.
930   　　O, hear me then, injurious, shifting Time!   *deceitful*
　　Be guilty of my death, since of my crime.

'Why hath thy servant Opportunity
Betrayed the hours thou gavest me to repose,
Cancelled my fortunes and enchained me
To endless date of never-ending woes?   *duration*
Time's office is to fine the hate of foes,   *finish*
　　To eat up errors by opinion bred,
　　Not spend the dowry of a lawful bed.

'Time's glory is to calm contending kings,
940   To unmask falsehood and bring truth to light,
To stamp the seal of time in aged things,
To wake the morn and sentinel the night,   *stand guard over*
To wrong the wronger till he render right,
　　To ruinate proud buildings with thy hours
　　And smear with dust their glitt'ring golden towers;

'To fill with worm-holes stately monuments,
To feed oblivion with decay of things,

To blot old books and alter their contents,   *efface*
To pluck the quills from ancient ravens' wings,[58]
950   To dry the old oak's sap and cherish springs,   *young plants*
   To spoil antiquities of hammered steel
   And turn the giddy round of Fortune's wheel;[59]

To show the beldam daughters of her daughter,   *grandmother*
To make the child a man, the man a child,
To slay the tiger that doth live by slaughter,
To tame the unicorn and lion wild,
To mock the subtle in themselves beguiled,   *wily*
   To cheer the ploughman with increaseful crops,
   And waste huge stones with little water-drops.

960   'Why work'st thou mischief in thy pilgrimage,
Unless thou couldst return to make amends?
One poor retiring minute in an age[60]
Would purchase thee a thousand thousand friends,
Lending him[61] wit that to bad debtors lends.
   O, this dread night, wouldst thou one hour come back,
   I could prevent this storm and shun thy wrack!   *anticipate*

'Thou ceaseless lackey to eternity,
With some mischance cross Tarquin in his flight;   *hinder*
Devise extremes beyond extremity,
970   To make him curse this cursed crimeful night;
Let ghastly shadows his lewd eyes affright,
   And the dire thought of his committed evil
   Shape every bush a hideous shapeless devil.

'Disturb his hours of rest with restless trances,   *states of dread*
Afflict him in his bed with bedrid groans;   *bedridden*
Let there bechance him pitiful mischances,
To make him moan, but pity not his moans.
Stone him with hard'ned hearts, harder than stones;
   And let mild women to him lose their mildness,
980   Wilder to him than tigers in their wildness.

'Let him have time to tear his curled hair,
Let him have time against himself to rave,
Let him have time of time's help to despair,
Let him have time to live a loathed slave,
Let him have time a beggar's orts to crave,   *scraps of food*
   And time to see one that by alms doth live
   Disdain to him disdained scraps to give.[62]

'Let him have time to see his friends his foes,
And merry fools to mock at him resort;   *frequent*
990   Let him have time to mark how slow time goes
In time of sorrow, and how swift and short
His time of folly and his time of sport;

---

58   Ravens were popularly believed to live much longer lives than human beings in Early Modern England.

59   Fortune is the female personification of the unpredictability of human life. She was usually represented with a wheel that could lift individuals up to the heights of worldly success, but just as easily bring them down to disgrace and ruin.

60   i.e. One minute that could be recalled, so that some human action could be changed.

61   i.e. A moneylender.

62   i.e. Let someone who lives by the charity of others (alms) refuse to give him food that even a beggar would not eat.

And ever let his unrecalling crime   *unable to be recalled*
Have time to wail th'abusing of his time.

'O Time, thou tutor both to good and bad,
Teach me to curse him that thou taught'st this ill!   *to whom*
At his own shadow let the thief run mad,
Himself himself seek every hour to kill!
Such wretched hands such wretched blood should spill;
1000   For who so base would such an office have
              As sland'rous deathsman to so base a slave?   *disreputable executioner*

'The baser is he, coming from a king,
To shame his hope[63] with deeds degenerate.
The mightier man, the mightier is the thing
That makes him honoured, or begets him hate;
For greatest scandal waits on greatest state.   *social position*
    The moon being clouded presently is missed,   *immediately*
    But little stars may hide them when they list.   *wish*

'The crow may bathe his coal-black wings in mire
1010   And unperceived fly with the filth away;
But if the like the snow-white swan desire,
The stain upon his silver down will stay.
Poor grooms are sightless night, kings glorious day.   *servants*
    Gnats are unnoted wheresoe'er they fly,
    But eagles gazed upon with every eye.

'Out, idle words, servants to shallow fools!
Unprofitable sounds, weak arbitrators!
Busy yourselves in skill-contending schools;   *universities*
Debate where leisure serves with dull debaters;
1020   To trembling clients be you mediators.   *lawyer's clients*
    For me, I force not argument a straw,   *care*
    Since that my case is past the help of law.

'In vain I rail at Opportunity,
At Time, at Tarquin, and uncheerful Night;
In vain I cavil with mine infamy,
In vain I spurn at my confirmed despite: *object to*
This helpless smoke of words doth me no right.   *reject/shameful injury*
    The remedy indeed to do me good
    Is to let forth my foul-defiled blood.

1030   'Poor hand, why quiver'st thou at this decree?
Honour thyself to rid me of this shame;
For if I die, my honour lives in thee,
But if I live, thou livest in my defame.   *shame*
Since thou couldst not defend thy loyal dame
    And wast afeard to scratch her wicked foe,
    Kill both thyself and her for yielding so.'

This said, from her betumbled couch she starteth,   *disorderly*
To find some desp'rate instrument of death.
But this no slaughterhouse no tool imparteth[64]
1040   To make more vent for passage of her breath,
Which, thronging through her lips, so vanisheth

---

63   See note 41 above.   64   The line implies "*being* no slaughterhouse ..."

As smoke from Etna, that in air consumes,   *dissolves*
Or that which from discharged cannon fumes.

'In vain,' quoth she, 'I live, and seek in vain
Some happy mean to end a hapless life.   *unlucky*
I feared by Tarquin's falchion to be slain,
Yet for the self-same purpose seek a knife;
But when I feared I was a loyal wife;
   So am I now – O no, that cannot be;
1050   Of that true type hath Tarquin rifled me.   *symbolic value/robbed*

'O, that is gone for which I sought to live,
And therefore now I need not fear to die.
To clear this spot by death, at least I give   *stain*
A badge of fame to slander's livery,   *noble servant's uniform*
A dying life to living infamy.
   Poor helpless help, the treasure stol'n away,
   To burn the guiltless casket where it lay!

'Well, well, dear Collatine, thou shalt not know
The stained taste of violated troth;
1060 I will not wrong thy true affection so,
To flatter thee with an infringed oath;
This bastard graff shall never come to growth;   *graff*
   He shall not boast who did thy stock pollute
   That thou art doting father of his fruit.

'Nor shall he smile at thee in secret thought,
Nor laugh with his companions at thy state;
But thou shalt know thy int'rest was not bought   *property*
Basely with gold, but stol'n from forth thy gate.
For me, I am the mistress of my fate,
1070   And with my trespass never will dispense,   *pardon*
   Till life to death acquit my forced offence.   *discharge*

'I will not poison thee with my attaint,   *taint*
Nor fold my fault in cleanly-coined excuses;   *counterfeited*
My sable ground[65] of sin I will not paint
To hide the truth of this false night's abuses.
My tongue shall utter all; mine eyes, like sluices,
   As from a mountain-spring that feeds a dale,
   Shall gush pure streams to purge my impure tale.'

By this, lamenting Philomel[66] had ended
1080 The well-tuned warble of her nightly sorrow,
And solemn night with slow sad gait descended
To ugly hell; when lo, the blushing morrow
Lends light to all fair eyes that light will borrow;   *use*
   But cloudy Lucrece shames herself to see,   *is ashamed*
   And therefore still in night would cloist'red be.

Revealing day through every cranny spies,
And seems to point her out where she sits weeping;
To whom she sobbing speaks: 'O eye of eyes,
Why pry'st thou through my window? leave thy peeping;

---

65 A black background to a heraldic device, and another of the   66 See gazetteer under Philomela.
common references to heraldry and coats of arms in this poem.

1090   Mock with thy tickling beams eyes that are sleeping;
             Brand not my forehead with thy piercing light,
             For day hath nought to do what's done by night.'   *to do with*

          Thus cavils she with every thing she sees.
          True grief is fond and testy as a child,   *foolish*
          Who wayward once, his mood with nought agrees.[67]
          Old woes, not infant sorrows, bear them mild;   *themselves*
          Continuance tames the one; the other wild,
             Like an unpractised swimmer plunging still
             With too much labour drowns for want of skill.

1100   So she, deep-drenched in a sea of care,
          Holds disputation with each thing she views,
          And to herself all sorrow doth compare;
          No object but her passion's strength renews,
          And as one shifts, another straight ensues.   *moves/straight away*
             Sometime her grief is dumb and hath no words;
             Sometime 'tis mad and too much talk affords.

          The little birds that tune their morning's joy
          Make her moans mad with their sweet melody;
          "For mirth doth search the bottom of annoy;   *explore the limit*
1110   "Sad souls are slain in merry company;
          "Grief best is pleased with grief's society.
             True sorrow then is feelingly sufficed   *appropriately satisfied*
             When with like semblance it is sympathized.   *harmonized*

          "'Tis double death to drown in ken of shore;   *sight*
          "He ten times pines that pines beholding food;
          "To see the salve doth make the wound ache more;   *medicine*
          "Great grief grieves most at that would do it good;   *which would*
          "Deep woes roll forward like a gentle flood,
             Who, being stopped, the bounding banks o'erflows;
1120   Grief dallied with nor law nor limit knows.[68]

          'You mocking-birds,' quoth she, 'your tunes entomb
          Within your hollow-swelling feathered breasts,
          And in my hearing be you mute and dumb.
          My restless discord loves no stops nor rests;[69]
          "A woeful hostess brooks not merry guests.   *tolerates*
             Relish your nimble notes to pleasing ears;   *Make pleasant*
             "Distress likes dumps when time is kept with tears.   *dejection*

          'Come, Philomel, that sing'st of ravishment,
          Make thy sad grove in my dishevelled hair.
1130   As the dank earth weeps at thy languishment,
          So I at each sad strain will strain a tear,   *melody*
          And with deep groans the diapason bear;   *harmony*
             For burden-wise I'll hum on Tarquin still,   *bass accompaniment*
             While thou on Tereus descants better skill.   *sings harmoniously with*

          'And whiles against a thorn thou bear'st thy part
          To keep thy sharp woes waking, wretched I,

---

67   i.e. Once it has become angry, grief agrees with nothing.
68   In keeping with note 57 above, "nor . . . nor . . ." means "neither
. . . nor . . ."

69   Shakespeare is punning on musical stops and rests, which the bird's
harmony introduces into Lucrece's "restless discord."

To imitate thee well, against my heart
Will fix a sharp knife to affright mine eye;
Who, if it wink, shall thereon fall and die.[70]
1140   These means, as frets[71] upon an instrument,
    Shall tune our heart-strings to true languishment.

'And for, poor bird, thou sing'st not in the day,[72]
As shaming any eye should thee behold,   *As if being ashamed*
Some dark deep desert, seated from the way,   *wilderness/located*
That knows not parching heat nor freezing cold,
Will we find out; and there we will unfold
    To creatures stern sad tunes, to change their kinds.   *natural dispositions*
    Since men prove beasts, let beasts bear gentle minds.'

As the poor frighted deer, that stands at gaze,   *gazing*
1150 Wildly determining which way to fly,
Or one encompassed with a winding maze
That cannot tread the way out readily;
So with herself is she in mutiny,
    To live or die which of the twain were better,
    When life is shamed and death reproach's debtor.[73]

'To kill myself,' quoth she, 'alack, what were it,
But with my body my poor soul's pollution?[74]
They that lose half with greater patience bear it
Than they whose whole is swallowed in confusion.   *ruin*
1160 That mother tries a merciless conclusion   *experiment*
    Who, having two sweet babes, when death takes one,
    Will slay the other and be nurse to none.

'My body or my soul, which was the dearer,
When the one pure, the other made divine?
Whose love of either to myself was nearer,
When both were kept for heaven and Collatine?
Ay me! the bark pilled from the lofty pine,   *peeled*
    His leaves will wither and his sap decay;
    So must my soul, her bark being pilled away.

1170 'Her house is sacked, her quiet interrupted,
Her mansion battered by the enemy;
Her sacred temple spotted, spoiled, corrupted,
Grossly engirt with daring infamy;   *encircled*
Then let it not be called impiety
    If in this blemished fort I make some hole
    Through which I may convey this troubled soul.   *release*

'Yet die I will not till my Collatine
Have heard the cause of my untimely death,
That he may vow, in that sad hour of mine,
1180 Revenge on him that made me stop my breath.
My stained blood to Tarquin I'll bequeath,
    Which by him tainted shall for him be spent,
    And as his due writ in my testament.   *will*

---

70 The line is ambiguous, but seems to mean "Which, if my eye closes, shall fall upon the knife and die."
71 The bars on the fingerboard of a stringed instrument.
72 It was believed at the time that nightingales sang only at night.

73 The last part of the line gives a reason not to commit suicide: it would incur reproach, since it is a sin.
74 Following her debate about suicide, she considers that it would infect her soul with the pollution that taints her body.

'My honour I'll bequeath unto the knife
That wounds my body so dishonoured.
'Tis honour to deprive dishonoured life;
The one will live, the other being dead.
So of shame's ashes shall my fame be bred;
 For in my death I murder shameful scorn.
1190 My shame so dead, mine honour is new born.

'Dear lord of that dear jewel I have lost,
What legacy shall I bequeath to thee?
My resolution, love, shall be thy boast,
By whose example thou revenged mayest be.
How Tarquin must be used, read it in me: *treated*
 Myself, thy friend, will kill myself, thy foe,
 And, for my sake, serve thou false Tarquin so.

'This brief abridgement of my will I make:
My soul and body to the skies and ground;
1200 My resolution, husband, do thou take;
Mine honour be the knife's that makes my wound;
My shame be his that did my fame confound;   *ruin*
 And all my fame that lives disbursed be   *paid out*
 To those that live and think no shame of me.

'Thou, Collatine, shalt oversee this will;
How was I overseen that thou shalt see it!   *neglected*
My blood shall wash the slander of mine ill;
My life's foul deed, my life's fair end shall free it.
Faint not, faint heart, but stoutly say "So be it".
1210 Yield to my hand; my hand shall conquer thee;
 Thou dead, both die and both shall victors be.'

This plot of death when sadly she had laid,
And wiped the brinish pearl from her bright eyes,
With untuned tongue she hoarsely calls her maid,
Whose swift obedience to her mistress hies;
"For fleet-winged duty with thought's feathers flies.
 Poor Lucrece' cheeks unto her maid seem so
 As winter meads when sun doth melt their snow.

Her mistress she doth give demure good-morrow *grave*
1220 With soft slow tongue, true mark of modesty,
And sorts a sad look to her lady's sorrow,   *adopts*
For why her face wore sorrow's livery,   *Because*
But durst not ask of her audaciously
 Why her two suns were cloud-eclipsed so,
 Nor why her fair cheeks over-washed with woe.

But as the earth doth weep, the sun being set,
Each flower moist'ned like a melting eye,
Even so the maid with swelling drops 'gan wet
Her circled eyne, enforced by sympathy   *rounded eyes*
1230 Of those fair suns set in her mistress' sky,
 Who in a salt-waved ocean quench their light,
 Which makes the maid weep like the dewy night.

A pretty while these pretty creatures stand,   *long*
Like ivory conduits coral cisterns filling.[75]
One justly weeps; the other takes in hand
No cause but company of her drops spilling:
Their gentle sex to weep are often willing,
  Grieving themselves to guess at others' smarts,   *griefs*
  And then they drown their eyes or break their hearts.

1240 For men have marble, women waxen, minds,
And therefore are they formed as marble will;   *wants*
The weak oppressed, th'impression of strange kinds *others' dispositions*
Is formed in them by force, by fraud, or skill.
Then call them not the authors of their ill,
  No more than wax shall be accounted evil
  Wherein is stamped the semblance of a devil.

Their smoothness, like a goodly champaign plain,   *level*
Lays open all the little worms that creep;   *Exposes*
In men, as in a rough-grown grove, remain
1250 Cave-keeping evils that obscurely sleep.   *dwelling/secretly*
Through crystal walls each little mote will peep.
  Though men can cover crimes with bold stern looks,
  Poor women's faces are their own faults' books.

No man inveigh against the withered flower,
But chide rough winter that the flower hath killed.
Not that devoured, but that which doth devour,
Is worthy blame. O, let it not be hild   *held*
Poor women's faults that they are so fulfilled   *filled up*
  With men's abuses: those proud lords to blame,
1260 Make weak-made women tenants to their shame.

The precedent whereof in Lucrece view,[76]   *sign*
Assail'd by night with circumstances strong
Of present death, and shame that might ensue
By that her death, to do her husband wrong.
Such danger to resistance did belong,
  That dying fear through all her body spread;   *mortal*
  And who cannot abuse a body dead?

By this, mild patience bid fair Lucrece speak   *By this time*
To the poor counterfeit of her complaining.   *image*
1270 'My girl,' quoth she, 'on what occasion break
Those tears from thee that down thy cheeks are raining?
If thou dost weep for grief of my sustaining,   *for grief of mine*
  Know, gentle wench, it small avails my mood;
  If tears could help, mine own would do me good.

'But tell me, girl, when went' – and there she stayed
Till after a deep groan – 'Tarquin from hence?'
'Madam, ere I was up,' replied the maid,
'The more to blame my sluggard negligence.   *idle*
Yet with the fault I thus far can dispense: *pardon*

75 A conduit was a fountain or water spout carved in the form of a human figure; the "coral cisterns" seem to allude to the women's red eyes.

76 This stanza summarizes the details of the rape and Tarquin's threats to Lucrece.

1280
Myself was stirring ere the break of day,
And ere I rose was Tarquin gone away.

'But, lady, if your maid may be so bold,
She would request to know your heaviness.'   *sadness*
'O, peace!' quoth Lucrece: 'if it should be told,
The repetition cannot make it less,
For more it is than I can well express;
  And that deep torture may be called a hell
  When more is felt than one hath power to tell.

'Go, get me hither paper, ink, and pen;
1290
Yet save that labour, for I have them here,
What should I say? One of my husband's men
Bid thou be ready by and by to bear   *immediately*
A letter to my lord, my love, my dear.
  Bid him with speed prepare to carry it;
  The cause craves haste, and it will soon be writ.'   *requires*

Her maid is gone, and she prepares to write,
First hovering o'er the paper with her quill.
Conceit and grief an eager combat fight;   *Thought*
What wit sets down is blotted straight with will;[77]
1300
This is too curious-good, this blunt and ill: *too crafted*
  Much like a press of people at a door,   *crowd*
  Throng her inventions, which shall go before.   *go through first*

At last she thus begins: 'Thou worthy lord
Of that unworthy wife that greeteth thee,
Health to thy person! next vouchsafe t'afford –
If ever, love, thy Lucrece thou wilt see –
Some present speed to come and visit me.
  So I commend me, from our house in grief;
  My woes are tedious, though my words are brief.'   *lengthy*

1310
Here folds she up the tenor of her woe,   *substance*
Her certain sorrow writ uncertainly.
By this short schedule Collatine may know   *summary*
Her grief, but not her grief's true quality;
She dares not thereof make discovery,
  Lest he should hold it her own gross abuse,[78]
  Ere she with blood had stained her stained excuse.

Besides, the life and feeling of her passion
She hoards, to spend when he is by to hear her,
When sighs and groans and tears may grace the fashion
1320
Of her disgrace, the better so to clear her
From that suspicion which the world might bear her.
  To shun this blot, she would not blot the letter   *stain*
  With words, till action might become them better.

To see sad sights moves more than hear them told;
For then the eye interprets to the ear

---

77   This line alludes to Early Modern notions of how the human soul was divided: "wit" was the intellectual faculty and "will" refers to the passions and emotions. Wit was, therefore, seen as the power of reason that helps us to rise above our animal natures and aspire to be worthy of God, whereas will represented our lower, more bestial urges. In the *Defense of Poesy*, Philip Sidney characterizes them as "erected wit" and "infected will."

78   i.e. Lest Collatine think that she had willingly betrayed him, before she sheds her own blood to excuse herself of blame.

The heavy motion that it doth behold,   *sad emotion*
When every part a part of woe doth bear.   *part of her*
'Tis but a part of sorrow that we hear:
    Deep sounds make lesser noise than shallow fords,   *waters*
1330   And sorrow ebbs, being blown with wind of words.   *recedes*

Her letter now is sealed, and on it writ
'At Ardea to my lord with more than haste.'
The post attends, and she delivers it,   *courier*
Charging the sour-faced groom to hie as fast
As lagging fowls before the northern blast.
    Speed more than speed but dull and slow she deems:
    Extremity still urgeth such extremes.

The homely villain curtsies[79] to her low,   *servant*
And blushing on her, with a steadfast eye
1340 Receives the scroll without or yea or no,
And forth with bashful innocence doth hie.   *modest/go*
But they whose guilt within their bosoms lie
    Imagine every eye beholds their blame;
    For Lucrece thought he blushed to see her shame:

When, silly groom, God wot, it was defect   *simple/knows*
Of spirit, life, and bold audacity.[80]
Such harmless creatures have a true respect
To talk in deeds, while others saucily
Promise more speed, but do it leisurely.
1350   Even so this pattern of the worn-out age   *model/bygone*
    Pawned honest looks, but laid no words to gage.[81]

His kindled duty kindled her mistrust,   *blushing obedience*
That two red fires in both their faces blazed;
She thought he blushed, as knowing Tarquin's lust,
And blushing with him, wistly on him gazed;   *intently*
Her earnest eye did make him more amazed;   *bewildered*
    The more she saw the blood his cheeks replenish,
    The more she thought he spied in her some blemish.

But long she thinks till he return again,[82]
1360 And yet the duteous vassal scarce is gone.
The weary time she cannot entertain,   *while away*
For now 'tis stale to sigh, to weep and groan;
So woe hath wearied woe, moan tired moan,
    That she her plaints a little while doth stay,   *stop*
    Pausing for means to mourn some newer way.

At last she calls to mind where hangs a piece
Of skilful painting, made for Priam's Troy,[83]
Before the which is drawn the power of Greece,
For Helen's rape the city to destroy,

79   Today we think of a "curtsy" as a woman's gesture of respect, but the word is an abbreviation of "courtesy" and in Shakespeare's day it referred to all gestures of respect from inferiors to superiors. Here, the male servant is bowing to Lucrece.
80   In other words, it was the servant's lack of "spirit, life and bold audacity" that caused him to blush.
81   i.e. Gave honest looks, but left no words as a pledge of his loyalty.

82   i.e. She thinks the time passes slowly until the servant returns.
83   From this point until line 1561, the poem focuses on Lucrece's description of and response to this painting of the Trojan War (see gazetteer). This kind of literary description of a piece of visual art is called an ecphrasis, and other prominent examples occur in *Iliad* 18, *Aeneid* 2, and Chaucer's *House of Fame*.

1370   Threat'ning cloud-kissing Ilion with annoy;   *Troy*
            Which the conceited painter drew so proud   *clever*
            As heaven, it seemed, to kiss the turrets bowed.

            A thousand lamentable objects there,
            In scorn of nature, art gave lifeless life:
            Many a dry drop seem'd a weeping tear,   *drop of paint*
            Shed for the slaught'red husband by the wife;
            The red blood reeked, to show the painter's strife;   *contest with Nature*
            And dying eyes gleamed forth their ashy lights,   *deathly pale*
            Like dying coals burnt out in tedious nights.

1380   There might you see the labouring pioneer   *engineer*
            Begrimed with sweat and smeared all with dust;
            And from the towers of Troy there would appear
            The very eyes of men through loop-holes thrust,
            Gazing upon the Greeks with little lust.   *pleasure*
            Such sweet observance in this work was had,   *verisimilitude*
            That one might see those far-off eyes look sad.

            In great commanders grace and majesty
            You might behold, triumphing in their faces;
            In youth, quick bearing and dexterity;   *vigorous*
1390   And here and there the painter interlaces
            Pale cowards marching on with trembling paces,
            Which heartless peasants did so well resemble   *cowardly*
            That one would swear he saw them quake and tremble.

            In Ajax[84] and Ulysses, O what art
            Of physiognomy[85] might one behold!
            The face of either ciphered either's heart;   *encoded*
            Their face their manners most expressly told: *forcefully*
            In Ajax' eyes blunt rage and rigour rolled;
            But the mild glance that sly Ulysses lent
1400   Showed deep regard and smiling government.   *thought/self-control*

            There pleading might you see grave Nestor[86] stand,
            As 'twere encouraging the Greeks to fight,
            Making such sober action with his hand
            That it beguiled attention, charmed the sight.
            In speech, it seemed, his beard all silver white
            Wagged up and down, and from his lips did fly
            Thin winding breath which purled up to the sky.   *flowed*

            About him were a press of gaping faces,
            Which seemed to swallow up his sound advice,
1410   All jointly list'ning, but with several graces,   *postures*
            As if some mermaid did their ears entice,
            Some high, some low, the painter was so nice;   *tall/short/precise*
            The scalps of many, almost hid behind,
            To jump up higher seemed, to mock the mind.

---

84   Ajax is one of the central Greek heroes of the Trojan War. Largely
as a result of Ovid's depiction of him in *Metamorphoses* 13, he has become
a literary exemplar of brawn without brains.

85   Physiognomy is a pseudo-science which claims to be able to learn
about the character and intellect of a person by "reading" their outward
appearance.

86   Nestor was an elderly counsellor in the Greek army at Troy; he
was immensely old, and was reputed to be very wise on the strength of
it.

Here one man's hand leaned on another's head,
His nose being shadowed by his neighbour's ear;
Here one being thronged bears back, all boll'n and red;   *crowded/swollen*
Another smothered seems to pelt and swear;   *speak angrily*
And in their rage such signs of rage they bear
    As, but for loss of Nestor's golden words,[87]
    It seemed they would debate with angry swords.

1420

For much imaginary work was there;
Conceit deceitful, so compact, so kind,   *Artifice/lifelike*
That for Achilles' image stood his spear[88]
Griped in an armed hand; himself behind
Was left unseen, save to the eye of mind:
    A hand, a foot, a face, a leg, a head,
    Stood for the whole to be imagined.

And from the walls of strong-besieged Troy
When their brave hope, bold Hector, marched to field,
Stood many Trojan mothers sharing joy
To see their youthful sons bright weapons wield;
And to their hope they such odd action yield,[89]
    That through their light joy seemed to appear,
    Like bright things stained, a kind of heavy fear.

1430

And from the strond of Dardan[90] where they fought,   *strand*
To Simois'[91] reedy banks the red blood ran,
Whose waves to imitate the battle sought
With swelling ridges; and their ranks began
To break upon the galled shore, and then   *unquiet*
    Retire again, till meeting greater ranks
    They join and shoot their foam at Simois' banks.

1440

To this well-painted piece is Lucrece come,
To find a face where all distress is stell'd.   *portrayed*
Many she sees where cares have carved some,
But none where all distress and dolour dwelled,
Till she despairing Hecuba[92] beheld,
    Staring on Priam's wounds with her old eyes,
    Which bleeding under Pyrrhus' proud foot lies.

In her the painter had anatomized   *dissected*
Time's ruin, beauty's wrack, and grim care's reign;
Her cheeks with chaps and wrinkles were disguised;
Of what she was no semblance did remain;
Her blue blood changed to black in every vein,
    Wanting the spring that those shrunk pipes had fed,
    Showed life imprisoned in a body dead.

1450

On this sad shadow Lucrece spends her eyes,   *image*
And shapes her sorrow to the beldam's woes,
Who nothing wants to answer her but cries,   *lacks*

---

87   i.e. As, except for their fear of missing Nestor's words.

88   This stanza exemplifies the rhetorical trope known as synecdoche, the substitution of a part for the whole.

89   i.e. Their expressed hope is accompanied by actions that do not signify hope (the "heavy fear" in line 1435).

90   "Dardania" is another name for the country around Troy.

91   A river near Troy.

92   Hecuba was the wife of King Priam of Troy and the mother of Hector. Pyrrhus (also called Neoptolemus) was the son of Achilles who, in Virgil's *Aeneid*, slaughtered Priam during the sack of Troy.

1460
And bitter words to ban her cruel foes: *curse*
The painter was no god to lend her those;
   And therefore Lucrece swears he did her wrong,
   To give her so much grief and not a tongue.

'Poor instrument,' quoth she, 'without a sound,
I'll tune thy woes with my lamenting tongue,
And drop sweet balm in Priam's painted wound,
And rail on Pyrrhus that hath done him wrong,
And with my tears quench Troy that burns so long;
   And with my knife scratch out the angry eyes
1470
   Of all the Greeks that are thine enemies.

'Show me the strumpet⁹³ that began this stir,   *prostitute*
That with my nails her beauty I may tear.
Thy heat of lust, fond Paris, did incur   *infatuated*
This load of wrath that burning Troy doth bear.
Thy eye kindled the fire that burneth here;
   And here in Troy, for trespass of thine eye,
   The sire, the son, the dame and daughter die.

'Why should the private pleasure of some one
Become the public plague of many moe?   *more*
1480
Let sin, alone committed, light alone   *rest*
Upon his head that hath transgressed so;
Let guiltless souls be freed from guilty woe.
   For one's offence why should so many fall,
   To plague a private sin in general?⁹⁴

'Lo, here weeps Hecuba, here Priam dies,
Here manly Hector faints, here Troilus⁹⁵ swounds,   *swoons*
Here friend by friend in bloody channel lies,   *gutter*
And friend to friend gives unadvised wounds,   *accidental*
And one man's lust these many lives confounds.   *ruins*
1490
   Had doting Priam checked his son's desire,   *Paris's*
   Troy had been bright with fame and not with fire.'

Here feelingly she weeps Troy's painted woes;
For sorrow, like a heavy-hanging bell,
Once set on ringing, with his own weight goes;
Then little strength rings out the doleful knell;
So Lucrece, set a-work, sad tales doth tell
   To pencilled pensiveness and coloured sorrow;   *painted*
   She lends them words, and she their looks doth borrow.

She throws her eyes about the painting round,
1500
And whom she finds forlorn she doth lament.
At last she sees a wretched image bound
That piteous looks to Phrygian shepherds lent;⁹⁶   *Trojan*
His face, though full of cares, yet showed content;
   Onward to Troy with the blunt swains he goes,   *shepherds*
   So mild that patience seemed to scorn his woes.   *his patience*

---

93   A reference to Helen of Troy (see gazetteer for her and Paris).
94   i.e. To punish a community for the sin of one person.
95   A Trojan hero whose love-affair with Cressida is depicted in a long
poem by Chaucer and a play by Shakespeare.

96   A reference to Sinon, the Greek soldier whose rhetoric and plausible lies convinced the Trojans to take the Trojan Horse into the city. See
Trojan War in the gazetteer. He was found by Trojan shepherds.

In him the painter laboured with his skill
To hide deceit and give the harmless show[97]
An humble gait, calm looks, eyes wailing still,   *ceaselessly*
A brow unbent that seemed to welcome woe;   *unwrinkled*

1510   Cheeks neither red nor pale, but mingled so
            That blushing red no guilty instance gave,   *sign*
            Nor ashy pale the fear that false hearts have.

But, like a constant and confirmed devil,
He entertained a show so seeming just,   *maintained*
And therein so ensconced his secret evil,
That jealousy itself could not mistrust   *suspicion*
False-creeping craft and perjury should thrust   *guile*
            Into so bright a day such black-faced storms,
            Or blot with hell-born sin such saint-like forms.

1520   The well-skilled workman this mild image drew
For perjured Sinon, whose enchanting story   *bewitching*
The credulous old Priam after slew;   *trusting*
Whose words, like wildfire, burnt the shining glory
Of rich-built Ilion, that the skies were sorry,   *Troy*
            And little stars shot from their fixed places,
            When their glass fell wherein they viewed their faces.   *mirror* (i.e. Troy)

This picture she advisedly perused,   *carefully examined*
And chid the painter for his wondrous skill,
Saying, some shape in Sinon's was abused;[98]
1530   So fair a form lodged not a mind so ill;   *body*
And still on him she gazed, and gazing still
            Such signs of truth in his plain face she spied
            That she concludes the picture was belied.   *shown to be untrue*

'It cannot be,' quoth she, 'that so much guile' –
She would have said 'can lurk in such a look';
But Tarquin's shape came in her mind the while,
And from her tongue 'can lurk' from 'cannot' took;
'It cannot be' she in that sense forsook,
            And turned it thus, 'It cannot be, I find,
1540   But such a face should bear a wicked mind;

'For even as subtle Sinon here is painted,
So sober-sad, so weary and so mild,   *serious*
As if with grief or travail he had fainted,
To me came Tarquin armed to beguiled[99]
With outward honesty, but yet defiled
            With inward vice. As Priam him did cherish,
            So did I Tarquin; so my Troy did perish.

'Look, look, how list'ning Priam wets his eyes,
To see those borrowed tears that Sinon sheds.   *temporarily adopted*
1550   Priam, why art thou old and yet not wise?
For every tear he falls a Trojan bleeds;   *Sinon*
His eye drops fire, no water thence proceeds;

97 "Harmless show" can refer to Sinon's harmless outward appearance or the harmless picture that Lucrece is studying.
98 i.e. Some other person's appearance was being used to represent Sinon.
99 A famously difficult line to understand or emend. The easiest reading is to substitute "beguile" for "beguiled."

Those round clear pearls of his that move thy pity
Are balls of quenchless fire to burn thy city.

'Such devils steal effects from lightless hell;
For Sinon in his fire doth quake with cold,
And in that cold hot-burning fire doth dwell;
These contraries such unity do hold
Only to flatter fools and make them bold;
    So Priam's trust false Sinon's tears doth flatter
    That he finds means to burn his Troy with water.'[100]

1560

Here, all enraged, such passion her assails,
That patience is quite beaten from her breast.   *driven*
She tears the senseless Sinon with her nails,   *inanimate*
Comparing him to that unhappy guest   *evil-causing*
Whose deed hath made herself herself detest.
    At last she smilingly with this gives o'er:
    'Fool, fool!' quoth she, 'his wounds will not be sore.'

Thus ebbs and flows the current of her sorrow,
And time doth weary time with her complaining.
She looks for night, and then she longs for morrow,
And both she thinks too long with her remaining.
Short time seems long in sorrow's sharp sustaining;   *in sharp sorrow*
    Though woe be heavy, yet it seldom sleeps,   *laborious*
    And they that watch see time how slow it creeps.   *stay awake*

1570

Which all this time hath overslipped her thought
That she with painted images hath spent,
Being from the feeling of her own grief brought
By deep surmise of others' detriment,   *conception*
Losing her woes in shows of discontent.   *images*
    It easeth some, though none it ever cured,
    To think their dolour others have endured.

1580

But now the mindful messenger come back   *heedful*
Brings home his lord and other company;
Who finds his Lucrece clad in mourning black,
And round about her tear-distained eye   *stained*
Blue circles streamed, like rainbows in the sky.
    These water-galls[101] in her dim element   *sky*
    Foretell new storms to those already spent.

Which when her sad-beholding husband saw,
Amazedly in her sad face he stares:
Her eyes, though sod in tears, looked red and raw,   *soaked*
Her lively colour killed with deadly cares.
He hath no power to ask her how she fares;
    Both stood, like old acquaintance in a trance,   *acquaintances*
    Met far from home, wond'ring each other's chance.

1590

At last he takes her by the bloodless hand,
And thus begins: 'What uncouth ill event   *unknown*
Hath thee befall'n, that thou dust trembling stand?
Sweet love, what spite hath thy fair colour spent?   *injury*

1600

---

100   i.e. As a result of Priam trusting Sinon's false tears, the city will   101   "A secondary or imperfectly-formed rainbow" (*OED*).
be burned down.

Why art thou thus attired in discontent?   *clothed*
   Unmask, dear dear, this moody heaviness,   *Uncover*
   And tell thy grief, that we may give redress.'   *relief*

Three times with sighs she gives her sorrow fire[102]
Ere once she can discharge one word of woe;
At length addressed to answer his desire,   *made ready*
She modestly prepares to let them know
Her honour is ta'en prisoner by the foe;
   While Collatine and his consorted lords   *associated*
1610   With sad attention long to hear her words.   *grave*

And now this pale swan in her wat'ry nest
Begins the sad dirge of her certain ending.[103]
'Few words,' quoth she, 'shall fit the trespass best,
Where no excuse can give the fault amending:
In me moe woes than words are now depending;   *more/pending*
   And my laments would be drawn out too long,
   To tell them all with one poor tired tongue.

'Then be this all the task it hath to say:
Dear husband, in the interest of thy bed   *legal right*
1620 A stranger came, and on that pillow lay
Where thou was wont to rest thy weary head;
And what wrong else may be imagined
   By foul enforcement might be done to me,
   From that, alas, thy Lucrece is not free.

'For in the dreadful dead of dark midnight,
With shining falchion in my chamber came
A creeping creature, with a flaming light,
And softly cried "Awake, thou Roman dame,
And entertain my love; else lasting shame   *receive*
1630   On thee and thine this night I will inflict,
   If thou my love's desire do contradict.

'"For some hard-favour'd groom of thine," quoth he,   *ugly*
"Unless thou yoke thy liking to my will,
I'll murder straight, and then I'll slaughter thee,   *immediately*
And swear I found you where you did fulfil
The loathsome act of lust, and so did kill
   The lechers in their deed: this act will be
   My fame, and thy perpetual infamy."

'With this, I did begin to start and cry,   *wake*
1640 And then against my heart he sets his sword,
Swearing, unless I took all patiently,
I should not live to speak another word;
So should my shame still rest upon record,
   And never be forgot in mighty Rome
   Th'adulterate death of Lucrece and her groom.   *adulterous*

'Mine enemy was strong, my poor self weak,
And far the weaker with so strong a fear.

---

102   The metaphor used in these two lines is taken from the firing of a cannon or musket: Lucrece begins (applies the match to the powder charge) three times before she can say a word (discharge).

103   In the Early Modern period, it was believed that swans (which do not sing at all) sang beautifully at the moment of their deaths.

My bloody judge forbade my tongue to speak;
No rightful plea might plead for justice there.
His scarlet lust came evidence to swear   *appeared as evidence*
   That my poor beauty had purloined his eyes,   *stolen*
   And when the judge is robbed, the prisoner dies.

'O, teach me how to make mine own excuse!
Or, at the least, this refuge let me find:
Though my gross blood be stained with this abuse,
Immaculate and spotless is my mind;
That was not forced; that never was inclined
   To accessory yieldings, but still pure   *consensual*
   Doth in her poisoned closet yet endure.'   *defiled body*

Lo, here, the hopeless merchant of this loss,   *owner*
With head declined, and voice dammed up with woe,   *looking down*
With sad-set eyes and wreathed arms across,[104]
From lips new waxen pale begins to blow   *newly become*
The grief away that stops his answer so;
   But, wretched as he is, he strives in vain;
   What he breathes out his breath drinks up again.

As through an arch the violent roaring tide   *arch of a bridge*
Outruns the eye that doth behold his haste,
Yet in the eddy boundeth in his pride
Back to the strait that forced him on so fast,   *confines*
In rage sent out, recalled in rage, being past;
   Even so his sighs, his sorrows, make a saw,[105]
   To push grief on, and back the same grief draw.

Which speechless woe of his poor she attendeth   *This speechless woe*
And his untimely frenzy thus awaketh: *delirium*
'Dear lord, thy sorrow to my sorrow lendeth
Another power; no flood by raining slaketh.   *diminishes*
My woe too sensible thy passion maketh   *deeply felt*
   More feeling-painful. Let it then suffice
   To drown one woe, one pair of weeping eyes.

'And for my sake, when I might charm thee so,[106]
For she that was thy Lucrece, now attend me:
Be suddenly revenged on my foe,
Thine, mine, his own; suppose thou dost defend me
From what is past. The help that thou shalt lend me
   Comes all too late, yet let the traitor die;
   "For sparing justice feeds iniquity.   *wickedness*

'But ere I name him, you fair lords,' quoth she,
Speaking to those that came with Collatine,
'Shall plight your honourable faiths to me,   *swear*
With swift pursuit to venge this wrong of mine;
For 'tis a meritorious fair design
   To chase injustice with revengeful arms:
   Knights, by their oaths, should right poor ladies' harms.'

1650

1660

1670

1680

1690

---

104 A sign of melancholy, as in note 51 above.   106 i.e. When I might have charmed you with my former virtues
105 The reference here is to the back and forth motion of using a   (before the rape).
handsaw.

At this request, with noble disposition
Each present lord began to promise aid,
As bound in knighthood to her imposition,
Longing to hear the hateful foe bewrayed.   *revealed*
But she, that yet her sad task hath not said,
    The protestation stops. 'O, speak,' quoth she,
1700   'How may this forced stain be wiped from me?

'What is the quality of mine offence,   *nature*
Being constrained with dreadful circumstance?
May my pure mind with the foul act dispense,   *be excused*
My low-declined honour to advance?
May any terms acquit me from this chance?   *conditions*
    The poisoned fountain clears itself again;
    And why not I from this compelled stain?'

With this, they all at once began to say,
1710 Her body's stain her mind untainted clears;
While with a joyless smile she turns away
The face, that map which deep impression bears
Of hard misfortune, carved in it with tears.
    'No, no,' quoth she, 'no dame, hereafter living
    By my excuse shall claim excuse's giving.'[107]

Here with a sigh, as if her heart would break,
She throws forth Tarquin's name; 'He, he,' she says,
But more than 'he' her poor tongue could not speak;
Till after many accents and delays,   *emotional sounds*
1720 Untimely breathings, sick and short assays,   *attempts*
    She utters this, 'He, he, fair lords, 'tis he,
    That guides this hand to give this wound to me.'

Even here she sheathed in her harmless breast
A harmful knife, that thence her soul unsheathed:
That blow did bail it from the deep unrest   *bail it out*
Of that polluted prison where it breathed.
Her contrite sighs unto the clouds bequeathed
    Her winged sprite, and through her wounds doth fly
    Life's lasting date from cancelled destiny.[108]   *everlasting time*

1730 Stone-still, astonished with this deadly deed,
Stood Collatine and all his lordly crew;
Till Lucrece' father, that beholds her bleed,
Himself on her self-slaught'red body threw;
And from the purple fountain Brutus[109] drew
    The murd'rous knife, and, as it left the place,
    Her blood, in poor revenge, held it in chase;

And bubbling from her breast, it doth divide
In two slow rivers, that the crimson blood
Circles her body in on every side,
1740 Who like a late-sacked island vastly stood   *recently/desolate*
Bare and unpeopled in this fearful flood.
    Some of her blood still pure and red remained,
    And some looked black, and that false Tarquin stained.

---

107   i.e. No woman will be able to use this excuse because of my example.

108   i.e. Lucrece's life is now everlasting, because her finite bodily life has been ended ("cancelled").

109   See Brutus, Lucius Junius in the gazetteer.

About the mourning and congealed face
Of that black blood a wat'ry rigol goes,[110]   *ring*
Which seems to weep upon the tainted place;
And ever since, as pitying Lucrece' woes,
Corrupted blood some watery token shows;
   And blood untainted still doth red abide,
1750   Blushing at that which is so putrefied.

'Daughter, dear daughter,' old Lucretius cries,
'That life was mine which thou hast here deprived.
If in the child the father's image lies,
Where shall I live now Lucrece is unlived?
Thou wast not to this end from me derived.
   If children predecease progenitors,
   We are their offspring, and they none of ours.

'Poor broken glass, I often did behold   *mirror*
In thy sweet semblance my old age new born;
1760   But now that fresh fair mirror, dim and old,
Shows me a bare-honed death by time out-worn;   *skull*
O, from thy cheeks my image thou hast torn,
   And shivered all the beauty of my glass,
   That I no more can see what once I was.

'O time, cease thou thy course and last no longer,
If they surcease to be that should survive.
Shall rotten death make conquest of the stronger   *cease*
And leave the falt'ring feeble souls alive?
The old bees die, the young possess their hive.
1770   Then live, sweet Lucrece, live again, and see
   Thy father die, and not thy father thee.'

By this, starts Collatine as from a dream,
And bids Lucretius give his sorrow place;   *precedence*
And then in key-cold[111] Lucrece' bleeding stream
He falls, and bathes the pale fear in his face,
And counterfeits to die with her a space;   *for a while*
   Till manly shame bids him possess his breath,
   And live to be revenged on her death.

The deep vexation of his inward soul
1780   Hath served a dumb arrest upon his tongue;[112]
Who, mad that sorrow should his use control
Or keep him from heart-easing words so long,
Begins to talk; but through his lips do throng
   Weak words, so thick come in his poor heart's aid   *so hurriedly come*
   That no man could distinguish what he said.

Yet sometime 'Tarquin' was pronounced plain,
But through his teeth, as if the name he tore.
This windy tempest, till it blow up rain,
Held back his sorrow's tide, to make it more;
1790   At last it rains, and busy winds give o'er;
   Then son and father weep with equal strife
   Who should weep most, for daughter or for wife.

---

110   This stanza refers to the separation between the clot and the
serum ("watery token") when blood is congealing.

111   i.e. Cold as steel; we would say "stone-cold."

112   i.e. Has made him silent, as if forced to by a legal warrant.

The one doth call her his, the other his,
Yet neither may possess the claim they lay.
The father says 'She's mine'. 'O, mine she is,'
Replies her husband: 'do not take away
My sorrow's interest; let no mourner say   *right of ownership*
    He weeps for her, for she was only mine,
    And only must be wailed by Collatine.'

1800   'O,' quoth Lucretius,' I did give that life
Which she too early and too late hath spilled.'   *recently*
'Woe, woe,' quoth Collatine, 'she was my wife;
I owed her, and 'tis mine that she hath killed.'   *owned*
'My daughter' and 'my wife' with clamours filled
    The dispersed air, who, holding Lucrece' life,
    Answer'd their cries, 'my daughter' and 'my wife'.

Brutus, who plucked the knife from Lucrece' side,
Seeing such emulation in their woe,   *likeness*
Began to clothe his wit in state and pride,
1810   Burying in Lucrece' wound his folly's show.[113]
He with the Romans was esteemed so
    As silly jeering idiots are with kings,   *court jesters*
    For sportive words and utt'ring foolish things.

But now he throws that shallow habit[114] by
Wherein deep policy did him disguise,   *prudence*
And armed his long-hid wits advisedly   *purposefully*
To check the tears in Collatinus' eyes.
'Thou wronged lord of Rome,' quoth he, 'arise;
    Let my unsounded self, supposed a fool,   *unexplored*
1820   Now set thy long-experienced wit to school.

'Why, Collatine, is woe the cure for woe?
Do wounds help wounds, or grief help grievous deeds?
Is it revenge to give thyself a blow
For his foul act by whom thy fair wife bleeds?
Such childish humour from weak minds proceeds.   *temperament*
    Thy wretched wife mistook the matter so
    To slay herself, that should have slain her foe.

'Courageous Roman, do not steep thy heart
In such relenting dew of lamentations,
1830   But kneel with me and help to bear thy part
To rouse our Roman gods with invocations
That they will suffer these abominations,   *permit*
    Since Rome herself in them doth stand disgraced,
    By our strong arms from forth her fair streets chased.   *to be chased*

'Now by the Capitol[115] that we adore,
And by this chaste blood so unjustly stained,
By heaven's fair sun that breeds the fat earth's store,   *fertile*
By all our country rights in Rome maintained,   *citizens' rights*
And by chaste Lucrece' soul that late complained
1840   Her wrongs to us, and by this bloody knife,
    We will revenge the death of this true wife.'

---

113 Brutus had pretended to be mad for many years in order to avoid being killed, as his brother was, for threatening the power of the Tarquins.

114 A pun on "habits" of behavior and "habit" as an outer garment.
115 The Capitoline hill in ancient Rome, site of the temple of Jupiter and the most sacred part of the city.

This said, he struck his hand upon his breast,
And kissed the fatal knife to end his vow,
And to his protestation urged the rest,
Who, wond'ring at him, did his words allow;   *approve*
Then jointly to the ground their knees they bow,
   And that deep vow which Brutus made before
   He doth again repeat, and that they swore.

When they had sworn to this advised doom,   *premeditated judgment*
1850   They did conclude to bear dead Lucrece thence,
To show her bleeding body thorough Rome,
And so to publish Tarquin's foul offence;
Which being done with speedy diligence,
   The Romans plausibly did give consent   *with applause*
   To Tarquin's everlasting banishment.

SONNETS

Dedication[1]

To The Only Begetter Of
These Ensuing Sonnets
Mr. W.H. All Happiness
And That Eternity
Promised
By
Our Ever-Living Poet
Wisheth
The Well-Wishing
Adventurer in
Setting
Forth

T. T.

I

From fairest creatures we desire increase,   *offspring*
That thereby beauty's rose might never die,
But as the riper should by time decease,   *older*
His tender heir might bear his memory;
But thou contracted to thine own bright eyes,   *engaged*
Feed'st thy light's flame with self-substantial fuel,   i.e. your own substance's
Making a famine where abundance lies,
Thyself thy foe, to thy sweet self too cruel.
Thou that art now the world's fresh ornament
10   And only herald to the gaudy spring   *colorful*
Within thine own bud buriest thy content,[2]
And, tender churl, mak'st waste in niggarding.[3]
   Pity the world, or else this glutton be:
   To eat the world's due, by the grave and thee.[4]

SONNETS

1 The dedication to the sonnets has caused an immense amount of speculation about the identity of "Mr. W. H.," but none of the theories advanced seems conclusive. "T. T." refers to the publisher of the sonnets, Thomas Thorpe.

2 Shakespeare is punning on content as "contentment" and "the contents within you."

3 i.e. And, like a young miser, create waste by being miserly.

4 i.e. To consume what you owe the world (some offspring), by your death and childless state.

2

When forty winters shall besiege thy brow   *wrinkles/face*
And dig deep trenches in thy beauty's field,
Thy youth's proud livery, so gazed on now,   *clothing*
Will be a tattered weed, of small worth held.   *rag*
Then being asked, where all thy beauty lies,
Where all the treasure of thy lusty days,   *energetic*
To say within thine own deep sunken eyes
Were an all-eating shame and thriftless praise.   *gluttonous/pointless*
How much more praise deserved thy beauty's use,   *would deserve*
If thou couldst answer 'This fair child of mine
Shall sum my count, and make my old excuse',[5]
Proving his beauty by succession thine.
    This were to be new made when thou art old,
    And see thy blood warm when thou feel'st it cold.

3

Look in thy glass, and tell the face thou viewest   *mirror*
Now is the time that face should form another,
Whose fresh repair if now thou not renewest   *youthful state*
Thou dost beguile the world, unbless some mother.   *cheat*
For where is she so fair whose uneared womb   *unseeded*
Disdains the tillage of thy husbandry?   *cultivation/labor*
Or who is he so fond will be the tomb   *foolish*
Of his self-love to stop posterity?
Thou art thy mother's glass, and she in thee   *image*
Calls back the lovely April of her prime;
So thou through windows of thine age shalt see,
Despite of wrinkles, this thy golden time.
    But if thou live remembered not to be,   *i.e. to be unremembered*
    Die single, and thine image dies with thee.

4

Unthrifty loveliness, why dost thou spend   *Wasteful*
Upon thyself thy beauty's legacy?
Nature's bequest gives nothing, but doth lend,
And being frank, she lends to those are free.   *generous/generous*
Then, beauteous niggard, why dost thou abuse   *miser*
The bounteous largess given thee to give?   *wealth*
Profitless usurer, why dost thou use[6]
So great a sum of sums yet canst not live?
For having traffic with thyself alone,   *interaction*
Thou of thyself thy sweet self dost deceive.
Then how when nature calls thee to be gone:
What acceptable audit canst thou leave?
    Thy unused beauty must be tombed with thee,
    Which used, lives th'executor to be.   *i.e. reproduced in a child*

5

Those hours that with gentle work did frame
The lovely gaze[7] where every eye doth dwell
Will play the tyrants to the very same,
And that unfair which fairly doth excel;   *make ugly*

---

5 i.e. "Shall clear my debt, and compensate for me growing old."
6 The verb "to use" meant "to lend money at interest" in Shakespeare's day (hence the term "usury") as well its common modern meaning. This early section of the sonnets uses many tropes of financial investment to represent the speaker's desire that the young man should preserve his beauty by having a child to reproduce it.
7 The word "gaze" here means "something looked at," a meaning which is now archaic.

For never-resting time leads summer on
To hideous winter, and confounds him there,   *destroys*
Sap checked with frost, and lusty leaves quite gone,   *youthful*
Beauty o'er-snowed, and bareness everywhere.
Then were not summer's distillation left
10   A liquid prisoner pent in walls of glass,[8]
Beauty's effect with beauty were bereft,   *would be lost*
Nor it nor no remembrance what it was.   *Neither . . . nor . . .*
   But flowers distilled, though they with winter meet,
   Leese but their show; their substance still lives sweet.   *Lose*

6

Then let not winter's ragged hand deface   *harsh*
In thee thy summer ere thou be distilled.
Make sweet some vial, treasure thou some place   *enrich*
With beauty's treasure ere it be self-killed.
That use is not forbidden usury   *investment*
Which happies those that pay the willing loan: *pleases/willingly pay*
That's for thyself to breed another thee,
Or ten times happier be it ten for one;
Ten times thyself were happier than thou art,
10   If ten of thine ten times refigured thee.   *represented you anew*
Then what could death do if thou shouldst depart,
Leaving thee living in posterity?
   Be not self-willed,[9] for thou art much too fair
   To be death's conquest and make worms thine heir.

7

Lo, in the orient when the gracious light   *east/sun*
Lifts up his burning head, each under eye   *eye below*
Doth homage to his new-appearing sight,
Serving with looks his sacred majesty,
And having climbed the steep-up heavenly hill,
Resembling strong youth in his middle age,
Yet mortal looks adore his beauty still,
Attending on his golden pilgrimage.
But when from highmost pitch with weary car,[10]
10   Like feeble age he reeleth from the day,   *falls hurriedly*
The eyes (fore duteous) now converted are   *before/turned away*
From his low tract and look another way.   *route*
   So thou, thyself out-going in thy noon,   *dying*
   Unlooked on diest unless thou get a son.

8

Music to hear,[11] why hear'st thou music sadly?
Sweets with sweets war not, joy delights in joy.
Why lov'st thou that which thou receiv'st not gladly,
Or else receiv'st with pleasure thine annoy?   *annoyance*
If the true concord of well-tuned sounds   *harmony*
By unions married do offend thine ear,
They do but sweetly chide thee, who confounds   *chastise/destroys*
In singleness the parts that thou shouldst bear.[12]

---

8   i.e. A perfume enclosed in a glass vial.
  9   Shakespeare is punning on a phrase meaning "stubborn" and, implicitly, "bequeathed to yourself."
10   "chariot"; in classical mythology, the sun was imagined to be a chariot pulled by a team of horses. See the gazetteer under *Phaethon*.

11   i.e. You who are music to hear . . .
12   This line puns on single and multiple musical parts in a harmony, and the single and married states.

Mark how one string, sweet husband to another,   *lute string*
10   Strikes each in each by mutual ordering,
Resembling sire, and child, and happy mother,
Who all in one one pleasing note do sing;
    Whose speechless song, being many, seeming one,
    Sings this to thee: 'Thou single wilt prove none.'

9

Is it for fear to wet a widow's eye
That thou consum'st thyself in single life?
Ah, if thou issueless shalt hap to die,   *childless*
The world will wail thee like a makeless wife.   *widowed*
The world will be thy widow and still weep
That thou no form of thee hast left behind,
When every private[13] widow well may keep
By children's eyes her husband's shape in mind.
Look what an unthrift in the world doth spend   *Whatever*
10   Shifts but his place, for still the world enjoys it;   *i.e. its place*
But beauty's waste hath in the world an end,
And kept unused, the user[14] so destroys it.
    No love toward others in that bosom sits
    That on himself such murd'rous shame commits.

10

For shame deny that thou bear'st love to any,
Who for thyself art so unprovident.   *rash*
Grant, if thou wilt, thou art beloved of many,
But that thou none lov'st is most evident;
For thou art so possessed with murd'rous hate
That 'gainst thyself thou stick'st not to conspire,   *hesitate*
Seeking that beauteous roof to ruinate   *dwelling*
Which to repair should be thy chief desire.
O, change thy thought, that I may change my mind!
10   Shall hate be fairer lodged than gentle love?
Be as thy presence is, gracious and kind,
Or to thyself at least kind-hearted prove.
    Make thee another self for love of me,
    That beauty still may live in thine or thee.

11

As fast as thou shalt wane, so fast thou grow'st
In one of thine from that which thou departest,[15]
And that fresh blood which youngly thou bestow'st   *in youth/give*
Thou mayst call thine when thou from youth convertest.   *change*
Herein lives wisdom, beauty, and increase;   *i.e. In your child*
Without this, folly, age, and cold decay.
If all were minded so, the times should cease,
And threescore year would make the world away.   *sixty*
Let those whom nature hath not made for store,   *supply*
10   Harsh, featureless, and rude, barrenly perish.   *Ill-featured/unfinished*
Look whom she best endowed, she gave thee more,   *Whomever*
Which bounteous gift thou shouldst in bounty cherish.   *generosity*
    She carved thee for her seal,[16] and meant thereby,   *Nature*
    Thou shouldst print more, not let that copy die.   *original*

---

13   The word "private" here means "not holding public office," that is, an ordinary individual, as opposed to the "world."
14   See note 6 above.

15   i.e. In a child of yours, from that which you are leaving (your youth).
16   A reference to the seals that were used to stamp an impression in wax and seal a document.

12

When I do count the clock that tells the time,
And see the brave day sunk in hideous night;   *shining*
When I behold the violet past prime,
And sable curls all silvered o'er with white;   *black*
When lofty trees I see barren of leaves,
Which erst from heat did canopy the herd,   *before*
And summer's green all girded up in sheaves   *gathered*
Borne on the bier with white and bristly beard: *farm cart*
Then of thy beauty do I question make   *i.e. do I consider*
10   That thou among the wastes of time must go,
Since sweets and beauties do themselves forsake,
And die as fast as they see others grow;
    And nothing 'gainst time's scythe can make defence
    Save breed to brave him when he takes thee hence.   *defy*

13

O that you were yourself! But, love, you are[17]
No longer yours, than you yourself here live.
Against this coming end you should prepare,   *Anticipating*
And your sweet semblance to some other give.
So should that beauty which you hold in lease
Find no determination; then you were   *termination*
Yourself again after your self's decease,
When your sweet issue your sweet form should bear.
Who lets so fair a house fall to decay,   *family*
10   Which husbandry in honour might uphold   *management*
Against the stormy gusts of winter's day,
And barren rage of death's eternal cold?
    O, none but unthrifts, dear my love, you know.   *wastrels*
    You had a father; let your son say so.

14

Not from the stars do I my judgement pluck,   *take*
And yet methinks I have astronomy;   *i.e. astrology*
But not to tell of good, or evil luck,
Of plagues, of dearths, or seasons' quality.
Nor can I fortune to brief minutes tell,[18]
'Pointing to each his thunder, rain, and wind,   *Assigning*
Or say with princes if it shall go well
By oft predict that I in heaven find;   *i.e. often predicting what*
But from thine eyes my knowledge I derive,
10   And, constant stars, in them I read such art
As truth and beauty shall together thrive
If from thyself to store thou wouldst convert.   *supply for the future*
    Or else of thee this I prognosticate: *foretell*
    Thy end is truth's and beauty's doom and date.   *end*

15

When I consider every thing that grows
Holds in perfection but a little moment,   *i.e. Remains perfect for*
That this huge state presenteth nought but shows   *i.e. the world*
Whereon the stars in secret influence comment;[19]
When I perceive that men as plants increase,   *breed*

---

17   i.e. Oh that your material self were your character (which is comprised of timeless, immaterial virtues) . . .

18   i.e. Nor can I predict exactly when things are going to happen.

19   In Shakespeare's day, it was still commonly believed that events in the heavens reflected (and could thus be used to predict) events on earth.

Cheered and checked even by the selfsame sky;   *Helped and hindered*
Vaunt in their youthful sap, at height decrease,   *Brag/energy*
And wear their brave state out of memory: *erode/showy*
Then the conceit of this inconstant stay   *concept/unpredictable mortal life*
10 Sets you most rich in youth before my sight,
Where wasteful time debateth with decay
To change your day of youth to sullied night;
   And all in war with time for love of you,
   As he takes from you, I engraft you new.   *replant*

16

But wherefore do not you a mightier way   *why/more effective*
Make war upon this bloody tyrant, time,
And fortify yourself in your decay
With means more blessed than my barren rhyme?
Now stand you on the top of happy hours,   *i.e. in your prime of youth*
And many maiden gardens yet unset   *unplanted*
With virtuous wish would bear you living flowers,   *i.e. children*
Much liker than your painted counterfeit,   *image*
So should the lines of life that life repair
10 Which this time's pencil or my pupil pen   *descriptive skill/inexpert*
Neither in inward worth nor outward fair   *beauty*
Can make you live yourself in eyes of men.
   To give away yourself keeps yourself still,   *i.e. To have children*
   And you must live drawn by your own sweet skill.

17

Who will believe my verse in time to come
If it were filled with your most high deserts? –   *merits*
Though yet, heaven knows, it is but as a tomb
Which hides your life, and shows not half your parts.   *abilities*
If I could write the beauty of your eyes
And in fresh numbers number all your graces,   *verses*
The age to come would say 'This poet lies;
Such heavenly touches ne'er touched earthly faces.'
So should my papers, yellowed with their age,
10 Be scorned, like old men of less truth than tongue,   *words*
And your true rights be termed a poet's rage   *inspiration*
And stretched metre of an antique song.   *strained*
   But were some child of yours alive that time,
   You should live twice: in it, and in my rhyme.

18

Shall I compare thee to a summer's day?
Thou art more lovely and more temperate.
Rough winds do shake the darling buds of May,
And summer's lease hath all too short a date.   *duration*
Sometime too hot the eye of heaven shines,   *the sun*
And often is his gold complexion dimmed,
And every fair from fair sometime declines,   *i.e. beauty from beauty*
By chance or nature's changing course untrimmed;   *stripped of ornament*
But thy eternal summer shall not fade
10 Nor lose possession of that fair thou ow'st,   *own*
Nor shall death brag thou wander'st in his shade
When in eternal lines to time thou grow'st.[20]
   So long as men can breathe or eyes can see,
   So long lives this, and this gives life to thee.   *i.e. this poem*

20 i.e. When in eternal lines of poetry you become part of time.

19

Devouring time, blunt thou the lion's paws,
And make the earth devour her own sweet brood;
Pluck the keen teeth from the fierce tiger's jaws,
And burn the long-lived phoenix, in her blood.[21]
Make glad and sorry seasons as thou fleet'st,   *i.e. you run*
And do whate'er thou wilt, swift-footed time,
To the wide world and all her fading sweets.
But I forbid thee one most heinous crime:
O, carve not with thy hours my love's fair brow,
10   Nor draw no lines there with thine antique[22] pen.   *wrinkles*
Him in thy course untainted do allow
For beauty's pattern to succeeding men.
  Yet do thy worst, old time; despite thy wrong
  My love shall in my verse ever live young.

20

A woman's face with nature's own hand painted
Hast thou, the master-mistress of my passion;
A woman's gentle heart, but not acquainted
With shifting change as is false women's fashion;   *habit*
An eye more bright than theirs, less false in rolling,   *wandering*
Gilding the object whereupon it gazeth;   *Brightening*
A man in hue, all hues in his controlling,   *appearance*
Which steals men's eyes and women's souls amazeth.   *infatuates*
And for a woman wert thou first created,   *i.e. as a woman*
10   Till nature as she wrought thee fell a-doting,   *infatuated*
And by addition me of thee defeated
By adding one thing to my purpose nothing.   *i.e. a penis*
  But since she pricked thee out for women's pleasure,
  Mine be thy love and thy love's use their treasure.

21

So is it not with me as with that muse   *i.e. a poet*
Stirred by a painted beauty to his verse,   *cosmetic-using*
Who heaven itself for ornament doth use,
And every fair with his fair doth rehearse,[23]
Making a couplement of proud compare   *comparison*
With sun and moon, with earth, and sea's rich gems,
With April's first-born flowers, and all things rare
That heaven's air in this huge rondure hems.   *sphere encloses*
O let me, true in love, but truly write,
10   And then believe me my love is as fair
As any mother's child, though not so bright
As those gold candles fixed in heaven's air.
  Let them say more that like of hearsay well;   *idle talk*
  I will not praise that purpose not to sell.[24]

22

My glass shall not persuade me I am old   *mirror*
So long as youth and thou are of one date;   *i.e. of the same age*
But when in thee time's furrows I behold,
Then look I death my days should expiate.   *I will look for/extinguish*
For all that beauty that doth cover thee

---

21   See Phoenix in the gazetteer.
22   A pun on "antique" meaning "old" and "antic" meaning "grotesque."
23   i.e. And compares every beautiful thing with his lady love.
24   i.e. I will not exaggerate, since I am not a trader trying to sell something.

Is but the seemly raiment of my heart,   *clothing*
Which in thy breast doth live, as thine in me;
How can I then be elder than thou art?
O therefore, love, be of thyself so wary   *careful*
10   As I, not for myself, but for thee will,
Bearing thy heart, which I will keep so chary   *carefully*
As tender nurse her babe from faring ill.
       Presume not on thy heart when mine is slain: *i.e. not to receive thy*
       Thou gav'st me thine not to give back again.

23

As an unperfect actor on the stage
Who with his fear is put besides his part,   *made to forget*
Or some fierce thing replete with too much rage
Whose strength's abundance weakens his own heart,
So I, for fear of trust, forget to say   *mistrusting/how to*
The perfect ceremony of love's rite,
And in mine own love's strength seem to decay,
O'ercharged with burthen of mine own love's might.   *burden*
O let my books be then the eloquence
10   And dumb presagers of my speaking breast,   *prophets*
Who plead for love, and look for recompense   *reward*
More than that tongue that more hath more expressed.[25]
       O learn to read what silent love hath writ;
       To hear with eyes belongs to love's fine wit.

24

Mine eye hath played the painter, and hath steeled   *engraved*
Thy beauty's form in table of my heart.   *wooden tablet*
My body is the frame wherein 'tis held,
And perspective[26] it is best painter's art;
For through the painter must you see his skill
To find where your true image pictured lies,
Which in my bosom's shop is hanging still,
That hath his windows glazed with thine eyes.[27]
Now see what good turns eyes for eyes have done:
10   Mine eyes have drawn thy shape, and thine for me
Are windows to my breast, wherethrough the sun
Delights to peep, to gaze therein on thee.
       Yet eyes this cunning want to grace their art: *skill*
       They draw but what they see, know not the heart.   *heart's feelings*

25

Let those who are in favour with their stars   *destiny*
Of public honour and proud titles boast,
Whilst I, whom fortune of such triumph bars,
Unlooked-for joy in that I honour most.   *i.e. enjoy that which*
Great princes' favourites their fair leaves spread[28]
But as the marigold at the sun's eye,
And in themselves their pride lies buried,
For at a frown they in their glory die.
The painful warrior famoused for might,   *diligent/made famous*
10   After a thousand victories once foiled   *defeated*

---

25   i.e. More than that tongue that has said more on many occasions.
26   An allusion to the painting technique of perspective, which is used
to create an impression of depth and distance in the two-dimensional
surface of a painting.

27   i.e. Because the young man's image is engraved in the poet's heart,
looking at that image allows direct access to the poet's heart.
28   The poet is comparing court favorites to flowers which turn to face
the sun (i.e. the monarch).

Is from the book of honour razed quite,   *erased*
And all the rest forgot for which he toiled.
  Then happy I, that love and am beloved
  Where I may not remove nor be removed.

26

Lord of my love, to whom in vassalage   *subjection*
Thy merit hath my duty strongly knit,
To thee I send this written embassage   *ambassador*
To witness duty, not to show my wit;   i.e. show duty
Duty so great which wit so poor as mine
May make seem bare in wanting words to show it,
But that I hope some good conceit of thine   *opinion*
In thy soul's thought, all naked, will bestow it,[29]
Till whatsoever star that guides my moving
10 Points on me graciously with fair aspect,   *influence*
And puts apparel on my tattered loving
To show me worthy of thy sweet respect.
  Then may I dare to boast how I do love thee;
  Till then, not show my head where thou mayst prove me.   *test*

27

Weary with toil I haste me to my bed,
The dear repose for limbs with travel tired;
But then begins a journey in my head
To work my mind, when body's work's expired;
For then my thoughts, from far where I abide,
Intend a zealous pilgrimage to thee,   *Proceed on*
And keep my drooping eyelids open wide,
Looking on darkness which the blind do see:
Save that my soul's imaginary sight
10 Presents thy shadow to my sightless view,   *image*
Which like a jewel hung in ghastly night
Makes black night beauteous, and her old face new.
  Lo, thus by day my limbs, by night my mind,
  For thee, and for myself, no quiet find.

28

How can I then return in happy plight,   *condition*
That am debarred the benefit of rest,
When day's oppression is not eased by night,
But day by night and night by day oppressed,
And each, though enemies to either's reign,
Do in consent shake hands to torture me,   *in agreement*
The one by toil, the other to complain[30]
How far I toil, still farther off from thee?
I tell the day to please him thou art bright,
10 And dost him grace when clouds do blot the heaven;[31]
So flatter I the swart-complexioned night   *dark*
When sparkling stars twire not thou gild'st the even.   *do not look down/evening*
  But day doth daily draw my sorrows longer,
  And night doth nightly make griefs strength seem stronger.

---

29 i.e. In thy soul's thought will house my unadorned ("naked") duty.   31 i.e. The young man's beauty substitutes for the sun when it is
30 i.e. The day by toil, the night by making me complain how much   covered by clouds.
I toil . . .

29

When, in disgrace with fortune and men's eyes,
I all alone beweep my outcast state,
And trouble deaf heaven with my bootless cries,   *futile*
And look upon myself and curse my fate,
Wishing me like to one more rich in hope,
Featured like him, like him with friends possessed,   *Looking*
Desiring this man's art and that man's scope,   *skill/mental capacity*
With what I most enjoy contented least:
Yet in these thoughts myself almost despising,
Haply I think on thee, and then my state,   *mental state*
Like to the lark at break of day arising
From sullen earth, sings hymns at heaven's gate;
    For thy sweet love remembered such wealth brings
    That then I scorn to change my state with kings'.

10

30

When to the sessions of sweet silent thought
I summon up remembrance of things past,[32]
I sigh the lack of many a thing I sought,
And with old woes new wail my dear time's waste.[33]
Then can I drown an eye unused to flow
For precious friends hid in death's dateless night,   *endless*
And weep afresh love's long since cancelled woe,
And moan th'expense of many a vanished sight.
Then can I grieve at grievances foregone,   *past*
And heavily from woe to woe tell o'er   *sadly/count*
The sad account of fore-bemoaned moan,
Which I new pay as if not paid before.
    But if the while I think on thee, dear friend,
    All losses are restored, and sorrows end.

10

31

Thy bosom is endeared with all hearts   *enriched/everyone*
Which I by lacking have supposed dead,
And there reigns love, and all love's loving parts,   *qualities*
And all those friends which I thought buried.
How many a holy and obsequious tear   *mourning*
Hath dear religious love stol'n from mine eye   *devout*
As interest of the dead,[34] which now appear
But things removed that hidden in thee lie!
Thou art the grave where buried love doth live,
Hung with the trophies of my lovers gone,
Who all their parts of me to thee did give:
That due of many now is thine alone.
    Their images I loved I view in thee,   *i.e. which I loved*
    And thou, all they,[35] hast all the all of me.

10

32

If thou survive my well-contented day
When that churl death my bones with dust shall cover,
And shalt by fortune once more resurvey
These poor rude lines of thy deceased lover,   *verses*
Compare them with the bett'ring of the time,   *better writing*

32   The "sessions" refers to Early Modern law courts, and the speaker   34   i.e. As what is owed to the dead.
is metaphorically summoning his memories to appear at trial.   35   i.e. And you, who are all of them.
33.   i.e. And with old woes complain afresh about the waste of pre-
cious time.

And though they be outstripped by every pen,
Reserve them for my love, not for their rhyme
Exceeded by the height of happier men.   *high rank/more fortunate*
O then vouchsafe me but this loving thought:
'Had my friend's muse grown with this growing age,
A dearer birth than this his love had brought   *better creation* (i.e. poems)
To march in ranks of better equipage;   *equipment*
    But since he died, and poets better prove,
    Theirs for their style I'll read, his for his love.'

33

Full many a glorious morning have I seen
Flatter the mountain tops with sovereign eye,
Kissing with golden face the meadows green,
Gilding pale streams with heavenly alchemy;
Anon permit the basest clouds to ride
With ugly rack on his celestial face,   *fog*
And from the forlorn world his visage hide,
Stealing unseen to west with this disgrace.
Even so my sun one early morn did shine
With all triumphant splendour on my brow;
But out, alas, he was but one hour mine;
The region cloud hath masked him from me now.   *That region's*
    Yet him for this, my love no whit disdaineth:
    Suns of the world may stain when heaven's sun staineth.

34

Why didst thou promise such a beauteous day
And make me travel forth without my cloak,
To let base clouds o'ertake me in my way,
Hiding thy brav'ry in their rotten smoke?   *finery/mist*
'Tis not enough that through the cloud thou break
To dry the rain on my storm-beaten face,
For no man well of such a salve can speak   *remedy*
That heals the wound and cures not the disgrace.   *scar*
Nor can thy shame give physic to my grief;   *cure*
Though thou repent, yet I have still the loss.
Th'offender's sorrow lends but weak relief
To him that bears the strong offence's cross.   *burden*
    Ah, but those tears are pearl which thy love sheds,
    And they are rich, and ransom all ill deeds.

35

No more be grieved at that which thou hast done:
Roses have thorns, and silver fountains mud.
Clouds and eclipses stain both moon and sun,
And loathsome canker lives in sweetest bud.   *worm*
All men make faults, and even I in this,
Authorizing thy trespass with compare,   *Justifying*
Myself corrupting salving thy amiss,[36]
Excusing thy sins more than thy sins are:
For to thy sensual fault I bring in sense –   *reason*
Thy adverse party is thy advocate –   *lawyer*
And 'gainst myself a lawful plea commence.

36   i.e. Corrupting myself by remedying your faults.

Such civil war is in my love and hate
That I an accessary needs must be
To that sweet thief which sourly robs from me.   *harshly*

36

Let me confess that we two must be twain   *separate*
Although our undivided loves are one;
So shall those blots that do with me remain   *faults*
Without thy help by me be borne alone.
In our two loves there is but one respect,   *reference*
Though in our lives a separable spite[37]
Which, though it alter not love's sole effect,   *unique*
Yet doth it steal sweet hours from love's delight.
I may not evermore acknowledge thee[38]
10   Lest my bewailed guilt should do thee shame,
Nor thou with public kindness honour me
Unless thou take that honour from thy name.
   But do not so. I love thee in such sort   *a way*
   As, thou being mine, mine is thy good report.[39]   *That/reputation*

37

As a decrepit father takes delight
To see his active child do deeds of youth,
So I, made lame by fortune's dearest spite,   *strongest*
Take all my comfort of thy worth and truth;
For whether beauty, birth, or wealth, or wit,
Or any of these all, or all, or more,
Entitled in thy parts do crowned sit,   *Privileged among/qualities*
I make my love engrafted to this store.   *attached/abundance*
So then I am not lame, poor, nor despised,
10   Whilst that this shadow doth such substance give   *image/reality*
That I in thy abundance am sufficed   *contented*
And by a part of all thy glory live.
   Look what is best, that best I wish in thee;
   This wish I have, then ten times happy me.   *i.e. This wish obtained,*

38

How can my muse want subject to invent   *lack/compose*
While thou dost breathe, that pour'st into my verse   *who*
Thine own sweet argument, too excellent
For every vulgar paper to rehearse?[40]
O, give thyself the thanks if aught in me   *anything*
Worthy perusal stand against thy sight;   *stands in*
For who's so dumb that cannot write to thee,   *silent*
When thou thyself dost give invention light?
Be thou the tenth muse, ten times more in worth
10   Than those old nine which rhymers invocate,   *i.e. the Muses*
And he that calls on thee, let him bring forth
Eternal numbers to outlive long date.   *verses/period of time*
   If my slight muse do please these curious days,   *exacting*
   The pain be mine, but thine shall be the praise.

---

37   "separable spite" refers to the malignant forces which keep the poet
and the young man apart.
38   i.e. I may never again be able to publicly acknowledge that I know
you.

39   This final couplet is repeated in Sonnet 96.
40   i.e. For every common piece of writing to repeat?

39

O, how thy worth with manners may I sing   *gracefulness*
When thou art all the better part of me?
What can mine own praise to mine own self bring,
And what is't but mine own when I praise thee?
Even for this let us divided live,   *i.e. this reason*
And our dear love lose name of single one,   *reputation*
That by this separation I may give
That due to thee which thou deserv'st alone.
O absence, what a torment wou!dst thou prove
10 Were it not thy sour leisure gave sweet leave   *permission*
To entertain the time with thoughts of love,   *occupy*
Which time and thoughts so sweetly doth deceive,   *i.e. you so*
   And that thou teachest how to make one twain   *Except that/into two*
   By praising him here who doth hence remain!⁴¹

40

Take all my loves, my love, yea take them all:
What hast thou then more than thou hadst before?
No love, my love, that thou mayst true love call –
All mine was thine before thou hadst this more.   *addition*
Then if for my love thou my love receivest,⁴²
I cannot blame thee for my love thou usest;⁴³
But yet be blamed if thou thyself deceivest
By wilful taste of what thyself refusest.⁴⁴
I do forgive thy robh'ry, gentle thief,
10 Although thou steal thee all my poverty;   *i.e. steal what little I have*
And yet love knows it is a greater grief
To bear greater wrong than hate's known injury.
   Lascivious grace,⁴⁵ in whom all ill well shows,
   Kill me with spites, yet we must not be foes.

41

Those pretty wrongs that liberty commits   *petty/license*
When I am sometime absent from thy heart
Thy beauty and thy years full well befits,
For still temptation follows where thou art.   *invariably*
Gentle thou art, and therefore to be won;
Beauteous thou art, therefore to be assailed;
And when a woman woos, what woman's son
Will sourly leave her till he have prevailed?   *harshly*
Ay me, but yet thou mightst my seat forbear,   *capital city (i.e. mistress)*
10 And chide thy beauty and thy straying youth
Who lead thee in their riot even there   *Which/dissipation*
Where thou art forced to break a twofold truth:
   Hers, by thy beauty tempting her to thee,
   Thine, by thy beauty being false to me.

42

That thou hast her, it is not all my grief,
And yet it may be said I loved her dearly;
That she hath thee is of my wailing chief,   *i.e. my chief complaint*
A loss in love that touches me more nearly.

41   i.e. By praising the image of the young man which is in me, even   44   A difficult line, which can perhaps best be glossed as "By wilfully
though he is far away.   tasting that which your reason refuses."
42   i.e. If, because you love me, you are gracious to the woman I love.   45   The young man, who is full of grace even when he is being lustful.
43   i.e. I cannot blame you for sexually using the woman I love.

Loving offenders, thus I will excuse ye:
Thou dost love her, because thou know'st I love her,
And for my sake even so doth she abuse me,   *betray*
Suff'ring my friend for my sake to approve her.   *Allowing/experience* (sexually)
If I lose thee, my loss is my love's gain,
10   And losing her, my friend hath found that loss:
Both find each other, and I lose both twain,
And both for my sake lay on me this cross.   *affliction*
    But here's the joy: my friend[46] and I are one,
    Sweet flattery! Then she loves but me alone.

43

When most I wink, then do mine eyes best see,   *close my eyes*
For all the day they view things unrespected;   *lightly valued*
But when I sleep, in dreams they look on thee,
And darkly bright, are bright in dark directed.[47]
Then thou, whose shadow shadows doth make bright,   *image*
How would thy shadow's form form happy show[48]
To the clear day with thy much clearer light,
When to unseeing eyes thy shade shines so!   *image*
How would, I say, mine eyes be blessed made
10   By looking on thee in the living day,
When in dead night thy fair imperfect shade   *incomplete*
Through heavy sleep on sightless eyes doth stay!
    All days are nights to see till I see thee,   *dark*
    And nights bright days when dreams do show thee me.   *to me*

44

If the dull substance of my flesh were thought,   *sluggish*
Injurious distance should not stop my way;
For then, despite of space, I would be brought   *i.e. in spite of distance*
From limits far remote, where thou dost stay.   *places/to where*
No matter then although my foot did stand
Upon the farthest earth removed from thee;   *place*
For nimble thought can jump both sea and land
As soon as think the place where he would be.   *it*
But ah, thought kills me that I am not thought,
10   To leap large lengths of miles when thou art gone,
But that, so much of earth and water wrought,[49]
I must attend time's leisure with my moan,   *await*
    Receiving nought by elements so slow
    But heavy tears, badges of either's[50] woe.

45

The other two, slight air and purging fire,   *i.e. two elements*
Are both with thee, wherever I abide;
The first my thought, the other my desire,
These present-absent with swift motion slide;[51]
For when these quicker elements are gone
In tender embassy of love to thee,   *diplomatic mission*

46   i.e. the young man. "Friendship" was a term almost exclusively reserved for close male/male relations in Early Modern England. As with the speaker and the young man in these sonnets, such friendships were often described in ambiguously sexual terms.

47   i.e. And, seeing well in that darkness, are directed to your brightness.

48   i.e. How would your real presence make a beautiful sight.

49   The four primary elements of matter were earth, air, fire, and water; earth and water, being the heavier two, are the main elements in the speaker's body, and prevent him from moving as fast as thought.

50   i.e. earth or water's (because the tears are "heavy" like earth and liquid like water).

51   i.e. These are present, and then instantly absent, with a swift movement.

My life, being made of four, with two alone
Sinks down to death, oppressed with melancholy,
Until life's composition be recured   *harmony/restored*
10   By those swift messengers returned from thee,
Who even but now come back again assured   *just now*
Of thy fair health, recounting it to me.
    This told, I joy; but then no longer glad,
    I send them back again and straight grow sad.

46

Mine eye and heart are at a mortal war   *deadly*
How to divide the conquest of thy sight.
Mine eye my heart thy picture's sight would bar,
My heart, mine eye the freedom of that right.[52]
My heart doth plead that thou in him dost lie,
A closet never pierced with crystal eyes;
But the defendant doth that plea deny,   *i.e. my eye*
And says in him thy fair appearance lies.
To 'cide this title is impanelled   *decide*
10   A quest of thoughts, all tenants to the heart,   *An inquest*
And by their verdict is determined
The clear eye's moiety and the dear heart's part,   *portion*
    As thus: mine eye's due is thy outward part,
    And my heart's right, thy inward love of heart.

47

Betwixt mine eye and heart a league is took,   *pact/agreed*
And each doth good turns now unto the other.
When that mine eye is famished for a look,
Or heart in love with sighs himself doth smother,   *suffocate*
With my love's picture then my eye doth feast,
And to the painted banquet bids my heart.   *i.e. picture*
Another time mine eye is my heart's guest
And in his thoughts of love doth share a part.
So either by thy picture or my love,
10   Thyself away art present still with me;
For thou not farther than my thoughts canst move,   *i.e. thou art not*
And I am still with them, and they with thee;
    Or if they sleep, thy picture in my sight
    Awakes my heart to heart's and eye's delight.

48

How careful was I when I took my way   *began my journey*
Each trifle under truest bars to thrust,   *trusted*
That to my use it might unused stay
From hands of falsehood, in sure wards of trust.   *i.e. thieves/custody*
But thou, to whom my jewels trifles are,   *compared to*
Most worthy comfort, now my greatest grief,   *precious*
Thou best of dearest and mine only care
Art left the prey of every vulgar thief.   *common*
Thee have I not looked up in any chest
10   Save where thou art not, though I feel thou art –
Within the gentle closure of my breast,
From whence at pleasure thou mayst come and part: *go*
    And even thence thou wilt be stol'n, I fear,
    For truth proves thievish for a prize so dear.   *becomes*

52   i.e. My eyes would bar your image from my heart, and my heart
would bar my eye the right to possess it.

49

Against that time – if ever that time come –   *In anticipation of*
When I shall see thee frown on my defects,
When as thy love hath cast his utmost sum,[53]
Called to that audit by advised respects;   *premeditated reasons*
Against that time when thou shalt strangely pass[54]
And scarcely greet me with that sun, thine eye,
When love converted from the thing it was
Shall reasons find of settled gravity: *known weightiness*
Against that time do I ensconce me here   *take refuge*
10   Within the knowledge of mine own desert,   *merit*
And this my hand against myself uprear   *raise up*
To guard the lawful reasons on thy part.   *protect/side*
   To leave poor me, thou hast the strength of laws,   *support*
   Since why to love I can allege no cause.   *i.e. to love me*

50

How heavy do I journey on the way,   *sad*
When what I seek – my weary travel's end –
Doth teach that case and that repose to say   *that end/rest*
'Thus far the miles are measured from thy friend.'
The beast that bears me, tired with my woe,
Plods dully on to bear that weight in me,
As if by some instinct the wretch did know
His rider loved not speed, being made from thee.   *directed away*
The bloody spur cannot provoke him on
10   That sometimes anger thrusts into his hide,
Which heavily he answers with a groan
More sharp to me than spurring to his side;
   For that same groan doth put this in my mind:
   My grief lies onward and my joy behind.

51

Thus can my love excuse the slow offence   *i.e. slowness*
Of my dull bearer when from thee I speed: *i.e. the horse*
From where thou art why should I haste me thence?
Till I return, of posting is no need.   *swiftness*
O what excuse will my poor beast then find
When swift extremity can seem but slow?   *extreme speed*
Then should I spur, though mounted on the wind;
In winged speed no motion shall I know.[55]
Then can no horse with my desire keep pace;
10   Therefore desire, of perfect'st love being made,
Shall neigh (no dull flesh) in his fiery race;   *immaterial kind*
But love, for love, thus shall excuse my jade: *slow, old horse*
   Since from thee going he went wilful-slow,
   Towards thee I'll run and give him leave to go.[56]

52

So am I as the rich whose blessed key   *i.e. like the rich man*
Can bring him to his sweet up-locked treasure,
The which he will not ev'ry hour survey,
For blunting the fine point of seldom pleasure.   *rare*
Therefore are feasts so solemn and so rare
Since, seldom coming, in that long year set

---

53   i.e. When your love has settled its account with me.   55   i.e. Even flight will seem like standing still.
54   i.e. When you shall pass me by as if I were a stranger.   56   i.e. I will run toward you, and let him go.

Like stones of worth they thinly placed are,	*gems/rarely*
Or captain jewels in the carcanet.	*necklace*
So is the time that keeps you as my chest,	*like*
10 Or as the wardrobe which the robe doth hide,	
To make some special instant special-blest	
By new unfolding his imprisoned pride.	*its*
Blessed are you whose worthiness gives scope,	*the possibility*
Being had, to triumph; being lacked, to hope.	

53

What is your substance, whereof are you made,	
That millions of strange shadows on you tend?	*wait*
Since every one, hath every one, one shade,	*shadow*
And you, but one, can every shadow lend.[57]	
Describe Adonis,[58] and the counterfeit	*image*
Is poorly imitated after you.	
On Helen's[59] cheek all art of beauty set,	
And you in Grecian tires are painted new.	*clothes*
Speak of the spring, and foison of the year:	*abundance* (i.e. harvest)
10 The one doth shadow of your beauty show,	
The other as your bounty doth appear;	*generosity*
And you in every blessed shape we know.	
In all external grace you have some part,	
But you like none, none you, for constant heart.	*like you*

54

O how much more doth beauty beauteous seem	
By that sweet ornament which truth doth give!	*With/fidelity*
The rose looks fair, but fairer we it deem	
For that sweet odour which doth in it live.	
The canker blooms have full as deep a dye	*dog-roses*
As the perfumed tincture of the roses,	*colour*
Hang on such thorns, and play as wantonly	*similar*
When summer's breath their masked buds discloses;	*opens up*
But for their virtue only is their show	*appearance*
10 They live unwooed and unrespected fade,	*unlooked at*
Die to themselves. Sweet roses do not so;	
Of their sweet deaths are sweetest odours made:	*perfumes*
And so of you, beauteous and lovely youth,	
When that shall fade, by verse distills your truth.[60]	

55

Not marble nor the gilded monuments	
Of princes shall outlive this powerful rhyme,	
But you shall shine more bright in these contents	i.e. of my poems
Than unswept stone besmeared with sluttish time.	*stone monument/dirty*
When wasteful war shall statues overturn,	
And broils root out the work of masonry,	*battles*
Nor Mars his sword nor war's quick fire shall burn	i.e. Neither Mars's
The living record of your memory.	
'Gainst death and all-oblivious enmity	*oblivion*
10 Shall you pace forth; your praise shall still find room	
Even in the eyes of all posterity	

---

57 i.e. And yet you, though only one person, can create many different reflections.
58 See the gazetteer.

59 See Helen of Troy in the gazetteer.
60 i.e. When your beauty and youth fade, my poetry will preserve
their essence.

That wear this world out to the ending doom.[61]
    So, till the judgment that yourself arise,   *Last Judgment/resurrects*
    You live in this, and dwell in lovers' eyes.

56

Sweet love, renew thy force. Be it not said
Thy edge should blunter be than appetite,   *desire*
Which but today by feeding is allayed,   *sated*
Tomorrow sharpened in his former might.   *its*
So, love, be thou: although today thou fill
Thy hungry eyes even till they wink with fullness,   *close*
Tomorrow see again, and do not kill
The spirit of love with a perpetual dullness.   *lack of interest*
Let this sad int'rim like the ocean be   *interval*
10   Which parts the shore where two contracted new   *newly engaged*
Come daily to the banks, that when they see
Return of love, more blessed may be the view;
    Or call it winter, which being full of care,
    Makes summer's welcome, thrice more wished, more rare.

57

Being your slave, what should I do but tend   *wait*
Upon the hours and times of your desire?
I have no precious time at all to spend,
Nor services to do, till you require;
Nor dare I chide the world-without-end hour   *never-coming*
Whilst I, my sovereign, watch the clock for you,
Nor think the bitterness of absence sour
When you have bid your servant once adieu.
Nor dare I question with my jealous thought
10   Where you may be, or your affairs suppose,   *imagine*
But like a sad slave stay and think of naught   *serious*
Save, where you are, how happy you make those.   *i.e. those with you*
    So true a fool is love that in your will,[62]
    Though you do anything, he thinks no ill.

58

That god forbid, that made me first your slave,
I should in thought control your times of pleasure,
Or at your hand th'account of hours to crave,[63]
Being your vassal bound to stay your leisure.   *wait at*
O let me suffer, being at your beck,   *call*
Th'imprisoned absence of your liberty,[64]
And patience, tame to sufferance, bide each check,
Without accusing you of injury.
Be where you list, your charter is so strong   *please/legal immunity*
10   That you yourself may privilege your time   *justify*
To what you will; to you it doth belong
Yourself to pardon of self-doing crime.
    I am to wait, though waiting so be hell,
    Not blame your pleasure, be it ill or well.

---

61 i.e. From now until the end of time.
62 Some editors see this as a pun on Shakespeare's name.
63 i.e. Or demand from you an account of how you spend your time.
64 i.e. The lack of freedom I endure because of your freedom. / And patience, accustomed to endure, accept each slight.

59

If there be nothing new, but that which is
Hath been before, how are our brains beguiled,
Which labouring for invention bear amiss   *miscarry*
The second burthen of a former child!   *pregnancy/previous*
O that record could with a backward look   *memory*
Even of five hundred courses of the sun   *years*
Show me your image in some antique book
Since mind at first in character was done,[65]
That I might see what the old world could say
10   To this composed wonder of your frame;   *harmonious/body*
Whether we are mended, or whether better they,   *improved*
Or whether revolution be the same.   i.e. life in time
    O sure I am the wits of former days
    To subjects worse have given admiring praise.

60

Like as the waves make towards the pebbled shore,
So do our minutes hasten to their end,
Each changing place with that which goes before;   i.e. Each minute
In sequent toil all forwards do contend.   *sequential*
Nativity, once in the main of light,   A *baby/expanse*
Crawls to maturity, wherewith being crowned
Crooked eclipses 'gainst his glory fight,   *malicious*
And time that gave, doth now his gift confound.   *ruin*
Time doth transfix the flourish set on youth,   *penetrate/varnish*
10   And delves the parallels in beauty's brow;   *wrinkles*
Feeds on the rarities of nature's truth,[66]
And nothing stands but for his scythe to mow.   i.e. Time's
    And yet to times in hope my verse shall stand,   *future time*
    Praising thy worth despite his cruel hand.

61

Is it thy will thy image should keep open
My heavy eyelids to the weary night?
Dost thou desire my slumbers should be broken
While shadows like to thee do mock my sight?
Is it thy spirit that thou send'st from thee
So far from home into my deeds to pry,
To find out shames and idle hours in me,
The scope and tenor of thy jealousy?   *condition*
O no; thy love though much, is not so great.
10   It is my love that keeps mine eye awake,
Mine own true love that doth my rest defeat,
To play the watchman ever for thy sake.[67]
    For thee watch I whilst thou dost wake elsewhere,   *carouse*
    From me far off, with others all too near.

62

Sin of self-love possesseth all mine eye,
And all my soul, and all my every part;   *single parts*
And for this sin there is no remedy,
It is so grounded inward in my heart.
Methinks no face so gracious is as mine,
No shape so true, no truth of such account,   *form/value*

65 i.e. Since thought was first expressed in writing.   67 Watchmen stay awake all night and record the hours.
66 i.e. Feeds on the valuable aspects of nature's genuine quality.

And for myself mine own worth do define
As I all other in all worths surmount.   *As if/others/qualities*
But when my glass shows me myself indeed,   *mirror*
Beated and chapped with tanned antiquity,   *old age*
10   Mine own self-love quite contrary I read;
Self so self-loving were iniquity.   *sinful*
   'Tis thee, my self, that for myself I praise,[68]
   Painting my age with beauty of thy days.   *youthful days*

63

Against my love shall be as I am now,   *Anticipating when*
With time's injurious hand crushed and o'erworn;
When hours have drained his blood and filled his brow
With lines and wrinkles; when his youthful morn
Hath travelled on to age's steepy night,   *steep*
And all those beauties whereof now he's king
Are vanishing, or vanished out of sight,
Stealing away the treasure of his spring:
For such a time do I now fortify   *erect defenses*
10   Against confounding age's cruel knife,   *destructive*
That he shall never cut from memory
My sweet love's beauty, though my lover's life.   *though he take*
   His beauty shall in these black lines be seen,
   And they shall live, and he in them still green.   *fresh*

64

When I have seen by time's fell hand defaced   *malignant*
The rich proud cost of outworn buried age;   *expense/past time*
When sometime-lofty towers I see down razed,   *once*
And brass eternal slave to mortal rage;[69]
When I have seen the hungry ocean gain
Advantage on the kingdom of the shore,   *i.e. At the expense of*
And the firm soil win of the wat'ry main,
Increasing store with loss and loss with store;[70]
When I have seen such interchange of state,   *condition*
10   Or state itself confounded to decay,   *mortal existence*
Ruin hath taught me thus to ruminate: *meditate*
That time will come and take my love away.
   This thought is as a death, which cannot choose   *and cannot*
   But weep to have that which it fears to lose.[71]

65

Since brass, nor stone, nor earth, nor boundless sea,   *i.e. Since there is neither*
But sad mortality o'ersways their power,
How with this rage shall beauty hold a plea,   *sustain*
Whose action is no stronger than a flower?
O how shall summer's honey breath hold out
Against the wrackful siege of battering days   *destructive*
When rocks impregnable are not so stout,
Nor gates of steel so strong, but time decays?
O fearful meditation! Where, alack,   *alas*
10   Shall time's best jewel from time's chest lie hid, *possession/lie hidden*
Or what strong hand can hold his swift foot back,
Or who his spoil of beauty can forbid?   *ruin*

---

68 i.e. It is you, who are myself, whom I praise in myself.   70 i.e. Exchanging gain for loss and loss for gain.
69 i.e. And brass, which never rusts, become prey to the fury of   71 i.e. But weep because it possesses that which it is afraid to lose.
mortality.

O none, unless this miracle have might:
That in black ink my love may still shine bright.

66

Tired with all these, for restful death I cry:
As, to behold desert a beggar born, *worthiness*
And needy nothing trimmed in jollity, *dressed/magnificence*
And purest faith unhappily forsworn, *betrayed*
And gilded honour shamefully misplaced,
And maiden virtue rudely strumpeted, *prostituted*
And right perfection wrongfully disgraced, *marred*
And strength by limping sway disabled, *feeble rule*
And art made tongue-tied by authority, *silent*
10 And folly, doctor-like, controlling skill, *imitating a doctor*
And simple truth miscalled simplicity, *foolishness*
And captive good attending captain ill. *evil*
    Tired with all these, from these would I be gone,
    Save that to die I leave my love alone.

67

Ah, wherefore with infection should he live *corruption*
And with his presence grace impiety,
That sin by him advantage should achieve
And lace itself with his society? *embroider*
Why should false painting imitate his cheek,
And steal dead seeming of his living hue? *from his*
Why should poor beauty indirectly seek
Roses of shadow, since his rose is true? *i.e. Counterfeit roses*
Why should he live now nature bankrupt is,
10 Beggared of blood to blush through lively veins, *Deprived*
For she hath no exchequer now but his, *treasury*
And proud of many, lives upon his gains?
    O, him she stores to show what wealth she had *keeps*
    In days long since, before these last so bad. *long ago*

68

Thus is his cheek the map of days outworn, *image/gone by*
When beauty lived and died as flowers do now,
Before these bastard signs of fair were born *corrupt shows*
Or durst inhabit on a living brow;
Before the golden tresses of the dead,
The right of sepulchres, were shorn away
To live a second life on second head; *i.e. as a wig*
Ere beauty's dead fleece made another gay. *Before*
In him those holy antique hours are seen *ancient times*
10 Without all ornament, itself and true,
Making no summer of another's green, *fertility*
Robbing no old to dress his beauty new;
    And him as for a map doth nature store,
    To show false art what beauty was of yore. *in the past*

69

Those parts of thee that the world's eye doth view *qualities*
Want nothing that the thought of hearts can mend *Lack*
All tongues, the voice of souls, give thee that due,
Uttering bare truth even so as foes commend.[72]

72 i.e. Uttering the bare minimum of truth, in the ways that enemies
praise.

Thy outward thus with outward praise is crowned,
But those same tongues that give thee so thine own   *what is yours*
In other accents do this praise confound   *tones*
By seeing farther than the eye hath shown.
They look into the beauty of thy mind,

10   And that in guess they measure by thy deeds.   *to guess*
Then, churls, their thoughts – although their eyes were kind –   *louts*
To thy fair flower add the rank smell of weeds.
     But why thy odour matcheth not thy show,   *appearance*
     The soil is this: that thou dost common[73] grow.   *source*

70

That thou art blamed shall not be thy defect,
For slander's mark was ever yet the fair,
The ornament of beauty is suspect,   *accompaniment/suspicion*
A crow that flies in heaven's sweetest air.[74]
So thou be good, slander doth but approve   *If/demonstrate*
Thy worth the greater, being wooed of time;
For canker vice the sweetest buds doth love,   *rose worm*
And thou present'st a pure unstained prime.   *youth*
Thou hast passed by the ambush of young days   *traps*

10   Either not assailed, or victor being charged;   *when attacked*
Yet this thy praise cannot be so thy praise   *be enough*
To tie up envy, evermore enlarged.   *always at large*
     If some suspect of ill masked not thy show,[75]
     Then thou alone kingdoms of hearts shouldst owe.   *own*

71

No longer mourn for me when I am dead
Than you shall hear the surly sullen bell
Give warning to the world that I am fled
From this vile world with vilest worms to dwell.
Nay, if you read this line, remember not
The hand that writ it; for I love you so
That I in your sweet thoughts would be forgot
If thinking on me then should make you woe.   *cause*
O, if, I say, you look upon this verse

10   When I perhaps compounded am with clay,   *mixed*
Do not so much as my poor name rehearse,   *repeat*
But let your love even with my life decay.
     Lest the wise world should look into your moan
     And mock you with me after I am gone.   *i.e. because of*

72

O, lest the world should task you to recite   *impose on*
What merit lived in me that you should love,
After my death, dear love, forget me quite;
For you in me can nothing worthy prove –   *show*
Unless you would devise some virtuous lie
To do more for me than mine own desert,
And hang more praise upon deceased I
Than niggard truth would willingly impart.   *miser*
O, lest your true love may seem false in this,

10   That you for love speak well of me untrue,   *falsely*
My name be buried where my body is,   *Let my*

---

73   "Common" here means both "of the lower class" (i.e. base, or
inferior) and "freely available."

74   i.e. It flies like an ugly crow in beauty's sweetest air.

75   i.e. If some suspicion of evil did not cover your beauty.

And live no more to shame nor me, nor you;   *neither*
  For I am shamed by that which I bring forth,   *write*
  And so should you, to love things nothing worth.   *would*

73

That time of year thou mayst in me behold
When yellow leaves, or none, or few, do hang
Upon those boughs which shake against the cold,
Bare ruined choirs[76] where late the sweet birds sang.   *lately*
In me thou seest the twilight of such day
As after sunset fadeth in the west,
Which by and by black night doth take away,
Death's second self, that seals up all in rest.
In me thou seest the glowing of such fire
That on the ashes of his youth doth lie
As the death-bed whereon it must expire,
Consumed with that which it was nourished by.
  This thou perceiv'st, which makes thy love more strong,
  To love that well which thou must leave ere long.

74

But be contented when that fell arrest   *Only/cruel death*
Without all bail shall carry me away.
My life hath in this line some interest,   *verse/legal right*
Which for memorial still with thee shall stay.
When thou reviewest this, thou dost review
The very part was consecrate to thee.   *that was*
The earth can have but earth, which is his due;
My spirit is thine, the better part of me.
So then thou hast but lost the dregs of life,
The prey of worms, my body being dead,
The coward conquest of a wretch's knife,[77]
Too base of thee to be remembered.   *by you*
  The worth of that is that which it contains,   *that body/that spirit*
  And that is this, and this with thee remains.   *this poetry*

75

So are you to my thoughts as food to life,   *i.e. You are to*
Or as sweet-seasoned showers are to the ground;
And for the peace of you I hold such strife[78]
As 'twixt a miser and his wealth is found:
Now proud as an enjoyer, and anon   *owner*
Doubting the filching age will steal his treasure;   *larcenous*
Now counting best to be with you alone,   *counting it*
Then bettered that the world may see my pleasure;
Sometime all full with feasting on your sight,
And by and by clean starved for a look;   *completely*
Possessing or pursuing no delight
Save what is had or must from you be took.
  Thus do I pine and surfeit day by day,
  Or gluttoning on all, or all away.[79]   *hunger*

76   The part of a church between the altar and the congregation where
the choir sits. The poet is imagining the bare trees to be a ruined
church.

77   i.e. The worthless possession of the coward who killed me
(death).

78   i.e. And for the peace you give me, I feel such conflict.

79   i.e. Either gorging on everything, or left hungry with nothing.

76

Why is my verse so barren of new pride,   *fashion*
So far from variation or quick change?   *newfangledness*
Why, with the time, do I not glance aside   *trend*
To new-found methods and to compounds strange?   *compositions*
Why write I still all one, ever the same,   *all the same*
And keep invention in a noted weed,   *habitual garment*
That every word doth almost tell my name,
Showing their birth and where they did proceed?   *from where*
O know, sweet love, I always write of you,
And you and love are still my argument;   *only subject*
So all my best is dressing old words new,
Spending again what is already spent;
    For as the sun is daily new and old,
    So is my love, still telling what is told.

77

Thy glass will show thee how thy beauties wear,   *mirror/fade*
Thy dial how thy precious minutes waste,   *sundial*
These vacant leaves thy mind's imprint will bear,   *blank pages/writing*
And of this book this learning mayst thou taste:
The wrinkles which thy glass will truly show
Of mouthed graves will give thee memory;   *open*
Thou by thy dial's shady stealth mayst know[80]
Time's thievish progress to eternity;
Look what thy memory cannot contain   *Whatever*
Commit to these waste blanks, and thou shalt find   *blank pages*
Those children nursed, delivered from thy brain,   *thoughts*
To take a new acquaintance of thy mind.   *be remembered by*
    These offices so oft as thou wilt look   *rituals*
    Shall profit thee and much enrich thy book.

78

So oft have I invoked thee for my muse
And found such fair assistance in my verse
As every alien pen hath got my use,[81]
And under thee their poesy disperse.   *your influence*
Thine eyes, that taught the dumb on high to sing   *out loud*
And heavy ignorance aloft to fly,   *dull*
Have added feathers to the learned's wing[82]
And given grace a double majesty.
Yet be most proud of that which I compile,   *compose*
Whose influence is thine, and born of thee.   *guide*
In others' works thou dost but mend the style,   *correct*
And arts with thy sweet graces graced be;   *learning*
    But thou art all my art, and dost advance   *raise up*
    As high as learning my rude ignorance.   *crude*

79

Whilst I alone did call upon thy aid   *i.e. invoke you as Muse*
My verse alone had all thy gentle grace;
But now my gracious numbers are decayed,   *verses*
And my sick muse doth give an other place.   *gives way to another*

---

80 i.e. By the slow movement of the shadow across the sundial.
81 i.e. That every other poet is copying this habit.
82 Early Modern poets, copying a classical metaphor, often compared
the experience of composing poetry to flying above the earth, borne by
their muses. Here, the young man is being compared to this divine
source of inspiration; in the next line he makes "grace" (poetic skill)
seem twice as great as it is by his presence as a theme.

I grant, sweet love, thy lovely argument
Deserves the travail of a worthier pen,   *labor*
Yet what of thee thy poet doth invent   *about thee*
He robs thee of, and pays it thee again.
He lends thee virtue, and he stole that word
10   From thy behaviour; beauty doth he give,
And found it in thy cheek: he can afford   *supply*
No praise to thee but what in thee doth live.
  Then thank him not for that which he doth say,
  Since what he owes thee thou thyself dost pay.   *i.e. inspiration*

80

O, how I faint when I of you do write,   *lose heart*
Knowing a better spirit doth use your name,   *i.e. better poet*
And in the praise thereof spends all his might,
To make me tongue-tied, speaking of your fame!
But since your worth, wide as the ocean is,
The humble as the proudest sail doth bear,   *as well as*
My saucy barque, inferior far to his,   *presumptuous ship*
On your broad main doth wilfully appear.   *ocean*
Your shallowest help will hold me up afloat
10   Whilst he upon your soundless deep doth ride;   *unmeasurable*
Or, being wrecked, I am a worthless boat,
He of tall building and of goodly pride.   *large/appearance*
  Then if he thrive and I be cast away,
  The worst was this: my love was my decay.

81

Or I shall live your epitaph to make,   *Whether*
Or you survive when I in earth am rotten.
From hence your memory death cannot take,   *i.e. this poetry*
Although in me each part will be forgotten.   *of me/quality*
Your name from hence immortal life shall have,   *now*
Though I, once gone, to all the world must die.
The earth can yield me but a common grave
When you entombed in men's eyes shall lie.
Your monument shall be my gentle verse,
10   Which eyes not yet created shall o'er-read,
And tongues to be your being shall rehearse[83]
When all the breathers of this world are dead.   *living/this time*
  You still shall live – such virtue hath my pen –
  Where breath most breathes, even in the mouths of men.

82

I grant thou wert not married to my muse,
And therefore mayst without attaint o'erlook   *discredit/read over*
The dedicated words which writers use   *other writers*
Of their fair subject, blessing every book.[84]
Thou art as fair in knowledge as in hue,   *appearance*
Finding thy worth a limit past my praise,
And therefore art enforced to seek anew
Some fresher stamp of the time-bettering days.[85]
And do so, love; yet when they have devised
10   What strained touches rhetoric can lend,   *artificial*
Thou, truly fair, wert truly sympathized   *represented*

83   i.e. And the tongues of people in the future shall recite your life.   85   i.e. Some newer imprint (book, writing) of the new, better age.
84   i.e. Blessing by your act of reading all of those books.

In true plain words by thy true-telling friend;
    And their gross painting might be better used   *i.e. cosmetics*
    Where cheeks need blood: in thee it is abused.

83

I never saw that you did painting need,   *make-up (i.e. exaggeration)*
And therefore to your fair no painting set.   *beauty*
I found – or thought I found – you did exceed
That barren tender of a poet's debt;   *poor payment*
And therefore have I slept in your report: *been slack/praise*
That you yourself, being extant, well might show   *Because/alive*
How far a modern quill doth come too short,   *miss the target*
Speaking of worth, what worth in you doth grow.   *of what*
This silence for my sin you did impute,[86]
10 Which shall be most my glory, being dumb;
For I impair not beauty, being mute,
When others would give life, and bring a tomb.   *i.e. and instead*
    There lives more life in one of your fair eyes
    Than both your poets can in praise devise.

84

Who is it that says most which can say more   *who*
Than this rich praise: that you alone are you,
In whose confine immured is the store   *person contained*
Which should example where your equal grew?[87]
Lean penury within that pen doth dwell   *poverty*
That to his subject lends not some small glory;   *adds*
But he that writes of you, if he can tell
That you are you, so dignifies his story.   *thus*
Let him but copy what in you is writ,
10 Not making worse what nature made so clear,
And such a counterpart shall fame his wit,   *copy/make famous*
Making his style admired everywhere.
    You to your beauteous blessings add a curse,
    Being fond on praise, which makes your praises worse.[88]

85

My tongue-tied muse in manners holds her still   *is politely quiet*
While comments of your praise richly compiled,   *in/composed*
Reserve their character with golden quill   *Preserve/depiction*
And precious phrase by all the muses filed.   *smoothed*
I think good thoughts, whilst other write good words,
And like unlettered clerk still cry 'Amen'[89]
To every hymn that able spirit affords   *i.e. poetic spirit offers*
In polished form of well-refined pen.   *from*
Hearing you praised I say ''Tis so, 'tis true,'
10 And to the most of praise add something more;   *height*
But that is in my thought, whose love to you,   *i.e. Only that which*
Though words come hindmost, holds his rank before.[90]
    Then others, for the breath of words respect,   *i.e. for respect of their words*
    Me for my dumb thoughts, speaking in effect.[91]

---

86 i.e. You imputed my silence to sin.

87 i.e. Which should set an example to one equal to you in qualities.

88 i.e. Being made foolish by flattery, which makes the poems in your praise worse (because they reflect you).

89 i.e. Like an illiterate parish clerk, I can only cry "Amen."

90 i.e. Though my words come last, my thought considers itself in the first rank.

91 i.e. Me, in my silent thoughts, speaking better than words can.

86

Was it the proud full sail of his great verse   *i.e. the other poet's*
Bound for the prize⁹² of all-too-precious you
That did my ripe thoughts in my brain inhearse,
Making their tomb the womb wherein they grew?
Was it his spirit, by spirits taught to write   *supernatural forces*
Above a mortal pitch, that struck me dead?   *elevation/silent*
No, neither he, nor his compeers by night   *attendant spirits*
Giving him aid my verse astonished.   *paralyzed*
He nor that affable familiar ghost
10 Which nightly gulls him with intelligence,   *deludes/information*
As victors, of my silence cannot boast;
I was not sick of any fear from thence.
  But when your countenance filled up his line,   *face's beauty*
  Then lacked I matter; that enfeebled mine.   *subject matter*

87

Farewell – thou art too dear for my possessing,   *expensive*
And like enough thou know'st thy estimate.   *value*
The charter of thy worth gives thee releasing;⁹³
My bonds in thee are all determinate.
For how do I hold thee but by thy granting,
And for that riches where is my deserving?   *those*
The cause of this fair gift in me is wanting,   *lacking*
And so my patent back again is swerving.   *turning*
Thyself thou gav'st, thy own worth then not knowing,   *at that time*
10 Or me to whom thou gav'st it else mistaking;⁹⁴
So thy great gift upon misprision growing,   *growing out of error*
Comes home again, on better judgement making.   *judgment's forming*
  Thus have I had thee as a dream doth flatter;
  In sleep a king, but waking no such matter.

88

When thou shalt be disposed to set me light   *value me lightly*
And place my merit in the eye of scorn,
Upon thy side against myself I'll fight,   *your cause*
And prove thee virtuous though thou art forsworn. *i.e. you have perjured yourself*
With mine own weakness being best acquainted,
Upon thy part I can set down a story
Of faults concealed wherein I am attainted,   *condemned*
That thou in losing me shalt win much glory;   *leaving*
And I by this will be a gainer too;
10 For bending all my loving thoughts on thee,
The injuries that to myself I do,
Doing thee vantage, double-vantage me.   *advantage*
  Such is my love, to thee I so belong,
  That for thy right, myself will bear all wrong.   *privilege*

89

Say that thou didst forsake me for some fault,
And I will comment upon that offence;   *expand*
Speak of my lameness, and I straight will halt,   *limp*

---

92 Ships captured in war were referred to as "prizes"; the rival poet is being compared to a pirate or privateer.

93 i.e. The legal privileges that your worth gives you release you from my love. This sonnet's dominant metaphors are drawn from legal documents: a "bond" (line 4) is a contract which is "determinate" when it expires; the speaker "holds" his beloved in the sense that a tenant holds a property, by the "granting" of the owner; and a "patent" is a royal grant of exclusive monopoly in some form of business.

94 i.e. Or mistakenly valuing me, to whom you gave yourself.

Against thy reasons making no defence.
Thou canst not, love, disgrace me half so ill,   *disparage*
To set a form upon desired change,[95]
As I'll myself disgrace, knowing thy will.
I will acquaintance strangle and look strange,[96]
Be absent from thy walks, and in my tongue
10   Thy sweet beloved name no more shall dwell,
Lest I, too much profane, should do it wrong,
And haply of our old acquaintance tell.   *by chance*
    For thee, against myself I'll vow debate;   *dispute*
    For I must ne'er love him whom thou dost hate.

90

Then hate me when thou wilt, if ever, now,
Now while the world is bent my deeds to cross,   *frustrate*
Join with the spite of fortune, make me bow,
And do not drop in for an after-loss.[97]
Ah do not, when my heart hath 'scaped this sorrow,
Come in the rearward of a conquered woe;[98]
Give not a windy night a rainy morrow   *morning*
To linger out a purposed overthrow.   *draw out/proposed*
If thou wilt leave me, do not leave me last,
10   When other petty griefs have done their spite,
But in the onset come; so shall I taste   *beginning*
At first the very worst of fortune's might,
    And other strains of woe, which now seem woe,   *breeds*
    Compared with loss of thee will not seem so.

91

Some glory in their birth, some in their skill,
Some in their wealth, some in their body's force,   *strength*
Some in their garments (though new-fangled ill),   *fashionably ugly*
Some in their hawks and hounds, some in their horse,
And every humour hath his adjunct pleasure   *temperament/appropriate*
Wherein it finds a joy above the rest.
But these particulars are not my measure;   *pleasures/judgment*
All these I better in one general best.   *surpass*
Thy love is better than high birth to me,
10   Richer than wealth, prouder than garments' costs,
Of more delight than hawks and horses be,
And having thee of all men's pride I boast,   *sources of pride*
    Wretched in this alone: that thou mayst take
    All this away, and me most wretched make.

92

But do thy worst to steal thyself away,
For term of life thou art assured mine,   *life's duration*
And life no longer than thy love will stay,
For it depends upon that love of thine.
Then need I not to fear the worst of wrongs
When in the least of them my life hath end.[99]
I see a better state to me belongs   *condition*
Than that which on thy humour doth depend.
Thou canst not vex me with inconstant mind,   *with your*

---

95   i.e. To provide an excuse for changing your feelings towards me.   97   i.e. And do not add to my woes later on.
96   i.e. I will kill friendship, and pretend not to know you when we   98   i.e. Come to me later after I have overcome my present woe.
meet.   99   i.e. When in the loss of your affection my life is over.

10   Since that my life on thy revolt doth lie.[100]
        O, what a happy title do I find –   *legal right*
        Happy to have thy love, happy to die!
            But what's so blessed-fair that fears no blot?   *taint*
            Thou mayst be false, and yet I know it not.

93

        So shall I live, supposing thou art true   *i.e. So I shall/faithful*
        Like a deceived husband; so love's face   *i.e. the appearance of love*
        May still seem love to me, though altered new –
        Thy looks with me, thy heart in other place.
        For there can live no hatred in thine eye,
        Therefore in that I cannot know thy change.   *learn of*
        In many's looks the false heart's history
        Is writ in moods and frowns and wrinkles strange;   *hostile*
        But heaven in thy creation did decree
10   That in thy face sweet love should ever dwell;
        Whate'er thy thoughts or thy heart's workings be,
        Thy looks should nothing thence but sweetness tell.   *from there (i.e. his face)*
            How like Eve's apple doth thy beauty grow
            If thy sweet virtue answer not thy show!   *matches/appearance*

94

        They that have power to hurt and will do none,
        That do not do the thing they most do show,   *seem to do*
        Who moving others are themselves as stone,   *inspiring*
        Unmoved, cold, and to temptation slow –
        They rightly do inherit heaven's graces,   *blessings*
        And husband nature's riches from expense;   *save/waste*
        They are the lords and owners of their faces,   *i.e. of how they appear*
        Others but stewards of their excellence.   *managers*
        The summer's flower is to the summer sweet
10   Though to itself it only live and die,   *by itself*
        But if that flower with base infection meet
        The basest weed outbraves his dignity;   *surpasses/merit*
            For sweetest things turn sourest by their deeds:
            Lilies that fester smell far worse than weeds.

95

        How sweet and lovely dost thou make the shame
        Which, like a canker in the fragrant rose,   *worm*
        Doth spot the beauty of thy budding name!   *stain/reputation*
        O, in what sweets dost thou thy sins enclose!   *sweetness*
        That tongue that tells the story of thy days,
        Making lascivious comments on thy sport,   *adventures*
        Cannot dispraise, but in a kind of praise,
        Naming thy name, blesses an ill report.   *reputation*
        O, what a mansion have those vices got
10   Which for their habitation chose out thee,
        Where beauty's veil doth cover every blot
        And all things turns to fair that eyes can see!
            Take heed, dear heart, of this large privilege: *your*
            The hardest knife ill-used doth lose his edge.

---

100   i.e. Since I would die if you ever rejected me (and would thus end
my suffering).

96

Some say thy fault is youth, some wantonness;   *lustfulness*
Some say thy grace is youth and gentle sport.   *amorous play*
Both grace and faults are loved of more and less;   *i.e. by the upper and lower class*
Thou mak'st faults graces that to thee resort.   *flock*
As on the finger of a throned queen
The basest jewel will be well esteemed,   *valued*
So are those errors that in thee are seen
To truths translated, and for true things deemed.   *transformed/named*
How many lambs might the stern wolf betray
If like a lamb he could his looks translate!
How many gazers mightst thou lead away
If thou wouldst use the strength of all thy state!   *power*
   But do not so: I love thee in such sort   *i.e. such a way*
   As, thou being mine, mine is thy good report.[101]   *That/reputation*

97

How like a winter hath my absence been
From thee, the pleasure of the fleeting year!
What freezings have I felt, what dark days seen,
What old December's bareness everywhere!
And yet this time removed was summer's time,   *away*
The teeming autumn big with rich increase,   *fertile/pregnant*
Bearing the wanton burden of the prime   *spring*
Like widowed wombs after their lords' decease.
Yet this abundant issue seemed to me   *offspring*
But hope of orphans, and unfathered fruit,   *parentless children*
For summer and his pleasures wait on thee,   *attend*
And thou away, the very birds are mute;
   Or if they sing, 'tis with so dull a cheer
   That leaves look pale, dreading the winter's near.   *is near*

98

From you have I been absent in the spring
When proud-pied April, dressed in all his trim,   *multi-coloured*
Hath put a spirit of youth in everything,
That heavy Saturn[102] laughed and leaped with him.   *So that/melancholy*
Yet nor the lays of birds nor the sweet smell   *songs*
Of different flowers in odour and in hue   *colour*
Could make me any summer's story tell,
Or from their proud lap pluck them where they grew;   *i.e. ground*
Nor did I wonder at the lily's white,
Nor praise the deep vermilion in the rose.
They were but sweet, but figures of delight   *images*
Drawn after you, you pattern of all those;
   Yet seemed it winter still, and you away,
   As with your shadow I with these did play.   *As if/portrait*

99

The forward violet thus did I chide: *early*
Sweet thief, whence didst thou steal thy sweet that smells,   *scent*
If not from my love's breath? The purple pride
Which on thy soft cheek for complexion dwells
In my love's veins thou hast too grossly dyed.   *From/blatantly*
The lily I condemned for thy hand,[103]

---

101 This final couplet is the same as in Sonnet 36.
102 This refers to Saturn not as a classical god but as a planet; in astrology, the influence of Saturn was said to make one melancholy.

103 i.e. The lily I condemned for stealing its whiteness from my beloved's hand.

And buds of marjoram had stol'n thy hair;
The roses fearfully on thorns did stand,   *thorny stalks*
One blushing shame, another white despair;
10 A third, nor red nor white, had stol'n of both,
And to his robb'ry had annexed thy breath;
But for his theft in pride of all his growth
A vengeful canker eat him up to death.   *worm*
    More flowers I noted, yet I none could see
    But sweet or colour it had stol'n from thee.   *Except*

100

Where art thou, muse, that thou forget'st so long
To speak of that which gives thee all thy might?
Spend'st thou thy fury on some worthless song,   *poetic inspiration*
Dark'ning thy power to lend base subjects light?   *Demeaning*
Return, forgetful muse, and straight redeem   *straightaway*
In gentle numbers time so idly spent;   *noble verses*
Sing to the ear that doth thy lays esteem   *songs*
And gives thy pen both skill and argument.   *subject matter*
Rise, resty muse, my love's sweet face survey   *lazy*
10 If time have any wrinkle graven there.
If any, be a satire to decay[104]
And make time's spoils despised everywhere.   *effects*
    Give my love fame faster than time wastes life;
    So, thou prevent'st his scythe and crooked knife.   *ward off*

101

O truant muse, what shall be thy amends
For thy neglect of truth in beauty dyed?
Both truth and beauty on my love depends;
So dost thou too, and therein dignified.   *and are*
Make answer, muse. Wilt thou not haply say   *perchance*
'Truth needs no colour with his colour fixed,'[105]
Beauty no pencil beauty's truth to lay,   *paint brush/apply*
But best is best if never intermixed'?
Because he needs no praise wilt thou be dumb?
10 Excuse not silence so, for't lies in thee
To make him much outlive a gilded tomb,
And to be praised of ages yet to be.
    Then do thy office, muse; I teach thee how   *job*
    To make him seem long hence as he shows now.[106]

102

My love is strengthened, though more weak in seeming.   *appearance*
I love not less, though less the show appear.
That love is merchandized whose rich esteeming   *valuation*
The owner's tongue doth publish everywhere.
Our love was new and then but in the spring
When I was wont to greet it with my lays,   *accustomed*
As Philomel[107] in summer's front doth sing,   *beginning*
And stops her pipe in growth of riper days –
Not that the summer is less pleasant now
10 Than when her mournful hymns did hush the night,
But that wild music burthens every bough,   i.e. that other birds' music
And sweets grown common lose their dear delight.

---

104 i.e. If there are any, write a satire against the decay caused by time.   106 i.e. To make him appear in the future the way he appears now.
105 i.e. Truth needs no artificial color to add to its true color.   107 See the gazetteer under Philomela.

Therefore like her I sometime hold my tongue,
Because I would not dull you with my song.   *blunt*

103

Alack, what poverty my muse brings forth   *poor verse*
That, having such a scope to show her pride,
The argument all bare is of more worth   *by itself*
Than when it hath my added praise beside!
O blame me not if I no more can write!
Look in your glass and there appears a face
That overgoes my blunt invention quite,   *outdoes/crude*
Dulling my lines and doing me disgrace.   *Making dull*
Were it not sinful then, striving to mend,
10   To mar the subject that before was well? –
For to no other pass my verses tend   *course of action*
Than of your graces and your gifts to tell;
      And more, much more, than in my verse can sit   *stay*
      Your own glass shows you when you look in it.

104

To me, fair friend, you never can be old;
For as you were when first your eye I eyed,
Such seems your beauty still. Three winters cold
Have from the forests shook three summers' pride;   *glory*
Three beauteous springs to yellow autumn turned
In process of the seasons have I seen,
Three April perfumes in three hot Junes burned
Since first I saw you fresh, which yet are green.
Ah yet doth beauty, like a dial hand,   *clock*
10   Steal from his figure and no pace perceived;[108]
So your sweet hue, which methinks still doth stand,   *appearance*
Hath motion, and mine eye may be deceived.
      For fear of which, hear this thou age unbred: *unborn* (i.e. future)
      Ere you were born was beauty's summer dead.   *Before*

105

Let not my love be called idolatry,
Nor my beloved as an idol show,
Since all alike my songs and praises be
To one, of one, still such, and ever so.   *always*
Kind is my love today, tomorrow kind,
Still constant in a wondrous excellence.
Therefore my verse, to constancy confined,
One thing expressing, leaves out difference.   *variety*
Fair, kind, and true, is all my argument,
10   'Fair, kind, and true' varying to other words,
And in this change is my invention spent,   *change of words/exhausted*
Three themes in one, which wondrous scope affords.
      Fair, kind, and true have often lived alone,   *apart*
      Which three till now never kept seat in one.   *lived*

106

When in the chronicle of wasted time   *past*
I see descriptions of the fairest wights,   *persons*
And beauty making beautiful old rhyme
In praise of ladies dead and lovely knights;

---

108   i.e. Move off the number on which it sits without seeming to move.

Then in the blazon of sweet beauty's best,[109]   *record*
Of hand, of foot, of lip, of eye, of brow,
I see their antique pen would have expressed
Ev'n such a beauty as you master now.   *control*
So all their praises are but prophecies
10   Of this our time, all you prefiguring,
And for they looked but with divining eyes   *conjecturing*
They had not skill enough your worth to sing;
      For we which now behold these present days
      Have eyes to wonder, but lack tongues to praise.

107

Not mine own fears, nor the prophetic soul
Of the wide world dreaming on things to come
Can yet the lease of my true love control,   *time span*
Supposed as forfeit to a confined doom.[110]
The mortal moon[111] hath her eclipse endured,
And the sad augurs mock their own presage;   *soothsayers/predictions*
Incertainties now crown themselves assured,[112]
And peace proclaims olives[113] of endless age.   *without end*
Now with the drops of this most balmy time
10   My love looks fresh, and death to me subscribes,   *consents*
Since spite of him I'll live in this poor rhyme   *in spite*
While he insults o'er dull and speechless tribes;[114]
      And thou in this shalt find thy monument
      When tyrants' crests and tombs of brass are spent.   *monuments/wasted away*

108

What's in the brain that ink may character   *write*
Which hath not figured to thee my true spirit?   *represented*
What's new to speak, what now to register,   *record*
That may express my love or thy dear merit?
Nothing, sweet boy; but yet like prayers divine
I must each day say o'er the very same,
Counting no old thing old, thou mine, I thine,[115]
Even as when first I hallowed thy fair name.   *blessed*
So that eternal love in love's fresh case   i.e. *garments*
10   Weighs not the dust and injury of age,   i.e. *Cares not for*
Nor gives to necessary wrinkles place,   *gives way to*
But makes antiquity for aye his page,   *ever/servant*
      Finding the first conceit of love there bred   *conception/i.e. in antiquity*
      Where time and outward form would show it dead.

109

O never say that I was false of heart,
Though absence seemed my flame to qualify –   *modify*
As easy might I from myself depart
As from my soul, which in thy breast doth lie.
That is my home of love. If I have ranged,   *wandered*
Like him that travels I return again,

---

109   This kind of itemized list of the beloved's excellencies is characteristic of Petrarchan love poetry, which was still a strong influence on
love poetry in Shakespeare's day (see the gazetteer under Petrarch).
110   i.e. Supposed to be in the power of finite destiny (mortality).
111   Some editors read this as a reference to the late Queen Elizabeth
I, who was often compared poetically to (and represented pictorially as)
the moon goddess Diana because of her virginity.

112   i.e. Uncertainties now declare themselves to be certainties.
113   The olive branch was then, as now, a symbol of peace.
114   i.e. While death exults over those who have no poetry to defy him
with.
115   i.e. Valuing no old thing as stale, since you have been mine and
I yours for a long time.

Just to the time, not with the time exchanged,   *Prompt/altered*
So that myself bring water for my stain.[116]
Never believe, though in my nature reigned
10   All frailties that besiege all kinds of blood,   *types of person*
That it could so preposterously be stained
To leave for nothing all thy sum of good;
    For nothing this wide universe I call
    Save thou my rose; in it thou art my all.

110

Alas, 'tis true, I have gone here and there
And made myself a motley to the view,   *jester*
Gored mine own thoughts, sold cheap what is most dear,   *Wounded*
Made old offences of affections new.[117]
Most true it is that I have looked on truth
Askance and strangely. But, by all above,   *Indirectly*
These blenches gave my heart another youth,   *side glances*
And worse essays proved thee my best of love.   *experiments*
Now all is done, have what shall have no end;   *take what*
10   Mine appetite I never more will grind   *desire/sharpen*
On newer proof to try an older friend,   *i.e. With a newer test*
A god in love, to whom I am confined.   *in his*
    Then give me welcome, next my heaven the best,   *next to*
    Even to thy pure and most most loving breast.

111

O, for my sake do you with fortune chide,
The guilty goddess of my harmful deeds,   *i.e. The goddess guilty of*
That did not better for my life provide
Than public means which public manners breeds.[118]
Thence comes it that my name receives a brand,   *mark of shame*
And almost thence my nature is subdued   *subordinated*
To what it works in, like the dyer's hand.
Pity me then, and wish I were renewed,   *restored*
Whilst like a willing patient I will drink
10   Potions of eisel 'gainst my strong infection;   *vinegar*
No bitterness that I will bitter think,
Nor double penance to correct correction.[119]
    Pity me then, dear friend, and I assure ye,
    Even that your pity is enough to cure me.

112

Your love and pity doth th'impression fill   *erase the mark*
Which vulgar scandal stamped upon my brow;
For what care I who calls me well or ill,
So you o'er-green my bad, my good allow?   *i.e. replace my bad qualities*
You are my all the world, and I must strive
To know my shames and praises from your tongue –   *learn*
None else to me, nor I to none alive,
That my steeled sense or changes, right or wrong.[120]
In so profound abyss I throw all care   *such a*
10   Of others' voices that my adder's sense[121]

---

116 i.e. So I myself bring the means to erase my sin (leaving you).

117 i.e. Offended my old affections by enthusiasms for new things.

118 i.e. Than a job in the public eye, which breeds manners that flatter the public. This line is often read as a reference to Shakespeare's career as an actor and playwright. The "brand" in line 5 would then refer to the low esteem in which the acting profession was held.

119 i.e. Nor a second cure, that could undo the good that the first one has done.

120 i.e. could change my fixed sensibilities, rightly or wrongly.

121 In Early Modern Europe, adders were popularly thought to be deaf, hence "adder's sense" would mean deaf ears.

To critic and to flatterer stopped are.   *blocked*
Mark how with my neglect I do dispense:[122]
    You are so strongly in my purpose bred   *nurtured*
    That all the world besides, methinks, they're dead.

113

Since I left you mine eye is in my mind,
And that which governs me to go about
Doth part his function and is partly blind,   *divide*
Seems seeing, but effectually is out;   *seems to see/blind*
For it no form delivers to the heart
Of bird, of flower, or shape which it doth latch.   *catch*
Of his quick objects hath the mind no part,   *living*
Nor his own vision holds what it doth catch;   *i.e. does my mind's eye hold*
For if it see the rud'st or gentlest sight,   *commonest/noblest*
10   The most sweet favour or deformed'st creature,   *appearance*
The mountain or the sea, the day or night,
The crow or dove, it shapes them to your feature.   *appearance*
    Incapable of more, replete with you,   *filled*
    My most true mind thus makes mine eye untrue.

114

Or whether doth my mind, being crowned with you,   *Whether my mind/raised by*
Drink up the monarch's plague, this flattery,   *curse*
Or whether shall I say mine eye saith true,
And that your love taught it this alchemy,[123]
To make of monsters and things indigest   *shapeless*
Such cherubins as your sweet self resemble,   *angels*
Creating every bad a perfect best   *Recreating*
As fast as objects to his beams assemble?   *eyesight*
O, 'tis the first, 'tis flatt'ry in my seeing,
10   And my great mind most kingly drinks it up.
Mine eye well knows what with his gust is 'greeing,   *taste*
And to his palate doth prepare the cup.   *according to*
    If it be poisoned, 'tis the lesser sin
    That mine eye loves it and doth first begin.   *Because/begin to drink*

115

Those lines that I before have writ do lie,
Even those that said I could not love you dearer;
Yet then my judgment knew no reason why
My most full flame should afterwards burn clearer.   *love/brighter*
But reckoning time, whose millioned accidents   *millions of*
Creep in 'twixt vows and change decrees of kings,
Tan sacred beauty, blunt the sharp'st intents,   *Darken*
Divert strong minds to th'course of alt'ring things –   *changeful*
Alas, why, fearing of time's tyranny,   *afraid of*
10   Might I not then say 'Now I love you best',
When I was certain o'er incertainty,
Crowning the present, doubting of the rest?   *Elevating*
    Love is a babe; then might I not say so,   *back then*
    To give full growth to that which still doth grow.   *allow*

---

122 i.e. See how I condone my lack of concern for what others think   123 "Alchemy" is often poetically used in the general sense of
of me.   "magic," but here it has its precise meaning as a form of magic which
focuses on transformation (especially of base metals into gold).

116

Let me not to the marriage of true minds
Admit impediments. Love is not love
Which alters when it alteration finds,
Or bends with the remover to remove.   *restless person*
O no, it is an ever-fixèd mark   *landmark*
That looks on tempests and is never shaken;
It is the star to every wand'ring barque,   *ship*
Whose worth's unknown although his height be taken.[124]
Love's not time's fool, though rosy lips and cheeks   *minion*
Within his bending sickle's compass come;   *time's/power*
Love alters not with his brief hours and weeks,
But bears it out even to the edge of doom.   *endures/Doomsday*
   If this be error and upon me proved,
   I never writ, nor no man ever loved.

10 (line 10 marker)

117

Accuse me thus: that I have scanted all   *withheld*
Wherein I should your great deserts repay,
Forgot upon your dearest love to call
Whereto all bonds do tie me day by day;
That I have frequent been with unknown minds,   *familiar/people*
And given to time your own dear-purchased right;[125]
That I have hoisted sail to all the winds
Which should transport me farthest from your sight.   *would*
Book both my wilfulness and errors down,   *Note*
And on just proof surmise accumulate;[126]
Bring me within the level of your frown,   *aim*
But shoot not at me in your wakened hate,
   Since my appeal says I did strive to prove   *legal appeal/test*
   The constancy and virtue of your love.

10 (line 10 marker)

118

Like as, to make our appetite more keen,   *i.e. Just as*
With eager compounds we our palate urge;   *strong-tasting/provoke*
As to prevent our maladies unseen
We sicken to shun sickness when we purge:[127]
Even so, being full of your ne'er cloying sweetness,   *excessive*
To bitter sauces did I frame my feeding,   *direct*
And, sick of welfare, found a kind of meetness   *health/fitness*
To be diseased ere that there was true needing.   *i.e. before there was need*
Thus policy in love, t' anticipate   *cunning*
The ills that were not, grew to faults assured,   *confirmed*
And brought to medicine a healthful state
Which, rank of goodness, would by ill be cured.   *swollen with*
   But thence I learn, and find the lesson true:
   Drugs poison him that so fell sick of you.   *i.e. that in this way*

10 (line 10 marker)

119

What potions have I drunk of siren tears[128]
Distilled from limbecks foul as hell within,   *stills*
Applying fears to hopes, and hopes to fears,
Still losing when I saw myself to win!

124   A reference to the practice of measuring the position of a star in the sky in order to determine a ship's position at sea.
125   i.e. And given to transient time the right to my attention that you have paid for.
126   i.e. And add suspicion to proved truth.
127   i.e. We make ourselves a little sick, by purging, to fend off greater sickness.
128   See the gazetteer under Sirens.

What wretched errors hath my heart committed
Whilst it hath thought itself so blessed never!   *i.e. never so blessed*
How have mine eyes out of their spheres been fitted   *sockets/forced*
In the distraction of this madding fever!
O benefit of ill! Now I find true   *evil*
That better is by evil still made better,   *made still*
And ruined love when it is built anew
Grows fairer than at first, more strong, far greater.
    So I return rebuked to my content,   *contentment*
    And gain by ills thrice more than I have spent.

120

That you were once unkind befriends me now,   *comforts*
And for that sorrow which I then did feel   *because of*
Needs must I under my transgression bow,   *offense*
Unless my nerves were brass or hammered steel.
For if you were by my unkindness shaken
As I by yours, you've passed a hell of time,
And I, a tyrant, have no leisure taken   *opportunity*
To weigh how once I suffered in your crime.   *consider*
O that our night of woe might have remembered   *period of suffering/reminded*
My deepest sense how hard true sorrow hits,   *sensibility*
And soon to you as you to me then tendered   *offered*
The humble salve which wounded bosoms fits!   *balm (i.e. remorse)*
    But that your trespass now becomes a fee;   *i.e. But your unkindness/payment*
    Mine ransoms yours, and yours must ransom me.   *rescues*

121

'Tis better to be vile than vile esteemed   *i.e. reputed to be vile*
When not to be receives reproach of being,
And the just pleasure lost, which is so deemed   *proper/reputed so*
Not by our feeling but by others' seeing.   *feelings/opinions*
For why should others' false adulterate eyes   *corrupted*
Give salutation to my sportive blood?   *greetings/amorous passion*
Or on my frailties why are frailer spies,   *weaknesses/i.e. why are there*
Which in their wills count bad what I think good?   *minds/consider*
No, I am that I am, and they that level   *what/take aim*
At my abuses reckon up their own.   *total*
I may be straight, though they themselves be bevel;   *slanted*
By their rank thoughts my deeds must not be shown,   *unpleasant*
    Unless this general evil they maintain: *reinforce*
    All men are bad and in their badness reign.

122

Thy gift, thy tables, are within my brain   *i.e. a notebook*
Full charactered with lasting memory,   *written*
Which shall above that idle rank remain   *worthless status*
Beyond all date, even to eternity;
Or at the least so long as brain and heart
Have faculty by nature to subsist,[129]
Till each to razed oblivion yield his part   *erasing*
Of thee, thy record never can be missed.   *lost*
That poor retention could not so much hold,   *mere records*
Nor need I tallies[130] thy dear love to score;
Therefore to give them from me was I bold,   *away from*

---

129 i.e. Have the capacity, because of their natures, to endure.

130 A "tally" was a notched stick used to keep a record of debts and numerical transactions.

To trust those tables that receive thee more. *i.e. tables of memory*
To keep an adjunct to remember thee *subordinate*
Were to import forgetfulness in me. *signify*

123

No, time, thou shalt not boast that I do change!
Thy pyramids built up with newer might *monuments/more recent*
To me are nothing novel, nothing strange, *alien*
They are but dressings of a former sight.[131]
Our dates are brief, and therefore we admire *i.e. lives are short*
What thou dost foist upon us that is old,
And rather make them born to our desire *i.e. imagine them created*
Than think that we before have heard them told.
Thy registers and thee I both defy,
10 Not wond'ring at the present nor the past;
For thy records and what we see doth lie,
Made more or less by thy continual haste. *i.e. more or less important*
   This I do vow, and this shall ever be:
   I will be true despite thy scythe and thee.

124

If my dear love were but the child of state[132]
It might for fortune's bastard be unfathered,
As subject to time's love or to time's hate,
Weeds among weeds or flowers with flowers gathered.[133]
No, it was builded far from accident; *chance events*
It suffers not in smiling pomp, nor falls *undergoes change*
Under the blow of thralled discontent *enslaved*
Whereto th'inviting time our fashion calls.[134]
It fears not policy, that heretic *insincerity*
10 Which works on leases of short-numbered hours,[135]
But all alone stands hugely politic, *prudent*
That it nor grows with heat nor drowns with showers. *i.e. prosperity/misfortune*
   To this I witness call the fools of time, *i.e. call to witness*
   Which die for goodness, who have lived for crime. *Who/in goodness/in crime*

125

Were't aught to me I bore the canopy,[136]
With my extern the outward honouring, *public acts/shows of power*
Or laid great bases for eternity *foundations/permanent monuments*
Which proves more short than waste or ruining? *i.e. lasts a shorter time*
Have I not seen dwellers on form and favour *ceremony/superficial appearances*
Lose all and more by paying too much rent,[137]
For compound sweet forgoing simple savour,[138]
Pitiful thrivers in their gazing spent?[139]
No, let me be obsequious in thy heart, *obedient*
10 And take thou my oblation, poor but free, *offering*

---

131 i.e. They are just redecorated versions of something old. Some scholars sense a reference here to the grandiose structures erected for the coronation of King James I in 1603.

132 i.e. If my feelings for you were the products of the changing state of things, then they might seem to exist only by chance.

133 i.e. Loved or hated, as the changing times dictate.

134 i.e. With which time tempts us by making them seem fashionable.

135 i.e. Which plans only for short periods of time (in other words, temporary gains).

136 i.e. What would it be to me if I bore the canopy. "Bearing the canopy" refers to the Early Modern practice of holding a cloth screen over the heads of monarchs as they went on public processions. It was considered an honor to hold one of the poles which kept the canopy up.

137 i.e. Lose all that they have by devoting too much energy to superficial things.

138 i.e. For elaborate compliments sacrificing plain speech.

139 i.e. drained by focusing ("gazing") on externalities.

Which is not mixed with seconds, knows no art   *defective matter/deceit*
But mutual render, only me for thee.   *mutual exchange*
  Hence, thou suborned informer! A true soul   *perjured*
  When most impeached stands least in thy control.   *accused*

126[140]

O thou my lovely boy who in thy power
Dost hold time's fickle glass, his sickle-hour;   *mirror/harvest time*
Who hast by waning grown, and therein show'st,   *i.e. by ageing grown young*
Thy lovers withering as thy sweet self grow'st —
If nature, sovereign mistress over wrack,   *decay*
As thou goest onwards still will pluck thee back,
She keeps thee to this purpose: that her skill   *for this*
May time disgrace, and wretched minutes kill.
Yet fear her, O thou minion of her pleasure!   *plaything*
She may detain but not still keep her treasure.   *i.e. Nature*
  Her audit, though delayed, answered must be,   *debt*
  And her quietus is to render thee.   *discharge/surrender*

127

In the old age black was not counted fair,   *past times*
Or if it were, it bore not beauty's name;
But now is black beauty's successive heir,   *succeeding*
And beauty slandered with a bastard shame: *i.e. illegitimacy*
For since each hand hath put on nature's power,   *taken*
Fairing the foul with art's false borrowed face,   *Beautifying/painted*
Sweet beauty hath no name, no holy bower,
But is profaned, if not lives in disgrace.   *corrupted*
Therefore my mistress' eyes are raven-black,
Her brow so suited, and they mourners seem   *matched*
At such who, not born fair, no beauty lack,   *For*
Sland'ring creation with a false esteem.   *reputation*
  Yet so they mourn, becoming of their woe,   *i.e. beautifying their*
  That every tongue says beauty should look so.

128

How oft, when thou, my music, music play'st
Upon that blessed wood whose motion sounds   *i.e. keyboard*
With thy sweet fingers when thou gently sway'st   *manage*
The wiry concord that mine ear confounds,   *string harmony/amazes*
Do I envy those jacks that nimble leap   *keys*
To kiss the tender inward of thy hand
Whilst my poor lips, which should that harvest reap,
At the wood's boldness by thee blushing stand!
To be so tickled they would change their state   *condition*
And situation with those dancing chips
O'er whom thy fingers walk with gentle gait,
Making dead wood more blest than living lips.
  Since saucy jacks so happy are in this,
  Give them thy fingers, me thy lips to kiss.

129[141]

Th' expense of spirit in a waste of shame   *expenditure of life energy*
Is lust in action; and till action, lust

---

140 This sonnet is written in six couplets, rather than the usual Shakespearean sonnet form.
141 Revulsion at sexual attraction was a common poetic theme in this period. Sometimes, as is the case here, they are inserted in sequences of poems that otherwise celebrate this subject. In other cases, poets famous for writing love poetry show equal skill in damning sensual love in favor of spiritual pursuits (see, for example, Philip Sidney's "Leave Me, O Love" on p. 583).

Is perjured, murd'rous, bloody, full of blame,
Savage, extreme, rude, cruel, not to trust,   *untrustworthy*
Enjoyed no sooner but despised straight,   *straightaway*
Past reason hunted, and no sooner had   *Furiously*
Past reason hated as a swallowed bait
On purpose laid to make the taker mad;
Mad in pursuit and in possession so,
Had, having, and in quest to have, extreme;
A bliss in proof and proved, a very woe;[142]
Before, a joy proposed; behind, a dream.
    All this the world well knows, yet none knows well
    To shun the heaven that leads men to this hell.

130

My mistress' eyes are nothing like the sun;
Coral is far more red, than her lips red.
If snow be white, why then her breasts are dun;   *grey-brown*
If hairs be wires, black wires grow on her head.
I have seen roses damasked, red and white,   *ornamented*
But no such roses see I in her cheeks;
And in some perfumes is there more delight
Than in the breath that from my mistress reeks.   *smells*
I love to hear her speak, yet well I know
That music hath a far more pleasing sound.
I grant I never saw a goddess go: *walk*
My mistress when she walks treads on the ground.
    And yet, by heaven, I think my love as rare
    As any she belied with false compare.   *woman/comparison*

131

Thou art as tyrannous so as thou art[143]
As those whose beauties proudly make them cruel,
For well thou know'st to my dear doting heart   *foolish*
Thou art the fairest and most precious jewel.
Yet, in good faith, some say that thee behold
Thy face hath not the power to make love groan.   *pine*
To say they err I dare not be so bold,
Although I swear it to myself alone;
And, to be sure that is not false I swear,   i.e. what I swear is not false
A thousand groans but thinking on thy face
One on another's neck do witness bear   *In quick succession*
Thy black is fairest in my judgment's place.
    In nothing art thou black save in thy deeds,
    And thence this slander, as I think, proceeds.   *from this*

132

Thine eyes I love, and they as pitying me –   *as if*
Knowing thy heart torments me with disdain –
Have put on black, and loving mourners be,
Looking with pretty ruth upon my pain;   *pity*
And truly, not the morning sun of heaven   *not even*
Better becomes the grey cheeks of the east,   i.e. clouds
Nor that full star that ushers in the even   *Venus/evening*
Doth half that glory to the sober west,
As those two mourning eyes become thy face.
O, let it then as well beseem thy heart   *befit*

---

142   i.e. A bliss while being enjoyed, but, once enjoyed, a woe.   143   i.e. You are as tyrannous, even the way you are.

To mourn for me, since mourning doth thee grace,
And suit thy pity like in every part.   *dress*
  Then will I swear beauty herself is black,
  And all they foul that thy complexion lack.

133

Beshrew that heart that makes my heart to groan   *Curse*
For that deep wound it gives my friend and me!
Is't not enough to torture me alone,
But slave to slavery my sweet'st friend must be?
Me from myself thy cruel eye hath taken,
And my next self thou harder hast engrossed.   *i.e. my friend/monopolized*
Of him, myself, and thee I am forsaken –
A torment thrice three-fold thus to be crossed.   *tormented*
Prison my heart in thy steel bosom's ward,
But then my friend's heart let my poor heart bail;   *bail out*
Whoe'er keeps me, let my heart be his guard;   *guards/prison*
Thou canst not then use rigour in my jail.
  And yet thou wilt for I being pent in thee,   *contained*
  Perforce am thine, and all that is in me.

134[144]

So, now I have confessed that he is thine,   *i.e. my heart*
And I myself am mortgaged to thy will,
Myself I'll forfeit, so that other mine   *that my friend*
Thou wilt restore to be my comfort still.   *release*
But thou wilt not, nor he will not be free,   *wants not*
For thou art covetous, and he is kind.   *sympathetic*
He learned but suretylike to write for me[145]
Under that bond that him as fast doth bind.
The statute of thy beauty thou wilt take,   *bond*
Thou usurer that putt'st forth all to use,[146]
And sue a friend came debtor for my sake;   *who became a*
So him I lose through my unkind abuse.
  Him have I lost; thou hast both him and me;
  He pays the whole, and yet am I not free.

135[147]

Whoever hath her wish, thou hast thy Will,
And Will to boot, and Will in overplus.
More than enough am I that vex thee still,   *always*
To thy sweet will making addition thus.
Wilt thou, whose will is large and spacious,
Not once vouchsafe to hide my will in thine?
Shall will in others seem right gracious,   *acceptable*
And in my will no fair acceptance shine?
The sea, all water, yet receives rain still,
And in abundance addeth to his store;

144   This sonnet uses a series of metaphors drawn from legal contracts to depict the speaker being replaced in his mistress's affections by the friend of the previous sonnet. The speaker mortgages himself for his friend, but his friend is "kind" (which here means in sympathy with the woman). The friend signs a bond to assume the speaker's responsibility, and the "Dark Lady" immediately calls in her "interest." Throughout the poem, the language of financial transactions is used to express sexual transactions.

145   i.e. He will sign the bond with you in my place.

146   The word "use" here means both "lend at interest" and "use sexually." It plays on the "bond" that binds the speaker to his friend in the previous line.

147   This sonnet and the one after it pun on the poet's first name and the various meanings of the word "will." The word is used to mean both what one wants and the psychological faculty that represents sensual desire (as opposed to reason, which was sometimes known as "wit"). Both sonnets contain double-entendres suggesting intercourse and, in the second one, allusions to the Dark Lady's indiscriminate sexual appetite and large number of lovers.

So thou, being rich in Will, add to thy Will
One will of mine to make thy large Will more.
 Let no unkind no fair beseechers kill;   *unkindness*
 Think all but one, and me in that one Will.   *all the same*

136

If thy soul check thee that I come so near,[148]
Swear to thy blind soul that I was thy Will,
And will, thy soul knows, is admitted there;
Thus far for love my love-suit, sweet, fulfill.
'Will' will fulfil the treasure of thy love,   *treasury*
Ay, fill it full with wills, and my will one.   *i.e. one among them*
In things of great receipt with ease we prove,   *capacity*
Among a number one is reckoned none.[149]
Then in the number let me pass untold,   *uncounted*
Though in thy store's account I one must be;   *inventory*
For nothing hold me, so it please thee hold,   *value me*
That nothing me a something, sweet, to thee.
 Make but my name thy love, and love that still,   *always*
 And then thou lov'st me for my name is Will.

137

Thou blind fool love, what dost thou to mine eyes
That they behold and see not what they see?
They know what beauty is, see where it lies,   *lives*
Yet what the best is take the worst to be.   *i.e. they take*
If eyes corrupt by over-partial looks   *fond*
Be anchored in the bay where all men ride,[150]
Why of eyes' falsehood hast thou forged hooks   *i.e. my eyes'*
Whereto the judgment of my heart is tied?
Why should my heart think that a several plot   *private field*
Which my heart knows the wide world's common place? –   *common ground*
Or mine eyes, seeing this, say this is not,   *i.e. should mine*
To put fair truth upon so foul a face?   *appearance*
 In things right true my heart and eyes have erred,
 And to this false plague are they now transferred.   *falseness*

138

When my love swears that she is made of truth
I do believe her though I know she lies,   *pretend to believe*
That she might think me some untutored youth
Unlearned in the world's false subtleties.
Thus vainly thinking that she thinks me young,
Although she knows my days are past the best,
Simply I credit her false-speaking tongue;   *Seeming foolish*
On both sides thus is simple truth suppressed.
But wherefore says she not she is unjust,   *why*
And wherefore say not I that I am old?
O, love's best habit is in seeming trust,   *superficial*
And age in love loves not to have years told.   *counted*
 Therefore I lie with her, and she with me,
 And in our faults by lies we flattered be.

148 i.e. If your soul reproves you because I have affected you deeply (with a punning sense of physical proximity).

149 i.e. In a large quantity, one is counted as nothing.

150 A famous image for the speaker's claim that he is only one of many lovers that his mistress has.

139

O, call not me to justify the wrong   *ask*
That thy unkindness lays upon my heart.   *promiscuity*
Wound me not with thine eye[151] but with thy tongue;
Use power with power, and slay me not by art.   *force/deceit*
Tell me thou lov'st elsewhere, but in my sight,
Dear heart, forbear to glance thine eye aside.
What need'st thou wound with cunning when thy might
Is more than my o'erpressed defence can bide?   *withstand*
Let me excuse thee: 'Ah, my love well knows
10   Her pretty looks have been mine enemies,
And therefore from my face she turns my foes,
That they elsewhere might dart their injuries.'
    Yet do not so; but since I am near slain,
    Kill me outright with looks, and rid my pain.   *end*

140

Be wise as thou art cruel; do not press
My tongue-tied patience with too much disdain,
Lest sorrow lend me words, and words express
The manner of my pity-wanting pain.   *i.e. lacking your pity*
If I might teach thee wit, better it were,   *reason*
Though not to love, yet, love, to tell me so –[152]
As testy sick men when their deaths be near   *irritable*
No news but health from their physicians know.   *learn*
For if I should despair I should grow mad,
10   And in my madness might speak ill of thee
Now this ill-wresting world is grown so bad   *misrecognizing*
Mad slanderers by mad ears believed be.
    That I may not be so, nor thou belied,   *slandered*
    Bear thine eyes straight, though thy proud heart go wide.   *i.e. straight at me/astray*

141

In faith, I do not love thee with mine eyes,
For they in thee a thousand errors note;
But 'tis my heart that loves what they despise,   *i.e. the eyes*
Who in despite of view is pleased to dote.   *Which*
Nor are mine ears with thy tongue's tune delighted,
Nor tender feeling to base touches prone;   *sense of touch/sexual*
Nor taste nor smell desire to be invited
To any sensual feast with thee alone;
But my five wits[153] nor my five senses can
10   Dissuade one foolish heart from serving thee,
Who leaves unswayed the likeness of a man,   *Which/ungoverned/image*
Thy proud heart's slave and vassal wretch to be.
    Only my plague thus far I count my gain: *account*
    That she that makes me sin awards me pain.

142

Love is my sin, and thy dear virtue hate,
Hate of my sin grounded on sinful loving.   *Your hate*
O, but with mine compare thou thine own state,   *condition*
And thou shalt find it merits not reproving;   *i.e. my state*
Or if it do, not from those lips of thine

151   The eye is the sense organ through which we see what we desire,   153   A reference to Early Modern concepts of intellectual activity. The
and is here being used as a figure for the Dark Lady's lust.   five faculties were memory, judgment, imagination, fancy, and common
152   i.e. It would teach you to tell me that you love, even though you   sense.
don't.

That have profaned their scarlet ornaments   *corrupted*
And sealed false bonds of love as oft as mine,   *promises*
Robbed others' beds' revenues of their rents.[154]
Be it lawful I love thee as thou lov'st those   *that I*
10   Whom thine eyes woo as mine importune thee.   *beseech*
Root pity in thy heart, that when it grows,
Thy pity may deserve to pitied be.   *i.e. to be pitied*
  If thou dost seek to have what thou dost hide,   *deny me*
  By self example mayst thou be denied!

143

Lo, as a careful housewife runs to catch
One of her feathered creatures broke away,
Sets down her babe and makes all swift dispatch
In pursuit of the thing she would have stay,
Whilst her neglected child holds her in chase,   *chases after her*
Cries to catch her whose busy care is bent
To follow that which flies before her face,   *in front of*
Not prizing her poor infant's discontent:
So run'st thou after that which flies from thee,
10   Whilst I, thy babe, chase thee afar behind;
But if thou catch thy hope, turn back to me
And play the mother's part: kiss me, be kind.
  So will I pray that thou mayst have thy Will,[155]
  If thou turn back and my loud crying still.   *silence*

144

Two loves I have of comfort and despair,
Which like two spirits do suggest me still.   *seduce*
The better angel is a man right fair,
The worser spirit a woman coloured ill.   *unfavorably*
To win me soon to hell my female evil
Tempteth my better angel from my side,
And would corrupt my saint to be a devil,
Wooing his purity with her foul pride;
And whether that my angel be turned fiend
10   Suspect I may, yet not directly tell;
But being both from me, both to each friend,   *away from/each other*
I guess one angel in another's hell.[156]
  Yet this shall I ne'er know, but live in doubt
  Till my bad angel fire my good one out   *expel*

145

Those lips that love's own hand did make
Breathed forth the sound that said 'I hate'
To me that languished for her sake;   *suffered*
But when she saw my woeful state,
Straight in her heart did mercy come,
Chiding that tongue that ever sweet   *always*
Was used in giving gentle doom,   *judgment*
And taught it thus anew to greet:
'I hate' she altered with an end
10   That followed it as gentle day
Doth follow night who, like a fiend,

---

154   i.e. You have received the marital obligations of several husbands in place of their wives.

155   Another pun on the author's name.

156   i.e. I suppose that the angel is in sexual congress with the evil woman. "Hell" was a common misogynist metaphor for the female genitals.

From heaven to hell is flown away.
'I hate' from hate away she threw,
And saved my life, saying 'not you.'

146

Poor soul, the centre of my sinful earth,   *i.e. body*
My sinful earth these rebel powers array;[157]   *clothe my desires*
Why dost thou pine within and suffer dearth,   *lack*
Painting thy outward walls so costly gay?   *expensively well*
Why so large cost, having so short a lease,   *time pertiod*
Dost thou upon thy fading mansion spend?   *i.e. the body*
Shall worms, inheritors of this excess,
Eat up thy charge? Is this thy body's end?   *expense*
Then, soul, live thou upon thy servant's loss,
10 And let that pine to aggravate thy store.   *diminish/increase*
Buy terms divine in selling hours of dross;   *i.e. by selling*
Within be fed, without be rich no more.
   So shall thou feed on death, that feeds on men,
   And death once dead, there's no more dying then.

147

My love is as a fever, longing still   *constantly*
For that which longer nurseth the disease,   *supports*
Feeding on that which doth preserve the ill,
Th'uncertain sickly appetite to please.
My reason, the physician to my love,
Angry that his prescriptions are not kept,
Hath left me, and I desperate now approve   *demonstrate*
Desire is death, which physic did except.[158]
Past cure I am, now reason is past care,   *caring*
10 And frantic mad with evermore unrest.   *perpetual*
My thoughts and my discourse as madmen's are,
At random from the truth vainly expressed;   *Divided from*
   For I have sworn thee fair, and thought thee bright,
   Who art as black as hell, as dark as night.

148

O me, what eyes hath love put in my head,
Which have no correspondence with true sight!
Or if they have, where is my judgment fled,
That censures falsely what they see aright?   *judges*
If that be fair whereon my false eyes dote,
What means the world to say it is not so?
If it be not, then love doth well denote
Love's eye is not so true as all men's. No,
How can it, O, how can love's eye be true,
10 That is so vexed with watching and with tears?   *sleeplessness*
No marvel then though I mistake my view: *if I/what I see*
The sun itself sees not, till heaven clears.
   O cunning love, with tears thou keep'st me blind
   Lest eyes, well seeing, thy foul faults should find!

149

Canst thou, O cruel, say I love thee not
When I against myself with thee partake?   *take sides*

157 This line appears in this form in the first quarto of Shakespeare's   158 i.e. That desire, which medicine did reject, is death.
complete works; "my sinful earth" may be only an editorial guess at
what Shakespeare intended.

Do I not think on thee when I forgot   *i.e. when I myself*
Am of myself, all-tyrant, for thy sake?   *over myself*
Who hateth thee that I do call my friend?
On whom frown'st thou that I do fawn upon?
Nay, if thou lour'st on me, do I not spend   *frown*
Revenge upon myself with present moan?   *suffering*
What merit do I in myself respect
That is so proud thy service to despise,
When all my best doth worship thy defect,   *best qualities*
Commanded by the motion of thine eyes?
    But, love, hate on; for now I know thy mind.
    Those that can see thou lov'st, and I am blind.[159]

          150

O, from what power hast thou this powerful might
With insufficiency my heart to sway,   *your faults/rule*
To make me give the lie to my true sight   *i.e. to accuse my sight of lying*
And swear that brightness doth not grace the day?   *daylight*
Whence hast thou this becoming of things ill,   *power to beautify*
That in the very refuse of thy deeds   *rubbish*
There is such strength and warrantise of skill   *warrant*
That in my mind thy worst all best exceeds?
Who taught thee how to make me love thee more
The more I hear and see just cause of hate?
O, though I love what others do abhor,
With others thou shouldst not abhor my state.   *condition*
    If thy unworthiness raised love in me,
    More worthy I to be beloved of thee.

          151

Love[160] is too young to know what conscience is,
Yet who knows not conscience is born of love?
Then, gentle cheater, urge not my amiss,   *sin*
Lest guilty of my faults thy sweet self prove.
For, thou betraying me, I do betray
My nobler part to my gross body's treason.   *My soul*
My soul doth tell my body that he may
Triumph in love; flesh stays no farther reason,   *waits for*
But rising at thy name doth point out thee
As his triumphant prize. Proud of this pride,
He is contented thy poor drudge to be,   *menial servant*
To stand in thy affairs, fall by thy side.
    No want of conscience hold it that I call   *lack*
    Her 'love' for whose dear love I rise and fall.

          152

In loving thee thou know'st I am forsworn,   *unfaithful*
But thou art twice forsworn to me love swearing:
In act thy bed-vow broke, and new faith torn   *marriage vow*
In vowing new hate after new love bearing.   *creating*
But why of two oaths' breach do I accuse thee
When I break twenty? I am perjured most,
For all my vows are oaths but to misuse thee,   *deceive*
And all my honest faith in thee is lost.
For I have sworn deep oaths of thy deep kindness,
Oaths of thy love, thy truth, thy constancy,

---

159 i.e. You love those who can see you properly, and I cannot.   160 "Love" is here being used as a name for Cupid (see the gazetteer).

And to enlighten thee gave eyes to blindness,   *i.e. to make you bright*
Or made them swear against the thing they see.
   For I have sworn thee fair – more perjured eye
   To swear against the truth so foul a lie.

153[161]

Cupid laid by his brand and fell asleep,   *torch*
A maid of Dian's this advantage found,   *Diana's (see gazetteer)*
And his love-kindling fire did quickly steep   *soak*
In a cold valley-fountain of that ground,   *that region*
Which borrowed from this holy fire of love
A dateless lively heat, still to endure,   *timeless/always*
And grew a seething bath which yet men prove   *hot spring*
Against strange maladies a sovereign cure.
But at my mistress' eye love's brand new fired,
10   The boy for trial needs would touch my breast.   *for experiment*
I, sick withal, the help of bath desired,
And thither hied a sad distempered guest,   *sickly*
   But found no cure; the bath for my help lies   *cure*
   Where Cupid got new fire: my mistress' eyes.

154

The little love-god lying once asleep   *i.e. Cupid*
Laid by his side his heart-inflaming brand,
Whilst many nymphs that vowed chaste life to keep
Came tripping by; but in her maiden hand
The fairest votary[162] took up that fire
Which many legions of true hearts had warmed,
And so the general of hot desire
Was sleeping by a virgin hand disarmed.
This brand she quenched in a cool well by,
10   Which from love's fire took heat perpetual,
Growing a bath and healthful remedy
For men diseased; but I my mistress' thrall,
Came there for cure; and this by that I prove:
Love's fire heats water, water cools not love.

Thomas Campion (1567–1620)

The relationship between music and words – sound and sense – has always been a complex matter, and and there was considerable controversy about it during the Renaissance. For example, Sir Frederick, one of the speakers in Castiglione's *Courtier* (1528) complains about the music drowning out the poetry in madrigals. In this respect he agrees with the great composer Monteverdi, who argued that the text should be the "master" rather than the "servant" of the music. Campion is on the same side in this argument in that he is suspicious of contrapuntal settings of verse. In his address "To the Reader" in *Two Bookes of Ayres* (1613?), Campion argues for a loving marriage of words and notes: "In these English Ayres, I have chiefly aymed to couple my Words and Notes lovingly together." What is ironic about this is that Campion's lyrics have often been ignored by later poets and readers who champion a more witty, metaphorical, and intellectual tradition in poetry, a tradition of which John Donne is the epitome. Campion, however, was a disciple of Sir Philip Sidney; and his work has an important relationship to the poetry of

161   The last two sonnets have nothing to do with the Dark Lady and are conventional retellings of a classical poetic conceit. Their function in the sonnets as a whole (and whether or not they were included mistakenly) has been much debated.

162   A "votary" is worshipper in a religion who has bound him- or herself to certain devotional practices by an oath.

Spenser and Milton, for whom the sound of poetry (its music) is almost as important as its visual imagery and its sense. Campion, therefore (as Walter R. Davis has written) "is the primary poet of the auditory imagination." He combined the arts of poet and composer in the same complementary way as William Blake, two centuries later, combined the arts of poet and painter. Neither poet allowed the words to be either "master" or "servant."

At least nine of Campion's ayres are spoken as though by female personae. Campion is not unique among English Renaissance poets in fictionalizing women speakers; but his women, unlike Donne's and Jonson's, for example, are far more individualized, rather than being generic women or

masks for the poet (see Reitenbach.) These nine poems are grouped together below.

READING

Bruce Pattison, *Music and Poetry of the English Renaissance.*
Gail Reitenbach, "'Maydes are simple, some men say': Thomas Campion's Female Persona Poems."
David A. Richardson, "The Golden Mean in Campion's Airs."
Hallett Smith, *Elizabethan Poetry.*

M. P.

A BOOKE OF AYRES

TO THE READER

WHAT Epigrams are in Poetrie, the same are Ayres in musicke, then in their chiefe perfection when they are short and well seasoned. But to clogg a light song with a long Praeludium,[1] is to corrupt the nature of it. Manie rests in Musicke were invented either for necessitie of the fuge,[2] or granted as a harmonicall licence in songs of many parts: but in Ayres I find no use they have, unlesse it be to make a vulgar and triviall modulation seeme to the ignorant strange, and to the judiciall tedious. A naked Ayre without guide, or prop, or colour but his owne, is easily censured of everie eare, and requires so much the more invention to make it please. And as *Martiall* speaks in defence of his short Epigrams, so may I say in th' apologie of Ayres, that where there is a full volume, there can be no imputation of shortnes.[3] The Lyricke Poets among the Greekes and Latines were first inventers of Ayres, tying themselves strictly to the number and value of their sillables, of which sort, you shall find here onely one song in Saphicke verse; the rest are after the fascion of the time, eare-pleasing rimes without Arte. The subject of them is for the most part amorous, and why not amorous songs, as well as amorous attires? Or why not new Ayres, as well as new fascions? For the Note and Tableture, if they satisfie the most, we have our desire; let expert masters please themselves with better. And if anie light error hath escaped us, the skilfull may easily correct it, the unskilfull will hardly perceive it. But there are some, who to appeare the more deepe and singular in their judgement, will admit no Musicke but that which is long, intricate, bated with fuge, chaind with sincopation, and where the nature of everie word is precisely exprest in the Note, like the old exploded action in Comedies, when if they did pronounce *Memini,*[4] they would point to the hinder part of their heads, if *Video,*[5] put their finger in their eye. But such childish observing of words is altogether ridiculous, and we ought to maintaine as well in Notes, as in action, a manly cariage, gracing no word, but that which is eminent, and emphaticall. Nevertheles, as in Poesie we give the prehemineuce to the Heroicall Poeme, so in Musicke we yeeld the chiefe place to the grave and well invented Motet, but not to every harsh and dull confused Fantasie, where in multitude of points the Harmonie is quite drowned. Ayres have both their Art and pleasure, and I will conclude of them, as the Poet did in his censure of *Catullus* the Lyricke, and *Vergil* the Heroicke writer:

Tantum magna suo debet Verona Catullo:
Quantum parva suo Mantua Vergilio.[6]

A BOOKE OF AYRES
1 *prelude.*
2 *fugue.* The rests allow the different voices in the fugue to be heard.
3 The reference here is to Martial, the Latin author of epigrams.
4 "I remember."

5 "I see."
6 The quotation is from Martial, *Epigrams,* 14. 115: "Great Verona owes as much to Catullus as little Mantua owes to her Virgil." Catullus is one of Campion's sources for his songs. Other Latin sources include Propertius and Horace.

I.

My sweetest Lesbia, let us live and love,
And, though the sager sort our deedes reprove,
Let us not way them: heav'ns great lampes doe dive
Into their west, and strait againe revive,
But, soone as once set is our little light,
Then must we sleepe one ever-during night.

If all would lead their lives in love like mee,
Then bloudie swords and armour should not be,
No drum nor trumpet peacefull sleepes should move,
Unles alar'me came from the campe of love:
But fooles do live, and wast their little light,
And seeke with paine their ever-during night.

When timely death my life and fortune ends,
Let not my hearse be vext with mourning friends,
But let all lovers, rich in triumph, come,
And with sweet pastimes grace my happie tombe;
And, Lesbia, close up thou my little light,
And crowne with love my ever-during night.

II.

Though, you are yoong and I am olde,
Though your vaines hot and my bloud colde,
Though youth is moist and age is drie,
Yet embers live when flames doe die.

The tender graft is easely broke,
But who shall shake the sturdie Oke?
You are more fresh and faire then I,
Yet stubs doe live, when flowers doe die.

Thou that thy youth doest vainely boast,
Know buds are soonest nipt with frost;
Thinke that thy fortune still doth crie,
Thou foole, tomorrow thou must die.

III.

I care not for these Ladies
That must be woode and praide,
Give me kind Amarillis
The wanton countrey maide;
Nature art disdaineth,
Her beautie is her owne;
  Her when we court and kisse,
  She cries, forsooth, let go:
  But when we come where comfort is,
  She never will say no.

If I love Amarillis,
She gives me fruit and flowers,
But if we love these Ladies,
We must give golden showers;
Give them gold that sell love,
Give me the Nutbrowne lasse,
  Who when we court and kisse,
  She cries, forsooth, let go:

But when we come where comfort is,
    She never will say no.

20

These Ladies must have pillowes,
And beds by strangers wrought,
Give me a Bower of willowes,
Of mosse and leaves unbought,
And fresh Amarillis,
With milke and honie fed,
    Who when we court and kisse,
    She cries, forsooth, let go:
    But when we come where comfort is,
    She never will say no.

30

IV.

Followe thy faire sunne, unhappy shaddowe:
Though thou be blacke as night,
And she made all of light,
Yet follow thy faire sunne, unhappie shaddowe.

Follow her whose light thy light depriveth:
Though here thou liv'st disgrac't,
And she in heaven is plac't,
Yet follow her whose light the world reviveth.

Follow those pure beames whose beautie burneth,
That so have scorched thee,
As thou still blacke must bee,
Til her kind beames thy black to brightnes turneth.

10

Follow her while yet her glorie shineth:
There comes a luckles night,
That will dim all her light;
And this the black unhappie shade devineth.

Follow still since so thy fates ordained:
The Sunne must have his shade,
Till both at once doe fade,
The Sun still prov'd, the shadow still disdained.   *approved*

20

V.

My love hath vowd hee will forsake mee,
And I am alreadie sped.
Far other promise he did make me
When he had my maidenhead.
If such danger be in playing,
And sport must to earnest turne;
I will go no more a-maying.

Had I foreseene what is ensued,
And what now with paine I prove,
Unhappie then I had eschewed
This unkind event of love:
Maides foreknow their own undooing,
But feare naught till all is done,
When a man alone is wooing.

10

Dissembling wretch, to gaine thy pleasure,
What didst thou not vow and sweare?
So didst thou rob me of the treasure
Which so long I held so deare;
Now thou prov'st to me a stranger,
20   Such is the vile guise of men
When a woman is in danger.

That hart is neerest to misfortune
That will trust a fained toong;
When flattring men our loves importune,
They entend us deepest wrong;
If this shame of loves betraying
But this once I cleanely shun,
I will go no more a-maying.

VI.

When to her lute Corrina sings,
Her voice revives the leaden stringes,
And doth in highest noates appeare
As any challeng'd eccho cleere;
But when she doth of mourning speake,
Ev'n with her sighes the strings do breake.

And, as her lute doth live or die,
Led by her passion, so must I:
For when of pleasure she doth sing,
10   My thoughts enjoy a sodaine spring;
But if she doth of sorrow speake,
Ev'n from my hart the strings doe breake.

VII.

Turne backe, you wanton flyer,
And answere my desire
With mutuall greeting;
Yet bende a little neerer,
True beauty stil shines cleerer
In closer meeting.
Harts with harts delighted
Should strive to be united,
Either others armes with armes enchayning:
10   Harts with a thought, rosie lips
With a kisse still entertaining.

What harvest halfe so sweete is
As still to reape the kisses
Growne ripe in sowing,
And straight to be receiver
Of that which thou art giver,
Rich in bestowing?
There's no strickt observing
Of times, or seasons changing,
20   There is ever one fresh spring abiding:
Then what we sow with our lips
Let us reape, loves gaines deviding.

VIII.

It fell on a sommers day,
While sweete Bessie sleeping laie

In her bowre, on her bed,
Light with curtaines shadowed;
Jamy came, shee him spies,
Opning halfe her heavie eies.

Jamy stole in through the dore,
She lay slumbring as before;
Softly to her he drew neere,
She heard him, yet would not heare;
Bessie vow'd not to speake,
He resolv'd that dumpe to breake.   *reverie*

First a soft kisse he doth take,
She lay still, and would not wake;
Then his hands learn'd to woo,
She dreamp't not what he would doo,
But still slept, while he smild
To see love by sleepe beguild.

Jamy then began to play,
Bessie as one buried lay,
Gladly still through this sleight
Deceiv'd in her owne deceit;
And, since this traunce begoon,
She sleepes ev'rie afternoone.

IX.

The Sypres curten⁷ of the night is spread,
And over all a silent dewe is cast.
The weaker cares by sleepe are conquered;
But I alone, with hidious griefe agast,
In spite of Morpheus charmes a watch doe keepe
Over mine eies, to banish carelesse sleepe.

Yet oft my trembling eyes through faintnes close,
And then the Mappe of hell before me stands,
Which Ghosts doe see, and I am one of those
Ordain'd to pine in sorrowes endles bands,
Since from my wretched soule all hopes are reft
And now no cause of life to me is left.

Griefe, ceaze my soule; for that will still endure
When my cras'd bodie is consum'd and gone;
Beare it to thy blacke denne, there keepe it sure,
Where thou ten thousand soules doest tyre upon:
Yet all doe not affoord such foode to thee
As this poore one, the worser part of mee.

X.

Follow your Saint, follow with accents sweet,
Haste you, sad noates, fall at her flying feete;
There, wrapt in cloud of sorrowe, pitie move,
And tell the ravisher of my soule I perish for her love.
But if she scorns my never-ceasing paine,
Then burst with sighing in her sight, and nere returne againe.

10

10

10

20

20

7   A thin, black mourning veil.

All that I soong still to her praise did tend,
Still she was first, still she my songs did end.
Yet she my love and Musicke both doeth flie,
10   The Musicke that her Eccho is, and beauties simpathie;
Then let my Noates pursue her scornefull flight:
It shall suffice that they were breath'd, and dyed, for her delight.

XI.

Faire, if you expect admiring,
Sweet, if you provoke desiring,
Grace deere love with kinde requiting.
Fond, but if thy sight be blindnes,
False, if thou affect unkindnes,
Flie both love and loves delighting.
Then when hope is lost and love is scorned,
Ile bury my desires, and quench the fires that ever yet in vaine have burned.

Fates, if you rule lovers fortune,
10   Stars, if men your powers importune,
Yield reliefe by your relenting.
Time, if sorrow be not endles,
Hope made vaine; and pittie friendles,
Helpe to ease my long lamenting.
But if griefes remaine still unredressed,
I'le flie to her againe, and sue for pitie to renue my hopes distressed.

XII.

Thou art not faire, for all thy red and white,
For all those rosie ornaments in thee;
Thou art not sweet, though made of meer delight,
Nor faire nor sweet, unlesse thou pitie mee.
I will not sooth thy fancies: thou shalt prove
That beauty is no beautie without love.

Yet love not me, nor seeke thou to allure
My thoughts with beautie, were it more devine;
Thy smiles and kisses I cannot endure,
10   I'le not be wrapt up in those armes of thine.
Now shew it, if thou be a woman right:
Embrace, and kisse; and love me, in despight.

XIII.

See where she flies enrag'd from me,
View her when she intends despite:
The winde is not more swift then shee,
Her furie mov'd such terror makes
As, to a fearfull guiltie sprite,
The voice of heav'ns huge thunder cracks.
But, when her appeased minde yeelds to delight,
All her thoughts are made of joyes,
Millions of delights inventing:
10   Other pleasures are but toies
To her beauties sweete contenting.

My fortune hangs upon her brow,
For, as she smiles or frownes on mee,
So must my blowne affections bow;
And her proude thoughts too well do find

With what unequall tyrannie
Her beauties doe command my mind.
Though, when her sad planet raignes, froward she bee,
She alone can pleasure move,
20   And displeasing sorrow banish:
May I but still hold her love,
Let all other comforts vanish.

XIV.

Blame not my cheeks, though pale with love they be;
The kindly heate unto my heart is flowne,
To cherish it that is dismaid by thee,
Who art so cruell and unsteedfast growne:
For nature, cald for by distressed harts,
Neglects and quite forsakes the outward partes.

But they whose cheekes with careles blood are stain'd
Nurse not one sparke of love within their harts,
And, when they woe, they speake with passion fain'd,
10   For their fat love lyes in their outward parts:
But in their brests, where love his court should hold,
Poore Cupid sits and blowes his nailes for cold.

XV.

When the God of merrie love
As yet in his cradle lay,
Thus his wither'd nurse did say:
Thou a wanton boy wilt prove
To deceive the powers above;
For by thy continuall smiling
I see thy power of beguiling.

Therewith she the babe did kisse;
When a sodaine fire out came
10   From those burning lips of his,
That did her with love enflame;
But none would regard the same,
So that, to her daie of dying,
The old wretch liv'd ever crying.

XVI.

Mistris, since you so much desire
To know the place of Cupids fire,
In your faire shrine that flame doth rest,
Yet never harbourd in your brest;
It bides not in your lips so sweete,
Nor where the rose and lillies meete,
But a little higher, but a little higher:
There, there, O there lies Cupids fire.

Even in those starrie pearcing eyes,
There Cupids sacred fire lyes;
10   Those eyes I strive not to enjoy,
For they have power to destroy;
Nor woe I for a smile, or kisse,
So meanely triumph's not my blisse;
But a little higher, but a little higher,
I climbe to crowne my chast desire.

XVII.

Your faire lookes enflame my desire:
    Quench it againe with love.
Stay, O strive not still to retire,
    Doe not inhumane prove.
If love may perswade,
    Loves pleasures, deere, denie not;
Heere is a silent grovie shade:
    O tarrie then, and flie not.

Have I seaz'd my heavenly delight
    In this unhaunted grove?
Time shall now her furie requite
    With the revenge of love.
Then come, sweetest, come,
    My lips with kisses gracing:
Here let us harbour all alone,
    Die, die in sweete embracing.

Will you now so timely depart,
    And not returne againe?
Your sight lends such life to my hart
    That to depart is paine.
Feare yeelds no delay,
    Securenes helpeth pleasure:
Then, till the time gives safer stay,
    O farewell, my lives treasure!

XVIII.

The man of life upright,
    Whose guiltlesse hart is free
From all dishonest deedes,
    Or thought of vanitie,

The man whose silent dayes
    In harmeles joyes are spent,
Whome hopes cannot delude,
    Nor sorrow discontent,

That man needes neither towers
    Nor armour for defence,
Nor secret vautes to flie
    From thunders violence.

Hee onely can behold
    With unafrighted eyes
The horrours of the deepe,
    And terrours of the Skies.

Thus, scorning all the cares
    That fate, or fortune brings,
He makes the heav'n his booke,
    His wisedome heev'nly things,

Good thoughts his onely friendes,
    His wealth a well-spent age,
The earth his sober Inne,
    And quiet Pilgrimage.

XIX.

Harke, al you ladies that do sleep:
  the fayry queen Proserpina
Bids you awake and pitie them that weep;
  you may doe in the darke
What the day doth forbid:
  feare not the dogs that barke,
        Night will have all hid.

But if you let your lovers mone,
  the Fairie Queene Proserpina
Will send abroad her Fairies ev'rie one,
  that shall pinch blacke and blew
Your white hands, and faire armes,
  that did not kindly rue
        Your Paramours harmes.

In Myrtle Arbours on the downes,
  the Fairie Queene Proserpina,
This night by moone-shine leading merrie rounds,
  holds a watch with sweet love;
Downe the dale, up the hill,
  no plaints or groanes may move
        Their holy vigill.

All you that will hold watch with love,
  the Fairie Queene Proserpina
Will make you fairer then Diones dove;
  Roses red, Lillies white,
And the cleare damaske hue,
  shall on your cheekes alight:
        Love will adorne you.

All you that love, or lov'd before,
  the Fairie Queene Proserpina
Bids you encrease that loving humour more:
  they that yet have not fed
On delight amorous,
  she vowes that they shall lead
        Apes in Avernus.[8]

XX.

When thou must home to shades of under ground,
And there ariv'd, a newe admired guest,
The beauteous spirits do ingirt thee round,
White Iope, blith Hellen, and the rest,
To heare the stories of thy finisht love,
From that smoothe toong whose musicke hell can move:

Then wilt thou speake of banqueting delights,
Of masks and revels which sweete youth did make,
Of Turnies and great challenges of knights,
And all these triumphes for thy beauties sake:
When thou hast told these honours done to thee,
Then tell, O tell, how thou didst murther me.

8 Leading apes in hell was a proverbial punishment for old maids.

XXI.

Come, let us sound with melody the praises
Of the kings king, th'omnipotent creator,
Author of number, that hath all the world in
        Harmonie framed.

Heav'n is his throne perpetually shining,
His devine power and glorie thence he thunders,
One in all, and all still in one abiding,
        Both Father, and Sonne.

O sacred sprite, invisible, eternall,
10   Ev'ry where, yet unlimited, that all things
Canst in one moment penetrate, revive me,
        O holy Spirit.

Rescue, O rescue me from earthly darknes,
Banish hence all these elementall objects,
Guide my soule that thirsts to the lively Fountaine
        Of thy devinenes.

Cleanse my soule, O God, thy bespotted Image,
Altered with sinne so that heav'nly purenes
Cannot acknowledge me but in thy mercies,
20   O Father of grace.

But when once thy beames do remove my darknes,
O then I'le shine forth as an Angell of light,
And record, with more than an earthly voice, thy
        Infinite honours.

[FEMALE PERSONA LYRICS]

2: IX.

Good men, shew, if you can tell,
Where doth humane pittie dwell?
Farre and neere her would I seeke,
So vext with sorrow is my brest.
She (they say) to all is meeke,
And onely makes th' unhappie blest.

Oh! if such a Saint there be,
Some hope yet remaines for me:
Prayer or sacrifice may gaine
10   From her implored grace reliefe,
To release mee of my paine,
Or at the least to ease my griefe.

Young am I, and farre from guile;
The more is my woe the while:
Falshood with a smooth disguise
My simple meaning hath abus'd,
Casting mists before mine eyes,
By which my senses are confus'd.

Faire he is, who vow'd to me
20   That he onely mine would be:

But, alas, his minde is caught
With ev'ry gaudie bait he sees.
And too late my flame is taught
That too much kindnesse makes men freese.

From me all my friends are gone,
While I pine for him alone;
And not one will rue my case,
But rather my distresse deride:
That I thinke there is no place
Where pittie ever yet did bide.

30

2: XV.

So many loves have I neglected
   Whose good parts might move mee,
That now I live of all rejected,
   There is none will love me.
Why is mayden heate so coy?
   It freezeth when it burneth,
Looseth what it might injoy,
   And, having lost it, mourneth.

Should I then wooe, that have been wooed,
   Seeking them that flye mee?
When I my faith with teares have vowed,
   And when all denye mee,
Who will pitty my disgrace,
   Which love might have prevented?
There is no submission base
   Where error is repented.

10

O happy men, whose hopes are licenc'd
   To discourse their passion,
While women are confin'd to silence,
   Loosing wisht occasion.
Yet our tongues then theirs, men say,
   Are apter to be moving:
Women are more dumbe then they,
   But in their thoughts more roving.

20

When I compare my former strangenesse
   With my present doting,
I pitty men that speake in plainenesse,
   Their true hearts devoting;
While wee with repentance jest
   At their submissive passion:
Maydes, I see, are never blest
   That strange be but for fashion,

30

3: IV.

Maydes are simple, some men say:
They, forsooth, will trust no men.
But, should they mens wils obey,
Maides were very simple then.

Truth a rare flower now is growne,
Few men weare it in their hearts;
Lovers are more easily knowne
By their follies, then deserts.

10 Safer may we credit give
To a faithlesse wandering Jew
Then a young mans vowes beleeve
When he sweares his love is true.

Love they make a poore blinde childe,
But let none trust such as hee:
Rather then to be beguil'd,
Ever let me simple be.

3: XVI.

If thou longst so much to learne (sweet boy) what 'tis to love,
Doe but fixe thy thought on mee, and thou shalt quickly prove.
Little sute, at first, shal win
Way to thy abasht desire,
But then will I hedge thee in,
Salamander-like, with fire.[9]

With thee dance I will, and sing, and thy fond dalliance beare;
Wee the grovy hils will climbe, and play the wantons there;
Other whiles wee'le gather flowres,
10   Lying dalying on the grasse,
And thus our delightfull howres
Full of waking dreames shall passe.

When thy joyes were thus at height, my love should turne from thee;
Old acquaintance then should grow as strange as strange might be;
Twenty rivals thou should'st finde
Breaking all their hearts for mee,
When to all Ile prove more kinde
And more forward then to thee.

Thus thy silly youth, enrag'd, would soone my love defie;
20 But, alas, poore soule, too late: clipt wings can never flye.
Those sweet houres which wee had past,
Cal'd to minde, thy heart would burne;
And, could'st thou flye ne'er so fast,
They would make thee straight returne.

3: XXVII.

Never love unlesse you can
Beare with all the faults of man:
Men sometimes will jealous bee
Though but little cause they see,
And hang the head, as discontent,
And speake what straight they will repent.

Men that but one Saint adore
Make a shew of love to more:
Beauty must be scorn'd in none,
Though but truely serv'd in one:
10   For what is courtship, but disguise?
True hearts may have dissembling eyes.

Men, when their affaires require,
Must a while themselves retire:

---

9 The salamander was thought to be able to live in fire.

Sometimes hunt, and sometimes hawke,
And not ever sit and talke.
    If these, and such like, you can beare,
    Then like, and love, and never feare.

4: IX.

Young and simple though I am,
I have heard of *Cupids* name:
Guesse I can what thing it is
Men desire when they doe kisse.
    Smoake can never burne, they say,
    But the flames that follow may.

I am not so foule or fayre
To be proud, nor to despayre;
Yet my lips have oft observ'd,
Men that kisse them presse them hard,
    As glad lovers use to doe
    When their new met loves they wooe.

Faith, 'tis but a foolish minde,
Yet, me thinkes, a heate I finde.
Like thirst longing, that doth bide
Ever on my weaker side,
    Where they say my heart doth move.
    Venus, grant it be not love.

If it be, alas, what then?
Were not women made for men?
As good 'twere a thing were past,
That must needes be done at last.
    Roses that are over-blowne
    Growe lesse sweet, then fall alone.

Yet nor Churle, nor silken Gull   *fop*
Shall my Mayden blossome pull:
Who shall not I soone can tell;
Who shall, would I could as well:
    This I know, who ere hee be,
    Love hee must, or flatter me.

4: XIII.

O Love, where are thy Shafts, thy Quiver, and thy Bow?
Shall my wounds onely weepe, and hee ungaged goe?   *unbound*
Be just, and strike him, to, that dares contemne thee so.

No eyes are like to thine, though men suppose thee blinde,
So fayre they levell when the marke they list to finde: *aim*
Then strike, o strike the heart that beares the cruell minde.

Is my fond sight deceived? or doe I *Cupid* spye
Close ayming at his breast, by whom despis'd I dye?
Shoot home, sweet *Love,* and wound him, that hee may not flye!

O then we both will sit in some unhaunted shade,
And heale each others wound which *Love* hath justly made:
O hope, o thought too vaine, how quickly dost thou fade!

At large he wanders still, his heart is free from paine,
While secret sighes I spend, and teares, but all in vaine:
Yet, *Love*, thou know'st, by right I should not thus complaine.

4: XVIII.

Think'st thou to seduce me then with words that have no meaning?
Parats so can learne to prate, our speech by pieces gleaning: *parrots*
Nurces teach their children so about the time of weaning.

Learne to speake first, then to wooe: to wooing much pertayneth:
Hee that courts us, wanting Arte, soone falters when he fayneth,
Lookes a-squint on his discourse, and smiles when hee complaineth.

Skilfull Anglers hide their hookes, fit baytes for every season;
But with crooked pins fish thou, as babes doe that want reason;
Gogians[10] onely can be caught with such poore trickes of treason.

10   Ruth forgive me, if I err'd from humane hearts compassion
When I laught sometimes too much to see thy foolish fashion:
But, alas, who lesse could doe that found so good occasion?

4: XXIV.

Faine would I wed a faire yong man that day and night
    could please mee,
When my mind or body grieved, that had the powre to ease
    mee.
Maids are full of longing thoughts that breed a bloudlesse
    sickenesse,
And that, oft I heare men say, is onely cur'd by quicknesse.
Oft have I beene woo'd and prai'd, but never could be
    moved:
Many for a day or so I have most dearely loved,
But this foolish mind of mine straight loaths the thing resolved.
If to love be sinne in mee, that sinne is soone absolved.
Sure, I thinke I shall at last flye to some holy Order;
10   When I once am setled there, then can I flye no farther.
Yet I would not dye a maid, because I had a mother:
As I was by one brought forth, I would bring forth another.

[FROM] THE THIRD BOOKE OF AYRES

3: XII.

Now winter nights enlarge
    The number of their houres,
And clouds their stormes discharge
    Upon the ayrie towres;
Let now the chimneys blaze
    And cups o'erflow with wine,
Let well-tun'd words amaze
    With harmonie divine.
Now yellow waxen lights
10   Shall waite on hunny Love,

---

10 Gudgeons are small fishes that are easy to catch and therefore thought to be gullible.

While youthfull Revels, Masks, and Courtly sights,
    Sleepes leaden spels remove.

This time doth well dispence
    With lovers long discourse;
Much speech hath some defence,
    Though beauty no remorse.
All doe not all things well:
    Some measures comely tread,
Some knotted Ridles tell,
20   Some Poems smoothly read.
The Summer hath his joyes,
    And Winter his delights;
Though Love and all his pleasures are but toyes,
    They shorten tedious nights.

Thomas Nashe (1567–1601)

Nashe was best known in his own day as a controversialist. His preface to Robert Greene's *Menaphon* (1589) attacked numerous contemporary writers (including Shakespeare) for their lack of originality, and *Piers Penniless His Supplication to the Devil* (1592) offered an episodic social satire targeting many aspects of contemporary England. When the Church of England found itself under attack from an anonymous group of Puritan pamphleteers which used the penname "Martin Marprelate" and needed to reply in a similarly scurrilous vein, it was to Nashe and others like him that it turned for help; Nashe's *An Almond for a Parrot* (1590) answered "Martin" in his own terms and was much more successful than the pompous replies that had been published by the bishops. His generically unclassifiable prose fiction *The Unfortunate Traveller* (1594) was a failure, but it has attracted a lot of critical attention in recent decades.

The Choice of Valentines belongs to Nashe's satiric corpus and was circulated in manuscript rather than printed. It burlesques Petrarchan themes and languages by applying the high-flown tropes of love poetry to an encounter in a brothel; it represents the kind of semi-pornographic light verse that was commonly written and read in the Renaissance, but is seldom edited or taught now. The occasional frank sexuality found in Marlowe, Sidney, Shakespeare, and others reminds us that this poem's gleeful vulgarity is far from anomalous in Renaissance culture. Nashe simply makes manifest what writers with more care for their public reputations could only hint.

READING

Lorna Hutson, *Thomas Nashe in Context*.
M. L. Stapleton, "Nashe and the Poetics of Obscenity: The Choise of Valentines."

J. H.

The Choice of Valentines[1]

To the Right Honourable the Lord S.[2]

Pardon, sweet flower of matchless poetry,
    And fairest bud the red rose ever bare,
Although my muse divorced from deeper care
    Presents thee with a wanton elegy.[3]

THE CHOICE OF VALENTINES
1   As unusual as this poem might appear to modern readers, male impotence was a well-established subject in classical poetry. Nashe himself alludes to one of the most famous expressions of this theme in line 124 below.

2   Probably a reference to Lord Strange, who was a patron of the theater and poets and a poet in his own right.
3   Nashe means "elegy" as a poem about love, as it was established by Ovid and others in classical Rome.

Ne blame my verse of loose unchastity
  For painting forth the things that hidden are,
  Since all men act what I in speech declare,
  Only induced by variety.
Complaints and praises everyone can write,
10   And passion out their pangs in stately rhymes,
  But of love's pleasures none did ever write
  That hath succeeded in these latter times.
Accept of it, dear Lord, in gentle gree,   *goodwill*
  And better lines ere long shall honour thee.

THE CHOOSING OF VALENTINES

It was the merry month of February,
  When young men in their jolly roguery
Rose early in the morn 'fore break of day
  To seek them valentines so trim and gay,
With whom they may consort in summer-sheen
And dance the heidegeies⁴ on our town-green,
As Ales at Easter or at Pentecost   *ale festivals*
  Perambulate the fields that flourish most,
And go to some village abordering near
10   To taste the cream and cakes and such good cheer,
Or see a play of strange morality
  Showen by bachelry of Manningtree;⁵   *young men*
Whereto the country franklins flock-meal swarm,   *freeholders/by groups*
  And John and Joan come marching arm in arm
Even on the hallows⁶ of that blessed saint
  That doth true lovers with those joys acquaint,
I went, poor pilgrim, to my lady's shrine
  To see if she would be my valentine.
But woe, alas, she was not be found,
20   For she was shifted to an Upper Ground.⁷
Good Justice Dudgeon-haft and Crabtree-Face⁸
  With bills and staves had scared her from the place;
And now she was compelled for sanctuary
  To fly unto an house of venery.   *i.e. a brothel*
Thither went I, boldly made enquire
  If they had hackneys⁹ to let out to hire,
And what they craved by order of their trade
  To let one ride a journey on a jade.
Therewith out stepped a foggy three-chinned dame,   *flabby*
30   That us'd to take young wenches for to tame,
And asked me if I meant as I professed,
  Or only asked a question but in jest,
'In jest?' quoth I. 'That term it as you will:
  I come for game, therefore give me my Jill.'
'Why sir,' quoth she, 'if that be your demand,
  Come, lay me a God's-penny in my hand;   *deposit*

---

4 Nashe's meaning is unknown here. It is possible that the text is
corrupt.
5 A town in Essex where medieval morality plays were still performed
in Nashe's day.
6 Usually this word would mean "shrine," but here it seems to mean
the eve of Valentine's Day.

7 A street in Southwark associated with prostitution.
8 Fictitious justices of the peace.
9 The word can mean both "horses" and "prostitutes."

For in our oratory sikerly   *certainly*
    None enters here to do his nicery
But he must pay his offertory first,
    And then perhaps we'll ease him of his thirst.'
40   I, hearing her so earnest for the box,[10]
    Gave her her due, and she the door unlocks.
In am I entered: Venus be my speed.
    But where's the female that must to this deed?
By blind meanders, and by crankled ways   *zig-zag*
    She leads me onward (as my author says),
Until we came within a shady loft
    Where Venus' bouncing vestals[11] skirmish oft.
And there she set me in a leather chair,
50   And brought me forth of pretty trulls a pair,   *prostitutes*
To choose of them which might content mine eye;
    But her I sought I could nowhere espy.
I spake them fair, and wished them well to fare,
    Yet so it is, I must have fresher ware.   *goods*
Wherefore, dame bawd, as dainty as you be,
    Fetch gentle Mistress Francis forth to me.
'By Halydame,' quoth she, 'and God's own mother,
    I well perceive you are a wily brother.
For if there be a morsel of more price,
60   You'll smell it out though I be never so nice.
As you desire, so shall you swive with her,   *copulate*
    But think your purse-strings shall abuy it dear;
For he that will eat quails must lavish crowns,
    And Mistress Francis in her velvet gowns,
And ruffs and periwigs as fresh as May
    Cannot be kept with half-a-crown a day.'
'Of price, good hostess, we will not debate,
    Though you assize me at the highest rate.   *assess*
Only conduct me to this bonny belle,
70   And ten good gobs I will unto thee tell   *lumps/pay out*
Of gold or silver, which shall like thee best,
    So much do I her company request.'
Away she went: so sweet a thing is gold
    That (mauger) will invade the strongest hold.   *in spite of everything*
Hey-ho, she comes, that hath my heart in keep:
    Sing lullaby, my cares, and fall asleep.
Sweeping she comes, as she would brush the ground:
    Her rattling silks my senses do confound.
Oh, I am ravished! Void the chamber straight,
80   For I must needs upon her with my weight.
'My Tomalin',[12] quoth she, and then she smiled
    'Ay, Ay', quoth I. So more men are beguiled
With smiles, with flattering words and feigned cheer,
    When in their deeds their falsehood doth appear.
'As how, my lambkin?' blushing she replied.
    'Because I in this dancing school abide?
If that be it that breeds this discontent,
    We will remove the camp incontinent.   *immediately*
For shelter only, sweetheart, came I hither,
90   And to avoid the troublous stormy weather.

10   Nashe is alluding to the offering box of a church.   12   A diminutive for "Thomas."
11   Prostitutes were often referred to as "Venus' nuns" in Nashe's day.

But now the coast is clear we will be gone,
    Since but thyself true lover have I none.
With that, she sprung full lightly to my lips,
    And fast about the neck me colls and clips.   *embraces*
She wanton faints and falls upon her bed,
    And often tosseth to and fro her head.
She shuts her eyes and waggles with her tongue:
    Oh, who is able to abstain so long?
I come, I come; sweet lining by thy leave.   *underwear*
100   Softly my fingers up these curtains heave
And make me happy stealing by degrees.
    First bare her legs, then creep up to her knees.
From thence ascend unto her manly thigh
    (A pox on lingering when I am so nigh).
Smock, climb a-pace, that I may see my joys.
    Oh, heaven and paradise are all but toys
Compared with this sight I now behold,
    Which well might keep a man from being old.
A pretty rising womb without a weam,   *blemish*
110   That shone as bright as any silver stream,
And bare out like the bending of an hill,
    At whose decline a fountain dwelleth still,
That hath his mouth beset with ugly briars
    Resembling much a dusky net of wires.
A lofty buttock barred with azure veins,
    Whose comely swelling, when my hand distrains,   *squeezes*
Or wanton checketh with a harmless stype,[13]
    It makes the fruits of love eftsoon be ripe,   *soon after*
And pleasure plucked too timely from the stem,   *early*
120   To die ere it hath seen Jerusalem.[14]
Oh gods, that ever anything so sweet
    So suddenly should fade away and fleet.   *disappear*
Her arms are spread, and I am all unarmed.
    Like one with Ovid's cursed hemlock charmed,[15]
So are my limbs unwieldly for the fight,
    That spend their strength in thought of their delight.
What shall I do to show myself a man?
    It will not be for aught that beauty can.
I kiss, I clap, I feel, I view at will,   *embrace*
130   Yet dead he lies not thinking good or ill.
'Unhappy me,' quoth she, 'and will it not stand?
    Come, let me rub and chafe it with my hand.
Perhaps the silly worm is labored sore,
    And wearied that it can do no more.
If it be so (as I am great a-dread)
    I wish ten thousand times that I were dead.
How e'er it is, no means shall want in me,
    That may avail to his recovery.'
Which said, she took and rolled it on her thigh,
140   And when she looked on it, she would weep and sigh,
And dandled it and danced it up and down,
    Not ceasing, till she raise it from his swoon.

---

13 Meaning unknown. Again, it is possible that the text is corrupt here.

14 The line has a double meaning: both a fruit that is dying because it was picked too soon, and a premature sexual climax ("die").

15 A reference to Ovid *Amores* 3.6, which is another poem about impotence. Ovid's speaker blames poison and witchcraft.

And then he flew on her as he were wood,   *mad*
   And on her breach did thack and foin a-good.   *hit/thrust*
He rubbed and pricked and pierced her to the bones,
   Digging as far as eath he might for stones.   *easily*
Now high, now low, now striking short and thick,
   Now diving deep he touched her to the quick.
Now with a gird he would his course rebate.   *sudden movement/abate*
   Straight would he take him to a stately gait.

150   Play while him list, and thrust he never so hard,
   Poor patient Grisel[16] lieth at his ward,
And gives and takes as blithe and free as May,
   And ever more meets him in the middle way.
On him her eyes continually were fixed,
   With her eye-beams his melting looks were mixed,[17]
Which like the sun, that twixt two glasses plays   *mirrors*
   From one to the other casts rebounding rays.
He like a star, that to reguild his beams
160   Sucks in the influence of Phoebus' streams,   *i.e. the Sun's*
Imbathes the lines of his descending light
   In the bright fountains of her clearest sight.
She fair as fairest planet in the sky
   Her purity to no man doth deny.
The very chamber, that enclouds her shine,
   Looks like the palace of that God divine,
Who leads the day about the zodiac,   *course*
   And every even descends to the ocean lake.   *evening*
So fierce and fervent is her radiance,
170   Such fiery stakes she darts at every glance,
She might enflame the icy limbs of age,
   And make pale death his surquedry assuage   *pride*
To stand and gaze upon her orient lamps
   Where Cupid all his chiefest joys encamps,
And sits and plays with every atomy   *dust mote*
   That in her sunbeams swarm abundantly.
Thus gazing, and thus striving we persevere,
   But what so firm that may continue ever?
'Oh, not so fast!' my ravished mistress cries,
180   'Lest my content, that on thy life relies,
Be brought too soon from his delightful seat,
   And me unwares of hoped bliss defeat.
Together let our equal motions stir;
   Together let us live and die, my dear.
Together let us march unto content,
   And be consumed with one blandishment.'
As she prescribed, so kept we crotchet-time,   *musical time*
   And every stroke in order like a chime.
Whilst she, that had preserved me by her pity,
190   Unto our music framed a groaning ditty.
Alas, alas, that love should be a sin,
   Even now my bliss and sorrow doth begin.
Hold wide thy lap, my love Danaë,[18]
   And entertain the golden shower so free,

16 A reference to the character Griselda, found in Chaucer and Boccaccio, who was the type of the long-suffering woman.
17 The long description of the power of Francis's glance uses many of
the conventions of more refined love poetry. Their presence here is part
of Nashe's humor.
18 One of Zeus' paramours. He came to her in the form of a golden
shower.

That trilling falls into thy treasury,
  As April-drops not half so pleasant be,
Nor Nilus' overflow to Egypt plains,   i.e. the Nile's
  As this sweet-stream, that all her joints imbanes.[19]
With 'Oh' and 'Oh', she itching moves her hips,
200   And to and fro full lightly starts and skips.
She jerks her legs, and sprawleth with her heels,
  No tongue may tell the solace that she feels.
'I faint, I yield: Oh, death rock me asleep.'
  'Sleep, sleep, desire, entombed in the deep.'
'Not so, my dear', my dearest saint replied,
  'For from us yet thy spirit may not glide
Until the sinowy channels of our blood
  Withhold their source from this imprisoned flood;
And then will we (that "then" will come too soon)
210   Dissolved lie as though our days were done,
The whilst I speak, my soul is fleeting hence,
  And life forsakes his fleshly residence.
Stay, stay, sweet joy, and leave me not forlorn.
  Why shouldst thou fade that art but newly born?
Stay but an hour; an hour is not so much.
  But half an hour, if that they haste be such.
Nay, but a quarter: I will ask no more,
  That thy departure (which torments me sore)
May be alightened with a little pause,
220   And take away this passion's sudden cause.
He hears me not, hard-hearted as he is:
  He is the son of Time and hates my bliss.
Time never looks back, the river never return;
  A second spring must help me or I burn.
No, no, the well is dry that should refresh me.
  The glass is run of all my destiny.
Nature of winter learneth niggardize,   miserliness
  Who, as he overbears the stream with ice,
That man nor beast may of their pleasance taste,
230   So shuts she up her conduit all in haste,
And will not let her nectar overflow,
  Lest mortal men immortal joys should know.
Adieu, unconstant love, to thy disport.
  Adieu, false mirth, and melody too short.
Adieu, faint-hearted instrument of lust,
  That falsely hast betrayed our equal trust.
Henceforth no more will I implore thine aid,
  Or thee, or men, of cowardize upbraid.
My little dildo shall supply their kind,
240   A knave that moves as light as leaves by wind,
That bendeth not, nor foldest any deal,
  But stands as stiff as he were made of steel,
And plays at peacock twixt my legs right blithe,
  And doth my tickling swage with many a sigh.   assuage
For, by Saint Runyon,[20] he'll refresh me well,
  And never make my tender belly swell.'
Poor Priapus,[21] whose triumph now must fall,
  Except thou thrust this weakling to the wall,

19 Unknown; possibly related to "embane," meaning to taint or
poison.
20 A term for the male organ.

21 A classical male fertility god, usually depicted with highly exaggerated genitals.

Behold how he usurps in bed and bower,
250   And undermines thy kingdom every hour.
How sly he creeps betwixt the bark and tree,
    And sucks the sap, whilst sleep detaineth thee.
He is my mistress' page at every stound,   *occasion*
    And soon will tent a deep intrenched wound.   *probe*
He waits on courtly nymphs that be so coy,
    And bids them scorn the blind-alluring boy.
He gives young girls their gamesome sustenance,
    And every gaping mouth his full sufficience.
He fortifies disdain with foreign arts,
260   And wanton-chaste deludes all loving hearts.
If any wight a cruel mistress serves,   *person*
    Or in despair, unhappy pines and sterves,   *dies*
Curse eunuch dildo, senseless, counterfeit,
    Who sooth may fill, but never can beget.
But if revenge enraged with despair
    That such a dwarf his welfare should impair,
Would fain this woman's secretary know,
    Let him attend the marks that I shall show.
He is a youth almost to handfuls high,
270   Straight, round, and plumb, yet having but one eye,   *upright*
Wherein the rheum so fervently doth rain,
    That Stygian gulf may scarce his tears contain;   *Hell's*
Attired in white velvet or in silk,
    And nourished with hot water or with milk;
Armed otherwhile in thick congealed glass,
    When he more glib to hell[22] below would pass,
Upon a chariot of five wheels he rides,   *i.e. fingers*
    The which an arm-strong driver steadfast guides,
And often alters pace as ways grow deep
280   (For who in paths unknown one gate can keep?).
Sometimes he smoothly slideth down the hill,
    Another while the stones his feet do kill.
In clammy ways he treadeth by and by,
    And plasheth and sprayeth all that be him nigh.
So fares this jolly rider in his race,
    Plunging and sourcing forward in like case,   *surging*
Bedashed, bespirted, and beplodded[23] foul,   *covered in filth*
    God give thee shame, thou blind misshapen owl.
Fie, fie, for grief: a lady's chamberlain,[24]
290   And canst not thou thy tattling tongue refrain?
I read thee, beardless blab, beware of stripes,   *advise/whippings*
    And be advised what thou vainly pipes.
Thou wilt be whipped with nettles for this gear,   *affair*
    If Cicely show but of thy knavery here.
Saint Denis shield me from such female sprites!
    Regard not, dames, what Cupid's poet writes.
I penned this story only for myself,
    Who giving suck unto a childish elf,
And quite discouraged in my nursery,
300   Since all my store seems to her penury.
I am not as was Hercules the stout,
    That to the seventh journey could hold out.

---

22 A common misogynist nickname for the female genitals.   24 A bedroom servant.
23 Meaning unclear.

I want those herbs and roots of Indian soil,
   That strengthen weary members in their toil.
Drugs and electuaries of new device   *i.e. aphrodisiacs*
   Do shun my purse, that trembles at the price.
Sufficeth, all I have I yield her whole,
   Which for a poor man is a princely dole.
I pay our hostess scot and lot at most,   *thoroughly*
310   And look as lean and lank as any ghost.
What can be added more to my renown?
   She lieth breathless; I am taken down.
The waves do swell, the tides climb over the banks,
   Judge, gentlemen, if I deserve not thanks.
And so good night unto you every one,
   For lo, our thread is spun, our play is done.
   Claudito iam rivos Priape, sat prata biberunt.

Thus hath my pen presum'd to please my friend;
   Oh mightst thou likewise please Apollo's eye.
320   No: Honour brooks no such impiety,
   Yet Ovid's wanton Muse did not offend.
He is the fountain whence my streams do flow –
   Forgive me if I speak as I was taught,
   Alike to women, utter all I know,
   As longing to unlade so bad a fraught.   *freight*
My mind once purg'd of such lascivious wit,
   With purified words and hallowed verse,
   Thy praises in large volumes shall rehearse,
   That better may thy graver view befit.
330 Meanwhile yet rests, you smile at what I write;
   Or, for attempting, banish me your sight.

Æmilia Lanyer (1569–1645)

Æmilia Bassano Lanyer was the first woman poet in England to publish her own volume of poetry with the intention of establishing herself as a professional writer. Her book, *Salve Deus Rex Judæorum*, was dated the same year (1611) as Lady Mary Wroth's prose romance, *Urania*; and, like Wroth's work, it is written from the narrative point of view of a woman. *Salve* opens with nine dedicatory poems to royal and noble ladies and a prose dedication to the Countess of Cumberland, who was also a patron of Edmund Spenser and Samuel Daniel. These dedications are important in their own right in helping to fashion a literary culture for women. They are followed by a prose epistle, "To the Vertuous Reader," which argues women's equality – or superiority – to men in spiritual and moral concerns. The title poem of 1056 lines is a meditation on the Passion and death of Christ, which emphasizes the good women who are associated with that story. This poem is contained within a frame of 776 lines that includes a tribute to Margaret Clifford (the Countess of Cumberland) as a virtuous follower of Christ. On her title page, Lanyer outlines the contents of the poem as follows:

1. The Passion of Christ.
2. Eves Apologie in defence of Women.
3. The Teares of the Daughters of Jerusalem.
4. The Salutation and Sorrow of the Virgine Marie.

Her book concludes with a country-house poem, "The Description of Cooke-ham," celebrating Margaret Clifford's estate as a paradise for literary women of spirit.

The remarkable achievement of *Salve Deus Rex Judæorum* lies in the simplicity of its narrative and the clarity of its point of view. The four Gospel accounts of the Passion are preserved in the New Testament for the obvious reason that each provides material that the others lack. It helps to read Lanyer's poem with at least a copy of the Gospels at hand, if not an even more helpful edition of the Parallel Gospels (such editions print the texts of the Gospels in parallel columns). The ambition of Lanyer's poem is nothing less than to cut back through 1,500 years of controversy about the Gospels in order to recover a story that can be told in such a way as to underscore the importance of women in that narrative without diminishing its central focus on Jesus. This she does with remarkable subtlety and charm. Nevertheless, she is very sophisticated in her understanding of such processes of biblical narrative and interpretation as typology, midrash, and allegory (for an excellent guide to these topics from a Renaissance point of view, see Shuger).

Æmilia Lanyer was the daughter of an English mother (probably Margaret Johnson, about whom little is known) and Baptista Bassano, a Jewish, Venetian-born, court musician. By her own account, Lanyer was educated under the direction of Susan Bertie, the dowager Countess of Kent, whose Protestant humanist circle had a profound influence on the young poet. In 1592, however, she was pregnant by Henry Carey, Lord Hunsdon, Queen Elizabeth's first cousin and her Lord Chamberlain, during a relationship that had lasted perhaps as long as four years. She was then in her twenties and he in his sixties. Her subsequent marriage to Alfonso Lanyer, also a court musician, is reported by Simon Forman, the astrologer whom she consulted, as having been

unhappy. However, if the picture that may be her portrait (*Unknown Woman in Black*, 1592, in Berkeley Castle) is in fact Lanyer, then her power can be easily imagined. She was apparently a young, beautiful, intelligent, and talented woman. That she was the "dark lady" of Shakespeare's sonnets (assuming there was such an historical person) is quite doubtful. Her connection with Shakespeare and other male writers appears to have been a literary one.

READING

Marshall Grossman, (ed.), *Æmilia Lanyer: Gender, Genre, and the Canon*.

Debora Kuller Shuger, *The Renaissance Bible: Scholarship, Sacrifice, and Subjectivity*.

Susanne Woods, *Lanyer: A Renaissance Woman Poet*.

M. P.

[FROM] SALVE DEUS REX JUDÆORUM

To the Vertuous Reader

Often have I heard, that it is the property of some women, not only to emulate the virtues and perfections of the rest, but also by all their powers of ill speaking, to ecclipse the brightnes of their deserved fame: now contrary to this custome, which men I hope unjustly lay to their charge, I have written this small volume, or little booke, for the generall use of all virtuous Ladies and Gentlewomen of this kingdome; and in commendation of some particular persons of our owne sexe, such as for the most part, are so well knowne to my selfe, and others, that I dare undertake Fame dares not to call any better. And this have I done, to make knowne to the world, that all women deserve not to be blamed though some forgetting they are women themselves, and in danger to be condemned by the words of their owne mouthes, fall into so great an errour, as to speake unadvisedly against the rest of their sexe; which if it be true, I am perswaded they can shew their owne imperfection in nothing more: and therefore could wish (for their owne ease, modesties, and credit) they would referre such points of folly, to be practised by evill disposed men, who forgetting they were borne of women, nourished of women, and that if it were not by the means of women, they would be quite extinguished out of the world, and a finall ende of them all, doe like Vipers deface the wombes wherein they were bred, onely to give way and utterance to their want of discretion and goodnesse. Such as these, were they that dishonoured Christ his Apostles and Prophets, putting them to shamefull deaths. Therefore we are not to regard any imputations, that they undeservedly lay upon us, no otherwise than to make use of them to our owne benefits, as spurres to vertue, making us flie all occasions that may colour their unjust speeches to passe currant. Especially considering that they have tempted even the patience of God himselfe, who gave power to wise and virtuous women, to bring downe their pride and arrogancie. As was cruell *Cesarus* by the discreet counsell of noble *Deborah*, Judge and Prophetesse of Israel: and resolution of *Jael* wife of *Heber* the Kenite: wicked *Haman*, by the divine prayers and prudent proceedings of beautiful *Hester*: blasphemous *Holofernes*, by the invincible courage, rare wisdome, and confident carriage of *Judeth*: & the unjust Judges, by the innocency of chast *Susanna*: with infinite others, which for brevitie sake I will omit.[1] As also in respect it pleased our Lord and Saviour Jesus Christ, without the assistance

---

[FROM] SALVE DEUS REX JUDÆORUM

1 These are all examples of female heroism. The story of Deborah and Cesarus (or Sisera) is in Judges 4:10–17; Heber and Jael in Judges 4:18–22; Hester and Haman in Esther 5–7; Judeth and Holofernes in the Apocryphal Book of Judith 8–13; and Susanna and the Judges in the Apocryphal History of Daniel and Susanna.

of man, beeing free from originall and all other sinnes, from the time of his conception, till the houre of his death, to be begotten of a woman, borne of a woman, nourished of a woman, obedient to a woman; and that he healed woman, pardoned women, comforted women: yea, even when he was in his greatest agonie and bloodie sweat, going to be crucified, and also in the last houre of his death, tooke care to dispose of a woman:[2] after his resurrection, appeared first to a woman, sent a woman to declare his most glorious resurrection to the rest of his Disciples.[3] Many other examples I could alleadge of divers faithfull and virtuous women, who have in all ages, not onely beene Confessors, but also indured most cruel martyrdome for their faith in Jesus Christ. All which is sufficient to inforce all good Christians and honourable minded men to speake reverently of our sexe, and especially of all virtuous and good women. To the modest sensures of both which, I refer these my imperfect indeavours, knowing that according to their owne excellent dispositions, they will rather, cherish, nourish, and increase the least sparke of virtue where they find it, by their favourable and best interpretations, than quench it by wrong constructions. To whom I wish all increase of virtue, and desire their best opinions.

SALVE DEUS REX JUDÆORUM

Sith *Cynthia*[4] is ascended to that rest
Of endlesse joy and true Eternitie,
That glorious place that cannot be exprest
By any wight clad in mortalitie,   *person*
In her almightie love so highly blest,
And crown'd with everlasting Sov'raigntie;
   Where Saints and Angells do attend her Throne,
   And she gives glorie unto God alone.

     To thee great Countesse now I will applie   *The Ladie*
10   My Pen, to write thy never dying fame;   *Margaret*
That when to Heav'n thy blessed Soule shall flie,   *Countesse*
These lines on earth record thy reverend name: *Dowager of*
And to this taske I meane my Muse to tie,   *Cumberland*
Though wanting skill I shall but purchase blame:
   Pardon (deere Ladie) want of womans wit
   To pen thy praise, when few can equall it.

And pardon (Madame) though I do not write
Those praisefull lines of that delightful place,
As you commaunded me in that faire night,
20   When shining *Phoebe* gave so great a grace,
Presenting *Paradice* to your sweet sight,
Unfolding all the beauty of her face
   With pleasant groves, hills, walks and stately trees,
   Which pleasures with retired minds agrees.

Whose Eagles eyes behold the glorious Sunne
Of th'all-creating Providence, reflecting
His blessed beames on all by him, begunne;
Increasing, strengthning, guiding and directing
All wordly creatures their due course to runne,
30   Unto His powrefull pleasure all subjecting:
   And thou (deere Ladie) by his special grace,
   In these his creatures dost behold his face.

2   Mary, his mother (John 19:25–27).

3   Mary Magdalene and "the other Mary" (Matthew 28:8–10).

4   Queen Elizabeth I was mythologized as the moon goddess and associated with Phoebe and Diana. She died in 1603.

Whose all-reviving beautie, yeelds such joyes
To thy sad Soule, plunged in waves of woe,
That worldly pleasures seemes to thee as toyes,
Onely thou seek'st Eternitie to know,
Respecting not the infinite annoyes
That Satan to thy well-staid mind can show;
   Ne can he quench in thee, the Spirit of Grace,
   Nor draw thee from beholding Heavens bright face.

40

Thy Mind so perfect by thy Maker fram'd
No vaine delights can harbour in thy heart,
With his sweet love, thou art so much inflam'd,
As of the world thou seem'st to have no part;
So, love him still, thou need'st not be asham'd,
Tis He that made thee, what thou wert, and art:
   Tis He that dries all teares from Orphans eies,
   And heares from heav'n the wofull widdows cries.

Tis He that doth behold thy inward cares,
And will regard the sorrowes of thy Soule;
Tis He that guides thy feet from Sathans snares,
And in his Wisedome, doth thy waies controule:
He through afflictions, still thy Minde prepares,
And all thy glorious Trials will enroule:
   That when darke daies of terror shall appeare,
   Thou as the Sunne shalt shine; or much more cleare.

50

The Heav'ns shall perish as a garment olde,
Or as a vesture by the maker chang'd,
And shall depart, as when a skrowle is rolde;   *scroll*
Yet thou from him shalt never be estrang'd,
When He shall come in glory, that was solde
For all our sinnes; we happily are chang'd,
   Who for our faults put on his righteousnesse,
   Although full oft his Lawes we doe transgresse.

60

Long mai'st thou joy in this almightie love,
Long may thy Soule be pleasing in his sight,
Long mai'st thou have true comforts from above,
Long mai'st thou set on him thy whole delight,
And patiently endure when he doth prove,
Knowing that He will surely do thee right:
   Thy patience, faith, long suffring, and thy love,
   He will reward with comforts from above.

70

With Majestie and Honour is He clad,
And deck'd with light, as with a garment faire;
He joyes the Meeke, and makes the Mightie sad,
Pulls downe the Prowd, and doth the Humble reare:
Who sees this Bridegroome,[5] never can be sad;
None lives that can his wondrous workes declare:
   Yea, looke how farre the Est is from the West,
   So farre he sets our sinnes that have transgrest.[6]

80

He rides upon the wings of all the windes,
And spreads the heav'ns with his all powrefull hand;

---

5 See the parable of the bridegroom in Matthew 25:1–13.   6 Allusions to the Psalms, especially 103 and 97, appear here and in the following lines.

Oh! who can loose when the Almightie bindes?
Or in his angry presence dares to stand?
He searcheth out the secrets of all mindes;
All those that feare him, shall possesse the Land:
   He is exceeding glorious to behold,
   Antient of Times; so faire, and yet so old.

He of the watry Cloudes his Chariot frames,
90   And makes his blessed Angels powrefull Spirits,
His Ministers are fearefull fiery flames,
Rewarding all according to their merits;
The Righteous for an heritage he claimes,
And registers the wrongs of humble spirits:
   Hills melt like wax, in presence of the Lord,
   So do all sinners, in his sight abhorr'd

He in the waters laies his chamber beames,
And cloudes of darkenesse compasse him about,
Consuming fire shall goe before in streames,
100   And burne up all his en'mies round about:
Yet on these Judgements worldlings never dreames,
Nor of these daungers never stand in doubt:
   While he shall rest within his holy Hill,
   That lives and dies according to his Will.

But woe to them that double-hearted bee,
Who with their tongues the righteous Soules doe slay;
Bending their bowes to shoot at all they see,
With upright hearts their Maker to obay;
And secretly doe let their arrowes flee,
110   To wound true hearted people any way:
   The Lord wil roote them out that speak prowd things,
   Deceitfull tongues are but false Slanders wings.

Froward are the ungodly from their berth,
No sooner borne, but they doe goe astray;
The Lord will roote them out from off the earth,
And give them to their en'mies for a pray,   *prey*
As venemous as Serpents is their breath,
With poysned lies to hurt in what they may
   The Innocent: who as a Dove shall flie
120   Unto the Lord, that he his cause may trie.

The righteous Lord doth righteousnesse allow,
His countenance will behold the thing that's just;
Unto the Meane he makes the Mightie bow,   *lowly*
And raiseth up the Poore out of the dust:
Yet makes no count to us, nor when, nor how,
But powres his grace on all, that puts their trust
   In him: that never will their hopes betray,
   Nor lets them perish that for mercie pray.

He shall within his Tabernacle dwell,
130   Whose life is uncorrupt before the Lord,
Who no untrueths of Innocents doth tell,
Nor wrongs his neighbour, nor in deed, nor word,
Nor in his pride with malice seems to swell,
Nor whets his tongue more sharper than a sword,

To wound the reputation of the Just;
Nor seekes to lay their glorie in the Dust.

That great *Jehova* King of heav'n and earth,
Will raine downe fire and brimstone from above,
Upon the wicked monsters in their berth
That storme and rage at those whom he doth love:
Snares, stormes, and tempests he will raine,
    and dearth,
Because he will himselfe almightie prove:
   And this shall be their portion they shall drinke,
   That thinkes the Lord is blind when he doth winke.

Pardon (good Madame) though I have digrest
From what I doe intend to write of thee,
To set his glorie forth whom thou lov'st best,
Whose wondrous works no mortall eie can see;
His special care on those whom he hath blest
From wicked worldlings, how he sets them free:
   And how such people he doth overthrow
   In all their waies, that they his powre may know.

The meditation of this Monarchs love,
Drawes thee from caring what this world can yield;
Of joyes and griefes both equall thou dost prove,
They have no force, to force thee from the field:
Thy constant faith like to the Turtle Dove
Continues combat, and will never yield
   To base affliction; or prowd pomps desire,
   That sets the weakest mindes so much on fire.

Thou from the Court to the Countrie art retir'd,
Leaving the world, before the world leaves thee:
That great Enchantresse of weake mindes admir'd,
Whose all-bewitching charmes so pleasing be
To worldly wantons; and too much desir'd
Of those that care not for Eternitie:
   But yeeld themselves as preys to Lust and Sinne,
   Loosing their hopes of Heav'n Hell paines to winne.

But thou, the wonder of our wanton age
Leav'st all delights to serve a heav'nly King:
Who is more wise? or who can be more sage,
Than she that doth Affection subject bring;
Not forcing for the world, or Satans rage,
But shrowding under the Almighties wing;
   Spending her yeares, moneths, daies,
      minutes, howres,
   In doing service to the heav'nly powres.

Thou faire example, live without compare,
With Honours triumphs seated in thy breast;
Pale Envy never can thy name empaire,
When in thy heart thou harbour'st such a guest:
Malice must live for ever in dispaire;
There's no revenge where Virtue still doth rest:
   All hearts must needs do homage unto thee,
   In whom all eies such rare perfection see.

To the
Countesse of
Cumberland.

That outward Beautie which the world commends,
Is not the subject I will write upon,
Whose date expir'd, that tyrant Time soone ends;
Those gawdie colours soone are spent and gone:
But those faire Virtues which on thee attends
190   Are alwaies fresh, they never are but one:
    They make thy Beautie fairer to behold,
    Than was that Queenes for whom prowd *Troy*
      was sold.

An Invective against outward beauty unaccompanied with virtue.

As for those matchlesse colours Red and White,
Or perfit features in a fading face,
Or due proportion pleasing to the sight;
All these doe draw but dangers and disgrace:
A mind enrich'd with Virtue, shines more bright,
Addes everlasting Beauty, gives true grace,
    Frames an immortall Goddesse on the earth,
200   Who though she dies, yet Fame gives her new berth.

That pride of Nature which adorns the faire,
Like blasing Comets to allure all eies,
Is but the thred, that weaves their web of Care,
Who glories most, where most their danger lies;
For greatest perills do attend the faire,
When men do seeke, attempt, plot and devise,
    How they may overthrow the chastest Dame,
    Whose Beautie is the White whereat they aime.

Twas Beaurie bred in *Troy* the ten yeares strife,
210   And carried *Hellen* from her lawfull Lord;
Twas Beautie made chaste *Lucrece* loose her life,
For which prowd *Tarquins* fact was so abhorr'd:
Beautie the cause *Antonius* wrong'd his wife,
Which could not be decided but by sword:
    Great *Cleopatraes* Beautie and defects
    Did worke *Octaviaes* wrongs, and his neglects.[7]

What fruit did yeeld that faire forbidden tree,
But blood, dishonour, infamie, and shame?
Poore blinded Queene, could'st thou no better see,
220   But entertaine disgrace, in stead of fame?
Doe these designes with Majestie agree?
To staine thy blood, and blot thy royall name.
    That heart that gave consent unto this ill,
    Did give consent that thou thy selfe should'st kill.

Faire *Rosamund*,[8] the wonder of her time,
Had bin much fairer, had shee not bin faire;
Beautie betraid her thoughts, aloft to clime,
To build strong castles in uncertaine aire,
Where th'infection of a wanton crime
230   Did worke her fall; first poyson, then despaire,
    With double death did kill her perjur'd soule,
    When heavenly Justice did her sinne controule.

Of Rosamund.

7 Cleopatra, Queen of Egypt, is here depicted as blind to the tragic effect her beauty has on her lover, Mark Antony, who was married to Octavia. Cleopatra and Antony committed suicide in 30 BCE.

8 Rosamund, the mistress of King Henry II, is reported to have been poisoned by Queen Eleanor of Aquitaine.

Holy *Matilda*[9] in a haplesse houre   *Of Matilda.*
Was borne to sorow and to discontent,
Beauty the cause that turn'd her Sweet to Sowre,
While Chastity sought Folly to prevent.
Lustfull King *John* refus'd, did use his powre,
By Fire and Sword, to compasse his content:
    But Friends disgrace, nor Fathers banishment,
    Nor Death it selfe, could purchase her consent.

240

Here Beauty in the height of all perfection,
Crown'd this faire Creatures everlasting fame,
Whose noble minde did scorne the base subjection
Of Feares, or Favours, to impaire her Name:
By heavenly grace, she had such true direction,
To die with Honour, not to live in Shame;
    And drinke that poyson with a cheerefull heart,
    That could all Heavenly grace to her impart.

This Grace great Lady, doth possesse thy Soule,   *To the*
250   And makes thee pleasing in thy Makers sight;   *Ladie of*
This Grace doth all imperfect Thoughts controule,   *Cumberland*
Directing thee to serve thy God aright;   *the Intro-*
Still reckoning him, the Husband of thy Soule,   *duction to*
Which is most pretious in his glorious sight: *the passion*
    Because the Worlds delights shee doth denie   *of Christ.*
    For him, who for her sake vouchsaf'd to die.

And dying made her Dowager of all;
Nay more, Co-heire of that eternall blisse
That Angels lost, and We by *Adams* fall;
260   Meere Cast-awaies, rais'd by a *Judas* kisse,
Christs bloody sweat, the Vineger, and Gall,
The Speare, Sponge, Nailes, his buffeting with Fists,
    His bitter Passion, Agony, and Death,
    Did gaine us Heaven when He did loose his breath.

These high deserts invites my lowely Muse   *A preamble*
To write of Him, and pardon crave of thee,   *of the*
For Time so spent, I need make no excuse,   *Author*
Knowing it doth with thy faire Minde agree   *before the*
So well, as thou no Labour wilt refuse,   *Passion.*
270   That to thy holy Love may pleasing be:
    His Death and Passion I desire to write,
    And thee to reade, the blessed Soules delight.

But my deare Muse, now whither wouldst thou flie,
Above the pitch of thy appointed straine?
With *Icarus* thou seekest now to trie,
Not waxen wings, but thy poore barren Braine,
Which farre too weake, these siely lines descrie;   *simple*
Yet cannot this thy forward Mind restraine,
    But thy poore Infant Verse must soare aloft,
280   Not fearing threat'ning dangers, happening oft.

Thinke when the eye of Wisdom shall discover
Thy weakling Muse to flie, that scarce could creepe,

9 Matilda, a virtuous woman, was pursued by King John.

And in the Ayre above the Clowdes to hover,
When better 'twere mued up, and fast asleepe;   *confined*
They'l thinke with *Phaeton,* thou canst neare recover,
But helplesse with that poore yong Lad to weepe:
 The little World of thy weake Wit on fire,
 Where thou wilt perish in thine owne desire.

290
But yet the Weaker thou doest seeme to be
In Sexe, or Sence, the more his Glory shines,
That doth infuze such powerfull Grace in thee,
To shew thy Love in these few humble Lines;
The Widowes Myte,[10] with this may well agree,
Her little All more worth than golden mynes,
 Beeing more deerer to our loving Lord,
 Than all the wealth that Kingdoms could affoard.

Therefore I humbly for his Grace will pray,
That he will give me Power and Strength to Write,
That what I have begun, so end I may,
300
As his great Glory may appeare more bright;
Yea in these Lines I may no further stray,
Than his most holy Spirit shall give me Light:
 That blindest Weakenesse be not over-bold,
 The manner of his Passion to unfold.

In other Phrases than may well agree
With his pure Doctrine, and most holy Writ,
That Heavens cleare eye, and all the World may see,
I seeke his Glory, rather than to get
The Vulgars breath, the seed of Vanitie,
310
Nor Fames lowd Trumpet care I to admit;
 But rather strive in plainest Words to showe,
 The Matter which I seeke to undergoe.

A Matter farre beyond my barren skill,
To shew with any Life this map of Death,
This Storie; that whole Worlds with Bookes would fill,
In these few Lines, will put me out of breath,
To run so swiftly up this mightie Hill,
I may behold it with the eye of Faith;
 But to present this pure unspotted Lambe,
320
 I must confesse, I farre unworthy am.

Yet if he please t'illuminate my Spirit,
And give me Wisdom from his holy Hill,
That I may Write part of his glorious Merit,
If he vouchsafe to guide my Hand and Quill,
To shew his Death, by which we doe inherit
Those endlesse Joyes that all our hearts doe fill;
 Then will I tell of that sad blacke fac'd Night,
 Whose mourning Mantle covered Heavenly Light.

That very Night our Saviour was betrayed,   *Here*
330
Oh night! exceeding all the nights of sorow,   *begins the*
When our most blessed Lord, although dismayed,   *Passion of*

---

10   The parable of the Widow's Mite is told in Mark 12:41–44 and
Luke 21:1–4.

Yet would not he one Minutes respite borrow,   *Christ.*
But to *Mount Olives* went, though sore afraid,
To welcome Night, and entertaine the Morrow;
    And as he oft unto that place did goe,
    So did he now, to meete his long nurst woe.

He told his deere Disciples that they all
Should be offended by him, that selfe night,
His Griefe was great, and theirs could not be small,
To part from him who was their sole Delight;
340 Saint *Peter* thought his Faith could never fall,
No mote could happen in so cleare a sight:
    Which made him say, though all men
        were offended,
    Yet would he never, though his life were ended.

But his deare Lord made answere, That before
The Cocke did crowe, he should deny him thrice;
This could not choose but grieve him very sore,
That his hot Love should proove more cold than Ice,
Denying him he did so much adore;
350 No imperfection in himselfe he spies,
    But faith againe, with him hee'l surely die,
    Rather than his deare Master once denie.

And all the rest (did likewise say the same)
Of his Disciples, at that instant time;
But yet poore *Peter*, he was most too blame,
That thought above them all, by Faith to clime;
His forward speech inflicted sinne and shame,
When Wisdoms eyes did looke and checke his crime:
    Who did foresee, and told it him before,
360 Yet would he needs averre it more and more.

Now went our Lord unto that holy place,
Sweet *Gethsemaine* hallowed by his presence,
That blessed Garden, which did now embrace
His holy corps, yet could make no defence   *body*
Against those Vipers, objects of disgrace,
Which sought that pure eternall Love to quench:
    Here his Disciples willed he to stay,
    Whilst he went further, where he meant to pray.

None were admitted with their Lord to goe,
370 But *Peter*, and the sonnes of *Zebed'us*,[11]
To them good *Jesus* opened all his woe,
He gave them leave his sorows to discusse,
His deepest griefes, he did not scorne to showe
These three deere friends, so much he did intrust:
    Beeing sorowfull, and overcharg'd with griefe,
    He told it them, yet look'd for no reliefe.

Sweet Lord, how couldst thou thus to flesh and blood
Communicate thy griefe? tell of thy woes?
Thou knew'st they had no powre to doe thee good.
380 But were the cause thou must endure these blowes,

11 James and John.

Beeing the Scorpions bred in *Adams* mud,
Whose poys'ned sinnes did worke among thy foes,
  To re-ore-charge thy over-burd'ned soule,
  Although the sorowes now they doe condole.

Yet didst thou tell them of thy troubled state,
Of thy Soules heavinesse unto the death,
So full of Love, so free wert thou from hate,
To bid them stay, whose sinnes did stop thy breath,
When thou wert entring at so straite a gate,
390   Yea entring even into the doore of Death,
    Thou bidst them tarry there, and watch with thee,
    Who from thy pretious blood-shed were not free.

Bidding them tarry, thou didst further goe,
To meet affliction in such gracefull sort,
As might moove pitie both in friend and foe,
Thy sorowes such, as none could them comport,
Such great Indurements who did ever know,
When to th' Almighty thou didst make resort?
400   And falling on thy face didst humbly pray,
    If 'twere his Will that Cup might passe away.

Saying, Not my will, but thy will Lord be done.
When as thou prayedst an Angel did appeare
From Heaven, to comfort thee Gods onely Sonne,
That thou thy Suffrings might'st the better beare,
Beeing in an agony, thy glasse neere run,   *time*
Thou prayedst more earnestly, in so great feare,
    That pretious sweat came trickling to the ground,
    Like drops of blood thy sences to confound.

Loe here his Will, not thy Will, Lord was done,
410   And thou content to undergoe all paines,
Sweet Lambe of God, his deare beloved Sonne,
By this great purchase, what to thee remaines?
Of Heaven and Earth thou hast a Kingdom wonne,
Thy Glory beeing equall with thy Gaines,
    In ratifying Gods promise on the Earth,
    Made many hundred yeares before thy birth.

But now returning to thy sleeping Friends,
That could not watch one houre for love of thee,
Even those three Friends, which on thy Grace depends,
420   Yet shut those Eies that should their Maker see;
What colour, what excuse, or what amends,
From thy Displeasure now can set them free?
    Yet thy pure Pietie bids them Watch and Pray,
    Lest in Temptation they be led away.

Although the Spirit was willing to obay,
Yet what great weakenesse in the Flesh was found!
They slept in Ease, whilst thou in Paine didst pray;
Loe, they in Sleepe, and thou in Sorow drown'd:
Yet Gods right Hand was unto thee a stay,
430   When horror, griefe, and sorow did abound:
    His Angel did appeare from Heaven to thee,
    To yeeld thee comfort in Extremitie.

But what could comfort then thy troubled Minde,
When Heaven and Earth were both against thee bent?
And thou no hope, no ease, no rest could'st finde,
But must restore that Life, which was but lent;
Was ever Creature in the World so kinde,
But he that from Eternitie was sent?
   To satisfie for many Worlds of Sinne,
440   Whose matchlesse Torments did but then begin.

If one Mans sinne doth challendge Death and Hell,
With all the Torments that belong thereto:
If for one sinne such Plagues on *David* fell,
As grieved him, and did his Seed undoe:[12]
If *Salomon*, for that he did not well,
Falling from Grace, did loose his Kingdome too:
   Ten Tribes beeing taken from his wilfull Sonne
   And Sinne the Cause that they were all undone.

What could thy Innocency now expect,
450 When all the Sinnes that ever were committed,
Were laid to thee, whom no man could detect?
Yet farre thou wert of Man from beeing pittied,
The Judge so just could yeeld thee no respect,
Nor would one jot of penance be remitted;
   But greater horror to thy Soule must rise,
   Than Heart can thinke, or any Wit devise.

Now drawes the houre of thy affliction neere,
And ugly Death presents himselfe before thee;
Thou now must leave those Friends thou held'st so deere,
460 Yea those Disciples, who did most adore thee;
Yet in thy countenance doth no Wrath appeare,
Although betrayd to those that did abhorre thee:
   Thou did'st vouchsafe to visit them againe,
   Who had no apprehension of thy paine.

Their eyes were heavie, and their hearts asleepe,
Nor knew they well what answere then to make thee;
Yet thou as Watchman, had'st a care to keepe
Those few from sinne, that shortly would forsake thee;
But now thou bidst them henceforth Rest and Sleepe,
470 Thy houre is come, and they at hand to take thee:
   The Sonne of God to Sinners made a pray,
   Oh hatefull houre! oh blest! oh cursed day!

Loe here thy great Humility was found,
Beeing King of Heaven, and Monarch of the Earth,
Yet well content to have thy Glory drownd,
By beeing counted of so meane a berth;
Grace, Love, and Mercy did so much abound,
Thou entertaindst the Crosse, even to the death:
   And nam'dst thy selfe, the sonne of Man to be,
480   To purge our pride by thy Humilitie.

But now thy friends whom thou didst call to goe,
Heavy Spectators of thy haplesse case,

---

12 See 1 Chronicles 21:1–17.

See thy Betrayer, whom too well they knowe,   *Judas*
One of the twelve, now object of disgrace,
A trothlesse traytor, and a mortall foe,
With fained kindnesse seekes thee to imbrace;
   And gives a kisse, whereby he may deceive thee,
   That in the hands of Sinners he might leave thee.

Now muster forth with Swords, with Staves, with Bils,   *axes*
490 High Priests and Scribes, and Elders of the Land,
Seeking by force to have their wicked Wils,
Which thou didst never purpose to withstand;
Now thou mak'st haste unto the worst of Ils,
And who they seeke, thou gently doest demand;
   This didst thou Lord, t'amaze these Fooles the more,
   T'inquire of that, thou knew'st so well before.

When loe these Monsters did not shame to tell,
His name they sought, and found, yet could not know
Jesus of Nazareth, at whose feet they fell,
500 When Heavenly Wisdome did descend so lowe
To speake to them: they knew they did not well,
Their great amazement made them backeward goe:
   Nay, though he said unto them, I am he,
   They could not know him, whom their eyes did see.

How blinde were they could not discerne the Light!
How dull! if not to understand the truth,
How weake! if meekenesse overcame their might;
How stony hearted, if not mov'd to ruth:
How void of Pitie, and how full of Spight,
510 Gainst him that was the Lord of Light and Truth:
   Here insolent Boldnesse checkt by Love and Grace,
   Retires, and falls before our Makers face.

For when he spake to this accursed crew,
And mildely made them know that it was he:
Presents himselfe, that they might take a view;
And what they doubted they might cleerely see;
Nay more, to re-assure that it was true,
He said: I say unto you, I am hee.
   If him they sought, he's willing to obay,
520   Onely desires the rest might goe their way.

Thus with a heart prepared to endure
The greatest wrongs Impietie could devise,
He was content to stoope unto their Lure,
Although his Greatnesse might doe otherwise:
Here Grace was seised on with hands impure,
And Virtue now must be supprest by Vice,
   Pure Innocencie made a prey to Sinne,
   Thus did his Torments and our Joyes beginne.

Here faire Obedience shined in his breast,
530 And did suppresse all feare of furure paine;
Love was his Leader unto this unrest,
Whil'st Righteousnesse doth carry up his Traine;
Mercy made way to make us highly blest,
When Patience beat downe Sorrow, Feare and Paine:

Justice sate looking with an angry brow,
On blessed misery appeering now.

More glorious than all the Conquerors
That ever liv'd within this Earthly round,
More powrefull than all Kings, or Governours
540   That ever yet within this World were found;
More valiant than the greatest Souldiers
That ever fought, to have their glory crown'd:
   For which of them, that ever yet tooke breath,
   Sought t'indure the doome of Heaven and Earth?

But our sweet Saviour whom these Jewes did name;
Yet could their learned Ignorance apprehend
No light of grace, to free themselves from blame:
Zeale, Lawes, Religion, now they doe pretend
Against the truth, untruths they seeke to frame:
Now al their powres, their wits, their strengths,
550   they bend
   Against one siely, weake, unarmed man,   *innocent*
   Who no resistance makes, though much he can,

To free himselfe from these unlearned men,
Who call'd him Saviour in his blessed name;
Yet farre from knowing him their Saviour then,
That came to save both them and theirs from blame;
Though they retire and fall, they come agen
To make a surer purchase of their shame:
   With lights and torches now they find the way,
560   To take the Shepheard whilst the sheep doe stray.

Why should unlawfull actions use the Light?
Inniquitie in Darkenesse seekes to dwell;
Sinne rides his circuit in the dead of Night,
Teaching all soules the ready waies to hell;
Sathan coms arm'd with all the powres of Spight,
Heartens his Champions, makes them rude and fell;
   Like rav'ning wolves, to shed his guiltlesse blood,
   Who thought no harme, but di'd to doe them good.

Here Falshood beares the shew of formall Right,
570   Base Treacherie hath gote a guard of men;
Tyranny attends, with all his strength and might,
To leade this siely Lamb to Lyons denne;
Yet he unmoov'd in this most wretched plight,
Goes on to meete them, knowes the houre, and when:
   The powre of darkenesse must expresse Gods ire,
   Therefore to save these few was his desire.

These few that wait on Poverty and Shame,
And offer to be sharers in his Ils;
These few that will be spreaders of his Fame,
580   He will not leave to Tyrants wicked wils;
But still desires to free them from all blame,
Yet Feare goes forward, Anger Patience kils:
   A Saint is mooved to revenge a wrong,
   And Mildnesse doth what doth to Wrath belong.

For *Peter* griev'd at what might then befall,
Yet knew not what to doe, nor what to thinke,
Thought something must be done; now, if at all,
To free his Master, that he might not drinke
This poys'ned draught, farre bitterer than gall,
590   For now he sees him at the very brinke
          Of griesly Death, who gins to shew his face,
          Clad in all colours of a deepe disgrace.

And now those hands, that never us'd to fight,
Or drawe a weapon in his owne defence,
Too forward is, to doe his Master right,
Since of his wrongs, hee feeles so true a sence:
But ah poore *Peter!* now thou wantest might,
And hee's resolv'd, with them he will goe hence:
600   To draw thy sword in such a helpelesse cause,
          Offends thy Lord, and is against the Lawes.

So much he hates Revenge, so farre from Hate,
That he vouchsafes to heale, whom thou dost wound;
His paths are Peace, with none he holdes Debate,
His Patience stands upon so sure a ground,
To counsell thee, although it comes too late:
Nay, to his foes, his mercies so abound,
          That he in pitty doth thy will restraine,
          And heales the hurt, and takes away the paine.

For willingly he will endure this wrong,
610   Although his pray'rs might have obtain'd such grace,
As to dissolve their plots though ne'r so strong,
And bring these wicked Actors in worse case
Than *Ægypts* King on whom Gods plagues did throng,
But that foregoing Scriptures must take place: *prophetic*
          If God by prayers had an army sent
          Of powrefull Angels, who could them prevent?

Yet mightie JESUS meekely ask'd, Why they
With Swords and Staves doe come as to a Thiefe?
Hee teaching in the Temple day by day
620   None did offend, or give him cause of griefe.
Now all are forward, glad is he that may
Give most offence, and yeeld him least reliefe:
          His hatefull foes are ready now to take him,
          And all his deere Disciples do forsake him.

Those deare Disciples that he most did love,
And were attendant at his becke and call,
When triall of affliction came to prove,
They first left him, who now must leave them all:
For they were earth, and he came from above,
630   Which made them apt to flie, and fit to fall:
          Though they protest they never will forsake him,
          They do like men, when dangers overtake them.

And he alone is bound to loose us all,
Whom with unhallowed hands they led along,
To wicked *Caiphas*[13] in the Judgement Hall,

---

13   High Priest of Jerusalem who presided over Jesus' trial.

Who studies onely how to doe him wrong;
High Priests and Elders, People great and small,
With all reprochfull words about him throng:
　　False Witnesses are now call'd in apace,
　　Whose trothlesse tongues must make pale
640　　　　death imbrace

The beauty of the World, Heavens chiefest Glory;
The mirrour of Martyrs, Crowne of holy Saints;
Love of th'Almighty, blessed Angels story;
Water of Life, which none that drinks it, faints;　　　　　　　*dies*
Guide of the Just, where all our Light we borrow;
Mercy of Mercies; Hearer of Complaints;
　　Triumpher over Death; Ransomer of Sinne;
　　Falsly accused: now his paines begin.

Their tongues doe serve him as a Passing bell,
650　For what they say is certainly beleeved;
So sound a tale unto the Judge they tell,
That he of Life must shortly be bereaved;
Their share of Heaven, they doe not care to sell,
So his afflicted Heart be throughly grieved:
　　They tell his Words, though farre from his intent,
　　And what his Speeches were, not what he meant.

That he Gods holy Temple could destroy,
And in three daies could build it up againe;
This seem'd to them a vaine and idle toy,
660　It would not sinke into their sinful braine:
Christs blessed body, al true Christians joy,
Should die, and in three dayes revive againe:
　　This did the Lord of Heaven and earth endure,
　　Unjustly to be charg'd by tongues impure.

And now they all doe give attentive eare,
To heare the answere, which he will not make;
The people wonder how he can forbeare,
And these great wrongs so patiently can take;
But yet he answers not, nor doth he care,
670　Much more he will endure for our sake:
　　Nor can their wisdoms any way discover,
　　Who he should be that proov'd so true a Lover.

To entertaine the sharpest pangs of death,
And fight a combate in the depth of hell,
For wretched Worldlings made of dust and earth,
Whose hard'ned hearts, with pride and mallice swell;
In midst of bloody sweat, and dying breath,
He had compassion on these tyrants fell:
　　And purchast them a place in Heav'n for ever,
680　　When they his Soule and Body sought to sever.

Sinnes ugly mists, so blinded had their eyes,
That at Noone dayes they could discerne no Light;
These were those fooles, that thought themselves so wise,
The Jewish wolves, that did our Saviour bite;
For now they use all meanes they can devise,
To beate downe truth, and goe against all right:
　　Yea now they take Gods holy name in vaine,
　　To know the truth, which truth they doe prophane.

690
The chiefest Hel-hounds of this hatefull crew,
Rose up to aske what answere he could make,
Against those false accusers in his view;
That by his speech, they might advantage take:
He held his peace, yet knew they said not true,
No answere would his holy wisdome make,
    Till he was charged in his glorious name,
    Whose pleasure 'twas he should endure this shame.

Then with so mild a Majestie he spake,
As they might easly know from whence he came,
His harmelesse tongue doth no exceptions take,
700
Nor Priests, nor People, meanes he now to blame;
But answers Folly, for true Wisdomes sake,
Beeing charged deeply by his powrefull name,
    To tell if Christ the Sonne of God he be,
    Who for our sinnes must die, to set us free.

To thee O *Caiphas* doth he answere give,
That thou hast said, what thou desir'st to know,
And yet thy malice will not let him live,
So much thou art unto thy selfe a foe;
He speakech truth, but thou wilt not beleeve,
710
Nor canst thou apprehend it to be so:
    Though he expresse his Glory unto thee,
    Thy Owly eies are blind, and cannot see.

Thou rend'st cloathes, in stead of thy false heart,
And on the guiltlesse lai'st thy guilty crime;
For thou blasphem'st, and he must feele the smart:
To sentence death, thou think'st it now high time;
No witnesse now thou need'st, for this fowle part,
Thou to the height of wickednesse canst clime:
    And give occasion to the ruder sort,
720
    To make afflictions, sorrows, follies sport.

Now when the dawne of day gins to appeare,
And all your wicked counsels have an end,
To end his Life, that holds you all so deere,
For to that purpose did your studies bend;
Proud *Pontius Pilate* must the matter heare,
To your untroths his eares he now must lend:
    Sweet *Jesus* bound, to him you led away,
    Of his most pretious blood to make your pray.

Which, when that wicked Caytife did perceive,   *slave (Judas)*
730
By whose lewd meanes he came to this distresse;
He brought the price of blood he did receive,
Thinking thereby to make his fault seeme lesse,
And with these Priests and Elders did it leave,
Confest his fault, wherein he did transgresse:
    But when he saw Repentance unrespected,
    He hang'd himselfe; of God and Man rejected.

By this Example, what can be expected
From wicked Man, which on the Earth doth live?
But faithlesse dealing, feare of God neglected;
740
Who for their private gaine cares not to sell

The Innocent Blood of Gods most deere elected,
As did that caytife wretch, now damn'd in Hell:
   If in Christs Schoole, he tooke so great a fall,
   What will they doe, that come not there at all.

Now *Pontius Pilate* is to judge the Cause
Of faultlesse *Jesus*, who before him stands;
Who neither hath offended Prince, nor Lawes,
Although he now be brought in woefull bands:
O noble Governour, make thou yet a pause,
750   Doe not in innocent blood imbrue thy hands;
   But heare the words of thy most worthy wife,
   Who sends to thee, to beg her Saviours life.

Let barb'rous crueltie farre depart from thee,
And in true Justice take afflictions part;
Open thine eies, that thou the truth mai'st see,
Doe not the thing that goes against thy heart,
Condemne not him that must thy Saviour be;
But, view his holy Life, his good desert.
   Let not us Women glory in Mens fall,
760   Who had power given to over-rule us all.

Till now your indiscretion sets us free,[14]   *Eve's*
And makes our former fault much lesse appease;   *Apologie.*
Our Mother *Eve*, who tasted of the Tree,
Giving to *Adam* what shee held most deare,
Was simply good, and had no powre to see,
The after-comming harme did not appeare:
   The subtile Serpent that our Sex betraide,
   Before our fall so sure a plot had laide.

That undiscerning Ignorance perceav'd
770   No guile, or craft that was by him intended;
For had she knowne, of what we were bereav'd,
To his request she had not condiscended.
But she (poore soule) by cunning was deceav'd,
No hurt therein her harmelesse Heart intended:
   For she alleadg'd Gods word, which he denies,
   That they should die, but even as Gods, be wise.

But surely *Adam* can not be excusde,
Her fault though great, yet hee was most too blame;
What Weaknesse offerd, Strength might have refusde,
780   Being Lord of all, the greater was his shame:
Although the Serpents craft had her abusde,
Gods holy word ought all his actions frame,
   For he was Lord and King of all the earth,
   Before poore *Eve* had either life or breath.

Who being fram'd by Gods eternall hand,
The perfect'st man that ever breath'd on earth;
And from Gods mouth receiv'd that strait command,
The breach whereof he knew was present death:

14   The crucifixion and resurrection of Jesus are often considered to have been necessitated by the temptation and fall of Adam and Eve; or, their temptation and fall provide the fortunate occasion for the display of God's love through the Passion of his son. These ideas are fundamental, for example, to Milton's *Paradise Lost.*

Yea having powre to rule both Sea and Land,
790   Yet with one Apple wonne to loose that breath
Which God had breathed in his beauteous face,
Bringing us all in danger and disgrace.

And then to lay the fault on Patience backe,
That we (poore women) must endure it all;
We know right well he did discretion lacke,
Beeing not perswaded thereunto at all;
If *Eve* did erre, it was for knowledge sake,
The fruit beeing faire perswaded him to fall:
No subtill Serpents falshood did betray him,
800   If he would eate it, who had powre to stay him?

Not *Eve*, whose fault was onely too much love,
Which made her give this present to her Deare,
That what shee tasted, he likewise might prove,
Whereby his knowledge might become more cleare;
He never sought her weakenesse to reprove,
With those sharpe words, which he of God did heare:
Yet Men will boast of Knowledge, which he tooke
From *Eves* faire hand, as from a learned Booke.

If any Evill did in her remaine,
810   Beeing made of him, he was the ground of all;
If one of many Worlds could lay a staine
Upon our Sexe, and worke so great a fall
To wretched Man, by Satans subtill traine;
What will so fowle a fault amongst you all?
Her weakenesse did the Serpents words obay;
But you in malice Gods deare Sonne betray.

Whom, if unjustly you condemne to die,
Her sinne was small, to what you doe commit;
All mortall sinnes that doe for vengeance crie,
820   Are not to be compared unto it:
If many worlds would altogether trie,
By all their sinnes the wrath of God to get;
This sinne of yours, surmounts them all as farre
As doth the Sunne, another little starre,

Then let us have our Libertie againe,
And challendge to your selves no Sov'raigntie;
You came not in the world without our paine,
Make that a barre against your crueltie;
Your fault beeing greater, why should you disdaine
830   Our beeing your equals, free from tyranny?
If one weake woman simply did offend,
This sinne of yours, hath no excuse, nor end.

To which (poore soules) we never gave consent,
Witnesse thy wife (O *Pilate*) speakes for all;
Who did but dreame, and yet a message sent,
That thou should'st have nothing to doe at all
With that just man; which, if thy heart relent,
Why wilt thou be a reprobate with *Saul*?[15]

15   Two Sauls are conflated here: Saul of 1 Samuel 22–23, who plots
to kill David; and Saul (Paul before his conversion) of Acts 9:1–31, who
plotted to kill Christians.

To seeke the death of him that is so good,
840   For thy soules health to shed his dearest blood.

Yea, so thou mai'st these sinful people please,
Thou art content against all truth and right,
To seale this act, that may procure thine ease
With blood, and wrong, with tyrannie, and might;
The multitude thou seekest to appease,
By base dejection of this heavenly Light:
    Demanding which of these that thou should'st loose,
    Whether the Thiefe, or Christ King of the Jewes.

Base *Barrabas* the Thiefe, they all desire,
850   And thou more base than he, perform'st their will;
Yet when thy thoughts backe to themselves retire,
Thou art unwilling to commit this ill:
Oh that thou couldst unto such grace aspire,
That thy polluted lips might never kill
    That Honour, which right Judgement ever graceth,
    To purchase shame, which all true worth defaceth.

Art thou a Judge, and asketh what to do
With one, in whom no fault there can be found?
The death of Christ wilt thou consent unto,
860   Finding no cause, no reason, nor no ground?
Shall he be scourg'd, and crucified too?
And must his miseries by thy meanes abound?
    Yet not asham'd to aske what he hath done,
    When thine owne conscience seeks this sinne
        to shunne.

Three times thou ask'st, What evill hath he done?
And saist, thou find'st in him no cause of death,
Yet wilt thou chasten Gods beloved Sonne,
Although to thee no word of ill he saith:
For Wrath must end, what Malice hath begunne,
870   And thou must yield to stop his guiltlesse breath.
    This rude tumultuous rowt doth presse so sore,
    That thou condemnest him thou shouldst adore.

Yet *Pilate*, this can yeeld thee no content,
To exercise thine owne authoritie,
But unto *Herod* he must needes be sent,
To reconcile thy selfe by tyrannie:
Was this the greatest good in Justice meant,
When thou perceiv'st no fault in him to be?
    If thou must make thy peace by Virtues fall,
880   Much better 'twere not to be friends all.

Yet neither thy sterne browe, nor his great place,
Can draw an answer from the Holy One:
His false accusers, nor his great disgrace,
Nor *Herods* scoffes; to him they are all one:
He neither cares, nor feares his owne ill case,
Though being despis'd and mockt of every one:
    King *Herods* gladnesse gives him little ease,
    Neither his anger seekes he to appease.

Yet this is strange, that base Impietie
890   Should yeeld those robes of honour, which were due;
Pure white, to shew his great Integritie,
His innocency, that all the world might view;
Perfections height in lowest penury,
Such glorious poverty as they never knew:
     Purple and Scarlet well might him beseeme,
     Whose pretious blood must all the world redeeme.

And that Imperiall Crowne of Thornes he wore,
Was much more pretious than the Diadem
Of any King that ever liv'd before,
900   Or since his time, their honour's but a dreame
To his eternall glory, beeing so poore,
To make a purchasse of that heavenly Realme;
     Where God with all his Angels lives in peace,
     No griefes, nor sorrowes, but all joyes increase.

Those royall robes, which they in scorne did give,
To make him odious to the common sort,
Yeeld light of Grace to those whose soules shall live
Within the harbour of this heavenly port;
Much doe they joy, and much more doe they grieve,
910   His death, their life, should make his foes such sport:
     With sharpest thornes to pricke his blessed face,
     Our joyfull sorrow, and his greater grace.

Three feares at once possessed *Pilates* heart;
The first, Christs innocencie, which so plaine appeares;
The next, That he which now must feele this smart,
Is Gods deare Sonne, for any thing he heares:
But that which proov'd the deepest wounding dart,
Is Peoples threat'nings, which he so much feares,
     That he to *Cæsar* could not be a friend,
920   Unlesse he sent sweet JESUS to his end.

Now *Pilate* thou art proov'd a painted wall,
A golden Sepulcher with rotten bones;
From right to wrong, from equitie to fall:
If none upbraid thee, yet the very stones
Will rise against thee, and in question call
His blood, his teares, his sighes, his bitter groanes:
     All these will witnesse at the latter day,
     When water cannot wash thy sinne away.

Canst thou be innocent, that gainst all right,
930   Wilt yeeld to what thy conscience doth withstand?
Beeing a man of knowledge, powre, and might,
To let the wicked carrie such a hand,
Before thy face to blindfold Heav'ns bright light,
And thou to yeeld to what they did demand?
     Washing thy hands, thy conscience cannot cleare,
     But to all worlds this staine must needs appeare.

For loe, the Guiltie doth accuse the Just,
And faultie Judge condemnes the Innocent;
And wilfull Jewes to exercise their lust,
940   With whips and taunts against their Lord are bent;

He basely used, blasphemed, scorn'd and curst,
Our heavenly King to death for us they sent:
  Reproches, slanders, spittings in his face,
  Spight doing all her worst in his disgrace.

And now this long expected houre drawes neere,   *Christ*
When blessed Saints with Angels doe condole;   *going to*
His holy march, soft pace, and heavy cheere,   *death.*
In humble sort to yeeld his glorious soule,
By his deserts the fowlest sinnes to cleare;
950 And in th'eternall booke of heaven to enroule
      A satisfaction till the generall doome,
      Of all sinnes past, and all that are to come.

They that had seene this pitifull Procession,
From *Pilates* Palace to Mount Calvarie,
Might thinke he answer'd for some great transgression,
Beeing in such odious sort condemn'd to die;
He plainely shewed that his own profession
Was virtue, patience, grace, love, piety:
      And how by suffering he could conquer more
960   Than all the Kings that ever liv'd before.

First went the Crier with open mouth proclayming
The heavy sentence of Iniquitie,
The Hangman next, by his base office clayming
His right in Hell, where sinners never die,
Carrying the nayles, the people still blaspheming
Their maker, using all impiety;
      The Thieves attending him on either side,   *The teares*
      The Serjeants watching, while the women cri'd.   *of the*
                                                          daughters
Thrice happy women that obtaind such grace   *of*
970 From him whose worth the world could not containe;   *Jerusalem.*
Immediately to turne about his face,
As not remembring his great griefe and paine,
To comfort you, whose teares powr'd forth apace
On *Flora's* bankes, like shewers of Aprils raine:
      Your cries inforced mercie, grace, and love
      From him, whom greatest Princes could not moove:

To speake one word, nor once to lift his eyes
Unto proud *Pilate*, no nor *Herod*, king;
By all the Questions that they could devise,
980 Could make him answere to no manner of thing;
Yet these poore women, by their pitious cries
Did moove their Lord, their Lover, and their King,
      To take compassion, turne about, and speake
      To them whose hearts were ready now to breake.

Most blessed daughters of Jerusalem,
Who found such favour in your Saviors sight,
To turne his face when you did pitie him;
Your tearefull eyes, beheld his eies more bright;
Your Faith and Love unto such grace did clime,
990 To have reflection from this Heav'nly Light:
      Your Eagles eyes did gaze against this Sunne,
      Your hearts did thinke, he dead, the world were done.

When spightfull men with torments did oppresse
Th'afflicted body of this innocent Dove,
Poore women seeing how much they did transgresse,
By teares, by sighes, by cries intreat, may prove,
What may be done among the thickest presse,
They labor still these tyrants hearts to move;
   In pitie and compassion to forbeare
   Their whipping, spurning, tearing of his haire.

1000

But all in vaine, their malice hath no end,
Their hearts more hard than flint, or marble stone;
Now to his griefe, his greatnesse they attend,
When he (God knowes) had rather be alone;
They are his guard, yet seeke all meanes to offend:
Well may he grieve, well may he sigh and groane,
   Under the burthen of a heavy crosse,
   He faintly goes to make their gaine his losse.

His woefull Mother wayting on her Sonne,   *The sorrow*

1010

All comfortlesse in depth of sorow drowned;   *of she*
Her griefes extreame, although but new begun,   *virgin*
To see his bleeding body oft shee swouned;   *Marie*
How could shee choose but thinke her selfe undone,
He dying, with whose glory shee was crowned?
   None ever lost so great a losse as shee,
   Beeing Sonne, and Father of Eternitie.

Her teares did wash away his pretious blood,
That sinners might not tread it under feet
To worship him, and that it did her good

1020

Upon her knees, although in open street,
Knowing he was the Jessie floure and bud,
That must be gath'red when it smell'd most sweet:
   Her Sonne, her Husband, Father, Saviour, King,
   Whose death killd Death, and tooke away his sting.

Most blessed Virgin, in whose faultlesse fruit,
All Nations of the earth must needes rejoyce,
No Creature having sence though ne'r so brute,
But joyes and trembles when they heare his voyce;
His wisedome strikes the wisest persons mute,

1030

Faire chosen vessell, happy in his choyce:
   Deere Mother of our Lord, whose reverend name,
   All people Blessed call, and spread thy fame.

For the Almightie magnified thee,
And looked downe upon thy meane estate;
Thy lowly mind, and unstain'd Chastitie
Did pleade for Love at great *Jehovaes* gate,
Who sending swift-wing'd *Gabriel* unto thee,
His holy will and pleasure to relate;
   To thee most beauteous Queene of Woman-kind,

1040

   The Angell did unfold his Makers mind.

He thus beganne, Haile *Mary* full of grace,   *The*
Thou freely art beloved of the Lord,   *salutation*
He is with thee, behold thy happy case;   *of the*
What endlesse comfort did these words afford   *virgin*

To thee that saw'st an Angell in the place   *Marie.*
Proclaime thy Virtues worth, and to record
  Thee blessed among women: that thy praise
  Should last so many worlds beyond thy daies.

Loe, this high message to thy troubled spirit,
1050   He doth deliver in the plainest sence;
Sayes, Thou shouldst beare a Sonne that shal inherit
His Father *Davids* throne, free from offence,
Call's him that Holy thing, by whose pure merit
We must be sav'd, tels what he is, of whence;
  His worth, his greatnesse, what his name must be,
  Who should be call'd the Sonne of the most High.

He cheeres thy troubled soule, bids thee not feare;
When thy pure thoughts could hardly apprehend
This salutation, when he did appeare;
Not couldst thou judge, whereto those words
1060   did tend;
His pure aspect did moove thy modest cheere
To muse, yet joy that God vouchsaf'd to send
  His glorious Angel; who did thee assure
  To beare a child, although a Virgin pure.

Nay more, thy Sonne should Rule and Raigne
    for ever;
Yea, of his Kingdom there should be no end;
Over the house of *Jacob*, Heavens great Giver   *Israel*
Would give him powre, and to that end did send
His faithfull servant *Gabriel* to deliver
1070   To thy chast eares no word that might offend:
  But that this blessed Infant borne of thee,
  Thy Sonne, The onely Sonne of God should be.

When on the knees of thy submissive heart
Thou humbly didst demand, How that should be?
Thy virgin thoughts did thinke, none could impart
This great good hap, and blessing unto thee;
Farre from desire of any man thou art,
Knowing not one, thou art from all men free:
  When he, to answere this thy chaste desire,
1080   Gives thee more cause to wonder and admire.

That thou a blessed Virgin shoulst remaine,
Yea that the holy Ghost should come on thee
A maiden Mother, subject to no paine,
For highest powre should overshadow thee:
Could thy faire eyes from teares of joy refraine,
When God look'd downe upon thy poore degree?
  Making thee Servant, Mother, Wife, and Nurse
  To Heavens bright King, that freed us from the curse.

Thus beeing crown'd with glory from above,
1090   Grace and Perfection resting in thy breast,
Thy humble answer doth approove thy Love,
And all these sayings in thy heart doe rest:
Thy Child a Lambe, and thou a Turtle dove,
Above all other women highly blest;

To find such favour in his glorious sight,
In whom thy heart and soule doe most delight.

What wonder in the world more strange could seeme,
Than that a Virgin could conceive and beare
Within her wombe a Sonne, That should redeeme
1100   All Nations on the earth, and should repaire
Our old decaies: who in such high esteeme,
Should prize all mortals, living in his feare;
    As not to shun Death, Povertie, and Shame,
    To save their soules, and spread his glorious Name.

And partly to fulfil his Fathers pleasure,
Whose powrefull hand allowes it not for strange,
If he vouchsafe the riches of his treasure,
Pure Righteousnesse to take such il exchange;
On all Iniquitie to make a seisure,
1110   Giving his snow-white Weed for ours in change   *clothing (body)*
    Our mortall garment in a skarlet Die,   *blood*
    Too base a roabe for Immortalitie.

Most happy news, that ever yet was brought,
When Poverty and Riches met together,
The wealth of Heaven, in our fraile clothing wrought
Salvation by his happy comming hither:
Mighty Messias, who so deerely bought
Us Slaves to sinne, farre lighter than a feather:
    Toss'd to and fro with every wicked wind,
1120   The world, the flesh, or Devill gives to blind.

Who on his shoulders our blacke sinnes doth beare
To that most blessed, yet accursed Crosse;
Where fastning them, he rids us of our feare,
Yea for our gaine he is content with losse,
Our ragged clothing scornes he not to weare,
Though foule, rent, torne, disgracefull, rough
      and grosse,
    Spunne by that monster Sinne, and weav'd by Shame,
    Which grace it selfe, disgrac'd with impure blame.

How canst thou choose (faire Virgin) then but mourne,
1130   When this sweet of-spring of thy body dies,
When thy faire eies beholds his bodie torne,
The peoples fury, heares the womens cries;
His holy name prophan'd, He made a scorne,
Abusde with all their hatefull slaunderous lies:
    Bleeding and fainting in such wondrous sort,
    As scarce his feeble limbes can him support.

Now *Simon* of *Cyrene* passeth them by,
Whom they compell sweet JESUS Crosse to beare
To *Golgatha*, there doe they meane to trie
1140   All cruell meanes to worke in him dispaire:
That odious place, where dead mens skulls did lie,
There must our Lord for present death prepare:
    His sacred blood must grace that loathsome field,
    To purge more filth, than that foule place could yield.

For now arriv'd unto this hatefull place,   *Christs*
In which his Crosse erected needes must bee,   *death.*
False hearts, and willing hands come on apace,
All prest to ill, and all desire to see:
Gracelesse themselves, still seeking to disgrace;
1150   Bidding him, If the Sonne of God he bee,
    To save himselfe, if he could others save,
    With all th'opprobrious words that might deprave.

His harmelesse hands unto the Crosse they nailde,
And feet that never trode in sinners trace,
Betweene two theeves, unpitied, unbewailde,
Save of some few possessors of his grace,
With sharpest pangs and terrors thus appailde,
Sterne Death makes way, that Life might give him place:
1160   His eyes with teares, his body full of wounds,
    Death last of paines his sorrows all confounds.

His joynts dis-joynted, and his legges hang downe,
His alablaster breast, his bloody side,
His members torne, and on his head a Crowne
Of sharpest Thorns, to satisfie for pride:
Anguish and Paine doe all his Sences drowne,
While they his holy garments do divide:
    His bowells drie, his heart full fraught with griefe,
    Crying to him that yeelds him no reliefe.

This with the eie of Faith thou maist behold,   *To my Ladie*
1170   Deere Spouse of Christ,[16] and more than I can write;   *of*
And here both Griefe and Joy thou maist unfold,   *Cumberland.*
To view thy Love in this most heavy plight,
Bowing his head, his bloodlesse body cold;
Those eies waxe dimme that gave us all our light,
    His count'nance pale, yet still continues sweet,
    His blessed blood watring his pierced feet.

O glorious miracle without compare!
Last, but not least which was by him effected;
Uniting death, life, misery, joy and care,
1180   By his sharpe passion in his deere elected:
Who doth the Badges of like Liveries weare,
Shall find how deere they are of him respected.
    No joy, griefe, paine, life, death, was like to his,
    Whose infinitie dolours wrought eternall blisse.

What creature on the earth did then remaine,   *The terror*
On whom the horror of this shamefull deed   *of all*
Did not inflict some violent touch, or straine,   *creatures*
To see the Lord of all the world to bleed?   *at that*
His dying breath did rend huge rockes in twaine,   *instant*
1190   The heavens betooke them to their mourning weed: *when*
    The Sunne grew darke, and scorn'd to give   *Christ died.*
        them light,
    Who durst ecclipse a glory farre more bright.

---

16   In the traditional allegorical sense that the Christian soul is the   the Song of Songs (Canticles), which is the text alluded to at length in
bride of Christ. This was the basis for Christian allegorical readings of   the following lines.

The Moone and Starres did hide themselves for shame,
The earth did tremble in her loyall feare,
The Temple vaile did rent to spread his fame,
The Monuments did open every where;
Dead Saints did rise forth of their graves, and came
To divers people that remained there
    Within that holy City; whose offence,
1200   Did put their Maker to this large expence.

Things reasonable, and reasonlesse possest
The terrible impression of this fact;
For his oppression made them all opprest,
When with his blood he seal'd so faire an act,
In restlesse miserie to procure our rest;
His glorious deedes that dreadfull prison sackt:
    When Death, Hell, Divells, using all their powre,
    Were overcome in that most blessed houre.

Being dead, he killed Death, and did survive
1210   That prowd insulting Tyrant: in whose place
He sends bright Immortalitie to revive
Those whom his yron armes did long embrace;
Who from their loathsome graves brings them alive
In glory to behold their Saviours face:
    Who tooke the keys of all Deaths powre away,
    Opening to those that would his name obay.

O wonder, more than man can comprehend,
Our Joy and Griefe both at one instant fram'd,
Compounded: Contrarieties contend
1220   Each to exceed, yet neither to be blam'd.
Our Griefe to see our Saviours wretched end,
Our Joy to know both Death and Hell he tam'd:
    That we may say, O Death, where is thy sting?
    Hell, yeeld thy victory to thy conq'ring King.

Can stony hearts refraine from shedding teares,
To view the life and death of this sweet Saint?
His austere course in yong and tender yeares,
When great indurements could not make him faint:
His wants, his paines, his torments, and his feares,
1230   All which he undertooke without constraint,
    To shew that infinite Goodnesse must restore,
    What infinite Justice looked for, and more.

Yet, had he beene but of a meane degree,
His suffrings had beene small to what they were;
Meane minds will shew of what meane mouldes
     they bee;
Small griefes seeme great, yet Use doth make them beare:
But ah! tis hard to stirre a sturdy tree;
Great dangers hardly puts great minds in feare:
    They will conceale their griefes which mightie grow
1240   In their stout hearts untill they overflow.

If then an earthly Prince may ill endure
The least of those afflictions which he bare,
How could this all-commaunding King procure

Such grievous torments with his mind to square,
Legions of Angells being at his Lure?
He might have liv'd in pleasure without care:
    None can conceive the bitter paines he felt,
    When God and man must suffer without guilt.

Take all the Suffrings Thoughts can thinke upon,
1250   In ev'ry man that this huge world hath bred;
Let all those Paines and Suffrings meet in one,
Yet are they not a Mite to that he did
Endure for us: Oh let us thinke thereon,
That God should have his pretious blood so shed:
    His Greatnesse clothed in our fraile attire,
    And pay so deare a ransome for the hire.

Loe, here was glorie, miserie, life and death,
An union of contraries did accord;
Gladnesse and sadnesse here had one berth,
1260   This wonder wrought the Passion of our Lord,
He suffring for all the sinnes of all th'earth,
No satisfaction could the world afford:
    But this rich Jewell, which from God was sent,
    To call all those that would in time repent.

Which I present (deare Lady) to your view,
Upon the Crosse depriv'd of life or breath,
To judge if ever Lover were so true,
To yeeld himselfe unto such shamefull death:
Now blessed *Joseph* doth both beg and sue,
1270   To have his body who possest his faith,
    And thinkes, if he this small request obtaines,
    He wins more wealth than in the world remaines.

Thus honourable *Joseph* is possest.
Of what his heart and soule so much desired,
And now he goes to give that body rest,
That all his life, with griefes and paines was tired;
He finds a Tombe, a Tombe most rarely blest,
In which was never creature yet interred;
    There this most pretious body he incloses,
1280   Imbalmd and deckt with Lillies and with Roses.

Loe here the Beautie of Heav'n and Earth is laid,
The purest coulers underneath the Sunne,
But in this place he cannot long be staid,
Glory must end what horror hath begun;
For he the furie of the Heavens obay'd,
And now he must possesse what he hath wonne:
    The *Maries* doe with pretious balmes attend,
    But beeing come, they find it to no end.

For he is rize from Death t'Eternall Life,
1290   And now those pretious oyntments he desires
Are brought unto him, by his faithfull Wife
The holy Church; who in those rich attires,
Of Patience, Love, Long suffring, Voide of strife,
Humbly presents those oyntments he requires:
    The oyles of Mercie, Charitie, and Faith,
    Shee onely gives that which no other hath.

*Christs
resurrection.*

These pretious balmes doe heale his grievous wounds,
And water of Compunction washeth cleane
The soares of sinnes, which in our Soules abounds;
1300 So faire it heales, no skarre is ever seene;
Yet all the glory unto Christ redounds,
His pretious blood is that which must redeeme;
    Those well may make us lovely in his sight,
    But cannot save without his powrefull might.

*A briefe
description
of his
beautie
upon the
Canticles*

This is that Bridegroome that appeares so faire,
So sweet, so lovely in his Spouses sight,
That unto Snowe we may his face compare,
His cheekes like skarlet, and his eyes so bright
As purest Doves that in the rivers are,
1310 Washed with milke, to give the more delight;
    His head is likened to the finest gold,
    His curled lockes so beauteous to behold;

Blacke as a Raven in her blackest hew;[17]
His lips like skarlet threeds, yet much more sweet
Than is the sweetest hony dropping dew,
Or hony combes, where all the Bees doe meet;
Yea, he is constant, and his words are true,
His cheekes are beds of spices, flowers sweet;
1320   His lips, like Lillies, dropping downe pure mirrhe,
    Whose love, before all worlds we doe preferre.

Ah! give me leave (good Lady) now to leave
This taske of Beauty which I tooke in hand,
I cannot wade so deepe, I may deceave
My selfe, before I can attaine the land;
Therefore (good Madame) in your heart I leave
His perfect picture, where it still shall stand,
    Deepely engraved in that holy shrine,
    Environed with Love and Thoughts divine.

*To my Ladie
of
Cumberland.*

There may you see him as a God in glory,
1330 And as a man in miserable case;
There may you reade his true and perfect storie,
His bleeding body there you may embrace,
And kisse his dying cheekes with teares of sorrow,
With joyfull griefe, you may intreat for grace;
    And all your prayers, and your almes-deeds
    May bring to stop his cruell wounds that bleeds.

Oft times hath he made triall of your love,
And in your Faith hath tooke no small delight,
By Crosses and Afflictions he doth prove,
1340 Yet still your heart remaineth firme and right;
Your love so strong, as nothing can remove,
Your thoughts beeing placed on him both day and night,
    Your constant soule doth lodge betweene her brests,
    This Sweet of sweets, in which all glory rests.

Sometime h'appeares to thee in Shepheards weed,
And so presents himselfe before thine eyes,

17   Cf. "I am black, but comely, O ye daughters of Jerusalem" (Song
of Songs 1:5).

A good old man; that goes his flocke to feed;
Thy colour changes, and thy heart doth rise;
Thou call'st, he comes, thou find'st tis he indeed,
Thy Soule conceaves that he is truely wise:
   Nay more, desires that he may be the Booke,
   Whereon thine eyes continually may looke.

1350

Sometime imprison'd, naked, poore, and bare,
Full of diseases, impotent, and lame,
Blind, deafe, and dumbe, he comes unto his faire,
To see if yet shee will remaine the same;
Nay sicke and wounded, now thou do'st prepare
To cherish him in thy dear Lovers name:
   Yea thou bestow'st all paines, all cost, all care,
   That may relieve him, and his health repaire.

1360

These workes of mercy are so sweete, so deare
To him that is the Lord of Life and Love,
That all thy prayers he vouchsafes to heare,
And sends his holy Spirit from above;
Thy eyes are op'ned, and thou seest so cleare,
No worldly thing can thy faire mind remove;
   Thy faith, thy prayers, and his speciall grace
   Doth open Heav'n, where thou behold'st his face.

These are those Keyes Saint *Peter* did possesse,
Which with a Spirituall powre are giv'n to thee,
To heale the soules of those that doe transgresse,
By thy faire virtues; which, if once they see,
Unto the like they doe their minds addresse,
Such as thou art, such they desire to be:
   If they be blind, thou giv'st to them their sight;
   If deafe or lame, they heare, and goe upright.

1370

Yea, if possest with any evill spirits,
Such powre thy faire examples have obtain'd
To cast them out, applying Christs pure merits,
By which they are bound, and of all hurt restrain'd:
If strangely taken, wanting sence or wits,
Thy faith appli'd unto their soules so pain'd,
   Healeth all griefes, and makes them grow so strong,
   As no defects can hang upon them long.

1380

Thou beeing thus rich, no riches do'st respect,
Nor do'st thou care for any outward showe;
The proud that doe faire Virtues rules neglect,
Desiring place, thou sittest them belowe:
All wealth and honour thou do'st quite reject,
If thou perceiv'st that once it prooves a foe
   To virtue, learning, and the powres divine,
   Thou mai'st convert, but never wilt incline

1390

To fowle disorder, or licentiousnesse
But in thy modest vaile do'st sweetly cover
The staines of other sinnes, to make themselves,
That by this meanes thou mai'st in time recover
Those weake lost sheepe that did so long transgresse,
Presenting them unto thy deerest Lover;

That when he brings them backe unto his fold,
1400   In their conversion then he may behold

Thy beauty shining brighter than the Sunne,
Thine honour more than ever Monarke gaind,
Thy wealth exceeding his that Kingdomes wonne,
Thy Love unto his Spouse, thy Faith unfaind,
Thy Constancy in what thou hast begun,
Till thou his heavenly Kingdom have obtaind;
    Respecting worldly wealth to be but drosse,
    Which, if abuz'd, doth proove the owners losse.

Great *Cleopatra's* love to *Anthony*,[18]
1410   Can no way be compared unto thine;
Shee left her Love in his extremitie,
When greatest need should cause her to combine
Her force with his, to get the Victory:
Her Love was earthly, and thy Love Divine;
    Her Love was onely to support her pride,
    Humilitie thy Love and Thee doth guide.

That glorious part of Death, which last shee plai'd,
T'appease the ghost of her deceased Love,
Had never needed, if shee could have stai'd
1420   When his extreames made triall, and did prove
Her leaden love unconstant, and afraid:
Their wicked warres the wrath of God might move
    To take revenge for chast *Octavia's* wrongs,
    Because shee enjoyes what unto her belongs.

No *Cleopatra*, though thou wert as faire
As any Creature in *Antonius* eyes;
Yea though thou wert as rich, as wise, as rare,
As any Pen could write, or Wit devise;
Yet with this Lady canst thou not compare,
1430   Whose inward virtues all thy worth denies:
    Yet thou a blacke Egyptian do'st appeare;
    Thou false, shee true; and to her Love more deere.

Shee sacrificeth to her deerest Love,
With flowres of Faith, and garlands of Good deeds;
Shee flies not from him when afflictions prove,
Shee beares his crosse, and stops his wounds that bleeds;
Shee love and lives chaste as the Turtle dove,
Shee attends upon him, and his flocke shee feeds;
    Yea for one touch of death which thou did'st trie,
1440   A thousand deaths shee every day doth die.

Her virtuous life exceeds thy worthy death,
Yea, she hath richer ornaments of state,
Shining more glorious than in dying breath
Thou didst; when either pride, or cruel fate,
Did worke thee to prevent a double death;
To stay the malice, scorne, and cruell hate
    Of Rome; that joy'd to see thy pride pull'd downe,
    Whose Beauty wrought the hazard of her Crowne.

18 See note 7.

Good Madame, though your modestie be such,
1450   Not to acknowledge what we know and find;
And that you thinke these prayses overmuch,
Which doe expresse the beautie of your mind;
Yet pardon me although I give a touch
Unto their eyes, that else would be so blind,
    As not to see thy store, and their owne wants,
    From whose faire seeds of Virtue spring these plants.

And knowe, when first into this world I came,
This charge was giv'n me by th'Eternall powres,
Th'everlasting Trophie of thy fame,
1460   To build and decke it with the sweetest flowres
That virtue yeelds; Then Madame, doe nor blame
Me, when I shew the World but what is yours,
    And decke you with that crowne which is your due,
    That of Heav'ns beauty Earth may take a view.

Though famous women elder times have knowne,
Whose glorious actions did appeare so bright,
That powrefull men by them were overthrowne,
And all their armies overcome in fight;
The Scythian women by their powre alone,
1470   Put king *Darius* unto shamefull flight:
    All Asia yeelded to their conq'ring hand,
    Great *Alexander* could not their powre withstand.[19]

Whose worth, though writ in lines of blood and fire,
Is not to be compared unto thine;
Their powre was small to overcome Desire,
Or to direct their wayes by Virtues line:
Were they alive, they would thy Life admire,
And unto thee their honours would resigne:
    For thou a greater conquest do'st obtaine,
1480   Than they who have so many thousands slaine.

Wise *Deborah* that judged Israel,
Nor valiant *Judeth* cannot equall thee,[20]
Unto the first, God did his will reveale,
And gave her powre to set his people free;
Yea *Judeth* had the powre likewise to queale   *quell*
Proud *Holifernes*, that the just might see
    What small defence vaine pride, and greatnesse hath
    Against the weapons of Gods word and faith.

But thou farre greater warre do'st still maintaine,
1490   Against that many headed monster Sinne,
Whose mortall sting hath many thousand slaine,
And every day fresh combates doe begin;
Yet cannot all his venome lay one staine
Upon thy Soule, thou do'st the conquest winne,
    Though all the world he daily doth devoure,
    Yet over thee he never could get powre.

---

19 Although Plutarch records the conquest of Darius, king of Persia, by Alexander the Great, Lanyer gives the credit to the women of Scythia.

20 On Deborah, a judge of Israel, see Judges 4:4; Judith saved Israel by beheading Holofernes, according to the Apocryphal book of Judith.

For that one worthy deed by *Deb'rah* done,
Thou hast performed many in thy time;
For that one Conquest that faire *Judeth* wonne,
1500   By which shee did the steps of honour clime;
Thou hast the Conquest of all Conquests wonne,
When to thy Conscience Hell can lay no crime:
    For that one head that *Judeth* bare away,
    Thou tak'st from Sinne a hundred heads a day.

Though virtuous *Hester* fasted three dayes space,[21]
And spent her time in prayers all that while,
That by Gods powre shee might obtaine such grace,
That shee and hers might not become a spoyle
To wicked *Hamon*, in whose crabbed face
1510   Was seene the map of malice, envie, guile;
    Her glorious garments though shee put apart,
    So to present a pure and single heart

To God, in sack-cloth, ashes, and with teares;
Yet must faire *Hester* needs give place to thee,
Who hath continu'd dayes, weekes, months, and yeares,
In Gods true service, yet thy heart beeing free
From doubt of death, or any other feares:
Fasting from sinne, thou pray'st thine eyes may see
    Him that hath full possession of thine heart,
1520   From whose sweet love thy Soule can never part.

His Love, not Feare, makes thee to fast and pray,
No kinsmans counsell needs thee to advise;
The sack-cloth thou do'st weare both night and day,
Is worldly troubles, which thy rest denies;
The ashes are the Vanities that play
Over thy head, and steale before thine eyes;
    Which thou shak'st off when mourning time is past,
    That royall roabes thou may'st put on at last.

Joachims wife,[22] that faire and constant Dame,
1530   Who rather chose a cruel death to die,
Than yeeld to those two Elders voide of shame,
When both at once her chastitie did trie,
Whose Innocencie bare away the blame,
Untill th'Almighty Lord had heard her crie;
    And rais'd the spirit of a Child to speake,
    Making the powrefull judged of the weake.

Although her virtue doe deserve to be
Writ by that hand that never purchas'd blame;
In holy Writ, where all the world may see
1540   Her perfit life, and ever honoured name:
Yet was she not to be compar'd to thee,
Whose many virtues doe increase thy fame:
    For shee oppos'd against old doting Lust,
    Who with lifes danger she did feare to trust.

But your chaste breast, guarded with strength of mind,
Hates the imbracements of unchaste desires;

---

21   See note 1.   22   Susanna; see note 1.

You loving God, live in your selfe confind
From unpure Love, your purest thoughts retires,
Your perfit sight could never be so blind,
To entertaine the old or yong desires
    Of idle Lovers; which the world presents,
    Whose base abuses worthy minds prevents.

1550

Even as the constant Lawrell, alwayes greene,   *laurel*
No parching heate of Summer can deface,
Nor pinching Winter ever yet was seene,
Whose nipping frosts could wither, or disgrace:
So you (deere Ladie) still remaine as Queene,
Subduing all affections that are base,
    Unalterable by the change of times,
    Not following, but lamenting others crimes.

1560

No feare of Death, or dread of open shame,
Hinders your perfect heart to give consent;
Nor loathsome age, whom Time could never tame
From ill designes, whereto their youth was bent;
But love of God, care to preserve your fame,
And spend that pretious time that God hath sent,
    In all good exercises of the minde,
    Whereto your noble nature is inclin'd.

That Ethyopian Queene did gaine great fame,
Who from the Southerne world, did come to see
Great *Salomon;* the glory of whose name
Had spread it selfe ore all the earth, to be
So great, that all the Princes thither came,
To be spectators of his royaltie:
    And this faire Queene of Sheba came from farre,
    To reverence this new appearing starre.[23]

1570

From th'utmost part of all the Earth shee came,
To heare the Wisdom of this worthy King;
To trie if Wonder did agree with Fame,
And many faire rich presents did she bring:
Yea many strange hard questions did shee frame,
All which were answer'd by this famous King:
    Nothing was hid that in her heart did rest,
    And all to proove this King so highly blest.

1580

Here Majestie with Majestie did meete,
Wisdome to Wisdome yeelded true content,
One Beauty did another Beauty greet,
Bounty to Bountie never could repent;
Here all distaste is troden under feet,
No losse of time, where time was so well spent
    In virtuous exercises of the minde,
    In which this Queene did much contentment finde.

1590

Spirits affect where they doe sympathize,
Wisdom desires Wisdome to embrace,
Virtue covets her like, and doth devize

23 For the story of Solomon and the Queen of Sheba, see 2 Samuel
10:1-13.

How she her friends may entertaine with grace;
Beauty sometime is pleas'd to feed her eyes,
With viewing Beautie in anothers face:
    Both good and bad in this point doe agree,
1600   That each desireth with his like to be.

And this Desire did worke a strange effect,
To drawe a Queene forth of her native Land,
Not yeelding to the nicenesse and respect
Of woman-kind; shee past both sea and land,
All feare of dangers shee did quite neglect,
Onely to see, to heare, and understand
    That beauty, wisedome, majestie, and glorie,
    That in her heart imprest his perfect storie.

Yet this faire map of majestie and might,
1610   Was but a figure of thy deerest Love,
Borne t'expresse that true and heavenly light,
That doth all other joyes imperfect prove;
If this faire Earthly starre did shine so bright,
What doth that glorious Sonne that is above?
    Who weares th'imperiall crowne of heaven and earth,
    And made all Christians blessed in his berth.

If that small sparke could yeeld so great a fire,
As to inflame the hearts of many Kings
To come to see, to heare, and to admire
1620   His wisdome, tending but to worldly things;
Then much more reason have we to desire
That heav'nly wisedome, which salvation brings;
    The Sonne of righteousnesse, that gives true joyes,
    When all they fought for, were but Earthly toyes.

No travels ought th'affected soule to shunne,
That this faire heavenly Light desires to see:
This King of kings to whom we all should runne,
To view his Glory and his Majestie;
He without whom we all had beene undone,
1630   He that from Sinne and Death hath set us free,
    And overcome Satan, the world, and sinne,
    That by his merits we those joyes might winne.

Prepar'd by him, whose everlasting throne
Is plac'd in heaven, above the starrie skies,
Where he that sate, was like the Jasper stone,[24]
Who rightly knowes him shall be truely wise,
A Rainebow round about his glorious throne;
Nay more, those winged beasts so full of eies,
    That never cease to glorifie his Name,
1640   Who was, and will be, and is now the same.

This is that great almightie Lord that made
Both heaven and earth, and lives for evermore;
By him the worlds foundation first was laid:

24   The description here alludes to St. John's vision of the enthroned
Jesus in Revelation 4ff.

He fram'd the things that never were before:
The Sea within his bounds by him is staid,
He judgeth all alike, both rich and poore:
    All might, all majestie, all love, all lawe
    Remaines in him that keepes all worlds in awe.

From his eternall throne the lightning came,
Thundrings and Voyces did from thence proceede;
And all the creatures glorifi'd his name,
In heaven, in earth, and seas, they all agreed,
When loe that spotlesse Lambe so voyd of blame,
That for us di'd, whose sinnes did make him bleed:
    That true Physition that so many heales,
    Opened the Booke, and did undoe the Seales.

He onely worthy to undoe the Booke
Of our charg'd soules, full of iniquitie,
Where with the eyes of mercy he doth looke
Upon our weakenesse and infirmitie;
This is that corner stone that was forsooke,
Who leaves it, trusts but to uncertaintie:
    This is Gods Sonne, in whom he is well pleased,
    His deere beloved, that his wrath appeased.

He that had powre to open all the Seales,
And summon up our sinnes of blood and wrong,
He unto whom the righteous soules appeales,
That have bin martyrd, and doe thinke it long,
To whom in mercie he his will reveales,
That they should rest a little in their wrong,
    Untill their fellow servants should be killed,
    Even as they were, and that they were fulfilled.

Pure thoughted Lady, blessed be thy choyce
Of this Almightie, everlasting King;
In thee his Saints and Angels doe rejoyce,
And to their Heav'nly Lord doe daily sing
Thy perfect praises in their lowdest voyce;
And all their harpes and golden vials bring
    Full of sweet odours, even thy holy prayers
    Unto that spotlesse Lambe, that all repaires.

*To the Lady
dowager of
Cumberland.*

Of whom that Heathen Queene obtain'd such grace,
By honouring but the shadow of his Love,
That great Judiciall day to have a place,
Condemning those that doe unfaithfull prove;
Among the haplesse, happie is her case,
That her deere Saviour spake for her behove;
    And that her memorable Act should be
    Writ by the hand of true Eternitie.

Yet this rare Phoenix of that worne-out age,
This great majesticke Queene comes short of thee,
Who to an earthly Prince did then ingage
Her hearts desires, her love, her libertie,
Acting her glorious part upon a Stage
Of weaknesse, frailtie, and infirmity:

1650

1660

1670

1680

1690

Giving all honour to a Creature, due
To her Creator, whom shee never knew.

But loe, a greater thou hast sought and found
Than *Salomon* in all his royaltie;
And unto him thy faith most firmely bound
1700   To serve and honour him continually;
That glorious God, whose terror doth confound
All sinfull workers of iniquitie:
    Him hast thou truely served all thy life,
    And for his love, liv'd with the world at strife.

To this great Lord, thou onely art affected,
Yet came he not in pompe or royaltie,
But in an humble habit, base, dejected;
A King, a God, clad in mortalitie,
He hath thy love, thou art by him directed,
1710   His perfect path was faire humilitie:
    Who being Monarke of heav'n, earth, and seas,
    Indur'd all wrongs, yet no man did displease.

Then how much more art thou to be commended,
That seek'st thy love in lowly shepheards weed?
A seeming Trades-mans sonne, of none attended,
Save of a few in povertie and need;
Poore Fishermen[25] that on his love attended,
His love that makes so many thousands bleed:
    Thus did he come, to trie our faiths the more,
1720   Possessing worlds, yet seeming extreame poore.

The Pilgrimes travels, and the Shepheards cares,
He tooke upon him to enlarge our soules,
What pride hath lost, humilitie repaires,
For by his glorious death he us inroules
In deepe Characters, writ with blood and teares,
Upon those blessed Everlasting scroules;
    His hands, his feete, his body, and his face,
    Whence freely flow'd the rivers of his grace.

Sweet holy rivers, pure celestiall springs,
1730   Proceeding from the fountaine of our life;
Swift sugred currents that salvation brings,
Cleare christall streames, purging all sinne and strife,
Faire floods, where souls do bathe their snow-white wings,
Before they flie to true eternall life:
    Sweet Nectar and Ambrosia, food of Saints,
    Which, whoso tasteth, never after faints.

This hony dropping dew of holy love,
Sweet milke, wherewith we weaklings are restored,
Who drinkes thereof, a world can never move,
1740   All earthly pleasures are of them abhorred;
This love made Martyrs many deaths to prove,
To taste his sweetnesse, whom they so adored:
    Sweetnesse that makes our flesh a burthen to us,
    Knowing it serves but onely to undoe us.

25   Peter, James, and John.

His sweetnesse sweet'ned all the sowre of death,
To faithful *Stephen* his appointed Saint;[26]
Who by the river stones did loose his breath,
When paines nor terrors could not make him faint:
So was this blessed Martyr turn'd to earth,
1750   To glorifie his soule by deaths attaint: *stigma*
    This holy Saint was humbled and cast downe,
    To winne in heaven an everlasting crowne.

Whose face repleat with Majestie and Sweetnesse,
Did as an Angel unto them appeare,
That sate in Counsell hearing his discreetnesse,
Seeing no change, or any signe of a feare;
But with a constant browe did there confesse
Christs high deserts, which were to him so deare:
    Yea when these Tyrants stormes did most oppresse,
1760   Christ did appeare to make his griefe the lesse.

For beeing filled with the holy Ghost,
Up unto Heav'n he look'd with stedfast eies,
Where God appeared with his heavenly hoste
In glory to this Saint before he dies;
Although he could no Earthly pleasures boast,
At Gods right hand sweet JESUS he espies;
    Bids them behold Heavens open, he doth see
    The Sonne of Man at Gods right hand to be.

Whose sweetnesse sweet'ned that short sowre of Life,
1770   Making all bitternesse delight his taste,
Yeelding sweet quietnesse in bitter strife,
And most contentment when he di'd disgrac'd;
Heaping up joyes where sorrows were most rife;
Such sweetnesse could not choose but be imbrac'd:
    The food of Soules, the Spirits onely treasure,
    The Paradise of our celestiall pleasure.

This Lambe of God, who di'd, and was alive,
Presenting us the bread of life Eternall,
His bruised body powrefull to revive
1780   Our sinking soules, out of the pit infernall;
For by this blessed food he did contrive
A worke of grace, by this his gift externall,
    With heav'nly Manna, food of his elected,
    To feed their soules, of whom he is respected.

This wheate of Heaven the blessed Angells bread,
Wherewith he feedes his deere adopted Heires;
Sweet foode of life that doth revive the dead,
And from the living takes away all cares;
To taste this sweet Saint *Laurence* did not dread,
1790   The broyling gridyorne cool'd with holy teares:
    Yeelding his naked body to the fire,
    To taste this sweetnesse, such was his desire.

26 According to Acts 6–7, Stephen was the first Christian martyr. The
martyrdoms of Laurence and Andrew followed.

Nay, what great sweetnesse did th'Apostles taste,
Condemn'd by Counsell, when they did returne;
Rejoycing that for him they di'd disgrac'd,
Whose sweetnes made their hearts and soules so burne
With holy zeale and love most pure and chaste;
For him they sought from whome they might not turne:
   Whose love made *Andrew* goe most joyfully,
1800   Unto the Crosse, on which he meant to die.

The Princes of th'Apostles were so filled
With the delicious sweetnes of his grace,
That willingly they yeelded to be killed,
Receiving deaths that were most vile and base,
For his name sake, that all might be fulfilled.
They with great joy all torments did imbrace:
   The ugli'st face that Death could ever yeeld,
   Could never feare these Champions from the field.

They still continued in their glorious fight,
1810 Against the enemies of flesh and blood;
And in Gods law did set their whole delight,
Suppressing evill, and erecting good:
Not sparing Kings in what they did not right;
Their noble Actes they seal'd with deerest blood:
   One chose the Gallowes,²⁷ that unseemely death,
   The other by the Sword²⁸ did loose his breath.

His Head did pay the dearest rate of sin,
Yeelding it joyfully unto the Sword,
To be cut off as he had never bin,
1820 For speaking truth according to Gods word,
Telling king *Herod* of incestuous sin,
That hatefull crime of God and man abhorr'd:
   His brothers wife, that prowd licentious Dame,
   Cut off his Head to take away his shame.

Loe Madame, heere you take a view of those,
Whose worthy steps you doe desire to tread,
Deckt in those colours which our Saviour chose;
The purest colours both of White and Red,   *Colours of*
Their freshest beauties would I faine disclose,   *Confessors*
1830 By which our Saviour most was honoured: *& Martirs.*
   But my weake Muse desireth now to rest,
   Folding up all their Beauties in your breast.

Whose excellence hath rais'd my sprites to write,
Of what my thoughts could hardly apprehend;
Your rarest Virtues did my soule delight,
Great Ladie of my heart: I must commend
You that appeare so faire in all mens sight:
On your Deserts my Muses doe attend:
   You are the Articke Starre that guides my hand,   *North Star*
1840   All what I am, I rest at your command.

27 Peter.
28 John the Baptist.

THE DESCRIPTION OF COOKE-HAM

Farewell (sweet *Cooke-ham*)[1] where I first obtain'd
Grace from that Grace where perfit Grace remain'd;
And where the Muses gave their full consent,
I should have powre the virtuous to content:
Where princely Palace will'd me to indite,   *write*
The sacred Storie of the Soules delight.
Farewell (sweet Place) where Virtue then did rest,
And all delights did harbour in her breast:
Never shall my sad eies againe behold
10   Those pleasures which my thoughts did then unfold:
Yet you (great Lady) Mistris of that Place,
From whose desires did spring this worke of Grace;
Vouchsafe to thinke upon those pleasures past,
As fleeting worldly Joyes that could not last:
Or, as dimme shadowes of celestiall pleasures,
Which are desir'd above all earthly treasures.
Oh how (me thought) against you thither came,
Each part did seeme some new delight to frame!
The House receiv'd all ornaments to grace it,
20   And would indure no foulenesse to deface it.
The Walkes put on their summer Liveries,
And all things else did hold like similies:
The Trees with leaves, with fruits, with flowers clad,
Embrac'd each other, seeming to be glad,
Turning themselves to beauteous Canopies,
To shade the bright Sunne from your brighter eies:
The cristall Streames with silver spangles graced,
While by the glorious Sunne they were embraced:
The little Birds in chirping notes did sing,
30   To entertaine both You and that sweet Spring.
And *Philomela* with her sundry leyes,   *nightingale/lays*
Both You and that delightfull Place did praise.
Oh how me thought each plant, each floure, each tree
Set forth their beauties then to welcome thee:
The very Hills right humbly did descend,
When you to tread upon them did intend.
And as you set your feete, they still did rise,
Glad that they could receive so rich a prise.
The gentle Windes did take delight to bee
40   Among those woods that were so grac'd by thee.
And in sad murmure utterd pleasing sound,   *deep*
That Pleasure in that place might more abound:
The swelling Bankes deliver'd all their pride,
When such a *Phœnix* once they had espide.
Each Arbor, Banke, each Seate, each stately Tree,
Thought themselves honor'd in supporting thee.
The pretty Birds would oft come to attend thee,
Yet flie away for feare they should offend thee:
The little creatures in the Burrough by
50   Would come abroad to sport them in your eye;

THE DESCRIPTION OF COOKE-HAM
1   Cookham is the royal country estate that was leased to the Count-   Her conversations there with the countess were among the most impor-
ess of Cumberland's brother. Lanyer spent some time there before 1609.   tant events in her life.

Yet fearefull of the Bowe in your faire Hand,
Would runne away when you did make a stand.
Now let me come unto that stately Tree,
Wherein such goodly Prospects you did see;
That Oake that did in height his fellowes passe,
As much as lofty trees, low growing grasse:
Much like a comely Cedar streight and tall,
Whose beauteous stature farre exceeded all:
How often did you visite this faire tree,
60   Which seeming joyfull in receiving thee,
Would like a Palme tree spread his armes abroad,
Desirous that you there should make abode:
Whose faire greene leaves much like a comely vaile,
Defended *Phebus* when he would assaile:
Whose pleasing boughes did yeeld a coole fresh ayre,
Joying his happinesse when you were there.
Where beeing seated, you might plainely see,
Hills, vales, and woods, as if on bended knee
They had appeard, your honour to salute,
70   Or to preferre some strange unlook'd for sute:
All interlac'd with brookes and christall springs,
A Prospect fit to please the eyes of Kings:
And thirteene shires appear'd all in your sight,
Europe could not affoard much more delight.
What was there then but gave you all content,
While you the time in meditation spent,
Of their Creators powre, which there you saw,
In all his Creatures held a perfit Law;
And in their beauties did you plaine descrie,
80   His beauty, wisdome, grace, love, majestie.
In these sweet woods how often did you walke,
With Christ and his Apostles there to talke;
Placing his holy Writ in some faire tree,
To meditate what you therein did see:
With *Moyses* you did mount his holy Hill,   *Moses*
To know his pleasure, and performe his Will.
With lovely *David* you did often sing,
His holy Hymnes to Heavens Eternall King.
And in sweet musicke did your soule delight,
90   To sound his prayses, morning, noone, and night.
With blessed *Joseph* you did often feed
Your pined brethren, when they stood in need.
And that sweet Lady sprung from *Cliffords* race,
Of noble *Bedfords* blood, faire steame of Grace;
To honourable *Dorset* now espows'd,[2]
In whose faire breast true virtue then was hous'd:
Oh what delight did my weake spirits find
In those pure parts of her well framed mind:
And yet it grieves me that I cannot be
100   Neere unto her, whose virtues did agree
With those faire ornaments of outward beauty,
Which did enforce from all both love and dutie.
Unconstant Fortune, thou art most too blame,
Who casts us downe into so lowe a frame:
Where our great friends we cannot dayly see,

---

2 Anne, Countess of Dorset, the daughter of the Countess of
Cumberland.

So great a diffrence is there in degree.
Many are placed in those Orbes of state,
Parters in honour, so ordain'd by Fate;
Neerer in show, yet farther off in love,
110   In which, the lowest alwayes are above.
But whither am I carried in conceit?   *thought*
My Wit too weake to conster of the great.   *understand*
Why not? although we are but borne of earth,
We may behold the Heavens, despising death;
And loving heaven that is so farre above,
May in the end vouchsafe us entire love.
Therefore sweet Memorie doe thou retaine
Those pleasures past, which will not turne againe:
Remember beauteous *Dorsets* former sports,
120   So farre from beeing toucht by ill reports;
Wherein my selfe did alwaies beare a part,
While reverend Love presented my true heart:
Those recreations let me beare in mind,
Which her sweet youth and noble thoughts did finde:
Whereof depriv'd, I evermore must grieve,
Hating blind Fortune, carelesse to relieve.
And you sweet Cooke-ham, whom these Ladies leave,
I now must tell the griefe you did conceave
At their departure; when they went away,
130   How every thing retaind a sad dismay:
Nay long before, when once an inkeling came,
Me thought each thing did unto sorrow frame:
The trees that were so glorious in our view,
Forsooke both flowres and fruit, when once they knew
Of your depart, their very leaves did wither,
Changing their colours as they grewe together.
But when they saw this had no powre to stay you,
They often wept, though speechlesse, could not pray you;
Letting their teares in your faire bosoms fall,
140   As if they said, Why will ye leave us all?
This being vaine, they cast their leaves away,
Hoping that pitie would have made you stay:
Their frozen tops like Ages hoarie haires,   *white*
Showes their disasters, languishing in feares:
A swarthy riveld ryne all over spread,
Their dying bodies halfe alive, halfe dead.
But your occasions call'd you so away,
That nothing there had power to make you stay:
Yet did I see a noble gratefull minde,
150   Requiting each according to their kind,
Forgetting not to turne and take your leave
Of these sad creatures, powrelesse to receive
Your favour when with griefe you did depart,
Placing their former pleasures in your heart;
Giving great charge to noble Memory,
There to preserve their love continually:
But specially the love of that faire tree,
That first and last you did vouchsafe to see:
In which it pleas'd you oft to take the ayre,
160   With noble *Dorset*, then a virgin faire:
Where many a learned Booke was read and skand
To this faire tree, taking me by the hand,
You did repeat the pleasures which had past,

Seeming to grieve they could no longer last.
And with a chaste, yet loving kisse tooke leave,
Of which sweet kisse I did it soone bereave:
Scorning a sencelesse creature should possesse
So rare a favour, so great happinesse.
No other kisse it could receive from me,
170   For feare to give backe what it tooke of thee:
So I ingratefull Creature did deceive it,
Of that which you vouchsaft in love to leave it.
And though it oft had giv'n me much content,
Yet this great wrong I never could repent:
But of the happiest made it most forlorne,
To shew that nothing's free from Fortunes scorne,
While all the rest with this most beauteous tree,
Made their sad consort Sorrowes harmony.
The floures that on the banks and walkes did grow,
180   Crept in the ground, the Grasse did weepe for woe.
The Windes and Waters seem'd to chide together,
Because you went away they know not whither:
And those sweet Brookes that ranne so faire and cleare,
With griefe and trouble wrinckled did appeare.
Those pretty Birds that wonted were to sing,   *accustomed*
Now neither sing, nor chirp, nor use their wing;
But with their tender feet on some bare spray,
Warble forth sorrow, and their owne dismay.
Faire *Philomela* leaves her mournefull Ditty,
190   Drownd in dead sleepe, yet can procure no pittie:
Each arbour, banke, each seate, each stately tree,
Lookes bare and desolate now for want of thee;
Turning greene tresses into frostie gray,
While in cold griefe they wither all away.
The Sunne grew weake, his beames no comfort gave,
While all greene things did make the earth their grave:
Each brier, each bramble, when you went away,
Caught fast your clothes, thinking to make you stay:
Delightfull Eccho wonted to reply
200   To our last words, did now for sorrow die:
The house cast off each garment that might grace it,
Putting on Dust and Cobwebs to deface it.
All desolation then there did appeare,
When you were going whom they held so deare.
This last farewell to *Cooke-ham* here I give,
When I am dead thy name in this may live,
Wherein I have perform'd her noble hest,
Whose virtues lodge in my unworthy breast,
And ever shall, so long as life remaines,
210   Tying my heart to her by those rich chaines.

To the doubtfull Reader

Gentle Reader, if thou desire to be resolved, why I give this Title, *Salve Deus Rex Judæorum*, know for certaine; that it was delivered unto me in sleepe many yeares before I had any intent to write in this maner, and was quite out of my memory, untill I had written the Passion of Christ, when immediately it came into my remembrance, what I had dreamed long before; and thinking it a significant token, that I was appointed to performe this Worke, I gave the very same words I received in sleepe as the fittest Title I could devise for this Booke.

Ben Jonson (1572–1637)

Like Shakespeare, Ben Jonson did not go to university, but produced a literary corpus that reflects immense reading. Unlike Shakespeare, Jonson used his learning to produce literature that ostentatiously positioned itself in literary traditions (many of his plays and poems adapt passages from classical authors) and in the social world of his own day (his works contain many more direct allusions to contemporary phenomena and his poems flatter many contemporary aristocrats). When scholars try to explain how his reputation, which equaled or excelled Shakespeare's in the seventeenth century, has fallen so far behind it in subsequent times, it is usually to these two factors that they turn. Shakespeare's poetry always somehow eludes or transforms the formal constraints within which he chose to work, whereas Jonson's always appears to inhabit them with a graceful ease – even when this appearance is misleading. Shakespeare's plays have a translatability that allows them to be readily reinterpreted for new cultural situations. Jonson's works read as historical artifacts, and he has attracted a largely historicist body of criticism.

The two writers also began as actors and used their playwriting success to rise in the world from undistinguished middle-class backgrounds. Jonson was the posthumous son of a minister, who got a grammar school education only by the intervention of an unknown benefactor. After some brief spells in other trades (probably his stepfather's trade of bricklaying and some service as a soldier), he turned to acting and writing around 1597. The next year, he was briefly imprisoned for his part in writing a lost play that was deemed seditious, and the year after that he was tried for murder after killing another actor; he was released after pleading "benefit of clergy," which meant that he could speak Latin. Shakespeare made enough money as a shareholder in his company to leave the public world of the theatre and retire to Stratford as a gentleman of means. Jonson, on the other hand, deliberately set out to become much more of a public figure. He wrote the text for many court masques, starting in about 1605, was granted a royal pension in 1616, and published a folio edition of his works during the same year. This was a very unusual act for a living writer at the time, and seemed even more presumptuous to his contemporaries because it included his plays (which did not then count as "respectable" literature). But Jonson manifested a very professional attitude to writing, and he wrote about the writing process a lot in his play prefaces and his commonplace book, *Timber; or Discoveries*. He also translated Horace's *Ars poetica*. A group of younger writers, who called themselves the "Tribe of Ben," used to meet regularly with him to drink and discuss poetry, and he clearly enjoyed his position as a literary arbiter.

The selection included here draws from his lyric poetry, but excludes his masques and plays. Throughout it all, Jonson is a consummate technician and very much a poet's poet. He eschews the ostentatious displays of artificial wit and conceptual brio that make Donne so appealing to modern readers, and instead uses what often appears, at first glance, to be a poetic version of ordinary language. The effects that his work creates are much more subtle than Donne's, and Epigram XXIII "To John Donne" is a good example of this difference. It looks like a very conventional poem of praise for a talented contemporary, but the more one reads it, the more ambivalent and complex its seemingly simple declarations of praise start to sound. When Jonson does choose to show off, it is by writing a poem like the Cary–Morison ode (*Underwood* 70). Very few of the many Renaissance attempts to write English verse in a complex classical form (in this case, the Pindaric ode) succeed half as well as this poem does, but it is a success that cannot be fully understood without knowing about its poetic antecedents. As usual with Jonson, its strengths are not obvious outside the context within which it was written. Another salient trait of Jonson's verse is the strong sense of an authorial persona within it. Because he lived a very public life and because he addressed contemporary issues and people in his verse, it is even harder than usual not to conflate the speaker's voice in his poems with Jonson's own voice; he seems to invite it. Added to the unusual amount of control he exercised over the arrangement and content of his published works, this deliberately fashioned literary self-image has influenced nearly all critical attempts to understand his work. Richard Harp and Stanley Stewart's anthology of critical essays confirms the extent to which even the very best criticism reads him within a very confined historical framework.

Recently, however, scholars have begun to ask whether we should accept Jonson's self-presentation and to begin a re-examination of the contexts in which it was produced. This provocative project can be understood as an attempt to free the poetry from the interpretive matrix that it seems to provide for itself and to open it up to the more variegated readings that other Renaissance poets have received. The extent to which this project succeeds will be a significant litmus test for the twenty-first century academy's response to the Renaissance as a historical period. Very few canonical writers have been so confined by their historical context as Jonson, and yet equally few can match his linguistic virtuosity and rhetorical self-awareness – the very qualities that usually encourage literary theoretical reflection.

READING

Bruce Thomas Boehrer, *"The Fury of Men's Gullets": Ben Jonson and the Digestive Canal.*

Martin Butler (ed.), *Re-presenting Ben Jonson: Text, History, Performance*

Richard Harp and Stanley Stewart (eds.), *Ben Jonson.*

Richard S. Peterson, *Imitation and Praise in the Poems of Ben Jonson.*

Julie Sanders, Kate Chedgzoy, and Susan Wiseman (eds.), *Refashioning Ben Jonson: Gender, Politics, and the Jonsonian Canon.*

J. H.

FROM *EPIGRAMS* (1616)

XI. ON SOMETHING THAT WALKS SOMEWHERE

At court I met it, in clothes brave enough   *showy*
   To be a courtier, and looks grave enough
To seem a statesman. As I near it came,
   It made me a great face; I asked the name;   *proud*
A lord, it cried, buried in flesh and blood,
   And such from whom let no man hope least good,
For I will do none; and as little ill,
   For I will dare none. Good lord, walk dead still.

XIV. TO WILLIAM CAMDEN[1]

Camden, most reverend head, to whom I owe
   All that I am in arts, all that I know,
(How nothing's that?) to whom my country owes
   The great renown and name wherewith she goes;
Than thee the age sees not that thing more grave,
   More high, more holy, that she more would crave.
What name, what skill, what faith hast thou in things!
   What sight in searching the most antique springs!
What weight, and what authority in thy speech!
10   Man scarce can make that doubt, but thou canst teach.
Pardon free truth, and let thy modesty,
   Which conquers all, be once overcome by thee.
Many of thine this better could than I;   *i.e. thy pupils*
   But for their powers accept my piety.

XXII. ON MY FIRST DAUGHTER

Here lies, to each her parents' ruth,   *sorrow*
   Mary, the daughter of their youth;
Yet, all heaven's gifts being heaven's due,
   It makes the father less to rue.
At six months' end she parted hence
   With safety of her innocence;
Whose soul heaven's Queen (whose name she bears),
   In comfort of her mother's tears,
Hath placed amongst her virgin train;

FROM EPIGRAMS (1616)
1   William Camden (1551–1623), an antiquary and schoolmaster. He taught Jonson at Westminster School.

10   Where, while that severed doth remain,   *i.e. the soul*
This grave partakes the fleshly birth;   *shares in*
Which cover lightly, gentle earth.

XXIII. TO JOHN DONNE

Donne, the delight of Phoebus and each muse,   *Apollo*
    Who, to thy one, all other brains refuse;
Whose every work of thy most early wit
    Came forth example,[2] and remains so yet;
Longer a-knowing than most wits do live;
    And which no affection praise enough can give!
To it, thy language, letters, arts, best life,
    Which might with half mankind maintain a strife;
All which I meant to praise, and yet I would,
    But leave, because I cannot as I should.

XLV. ON MY FIRST SON

Farewell, thou child of my right hand,[3] and joy;
    My sin was too much hope of thee, loved boy.
Seven years thou wert lent to me, and I thee pay,
    Exacted by thy fate, on the just day.
Oh, could I lose all father[4] now! For why
    Will man lament the state he should envy?
To have so soon 'scaped world's and flesh's rage,
    And, if no other misery, yet age?
Rest in soft peace, and, asked, say here doth lie
10   Ben Jonson his best piece of poetry;[5]
For whose sake, henceforth, all his vows be such,
    As what he loves may never like too much.

LII. TO CENSORIOUS COURTLING[6]

Courtling, I rather thou shouldst utterly
    Dispraise my work than praise it frostily:
When I am read thou feign'st a weak applause,
    As if thou wert my friend, but lack'dst a cause.
This but thy judgement fools; the other way
    Would both thy folly and thy spite betray.

LXII. TO FINE LADY WOULD-BE

Fine Madam Would-Be, wherefore should you fear,
    That love to make so well,[7] a child to bear?
The world reputes you barren; but I know
    Your 'pothecary, and his drug says no.   *druggist*

---

2 i.e. Came forth as an example for others to follow.
3 In Hebrew, the name "Benjamin" means "son of the right hand."
4 i.e. lose all of the feelings associated with fatherhood.
5 Jonson is playing on the Greek root of this English word (*poïēsis*) which means "making."

6 i.e. One who frequents the court. Usually used as a term of abuse.
7 i.e. That enjoy sex so well. This phrase uses the same terms as the "poetry" on "On My First Son" (q.v.) but with completely opposite effects.

Is it the pain affrights? That's soon forgot.
　　Or your complexion's loss? You have a pot
That can restore that. Will it hurt your feature?
　　To make amends, you're thought a wholesome creature.
What should the cause be? Oh, you live at court:
　　And there's both loss of time and loss of sport
In a great belly. Write, then, on thy womb:
　　Of the not born, yet buried, here's the tomb.

10

LXXVI. ON LUCY, COUNTESS OF BEDFORD[8]

This morning, timely rapt with holy fire,[9]
　　I thought to form unto my zealous muse
What kind of creature I could most desire
　　To honour, serve and love, as poets use.
I meant to make her fair, and free, and wise,
　　Of greatest blood, and yet more good than great;
I meant the day-star should not brighter rise,
　　Nor lend like influence from his lucent seat.　　*shining*
I meant she should be courteous, facile, sweet,　　*affable*
　　Hating that solemn vice of greatness, pride;
I meant each softest virtue there should meet,
　　Fit in that softer bosom to reside.
Only a learnèd and a manly soul
　　I purposed her, that should, with even powers,　　*i.e. intended for*
The rock, the spindle and the shears[10] control
　　Of destiny, and spin her own free hours.
Such when I meant to feign and wished to see,
　　My muse bade, *Bedford* write, and that was she.

10

LXXXIII. TO A FRIEND

To put out the word 'whore' thou dost me woo,
　　Throughout my book. Troth, put out 'woman' too.

LXXXIX. TO EDWARD ALLEYN[11]

If Rome so great, and in her wisest age,
　　Feared not to boast the glories of her stage,
As skilful Roscius and grave Aesop,[12] men
　　Yet crowned with honours as with riches then,
Who had no less a trumpet of their name
　　Than Cicero, whose every breath was fame:
How can so great example die in me,
　　That, Alleyn, I should pause to publish thee?
Who both their graces in thyself hast more
　　Out-stripped, than they did all that went before;

10

8　The Countess of Bedford (*c.*1581–1627) was a friend and patron
to Jonson and several other poets.
9　A common classical image for feeling poetic inspiration. Its most
famous articulation is in Plato's *Phaedrus* 245a.
10　Three iconographic symbols of the Fates, the classical goddesses
who were said to determine mortal destinies (see gazetteer).

11　Edward Alleyn (1566–1625) was a famous contemporary actor who
performed in plays by Marlowe, Jonson, and many others.
12　Classical Roman actors, both of whom were written about by the
Roman statesman Cicero (see gazetteer).

And present worth in all dost so contract,
    As other speak, but only thou dost act.
Wear this renown. 'Tis just that who did give
    So many poets life, by one should live.

combine

CI. INVITING A FRIEND TO SUPPER[13]

Tonight, grave sir, both my poor house and I
    Do equally desire your company;
Not that we think us worthy such a guest,
    But that your worth will dignify our feast
With those that come; whose grace may make that seem
    Something, which else could hope for no esteem.
It is the fair acceptance, sir, creates
    The entertainment perfect, not the cates.   *food*
Yet shall you have, to rectify your palate,
10   An olive, capers, or some better salad
Ushering the mutton; with a short-legged hen,
    If we can get her, full of eggs, and then
Lemons, and wine for sauce; to these, a coney   *rabbit*
    Is not to be despaired of, for our money;
And though fowl now be scarce, yet there are clerks,
    The sky not falling, think we may have larks.[14]
I'll tell you of more, and lie, so you will come:
    Of partridge,[15] pheasant, woodcock, of which some
May yet be there; and godwit, if we can;
20   Knat, rail and ruff, too. Howsoe'er, my man
Shall read a piece of Virgil, Tacitus,
    Livy,[16] or of some better book to us,
Of which we'll speak our minds, amidst our meat;
    And I'll profess no verses to repeat;
To this, if aught appear which I not know of,
    That will the pastry, not my paper, show of.
Digestive cheese and fruit there sure will be;
    But that which most doth take my muse and me
Is a pure cup of rich Canary wine,
30   Which is the Mermaid's[17] now, but shall be mine;
Of which had Horace or Anacreon[18] tasted,
    Their lives, as do their lines, till now had lasted.
Tobacco, nectar, or the Thespian spring[19]
    Are all but Luther's beer[20] to this I sing.
Of this we will sup free, but moderately;
    And we will have no Poley or Parrot[21] by;
Nor shall our cups make any guilty men,
    But at our parting we will be as when
We innocently met. No simple word
40   That shall be uttered at our mirthful board

13 The poem of invitation was a stock theme of classical Roman literature which Jonson here reproduces in English.
14 An allusion to a contemporary proverb that promised a ready supply of larks if the sky fell. "Clerks" is here used as a term for anyone learned.
15 All the names in the next three lines refer to different kinds of edible birds.
16 A great Roman poet and two Roman historians. See gazetteer.
17 A well-known tavern in Cheapside which Jonson and his friends frequented.

18 Two classical poets, Roman and Greek respectively, who wrote in praise of wine.
19 The spring on Mt. Helicon, the home of the Muses (see gazetteer).
20 Continental European beer (here named for Martin Luther) was weaker than its English counterpart.
21 "Poley" and "Parrot" refer to two government informers who were at work in Jonson's day. Conveniently for Jonson's purposes, their surnames also evoke a bird which repeats human speech without understanding it.

Shall make us sad next morning, or affright
The liberty that we'll enjoy tonight.

CII. TO WILLIAM, EARL OF PEMBROKE[22]

I do but name thee, Pembroke, and I find
    It is an epigram on all mankind,
Against the bad, but of and to be good;
    Both which are asked, to have thee understood.
Nor could the age have missed thee, in this strife
    Of vice and virtue, wherein all great life,
Almost, is exercised; and scarce one knows
    To which yet of the sides himself he owes.
They follow virtue for reward today,
    Tomorrow vice, if she give better pay;
And are so good and bad, just at a price,
    As nothing else discerns the virtue or vice.
But thou, whose noblesse keeps one stature still,
    And one true posture, though besieged with ill
Of what ambition, faction, pride can raise,
    Whose life even they that envy it must praise,
That art so reverenced, as thy coming in
    But in the view doth interrupt their sin:
Thou must draw more; and they that hope to see   *attract*
    The commonwealth still safe must study thee.

10

20

CV. TO MARY, LADY WROTH[23]

Madam, had all antiquity been lost,
    All history sealed up and fables crossed;   *erased*
That we had left us, nor by time nor place,
    Least mention of a nymph, a muse, a grace,[24]
But even their names were to be made anew:
    Who could not but create them all from you?
He that but saw you wear the wheaten hat
    Would call you more than Ceres,[25] if not that;
And, dressed in shepherd's 'tire, who would not say
    You were the bright Oenone,[26] Flora,[27] or May?
If dancing, all would cry the Idalian queen   *i.e. Venus*
    Were leading forth the graces on the green;
And, armèd to the chase, so bare her bow
    Diana[28] alone, so hit, and hunted so.
There's none so dull that for your style would ask   *distinguishing title*
    That saw you put on Pallas' plumèd casque;[29]

10

22   William, third Earl of Pembroke (1580–1630), was a poet and
patron of learning who gave his name to Pembroke College, Oxford.
Jonson's poem glides over his notorious extramarital affairs.
23   A poet and writer whose long prose romance *Urania* was suppressed almost as soon as it was published (1621). Contained within the
text is a sonnet sequence, "Pamphilia to Amphilanthus," which is often
excerpted on its own. She was the niece of Philip Sidney (q.v.), whose
Arcadia was a model for the *Urania*.
24   Nymphs, muses, and graces were all classical female divinities.

25   A Roman fertility goddess (see gazetteer).
26   Trojan nymph who was abandoned by Paris (see gazetteer) in favour
of Helen of Troy.
27   Flora and May (Latin *Maia*) are the Roman goddesses of flowers
and living things respectively.
28   Roman goddess of the hunt (see gazetteer).
29   The goddess Athena (sometimes known as Pallas Athena) is usually
represented in classical art wearing a plumed helmet.

Or, keeping your due state, that would not cry
There Juno[30] sat, and yet no peacock by.
So are you nature's index, and restore
20   In yourself all treasure lost of the age before.

CX. TO CLEMENT EDMONDES, *ON HIS CAESAR'S COMMENTARIES OBSERVED AND TRANSLATED*[31]

Not Caesar's deeds, nor all his honours won
    In these west parts; nor when that war was done,
The name of Pompey[32] for an enemy,
    Cato's to boot, Rome and her liberty
All yielding to his fortune; nor, the while,
    To have engraved these acts with his own style,
And that so strong and deep as't might be thought
    He wrote with the same spirit that he fought;
Nor that his work lived in the hands of foes,
10   Unargued then, and yet hath fame from those:
Not all these, Edmondes, or what else put to,
    Can so speak Caesar as thy labours do.
For, where his person lived but one just age,
    And that midst envy and parts, then fell by rage: *factions*
His deeds too dying, but in books (whose good
    How few have read, how fewer understood!)
Thy learnèd hand and true Promethean[33] art
    (As by a new creation) part by part,
In every counsel, stratagem, design,
20   Action or engine worth a note of thine,   *skill*
To all future time not only doth restore
    His life, but makes that he can die no more.

CXVIII. ON GUT

Gut eats all day, and lechers all the night,
    So all his meat he tasteth over, twice;
And striving so to double his delight,
    He makes himself a thoroughfare of vice.
Thus in his belly can he change a sin:
    Lust it comes out, that gluttony went in.

CXXXIV. ON THE FAMOUS VOYAGE[34]

No more let Greece her bolder fables tell
    Of Hercules or Theseus going to hell,[35]

---

30 Jupiter's wife, and the goddess of childbirth and marriage. The peacock was one of her iconographic symbols.
31 Edmondes (*c.*1564–1622) was a government official whose commentary on Caesar's book first appeared in 1600.
32 "Pompey" is the common English abbreviation for Gnaeus Pompeius Magnus (106–48 BC), a Roman general and politician. After he had been Julius Caesar's ally for many years, the two fought a civil war which ended with Pompey's defeat at Pharsalus in 48 BC. For Cato, see the gazetteer.

33 See gazetteer entry for Prometheus.
34 As the opening lines make clear, this poem is a comic burlesque of the many journeys to the Underworld found in classical literature and myth. Here, a journey in a small boat up the Fleet River in London is retold as an epic voyage. As Jonson implies, the Fleet River was so infested with garbage as to be more or less an open sewer.
35 Hercules went to the Underworld to capture its guardian monster, Cerberus, and to free Theseus, who had accompanied King Pirithous of the Lapiths in an expedition to free Persephone (see gazetteer).

Orpheus, Ulysses; or the Latin muse
　　With tales of Troy's just knight our faiths abuse:[36]
We have a Sheldon and a Heydon[37] got,
　　Had power to act what they to feign had not.
All that they boast of Styx, of Acheron,
　　Cocytus, Phlegethon,[38] our have proved in one:
The filth, stench, noise; save only what was there

10　　Subtly distinguished, was confusèd here.
Their wherry had no sail, too; ours had none;　　　　　　　*rowing boat*
　　And in it two more horrid knaves than Charon.[39]
Arses were heard to croak instead of frogs,
　　And for one Cerberus,[40] the whole coast was dogs.
Furies there wanted not; each scold was ten;
　　And for the cries of ghosts, women and men
Laden with plague-sores and their sins were heard,
　　Lashed by their consciences; to die, afeard.　　　　　　　*afraid*
Then let the former age with this content her:

20　　She brought the poets forth, but ours the adventer.　　*adventure*

The Voyage Itself

I sing the brave adventure of two wights,　　　　　　　　*people*
And pity 'tis, I cannot call 'em knights:
One was; and he for brawn and brain right able
To have been stylèd of King Arthur's table.　　　　　　　*honored*
The other was a squire of fair degree,
But in the action greater man than he,
Who gave, to take at his return from hell,
His three for one.[41] Now, lordlings, listen well.
　　It was the day, what time the powerful moon[42]

30　Makes the poor Bankside creature wet it' shoon　　　　　*shoes*
In it' own hall, when these (in worthy scorn
Of those that put out moneys on return
From Venice, Paris, or some inland passage
Of six times to and fro without embassage,　　　　　　　*mission*
Or him that backward went to Berwick, or which
Did dance the famous morris, unto Norwich)[43]
At Bread Street's Mermaid having dined, and merry,
Proposed to go to Holborn[44] in a wherry:
A harder task than either his to Bristo',

40　Or his to Antwerp.[45] Therefore, once more, list ho'!
　　A dock there is that callèd is Avernus,
Of some, Bridewel,[46] and may in time concern us

36　Orpheus, Ulysses, and Virgil's hero Aeneas (in *Aeneid* 6) all jour-
neyed to the underworld (see the gazetteer for all three).

37　The precise identities of the two protagonists have never been
known with absolute certainty, nor would such certainty add much to
interpretations of the poem. It seems clear, however, that they are meant
to be as unheroic as their classical counterparts are heroic.

38　Four of the rivers in the classical Underworld, here conflated with
the foul-smelling River Thames in London.

39　In classical mythology, the boatman who ferries the souls of the
dead across the Styx.

40　A three-headed dog which guarded the Underworld, partly to
prevent incursions from living souls.

41　A reference to bets made against a traveller's return from a journey
abroad and to commercial investments in merchant ship ventures to
foreign destinations (such as Venice and Paris in line 33).

42　The moon is invoked here as the force that controls tides,
especially in low-lying areas near the Thames such as Bankside.

43　References to two contemporary publicity stunts: William Kemp,
an actor and jester, did a morris dance while walking from London to
Norwich in 1599. The other reference has not been traced.

44　A neighborhood west of the City of London, reachable by using
the Fleet River.

45　References to two famous contemporary voyages from London in
small boats, one to Bristol and one (not traced) to Antwerp.

46　Avernus is the name of the lake near Naples by which Aeneas found
an entrance to the Underworld. Bridewell, to complete the burlesque
comparison, was a dock situated where the Fleet River joins the Thames.

All that are readers; but methinks 'tis odd
That all this while I have forgot some god
Or goddess to invoke, to stuff my verse,
And with both bombard-style and phrase rehearse   *bombast*
The many perils of this port, and how
Sans help of sibyl or a golden bough[47]
Or magic sacrifice, they past along.
50   Alcides, be thou succouring to my song!   i.e. Hercules
Thou hast seen hell, some say, and know'st all nooks there,
Canst tell me best how every fury looks there,
And art a god, if fame thee not abuses,
Always at hand to aid the merry muses.
Great Club-fist,[48] though thy back and bones be sore
Still, with thy former labours, yet once more
Act a brave work, call it thy last adventry;   *adventure*
But hold my torch while I describe the entry
To this dire passage. Say thou stop thy nose:
60   'Tis but light pains: indeed this dock's no rose.
    In the first jaws appeared that ugly monster
Yclepèd Mud, which when their oars did once stir,   *Named*
Belched forth an air as hot as at the muster
Of all your night-tubs,[49] when the carts do cluster,
Who shall discharge first his merd-urinous[50] load:
Thorough her womb they make their famous road
Between two walls, where on one side, to scar men   *scare*
Were seen your ugly centaurs ye call car-men,   *cart drivers*
Gorgonian scolds and harpies;[51] on the other
70   Hung stench, diseases, and old filth, their mother,
With famine, wants and sorrows many a dozen,
The least of which was to the plague a cousin.
But they unfrighted pass, though many a privy
Spake to 'em louder than the ox in Livy,[52]
And many a sink poured out her rage anenst 'em;   *sewer/against*
But still their valour and their virtue fenced 'em,
And on they went, like Castor brave and Pollux,[53]
Ploughing the main. When see (the worst of all lucks)
They met the second prodigy, would fear a   *frighten*
80   Man that had never heard of a Chimaera.[54]
One said it was bold Briareus, or the beadle[55]
(Who hath the hundred hands when he doth meddle);
The other thought it Hydra,[56] or the rock
Made of the trull that cut her father's lock;[57]   *whore*
But coming near, they found it but a lighter,   *barge*
So huge, it seemed, they could by no means quite her.   *escape*
Back, cried their brace of Charons; they cried, No,   i.e. their boatmen

47   In the *Aeneid*, Aeneas receives guidance from the immortal Sibyl
of Cumae. He is directed by her to a golden bough which he uses as a
means to convince Charon to ferry him across the Styx.
48   Hercules is often represented carrying a large club.
49   Containers of human waste that were put out to be collected at
night.
50   Pertaining to feces and urine.
51   Two forms of mythical female monsters; here, the terms are used
to describe the female inhabitants of this part of London.
52   A reference to a story in Livy's history of Rome (35.21; see
gazetteer) in which a cow warns a Roman consul that the city should
beware.

53   In classical mythology, the twin sons who were born, along with
Helen of Troy, to Zeus and Leda (see Leda in the gazetteer). They sailed
with Jason on the voyage of the Argonauts.
54   A mythical monster with the head of a lion, the body of a goat and
the tail of a snake.
55   Briareus was a 100-handed giant in classical mythology; a beadle
was a form of bailiff who served warrants for petty crimes.
56   A mythical monster with 100 heads which was finally killed by
Hercules.
57   Like many Early Modern authors, Jonson mistakenly conflates two
Scyllas from classical myth: the monster from the *Odyssey* who is finally
turned into rocks, and the woman who cut a magic lock of hair from
her father's head, thus causing their city to fall.

No going back! On still, you rogues, and row.

How hight the place? A voice was heard: Cocytus. *named*

90 Row close then, slaves! Alas, they will beshite us.

No matter, stinkards, row! What croaking sound

Is this we hear? Of frogs? No, guts wind-bound,

Over your heads. Well, row! At this a loud

Crack did report itself, as if a cloud

Had burst with storm, and down fell *ab excelsis* i.e. from on high

Poor Mercury, crying out on Paracelsus[58]

And all his followers, that had so abused him,

And in so shitten sort so long had used him; *disgusting*

For (where he was the god of eloquence,

100 And subtlety of metals) they dispense

His spirits now in pills and eke in potions,

Suppositories, cataplasms and lotions. *poultices*

But many moons there shall not wane, quoth he,

(In the meantime let 'em imprison me)

But I will speak – and know I shall be heard –

Touching this cause, where they will be afeard

To answer me. And sure, it was the intent

Of the grave fart, late let in parliament,[59]

Had it been seconded, and not in fume

110 Vanished away: as you must all presume

Their Mercury did now. By this, the stem *prow*

Of the hulk touched and, as by Polypheme[60] *boat*

The sly Ulysses stole in a sheepskin,

The well-greased wherry now had got between,

And bade her farewell sough unto the lurdan. *sigh/loafer*

Never did bottom more betray her burden:

The meat-boat of Bears' College, Paris Garden,[61]

Stunk not so ill; nor, when she kissed, Kate Arden.[62]

Yet one day in the year for sweet 'tis voiced,

120 And that is when it is the Lord Mayor's foist.[63]

By this time had they reached the Stygian pool

By which the masters swear when, on the stool

Of worship, they their nodding chins do hit

Against their breasts. Here several ghosts did flit

About the shore, of farts but late departed,

White, black, blue, green, and in more forms out-started[64]

Than all those atomi ridiculous *atoms*

Whereof old Democrite and Hill Nicholas,[65]

One said, the other swore, the world consists.

130 These be the cause of those thick frequent mists

Arising in that place, through which who goes

Must try the unused valour of a nose:

And that ours did. For yet no nare was tainted, *nostril*

Nor thumb nor finger to the stop acquainted,

---

58 Paracelsus was a common name for the alchemist Theophrastus Bombastus von Hohenheim (1493–1541). The reference to Mercury is explained in the next ten lines as the god is conflated with the physical substance of the same name; mercury was often used in preparing medicines and in alchemical experiments.

59 A reference to an incident in Parliament in 1607, when an MP (Henry Ludlow) broke wind in response to a message from the Sergeant of the House of Lords.

60 In the *Odyssey* 9, Polyphemus is the cannibalistic Cyclops whom Odysseus escapes by hiding under a ram.

61 A reference to the practice of shipping offal from London butchers to the Paris Garden on Bankside, where bull- and bear-baiting contests were staged.

62 A famous London prostitute.

63 The word means both "barge" and "fart."

64 Jonson is here playing on classical descriptions of the souls of the dead as wispy and insubstantial.

65 Democritus (460–c.357 BC) was an ancient Greek philosopher who held an atomic theory of the composition of matter. Nicholas Hill was a contemporary scholar who published a justification of Democritus' theory.

But open and unarmed encountered all.
Whether it languishing stuck upon the wall
Or were precipitated down the jakes,   *toilet*
And after swom abroad in ample flakes,   *swam/streaks of cloud*
Or that it lay heaped like an usurer's mass,
140   All was to them the same: they were to pass,
And so they did, from Styx to Acheron,
The ever-boiling flood; whose banks upon
Your Fleet Lane furies and hot cooks do dwell,
That with still-scalding steams make the place hell.
The sinks ran grease, and hair of measled hogs,   *diseased*
The heads, houghs, entrails, and the hides of dogs: *joints*
For, to say truth, what scullion is so nasty   *kitchen servant*
To put the skins and offal in a pasty?
Cats there lay divers had been flayed and roasted
150   And, after mouldy grown, again were toasted;
Then selling not, a dish was ta'en to mince 'em,
But still, it seemed, the rankness did convince 'em.   *odor/expose*
For here they were thrown in wi' the melted pewter,
Yet drowned they not. They had five lives in future.
      But 'mongst these Tiberts, who d'you think there was?   *i.e. cats*
Old Banks[66] the juggler, our Pythagoras,
Grave tutor to the learnèd horse: both which
Being, beyond sea, burned for one witch,[67]
Their spirits transmigrated to a cat;
160   And now, above the pool, a face right fat,
With great gray eyes, are lifted up, and mewed;
Thrice did it spit, thrice dived. At last it viewed
Our brave heroes with a milder glare,
And in a piteous tune began: How dare
Your dainty nostrils (in so hot a season,
When every clerk eats artichokes and peason,   *peas*
Laxative lettuce, and such windy meat)
'Tempt such a passage? When each privy's seat
Is filled with buttock, and the walls do sweat
170   Urine and plasters? When the noise doth beat   *excrement*
Upon your ears of discords so unsweet,
And outcries of the damnèd in the Fleet?[68]
Cannot the plague-bill[69] keep you back? nor bells
Of loud Sepulchre's,[70] with their hourly knells,
But you will visit grisly Pluto's[71] hall?
Behold where Cerberus, reared on the wall
Of Holborn (three sergeants' heads) looks o'er,
And stays but till you come unto the door!
Tempt not his fury; Pluto is away,
180   And Madame Caesar,[72] great Proserpina,[73]
Is now from home. You lose your labours quite,
Were you Jove's sons, or had Alcides' might.
They cried out, Puss! He told them he was Banks,
That had so often showed 'em merry pranks.
They laughed at his laugh-worthy fate; and passed

66   A contemporary entertainer famous for his trained horse which, he claimed, could count.
67   Jonson here repeats a false rumor that both Banks and his horse were burned as witches in Rome.
68   A famous prison in Jonson's day that abutted the river.
69   The official record of the dead in an outbreak of the plague.
70   A reference to the bells of St. Sepulchre's, which tolled for prisoners being executed.
71   Classical god of the Underworld (see gazetteer).
72   A contemporary brothel-keeper.
73   Pluto's consort, whom he kidnapped from the world of the living (see gazetteer).

The triple head without a sop.[74] At last,
Calling for Rhadamanthus,[75] that dwelt by,
A soap-boiler, and Aeacus him nigh,
Who kept an ale-house, with my little Minos,
190   An ancient purblind fletcher with a high nose,[76]
They took 'em all to witness of their action,
And so went bravely back, without protraction,   *delay*
   In memory of which most liquid deed,   *watery*
The city since hath raised a pyramid.
And I could wish for their eternized sakes,
My muse had ploughed with his that sung A-jax.[77]

FROM *THE FOREST* (1616)

I. WHY I WRITE NOT OF LOVE[1]

Some act of Love's bound to rehearse,   *relate*
I thought to bind him in my verse;
Which when he felt, Away! quoth he,[2]
Can poets hope to fetter me?
It is enough they once did get
Mars and my mother in their net:[3]
I wear not these my wings in vain.
With which he fled me; and again
Into my rhymes could ne'er be got
10   By any art. Then wonder not
That since, my numbers are so cold,   *verses*
When Love is fled, and I grow old.

II. TO PENSHURST[4]

Thou art not, Penshurst, built to envious show
   Of touch or marble, nor canst boast a row   *black marble*
Of polished pillars, or a roof of gold;
   Thou hast no lantern[5] whereof tales are told,
Or stair, or courts; but stand'st an ancient pile,
   And these grudged at, art reverenced the while.
Thou joy'st in better marks, of soil, of air,
   Of wood, of water; therein thou art fair.
Thou hast thy walks for health as well as sport:
10   Thy Mount, to which the dryads[6] do resort,

---

74 A bribe of food to placate triple-headed Cerberus and allow one into Hades.

75 Rhadamanthus, Aeacus, and Minos were the judges of the dead in the classical Underworld.

76 i.e. a blind arrow-maker, who compensates by having a keen sense of smell ("high nose").

77 A reference to the contemporary poet Sir John Harrington, who had written a satirical treatise on toilets which used the Ajax/a jakes pun in its title.

THE FOREST

1 This poem alludes to (and reverses) the beginning of Ovid's *Amores*, in which the speaker tries to write about subjects other than love but is compelled to serve Love.

2 As is often the case in classical and Early Modern literature, Cupid is described as Love personified.

3 See Ares in the gazetteer.

4 The family home of the Sidney family in Kent. The current "lord" of the place was Robert Sidney, Philip Sidney's younger brother. The poem is full of classical allusions, especially to Martial's *Epigrams*.

5 A turret with glazed windows, designed to admit light to the room below.

6 Dryads were mythical tree nymphs; Pan and Bacchus, in the next line, are classical forest gods (see gazetteer).

Where Pan and Bacchus their high feasts have made,
    Beneath the broad beech, and the chestnut shade;
That taller tree, which of a nut was set
    At his great birth, where all the muses met.[7]
There, in the writhèd bark, are cut the names
    Of many a sylvan[8] taken with his flames;
And thence the ruddy satyrs[9] oft provoke
    The lighter fauns to reach thy lady's oak.
Thy copse, too, named of Gamage,[10] thou hast there,
20   That never fails to serve thee seasoned deer
When thou wouldst feast or exercise thy friends.
    The lower land, that to the river bends,
Thy sheep, thy bullocks, kine and calves do feed;   *cows*
    The middle grounds thy mares and horses breed.
Each bank doth yield thee conies, and the tops,   *rabbits*
    Fertile of wood, Ashour, and Sidney's copse,[11]
To crown thy open table, doth provide
    The purpled pheasant with the speckled side;
The painted partridge lies in every field,
30   And for thy mess is willing to be killed.
And if the high-swoll'n Medway[12] fail thy dish,
    Thou hast thy ponds that pay thee tribute fish:
Fat, agèd carps, that run into thy net;
    And pikes, now weary their own kind to eat,
As loath the second draught[13] or cast to stay,
    Officiously, at first, themselves betray;
Bright eels, that emulate them, and leap on land
    Before the fisher, or into his hand.
Then hath thy orchard fruit, thy garden flowers,
40   Fresh as the air and new as are the hours:[14]
The early cherry, with the later plum,
    Fig, grape and quince, each in his time doth come;
The blushing apricot and woolly peach
    Hang on thy walls, that every child may reach.
And though thy walls be of the country stone,
    They're reared with no man's ruin, no man's groan;[15]
There's none that dwell about them wish them down,
    But all come in, the farmer and the clown,   *peasant*
And no one empty-handed, to salute
50   Thy lord and lady, though they have no suit.
Some bring a capon, some a rural cake,   *castrated cock*
    Some nuts, some apples; some that think they make
The better cheeses, bring 'em; or else send
    By their ripe daughters, whom they would commend
This way to husbands; and whose baskets bear
    An emblem of themselves, in plum or pear.
But what can this (more than express their love)
    Add to thy free provisions, far above
The need of such? whose liberal board doth flow   *table*
60   With all that hospitality doth know!

---

7 A reference to Philip Sidney. Jonson is here alluding to a similar tree-planting for the birth of the poet Virgil as described by Suetonius (*Vita Virgili* 5).

8 "Sylvan" is here used as a catch-all term for rustic lovers.

9 See gazetteer.

10 A reference to Barbara Gamage, who married Robert Sidney in 1584; she is also the lady of "my lady's oak," following a tradition that she once went into labor under an oak tree.

11 Features of the Penshurst estate.

12 A nearby river.

13 A reference to fishing with a net.

14 A play on the Hours, classical goddesses who governed the changing of the seasons.

15 An indirect reference to the common (and illegal) practice of enclosing common land with fences. This was all too common in 16th- and 17th-century England.

Where comes no guest but is allowed to eat
    Without his fear, and of thy lord's own meat;
Where the same beer and bread and self-same wine
    That is his lordship's shall be also mine;
And I not fain to sit, as some this day
    At great men's tables, and yet dine away.[16]
Here no man tells my cups, nor, standing by,   *counts*
    A waiter, doth my gluttony envy,
But gives me what I call, and lets me eat;
70   He knows below he shall find plenty of meat,
Thy tables hoard not up for the next day.
    Nor, when I take my lodging, need I pray
For fire or lights or livery: all is there,   *provisions*
    As if thou then wert mine, or I reigned here;
There's nothing I can wish, for which I stay.
    That found King James, when, hunting late this way
With his brave son, the Prince, they saw thy fires
    Shine bright on every hearth as the desires
Of thy Penates[17] had been set on flame
80   To entertain them; or the country came
With all their zeal to warm their welcome here.
    What (great, I will not say, but) sudden cheer
Didst thou then make 'em! and what praise was heaped
    On thy good lady then! who therein reaped
The just reward of her high housewifery:
    To have her linen, plate, and all things nigh
When she was far; and not a room but dressed
    As if it had expected such a guest!
These, Penshurst, are thy praise, and yet not all.
90   Thy lady's noble, fruitful, chaste withal;
His children thy great lord may call his own,
    A fortune in this age but rarely known.
They are and have been taught religion; thence
    Their gentler spirits have sucked innocence.
Each morn and even they are taught to pray
    With the whole household, and may every day
Read in their virtuous parents' noble parts   *qualities*
    The mysteries of manners, arms and arts.   *skills*
Now, Penshurst, they that will proportion thee
100   With other edifices, when they see
Those proud, ambitious heaps, and nothing else,
    May say, their lords have built, but thy lord dwells.

IV. TO THE WORLD

A Farewell for a Gentlewoman, Virtuous and Noble

False world, good night. Since thou hast brought
    That hour upon my morn of age,
Henceforth I quit thee from my thought;
    My part is ended on thy stage.
Do not once hope that thou canst tempt
    A spirit so resolved to tread

16 i.e. He is not invited to dine with a lord and then shown to an inferior table.

17 The household gods in a classical Roman home. Their images were kept in a shrine near the front door.

Upon thy throat and live exempt
  From all the nets that thou canst spread.
I know thy forms are studied arts,
  Thy subtle ways be narrow straits,
Thy courtesy but sudden starts,
  And what thou call'st thy gifts are baits.
I know too, though thou strut and paint,[18]
  Yet art thou both shrunk up and old;
That only fools make thee a saint,
  And all thy good is to be sold.
I know thou whole art but a shop
  Of toys and trifles, traps and snares,
To take the weak, or make them stop;
  Yet art thou falser than thy wares.
And knowing this, should I yet stay,
  Like such as blow away their lives
And never will redeem a day,
  Enamoured of their golden gyves?   *shackles*
Or, having 'scaped, shall I return
  And thrust my neck into the noose
From whence so lately I did burn
  With all my powers myself to loose?
What bird or beast is known so dull
  That, fled his cage, or broke his chain,
And tasting air and freedom, wull   *will*
  Render his head in there again?
If these, who have but sense, can shun
  The engines that have them annoyed,
Little for me had reason done,
  If I could not thy gins avoid.   *snares*
Yes, threaten, do. Alas, I fear
  As little as I hope from thee;
I know thou canst nor show nor bear
  More hatred than thou hast to me.
My tender, first, and simple years
  Thou didst abuse, and then betray;
Since stirredst up jealousies and fears,
  When all the causes were away.
Then in a soil hast planted me
  Where breathe the basest of thy fools,
Where envious arts professèd be,
  And pride and ignorance the schools;
Where nothing is examined, weighed,
  But, as 'tis rumoured, so believed;
Where every freedom is betrayed,
  And every goodness taxed or grieved.
But what we're born for we must bear:
  Our frail condition it is such
That, what to all may happen here,
  If't chance to me, I must not grutch.   *complain*
Else I my state should much mistake,
  To harbour a divided thought
From all my kind; that, for my sake,
  There should a miracle be wrought.
No, I do know that I was born
  To age, misfortune, sickness, grief;

---

18 i.e. conceal your true nature behind false appearances.

But I will bear these with that scorn
    As shall not need thy false relief.
Nor for my peace will I go far,
    As wanderers do that still do roam,
But make my strengths, such as they are,
    Here in my bosom, and at home.

V. SONG

To Celia[19]

Come, my Celia, let us prove,   *experience*
While we may, the sports of love;
Time will not be ours for ever;
He at length our good will sever.
Spend not then his gifts in vain.
Suns that set may rise again;
But if once we lose this light,
'Tis with us perpetual night.
Why should we defer our joys?
Fame and rumour are but toys.   *Reputation*
Cannot we delude the eyes
Of a few poor household spies?
Or his easier ears beguile,
So removèd by our wile?
'Tis no sin love's fruit to steal,
But the sweet theft to reveal:
To be taken, to be seen,
These have crimes accounted been.

IX. SONG

To Celia[20]

Drink to me only with thine eyes,
    And I will pledge with mine;   *drink a toast*
Or leave a kiss but in the cup,
    And I'll not look for wine.
The thirst that from the soul doth rise
    Doth ask a drink divine;
But might I of Jove's nectar[21] sup,
    I would not change for thine.
I sent thee late a rosy wreath,
    Not so much honouring thee
As giving it a hope that there
    It could not withered be.
But thou thereon didst only breathe,
    And sent'st it back to me;
Since when it grows, and smells, I swear,
    Not of itself, but thee.

19   In Jonson's play *Volpone*, this song is sung to Celia by the title   20   Like the previous poem, this is taken from the play *Volpone*.
character. It is adapted from a poem by the Roman love poet Catullus.   21   The drink of the classical gods. Their food was ambrosia.

XV. TO HEAVEN

Good and great God, can I not think of thee,
　　But it must straight my melancholy be?
Is it interpreted in me disease
　　That, laden with my sins, I seek for ease?
Oh, be thou witness, that the reins dost know   *passions*
　　And hearts of all, if I be sad for show;
And judge me after, if I dare pretend
　　To aught but grace, or aim at other end.
As thou art all, so be thou all to me,
　　First, midst, and last; converted one and three;[22]
10　My faith, my hope, my love; and in this state,
　　My judge, my witness, and my advocate.
Where have I been this while exiled from thee?
　　And whither rapt, now thou but stoop'st to me?   *carried away*
Dwell, dwell here still: Oh, being everywhere,
　　How can I doubt to find thee ever here?
I know my state, both full of shame and scorn,
　　Conceived in sin, and unto labour born,
Standing with fear, and must with horror fall,
　　And destined unto judgement, after all.
20　I feel my griefs too, and there scarce is ground
　　Upon my flesh to inflict another wound.
Yet dare I not complain, or wish for death
　　With holy Paul,[23] lest it be thought the breath
Of discontent; or that these prayers be
　　For weariness of life, not love of thee.

FROM *UNDERWOODS* (1640)

2. A CELEBRATION OF CHARIS[1] IN TEN LYRIC PIECES

I

His Excuse for loving

Let it not your wonder move,
Less your laughter, that I love.
Though I now write fifty years,
I have had, and have, my peers;   i.e. other poets
Poets, though divine, are men:
Some have loved as old again.
And it is not always face,
Clothes, or fortune gives the grace,
Or the feature, or the youth;   *appearance*
But the language, and the truth,
10　With the ardour and the passion,
Gives the lover weight and fashion.
If you then will read the story,

22　A reference to the Christian doctrine of the Trinity, in which God is both one and three (Father, Son, and Holy Ghost).

23　A reference to Romans 7:24.

2. A CELEBRATION OF CHARIS IN TEN LYRIC PIECES

1　The name "Charis" is the singular form of the Greek *Charitēs*, or "Graces." These three classical goddesses were bringers of grace and harmony to human life and work. One of them was married to the god Hephaestus, and Jonson plays on this association at various moments in these poems.

First prepare you to be sorry
That you never knew till now
Either whom to love, or how;
But be glad as soon with me,
When you know that this is she,
Of whose beauty it was sung,
She shall make the old man young,
20   Keep the middle age at stay,
And let nothing high decay,
Till she be the reason why
All the world for love may die.

IV

Her Triumph[2]

See the chariot at hand here of Love,[3]
   Wherein my lady rideth!
Each that draws is a swan or a dove,
   And well the car Love guideth.
As she goes, all hearts do duty   *pay homage*
   Unto her beauty;
And enamoured, do wish, so they might
   But enjoy such a sight,
That they still were, to run by her side,
10   Through swords, through seas, whither she would ride.

Do but look on her eyes, they do light
   All that Love's world compriseth!
Do but look on her hair, it is bright
   As Love's star when it riseth!   *i.e. the planet Venus*
Do but mark, her forehead's smoother   *observe*
   Than words that soothe her!
And from her arched brows, such a grace
   Sheds itself through the face,
As alone there triumphs to the life
20   All the gain, all the good, of the elements' strife.

Have you seen but a bright lily grow,
   Before rude hands have touched it?
Have you marked but the fall o' the snow,
   Before the soil hath smutched it?   *dirtied*
Have you felt the wool o' the beaver?
   Or swan's down ever?
Or have smelled o' the bud o' the briar?
   Or the nard i' the fire?   *aromatic balsam*
   Or have tasted the bag o' the bee?
30   O so white! o so soft! o so sweet is she!

V

His discourse with Cupid[4]

Noblest Charis, you that are
Both my fortune and my star!

---

2   The title refers to the ancient Roman custom of granting a victorious general a triumphal procession through the streets of the city.
The Roman poet Ovid popularized the tradition of comparing love's
triumph in the heart to a military conquest.

3   Venus was often represented in a chariot pulled by doves (her sacred
birds; see gazetteer).

4   As in many other Early Modern poems, Cupid, the son of Venus, is
here called Love and treated as its personification.

And do govern more my blood
Than the various moon the flood!
Hear what late discourse of you
Love and I have had, and true.
'Mongst my muses finding me,
Where he chanced your name to see
Set, and to this softer strain: *melody*
10   Sure, said he, if I have brain,
This, here sung, can be no other
By description but my mother!
So hath Homer praised her hair,⁵
So Anacreon drawn the air
Of her face, and made to rise,
Just about her sparkling eyes,
Both her brows, bent like my bow.
By her looks I do her know,
Which you call my shafts. And see!   *arrows*
20   Such my mother's blushes be,
As the bath your verse discloses
In her cheeks, of milk and roses;
Such as oft I wanton in!   *play*
And, above her even chin,
Have you placed the bank of kisses,
Where, you say, men gather blisses,
Ripened with a breath more sweet,
Then when flowers and west winds meet.
Nay, her white and polished neck,
30   With the lace that doth it deck,
Is my mother's! Hearts of slain
Lovers, made into a chain!
And between each rising breast
Lies the valley called my nest,
Where I sit and proyne my wings   *preen*
After flight, and put new stings
To my shafts! Her very name
With my mother's is the same.
I confess all, I replied,
40   And the glass hangs by her side,   *mirror*
And the girdle 'bout her waist:
All is Venus, save unchaste.
But alas, thou seest the least
Of her good, who is the best
Of her sex; But could'st thou, Love,
Call to mind the forms that strove
For the apple⁶ and those three
Make in one, the same were she.
For this beauty yet doth hide
50   Something more than thou hast spied.
Outward grace weak love beguiles;
She is Venus, when she smiles,
But she's Juno,⁷ when she walks,
And Minerva, when she talks.

---

5 In *Iliad* 17.51; the Anacreon reference in the following line is to
Anacreontea 15 (part of a body of imitations of, rather than products of,
Anacreon).

6 A reference to the Judgment of Paris; see Paris in the gazetteer.
7 Juno and Minerva were the other two goddesses in the competition
with Venus.

9. MY PICTURE LEFT IN SCOTLAND

I now think Love is rather deaf than blind,
  For else it could not be
    That she
Whom I adore so much should so slight me,
  And cast my love behind;
I'm sure my language to her was as sweet,
    And every close did meet   *cadence*
    In sentence of as subtle feet,   i.e. metrical feet
    As hath the youngest he
10   That sits in shadow of Apollo's tree.   i.e. other poets

    Oh, but my conscious fears
      That fly my thoughts between,
    Tell me that she hath seen
    My hundred of grey hairs,
    Told seven-and-forty years,
Read so much waste, as she cannot embrace
My mountain belly, and my rocky face;
And all these through her eyes have stopped her ears.

23. AN ODE. TO HIMSELF

Where dost thou careless lie,
  Buried in ease and sloth?
Knowledge that sleeps doth die;
  And this security,
    It is the common moth
That eats on wits and arts, and oft destroys them both.

    Are all the Aonian springs[8]
      Dried up? Lies Thespia waste?
    Doth Clarius' harp want strings,   *Apollo's*
10   That not a nymph now sings?
      Or droop they, as disgraced
To see their seats and bowers by chattering pies defaced?   *magpies*

    If hence thy silence be,
      As 'tis too just a cause,
    Let this thought quicken thee: *energize*
    Minds that are great and free,
      Should not on fortune pause;
'Tis crown enough to virtue still, her own applause.

    What though the greedy fry[9]
20   Be taken with false baits
    Of worded balladry,
    And think it poesy?
      They die with their conceits,   *affectations*
And only piteous scorn upon their folly waits.

---

8   The Aonian springs and, in the next line, Thespia were both associated with the Muses (see gazetteer).

9   "Fry" is a term for an animal's young, especially fish; Jonson is here
using it scornfully to refer to his young contemporaries and their taste
in poetry.

Then take in hand thy lyre,
    Strike in thy proper strain;
With Japhet's[10] line, aspire
Sol's chariot for new fire   *The Sun's*
    To give the world again;
Who aided him, will thee, the issue of Jove's brain.[11]

30

And since our dainty age
    Cannot endure reproof,
Make not thyself a page   *servant*
To that strumpet, the stage;
    But sing high and aloof,
Safe from the wolf's black jaw, and the dull ass's hoof.[12]

29. A Fit of Rhyme against Rhyme

Rhyme, the rack of finest wits
That expresseth but by fits[13]
    True conceit;   *thought*
Spoiling senses of their treasure,
Cozening judgement with a measure   *meter*
    But false weight.   i.e. value
Wresting words from their true calling,
Propping verse for fear of falling
    To the ground.
10 Jointing syllabes, drowning letters,   *Dividing*
Fastening vowels, as with fetters
    They were bound!
Soon as lazy thou wert known,
All good poetry hence was flown,
    And art banished.
For a thousand years together
All Parnassus'[14] green did wither,
    And wit vanished.
Pegasus[15] did fly away,
20 At the well no muse did stay,
    But bewailed
So to see the fountain dry,
And Apollo's music die,
    All light failed!
Starveling rhymes did fill the stage,
Not a poet in an age
    Worth crowning.
Not a work deserving bays,   *laurels*
Nor a line deserving praise,
30   Pallas[16] frowning.
Greek was free from rhyme's infection,
Happy Greek by this protection,
    Was not spoiled.
Whilst the Latin, queen of tongues,[17]

---

10 A reference to Iapetus, the father of Prometheus (see gazetteer).

11 A reference to Athena, who was born from Zeus' forehead.

12 Figures for harsh critics and ignorant audiences respectively.

13 A "fit" is a term for a section of a poem, but Jonson is also alluding (as he does in the title) to the paroxysms of madness or passion that the word also denotes.

14 The sacred mountain of the Muses.

15 The winged horse Pegasus was said to have created a spring on Mt. Helicon, another home of the muses, by stamping its foot.

16 See Athena in the gazetteer.

17 Classical Latin poetry never rhymes, but some Early Modern writers did produce rhyming Latin verse.

Is not yet free from rhyme's wrongs,
  But rests foiled.   *besmirched*
Scarce the hill again doth flourish,
Scarce the world a wit doth nourish,
  To restore
40 Phoebus to his crown again,
And the muses to their brain,
  As before.
Vulgar languages that want   *Vernacular*
Words and sweetness, and be scant
  Of true measure,
Tyrant rhyme hath so abused,
That they long since have refused
  Other ceasure.   *metrical pause*
He that first invented thee,
50 May his joints tormented be,
  Cramped for ever;
Still may syllabes jar with time,
Still may reason war with rhyme,
  Resting never.
May his sense, when it would meet
The cold tumour in his feet,[18]
  Grow unsounder.
And his title be long fool,
That in rearing such a school,
60 Was the founder.

47. AN EPISTLE ANSWERING TO ONE THAT ASKED TO BE SEALED[19] OF THE TRIBE OF BEN[20]

Men that are safe and sure in all they do
 Care not what trials they are put unto;
They meet the fire, the test, as martyrs would,
 And though opinion stamp them not, are gold.[21]
I could say more of such, but that I fly
 To speak myself out too ambitiously,
And showing so weak an act to vulgar eyes,
 Put conscience and my right to compromise.
Let those that merely talk, and never think,
10 That live in the wild anarchy of drink,
Subject to quarrel only, or else such
 As make it their proficiency how much
They have glutted in and lechered out that week,
 That never yet did friend or friendship seek
But for a sealing: let these men protest.
 Or the other on their borders, that will jest
On all souls that are absent, even the dead,
 Like flies or worms which man's corrupt parts fed:
That to speak well, think it above all sin,
20 Of any company but that they are in;

---

18   This line has a double meaning: it literally refers to a swelling in the feet, but "tumour" can also mean "inflated language" and "feet" can be metrical as well as bodily.

19   i.e. certified or publicly welcomed.

20   The "Tribe of Ben" was a group of younger writers who met regularly with Jonson, first at the Mermaid Tavern, and later at the Devil and St. Dunstan.

21   A reference to testing the quality of gold by a touchstone.

Call every night to supper in these fits,
    And are received for the covey of wits;   *company*
That censure all the town, and all the affairs,
    And know whose ignorance is more than theirs;
Let these men have their ways, and take their times
    To vent their libels, and to issue rhymes,
I have no portion in them, nor their deal
    Of news they get to strew out the long meal;
I study other friendships, and more one
30   Than these can ever be; or else wish none.
What is't to me whether the French design[22]
    Be, or be not, to get the Valtelline?
Or the States' ships sent forth belike to meet
    Some hopes of Spain in their West Indian Fleet?
Whether the dispensation yet be sent,
    Or that the match from Spain was ever meant?
I wish all well, and pray high heaven conspire
    My prince's safety and my king's desire;
But if, for honour, we must draw the sword,
40   And force back that which will not be restored,[23]
I have a body yet that spirit draws
    To live, or fall a carcass in the cause.
So far without inquiry what the States,
    Brunsfield,[24] and Mansfield, do this year, my fates
Shall carry me at call, and I'll be well,
    Though I do neither hear these news, nor tell
Of Spain or France, or were not pricked down one   *marked*
    Of the late mystery of reception,[25]
Although my fame to his not under-hears,   i.e. is not inferior
50   That guides the motions and directs the bears.
But that's a blow by which in time I may
    Lose all my credit with my Christmas clay[26]
And animated porcelain of the court;
    Aye, and for this neglect, the coarser sort
Of earthen jars there may molest me too:
    Well, with mine own frail pitcher, what to do
I have decreed; keep it from waves and press,
    Lest it be jostled, cracked, made naught, or less;
Live to that point I will, for which I am man,
60   And dwell as in my centre as I can,
Still looking to, and ever loving, heaven;
    With reverence using all the gifts thence given.
'Mongst which, if I have any friendships sent,
    Such as are square, well-tagged, and permanent,   *equal/well-fastened*
Not built with canvas, paper, and false lights,[27]
    As are the glorious scenes at the great sights,

---

22 The next six lines refer to contemporary international issues about which Jonson professes not to care. The Valtelline was a strategically important transport route which the French captured; "States" refers to Holland; and the "match from Spain" was the projected marriage of Prince Charles and the Infanta of Spain.

23 A reference to the invasion of the Palatinate, a German territory in the Rhineland ruled by Elector Frederick V, son-in-law to James I of England. The invasion of this territory in 1619 marked the military beginning of the Thirty Years War.

24 Brunsfield is unknown, but Mansfield refers to a general in the service of the Elector Palatine.

25 A reference to the elaborate theatrical celebrations planned to greet the Infanta of Spain upon her arrival in England. Jonson's rival Inigo Jones was in charge of these pageants, and the poet is sniping at Jones in these lines.

26 The next seven lines use a metaphor of creating pottery for creating poetry. As a writer of masques with Inigo Jones, Jonson had created poetry to accompany a visual spectacle, but by the year this poem was written he had fallen out of favor at court. Here he contrasts his plain products with the "animated porcelain" of court entertainment.

27 In the next two lines, Jonson is again referring to court spectacles and their elaborate scenery and "special effects."

And that there be no fevery heats, nor colds,
   Oily expansions, or shrunk dirty folds,
But all so clear and led by reason's flame,
70   As but to stumble in her sight were shame;
These I will honour, love, embrace, and serve,
   And free it from all question to preserve,
So short you read my character, and theirs   *inadequately*
   I would call mine, to which not many stairs
Are asked to climb. First give me faith, who know
   Myself a little. I will take you so,
As you have writ yourself. Now stand, and then,
   Sir, you are sealèd of the tribe of Ben.

70. TO THE IMMORTAL MEMORY AND FRIENDSHIP OF THAT NOBLE PAIR, SIR LUCIUS CARY AND SIR H. MORISON[28]

The Turn

Brave Infant of Saguntum,[29] clear
Thy coming forth in that great year
When the prodigious Hannibal did crown
His rage with razing your immortal town.
Thou, looking then about,
Ere thou wert half got out,
Wise child, didst hastily return,
And mad'st thy mother's womb thine urn.   *grave*
How summed a circle didst thou leave mankind   *complete*
10 Of deepest lore, could we the centre find!

The Counter-turn

Did wiser nature draw thee back
From out the horror of that sack?   *i.e. sack of the city*
Where shame, faith, honour, and regard of right
Lay trampled on; the deeds of death and night
Urged, hurried forth, and hurled
Upon the affrighted world:
Sword, fire, and famine with fell fury met,
And all on utmost ruin set;
As, could they but life's miseries foresee,
20 No doubt all infants would return like thee.

The Stand

For what is life, if measured by the space,   *duration*
Not by the act?
Or maskèd man, if valued by his face
Above his fact?

28 Cary and Morison were friends until Morison's death in 1629. This poem represents the first attempt in English to reproduce the structure of a Pindaric ode. Pindar (518–*c*.440 BC) was a lyric poet famous for his odes celebrating the victors in athletic contests. Pindaric odes were divided into three sections called strophe, antistrophe, and epode (here called turn, counter-turn, and stand). There were also metrically complex and featured lines of varying lengths, another feature that Jonson reproduces here. The reflections about the quality of life being more important than its length are adapted from Seneca, *Epistles* 93.

29 This stanza refers to a city attacked by the Carthaginian general Hannibal in 219 BCE, an event which started the Second Punic War between Rome and Carthage. The story of the child returning to the womb is told by the Roman historian Pliny in *Natural History* 7.3.39.

Here's one[30] outlived his peers
And told forth fourscore years;
He vexèd time, and busied the whole state;
Troubled both foes and friends,
But ever to no ends;
What did this stirrer, but die late?   *trouble-maker*
How well at twenty had he fallen or stood!
For three of his four score he did no good.

The Turn

He entered well by virtuous parts,
Got up and thrived with honest arts;   *Brought up*
He purchased friends and fame and honours then,
And had his noble name advanced with men;
But weary of that flight,
He stooped in all men's sight
To sordid flatteries, acts of strife,
And sunk in that dead sea of life
So deep, as he did then death's waters sup,
But that the cork of title buoyed him up.

The Counter-turn

Alas, but Morison fell young!
He never fell: thou fall'st, my tongue.
He stood, a soldier to the last right end,
A perfect patriot, and a noble friend;
But most, a virtuous son.
All offices were done
By him so ample, full, and round,   *complete*
In weight, in measure, number, sound,
As, though his age imperfect might appear,
His life was of humanity the sphere.   *perfection*

The Stand

Go now, and tell out days summed up with fears;   *count*
And make them years;
Produce thy mass of miseries on the stage,
To swell thine age;
Repeat of things a throng,
To show thou hast been long,
Not lived; for life doth her great actions spell
By what was done and wrought
In season, and so brought
To light: her measures[31] are, how well
Each syllabe answered, and was formed, how fair;   *syllable*
These make the lines of life, and that's her air.   *tune*

The Turn

It is not growing like a tree
In bulk, doth make man better be;

---

30 Jonson's instance is a hypothetical one.

31 Jonson is punning on "measures" which means both "standards" and "metrical units."

Or standing long an oak, three hundred year,
To fall a log at last, dry, bald, and sere: *withered*
A lily of a day
70   Is fairer far, in May,
Although it fall and die that night;
It was the plant and flower of light.
In small proportions we just beauty see,
And in short measures life may perfect be.

The Counter-turn

Call, noble Lucius, then for wine,
And let thy looks with gladness shine;
Accept this garland, plant it on thy head;
And think, nay know, thy Morison's not dead.
He leaped the present age,
80   Possessed with holy rage   *ardor*
To see that bright eternal day,
Of which we priests and poets say
Such truths as we expect for happy men;
And there he lives with memory, and Ben

The Stand

Jonson, who sung this of him, ere he went
himself to rest,
Or taste a part of that full joy he meant
To have expressed
In this bright asterism;   *constellation*
90   Where it were friendship's schism
(Were not his Lucius long with us to tarry)
To separate these twi-
Lights, the Dioscuri;[32]
And keep the one half from his Harry.   *i.e. Morison*
But fate doth so alternate the design,
Whilst that in heaven, this light on earth must shine.

The Turn

And shine as you exalted are;
Two names of friendship, but one star:
Of hearts the union. And those not by chance
100   Made, or indentured, or leased out to advance   *contracted*
The profits for a time.
No pleasures vain did chime,
Of rhymes, or riots, at your feasts,
Orgies of drink, or feigned protests:
But simple love of greatness, and of good;
That knits brave minds and manners, more than blood.

The Counter-turn

This made you first to know the why
You liked; then after to apply

32   A reference to the twin sons of Zeus and Leda, Castor and Pollux.
They were worshiped as gods in Sparta and later in Rome.

drawn/desire

110   That liking; and approach so one the tother,
Till either grew a portion of the other:
Each stylèd, by his end,
The copy of his friend.
You lived to be the great surnames
And titles by which all made claims
Unto the virtue. Nothing perfect done
But as a Cary, or a Morison.

The Stand

And such a force the fair example had,
As they that saw
The good and durst not practise it, were glad
120   That such a law
Was left yet to mankind;
Where they might read and find
Friendship in deed was written, not in words;
And with the heart, not pen,
Of two so early men
Whose lines her rolls were, and records.
Who, ere the first down bloomèd on the chin,
Had sowed these fruits, and got the harvest in.

young
lives/register

MISCELLANEOUS POEMS

TO THE MEMORY OF MY BELOVED, THE AUTHOR, MR. WILLIAM SHAKESPEARE, AND WHAT HE HATH LEFT US[1]

To draw no envy, Shakespeare, on thy name,
   Am I thus ample to thy book and fame;   *copious*
While I confess thy writings to be such
   As neither man nor muse can praise too much:
'Tis true, and all men's suffrage. But these ways   *opinion*
   Were not the paths I meant unto thy praise:
For silliest ignorance on these may light,   *arrive*
   Which, when it sounds at best, but echoes right;
Or blind affection, which doth ne'er advance
10   The truth, but gropes, and urgeth all by chance;
Or crafty malice might pretend this praise,
   And think to ruin where it seemed to raise.
These are as some infamous bawd or whore
   Should praise a matron: what could hurt her more?
But thou art proof against them, and indeed
   Above the ill fortune of them, or the need.
I therefore will begin. Soul of the age!
   The applause, delight, the wonder of our stage!
My Shakespeare, rise: I will not lodge thee by
20   Chaucer or Spenser, or bid Beaumont[2] lie
A little further, to make thee a room;
   Thou art a monument without a tomb,

TO THE MEMORY OF MY BELOVED, THE AUTHOR, MR. WILLIAM SHAKESPEARE, AND WHAT HE HATH LEFT US
1   This poem was originally published in the first folio of Shakespeare's works in 1618.

2   Geoffrey Chaucer, Edmund Spenser, and the playwright Francis Beaumont were all associated with Shakespeare in William Basse's "Elegy on Shakespeare" (1622).

And art alive still while thy book doth live,
    And we have wits to read, and praise to give.
That I not mix thee so, my brain excuses:
    I mean with great, but disproportioned, muses;[3]
For if I thought my judgement were of years
    I should commit thee surely with thy peers: *compare*
And tell how far thou didst our Lyly[4] outshine,
30   Or sporting Kyd, or Marlowe's mighty line.[5]
And though thou hadst small Latin, and less Greek,
    From thence to honour thee I would not seek
For names, but call forth thundering Aeschylus,[6]
    Euripides, and Sophocles to us,
Pacuvius,[7] Accius, him of Cordova dead,
    To life again, to hear thy buskin[8] tread,
And shake a stage; or, when thy socks were on,
    Leave thee alone for the comparison
Of all that insolent Greece or haughty Rome
40   Sent forth, or since did from their ashes come.
Triumph, my Britain, thou hast one to show
    To whom all scenes of Europe homage owe.
He was not of an age, but for all time!
    And all the muses still were in their prime
When like Apollo he came forth to warm
    Our ears, or like a Mercury to charm![9]
Nature herself was proud of his designs,
    And joyed to wear the dressing of his lines,
Which were so richly spun and woven so fit
50   As, since, she will vouchsafe no other wit.
The merry Greek, tart Aristophanes,
    Neat Terence, witty Plautus,[10] now not please,
But antiquated and deserted lie
    As they were not of nature's family.
Yet must I not give nature all: thy art,
    My gentle Shakespeare, must enjoy a part.
For though the poet's matter nature be,
    His art doth give the fashion. And that he
Who casts to write a living line must sweat
60   (Such as thine are) and strike the second heat
Upon the muses' anvil: turn the same
    (And himself with it) that he thinks to frame;
Or for the laurel he may gain a scorn:
    For a good poet's made, as well as born;
And such wert thou. Look how the father's face
    Lives in his issue: even so, the race
Of Shakespeare's mind and manners brightly shines
    In his well-turnèd and true-filèd lines: *polished*
In each of which he seems to shake a lance,
70   As brandished at the eyes of ignorance.
Sweet swan of Avon! What a sight it were
    To see thee in our waters yet appear,

---

3   i.e. With poets who are great, but not close to your ability.

4   John Lyly (c.1554–1606), who is represented in this anthology as a prose writer, was also a playwright.

5   Thomas Kyd (1558–94) and Christopher Marlowe (1564–93) were other successful contemporary playwrights.

6   Aeschylus, Euripides, and Sophocles were all Greek tragic playwrights. While famous today, their direct influence on Early Modern English drama is actually very slight.

7   Pacuvius and Accius were classical Roman tragic dramatists; "him of Cordova" refers to Seneca (see gazetteer).

8   The "buskin" is the English term for the footwear of classical tragic actors. Comic actors wore a kind of slipper known in English as a "sock."

9   Apollo was the classical god of music and Mercury of rhetoric.

10   Aristophanes, Terence, and Plautus were all classical comic dramatists.

And make those flights upon the banks of Thames
  That so did take Eliza, and our James!
But stay, I see thee in the hemisphere
  Advanced, and made a constellation there!
Shine forth, thou star of poets, and with rage   *inspiration*
  Or influence chide or cheer the drooping stage;
Which, since thy flight from hence, hath mourned like night,
80   And despairs day, but for thy volume's light.

TO A FRIEND

AN EPIGRAM OF HIM[11]

Sir Inigo doth fear it, as I hear,
And labours to seem worthy of that fear,
That I should write upon him some sharp verse
Able to eat into his bones, and pierce
The marrow. Wretch, I quit thee of thy pain: *release*
Thou'rt too ambitious, and dost fear in vain!
The Libyan lion hunts no butterflies,
He makes the camel and dull ass his prize.
If thou be so desirous to be read
10   Seek out some hungry painter, that for bread
With rotten chalk or coal upon a wall
Will well design thee, to be viewed of all   *represent*
That sit upon the common draught or strand: *privy/gutter*
Thy forehead is too narrow for my brand.

ODE

If men and times were now
  Of that true face   *appearance*
As when they both were great, and both knew how
  That fortune to embrace
By cherishing the spirits that gave their greatness grace:
  I then could raise my notes
  Loud to the wondering throng
And better blazon them than all their coats,[12]
  That were the happy subject of my song.   *display*

10 But clownish pride hath got
  So much the start   *advantage*
Of civil virtue, that he now is not
  Nor can be of desert   *worth*
That hath not a country impudence enough to laugh at art:
  Whilst like a blaze of straw
  He dies with an ill scent
To every sense, and scorn to those that saw
How soon with a self-tickling he was spent.[13]

11 The "friend" in question is Inigo Jones (1573–1652), Jonson's one-time collaborator in producing masques for the royal court. They quarreled after many years of working together, and Jonson lost his royal patronage as a result. The poem is an adaptation of Martial, *Epigrams* 12.41.

12 i.e. heraldic coats of arms.

13 i.e. How soon his self-regarding products become tiresome.

20

Break then thy quills, blot out
    Thy long-watched verse,
And rather to the fire than to the rout
    Thy laboured tunes rehearse,   *finely wrought*
Whose air will sooner hell, than their dull senses, pierce:
    Thou that dost spend thy days
    To get thee a lean face
And come forth worthy ivy or the bays,   *i.e. poetic rewards*
And, in this age, canst hope no other grace.

30

Yet since the bright and wise
    Minerva[14] deigns
Upon so humbled earth to cast her eyes,   *i.e. body*
    We'll rip our richest veins
And once more strike the ear of time with those fresh strains
    As shall, besides delight
    And cunning of their ground,   *melody*
Give cause to some of wonder, some despite,
But unto more, despair to imitate their sound.

40

Throw, holy virgin, then
    Thy crystal shield[15]
About this isle, and charm the round,[16] as when
    Thou mad'st in open field
The rebel giants stoop,[17] and gorgon envy yield;
    Cause reverence, if not fear,
    Throughout their general breasts,
And, by their taking, let it once appear
Who worthy win, who not, to be wise Paleas' guests.   *i.e. Athena's*

John Donne (1572–1631)

Donne was related both from birth and by marriage to the most celebrated Roman Catholic of the English Renaissance, Thomas More. But Donne formally rejected Catholicism and became one of the greatest Protestant preachers in the history of the English Church. His father, a tradesman, died when he was three years old, leaving him (so he later thought) to be indoctrinated by Jesuits. The suppression of Roman Catholicism under Elizabeth led the Jesuits, mistakenly in Donne's view, to become infatuated with martyrdom. His own place in these conflicts led him to the interest in suicide that he records in *Biathanatos*. John Carey is not alone among Donne's biographers in thinking that his apostasy shaped his life and his thought. His early education was at Hart Hall, Oxford, and Lincoln's Inn. Before his secret marriage to Anne More in 1601, after which her father had him imprisoned for two months, he accompanied the Earl of Essex to the Azores. In 1615 he

was ordained and received his Doctorate of Divinity at Cambridge. Six years later he was named Dean of St. Paul's, a post he held for the next decade, until his death. The brilliant sermons he preached contributed as much to his fame as the poems he wrote, especially one of his final performances in which he wore his death shroud into the pulpit. This sense of a divided persona – Doctor John Donne, Dean of St. Paul's Cathedral, London; and Jack Donne, author of some of the most sexually explicit love poems in English – is not a misleading way to think of the man and his work.

Two hundred years after Donne's birth, Samuel Johnson coined the term "metaphysical poets" to account for Abraham Cowley, Donne, and others. They were "men of learning, and to show their learning was their whole endeavour," according to Johnson. The way they did this was by wit, "philosophically considered as a kind of *dis-*

---

14 The goddess of wisdom (see gazetteer).
15 Minerva gave a mirrored shield to Perseus to help him kill the gorgon Medusa, whose glance turned people to stone.

16 The word "round" here means both "the whole country" and a type of song.
17 A reference to the giants who rebelled against the rule of the Olympian gods.

cordia concors; a combination of dissimilar images, or discovery of occult resemblances in things apparently unlike." In other words, Donne stretches the ground of comparison between the two parts of his metaphors (tenor and vehicle) to such an extreme that they seemed to Johnson to be "yoked by violence together." That in Donne which was infuriating to Johnson's neo-classical sensibility became highly prized by such modern poets as T. S. Eliot. But Eliot may have been as extreme in his admiration as Johnson was in his condemnation, for in Eliot's view Donne represents a key point in the history of Western consciousness. Unlike later poets who dissociate feeling from thought, Donne's sensibility was undissociated; for him thought was an experience that modified his sensibility. In Donne's poetry, the more intense the thought the more intense the feeling.

That is why it is often productive to paraphrase his poems, as here for "Air and Angels":

I loved you two or three times before I knew your face or your name. So it is that angels – in a voice or a flame – affect us and are worshiped. Nevertheless, when I came to where you were, I saw there "some lovely glorious nothing." But since my soul, whose child is love, assumes a body of flesh (without which it could do nothing); and since love (my soul's child) is subtler than my soul, who is its parent – love must not just be, but also take on bodily form. Therefore, I direct love to ask what you were and who you are, so that love {my soul's offspring} might assume a body and "fix" itself "in thy lip, eye, and brow."

Thus, while I thought to "ballast" love by returning it to bodies in order to stabilize it with cargo {"wares"} that would sink admiration by transforming it into desire, I recognized that I had overloaded love's boat. Even a single strand of your hair for love to work upon is too much, and so something "fitter must be sought." Neither in nothing but in things, neither in extremely intense nor in scattered light can love inhere." Therefore, as an angel wears a face and wings of air, so your love may be my love's celestial sphere.

Exactly such a disparity as exists between the purity of air and that of angels exists forever between women's love and men's.

Just as there is no antipathy between emotion and thought in Donne's poetry, so is there none between faith and spiritual method. As powerfully as Donne resisted the

Jesuits' thinking about martyrdom, he welcomed and incorporated their spiritual exercises into his poetic practice. Soon after their composition in 1521–41, the *Spiritual Exercises* of St. Ignatius Loyola were employed throughout Europe, typically for morning and afternoon meditation, with a special four-week period set aside each year for more intense practice. The *Exercises* were adapted in various ways, but the meditative sequence of Fray Luis de Granada appears to have been typical: "(1) the knowledge of ourselves and of our sins; (2) the miseries of this life; (3) the hour of death; (4) the Day of Judgement; (5) the pains of Hell; (6) the glory and felicity of the Kingdom of Heaven; (7) the benefits of God" (Martz, p. 26). These exercises are often presupposed in Donne's religious poetry, especially in his "Holy Sonnets" (which are titled "Devine Meditations" in some of the early manuscripts) and in "Good Friday, 1613. Riding Westward."

The meditative tradition left its mark on Donne's prose as well. Each of his *Devotions* (1624), for example, follows the same structural sequence as illustrated in XVII. Nunc Lento Solitu Dicunt, Morieris ("Now this bell tolling softly for another, says to me: Thou must die"). Each of the *Devotions* opens with a meditation on the human condition, which is then followed by an expostulation and a prayer. Izaak Walton, one of Donne's earliest biographers, described the *Devotions* as "A sacred picture of spiritual ecstasies writ on his sick-bed, herein imitating the holy Patriarchs, who were wont to build their altars in that place where they had received their blessings." Donne died seven years later, soon after posing for a drawing of himself in his shroud.

READING

John Carey, *John Donne: Life, Mind, and Art*.
Thomas Docherty, *John Donne Undone*.
T. S. Eliot, "The Metaphysical Poets."
Samuel Johnson, *The Lives of the Poets*.
Louis L. Martz, *The Poetry of Meditation*.

M. P.

SONGS AND SONNETS

AIR AND ANGELS

Twice or thrice had I loved thee
Before I knew thy face or name;
So in a voice, so in a shapeless flame,
Angels affect us oft, and worshipped be;
    Still when to where thou wert I came
Some lovely glorious nothing I did see;
    But since my soul, whose child love is,
Takes limbs of flesh, and else could nothing do,
    More subtle than the parent is

10   Love must not be, but take a body too,
 And therefore what thou wert and who
  I bid love ask, and now
 That it assume thy body I allow,
 And fix itself in thy lip, eye, and brow.

 Whilst thus to ballast love I thought,
 And so more steadily to have gone,
  With wares which would sink admiration
 I saw I had love's pinnace overfraught: *sailboat*
  Every thy hair for love to work upon
20   Is much too much, some fitter must be sought;
  For nor in nothing nor in things
 Extreme and scatt'ring bright can love inhere;
  Then as an angel face and wings
 Of air – not pure as it, yet pure – doth wear,
  So thy love may be my love's sphere;
   Just such disparity
 As is 'twixt air and angels' purity
 'Twixt women's love and men's will ever be.

THE ANNIVERSARY

 All kings, and all their favourites,
 All glory of honours, beauties, wits,
The sun itself, which makes times as they pass,
Is elder by a year, now, than it was
 When thou and I first one another saw.
All other things to their destruction draw;
 Only our love hath no decay;
This no tomorrow hath, nor yesterday;
Running it never runs from us away,
10   But truly keeps his first, last, everlasting day.

 Two graves must hide thine and my corse;
 If one might, death were no divorce.
Alas, as well as other princes, we
(Who prince enough in one another be)
 Must leave at last in death these eyes and ears
Oft fed with true oaths and with sweet salt tears;
 But souls where nothing dwells but love
(All other thoughts being inmates) then shall prove
This or a love increasèd there above,
20   When bodies to their graves, souls from their graves remove.

 And then we shall be throughly bless'd,
 But we no more than all the rest.
Here upon earth we're kings, and none but we
Can be such kings, nor of such subjects be;
 Who is so safe as we, where none can do
Treason to us except one of us two?
 True and false fears let us refrain;
Let us love nobly, and live, and add again
Years and years unto years, till we attain
30   To write threescore; this is the second of our reign.

THE APPARITION

When by thy scorn, O murd'ress, I am dead,
And that thou think'st thee free
From all solicitation from me,
Then shall my ghost come to thy bed,
And thee, feigned vestal, in worse arms shall see.
Then thy sick taper will begin to wink,
And he whose thou art then, being tired before,
Will, if thou stir, or pinch to wake him, think
    Thou call'st for more,
10   And in false sleep will from thee shrink.
And then, poor aspen wretch, neglected thou   *trembling*
Bathed in a cold quicksilver sweat wilt lie
    A verier ghost than I.
What I will say, I will not tell thee now,
Lest that preserve thee; and since my love is spent,
I had rather thou shouldst painfully repent,
Than by my threatenings rest still innocent.

THE BAIT[1]

Come live with me, and be my love,
And we will some new pleasures prove
Of golden sands, and crystal brooks,
With silken lines, and silver hooks.

There will the river whispering run
Warmed by thy eyes more than the sun.
And there the enamoured fish will stay,
Begging themselves they may betray.

When thou wilt swim in that live bath,
Each fish, which every channel hath,
10   Will amorously to thee swim,
Gladder to catch thee than thou him.

If thou to be so seen be'st loath
By sun or moon, thou dark'nest both,
And if myself have leave to see,
I need not their light, having thee.

Let others freeze with angling reeds,
And cut their legs with shells and weeds,
Or treacherously poor fish beset
20   With strangling snare or windowy net;

Let coarse bold hands from slimy nest
The bedded fish in banks outwrest,
Or curious traitors, sleavesilk flies,[2]
Bewitch poor fishes' wandering eyes.

THE BAIT
1 This poem parodies Marlowe's "The Passionate Shepherd to his
Love" (1599) and Raleigh's "The Nymph's Reply" (1600).

2 Artificial flies made out of unraveled silk.

For thee, thou need'st no such deceit,
For thou thyself art thine own bait;
That fish that is not catched thereby,
Alas, is wiser far than I.

THE BLOSSOM

Little think'st thou, poor flower,
    Whom I have watched six or seven days,
And seen thy birth, and seen what every hour
Gave to thy growth, thee to this height to raise,
And now dost laugh and triumph on this bough,
    Little think'st thou
That it will freeze anon, and that I shall
Tomorrow find thee fall'n, or not at all.

Little think'st thou, poor heart,
    That labour'st yet to nestle thee,
And think'st by hovering here to get a part
In a forbidden or forbidding tree,
And hop'st her stiffness by long siege to bow,
    Little think'st thou,
That thou tomorrow, ere that sun doth wake,
Must with this sun and me a journey take.

But thou, which lov'st to be
    Subtle to plague thyself, wilt say,
'Alas, if you must go, what's that to me?
Here lies my business, and here I will stay.
You go to friends, whose love and means present
    Various content
To your eyes, ears, and tongue, and every part.
If then your body go, what need you a heart?'

Well then, stay here; but know,
    When thou hast stayed and done thy most,
A naked thinking heart, that makes no show,
Is to a woman but a kind of ghost;
How shall she know my heart, or, having none,
    Know thee for one?
Practice may make her know some other part,
But take my word, she doth not know a heart.

Meet me at London, then,
    Twenty days hence, and thou shalt see
Me fresher, and more fat, by being with men,
Than if I had stayed still with her and thee.
For God's sake, if you can, be you so too:
    I would give you,
There, to another friend, whom we shall find
As glad to have my body as my mind.

BREAK OF DAY

'Tis true, 'tis day, what though it be?
O wilt thou therefore rise from me?

Why should we rise, because 'tis light?
Did we lie down because 'twas night?
Love, which in spite of darkness brought us hither,
Should in despite of light keep us together.

Light hath no tongue, but is all eye;
If it could speak as well as spy,
This were the worst that it could say,
That, being well, I fain would stay,
And that I loved my heart and honour so,
That I would not from him that had them go.

Must business thee from hence remove?
Oh, that's the worst disease of love;
The poor, the foul, the false, love can
Admit, but not the busied man.
He which hath business, and makes love, doth do
Such wrong as when a married man doth woo.

THE BROKEN HEART

He is stark mad, whoever says
    That he hath been in love an hour;
Yet not that love so soon decays,
    But that it can ten in less space devour;
Who will believe me if I swear
That I have had the plague a year?
    Who would not laugh at me if I should say
    I saw a flask of powder burn a day?

Ah, what a trifle is a heart,
    If once into Love's hands it come!
All other griefs allow a part
    To other griefs, and ask themselves but some;
They come to us, but us Love draws;
He swallows us, and never chaws;
    By him, as by chained shot, whole ranks do die;
    He is the tyrant pike, our hearts the fry.

If 'twere not so, what did become
    Of my heart when I first saw thee?
I brought a heart into the room,
    But from the room I carried none with me;
If it had gone to thee, I know
Mine would have taught thy heart to show
    More pity unto me; but Love, alas,
    At one first blow did shiver it as glass.

Yet nothing can to nothing fall,
    Nor any place be empty quite;
Therefore I think my breast hath all
    Those pieces still, though they be not unite;
And now, as broken glasses show
A hundred lesser faces, so
    My rags of heart can like, wish, and adore,
    But after one such love can love no more.

THE CANONIZATION

For God's sake hold your tongue, and let me love,
  Or chide my palsy or my gout,
My five grey hairs or ruined fortune flout;
    With wealth your state, your mind with arts improve;
      Take you a course, get you a place,
      Observe his Honour, or his Grace,
Or the King's real, or his stamped face
    Contemplate; what you will, approve,
    So you will let me love.

10   Alas, alas, who's injured by my love?
    What merchant's ships have my sighs drowned?
Who says my tears have overflowed his ground?
    When did my colds a forward spring remove?
      When did the heats which my veins fill
      Add one more to the plaguy bill?
Soldiers find wars, and lawyers find out still
    Litigious men which quarrels move,
    Though she and I do love.

Call us what you will, we are made such by love;
20   Call her one, me another fly;
We 're tapers too, and at our own cost die,
    And we in us find the eagle and the dove.
      The phoenix riddle hath more wit
      By us; we two, being one, are it.
So to one neutral thing both sexes fit.
    We die and rise the same, and prove
    Mysterious by this love.

We can die by it, if not live by love;
    And if unfit for tombs and hearse
30   Our legend be, it will be fit for verse;
    And if no piece of chronicle we prove,
      We'll build in sonnets pretty rooms;
      As well a well-wrought urn becomes   *befits*
The greatest ashes as half-acre tombs.
    And by these hymns, all shall approve
    Us canonized for love:

And thus invoke us: 'You whom reverend love
    Made one another's hermitage;
You to whom love was peace, that now is rage;
40   Who did the whole world's soul contract, and drove
      Into the glasses of your eyes
      (So made such mirrors and such spies
That they did all to you epitomize)
    Countries, towns, courts: beg from above
    A pattern of your love!'

COMMUNITY

Good we must love, and must hate ill,
For ill is ill and good good still;

But there are things indifferent,
Which we may neither hate nor love,
But one and then another prove,
    As we shall find our fancy bent.

If then at first wise Nature had
Made women either good or bad,
    Then some we might hate and some choose;
10 But since she did them so create
That we may neither love nor hate,
    Only this rests, all all may use.

If they were good it would be seen;
Good is as visible as green,
    And to all eyes itself betrays.
If they were bad they could not last;
Bad doth itself and others waste.
    So they deserve nor blame nor praise.

But they are ours as fruits are ours;
20 He that but tastes, he that devours,
    And he that leaves all, doth as well.
Changed loves are but changed sorts of meat,
And when he hath the kernel eat,
    Who doth not fling away the shell?

The Computation

For the first twenty years since yesterday
    I scarce believed thou couldst be gone away.
For forty more I fed on favours past,
    And forty on hopes that thou wouldst they might last.
Tears drowned one hundred, and sighs blew out two;
    A thousand I did neither think nor do,
    Or not divide, all being one thought of you;
    Or in a thousand more, forgot that too.
Yet call not this long life; but think that I
10 Am, by being dead, immortal; can ghosts die?

The Curse

Whoever guesses, thinks, or dreams he knows
Who is my mistress, wither by this curse:
    His only, and only his purse
    May some dull heart to love dispose,
And she yield then to all that are his foes;
    May he be scorned by one whom all else scorn,
    Forswear to others what to her he hath sworn,
    With fear of missing, shame of getting, torn;

Madness his sorrow, gout his cramps, may he
10 Make, by but thinking who hath made him such:
    And may he feel no touch
    Of conscience but of fame, and be
Anguished not that 'twas sin, but that 'twas she;

In early and long scarceness may he rot,
For land which had been his, if he had not
Himself incestuously an heir begot;

May he dream treason, and believe that he
Meant to perform it, and confess, and die,
    And no record tell why;
20   His sons, which none of his may be,
Inherit nothing but his infamy;
    Or may he so long parasites have fed,
That he would fain be theirs whom he hath bred,
And at the last be circumcized for bread;

The venom of all stepdames, gamesters' gall,
What tyrants and their subjects interwish,
      What plants, mines, beasts, fowl, fish,
      Can contribute, all ill which all
Prophets or poets spake; and all which shall
30   Be annexed in schedules unto this by me,
    Fall on that man; for if it be a she
    Nature beforehand hath outcursèd me.

The Damp

When I am dead, and doctors know not why,
    And my friends' curiosity
Will have me cut up to survey each part,
When they shall find your picture in my heart,
      You think a sudden damp of love   *noxious fume*
      Will thorough all their senses move,
And work on them as me, and so prefer
Your murder to the name of massacre.

Poor victories; but if you dare be brave,
10   And pleasure in your conquest have,
First kill th' enormous giant your Disdain,
And let th' enchantress Honour next be slain,
      And like a Goth and Vandal rise,
      Deface records and histories
Of your own arts and triumphs over men,
And without such advantage kill me then.

For I could muster up as well as you
    My giants and my witches too,
Which are vast Constancy and Secretness,
20 But these I neither look for nor profess;
      Kill me as woman, let me die
      As a mere man; do you but try
Your passive valour, and you shall find then,
Naked you've odds enough of any man.

The Dissolution

She's dead; and all which die
    To their first elements resolve;

And we were mutual elements to us,
    And made of one another.
    My body then doth hers involve,
And those things whereof I consist hereby
In me abundant grow and burdenous,
    And nourish not, but smother.
    My fire of passion, sighs of air,
Water of tears, and earthy sad despair,
    Which my materials be,
But near worn out by love's security,
She, to my loss, doth by her death repair,
    And I might live long wretched so
But that my fire doth with my fuel grow.
    Now as those active kings
    Whose foreign conquest treasure brings
Receive more, and spend more, and soonest break:
This (which I am amazed that I can speak)
    This death hath with my store
    My use increased.
And so my soul more earnestly released,
Will outstrip hers; as bullets flown before
A latter bullet may o'ertake, the powder being more.

THE DREAM

Dear love, for nothing less than thee
Would I have broke this happy dream.
    It was a theme
For reason, much too strong for fantasy,
Therefore thou waked'st me wisely; yet
My dream thou brok'st not, but continued'st it;
Thou art so true, that thoughts of thee suffice,
To make dreams truths, and fables histories;
Enter these arms, for since thou thought'st it best
Not to dream all my dream, let's act the rest.

As lightning, or a taper's light,
Thine eyes and not thy noise waked me;
    Yet I thought thee
(For thou lov'st truth) an angel, at first sight;
But when I saw thou saw'st my heart,
And knew'st my thoughts, beyond an angel's art,
When thou knew'st what I dreamt, when thou knew'st
    when
Excess of joy would wake me, and cam'st then,
I must confess it could not choose but be
Profane to think thee anything but thee.

Coming and staying showed thee thee,
But rising makes me doubt that now
    Thou art not thou.
That love is weak where fear's as strong as he;
'Tis not all spirit, pure, and brave,
If mixture it of fear, shame, honour, have.
Perchance as torches which must ready be
Men light and put out, so thou deal'st with me;

Thou cam' st to kindle, go'st to come; then I
Will dream that hope again, but else would die.

THE ECSTASY[3]

Where, like a pillow on a bed,
   A pregnant bank swelled up, to rest
The violet's reclining head,
   Sat we two, one another's best;

Our hands were firmly cemented
   With a fast balm which thence did spring;
Our eye-beams twisted, and did thread
   Our eyes upon one double string;

So to intergraft our hands, as yet,
10   Was all our means to make us one,
And pictures in our eyes to get
   Was all our propagation.

As 'twixt two equal armies Fate
   Suspends uncertain victory,
Our souls, which to advance their state
   Were gone out, hung 'twixt her and me;

And whilst our souls negotiate there,
   We like sepulchral statues lay;
All day the same our postures were,
20   And we said nothing all the day.

If any, so by love refined
   That he souls' language understood,
And by good love were grown all mind,
   Within convenient distance stood,

He (though he knew not which soul spake,
   Because both meant, both spake the same)
Might thence a new concoction take,
   And part far purer than he came.

This ecstasy doth unperplex
30   (We said) and tell us what we love;
We see by this, it was not sex,
   We see, we saw not what did move;

But as all several souls contain   *distinct*
   Mixture of things, they know not what,
Love these mixed souls doth mix again,
   And makes both one, each this and that.

A single violet transplant,
   The strength, the colour, and the size,
All which before was poor and scant,
40   Redoubles still and multiplies.

3 A mystically transcendent, out-of-body experience; rapture.

When love with one another so
  Interinanimates two souls,
That abler soul which thence doth flow
  Defects of loneliness controls.

We, then, who are this new soul, know
  Of what we are composed and made,
For th' atomies of which we grow
  Are souls whom no change can invade.

But O, alas, so long, so far,
50 Our bodies why do we forbear?
They're ours, though they're not we, we are
  The intelligences, they the sphere.

We owe them thanks because they thus
  Did us to us at first convey,
Yielded their forces, sense, to us,
  Nor are dross to us, but allay.   *alloy*

On man heaven's influence works not so
  But that it first imprints the air;
So soul into the soul may flow,
60 Though it to body first repair.

As our blood labours to beget
  Spirits as like souls as it can,
Because such fingers need to knit
  That subtle knot which makes us man,

So must pure lovers' souls descend
  To affections, and to faculties,
Which sense may reach and apprehend,
  Else a great prince in prison lies.

To our bodies turn we then, that so
70 Weak men on love revealed may look;
Love's mysteries in souls do grow,
  But yet the body is his book.

And if some lover such as we
  Have heard this dialogue of one,
Let him still mark us, he shall see
  Small change when we're to bodies gone.

THE EXPIRATION

So, so, break off this last lamenting kiss,
  Which sucks two souls, and vapours both away;
Turn thou ghost that way, and let me turn this,
  And let ourselves benight our happiest day.
We asked none leave to love; nor will we owe
  Any so cheap a death as saying, Go.

Go; and if that word have not quite killed thee,
  Ease me with death by bidding me go too.

10   Or if it have, let my word work on me,
          And a just office on a murderer do.
     Except it be too late to kill me so,
          Being double dead, going and bidding go.

A FEVER

O do not die, for I shall hate
     All women so, when thou art gone,
That thee I shall not celebrate
     When I remember thou wast one.

But yet thou canst not die, I know;
     To leave this world behind is death,
But when thou from this world wilt go
     The whole world vapours with thy breath.

10   Or if, when thou, the world's soul, go'st,
          It stay, 'tis but thy carcass then,
     The fairest woman but thy ghost,
          But corrupt worms the worthiest men.

O wrangling schools, that search what fire
     Shall burn this world, had none the wit
Unto this knowledge to aspire,
     That this her fever might be it?

And yet she cannot waste by this,
     Nor long bear this torturing wrong,
For much corruption needful is
20   To fuel such a fever long.

These burning fits but meteors be,
     Whose matter in thee is soon spent.
Thy beauty and all parts which are thee
     Are unchangeable firmament.

Yet 'twas of my mind, seizing thee,
     Though it in thee cannot persever.
For I had rather owner be
     Of thee one hour, than all else ever.

THE FLEA

Mark but this flea, and mark in this,
How little that which thou deny'st me is;
It sucked me first, and now sucks thee,
And in this flea our two bloods mingled be;[4]
Thou know'st that this cannot be said
A sin, nor shame, nor loss of maidenhead,
     Yet this enjoys before it woo,
     And pampered swells with one blood made of two,
     And this, alas, is more than we would do.

4   An Aristotelian tradition held that intercourse involved a mingling
of bloods.

10

Oh stay, three lives in one flea spare,
Where we almost, nay more than married are.
This flea is you and I, and this
Our marriage bed and marriage temple is;
Though parents grudge, and you, we're met
And cloistered in these living walls of jet.
      Though use make you apt to kill me,
      Let not to this self-murder added be,
      And sacrilege, three sins in killing three.

20

Cruel and sudden, hast thou since
Purpled thy nail in blood of innocence?
Wherein could this flea guilty be
Except in that drop which it sucked from thee?
Yet thou triumph'st, and say'st that thou
Find'st not thyself nor me the weaker now.
      'Tis true; then learn how false fears be;
      Just so much honour, when thou yield'st to me,
      Will waste as this flea's death took life from thee.

The Funeral

Whoever comes to shroud me, do not harm
      Nor question much
That subtle wreath of hair, which crowns my arm,   *fine*
The mystery, the sign you must not touch;
      For 'tis my outward soul,
Viceroy to that which, then to heaven being gone,
      Will leave this to control
And keep these limbs, her provinces, from dissolution.

10

For if the sinewy thread my brain lets fall
      Through every part
Can tie those parts, and make me one of all,
These hairs which upward grew, and strength and art
      Have from a better brain,
Can better do't; except she meant that I
      By this should know my pain,
As prisoners then are manacled when they're condemned to
   die.

20

What'er she meant by't, bury it with me,
      For since I am
Love's martyr, it might breed idolatry
If into others' hands these relics came;
      As 'twas humility
To afford to it all that a soul can do,
      So 'tis some bravery
That since you would save none of me I bury some of you.

The Good-Morrow

I wonder, by my troth, what thou and I
      Did till we loved? were we not weaned till then,
But sucked on country pleasures, childishly?   *nursed*

Or snorted we in the seven sleepers' den?
'Twas so; but this, all pleasures fancies be.
If ever any beauty I did see,
Which I desired, and got, 'twas but a dream of thee.

And now good-morrow to our waking souls,
    Which watch not one another out of fear;
For love all love of other sights controls,
    And makes one little room an everywhere.
Let sea-discoverers to new worlds have gone,
Let maps to others worlds on worlds have shown,
Let us possess one world, each hath one, and is one.

My face in thine eye, thine in mine appears,
    And true plain hearts do in the faces rest;
Where can we find two better hemispheres
    Without sharp north, without declining west?
Whatever dies, was not mixed equally;
    If our two loves be one, or thou and I
Love so alike that none do slacken, none can die.

THE INDIFFERENT

I can love both fair and brown,
Her whom abundance melts, and her whom want betrays,
Her who loves loneness best, and her who masques and plays,
Her whom the country formed, and whom the town,
Her who believes, and her who tries,
Her who still weeps with spongy eyes,
And her who is dry cork and never cries;
I can love her and her, and you and you;
I can love any, so she be not true.

Will no other vice content you?
Will it not serve your turn to do as did your mothers?
Have you old vices spent, and now would find out others?
Or doth a fear that men are true torment you?
Oh we are not, be not you so,
Let me, and do you, twenty know.
Rob me, but bind me not, and let me go.
Must I, who came to travel thorough you,
Grow your fixed subject because you are true?

Venus heard me sigh this song,
And by love's sweetest part, variety, she swore
She heard not this till now; it should be so no more.
She went, examined, and returned ere long,
And said, 'Alas, some two or three
Poor heretics in love there be,
Which think to stablish dangerous constancy.
But I have told them, "Since you will be true,
You shall be true to them, who're false to you." '

A LECTURE UPON THE SHADOW

Stand still, and I will read to thee
A lecture, love, in love's philosophy.

These three hours that we have spent
    Walking here, two shadows went
Along with us, which we ourselves produced;
But now the sun is just above our head
    We do those shadows tread,
    And to brave clearness all things are reduced.
So whilst our infant loves did grow,
Disguises did, and shadows, flow
From us and our care; but now 'tis not so.

That love hath not attained the high'st degree,
Which is still diligent lest others see.

Except our loves at this noon stay,
We shall new shadows make the other way.
    As the first were made to blind
    Others, these which come behind
Will work upon ourselves, and blind our eyes.
If our loves faint, and westwardly decline,
    To me thou, falsely, thine,
    And I to thee mine actions shall disguise.
The morning shadows wear away,
But these grow longer all the day,
But oh, love's day is short, if love decay.

Love is a growing or full constant light,
And his first minute after noon is night.

THE LEGACY

When I died last (and, dear, I die
    As often as from thee I go),
    Though it be an hour ago,
And lovers' hours be full eternity,
I can remember yet that I
    Something did say, and something did bestow;
Though I be dead which sent me, I should be
Mine own executor and legacy.

I heard me say, 'Tell her anon,
    That my self' (that's you, not I)
    'Did kill me,' and when I felt me die,
I bid me send my heart, when I was gone;
But I alas could there find none,
    When I had ripped me, and searched where hearts should
        lie;
It killed me again, that I, who still was true
In life, in my last will should cozen you.   *deceive*

Yet I found something like a heart,
    But colours it and corners had;
    It was not good, it was not bad;
It was entire to none, and few had part.
As good as could be made by art
    It seemed; and therefore, for our losses sad,
I meant to send this heart instead of mine,
But oh, no man could hold it, for 'twas thine.

LOVERS' INFINITENESS

If yet I have not all thy love,
Dear, I shall never have it all;
I cannot breathe one other sigh, to move,
Nor can entreat one other tear to fall;
All my treasure, which should purchase thee,
Sighs, tears, and oaths, and letters, I have spent;
Yet no more can be due to me,
Than at the bargain made was meant.
If then thy gift of love were partial,
That some to me, some should to others fall,
    Dear, I shall never have thee all.

Or if then thou gav'st me all,
All was but all which thou hadst then;
But if in thy heart, since, there be or shall
New love created be by other men,
Which have their stocks entire, and can in tears,
In sighs, in oaths, and letters, outbid me,
This new love may beget new fears,
For this love was not vowed by thee.
And yet it was, thy gift being general;
The ground, thy heart, is mine; whatever shall
    Grow there, dear, I should have it all.

Yet I would not have all yet,
He that hath all can have no more,
And since my love doth every day admit
New growth, thou shouldst have new rewards in store.
Thou canst not every day give me thy heart:
If thou canst give it, then thou never gav'st it.
Love's riddles are that though thy heart depart
It stays at home, and thou with losing sav'st it;
But we will have a way more liberal
Than changing hearts, to join them; so we shall
    Be one, and one another's all.

LOVE'S ALCHEMY

Some that have deeper digged love's mine than I,
Say where his centric happiness doth lie.   *essential*
    I have loved, and got, and told,
But should I love, get, tell, till I were old,
I should not find that hidden mystery;
    Oh, 'tis imposture all.
And as no chemic yet the elixir got,   *alchemist*
    But glorifies his pregnant pot
    If by the way to him befall
Some odoriferous thing, or med'cinal,
    So lovers dream a rich and long delight,
    But get a winter-seeming summer's night.

Our ease, our thrift, our honour, and our day,
Shall we for this vain bubble's shadow pay?
    Ends love in this, that any man

Can be as happy as I can, if he can
Endure the short scorn of a bridegroom's play?
   That loving wretch that swears
'Tis not the bodies marry, but the minds,
    Which he in her angelic finds,
   Would swear as justly that he hears
In that day's rude hoarse minstrelsy the spheres.
   Hope not for mind in women; at their best
   Sweetness and wit, they're but mummy, possessed.

LOVE'S DEITY

I long to talk with some old lover's ghost
   Who died before the god of love was born:
I cannot think that he who then loved most
   Sunk so low as to love one which did scorn.
But since this god produced a destiny,
And that vice-nature custom lets it be,
   I must love her that loves not me.

Sure, they which made him god meant not so much,
   Nor he in his young godhead practised it,
But when an even flame two hearts did touch,
   His office was indulgently to fit
Actives to passives. Correspondency
Only his subject was; it cannot be
   Love, till I love her that loves me.

But every modern god will now extend
   His vast prerogative as far as Jove.
To rage, to lust, to write to, to commend,
   All is the purlieu of the god of love.
O, were we wakened by this tyranny
To ungod this child again, it could not be
   I should love her who loves not me.

Rebel and atheist too, why murmur I,
   As though I felt the worst that love could do?
Love might make me leave loving, or might try
   A deeper plague, to make her love me too,
Which, since she loves before, I'm loath to see;
Falsehood is worse than hate; and that must be,
   If she whom I love should love me.

LOVE'S DIET

To what a cumbersome unwieldiness
And burdenous corpulence my love had grown,
   But that I did, to make it less,
   And keep it in proportion,
Give it a diet, made it feed upon
That which love worst endures, discretion.

Above one sigh a day I allowed him not,
Of which my fortune and my faults had part;

And if sometimes by stealth he got
10   A she-sigh from my mistress' heart,
    And thought to feast on that, I let him see
    'Twas neither very sound, nor meant to me.   *genuine*

If he wrung from me a tear, I brined it so
With scorn or shame, that him it nourished not;
    If he sucked hers, I let him know
    'Twas not a tear which he had got;
His drink was counterfeit, as was his meat;
For eyes which roll towards all weep not, but sweat.

Whatever he would dictate, I writ that,
20   But burnt my letters; when she writ to me,
    And that that favour made him fat,
    I said, 'If any title be
Conveyed by this, ah, what doth it avail,
To be the fortieth name in an entail?'

Thus I reclaimed my buzzard love, to fly
At what, and when, and how, and where I choose;
    Now negligent of sport I lie,
    And now, as other falconers use,
I spring a mistress, swear, write, sigh and weep,
30 And, the game killed or lost, go talk and sleep.

LOVE'S EXCHANGE

    Love, any devil else but you,
Would for a given soul give something too.
    At court your fellows every day
Give th' art of rhyming, huntsmanship, and play,
    For them who were their own before;
    Only I have nothing which gave more,
But am, alas, by being lowly, lower.

    I ask not dispensation now
To falsify a tear, or sigh, or vow;
10   I do not sue from thee to draw
A *non obstante* on nature's law;
    These are prerogatives, they inhere
    In thee and thine; none should forswear
Except that he Love's minion were.

    Give me thy weakness, make me blind
Both ways, as thou and thine, in eyes and mind;
    Love, let me never know that this
Is love, or that love childish is.
    Let me not know that others know
20   That she knows my pain, lest that so
A tender shame make me mine own new woe.

    If thou give nothing, yet thou'rt just,
Because I would not thy first motions trust;
    Small towns which stand stiff till great shot
Enforce them, by war's law condition not.

Such in love's warfare is my case,
 I may not article for grace,
Having put Love at last to show this face.

 This face by which he could command
And change the idolatry of any land,
 This face which wheresoe'er it comes
Can call vowed men from cloisters, dead from tombs,
  And melt both poles at once, and store
  Deserts with cities, and make more
Mines in the earth, than quarries were before.

 For this Love is enraged with me,
Yet kills not. If I must example be
 To future rebels, if th' unborn
Must learn by my being cut up and torn,
  Kill and dissect me, Love, for this
  Torture against thine own end is:
Racked carcasses make ill anatomies.[5]

LOVE'S GROWTH

I scarce believe my love to be so pure
  As I had thought it was,
  Because it doth endure
Vicissitude and season, as the grass;
Methinks I lied all winter, when I swore
My love was infinite, if spring make it more.
But if this medicine love, which cures all sorrow
With more, not only be no quintessence,
But mixed of all stuffs paining soul or sense,
And of the sun his working vigour borrow,
Love's not so pure and abstract as they use
To say which have no mistress but their Muse,
But as all else, being elemented too,
Love sometimes would contemplate, sometimes do.

And yet not greater, but more eminent,
  Love by the spring is grown;
  As, in the firmament,
Stars by the sun are not enlarged, but shown.
Gentle love-deeds, as blossoms on a bough,
From love's awakened root do bud out now.
If, as in water stirred more circles be
Produced by one, love such additions take,
Those, like so many spheres, but one heaven make,
For they are all concentric unto thee;
And though each spring do add to love new heat,
As princes do in times of action get
New taxes, and remit them not in peace,
No winter shall abate the spring's increase.

5 Bodies that have been stretched on the rack are ill suited for
anatomical dissection.

LOVE'S USURY

For every hour that thou wilt spare me now,
    I will allow,
Usurious God of Love, twenty to thee,
When with my brown my grey hairs equal be;
Till then, Love, let my body reign, and let
Me travel, sojourn, snatch, plot, have, forget,
Resume my last year's relict, think that yet   *remains*
    We'd never met.

Let me think any rival's letter mine,
    And at next nine
Keep midnight's promise; mistake by the way
The maid, and tell the lady of that delay;
Only let me love none, no, not the sport;
From country grass to comfitures of court
Or city's *quelque-choses*, let report
    My mind transport.

This bargain's good; if when I'm old, I be
    Inflamed by thee,
If thine own honour, or my shame, or pain,
Thou covet, most at that age thou shalt gain.
Do thy will then, then subject and degree
And fruit of love, Love, I submit to thee;
Spare me till then, I'll bear it, though she be
    One that loves me.

THE MESSAGE

Send home my long-strayed eyes to me,
Which, O, too long have dwelt on thee.
Yet since there they've learned such ill,
    Such forced fashions
    And false passions
      That they be
      Made by thee
Fit for no good sight, keep them still.

Send home my harmless heart again,
Which no unworthy thought could stain.
But if it be taught by thine
    To make jestings
    Of protestings,
      And cross both
      Word and oath,
Keep it, for then 'tis none of mine.

Yet send me back my heart and eyes,
That I may know and see thy lies,
And may laugh and joy when thou
    Art in anguish
    And dost languish
      For some one
      That will none,
Or prove as false as thou art now.

NEGATIVE LOVE

I never stooped so low as they
Which on an eye, cheek, lip, can prey;
   Seldom to them which soar no higher
   Than virtue or the mind to admire;
For sense and understanding may
   Know what gives fuel to their fire.
My love, though silly, is more brave,   *foolish*
For may I miss whene'er I crave,
If I know yet what I would have.

10   If that be simply perfectest
Which can by no way be expressed
   But negatives, my love is so.
   To all which all love I say no.
If any who decipher best
   What we know not, ourselves, can know,
Let him teach me that nothing; this
As yet my ease and comfort is,
Though I speed not, I cannot miss.

A NOCTURNAL UPON ST LUCY'S DAY, BEING THE SHORTEST DAY[6]

'Tis the year's midnight, and it is the day's,
Lucy's, who scarce seven hours herself unmasks;
   The sun is spent, and now his flasks
   Send forth light squibs, no constant rays;
     The world's whole sap is sunk:
The general balm th' hydroptic earth hath drunk,
Whither, as to the bed's-feet, life is shrunk,
Dead and interred; yet all these seem to laugh,
Compared with me, who am their epitaph.

10   Study me then, you who shall lovers be
At the next world, that is, at the next spring:
   For I am every dead thing
   In whom Love wrought new alchemy.
     For his art did express
A quintessence even from nothingness,
From dull privations, and lean emptiness;
He ruined me, and I am re-begot
Of absence, darkness, death; things which are not.

20   All others from all things draw all that's good,
Life, soul, form, spirit, whence they being have;
   I, by love's limbeck, am the grave   *alembic*
   Of all that's nothing. Oft a flood
     Have we two wept, and so
Drowned the whole world, us two; oft did we grow
To be two chaoses, when we did show

6 December 13th was mistakenly thought to be the shortest day of
the year (the winter solstice).

Care to aught else; and often absences
Withdrew our souls, and made us carcasses.

But I am by her death (which word wrongs her)
Of the first nothing the elixir grown;
30   Were I a man, that I were one
    I needs must know; I should prefer,
        If I were any beast,
Some ends, some means; yea plants, yea stones detest,
And love; all, all some properties invest;
If I an ordinary nothing were,
As shadow, a light and body must be here.

But I am none; nor will my sun renew.
You lovers, for whose sake the lesser sun
    At this time to the Goat is run
40   To fetch new lust, and give it you,
        Enjoy your summer all;
Since she enjoys her long night's festival,
Let me prepare towards her, and let me call
This hour her vigil and her eve, since this
Both the year's and the day's deep midnight is.

THE PARADOX

No lover saith 'I love', nor any other
    Can judge a perfect lover;
He thinks that else none can, nor will agree
    That any loves but he:
I cannot say I loved, for who can say
    He was killed yesterday?
Love with excess of heat, more young than old,
    Death kills with too much cold;
We die but once, and who loved last did die,
10   He that saith twice, doth lie:
For though he seem to move and stir a while,
    It doth the sense beguile.
Such life is like the light which bideth yet
    When the light's life is set,
Or like the heat which fire in solid matter
    Leaves behind two hours after.
Once I loved and died; and am now become
    Mine epitaph and tomb.
Here dead men speak their last, and so do I;
20   Love-slain, lo, here I lie.

THE PRIMROSE

Upon this primrose hill,
    Where, if heaven would distil
A shower of rain, each several drop might go
To his own primrose, and grow manna so,
And where their form and their infinity
    Make a terrestrial galaxy,
    As the small stars do in the sky,

I walk to find a true-love; and I see
That 'tis not a mere woman that is she,
10   But must or more or less than woman be.

Yet know I not which flower
I wish; a six, or fours.[7]
For should my true-love less than woman be,
She were scarce anything; and then, should she
Be more than woman, she would get above
All thought of sex, and think to move
My heart to study her, and not to love.
Both these were monsters; since there must reside
Falsehood in woman, I could more abide
20   She were by art than nature falsified.

Live, primrose, then, and thrive
With thy true number, five;
And women, whom this flower doth represent,
With this mysterious number be content.
Ten is the farthest number; if half ten
Belong unto each woman, then
Each woman may take half us men;
Or if this will not serve their turn, since all
Numbers are odd or even, and they fall
30   First into this, five, women may take us all.

THE PROHIBITION

Take heed of loving me;
At least remember I forbade it thee;
Not that I shall repair my unthrifty waste
Of breath and blood upon thy sighs and tears
By being to thee then what to me thou wast;
But so great joy our life at once outwears.
Then lest thy love by my death frustrate be,
If thou love me, take heed of loving me.

Take heed of hating me,
10   Or too much triumph in the victory;
Not that I shall be mine own officer,
And hate with hate again retaliate;
But thou wilt lose the style of conqueror
If I, thy conquest, perish by thy hate.
Then lest my being nothing lessen thee,
If thou hate me, take heed of hating me.

Yet love and hate me too;
So these extremes shall neither's office do;
Love me, that I may die the gentler way;   i.e. by orgasm
20   Hate me, because thy love's too great for me;
Or let these two themselves, not me, decay;
So shall I live thy stay, not triumph be.
Lest thou thy love and hate and me undo,
To let me live, O, love and hate me too.

7 Six-petaled, four-petaled, whereas primroses commonly are
five-petaled.

THE RELIC

When my grave is broke up again
Some second guest to entertain
(For graves have learned that womanhead
To be to more than one a bed),
    And he that digs it spies
A bracelet of bright hair about the bone,
    Will he not let's alone,
And think that there a loving couple lies,
Who thought that this device might be some way
10   To make their souls, at the last busy day,
Meet at this grave, and make a little stay?

    If this fall in a time or land
    Where mis-devotion doth command,
    Then he that digs us up will bring
    Us to the bishop and the king,
        To make us relics; then
Thou shalt be a Mary Magdalen,[8] and I
    A something else thereby;
All women shall adore us, and some men;
20   And since at such time miracles are sought,
I would have that age by this paper taught
What miracles we harmless lovers wrought.

    First, we loved well and faithfully,
    Yet knew not what we loved, nor why.
    Difference of sex no more we knew,
    Than our guardian angels do.
        Coming and going, we
Perchance might kiss, but not between those meals.
        Our hands ne'er touched the seals
30   Which nature, injured by late law, sets free.
These miracles we did; but now, alas,
All measure and all language I should pass,
Should I tell what a miracle she was.

SONG

Go and catch a falling star,
    Get with child a mandrake root,   *fork-rooted plant*
Tell me where all past years are,
    Or who cleft the Devil's foot,
Teach me to hear mermaids singing,
Or to keep off envy's stinging,
        And find
        What wind
Serves to advance an honest mind.

10   If thou be'st borne to strange sights,
    Things invisible to see,
Ride ten thousand days and nights,
    Till age snow white hairs on thee;

---

8   A sexually attractive saint.

Thou, when thou return'st, wilt tell me
All strange wonders that befell thee,
    And swear
    Nowhere
Lives a woman true and fair.

If thou find'st one, let me know;
  Such a pilgrimage were sweet.
Yet do not, I would not go,
  Though at next door we might meet.
Though she were true when you met her,
And last till you write your letter,
    Yet she
    Will be
False, ere I come, to two or three.

SONG

Sweetest love, I do not go
  For weariness of thee,
Nor in hope the world can show
  A fitter love for me;
    But since that I
Must die at last, 'tis best
To use my self in jest
    Thus by feigned deaths to die.

Yesternight the sun went hence,
  And yet is here today;
He hath no desire nor sense,
  Nor half so short a way;
    Then fear not me,
But believe that I shall make
Speedier journeys, since I take
    More wings and spurs than he.

O how feeble is man's power,
  That if good fortune fall,
Cannot add another hour,
  Nor a lost hour recall!
    But come bad chance,
And we join to it our strength,
And we teach it art and length,
    Itself o'er us t'advance.

When thou sigh'st, thou sigh'st not wind,
  But sigh'st my soul away,
When thou weep'st, unkindly kind,
  My life's blood doth decay.
    It cannot be
That thou lov'st me, as thou say'st,
If in thine my life thou waste:
    Thou art the best of me.

Let not thy divining heart
  Forethink me any ill;
                                         foreseeing

Destiny may take thy part,
And may thy fears fulfil.
But think that we
Are but turned aside to sleep;
They who one another keep
40   Alive ne'er parted be.

THE SUN RISING

Busy old fool, unruly sun,
Why dost thou thus
Through windows and through curtains call on us?
Must to thy motions lovers' seasons run?
Saucy pedantic wretch, go chide
Late schoolboys and sour prentices;
Go tell court-huntsmen that the king will ride;
Call country ants to harvest offices;
Love, all alike, no season knows nor clime,
10   Nor hours, days, months, which are the rags of time.

Thy beams so reverend and strong
Why shouldst thou think?
I could eclipse and cloud them with a wink,
But that I would not lose her sight so long.
If her eyes have not blinded thine,
Look, and tomorrow late, tell me;
Whether both th' Indias, of spice and mine,
Be where thou left'st them, or lie here with me.
Ask for those kings whom thou saw'st yesterday,
20   And thou shalt hear, all here in one bed lay.

She's all states, and all princes I;
Nothing else is.
Princes do but play us; compared to this,
All honour's mimic, all wealth alchemy.
Thou, sun, art half as happy as we,
In that the world's contracted thus;
Thine age asks ease, and since thy duties be
To warm the world, that's done in warming us.
Shine here to us, and thou art everywhere;
30   This bed thy centre is, these walls thy sphere.

TWICKENHAM GARDEN[9]

Blasted with sighs and surrounded with tears,
Hither I come to seek the spring,
And at mine eyes and at mine ears
Receive such balms as else cure everything;
But O, self-traitor, I do bring
The spider love, which transubstantiates all,
And can convert manna to gall,
And that this place may thoroughly be thought
True paradise, I have the serpent brought.

9   From 1607 to 1618 Twickenham Park was the home of Donne's
patroness, Lucy Countess of Bedford.

10 'Twere wholesomer for me that winter did
  Benight the glory of this place,
  And that a grave frost did forbid
These trees to laugh and mock me to my face;
  But that I may not this disgrace
Endure, nor yet leave loving, Love, let me
  Some senseless piece of this place be:
Make me a mandrake, so I may groan here,
  Or a stone fountain weeping out my year.

20 Hither with crystal vials, lovers, come,
  And take my tears, which are love's wine,
  And try your mistress' tears at home,
For all are false that taste not just like mine;
  Alas, hearts do not in eyes shine,
Nor can you more judge woman's thoughts by tears
  Than by her shadow what she wears.
O perverse sex, where none is true but she,
  Who's therefore true, because her truth kills me.

THE UNDERTAKING

I have done one braver thing
  Than all the Worthies did,   *celebrated warriors*
And yet a braver thence doth spring,
  Which is, to keep that hid.

It were but madness now t' impart
  The skill of specular stone,
When he which can have learned the art
  To cut it can find none.

10 So if I now should utter this,
  Others (because no more
Such stuff to work upon there is)
  Would love but as before.

But he who loveliness within
  Hath found all outward loathes,
For he who colour loves, and skin,
  Loves but her oldest clothes.

If, as I have, you also do
  Virtue attired in woman see,
And dare love that, and say so too,
20   And forget the He and She;

And if this love, though placèd so,
  From profane men you hide,
Which will no faith on this bestow,
  Or, if they do, deride:

Then you have done a braver thing
  Than all the Worthies did,
And a braver thence will spring,
  Which is, to keep that hid.

A VALEDICTION: FORBIDDING MOURNING

As virtuous men pass mildly away,
    And whisper to their souls to go,
Whilst some of their sad friends do say,
    The breath goes now, and some say, no,

So let us melt, and make no noise,
    No tear-floods nor sigh-tempests move;
'Twere profanation of our joys
    To tell the laity our love.

Moving of th' earth brings harms and fears,
10   Men reckon what it did and meant,
But trepidation of the spheres,
    Though greater far, is innocent.

Dull sublunary lovers' love
    (Whose soul is sense) cannot admit
Absence, because it doth remove
    Those things which elemented it.

But we, by a love so much refined
    That ourselves know not what it is
Inter-assurèd of the mind,
20   Care less eyes, lips, and hands to miss.

Our two souls, therefore, which are one,
    Though I must go, endure not yet
A breach, but an expansion,
    Like gold to airy thinness beat.

If they be two, they are two so
    As stiff twin compasses are two;   *dividers*
Thy soul, the fixed foot, makes no show
    To move, but doth, if th' other do.

And though it in the centre sit,
30   Yet when the other far doth roam,
It leans and hearkens after it,
    And grows erect as that comes home.

Such wilt thou be to me, who must
    Like th' other foot obliquely run;
Thy firmness makes my circle just,
    And makes me end where I begun.

A VALEDICTION: OF WEEPING

Let me pour forth
My tears before thy face, whilst I stay here,
For thy face coins them, and thy stamp they bear,
And by this mintage they are something worth,
    For thus they be
    Pregnant of thee;

Fruits of much grief they are, emblems of more;
When a tear falls, that thou falls which it bore;
So thou and I are nothing then, when on a diverse shore.

10   On a round ball
A workman that hath copies by can lay
An Europe, Afric, and an Asia,
And quickly make that which was nothing all;
   So doth each tear,
   Which thee doth wear,
A globe, yea world, by that impression grow,
Till thy tears mixed with mine do overflow
This world, by waters sent from thee, my heaven dissolvèd so.

     O more than moon,
20 Draw not up seas to drown me in thy sphere,
Weep me not dead in thine arms, but forbear
To teach the sea what it may do too soon;
   Let not the wind
   Example find
To do me more harm than it purposeth;
Since thou and I sigh one another's breath,
Whoe'er sighs most is cruellest, and hastes the other's death.

THE WILL

Before I sigh my last gasp, let me breathe,
Great Love, some legacies; here I bequeath
Mine eyes to Argus,[10] if mine eyes can see;
If they be blind, then, Love, I give them thee;
My tongue to Fame; to ambassadors mine ears;
   To women or the sea my tears.
Thou, Love, hast taught me heretofore,
By making me serve her who had twenty more,
That I should give to none but such as had too much before.

10   My constancy I to the planets give;
My truth to them who at the court do live;
Mine ingenuity and openness
To Jesuits;[11] to buffoons my pensiveness;
My silence to any who abroad hath been;
   My money to a Capuchin.[12]
Thou, Love, taught'st me, by appointing me
To love there where no love received can be,
Only to give to such as have an incapacity.

   My faith I give to Roman Catholics;
20 All my good works unto the schismatics
Of Amsterdam; my best civility
And courtship to an university;
My modesty I give to soldiers bare;
   My patience let gamesters share.

10 A mythological giant with eyes all over his body, making him the
spy of the gods; he was killed for spying on Jove's mistress.

11 Members of the Jesuit Order with a reputation for casuistry.

12 Capuchins take a vow of poverty.

Thou, Love, taught'st me, by making me
Love her that holds my love disparity,
Only to give to those that count my gifts indignity.

I give my reputation to those
Which were my friends; mine industry to foes;
30   To schoolmen I bequeath my doubtfulness;
My sickness to physicians, or excess;
To Nature, all that I in rhyme have writ;
     And to my company my wit.
Thou, Love, by making me adore
Her who begot this love in me before,
Taught'st me to make as though I gave, when I did but
     restore.

To him for whom the passing bell next tolls,
I give my physic books; my written rolls   *medical*
Of moral counsels I to Bedlam[13] give;
40   My brazen medals unto them which live
In want of bread; to them which pass among
     All foreigners mine English tongue.
Thou, Love, by making me love one
Who thinks her friendship a fit portion
For younger lovers, dost my gifts thus disproportion.

Therefore I'll give no more; but I'll undo
The world by dying; because Love dies too.
Then all your beauties will be no more worth
Than gold in mines, where none doth draw it forth;
50   And all your graces no more use shall have
     Than a sundial in a grave.
Thou, Love, taught'st me, by making me
Love her who doth neglect both me and thee,
T' invent and practise this one way t' annihilate all three.

WOMAN'S CONSTANCY

Now thou hast loved me one whole day,
Tomorrow, when thou leav'st, what wilt thou say?
Wilt thou then antedate some new-made vow?
     Or say that now
We are not just those persons which we were?
Or that oaths made in reverential fear
Of Love, and his wrath, any may forswear?
Or as true deaths true marriages untie,
So lovers' contracts, images of those,
10   Bind but till sleep, death's image, them unloose?
     Or, your own end to justify,
For having purposed change and falsehood, you
Can have no way but falsehood to be true?
Vain lunatic, against these 'scapes I could
     Dispute, and conquer, if I would,
     Which I abstain to do,
For by tomorrow I may think so too.

---

13   Bethlehem Hospital for the insane in London.

ELEGIES

ELEGY 1 JEALOUSY

Fond woman, which wouldst have thy husband die,
And yet complain'st of his great jealousy;
If swoll'n with poison he lay in his last bed,
His body with a sere-bark coverèd,
Drawing his breath as thick and short as can
The nimblest crotcheting musician,
Ready with loathsome vomiting to spew
His soul out of one hell into a new,
Made deaf with his poor kindred's howling cries,
10   Begging with few feigned tears great legacies,
Thou wouldst not weep, but jolly and frolic be
As a slave which tomorrow should be free;
Yet weep'st thou when thou seest him hungerly
Swallow his own death, heart's-bane jealousy.
O give him many thanks, he's courteous,
That in suspecting kindly warneth us.
We must not, as we used, flout openly,
In scoffing riddles, his deformity;
Nor at his board together being sat,
20   With words, nor touch, scarce looks adulterate;
Nor when he, swoll'n and pampered with great fare,
Sits down and snorts, caged in his basket chair,
Must we usurp his own bed any more,
Nor kiss and play in his house, as before.
Now I see many dangers; for that is
His realm, his castle, and his diocese.
But if, as envious men, which would revile
Their prince, or coin his gold, themselves exile
Into another country, and do it there,
30   We play in another house, what should we fear?
There we will scorn his household policies,
His silly plots, and pensionary spies,
As the inhabitants of Thames' right side
Do London's Mayor; or Germans, the Pope's pride.[1]

ELEGY 2 THE ANAGRAM

Marry and love thy Flavia, for she
Hath all things whereby others beauteous be;
For, though her eyes be small, her mouth is great;
Though they be ivory, yet her teeth are jet;
Though they be dim, yet she is light enough;   *wanton*
And though her harsh hair fall, her skin is rough;
What though her cheeks be yellow, her hair's red;
Give her thine, and she hath a maidenhead.
These things are beauty's elements; where these

ELEGIES

ELEGY 1 JEALOUSY

1.   Southwark was the only part of the South Bank of the Thames that
fell under the Lord Mayor's control; in the 16th century the German
states led in opposing the Pope.

10   Meet in one, that one must, as perfect, please.
If red and white and each good quality
Be in thy wench, ne'er ask where it doth lie.
In buying things perfumed, we ask if there
Be musk and amber in it, but not where.
Though all her parts be not in th' usual place,
She hath yet an anagram of a good face.
If we might put the letters but one way,
One like none, and liked of none, fittest were,
For things in fashion every man will wear.

ELEGY 3 CHANGE

Although thy hand and faith, and good works too,
Have sealed thy love which nothing should undo,
Yea though thou fall back, that apostasy
Confirm thy love; yet much, much I fear thee.
Women are like the arts, forced unto none,
Open to all searchers, unprized if unknown.
If I have caught a bird, and let him fly,
Another fowler using these means, as I,
May catch the same bird; and, as these things be,
10   Women are made for men, not him, nor me.
Foxes and goats, all beasts change when they please;
Shall women, more hot, wily, wild than these,
Be bound to one man, and did Nature then
Idly make them apter t' endure than men?
They're our clogs, not their own; if a man be
Chained to a galley, yet the galley's free;
Who hath a plough-land casts all his seed corn there,
And yet allows his ground more corn should bear;
Though Danuby into the sea must flow,
20   The sea receives the Rhine, Volga, and Po.
By nature, which gave it, this liberty
Thou lov'st, but O, canst thou love it and me?
Likeness glues love: then, if so thou do,
To make us like and love, must I change too?
More than thy hate I hate it; rather let me
Allow her change, than change as oft as she,
And so not teach but force my opinion
To love not any one, nor every one.
To live in one land is captivity;
30   To run all countries, a wild roguery;
Waters stink soon if in one place they bide,
And in the vast sea are worse putrefied:
But when they kiss one bank and, leaving this,
Never look back, but the next bank do kiss,
Then are they purest; change is the nursery
Of music, joy, life and eternity.

ELEGY 9 THE AUTUMNAL

No spring nor summer beauty hath such grace
As I have seen in one autumnal face.
Young beauties force your love, and that's a rape;

This doth but counsel, yet you cannot scape.
If 'twere a shame to love, here 'twere no shame;
Affection here takes reverence's name.
Were her first years the Golden Age, that's true,
But now she's gold oft tried, and ever new.
That was her torrid and inflaming time,
This is her tolerable tropic clime.
Fair eyes, who asks more heat than comes from hence,
He in a fever wishes pestilence.
Call not these wrinkles graves; if graves they were,
They were Love's graves, for else he is nowhere.
Yet lies not Love dead here, but here doth sit
Vowed to this trench, like an anachorit.   *anchorite*
And here, till hers, which must be his death, come,
He doth not dig a grave, but build a tomb.
Here dwells he; though he sojourn everywhere
In progress, yet his standing house is here,
Here, where still evening is; not noon, nor night;
Where no voluptuousness, yet all delight.
In all her words, unto all hearers fit,
You may at revels, you at council, sit.
This is Love's timber, youth his underwood;
There he, as wine in June, enrages blood,
Which then comes seasonabliest, when our taste
And appetite to other things is past.
Xerxes' strange Lydian love, the platane tree,[2]
Was loved for age, none being so large as she,
Or else because, being young, nature did bless
Her youth with age's glory, barrenness.
If we love things long sought, age is a thing
Which we are fifty years in compassing;
If transitory things, which soon decay,
Age must be loveliest at the latest day.
But name not winter-faces, whose skin's slack;
Lank as an unthrift's purse; but a soul's sack;
Whose eyes seek light within, for all here's shade;
Whose mouths are holes, rather worn out than made;
Whose every tooth to a several place is gone,
To vex their souls at resurrection;
Name not these living death's-heads unto me,
For these not ancient but antics be.
I hate extremes; yet I had rather stay
With tombs than cradles, to wear out a day.
Since such love's natural lation[3] is, may still
My love descend and journey down the hill,
Not panting after growing beauties, so,
I shall ebb on with them who homeward go.

10
20
30
40
50

ELEGY 16 ON HIS MISTRESS

By our first strange and fatal interview,
By all desires which thereof did ensue,
By our long starving hopes, by that remorse

2 According to Herodotus, Xerxes greatly loved a plane tree that he   3 Astronomical term for the movement of a body.
found in Lydia.

Which my words' masculine persuasive force
Begot in thee, and by the memory
Of hurts which spies and rivals threatened me,
I calmly beg; but by thy parents' wrath,
By all pains which want and divorcement hath,
I conjure thee; and all those oaths which I
10   And thou have sworn to seal joint constancy,
Here I unswear, and overswear them thus,
Thou shalt not love by means so dangerous.
Temper, O fair love, love's impetuous rage,
Be my true mistress still, not my feigned page.
I'll go, and, by thy kind leave, leave behind
Thee, only worthy to nurse in my mind
Thirst to come back; O, if thou die before,
From other lands my soul towards thee shall soar.
Thy else almighty beauty cannot move
20   Rage from the seas, nor thy love teach them love,
Nor tame wild Boreas' harshness; thou hast read
How roughly he in pieces shiverèd
Fair Orithea, whom he swore he loved.[4]
Fall ill or good, 'tis madness to have proved
Dangers unurged; feed on this flattery,
That absent lovers one in th' other be.
Dissemble nothing, not a boy, nor change
Thy body's habit, nor mind's; be not strange
To thy self only; all will spy in thy face
30   A blushing womanly discovering grace;
Richly clothed apes are called apes, and as soon
Eclipsed as bright we call the moon the moon.
Men of France, changeable chameleons,
Spitals of diseases, shops of fashions,   *Hospitals*
Love's fuellers, and the rightest company
Of players which upon the world's stage be,
Will quickly know thee, and know thee; and, alas,
Th' indifferent Italian, as we pass
His warm land, well content to think thee page,
40   Will haunt thee with such lust and hideous rage
As Lot's fair guests were vexed. But none of these,
Nor spongy hydroptic Dutch, shall thee displease   *insatiably thirsty*
If thou stay here. Oh stay here, for for thee
England is only a worthy gallery,
To walk in expectation, till from thence
Our great King call thee into his presence.
When I am gone, dream me some happiness,
Nor let thy looks our long-hid love confess,
Nor praise nor dispraise me, nor bless nor curse
50   Openly love's force, nor in bed fright thy nurse
With midnight's startings, crying out, 'Oh, oh,
Nurse, O my love is slain, I saw him go
O'er the white Alps alone; I saw him, I,
Assailed, fight, taken, stabbed, bleed, fall, and die.'
Augur me better chance, except dread Jove
Think it enough for me to have had thy love.

4   Boreas, the god of the north wind in Greek mythology, kidnapped
Orithyia when her father refused to allow them to marry.

ELEGY 18 LOVE'S PROGRESS

Whoever loves, if he do not propose
The right true end of love, he's one that goes
To sea for nothing but to make him sick.
Love is a bear-whelp born; if we over-lick
Our love, and force it new strange shapes to take,
We err, and of a lump a monster make.
Were not a calf a monster that were grown
Faced like a man, though better than his own?
Perfection is in unity: prefer

10 One woman first, and then one thing in her.
I, when I value gold, may think upon
The ductileness, the application,
The wholesomeness, the ingenuity,
From rust, from soil, from fire ever free,
But if I love it, 'tis because 'tis made
By our new nature, use, the soul of trade.
    All these in women we might think upon
(If women had them) and yet love but one.
Can men more injure women than to say

20 They love them for that by which they are not they?
Makes virtue woman? must I cool my blood
Till I both be and find one wise and good?
May barren angels love so. But if we
Make love to woman, virtue is not she,
As beauty's not, nor wealth. He that strays thus
From her to hers, is more adulterous
Than if he took her maid. Search every sphere
And firmament, our Cupid is not there.
He's an infernal god and underground

30 With Pluto dwells, where gold and fire abound.
Men to such gods their sacrificing coals
Did not in altars lay, but pits and holes.
Although we see celestial bodies move
Above the earth, the earth we till and love:
So we her airs contemplate, words and heart,
And virtues; but we love the centric part.
    Nor is the soul more worthy or more fit
For love than this, as infinite as it.
But in attaining this desirèd place

40 How much they stray, that set out at the face!
The hair a forest is of ambushes,
Of springes, snares, fetters and manacles;
The brow becalms us when 'tis smooth and plain,
And when 'tis wrinkled shipwrecks us again;
Smooth, 'tis a paradise, where we would have
Immortal stay, and wrinkled 'tis our grave.
The nose like to the first meridian runs
Not 'twixt an east and west, but 'twixt two suns;
It leaves a cheek, a rosy hemisphere,

50 On either side, and then directs us where
Upon the Islands Fortunate we fall
(Not faint Canaries, but Ambrosial),
Her swelling lips; to which when we are come,
We anchor there, and think ourselves at home,
For they seem all: there sirens' songs, and there

Wise Delphic oracles do fill the ear;
There in a creek where chosen pearls do swell,
The remora, her cleaving tongue, doth dwell.
These, and the glorious promontory, her chin,
60 O'erpast, and the strait Hellespont between
The Sestos and Abydos of her breasts,
(Not of two lovers, but two Loves the nests)
Succeeds a boundless sea, but that thine eye
Some island moles may scattered there descry,
And sailing towards her India, in that way
Shall at her fair Atlantic navel stay;
Though thence the current be thy pilot made,
Yet ere thou be where thou wouldst be embayed,
Thou shalt upon another forest set,
70 Where many shipwreck, and no further get.
When thou art there, consider what this chase
Misspent by thy beginning at the face.
　　Rather set out below, practise my art.
Some symmetry the foot hath with that part
Which thou dost seek, and is thy map for that,
Lovely enough to stop, but not stay at;
Least subject to disguise and change it is;
Men say the Devil never can change his;
It is the emblem that hath figurèd
80 Firmness; 'tis the first part that comes to bed.　　　　*stability*
Civility, we see, refined the kiss,
Which, at the face begun, transplanted is
Since to the hand, since to the imperial knee,
Now at the papal foot delights to be.
If kings think that the nearer way, and do
Rise from the foot, lovers may do so too;
For as free spheres move faster far than can
Birds, whom the air resists, so may that man
Which goes this empty and ethereal way,
90 Than if at beauty's elements he stay.
Rich Nature hath in women wisely made
Two purses, and their mouths aversely laid;
They then, which to the lower tribute owe,
That way which that exchequer looks must go.
He which doth not, his error is as great
As who by clyster gave the stomach meat.

ELEGY 19 TO HIS MISTRESS GOING TO BED

Come, Madam, come, all rest my powers defy;
Until I labour, I in labour lie.
The foe oft-times, having the foe in sight,
Is tired with standing though he never fight.
Off with that girdle, like heaven's zone glistering,
But a far fairer world encompassing.
Unpin that spangled breastplate which you wear　　　　*stomacher*
That th' eyes of busy fools may be stopped there.
Unlace yourself, for that harmonious chime
10 Tells me from you, that now 'tis your bed time.
Off with that happy busk, which I envy,
That still can be, and still can stand so nigh.
Your gown going off, such beauteous state reveals

As when from flowery meads th' hills' shadow steals.
Off with that wiry coronet and show
The hairy diadem which on you doth grow;
Now off with those shoes, and then safely tread
In this Love's hallowed temple, this soft bed.
In such white robes heaven's angels used to be
20 Received by men; thou angel bring'st with thee
A heaven like Mahomet's paradise; and though
Ill spirits walk in white, we easily know
By this these angels from an evil sprite —   *women*
Those set our hairs, but these our flesh upright.
 Licence my roving hands, and let them go
Before, behind, between, above, below.
O my America, my new found land,
My kingdom, safeliest when with one man manned,
My mine of precious stones, my empery,
30 How bless'd am I in this discovering thee!
To enter in these bonds is to be free;
Then where my hand is set my seal shall be.
 Full nakedness, all joys are due to thee.
As souls unbodied, bodies unclothed must be,
To taste whole joys. Gems which you women use
Are like Atlanta's balls, cast in men's views,
That when a fool's eye lighteth on a gem,
His earthly soul may covet theirs, not them.
Like pictures, or like books' gay coverings made
40 For laymen, are all women thus arrayed;
Themselves are mystic books, which only we
Whom their imputed grace will dignify
Must see revealed. Then since that I may know,
As liberally as to a midwife show
Thyself: cast all, yea, this white linen hence;
There is no penance due to innocence.
 To teach thee, I am naked first; why then,
What need'st thou have more covering than a man?

THE FIRST ANNIVERSARY: AN ANATOMY OF THE WORLD

WHEREIN, BY OCCASION OF THE
UNTIMELY DEATH OF MISTRESS
ELIZABETH DRURY,[1] THE FRAILTY
AND THE DECAY OF THIS WHOLE
WORLD IS REPRESENTED

When that rich soul which to her heaven is gone,
Whom all they celebrate who know they 've one
(For who is sure he hath a soul, unless
It see, and judge, and follow worthiness,
And by deeds praise it? he who doth not this,
May lodge an inmate soul, but 'tis not his),
When that queen ended here her progress time,   *ceremonial journey*

THE FIRST ANNIVERSARY: AN ANATOMY OF THE WORLD
1 Elizabeth Drury, daughter of Sir Robert Drury, died early in December 1610, shortly before her fifteenth birthday. Donne did not know her, which allowed him, as he explained to Ben Jonson, to treat her as "the Idea of a Woman and not as she was." In his definitive study of the poem, Frank Manley observes that the poem consists of a succession of three structural units: (1) a meditation on the decay of the world; (2) a eulogy for Elizabeth Drury as a lost pattern of virtue; and (3) a moral, urging the reader to forget the dying world. Each of these recurrent parts corresponds to a portion of the rational soul: memory, understanding, and will.

And, as t' her standing house, to heaven did climb,
Where loath to make the saints attend her long,
10 She's now a part both of the choir and song,
This world in that great earthquake languishèd;
For in a common bath of tears it bled,
Which drew the strongest vital spirits out.
But succoured then with a perplexèd doubt,
Whether the world did lose or gain in this
(Because since now no other way there is
But goodness, to see her whom all would see,
All must endeavour to be good as she),
This great consumption to a fever turned,
20 And so the world had fits; it joyed, it mourned.
And as men think that agues physic are,
And, th' ague being spent, give over care,
So thou, sick world, mistak'st thyself to be
Well, when, alas, thou'rt in a lethargy.
Her death did wound and tame thee then, and then
Thou mightst have better spared the sun, or man.
That wound was deep, but 'tis more misery
That thou hast lost thy sense and memory.
'Twas heavy then to hear thy voice of moan,
30 But this is worse, that thou art speechless grown.
Thou hast forgot thy name thou hadst; thou wast
Nothing but she, and her thou hast o'erpast.
For as a child kept from the font until
A prince, expected long, come to fulfil
The ceremonies, thou unnamed hadst laid,
Had not her coming thee her palace made:
Her name defined thee, gave thee form and frame,
And thou forget'st to celebrate thy name.
Some months she hath been dead (but being dead,
40 Measures of times are all determinèd),
But long she hath been away, long, long, yet none
Offers to tell us who it is that's gone.
But as in states doubtful of future heirs,
When sickness without remedy impairs
The present prince, they're loath it should be said
The prince doth languish, or the prince is dead,
So mankind feeling now a general thaw,
A strong example gone, equal to law,
The cement which did faithfully compact
50 And glue all virtues, now resolved and slacked,
Thought it some blasphemy to say she was dead;
Or that our weakness was discoverèd
In that confession; therefore spoke no more
Than tongues, the soul being gone, the loss deplore.
But though it be too late to succour thee,
Sick world, yea dead, yea putrefied, since she
Thy intrinsic balm and thy preservative
Can never be renewed, thou never live,
I (since no man can make thee live) will try
60 What we may gain by thy anatomy.
Her death hath taught us dearly that thou art
Corrupt and mortal in thy purest part.
Let no man say, the world itself being dead,
'Tis labour lost to have discoverèd
The world's infirmities, since there is none

Alive to study this dissection;
For there's a kind of world remaining still;
Though she which did inanimate and fill
The world be gone, yet in this last long night
Her ghost doth walk; that is, a glimmering light,
A faint weak love of virtue and of good
Reflects from her on them which understood
Her worth; and though she have shut in all day,
The twilight of her memory doth stay;
Which, from the carcass of the old world free,
Creates a new world; and new creatures be
Produced; the matter and the stuff of this,
Her virtue, and the form our practice is.
And though to be thus elemented arm
These creatures from home-born intrinsic harm
(For all assumed unto this dignity,
So many weedless paradises be,
Which of themselves produce no venomous sin,
Except some foreign serpent bring it in),
Yet, because outward storms the strongest break,
And strength itself by confidence grows weak,
This new world may be safer, being told
The dangers and diseases of the old:
For with due temper men do then forgo
Or covet things, when they their true worth know.
There is no health; physicians say that we
At best enjoy but a neutrality.
And can there be worse sickness than to know
That we are never well, nor can be so?
We are born ruinous: poor mothers cry
That children come not right nor orderly
Except they headlong come, and fall upon
An ominous precipitation.
How witty's ruin! how importunate
Upon mankind! It laboured to frustrate
Even God's purpose; and made woman, sent
For man's relief, cause of his languishment.
They were to good ends, and they are so still,
But accessory and principal in ill.
For that first marriage was our funeral:
One woman at one blow then killed us all,
And singly, one by one, they kill us now.
We do delightfully ourselves allow
To that consumption; and, profusely blind,
We kill ourselves, to propagate our kind.
And yet we do not that; we are not men:
There is not now that mankind which was then,
Whenas the sun and man did seem to strive
(Joint tenants of the world) who should survive;
When stag, and raven, and the long-lived tree,
Compared with man, died in minority;
When, if a slow-paced star had stol'n away
From the observer's marking, he might stay
Two or three hundred years to see't again,
And then make up his observation plain;
When, as the age was long, the size was great;
Man's growth confessed, and recompensed the meat;
So spacious and large that every soul

Did a fair kingdom and large realm control;
And when the very stature, thus erect,
Did that soul a good way towards heaven direct.
Where is this mankind now? Who lives to age
Fit to be made Methusalem[2] his page?
Alas, we scarce live long enough to try

130   Whether a new-made clock run right or lie.
Old grandsires talk of yesterday with sorrow,
And for our children we reserve tomorrow.
So short is life, that every peasant strives
In a torn house or field to have three lives.
And as in lasting, so in length is man
Contracted to an inch, who was a span;
For had a man at first in forests strayed,
Or shipwrecked in the sea, one would have laid
A wager that an elephant or whale

140   That met him would not hastily assail
A thing so equal to him; now, alas,
The fairies and the pygmies well may pass
As credible; mankind decays so soon,
We're scarce our fathers' shadows cast at noon.
Only death adds t' our length: nor are we grown
In stature to be men, till we are none.
But this were light, did our less volume hold
All the old text; or had we changed to gold
Their silver; or disposed into less glass

150   Spirits of virtue which then scattered was.
But 'tis not so: we're not retired, but damped;   *concentrated*
And as our bodies, so our minds are cramped;
'Tis shrinking, not close weaving, that hath thus
In mind and body both bedwarfèd us.
We seem ambitious God's whole work t' undo;
Of nothing he made us, and we strive too
To bring ourselves to nothing back; and we
Do what we can, to do't so soon as he.
With new diseases on ourselves we war,

160   And with new physic,[3] a worse engine far.
Thus man, this world's vice-emperor, in whom
All faculties, all graces are at home –
And if in other creatures they appear,
They're but man's ministers and legates there,
To work on their rebellions, and reduce
Them to civility and to man's use –
This man, whom God did woo, and loath t' attend
Till man came up, did down to man descend,
This man, so great that all that is is his,

170   Oh what a trifle and poor thing he is!
If man were anything, he's nothing now:
Help, or at least some time to waste, allow
T' his other wants, yet when he did depart
With her whom we lament, he lost his heart.
She of whom th' ancients seemed to prophesy,
When they called virtues by the name of she;
She in whom virtue was so much refined,
That for allay unto so pure a mind
She took the weaker sex; she that could drive

2   According to Genesis 5:27, he lived 969 years.   3   Medical writings of Paracelsus.

180   The poisonous tincture and the stain of Eve
         Out of her thoughts and deeds, and purify
         All, by a true religious alchemy;
         She, she is dead; she's dead: when thou know'st this,
         Thou know'st how poor a trifling thing man is,
         And learn'st thus much by our anatomy,
         The heart being perished, no part can be free.
         And that except thou feed (not banquet) on
         The supernatural food, religion,
         Thy better growth grows witherèd and scant;
190   Be more than man, or thou'rt less than an ant.
         Then, as mankind, so is the world's whole frame
         Quite out of joint, almost created lame:
         For before God had made up all the rest,
         Corruption entered, and depraved the best:
         It seized the angels, and then first of all
         The world did in her cradle take a fall,
         And turned her brains, and took a general maim
         Wronging each joint of th' universal frame.
         The noblest part, man, felt it first; and then
200   Both beasts and plants, cursed in the curse of man.
         So did the world from the first hour decay,
         That evening was beginning of the day,
         And now the springs and summers which we see
         Like sons of women after fifty be.
         And new philosophy calls all in doubt;[4]
         The element of fire is quite put out;
         The sun is lost, and th' earth, and no man's wit
         Can well direct him where to look for it.
         And freely men confess that this world's spent,
210   When in the planets and the firmament
         They seek so many new; they see that this
         Is crumbled out again to his atomies.   *atoms*
         'Tis all in pieces, all coherence gone,
         All just supply, and all relation:
         Prince, subject, father, son, are things forgot,
         For every man alone thinks he hath got
         To be a phoenix, and that there can be
         None of that kind of which he is, but he.
         This is the world's condition now, and now
220   She that should all parts to reunion bow,
         She that had all magnetic force alone
         To draw and fasten sundered parts in one;
         She whom wise nature had invented then
         When she observed that every sort of men
         Did in their voyage in this world's sea stray,
         And needed a new compass for their way;
         She that was best and first original
         Of all fair copies; and the general
         Steward to Fate; she whose rich eyes, and breast,
230   Gilt the West Indies, and perfumed the East;
         Whose having breathed in this world did bestow
         Spice on those isles, and bade them still smell so,   *East Indies*
         And that rich Indy which doth gold inter
         Is but as single money coined from her;
         She to whom this world must itself refer,

4   See the introduction to this volume.

As suburbs, or the microcosm of her,
She, she is dead; she's dead: when thou know'st this,
Thou know'st how lame a cripple this world is,
And learn'st thus much by our anatomy,
240   That this world's general sickness doth not lie
In any humour, or one certain part;
But as thou saw'st it rotten at the heart,
Thou seest a hectic fever hath got hold
Of the whole substance, not to be controlled,
And that thou hast but one way not to admit
The world's infection, to be none of it.
For the world's subtlest immaterial parts
Feel this consuming wound, and age's darts.
For the world's beauty is decayed or gone,
250   Beauty, that's colour and proportion.
We think the heavens enjoy their spherical,
Their round proportion embracing all,
But yet their various and perplexèd course,
Observed in diverse ages, doth enforce
Men to find out so many eccentric parts,
Such diverse downright lines, such overthwarts,
As disproportion that pure form. It tears
The firmament in eight-and-forty shares,[5]
And in those constellations there arise
260   New stars, and old do vanish from our eyes,
As though heaven suffered earthquakes, peace or war,
When new towns rise, and old demolished are.
They have impaled within a zodiac
The free-born sun, and keep twelve signs awake
To watch his steps; the goat and crab control,
And fright him back, who else to either pole
(Did not these tropics fetter him) might run:
For his course is not round; nor can the sun
Perfect a circle, or maintain his way
270   One inch direct; but where he rose today
He comes no more, but with a cozening line,
Steals by that point, and so is serpentine:
And seeming weary with his reeling thus,
He means to sleep, being now fall'n nearer us.
So, of the stars which boast that they do run
In circle still, none ends where he begun;
All their proportion's lame, it sinks, it swells,
For of meridians and parallels
Man hath weaved out a net, and this net thrown
280   Upon the heavens, and now they are his own.
Loath to go up the hill, or labour thus
To go to heaven, we make heaven come to us.
We spur, we rein the stars, and in their race
They're diversely content to obey our pace.
But keeps the earth her round proportion still?
Doth not a Tenerife,[6] or higher hill,
Rise so high like a rock, that one might think
The floating moon would shipwreck there, and sink?
Seas are so deep, that whales being struck today,
290   Perchance tomorrow, scarce at middle way
Of their wished journey's end, the bottom, die.

---

5   Ptolemy divided the stars into 48 constellations.   6   Volcanic peak, the Pico de Teyde, on the island of Tenerife.

And men, to sound depths, so much line untie
As one might justly think that there would rise
At end thereof one of th' Antipodes:
If under all a vault infernal be
(Which sure is spacious, except that we
Invent another torment, that there must
Millions into a strait hot room be thrust),
Then solidness and roundness have no place.
300 Are these but warts and pock-holes in the face
Of th' earth? Think so: but yet confess, in this
The world's proportion disfigured is,
That those two legs whereon it doth rely,
Reward and punishment, are bent awry.
And, O, it can no more be questionèd,
That beauty's best, proportion, is dead,
Since even grief itself, which now alone
Is left us, is without proportion.
She by whose lines proportion should be
310 Examined, measure of all symmetry,
Whom had that ancient seen, who thought souls made
Of harmony, he would at next have said
That harmony was she, and thence infer
That souls were but resultances from her,
And did from her into our bodies go,
As to our eyes the forms from objects flow:
She, who if those great doctors truly said
That th' Ark to man's proportions was made,
Had been a type for that, as that might be
320 A type of her in this, that contrary
Both elements and passions lived at peace
In her, who caused all civil war to cease.
She, after whom, what form soe'er we see
Is discord and rude incongruity;
She, she is dead; she's dead; when thou know'st this,
Thou know'st how ugly a monster this world is,
And learn'st thus much by our anatomy,
That here is nothing to enamour thee,
And that not only faults in inward parts,
330 Corruptions in our brains, or in our hearts,
Poisoning the fountains whence our actions spring,
Endanger us; but that if everything
Be not done fitly and in proportion,
To satisfy wise and good lookers-on
(Since most men be such as most think they be),
They're loathsome too, by this deformity.
For good and well must in our actions meet;
Wicked is not much worse than indiscreet.
But beauty's other second element,
340 Colour and lustre, now is as near spent,
And had the world his just proportion,
Were it a ring still, yet the stone is gone.
As a compassionate turquoise which doth tell,
By looking pale, the wearer is not well,
As gold falls sick being stung with mercury,
All the world's parts of such complexion be.
When nature was most busy, the first week,
Swaddling the new-born earth, God seemed to like
That she should sport herself sometimes and play,

350 To mingle and vary colours every day:
And then, as though she could not make enow,
Himself his various rainbow did allow.
Sight is the noblest sense of any one,
Yet sight hath only colour to feed on,
And colour is decayed: summer's robe grows
Dusky, and like an oft-dyed garment shows.
Our blushing red, which used in cheeks to spread,
Is inward sunk, and only our souls are red.
Perchance the world might have recoverèd,
360 If she whom we lament had not been dead:
But she, in whom all white, and red, and blue
(Beauty's ingredients) voluntary grew,
As in an unvexed paradise; from whom
Did all things' verdure and their lustre come,
Whose composition was miraculous,
Being all colour, all diaphanous
(For air and fire but thick gross bodies were,
And liveliest stones but drowsy and pale to her)
She, she is dead; she's dead: when thou know'st this,
370 Thou know'st how wan a ghost this our world is,
And learn'st thus much by our anatomy,
That it should more affright than pleasure thee;
And that, since all fair colour then did sink,
'Tis now but wicked vanity to think
To colour vicious deeds with good pretence,
Or with bought colours to illude men's sense.
Nor in aught more this world's decay appears,
Than that her influence the heaven forbears,
Or that the elements do not feel this,
380 The father or the mother barren is.
The clouds conceive not rain, or do not pour,
In the due birth-time, down the balmy shower.
Th' air doth not motherly sit on the earth,
To hatch her seasons, and give all things birth.
Spring-times were common cradles, but are tombs;
And false conceptions fill the general wombs.
Th' air shows such meteors, as none can see
Not only what they mean but what they be;
Earth such new worms, as would have troubled much
390 Th' Egyptian mages to have made more such.[7]   *magicians*
What artist now dares boast that he can bring
Heaven hither, or constellate anything,
So as the influence of those stars may be
Imprisoned in an herb, or charm, or tree,
And do by touch all which those stars could do?
The art is lost, and correspondence too.
For heaven gives little, and the earth takes less,
And man least knows their trade and purposes.
If this commerce 'twixt heaven and earth were not
400 Embarred, and all this traffic quite forgot,
She, for whose loss we have lamented thus,
Would work more fully and powerfully on us.
Since herbs and roots by dying lose not all,
But they, yea ashes too, are med'cinal,

7 See Exodus 7:10–12.

Death could not quench her virtue so, but that
It would be (if not followed) wondered at,
And all the world would be one dying swan,
To sing her funeral praise, and vanish then.
But as some serpents' poison hurteth not,
410   Except it be from the live serpent shot,
So doth her virtue need her here, to fit
That unto us; she working more than it.
But she, in whom to such maturity
Virtue was grown, past growth, that it must die;
She, from whose influence all impressions came,
But, by receivers' impotencies, lame;
Who, though she could not transubstantiate
All states to gold, yet gilded every state,
So that some princes have some temperance,
420   Some counsellors some purpose to advance
The common profit, and some people have
Some stay, no more than kings should give to crave,
Some women have some taciturnity,
Some nunneries some grains of chastity;
She that did thus much, and much more could do,
But that our age was iron, and rusty too,
She, she is dead; she's dead; when thou know'st this,
Thou know'st how dry a cinder this world is,
And learn'st thus much by our anatomy,
430   That 'tis in vain to dew or mollify
It with thy tears, or sweat, or blood: nothing
Is worth our travail, grief, or perishing,
But those rich joys, which did possess her heart,
Of which she's now partaker, and a part.
But as in cutting up a man that's dead,
The body will not last out to have read
On every part, and therefore men direct
Their speech to parts that are of most effect;
So the world's carcass would not last, if I
440   Were punctual in this anatomy.
Nor smells it well to hearers if one tell
Them their disease, who fain would think they're well.
Here therefore be the end: and blessed maid,
Of whom is meant whatever hath been said,
Or shall be spoken well by any tongue,
Whose name refines coarse lines, and makes prose song,
Accept this tribute, and his first year's rent,
Who till his dark short taper's end be spent,
As oft as thy feast sees this widowed earth,
450   Will yearly celebrate thy second birth,
That is, thy death. For though the soul of man
Be got when man is made, 'tis born but then
When man doth die. Our body's as the womb,
And as a midwife death directs it home.
And you her creatures, whom she works upon,
And have your last and best concoction
From her example and her virtue, if you
In reverence to her do think it due
That no one should her praises thus rehearse
460   (As matter fit for chronicle, not verse),
Vouchsafe to call to mind that God did make

A last and lasting'st piece, a song. He spake
To Moses,[8] to deliver unto all
That song, because he knew they would let fall
The Law, the prophets, and the history,
But keep the song still in their memory.
Such an opinion (in due measure) made
Me this great office boldly to invade.
Nor could incomprehensibleness deter
Me from thus trying to imprison her.
Which when I saw that a strict grave could do,
I saw not why verse might not do so too.
Verse hath a middle nature: heaven keeps souls,
The grave keeps bodies, verse the fame enrols.

RELIGIOUS POEMS

HOLY SONNETS

1

Thou hast made me, and shall thy work decay?
Repair me now, for now mine end doth haste;
I run to death, and death meets me as fast,
And all my pleasures are like yesterday;
I dare not move my dim eyes any way,
Despair behind and death before doth cast
Such terror, and my feeble flesh doth waste
By sin in it, which it towards hell doth weigh;
Only thou art above, and when towards thee

10   By thy leave I can look, I rise again;
But our old subtle foe so tempteth me,
That not one hour I can myself sustain;
Thy grace may wing me to prevent his art,
And thou like adamant draw mine iron heart.

2

As due by many titles I resign   *legal titles*
Myself to thee, O God; first I was made
And gluttonous death will instantly unjoint
My body and soul, and I shall sleep a space,
But my ever-waking part shall see that face
Whose fear already shakes my every joint:
Then, as my soul t' heaven her first seat takes flight,

10   And earth-born body in the earth shall dwell,
So fall my sins, that all may have their right,
To where they 're bred, and would press me, to hell.
Impute me righteous, thus purged of evil,
For thus I leave the world, the flesh, the Devil.

7

At the round earth's imagined corners, blow
Your trumpets, angels, and arise, arise
From death, you numberless infinities
Of souls, and to your scattered bodies go,
All whom the flood did, and fire shall o'erthrow,
All whom war, dearth, age, agues, tyrannies,
Despair, law, chance, hath slain, and you whose eyes

8 See Deuteronomy 32:1–43.

Shall behold God, and never taste death's woe.
But let them sleep, Lord, and me mourn a space,
10 For if above all these my sins abound,
'Tis late to ask abundance of thy grace,
When we are there; here on this lowly ground,
Teach me how to repent; for that's as good
As if thou'dst sealed my pardon with thy blood.

9

If poisonous minerals, and if that tree,
Whose fruit threw death on else immortal us,
If lecherous goats, if serpents envious
Cannot be damned, alas, why should I be?
Why should intent or reason, born in me,
Make sins, else equal, in me more heinous?
And mercy being easy and glorious
To God, in his stern wrath why threatens he?
But who am I, that dare dispute with thee,
O God? O, of thine only worthy blood
And my tears make a heavenly Lethean flood,¹
And drown in it my sins' black memory;
That thou remember them some claim as debt;
I think it mercy if thou wilt forget.

10

Death, be not proud, though some have callèd thee
Mighty and dreadful, for thou art not so,
For those whom thou think'st thou dost overthrow
Die not, poor Death, nor yet canst thou kill me;
From rest and sleep, which but thy pictures be,
Much pleasure, then from thee much more must flow,
And soonest our best men with thee do go,
Rest of their bones, and souls' delivery.
Thou 'rt slave to fate, chance, kings, and desperate men,
10 And dost with poison, war, and sickness dwell,
And poppy or charms can make us sleep as well,
And better than thy stroke; why swell'st thou then?
One short sleep past, we wake eternally,
And death shall be no more; Death, thou shalt die.

11

Spit in my face, ye Jews, and pierce my side,
Buffet, and scoff, scourge and crucify me,
For I have sinned, and sinned, and only he
Who could do no iniquity hath died:
But by my death cannot be satisfied
My sins, which pass the Jews' impiety:
They killed once an inglorious man, but I
Crucify him daily, being now glorified.
O, let me then his strange love still admire:
10 Kings pardon, but he bore our punishment.
And Jacob came clothed in vile harsh attire
But to supplant, and with gainful intent:

RELIGIOUS POEMS
HOLY SONNETS
1 Mythological river of forgetfulness.

God clothed himself in vile man's flesh, that so
He might be weak enough to suffer woe.

13

What if this present were the world's last night?
Mark in my heart, O soul, where thou dost dwell,
The picture of Christ crucified, and tell
Whether that countenance can thee affright;
Tears in his eyes quench the amazing light,
Blood fills his frowns, which from his pierced head fell,
And can that tongue adjudge thee unto hell,
Which prayed forgiveness for his foes' fierce spite?
No, no; but as in my idolatry
I said to all my profane mistresses,
'Beauty, of pity, foulness only is
A sign of rigour', so I say to thee,
'To wicked spirits are horrid shapes assigned;
This beauteous form assures a piteous mind.'

14

Batter my heart, three-personed God; for you
As yet but knock, breathe, shine, and seek to mend;
That I may rise and stand, o'erthrow me, and bend
Your force to break, blow, burn, and make me new.
I, like an usurped town, to another due,
Labour to admit you, but O, to no end;
Reason, your viceroy in me, me should defend,
But is captived, and proves weak or untrue;
Yet dearly I love you, and would be loved fain,
But am betrothed unto your enemy;
Divorce me, untie, or break that knot again,
Take me to you, imprison me, for I,
Except you enthral me, never shall be free,
Nor ever chaste, except you ravish me.

17

Since she whom I loved hath paid her last debt
To nature, and to hers and my good is dead,
And her soul early into heaven ravishèd,
Wholly in heavenly things my mind is set.
Here the admiring her my mind did whet
To seek thee, God; so streams do show the head;
But though I 've found thee, and thou my thirst hast fed,
A holy thirsty dropsy melts me yet.
But why should I beg more love, whenas thou
Dost woo my soul, for hers offering all thine:
And dost not only fear lest I allow
My love to saints and angels, things divine,
But in thy tender jealousy dost doubt
Lest the world, flesh, yea Devil put thee out?

GOOD FRIDAY, 1613. RIDING WESTWARD[2]

Let man's soul be a sphere, and then, in this,
The intelligence that moves, devotion is;[3]

2 The occasion is Donne's riding westward on Good Friday, April 3, 1613, from Sir Henry Goodyer's house at Polesworth to Sir Edward Herbert's house at Montgomery.

3 The analogy here is between the angels inhabiting and guiding the heavenly spheres and devotion guiding the soul.

And as the other spheres, by being grown
Subject to foreign motions, lose their own,
And being by others hurried every day,
Scarce in a year their natural form obey,
Pleasure or business, so, our souls admit
For their first mover, and are whirled by it.
Hence is't that I am carried towards the west
10   This day, when my soul's form bends toward the east.
There I should see a sun by rising set,
And by that setting endless day beget;
But that Christ on this Cross did rise and fall,
Sin had eternally benighted all.
Yet dare I almost be glad I do not see
That spectacle of too much weight for me.
Who sees God's face, that is self life, must die;
What a death were it then to see God die?
It made his own lieutenant Nature shrink,
20   It made his footstool crack, and the sun wink.
Could I behold those hands which span the poles,
And turn all spheres at once, pierced with those holes?
Could I behold that endless height which is
Zenith to us and t' our antipodes,
Humbled below us? or that blood which is
The seat of all our souls, if not of his,
Make dirt of dust, or that flesh which was worn
By God for his apparel, ragg'd, and torn?
If on these things I durst not look, durst I
30   Upon his miserable mother cast mine eye,
Who was God's partner here, and furnished thus
Half of that sacrifice which ransomed us?
Though these things, as I ride, be from mine eye,
They are present yet unto my memory,
For that looks towards them; and thou look'st towards me,
O Saviour, as thou hang'st upon the tree;
I turn my back to thee but to receive
Corrections, till thy mercies bid thee leave.
O think me worth thine anger, punish me,
40   Burn off my rusts and my deformity,
Restore thine image, so much, by thy grace,
That thou mayst know me, and I'll turn my face.

Hymn to God My God, in My Sickness

Since I am coming to that holy room   *heaven*
  Where, with thy choir of saints for evermore,
I shall be made thy music, as I come
  I tune the instrument here at the door,
  And what I must do then, think now before.

Whilst my physicians by their love are grown
  Cosmographers, and I their map, who lie
Flat on this bed, that by them may be shown
  That this is my south-west discovery
10   *Per fretum febris*,[4] by these straits to die,

---

4 By the heat and strait of fever.

I joy that in these straits I see my west;
    For though their currents yield return to none,
What shall my west hurt me? As west and east
    In all flat maps (and I am one) are one,
    So death doth touch the resurrection.

Is the Pacific Sea my home? Or are
    The eastern riches? Is Jerusalem?
Anyan,[5] and Magellan, and Gibraltar,
    All straits, and none but straits, are ways to them,
20   Whether where Japhet dwelt, or Cham, or Shem.[6]

We think that Paradise and Calvary,
    Christ's Cross and Adam's tree, stood in one place;
Look, Lord, and find both Adams met in me;
    As the first Adam's sweat surrounds my face,
    May the last Adam's blood my soul embrace.

So in his purple wrapped receive me, Lord,
    By these his thorns give me his other crown;
And as to others' souls I preached thy word,
    Be this my text, my sermon to mine own:
30   'Therefore that he may raise the Lord throws down.'

[FROM] DEVOTIONS

XVII. NUNC LENTO SONITU DICUNT, MORIERIS.

Now, this bell tolling softly for another, says to me:
Thou must die.

XVII. MEDITATION.

Perchance he for whom this bell tolls may be so ill, as that he knows not it tolls for him; and perchance I may think myself so much better than I am, as that they who are about me, and see my state, may have caused it to toll for me, and I know not that. The church is catholic, universal, so are all her actions; all that she does belongs to all. When she baptizes a child, that action concerns me; for that child is thereby connected to that body which is my head too, and ingrafted into that body whereof I am a member. And when she buries a man, that action concerns me: all mankind is of one author, and is one volume; when one man dies, one chapter is not torn out of the book, but translated into a better language; and every chapter must be so translated; God employs several translators; some pieces are translated by age, some by sickness, some by war, some by justice; but God's hand is in every translation, and his hand shall bind up all our scattered leaves again for that library where every book shall lie open to one another. As therefore the bell that rings to a sermon calls not upon the preacher only, but upon the congregation to come, so this bell calls us all; but how much more me, who am brought so near the door by this sickness. There was a contention as far as a suit (in which both piety and dignity, religion and estimation, were mingled), which of the religious orders should ring to prayers first in the morning; and it was determined, that they should ring first that rose earliest. If we understand aright the dignity of this bell that tolls for our evening prayer, we would be glad to make it ours by rising early, in that application, that it might be ours as well as his, whose indeed it is. The bell doth toll for him that thinks it doth; and though it intermit again, yet from that minute that that occasion wrought upon him, he is united to God.

---

5 Modern Anyan, the name of the strait that supposedly divided America from Asia.   6 The sons of Noah among whom the world was supposedly divided.

Who casts not up his eye to the sun when it rises? but who takes off his eye from a comet when that breaks out? Who bends not his ear to any bell which upon any occasion rings? but who can remove it from that bell which is passing a piece of himself out of this world? No man is an island, entire of itself; every man is a piece of the continent, a part of the main. If a clod be washed away by the sea, Europe is the less, as well as if a promontory were, as well as if a manor of thy friend's or of thine own were: any man's death diminishes me, because I am involved in mankind, and therefore never send to know for whom the bells tolls; it tolls for thee. Neither can we call this a begging of misery, or a borrowing of misery, as though we were not miserable enough of ourselves, but must fetch in more from the next house, in taking upon us the misery of our neighbours. Truly it were an excusable covetousness if we did, for affliction is a treasure, and scarce any man hath enough of it. No man hath affliction enough that is not matured and ripened by it, and made fit for God by that affliction. If a man carry treasure in bullion, or in a wedge of gold, and have none coined into current money, his treasure will not defray him as he travels. Tribulation is treasure in the nature of it, but it is not current money in the use of it, except we get nearer and nearer our home, heaven, by it. Another man may be sick too, and sick to death, and this affliction may lie in his bowels, as gold in a mine, and be of no use to him; but this bell, that tells me of his affliction, digs out and applies that gold to me: if by this consideration of another's danger I take mine own into contemplation, and so secure myself, by making my recourse to my God, who is our only security.

XVII. EXPOSTULATION.

My God, my God, is this one of thy ways of drawing light out of darkness, to make him for whom this bell tolls, now in this dimness of his sight, to become a superintendent, an overseer, a bishop, to as many as hear his voice in this bell, and to give us a confirmation in this action? Is this one of thy ways, to raise strength out of weakness, to make him who cannot rise from his bed, nor stir in his bed, come home to me, and in this sound give me the strength of healthy and vigorous instructions? O my God, my God, what thunder is not a well-tuned cymbal, what hoarseness, what harshness, is not a clear organ, if thou be pleased to set thy voice to it? And what organ is not well played on if thy hand be upon it? Thy voice, thy hand, is in this sound, and in this one sound I hear this whole concert. I hear thy Jacob call unto his sons and say, *Gather yourselves together, that I may tell you what shall befall you in the last days*:[1] he says, That which I am now, you must be then. I hear thy Moses telling me, and all within the compass of this sound, *This is the blessing wherewith I bless you before my death*;[2] this, that before your death, you would consider your own in mine. I hear thy prophet saying to Hezekiah, *Set thy house in order, for thou shalt die, and not live*:[3] he makes use of his family, and calls this a setting of his house in order, to compose us to the meditation of death. I hear thy apostle saying, *I think it meet to put you in remembrance, knowing that shortly I must go out of this tabernacle*:[4] this is the publishing of his will, and this bell is our legacy, the applying of his present condition to our use. I hear that which makes all sounds music, and all music perfect; I hear thy Son himself saying, *Let not your hearts be troubled*;[5] only I hear this change, that whereas thy Son says there, *I go to prepare a place for you*, this man in this sound says, I send to prepare you for a place, for a grave. But, O my God, my God, since heaven is glory and joy, why do not glorious and joyful things lead us, induce us to heaven? Thy legacies in thy first will, in the Old Testament, were plenty and victory, wine and oil, milk and honey, alliances of friends, ruin of enemies, peaceful hearts and cheerful countenances, and by these galleries thou broughtest them into thy bedchamber, by these glories and joys, to the joys and glories of heaven. Why hast thou changed thine old way, and carried us by the ways of discipline and mortification, by the ways of mourning and lamentation, by the ways of miserable ends and miserable anticipations of those miseries,

[FROM] DEVOTIONS
XVII. NUNC LENTO SONITU DICUNT, MORIERIS
1 Genesis 49:1.
2 Deuteronomy 33:1.
3 2 Kings 20:1.
4 2 Peter 1:13.
5 John 14:1.

in appropriating the exemplar miseries of others to ourselves, and usurping upon their miseries as our own, to our prejudice? Is the glory of heaven no perfecter in itself, but that it needs a foil of depression and ingloriousness in this world, to set it off? Is the joy of heaven no perfecter in itself, but that it needs the sourness of this life to give it a taste? Is that joy and that glory but a comparative glory and a comparative joy? not such in itself, but such in comparison of the joylessness and the ingloriousness of this world? I know, my God, it is far, far otherwise. As thou thyself, who art all, art made of no substances, so the joys and glory which are with thee are made of none of these circumstances, essential joy, and glory essential. But why then, my God, wilt thou not begin them here? Pardon, O God, this unthankful rashness; I that ask why thou dost not, find even now in myself, that thou dost; such joy, such glory, as that I conclude upon myself, upon all, they that find not joys in their sorrows, glory in their dejections in this world, are in a fearful danger of missing both in the next.

Richard Barnfield (1574–1627)

Several of Barnfield's poems were first published in the popular anthologies *The Passionate Pilgrim* (1599) and *England's Helicon* (1600), where they are mistakenly attributed to Shakespeare. *The Affectionate Shepheard*, in which Daphnis, the mythic founder of pastoral poetry, addresses the unattainable male object of his desire, provides an important context for the first 126 sonnets in Shakespeare's sequence, which was published 15 years later. There are also shared images of love as both sweet and bitter and of sexual pursuit as a fishing sport. Early assessments of Barnfield's work were high, including Francis Meres's comment in 1598 that, along with Sidney and Spenser, he was one of

the best writers of pastoral. Now known as a writer of homoerotic poetry, Barnfield was haughtily dismissed by C. S. Lewis as suffering "from the most uninteresting of all misfortunes" (Lewis 1954, p. 497). Barnfield is given a slightly more sympathetic reading by Bruce R. Smith, who sees him, nonetheless, as a self-absorbed poet of masturbation (p. 112). Barnfield's 1936 editor, Montague Summers, makes an early and brave case for his sincerity. *The Affectionate Shepheard* was published in 1594 and the *Sonnets* a year later as an addition to *Cynthia*. There is an important and relevant discussion of gender as a matter of performance or impersonation in Stephen Orgel's *Impersonations*.

THE AFFECTIONATE SHEPHEARD

Containing the Complaint of *Daphnis*[1] for the loue of *Ganymede*[2]

To the Right Excellent and most beautifull Lady, the Ladie
PENELOPE RITCH.[3]

> *Fayre louely Ladie, whose Angelique eyes*
> *Are Vestall Candles of sweet Beauties Treasure,*
> *Whose speech is able to inchaunt the wise,*
> *Conuerting Ioy to Paine, and Paine to Pleasure;*
>   *Accept this simply Toy of my Soules Dutie,*
>   *Which I present vnto thy matchles Beautie.*
>
> *And albeit the gift be all too meane,*
> *Too meane an Offring for thine Iuorie Shrine,*

THE AFFECTIONATE SHEPHEARD

1 The legends of Daphnis include Theocritus' story that because of his refusal to love, Aphrodite punished Daphnis with unattainable desire. The outcome of his longing is pastoral poetry, which he is said to have invented.

2 According to Ovid, he is the cup-bearer to Zeus and the ideal of youthful male beauty.

3 Penelope Devereux, Lady Rich, sister of the Earl of Essex and the historical Stella of Sidney's sonnet sequence.

Yet must thy Beautie my iust blame susteane,
Since it is mortall, but thy selfe diuine.
    Then (Noble Ladie) take in gentle worth,
    This new-borne Babe which here my Muse brings forth.

Your Honours most affectionate and perpetually
deuoted Shepheard: *DAPHNIS*.

THE TEARS OF AN AFFECTIONATE SHEPHEARD SICKE FOR LOUE OR THE COMPLAINT OF DAPHNIS FOR THE LOUE OF GANIMEDE

Scarce had the morning Starre hid from the light
Heauens crimson Canopie with stars bespangled,
But I began to rue th'vnhappy sight
Of that faire Boy that had my hart intangled;
    Cursing the Time, the Place, the sense, the sin;
    I came, I saw, I viewd, I slipped in.

If it be sinne to loue a sweet-fac'd Boy,
(Whose amber locks trust vp in golden tramels
Dangle adowne his louely cheekes with ioy,
When pearle and flowers his faire haire enamels)
    If it be sinne to loue a louely Lad;
    Oh then sinne I, for whom my soule is sad.

His Iuory-white and Alabaster skin
Is stained throughout with rare Vermillion red,
Whose twinckling starrie lights do neuer blin
To shine on louely *Venus* (Beauties bed:)
    But as the Lillie and the blushing Rose,
    So white and red on him in order growes.

Vpon a time the Nymphs bestird them-selues
To trie who could his beautie soonest win:
But he accounted them but all as Elues,
Except it were the faire Queene *Guendolen*,[4]
    Her he embrac'd, of her was beloued,
    With plaints he proued, and with teares he moued.

But her an Old-Man had beene sutor too,
That in his age began to doate againe;
Her would he often pray, and often woo,
When through old-age enfeebled was his Braine:
    But she before had lou'd a lustie youth
    That now was dead, the cause of all her ruth.

And thus it hapned, Death and *Cupid* met
Vpon a time at swilling *Bacchus* house,
Where daintie cates vpon the Board were set,
And Goblets full of wine to drinke carouse:
    Where Loue and Death did loue the licor so,
    That out they fall and to the fray they goe.

10

20

30

---

4   According to Geoffrey of Monmouth, the legendary queen of Britain
who divorced her unfaithful husband.

And hauing both their Quiuers at their backe
Fild full of Arrows; Th'one of fatall steele,
The other all of gold; Deaths shaft was black,
But Loues was yellow: Fortune turnd her wheele;
 And from Deaths Quiuer fell a fatall shaft,
 That vnder *Cupid* by the wine was waft.

And at the same time by ill hap there fell
Another Arrow out of *Cupids* Quiuer;
The which was carried by the winde at will,
And vnder Death, the amorous shaft did shiuer:
 They being parted, Loue tooke vp Deaths dart,
 And Death tooke vp Loues Arrow (for his part).

Thus as they wandred both about the world,
At last Death met with one of feeble age:
Wherewith he drew a shaft and at him hurld
The vnknowne Arrow; (with a furious rage)
 Thinking to strike him dead with Deaths blacke dart,
 But he (alas) with Loue did wound his hart.

This was the doting foole, this was the man
That lou'd faire *Guendolena* Queene of Beautie;
Shee cannot shake him off, doo what she can,
For he hath vowd to her his soules last duety:
 Making him trim vpon the holy-daies;
 And crownes his Loue with Garlands made of Baies.

Now doth he stroke his Beard; and now (againe)
He wipes the driuel from his filthy chin;
Now offers he a kisse; but high Disdaine
Will not permit her hart to pity him:
 Her hart more hard than Adamant or steele,
 Her hart more changeable than Fortunes wheele.

But leaue we him in loue (vp to the eares)
And tell how Loue behau'd himselfe abroad;
Who seeing one that mourned still in teares
(a young-man groaning vnder Loues great Load)
 Thinking to ease his Burden, rid his paines:
 For men haue griefe as long as life remaines.

Alas (the while) that vnawares he drue
The fatall shaft that Death had dropt before;
By which deceit great harme did then insue,
Stayning his face with blood and filthy goare.
 His face, that was to *Guendolen* more deere
 Than loue of Lords, or any lordly Peere.

This was that faire and beautifull young-man,
Whom *Guendolena* so lamented for;
This is that Loue whom she doth curse and ban,
Because she doth that dismall chaunce abhor:
 And if it were not for his Mothers sake,
 Euen *Ganimede* himselfe she would forsake.

Oh would shee would forsake my *Ganimede*,
Whose sugred loue is full of sweete delight,

40

50

60

70

80

Vpon whose fore-head you may plainely reade
Loues Pleasure, grau'd in yuorie Tables bright:
  In whose faire eye-balls you may clearely see
90   Base Loue still staind with foule indignitie.

Oh would to God he would but pitty mee,
That loue him more than any mortall wight;
Then he and I with loue would soone agree,
That now cannot abide his Sutors sight.
  O would to God (so I might haue my fee)
  My lips were honey, and thy mouth a Bee.

Then shouldst thou sucke my sweete and my faire flower
That now is ripe, and full of honey-berries:
Then would I leade thee to my pleasant Bower
100 Fild full of Grapes, of Mulberries, and Cherries;
  Then shouldst thou be my Waspe or else my Bee,
  I would thy hiue, and thou my honey bee.

I would put amber Bracelets on thy wrests,
Crownets of Pearle about thy naked Armes:
And when thou sitst at swilling *Bacchus* feasts
My lips with charmes should saue thee from all harmes:
  And when in sleepe thou tookst thy chiefest Pleasure,
  Mine eyes should gaze vpon thine eye-lids Treasure.

And euery Morne by dawning of the day,
110 When *Phœbus* riseth with a blushing face,
Siluanus Chappel-Clarkes shall chaunt a Lay,
And play thee hunts-vp in thy resting place:
  My Coote thy Chamber, my bosome thy Bed;
  Shall be appointed for thy sleepy head.

And when it pleaseth thee to walke abroad,
(Abroad into the fields to take fresh ayre:)
The Meades with *Floras* treasure should be strowde,
(The mantled meaddowes, and the fields so fayre.)
  And by a siluer Well (with golden sands)
120 Ile sit me downe, and wash thine yuory hands.

And in the sweltring heate of summer time,
I would make Cabinets for thee (my Loue:)
Sweet-smelling Arbours made of Eglantine
Should be thy shrine, and I would be thy Doue.
  Coole Cabinets of fresh greene Laurell boughs
  Should shadow vs, ore-set with thicke-set Eughes.

Or if thou list to bathe thy naked limbs,
Within the Christall of a Pearle-bright brooke,
Paued with dainty pibbles to the brims;
130 Or cleare, wherein thyselfe thy selfe mayst looke;
  Weele goe to *Ladon*,[5] whose still trickling noyse,
  Will lull thee fast asleepe amids thy ioyes.

Or if thoult goe vnto the Riuer side,
To angle for the sweet fresh-water fish:

5 A river in Arcadia.

Arm'd with thy implements that will abide
(Thy rod, hooke, line) to take a dainty dish;
   Thy rods shall be of cane, thy lines of silke,
   Thy hooks of siluer, and thy bayts of milke.

Or if thou lou'st to heare sweet Melodic,
140   Or pipe a Round vpon an Oaten Reede,
Or make thy selfe glad with some myrthfull glee,
Or play them Musicke whilst thy flocke doth feede;
   To *Pans* owne Pipe Ile helpe my louely Lad,
   (*Pans* golden Pype) which he of *Syrinx* had.[6]

Or if thou dar'st to climbe the highest Trees
For Apples, Cherries, Medlars, Peares, or Plumbs,
Nuts, Walnuts, Filbeards, Chest-nuts, Ceruices,
The hoary Peach, when snowy winter comes;
150   I haue fine Orchards full of mellowed frute;
   Which I will giue thee to obtain my sute.

Not proud *Alcynous*[7] himselfe can vaunt,
Of goodlier Orchards or of brauer Trees
Than I haue planted; yet thou wilt not graunt
My simple sute; but like the honey Bees
   Thou suckst the flowre till all the sweet be gone;
   And lou'st mee for my Coyne till I haue none.

Leaue *Guendolen* (sweet hart) though she be faire
160   Yet is she light; not light in vertue shining:
But light in her bahauiour, to impaire
Her honour in her Chastities declining;
   Trust not her teares, for they can watonnize,
   When teares in pearle are trickling from her eyes.

If thou wilt come and dwell with me at home;
My sheep-cote shall be strowd with new greene rushes
Weele haunt the trembling Prickets as they rome
About the fields, along the hauthorne bushes;
   I haue a pie-bald Curre to hunt the Hare: *mongrel*
   So we will liue with daintie forrest fare.

170   Nay more than this, I haue a Garden-plot,
Wherein there wants nor hearbs, nor roots, nor flowers;
(Flowers to smell, roots to eate, hearbs for the pot,)
And dainty Shelters when the Welkin lowers:
   Sweet-smelling Beds of Lillies and of Roses,
   Which Rosemary banks and Lauender incloses.

There growes the Gilliflowre, the Mynt, the Dayzie
(Both red and white,) the blew-veynd-Violet:
The purple Hyacinth, the Spyke to please thee,
The scarlet dyde Carnation bleeding yet;
180   The Sage, the Sauery, and sweet Margerum,
   Isop, Tyme, and Eye-bright, good for the blinde and dumbe.

---

6 According to Ovid, Pan pursued the nymph Syrinx, who was trans-   7 Ruler of the Phaeacians in Homer's *Odyssey*.
formed into a reed in order to escape him. The musical pipe of seven
reeds, which Pan is said to have invented, is named for her.

The Pinke, the Primrose, Cowslip, and Daffadilly,
The Hare-bell blue, the crimson Cullumbine,
Sage, Lettis, Parsley, and the milke-white Lilly,
The Rose, and speckled flowre cald Sops-in-wine,
    Fine pretie King-cups, and the yellow Bootes,
    That growes by Riuers, and by shallow Brookes.

And manie thousand moe (I cannot name)
Of hearbs and flowers that in gardens grow,
I haue for thee; and Coneyes that be tame,
Yong Rabbets, white as Swan, and blacke as Crow,
    Some speckled here and there with daintie spots:
    And more I haue two mylch and milke-white Goates.

All these, and more, Ile giue thee for thy loue;
If these, and more, may tyce thy loue away:
I haue a Pidgeon-house, in it a Doue,
Which I loue more than mortall tongue can say:
    And last of all, Ile giue thee a little Lambe
    To play withall, new weaned from her Dam.

But if thou wilt not pittie my Complaint,
My Teares, nor Vowes, nor Oathes, made to thy Beautie:
What shall I doo? But languish, die, or faint,
Since thou dost scorne my Teares, and my Soules Duetie:
    And Teares contemned, Vowes and Oaths must faile;
    For where Teares cannot, nothing can preuaile.

Compare the loue of faire Queene *Guendolin*
With mine, and thou shalt see how she doth loue thee
I loue thee for thy qualities diuine,
But she doth loue another Swaine aboue thee:
    I loue thee for thy gifts, She for hir pleasure;
    I for thy Vertue, She for Beauties treasure.

And alwaies (I am sure) it cannot last,
But sometimes Nature will denie those dimples:
Insteed of Beautie (when thy Blossom's past)
Thy face will be deformed, full of wrinckles:
    Then She that lou'd thee for thy Beauties sake,
    When Age drawes on, thy loue will soone forsake.

But I that lou'd thee for thy gifts diuine,
In the December of thy Beauties waning,
Will still admire (with ioy) those louely eine,
That now behold me with their beauties baning:
    Though Ianuarie will neuer come againe,
    Yet Aprill yeres will come in showers of raine.

When will my May come, that I may embrace thee?
When will the hower be of my soules ioying?
Why dost thou seeke in mirthe still to disgrace mee?
Whose mirth's my health, whose griefe's my harts annoying
    Thy bane my bale, thy blisse my blessednes,
    Thy ill my hell, thy weale my welfare is.

Thus doo I honour thee that loue thee so,
And loue thee so, that so doo honour thee

Much more than anie mortall man doth know,
Or can discerne by Loue or Iealozie:
   But if that thou disdainst my louing euer;
   Oh happie I, if I had loued neuer. *Finis.*

Plus fellis quam mellis Amor.[8]

SONNETS

Sonnet I.

Sporting at fancie, setting light by loue,
   There came a theefe, and stole away my heart,
   (And therefore robd me of my chiefest part)
Yet cannot Reason him a felon proue.
For why his beauty (my hearts thiefe) affirmeth,
   Piercing no skin (the bodies fensiue wall)
   And hauing leaue, and free consent withall,
Himselfe not guilty, from loue guilty tearmeth,
Conscience the Iudge, twelue Reasons are the Iurie,
   They finde mine eies the beutie t' haue let in,
   And on this verdict giuen, agreed they bin,
VVherefore, because his beauty did allure yee,
   Your Doome is this: in teares still to be drowned,
   VVhen his faire forehead with disdain is frowned.

Sonnet II.

Beuty and Maiesty are falne at ods,   *fallen*
Th'one claimes his cheeke, the other claimes his chin;
   Then Vertue comes, and puts her title in.
(Quoth she) I make him like th'immortall Gods.
(Quoth Maiestie) I owne his lookes, his Brow,
   His lips, (quoth Loue) his eies, his faire is mine.
   And yet (quoth Maiesty) he is not thine,
I mixe Disdaine with Loues congealed Snow.
I, but (quoth Loue) his locks are mine (by right)
   His stately gate is mine (quoth Maiestie),
   And mine (quoth Vertue) is his Modestie.
Thus as they striue about this heauenly wight,
   At last the other two to Vertue yeeld,
   The lists of Loue, fought in faire Beauties field.

Sonnet III.

The Stoicks thinke, (and they come neere the truth,)
   That vertue is the chiefest good of all,
   The Academicks on *Idea* call.
The Epicures in pleasure spend their youth,
The Perrepatetickes iudge felicitie,   *Peripatetics*
   To be the chiefest good aboue all other,
   One man, thinks this: and that conceaues another:
So that in one thing very few agree.
Let Stoicks haue their Vertue if they will,

8 "More bitter than sweet. Love."

And all the rest their chiefe-supposed good,
Let cruell Martialists delight in blood,
And Mysers ioy their bags with gold to fill:
My chiefest good, my chiefe felicity,
Is to be gazing on my loues faire eie.

Sonnet IIII.

Two stars there are in one faire firmament,
(Of some intitled *Ganymedes* sweet face),
VVhich other stars in brightnes doe disgrace,
As much as *Po* in clearenes passeth *Trent*.
Nor are they common natur'd stars: for why,
These stars when other shine vaile their pure light,
And when all other vanish out of sight,
They adde a glory to the worlds great eie.
By these two stars my life is onely led,
In them I place my ioy, in them my pleasure,
Loue's piercing Darts, and Natures precious treasure
With their sweet foode my fainting soule is fed:
Then when my sunne is absent from my sight
How can it chuse (with me) but be dark night?

Sonnet V.

It is reported of faire *Thetis* Sonne,
(*Achilles* famous for his chiualry,
His noble minde and magnanimity,)
That when the Troian wars were new begun,
Whos'euer was deepe-wounded with his speare,
Could neuer be recured of his maime,
Nor euer after be made whole againe:
Except with that speares rust he holpen were
Euen so it fareth with my fortune now,
Who being wounded with his piercing eie,
Must either thereby finde a remedy,
Or els to be releeu'd, I know not how.
Then if thou hast a minde still to annoy me,
Kill me with kisses, if thou wilt destroy me.

Sonnet VI.

Sweet Corrall lips, where Nature's treasure lies,
The balme of blisse, the soueraigne salue of sorrow,
The secret touch of loues heart-burning arrow,
Come quench my thirst or els poor *Daphnis* dies.
One night I dream'd (alas twas but a Dreame)
That I did feele the sweetnes of the same,
Where-with inspir'd, I young againe became,
And from my heart a spring of blood did streame,
But when I wak't, I found it nothing so,
Saue that my limbs (me thought) did waxe more strong
And I more lusty far, and far more yong.
This gift on him rich Nature did bestow.
Then if in dreaming so, I so did speede,
What should I doe, if I did so indeede?

Sonnet VII.

Sweet *Thames* I honour thee, not for thou art
   The chiefest Riuer of the fairest Ile,
   Nor for thou dost admirers eies beguile,
But for thou hold'st the keeper of my heart,
For on thy waues, (thy Christal-billow'd waues),
   My fairest faire, my siluer Swan is swimming:
   Against the sunne his pruned feathers trimming:
Whilst *Neptune* his faire feete with water laues,
Neptune, I feare not thee, not yet thine eie,
   And yet (alas) *Apollo* lou'd a boy,
   And *Cyparissus* was *Siluanus* ioy.[1]
No, no, I feare none but faire *Thetis*,[2] I,
   For if she spie my Loue, (alas) aie me,
   My mirth is turn'd to extreame miserie.

Sonnet VIII.

Sometimes I wish that I his pillow were,
   So might I steale a kisse, and yet not seene,
   So might I gaze vpon his sleeping eine,
Although I did it with a panting feare:
But when I well consider how vaine my wish is,
   Ah foolish Bees (thinke I) that doe not sucke
   His lips for hony; but poore flowers doe plucke
Which haue no sweet in them: when his sole kisses,
Are able to reuiue a dying soule.
   Kisse him, but sting him not, for if you doe,
   His angry voice your flying will pursue:
But when they heare his tongue, what can controule,
   Their back-returne? for then they plaine may see,
   How hony-combs from his lips dropping bee.

Sonnet IX.

Diana[3] (on a time) walking the wood,
   To sport herselfe, of her faire traine forlorne,
   Chaunc't for to pricke her foote against a thorne,
And from thence issu'd out a streame of blood.
No sooner shee was vanisht out of sight,
   But loues faire Queen came there away by chance,   *Venus*
   And hauing of this hap a glym'ring glance,
She put the blood into a christall bright,
When being now come vnto mount *Rhodope*,
   With her faire bands she formes a shape of Snow,
   And blends it with this blood; from whence doth grow
A louely creature, brighter than the Dey.
   And being christned in faire *Paphos*[4] shrine,
   She call'd him *Ganymede*: as all diuine.

SONNETS

1 According to Ovid, Cyparissus was a handsome youth who loved a great stag, which he accidentally killed with an arrow. In his excessive grief for the stag, Cyparissus is transformed into the cypress, the tree of mourning. In Roman religion Silvanus was a spirit of the forest.

2 According to Ovid, Thetis was loved by Peleus and gave birth to Achilles.

3 According to Ovid, Diana is the goddess of hunting and of virgins.

4 Paphos in Cyprus is where Aphrodite (Venus) emerged from the sea.

Sonnet X.

Thus was my loue, thus was my *Ganymed*,
   (Heauens ioy, worlds wonder, natures fairest work,
   In whose aspect Hope and Dispaire doe lurke)
Made of pure blood in whitest snow yshed,
And for sweete *Venus* only form'd his face,
   And his each member delicately framed,
   And last of all faire *Ganymede* him named,
His limbs (as their Creatrix) her imbrace.
But as for his pure, spotles, vertuous minde,
   Because it sprung of chaste *Dianaes* blood,
   (Goddesse of Maides, directresse of all good,)
It wholy is to chastity inclinde.
   And thus it is: as far as I can proue,
   He loues to be beloued, but not to loue.

Sonnet XI.

Sighing, and sadly sitting by my Loue,
   He ask't the cause of my hearts sorrowing,
   Coniuring me by heauens eternall King
To tell the cause which me so much did moue.
Compell'd: (quoth I) to thee will I confesse,
   Loue is the cause; and only loue it is
   That doth depriue me of my heauenly blisse.
Loue is the paine that doth my heart oppresse.
And what is she (quoth he) whom thou dos't loue?
   Looke in this glasse (quoth I) there shalt thou see
   The perfect forme of my fælicitie.
When, thinking that it would strange Magique proue,
   He open'd it: and taking of the couer,
   He straight perceau'd himselfe to be my Louer.

Sonnet XII.

Some talke of *Ganymede* th' *Idalian* Boy,
   And some of faire *Adonis* make their boast,
   Some talke of him whom louely *Læda* lost,[5]
And some of *Ecchoes*[6] loue that was so coy.
They speake by heere-say, I of perfect truth,
   They partially commend the persons named,
   And for them, sweet Encomions haue framed:
I onely t'him haue sacrifized my youth.
As for those wonders of antiquitie,
   And those whom later ages haue inioy'd,
   (But ah what hath not cruell death destroide?
Death, that enuies this worlds felicitie),
   They were (perhaps) lesse faire then Poets write.
   But he is fairer then I can indite.

---

5 Leda was loved by Zeus (Jove) when he took the form of a swan.

6 The nymph Echo fell in love with Narcissus but was rejected by him. Aphrodite punished him by making him fall in love with his own reflection in a fountain.

Sonnet XIII.

Speake Eccho, tell; how may I call my loue?
   But how his Lamps that are so christaline?   *eyes*
   Oh happy starrs that make your heauens diuine:
And happy Iems that admiration moue.
How tearm'st his golden tresses wau'd with aire?   *hair*
   Oh louely haire of your more-louely Maister,
   Image of loue, faire shape of Alablaster,
Why do'st thou driue thy Louer to dispaire?
How do'st thou cal the bed wher beuty grows?
   Faire virgine-Rose, whose mayden blossoms couer
   The milke-white Lilly, thy imbracing Louer:
Whose kisses makes thee oft thy red to lose.
   And blushing oft for shame, when he hath kist thee,
   He vades away, and thou raing'st where it list thee.

Sonnet XIIII.

Here, hold this gloue (this milk-white cheueril gloue)   *kid-leather*
   Not quaintly ouer-wrought with curious knots,
   Not deckt with golden spangs, nor siluer spots,
Yet wholesome for thy hand as thou shalt proue.
Ah no; (sweet boy) place this gloue neere thy heart,
   Weare it, and lodge it still within thy brest,
   So shalt thou make me (most vnhappy), blest.
So shalt thou rid my paine, and ease my smart:
How can that be (perhaps) thou wilt reply,
   A gloue is for the hand not for the heart,
   Nor can it well be prou'd by common art,
Nor reasons rule. To this, thus answere I:
   If thou from gloue do'st take away the g,
   Then gloue is loue: and so I send it thee.

Sonnet XV.

A[h] fairest *Ganymede*, disdaine me not,
   Though silly Sheepeheard I, presume to loue thee,
   Though my harsh songs and Sonnets cannot moue thee,
Yet to thy beauty is my loue no blot.
Apollo, Ioue, and many Gods beside,
   S' daind not the name of cuntry shepheards swains,
   Nor want we pleasure, though we take some pains,
We liue contentedly: a thing call'd pride,
Which so corrupts the Court and euery place,
   (Each place I meane where learning is neglected,
   And yet of late, euen learnings selfe's infected)
I know not what it meanes, in any case:
   Wee onely (when *Molorchus*[7] gins to peepe)
   Learne for to folde, and to vnfold our sheepe.

7   According to Virgil, Molorchus was a poor vine-dresser who helped
Hercules when he slew the Nemean lion. Here he seems to be also a
rustic poet.

Sonnet XVI.

Long haue I long'd to see my Loue againe,
  Still haue I wisht, but neuer could obtaine it;
  Rather than all the world (if I might gaine it)
Would I desire my loues sweet precious gaine.
Yet in my soule I see him euerie day,
  See him, and see his still sterne countenaunce,
  But (ah) what is of long continuance,
Where Maiestie and Beautie beares the sway?
Sometimes, when I imagine that I see him,
  (As loue is full of foolish fantasies)
  Weening to kisse his lips, as my loues fee's,
I feele but Aire: nothing but Aire to bee him.
  Thus with *Ixion*,[8] kisse I clouds in vaine:
  Thus with *Ixion*, feele I endles paine.

Sonnet XVII.

Cherry-lipt *Adonis* in his snowie shape,
  Might not compare with his pure Iuorie white,
  On whose faire front a Poets pen may write,
Whose rosiate red excels the crimson grape,
His loue-enticing delicate soft limbs,
  Are rarely fram'd t'intrap poore gazing eies:
  His cheekes, the Lillie and Carnation dies,
With louely tincture which *Apolloes* dims.
His lips ripe strawberries in Nectar wet,
  His mouth a Hiue, his tongue a hony-combe,
  Where Muses (like Bees) make their mansion.
His teeth pure Pearle in blushing Correll set.
  Oh how can such a body sinne-procuring,
  Be slow to loue, and quicke to hate, enduring?

Sonnet XVIII.

Not *Megabœtes* nor *Cleonymus*,[9]
  (Of whom great *Plutarch* makes such mention,
  Praysing their faire with rare inuention)
As *Ganymede* were halfe so beauteous.
They onely pleas'd the eies of two great Kings,
  But all the worlde at my loue stands amazed,
  Nor one that on his Angels face hath gazed,
But (rauisht with delight) him Presents brings.
Some weaning Lambs, and some a suckling Kyd,
  Some Nuts, and fil-beards, others Peares and Plums,
  Another with a milk-white Heyfar comes;
As lately *Ægons* man (*Damœtas*) did:
  But neither he, nor all the Nymphs beside,
  Can win my *Ganymede*, with them t'abide.

8 In Greek mythology Ixion tried to love Hera, whose likeness her husband Zeus shaped out of a cloud. Ixion is punished in the underworld on a wheel that turns forever.

9 See Plutarch's *Lives*, 5.28, 9.404.

Sonnet XIX.

Ah no; nor I my selfe: though my pure loue
  (Sweete *Ganymede*) to thee hath still beene pure,
  And euen till my last gaspe shall aie endure,
Could euer thy obdurate beuty moue:
Then cease oh Goddesse sonne (for sure thou art,
  A Goddesse sonne that canst resist desire)
  Cease thy hard heart, and entertaine loues fire,
Within thy sacred breast: by Natures art.
And as I loue thee more then any Creature,
  (Loue thee, because thy beautie is diuine;
  Loue thee, because my selfe, my soule is thine:
Wholie deuoted to thy louelie feature),
  Euen so of all the vowels, I and V,   i.e. U
  Are dearest vnto me, as doth ensue.

Sonnet XX.

But now my Muse toyld with continuall care,
  Begins to faint, and slacke her former pace,
  Expecting fauour from that heauenly grace,
That maie (in time) her feeble strength repaire.
Till when (sweete youth) th'essence of my soule,
  (Thou that dost sit and sing at my hearts griefe.
  Thou that dost send thy shepheard no reliefe)
Beholde, these lines; the sonnes of Teares and Dole.
Ah had great *Colin* chiefe of sheepheards all,
  Or gentle *Rowland*, my professed friend,
  Had they thy beautie, or my pennance pend,
Greater had beene thy fame, and lesse my fall:
  But since that euerie one cannot be wittie,
  Pardon I craue of them, and of thee, pitty.

John Marston (1576–1634)

Marston is best remembered today as a successful playwright from the early seventeenth century. He wrote or collaborated on ten plays in the period between 1599 and 1608, and one of them (*The Malcontent*) is one of the best tragicomedies of the period. In 1609 he was ordained as a minister, and he lived quietly in the country for the rest of his life.

Before any of this, however, he had already become infamous as one of the earliest Juvenalian satirists in Early Modern England. The Roman poet Juvenal (fl. second century CE) bequeathed to the Renaissance a model for satire that was coarse, pessimistic, and full of invective against popular trends and corrupt authority. In the late 1590s, a small group of poets took up this model and began imitating them in English, and at the forefront of this vogue was John Marston. His *Certain Satires* and

Scourge of Villanie (both 1598) were caustic critiques of contemporary English life, but they attracted official disapproval: in 1599 all of Marston's works, and those of a few other writers in the same vein, were burned on the orders of the Archbishop of Canterbury and the Bishop of London. All further publication was banned, and Marston quickly turned to the theater as a means to make a living as a writer.

It is this short-lived vogue for satire that is represented in the selection below. "Satire II" follows Marston's usual technique of attaching classical Latin names and concepts to people and places that are obviously meant to evoke contemporary London. His theme of how the shifting surfaces that people present to the world do not match their inner states is taken up in many different Renaissance poems and plays, but rarely with as much savage energy as Marston musters. It is his insistence on the direct applicability of his satires to his society that forced the authorities to ban his works: there could be no ambiguity about the targets of his attacks, and his poems offer a fine example of the kind of critical political discourse that the government was unwilling to tolerate.

READING

T. E. Wharton, "'Furor Poeticus': Marston and His Contemporaries."

J. H.

[FROM] *THE METAMORPHOSIS OF PYGMALION'S IMAGE AND CERTAIN SATIRES* (1598)

SATIRE II

Quedam sunt, et non videntur[1]

I that even now lisped like an amorist,	
Am turned into a snaphance satirist.	*i.e. snapping*
O title, which my judgment doth adore!	
But I dull-sprighted fat Boetian boor,[2]	*spirited*
Do far of honour that Censorian seat.[3]	
But if I could in milk-white robes entreat	
Plebeians' favour, I would show to be	*Common people's*
Tribunus plebis, 'gainst the villainy	
Of these same *Proteans*,[4] whose hypocrisy,	
Doth still abuse our fond credulity.	*naïve*
But since my self am not immaculate,	*unspotted*
But many spots my mind doth vitiate,	*impair*
I'll leave the white robe, and the biting rhymes	
Unto our modern satire's sharpest lines;[5]	
Whose hungry fangs snarl at some secret sin.	
And in such pitchy clouds enwrapped been	*black*
His *Sphinxian* riddles, that old *Oedipus*[6]	*i.e. Hall's*
Would be amazed and take it in foul snuffs	*i.e. take offense*
That such *Cimmerian*[7] darkness should involve	
A quaint conceit, that he could not resolve.	*device*
O darkness palpable! Egypt's black night![8]	
My wit is stricken blind, hath lost his sight.	
My shins are broke, with groping for some sense	
To know to what his words have reference.[9]	
Certes (*sunt*) but (*non videntur*) that I know.	*Surely*
Reach me some Poet's Index[10] that will show.	
Imagines Deorum. Book of Epithets,	

Line numbers: 10, 20

FROM THE METAMORPHOSIS OF PYGMALION'S IMAGE AND
  CERTAIN SATIRES (1598)
SATIRE II
1 "Some are, and do not appear to be."
2 Boeotians were proverbially rustic and unrefined.
3 i.e. Do far from honor that position. A Censor was a title for a magistrate in ancient Rome, hence Marston's allusions to the white togas that candidates for public office wore there. *Tribunis plebis* means "tribune of the people," an official elected by the common people.
4 Literally "shape shifters." Here used for hypocrites or people who change their views to suit the times.

5 A reference to Marston's contemporary Joseph Hall, who published two volumes of satires (1597 and 1598).
6 A reference to the myth of Oedipus and the Sphinx. Following Marston's theme, the Sphinx's riddle poses man as an animal with a different form in each stage of life.
7 In Homer's *Odyssey* 11, the Cimmerians are a people who live in a land of perpetual darkness.
8 See Exodus 10:21–22.
9 The speaker is complaining that Hall's satires are so obscure as to leave the reader wondering whom or what is being satirized.
10 The next few lines refer to reference works that explain classical culture or religion.

Natales Comes, thou I know recites,
And makest anatomy of poesy.

30 Help to unmask the satire's secresy.
Delphic *Apollo*, aid me to unrip,   *lay open*
These intricate deep oracles of wit.
These dark enigmas, and strange riddling sense
Which pass my dullard brain's intelligence.
Fie on my senseless pate; Now I can show   *brain*
Thou writest that which I, nor thou, dost know.
Who would imagine that such squint-eyed sight
Could strike the world's deformities so right.
But take heed *Pallas*,[11] lest thou aim awry

40 Love, nor Hate, had e'er true judging eye.
Who would once dream that that same elegy,
That fair framed piece of sweetest poesy,
Which *Muto*[12] put betwixt his Mistress' paps,
(When he (quick-witted) called her *Cruel chaps*,   *mouth*
And told her, there she might his dolors read   *woes*
Which she, oh she, upon his heart had spread)
Was penned by *Roscio* the Tragedian.[13]
Yet *Muto*, like a good *Vulcanian*,[14]
An honest cuckold, calls the bastard son,

50 And brags of that which others for him done.
Satire thou liest, for that same elegy
Is Muto's *own, his own dear Poesy:*
Why tis his own, and dear, for he did pay
Ten crowns for it, as I heard *Roscius* say.
Who would imagine yonder sober man,
That same devout meal-mouthed Precisian,   *Puritan*
That cries *good brother, kind sister*, makes a duck   *bow*
After the antique grace, can always pluck   i.e. old-fashioned manner
A sacred book, out of his civil hose,   *plain*

60 And at th'opening, and at our stomachs close[15]
Says with a turned-up eye a solemn grace
Of half an hour, then with his silken face   *ingratiating*
Smile on the holy crew, And then doth cry
O manners! O times of impurity![16]
With that depaints a church reformed state,   *depicts*
The which the female tongues magnificate: *praise*
Because that Plato's odd opinion,
Of all things common[17] hath strong motion
In their weak minds. Who thinks that this good man

70 Is a vile, sober, damned, Politician?
Not I, till with his bait of purity
He bit me sore in deepest usury.
No Jew, no Turk, would use a Christian
So inhumanely as this Puritan.
Diomedes Iades[18] were not so bestial
As this same seeming-saint, vile cannibal.
Take heed O world, take heed advisedly

---

11 Athena, goddess of wisdom, is conventionally armed with a spear.
12 A fictional lover whose name means "mute."
13 A reference to Roscius, a famous classical tragic actor; here, his name stands for a generic actor. Muto is paying an actor for poems to pass off as his own.
14 See gazetteer under Hephaestus (i.e. Vulcan). The reference is to the affair between Mars and Venus, the result of which was Cupid.

15 i.e. At the beginning and end of a meal.
16 A translation of Cicero's *O tempora, O mores.*
17 i.e. Holding all goods in common, an idea Plato explores in the *Republic.*
18 An evil monarch in classical myth who fed human flesh to his horses. He was killed and fed to his own horses by Hercules.

Of these same damned anthropophagi.   *cannibals*
I had rather be within a Harpy's[19] claws
80   Then trust myself in their devouring jaws.
Who all confusion to the world would bring
Under the form of their new discipline.   *i.e. church organization*
O I could say, *Briareus* hundred hands
Were not so ready to bring *Jove* in bands[20]   *chains*
As these to set endless contentious strife
Betwixt *Jehouah*, and his sacred wife.   *i.e. God and the Church*
    But see who's yonder, true Humility
The perfect image of fair Courtesy.
See, he doth deign to be in servitude
90   Where he hath no promotions livelihood.[21]
Mark, he doth curtsy, and salutes a block,
Will seem to wonder at a weathercock,
Trenchmore[22] with apes, play music to an owl,
Bless his sweet honour's running brazil bowl:[23]
Cries *Bravely broke* when that his Lordship missed,[24]
And is of all the thronged scaffold hissed.   *crowded gallery*
O is not this a courteous minded man?
No fool, no, a damned Machiavellian.
Holds candle to the devil for a while,   *i.e. Helps the devil*
100   That he the better may the world beguile
That's fed with shows. He hopes though some repine,   *grudge*
When sun is set, the lesser stars will shine:
He is within a haughty malcontent,
Though he do use such humble blandishment.
But bold-faced satire, strain not over high,
But laugh and chuck at meaner gullery.   *chuckle/deceit*
    In faith yon is a well-faced gentleman,[25]
See how he paces like a Cyprian: *i.e. follower of Venus*
Fair amber tresses of the fairest hair
110   That e'er were waved by our London air,
Rich laced suit, all spruce, all neat in truth.
Ho *Lynceus!*[26] What's yonder brisk neat youth
'Bout whom yon troupe of gallants flocken so?   *men of fashion*
And now together to *Browns* common[27] go?
Thou knowst I am sure, for thou canst cast thine eye
Through nine mud walls, or else odd Poets lie.   *eminent*
'Tis loose legged *Lais*,[28] that same common *Drab*,
For whom good Tubrio[29] *took the moral stab.*
Ha ha, Nay then I'll never rail at those
120   That wear a codpiece, thereby to disclose
What sex they are, since strumpets' breeches use,   *wear*
And all men's eyes save *Lynceus* can abuse.   *deceive*
Nay steed of shadow, lay the substance out,
Or else fair *Briscus*[30] I shall stand in doubt
What sex thou art, since such Hermaphrodites
Such *Protean* shadows so delude our sights.
    Look, look, with what a discontented grace

---

19 A mythical monster with the body of a bird and the face of a
woman.
20 Briareus was a hundred-handed giant in classical myth. In some
stories, he rebelled against Zeus and was punished. In others, however,
he aided Zeus.
21 i.e. He has no chance of promotion.
22 A boisterous rustic dance.
23 i.e. He will bless his master's bowling ball.

24 Cheers when his master misses his opponent while jousting.
25 This passage attacks women who cross-dress as men.
26 The name means "sharp-eyed."
27 This could be an eating house or a brothel.
28 Lais was a famous courtesan in classical antiquity.
29 It is unclear if anyone particular is being referred to here.
30 Again, the specific reference of this name is not known.

Bruto the traveller doth sadly pace

130   Long Westminster, O civil seeming shade,   *ghost*

Mark his sad colors, how demurely clad,

Staidness itself, and *Nestor's*[31] gravity

Are but the shade of his civility.   *shadow*

And now he sighs. *O thou corrupted age,*

Which slight regard'st men of sound carriage,   *conduct*

Virtue, knowledge, fly to heaven again

Deign not among these ungrateful sots remain.

Well, some tongues I know, some Countries I have seen   *languages*

And yet these oily Snails respectless been

Of my good parts. O worthless puffy slave!   *vain*

140   Did'st thou to *Venice* go ought else to have?

But buy a lute and use a courtesan?

And there to live like a Cyllenian?   i.e. follower of Venus

And now from thence what hither dost thou bring?

But surflings, new paints and poisonings?   *cosmetics*

Aretine's pictures,[32] some strange luxury?

And new found use of *Venus'* venery?   *lechery*

What art thou but black clothes? Say *Bruto* say

Art any thing but only sad array?   *sober*

Which I am sure is all thou brought from France,

150   Save Naples' pox, and Frenchmen's dalliance.

From haughty Spain, what brought thou else beside,

But lofty looks, and their Lucifrian pride?   *diabolical*

From Belgia what? But their deep bezeling,   *Belgium/drinking*

Their boot-carouse, and their beer-buttering.[33]

Well then exclaim not on our age good man,

But hence polluted Neopolitan.[34]

Now Satire cease to rub our galled skins,   *chapped*

And to unmask the world's destested sins.

Thou shalt as soon draw *Nilus* river dry,   *Nile's*

160   As cleanse the world from foul impiety.

MISCELLANEOUS POEMS

TO EVERLASTING OBLIVION[1]

Thou mighty gulf, insatiate cormorant,   i.e. monster of greed

Deride me not, though I seem petulant

To fall into thy chops. Let others pray   *jaws*

Forever their fair poems flourish may.

But as for me, hungry *Oblivion*

Devour me quick, accept my orison: *prayer*

My earnest prayers, which do importune thee,

With gloomy shade of thy still empery,   *kingdom*

To veil both me and my rude poesy.

10   Far worthier lines in silence of thy state

Do sleep securely free from love or hate,

---

31   The proverbially wise counselor of the Greeks in Homer.

32   The artist Giulio Romano made some infamous pornographic illustrations for Pietro Aretino's equally infamous sonnets.

33   i.e. Drinking out of boots and adding butter to beer.

34   Italy was a by-word for vice in Early Modern England.

MISCELLANEOUS POEMS
TO EVERLASTING OBLIVION

1   The word means "forgetfulness" or, in literary terms, going unread.

From which this living, ne'er can be exempt,
But whilst it breathes will hate and fury tempt.
Then close his eyes with thy all-dimming hand,
Which not right glorious actions can withstand.
Peace hateful tongues, I now in silence pace,
Unless some hound do wake me from my place,
   I with this sharp, yet well meant poesy,
   Will sleep secure, right free from injury
20   Of cankered hate, or rankest villainy.   *corrupt*

Martha Moulsworth (1577–?)

Martha Moulsworth's "Memorandum" is one of the earliest known autobiographical poems by a woman in the English language. Little is known about its author outside what is in the poem. (Her husband, Bevill Mowlsworth, for example, is mentioned briefly in a letter dated 1603 by Sir Robert Cecil, concerning the maintenance of Cecil's silk farm.) Her poem offers a brief but uniquely important glimpse of a woman's life during the English Renaissance. It also preserves a wonderful sense of her wit and intellectual vitality, which survived the deaths of three husbands and her children. In part, the poem is a celebration (or defense) of widowhood. As such, it raises important issues concerning women's writing, feminist theory, and the art of autobiography as a means of constructing the self.

READING

Robert C. Evans and Barbara Wiedemann (eds.), *"My Name Was Martha": A Renaissance Woman's Autobiographical Poem.*

M. P.

NOUEMBER THE 10th 1632

THE MEMORANDUM OF MARTHA MOULSWORTH

WIDDOWE

The tenth day of the winter month Nouember
A day which I must duely still remember
did open first theis eis, and shewed this light
Now on thatt day* vppon thatt daie I write   *Nouember 10th 1632   *about*

This season fitly willinglie combines
the birth day of my selfe, & of theis lynes
The tyme the clocke, the yearly stroke is one   my muse is a tell
thatt clocke by ffiftie fiue retourns hath gonn   clocke, & echoeth
How ffew, how many warnings itt will giue   euerie stroke wth
10   he only knowes in whome we are, & liue   a coupled ryme
                                                so many tymes
                                              viz 55
                                              Acts 17:28 &[c]

In carnall state of sin originall
I did nott stay one whole day naturall
The seale of grace in Sacramentall water
so soone had I, so soone become the daughter
of earthly parents, & of heauenlie ffather
some christen late for state, the wiser rather.   *earlier*

My Name was Martha, Martha tooke much payne   Luke 10:14[1]
our Sauiour christ her guess[t] to entertayne
God gyue me grace my Inward house to dight   *prepare*
20   That he wth me may supp, & stay all night   Reuel 3:20

My ffather was a Man of spottles ffame   Luke 24:29
of gentle Birth, & Dorsett was his name
He had, & left lands of his owne possession
he was of Leuies tribe by his profession[2]   *Levi's*
his Mother oxford knowenge well his worth
arayd in scarlett Robe[3] did send him fforth.
By him I was brought vpp in godlie pietie
In modest chearefullnes, & sad sobrietie
Noat onlie so, Beyond my sex & kind
30   he did wth learning Lattin decke [my] mind
And whie nott so? The muses ffemalls are
and therfore of Vs ffemales take some care
Two Vniuersities we haue of men
o thatt we had but one of women then
O then thatt would in witt, and tongs surpasse
All art of men thatt is, or euer was
But I of Lattin haue no cause to boast
ffor want of vse, I longe agoe itt lost   Lattin is not the most
                                                 marketable mariadge
                                                 mettall

Had I no other portion of my dowre
40   I might have stood a virgin to this houre
Butt though the virgin Muses I loue well
I haue longe since Bid virgin life ffarewell

Thrice this Right hand did holly wedlocke plight
And thrice this Left with pledged ringe was dight
three husbands me, & I haue them enioyde
all louely, lovinge all, some more, some lesse
though gonn their loue, & memorie I blesse.
Vntill my one & twentieth yeare of Age   1 Husband, Mr Nicolas
                                                Prynne, Aprill 18 1598

50   I did nott bind my selfe in Mariadge
My springe was late, some thinke thatt sooner loue
butt backward springs doe oft the kindest proue
My first knott held fiue yeares, & eight months more
then was a yeare sett on my mourninge score
My second bond tenn years nine months did last   2d Mr Tho: Througood
                                                        Ffebruary 3 1604
three years eight Months I kept a widowes ffast

The third I tooke a louely man, & kind
such comlines in age we seldome ffind   3d Mr Beuill Moulswoorth
                                               June 15, 1619
ffrom Mortimers he drewe his pedigre
60   their Arms he bore, not bought wth Heraulds fee[4]
third wife I was to him, as he to me

NOUEMBER THE 10TH 1632
1   The story of Mary and Martha is at Luke 10:41.
2   Her father was presumably a clergyman.

3   Scarlet academic gowns were awarded for degrees in divinity or law.
4   His family's coat of arms was not purchased.

third husband was, in nomber we agree
eleuen years, & eight mongths his autume lasted
a second spring to soone awaie it hasted
was neuer man so Buxome to his wife
wth him I led an easie darlings life.
I had my will in house, in purse in Store⁵
what would a women old or yong haue more?

Two years Almost outwearinge since he died
70 And yett, & yett my tears ffor him nott dried
I by the ffirst, & last some Issue had
butt roote, & ffruite is dead wch makes me sad

My husbands all on holly dayes did die
Such day, such waie, they to the Sts did hye
This life is worke-day euen att the Best
but christian death, an holly day of Rest
the ffirst, the ffirst of Martirs did befall
St Stevens ffeast⁶ to him was ffunerall   Niceph: Histo:⁷
the morrowe after christ our fflesh did take
80 this husband did his mortall fflesh fforsake
the second on a double sainted day
to Jude, & Symon tooke his happy way
This Symon as an auncient Story Sayth
did ffirst in England plant the Christian ffayth
Most sure itt is that Jude in holy writt   Jude ver: 3
doth warne vs to Mayntayne, & ffight ffor itt
In wch all those that liue, & die, may well
Hope wth the Sts eternally to dwell
The last on St Mathias day⁸ did wend
90 vnto his home, & pilgrimages ende
this feast comes in that season wch doth bringe
vppon dead Winters cold, a lyvelie Springe
His Bodie winteringe in the lodge of death
Shall ffeele A springe, wth budd of life, & Breath
And Rise in incorruption, glorie power   corrin: 15:42
Like to the Bodie of our Sauiour   phillip: 3:21
In vayne itt were, prophane itt were ffor me
W^th Sadnes⁹ to aske wch of theis three   Matt: 22:18   Sadducees
I shall call husband in ye Resurrection
100 ffor then shall all in glorious perfection
Like to th'immortall heauenlie Angells liue
who wedlocks bonds doe neither take nor giue   verse 30

But in the Meane tyme this must be my care
of knittinge here a fourth knott to beware
A threefold cord though hardlie yett is broken
Another Auncient storie doth betoken   Ecclesiast 4:12
thatt seldome comes A Better;¹⁰ whie should I
then putt my Widowehood in jeopardy?
the Virgins life is gold, as Clarks vs tell
110 the Widowes siluar, I loue siluar well.

5 In the maintenance of household provisions.
6 December 26th.
7 Nicephorus Callistus's *Church History* was translated into Latin in 1555. Perhaps Moulsworth exaggerates her neglect of Latin.
8 February 24th.

9 Matthew 21:23ff. concerns the Sadducees' denial of resurrection and their questioning Jesus about what will happen, assuming the resurrection of the dead, to a wife who was married more than once.
10 A 16th-century proverb. See Tilley, *A Dictionary of the Proverbs in England in the Sixteenth and Seventeenth Centuries*, p. 46.

Elizabeth (Tanfield) Cary, Lady Falkland
(1585–1639)

Elizabeth Cary was the first Englishwoman to write a tragedy. *The Tragedy of Mariam* (*c*.1606), which is based on Seneca's classical Roman models, is the only one of her plays to have survived; but it appears from a reference in the dedicatory sonnet to that play that she had written an earlier (lost) tragedy set in Sicily. Cary's *History of the Life, Reign, and Death of Edward II* (1627), based on the model of Tacitus' Roman histories, is also the first significant historical work written by an Englishwoman. Both of these works – because of rather than despite their classical influences – were doubtless read as more radical texts than they seem today. Barbara Lewalski points out that "contemporary Senecan dramas and histories written in the Tacitean mode . . . [were] often perceived as dangerous by Elizabethan and Jacobean censors precisely because they allow for the clash of ideological positions and for the sympathetic representation of resistance and rebellion" (p. 179).

Cary's father, Sir Lawrence Tanfield, was a highly successful lawyer, judge, and courtier; and her mother, Elizabeth Symondes, was a descendant of country gentry. An only child, Cary learned to read when she was very young; and she showed a marked talent for languages. According to her daughter's biography of her mother (it remains uncertain whether the author was Anne or Lucy), Cary was largely self-taught in French, Spanish, Italian, Latin, Hebrew, and Transylvanian. But she was also the pupil of John Davies, who thought her a peer of Mary, Countess of Pembroke, and Lucy, Countess of Bedford. Her extraordinary intelligence is the subject of Davies' encomium:

> Art, Language; yea, abstruse and holy Tones,
>   Thy Wit and Grace acquir'd thy Fame to raise;
> And still to fill thine owne, and others Songs;
>   Thine, with thy Parts, and others, with thy praise.

Such nervy Limbes of Art, and Straines of Wit
    Times past ne'er knew the weaker Sexe to have;
And Times to come, will hardly credit it,
    If thus thou give they Workes both Birth and Grave.

These words may have prompted Cary to publish *Mariam* in 1613.

The plot of the tragedy is symmetrical. King Herod is first thought to be dead, which has an immediately liberating effect on his family and servants; but when he unexpectedly returns and reestablishes his patriarchal authority, six characters pay with their lives. The two states of Judean society – with and without Herod in control – allow for an exploration of women's integrity and virtue by exposing and rejecting the equation of outspokenness with sexual promiscuity. Here the central contrast is between the integrity of Mariam and the duplicity of Salome. The plot echoes in many ways Cary's oppressive treatment at the hands of her husband, Sir Henry Cary, who eventually disowned her when she converted to Catholicism in 1626. Her sons' conversions led to Cary's being threatened with imprisonment in the Tower. Patrick and Henry eventually travelled to the Continent where, before their mother's death, they took holy orders. The circumstances of Elizabeth Cary's death are unknown.

READING

Elizabeth Cary, *The Tragedy of Mariam*, ed. Barry Weller and Margaret W. Ferguson.
Elizabeth Cary, *The Tragedy of Mariam*, ed. Stephanie Hodgson-Wright.
Barbara Lewalski, *Writing Women in Jacobean England*.

M. P.

[FROM] THE TRAGEDY OF MARIAM, THE FAIR QUEEN OF JEWRY

To Diana's Earthly Deputess, and My Worthy Sister, Mistress Elizabeth Cary[1]

When cheerful Phoebus his full course hath run,
    His sister's fainter beams our hearts doth cheer:

[FROM] TRAGEDY OF MARIAM, THE FAIR QUEEN OF JEWRY
1 Possibly the sister-in-law of the author.

So your fair brother is to me the sun,
And you his sister as my moon appear.

You are my next belov'd, my second friend,
For when my Phoebus' absence makes it night,
Whilst to th' antipodes[2] his beams do bend,
From you, my Phoebe,[3] shines my second light.

10   He like to Sol, clear-sighted, constant, free,
      You Luna-like, unspotted, chaste, divine:
      He shone on Sicily,[4] you destin'd be
      T'illumine the now obscurèd Palestine.
      My first was consecrated to Apollo,
      My second to Diana now shall follow.

The Argument

Herod, the son of Antipater (an Idumean), having crept by the favour of the Romans, into the Jewish monarchy, married Mariam, the granddaughter of Hircanus, the rightful king and priest, and for her (besides her high blood, being of singular beauty) he repudiated Doris, his former wife, by whom he had children.[5]

This Mariam had a brother called Aristobulus, and next him and Hircanus, his grandfather, Herod in his wife's right had the best title. Therefore to remove them, he charged the second with treason, and put him to death; and drowned the first under colour of sport. Alexandra, daughter to the one, and mother to the other, accused him for their deaths before Anthony.

So when he was forced to go answer this accusation at Rome, he left the custody of his wife to Josephus, his uncle, that had married his sister Salome, and out of a violent affection (unwilling that any should enjoy her after him) he gave strict and private commandment, that if he were slain, she should be put to death. But he returned with much honour, yet found his wife extremely discontented, to whom Josephus had (meaning it for the best, to prove Herod loved her) revealed his charge.

So by Salome's accusation he put Josephus to death, but was reconciled to Mariam, who still bare the death of her friends exceeding hardly.

In this meantime Herod was again necessarily to revisit Rome, for Caesar having overthrown Anthony, his great friend, was likely to make an alteration of his[6] fortune.

In his absence, news came to Jerusalem that Caesar had put him to death; their willingness it should be so, together with the likelihood, gave this rumour so good credit, as Sohemus, that had succeeded Josephus' charge, succeeded him likewise in revealing it. So at Herod's return, which was speedy and unexpected, he found Mariam so far from joy, that she showed apparent signs of sorrow. He still desiring to win her to a better humour, she, being very unable to conceal her passion, fell to upbraiding him with her brother's death. As they were thus debating, came in a fellow with a cup of wine, who, hired by Salome, said first, it was a love potion, which Mariam desired to deliver to the king: but afterwards he affirmed that it was a poison, and that Sohemus had told her somewhat which procured the vehement hate in her.

The king hearing this, more moved with jealousy of Sohemus, than with this intent of poison, sent her away, and presently after by the instigation of Salome, she was beheaded. Which rashness was afterward punished in him, with an intolerable and almost frantic passion for her death.

---

2   The other side of the earth.
3   Phoebe, Luna, and Diana, by association with the moon, are figures of chastity. The corresponding mythological figures for the sun are Sol and Apollo.

4   Cary had written an earlier tragedy set in Sicily. No copies of the earlier work appear to have survived.
5   Josephus' *Antiquities* is Cary's principal historical source.
6   i.e. Herod's.

Actus Primus. Scena Prima

Mariam sola

Mariam. How oft have I with public voice run on
To censure Rome's last hero for deceit:
Because he wept when Pompey's life was gone,
Yet when he liv'd, he thought his name too great.
But now I do recant, and, Roman lord,[7]
Excuse too rash a judgement in a woman:
My sex pleads pardon, pardon then afford,
Mistaking is with us but too too common.
Now do I find, by self-experience taught,

10   One object yields both grief and joy:
You wept indeed, when on his worth you thought,
But joy'd that slaughter and your foe destroy.
So at his death your eyes true drops did rain,
Whom dead, you did not wish alive again.
When Herod liv'd, that now is done to death,
Oft have I wish'd that I from him were free:
Oft have I wish'd that he might lose his breath,
Oft have I wish'd his carcass dead to see.
Then rage and scorn had put my love to flight,

20   That love which once on him was firmly set:
Hate hid his true affection from my sight,
And kept my heart from paying him his debt.
And blame me not, for Herod's jealousy
Had power even constancy itself to change:
For he, by barring me from liberty,   *prevent*
To shun my ranging, taught me first to range.
But yet too chaste a scholar was my heart,
To learn to love another than my lord:
To leave his love, my lesson's former part,

30   I quickly learn'd, the other I abhorr'd.
But now his death to memory doth call
The tender love that he to Mariam bare.
And mine to him; this makes those rivers fall,
Which by another thought unmoisten'd are.
For Aristobulus, the loveliest youth
That ever did in angel's shape appear,
The cruel Herod was not mov'd to ruth;
Then why grieves Mariam Herod's death to hear?
Why joy I not the tongue no more shall speak,

40   That yielded forth my brother's latest doom:
Both youth and beauty might thy fury break,
And both in him did ill befit a tomb.
And, worthy grandsire, ill did he requite
His high ascent, alone by thee procur'd,
Except he murder'd thee to free the sprite
Which still he thought on earth too long immur'd.
How happy was it that Sohemus' mind
Was mov'd to pity my distress'd estate!
Might Herod's life a trusty servant find,

50   My death to his had been unseparate.
These thoughts have power, his death to make me bear,
Nay more, to wish the news may firmly hold:

7 An apostrophe to Julius Caesar.

Yet cannot this repulse some falling tear,
That will against my will some grief unfold.
And more I owe him for his love to me,
The deepest love that ever yet was seen:
Yet had I rather much a milkmaid be,
Than be the monarch of Judea's queen.
It was for nought but love he wish'd his end
60   Might to my death but the vaunt-courier prove: *forerunner*
But I had rather still be foe than friend,
To him that saves for hate, and kills for love.
Hard-hearted Mariam, at thy discontent
What floods of tears have drench'd his manly face!
How canst thou then so faintly now lament
Thy truest lover's death, a death's disgrace:
Ay, now, mine eyes, you do begin to right
The wrongs of your admirer and my lord.
Long since you should have put your smiles to flight,
70   Ill doth a widowed eye with joy accord.
Why, now methinks the love I bare him then,
When virgin freedom left me unrestrain'd,
Doth to my heart begin to creep again,
My passion now is far from being feign'd
But, tears, fly back, and hide you in your banks,
You must not be to Alexandra seen:
For if my moan be spied, but little thanks
Shall Mariam have, from that incensèd queen.

Lady Mary (Sidney) Wroth (1586?–1651?)

One of the most accomplished and innovative women writers of the English Renaissance, Lady Mary Wroth was born into an aristocratic family of men and women who made major contributions to English literature and who also played active parts in the court life of the reigns of Elizabeth and James I. If she was indeed born in 1586 – there is no record of her birth in the parish registers of Penshurst, the Sidney family estate – then she would have been born in the year of the death of her uncle Sir Philip Sidney, whose complex literary legacy of achievement and unfulfilled promise exerted a powerful influence over her career as a writer. Lady Mary's principal works are in some sense a creatively ironic response to her uncle's texts: thus, *Urania*, apparently the earliest published work of prose fiction in English written by a woman, in some ways continues the otherwise incomplete *Arcadia* (however carefully and lovingly it was edited by her aunt) and transforms it into a work of female eroticism and heroism, just as *Pamphilia to Amphilanthus* appropriates and inverts *Astrophil and Stella*. Her father, Sir Robert Sidney, and her aunt, Mary, Countess of Pembroke, were also accomplished writers; her mother, Lady Barbara Gamage, was first cousin to Sir Walter Raleigh; and her first cousin, William Herbert, third Earl of Pembroke, by whom Lady Mary had two illegitimate children, was a poet and distinguished patron of Shakespeare's first folio and the works of Jonson. Jonson's poem *"To Penshurst"* provides brief glimpses of life in this devoutly Protestant literary family:

Each morne, and even, they are taught to pray,
    With the whole houshold, and may, every day,
Reade, in their virtuous parents noble parts,
    The mysteries of manners, armes, and arts.

The Sidneys' status, affluence, and learning did not protect them from conflict, tragedy, and unhappiness: the Queen at first vigorously opposed the marriage of Lady Mary's parents; her uncle, Sir Philip, died young defending the Protestant cause in the Netherlands and was immediately appropriated and transformed into a national icon; her marriage to Sir Robert Wroth was a traditional marriage of family convenience but was predictably unhappy; after his death Lady Mary inherited enormous financial troubles, while simultaneously suffering the loss of her infant son James. Nevertheless, her extraordinary accomplishments as a writer were celebrated by such contemporaries as Jonson, Chapman, George Wither, Joshua Sylvester, and others.

Lady Mary lived in what might be conceived as two very different circles of patriarchy. The most immediate, her family, was largely one of attenuated male authority: her uncle's untimely death but early accomplishment as a writer left her an example to rival and a family tradition to complete; her father's writing, lost until recently, suggests a serious poetic ambition but a limited achievement in marked contrast to hers; then there was the example of her aunt (also a Mary) the Countess of Pembroke, her lover's mother, who edited her dead uncle's *Arcadia* and produced important writing of her own, while giving Lady Mary access to the literary and intellectual circle of her own estate at Wilton. But perhaps most importantly, the Countess of Pembroke provided Lady Mary with an immediate, family example of female authorship of high and learned achievement. The second patriarchal circle was that of the court of the misogynistic James I, who ordered the Bishop of London to instruct the clergy to "inveigh vehemently and bitterly in theyre sermons against the insolencie of our women," particularly to condemn "cross-dressing" or the assumption of "male" attire by women. In such writings as "A Satire against Woemen" (even his spelling is significant), James exhibited his contempt for women and perhaps his antagonism to his own queen, with whom Lady Mary became closely associated. At least part of the social context, here, however, as Lawrence Stone (1990) has estimated, is that a crisis of the aristocracy, like that taking place in Lady Mary's own marriage, was underway, in which perhaps as many as one-third of aristocratic marriages in England were on the verge of collapse.

Pamphilia to Amphilanthus, which is likely to be her most lasting legacy to English literature, was written over a period of several years, with some of the poems in circulation before 1613. They were arranged with obvious care and were appended to Part I of *Urania* in 1621. Pamphilia ("all-loving") and Amphilanthus ("lover of two") are in some ways fictional extensions of Lady Mary and William Herbert (thus, such puns on his name as "best pleasing will" in Sonnet 48). In their fictional context in *Urania*, Pamphilia's 48 sonnets and their six interspersed songs are those that Amphilanthus finds in circumstances that lead to his and Pamphilia's mutual confession of love. Some of the key features of Wroth's relationship to male poetic traditions are her critical incorporation of the work of Dante and Petrarch; her development of a distinctively dramatic female persona, which in its virtuosity recalls Shakespeare's fictional poet in his sonnet sequence; and her elision of the secular and the sacred, as in the poetry of Donne.

Urania – like such other massive narratives of the English Renaissance as Spenser's *Faerie Queene*, Raleigh's *History of the World*, and Sidney's *New Arcadia* – is incomplete. Like her uncle's second version of the *Arcadia*, Lady Mary's 1621 *Urania* stops in mid-sentence, appropriately ending with the word "and." Inspired, perhaps, by the all-encompassing narrative structure of the Old and New Testaments, Spenser, Raleigh, Sidney, and Wroth desired to tell a complete story that left nothing out. Lady Mary wrote a continuation of *Urania*, commonly referred to as the "Newberry manuscript," which she did not publish (a modern edition is in preparation). The title of the published version honors Lady Mary's friend and neighbor, Susan de Vere, who was William Herbert's sister-in-law and also a patroness of John Donne. In 1605, the Countess of Montgomery and Lady Mary had appeared together in the court performance of Jonson's *The Masque of Blackness*, and their friendship continued beyond the dissolution of the circle of women that had formed around Queen Anne, who died in 1619.

A recent study of *Urania* by Jennifer Lee Carrell convincingly argues that it simultaneously is a fictional transformation of Lady Mary's life, a creatively critical response to the gender debates of its time, and an imaginative intervention in contemporaneous experimentation with the art of prose fiction that also included the English translation of Cervantes's *Don Quixote* (1612, 1620). As a fictional version of her autobiography, Wroth dismembers, displaces, repeats, and in a sense represses a story that keeps being almost told in various episodes of her book but is never quite explicitly narrated. This is Carrell's helpful reconstruction of this "ur-tale":

> A young woman grows up in close proximity to a young nobleman, and she realizes that she loves him long before he returns that love, They marry, but not each other – the woman especially unworthily, "on a jealous husband." At court, however, the old friends see each other and fall in love – a chaste love for married folk. Nevertheless, this love provokes the suspicion and jealousy of the queen, and the lady eventually loses her position at court and retreats to her husband's home in the country. The husband dies, but instead of this opening a window for bliss, she finds that her love has deserted her for another woman. His infidelity does nothing to shake her constancy, though it produces reams of poetic love complaints. Despite tears and poetry, her lover cruelly scorns her. However, he returns to her briefly, and their relationship blooms again, before he leaves her again, once more for another woman. Despite continual betrayal, the lady, who has lost her beauty due to continual weeping, declares that she will remain forever constant to her first and greatest love. (Carrell, p. 94)

The episodes from *Urania* reprinted here provide a sense of Pamphilia's strong, creative persona; Amphilanthus's role as a "Shepheard knight" which was an epithet of Sir Philip Sidney's; Pamphilia's use of her poetry as love tokens; and Lady Mary's interest in framed narrative, in which the lovers overhear a young shepherd-poet.

READING

Elaine V. Beilin, *Redeeming Eve: Women Writers of the English Renaissance*.

Jennifer Lee Carrell, "*Urania*'s Magic Mirror of Romance."

Naomi J. Miller and Gary Waller (eds.), *Reading Mary Wroth: Representing Alternatives in Early Modern England*.

Josephine A. Roberts (ed.), *The Poems of Lady Mary Wroth*.

——— *The First Part of the Countess of Montgomery's Urania*.

Gary Waller, *The Sidney Family Romance: Mary Wroth, William Herbert, and the Early Modern Construction of Gender*.

M. P.

PAMPHILIA TO AMPHILANTHUS

{PART ONE}

I.

When nights black mantle could most darknes prove,
    And sleepe deaths Image did my senses hire
    From knowledg of my self, then thoughts did move
    Swifter then those most swiftnes need require:

In sleepe, a Chariot drawne by wing'd desire
    I sawe: wher sate bright Venus Queene of love,
    And att her feete her sonne, still adding fire
    To burning hearts which she did hold above,

Butt one hart flaming more then all the rest
10   The goddess held, and putt itt to my brest,[1]
    Deare sonne, now shutt sayd she: thus must wee winn;

Hee her obay'd, and martir'd my poore hart,
    I, waking hop'd as dreames itt would depart
    Yett since: O mee: a lover I have binn.

2.

Deare eyes how well (indeed) you doe adorne
    That blessed sphaere, which gazing soules hold deere:
    The loved place of sought for triumphs neere:
    The court of glory, wher Loves force was borne:

How may they terme you Aprills sweetest morne
    When pleasing looks from those bright lights apeere:
    A sun-shine day; from clouds, and mists still cleere
    Kind nursing fires for wishes yett unborne!

Two starrs of Heaven, sent downe to grace the Earthe,
10   Plac'd in that throne which gives all joyes theyr birthe;
    Shining, and burning; pleasing yett theyr charmes;

Which wounding, even in hurts are deem'd delights,
    Soe pleasant is ther force! Soe great theyr mights
    As, happy, they can triumph in theyr harmes.

3.

Yett is ther hope: Then Love butt play thy part
    Remember well thy self, and think on mee;
    Shine in those eyes which conquer'd have my hart;
    And see if mine bee slack to answere thee:

Lodg in that brest, and pitty moving see
    For flames which in mine burne in truest smart
    Exiling thoughts that touch inconstancie,
    Or those which waste nott in the constant art,

Watch butt my sleepe, if I take any rest
10   For thought of you, my spiritt soe distrest
    As pale, and famish'd, I, for mercy cry;

PAMPHILIA TO AMPHILANTHUS
1 Venus holding a flaming heart appears on the title page illustration
of *Urania*.

Will you your servant leave? Think butt on this;
    Who weares loves crowne, must nott doe soe amiss,
    Butt seeke theyr good, who on thy force doe lye.

4.

Forbeare darke night, my joyes now budd againe,
    Lately growne dead, while cold aspects, did chill
    The roote at heart, and my chiefe hope quite kill,
    And thunders strooke me in my pleasures waine.

Then I alas with bitter sobs, and paine,
    Privately groan'd, my Fortunes present ill;
    All light of comfort dimb'd, woes in prides fill,
    With strange encrease of griefe, I griev'd in vaine,

And most, when as a memory to good
10   Molested me, which still as witnes stood,
    Of those best dayes, in former time I knew:

Late gone as wonders past, like the great Snow,[2]
    Melted and wasted, with what, change must know:
    Now backe the life comes where as once it grew.

5.

Can pleasing sight, misfortune ever bring?
    Can firme desire a painefull torment try?
    Can winning eyes prove to the hart a sting?
    Or can sweet lips in treason hidden ly?

The Sun most pleasing blinds the strongest eye
    If too much look'd on, breaking the sights string;[3]
    Desires still crost, must unto mischiefe hye,
    And as dispaire, a luckles chance may fling.

Eyes, having wunn, rejecting proves a sting
    Killing the bud beefor the tree doth spring;
10   Sweet lips nott loving doe as poyson prove:

Desire, sight, Eyes, lips, seeke, see, prove, and find
    You love may winn, butt curses if unkind:
    Then show you harrnes dislike, and joye in Love.

6.

Ô strive nott still to heape disdaine on mee
    Nor pleasure take your cruelty to show
    On haples mee, on whom all sorrowes flow,
    And byding make: as given, and lost by thee,

Alas; ev'ne griefe is growne to pitty mee;
    Scorne cries out 'gainst itt self such ill to show,
    And would give place for joyes delights to flow;
    Yett wreched I, all torturs beare from thee,

Long have I suffer'd, and esteem'd itt deere
10   Since such thy will; yett grew my paine more neere:
    Wish you my end? say soe, you shall itt have;

---

2   The first decade of the seventeenth century was marked by unusu-
ally cold weather in England. See Thomas Dekker, *The Great Frost: Cold
Doings in London* (1608) and a fictional elaboration in Virginia Woolf's
Orlando.

3   The invisible beam of light that some Renaissance thinkers believed
to be projected by the eye onto objects of sight.

For all the depth of my hart-held dispaire
    Is that for you I feele nott death for care;
    Butt now I'le seeke itt, since you will nott save.

Song. 1

The spring now come att last
    To trees, fields, to flowers,
And medowes makes to tast
    His pride, while sad showers
Which from mine eyes do flow
    Makes knowne with cruell paines
Colde winter yett remaines
    Noe signe of spring wee know.

The Sunn which to the Earth
    Gives heate, light, and pleasure,
Joyes in spring, hateth dearth,
    Plenty makes his treasure.
His heat to mee is colde,
    His light all darknes is
Since I am bar'd of bliss
    I heate nor light beeholde.

A sheapherdess thus sayd
    Who was with griefe oprest
For truest love beetraid
    Bard her from quiett rest
And weeping thus sayd she
    My end aprocheth neere
Now willow must I weare
    My fortune soe will bee.

With branches of this tree
    I'le dress my haples head
Which shall my wittnes bee
    My hopes in love ar dead;
My clothes imbroder'd all
    Shall bee with Gyrlands round .
Some scater'd, others bound
    Some ti'de, some like to fall.

The barck my booke shall bee
    Wher dayly I will wright
This tale of haples mee
    True slave to fortunes spight;
The roote shall bee my bed
    Wher nightly I will lye,
Wayling inconstancy
    Since all true love is dead.

And thes lines I will leave
    If some such lover come
Who may them right conseave,
    And place them on my tombe:
She who still constant lov'd
    Now dead with cruell care
Kil'd with unkind dispaire,
    And change, her end heere prov'd.

7.

Love leave to urge, thou know'st thou hast the hand;
  'T'is cowardise, to strive wher none resist:
  Pray thee leave off, I yeeld unto thy band;
  Doe nott thus, still, in thine owne powre persist,

Beehold I yeeld: lett forces bee dismist;
  I ame thy subject, conquer'd, bound to stand,
  Never thy foe, butt did thy claime assist
  Seeking thy due of those who did withstand;

Butt now, itt seemes, thou would'st I should thee love;
  I doe confess, t'was thy will made mee chuse;
  And thy faire showes made mee a lover prove
  When I my freedome did, for paine refuse.

Yett this Sir God, your boyship I dispise;
Your charmes I obay, butt love nott want of eyes.

8.

Led by the powre of griefe, to waylings brought
  By faulce consiete of change fall'ne on my part,
  I seeke for some smale ease by lines, which bought
  Increase the paine; griefe is nott cur'd by art:

Ah! how unkindnes moves within the hart
  Which still is true, and free from changing thought:
  What unknowne woe itt breeds; what endles smart
  With ceasles teares which causelessly ar wrought.

Itt makes mee now to shunn all shining light,
  And seeke for blackest clouds mee light to give,

  Which to all others, only darknes drive,
  They on mee shine, for sunn disdaines my sight.

Yett though I darke do live I triumph may;
Unkindnes, nor this wrong shall love allay.

9.

Bee you all pleas'd? your pleasures grieve nott mee:
  Doe you delight? I envy nott your joy:
  Have you content? contentment with you bee:
  Hope you for bliss? hope still, and still injoye:

Lett sad misfortune, haples mee destroy.
  Leave crosses to rule mee, and still rule free,
  While all delights theyr contrairies imploy
  To keepe good back, and I butt torments see,

Joyes are beereav'd, harmes doe only tarry;
  Dispaire takes place, disdaine hath gott the hand;
  Yett firme love holds my sences in such band
  As since dispis'ed, I with sorrow marry;

Then if with griefe I now must coupled bee
Sorrow I'le wed: Dispaire thus governs mee.

10.

The weary traveller who tired sought
  In places distant farr, yett found noe end
  Of paine, or labour, nor his state to mend,
  Att last with joy is to his home back brought;

Finds nott more ease, though hee with joy bee fraught;
   When past is feare, content like soules assend;
   Then I, on whom new pleasures doe dessend
   Which now as high as first borne bliss is wrought;

Hee tired with his paines, I, with my mind;
   Hee all content receaves by ease of limms;
   I, greatest hapines that I doe find
   Beeleefe for fayth, while hope in pleasure swimms;

Truth saith t'was wrong conseite bred my despite
Which once acknowledg'd, brings my harts delight.

11.

You endless torments that my rest opress
   How long will you delight in my sad paine?
   Will never love your favour more express?
   Shall I still live, and ever feele disdaine?

Alass now stay, and lett my griefe obtaine
   Some end; feede nott my hart with sharpe distress:
   Lett mee once see my cruell fortunes gaine
   Att least release, and long felt woes redress;

Lett nott the blame of cruelty disgrace
   The honor'd title of your Godhed, Love:
   Give nott just cause for mee to say a place
   Is found for rage alone on mee to move;

O quickly end, and doe nott long debate
My needfull ayde, least help do come too late.

12.

Cloy'd with the torments of a tedious night
   I wish for day; which come, I hope for joy:
   When cross I finde new tortures to destroy
   My woe-kil'd hart, first hurt by mischiefs might,

Then cry for night, and once mote day takes flight
   And brightnes gon; what rest should heere injoy
   Usurped is; hate will her force imploy;
   Night can nott griefe intombe though black as spite.

My thoughts are sad; her face as sad doth seeme:
   My paines are long; Her houers taedious are:
   My griefe is great, and endles is my care:
   Her face, her force, and all of woes esteeme:

Then wellcome Night, and farwell flattring day
Which all hopes breed, and yett our joyes delay.

Song. 2.

All night I weepe, all day I cry, Ay mee;
I still doe wish though yett deny, Ay mee;
I sigh, I mourne, I say that still
I only ame the store for ill, Ay mee;

In coldest hopes I freeze, yett burne Ay mee;
From flames I strive to fly, yett turne Ay mee;
From griefe I haste butt sorrowes hy,
And on my hart all woes doe ly Ay mee;

From contraries I seeke to runn Ay mee;
10   Butt contraries I can nott shunn Ay mee;
     For they delight theyr force to try,
     And to despaire my thoughts doe ty Ay mee;

Whether (alass) then shall I goe Ay mee;
     When as dispaire all hopes outgoe Ay mee;
     Iff to the Forest, Cupid hyes,
     And my poore soule to his lawe ties Ay me;

To the Court? O no. Hee crys fy Ay mee;
     Ther no true love you shall espy Ay mee;
     Leave that place to faulscest lovers
20   Your true love all truth discovers Ay mee;

Then quiett rest, and noe more prove Ay mee;
     All places ar alike to love Ay mee;
     And constant bee in this beegunn
     Yett say, till lyfe with love be dunn Ay mee.

13.

Deare fammish nott what you your self gave food;
     Destroy nott what your glory is to save;
     Kill nott that soule to which you spiritt gave;
     In pitty, nott disdaine your triumph stood;

An easy thing itt is to shed the blood
     Of one, who att your will, yeelds to the grave;
     Butt more you may true worthe by mercy crave
     When you preserve, nott spoyle, butt nurrish good;

Your sight is all the food I doe desire;
10   Then sacrifies mee nott in hidden fire,
     Or stop the breath which did your prayses move:

Think butt how easy t'is a sight to give;
     Nay ev'n deserte; since by itt I doe live,
     I butt Camaelion-like would live, and love.[4]

14.

Am I thus conquer'd? have I lost the powers
     That to withstand, which joy's to ruin mee?
     Must I bee still while itt my strength devowres
     And captive leads mee prisoner, bound, unfree?

Love first shall leave mens phant'sies to them free,
     Desire shall quench loves flames, spring hate sweet showres,
     Love shall loose all his darts, have sight, and see
     His shame, and wishings hinder happy howres;

Why should wee nott loves purblind charmes resist?   *totally blind*
10   Must wee bee servile, doing what hee list?
     Noe, seeke some hoste to harbour thee: I fly

Thy babish trickes, and freedome doe profess;
     Butt Ô my hurt, makes my lost hart confess
     I love, and must: So farwell liberty.

---

4 Because it can live for long periods without food, the chameleon was thought by Pliny, Erasmus, and other authorities to live on air.

15.

Truly poore Night thou wellcome art to mee:
    I love thee better in this sad attire
    Then that which raiseth some mens phant'sies higher
    Like painted outsids which foule inward bee;

I love thy grave, and saddest lookes to see,
    Which seems my soule, and dying hart intire,
    Like to the ashes of some happy fire
    That flam'd in joy, butt quench'd in miserie:

I love thy count'nance, and thy sober pace
10   Which evenly goes, and as of loving grace
    To uss, and mee among the rest oprest

Gives quiet, peace to my poore self alone,
    And freely grants day leave when thou art gone
    To give cleere light to see all ill redrest.

16.

Sleepe fy possess mee nott, nor doe nott fright
    Mee with thy heavy, and thy deathlike might
    For counterfetting's vilder then deaths sight,
    And such deluding more my thoughts doe spite.

Thou suff'rest faulsest shapes my soule t'affright
    Some times in liknes of a hopefull spright,
    And oft times like my love as in dispite
    Joying thou canst with mallice kill delight,

When I (a poore foole made by thee) think joy
10   Doth flow, when thy fond shadows doe destroy
    My that while senceles self, left free to thee,

Butt now doe well, lett mee for ever sleepe,
    And soe for ever that deare Image keepe,
    Or still wake, that my sences may bee free.

17.

Sweet shades why doe you seeke to give delight
    To mee who deeme delight in this vilde place
    Butt torment, sorrow, and mine owne disgrace
    To taste of joy, or your vaine pleasing sight;

Show them your pleasures who saw never night
    Of griefe, wher joyings fauning, smiling face
    Appeers as day, wher griefe found never space
    Yett for a sigh, a grone, or envies spite;

Butt O on mee a world of woes doe ly,
10   Or els on mee all harmes strive to rely,
    And to attend like servants bound to mee,

Heat in desire, while frosts of care I prove,
    Wanting my love, yett surfett doe with love
    Burne, and yett freeze, better in hell to bee.

18.

Which should I better like of, day, or night
    Since all the day I live in bitter woe
    Injoying light more cleere my wrongs to know,
    And yett most sad, feeling in itt all spite;

In night, when darknes doth forbid all light
 Yett see I griefe aparant to the show
 Follow'd by jealousie whose fond tricks flow,
 And on unconstant waves of doubt allight,

I can beehold rage cowardly to feede
 Upon foule error which thes humours breed
 Shame, doubt, and feare, yett boldly will think ill,

All those in both I feele, then which is best
 Darke to joy by day, light in night oprest
 Leave both, and end, thes butt each other spill.

10

Song. 3.

Stay, my thoughts, do nott aspire
 To vaine hopes of high desire:
 See you nott all meanes bereft
 To injoye? noe joye is left;
 Yett still mee thinks my thoughts doe say
 Some hopes do live amid dismay;

Hope, then once more hope for joy;
 Bury feare which joyes destroy;
 Thought hath yett some comfort giv'ne
 Which dispaire hath from us drivn;
 Therfor deerly my thoughts cherish
 Never lett such thinking perish;

10

'Tis an idle thing to plaine
 Odder farr to dy for paine,
 Thinke, and see how thoughts do rise
 Winning wher ther noe hope lies:
 Which alone is lovers treasure
 For by thoughts wee love doe measure:

Then kinde thought my phant'sie guide
 Lett mee never haples slide;
 Still maintaine thy force in mee,
 Lett mee thinking still bee free:
 Nor leave thy might untill my death
 Butt lett mee thinking yeeld up breath.

20

19.

Come darkest night, beecoming sorrow best;
 Light; leave thy light; fitt for a lightsome soule;
 Darknes doth truly sute with mee oprest
 Whom absence power doth from mirthe controle:

The very trees with hanging heads condole
 Sweet sommers parting, and of leaves distrest
 In dying coulers make a griefe-full role;
 Soe much (alas) to sorrow are they prest.

Thus of dead leaves her farewell carpett's made:
 Theyr fall, theyr branches, all theyr mournings prove;
 With leavles, naked bodies, whose huese vade   *decay*
 From hopefull greene, to wither in theyr love,

10

If trees, and leaves for absence, mourners bee
Noe mervaile that I grieve, who like want see.

20.

The Sunn which glads, the earth att his bright sight
    When in the morne hee showes his golden face,
    And takes the place from taedious drowsy night
    Making the world still happy in his grace;

Shewes hapines remaines nott in one place,
    Nor may the heavens alone to us give light,
    Butt hide that cheerfull face, though noe long space,
    Yett long enough for triall of theyr might;

Butt never sunn-sett could bee soe obscure
    No desart ever had a shade soe sadd,
    Nor could black darknes ever prove soe badd
    As paines which absence makes mee now indure;

The missing of the sunn awhile makes night
Butt absence of my joy sees never Light.

21.

When last I saw thee, I did nott thee see,
    Itt was thine Image, which in my thoughts lay
    Soe lively figur'd, as noe times delay
    Could suffer mee in hart to parted bee;

And sleepe soe favorable is to mee,
    As nott to lett thy lov'd remembrance stray,
    Least that I waking might have cause to say
    Ther was one minute found to forgett thee;

Then since my faith is such, soe kind my sleepe
    That gladly thee presents into my thought:
    And still true lover like thy face doth keepe
    Soe as some pleasure shadowe-like is wrought.

Pitty my loving, nay of consience give
Reward to mee in whom thy self doth live.

22.

Like to the Indians, scorched with the sunne,
    The sunn which they doe as theyr God adore
    Soe ame I us'd by love, for ever more
    I worship him, less favors have I wunn,

Better are they who thus to blacknes runn,[5]
    And soe can only whitenes want deplore
    Then I who pale, and white ame with griefs store,
    Nor can have hope, butt to see hopes undunn;

Beesids theyr sacrifies receavd's in sight   *received is*
    Of theyr chose sainte: Mine hid as worthles rite;
    Grant mee to see wher I my offrings give,

Then lett mee weare the marke of Cupids might
    In hart as they in skin of Phoebus light
    Nott ceasing offrings to love while I Live.

23.

When every one to pleasing pastime hies
    Some hunt, some hauke, some play, while some delight

---

5   Possibly an allusion to Jonson's *Masque of Blackness* (1606) in which
Lady Mary had participated.

In sweet discourse, and musique showes joys might
Yett I my thoughts doe farr above thes prise.

The joy which I take, is that free from eyes
　　I sitt, and wunder att this daylike night
　　Soe to dispose them-selves, as voyd of right;
And leave true pleasure for poore vanities;

When others hunt, my thoughts I have in chase;
　　If hauke, my minde att wished end doth fly,
　　Discourse, I with my spiritt tauke, and cry
While others, musique choose as greatest grace.

O God, say I, can thes fond pleasures move?
Or musique bee butt in sweet thoughts of love?

24.

Once did I heere an aged father say
　　Unto his sonn who with attention hears
　　What age, and wise experience ever clears
From doubts of feare, or reason to betray,

My Sonn sayd hee, beehold thy father, gray,
　　I once had as thou hast, fresh tender years,
　　And like thee sported, destitude of feares
Butt my young faults made mee too soone decay,

Love once I did, and like thee fear'd my love,
　　Led by the hatefull thread of Jelousy,
　　Striving to keepe, I lost my liberty,
And gain'd my griefe which still my sorrowes move,

In time shunn this; To love is noe offence
Butt doubt in youth, in age breeds penitence.

Song. 4.

Sweetest love returne againe
　　Make nott too long stay:
Killing mirthe, and forceing paine
　　Sorrow leading way:
Lett us nott thus parted bee
Love, and absence ne're agree;

Butt since you must needs depart,
　　And mee haples leave,
In your journey take my hart
　　Which will nott deseave
Yours itt is, to you itt flyes
Joying in those loved eyes,

Soe in part, wee shall nott part
　　Though wee absent bee;
Time, nor place, nor greatest smart
　　Shall my bands make free
Ty'de I ame, yett thinke itt gaine;
In such knotts I feele noe paine.

Butt can I live having lost
  Chiefest part of mee
Hart is fled, and sight is crost
  These my fortunes bee
Yett deere hart goe, soone returne
As good there, as heere to burne.

25.

Poore eyes bee blind, the light behold noe more
  Since that is gon which is your deere delight
  Ravish'd from you by greater powre, and might
  Making your loss a gaine to others store,

Oreflowe, and drowne, till sight to you restore
  That blessed star, and as in hatefull spite
  Send forth your teares in flouds, to kill all sight,
  And looks, that lost, wherin you joy'd before.

Bury thes beames, which in some kindled fires,
  And conquer'd have theyr love-burnt-harts desires
  Loosing, and yett noe gaine by you esteem'd,

Till that bright starr doe once againe apeere
  Brighter then Mars when hee doth shine most cleere
  See nott: then by his might bee you redeem'd.

26.

Deare cherish this, and with itt my soules will,
  Nor for itt rann away doe itt abuse,
  Alas itt left poore mee your brest to chuse
  As the blest shrine wher itt would harbour still;

Then favor shew, and nott unkindly kill
  The hart which fled to you, butt doe excuse
  That which for better, did the wurse refuse,
  And pleas'd I'le bee, though hartles my lyfe spill,

Butt if you will bee kind, and just indeed,
  Send mee your hart which in mines place shall feed
  On faithfull love to your devotion bound;

Ther shall itt see the sacrifises made
  Of pure, and spottles love which shall nott vade
  While soule, and body are together found.

27.

Fy tedious Hope, why doe you still rebell?
  Is itt nott yett enough you flatterd mee?
  Butt cuningly you seeke to use a spell
  How to beetray, must thes your trophies bee?

I look'd from you farr sweeter fruite to see
  Butt blasted were your blossoms when they fell,
  And those delights expected from hands free
  Wither'd, and dead, and what seem'd bliss proves Hell.

Noe towne was wunn by a more plotted slight
  Then I by you, who may my fortune write
  In embers of that fire which ruind mee,

Thus Hope, your faulshood calls you to bee tride
   You're loth I see the triall to abide;
   Prove true att last, and gaine your liberty.

28.

Griefe, killing griefe: have nott my torments binn
   Allreddy great, and strong enough: butt still
   Thou dost increase, nay glory in mine ill,
   And woes new past affresh new woes beeginn!

Am I the only purchase thou canst winn?
   Was I ordain'd to give dispaire her fill
   Or fittest I should mounte misfortunes hill
   Who in the plaine of joy can-nott live in?

If itt bee soe: Griefe come as wellcome ghest
10   Since I must suffer, for an others rest:
   Yett this good griefe, lett mee intreat of thee,

Use still thy force, butt nott from those I love
   Lett mee all paines, and lasting torments prove
   Soe I miss thes, lay all thy waits on mee.

29.

Fly hence O! joy noe longer heere abide
   Too great thy pleasures ar for my dispaire
   To looke on, losses now must prove my fare
   Who nott long since, on better foode relide;

Butt foole, how oft had I heavns changing spide
   Beefore of mine owne fate I could have care,
   Yett now past time, I can too late beeware
   When nothing's left butt sorrowes faster tyde;

While I injoy'd that sunn whose sight did lend
10   Mee joy, I thought, that day, could have noe end
   Butt soone a night came cloth'd in absence darke,

Absence more sad, more bitter then is gall
   Or death, when on true lovers itt doth fall
   Whose fires of love, disdaine rests poorer sparke.

30.

You blessed shades, which give mee silent rest,
   Wittnes butt this when death hath clos'd mine eyes,
   And separated mee from earthly ties,
   Beeing from hence to higher place adrest;

How oft in you I have laine heere oprest,
   And have my miseries in woefull cries
   Deliver'd forth, mounting up to the skies
   Yett helples back returnd to wound my brest,

Which wounds did butt strive how, to breed more harme
10   To mee, who, can bee cur'de by noe one charme
   Butt that of love, which yett may mee releeve;

If nott, lett death my former paines redeeme,
   My trusty freinds, my faith untouch'd esteeme
   And wittnes I could love, who soe could greeve.

Song. 5.

Time only cause of my unrest
By whom I hop'd once to bee blest
   How cruell art thou turned?
That first gav'st lyfe unto my love,
And still a pleasure nott to move
   Or change though ever burned;

Have I thee slack'd, or left undun
One loving rite, and soe have wunn
   Thy rage or bitter changing?
That now noe minutes I shall see,
Wherin I may least happy bee
   Thy favors soe estranging.

Blame thy self, and nott my folly,
Time gave time butt to bee holly;
   True love such ends best loveth,
Unworthy love doth seeke for ends
A worthy love butt worth pretends
   Nor other thoughts itt proveth:

Then stay thy swiftnes cruell time,
And lett mee once more blessed clime
   To joy, that I may prayse thee:

Lett mee pleasure sweetly tasting
Joy in love, and faith nott wasting
   And on fames wings I'le rayse thee:

Never shall thy glory dying
Bee untill thine owne untying
   That time noe longer liveth;
T'is a gaine such tyme to lend:
Since soe thy fame shall never end
   Butt joy for what she giveth.

31.

After long trouble in a taedious way
   Of loves unrest, lay'd downe to ease my paine
   Hopeing for rest, new torments I did gaine
   Possessing mee as if I ought t'obay:

When Fortune came, though blinded, yett did stay,
   And in her blesse'd armes did mee inchaine:
   I, colde with griefe, thought noe warmth to obtaine
   Or to dissolve that ice of joyes decay;

Till, 'rise sayd she, Reward to thee doth send
   By mee the servante of true lovers, joy:
   Bannish all clowds of doubt, all feares destroy,
   And now on fortune, and on Love depend.

I, her obay'd, and rising felt that love
Indeed was best, when I did least itt move.

32.

How fast thou fliest, O Time, on loves swift wings
   To hopes of joy, that flatters our desire
   Which to a lover, still, contentment brings!
   Yett, when wee should injoy thou dost retire,

Thou stay'st thy pace faulse time from our desire,
   When to our ill thou hast'st with Eagles wings.
   Slowe, only to make us see thy retire
   Was for dispayre, and harme, which sorrowe brings;

O! slacke thy pase, and milder pass to love;
   Bee like the Bee, whose wings she doth butt use
   To bring home profitt, masters good to prove
   Laden, and weary, yett againe pursues,

Soe lade thy self with honnye of sweet joye,
And doe nott mee the Hive of love destroy.

33.

How many eyes poore Love hast thou to guard
   Thee, from thy most desired wish, and end?
   Is itt because some say thou'art blind, that bard
   From sight, thou should'st noe hapines attend?

Who blame thee soe, smale justice can pretend
   Since 'twixt thee, and the sunn noe question hard
   Can bee, his sight butt outward, thou canst bend
   The hart, and guide itt freely; thus unbard

Art thou, while wee both blind, and bold oft dare
   Accuse thee of the harmes, our selves should find
   Who led with folly, and by rashnes blind
   Thy sacred powre, doe with a childs compare.

Yett Love this boldnes pardon: for admire
Thee sure wee must, or bee borne without fire.

34.

Take heed mine eyes, how you your lookes doe cast
   Least they beetray my harts most secrett thought;
   Bee true unto your selves for nothings bought
   More deere then doubt which brings a lovers fast.

Catch you all waching eyes, ere they bee past,
   Or take yours fixt wher your best love hath sought
   The pride of your desires; lett them bee taught
   Theyr faults for shame, they could noe truer last;

Then looke, and looke with joye for conquest wunn
   Of those that search'd your hurt in double kinde;
   Soe you kept safe, lett them themselves looke blinde
   Watch, gaze, and marke till they to madnes runn,

While you, mine eyes injoye full sight of love
Contented that such hapinesses move.

35.

Faulce hope which feeds butt to destroy, and spill
    What itt first breeds; unaturall to the birth
    Of thine owne wombe; conceaving butt to kill,
    And plenty gives to make the greater dearth,

Soe Tirants doe who faulsly ruling earth
    Outwardly grace them, and with profitts fill
    Advance those who appointed are to death
    To make theyr greater falle to please theyr will.

Thus shadow they theyr wicked vile intent
    Coulering evill with a show of good
    While in faire showes theyr malice soe is spent;
    Hope kills the hart, and tirants shed the blood.

For hope deluding brings us to the pride
Of our desires the farder downe to slide.

10

36.

How well poore hart thou wittnes canst I love,
    How oft my griefe hath made thee shed for teares
    Drops of thy deerest blood, and how oft feares
    Borne testimony of the paines I prove,

What torments hast thou sufferd while above
    Joy, thou tortur'd wert with racks which longing beares
    Pinch'd with desires which yett butt wishing reares
    Firme in my faith, in constancy to move,

Yett is itt sayd that sure love can nott bee
    Wher soe small showe of passion is descrid,
    When thy chiefe paine is that I must itt hide
    From all save only one who showld itt see.

For know more passion in my hart doth move
Then in a million that make show of love.

10

Song. 6.

You happy blessed eyes,
Which in that ruling place
Have force both to delight, and to disgrace,
Whose light allures, and ties
All harts to your command
O! looke on mee, who doe att mercy stand:

T'is you that rule my lyfe
T'is you my comforts give;
Then lett nott scorne to mee my ending drive,
Nor lett the frownes of stryfe
Have might to hurt those lights
Which while they shine they are true loves delights;

See butt, when Night appeares,
And Sunn hath lost his force
How his loss doth all joye from us divorce;

10

And when hee shines, and cleares
The heav'ns from clowds of night
How happy then is made our gazing sight,

Butt more then Sunns faire light
20   Your beames doe seeme to mee,
Whose sweetest lookes doe tye and yett make free;
Why should you then soe spite
Poore mee as to destroy
The only pleasure that I taste of joye?

Shine then, O deerest lights
With favor, and with love,
And lett noe cause, your cause of frownings move
Butt as the soules delights
Soe bless my then-bless'd eyes
30   Which unto you theyr true affection tyes.

Then shall the Sunn give place
As to your greater might,
Yeelding that you doe show more parfect light,
O, then, butt grant this grace
Unto your love-tied slave
To shine on mee, who to you all fayth gave;

And when you please to frowne
Use your most killing eyes
On them, who in untruth and faulcehood lyes;
40   Butt (deare) on mee cast downe
Sweet lookes for true desire
That bannish doe all thoughts of fayned fire.

37.

Night, welcome art thou to my mind destrest
  Darke, heavy, sad, yett nott more sad then I
  Never could'st thou find fitter company
For thine owne humor then I thus oprest.

If thou beest dark, my wrongs still unredrest
  Saw never light, nor smalest bliss can spy;
  If heavy, joy from mee too fast doth hy
And care outgoes my hope of quiett rest,

Then now in freindship joine with haples mee,
10   Who ame as sad, and dark as thou cansr bee
  Hating all pleasure, or delight of lyfe;

Silence, and griefe, with thee I best doe love
  And from you three, I know I can nott move,
  Then lett us live companions without strife.

38.

What pleasure can a bannish'd creature have
  In all the pastimes that invented arr
  By witt or learning, absence making warr
Against all peace that may a biding crave;   *shelter*

Can wee delight butt in a wellcome grave
  Wher wee may bury paines, and soe bee farr
  From lothed company who allways jarr
  Upon the string of mirthe that pastime gave;

The knowing part of joye is deem'd the hart;
  If that bee gon, what joy can joy impart
  When senceless is the feeler of our mirthe;

Noe, I ame bannish'd, and no good shall find
  Butt all my fortunes must with mischief bind
  Who butt for miserie did gaine a birth.

39.

Iff I were giv'n to mirthe 't'wowld bee more cross
  Thus to bee robbed of my chiefest joy;
  Butt silently I beare my greatest loss
  Who's us'd to sorrow, griefe will nott destroy;

Nor can I as those pleasant witts injoy
  My owne fram'd words, which I account the dross
  Of purer thoughts, or recken them as moss
  While they (witt sick) them selves to breath imploy,

Alas, think I, your plenty shewes your want,
  For wher most feeling is, words are more scant,
  Yett pardon mee, Live, and your pleasure take,

Grudg nott, if I neglected, envy show
  'T'is nott to you that I dislike doe owe
  Butt crost my self, wish some like mee to make.

40.

Itt is nott love which you poore fooles do deeme
  That doth apeare by fond, and outward showes
  Of kissing, toying, or by swearings glose,   *conceal*
  O noe thes are farr off from loves esteeme;

Alas they ar nott such that can redeeme
  Love lost, or wining keepe those chosen blowes
  Though oft with face, and lookes love overthrowse
  Yett soe slight conquest doth nott him beeseeme,

'T'is nott a showe of sighes, or teares can prove
  Who loves indeed which blasts of fained love
  Increase, or dy as favors from them slide;

Butt in the soule true love in safety lies
  Guarded by faith which to desart still hies,
  And yett kinde lookes doe many blessings hide.

41.

You blessed starrs which doe heavns glory show,
  And att your brightnes makes our eyes admire
  Yett envy nott though I on earth beelow
  Injoy a sight which moves in mee more fire;

I doe confess such beauty breeds desire,
 You shine, and cleerest light on us beestow,
 Yett doth a sight on earth more warmth inspire
 Into my loving soule, his grace to knowe;

Cleere, bright, and shining as you are, is this
 Light of my joye, fixt stedfast nor will move
 His light from mee, nor I chang from his love,
 Butt still increase as th'eith of all my bliss.   *the height*

His sight gives lyfe unto my love-rulde eyes
My love content beecause in his, love lies.

42.

If ever love had force in humaine brest?
 If ever hee could move in pensive hart?
 Or if that hee such powre could butt impart
 To breed those flames whose heat brings joys unrest.

Then looke on mee; I ame to thes adrest,
 I, ame the soule that feeles the greatest smart;
 I, ame that hartles trunk of harts depart
 And I, that one, by love, and griefe oprest;

Non ever felt the truth of loves great miss
 Of eyes, till I deprived was of bliss;
 For had hee seene, hee must have pitty show'd;

I should nott have bin made this stage of woe
 Wher sad disasters have theyr open showe
 O noe, more pitty hee had sure beestow'd.

Song. 7.

Sorrow, I yeeld, and greive that I did miss:
Will nott thy rage bee satisfied with this?
 As sad a Divell as thee,
 Made mee unhapy bee.
Wilt thou nott yett consent to leave, butt still
Strive how to showe thy cursed, devilsh skill;

I mourne, and dying am; what would you more?
My soule attends, to leave this cursed shore
 Wher harmes doe only flow
 Which teach mee butt to know
The sadest howres of my lives unrest,
And tired minutes with griefs hand oprest:

Yett all this will nott pacefy thy spite;
No, nothing can bring ease butt my last night.
 Then quickly lett itt bee
 While I unhappy see
That time, soe sparing to grant lovers bliss
Will see for time lost, ther shall noe grief miss,

Nor lett mee ever cease from lasting griefe,
Butt endless lett itt bee without reliefe:

    To winn againe of love,
      The favor I did prove;
And with my end please him; since dying I
Have him offended, yett unwillingly.

43.

O dearest eyes the lights, and guids of love,
    The joyes of Cupid who himself borne blind
    To your bright shining doth his triumphs bind
    For in your seeing doth his glory move;

How happy are those places wher you prove
    Your heavnly beames which makes the sunn to find
    Envy, and grudging hee soe long hath shind
    For your cleer lights, to mach his beames above.

Butt now, Alas, your sight is heere forbid
    And darknes must thes poore lost roomes possess
    Soe bee all blessed lights from henceforth hid
    That this black deed of darknes have excess,

For why showld heaven afford least light to those
Who for my misery such darcknes chose.

44.

How fast thou hast'st (O spring) with sweetest speed
    To catch thy waters which befor are runn,
    And of the greater rivers wellcom wunn,
    'Ere thes thy new borne streames thes places feed,

Yett you doe well least staying heere might breed
    Dangerous fluds your sweetest banks t'orerunn,
    And yett much better my distress to shunn
    Which makes my teares your swiftest course succeed,

Butt best you doe when with soe hasty flight,
    You fly my ills which now my self outgoe,
    Whose broken hart can testify such woe,
    That soe o'recharg'd my lyfe blood wasteth quite.

Sweet spring then keepe your way, bee never spent
And my ill days, or griefs assunder rent.

45.

Good now bee still, and doe nott mee torment
    With multituds of questions, bee att rest,
    And only lett mee quarrell with my brest
    Which still letts in new stormes my soule to rent:

Fy, will you still my mischiefs more augment?
    You say I answere cross, I that confest
    Long since, yett must I ever bee oprest
    With your toungue torture which will ne're bee spent?

Well then I see noe way butt this will fright
    That Divell speach; Alas I ame possesst,
    And mad folks senceles ar of wisdomes right,

The hellish speritt absence doth arest
   All my poore sences to his cruell might,
   Spare mee then till I ame my self, and blest.

46.

Love, thou hast all, for now thou hast mee made
   Soe thine, as if for thee I were ordain'd;
   Then take thy conquest, nor lett mee bee pain'd
   More in thy sunn, when I doe seeke thy shade,

Noe place for help have I left to invade,
   That show'de a face wher least ease might bee gain'd;
   Yett found I paine increase, and butt obtain'd
   That this noe way was to have love allayd,

When hott and thirsty to a well I came
10   Trusting by that to quench part of my flame.
   Butt ther I was by love afresh imbrac'd;

Drinke I could nott, butt in itt I did see
   My self a living glass as well as shee
   For love to see him self in truly plac'd.

47.

O stay mine eyes, shed nott thes fruitles teares
   Since hope is past to winn you back againe
   That treasure which beeing lost breeds all your paine,
   Cease from this poore betraying of your feares,

Think this too childish is, for wher griefe reares
   Soe high a powre, for such a wreched gaine;
   Sighs, nor laments should thus bee spent in vaine:
   True sorrow, never outward wayling beares;

Bee rul'd by mee, keepe all the rest in store,
10   Till noe roome is that may containe one more,
   Then in that sea of teares, drowne haples mee,

And I'le provide such store of sighs as part
   Shalbee enough to breake the strongest hart,
   This dunn, wee shall from torments freed bee.

48.

How like a fire doth love increase in mee,
   The longer that itt lasts, the stronger still,
   The greater purer, brighter, and doth fill
   Not eye with wunder more, then hopes still bee

Bred in my brest, when fires of love are free
   To use that part to theyr best pleasing will,
   And now impossible itt is to kill
   The heat soe great wher Love his strength doth see.

Mine eyes can scarce sustaine the flames my hart
10   Doth trust in them my passions to impart,
   And languishingly strive to show my love;

My breath nott able is to breathe least part
Of that increasing fuell of my smart;
Yett love I will till I butt ashes prove.

Pamphilia.

[FROM] THE COUNTESS OF MONTGOMERY'S URANIA

{PAMPHILIA'S SOLITARY WALKS}

Here was a fine grove of Bushes, their roots made rich with the sweetest flowres for smell, and colour. There a Plaine, here a Wood, fine hills to behold, as placed, that her sight need not, for natural content, stray further then due bounds. At their bottomes delicate Valleyes, adorn'd with severall delightfull objects. But what were all these to a loving heart? Alas, meerely occasions to increase sorrow, Love being so cruell, as to turne pleasures in this nature, to the contrary course, making the knowledge of their delights, but serve to set forth the perfecter mourning, tryumphing in such glory, where his power rules, not onely over mindes, but on the best of mindes: and this felt the perplexed Pamphilia, who with a Booke in her hand, not that shee troubled it with reading, but for a colour of her solitarinesse, shee walked beholding these pleasures, till griefe brought this Issue.

Seeing this place delicate without, as shee was faire, and darke within as her sorrowes, shee went into the thickest part of it, being such, as if Phoebus durst not there shew his face, for feare of offending the sadd Princesse; but a little glimmeringly, as desirous to see, and fearing to bee seene, stole heere, and there a little sight of that all-deserving Lady, whose beames sometimes ambitiously touching her, did seeme as if he shin'd on purest gold, whose brightnesse did strive with him, and so did her excellencie encounter his raies: The tops of the trees joyning so close, as if in love with each other, could not but affectionatly embrace. The ground in this place, where shee stayed was plaine, covered with greene grasse, which being low and thicke, looked as if of purpose it had beene covered with a greene Velvet Carpet, to entertaine this melancholy Lady, for her the softer to tread, loth to hurt her feet, lest that might make her leave it; this care prov'd so happy, as heere shee tooke what delight it was possible for her to take in such kinde of pleasures: walking up and downe a pretty space, blaming her fortune, but more accusing her love, who had the heart to grieve her, while shee might more justly have chid her selfe, whose feare had forc'd her to too curious a secrecie: Cupid, in her, onely seeking to conquer, but not respecting his victory so farre, as to allow so much favour, as to helpe the vanquished, or rather his power being onely able to extend to her yeelding, but not to master her spirit.

Oft would shee blame his cruelty, but that againe shee would salve with his being ignorant of her paine: then justly accuse her selfe, who in so long time, and many yeares could not make him discerne her affections, (though not by words plainely spoken;) but soone was that thought recalled, and blamed with the greatest condemnation, acknowledging her losse in this kinde to proceed from vertue. Then shee considered, hee lov'd another, this put her beyond all patience, wishing her sudden end, cursing her dayes, fortune, and affection, which cast her upon this rocke of mischiefe. Oft would shee wish her dead, or her beauty marr'd, but that she recall'd againe; loving so much, as yet in pitty shee would not wish what might trouble him, but rather continued according to her owne wish; complaining, fearing, and loving the most distressed, secret, and constant Lover that ever Venus, or her blind Sonne bestowed a wound or dart upon.

In this estate shee stayed a while in the wood, gathering sometimes flowres which there grew; the names of which began with the letters of his name, and so placing them about her.

"Well Pamphilia," said she, "for all these disorderly passions, keepe still thy soule from thought of change, and if thou blame any thing, let it be absence, since his presence will give thee againe thy fill of delight. And yet what torment will that prove, when I shall with him see his hopes, his joyes, and content come from another? O Love, O froward fortune, which of you two should I most curse? You are both cruell to me, but both alas are blinde, and therefore let me rather hate my selfe for this unquietnesse; and yet unjustly shall I doe too in that, since how can I condemne my heart, for having vertuously and worthily chosen? Which very choice shall satisfie mee with as much comfort, as I felt despaire. And now poore grasse," said shee, "thou shalt suffer for my paine, my love-smarting body thus pressing thee."

Then laid shee her excelling selfe upon that (then most blessed ground), "And in compassion give mee some rest," said shee, "on you, which well you may doe being honor'd with the weight of the loyallest, but most afflicted Princesse that ever this Kingdome knew: Joy in this and flourish still, in hope to beare this vertuous affliction. O Morea, a place accounted full of Love, why is Love in thee thus terribly oppressed, and cruelly rewarded? Am I the first unfortunate Woman that bashfulnesse hath undone? If so, I suffer for a vertue, yet gentle pitty were a sweeter lot. Sweet Land, and thou more sweet Love, pardon me, heare me, and commiserate my woe."

Then hastily rising from her low greene bed; "Nay," said shee, "since I finde no redresse, I will make others in part taste my paine, and make them dumbe partakers of my griefe." Then taking a knife, shee finished a Sonnet, which at other times shee had begunne to ingrave in the barke of one of those fayre and straight Ashes, causing that sapp to accompany her teares for love, that for unkindnesse.[1]

> Beare part with me most straight and pleasant Tree,
>   And imitate the Torments of my smart
>   Which cruell Love doth send into my heart,
>   Keepe in thy skin this testament of me:
>
> Which Love ingraven hath with miserie,
>   Cutting with griefe the unresisting part,
>   Which would with pleasure soone have learnd loves art
>   But wounds still curelesse, must my rulers bee.
>
> Thy sap doth weepingly bewray thy paine,
> 10 My heart-blood drops with stormes it doth sustaine,
>   Love sencelesse, neither good nor mercy knowes
>   Pitiles I doe wound thee, while that I
>   Unpitied, and unthought on, wounded crie:
>   Then out-live me, and testifie my woes.

And on the rootes, whereon she had laid her head, serving (though hard) for a pillow at that time, to uphold the richest World of wisdome in her sex, she writ this.

> My thoughts thou hast supported without rest,
> My tyred body here hath laine opprest
> With love, and feare: yet be thou ever blest;
> Spring, prosper, last; I am alone unblest.

Having ended it, againe laying her sad perfections on the grasse, to see if then some rest would have favourd her, and have thought travel had enough disturbed her, she presently found, passion had not yet allowed time for her quiet, wherefore rising, and giving as kind a farwell-looke to the tree, as one would doe to a trusty friend, she went to the brooke, upon the banke whereof were some fine shadie trees, and choice thorne bushes, which might as they were mixt, obtaine the name of a pretty Grove, whereinto she went, and sitting downe under a Willow,[2] there anew began her complaints; pulling off those branches, sometimes putting them on her head: but remembring her selfe, she quickly threw them off, vowing how ever her chance was, not to carry the tokens of her losse openly on her browes, but rather weare them privately in her heart.

[FROM] THE COUNTESS OF MONTGOMERY'S URANIA
1   Compare a similar act of poetic engraving by Pamela in Sidney's *Old Arcadia*, p. 198.
2   The willow is traditionally associated with the sadness of unrequited love, most famously in Desdemona's willow song in *Othello*, IV.iii.51.

{PAMPHLLIA AND AMPHILANTHUS VISIT THE THRONE OF LOVE}

Then came the Shepheard knight[3] (for so they cald him) all in Ash-colour,[4] no plume nor favour, onely favourd with his Ladies best wishes (the best of favours). The encounter was strong and delightful, shivers of their speares ascending into the aire, like sparkes of a triumph fire: fowre courses they ran, without any difference for advantage; the fift, the Knight of Victorie lost both stirrops, and a little yeelded with his body; the other passing with the losse of one stirrop; the sixth and last, being (if it were possible) a more strong, and excellent course: their ambitions equall to honour, glorious to love, and covetous of gaine before their Ladies, scorning any place lower then the face. Both hit so luckely and equally, as their beavers flew up, the Knight of Victorie being knowne to be Perissus, the other Amphilanthus, who confident that now he had truth on his side, and desirous once more to trie the strength of the other, while most eyes were on the Champion, he stole away, and arm'd himselfe. Amphilanthus at first knew not Perissus, many yeares having past since their last meeting: but when he heard Perissus nam'd, with what joy did he embrace him, being the man, who from his youth, hee had like himselfe loved, admiring his vertues, and loving his person. This done, they went to Pamphilia's tent, where shee gave Amphilanthus infinite thanks for the honour hee had done her.

"But yet my Lord," said she, "I must blame my poore beauty for the delay you had in your Victory, which I confessed, when I saw so long differring of your overcomming, grieving then for that want, which brought your stay in winning."

"Detract not from your beauty, which all judgements know without equall," said hee, "nor from the bountie of the renowned and famous Perissus, but give the reason where it is, which is want in my fortune to obtaine any thing that most I desire, or seek, such crosses hitherunto accompanied my life."

Then did Pamphilia intreat him to take knowledge of the other knight, whose name was Melisander, Duke of Pergamus[5] and her subject, whose father, though newly dead, and therefore wore that mourning armour, yet would not stay, but attend her thither; then Amphilanthus desired to know how it came about, that she honoured that place with her presence. The Queene willing to satisfie his demand began her discourse in this manner.

"Mine Uncle King of Pamphilia, comming for me to carry me into his Country, and there to settle me (as long since he resolv'd) by the consent and leave of my father, I went with him, by the way winning the happines of the companies of these excellent Princes, Perissus and Limena: after our arrivall I was crowned, and being peaceably setled, mine Uncle retired into a Religious house, where he will end his dayes: I heard still the fame of this enchantment, of which I had understood by my brother Parselius, who had himselfe got some unfortunate knowledge of it; I desired to adventure it, being assured that I was able for one part to conclude it, since it is to be finished by that vertue I may most justly boast of. Thus resolved (honoured with the presence likewise of this excellent King, and vertuous Queene, with the consent of my people, leaving the government for this time with the Councell) we came to adventure for the Throne of Love."

"Which," said Amphilanthus, "I am also to trie; wherefore let me be so much favoured, as I may bee the Knight to adventure with you, and you shall see, I want not so much constancy, as not to bring it to end, though it pleased you lately to taxe me with it."

"My Lord," said she, "I taxed you onely for Antissia's sake, who (poore Lady) would die, if shee thought that you had chang'd, shee so entirely loveth you."

"Hath she spoken to you to speake for her?" said hee. "In truth shee did well, since love much better suites with your lippes then her owne: but shall I have the honour that I seeke?"

"You shall command my Lord," said shee, "and wee will surely bring an end to it; your valour, and my loyalty being met together."

3 This disguise recalls Sir Philip Sidney's performance as the shepherd-knight in the Accession Day tilts, which continued to be commemorated after his death (see Roger Howell, *Sir Philip Sidney, the Shepherd Knight*).

4 Traditional symbol of repentance.

5 A city north of Smyrna in Asia Minor. The geography of *Urania* blends fact and fiction, just as it does biography, history, and romantic invention.

He made no other answere then with his eyes, so for that night they all parted, every one expecting the next mornings fortune, when the Throne should be so bravely adventur'd for. All that would trie their fortunes had free libertie; so six couples ventur'd before the peerelesse payre; but all were imprisoned, to be honord the more, with having their delivery by the power of the most excellent, who being ready to adventure, they were hindred a little by the comming of a Gentleman in white armour richly set forth, and bravely accompanied, who comming directly to Amphilanthus desired the honour of Knighthood, telling him hee had sought many places, and passed many Countries to receive that favour from him, which, but from him hee would not accept, withall pulling off his helme, which presently made him to be knowne to be Antissius King of Romania. Amphilanthus with due respect to him welcomd him, protesting he could never merit so high an honor as this was unto him, wherefore without delay in the sight of all that Princely company, he girt the sword to him, and he with Perissus put on his spurs; then came Allimarlus to kisse his hands, who most kindly he received.

"And now my Lord," said hee, "you are very fitly come to see the Throne of Love wonne (I hope) by this surpassing Queene, and your servant my selfe."

Antissius went to salute the Queene, so together they passed towards the Bridge. Antissius and Ollorandus going together, twind in each others armes, Pamphilia being thus appareld in a Gowne of light Tawny or Murrey,[6] embroidered with the richest, and perfectest Pearle for roundnesse and whitenes,[7] the work contrived into knots and Garlands; on her head she wore a crowne of Diamonds, without foiles, to shew her clearenesse, such as needed no foile to set forth the true brightnesse of it: her haire (alas that plainely I must call that haire, which no earthly riches could value, nor heavenly resemblance counterfeit) was prettily intertwind betweene the Diamonds in many places, making them (though of the greatest value) appeare but like glasse set in gold. Her necke was modestly bare, yet made all discerne, it was not to be beheld with eyes of freedome: her left Glove was off, holding the King by the hand, who held most hearts.

He was in Ashcolour, witnessing his repentance, yet was his cloake, and the rest of his suite so sumptuously embroidred with gold, as spake for him, that his repentance was most glorious; thus they passed unto the first Tower, where in letters of Gold they saw written, *Desire.* Amphilanthus knew he had as much strength in desire as any, wherefore he knocked with assured confidence at the Gate, which opened, and they with their royall companions passed to the next Tower, where in letters of Rubies they read *Love.*

"What say you to this, brave Queene?" said hee. "Have you so much love, as can warrant you to adventure for this?"

"I have," answerd shee, "as much as will bring me to the next Tower; where I must (I believe) first adventure for that."

Both then at once extremely loving, and love in extremity in them, made the Gate flie open to them, who passed to the last Tower, where *Constancy* stood holding the keyes, which Pamphilia tooke; at which instant *Constancy* vanished, as metamorphosing her self into her breast:[8] then did the excellent Queene deliver them to Amphilanthus, who joyfully receiving them, opened the Gate; then passed they into the Gardens, where round about a curious Fountaine were fine seates of white Marble, which after, or rather with the sound of rare and heavenly musick, were filled with those poore lovers who were there imprisoned, all chain'd one unto another with linkes of gold, enamiled with Roses and other flowers dedicated to *Love:* then was a voyce heard, which delivered these wordes:

"Loyallest, and therefore most incomparable Pamphilia release the Ladies, who must to your worth, with all other of your sexe, yeeld right preheminence: and thou Amphilanthus, the valliantest and worthiest of thy sexe, give freedome to the Knights, who with all other, must confesse thee matchlesse; and thus is *Love* by love and worth released."

Then did the musick play againe, and in that time the Pallace and all vanished, the Knights and Ladies with admiration beholding each other.[9] Then Pamphilia tooke Urania, and with affec-

---

6 Traditional symbol of despair.
7 As in the Rainbow and Ermine portraits of Queen Elizabeth at Hatfield House.

8 Cf. Matthew 6:21: "For where your treasure is, there will your heart be also."
9 As in a court masque.

tion kissing her, told her, the worth which shee knew to bee in her, had long since bound her love to her, and had caus'd that journey of purpose to doe her service. Then came Perissus, bringing Limena to thanke her, who heartilty did it as shee deserved, since from her counsell her fortunes did arise. Amphilanthus likewise saluted her, having the same conceit of resemblance between her and Leonius, as Parselius had, and so told her with exceeding joy, all after one another comming to her, and the rest. Antissius casting his eye upon Selarina, fixed it so, as it was but as the setting of a branch, to make a tree spring of it: so did his love increase to full perfection.

Then all desir'd by Pamphilia tooke their way to her Tent, everyone conducting his Lady, Amphilanthus, Pamphilia; Perissus, his Limena; Ollorandus, Urania; Antissius, Selarina; the King of Cyprus, his Queene; his brave base Sonne Polarchos, the Lady hee only lov'd, who was Princesse of Rodes.[10] Many other great Princes, and Princesses there were, both Greekes and Italians; Allimarlus for old acquaintance leading Urania's maide: thus to Pamphilia's tent they came, where most sumptuously shee entertain'd them: then did all the great Princes feast each other, the last being made by the King of Ciprus, who out of love to the Christian Faith, which before he contemned, seeing such excellent, and happy Princes professors of it, desired to receive it, which Amphilanthus infinitly rejoycing at, and all the rest, Christned him with his wife, excellently faire daughter, and Polarchos his valiant Sonne, and so became the whole Island Christians.

Then came he unto Amphilanthus, humbly telling him that the disgrace he had from him receiv'd, he esteemed as a favour, and honour sufficient, to be overcome by the valiantest King, who none must resist; to manifest which, he besought him to accept him unto his servant, and friend, with whom hee resolved to end his daies.

Amphilanthus replied, the honor was his, to gaine so brave a gentleman to his friendship, who should ever finde him ambitious to express his love to him.

"But," said he, "assuredly you never adventured the throne, but that you were in love."

He blushing, told him it was true, "But (alas) my Lord," said he, "I have no hope now to winne her." Then told he the King, the whole story of his love, beseeching him to assist him, which he promised to doe, and for that purpose to take their way by Rodes, and so at the delivering of her to her Father, to sollicit his suit for him, she extreamly loving him, hee kissed the Kings hands for it. And thus every one remain'd contented, Urania, longing to see Parselius, and yet not daring to demand any thing of him, till one day, (and the first of their journey) shee prettily began with Pamphilia, taking occasion upon her owne discourse as you shall heare.

But now that every one resolves of going homeward, what can bee imagin'd of loving Lucenia? Whose heart is now almost burst with spite, and rage, which she shewed to the King himselfe, when he came to take leave of her, telling her that it must be his ill fortune to part with her, that being finished which brought him thither. She answer'd, it was true, it was finished now to her knowledge, which she doubted not had had many ends with such foolish creatures as her selfe, "Els," said she, "had I never beene deluded with your flatteries."

"I never," said he, "protested more then I perform'd."

"It was my folly then," said she, "to deceive my selfe, and wrong mine owne worth, with letting my love too much express it selfe, to give advantage for my losse, when as if you had first sued, your now leaving mee might have beene falshood, where as it is onely turnd to my shame, and losse."

"I am sorry," said hee, "I shall part thus much in your displeasure, since I know I once was more favour'd of you."

"You cannot right me more," said shee, "then to goe, and gone, never more to thinke of me, unlesse your owne Conscience call upon you."

"It will not I hope," reply'd Amphilanthus, "be overburdened with this weight, since I will (now as ever I did) obey you, and so brave Lady farewell."

Shee would not wish him so much good, who now shee hated, so as onely making him a small reverence they parted, the Prince going to the Kings and Queenes who attended for him, the King of Cyprus bringing them to the Sea, the morning before their taking Shipp, presenting them with

10 Rhodes.

the Shepherds, and Shepherdesses of those Plaines, who after their manner sang and sported before
them, to the great delight of all, especially Pamphilia, who much loving Poetry, liked their pretie
expressions in their loves, some of which she caused to be twice sung, and those that were at the
banquet, (which was made upon the Sands, they being serv'd by those harmelesse people) to be
written out, which were two songes, and one Dialogue delivered betweene a neate, and fine
Shepheard, and a dainty loving Lasse, it was this.

Sh.	Deare, how doe thy winning eyes	
	my senses wholly tye?	
She.	Sense of sight wherein most lyes	
	change, and Variety.	
Sh.	Change in me?	
She.	Choice in thee some new delights to try.	
Sh.	When I change or choose but thee	
	then changed be mine eyes.	
She.	When you absent, see not me,	
	will you not breake these tyes?	
Sh.	How can I,	
	ever flye, where such perfection lies?	
She.	I must yet more try thy love,	
	how if that I should change?	
Sh.	In thy heart can never moove	
	a thought so ill, so strange.	
She.	Say I dye?	
Sh.	Never I, could from thy love estrange.	
She.	Dead, what canst thou love in me,	
	when hope, with life is fledd?	
Sh.	Vertue, beauty, faith in thee,	
	which live will, though thou dead,	
She.	Beauty dyes.	
Sh.	Not where lyes a minde so richly spedd.	
She.	Thou do'st speake so faire, so kind,	
	I cannot chose but trust,	
Sh.	None unto so chaste a minde	
	should ever be unjust.	
She.	Then thus rest,	
	true possest, of love without mistrust.	

An other delicate Mayd, with as sweet a voyce, as her owne lovely sweetnes, which was in her,
in more then usuall plentifulnesse, sang this Song, being as it seemd falne out with Love, or having
some great quarell to him.

　　　　Love what art thou? A vaine thought,
　　　　　In our mindes by fancy wrought,
　　　　　Idle smiles did thee beget,
　　　　　While fond wishes made the nett
　　　　　Which so many fooles have caught.

　　　　Love what art thou? light, and faire,
　　　　　Fresh as morning, cleere as th' ayre:
　　　　　But too soone thy evening change,
　　　　　Makes thy worth with coldnesse range,
　　　　　Still thy joy is mixt with care.

　　　　Love what art thou? a sweet flowre,
　　　　　Once full blowne, dead in an houre.
　　　　　Dust in winde as staid remaines

As thy pleasure, or our gaines,
If thy humour change to lowre.

Love what art thou? Childish, vaine,
    Firme as bubbles made by raine:
    Wantonnesse thy greatest pride,
    These foule faults thy vertues hide,
20 But babes can no staydnesse gaine.

Love what art thou? Causelesse curst,
    Yet alas these not the worst,
    Much more of thee may bee said,
    But thy Law I once obay'd,
    Therefore say no more at first.

This was much commended, and by the Ladies well liked of, onely Amphilanthus seem'd to take Loves part, and blame the mayde for accusing him unjustly, especially, for describing him with so much lightnesse. Then to satisfie him, a spruce Shepherd began a Song, all the others keeping the burden[11] of it, with which they did begin.

Who can blame me if I love?
    Since Love before the World did move.
When I loved not, I despair'd,
Scarce for handsomenesse I car'd;
Since so much I am refin'd,
As new fram'd of state, and mind,
        Who can blame me if I love,
        Since Love before the World did move.

Some in truth of Love beguil'd
10 Have him blinde and Childish stil'd:
But let none in these persist,
Since so judging judgement mist,
        Who can blame me?

Love in Chaos did appeare
When nothing was, yet he seemd cleare:
Nor when light could be describe,
To his crowne a light was tide.
        Who can blame me?

Love is truth, and doth delight,
20 Where as honour shines most bright:
Reason's selfe doth love approve,
Which makes us our selves to love.
        Who can blame me?

Could I my past time begin,
    I would not commit such sin
To live an houre, and not to love,
Since love makes us perfect prove,
        Who can blame me?

This did infinitely please the brave King; so cunningly, and with so many sweet voyces it was sung: then the banquet ended, they tooke leave of the kind King of Ciprus, and his company, all the rest taking ship with Pamphilia, sailing directly to Rodes, where they received unspeakable welcome, being feasted there eight dayes together, and for show of their true welcome, the Duke

11   Refrain (see headnote to Carols, p. 188.)

of that Iland bestowed his consent for marriage of his daughter, with her long beloved friend Polarchos, whose joy and content was such, as the other amorous Knights wisht to know. Then tooke they their leaves of the Duke, and all the Rodean Knights and Ladies, taking their way to Delos, Polarchos promising within short time to attend them in Morea.

{PAMPHILIA GIVES HER POEMS TO AMPHILANTUHS}

. . . Now the time for the Kings departure drew neere, the day before which hee spake to Pamphilia for some Verses of hers, which he had heard of. She granted them, and going into her Cabinet to fetch them, he would needs accompany her; shee that was the discreetest fashiond woman, would not deny so small a favour. When they were there, she tooke a deske, wherein her papers lay, and kissing them, delivered all shee had saved from the fire, being in her owne hand unto him, yet blushing told him, she was ashamed, so much of her folly should present her selfe unto his eyes.

He told her, that for any other, they might speake for their excellencies, yet in comparison of her excelling vertues, they were but shadowes to set the others forth withall, and yet the best he had seene made by woman: "But one thing," said he, "I must find fault with, that you counterfeit loving so well, as if you were a lover, and as we are, yet you are free; pitie it is you suffer not, that can faigne so well."

She smild, and blusht, and softly said (fearing that he or her selfe should heare her say so much), "Alas my Lord, you are deceived in this for I doe love."

He caught her in his armes, she chid him not, nor did so much as frowne, which shewed she was betrayd.

In the same boxe also he saw a little tablet lie, which, his unlooked for discourse had so surprised her, as shee had forgot to lay aside. He tooke it up, and looking in it, found her picture curiously drawne by the best hand of that time; her haire was downe, some part curld, some more plaine, as naturally it hung, of great length it seemd to bee, some of it comming up againe, shee held in her right hand, which also she held upon her heart, a wastcoate shee had of needle worke, wrought with those flowers she loved best.[12] He beheld it a good space, at last shutting it up, told her, he must have that to carry with him to the field. She said, it was made for her sister.

"Shee may have others," said he, "let me have this."

"You may command, my Lord," said she.

This done, they came forth againe, and so went to find Antissia, who was gone into the Parke, they followed her, and overtooke her in the Wood, where they sat downe, every one discoursing of poore Love, made poore by such perpetuall using his name. Amphilanthus began, but so sparingly he spake, as one would doe, who would rather cleare, then condemne a friend. Pamphilia followed, and much in the same kind. Antissia was the last, and spake enough for them both, beginning her story thus.

"I was till sixteene yeares of age so troubled, or busied with continuall misfortunes, as I was ingrafted into them; I saw no face that me thought brought not new, or rather continuance of perplexity, how was libertie then priz'd by me? envy almost creeping into me against such, as felt freedome; for none was so slavish as I deemd my selfe; betraid, sold, stolne, almost dishonored, these adverse fortunes I ranne, but from the last you rescued me, and saved your servant Antissia, to live fit to be commanded by you; yet gave you not so great a blessing alone, but mixt it, or suffered mixture in it: for no sooner was I safe, but I was as with one breath pardoned, and condemned againe subject, and in a farre stricter subjection: you brave King deliverd mee from the hands of

---

12   The handling of Pamphilia's miniature by Amphilanthus supports the view that these jewel-like objects were icons of the private self and were kept from public view, unlike the general display of the self in fashion and other public cultural forms during the English Renaissance. The hand over the heart, a common pose in miniatures by Nicholas Hilliard and Isaac Oliver, further emphasizes this sense of the private, inward self.

Villans, into the power of Love; whither imagine you, is the greater bondage, the latter the nobler, but without question as full of vexation.

"But to leave these things, love possessed me, love tirannized, and doth command me; many of those passions I felt in Morea, and whereof you most excellent Queene have been witnesse, but none so terrible, as absence hath since wrought in me, Romania being to me like the prison, appointed to containe me, and my sorrowes. One day among many other, I went to the sea side through a Walke, which was private and delicate, leading from the Court at Constantinople to the sea; there I used to walke, and passe much time upon the sands, beholding ships that came in, and boates that came ashoare, and many times fine passengers in them, with whom I would discourse as an indifferent woman, not acknowledging my greatnes, which brought mee to the knowledge of many pretty adventures, but one especially, which happened in this kind.

"A ship comming into the Harbor, but being of too great burden to come ashoare, in the long-boat the passengers came, and landed on the sands; I beheld them, among whom was one, whose face promised an excellent wit and spirit, but that beauty she had had, was diminished, so much only left, as to shew she had been beautifull. Her fashion was brave, and confident; her countenance sweet, and grave; her speech mild and discreet; the company with her were some twenty that accompanied her, the number of servants answerable to their qualities. Thus they came on towards us; I sent to know who they were, and of what Country (for their habits said, they were not Greekes). The reply was they were of Great Brittany, and that the chiefe Lady was a widdow, and sister to the Embassador that lay Leigeir there for the King of that Countrey. I had heard much fame of the Ladies of that Kingdome for all excellencies, which made mee the more desire to bee acquainted with her, yet for that time let it passe, till a fitter opportunity, which was soone offered me, for within few dayes she desired to bee permitted to kisse my hands. I willingly granted it, longing to heare some things of Brittany; when she came, I protest, shee behaved her selfe so excellently finely, as me thought, I envied that Countrey where such good fashion was.

"After this, shee desirous of the honour to be with me often, and I embracing her desire, loving her conversation, we grew so neere in affection, as wee were friends, the neerest degree that may be. Many times we walked together, and downe the same walke where first we met with our eyes; one day wee fell into discourse of the same subject we now are in, freely speaking as wee might, who so well knew each other, she related the story of her love thus.

"'I was,' said shee, 'sought of many, and beloved (as they said) by them, I was apt enough to beleeve them, having none of the worst opinions of my selfe, yet not so good an one as aspired to pride; and well enough I was pleased to see their paines, and without pitty to be pleased with them: but then love saw with just eyes of judgement that I deserved punishment for so much guilty neglect, wherefore in fury he gave me that cruell wound with a poysoned dart; which yet is uncured in my heart; for being free, and bold in my freedome, I gloried like a Marygold[13] in the Sun: but long this continued not, my end succeeding, like the cloasing of that flowre with the Sunnes setting. What shal I say, brave Princess? I lov'd, and yet continue it, all the passions which they felt for me; I grew to commiserat, and compare with mine; free I was in discourse with my rejected suiters, but onely because I desired to heare of it, which so much rul'd me, like a Souldier that joyes in the trumpet which summons him to death.

"'Those houres I had alone, how spent I them? if otherwise then in deare thoughts of love, I had deserved to have beene forsaken. Sometimes I studied on my present joyes, then gloried in my absent: triumphed to thinke how I was sought, how by himselfe invited, nay implor'd to pitty him, I must confesse not wonne, as most of us by words, or dainty fashion, rich cloathes, curiositie, in curiousnes, these wonne me not; but a noble mind, a free disposition, a brave, and manly counte-nance, excellent discourse, wit beyond compare, all these joynd with a sweete, and yet not Courtier-like dainty Courtship, but a respective love and neglective affection conquered me. He shewed enough to make me see he would rather aske then deny, yet did not, scorning refusall as well he

---

13 Perhaps a symbol of marriage.

might; free gift was what he wished, and welcom'd, daintynes had lost him, for none could winne or hold him, that came not halfe way at the least to meete his love, I came much more, and more I lov'd, I still was brought more to confirme his by my obedience. I may boldly, and truly confesse, that what with his liking, and observing, I lived as happy in his love as ever any did, and bless'd with blessings, as if with fasts, and prayers obtain'd.

" 'This happines set those poore witts I have to worke, and so to set in some brave manner forth my true-felt blisse, among the cheifest wayes I found expression in verse, a fine and principall one, that I followed, for he loved verse, and any thing that worthy was or good, or goodnes loved him so much as she dwelt in him, and as from ancient Oracles the people tooke direction, so governd he the rest by his example or precept, and from the continual flowing of his vertues was the Country inriched, as Egypt by the flowing of Nile gaines plenty to her fields: But I a poore weake creature, like the Ant, that though she know how to provide, yet doth it so, as all discerne her craft:[14] so I, although I sought the meanes to keepe this treasure, and my selfe from sterving, yet so foolishly I behaved my selfe, as indaingerd my losse, and wonne all envy to mee; I considered not, I might have kept, and saved, but I would make provision before such, as might be certaine of my riches. This undid mee, carrying a burthen, which not weightyer then I might wel beare, was not too much seene, an empty trunke is more trobesome then a bag of gold; so did my empty wit lead me to the trouble of discovery, and changing the golden waight of joy to the leaden, and heavy dispaire; but that came many yeares after my happines, for seaven yeares I was blest,[15] but then, O me, pardon me great Princesse,' cryd shee, 'I must not proceed, for never shall these lipps that spake his love, that kiss'd his love, discover what befell me.'

" 'Speake then,' said I, 'of these sweete dayes you knew, and touch not on his fault.'

" 'On mine deere Lady,' cryed shee, 'it of force must be, he could not err, I did, he was and is true worth, I folly, ill desert; he bravens mixt with gentle sweetnes, I ignorance, and weaknesse; hee wisdoms selfe, I follyes Mistris.'

" 'Why what offence gave you?' said I, 'speake of your owne.'

" 'I cannot name that, but it must,' replid she, 'bring the other on, for how can I say I saw the clowd, but I must feele the showre, therefore O pardon mee, I will not blame him, I alone did ill, and suffer still, yet thus farre I will satisfie you. Having search'd with curious, and unpartiall judgment, what I did, and how I had offended him, I found I was to busie, and did take a course to give offence, when most I hoped to keepe, I grew to doubt him to, if justly, yet I did amisse, and rather should have suffered then disliked. I thought by often letting him behold the paine I did endure for being blessd, tooke away al the blessing, wearying him, when that I hoped should have indeered him: but that though somtimes is a way, yet not alwayes to be practised, too much businesse, and too many excuses, made me past excuse. I thought, or feard, or foolishly mistrusted, hee had got an other love; I under other mens reports as I did faigne did speake my owne mistrust, whether he found it, or being not so hot in flames of yong affection, (growne now old to me) as once he was, gave not such satisfaction, as I hoped to have, but coldly bidde mee be assur'd, hee lov'd mee still, and seem'd to blame me, said I slact my love, and told mee I was not so fond.

" 'This I did falsly take like a false fier, and did worke on that, so as one night hee comming to my Chamber as hee used, after a little talke hee was to goe, and at his going stoop'd and kiss'd mee. I did answere that so foolishly, (for modestly I cannot call it, since it was a favour I esteem'd, and nere refus'd to take:) hee apprehended it for scorne, and started back, but from that time, unfortunate I, lived but little happier then you see me now.' "

Pamphilia smild to heare her come to that; the King was forc'd to cover his conceits, and wish her to proceed. She tooke her selfe, "Pray God," said shee, "I doe not play the Brittaine Lady now." They both then did intreat to heare the rest.

---

14 An allusion to Aesop's fable of the ant.

15 Josephine Roberts in her commentary (pp. 753–5) suggests that the dates in Antissia's narrative correspond with Mary Fitton's relationship with Pembroke, which ended in his imprisonment in 1601.

"That soone you may," said shee, "for this was all, only in a finer manner," and with greater passion shee did then conclude.

They found she was not pleas'd, therefore they sought some other way to please, and rising walked into an other wood, and so unto a pond, which they did fish, and passe the time with all, while poore Antissia thought her selfe each fish, and Amphilanthus stil the nette that caught her, in all shapes, or fashions she could be framed in.

Then came his going, all the night before, his whole discourse, and manner was to purchase still more love, greedy, as covetous of such gaine; hee wished not any thing that he enjoyed not, all was as hee wished. At supper poore Antissias eyes were never off from him, she did lament his going, her heart wept; hee looked as glad to see she lov'd him still, (for what man lives, that glories not in multitudes of womens loves?)[16] so he, though now neither fond nor loving to her, yet seem'd to like her love, if only that his might be the more prized, wonne from so brave and passionate a Lady; and thus she often caught his eyes, which on what condition soever, yet being on her, were esteem'd, and gave content, as debters doe with faire words, to procure their Creditors to stay a longer time: so did she, but prolonging the time in her torments to her greater losse.

Amphilanthus being to depart, offer'd to take his leave, but Pamphilia refused it, telling him she would bee ready the next morning before his going, which she was, and with Antissia, brought him a mile or more from the Court into a Forrest, then tooke leave, hee making all hast to the Campe.

George Wither (1588–1667)

A poet and pamphleteer, Wither was educated at Magdalen College, Oxford, and entered Lincoln's Inn in 1615. He published a wide range of satires, hymns, political diatribes, and a metrical Psalm book. He became a Puritan, serving as a military officer on the side of Parliament in 1642. His emblem book consists of a set of engravings that were first printed in *Nucleus emblematum selectissimorum* by Gabriel Rollenhagen, possibly in 1611 and 1613 in Utrecht. Wither proceeded to write what he called "Illustrations – poetic elaborations of the moral of each emblem – taking his clue from the Latin, Greek, or Italian mottoes in Rollenhagen's Dutch engravings. But Withers verses might be said to far exceed the engravings that inspire them in that they often expound a determined Christian allegory. Nevertheless, there is an appealing roughness in the verses (and in their printing), which contrasts with the more technically refined engravings. Elizabeth Eisenstein comments (1, p. 69) on the use of printed images as

mnemonic devices and suggests an important connection between emblem books, the art of memory tradition, and the increasing use of visual materials in printed books during the Renaissance. The reciprocal process of introducing verbal texts into painting is one of the themes of Svetlana Alpers's *The Art of Describing*.

READING

Svetlana Alpers, *The Art of Describing*.
Elizabeth L. Eisenstein, *The Printing Press as an Agent of Change*.
Rosemary Freeman, *English Emblem Books*.
Charles S. Hensley (ed.), *A Collection of Emblemes, Ancient and Moderne (1635)* by George Wither.

M. P.

16   A thinly veiled reference to Amphilanthus himself.

FROM A COLLECTION OF EMBLEMES, ANCIENT AND MODERNE

As soone, as wee to bee, begunne;
We did beginne, to be Vndone.

ILLVSTR. XLV.   *Book.* I

When fome, in former Ages, had a meaning
An *Emblem*, of *Mortality*, to make,
They form'd an *Infant*, on a *Deaths-head* leaning,
And, round about, encircled with a *Snake*.
The *Childe* fo pictur'd, was to fignifie,
That, from our very *Birth*, our *Dying* fprings:
The *Snake*, her *Taile* devouring, doth implie
The *Revolution*, of all Earthly things.
For, whatfoever hath *beginning*, here,
Beginnes, immediately, to vary from
The fame it was; and, doth at laft appeare
What very few did thinke it fhould become.
   The folid *Stone*, doth molder into *Earth*,
That *Earth*, e're long, to *Water*, rarifies;
That *Water*, gives an *Airy Vapour* birth,
And, thence, a *Fiery-Comet* doth arife:
That, moves, untill it felfe it fo impaire,
That from a *burning-Meteor*, backe againe,
It finketh downe, and thickens into *Aire*;
That *Aire*, becomes a *Cloud*; then, *Drops of Raine*:
Thofe *Drops*, defcending on a *Rocky-Ground*,
There, fettle into *Earth*, which more and more,

Doth harden, ſtill; ſo, running out the *round*,
It growes to be the *Stone* it was before.
    Thus, All things wheele about; and, each *Beginning*,
Made entrance to it owne *Deſtruction*, hath.
The *Life* of *Nature*, entreth in with *Sinning*;
And, is for ever, wayted on by *Death*:
    The *Life* of *Grace*, is form'd by *Death* to *Sinne*;
    And, there, doth *Life-eternall*, ſtraight beginne.

ILLVSTR. XLIII.   *Book.* 2

This is the *Poets-horſe*; a *Palfray*, SIRS,
(That may be ridden, without rod or ſpurres)
Abroad, more famous then *Buccephalsus*,
Though, not ſo knowne, as *Banks* his horſe, with us;
Or ſome of thoſe *fleet-horſes*, which of late,
Have runne their *Maſters*, out of their eſate.
For, thoſe, and *Hobby-horſes*, beſt befit
The note, and practice of their moderne wit,
Who, what this *Horſe* might meane, no knowledge had,
Vntill, a *Taverne-ſigne*, they ſaw it made.
    Yer, this old *Emblem* (worthy veneration)
Doth figure out, that *winged-contemplation*,
On which the *Learned* mount their beſt *Invention*,
And, climbe the *Hills* of higheſt Apprehenſion.
This is the nimble *Gennet*, which doth carry,
Their *Fancie*, thorow *Worlds* imaginary;

And, by *Ideas* feigned, fhewes them there,
The nature of thofe *Truths*, that reall are.
By meanes of *this*, our *Soules* doe come to know
A thoufand fecrets, in the *Deeps* below;
Things, here on *Earth*, and, things above the *Skyes*,
On which, we never fixed, yet, our eyes.
    No thorny, miery, fteepe, nor craggy place,
Can interrupt this *Courfer*, in his race:
For, that, which others, in their paffage troubles,
Augments his courage, and his vigour doubles.
Thus, fares the Minde, *infus'd with brave defires;*
It flies through Darkeneffe, Dangers, Flouds, and Fires:
    And, in defpight of what her ayme refifteth:
    Purfues her hopes, and takes the way fhe lifieth.

Live, *ever mindfull of thy* **dying;**
For, Time *is* **alwayes** *from thee* **flying.**

HORA ◉ VIVE MEMOR LETHI · FUGIT

ILLVSTR. XXVII.   *Book.* 4

This vulgar *Figure* of a *winged glaffe*,
Doth fignifie, how fwiftly *Time* doth paffe.
By that leane *Scull*, which to this *houre-glaffe* clings,
We are informed what effect it brings;
And, by the *Words* about it, wee are taught
To keepe our latter ending ftill in thought.
The common *houre-glaffe*, of the *Life* of *Man*,
Exceedeth not the largeneffe of a *fpan*.
The *Sand*-like *Minutes*, flye away fo faft,

That, *yeares* are out, e're wee thinke *months* are paſt:
Yea, many times, our *nat'rall day* is gone,
Before wee look'd for *twelve a clocke at Noone*;
And, where wee ſought for *Beautie, at the Full*,
Wee finde the *Fleſh* quite rotted from the *Skull*.

Let theſe Expreſſions of *Times* paſſage, bee
Remembrancers for ever, *Lord*, to mee;
That, I may ſtill bee guiltleſſe of their crime,
Who fruitleſly conſume their precious *Time*:
And, minde my *Death*; not with a ſlaviſh feare,
But, with a thankfull uſe, of *life-time*, here:
Not grieving, that my *dayes* away doe poſt;
But, caring rather, that they bee not loſt,
And, lab'ring with Diſceretion, how I may
Redeeme the *Time*, that's vainely ſlipt away.
So, when that *moment* comes, which others dread,
I, undiſmay'd, ſhall climbe my *dying bed*;
With joyfull *Hopes*, my *Fleſh* to duſt commend;
In *Spirit*, with a ſtedfaſt *Faith* aſcend;
  And, whilſt I *living* am, to ſinne ſo *dye*,
  That *dying*, I may live eternally.

For whatſoever, Man doth ſtrive,
The Conqueſt, God alone, doth give.

ILLVSTR. XXXIII.   *Book.* 4

When on the *Sword*, the *Olive-branch* attends,
(That is, when bloody *Warres*, have peacefull *Ends*)

And, whenfoever *Victories* are gained;
This *Emblem* fhewes, by whom they are obtained:
For, that all *Victorie*, doth onely from
The pow'rfull hand of *God-Almighite*, come,
The Boughes of *Bayes* and *Olives*, doe declare,
Which round the *Tetragrammaton* appeare.
Nor muft we thinke, that God beftowes, alone,
The *Victories* of Warre, on any one;
But, that, when we contend in other things,
From him, th'event that's wifht for, alfo fprings.
  This being fo, how dare wee, by the *Lawes*,
Or, by the *Sword*, purfue a wicked Caufe:
How dare wee bring a matter that's unjuft,
Where hee (though few perceive him) judge it muft:
Or, profecute with fury, or defpite,
Againft the perfon of his *Favourite?*
What Fooles are they, who feeke the *Conquest*, by
Oppreffion, Fraud, or hellifh Perjurie?
How mad are thofe, who to the *Warres* prepare,
For nothing, but to fpoyle and murther there?
Who, nor ingag'd by Faith to their *Alies*,
Nor urg'd by any private injuries,
Nor fent, nor tolerated, by their *Prince*,
Nor caring whether fide hath giv'n offence,
Run rambling through the World, to kill and flay,
Like needie Butchers, for two groats a day?
  Thefe men may fide, where *Conquefts*, God beftowes;
  Yet, when the *Field* is wonne, thefe men doe lofe.

How ever thou the Viper take,
A dang'rous hazzard thou doſt make.

ILLVSTR. XXXIX.

Book. 4

This *Figure* warnes us, that wee meddle not
With matters, whereby nothing may bee got,
Save *harme* or *loſſe*; and, ſuch as once begun,
Wee may, nor ſafely *doe*, nor leave *undone*.
I ſhould bee loath to meddle in the ſtrife
Ariſing 'twixt a *Husband*, and his *Wife*;
For, *Truth* conceal'd, or ſpoke, on either ſide,
May one or th'other grieve, or both divide.
I would not with my moſt familiar *Mate*,
Be *Partner* in the whole of my eſtate;
Leſt I, by others errors, might offend,
Or, wrong my Family, or, loſe my *Friend*.
I would not, willingly, in my diſtreſſe,
From an unworthy hand, receive redreſſe;
Nor, when I need a *Suretie*, would I call
An *Vnthrift*, or a roaring *Prodigall*:
For, either theſe I thankleſly muſt ſhun,
Or, humour them, and be perhaps undone.
I would not heare my *Friend* unwiſely prate
Thoſe things, of which I muſt informe the *State*:
And, ſeeme unfriendly; or elſe leave to doe,
That, which a ſtronger *Band* obligeth to.
  Nor would I, for the world, my heart ſhould bee
Enthrald by one, that might not *marry* mee;

Or, fuch like *paſsions*, bee perplexed in,
As hang betwixt a *Vertue*, and a *Sinne*;
Or, fuch, as whether way foe're I went,
Occafion'd guilt, or fhame, or difcontent:
    For, howfoe're wee mannage fuch like things,
    Wee handle winding *Vipers*, that have ftings.

In all thine Actions , have a care,
That no unfeemlineſſe appeare.

ILLVSTR. XLV.

Book. 4

The *Virgine*, or the *Wife*, that much defires
To pleafe her *Lovers*, or her *Husband's* Eyes,
In all her coſtl'eſt *Robes*, her felfe attires;
And, feekes the coml'eſt *Dreſe*, fhee can devife.
Then, to her truſtie *Looking-glaſſe*, fhee goes,
(Where, often, fhee her perfon turnes and winds)
To view, how feemely her attiring fhowes;
Or, whether ought amiſſe therein fhe finds.
Which praifefull *Diligence*, is figur'd thus
In this our *Emblem*; that, it may be made
A documentall figne, remembring us,
What care of all our *Actions*, muſt bee had.
For, hee that in *God's* prefence would appeare
An acceptable *Soule*; or, gracious grow
With men, that of approv'd conditions are,
Muſt by fome faithfull *Glaſſe*, be trimmed fo,

The good Examples of thofe pious men,
Who liv'd in elder times, may much availe:
Yea, and by others evills, now and then,
Men fee how groffely, they themfelves, doe faile.
  A wife Companion, and, a loving Friend,
Stands nearer, than thofe ancient glaffes doe;
And, ferveth well to fuch an ufefull end:
For hee may bee thy *Glaffe*, and *Fountaine* too.
His good *Example*, fhewes thee what is fit;
His *Admonition*, checks what is awry;
Hee, by his *Good-advife*, reformeth it;
And, by his *Love*, thou mend'ft it pleafedly.
    But, if thou doe defire the perfect'ft *Glaffe*,
    Ioyne to the *Morrall-Law*, the *Law of Grace*.

Anonymous Ballads (*c.*1590)

Ballads are a form of narrative song that were passed on orally from as early as the Middle Ages. They deal with a wide range of subjects derived from historical events to legends and supernatural occurrences to the details of domestic life. The most common form is the ballad of common meter, a four-line strophe with alternating lines of eight and six syllables. Nonsense refrain lines are also common. During the sixteenth century broadside ballads became particularly popular in England. They were commonly printed on one side of a folio page and were sold at fairs and bookstalls or displayed at inns and taverns. Because they were quickly absorbed into oral tradition, ballads were naturally subject to a wide range of variation and improvization. The scholarly interest in ballads did not begin until the eighteenth century, which accounts for the fact that the surviving texts are often of a much later date than that of their original composition.

READING

Francis J. Child (ed.), *English and Scottish Popular Ballads*.

M. P.

MY LADY GREENSLEEVES

ALAS! my love, you do me wrong
    To cast me off discourteously;
And I have lovèd you so long,
    Delighting in your company.

    Greensleeves was all my joy!
    Greensleeves was my delight!
    Greensleeves was my heart of gold!
        And who but my Lady Greensleeves!

I bought thee petticoats of the best,
    The cloth so fine as fine as might be;
I gave thee jewels for thy chest,
    And all this cost I spent on thee.
        Greensleeves, etc.

Thy smock of silk, both fair and white,
    With gold embroidered gorgeously;
Thy petticoat of sendal right: *silk*

10

And these I bought thee gladly.
    Greensleeves, etc.

20
Thy gown was of the grassy green,
    The sleeves of satin hanging by;
Which made thee be our harvest queen:
    And yet thou wouldest not love me!
        Greensleeves, etc.

Greensleeves now farewell! adieu!
    God I pray to prosper thee!
For I am still thy lover true:
    Come once again and love me!
        Greensleeves was all my joy!
        Greensleeves was my delight!
30
        Greensleeves was my heart of gold!
        And who but Lady Greensleeves!

IN PRAISE OF ALE

WHEN the chill Charoko blows,   *Sirocco*
    And Winter tells a heavy tale,
And pyes and daws and rooks and crows
Do sit and curse the frosts and snows;
    Then give me ale.

Ale in a Saxon rumkin then,
    Such as will make grim Malkin prate;   *slut*
Bids valour burgeon in tall men,
Quickens the poet's wits and pen,
10
    Despises fate.

Ale, that the absent battle fights,
    And forms the march of Swedish drum,
Disputes the princes' laws, and rights,
What's past and done tells mortal wights,
    And what's to come.

Ale, that the plowman's heart up-keeps
    And equals it to tyrants' thrones,
That wipes the eye that ever-weeps,
And lulls in sweet and dainty sleeps
    Their very bones.

Grandchild of Ceres, Bacchus' daughter,
    Wine's emulous neighbour, though but stale,
Ennobling all the nymphs of water,
And filling each man's heart with laughter —
    Ha! Ha! give me ale!

ROBIN GOODFELLOW

FROM Oberon, in fairy land,
    The king of ghosts and shadows there,
Mad Robin I, at his command,
    Am sent to view the night-sports here.

What revel rout
Is kept about,
In every corner where I go,
I will o'ersee,
And merry be,
And make good sport, with ho, ho, ho!

More swift than lightning can I fly
About this airy welkin soon,
And, in a minute's space, descry
Each thing that's done below the moon.
There's not a hag
Or ghost shall wag,
Or cry, 'ware goblins! where I go;
But Robin I
Their feasts will spy,
And send them home with ho, ho, ho!

Whene'er such wanderers I meet,
As from their night-sports they trudge home,
With counterfeiting voice I greet,
And call them on with me to roam:
Through woods, through lakes,
Through bogs, through brakes;
Or else, unseen with them I go,
All in the nick,
To play some trick,
And frolic it, with ho, ho, ho!

Sometimes I meet them like a man,
Sometimes an ox, sometimes a hound;
And to a horse I turn me can,
To trip and trot about them round.
But if to ride
My back they stride,
More swift than wind away I go:
O'er hedge and lands,
Through pools and ponds
I hurry, laughing, ho, ho, ho!

When lads and lasses merry be,
With possets and with junkets fine;
Unseen of all the company,
I eat their cakes and sip their wine!
And, to make sport,
I puff and snort:
And out the candles I do blow:
The maids I kiss,
They shriek—Who's this?
I answer nought but ho, ho, ho!

Yet now and then, the maids to please,
At midnight I card up their wool;
And, while they sleep and take their ease,
With wheel to threads their flax I pull.
I grind at mill
Their malt up still;
I dress their hemp; I spin their tow;

                    If any wake,
                    And would me take,
60   I wend me, laughing, ho, ho, ho!

When any need to borrow aught,
        We lend them what they do require:
And for the use demand we nought;
        Our own is all we do desire.
                If to repay
                They do delay,
        Abroad amongst them then I go,
                And night by night
                I them affright
70   With pinchings, dreams, and ho, ho, ho!

When lazy queans have nought to do,
        But study how to cheat and lie:
To make debate and mischief too,
        'Twixt one another secretly:
                I mark their gloze,
                And it disclose
        To them whom they have wrongèd so:
                When I have done,
                I get me gone,
80   And leave them scolding, ho, ho, ho!

When men do traps and engines set
        In loop-holes, where the vermin creep,
Who from their folds and houses get
        Their ducks and geese, and lambs and sheep;
                I spy the gin,
                And enter in,
        And seem a vermin taken so;
                But when they there
                Approach me near,
90   I leap out laughing ho, ho, ho!

By wells and rills in meadows green,
        We nightly dance our heyday guise;
And to our fairy king and queen
        We chant our moonlight minstrelsies.
                When larks 'gin sing,
                Away we fling;
        And babes newborn steal as we go;
                And elf in bed
                We leave instead,
100   And wend us laughing, ho, ho, ho!

From hag-bred Merlin's time, have I
        Thus nightly revelled to and fro;
And for my pranks men call me by
        The name of Robin Goodfellow.
                Fiends, ghosts, and sprites,
                Who haunt the nights,
        The hags and goblins do me know;
                And beldames old
                My feats have told,
110   So vale, vale; ho, ho, ho!

THE SPANISH ARMADO[1]

SOME years of late, in eighty-eight,
   As I do well remember,
It was, some say, the middle of May,
   And some say in September,
     And some say in September.

The Spanish train launched forth amain,
   With many a fine bravado,
Their (as they thought, but it proved not)
   Invincible Armado,
10   Invincible Armado.

There was a man that dwelt in Spain
   Who shot well with a gun a,
Don Pedro[2] hight, as black a wight   *called*
   As the Knight of the Sun a,
     As the Knight of the Sun a.

King Philip[3] made him Admiral,
   And bid him not to stay a,
But to destroy both man and boy
   And so to come away a,
20   And so to come away a.

Their navy was well victualled
   With biscuit, pease, and bacon,
They brought two ships, well fraught with whips,
   But I think they were mistaken,
     But I think they were mistaken.

Their men were young, munition strong,
   And to do us more harm a,
They thought it meet to join their fleet
   All with the Prince of Parma,[4]
30   All with the Prince of Parma.

They coasted round about our land,
   And so came in by Dover:
But we had men set on 'em then,
   And threw the rascals over,
     And threw the rascals over.

The Queen was then at Tilbury,[5]
   What could we more desire a?
Sir Francis Drake[6] for her sweet sake
   Did set them all on fire a,
40   Did set them all on fire a.

Then straight they fled by sea and land,
   That one man killed threescore a,

The Spanish Armado
1 The Spanish Armada, also called the Invincible Armada, was launched against England in 1588 and was utterly destroyed.
2 Don Pedro de Valdes, one of the Spanish commanders.
3 Phillip II, King of Spain.

4 The fleet was to have met with the army of the Duke of Parma to invade England and capture the English throne for Philip.
5 Queen Elizabeth reviewed her troops at Tilbury on August 18th.
6 Drake was a principal leader of the English fleet.

And had not they all run away,
  In truth he had killed more a,
    In truth he had killed more a.

Then let them neither bray nor boast,
  But if they come again a,
Let them take heed they do not speed
  As they did you know when a,
50   As they did you know when a.

George Herbert (1593–1633)

Although his earliest biographer, Izaak Walton, captured much that is still important for an understanding of Herbert's life, thought, and art, he has suffered somewhat, as Emily Dickinson once did, from the myth of the reclusive, pious, and simple poet. In the work of both writers there is a lyrical intensity, a power of imaginative intelligence, and a relentless conviction that refuses to be sentimentalized. One of the greatest lyric poets to have written in English, Herbert survived with tough-minded determination some of the most powerful religious conflicts of his time. What Donne wrote in praise of Herbert's mother, Magdalene Herbert, applies with equal force to him: "For, as the rule of all her civil actions was Religion, so, the rule of her Religion, was the Scripture; and her rule, for her particular understanding of the Scripture, was the Church. She never diverted towards the Papist, in undervaluing the Scripture; nor towards the Separatist, in undervaluing the Church" (A Sermon of Commemoration). Herbert was well acquainted with many of the principal figures in the religious factions of his time (his oldest brother was famously unorthodox and his stepfather a leading regicide), but he managed to maintain his independence from them.

His father, Richard Herbert, died when Herbert was four, leaving his mother to manage her large and distinguished family (she had seven sons and three daughters). The home that Magdalene Herbert provided was witty and learned, as well as pious. She herself provided primary instruction in the Bible and the classics, and Donne, who knew her well, described her temperament as "naturally cheerful, and merry, and loving facetiousness, and sharpness of wit." When he was about 12 years old, George Herbert was sent to Westminster School, where his brother Charles was already a student. From Westminster he went to Trinity College, Cambridge. After receiving his BA, he progressed through his master's degree in 1616 (the year of Shakespeare's death), by which time he was already a Fellow of Trinity, where he was soon to become University Orator. In 1624 he was elected a Member of Parliament for Montgomery, for which he took a leave of absence from the University. Two years after his mother's death in 1627, he married and accepted an offer from the church at Bemerton. Most of the poems in The Temple were written during the last three hectic years of his life.

READING

Stanley Fish, Living Temple: George Herbert and Catechizing.
Joseph Summers, George Herbert: His Religion and Art.
Helen Vendler, The Poetry of George Herbert.

M. P.

[FROM] THE TEMPLE

The Altar

A broken ALTAR, Lord, thy servant rears,
  Made of a heart, and cemented with tears;
    Whose parts are as thy hand did frame;
    No workman's tool hath touched the same.
        A HEART alone
        Is such a stone,

As nothing but
Thy pow'r doth cut.
Wherefore each part
10   Of my hard heart
Meets in this frame,
To praise thy name.
That, if I chance to hold my peace,
These stones to praise thee may not cease.
O let thy blessed SACRIFICE be mine,
And sanctify this ALTAR to be thine.

The Sacrifice

Oh, all ye, who pass by, whose eyes and mind
To worldly things are sharp, but to me blind,
To me, who took eyes that I might you find:
                    Was ever grief like mine?

The Princes of my people make a head
Against their Maker: they do wish me dead,
Who cannot wish, except I give them bread:
                    Was ever grief like mine?

Without me each one, who doth now me brave,
10   Had to this day been an Egyptian slave.
They use that power against me, which I gave:
                    Was ever grief like mine?

Mine own Apostle, who the bag did bear,
Though he had all I had, did not forbear
To sell me also, and to put me there:
                    Was ever grief like mine?

For thirty pence he did my death devise,
Who at three hundred did the ointment prize,
Not half so sweet as my sweet sacrifice:
20   Was ever grief, &c.

Therefore my soul melts, and my heart's dear treasure
Drops blood (the only beads) my words to measure:
O let this cup pass, if it be thy pleasure:
                    Was ever grief, &c.

These drops being tempered with a sinner's tears
A balsam are for both the hemispheres:
Curing all wounds, but mine, all, but my fears:
                    Was ever grief, &c.

Yet my Disciples sleep: I cannot gain
30   One hour of watching, but their drowsy brain
Comforts not me, and doth my doctrine stain:
                    Was ever grief, &c.

Arise, arise, they come. Look how they run.
Alas! what haste they make to be undone!
How with their lanterns do they seek the sun!
                    Was ever grief, &c.

With clubs and staves they seek me, as a thief,
Who am the way of Truth, the true relief,
Most true to those, who are my greatest grief:
      Was ever grief, &c.

40

Judas, dost thou betray me with a kiss?
Canst thou find hell about my lips? and miss
Of life, just at the gates of life and bliss?
      Was ever grief, &c.

See, they lay hold on me, not with the hands
Of faith, but fury: yet at their commands
I suffer binding, who have loosed their bands:
      Was ever grief, &c.

All my Disciples fly; fear puts a bar

50

Betwixt my friends and me. They leave the star,
That brought the wise men of the East from far.
      Was ever grief like mine?

Then from one ruler to another bound
They lead me, urging, that it was not sound
What I taught: Comments would the text confound.
      Was ever grief, &c.

The Priests and rulers all false witness seek
'Gainst him, who seeks not life, but is the meek
And ready Paschal Lamb of this great week:

60

      Was ever grief, &c.

Then they accuse me of great blasphemy,
That I did thrust into the Deity,
Who never thought that any robbery:
      Was ever grief, &c.

Some said, that I the Temple to the floor
In three days razed, and raised as before.
Why, he that built the world can do much more:
      Was ever grief, &c.

Then they condemn me all with that same breath,

70

Which I do give them daily, unto death.
Thus *Adam* my first breathing rendereth:
      Was ever grief, &c.

They bind, and lead me unto *Herod*: he
Sends me to *Pilate*. This makes them agree;
But yet their friendship is my enmity:
      Was ever grief, &c.

Herod and all his bands do set me light,
Who teach all hands to war, fingers to fight,
And only am the Lord of Hosts and might:

80

      Was ever grief, &c.

Herod in judgement sits while I do stand,
Examines me with a censorious hand:
I him obey, who all things else command:
      Was ever grief, &c.

The *Jews* accuse me with despitefulness,
And vying malice with my gentleness,
Pick quarrels with their only happiness:
Was ever grief like mine?

I answer nothing, but with patience prove
90   If stony hearts will melt with gentle love.
But who does hawk at eagles with a dove?
Was ever grief, &c.

My silence rather doth augment their cry;
My dove doth back into my bosom fly,
Because the raging waters still are high:
Was ever grief, &c.

Hark how they cry aloud still, *Crucify*:
It is not fit he live a day, they cry,
Who cannot live less than eternally:
100   Was ever grief, &c.

Pilate a stranger holdeth off; but they,
Mine own dear people, cry, *Away, away*,
With noises confused frighting the day:
Was ever grief, &c.

Yet still they shout, and cry, and stop their ears,
Putting my life among their sins and fears,
And therefore wish *my blood on them and theirs*:
Was ever grief, &c.

See how spite cankers things. These words aright
110   Used, and wished, are the whole world's light:
But honey is their gall, brightness their night:
Was ever grief, &c.

They choose a murderer, and all agree
In him to do themselves a courtesy:
For it was their own cause who killed me:
Was ever grief, &c.

And a seditious murderer he was:
But I the Prince of peace, peace that doth pass
All understanding, more than heav'n doth glass:
120   Was ever grief, &c.

Why, Caesar is their only King, not I:
He clave the stony rock, when they were dry;
But surely not their hearts, as I well try:
Was ever grief like mine?

Ah! how they scourge me! yet my tenderness
Doubles each lash: and yet their bitterness
Winds up my grief to a mysteriousness:
Was ever grief, &c.

They buffet him, and box him as they list,
130   Who grasps the earth and heaven with his fist,
And never yet, whom he would punish, missed:
Was ever grief, &c.

Behold, they spit on me in scornful wise,
Who by my spittle gave the blind man eyes,
Leaving his blindness to my enemies:
                    Was ever grief, &c.

My face they cover, though it be divine.
As *Moses'* face was vailed so is mine,
Lest on their double-dark souls either shine:
140   Was ever grief, &c.

Servants and abjects flout me; they are witty:
Now prophesy who strikes thee, is their ditty.
So they in me deny themselves all pity:
                    Was ever grief, &c.

And now I am delivered unto death,
Which each one calls for so with utmost breath,
That he before me well nigh suffereth:
                    Was ever grief, &c.

Weep not, dear friends, since I for both have wept
150   When all my tears were blood, the while you slept:
Your tears for your own fortunes should be kept:
                    Was ever grief like mine?

The soldiers lead me to the common hall;
There they deride me, they abuse me all:
Yet for twelve heav'nly legions I could call:
                    Was ever grief, &c.

Then with a scarlet robe they me array:
Which shows my blood to be the only way,
And cordial left to repair man's decay:
160   Was ever grief, &c.

Then on my head a crown of thorns I wear:
For these are all the grapes *Sion* doth bear,
Though I my vine planted and watered there:
                    Was ever grief, &c.

So sits the earth's great curse in *Adam's* fall
Upon my head: so I remove it all
From th' earth unto my brows, and bear the thrall:
                    Was ever grief, &c.

Then with the reed they gave to me before,
170   They strike my head, the rock from whence all store
Of heav'nly blessings issue evermore:
                    Was ever grief, &c.

They bow their knees to me, and cry, *Hail king*:
Whatever scoffs and scornfulness can bring,
I am the floor, the sink, where they it fling:
                    Was ever grief, &c.

Yet since man's scepters are as frail as reeds,
And thorny all their crowns, bloody their weeds,   *clothing*
I, who am Truth, turn into truth their deeds:
180   Was ever grief, &c.

The soldiers also spit upon that face,
Which Angels did desire to have the grace,
And Prophets once to see, but found no place:
     Was ever grief, &c.

Thus trimmed, forth they bring me to the rout,
Who *Crucify him*, cry with one strong shout.
God holds his peace at man, and man cries out:
     Was ever grief, &c.

190
They lead me in once more, and putting then
Mine own clothes on, they lead me out again.
Whom devils fly, thus is he tossed of men:
     Was ever grief like mine?

And now weary of sport, glad to engross   *concentrate*
All spite in one, counting my life their loss,
They carry me to my most bitter cross:
     Was ever grief, &c.

My cross I bear my self, until I faint:
Then Simon bears it for me by constraint,
The decreed burden of each mortal saint:
200
     Was ever grief, &c.

O all ye who pass by, behold and see;
Man stole the fruit, but I must climb the tree,
The tree of life to all, but only me:
     Was ever grief, &c.

Lo, here I hang, charged with a world of sin,
The greater world o'th' two; for that came in
By words, but this by sorrow I must win:
     Was ever grief, &c.

210
Such sorrow as, if sinful man could feel,
Or feel his part, he would not cease to kneel,
Till all were melted, though he were all steel:
     Was ever grief, &c.

But, *O my God, my God!* why leav'st thou me,
The Son, in whom thou dost delight to be?
My God, my God –
     Never was grief like mine.

Shame tears my soul, my body many a wound,
Sharp nails pierce this, but sharper that confound,
Reproaches, which are free, while I am bound.
220
     Was ever grief, &c.

Now heal thy self, Physician; now come down.
Alas! I did so, when I left my crown
And father's smile for you, to feel his frown:
     Was ever grief, &c.

In healing not my self, there doth consist
All that salvation, which ye now resist;
Your safety in my sickness doth subsist:
     Was ever grief like mine?

Betwixt two thieves I spend my utmost breath,
230   As he that for some robbery suffereth.
Alas! what have I stolen from you? death:
                 Was ever grief, &c.

A King my title is, prefixt on high,
Yet by my subjects am condemned to die
A servile death in servile company:
                 Was ever grief, &c.

They give me vinegar mingled with gall,
But more with malice: yet, when they did call,
With Manna, Angels' food, I fed them all:
240   Was ever grief, &c.

They part my garments, and by lot dispose
My coat, the type of love, which once cured those
Who sought for help, never malicious foes:
                 Was ever grief, &c.

Nay, after death their spite shall further go
For they will pierce my side, I full well know;
That as sin came, so Sacraments might flow:
                 Was ever grief, &c.

But now I die; now all is finished.
250   My woe, man's weal: and now I bow my head.
Only let others say, when I am dead,
                 Never was grief like mine.

The Thanksgiving

Oh King of grief! (a title strange, yet true,
    To thee of all kings only due)
Oh King of wounds! how shall I grieve for thee,
    Who in all grief preventest me?
Shall I weep blood? Why thou hast wept such store
    That all thy body was one door
Shall I be scourged, flouted, boxed, sold?
    'Tis but to tell the tale is told.
My God, my God, why dost thou part from me?
10   Was such a grief as cannot be.
Shall I then sing, skipping thy doleful story,
    And side with thy triumphant glory?
Shall thy strokes be my stroking? thorns, my flower?
    Thy rod, my posy? cross, my bower?
But how then shall I imitate thee, and
    Copy thy fair, though bloody hand?
Surely I will revenge me on thy love,
    And try who shall victorious prove.
If thou dost give me wealth, I will restore
20   All back unto thee by the poor.
If thou dost give me honour, men shall see,
    The honour doth belong to thee.
I will not marry; or, if she be mine,
    She and her children shall be thine.
My bosom friend, if he blaspheme thy name,
    I will tear thence his love and fame.

One half of me being gone, the rest I give
        Unto some Chapel, die or live.
As for thy passion – But of that anon,
        When with the other I have done.
For thy predestination I'll contrive,
        That three years hence, if I survive,
I'll build a spittle, or mend common ways,   *hospital*
        But mend mine own without delays.
Then I will use the works of thy creation,
        As if I used them but for fashion.
The world and I will quarrel; and the year
        Shall not perceive, that I am here.
My music shall find thee, and ev'ry string
        Shall have his attribute to sing;
That all together may accord in thee,
        And prove one God, one harmony.
If thou shalt give me wit, it shall appear,
        If thou hast giv'n it me, 'tis here.
Nay, I will read thy book, and never move
        Till I have found therein thy love;
Thy art of love, which I'll turn back on thee,
        O my dear Saviour, Victory!
Then for thy passion – I will do for that –
        Alas, my God, I know not what.

The Reprisal

      I have considered it, and find
There is no dealing with thy mighty passion:
For though I die for thee, I am behind;
      My sins deserve the condemnation.

      O make me innocent, that I
May give a disentangled state and free:
And yet thy wounds still my attempts defy,
      For by thy death I die for thee.

      Ah! was it not enough that thou
By thy eternal glory didst outgo me?
Couldst thou not grief's sad conquests me allow,
      But in all vict'ries overthrow me?

      Yet by confession will I come
Into thy conquest: though I can do nought
Against thee, in thee I will overcome
      The man, who once against thee fought.

The Agony

      Philosophers have measured mountains,
Fathomed the depths of seas, of states, and kings,
Walked with a staff to heav'n, and traced fountains:
      But there are two vast, spacious things,
The which to measure it doth more behove:
Yet few there are that sound them; Sin and Love.

Who would know Sin, let him repair
Unto Mount Olivet; there shall he see
A man so wrung with pains, that all his hair,
His skin, his garments bloody be.
Sin is that press and vice, which forceth pain
To hunt his cruel food through ev'ry vein.

Who knows not Love, let him assay
And taste that juice, which on the cross a pike
Did set again abroach; then let him say   *open up again*
If ever he did taste the like.
Love is that liquor sweet and most divine,
Which my God feels as blood; but I, as wine.

Good Friday

O my chief good,
How shall I measure out thy blood?
How shall I count what thee befell,
And each grief tell?

Shall I thy woes
Number according to thy foes?
Or, since one star showed thy first breath,
Shall all thy death?

Or shall each leaf,
Which falls in Autumn, score a grief?
Or cannot leaves, but fruit, be sign
Of the true vine?

Then let each hour
Of my whole life one grief devour;
That thy distress through all may run,
And be my sun.

Or rather let
My several sins their sorrows get;
That as each beast his cure doth know,
Each sin may so.

Since blood is fittest, Lord, to write
Thy sorrows in, and bloody fight;
My heart hath store, write there, where in
One box doth lie both ink and sin:

That when sin spies so many foes,
Thy whips, thy nails, thy wounds, thy woes,
All come to lodge there, sin may say,
No room for me, and fly away.

Sin being gone, oh fill the place,
And keep possession with thy grace;
Lest sin take courage and return,
And all the writings blot or burn.

Redemption

Having been tenant long to a rich Lord,
     Not thriving, I resolved to be bold,
     And make a suit unto him, to afford
A new small-rented lease, and cancel th'old.
In heaven at his manor I him sought:
     They told me there, that he was lately gone
     About some land, which he had dearly bought
Long since on earth, to take possession.
I straight returned, and knowing his great birth,
     Sought him accordingly in great resorts,
     In cities, theatres, gardens, parks, and courts:
At length I heard a ragged noise and mirth
     Of thieves and murderers: there I him espied,
     Who straight, *Your suit is granted*, said, and died.

Sepulchre

O blessed body! Whither art thou thrown?
No lodging for thee, but a cold hard stone?
So many hearts on earth, and yet not one
          Receive thee?

Sure there is room within our hearts good store;
For they can lodge transgressions by the score:
Thousands of toys dwell there, yet out of door
          They leave thee.

But that which shows them large, shows them unfit.
What ever sin did this pure rock commit,
Which holds thee now? Who hath indicted it
          Of murder?

Where our hard hearts have took up stones to brain thee,
And missing this, most falsely did arraign thee,
Only these stones in quiet entertain thee,
          And order.

And as of old, the Law by heav'nly art
Was writ in stone; so thou, which also art
The letter of the word, find'st no fit heart
          To hold thee.

Yet do we still persist as we began,
And so should perish, but that nothing can,
Though it be cold, hard, foul, from loving man
          Withhold thee.

Easter Wings

Lord, who createdst man in wealth and store,
     Though foolishly he lost the same,
       Decaying more and more,
         Till he became
          Most poor:
          With thee
         O let me rise

As larks, harmoniously,
And sing this day thy victories:
Then shall the fall further the flight in me.

My tender age in sorrow did begin:
And still with sickness and shame
Thou didst so punish sin,
That I became
Most thin.
With thee
Let me combine,
And feel this day thy victory:
For, if I imp my wing on thine,   *graft*
20   Affliction shall advance the flight in me.

Easter

Rise heart; thy Lord is risen. Sing his praise
             Without delays,
Who takes thee by the hand, that thou likewise
             With him mayst rise:
That, as his death calcined thee to dust,
His life may make thee gold, and much more, just.
Awake, my lute, and struggle for thy part
             With all thy art.
The cross taught all wood to resound his name,
10   Who bore the same.
His stretched sinews taught all strings, what key
Is best to celebrate this most high day.

Consort both heart and lute, and twist a song
             Pleasant and long:
Or since all music is but three parts vied
             And multiplied,
O let thy blessed Spirit bear a part,
And make up our defects with his sweet art.

I got me flowers to straw thy way,   *strew*
20 I got me boughs off many a tree:
But thou wast up by break of day,
And brought'st thy sweets along with thee.

The Sun arising in the East,
Though he give light, and th' East perfume;
If they should offer to contest
With thy arising, they presume.

Can there be any day but this,
Though many suns to shine endeavour?
We count three hundred, but we miss:
30 There is but one, and that one ever.

H. Baptism (I)

As he that sees a dark and shady grove,
    Stays not, but looks beyond it on the sky;
So when I view my sins, mine eyes remove
More backward still, and to that water fly,

Which is above the heav'ns, whose spring and vent
　　　Is in my dear Redeemer's pierced side.
　　　O blessed streams! either ye do prevent
And stop our sins from growing thick and wide,

Or else give tears to drown them, as they grow.
　　　In you Redemption measures all my time,
　　　And spreads the plaster equal to the crime.
You taught the *Book of Life* my name, that so

　　　What ever future sins should me miscall,
　　　Your first acquaintance might discredit all.

H. Baptism (II)

　　　　　Since, Lord, to thee
　　　A narrow way and little gate
Is all the passage, on my infancy
　　　Though didst lay hold, and antedate
　　　　　My faith in me.

　　　　　O let me still
　　　Write thee great God, and me a child:
Let me be soft and supple to thy will;
　　　Small to my self, to others mild,
　　　　　Behither ill.

　　　　　Although by stealth
　　　My flesh get on, yet let her sister
My soul bid nothing, but preserve her wealth:
　　　The growth of flesh is but a blister,
　　　　　Childhood is health.

Sin (I)

Lord, with what care hast thou begirt us round!
　　　Parents first season us: then schoolmasters
　　　Deliver us to laws; they send us bound
To rules of reason, holy messengers,
Pulpits and Sundays, sorrow dogging sin,
　　　Afflictions sorted, anguish of all sizes,
　　　Fine nets and stratagems to catch us in,
Bibles laid open, millions of surprises,
Blessings beforehand, ties of gratefulness,
　　　The sound of glory ringing in our ears:
　　　Without, our shame; within, our consciences;
Angels and grace, eternal hopes and fears.
　　　Yet all these fences and their whole array
　　　One cunning bosom-sin blows quite away.

Affliction (I)

When first thou didst entice to thee my heart,
　　　I thought the service brave:　　　　　　　　*splendid*
So many joys I writ down for my part,
　　　Besides what I might have

Out of my stock of natural delights,
Augmented with thy gracious benefits.

I looked on thy furniture so fine,
                And made it fine to me:
Thy glorious household-stuff did me entwine,
                And 'tice me unto thee.
Such stars I counted mine: both heav'n and earth
Paid me my wages in a world of mirth.

What pleasures could I want, whose King I served,
                Where joys my fellows were?
Thus argued into hopes, my thoughts reserved
                No place for grief or fear.
Therefore my sudden soul caught at the place,
And made her youth and fierceness seek thy face.

At first thou gav'st me milk and sweetnesses,
                I had my wish and way:
My days were strawed with flow'rs and happiness,
                There was no month but May.
But with my years sorrow did twist and grow,
And made a party unawares for woe.

My flesh began unto my soul in pain,
                Sicknesses cleave my bones;
Consuming agues dwell in ev'ry vein,
                And tune my breath to groans.
Sorrow was all my soul; I scarce believed,
Till grief did tell me roundly, that I lived.

When I got health, thou took'st away my life,
                And more; for my friends die:
My mirth and edge was lost; a blunted knife
                Was of more use than I.
Thus thin and lean without a fence or friend,
I was blown through with ev'ry storm and wind.

Whereas my birth and spirit rather took
                The way that takes the town,
Thou didst betray me to a ling'ring book,
                And wrap me in a gown.
I was entangled in the world of strife,
Before I had the power to change my life.

Yet, for I threat'ned oft the siege to raise,
                Not simp'ring all mine age,
Thou often didst with Academic praise
                Melt and dissolve my rage.
I took thy sweet'ned pill? till I came where
I could not go away, nor persevere.

Yet lest perchance I should too happy be
                In my unhappiness,
Turning my purge to food, thou throwest me
                Into more sicknesses.
Thus doth thy power cross-bias me, not making
Thine own gift good, yet me from my ways taking.

Now I am here, what thou wilt do with me
             None of my books will show:
I read, and sigh, and wish I were a tree;
             For sure then I should grow
To fruit or shade: at least some bird would trust
Her household to me, and I should be just.

Yet, though thou troublest me, I must be meek;
             In weakness must be stout.
Well, I will change the service, and go seek
             Some other master out.
Ah my dear God! though I am clean forgot,
Let me not love thee, if I love thee not.

Prayer (I)

Prayer the Church's banquet, Angels' age,
             God's breath in man returning to his birth,
             The soul in paraphrase, heart in pilgrimage,
The Christian plummet sounding heav'n and earth;
Engine against th' Almighty, sinners' tower,
             Reversed thunder, Christ-side-piercing spear,
             The six-days' world transposing in an hour,
A kind of tune, which all things hear and fear;
Softness, and peace, and joy, and love, and bliss,
             Exalted Manna, gladness of the best,
             Heaven in ordinary, man well drest,
The milky way, the bird of Paradise,
             Church-bells beyond the stars heard, the soul's blood,
             The land of spices; something understood.

Prayer (II)

I know it is my sin, which locks thine ears,
             And binds thy hands,
Out-crying my requests, drowning my tears;
Or else the chillness of my faint demands.

But as cold hands are angry with the fire,
             And mend it still;
So I do lay the want of my desire,
Not on my sins, or coldness, but thy will.

Yet hear, O God, only for his blood's sake
             Which pleads for me:
For though sins plead too, yet like stones they make
His blood's sweet current much more loud to be.

The H. Communion

Not in rich furniture, or fine array,
             Nor in a wedge of gold,
             Thou, who for me wast sold,
To me dost now thy self convey;
For so thou should'st without me still have been,
             Leaving within me sin.

But by the way of nourishment and strength
        Thou creep'st into my breast,
        Making thy way my rest,
        And thy small quantities my length,
Which spread their forces into every part,
        Meeting sin's force and art.

Yet can these not get over to my soul,
        Leaping the wall that parts
        Our souls and fleshy hearts;
        But as th'outworks, they may control
My rebel flesh, and carrying thy Name
        Affright both sin and shame.

Only thy grace, which with these elements comes,
        Knoweth the ready way,
        And hath the privy key
        Op'ning the soul's most subtle rooms;
While those to spirits refin'd, at door attend
        Dispatches from their friend.

Church Lock-and-Key

Give me my captive soul, or take
        My body also thither.
Another lift like this will make
        Them both to be together.

Before that sin turned flesh to stone,
        And all our lump to leaven,
A fervent sigh might well have blown
        Our innocent earth to heaven.

For sure when Adam did not know
        To sin, or sin to smother,
He might to heav'n from Paradise go,
        As from one room t'another.

Thou hast restored us to this ease
        By this thy heav'nly blood,
Which I can go to, when I please,
        And leave th'earth to their food.

Love I

Immortal Love, author of this great frame,
        Sprung from that beauty which can never fade;
        How hath man parceled out thy glorious name,
And thrown it on that dust which thou hast made,

While mortal love doth all the title gain!
        Which siding with invention, they together
        Bear all the sway, possessing heart and brain,
(Thy workmanship) and give thee share in neither.

Wit fancies beauty, beauty raiseth wit:
      The world is theirs; they two play out the game,
      Thou standing by: and though thy glorious name
Wrought our deliverance from th' infernal pit,

      Who sings thy praise? only a scarf or glove
      Doth warm our hands, and make them write of love.

Love II

Immortal Heat, O let thy greater flame
      Attract the lesser to it: let those fires,
      Which shall consume the world, first make it tame,
And kindle in our hearts such true desires,

As may consume our lusts, and make thee way:
      Then shall our hearts pant thee; then shall our brain
      All her invention on thine Altar lay,
And there in hymns send back thy fire again.

Our eyes shall see thee, which before saw dust;
      Dust blown by wit, till that they both were blind:
      Thou shalt recover all thy goods in kind,
Who wert disseized by usurping lust: *dispossessed*

      All knees shall bow to thee, all wits shall rise,
      And praise him who did make and mend our eyes.

The Temper (I)

How should I praise thee, Lord! how should my rimes
    Gladly engrave thy love in steel,
    If what my soul doth feel sometimes,
      My soul might ever feel!

Although there were some forty heav'ns, or more,
    Sometimes I peer above them all;
    Sometimes I hardly reach a score,
      Sometimes to Hell I fall.

O rack me not to such a vast extent;
    Those distances belong to thee:
    The world's too little for thy tent,
      A grave too big for me.

Wilt thou meet arms with man, that thou dost stretch
    A crumb of dust from heav'n to hell?
    Will great God measure with a wretch?
      Shall he thy stature spell?

O let me, when thy roof my soul hath hid,
    O let me roost and nestle there:
    Then of a sinner thou art rid,
      And I of hope and fear.

Yet take thy way; for sure thy way is best:
    Stretch or contract me, thy poor debter:
    This is but tuning of my breast,
        To make the music better.

Whether I fly with angels, fall with dust,
    Thy hands made both, and I am there:
    Thy power and love, my love and trust
        Make one place ev'ry where.

The Temper (II)

It cannot be. Where is that mighty joy,
    Which just now took up all my heart?
    Lord, if thou must needs use thy dart,
Save that, and me; or sin for both destroy.

The grosser world stands to thy word and art;
    But thy diviner world of grace
    Thou suddenly dost raise and race,
And ev'ry day a new Creator art.

O fix thy chair of grace, that all my powers
    May also fix their reverence:
    For when thou dost depart from hence,
They grow unruly, and sit in thy bowers.

Scatter, or bind them all to bend to thee:
    Though elements change, and heaven move,
    Let not thy higher Court remove,
But keep a standing Majesty in me.

Jordan (I)

Who says that fictions only and false hair
Become a verse? Is there in truth no beauty?
Is all good structure in a winding stair?
May no lines pass, except they do their duty
    Not to a true but painted chair?

Is it no verse, except enchanted groves
And sudden arbours shadow coarse-spun lines?
Must purling streams refresh a lover's loves?
Must all be vailed, while he that reads, divines,
    Catching the sense at two removes?

Shepherds are honest people, let them sing:
Riddle who list, for me, and pull for Prime:
I envy no man's nightingale or spring
Nor let them punish me with loss of rime
    Who plainly say, *My God, My King.*

Employment (I)

If as a flower doth spread and die,
    Thou wouldst extend me to some good,
Before I were by frost's extremity
           Nipt in the bud;

The sweetness and the praise were thine;
    But the extension and the room,
Which in thy garland I should fill, were mine
        At thy great doom.

For as thou dost impart thy grace,
    The greater shall our glory be.
The measure of our joys is in this place,
        The stuff with thee.

Let me not languish then, and spend
    A life as barren to thy praise,
As is the dust, to which that life doth tend,
        But with delays.

All things are busy; only I
    Neither bring honey with the bees,
Nor flowers to make that, nor the husbandry
        To water these.

I am no link of thy great chain,
    But all my company is a weed.
Lord place me in thy consort; give one strain
        To my poor reed.

The H. Scriptures I

Oh Book! infinite sweetness! let my heart
    Suck ev'ry letter, and a honey gain,
    Precious for any grief in any part
To clear the breast, to mollify all pain.
    Thou art all health, health thriving till it make
    A full eternity: thou art a mass
    Of strange delights, where we may wish and take.
Ladies, look here; this is the thankful glass,
That mends the looker's eyes: this is the well
    That washes what it shows. Who can endear
    Thy praise too much? thou art heav'n's Lidger here,   *ambassador*
Working against the states of death and hell.
    Thou art joy's handsel: heav'n lies flat in thee,   *gift*
    Subject to ev'ry mounter's bended knee.

The H. Scriptures II

Oh that I knew how all thy lights combine,
    And the configurations of their glory!
    Seeing not only how each verse doth shine,
But all the constellations of the story.
    This verse marks that, and both do make a motion
    Unto a third, that ten leaves off doth lie:
    Then as dispersed herbs do watch a potion,
These three make up some Christian's destiny:
Such are thy secrets, which my life makes good,
    And comments on thee: for in ev'ry thing
    Thy words do find me out, and parallels bring,

And in another make me understood.
Stars are poor books, and oftentimes do miss:
This book of stars lights to eternal bliss.

Whitsunday

Listen sweet Dove unto my song,
And spread thy golden wings in me;
Hatching my tender heart so long,
Till it get wing, and fly away with thee.

Where is that fire which once descended
On thy Apostles? thou didst then
Keep open house, richly attended,
Feasting all comers by twelve chosen men.

Such glorious gifts thou didst bestow,
That th'earth did like a heav'n appear;
The stars were coming down to know
If they might mend their wages, and serve here.

The sun, which once did shine alone,
Hung down his head, and wished for night,
When he beheld twelve suns for one
Going about the world, and giving light.

But since those pipes of gold, which brought
That cordial water to our ground,
Were cut and martyred by the fault
Of those, who did themselves through their side wound

Thou shut'st the door, and keep'st within,
Scarce a good joy creeps through the chink:
And if the braves of conqu'ring sin
Did not excite thee, we should wholly sink.

Lord, though we change, thou art the same;
The same sweet God of love and light:
Restore this day for thy great name
Unto his ancient and miraculous right.

Grace

My stock lies dead, and no increase
Doth my dull husbandry improve:
O let thy graces without cease
                    Drop from above!

If still the sun should hide his face,
Thy house would but a dungeon prove,
Thy works night's captives: O let grace
                    Drop from above!
The dew doth ev'ry morning fall,
And shall the dew outstrip thy dove?
The dew, for which grass cannot call,
                    Drop from above.

Death is still working like a mole,
And digs my grave at each remove:
Let grace work too, and on my soul
                    Drop from above.

Sin is still hammering my heart
Unto a hardness, void of love:
Let suppling grace, to cross his art,
                    Drop from above.

O come! for thou dost know the way:
Or if to me thou wilt not move,
Remove me, where I need not say,
                    Drop from above.

Church Monuments

While that my soul repairs to her devotion,
Here I entomb my flesh, that it betimes
May take acquaintance of this heap of dust,
To which the blast of death's incessant motion,
Fed with the exhalation of our crimes,
Drives all at last. Therefore I gladly trust

My body to this school, that it may learn
To spell his elements, and find his birth
Written in dusty heraldry and lines;
Which dissolution sure doth best discern,
Comparing dust with dust, and earth with earth.
These laugh at Jet and Marble put for signs,

To sever the good fellowship of dust,
And spoil the meeting. What shall point out them,
When they shall bow, and kneel, and fall down flat
To kiss those heaps, which now they have in trust?
Dear flesh, while I do pray, learn here thy stem
And true descent: that when thou shalt grow fat,

And wanton in thy cravings, thou mayst know,
That flesh is but the glass, which holds the dust
That measures all our time; which also shall
Be crumbled into dust. Mark here below
How tame these ashes are, how free from lust,
That thou mayst fit thy self against thy fall.

Church Music

Sweetest of sweets, I thank you. When displeasure
                    Did through my body wound my mind,
You took me thence, and in your house of pleasure
                    A dainty lodging me assigned.

Now I in you without a body move,
                    Rising and falling with your wings:
We both together sweetly live and love,
                    Yet say sometimes, *God help poor Kings.*

Comfort, I'll die; for if you post from me,
        Sure I shall do so, and much more:
But if I travel in your company,
        You know the way to heaven's door.

The Windows

Lord, how can man preach thy eternal word?
        He is a brittle crazy glass:
Yet in thy temple thou dost him afford
        This glorious and transcendent place,
        To be a window through thy grace.

But when thou dust anneal in glass thy story,   *bake*
        Making thy life to shine within
The holy Preacher's; then the light and glory
        More rev'rend grows, and more doth win:
        Which else shows wat'rish, bleak, and thin.

Doctrine and life, colours and light, in one
        When they combine and mingle, bring
A strong regard and awe: but speech alone
        Doth vanish like a flaring thing,
        And in the ear, not conscience ring.

The Quiddity

My God, a verse is not a crown,
No point of honour, or gay suit,
No hawk, or banquet, or renown,
Nor a good sword, nor yet a lute:

It cannot vault, or dance or play,
It never was, in *France* or *Spain*,
Nor can it entertain the day
With my great stable or domain.

It is no office, art, or news,
Nor the Exchange or busy hall,
But it is that, which while I use
I am with thee, and must take all.

Sunday

O day most calm, most bright,
The fruit of this, the next world's bud,
Th' indorsement of supreme delight,
Writ by a friend, and with his blood;
The couch of time; care's balm and bay:
The week were dark, but for thy light:
        Thy torch doth show the way.

The other days and thou
Make up one man; whose face thou art,
Knocking at heaven with thy brow:
The worky-days are the back-part,
The burden of the week lies there,

Making the whole to stoop and bow,
    Till thy release appear.

      Man had straight forward gone
To endless death: but thou dust pull
And turn us round to look on one,
Whom, if we were not very dull,
We could not choose but look on still;
Since there is no place so alone,
    The which he doth not fill.

      Sundays the pillars are,
On which heav'n's palace arched lies:
The other days fill up the spare
And hollow room with vanities.
They are the fruitful beds and borders
In God's rich garden: that is bare,
    Which parts their ranks and orders.

      The Sundays of man's life,
Threaded together on time's string,
Make bracelets to adorn the wife
Of the eternal glorious King.
On Sunday heaven's gate stands ope';
Blessings are plentiful and rife,
    More plentiful than hope.

      This day my Saviour rose,
And did inclose this light for his:
That, as each beast his manger knows,
Man might not of his fodder miss.
Christ hath took in this piece of ground,
And made a garden there for those
    Who want herbs for their wound.

      The rest of our Creation
Our great Redeemer did remove
With the same shake, which at his passion
Did th' earth and all things with it move.
As Samson bore the doors away,
Christ's hands, though nailed, wrought our salvation,
    And did unhinge that day.

      The brightness of that day
We sullied by our foul offence:
Wherefore that robe we cast away,
Having a new at his expense,
Whose drops of blood paid the full price,
That was required to make us gay,
    And fit for Paradise.

      Thou art a day of mirth:
And where the weekdays trail on ground,
Thy flight is higher, as thy birth.
O let me take thee at the bound,
Leaping with thee from sev'n to sev'n,
Till that we both, being tossed from earth,
    Fly hand in hand to heav'n!

Employment (II)

He that is weary, let him sit.
　　　　My soul would stir
And trade in courtesies and wit,
　　　　Quitting the fur
To cold complexions needing it.

Man is no star, but a quick coal
　　　　Of mortal fire:
Who blows it not, nor doth control
　　　　A faint desire,
Lets his own ashes choke his soul.

When the'elements did for place contest
　　　　With him, whose will
Ordained the highest to be best;
　　　　The earth sat still,
And by the others is opprest.

Life is a business, not good cheer;
　　　　Ever in wars.
The sun still shineth there or here,
　　　　Whereas the stars
Watch an advantage to appear.

Oh that I were an Orange-tree,
　　　　That busy plant!
Then should I ever laden be,
　　　　And never want
Some fruit for him that dressed me.

But we are still too young or old;
　　　　The Man is gone,
Before we do our wares unfold:
　　　　So we freeze on,
Until the grave increase our cold.

Denial

When my devotions could not pierce
　　　　Thy silent ears;
Then was my heart broken, as was my verse:
　　　　My breast was full of fears
　　　　　　　And disorder:

My bent thoughts, like a brittle bow,
　　　　Did fly asunder:
Each took his way; some would to pleasures go,
　　　　Some to the wars and thunder
　　　　　　　Of alarms.

As good go any where, they say,
　　　　As to benumb
Both knees and heart, in crying night and day,
　　　　Come, come, my God, O come,
　　　　　　　But no hearing.

O that thou shouldst give dust a tongue
　　　　　To cry to thee,
And then not hear it crying! all day long
　　　My heart was in my knee,
20 　　　　　　But no hearing.

　　Therefore my soul lay out of sight,
　　　　　　Untuned, unstrung:
My feeble spirit, unable to look right,
　　　Like a nipt blossom, hung
　　　　　　Discontented.

　　O cheer and tune my heartless breast,
　　　　　Defer no time;
That so thy favours granting my request,
　　　They and my mind may chime,
30 　　　　　And mend my rime.

Christmas

All after pleasures as I rid one day,　　　　　　　　　　　　*rode*
　　　My horse and I, both tired, body and mind,
　　　With full cry of affections, quite astray,
I took up in the next inn I could find.　　　　　　　　　　　*lodged*
There when I came, whom found I but my dear,
　　　My dearest Lord, expecting till the grief
　　　Of pleasures brought me to him, ready there
To be all passengers' most sweet relief?
O Thou, whose glorious, yet contracted light,
10 　　　Wrapt in night's mantle, stole into a manger;
　　　Since my dark soul and brutish is thy right,
To man of all beasts be not thou a stranger:
　　　Furnish and deck my soul, that thou mayst have
　　　A better lodging, than a rack or grave.　　　　　　　　*hay rack*

　　The shepherds sing; and shall I silent be?
　　　　　My God, no hymn for thee?
My soul's a shepherd too; a flock it feeds
　　　　　Of thoughts, and words, and deeds.
The pasture is thy word: the streams, thy grace
20 　　　Enriching all the place.

Shepherd and flock shall sing, and all my powers
　　　Outsing the daylight hours.
Then we will chide the sun for letting night
　　　Take up his place and right:
We sing one common Lord; wherefore he should
　　　Himself the candle hold.
I will go searching, till I find a sun
　　　Shall stay, till we have done;
A willing shiner, that shall shine as gladly,
30 　　　As frost-nipt suns look sadly.
Then we will sing, and shine all our own day,
　　　And one another pay:
His beams shall cheer my breast, and both so twine,
Till ev'n his beams sing, and my music shine.

The World

Love built a stately house; where *Fortune* came,
And spinning fancies, she was heard to say,
That her fine cobwebs did support the frame,
Whereas they were supported by the same:
But *Wisdom* quickly swept them all away.

Then *Pleasure* came, who, liking not the fashion,
Began to make *Balconies, Terraces,*
Till she had weakened all by alteration:
But rev'rend *laws,* and many a *proclamation*
10   Reformed all at length with menaces.

Then entered *Sin,* and with that Sycamore,
Whose leaves first sheltered man from drought and dew,
Working and winding slily evermore,
The inward walls and sommers cleft and tore: *girders*
But *Grace* shored these, and cut that as it grew.

Then *Sin* combined with *Death* in a firm band
To raze the building to the very floor:
Which they effected, none could them withstand.
But *Love* and *Grace* took *Glory* by the hand,
20   And built a braver Palace than before.

Vanity (I)

The fleet Astronomer can bore,
And thread the spheres with his quick-piercing mind:
He views their stations, walks from door to door,
    Surveys, as if he had designed
To make a purchase there: he sees their dances,
    And knoweth long before,
Both their full-eyed aspects, and secret glances.

The nimble Diver with his side
Cuts through the working waves, that he may fetch
10   His dearly-earned pearl, which God did hide
    On purpose from the vent'rous wretch;
That he might save his life, and also hers,
    Who with excessive pride
Her own destruction and his danger wears.

The subtle Chymick can devest   *chemist*
And strip the creature naked, till he find
The callow principles within their nest: *stripped*
    There he imparts to them his mind,
Admitted to their bed-chamber, before
20   They appear trim and drest
To ordinary suitors at the door.

What hath not Man sought out and found,
But his dear God? who yet his glorious law
Embosoms in us, mellowing the ground
    With showers and frosts, with love and awe,
So that we need not say, Where's this command?
    Poor Man, thou searchest round
To find out *death*; but missest *life* at hand.

Virtue

Sweet day, so cool, so calm, so bright,
The bridal of the earth and sky:
The dew shall weep thy fall to night;
        For thou must die.

Sweet rose, whose hue angry and brave
Bids the rash gazer wipe his eye:
Thy root is ever in its grave,
        And thou must die.

Sweet spring, full of sweet days and roses,
A box where sweets compacted lie;
My music shows ye have your closes,
        And all must die.

Only a sweet and virtuous soul,
Like seasoned timber, never gives;
But though the whole world turn to coal,
        Then chiefly lives.

The Pearl. Matth. 13. 45

I know the ways of Learning; both the head
And pipes that feed the press, and make it run;
What reason hath from nature borrowed,
Or of it self, like a good housewife, spun
In laws and policy; what the stars conspire,
What willing nature speaks, what forced by fire;
Both th'old discoveries, and the new-found seas,
The stock and surplus, cause and history:
All these stand open, or I have the keys:
        Yet I love thee.

I know the ways of Honour, what maintains
The quick returns of courtesy and wit:
In vies of favours whether party gains,
When glory swells the heart, and moldeth it
To all expressions both of hand and eye,
Which on the world a true-love-knot may tie,
And bear the bundle, wheresoe'er it goes.   *of favors*
How many drams of spirit there must be
To sell my life unto my friends or foes:
        Yet I love thee.

I know the ways of Pleasure, the sweet strains,
The lullings and the relishes of it;
The propositions of hot blood and brains;
What mirth and music mean; what love and wit
Have done these twenty hundred years, and more:
I know the projects of unbridled store:
My stuff is flesh, not brass; my senses live,
And grumble oft, that they have more in me
Than he that curbs them, being but one to five:
        Yet I love thee.

I know all these, and have them in my hand:
Therefore not seeled, but with open eyes
I fly to thee, and fully understand
Both the main sale, and the commodities;
And at what rate and price I have thy love
With all the circumstances that may move:
Yet through these labyrinths, not my groveling wit,
But thy silk twist let down from heav'n to me,
Did both conduct and teach me, how by it
40   To climb to thee.

Affliction (IV)

Broken in pieces all asunder,
        Lord, hunt me not,
        A thing forgot,
Once a poor creature, now a wonder,
        A wonder tortured in the space
        Betwixt this world and that of grace.

My thoughts are all a case of knives,
        Wounding my heart
        With scattered smart,
10   As wat'ring pots give flowers their lives.
        Nothing their fury can control,
        While they do wound and pink my soul.

All my attendants are at strife,
        Quitting their place
        Unto my face:
Nothing performs the task of life:
        The elements are let loose to fight,
        And while I live, try out their right.

Oh help, my God! let not their plot
20   Kill them and me,
        And also thee,
Who art my life: dissolve the knot,
        As the sun scatters by his light
        All the rebellions of the night.

Then shall those powers, which work for grief,
        Enter thy pay,
        And day by day
Labour thy praise, and my relief;
        With care and courage building me,
30   Till I reach heav'n, and much more, thee.

Man

My God, I heard this day,
That none doth build a stately habitation,
        But he that means to dwell therein.
        What house more stately hath there been,
Or can be, than is Man? to whose creation
        All things are in decay.

For Man is ev'ry thing,
And more: he is a tree, yet bears more fruit;
A beast, yet is, or should be more:
Reason and speech we only bring.
Parrots may thank us, if they are not mute,
They go upon the score.

Man is all symmetry,
Full of proportions, one limb to another,
And all to all the world besides:
Each part may call the farthest, brother:
For head with foot hath private amity,
And both with moons and tides.

Nothing hath got so far,
But Man hath caught and kept it, as his prey.
His eyes dismount the highest star:
He is in little all the sphere.
Herbs gladly cure our flesh; because that they
Find their acquaintance there.

For us the winds do blow,
The earth doth rest, heav'n move, and fountains flow.
Nothing we see, but means our good,
As our *delight*, or as our *treasure*:
The whole is, either our cupboard of *food*,
Or cabinet of *pleasure*.

The stars have us to bed;
Night draws the curtain, which the sun withdraws;
Music and light attend our head.
All things unto our *flesh* are kind   *akin*
In their *descent* and *being*; to our *mind*
In their *ascent* and *cause*.

Each thing is full of duty:
Waters united are our navigation;
Distinguished, our habitation;
Below, our drink; above, our meat;
Both are our cleanliness. Hath one such beauty?
Then how are all things neat!

More servants wait on Man,
Than he'll take notice of: in ev'ry path
He treads down that which doth befriend him,
When sickness makes him pale and wan.
Oh mighty love! Man is one world, and hath
Another to attend him.

Since then, my God, thou hast
So brave a Palace built; O dwell in it,
That it may dwell with thee at last!
Till then, afford us so much wit,
That, as the world serves us, we may serve thee,
And both thy servants be.

Life

I made a posy, while the day ran by:
Here will I smell my remnant out, and tie
        My life within this band.
But time did beckon to the flowers, and they
By noon most cunningly did steal away,
        And withered in my hand.

My hand was next to them, and then my heart:
I took, without more thinking, in good part
        Time's gentle admonition:
10   Who did so sweetly death's sad taste convey,
Making my mind to smell my fatal day;
        Yet sug'ring the suspicion.

Farewell dear flowers, sweetly your time ye spent,
Fit, while ye lived, for smell or ornament,
        And after death for cures.
I follow straight without complaints or grief,
Since if my scent be good, I care not, if
        It be as short as yours.

Mortification

How soon doth man decay!
When clothes are taken from a chest of sweets   *perfumes*
    To swaddle infants, whose young breath
        Scarce knows the way;
    Those clouts are little winding sheets,   *swaddling clothes*
Which do consign and send them unto death.

    When boys go first to bed,
They step into their voluntary graves,
    Sleep binds them fast; only their breath
10   Makes them not dead.
    Successive nights like rolling waves,
Convey them quickly, who are bound for death.

    When youth is frank and free,
And calls for music, while his veins do swell,
    All day exchanging mirth and breath
        In company;
    That music summons to the knell,
Which shall befriend him at the house of death.

    When man grows staid and wise,
20   Getting a house and home, where he may move
    Within the circle of his breath,
        Schooling his eyes;
    That dumb inclosure maketh love
Unto the coffin, that attends his death.

    When age grows low and weak,
Marking his grave, and thawing ev'ry year,
    Till all do melt, and drown his breath
        When he would speak;

> A chair or litter shows the bier,
30   Which shall convey him to the house of death.

> Man, ere he is aware,
> Hath put together a solemnity,
>   And drest his hearse, while he has breath
>   As yet to spare:
>   Yet Lord, instruct us so to die,
> That all these dyings may be life in death.

Jordan (II)

When first my lines of heav'nly joys made mention,
Such was their luster, they did so excel,
That I sought out quaint words, and trim invention,
My thoughts began to burnish, sprout, and swell,
Curling with metaphors a plain intention,
Decking the sense, as if it were to sell.

Thousands of notions in my brain did run,
Off'ring their service, if I were not sped:
I often blotted what I had begun;
10   This was not quick enough, and that was dead.
Nothing could seem too rich to clothe the sun,
Much less those joys which trample on his head.

As flames do work and wind, when they ascend,
So did I weave my self into the sense.
But while I bustled, I might hear a friend
Whisper, *How wide is all this long pretence!*
There is in love a sweetness ready penned:
Copy out only that, and save expense.

Obedience

> My God, if writings may
> Convey a lordship any way
> Whither the buyer and the seller please;
>   Let it not thee displease,
> If this poor paper do as much as they.

>   On it my heart doth bleed
>   As many lines, as there doth need
> To pass it self and all it hath to thee.
>   To which I do agree,
10   And here present it as my special Deed.

>   If that hereafter Pleasure
>   Cavil, and claim her part and measure,
> As if this passed with a reservation,
>   Or some such words in fashion;
> I here exclude the wrangler from thy treasure.

>   O let thy sacred will
>   All thy delight in me fulfill!
> Let me not think an action mine own way,
>   But as thy love shall sway,
20   Resigning up the rudder to thy skill.

Lord, what is man to thee,
That thou shouldst mind a rotten tree?
Yet since thou canst not choose but see my actions,
So great are thy perfections,
Thou mayst as well my actions guide, as see.

Besides, thy death and blood
Showed a strange love to all our good:
Thy sorrows were in earnest; no faint proffer,
Or superficial offer
30   Of what we might not take, or be withstood.

Wherefore I all forego:
To one word only I say, No:
Where in the deed there was an intimation
Of a *gift* or *donation*,
Lord, let it now by way of *purchase* go.

He that will pass his land,
As I have mine, may set his hand
And heart unto this deed, when he hath read,
And make the purchase spread
40   To both our goods, if he to it will stand.

How happy were my part,
If some kind man would thrust his heart
Into these lines; till in heav'n's Court of Rolls
They were by winged souls
Entered for both, far above their desert!

The British Church

I joy, dear Mother, when I view
Thy perfect lineaments and hue
Both sweet and bright.

Beauty in thee takes up her place,
And dates her letters from thy face,
When she doth write.

A fine aspect in fit array,
Neither too mean, not yet too gay,
Shows who is best.

10   Outlandish looks may not compare: *Foreign*
For all they either painted are,
Or else undrest.

She on the hills, which wantonly
Allureth all in hope to be
By her preferred,

Hath kissed so long her painted shrines,
That ev'n her face by kissing shines,
For her reward.

She in the valley is so shy
20   Of dressing, that her hair doth lie
About her ears:

While she avoids her neighbour's pride,
She wholly goes on th'other side,
                    And nothing wears.

But dearest Mother, (what those miss)
The mean thy praise and glory is,
                    And long may be.

Blessed be God, whose love it was
To double-moat thee with his grace,
30   And none but thee.

The Quip

The merry world did on a day
With his train-bands and mates agree
To meet together, where I lay,
And all in sport to jeer at me.

First, Beauty crept into a rose,
Which when I plucked not, Sir, said she,
Tell me, I pray, Whose hands are those?
But thou shalt answer, Lord, for me.

Then Money came, and chinking still,
10   What tune is this, poor man? said he:
I heard in Music you had skill.
But thou shalt answer, Lord, for me.

Then came brave Glory puffing by
In silks that whistled, who but he?
He scarce allowed me half an eye.
But thou shalt answer, Lord, for me.

Then came quick Wit-and-Conversation,
And he would needs a comfort be,
And, to be short, make an oration.
20   *But thou shalt answer, Lord, for me.*

Yet when the hour of thy design
To answer these fine things shall come,
Speak not at large; say, I am thine:
And then they have their answer home.

Iesu

Iesu is in my heart, his sacred name
Is deeply carved there: but th'other week
A great affliction broke the little frame,
Ev'n all to pieces: which I went to seek:
And first I found the corner, where was *I*,
After, where *ES*, and next where *U* was graved.
When I had got these parcels, instantly
I sat me down to spell them, and perceived
That to my broken heart he was *I ease you*,
10   And to my whole is *IESU*.

Dialogue

Sweetest Saviour, if my soul
    Were but worth the having,
Quickly should I then control
    Any thought of waving.   *waiv{er}ing*
But when all my care and pains
Cannot give the name of gains
To thy wretch so full of stains,
What delight or hope remains?

What (child) is the balance thine,
    Thine the poise and measure?
If I say, Thou shalt be mine,
    Finger not my treasure.
What the gains in having thee
Do amount to, only he,
Who for man was sold, can see;
That transferred th' accounts to me.

But as I can see no merit,
    Leading to this favour:
So the way to fit me for it
    Is beyond my savour.   *understanding*
As the reason then is thine;
So the way is none of mine:
I disclaim the whole design:
Sin disclaims and I resign.

That is all, if that I could
    Get without repining,
And my clay my creature would
    Follow my resigning.
That as I did freely part
With my glory and desert,
Left all joys to feel all smart—— —
    Ah! no more: thou break'st my heart.

Dullness

Why do I languish thus drooping and dull,
    As if I were all earth?
O give me quickness, that I may with mirth
    Praise thee brim-full!

The wanton lover in a curious strain
    Can praise his fairest fair;
And with quaint metaphors her curled hair
    Curl o'er again.

Thou art my loveliness, my life, my light,
    Beauty alone to me:
Thy bloody death and undeserved, makes thee
    Pure red and white.

When all perfections as but one appear,
    That those thy form doth show,
The very dust, where thou dost tread and go,
    Makes beauties here.

Where are my lines then? my approaches? views?
      Where are my window-songs?   *serenades*
Lovers are still pretending, and ev'n wrongs
20   Sharpen their Muse:

But I am lost in flesh, whose sugared lies
      Still mock me, and grow bold:
Sure thou didst put a mind there, if I could
        Find where it lies.

Lord, clear thy gift, that with a constant wit
      I may but look towards thee:
Look only; for to *love* thee, who can be,
        What angel fit?

Sin's Round

Sorry I am, my God, sorry I am,
That my offences course it in a ring.
My thoughts are working like a busy flame,
Until their cockatrice they hatch and bring:
And when they once have perfected their draughts,
My words take fire from my inflamed thoughts.

My words take fire from my inflamed thoughts,
Which spit it forth like the Sicilian Hill.
They vent the wares, and pass them with their faults,
10 And by their breathing ventilate the ill.
But words suffice not, where are lewd intentions:
My hands do join to finish the inventions:

My hands do join to finish the inventions:
And so my sins ascend three stories high,
As Babel grew, before there were dissensions.
Yet ill deeds loiter not: for they supply
New thoughts of sinning: wherefore, to my shame,
Sorry I am, my God, sorry I am.

Peace

Sweet Peace, where dost thou dwell, I humbly crave,
      Let me once know.
  I sought thee in a secret cave,
      And asked if Peace were there.
A hollow wind did seem to answer, No:
      Go seek elsewhere.

I did; and going did a rainbow note:
      Surely, thought I,
  This is the lace of Peace's coat:
      I will search out the matter.
10 But while I looked, the clouds immediately
      Did break and scatter.

Then went I to a garden, and did spy
      A gallant flower,
  The Crown Imperial: Sure, said I,

Peace at the root must dwell.
But when I digged, I saw a worm devour
                    What showed so well.

At length I met a rev'rend good old man,
                    Whom when for Peace
     I did demand, he thus began:
          There was a Prince of old
At Salem dwelt, who lived with good increase
                    Of flock and fold.

He sweetly lived; yet sweetness did not save
                    His life from foes.
     But after death out of his grave
          There sprang twelve stalks of wheat:
Which many wond'ring at, got some of those
                    To plant and set.

It prospered strangely, and did soon disperse
                    Through all the earth:
     For they that taste it do rehearse,
          That virtue lies therein,
A secret virtue bringing peace and mirth
                    By flight of sin.

Take of this grain, which in my garden grows.
                    And grows for you;
     Make bread of it: and that repose
          And peace which ev'ry where
With so much earnestness you do pursue,
                    Is only there.

The Bunch of Grapes

Joy, I did lock thee up. But some bad man
               Hath let thee out again,
And now, me thinks, I am where I began
               Sev'n years ago: one vogue and vein,
               One air of thoughts usurps my brain.
I did towards Canaan draw, but now I am
Brought back to the Red Sea, the sea of shame.

For as the Jews of old by God's command
               Travelled, and saw no town:
So now each Christian hath his journeys spanned:
               Their story pens and sets us down.
               A single deed is small renown.
God's works are wide, and let in future times;
His ancient justice overflows our crimes.

Then have we too our guardian fires and clouds;
               Our Scripture-dew drops fast:
We have our sands and serpents, tents and shrouds;
               Alas! our murmurings come not last.
               But where's the cluster? where's the taste
Of mine inheritance? Lord, if I must borrow,
Let me as well take up their joy, as sorrow.

But can he want the grape, who hath the wine?
   I have their fruit and more.
Blessed be God, who prospered *Noah's* vine,
    And made it bring forth grapes good store.
    But much more him I must adore.
Who of the Law's sour juice sweet wine did make,
Ev'n God himself being pressed for my sake.

The Storm

If as the winds and waters here below
     Do fly and flow,
My sighs and tears as busy were above;
      Sure they would move
And much affect thee, as tempestuous times
Amaze poor mortals, and object their crimes.

Stars have their storms, ev'n in a high degree,
     As well as we.
A throbbing conscience spurred by remorse
      Hath a strange force:
It quits the earth, and mounting more and more
Dares to assault thee, and besiege thy door.

There it stands knocking, to thy music's wrong,
     And drowns the song.
Glory and honour are set by, till it
      An answer get.
Poets have wronged poor storms: such days are best;
They purge the air without, within the breast.

Paradise

 I bless thee, Lord, because I GROW
 Among thy trees, which in a ROW
 To thee both fruit and order OW.

 What open force, or hidden CHARM
 Can blast my fruit, or bring me HARM
 While the inclosure is thine ARM?

 Inclose me still for fear I START.
 Be to me rather sharp and TART,
 Than let me want thy hand and ART.

 When thou dost greater judgements SPARE,
 And with thy knife but prune and PARE;
 Ev'n fruitful trees more fruitful ARE.

 Such sharpness shows the sweetest FRIEND:
 Such cuttings rather heal than REND:
 And such beginnings touch their END.

The Size

 Content thee, greedy heart.
Modest and moderate joys to those, that have

Title to more hereafter when they part,
   Are passing brave.
Let th'upper springs into the low
Descend and fall, and thou dost flow.

   What though some have a fraught   *freight*
Of cloves and nutmegs, and in cinnamon sail;
If thou hast wherewithall to spice a draught,
   When griefs prevail,
  And for the future time art heir
  To th' Isle of spices? Is't not fair?

   To be in both worlds full
Is more than God was, who was hungry here.
Wouldst thou his laws of fasting disannul?
   Enact good cheer?
  Lay out thy joy, yet hope to save it?
  Wouldst thou both eat thy cake, and have it?

   Great joys are all at once;
But little do reserve themselves for more:
Those have their hopes; these what they have renounce,
   And live on score: *credit*
  Those are at home; these journey still,
  And meet the rest on Sion's hill.

   Thy Saviour sentenced joy,
And in the flesh condemned it as unfit,
At least in lump: for such doth oft destroy;
   Whereas a bit
  Doth tice us on to hopes of more,   *entice*
  And for the present health restore.

   A Christian's state and case
Is not a corpulent, but a thin and spare,
Yet active strength: whose long and bony face
   Content and care
  Do seem to equally divide,
  Like a pretender, not a bride.   *wooer*

   Wherefore sit down, good heart;
Grasp not at much, for fear thou losest all.
If comforts fell according to desert,
   They would great frosts and snows destroy:
  For we should count, since the last joy.

   Then close again the seam,
Which thou hast opened: do not spread thy robe
In hope of great things. Call to mind thy dream,
   An earthly globe,
  On whose meridian was engraven,
  These seas are tears, and heav'n the haven.

Artillery

As I one ev'ning sat before my cell,
Me thoughts a star did shoot into my lap.
I rose, and shook my clothes, as knowing well,

That from small fires comes oft no small mishap.
  When suddenly I heard one say,
   Do as thou usest, disobey,
   Expel good motions from thy breast,
Which have the face of fire, but end in rest.

I, who had heard of music in the spheres,
But not of speech in stars, began to muse:
But turning to my God, whose ministers
The stars and all things are; If I refuse,
   Dread Lord, said I, so oft my good;
   Then I refuse not ev'n with blood
   To wash away my stubborn thought:
For I will do or suffer what I ought.

But I have also stars and shooters too,   *shooting stars*
Born where thy servants both artilleries use.
My tears and prayers night and day do woo,
And work up to thee; yet thou dost refuse.
   Not, but I am (I must say still)
   Much more obliged to do thy will,
   Than thou to grant mine: but because
Thy promise now hath ev'n set thee thy laws.

Then we are shooters both, and thou dost deign
To enter combat with us, and contest
With thine own clay. But I would parley fain:
Shun not my arrows, and behold my breast.
   Yet if thou shunnest, I am thine:
   I must be so, if I am mine.
   There is no articling with thee: *negotiating*
I am but finite, yet thine infinitely.

The Pilgrimage

I travelled on, seeing the hill, where lay
    My expectation.
  A long it was and weary way.
   The gloomy cave of Desperation
I left on th' one, and on the other side
    The rock of Pride.

And so I came to Fancy's meadow strowed
    With many a flower;
  Fain would I here have made abode,
   But I was quickened by my hour.
So to Care's copse I came, and there got through
    With much ado.

That led me to the wild of Passion, which
    Some call the wold;   *moor*
  A wasted place, but sometimes rich.
   Here I was robbed of all my gold,
Save one good Angel, which a friend had tied   *gold coin*
    Close to my side.

At length I got unto the gladsome hill,
    Where lay my hope,

Where lay my heart; and climbing still,
When I had gained the brow and top,
A lake of brackish waters on the ground
Was all I found.

With that abashed and struck with many a sting
Of swarming fears,
I fell, and cried, Alas my King,
Can both the way and end be tears?
Yet taking heart I rose, and then perceived
I was deceived:

My hill was further: so I flung away,
Yet heard a cry
Just as I went, *None goes that way*
And lives: If that be all said I,
After so foul a journey death is fair,
And but a chair.

The Bag

Away despair! my gracious Lord doth hear.
Though winds and waves assault my keel,
He doth preserve it: he doth steer,
Ev'n when the boat seems most to reel.
Storms are the triumph of his art:
Well may he close his eyes, but not his heart.

Hast thou not heard, that my Lord JESUS died?
Then let me tell thee a strange story.
The God of power, as he did ride
In his majestic robes of glory,
Resolved to light; and so one day
He did descend, undressing all the way.

The stars his tire of light and rings obtained,   *tiara*
The cloud his bow, the fire his spear,
The sky his azure mantle gained.
And when they asked, what he would wear;
He smiled and said as he did go,
He had new clothes a making here below.

When he was come, as travellers are wont,
He did repair unto an inn.
Both then, and after, many a brunt
He did endure to cancel sin:
And having giv'n the rest before,
Here he gave up his life to pay our score.

But as he was returning, there came one
That ran upon him with a spear.
He, who came hither all alone,
Bringing nor man, nor arms, nor fear,
Received the blow upon his side,
And straight he turned, and to his brethren cried,

If ye have any thing to send or write,
(I have no bag, but here is room)
Unto my Father's hands and sight,

30

10

20

30

(Believe me) it shall safely come.
That I shall mind, what you impart;
Look, you may put it very near my heart.

Or if hereafter any of my friends
Will use me in this kind, the door
Shall still be open; what he sends
40   I will present, and somewhat more,
Not to his hurt. Sighs will convey
Any thing to me. Hark, Despair away.

The Collar   *yoke/choler*

I struck the board, and cried, No more.
I will abroad.
What? shall I ever sigh and pine?
My lines and life are free; free as the road,
Loose as the wind, as large as store.
Shall I be still in suit?
Have I no harvest but a thorn
To let me blood, and not restore
What I have lost with cordial fruit?
10   Sure there was wine
Before my sighs did dry it: there was corn
Before my tears did drown it.
Is the year only lost to me?
Have I no bays to crown it?
No flowers, no garlands gay? all blasted?
All wasted?
Not so, my heart: but there is fruit,
And thou hast hands.
Recover all thy sigh-blown age
20   On double pleasures: leave thy cold dispute
Of what is fit, and not. Forsake thy cage,
Thy rope of sands,
Which petty thoughts have made, and made to thee
Good cable, to enforce and draw,
And be thy law,
While thou didst wink and wouldst not see.
Away; take heed,
I will abroad.
Call in thy death's head there: tie up thy fears.
30   He that forbears
To suit and serve his need,
Deserves his load.
But as I raved and grew more fierce and wild
At every word,
Me thoughts I heard one calling, *Child:*
And I replied, *My Lord.*

Joseph's Coat

Wounded I sing, tormented I indite,
Thrown down I fall into a bed, and rest:
Sorrow hath changed its note: such is his will,
Who changeth all things, as him pleaseth best.
For well he knows, if but one grief and smart

Among my many had his full career,
Sure it would carry with it ev'n my heart,
And both would run until they found a bier
        To fetch the body; both being due to grief.
But he hath spoiled the race; and giv'n to anguish
One of Joy's coats, ticing it with relief
To linger in me, and together languish.
        I live to show his power, who once did bring
        My *joys* to *weep*, and now my *griefs* to *sing*.

The Pulley

        When God at first made man,
Having a glass of blessings standing by;
Let us (said he) pour on him all we can:
Let the world's riches, which dispersed lie,
        Contract into a span.

        So strength first made a way;
Then beauty flowed, then wisdom, honour, pleasure:
When almost all was out, God made a stay,
Perceiving that alone of all his treasure
10   Rest in the bottom lay.

        For if I should (said he)
Bestow this jewel also on my creature,
He would adore my gifts instead of me,
And rest in Nature, not the God of Nature:
        So both should losers be.

        Yet let him keep the rest,
But keep them with repining restlessness:
Let him be rich and weary, that at least,
If goodness lead him not, yet weariness
20   May toss him to my breast.

The Search

        Whither, O, whither art thou fled,
                My Lord, my Love?
        My searches are my daily bread;
                Yet never prove.

        My knees pierce th' earth, mine eyes the sky;
                And yet the sphere
        And centre both to me deny
                That thou art there.

        Yet can I mark how herbs below
10   Grow green and gay,
        As if to meet thee they did know,
                While I decay.

        Yet can I mark how stars above
                Simper and shine,   *Glimmer*
        As having keys unto thy love,
                While poor I pine.

I sent a sigh to seek thee out,
          Deep drawn in pain,
Winged like an arrow: but my scout
20   Returns in vain.

I tuned another (having store)
          Into a groan;
Because the search was dumb before:
          But all was one.

Lord, dost thou some new fabric mould,
          Which favour wins,
And keeps thee present, leaving th'old
          Unto their sins?

Where is my God? what hidden place
30   Conceals thee still?
What covert dare eclipse thy face?
          Is it thy will?

O let not that of any thing;
          Let rather brass,
Or steel, or mountains be thy ring,
          And I will pass.

Thy will such an entrenching is,
          As passeth thought:
To it all strength, all subtleties
40   Are things of nought.

Thy will such a strange distance is,
          As that to it
East and West touch, the poles do kiss,
          And parallels meet.

Since then my grief must be as large,
          As is thy space,
Thy distance from me; see my charge,
          Lord, see my case.

O take these bars, these lengths away,
50   Turn, and restore me:
Be not Almighty, let me say,
          Against, but for me.

When thou dost turn, and wilt be near,
          What edge so keen,
What point so piercing can appear
          To come between?

For as thy absence doth excell
          All distance known:
So doth thy nearness bear the bell,
60   Making two one.

The Flower

How fresh, O Lord, how sweet and clean
Are thy returns! ev'n as the flowers in spring;

To which, besides their own demean,   *demeanor*
The late-past frosts tributes of pleasure bring.
Grief melts away
Like snow in May,
As if there were no such cold thing.

Who would have thought my shriveled heart
Could have recovered greenness? It was gone
10   Quite under ground; as flowers depart
To see their mother-root, when they have blown,   *bloomed*
Where they together
All the hard weather,
Dead to the world, keep house unknown.

These are thy wonders, *Lord of power*,
Killing and quick'ning, bringing down to hell
And up to heaven in an hour;
Making a chiming of a passing-bell.
We say amiss,
20   This or that is:
Thy word is all, if we could spell.

O that I once past changing were,
Fast in thy Paradise, where no flower can wither!
Many a spring I shoot up fair,
Off'ring at heav'n, growing and groaning thither:
Nor doth my flower
Want a spring-shower,
My sins and I joining together.

But while I grow in a straight line,
30   Still upwards bent, as if heav'n were mine own,
Thy anger comes, and I decline:
What frost to that? what pole is not the zone
Where all things burn,
When thou dost turn
And the least frown of thine is shown?

And now in age I bud again,
After so many deaths I live and write,
I once more smell the dew and rain,
And relish versing: O my only light,
40   It cannot be
That I am he
On whom thy tempests fell all night.

These are thy wonders, *Lord of love*,
To make us see we are but flowers that glide:
Which when we once can find and prove,
Thou hast a garden for us, where to bide.
Who would be more,
Swelling through store,
Forfeit their Paradise by their pride.

The Son

Let foreign nations of their language boast,
What fine variety each tongue affords:

I like our language, as our men and coast:
Who cannot dress it well, want wit, not words.
How neatly do we give one only name
To parent's issue and the sun's bright star!
A son is light and fruit; a fruitful flame
Chasing the father's dimness, carried far   *dispelling*
From the first man in th' East, to fresh and new
Western discov'ries of posterity.
So in one word our Lord's humility
We turn upon him in a sense most true:
    For what Christ once in humbleness began,
    We him in glory call, *The Son of Man.*

10

A True Hymn

    My joy, my life, my crown!
    My heart was meaning all the day,
      Somewhat it fain would say:
And still it runneth mutt'ring up and down
With only this, *My joy, my life, my crown.*

    Yet slight not these few words:
    If truly said, they may take part
      Among the best in art.
The fineness which a hymn or psalm affords,
Is, when the soul unto the lines accords.

10

    He who craves all the mind,
    And all the soul, and strength, and time,
      If the words only rime,
Justly complains, that somewhat is behind   *insufficient*
To make his verse, or write a hymn in kind.

    Whereas if th' heart be moved,
    Although the verse be somewhat scant,
      God doth supply the want.
As when th' heart says (sighing to be approved)
O, could I love! and stops: God writeth, *Loved.*

20

Bitter-sweet

    Ah my dear angry Lord,
    Since thou dost love, yet strike,
    Cast down, yet help afford,
    Sure I will do the like.

    I will complain, yet praise;
    I will bewail, approve;
    And all my sour-sweet days
    I will lament, and love.

Aaron

    Holiness on the head,
    Light and perfections on the breast,
Harmonious bells below, raising the dead
    To lead them unto life and rest.
    Thus are true Aarons drest.

Profaneness in my head,
Defects and darkness in my breast,
A noise of passions ringing me for dead
Unto a place where is no rest.
Poor priest thus am I drest.

Only another head
I have, another heart and breast,
Another music, making live not dead,
Without whom I could have no rest:
In him I am well drest.

Christ is my only head,
My alone only heart and breast,
My only music, striking me ev'n dead,
That to the old man I may rest,
And be in him new drest.

So holy in my head,
Perfect and light in my dear breast,
My doctrine tuned by Christ, (who is not dead
But lives in me while I do rest)
Come people; Aaron's drest.

10

20

The Forerunners

The harbingers are come. See, see their mark,
White is their colour, and behold my head.
But must they have my brain? must they dispark
Those sparkling notions, which therein were bred?
Must dulness turn me to a clod?
Yet have they left me, *Thou art still my God.*

Good men ye be, to leave me my best room,
Ev'n all my heart, and what is lodged there:
I pass not, I, what of the rest become,   *care not*
So *Thou art still my God* be out of fear.
He will be pleased with that ditty;
And if I please him, I write fine and witty.

Farewell sweet phrases, lovely metaphors.
But will ye leave me thus? when ye before
Of stews and brothels only knew the doors,
Then did I wash you with my tears, and more,
Brought you to Church well drest and clad:
My God must have my best, ev'n all I had.

Lovely enchanting language, sugar-cane,
Honey of roses, whither wilt thou fly?
Hath some fond lover ticed thee to thy bane?
And wilt thou leave the Church, and love a sty?
Fie, thou wilt soil thy broidered coat,
And hurt thy self, and him that sings thy note.

Let foolish lovers, if they will love dung,
With canvas, not with arras clothe their shame:
Let folly speak in her own native tongue.
True beauty dwells on high: ours is a flame

10

20

But borrowed thence to light us thither.
30   Beauty and beauteous words should go together.

Yet if you go, I pass not; take your way:
For *Thou art still my God* is all that ye
Perhaps with more embellishment can say.
Go birds of spring: let winter have his fee:
        Let a bleak paleness chalk the door,
So all within be livelier than before.

Discipline

Throw away thy rod,
Throw away thy wrath:
      O my God,
Take the gentle path.

For my heart's desire
Unto thine is bent:
      I aspire
To a full consent.

Not a word or look
10   I affect to own,
      But by book,
And thy book alone.

Though I fail, I weep:
Though I halt in pace,
      Yet I creep
To the throne of grace.

Then let wrath remove;
Love will do the deed;
      For with love
20   Stony hearts will bleed.

Love is swift of foot;
Love's a man of war,
      And can shoot,
And can hit from far.

Who can scape his bow?
That which wrought on thee,
      Brought thee low,
Needs must work on me.

Throw away thy rod;
30   Though man frailties hath,
      Thou art God:
Throw away thy wrath.

The Banquet

Welcome sweet and sacred cheer,
          Welcome dear,
With me, in me, live and dwell:

For thy neatness passeth sight,
                              Thy delight
Passeth tongue to taste or tell.

O what sweetness from the bowl
                              Fills my soul,
Such as is, and makes divine!
Is some star (fled from the sphere)
                              Melted there,
As we sugar melt in wine?

Or hath sweetness in the bread
                              Made a head
To subdue the smell of sin;
Flowers, and gums, and powders giving
                              All their living,
Lest the enemy should win?

Doubtless, neither star nor flower
                              Hath the power
Such a sweetness to impart:
Only God, who gives perfumes,
                              Flesh assumes,
And with it perfumes my heart.

But as Pomanders and wood
                              Still are good,
Yet being bruised are better scented:
God, to show how far his love
                              Could improve,
Here, as broken, is presented.

When I had forgot my birth,
                              And on earth
In delights of earth was drowned;
God took blood, and needs would be
                              Spilt with me,
And so found me on the ground.

Having raised me to look up,
                              In a cup
Sweetly he doth meet my taste.
But I still being low and short,
                              Far from court,
Wine becomes a wing at last.

For with it alone I fly
                              To the sky:
Where I wipe mine eyes, and see
What I seek, for what I sue;
                              Him I view,
Who hath done so much for me.

Let the wonder of this pity
                              Be my ditty,
And take up my lines and life:
Hearken under pain of death,
                              Hands and breath;
Strive in this, and love the strife.

The Elixir

Teach me, my God and King,
In all things thee to see,
And what I do in any thing,
To do it as for thee:

Not rudely as a beast,
To run into an action;
But still to make thee prepossest,
And give it his perfection.

A man that looks on glass,
On it may stay his eye;
Or if he pleaseth, through it pass,
And then the heav'n espy.

All may of thee partake:
Nothing can be so mean,
Which with his tincture (for thy sake)
Will not grow bright and clean.

A servant with this clause
Makes drudgery divine:
Who sweeps a room, as for thy laws,
Makes that and th'action fine.

This is the famous stone
That turneth all to gold:
For that which God doth touch and own
Cannot for less be told.

A Wreath

A wreathed garland of deserved praise,
Of praise deserved, unto thee I give,
I give to thee, who knowest all my ways,
My crooked winding ways, wherein I live,
Wherein I die, not live: for life is straight,
Straight as a line, and ever tends to thee,
To thee, who art more far above deceit,
Than deceit seems above simplicity.
Give me simplicity, that I may live,
So live and like, that I may know thy ways,
Know them and practise them: then shall I give
For this poor wreath, give thee a crown of praise.

Death

Death, thou wast once an uncouth hideous thing,
                    Nothing but bones,
        The sad effect of sadder groans:
Thy mouth was open, but thou couldst not sing.

For we considered thee as at some six
                    Or ten years hence,
        After the loss of life and sense,
Flesh being turned to dust, and bones to sticks.

We look on this side of thee, shooting short,
     Where we did find
  The shells of fledge souls left behind,
Dry dust, which sheds no tears, but may extort.

But since our Saviour's death did put some blood
     Into thy face;
  Thou art grown fair and full of grace,
Much in request, much sought for as a good.

For we do now behold thee gay and glad,
     As at Doomsday;
  When souls shall wear their new array,
And all thy bones with beauty shall be clad.

Therefore we can go die as sleep, and trust
     Half that we have
  Unto an honest faithful grave;
Making our pillows either down, or dust.

Doomsday

     Come away,
   Make no delay.
Summon all the dust to rise,
Till it stir, and rub the eyes;
While this member jogs the other,
Each one whisp'ring, *Live you brother?*

     Come away,
   Make this the day.
Dust, alas, no music feels,
But thy trumpet: then it kneels,
As peculiar notes and strains
Cure Tarantula's raging pains.

     Come away,
   O make no stay!
Let the graves make their confession,
Lest at length they plead possession:
Flesh's stubbornness may have
Read that lesson to the grave.

     Come away,
   Thy flock doth stray.
Some to winds their body lend,
And in them may drown a friend:
Some in noisome vapours grow
To a plague and public woe.

     Come away,
   Help our decay.
Man is out of order hurled,
Parceled out to all the world.
Lord, thy broken consort raise,
And the music shall be praise.

Judgement

Almighty Judge, how shall poor wretches brook
              Thy dreadful look,
Able a heart of iron to appall,
              When thou shalt call
For every man's peculiar book?

What others mean to do, I know not well;
              Yet I hear tell,
That some will turn thee to some leaves therein
              So void of sin,
That they in merit shall excell.

But I resolve, when thou shalt call for mine,
              That to decline,
And thrust a Testament into thy hand:
              Let that be scanned.
There thou shalt find my faults are thine.

Heaven

O who will show me those delights on high?
      Echo.   *I.*
Thou Echo, thou art mortal, all men know.
      Echo.   *No.*
Wert thou not born among the trees and leaves?
      Echo.   *Leaves.*
And are there any leaves, that still abide?
      Echo.   *Bide.*
What leaves are they? impart the matter wholly.
      Echo.   *Holy.*
Are holy leaves the Echo then of bliss?
      Echo.   *Yes.*
Then tell me, what is that supreme delight?
      Echo.   *Light.*
Light to the mind: what shall the will enjoy?
      Echo.   *Joy.*
But are there cares and business with the pleasure?
      Echo.   *Leisure.*
Light, joy, and leisure; but shall they persever?
      Echo.   *Ever.*

Love (III)

Love bade me welcome. Yet my soul drew back
              Guilty of dust and sin.
But quick-eyed Love, observing me grow slack
              From my first entrance in,
Drew nearer to me, sweetly questioning,
              If I lacked any thing.

A guest, I answered, worthy to be here:
              Love said, You shall be he.
I the unkind, ungrateful? Ah my dear,
              I cannot look on thee.
Love took my hand, and smiling did reply,
              Who made the eyes but I?

Truth Lord, but I have marred them: let my shame
Go where it doth deserve.
And know you not, says Love, who bore the blame?
My dear, then I will serve.
You must sit down, says Love, and taste my meat:
So I did sit and eat.

Finis
Glory be to God on high
And on earth peace
Good will towards men.

Izaak Walton (1593–1683)

Although he also wrote several literary biographies – of John Donne, Sir Henry Wotton, Richard Hooker, George Herbert, and Bishop Robert Sanderson – Walton's *The Compleat Angler*, which first appeared in 1653, is his masterpiece. Chapter VII of Part II is a simple account of the sorts of artificial flies that are best for fishing between the months of January and May. But it is also a subtle piece of literary art on however a small scale. Not only is it an ostensible dialogue, it is also a piece of pastoral literature in calendar form, like Spenser's *The Shepheardes Calendar*. Walton was born in Stafford, was apprenticed to an iron-monger in London, and went into business for himself in 1614. When the English Revolution erupted, he sided with the royalists in 1642. *The Compleat Angler* is one of the best-selling books of all time. His motto, "Study to be quiet," affirms a simplicity that in some ways anticipates

Thoreau's, although it is hardly imaginable that they would have had much else in common. In a single sentence Douglas Bush captures the relationship between the subject matter of Walton's famous book and his inner life: "A love of angling is an outward and visible sign of an inward and spiritual grace, of a gentle, contemplative benignity of soul which abhors dissension and loves good old ways, whether in the choice of bait or ballads or barley-wine or the worship of the Creator" (p. 225).

READING

Douglas Bush, *English Literature in the Earlier Seventeenth Century.*

M. P.

THE COMPLEAT ANGLER

Part II: CHAP. VII.

Viat. Come Sir, having now well din'd, and being again set in your little House; I will now challenge your promise, and entreat you to proceed in your instruction for Flie-fishing, which, that you may be the better encourag'd to do, I will assure you, that I have not lost, I think, one sylla-ble of what you have told me: but very well retain all your directions both for the Rod, Line, and making a Flie, and now desire an account of the Flies themselves.

Pisc. Why Sir, I am ready to give it you, and shall have the whole afternoon to do it in, if no body come in to interrupt us; for you must know (besides the unfitness of the day) that the after-noons so early in *March* signifie very little to Angling with a Flie, though with a Minnow, or a Worm something might (I confess) be done.

To begin then where I left off, my father *Walton* tells us but of 12 Artificial flies only, to Angle with at the top, and gives their names; of which some are common with us here; and I think I guess at most of them by his description, and I believe they all breed, and are taken in our Rivers, though we do not make them either of the same Dubbing, or fashion. And it may be in the Rivers about *London*, which I presume he has most frequented, and where 'tis likely he has done most exe-cution, there is not much notice taken of many more: but we are acquainted with several others here (though perhaps I may reckon some of his by other names too) but if I do, I shall make you amends by an addition to his Catalogue. And although the forenamed great Master in the Art of Angling (for so in truth he is) tells you that no man should in honesty catch a Trout till the middle of *March*, yet I hope he will give a man leave sooner to take a Grayling, which, as I told you, is in the dead Months in his best season; and do assure you (which I remember by a very remarkable token) I did once take upon the sixt day of December one, and only one, of the biggest Graylings and the best in season, that ever I yet saw, or tasted; and do usually take Trouts too, and with a Flie, not only before the middle of this Month, but almost every year in *February*, unless it be a very ill spring indeed, and have sometimes in *January*, so early as New-years-tide, and in frost and snow taken Grayling in a warm sunshine day for an hour or two about Noon: and to fish for him with a Grub it is then the best time of all.

I shall therefore begin my Flie-fishing with that Month (though I confess very few begin so soon, and that such as are so fond of the sport as to embrace all opportunities, can rarely in that Month find a day fit for their purpose) and tell you, that upon my knowledg these Flies in a warm sun, for an hour or two in the day, are certainly taken.

January

1. A red-brown with wings of the Male of a Malard almost white: the dubbing of the tail of a black long coated Cur, such as they commonly make muffs of: for the hair on the tail of such a Dog dies, and turns to a red Brown, but the hair of a smoth coated Dog of the same colour will not do, because it will not dye, but retains its natural colour, and this flie is taken in a warm sun, this whole Month thorough.[1]

2. There is also a very little bright Dun Gnat, as little as can possibly be made, so little as never to be fisht with, with above one hair next the hook, and this is to be made of a mixt dubbing of Martins fur, and the white of a Hares scut; with a very white, and small wing; and 'tis no great matter how fine you fish, for nothing will rise in this Month but a Grayling, and of them I never at this season saw any taken with a Flie, of above a foot long in my life: but of little ones about the bigness of a smelt in a warm day, and a glowing Sun, you may take enough with these two flies, and they are both taken the whole North through.

February

1. Where the Red-brown of the last Month ends, another almost of the same colour begins with this, saving that the dubbing of this must be of something a blacker colour, and both of them warpt on with red silk: the dubbing that should make this Flie, and that is the truest colour, is to be got of the black spot of a Hog's ear: not that a black spot in any part of the Hog will not afford the same colour; but that the hair in that place is by many degrees softer, and more fit for the purpose: his wing must be as the other, and this kills all this Month, and is call'd the lesser Red-brown.

2. This Month also a plain Hackle, or palmer-Flie, made with a rough black body, either of black Spaniels furr, or the whirl of an *Estridg*[2] feather, and the red Hackle of a Capon over all, will kill, and if the weather be right make very good sport.

3. Also a lesser Hackle with a black body also, silver twist over that, and a red feather over all, will fill your pannier if the Month be open, and not bound up in Ice, and snow, with very good Fish; but in case of a frost and snow, you are to Angle only with the smallest Gnats, Browns and Duns you can make, and with those are only to expect Graylings no bigger, than sprats.

4. In this Month, upon a whirling round water, we have a great Hackle, the body black, and wrapped with a red feather of a Capon untrim'd: that is, the whole length of the Hackle staring out (for we sometimes barb the Hackle feather short all over; sometimes barb it only a little, and sometimes barb it close underneath, leaving the whole length of the feather on the top, or back of the Flie which makes it swim better, and as occasion serves kills very great Fish.

THE COMPLEAT ANGLER   2   *ostrich.*

1   Materials for making an artificial fly.

5. We make use also in this Month of another great Hackle the body black, and rib'd over with Gold twist, and a red feather over all, which also does great execution.

6. Also a great Dun, made with Dun Bears Hair, and the wings of the grey feather of a Mallard near unto his tail, which is absolutely the best Flie can be thrown upon a River this Month, and with which an Angler shall have admirable sport.

7. We have also this Month the great blew Dun, the dubbing of the bottom of Bears hair next to the roots, mixt with a little blue Camlet, the wings of the dark grey feather of a Mallard.

8. We have also this Month a Dark-Brown, the dubbing of the brown hair of the Flanck of a brended Cow, and the wings of the grey-Drakes feather.

And note, that these several Hackels, or Palmer Flies, are some for one Water, and one Skye, and some for another, and according to the change of those, we alter their size, and colour, and note also, that both in this, and all other Months of the Year, when you do not certainly know what Flie is taken; or cannot see any Fish to rise, you are then to put on a small Hackle, if the Water be clear, or a bigger if something dark, untill you have taken one, and then thrusting your finger thorough his Guills,[3] to pull out his Gorge, which being opened with your knife, you will then discover what Flie is taken, and may fit your self accordingly.

For the making of a Hackle, or Palmer Flie, my father *Walton* has already given you sufficient direction.

March

For this Month you are to use all the same Hackels, and Flies with the other, but you are to make them less.

1. We have besides, for this Month a little Dun call'd a whirling Dun (though it is not the whirling Dun, indeed, which is one of the best flies we have) and for this the dubbing must be of the bottom fur of a Squirrels tail and the wing of the grey feather of a Drake.

2. Also a bright brown, the dubbing either of the brown of a Spaniel, or that of a Cows flanck, with a grey wing.

3. Also a whitish Dun made of the roots of Camels hair, and the wings of the grey feather of a Mallard.

4. There is also for this Month a Flie, call'd the Thorn Tree Flie; the dubbing an absolute black mixt with eight or ten hairs of *Isabella* coloured Mohair, the body as little as can be made, and the wings of a bright Malards feather, an admirable Flie, and in great repute amongst us for a killer.

5. There is besides this another blew Dun, the dubbing of which it is made being thus to be got. Take a small tooth comb, and with it comb the neck of a black Grey hound, and the down that sticks in the teeth, will be the finest blew, that ever you saw. The wings of this Flie can hardly be too white, and he is taken about the tenth of this Month, and lasteth till the four and twentieth.

6. From the tenth of this Month also till towards the end, is taken a little black Gnat; the dubbing either of the fur of a black water-Dog, or the down of a young black water-Coot; the wings of the Male of a Mallard as white as may be, the body as little as you can possibly make it, and the wings as short as his body.

7. From the Sixteenth of this Month also to the end of it, we use a bright brown, the dubbing for which, is to be had out of a Skinners Lime-pits, and of the hair of an abortive Calf, which the lime will turn to be so bright, as to shine like Gold, for the wings of this Flie, the feather of a brown Hen is best; which Flie is also taken till the tenth of *April*.

April

All the same Hackles, and Flies that were taken in *March* will be taken in this Month also, with this distinction only concerning the Flies, that all the browns be lapt with red silk, and the Duns with yellow.

---

3   *gills.*

1. To these a small bright-brown, made of Spaniels fur, with a light grey wing; in a bright day, and a clear water is very well taken.

2. We have too a little dark brown, the dubbing of that colour, and some violet Camlet mixt, and the wing of the grey feather of a Mallard.

3. From the sixth of this Month to the tenth, we have also a Flie called the violet Flie, made of a dark violet stuff, with the wings of the grey feather of a Mallard.

4. About the twelfth of this Month comes in the Flie call'd the whirling Dun, which is taken every day about the mid time of day all this Month through, and by fits from thence to the end of *June*, and is commonly made of the down of a Fox Cub, which is of an Ash colour at the roots, next the skin, and ribb'd about with yellow silk, the wings of the pale grey feather of a Mallard.

5. There is also a yellow Dun, the dubbing of Camels hair, and yellow Camlet, or wool mixt, and a white grey wing.

6. There is also this Month another little brown, besides that mention'd before, made with a very slender body, the dubbing of dark brown, and violet Camlet mixt, and a grey wing; which though the direction for the making be near the other, is yet another Flie, and will take when the other will not, especially in a bright day, and a clear water.

7. About the twentieth of this Month comes in a Flie call'd the Horse-flesh Flie, the dubbing of which is a blew Mohair, with pink colour'd, and red Tammy[4] mixt, a light coloured wing, and a dark brown head. This flie is taken best in an Evening, and kills from two hours before Sun set till twilight, and is taken the Month thorough.

May

And now Sir, that we are entring into the Month of *May*, I think it requisite to beg not only your attention; but also your best patience; for I must now be a little tedious with you, and dwell upon this Month longer than ordinary: which that you may the better endure, I must tell you, this Month deserves, and requires to be insisted on, for as much as it alone, and the next following afford more pleasure to the Flie-Angler than all the rest; and here it is that you are to expect an account of the Green Drake and stone-flie, promis'd you so long ago, and some others that are peculiar to this Month and part of the month following, and that (though not so great either in bulk, or name) do yet stand in competition with the two before named, and so, that it is yet undecided amongst the Anglers to which of the pretenders to the Title of the May-flie, it does properly, and duly belong, neither dare I (where so many of the learned in this Art of Angling are got in dispute about the controversie) take upon me to determine; but I think I ought to have a vote amongst them, and according to that priviledg shall give you my free opinion, and peradventure when I have told you all, you may incline to think me in the right.

Viat. I have so great a deference to your judgment in these matters, that I must always be of your opinion; and the more you speak, the faster I grow to my attention, for I can never be weary of hearing you upon this Subject.

Pisc. Why that's encouragement enough: and now prepare your self for a tedious Lecture: but I will first begin with the flies of less esteem (though almost any thing will take a Trout in *May*) that I may afterwards insist the longer upon those of greater note and reputation: know therefore that the first flie we take notice of in this Month, is call'd the Turky-Flie.

1. The dubbing ravell'd out of some blew stuff, and lapt about with yellow silk, the wings of a grey Mallards feather.

2. Next a great Hackle: or Palmer-flie, with a yellow body ribb'd with Gold twist, and large wings of a Mallards feather dyed yellow, with a red Capons Hackle over all.

3. Then a black flie, the dubbing of a black Spaniels fur, and the wings of a grey Mallards feather.

4. After that a light brown with a slender body, the dubbing twirl'd upon small red silk, and rais'd with the point of a needle, that the ribs or rows of silk may appear through the wings of the grey feather of a Mallard.

4 Worsted cloth with a glaze finish.

5. Next a little Dun, the dubbing of a Bears dun whirl'd upon yellow silk, the wings of the grey feather of a Mallard.

6. Then a white Gnat, with a pale wing, and a black head.

7. There is also this Month a flie called the Peacock-flie, the body made of a whirl of a Peacocks feather, with a red head, and wings of a Mallards feather.

8. We have then another very killing flie, known by the name of the Dun-Cut, the dubbing of which is a Bears dun, with a little blew, and yellow mixt with it, a large dun wing, and two horns at the head, made of the hairs of a Squirrels tail.

9. The next is the Cow-Lady, a little flie, the body of a Peacocks feather, the wing of a red feather, or strips of the red hackle of a Cock.

10. We have then the Cow-turd flie; the dubbing light brown, and yellow mixt, the wing the dark grey feather of a Mallard. And note that besides these abovementioned, all the same Hackles and Flies, the Hackles only brighter, and the Flies smaller, that are taken in *April*, will also be taken this Month, as also all Browns and Duns; and now I come to my Stone-flie, and Green-Drake, which are the Matadores for Trout and Grayling, and in their season kill more fish in our *Derbyshire* Rivers, than all the rest past, and to come, in the whole year besides.

But first I am to tell you, that we have four several flies which contend for the Title of the May-Flie, namely,

> *The Green-Drake,*
> *The Stone-Flie,*
> *The Black-Flie, and*
> *The little yellow May-Flie.*

And all these have their Champions and Advocates to dispute, and plead their priority; though I do not understand why the two last named should; the first two having so manifestly the advantage, both in their beauty, and the wonderful execution they do in their season.

11. Of these the Green-Drake comes in about the twentieth of this Month, or betwixt that, and the latter end (for they are sometimes sooner and sometimes later according to the quality of the Year) but never well taken till towards the end of this Month, and the beginning of *June*. The Stone-Flie comes much sooner, so early as the middle of *April*; but is never well taken till towards the middle of *May*, and continues to kill much longer than the Green-Drake stays with us, so long as to the end almost of *June*; and indeed, so long as there are any of them to be seen upon the water; and sometimes in an Artificial Flie, and late at night, or before Sun rise in a morning, longer.

Now both these Flies (and I believe many others, though I think not all) are certainly, and demonstratively bred in the very Rivers where they are taken, our Caddis or Cod-bait which lye under stones in the bottom of the water, most of them turning into those two Flies, and being gather'd in the husk, or crust, near the time of their maturity, are very easily known, and distinguisht, and are of all other the most remarkable, both for their size, as being of all other the biggest (the shortest of them being a full inch long, or more) and for the execution they do, the Trout and Grayling being much more greedy of them, than of any others: and indeed the Trout never feeds fat, nor comes into his perfect season, till these Flies come in.

Of these the Green-Drake never discloses from his husk, till he be first there grown to full maturity, body, wings, and all, and then he creeps out of his cell, but with his wings so crimpt, and ruffled, by being prest together in that narrow room, that they are for some hours totally useless to him, by which means he is compelled either to creep upon the flags, sedges, and blades of grass (if his first rising from the bottom of the water be near the banks of the River) till the Air, and Sun, stiffen and smooth them! or if his first appearance above water happen to be in the middle, he then lies upon the surface of the water like a Ship at Hull (for his feet are totally useless to him there, and he cannot creep upon the water as the Stone-Flie can) untill his wings have got stiffness to fly with, if by some Trout, or Grayling he be not taken in the interim (which ten to one he is) and then his wings stand high, and clos'd exact upon his back, like the Butterfly, and his motion in flying is the same. His body is in some of a paler, in others of a darker yellow (for they are not all exactly of a colour) rib'd with rows of green, long, slender, and growing sharp towards the tail, at the end of which he has three long small whisks of a very dark colour, almost black, and his tail turns up towards his back like a Mallard, from whence questionless he has his name of the green-Drake. These (as I think I told you before) we commonly dape, or dibble with, and having gathered great store of them into a long draw box, with holes in the Cover to give them Air (where also they will continue fresh, and vigorous a night or more) we take them out thence by the wings, and bait them thus upon the Hook. We first take one (for we commonly fish with two of them at a time) and putting the point of the Hook into the thickest part of his Body under one of his wings, run it directly through and out at the other side, leaving him spitted cross upon the Hook, and then taking the other, put him on after the same manner, but with his head the contrary way, in which posture they will live upon the Hook, and play with their wings for a quarter of an hour, or more: but you must have a care to keep their wings dry, both from the water, and also that your fingers be not wet when you take them out to bait them: for then your bait is spoil'd.

Having now told you how to Angle with this Flie alive; I am now to tell you next, how to make an Artificial Flie, that will so perfectly resemble him, as to be taken in a rough windy day, when no Flies can lye upon the water; nor are to be found about the Banks and sides of the River, to a wonder, and with which you shall certainly kill the best Trout, and Grayling in the River.

The Artificial Green-Drake then is made upon a large Hook, the Dubbing, Camels hair, bright Bears hair, the soft down that is comb'd from a Hogs bristles, and yellow Camlet, well mixt together, the body long, and ribb'd about with green silk, or rather yellow waxt with green-wax, the whisks of the tail of the long hairs of sables, or fitchet, and the wings of the white grey feather of a Mallard dyed yellow, which also is to be dyed thus.

Take the root of a Barbary Tree, and shave it, and put to it Woody viss, with as much Alum as a Walnut, and boyl your feathers in it with Rain water; and they will be of a very fine yellow.

I have now done with the Green-drake, excepting to tell you, that he is taken at all hours during his season, whilst there is any day upon the Sky; and with a made Flie, I once took, ten days after he was absolutely gone, in a Cloudy day, after a showr, and in a whistling wind, five and thirty very great Trouts, and Graylings betwixt five, and eight of the Clock in the Evening, and had no less than five, or six Flies with three good hairs a piece taken from me in despite of my heart, besides.

12. I should now come next to the Stone-Flie, but there is another Gentleman in my way: that must of necessity come in between, and that is the Grey-Drake, which in all shapes, and dimensions is perfectly the same with the other, but quite almost of another colour, being of a paler, and more livid yellow, and green, and ribb'd with black quite down his body, with black shining wings, and so diaphanous and tender, cob-web like, that they are of no manner of use for Daping; but come in, and are taken after the Green-Drake, and in an Artificial Flie kill very well, which Flie is thus made, the Dubbing of the down of a Hogs bristles, and black Spaniels fur mixt, and ribb'd down the body with black silk, the whisks of the hairs of the beard of a black Cat, and the wings of the black grey feather of a Mallard.

And now I come to the Stone-Flie, but am afraid I have already wearied your patience, which if I have, I beseech you freely tell me so, and I will defer the remaining instructions for Flie-Angling till some other time.

Viat. No truly Sir, I can never be weary of hearing you: but if you think fit, because I am afraid I am too troublesom, to refresh your self with a glass, and a pipe; and may afterwards proceed, and I shall be exceedingly pleas'd to hear you.

Pisc. I thank you Sir for that motion; for believe me I am dry with talking, Here Boy, give us here a Bottle, and a Glass; and *Sir*, my service to you, and to all our friends in the South.

Viat. Your Servant *Sir*, and I'le pledg you as heartily; for the good powder'd beef I eat at Dinner, or something else, has made me thirsty.

Rachel Speght (1597–?)

The year of Rachel Speght's birth is uncertain and the year of her death unknown. The daughter of the Calvinist minister James Speght, she received a classical education from her father. Although in her autobiographical writings she gives her mother major credit for her development, not even her mother's name survives. At age 19 she made her intervention into the gender wars with her tract *A Mouzell for Melastomus {A Muzzle for Black Mouth}* (1617), which makes her the first Englishwoman to identify herself by name as an opponent of patriarchal ideology. At age 24 and with her father's consent she married William Procter, also a minister. They had two children, a boy and a girl, each named for their parents.

Her tract is directed against an anonymous and perhaps intentionally outrageous attack on women by Joseph Swetnam, a fencing master. His *Araignment of Lewde, Idle, Froward, and Unconstant Women* appeared in 1615. His text is part of what is sometimes referred to as the *querelle des femmes,* an ongoing rhetorical battle that may have been fuelled as much by the love of debate as by real misogyny. This is suggested by Swetnam's invitation to receive responses from women and their defenders. Nevertheless, a powerful challenge to strict gender definitions was taking place during the reign of James I. His wife, Queen Anne, was an active participant in a fad of female cross-dressing, which also transcended class lines to include such lower-class girls as Moll Cutpurse and Long Meg of Westminster. In retrospect it is easy to see these controversies as a con-tinuation of the whole project of self-fashioning that was fundamental to the European Renaissance, here being tentatively extended to women.

As a text, Rachel Speght's defense of women is a brilliant demonstration of Swetnam's ignorance of the Bible and the classical sources that he mistakenly thinks support his negative views of women. Her defense is launched from within a more thorough and meticulous grounding in scripture and humanistic learning. Rhetorically she assumes a David to his Goliath, but in fact he is no intellectual match for this 19-year-old woman. She defeats him easily, with wit to spare. With the force of learning and eloquence on her side, she reverses the power structure.

Her text includes a dedicatory epistle to all virtuous women, an address to Swetnam in the form of a Preface, the tract itself, and an appended tract, *Certaine Quaeres to the Bayter of Women*, which is more personally addressed to him.

READING

Barbara Kiefer Lewalski, *Writing Women in Jacobean England.*
Barbara Kiefer Lewalski (ed.), *The Polemics and Poems of Rachel Speght.*
Stephen Orgel, *Impersonations: The Performance of Gender in Shakespeare's England.*

M. P.

A MOVZELL FOR MELASTOMVS[1]

To all vertuous Ladies Honour*able or Worshipfull, and
to all other of* Hevahs *sex fearing God, and loving their
just reputation, grace and peace through*
Christ, *to eternall glory.*

It was the similie of that wise and learned *Lactantius,*[2] that if fire, though but with a small sparke kindled, bee not at the first quenched, it may worke great mischiefe and dammage: So likewise may the scandals and defamations of the malevolent in time prove pernitious, if they bee not nipt in the head at their first appearance. The consideration of this (right Honourable and Worshipfull Ladies) hath incited me (though yong, and the unworthiest of thousands) to encounter with a furious enemy to our sexe, least if his unjust imputations should continue without answere, he might insult and account himselfe a victor; and by such a conceit deale, as Historiographers report the viper to

---

A MOVZELL FOR MELASTOMUS
1 A muzzle for the black mouth.

2 Eloquent Latin Church Father.

doe, who in the Winter time doth vomit forth her poyson, and in the spring time sucketh the same up againe, which becommeth twise as deadly as the former: And this our pestiferous enemy, by thinking to provide a more deadly poyson for women, then already he hath foamed forth, may evaporate, by an addition unto his former illeterate Pamphlet (intituled *The Arraignement of Women*) a more contagious obtrectation[3] then he hath already done, and indeed hath threatned to doe. Secondly, if it should have had free passage without any answere at all (seeing that *Tacere* is, *quasi consentire*[4]) the vulgar ignorant might have beleeved his Diabolicall infamies to be infallible truths, not to bee infringed; whereas now they may plainely perceive them to bee but the scumme of Heathenish braines, or a building raised without a foundation (at least from sacred Scripture) which the winde of Gods truth must needs cast downe to the ground. A third reason why I have adventured to fling this stone at vaunting *Goliah* is, to comfort the mindes of all *Hevahs*[5] sex, both rich and poore, learned and unlearned, with this Antidote, that if the feare of God reside in their hearts, maugre all adversaries, they are highly esteemed and accounted of in the eies of their gracious Redeemer, so that they need not feare the darts of envy or obtrectators: For shame and disgrace (saith *Aristotle*) is the end of them that shoote such poysoned shafts. Worthy therefore of imitation is that example of *Seneca*, who when he was told that a certaine man did exclaime and raile against him, made this milde answere; Some dogs barke more upon custome then curstnesse; and some speake evill of others, not that the defamed deserve it, but because through custome and corruption of their hearts they cannot speake well of any. This I alleage as a paradigmatical patterne for all women, noble and ignoble to follow, that they be not enflamed with choler against this our enraged adversarie, but patiently consider of him according to the portraiture which he hath drawne of himselfe, his Writings being the very embleme of a monster.

This my briefe Apologie (Right Honourable and Worshipfull) did I enterprise, not as thinking my selfe more fit then others to undertake such a taske, but as one, who not perceiving any of our Sex to enter the Lists of encountring with this our grand enemy among men, I being out of all feare, because armed with the truth, which though often blamed, yet can never be shamed, and the Word of Gods Spirit, together with the example of vertues Pupils for a Buckler, did no whit dread to combate with our said malevolent adversarie. And if in so doing I shall bee censured by the judicious to have the victorie, and shall have given content unto the wronged, I have both hit the marke whereat I aymed, and obtained that prize which I desired. But if *Zoilus*[6] shall adjudge me presumptuous in Dedicating this my *Chirograph* unto personages of so high ranke; both because of my insufficiency in literature and tendernesse in yeares: I thus Apologize for my selfe; that seeing the *Bayter of Women* hath opened his mouth against noble as well as ignoble, against the rich as well as the poore; therefore meete it is that they should be joynt spectators of this encounter: And withall in regard of my imperfection both in learning and age, I need so much the more to impetrate patronage from some of power to sheild mee from the biting wrongs of *Momus*,[7] who oftentimes setteth a rankling tooth into the sides of truth. Wherefore I being of *Decius*[8] his mind, who deemed himselfe safe under the shield of *Cæsar*, have presumed to shelter my selfe under the wings of you (Honourable personages) against the persecuting heate of this fierie and furious Dragon; desiring that you would be pleased, not to looke so much *ad opus,* as *ad animum:*[9] And so not doubting of the favourable acceptance and censure of all vertuously affected, I rest

Your Honours and Worships
Humbly at commandement,
Rachel Speght.

---

3   Slander.
4   Silence implies consent.
5   Eve's.
6   Greek rhetorician and malignant critic of Plato and Homer.

7   Mythical son of Night who lampooned the gods.
8   Perhaps the supporter of Antony during the Roman civil wars.
9   Not to look so much at the work as at the intention.

I   f Reason had but curb'd thy witlesse will
O   r feare of God restrain'd thy raving quill,
S   uch venime fowle thou would'st have blusht to spue,
E   xcept that Grace have hidden thee adue:
P   rowesse disdaines to wrastle with the weake,
H   eathenish affected, care not what they speake.

S   educer of the vulgar sort of men,
W   as Sathan crept into thy filthie Pen,
E   nflaming thee with such infernall smoake,
10   *T   hat (if thou had'st thy will) should women choake?*
N   efarious fiends thy sence heerein deluded,
A   nd from thee all humanitie excluded.
M   onster of men, worthie no other name,
   For that thou did'st assay our Sex to shame.

RA. SP.

Not unto the veriest Ideot that *ever set Pen to Paper, but
to the* Cynicall Bayter of Women, or *metamorphosed
Misogunes,*[10] Joseph Swetnam.

From standing water, which soon putrifies, can no good fish be expected; for it produceth no other creatures but those that are venemous or noisome, as snakes, adders, and such like. Semblably, no better streame can we looke, should issue from your idle corrupt braine, then that whereto the ruffe of your fury (to use your owne words) hath moved you to open the sluce. In which excrement of your roaving cogitations you have used such irregularities touching concordance, and observed so disordered a methode, as I doubt not to tel you, that a very Accidence Schollar[11] would have quite put you downe in both. You appeare heerein not unlike that Painter, who seriously indevouring to pourtray *Cupids* Bowe, forgot the String: for you beeing greedie to botch up your mingle mangle invective against Women, have not therein observed, in many places, so much as a Grammer sense. But the emptiest Barrell makes the lowdest sound; and so we wil account of you.

Many propositions have you framed, which (as you thinke) make much against Women, but if one would make a Logicall assumption, the conclusion would be flat against your owne Sex. Your dealing wants so much discretion, that I doubt whether to bestow so good a name as the Dunce upon you: but Minority bids me keepe within my bounds; and therefore I onlie say unto you, that your corrupt Heart and railing Tongue, hath made you a fit scribe for the Divell.

In that you have termed your virulent foame, *the Beare-bayting of Women,* you have plainely displayed your owne disposition to be Cynicall, in that there appeares no other Dogge or Bull, to bayte them, but your selfe. Good had it beene for you to have put on that Muzzell, which Saint *James* would have all Christians to weare; *Speake not evill one of another:*[12] and then had you not seemed so like the Serpent *Porphirus*, as now you doe; which, though full of deadly poyson, yet being tooth-lesse, hurteth none so much as himselfe. For you having gone beyond the limits not of *Humanitie* alone, but of Christianitie, have done greater harme unto your owne soule, then unto women, as may plainely appeare. First, in dishonoring of God by palpable blasphemy, wresting and pervert-ing everie place of Scripture, that you have alleadged; which by the testimony of Saint *Peter*, is to the destruction of them that so doe.[13] Secondly, it appeares by your disparaging of, and opprobri-ous speeches against that excellent worke of Gods hands, which in his great love he perfected for the comfort of man. Thirdly, and lastly, by this your hodge-podge of heathenish Sentences, Simi-lies, and Examples, you have set forth your selfe in your right colours, unto the view of the world: and I doubt not but the Judicious will account of you according to your demerit: As for the Vulgar sort, which have no more learning then you have shewed in your Booke, it is likely they will applaud you for your paines.

10 Hater of women.
11 Latin grammar schoolboy.

12 James 4:11 (marginal citation).
13 1 Peter 3:16 (marginal citation).

As for your *Bugge-beare* or advice unto Women, that whatsoever they doe thinke of your Worke, they should conceale it, lest in finding fault, they bewray their galled backes to the world; in which you allude to that Proverbe, *Rubbe a galled horse, and he will kicke:* Unto it I answere by way of Apologie, that though everie galled horse, being touched, doth kicke; yet every one that kickes, is not galled: so that you might as well have said, that because burnt folks dread the fire, therfore none feare fire but those that are burnt, as made that illiterate conclusion which you have absurdly inferred.

In your Title Leafe, you arraigne none but lewd, idle, froward and unconstant women, but in the Sequele (through defect of memorie as it seemeth) forgetting that you had made a distinction of good from badde, condemning all in generall, you advise men to beware of, and not to match with any of these sixe sorts of women, *viz.* Good and *Badde, Faire* and *Foule, Rich* and *Poore:* But this doctrine of Divells Saint *Paul* foreseeing would be broached in the latter times, gives warning of.[14]

There also you promise a Commendation of wise, vertuous, and honest women, when as in the subsequent, the worst words, and filthiest Epithites that you can devise, you bestow on them in generall, excepting no sort of Women. Heerein may you be likened unto a man, which upon the doore of a scurvie house sets this Superscription, *Heere is a very faire house to be let:* whereas the doore being opened, it is no better then a dogge-hole and darke dungeon.

Further, if your owne words be true, that you wrote with your hand, but not with your heart, then are you an hypocrite in Print: but it is rather to be thought that your Pen was the bewrayer of the abundance of your minde, and that this was but a little morter to dawbe up agayne the wall, which you intended to breake downe.

The revenge of your rayling Worke wee leave to Him, who hath appropriated vengeance unto himselfe, whose Pen-man hath included Raylers in the Catalogue of them, that shall not inherite Gods Kingdome, and your selfe unto the mercie of that just Judge, who is able to save and to destroy.

Your undeserved friend,
RACHEL SPEGHT.

In praise of the Author and her Worke

If little David *that for* Israels *sake,*
   esteemed neyther life nor limbe too deare,
In that he did adventure without dread,
   to cast at him, whom all the hoste did feare,
A stone, which brought Goliah *to the ground,*
Obtain'd applause with Songs and Timbrels sound.

Then let another young encombatant
   receive applause, and thanks, as well as hee:
For with an enemie to Women kinde,
   she hath encountred, as each wight may see:
And with the fruit of her industrious toyle,
To this Goliah *she hath given the foyle.*

Admire her much I may, both for her age,
   and this her Mouzell *for blacke-mouth'd wight,*
But praise her, and her worke, to that desert,
   which unto them belongs of equall right
I cannot, onely this I say, and end,
Shee is unto her Sex a faithfull friend.
                   PHILALETHES.[15]

If he that for his Countrie doth expose
   himselfe unto the furie of his foe,

10

---

14   1 Tim. 4:3 (marginal citation).   15   Lover of truth.

Doth merite praise and due respect of those,
    for whom he did that perill undergoe:
Then let the Author of this Mouzell true
Receive the like, of right it is her due.

For she to shield her Sex from Slaunders Dart,
    and from invective obtrectation,
Hath ventured by force of Learnings Art,
    (in which she hath had education)
To combate with him, which doth shame his Sex,
By offring feeble women to perplex.

PHILOMATHES.[16]

Praise is a debt, which doth of due belong
To those, that take the path of Vertues trace,
Meating[17] their wayes and workes by Reasons rule,
Having their hearts so lightned with Gods grace,
    That willingly they would not him offend,
    But holily their lives beginne and end.

Of such a Pupill unto Pietie
As is describ'd, I doe intend to speake,
A Virgin young, and of such tender age,
As for encounter may be deemd too weake,
    Shee having not as yet seene twenty yeares,
    Though in her carriage older she appeares.

Her wit and learning in this present Worke,
More praise doth merit, then my quill can write:
Her magnanimitie deserves applaud,
In ventring with a fierie foe to fight:
    And now in fine, what shall I further say?
    But that she beares the triumph quite away.

FAVOUR B.[18]

A MOUZELL FOR MELASTOMUS THE CYNICALL BAYTER OF, AND FOULE-MOUTHED BARKER AGAINST EVAHS SEX

PROVERBS 18. 22.
He that findeth a wife, findeth a good thing, and
receiveth favour of the Lord.

If lawfull it bee to compare the *Potter* with his *Clay*, or the *Architect* with the *Edifice*; then may I, in some sort, resemble that love of God towards man, in creating woman, unto the affectionate care of *Abraham* for his sonne *Isaac*, who that hee might not take to wife one of the daughters of the *Canaanites*, did provide him one of his owne kindred.[19]

Almighty God, who is rich in mercie,[20] having made all things of nothing, and created man in his owne image: that is, (as the Apostle expounds it) *In wisedome, righteousnesse and true holinesse; making him Lord over all:*[21] to avoide that solitarie condition that hee was then in,[22] having none to commerce or converse withall but dumbe creatures, it seemed good unto the Lord, that as of every

---

16 Lover of knowledge.
17 Measuring.
18 Supporter B.
19 Gen. 24:4 (marginal citation).

20 Ephe. 2:4 (marginal citation).
21 Col. 3:[3] (marginal citation).
22 Ephe. 4:24 (marginal citation).

creature hee had made male and female, and man onely being alone without mate, so likewise to forme an helpe meete for him.[23] *Adam* for this cause being cast into a heavy sleepe, God extracting a rib from his side, thereof made, or built, Woman; shewing thereby, that man was as an unperfect building afore woman was made; and bringing her unto *Adam*, united and married them together.

Thus the resplendent love of God toward man appeared, in taking care to provide him an helper before hee saw his owne want, and in providing him such an helper as should bee meete for him. Soveraignety had hee over all creatures, and they were all serviceable unto him; but yet afore woman was formed, there was not a meete helpe found for *Adam*.[24] Mans worthinesse not meriting this great favour at Gods hands, but his mercie onely moving him thereunto: I may use those words which the *Jewes* uttered when they saw Christ weepe for *Lazarus, Behold how hee loved him*.[25] Behold, and that with good regard, Gods love; yea his great love, which from the beginning hee hath borne unto man: which, as it appeares in all things; so next, his love in Christ Jesus apparantly in this; that for mans sake, that hee might not be an unite, when all other creatures were for procreation duall, hee created woman to bee a solace unto him, to participate of his sorrowes, partake of his pleasures, and as a good yokefellow beare part of his burthen.[26] Of the excellencie of this Structure, I meane of Women, whose foundation and original of creation, was Gods love, do I intend to dilate.

Of Womans Excellency, with the causes of her creation, and of the sympathie which ought to be in man and wife each toward other.

The worke of Creation being finished, this approbation thereof was given by God himselfe, That *All was very good:*[27] If All, then *Woman*, who, excepting man, is the most excellent creature under the Canopie of heaven. But if it be objected by any.

First, that woman, though created good, yet by giving eare to Sathans temptations, brought death and misery upon all her posterity.

Secondly, That *Adam was not deceived, but that the woman was deceived, and was in the transgression.*[28]

Thirdly, that Saint *Paul* saith, *It were good for a man not to touch a woman.*[29]

Fourthly, and lastly, that of *Salomon*, who seemes to speake against all of our sex; *I have found one man of a thousand, but a woman among them all have I not found,*[30] whereof in its due place.

To the first of these objections I answere; that Sathan first assailed the woman, because where the hedge is lowest, most easie it is to get over, and she being the weaker vessell[31] was with more facility to be seduced: Like as a Cristall glasse sooner receives a cracke then a strong stone pot. Yet we shall finde the offence of *Adam* and *Eve* almost to paralell: For as an ambitious desire of being made like unto God, was the motive which caused her to eate, so likewise was it his; as may plainely appeare by that *Ironia,*[32] *Behold, man is become as one of us:*[33] Not that hee was so indeed; but heereby his desire to attaine a greater perfection then God had given him, was reproved. Woman sinned, it is true, by her infidelitie in not beleeving the Word of God, but giving credite to Sathans faire promises, that *shee should not die,*[34] but so did the man too: And if *Adam* had not approoved of that deed which *Eve* had done, and beene willing to treade the steps which she had gone, hee being her Head would have reproved her, and have made the commandement a bit to restraine him from breaking his Makers Injunction: For if a man burne his hand in the fire, the bellowes that blowed the fire are not to be blamed, but himselfe rather, for not being carefull to avoyde the danger: Yet if the bellowes had not blowed, the fire had not burnt; no more is woman simply to bee condemned

23 Gen. 2:20 (marginal citation).
24 Gen. 2:20 (marginal citation).
25 John 11:36 (marginal citation).
26 1 Cor. 11:9 (marginal citation).
27 Gen. 1:31 (marginal citation).
28 1 Tim. 2:14 (marginal citation).
29 1 Cor. 7:1 (marginal citation).

30 Eccles. 7:30 (marginal citation).
31 1 Peter 3:7.
32 Irony (called "dry mock" by George Puttenham in *The Arte of English Poesie* [1589]).
33 Gen. 3:22 (marginal citation).
34 Gen. 3:4 (marginal citation).

for mans transgression: for by the free will, which before his fall hee enjoyed, hee might have avoyded, and beene free from beeing burnt, or singed with that fire which was kindled by Sathan, and blowne by *Eve*. It therefore served not his turne a whit, afterwardes to say, *The woman which thou gavest mee, gave mee of the tree, and I did eate:*[35] For a penalty was inflicted upon him, as well as on the woman, the punishment of her transgression being particular to her owne sex, and to none but the female kinde: but for the sinne of man the whole earth was cursed. And he being better able, then the woman, to have resisted temptation, because the stronger vessell, was first called to account,[36] to shew, that to whom much is given, of them much is required;[37] and that he who was the soveraigne of all creatures visible, should have yeelded greatest obedience to God.

True it is (as is already confessed) that woman first sinned, yet finde wee no mention of spiri-tuall nakednesse till man had sinned: then it is said, *Their eyes were opened,*[38] the eies of their mind and conscience; and then perceived they themselves naked, that is, not onely bereft of that integri-tie, which they originally had, but felt the rebellion and disobedience of their members in the dis-ordered motions of their now corrupt nature, which made them for shame to cover their nakednesse: then (and not afore) is it said that they saw it, as if sinne were imperfect, and unable to bring a deprivation of a blessing received, or death on all mankind, till man (in whom lay the active power of generation) had transgressed. The offence therefore of *Adam* and *Eve* is by Saint *Austin* thus dis-tinguished, *the man sinned against God and himselfe, the woman against God, her selfe, and her husband:*[39] yet in her giving of the fruit to eate had she no malicious intent towardes him, but did therein shew a desire to make her husband partaker of that happinesse, which she thought by their eating they should both have enjoyed. This her giving *Adam* of that sawce, wherewith Sathan had served her, whose sowrenesse afore he had eaten, she did not perceive, was that, which made her sinne to exceede his; wherefore, that she might not of him, who ought to honour her,[40] be abhorred, the first promise that was made in Paradise, God makes to woman, that by her Seede should the Serpents head be broken:[41] whereupon *Adam* calles her *Hevah, life*, that as the woman had beene an occasion of his sinne, so should woman bring foorth the Saviour from sinne, which was in the full-nesse of time accomplished; by which was manifested, that he is a Saviour of beleeving women,[42] no lesse then of men, that so the blame of sinne may not be imputed to his creature, which is good; but to the will by which *Eve* sinned, and yet by Christs assuming the shape of man was it declared, that his mercie was equivalent to both Sexes; so that by *Hevahs* blessed Seed (as Saint *Paul* affirmes) it is brought to passe, that *male and female are all one in Christ Jesus.*[43]

To the second objection I answer, That the Apostle doth not heereby exempt man from sinne, but onely giveth to understand, that the woman was the primarie transgressour; and not the man, but that man was not at all deceived, was farre from his meaning: for he afterward expresly saith, that as *in Adam all die, so in Christ shall all be made alive.*[44]

For the third objection, *It is good for a man not to touch a woman:* The Apostle makes it not a posi-tive prohibition, but speakes it onelie because of the *Corinths* present necessitie,[45] who were then persecuted by the enemies of the Church, for which cause, and no other, hee saith, *Art thou loosed from a wife? seeke not a wife:* meaning whilst the time of these perturbations should continue in their heate; *but if thou art bound, seeke not to be loosed: if thou marriest, thou sinnest not,* only increasest thy care: *for the married careth for the things of this world, And I wish that you were without care, that yee might cleave fast unto the Lord without separation: For the time remaineth, that they which have wives be as though they had none:* for the persecuters shall deprive you of them, eyther by imprisonment, banishment, or death; so that manifest it is, that the Apostle doth not heereby forbid marriage, but onely adviseth the *Corinths* to forbeare a while, till God in mercie should curbe the fury of their adversaries. For (as *Eusebius*[46] writeth) *Paul* was afterward married himselfe, the which is very

---

35   Gen. 3:12 (marginal citation).
36   Gen. 3:17 (marginal citation).
37   See Luke 12:48.
38   Gen. 3:7 (marginal citation).
39   Derived from St. Augustine's "De Adam et Eva et Sancta Maria."
40   1 Pet. 3:7 (marginal citation).
41   Gen. 3:15 (marginal citation).

42   Galat. 4:4 (marginal citation).
43   Galat. 3:28 (marginal citation).
44   1 Cor. 15:22 (marginal citation).
45   1 Cor. 7 (marginal citation).
46   Eusebius (AD 260–340), the author of *Ecclesiastical History*, which refers to Paul's marriage (3:30).

probable, being that interrogatively he saith, *Have we not*[47] *power to leade about a wife, being a sister, as well as the rest of the Apostles, and as the brethren of the Lord and Cephas?*[48]

The fourth and last objection, is that of *Salomon, I have found one man among a thousand, but a woman among them all have I not found:*[49] for answere of which, if we looke into the storie of his life, wee shall finde therein a Commentary upon this enigmaticall Sentence included: for it is there said, that *Salomon* had seven hundred wives, and three hundred concubines, which number connexed make one thousand. These women turning his heart away from being perfect with the Lord his God,[50] sufficient cause had hee to say, that among the said thousand women found he not one upright.[51] Hee saith not, that among a thousand women never any man found one worthy of commendation, but speakes in the first person singularly, *I have not found*, meaning in his owne experience: for this assertion is to be holden a part of the confession of his former follies, and no otherwise, his repentance being the intended drift of *Ecclesiastes*.

Thus having (by Gods assistance) removed those stones, whereat some have stumbled, others broken their shinnes, I will proceede toward the period of my intended taske, which is, to decipher the excellency of women: of whose Creation I will, for orders sake observe; First, the efficient cause,[52] which was God; Secondly, the materiall cause, or that whereof shee was made; Thirdly, the formall cause, or fashion, and proportion of her feature; Fourthly and lastly, the finall cause, the end or purpose for which she was made. To beginne with the first.

The efficient cause of womans creation, was *Jehovah* the *Eternall*; the truth of which is manifest in *Moses* his narration of the six dayes workes, where he saith, *God created them male and female*:[53] And *David* exhorting all *the earth to sing unto the Lord*; meaning, by a Metonimie,[54] *earth*, all creatures that live on the earth, of what nation or Sex soever, gives this reason, *For the Lord hath made us.*[55] That worke then can not chuse but be good, yea very good, which is wrought by so excellent a workeman as the Lord: for he being a glorious Creator, must needes effect a worthie creature. Bitter water can not proceede from a pleasant sweete fountaine,[56] nor bad worke from that workman which is perfectly good, and in proprietie, none but he.[57]

Secondly, the materiall cause, or matter whereof woman was made, was of a refined mould, if I may so speake: for man was created of the dust of the earth, but woman was made of a part of man,[58] after that he was a living soule: yet was shee not produced from *Adams* foote, to be his too low inferiour; nor from his head to be his superiour, but from his side, neare his heart, to be his equall; that where he is Lord, she may be Lady: and therefore saith God concerning man and woman jointly, *Let them rule over the fish of the Sea, and over the foules of the Heaven, and over every beast that moveth upon the earth:*[59] By which words, he makes their authority equall, and all creatures to be in subjection unto them both. This being rightly considered, doth teach men to make such account of their wives, as *Adam* did of *Eve, This is bone of my bone, and flesh of my flesh:*[60] As also, that they neyther doe or wish any more hurt unto them, then unto their owne bodies: for men ought to love their wives as themselves, because hee that loves his wife, loves himselfe:[61] And never man hated his owne flesh (which the woman is) unlesse a monster in nature.

Thirdly, the formall cause, fashion, and proportion of woman was excellent: For she was neyther like the beasts of the earth, foules of the ayre, fishes of the Sea, or any other inferiour creature, but Man was the onely object, which she did resemble. For as God gave man a lofty countenance, that hee might looke up toward Heaven, so did he likewise give unto woman. And as the temperature of mans body is excellent, so is womans.[62] For whereas other Creatures, by reason of their grosse

---

47 1 Corint. 9:5 (marginal citation).
48 Another name for the Apostle Peter.
49 Eccles. 7:30 (marginal citation).
50 1 King. 11:3 (marginal citation).
51 Pagnine [pagan] (marginal note).
52 Aristotle's concept of three causes (*Physics*, 2.3) distinguishes among the agent (efficient cause), the matter (material cause), and the form (formal cause).
53 Genesis 1:28 (marginal citation).
54 Metonymy is a figure of speech that refers to the whole by means of a part.

55 Psal. 100:3 (marginal citation).
56 Psal. 100:[5] (marginal citation).
57 Math. 19:17 (marginal citation).
58 Genesis 2:7 (marginal citation).
59 Genesis 1:26 (marginal citation).
60 Genesis 2:23 (marginal citation).
61 Ephes. 5:28 (marginal citation).
62 A physiological argument for the inferiority of women was based on the supposition that women are cold and wet, unlike men, who were supposed hot and dry.

humours, have excrements for their habite, as foules, their feathers, beasts, their haire, fishes, their scales, man and woman onely, have their skinne cleare and smoothe. And (that more is) in the Image of God were they both created;[63] yea and to be briefe, all the parts of their bodies, both externall and internall, were correspondent and meete each for other.

Fourthly and lastly, the finall cause, or end, for which woman was made, was to glorifie God, and to be a collaterall companion for man to glorifie God, in using her bodie, and all the parts, powers, and faculties thereof, as instruments for his honour: As with her voice to sound foorth his prayses, like *Miriam*, and the rest of her company;[64] with her tongue not to utter words of strife, but to give good councell unto her husband, the which hee must not despise. For *Abraham* was bidden to give eare to *Sarah* his wife.[65] *Pilate* was willed by his wife not to have anie hand in the condemning of CHRIST;[66] and a sinne it was in him, that hee listned not to her: *Leah* and *Rachel* councelled *Jaacob* to do according to the word of the Lord:[67] and the Shunamite put her husband in mind of harbouring the Prophet *Elisha*:[68] her hands shold be open according to her abilitie, in contributing towards Gods service, and distressed servants, like to that poore widdow, which cast two mites into the Treasurie;[69] and as *Marie Magdalen, Susanna,* and *Joanna* the wife of *Herods* Steward, with many other, which of their substance ministred unto CHRIST.[70] Her heart should be a receptacle for Gods Word, like *Mary* that treasured up the sayings of CHRIST in her heart.[71] Her feete should be swift in going to seeke the Lord in his Sanctuarie, as *Marie Magdalen* made haste to seeke CHRIST at his Sepulchre.[72] Finally, no power externall or internall ought woman to keep idle, but to imploy it in some service of GOD, to the glorie of her Creator, and comfort of her owne soule.

The other end for which woman was made, was to be a Companion and *helper* for man; and if she must be an *helper*, and but an *helper*, then are those husbands to be blamed, which lay the whole burthen of domesticall affaires and maintenance on the shoulders of their wives. For, as yoake-fellowes they are to sustayne part of each others cares, griefs, and calamities: But as if two Oxen be put in one yoke, the one being bigger then the other, the greater beares most weight; so the Husband being the stronger vessell is to beare a greater burthen then his wife; And therefore the Lord said to *Adam, In the sweate of thy face shalt thou eate thy bread, till thou returne to the dust.*[73] And Saint *Paul* saith, *That he that provideth not for his houshold is worse then an Infidel.*[74] Nature hath taught senselesse creatures to helpe one another; as the Male Pigeon, when his Hen is weary with sitting on her egges, and comes off from them, supplies her place, that in her absence they may receive no harme, untill such time as she is fully refreshed.[75] Of small Birds the Cocke alwaies helpes his Hen to build her nest; and while she sits upon her egges, he flies abroad to get meat for her, who cannot then provide any for her selfe. The crowing Cockrell helpes his Hen to defend her Chickens from perill, and will indanger himselfe to save her and them from harme.[76] Seeing then that these unreasonable creatures, by the instinct of nature, beare such affection each to other, that without any grudge, they willingly, according to their kind, helpe one another, I may reason *à minore ad maius,*[77] that much more should man and woman, which are reasonable creatures, be helpers each to other in all things lawfull, they having the Law of God to guide them, his Word to bee a Lanthorne unto their feete, and a Light unto their pathes, by which they are excited to a farre more mutual participation of each others burthen, then other creatures.[78] So that neither the wife may say to her husband, nor the husband unto his wife, I have no need of thee, no more then the members of the body may so say each to other, betweene whom there is such a sympathie, that if one member suffer, all suffer with it: Therefore though God bade *Abraham* forsake his Countrey and Kindred, yet he bade him not forsake his wife, who being *Flesh of his flesh, and bone of his bone,*

63   Gen. 1:26 (marginal citation).
64   Exod. 15:20 (marginal citation).
65   Gen. 21:12 (marginal citation).
66   Math. 25:19 (marginal citation).
67   Gen. 31:16 (marginal citation).
68   2 Kings 4:9 (marginal citation).
69   See Luke 21:1–4; Luke 8 (marginal citation).
70   On these women's aid to Christ, see Luke 8:1–3.

71   Luke 1:51 (marginal citation).
72   John 20:1 (marginal citation).
73   Gen. 3:19 (marginal citation).
74   1 Tim. 5:8 (marginal citation).
75   See Pliny, *Historia Naturalis,* 10.79.
76   Ibid., 10.52.
77   From the lesser to the greater.
78   1 Cor. 12:21 (marginal citation).

was to bee copartner with him of whatsoever did betide him, whether joy or sorrow. Wherefore *Salomon* saith, *Woe to him that is alone*;[79] for when thoughts of discomfort, troubles of this world, and feare of dangers do possesse him, he wants a companion to lift him up from the pit of perplexitie, into which hee is fallen:[80] for a good wife, saith *Plautus*, is the wealth of the minde, and the welfare of the heart; and therefore a meete associate for her husband;[81] And *Woman*, saith *Paul*, *is the glorie of the man*.[82]

Marriage is a merri-age, and this worlds Paradise, where there is mutuall love. Our blessed Saviour vouchsafed to honour a marriage with the first miracle that he wrought,[83] unto which miracle matrimoniall estate may not unfitly bee resembled: For as Christ turned water into wine, a farre more excellent liquor; which, as the Psalmist saith, *Makes glad the heart of man*;[84] So the single man is by marriage changed from a Batchelour to a Husband, a farre more excellent title: from a solitarie life unto a joyfull union and conjunction, with such a creature as God hath made meete for man, for whom none was meete till she was made. The enjoying of this great blessing made *Pericles* more unwilling to part from his wife, then to die for his Countrie; And *Antoninus Pius* to poure forth that patheticall exclamation against death, for depriving him of his deerely beloved wife,[85] *O cruell hard-hearted death in bereaving mee of her whom I esteemed more then my owne life! A vertuous woman*, saith *Salomon*, *is the Crowne of her husband*;[86] By which metaphor hee sheweth both the excellencie of such a wife, and what account her husband is to make of her: For a King doth not trample his Crowne under his feete, but highly esteemes of it, gently handles it, and carefully laies it up, as the evidence of his Kingdome; and therefore when *David* destroyed *Rabbah* hee tooke off the Crowne from their Kings head:[87] So husbands should not account their wives as their vassals, but as those that are heires together of the grace of life,[88] and with all lenitie and milde perswasions set their feete in the right way, if they happen to tread awry, bearing with their infirmities, as Elkanah did with his wives barrennesse.

The Kingdome of God is compared unto the marriage of a Kings sonne:[89] *John* calleth the conjunction of Christ and his Chosen, a Marriage:[90] And not few, but many times, doth our blessed Saviour in the Canticles,[91] set forth his unspeakeable love towards his Church under the title of an Husband rejoycing with his Wife; and often vouchsafeth to call her his Sister and Spouse,[92] by which is shewed that with *God is no respect of persons*,[93] Nations, or Sexes: For whosoever, whether it be man or woman, that doth *beleeve in the Lord Jesus*, such *shall bee saved*.[94] And if Gods love even from the beginning, had not beene as great toward woman as to man, then would hee not have preserved from the deluge of the old world as many women as men; nor would Christ after his Resurrection have appeared unto a woman first of all other, had it not beene to declare thereby, that the benefites of his death and resurrection, are as availeable, by beleefe, for women as for men; for hee indifferently died for the one sex as well as the other: Yet a truth ungainesayable is it, that the *Man is the Womans Head*;[95] by which title yet of Supremacie, no authoritie hath hee given him to domineere, or basely command and imploy his wife, as a servant; but hereby is he taught the duties which hee oweth unto her: For as the head of a man is the imaginer and contriver of projects profitable for the safety of his whole body; so the Husband must protect and defend his Wife from injuries: For he is her *Head, as Christ is the Head of his Church*,[96] which hee entirely loveth, and for which hee gave his very life;[97] the deerest thing any man hath in this world; *Greater love then this hath no man, when he bestoweth his life for his friend*, saith our Saviour.[98] This president[99] passeth all

79 Eccles. 4:10 (marginal citation).
80 Eccles. 4:10 (marginal citation).
81 See Plautus, *Amphitryon*, 2.839–42.
82 1 Cor. 11:7 (marginal citation).
83 John 2 (marginal citation).
84 Psal. 104:15 (marginal citation).
85 Plutarch, "Life of Pericles," 24.
86 Prov. 12:4 (marginal citation).
87 1 Chron. 20:2 (marginal citation).
88 1 Pet. 3:7 (marginal citation).
89 1 Sam. 1:17 (marginal citation).

90 Math. 22 (marginal citation).
91 Rev. 19:7 (marginal citation).
92 Song of Songs.
93 Rom. 2:11 (marginal citation).
94 John 3:18 (marginal citation).
95 1 Cor. 11:3 (marginal citation).
96 Ephe. 5:23 (marginal citation).
97 Job 2:4 (marginal citation).
98 John 15:13 (marginal citation).
99 *precedent*.

other patternes, it requireth great benignity, and enjoyneth an extraordinary affection, For *men must love their wives, even as Christ loved his Church*.[100] Secondly, as the Head doth not jarre or contend with the members, which *being many*, as the Apostle saith, *yet make but one bodie*;[101] no more must the husband with the wife, but expelling all bitternesse and cruelty hee must live with her lovingly, and religiously, honouring her as the weaker vessell.[102] Thirdly, and lastly, as hee is her Head, hee must, by instruction, bring her to the knowledge of her Creator, that so she may be a fit stone for the Lords building.[103] Women for this end must have an especiall care to set their affections upon such as are able to teach them, that as they *grow in yeares, they may grow in grace, and in the knowledge of Christ Jesus our Lord*.[104]

Thus if men would remember the duties they are to performe in being heads, some would not stand a tip-toe as they doe, thinking themselves Lords and Rulers, and account every omission of performing whatsoever they command, whether lawfull or not, to be matter of great disparagement, and indignity done them; whereas they should consider, that women are enjoyned to submit themselves unto their husbands no otherwaies then as to *the Lord*;[105] so that from hence, for man, ariseth a lesson not to bee forgotten, that as the Lord commandeth nothing to be done, but that which is right and good, no more must the husband; for if a wife fulfill the evill command of her husband, shee obeies him as a tempter, as *Saphira* did *Ananias*.[106] But least I should seeme too partiall in praysing women so much as I have (though no more then warrant from Scripture doth allow) I adde to the premises, that I say not, all women are vertuous, for then they should be more excellent then men, sith of *Adams* sonnes there was *Cain* as well as *Abel*, and of *Noahs*, *Cham* as well as *Sem*;[107] so that of men as of women, there are two sorts, namely, good and bad, which in *Mathew* the five and twenty chapter, are comprehended under the name of *Sheepe* and *Goats*. And if women were not sinfull, then should they not need a Saviour: but the Virgin *Mary* a patterne of piety, *rejoyced in God her Saviour: Ergo*, she was a sinner.[108] In the *Revelation* the Church is called the Spouse of Christ; and in *Zachariah*, wickednesse is called a woman,[109] to shew that of women there are both godly and ungodly: For Christ would not *Purge his Floore*[110] if there were not Chaffe among the Wheate; nor should gold neede to bee fined, if among it there were no drosse. But farre be it from any one, to condemne the righteous with the wicked, or good women with the bad[111] (as the Bayter of women doth:) For though there are some scabbed sheepe in a Flocke, we must not therefore conclude all the rest to bee mangie: And though some men, through excesse, abuse Gods creatures, wee must not imagine that all men are Gluttons; the which wee may with as good reason do, as condemne all women in generall, for the offences of some particulars. Of the good sort is it that I have in this booke spoken, and so would I that all that reade it should so understand me: for if otherwise I had done, I should have incurred that woe, which by the Prophet *Isaiah* is pronounced against them that *speake well of evill*,[112] and should have *justified the wicked, which thing is abhominable to the Lord*.[113]

The Epilogue or upshut of the premises.

Great was the unthankefulnesse of *Pharaohs* Butler unto *Joseph*; for though hee had done him a great pleasure, of which the Butler promised requitall, yet was hee quite forgotten of him:[114] But farre greater is the ingratitude of those men toward God, that dare presume to speake and exclaime against *Woman*, whom God did create for mans comfort. What greater discredit can redound to a workeman, then to have the man, for whom hee hath made it, say, it is naught? or what greater discurtesie can be offered to one, that bestoweth a gift, then to have the receiver give out, that hee

100	1 Cor. 12:20 (marginal citation).		108	Luke 1:47 (marginal citation).
101	Col. 3:19 (marginal citation).		109	Zach. 5:7 (marginal citation).
102	1 Pet. 3:7 (marginal citation).		110	See Luke 3:16–17.
103	1 Cor. 14:35 (marginal citation).		111	Gen. 18:25 (marginal citation).
104	1 Pet. 3:18 (marginal citation).		112	Essay. 5:20 (marginal citation).
105	Ephes. 5 (marginal citation).		113	Prov. 17:15 (marginal citation).
106	Actes. 5:2 (marginal citation).		114	Gen. 40:23 (marginal citation).
107	See Gen. 4:1–14.			

cares not for it: For he needes it not? And what greater ingratitude can bee shewed unto GOD then the opprobrious speeches and disgracefull invectives, which some diabolicall natures doe frame against women?

Ingratitude is, and always hath beene accounted so odious a vice, that *Cicero* saith, *If one doubt what name to give a wicked man, let him call him an ungratefull person, and then hee hath said enough.*[115] It was so detested among the *Persians*, as that by a Law they provided, that such should suffer death as felons, which prooved unthankefull for any gift received. And *Love* (saith the Apostle) *is the ful-filling of the Lawe*:[116] But where Ingratitude is harbored, there Love is banished. Let men therefore beware of all unthankefulnesse, but especially of the superlative ingratitude, that which is towards God, which is no way more palpably declared, then by the contemning of, and rayling against women, which sinne, of some men (if to be termed men) no doubt but God will one day avenge, when they shall plainely perceive, that it had been better for them to have been borne dumbe and lame, then to have used their tongues and hands, the one in repugning, the other in writing against Gods handie worke, their owne flesh, women I meane, whom God hath made equall with them-selves in dignity, both temporally and eternally, if they continue in the faith: which God for his mercie sake graunt they alwayes may, to the glory of their Creator, and comfort of their owne soules, through Christ Amen.

To God onely wise be glorie now and for ever, AMEN.

England's Helicon (1600)

One of the finest anthologies of sixteenth-century lyric poetry, *England's Helicon* follows in the wake of several other anthologies that made commercially available some of the best poetry of the English Renaissance: *Tottel's Miscellany* (1557), *A Handful of Pleasant Delights* (1584), and *The Phoenix Nest* (1593). This last volume promises not only to be "built up with the most rare and refined workes of Noblemen, woorthy Knights, gallant Gentlemen, Masters of Arts, and braue Schollers" but also to be "full of varietie, excellent inuention, and singular delight." At first the claims of *England's Helicon* would seem to be more modest. The poems collected there deal more with shepherds' lives than with courtiers' and more with the simplicities of nature than with the interests of knights, gentlemen, and scholars. But this is only an apparent difference. In fact, *England's Helicon* is largely a collection of pastoral poetry.

One of the best brief statements about pastoral poetry is this one by Frank Kermode:

> The first condition of pastoral poetry is that there should be a sharp difference between two ways of life, the rustic and the urban. The city is an artificial product, and the pastoral poet invariably lives in it, or is the product of its schools and universities. Considerable animosity may exist between the townsman and the countryman. Thus the 'primitive' may be sceptical about the justice of a state of affairs which makes him live under rude conditions while the town-poet lives in polite society. On the other hand, the town- or court-poet has a certain contempt for the peasant (sometimes very strong); and both primitive and court-poet write verse which reflects these attitudes. Occa-sionally there is a certain similarity of subject. Townsman and rustic alike may consider the idea that at a remote period in history nature gave forth her fruits without the aid of man's labour and worship. Perhaps, somewhere, she still does so. This idea that the world has been a better place and that men have degenerated is remarkably wide-spread, and a regular feature of pastoral poetry . . . The first condition of Pastoral is that it is an urban product. (1952: 14)

This implies an inescapable ironic distance between the assumed urban, sophisticated point of view and the rustic, natural subjects of the poetry. It also assumes a degree of nostalgia for a lost cultural innocence that is being fiction-ally recreated.

Most of the poems in *England's Helicon* are attributed (not always accurately) to such poets as Sidney, Spenser, Drayton, Greene, Lodge, Surrey, Shakespeare, and Marlowe. The poems that appear below, however, are either by unknown or anonymous authors. Most of these were gath-ered by their Renaissance editor (who was perhaps John Bodenham [*c.*1558–1610]) from song books that were com-piled by Byrd, Dowland, Morley, and Young. In the First Book of Castiglione's *Courtier* the argument goes that "it hath bene the opinion of most wise Philosophers that the world is made of musick, and the heavens in their moving

---

115   See Cicero's *De Officiis*, 2.18.63.

116   Rom. 13:10 (marginal citation).

make a melody, and our soule framed after the very same sort, and therfore lifteth up it self and (as it were) reviveth the vertues and force of it with musick." Although a source of pleasure and joy, music was considered by Renaissance thinkers an essential part of life. Just as pastoral poetry longed to reclaim a fleeting paradise that partly survives in the simple, natural life, so does music recall the original harmony of the world before the fall of man.

READING

John Hollander, *The Untuning of the Sky: Ideas of Music in English Poetry, 1500–1700.*
Frank Kermode (ed.), *English Pastoral Poetry from the Beginnings to Marvell*
Hallett Smith, *Elizabethan Poetry.*

M. P.

[SONGS FROM ENGLANDS HELICON]

THE UNKNOWNE SHEEPHEARDS COMPLAINT

My Flocks feede not, my Ewes breede not,
My Rammes speede not, all is amisse:
Love is denying, Faith is defying,
Harts renying, causer of this.
All my merry Jiggs are quite forgot,
All my Ladies love is lost God wot.
Where her faith was firmely fixt in love,
There a nay is plac'd without remove.
    One silly crosse, wrought all my losse,
10   O frowning Fortune, cursed fickle Dame:
    For now I see, inconstancie
    More in women then in men remaine.

In black mourne I, all feares scorne I,
Love hath forlorne me, living in thrall:
Hart is bleeding, all helpe needing,
O cruell speeding, fraughted with gall.
My Sheepheards pipe can sound no deale,
My Weathers bell rings dolefull knell:
My curtaile dogge that wont to have plaide,
20 Playes not at all, but seemes afraide
    With sighs so deepe, procures to weepe,
    In howling-wise, to see my dolefull plight:
    How sighs resound, through hartlesse ground,
    Like a thousand vanquish'd men in bloody fight.

Cleare Wells spring not, sweet birds sing not,
Greene plants bring not foorth their die:
Heards stand weeping, Flocks all sleeping,
Nimphs back peeping fearefully.
All our pleasure knowne to us poore Swaines,
30 All our merry meeting on the Plaines.
All our evening sports from us are fled,
All our love is lost, for Love is dead.
    Farewell sweete Love, thy like nere was,
    For sweete content, the cause of all my moane:
    Poore *Coridon* must live alone,
    Other helpe for him, I see that there is none.

Ignoto

ANOTHER OF THE SAME SHEEPHEARDS

As it fell upon a day,
In the merry moneth of May,
Sitting in a pleasant shade,
Which a grove of Mirtles made.
Beasts did leape, and birds did sing,
Trees did grow, and plants did spring.
Every thing did banish moane,
Save the Nightingale alone.
Shee poore bird, as all forlorne,
10   Lean'd her breast against a thorne,
And there sung the dolefull'st Ditty,
That to heare it was great pitty.
Fie, fie, fie, now would she crie
Teru, Teru, by and by.
That to heare her so complaine.
Scarse I could from teares refraine.
For her greefes so lively showne,
Made me thinke upon mine owne.
Ah (thought I) thou mourn'st in vaine,
20   None takes pitty on thy paine.
Sencelesse trees, they cannot heare thee,
Ruthlesse beasts, they will not cheere thee.
King *Pandion* he is dead,
All thy friends are lapt in Lead.
All thy fellow birds doo sing,
Carelesse of thy sorrowing.
Even so poore bird like thee,
None a-live will pitty mee.

Ignoto

PHILLIDAES LOVE-CALL TO HER CORIDON, AND HIS REPLYING

Phil. *Coridon*, arise my *Coridon*,
        Titan shineth cleare:
Cor. Who is it that calleth *Coridon*,
        who is it that I heare?
Phil. *Phillida* thy true-Love calleth thee,
        arise then, arise then;
                arise and keepe thy flock with me:
Cor. *Phillida* my true-Love, is it she?
        I come then, I come then,
10   I come and keepe my flock with thee.

Phil. Heere are cherries ripe my *Coridon*,
        eate them for my sake:
Cor. Heere's my Oaten pipe my lovely one,
        sport for thee to make.
Phil. Heere are threeds my true-Love, fine as silke,
        to knit thee, to knit thee
                a paire of stockings white as milke.
Cor. Heere are Reedes my true-Love, fine and neate,
        to make thee, to make thee
20   a Bonnet to with-stand the heate.

Phil. I will gather flowers my *Coridon*,
        to set in thy cap:

Cor. I will gather Peares my lovely one,
    to put in thy lap.
Phil. I will buy my true-Love Garters gay,
    for Sundayes, for Sundayes,
        to weare about his legs so tall:
Cor. I will buy my true-Love yellow Say,
    for Sundayes, for Sundayes.
30   to weare about her middle small.

Phil. When my *Coridon* sits on a hill,
    making melodie:
Cor. When my lovely one goes to her wheele
    singing cherilie.
Phil. Sure me thinks my true-Love dooth excell
    for sweetnes, for sweetnes,
        our *Pan* that old Arcadian Knight:
Cor. And me thinks my true-Love beares the bell
    for clearenes, for clearenes,
40   beyond the Nimphs that be so bright.

Phil. Had my *Coridon*, my *Coridon*,
    beene (alack) my Swaine:
Cor. Had my lovely one, my lovely one,
    beene in *Ida* plaine.
Phil. Cinthia Endimion had refus'd,
    preferring, preferring
        my *Coridon* to play with-all:
Cor. The Queene of Love had beene excus'd,
    bequeathing, bequeathing,
50   my *Phillida* the golden ball.

Phil. Yonder comes my Mother, *Coridon*,
    whether shall I flie?
Cor. Under yonder Beech my lovely one,
    while she passeth by.
Say to her thy true-Love was not heere,
    remember, remember,
        to morrow is another day:
Phil. Doubt me not, my true-Love, doo not feare,
    farewell then, farewell then,
60   heaven keepe our loves alway.
                    Ignoto

THE SHEEPHEARDS DESCRIPTION OF LOVE

Melibeus. Sheepheard, what's Love, I pray thee tell?
Faustus.   It is that Fountaine, and that Well,
      Where pleasure and repentance dwell.
      It is perhaps that sauncing bell,
         That toules all into heaven or hell,
         And this is Love as I heard tell.
Meli.   Yet what is Love, I pre-thee say?
Fau.   It is a worke on holy-day,
      It is December match'd with May,
10   When lustie-bloods in fresh aray,
         Heare ten moneths after of the play,
         And this is Love, as I heare say.
Meli.   Yet what is Love, good Sheepheard saine?

Fau.	It is a Sun-shine mixt with raine,
	It is a tooth-ach, or like paine,
	It is a game where none dooth gaine,
	The Lasse saith no, and would full faine:
	And this is Love, as I heare saine.
Meli.	Yet Sheepheard, what is Love, I pray?
Fau.	It is a yea, it is a nay,
	A pretty kind of sporting fray,
	It is a thing will soone away,
	Then Nimphs take vantage while ye may:
	And this is love as I heare say.
Meli.	Yet what is love, good Sheepheard show?
Fau.	A thing that creepes, it cannot goe,
	A prize that passeth too and fro,
	A thing for one, a thing for moe,
	And he that prooves shall finde it so;
	And Sheepheard this is love I troe.

Ignoto

THE SHEEPHEARDS SORROW FOR HIS PHÆBES DISDAINE

Oh Woods unto your walks my body hies,
To loose the trayterous bonds of tyring Love,
    Where trees, where hearbs, where flowers,
    Their native moisture poures
From foorth their tender stalkes, to helpe mine eyes,
Yet their united teares may nothing move.

When I behold the faire adorned tree,
Which lightnings force and Winters frost resists,
    Then *Daphnes* ill betide,
    And *Phœbus* lawlesse pride
Enforce me say, even such my sorrowes be:
For selfe disdaine in *Phœbes* hart consists.

If I behold the flowers by morning teares
Looke lovely sweete: Ah then forlorne I crie
    Sweete showers for *Memnon* shed,
    All flowers by you are fed.
Whereas my pittious plaint that still appeares,
Yeelds vigor to her scornes, and makes me die.

When I regard the pretty glee-full bird,
With teare-full (yet delightfull) notes complaine:
    I yeeld a terror with my teares,
    And while her musique wounds mine eares,
Alas say I, when will my notes afford
Such like remorce, who still beweepe my paine?

When I behold upon the leafe-lesse bow
The haplesse bird lament her Loves depart:
    I draw her biding nigh,
    And sitting downe I sigh,
And sighing say: Alas, that birds avow
A setled faith, yet *Phœbe* scornes my smart.

Thus wearie in my walke, and wofull too,
I spend the day, fore-spent with daily greefe:
    Each object of distresse

My sorrow dooth expresse
I doate on that which dooth my hart undoo:
And honour her that scornes to yeeld releefe.

Ignoto

OLDE MELIBEUS SONG, COURTING HIS NIMPH

Loves Queene long wayting for her true-Love,
　Slaine by a Boare which he had chased,
　Left off her teares, and me embraced,
She kist me sweete, and call'd me new-Love.
　　With my silver haire she toyed,
　　In my stayed lookes she joyed.
　　Boyes (she sayd) breede beauties sorrow:
　　Olde men cheere it even and morrow.

My face she nam'd the seate of favour,
10　All my defects her tongue defended,
　My shape she prais'd, but most commended
My breath more sweete then Balme in savour.
　　Be old man with me delighted,
　　Love for love shall be requited.
　　With her toyes at last she wone me:
　　Now she coyes that hath undone me.

Ignoto

A NIMPHS DISDAINE OF LOVE

Hey downe a downe did *Dian* sing,
　　amongst her Virgins sitting:
Then love there is no vainer thing,
　　for Maydens most unfitting.
　　And so think I, with a downe downe derrie.

When women knew no woe,
　　but liv'd them-selves to please:
Mens fayning guiles they did not know,
　　the ground of their disease.
10　Unborne was false suspect,
　　no thought of jealousie:
From wanton toyes and fond affect,
　　the Virgins life was free.
　　Hey downe a downe did *Dian* sing, &c.

At length men used charmes,
　　to which what Maides gave eare:
Embracing gladly endlesse harmes,
　　anone enthralled were.
Thus women welcom'd woe,
20　　disguis'd in name of love:
A jealous hell, a painted show,
　　so shall they finde that prove.

Hey downe a downe did *Dian* sing,
　　amongst her Virgins sitting:
Then love there is no vainer thing,
　　for Maydens most unfitting.
And so think I, with a downe downe derrie.

Ignoto

THE SHEEPHEARD TO THE FLOWERS

Sweet Violets (Loves Paradise) that spread
Your gracious odours, which you couched beare
     Within your palie faces.
Upon the gentle wing of some calme-breathing-winde
     That playes amidst the Plaine,
     If by the favour of propitious starres you gaine
Such grace as in my Ladies bosome place to finde:
     Be proude to touch those places.
And when her warmth your moysture foorth dooth weare,
10 Whereby her daintie parts are sweetly fed:
     Your honours of the flowrie Meades I pray
     You prettie daughters of the earth and Sunne:
     With mild and seemely breathing straite display
     My bitter sighs, that have my hart undone.

Vermillion Roses, that with new dayes rise
Display your crimson folds fresh looking faire,
     Whose radiant bright, disgraces
The rich adorned rayes of roseate rising morne,
     Ah if her Virgins hand
20   Doo pluck your pure, ere *Phœbus* view the land,
And paile your gracious pompe in lovely Natures scorne.
     If chaunce my Mistres traces
Fast by your flowers to take the Sommers ayre:
Then wofull blushing tempt her glorious eyes,
     To spread their teares, *Adonis* death reporting,
     And tell Loves torments, sorrowing for her friend:
     Whose drops of blood within your leaves consorting,
     Report faire *Venus* moanes to have no end.
Then may remorce, in pittying of my smart:
30 Drie up my teares, and dwell within her hart.

                                Ignoto

THE SHEEPHEARDS SLUMBER

In Pescod time, when Hound to horne,   *peascod*
     gives eare till Buck be kild:
And little Lads with pipes of corne,
     sate keeping beasts a field.
I went to gather Strawberies tho,
     by Woods and Groaves full faire:
And parcht my face with *Phœbus* so,
     in walking in the ayre.
That downe I layde me by a streame,
10   with boughs all over-clad:
And there I met the straungest dreame,
     That ever Sheepheard had.
Me thought I saw each Christmas game,
     each revell all and some:
And every thing that I can name,
     or may in fancie come.
The substance of the sights I saw,
     in silence passe they shall:

Because I lack the skill to draw,
    the order of them all.
But *Venus* shall not passe my pen,
    whose maydens in disdaine:
Did feed upon the harts of men,
    that *Cupids* bowe had slaine.
And that blinde boy was all in blood,
    be-bath'd to the eares:
And like a Conquerour he stood,
    and scorned Lovers teares.
I have (quoth he) more harts at call,
    then *Cæsar* could commaund:
And like the Deare I make them fall,
    that runneth o're the lawnd.
One drops downe heere, another there,
    in bushes as they groane;
I bend a scornfull carelesse care,
    to heare them make their moane.
Ah Sir (quoth *Honest Meaning*) then,
    thy boy-like brags I heare:
When thou hast wounded many a man,
    as Hunts-man doth the Deare.
Becomes it thee to triumph so?
    thy Mother wills it not:
For she had rather breake thy bowe,
    then thou shouldst play the sot.
What saucie merchant speaketh now,
    sayd *Venus* in her rage:
Art thou so blinde thou knowest not how
    I governe every age?
My Sonne doth shoote no shaft in wast,
    to me the boy is bound:
He never found a hart so chast,
    but he had power to wound,
Not so faire Goddesse (quoth *Free-will*,)
    in me there is a choise:
And cause I am of mine owne ill,
    if I in thee rejoyce.
And when I yeeld my selfe a slave,
    to thee, or to thy Sonne:
Such recompence I ought not have,
    if things be rightly done.
Why foole stept forth *Delight*, and said,
    when thou art conquer'd thus:
Then loe dame *Lust*, that wanton maide,
    thy Mistresse is iwus.
And *Lust* is *Cupids* darling deere,
    behold her where she goes:
She creepes the milk-warme flesh so neere,
    she hides her under close.
Where many privie thoughts doo dwell,
    a heaven heere on earth:
For they have never minde of hell,
    they thinke so much on mirth.
Be still *Good Meaning*, quoth *Good Sport*,
    let *Cupid* triumph make:
For sure his Kingdome shall be short
    if we no pleasure take.

Faire *Beautie*, and her play-feares gay,
    the virgins *Vestalles* too:
Shall sit and with their fingers play,
    as idle people doo,
80
If *Honest Meaning* fall to frowne,
    and I *Good Sport* decay:
Then *Venus* glory will come downe,
    and they will pine away.
Indeede (quoth *Wit*) this your device,
    with straungenes must be wrought,
And where you see these women nice,
    and looking to be sought:
With scowling browes their follies check,
90
    and so give them the Fig:
Let *Fancie* be no more at beck,
    when *Beautie* lookes so big.
When *Venus* heard how they conspir'd,
    to murther women so:
Me thought indeede the house was fier'd,
    with stormes and lightning tho.
The thunder-bolt through windowes burst,
    and in their steps a wight:
Which seem'd some soule or sprite accurst,
100
    so ugly was the sight.
I charge you Ladies all (quoth he)
    looke to your selves in hast:
For if that men so wilfull be,
    and have their thoughts so chast;
And they can tread on *Cupids* brest,
    and martch on *Venus* face:
Then they shall sleepe in quiet rest,
    when you shall waile your case.
With that had *Venus* all in spight,
110
    stir'd up the Dames to ire:
And *Lust* fell cold, and *Beautie* white,
    sate babling with *Desire*.
Whose mutt' ring words I might not marke,
    much whispering there arose:
The day did lower, the Sunne wext darke,
    away each Lady goes.
But whether went this angry flock,
    our Lord him-selfe doth know:
Where-with full lowdly crewe the Cock,
120
    and I awaked so.
A dreame (quoth I?) a dogge it is,
    I take thereon no keepe:
I gage my head, such toyes as this,
    dooth spring from lack of sleepe.

Ignoto

ANOTHER OF THE SAME NATURE, MADE SINCE

Come live with mee, and be my deere,
And we will revell all the yeere,
In plaines and groaves, on hills and dales:
Where fragrant ayre breedes sweetest gales.

There shall you have the beauteous Pine,
The Cedar, and the spreading Vine,
And all the woods to be a Skreene:
Least *Phœbus* kisse my Sommers Queene.

10

The seate for your disport shall be
Over some River in a tree,
Where silver sands, and pebbles sing,
Eternall ditties with the spring.

There shall you see the Nimphs at play,
And how the Satires spend the day,
The fishes gliding on the sands:
Offering their bellies to your hands.

The birds with heavenly tuned throates,
Possesse woods Ecchoes with sweet noates,
Which to your sences will impart,

20

A musique to enflame the hart.

Upon the bare and leafe-lesse Oake,
The Ring-Doves wooings will provoke
A colder blood then you possesse,
To play with me and doo no lesse.

In bowers of Laurell trimly dight,
We will out-weare the silent night,
While *Flora* busie is to spread:
Her richest treasure on our bed.

Ten thousand Glow-wormes shall attend,

30

And all their sparkling lights shall spend,
All to adorne and beautifie:
Your lodging with most majestie.

Then in mine armes will I enclose
Lillies faire mixture with the Rose,
Whose nice perfections in loves play:
Shall tune me to the highest key.

Thus as we passe the welcome night,
In sportfull pleasures and delight,
The nimble Fairies on the grounds,

40

Shall daunce and sing mellodious sounds,

If these may serve for to entice,
Your presence to Loves Paradice,
Then come with me, and be my Deare:
And we will straite begin the yeare.

Ignoto

THIRSIS THE SHEEPHEARD, TO HIS PIPE

Like Desert woods, with darksome shades obscured,
Where dreadfull beasts, where hatefull horror raigneth
Such is my wounded hart, whom sorrow payneth,

The Trees are fatall shaft, to death inured,
That cruell love within my breast maintaineth,
To whet my greefe, when as my sorrow wayneth.

The ghastly beasts, my thoughts in cares assured,
Which wage me warre, while hart no succour gaineth:
With false suspect, and feare that still remaineth.

10   The horrors, burning sighs by cares procured,
Which foorth I send, whilst weeping eye complaineth:
To coole the heate, the helplesse hart containeth.

But shafts, but cares, but sighs, horrors unrecured,
Were nought esteem'd, if for these paines awarded:
My faithfull love by her might be regarded.

Ignoto

DISPRAISE OF LOVE, AND LOVERS FOLLIES

If Love be life, I long to die,
        Live they that list for me:
And he that gaines the most thereby,
        A foole at least shall be.
But he that feeles the sorest fits,
Scapes with no lesse than losse of wits,
        Unhappy life they gaine,
        Which Love doe entertaine.

10   In day by fained lookes they live,
        By lying dreames in night,
Each frowne a deadly wound doth give,
        Each smile a false delight.
If't hap their Lady pleasant seeme,
It is for others love they deeme:
        If voide she seeme of joy,
        Disdaine doth make her coy.

Such is the peace that Lovers finde,
        Such is the life they leade.
Blowne here and there with every winde
20   Like flowers in the Mead.
Now warre, now peace, now warre againe,
Desire, despaire, delight, disdaine,
        Though dead in midst of life,
        In peace, and yet at strife.

Ignoto

AN HEROICALL POEME

My wanton Muse that whilome wont to sing,
Faire beauties praise and Venus sweet delight,
Of late hath chang'd the tenor of her string
To higher tunes than serve for Cupids fight.
    Shrill Trumpets sound, sharpe swords, and Lances strong,
    Warre, bloud and death, were matter of her song.

The God of Love by chance had heard thereof,
That I was prov'd a rebell to his crowne,
Fit words for warre, quoth he, with angry scoffe,
A likely man to write of Mars his frowne.
    Well are they sped whose praises he shall write,
    Whose wanton Pen can nought but love indite.

This said, he whiskt his party-colour'd wings,
And downe to earth he comes more swift then thought,
Then to my heart in angry haste he flings,
To see what change these newes of warres had wrought.
    He pries, and lookes, he ransacks every vaine,
    Yet finds he nought, save love, and lovers paine.

Then I that now perceiv'd his needlesse feare,
With heavie smile began to plead my cause:
In vaine (quoth I) this endlesse griefe I beare,
In vaine I strive to keepe thy grievous Lawes,
    If after proofe, so often trusty found,
    Unjust suspect condemne me as unsound.

Is this the guerdon of my faithfull heart?   *reward*
Is this the hope on which my life is staide?
Is this the ease of never-ceasing smart?
Is this the price that for my paines is paide?
    Yet better serve fierce Mars in bloudie field,
    Where death, or conquest, end or joy doth yeeld.

Long have I serv'd, what is my pay but paine?
Oft have I sude, what gaine I but delay?
My faithfull love is quited with disdaine,
My griefe a game, my pen is made a play.
    Yea love that doth in other favour finde,
    In me is counted madnesse out of kinde.

And last of all, but grievous most of all,
Thy self, sweet love, hath kild me with suspect:
Could love beleeve, that I from love would fall?
Is warre of force to make me love neglect.
    No, Cupid knowes, my minde is faster set,
    Than that by warre I should my love forget.

My Muse indeed to warre enclines her minde,
The famous acts of worthy *Brute* to write:
To whom the Gods this Ilands rule assignde,
Which long he sought by Seas through Neptunes spight,
    With such conceits my busie head doth swell.
    But in my heart nought else but love doth dwell.

And in this warre thy part is not the least,
Here shall my Muse *Brutes* noble Love declare:
Here shalt thou see thy double love increast,
Of fairest twins that ever Lady bare:
    Let Mars triumph in armour shining bright,
    His conquerd armes shall be thy triumphs light.

As he the world, so thou shalt him subdue,
And I thy glory through the world will ring,

So by my paines, thou wilt vouchsafe to rue,
And kill despaire. With that he whiskt his wing.
And bid me write, and promist wished rest,
60   But sore I feare false hope will be the best.

Ignoto

THE LOVERS ABSENCE KILS ME, HER PRESENCE KILS ME

The frozen snake, opprest with heaped snow
By strugling hard gets out her tender head,
And spies farre off from where she lies below
The winter Sunne that from the North is fled.
    But all in vaine she lookes upon the light,
    Where heate is wanting to restore her might.

What doth it helpe a wretch in prison pent,
Long time with biting hunger over-prest,
To see without, or smell within, the sent,
10 Of daintie fare for others tables drest?
    Yet Snake and pris'ner both behold the thing,
    The which (but not with sight) might comfort bring.

Such is my state, or worse if worse may be,
My hart opprest with heavie frost of care,
Debar'd of that which is most deere to me,
Kild up with cold, and pinde with evill fare,
    And yet I see the thing might yeelde reliefe,
    And yet the sight doth breed my greater griefe.

So *Thisbe* saw her Lover through the wall,
20 And saw thereby she wanted that she saw,
And so I see, and seeing want withall,
And wanting so, unto my death I draw.
    And so my death were twenty times my friend,
    If with this verse my hated life might end.

Ignoto

LOVE THE ONLY PRICE OF LOVE

The fairest Pearles that Northerne Seas doe breed,
For precious stones from Easterne coasts are sold.
Nought yields the earth that from exchange is freed,
Gold values all, and all things value Gold.
    Where goodnes wants an equall change to make,
    There greatnesse serves, or number place doth take.

No mortall thing can beare so high a price,
But that with mortall thing it may be bought,
The corne of Sicill buies the Westerne spice,
10 French wine of us, of them our cloath is sought.
    No pearles, no gold, no stones, no corne, no spice.
    No cloath, no wine, of love can pay the price.

What thing is love, which nought can countervaile?
Nought save itself, ev'n such a thing is love.
All worldly wealth in worth as farre doth faile,
As lowest earth doth yeeld to heav'n above.
    Divine is love, and scorneth worldly pelfe,
    And can be bought with nothing, but with selfe.

Such is the price my loving heart would pay,
20   Such is the pay thy love doth claime as due.
Thy due is love, which I (poore I) assay,
In vaine assay to quite with friendship true:
    True is my love, and true shall ever be,
    And truest love is farre too base for thee.

Love but thy selfe, and love thy self alone,
For save thy self, none can thy love requite:
All mine thou hast, but all as good as none,
My small desart must take a lower flight.
    Yet if thou wilt vouchsafe my heart such blisse,
30   Accept it for thy prisoner as it is.

Ignoto

A Defiance to Disdainefull Love

Now have I learn'd with much adoe at last,
    By true disdaine to kill desire,
This was the marke at which I shot so fast,
    Unto this height I did aspire.
Proud Love, now doe thy worst, and spare not,
For thee and all thy shafts I care not.

What hast thou left wherewith to move my minde?
    What life to quicken dead desire?
I count thy wordes and oathes as light as winde,
10   I feele no heate in all thy fire.
Goe change thy bow, and get a stronger,
Goe breake thy shafts, and buy thee longer.

In vaine thou bait'st thy hooke with beauties blaze,
    In vaine thy wanton eyes allure.
These are but toyes, for them that love to gaze,
    I know what harme thy lookes procure:
Some strange conceit must be devised,
Or thou and all thy skill despised.

Ignoto

Philistus Farewell to False Clorinda

Clorinda false adiew, thy love torments me:
Let *Thirsis* have thy hart, since he contents thee.
    Oh greefe and bitter anguish,
      For thee I languish,
    Faine I (alas) would hide it,
      Oh, but who can abide it.
    I can, I cannot I abide it?

Adiew, adiew then,
　　Farewell,
10　Leave my death now desiring:
For thou hast thy requiring.
Thus spake *Philistus,* on his hooke relying:
　　And sweetly fell a dying.

Out of M. Morleyes *Madrigalls*

LYCORIS THE NIMPH, HER SAD SONG

In dewe of Roses, steeping her lovely cheekes,
　　Lycoris thus sate weeping.
Ah *Dorus* false, that hast my hart bereft me,
And now unkinde hast left me.
　　Heare alas, oh heare me,
　　　　Aye me, aye me,
　　Cannot my beautie moove thee?
　　Pitty, yet pitty me,
　　　　Because I love thee.
10　Aye me, thou scorn'st the more I pray thee:
And this thou doo'st, and all to slay me.
　　　　Why doo then,
　　Kill me, and vaunt thee:
　　　　Yet my Ghoast
　　Still shall haunt thee.

Out of M. Morleyes *Madrigalls*

THE SHEEPHEARDS CONSORT

Harke jollie Sheepheards,
　　harke yond lustie ringing:
How cheerefully the bells daunce,
　　the whilst the Lads are springing?
Goe we then, why sit we here delaying:
And all yond mery wanton lasses playing?
　　How gailie *Flora* leades it,
　　　　and sweetly treads it?
　　The woods and groaves they ring,
　　　　lovely resounding:
　　With Ecchoes sweet rebounding.

Out of M. Morleyes *Madrigalls*

THE HEARD-MANS HAPPIE LIFE

What pleasure have great Princes,
　　more daintie to their choice,
Then Heardmen wilde, who carelesse,
　　in quiet life rejoyce?
And Fortunes Fate not fearing,
Sing sweet in Sommer morning.

Their dealings plaine and rightfull
    are voide of all deceite:
They never know how spightfull,
    it is to kneele and waite;
On favourite presumptuous,
    Whose pride is vaine and sumptuous.

All day theyr flocks each tendeth,
    at night they take their rest:
More quiet then who sendeth
    his ship into the East;
Where gold and pearle are plentie,
But getting very daintie.

For Lawyers and their pleading,
    they'steeme it not a straw:
They thinke that honest meaning,
    is of it selfe a law;
Where conscience judgeth plainely,
They spend no money vainely.

Oh happy who thus liveth,
    not caring much for gold:
With cloathing which suffiseth,
    to keepe him from the cold.
Though poore and plaine his diet:
    Yet merrie it is and quiet.

            Out of M. Birds *set Songs*

TO AMARILLIS

THOUGH *Amarillis* daunce in greene,
    Like Faierie Queene,
    And sing full cleere,
    With smiling cheere.
Yet since her eyes make hart so sore,
    hey hoe, chill love no more.

My Sheepe are lost for want of foode
    And I so wood
    That all the day:
I sit and watch a Heard-mayde gay
Who laughs to see me sigh so sore:
    hey hoe, chill love no more.

Her loving lookes, her beautie bright,
    Is such delight,
    That all in vaine:
I love to like, and loose my gaine,
For her that thanks me not therefore,
    hey hoe, chill love no more.

Ah wanton eyes, my friendly foes,
    And cause of woes,
    Your sweet desire
Breedes flames of ice, and freeze in fire.

You scorne to see me weepe so sore:
      hey hoe, chill love no more.

Love ye who list, I force him not,
      Sith God it wot
      The more I waile:
The lesse my sighs and teares prevaile.
What shall I doo, but say therefore,
      hey hoe, chill love no more?

30

Out of M. Birds *set Songs*

OF PHILLIDA

As I beheld, I saw a Heardman wilde,
    with his sheep-hooke a picture fine deface:
Which he sometime his fancie to beguile,
    had carv'd on bark of Beech in secret place.
And with despight of most afflicted minde,
    through deepe dispaire of hart, for love dismaid
He pull'd even from the tree the carved rinde,
    and weeping sore, these wofull words he said.
Ah *Phillida*, would God thy picture faire,
10   I could as lightly blot out of my brest:
Then should I not thus rage in deepe dispaire,
    and teare the thing sometime I liked best.
But all in vaine, it booteth not God wot:
    What printed is in hart, on tree to blot.

Out of M. Birds *set Songs*

PHILON THE SHEEPHEARD, HIS SONG

WHILE that the Sunne with his beames hot,
Scorched the fruites in vale and mountaine:
Philon the Sheepheard late forgot,
Sitting besides a Christall Fountaine:
      In shaddow of a greene Oake tree,
      Upon his Pipe this Song plaid he.
Adiew Love, adiew Love, untrue Love,
Untrue Love, untrue Love, adiew Love:
Your minde is light, soone lost for new love.

10 So long as I was in your sight,
I was as your hart, your soule, and treasure:
And evermore you sob'd and sigh'd,
Burning in flames beyond all measure.
      Three dayes endured your love to me:
      And it was lost in other three.
Adiew Love, adiew Love, untrue Love. &c.

Another Sheepheard you did see,
To whom your hart was soone enchained:
Full soone your love was leapt from me,
20 Full soone my place he had obtained.
      Soone came a third, your love to win:

> And we were out, and he was in.
> Adiew Love. &c.

> Sure you have made me passing glad,
> That you your minde so soone removed:
> Before that I the Ieysure had,
> To choose you for my best beloved.
> For all my love was past and done:
> Two dayes before it was begun.
> Adiew Love. &c.

Out of M. Birds set Songs

Myles Smith (d. 1624)

At the time of the preparation of the Authorized Version of the Bible in English, Myles Smith was a Fellow of Brasenose College, Oxford, and the greatest scholar of Near-Eastern languages (Chaldaic, Syriac, Arabic, and Hebrew) in England. Along with Thomas Bilson, he was one of the general editors of the translation as a whole, and was entrusted with the task of writing the preface to the reader.

It is a curious accident of publishing history that the dedication to King James (which is a perfunctory piece of flattery) survives in most printed editions of the Authorized Version to this day, whereas Smith's preface (which is vastly more interesting and important) does not. Apparently considered to be too long, too scholarly, and too remote from modern readers to be worth keeping, it is in fact a vividly written document which deals with issues relevant to students of the period and lay readers of the Bible alike. Smith's arguments are buttressed by a wealth of scholarly citations, but they do not interfere with the clarity of his ideas. His task was no less than to justify the translation of the Bible into the English vernacular, to locate the Authorized Version in the context of other English translations, and to explain the principles by which the translators went about their work. In the course of doing so, his preface also produces memorable considerations of the dangers and rewards of any innovation in the arena of religion (which, for the seventeenth century, implied the arena of politics as well) and of how ambiguous passages in the Bible are to be interpreted. Smith was himself a moderate Puritan, but his preface tries to chart a middle course between the Roman Catholicism of England's European enemies and the Puritan critics of James I's religious policies at home. Obliged by his position to condemn the Church of Rome in conventional Protestant terms, he manages to avoid the sectarian extremes that were common in religious polemics of his day.

The omission of Smith's careful, broad-minded preface has, ironically, led to at least one notable example of religious intolerance. In the twentieth century, there has been a marked tendency in evangelical Protestantism (especially in America) to privilege the Authorized Version as superior to all other biblical translations in English before or since. No one who reads Smith's words, however, can possibly imagine him agreeing with this position. He speaks respectfully and gratefully about all previous translators of the Bible (of whatever denomination), and implicitly recognizes that the day will come when the Authorized Version is itself superseded by advances in historical or linguistic knowledge. Against "literal" fundamentalist readings of the text, he advocates tolerance for multiple interpretations and a recognition that some ambiguities in the Bible cannot be neatly resolved. It is also notable that he does not hesitate to cite pagan writers in support of his arguments about the Christian Bible and sees no contradiction in doing so. Reading Smith today is a sobering reminder that intellectual and religious tolerance is not necessarily more widespread now than it was in the Early Modern period.

Unless otherwise indicated, the notes in the text are Smith's.

READING

Olga S. Opfell, *The King James Bible Translators.*
A. T. Partridge, *English Biblical Translation.*
Erroll F. Rhodes and Liana Lupas (eds.), *The Translators to the Reader – The Original Preface of the KING JAMES VERSION of 1611 Revisited.*

J. H.

THE TRANSLATORS TO THE READER – THE PREFACE TO THE
AUTHORIZED VERSION (KING JAMES BIBLE) (1611)

Zeal to promote the common good, whether it be by devising anything ourselves, or revising that which hath been laboured by others, deserveth certainly much respect and esteem, but yet findeth but cold entertainment in the world. It is welcomed with suspicion instead of love, and with emulation instead of thanks: and if there be any hole left for cavil to enter (and cavil, if it do not find an hole, will make one) it is sure to be misconstrued, and in danger to be condemned. This will easily be granted by as many as know story, or have any experience. For was there ever any thing projected, that savoured any way of newness or renewing, but the same endured many a storm of gainsaying or opposition? A man would think that civility, wholesome laws, learning and eloquence, synods, and Church maintenance, (that we speak of no more things of this kind) should be as safe as a sanctuary, and out of shot, as they say, that no man would lift up the heel, no, nor dog move his tongue against the motioners of them. For by the first we are distinguished from brute beasts led with sensuality: by the second we are bridled and restrained from outrageous behaviour, and from doing of injuries, whether by fraud or by violence: by the third we are enabled to inform and reform others by the light and feeling that we have attained unto ourselves: briefly, by the fourth, being brought together to a parley face to face, we sooner compose our differences, than by writings which are endless: and lastly, that the Church be sufficiently provided for is so agreeable to good reason and conscience, that those mothers are holden to be less cruel, that kill their children as soon as they are born, than those nursing fathers and mothers (wheresoever they be) that withdraw from them who hang upon their breasts (and upon whose breasts again themselves do hang to receive the spiritual and sincere milk of the word) livelihood and support fit for their estates. Thus it is apparent, that these things which we speak of are of most necessary use, and therefore that none, either without absurdity can speak against them, or without note of wickedness can spurn against them.

Yet for all that, the learned know, that certain worthy men[1] have been brought to untimely death for none other fault, but for seeking to reduce their countrymen to good order and discipline: and that in some Commonwealths[2] it was made a capital crime, once to motion the making of a new law for the abrogating of an old, though the same were most pernicious: and that certain,[3] which would be counted pillars of the State, and patterns of virtue and prudence, could not be brought for a long time to give way to good letters and refined speech; but bare themselves as averse from them, as from rocks or boxes of poison: and fourthly, that he was no babe, but a great Clerk,[4] that gave forth, (and in writing to remain to posterity,) in passion peradventure, but yet he gave forth, That he had not seen any profit to come by any synod, or meeting of the Clergy, but rather the contrary: and lastly, against Church-maintenance and allowance, in such sort, as the ambassadors and messengers of the great King of kings should be furnished, it is not unknown what a fiction or fable (so it is esteemed, and for no better by the reporter himself,[5] though superstitious) was devised: namely, That at such a time as the professors and teachers of Christianity in the Church of Rome, then a true Church, were liberally endowed, a voice forsooth was heard from heaven, saying, Now is poison poured down into the Church, etc. Thus not only as oft as we speak, as one saith, but also as oft as we do anything of note or consequence, we subject ourselves to everyone's censure, and happy is he that is least tossed upon tongues; for utterly to escape the snatch of

---

THE TRANSLATORS TO THE READER – THE PREFACE TO THE
AUTHORIZED VERSION (KING JAMES BIBLE) (1611)

1   Anacharsis with others. *Editor's Note*: Anacharsis was a Scythian prince from the 6th century BCE whose deeds, recorded in Herodotus, may well be pure fiction. After travelling to Greece, he was put to death upon his return to Scythia for trying to introduce Greek religious practices to his native land.

2   Locri Epizephyrii. *Editor's Note*: a Sicilian Greek colony of people from the Locris region of central Greece. Its chief lawgiver Zaleucus (7th

century BC) was famous for the severity and conservatism of his legal code.

3   Cato the Elder. *Editor's Note*: See the gazetteer under Cato "the Censor".

4   Gregory the Divine. *Editor's Note*: Gregory Nazianzen (329–89), *Epistle* 130.

5   Nauclerus. *Editor's Note*: Johannes Nauclerus's *Chronica* (1516) was a widely read universal history in Early Modern Europe.

them it is impossible. If any man conceit, that this is the lot and portion of the meaner sort only, and that Princes are privileged by their high estate, he is deceived. As *the sword devoureth as well one as the other*, as it is in *Samuel*;[6] nay, as the great Commander charged his soldiers in a certain battle to strike at no part of the enemy but at the face; and as the king of Syria commanded his chief Captains *to fight neither with small nor great, save only against the King of Israel*:[7] so it is too true, that envy striketh most spitefully at the fairest, and at the chiefest. *David* was a worthy prince, and no man to be compared to him for his first deeds; and yet for as worthy as act as ever he did, even for bringing back the Ark of God in solemnity, he was scorned and scoffed at by his own wife.[8] *Solomon* was greater than *David*, though not in virtue, yet in power; and by his power and wisdom he built a Temple to the Lord, such an one as was the glory of the land of *Israel*, and the wonder of the whole world. But was that his magnificence liked of by all? We doubt of it. Otherwise why do they lay it in his son's dish, and call unto him for easing of the burden? *Make*, say they, *the grievous servitude of thy father, and his sore yoke, lighter*.[9] Belike he had charged them with some levies, and troubled them with some carriages; hereupon they raise up a tragedy, and wish in their heart the temple had never been built. So hard a thing it is to please all, even when we please God best, and do seek to approve ourselves to everyone's conscience.

If we will descend to latter times, we shall find many the like examples of such kind, or rather unkind acceptance. The first Roman Emperor[10] did never do a more pleasing deed to the learned, nor more profitable to posterity, for conserving the record of times in true supputation, than when he corrected the Calendar, and ordered the year according to the course of the sun: and yet this was imputed to him for novelty, and arrogance, and procured to him great obloquy. So the first Christened Emperor[11] (at the leastwise, that openly professed the faith himself, and allowed others to do the like) for strengthening the empire at his great charges, and providing for the Church, as he did, got for his labour the name *Pupillus*, as who would say, a wasteful Prince, that had need of a guardian or overseer.[12] So the best Christened Emperor,[13] for the love that he bare unto peace, thereby to enrich both himself and his subjects, and because he did not seek war but find it, was judged to be no man at arms,[14] (though indeed he excelled in feats of chivalry, and showed so much when he was provoked,) and condemned for giving himself to his ease, and to his pleasure. To be short, the most learned Emperor of former times,[15] (at the least, the greatest politician,) what thanks had he for cutting off the superfluities of the laws, and digesting them into some order and method? This, that he had been blotted by some to be an Epitomist, that is, one that extinguishes worthy whole volumes, to bring his abridgments into request. This is the measure that hath been rendered to excellent Princes in former times, even, *Cum bene facerent, male audire*, for their good deeds to be evil spoken of. Neither is there any likelihood, that envy and malignity died, and were buried with the ancient. No, no, the reproof of *Moses* taketh hold of most ages, *Ye are risen up in your fathers' stead, an increase of sinful men*.[16] *What is that that hath been done? that which shall be done: and there is no new thing under the sun*, saith the wise man.[17] And St. *Stephen*, *As your fathers did, so do ye*.[18] This, and more to this purpose, his Majesty that now reigneth (and long, and long, may he reign, and his offspring forever, *Himself and children, and children's children always!*) knew full well, according to the singular wisdom given unto him by God, and the rare learning and experience that he hath attained unto; namely, That whosoever attempteth anything for the public (especially if it pertain to religion, and to the opening and clearing of the word of God,) the same setteth himself upon a

6   2 Sam. 11:25.
7   1 Kings 22:31.
8   2 Sam. 6:16.
9   1 Kings 12:4.
10   C. Caesar. Plutarch. *Editor's Note*: Julius Caesar did introduce the Julian Calendar, as Plutarch records, but is not considered to be the first Roman emperor; that title is given to his grand-nephew, Augustus Caesar.
11   Constantine. *Editor's Note*: See the gazetteer.
12   Aurelius Victor. *Editor's Note*: a late Roman politician and historian who published *De Caesaribus* ("On the Caesars") some time after 360 AD.

13   Theodosius. *Editor's Note*: Theodosius the Great (ruled 388–95 AD) was the Roman emperor who forbade all public religious practices except Christianity, effectively making it the state religion of the Roman empire.
14   Zosimus. *Editor's Note*: a Greek historian of the 6th century CE who was notably hostile to Christianity in his writings.
15   Justinian. *Editor's Note*: Eastern Roman emperor (ruled 527–65 AD) who tried to abridge the vast mass of Roman law and tradition into a manageable, comprehensible form.
16   Num. 32:14.
17   Eccles 1:9.
18   Acts 7:51.

stage to be glouted[19] upon by every evil eye; yea, he casteth himself headlong upon pikes, to be gored by every sharp tongue. For he that meddleth with men's religion in any part meddleth with their custom, nay, with their freehold; and though they find no content in that which they have, yet they cannot abide to hear of altering. Notwithstanding his royal heart was not daunted or discouraged for this or that colour, but stood resolute, *as a statue immovable, and an anvil not easy to be beaten into plates*, as one saith;[20] he knew who had chosen him to be a soldier, or rather a captain, and being assured that the course which he intended made much for the glory of God, and the building up of his Church, he would not suffer it to be broken off for whatsoever speeches or practices. It doth certainly belong unto kings, yea, it doth specially belong unto them, to have care of religion, yea, to know it aright, yea, to profess it zealously, yea, to promote it to the uttermost of their power. This is their glory before all nations which mean well, and this will bring unto them a far most excellent weight of glory in the day of the Lord Jesus. For the Scripture saith not in vain, *Them that honour me, I will honour*:[21] neither was it a vain word that *Eusebius* delivered long ago, That piety towards God was the weapon, and the only weapon, that both preserved *Constantine's* person, and avenged him of his enemies.[22]

But now what piety without truth? What truth, what saving truth, without the word of God? What word of God, whereof we may be sure, without the Scripture? The Scriptures we are commanded to search, *John* 5:39. *Isaiah* 8:20. They are commended that searched and studied them, *Acts* 17:11 and 8:28, 29. They are reproved that were unskillful in them, or slow to believe them, *Matt.* 22:29. *Luke* 24:25. They can make us wise unto salvation, 2 *Tim.* 3:15. If we be ignorant, they will instruct us; if out of the way, they will bring us home; if out of order, they will reform us; if in heaviness, comfort us; if dull, quicken us; if cold, inflame us. *Tolle, lege; Tolle, lege,* Take up and read, take up and read the Scriptures,[23] (for unto them was the direction,) it was said unto St. *Augustine* by a supernatural voice. *Whatsoever is in the Scriptures, believe me*, saith the same St. *Augustine, is high and divine; there is verily truth, and a doctrine most fit for the refreshing of men's minds, and truly so tempered, that everyone may draw from thence that which is sufficient for him, if he come to draw with a devout and pious mind, as true religion requireth.*[24] Thus St. *Augustine.* And St. *Jerome, Ama scripturas, et amabit te sapientia, etc.*[25] Love the Scriptures, and wisdom will love thee. And St. *Cyril* against *Julian, Even boys that are bred up in the Scriptures, become most religious, etc.*[26] But what mention we three or four uses of the Scripture, whereas whatsoever is to be believed, or practiced, or hoped for, is contained in them? or three or four sentences of the Fathers,[27] since whosoever is worthy the name of a Father, from Christ's time downward, hath likewise written not only of the riches, but also of the perfection of the Scripture? *I adore the fullness of the Scripture*, saith *Tertullian* against *Hermogenes.*[28] And again, to *Apelles* an heretic of the like stamp he saith, *I do not admit that which thou bringest in* (or concludest) *of thine own* (head or store, *de tuo*) *without Scripture.*[29] So St. *Justin Martyr* before him; *We must know by all means* (saith he) *that it is not lawful* (or possible) *to learn* (anything) *of God or of right piety, save only out of the Prophets, who teach us by divine inspiration.*[30] So St. *Basil* after *Tertullian, It is a manifest falling away from the faith, and a fault of presumption, either to reject any of those things that are written, or to bring in* (upon the head of them, επεισαγειν) *any of those things that are not written.*[31] We omit to cite to the same effect, St. *Cyril*, Bishop of Jerusalem in his Fourth *Catachetical Lecture*, St. *Jerome* against *Helvidius*, St.

---

19 *Editor's Note:* "frowned or scowled upon" (*OED*).

20 Suidas. *Editor's Note:* a tenth-century Byzantine Greek, compiler of an important reference work on Greek language and literary culture.

21 1 Sam. 2:30.

22 Eusebius, *Ecclesiastical History* 10.8.6.

23 St. Augustine, *Confessions* 8:12.

24 St. Augustine, *De utilitate credendi* ("On the Profit of Believing") 6:13.

25 St. Jerome, *Ad Demetriad* ("To Demetrias").

26 St. Cyril, *Contra Iulianum* ("Against Julian"). *Editor's Note:* Cyril of Alexandria (died 444 CE) wrote this treatise against the ideas of Julian the Apostate (ruled AD 361–3), a Roman emperor who overturned the law making Christianity the sole legal religion in the Roman empire.

27 *Editor's Note:* The "Fathers of the Church" is a collective term usually applied to Christian writers of the first through the fifth centuries. All of the writers whom Smith cites in this paragraph are Church Fathers.

28 Tertullian, *Adversus Hermogenum* ("Against Hermogenes") 22.5.

29 Tertullian, *De carne Christi* ("On the Body of Christ") 7.3.

30 *Editor's Note:* Justin Martyr (AD 100–165) was an early Christian apologist whose works try to uncover the similarities between Christianity and the other religions of his day. He was executed in Rome.

31 *Editor's Note:* St. Basil (AD c.330–79) was a bishop of Caesaria and an important advocate of monastic life.

Augustine in his third book against the letters of *Petilian*, and in very many other places of his works. Also we forbear to descend to later Fathers, because we will not weary the reader. The Scriptures then being acknowledged to be so full and so perfect, how can we excuse ourselves of negligence, if we do not study them? of curiosity, if we be not content with them? Men talk much of ειρεσιωνη,[32] how many sweet and goodly things it had hanging on it; of the Philosophers' stone,[33] that it turneth copper into gold; of *Cornu-copia*,[34] that it had all things necessary for food in it; of *Panaces* the herb,[35] that it was good for all diseases; of *Catholicon*[36] the drug, that it is instead of all purges; of *Vulcan's* armour, that it was an armour of proof against all thrusts, and all blows,[37] etc. Well, that which they falsely or vainly attributed to these things for bodily good, we may justly and with full measure ascribe unto the Scripture for spiritual. It is not only an armour, but also a whole armoury of weapons, both offensive and defensive; whereby we may save ourselves and put the enemy to flight. It is not an herb, but a tree, or rather a whole paradise of trees of life, which bring forth fruit every month, and the fruit thereof is for meat, and the leaves for medicine. It is not a pot of *Manna*, or a cruse of oil, which were for memory only, or for a meal's meat or two; but, as it were, a shower of heavenly bread sufficient for a whole host, be it never so great;[38] and as it were a whole cellar full of oil vessels; whereby all our necessities may be provided for, and our debts discharged. In a word, it is a panary[39] of wholesome food against fenowed[40] traditions; a physician's shop (St. *Basil* calls it[41]) of preservatives against poisoned heresies; a pandect[42] of profitable laws against rebellious spirits; a treasury of most costly jewels against beggarly rudiments; finally, a fountain of most pure water springing up unto everlasting life. And what marvel? the original thereof being from heaven, not from earth; the author being God, not man; the inditer, the Holy Spirit, not the wit of the Apostles or Prophets; the penmen, such as were sanctified from the womb, and endued with a principal portion of God's spirit; the matter, verity, piety, purity, uprightness; the form, God's word, God's testimony, God's oracles, the word of truth, the word of salvation, etc.; the effects, light of understanding, stableness of persuasion, repentance from dead works, newness of life, holiness, peace, joy in the Holy Ghost; lastly, the end and reward of the study thereof, fellowship with the saints, participation of the heavenly nature, fruition of an inheritance immortal, undefiled, and that never shall fade away. Happy is the man that delighteth in the Scripture, and thrice happy that meditateth in it day and night.

But how shall men meditate in that which they cannot understand? How shall they understand that which is kept close in an unknown tongue? as it is written, *Except I know the power of the voice, I shall be to him that speaketh a barbarian, and he that speaketh shall be a barbarian to me.*[43] The Apostle excepteth no tongue; not *Hebrew* the ancientest, not *Greek* the most copious, not *Latin* the finest. Nature taught a natural man to confess, that all of us in those tongues which we do not understand are plainly deaf; we may turn the deaf ear unto them. The *Scythian* counted the *Athenian*, whom he did not understand, barbarous:[44] so the *Roman* did the *Syrian*, and the *Jew*: (even St. *Jerome* himself calleth the *Hebrew* tongue barbarous; belike, because it was strange to so many:)[45] so the Emperor of *Constantinople*[46] calleth the *Latin* tongue barbarous, though Pope *Nicolas* do storm at it:[47] so the *Jews* long before *Christ*, called all other nations, *Lognasim*, which is little better than

---

32   An olive bow wrapped about with wool, whereupon did hang figs, and bread, honey in a pot, and oil. *Editor's Note*: The reference here is to Plutarch, *Theseus* 22.5.

33   *Editor's Note*: An imaginary substance which turns ordinary metals into gold or silver; finding this substance was the highest goal of alchemy.

34   *Editor's Note*: "The horn of plenty; a goat's horn represented in art as overflowing with flowers, fruit, and corn" (*OED*).

35   *Editor's Note*: origin of the modern word "panacea," meaning a "cure-all."

36   *Editor's Note*: "an electuary supposed to be capable of evacuating all humours; a universal remedy or prophylactic" (*OED*).

37   *Editor's Note*: In Book 18 of Homer's *Iliad*, the god Hephaestus (the Roman "Vulcan") forges a new set of armour for the Greek hero Achilles.

38   *Editor's Note*: See Exodus 16:5–6 and Numbers 11:6 for the biblical stories that ground this reference.

39   *Editor's Note*: "a storehouse for bread" (*OED*).

40   *Editor's Note*: variant of "finew" which means "to become mouldy or musty" (*OED*).

41   St. Basil, *Exegetic Homilies* 10.1, *On Psalm 1*.

42   *Editor's Note*: "A complete body of the laws of any country or of any system of law" (*OED*).

43   1 Cor. 14:11.

44   Clement of Alexandria, *Stromateis* 1.77.3.

45   St. Jerome, *Epistles* 20.4.1.

46   Michael, son of Theophilus. *Editor's Note*: the Byzantine Emperor Michael III (842–67) broke with Pope Nicholas I on the issue of how much power the Roman Church had in Byzantine lands. This eventually led to the schism between the Roman Catholic and Greek Orthodox churches.

47   Petrus Crabbe (ed.), *Conciliorum omnium . . .* , Book 2 (1538).

barbarous. Therefore as one complaineth that always in the Senate of *Rome* there was one or other that called for an interpreter;[48] so lest the Church be driven to the like exigent, it is necessary to have translations in a readiness, translation it is that openeth the window, to let in the light; that breaketh the shell, that we may eat the kernel; that putteth aside the curtain, that we may look into the most holy place; that removeth the cover of the well, that we may come by the water; even as *Jacob* rolled away the stone from the mouth of the well, by which means the flocks of *Laban* were watered.[49] Indeed without translation into the vulgar tongue, the unlearned are but like children at *Jacob's* well (which was deep)[50] without a bucket or something to draw with: or as that person mentioned by *Isaiah*, to whom when a sealed book was delivered with this motion, *Read this, I pray thee*, he was fain to make this answer, *I cannot, for it is sealed.*[51]

While God would be known only in *Jacob*, and have his name great in *Israel*, and in none other place; while the dew lay on *Gideon's* fleece only, and all the earth besides was dry; then for one and the same people, which spake all of them the language of *Canaan*, that is, *Hebrew*, one and the same original in *Hebrew* was sufficient.[52] But when the fulness of time drew near, that the Sun of righteousness, the Son of God should come into the world, whom God ordained to be a reconciliation through faith in his blood, not of the *Jew* only, but also of the *Greek*, yea, of all them that were scattered abroad; then, lo, it pleased the Lord. to stir up the spirit of a *Greek* prince, (*Greek* for descent and language,) even of *Ptolemy Philadelph* king of *Egypt*, to procure the translating of the Book of God out of *Hebrew* into *Greek*. This is the translation of the *Seventy* Interpreters, commonly so called,[53] which prepared the way for our Saviour among the *Gentiles*[54] by written preaching, as St. *John Baptist* did among the *Jews* by vocal. For the *Grecians*, being desirous of learning, were not wont to suffer books of worth to lie moulding in kings' libraries, but had many of their servants, ready scribes, to copy them out, and so they were dispersed and made common. Again, the *Greek* tongue was well known and made familiar to most inhabitants in *Asia*, by reason of the conquest that there the *Grecians* had made, as also by the colonies which thither they had sent. For the same causes also it was well understood in many places of Europe, yea, and of *Africa* too. Therefore the word of God, being set forth in *Greek*, becometh hereby like a candle set upon a candlestick, which giveth light to all that are in the house; or like a proclamation sounded forth in the market place, which most men presently take knowledge of; and therefore that language was fittest to contain the Scriptures, both for the first preachers of the Gospel to appeal unto for witness, and for the learners also of those times to make search and trial by. It is certain, that that translation was not so sound and so perfect, but that it needed in many places correction; and who had been so sufficient for this work as the Apostles or apostolic men? Yet it seemed good to the Holy Ghost and to them to take that which they found, (the same being for the greatest part true and sufficient,) rather than by making a new, in that new world and green age of the Church, to expose themselves to many exceptions and cavillations, as though they made a translation to serve their own turn; and therefore bearing witness to themselves, their witness not to be regarded. This may be supposed to be some cause, why the translation of the *Seventy* was allowed to pass for current. Notwithstanding, though it was commended generally, yet it did not fully content the learned, no not of the *Jews*. For not long after *Christ*, *Aquila* fell in hand with a new translation, and after him *Theodotion*, and after him *Symmachus*:[55] yea, there was a fifth, and a sixth edition, the authors whereof were not known.[56] These with the *Seventy* made up the *Hexapla*, and were worthily and to great

48   Cicero, *De finibus bonorum et malorum* 5.28.89.

49   Gen. 29:10.

50   John 4:11.

51   Isaiah 29:11.

52   St. Augustine, *Contra Faustum Manichœum* ("Against Faustus the Manichean") 12.32.

53   *Editor's Note*: The *Septuagint*, which means "Seventy," is the name given to the translation of the Hebrew Scriptures (the Christian Old Testament) into Greek. According to legend, King Ptolemy II of Egypt commissioned 72 Jewish scholars to translate the Law (Torah) for the

royal library some time in the 2nd century BCE. They are supposed to have completed their work in 72 days. Ptolemy's commission of the work is accepted as genuine, but the rest of the story's details are probably pure fiction.

54   *Editor's Note*: originally, a "Gentile" referred to anyone who was not a Jew; later, it came also to be a synonym for "heathen" or "pagan."

55   *Editor's Note*: these references to early translations of the Bible are all preserved by Epiphanius; as Smith goes on to say, the Septuagint rapidly became the standard Greek version.

56   Epiphanius, *De mensuris et ponderibus* 17.

purpose compiled together by *Origen*.[57] Howbeit the edition of the *Seventy* went away with the credit, and therefore not only was placed in the midst by *Origen*, (for the worth and excellency thereof above the rest, as *Epiphanius* gathereth,) but also was used by the *Greek* Fathers for the ground and foundation of their Commentaries. Yea, *Epiphanius* above named doth attribute so much unto it, that he holdeth the authors thereof not only for interpreters, but also for prophets in some respect:[58] and *Justinian* the Emperor enjoining the *Jews* his subjects to use especially the translation of the *Seventy*, rendereth this reason thereof, Because they were, as it were, enlightened with prophetical grace. Yet for all that, as the *Egyptians* are said of the Prophet to be men and not God, and their horses flesh and not spirit:[59] so it is evident, (and St. *Jerome* affirmeth as much,)[60] that the *Seventy* were interpreters, they were not prophets. They did many things well, as learned men; but yet as men they stumbled and fell, one while through oversight, another while through ignorance; yea, sometimes they may be noted to add to the original, and sometimes to take from it: which made the Apostles to leave them many times, when they left the *Hebrew*, and to deliver the sense thereof according to the truth of the word, as the Spirit gave them utterance. This may suffice touching the *Greek* translations of the Old Testament.

There were also within a few hundred years after *Christ* translations many into the *Latin* tongue: for this tongue also was very fit to convey the Law and the Gospel by, because in those times very many Countries of the West, yea of the South, East and North, spake or understood *Latin*, being made provinces to the *Romans*. But now the *Latin* translations were too many to be all good: for they were infinite; (*Latini interpretes nullo modo numerari possunt*, saith St. *Augustine*.)[61] Again, they were not out of the *Hebrew* fountain, (we speak of the *Latin* translations of the Old Testament,) but out of the *Greek* stream; therefore the *Greek* being not altogether clear, the *Latin* derived from it must needs be muddy. This moved St. *Jerome*, a most learned Father, and the best linguist without controversy of his age, or of any that went before him, to undertake the translating of the Old Testament out of the very fountains themselves; which he performed with that evidence of great learning, judgement, industry, and faithfulness, that he had forever bound the Church unto him in a debt of special remembrance and thankfulness.

Now though the Church were thus furnished with *Greek* and *Latin* translations, even before the faith of *Christ* was generally embraced in the Empire: (for the learned know that even in St. *Jerome's* time, the Consul of *Rome* and his wife were both Ethnics,[62] and about the same time the greatest part of the Senate also:)[63] yet for all that the godly-learned were not content to have the Scriptures in the language which they themselves understood, *Greek* and *Latin*, (as the good lepers were not content to fare well themselves, but acquainted their neighbours with the store that God had sent, that they also might provide for themselves;)[64] but also for the behoof and edifying of the unlearned, which hungered and thirsted after righteousness, and had souls to be saved as well as they, they provided translations into the vulgar for their countrymen, insomuch that most nations under heaven did shortly after their conversion hear *Christ* speaking unto them in their mother tongue, not by the voice of their minister only, but also by the written word translated. If any doubt hereof, he may be satisfied by examples enough, if enough will serve the turn. First St. *Jerome* saith, *Multarum gentium linguis Scriptura ante translata docet falsa esse quae addita sunt, etc.* that is, *The Scripture being translated before in the languages of many nations doth show that those things that were added* (by *Lucian* and *Hesychius*) *are false.*[65] So St. *Jerome* in that place. The same *Jerome* elsewhere affirmeth that he, the time was, had set forth the translation of the *Seventy, suae linguae hominibus*, that is, for his

57   *Editor's Note*: Origen (*c.*184–255 CE) was an important early Church Father from Alexandria who was learned in pagan philosophy as well as Christianity. He was a pioneer in biblical commentary and textual criticism.

58   St. Augustine, *De doctrine Christiana* ("On Christian Doctrine") 2.15.22.

59   Isaiah 31:3.

60   St. Jerome, *De optimo genere interpretandi* ("On the Best Method of Translating").

61   St. Augustine, *De doctrina Christiana* 2.11.16. *Editor's Note*: Smith has reproduced the spirit, but not the letter, of Augustine's text. This fragment translates as "The Latin translators are innumerable."

62   *Editor's Note*: "Pertaining to nations not Christian or Jewish; Gentile, heathen, pagan" (*OED*).

63   St. Jerome. Ammianus Marcellinus. Zosimus. *Editor's Note*: the precise referents for this note are not at all clear.

64   2 Kings 7:9.

65   St. Jerome, *Praefatio . . . in Evangelio*.

countrymen of *Dalmatia*.[66] Which words not only *Erasmus* doth understand to purport, that St. *Jerome* translated the Scripture into the *Dalmatian* tongue, but also *Sixtus Senensis*,[67] and *Alphonsus à Castro*,[68] (that we speak of no more,) men not to be excepted against by them of *Rome*, do ingenuously confess as much. So, St. *Chrysostom*, that lived in St. *Jerome's* time, giveth evidence with him: *The doctrine of St. John* (saith he) *did not in such sort* (as the Philosophers' did) *vanish away: but the Syrians, Egyptians, Indians, Persians, Ethiopians, and infinite other nations, being barbarous people, translated it into their (mother) tongue, and have learned to be (true) Philosophers*, he meaneth Christians.[69] To this may be added *Theodoret*, as next unto him both for antiquity, and for learning. His words be these, *Every Country that is under the sun is full of these words* (of the Apostles and Prophets;) *and the Hebrew tongue* (he meaneth the Scriptures in the *Hebrew* tongue) *is turned not only into the language of the Grecians, but also of the Romans, and Egyptians, and Persians, and Indians, and Armenians, and Scythians, and Sauromatians, and, briefly, into all the languages that any nation useth*.[70] So he. In like manner, *Ulfilas* is reported by *Paulus Diaconus* and *Isidore*, and before them by *Sozomen*, to have translated the Scriptures into the *Gothic* tongue:[71] *John* Bishop of *Seville* by *Vasseus*, to have turned them into *Arabic*, about the year of our Lord 717:[72] *Bede* by *Cistertiensis*, to have turned a great part of them into *Saxon*: *Efnard* by *Trithemius*, to have abridged the French Psalter (as Bede had done the *Hebrew*) about the year 800:[73] King *Alfred* by the said *Cistertiensis*, to have turned the Psalter into *Saxon*:[74] *Methodius* by *Aventinus* (printed at *Ingolstadt*) to have turned the Scriptures into *Slavonian*:[75] *Valdo*, Bishop of *Frising* by *Beatus Rhenanus*, to have caused about that time, the Gospels to be translated into *Dutch* rhyme, yet extant in the Library of Corbinian:[76] *Valdus*, by divers, to have turned them himself, or to have gotten them turned, into *French*, about the year 1160: *Charles* the Fifth of that name, surnamed *the Wise*, to have caused them to be turned into *French* about 200 years after *Valdus* his time; of which translation there be many copies yet extant, as witnesseth *Beroaldus*.[77] Much about that time, even in our King *Richard* the Second's days, *John Trevisa* translated them into *English*, and many *English* Bibles in written hand are yet to be seen with divers; translated, as it is very probable, in that age. So the *Syrian* translation of the New Testament is in most learned men's libraries, of *Widminstadius* his setting forth; and the Psalter in *Arabic* is with many, of *Augustinus Nebiensis*' setting forth. So *Postel* affirmeth, that in his travel he saw the Gospels in the *Ethiopian* tongue: And *Ambrose Thesius* allegeth the Psalter of the *Indians*, which he testifieth to have been set forth by *Potken* in *Syrian* characters. So that to have the Scriptures in the mother tongue is not a quaint conceit lately taken up, either by the Lord *Cromwell* in *England*,[78] or by the Lord *Radevile* in *Poland*, or by the Lord *Ungnadius in* the Emperor's dominion, but hath been thought upon, and put in practice of old, even from the first times of the conversion of any nation; no doubt, because it was esteemed most profitable to cause faith to grow in men's hearts the sooner, and to make them to be able to say with the words of the Psalm, *As we have heard, so we have seen*.[79]

Now the church of *Rome* would seem at the length to bear a motherly affection towards her children, and to allow them the Scriptures in their mother tongue: but indeed it is a gift, not deserving to be called a gift, an unprofitable gift:[80] they must first get a license in writing before they may use them; and to get that, they must approve themselves to their Confessor, that is, to be such as are, if not frozen in the dregs, yet soured with the leaven of their superstition. Howbeit it seemed too much to *Clement* the Eighth, that there should be any license granted to have them in the vulgar

66   St. Jerome, *Preface to Sophronius on the Psalms*.

67   Sisto da Siena, *Biblioteca Sancta*, Bk 4.

68   Alfonso de Castro, *Adversus omnes haereses* ("Against All Heresies"), 1.13.

69   St. Chrysostom, *Homilies on the Gospel According to St. John* 2.2.

70   Theodoret of Cyrrhus, *Graecarum affectionem curatio* 5.66.

71   Paulus Diaconus, *Historia miscella* 12.

72   Joannes Vassaeus, *Rerum Hispaniae memorabilium annales*.

73   *Editor's Note:* King Alfred the Great (848–99) was king of the West Saxons from 871 onward; he was a diligent translator and patron of learning during his reign. The Venerable Bede (673–735) was an English monk and scholar who is famous for writing a Latin history of England from Julius Caesar's day until his own.

74   Polydor Vergil, *Anglicae Historiae Libri* XXVI.5.

75   Aventinus, *Annales Boiorum* 4.

76   Around the year 900. Beatus Rhenanus, *Rerum Germanicarum* 2.

77   Beroaldus, *Chronicum Scripturae sacrae* 4.8.

78   *Editor's Note:* Thomas Cromwell, Earl of Essex (c. 1485–1540) was an important figure in the printing of English Bibles under Henry VIII. Likewise, Mikolaj Radziwill and Baron Ungnad were sponsors of Bible translations into Polish and other Slavic languages.

79   Psalms 48:8.

80   Adapted from Sophocles, *Ajax* 655.

tongue, and therefore he overruleth and frustrateth the grant of *Pius* the Fourth.[81] So much are they afraid of the light of the Scripture, (*Lucifugae Scripturarum,*[82] as *Tertullian* speaketh,) that they will not trust the people with it, no not as it is set forth by their own sworn men, no not with the license of their own Bishops and Inquisitors. Yea, so unwilling they are to communicate the Scriptures to the people's understanding in any sort, that they are not ashamed to confess, that we forced them to translate it into *English* against their wills. This seemeth to argue a bad cause, or a bad conscience, or both. Sure we are, that it is not he that hath good gold, that is afraid to bring it to the touchstone, but he that hath the counterfeit; neither is it the true man that shunneth the light, but the malefactor, lest his deeds should be reproved;[83] neither is it the plain-dealing merchant that is unwilling to have the weights, or the meteyard,[84] brought in place, but he that useth deceit. But we will let them alone for this fault, and return to translation.

Many men's mouths have been open a good while (and yet are not stopped) with speeches about the translation so long in hand, or rather perusals of translations made before: and ask what may be the reason, what the necessity of the employment. Hath the Church been deceived, say they, all this while? Hath her sweet bread been mingled with leaven, her silver with dross, her wine with water, her milk with lime? (*lacte gypsum male miscetur,* saith St. *Irenaeus.*)[85] We hoped that we had been in the right way, that we had the Oracles of God delivered unto us, and that though all the world had cause to be offended, and to complain, yet that we had none. Hath the nurse holden out the breast, and nothing but wind in it? Hath the bread been delivered by the Fathers of the Church, and the same proved to be *lapidosus,* as Seneca speaketh?[86] What is it to handle the word of God deceitfully, if this be not? Thus certain brethren. Also the adversaries of *Judah* and *Jerusalem,* like *Sanballat* in *Nehemiah,* mock, as we hear, both at the work and the workmen, saying, *What do these weak Jews, etc. will they make the stones whole again out of the heaps of dust which are burnt? although they build, yet if a fox go up, he shall even break down their stony wall.*[87] Was their translation good before? Why do they now mend it? Was it not good? Why then was it obtruded to the people? Yea, why did the Catholics (meaning Popish *Romanists*) always go in jeopardy for refusing to go to hear it? Nay, if it must be translated into *English,* Catholics are fittest to do it. They have learning, and they know when a thing is well, they can *manum de tabula.*[88] We will answer them both briefly: and the former, being brethren, thus, with St. *Jerome, Damnamus veteres? Minime, sed post priorum studia in domo Domini quod possumus laboramus.*[89] That is, *Do we condemn the ancient? In no case: but after the endeavours of them that were before us, we take the best pains we can in the house of God.* As if he said, Being provoked by the example of the learned that lived before my time, I have thought it my duty to assay, whether my talent in the knowledge of the tongues may be profitable in any measure to God's Church, lest I should seem to have laboured in them in vain, and lest I should be thought to glory in men (although ancient) above that which was in them. Thus St. *Jerome* may be thought to speak.

And to the same effect say we, that we are so far off from condemning any of their labours that travailed before us in this kind, either in this land, or beyond sea, either in King *Henry's* time, or King *Edward's,* (if there were any translation, or correction of a translation in his time,) or Queen *Elizabeth's* of ever-renowned memory, that we acknowledge them to have been raised up of God for the building and furnishing of his Church, and that they deserve to be had of us and of posterity in everlasting remembrance.[90] The judgement of *Aristotle* is worthy and well known: *If Timotheus had not been, we had not had much sweet music: but if Phrynis* (Timotheus his master) *had not been, we had not had Timotheus.*[91] Therefore blessed be they, and most honoured be their name, that break

81 See the observation (set forth by Clement VIII's authority) upon the fourth rule of Pius IV's making in the *Index librorum prohibitorum.* *Editor's Note:* the Catholic Church's list of forbidden books is still commonly known as "the Index."

82 "running away from the light of the Scriptures"; Tertullian, *De resurrectione mortuorum* 47.

83 John 3:20.

84 *Editor's Note:* yard-stick.

85 St. Irenaeus, *Contra haereses* 3.17.4.

86 "stony"; Seneca, *De beneficiis* 1.5.91.

87 Nehemiah 4:3.

88 "hands off the tablet."

89 St. Jerome, *Contra Rufinum* 2.25.

90 *Editor's Note:* This paragraph is intended to answer the objections of the English Puritans, who called for a new translation of the Bible at the Hampton Court Conference of 1604. See note 99.

91 Aristotle, *Metaphysics* 2.1.4.

the ice, and giveth onset upon that which helpeth forward to the saving of souls. Now what can be more available thereto, than to deliver God's book unto God's people in a tongue which they understand? Since of an hidden treasure, and of a fountain that is sealed, there is no profit, as *Ptolemy Philadelph* wrote to the Rabbins or masters of the *Jews*, as witnesseth *Epiphanius*:[92] and as St. *Augustine* saith, *A man had rather be with his dog than with a stranger* (whose tongue is strange unto him).[93] Yet for all that, as nothing is begun and perfected at the same time, and the latter thoughts are thought to be the wiser: so, if we building upon their foundation that went before us, and being holpen by their labours, do endeavour to make that better which they left so good; no man, we are sure, hath cause to mislike us; they, we persuade ourselves, if they were alive, would thank us. The vintage of *Abiezer*, that strake the stroke: yet the gleaning of grapes of *Ephraim* was not to be despised. See *Judges* 8:2. *Joash* the king of *Israel* did not satisfy himself till he had smitten the ground three times; and yet he offended the Prophet for giving over then.[94] *Aquila*, of whom we spake before, translated the Bible as carefully, and as skillfully as he could; and yet he thought good to go over it again, and then it got the credit with the *Jews*, to be called κατ' ακριβειαν, that is, accurately, done, as *St. Jerome* witnesseth.[95] How many books of profane learning have been gone over again and again, by the same translators, by others? Of one and the same book of *Aristotle's* Ethics, there are extant not so few as six or seven several translations. Now if this cost may be bestowed upon the gourd, which affordeth us a little shade, and which today flourisheth, but tomorrow is cut down; what may we bestow, nay, what ought we not to bestow, upon the vine, the fruit whereof maketh glad the conscience of man, and the stem whereof abideth forever? And this is the word of God, which we translate. *What is the chaff to the wheat, saith the Lord?*[96] *Tanti vitreum, quanti verum margaritum!* (saith *Tertullian.*)[97] If a toy of glass be of that reckoning with us, how ought we to value the true pearl! Therefore let no man's eye be evil, because his Majesty's is good; neither let any be grieved, that we have a Prince that seeketh the increase of the spiritual wealth of *Israel*; (let *Sanballats* and *Tobiahs*[98] do so, which therefore do bear their just reproof;) but let us rather bless God from the ground of our heart for working this religious care in him to have the translations of the Bible maturely considered of and examined. For by this means it cometh to pass, that whatsoever is sound already, (and all is sound for substance, in one or other of our editions, and the worst of ours far better than their authentic vulgar) the same will shine as gold more brightly, being rubbed and polished; also, if anything be halting, or superfluous, or not so agreeable to the original, the same may be corrected, and the truth set in place. And what can the King command to be done, that will bring him more true honour than this? And wherein could they that have been set a work, approve their duty to the King, yea, their obedience to God, and love to his Saints, more, than by yielding their service, and all that is within them, for the furnishing of the work? But besides all this, they were the principal motives of it, and therefore ought least to quarrel it. For the very historical truth is, that upon the importunate petitions of the Puritans at his Majesty's coming to this crown, the conference at *Hampton Court* having been appointed for hearing their complaints,[99] when by force of reason they were put from other grounds, they had recourse at the last to this shift, that they could not with good conscience subscribe to the communion book, since it maintained the Bible as it was there translated, which was, as they said, a most corrupted translation. And although this was judged to be but a very poor and empty shift, yet even hereupon did his Majesty begin to bethink himself of the good that might ensue by a new translation, and presently after gave order for this translation which is now presented unto thee. Thus much to satisfy our scrupulous brethren.[100]

92 Epiphanius, *De mensuris et ponderibus* 11.

93 St. Augustine, *De civitate Dei* ("The City of God") 19.7.

94 2 Kings 13:18–19.

95 St. Jerome, *Commentarii in Ezechielem* 3.15.

96 Jeremiah 23:28.

97 Tertullian, *Ad martyras* 4.9. Jerome, *Ad Salvinam.*

98 *Editor's Note:* See Nehemiah 4:1–3.

99 *Editor's Note:* the Hampton Court Conference was held in 1604, soon after King James I ascended the throne of England. Its purpose was to hear out and settle points of contention between the episcopal majority of the Church of England and the Puritans, who wanted more reforms enacted. It was at this conference that James decided to order the new translation of the Bible that became the Authorized Version.

100 "Scrupulous brethren" was a phrase which would have immediately connoted Puritanism to a 17th-century English reader.

Now to the latter we answer,[101] That we do not deny, nay we affirm and avow, that the very meanest translation of the Bible in *English*, set forth by men of our profession, (for we have seen none of theirs of the whole Bible as yet) containeth the word of God, nay, is the word of God: As the King's speech which he uttereth in Parliament, being translated into *French, Dutch, Italian*, and *Latin*, is still the King's speech, though it be not interpreted by every translator with the like grace, nor peradventure so fitly for phrase, nor so expressly for sense, everywhere. For it is confessed, that things are to take their denomination of the greater part; and a natural man could say, *Verum ubi multa nitent in carmine, non ego paucis offendor maculis, etc.*[102] A man may be counted a virtuous man, though he have made many slips in his life, (else, there were none virtuous, for *in many things we offend all*,)[103] also a comely man and lovely, though he have some warts upon his hand; yea, not only freckles upon his face, but also scars. No cause therefore why the word translated should be denied to be the word, or forbidden to be current, notwithstanding that some imperfections and blemishes may be noted in the setting forth of it. For whatever was perfect under the sun, where Apostles or apostolic men, that is, men endued with an extraordinary measure of God's Spirit, and privileged with the privilege of infallibility, had not their hand? The Romanists therefore in refusing to hear, and daring to burn the word translated, did no less than despite the Spirit of grace, from whom originally it proceeded, and whose sense and meaning, as well as man's weakness would enable, it did express. Judge by an example or two. *Plutarch* writeth, that after that *Rome* had been burnt by the *Gauls*, they fell soon to build it again: but doing it in haste, they did not cast the streets, nor proportion the houses in such comely fashion, as had been most slightly and convenient.[104] Was Catiline[105] therefore an honest man, or a good patriot, that sought to bring it to a combustion? Or *Nero*[106] a good Prince, that did indeed set it on fire? So by the story of *Ezra*, and the prophecy of *Haggai* it may be gathered, that the temple built by *Zerubbabel* after the return from *Babylon* was by no means to be compared to the former built by *Solomon:* for they that remembered the former wept when they considered the latter.[107] Notwithstanding might this latter either have been abhorred and forsaken by the *Jews*, or profaned by the *Greeks?* The like we are to think of translations. The translation of the *Seventy* dissenteth from the Original in many places, neither doth it come near it, for perspicuity, gravity, majesty. Yet which of the Apostles did condemn it? Condemn it? Nay, they used it, (as it is apparent, and as St. *Jerome* and most learned men do confess;) which they would not have done, nor by their example of using it so grace and commend it to the Church, if it had been unworthy of the appellation and name of the word of God. And whereas they urge for their second defence of their vilifying and abusing of the *English* Bibles, or some pieces thereof, which they meet with, for that heretics forsooth were the authors of the translations: heretics they call us by the same right that they call themselves Catholics, both being wrong:) we marvel what divinity taught them so. We are sure *Tertullian* was of another mind: *Ex personis probamus fidem, an ex fide personas?*[108] Do we try men's faith by their persons? We should try their persons by their faith. Also St. *Augustine* was of another mind: for he, lighting upon certain rules made by *Tychonius* a *Donatist*[109] for the better understanding of the word, was not ashamed to make use of them, yea, to insert them into his own book, with giving commendation to them so far forth as they were worthy to be commended, as is to be seen in St. *Augustine*'s third book *De doctrina Christiana.*[110] To be short, *Origen*, and the whole Church of God for certain hundred years, were of another mind: for they were so far from treading under foot (much more from burning) the translation of *Aquila* a proselyte, that is, one that had turned *Jew*, of *Symmachus*, and *Theodotion*, both *Ebionites*,[111]

---

101   *Editor's Note*: This paragraph is aimed at the objections to vernacular translations by those English Catholics who had fled into exile on the Continent because of persecution under Protestant English monarchs.

102   Horace, *Ars poetica* ("On the Art of Poetry").

103   James 3:2.

104   Plutarch, *Camillus* 32.3.

105   *Editor's Note*: See gazetteer.

106   *Editor's Note*: The Roman emperor Nero (ruled AD 54–68) was reputed to have started a disastrous fire, which destroyed half of the city in AD 64. The story is probably false.

107   Ezra 3:12.

108   Tertullian, *De praescriptione haereticorum* 3.15.

109   *Editor's Note*: The Donatists were a group of 4th-century African Christians who separated from the main body of the Catholic Church. St. Augustine wrote many treatises against their beliefs.

110   St. Augustine, *De doctrina Christiana* 3.30.

111   *Editor's Note*: A sect of Jewish Christians who held unorthodox views on several doctrinal points.

that is, most vile heretics, that they joined together with the *Hebrew* original, and the translation
of the *Seventy* (as hath been before signified out of *Epiphanius*,) and set them forth openly to be considered of and perused by all. But we weary the unlearned, who need not know so much: and trouble
the learned, who know it already.

Yet before we end, we must answer a third cavil and objection of theirs against us, for altering
and amending our translations so oft; wherein truly they deal hardly, and strangely with us. For to
whomever was it imputed for a fault, (by such as were wise,) to go over that which he had done,
and to amend it where he saw cause? St. *Augustine* was not afraid to exhort St. *Jerome* to a *Palinodia*
or recantation.[112] The same St. *Augustine* was not ashamed to retractate, we might say revoke, many
things that had passed him, and doth even glory that he seeth his infirmities.[113] If we will be sons
of the truth, we must consider what it speaketh, and trample upon our own credit, yea, and upon
other men's too, if either be any way an hindrance to it. This to the cause. Then to the persons we
say, that of all men they ought to be most silent in this case. For what varieties have they, and what
alterations have they made, not only of their service books, portesses, and breviaries,[114] but also of
their *Latin* translation? The service book supposed to be made by St. *Ambrose*, (*Officium
Ambrosianum*,) was a great while in special use and request: but Pope *Hadrian* calling a council with
the aid of *Charles* the Emperor, abolished it, yea, burnt it, and commanded the service book of St.
Gregory universally to be used.[115] Well, *Officium Gregorianum* gets by this means to be in credit; but
doth it continue without change or altering? No, the very *Roman* service was of two fashions; the
new fashion, and the old, the one used in one Church, the other in another; as is to be seen in
Pamelius a Romanist, his preface before *Micrologus*.[116] The same *Pamelius* reporteth out *Radulphus de
Rivo*, that about the year of our Lord 1277 Pope *Nicholas* the Third removed out of the churches
of *Rome* the more ancient books (of service) and brought into use the missals of the Friars Minorites,
and commanded them to be observed there; insomuch that about an hundred years after, when the
above-named *Radulphus* happened to be at *Rome*, he found all the books to be new, of the new stamp.
Neither was there this chopping and changing in the more ancient times only, but also of late. *Pius
Quintus* himself confesseth, that every bishopric almost had a peculiar kind of service, most unlike
to that which others had; which moved him to abolish all other breviaries, though never so ancient,
and privileged and published by Bishops in their Dioceses, and to establish and ratify that only
which was of his own setting forth in the year 1568. Now when the Father of their Church, who
gladly would heal the sore of the daughter of his people softly and sleightly, and make the best of
it, findeth so great fault with them for their odds and jarring; we hope the children have no great
cause to vaunt of their uniformity. But the difference that appeareth between our translations, and
our often correcting of them, is the thing that we are specially charged with; let us see therefore
whether they themselves be without fault this way, (if it be to be counted a fault, to correct,) and
whether they be fit men to throw stones at us: *O tandem maior parcas insane minori*: They that are
less sound themselves, ought not to object infirmities to others.[117] If we should tell them that *Valla*,
Stapulensis, *Erasmus*, and *Vives*,[118] found fault with their vulgar translation, and consequently wished
the same to be mended, or a new one to be made; they would answer peradventure, that we produced their enemies for witnesses against them; albeit, they were in no other sort enemies, than as
St. *Paul* was to the *Galatians*, for telling them the truth:[119] and it were to be wished, that they had
dared to tell it them plainlier and oftener. But what will they say to this, That Pope *Leo* the Tenth
allowed *Erasmus'* translation of the New Testament, so much different from the vulgar, by his apostolic letter and bull? That the same *Leo* exhorted *Pagnine* to translate the whole Bible, and bare
whatsoever charges was necessary for the work?[120] Surely, as the apostle reasoneth to the *Hebrews*,

112   St. Augustine, *Epistles* 40.7.

113   St. Augustine, *Retractiones* ("Reconsiderations").

114   *Editor's Note*: In the Roman Catholic church, a breviary is "the
book containing the 'Divine Office' for each day, which those who are
in orders are bound to recite" (*OED*); a "portess" is a portable breviary.

115   Guillaume Durand, *Rationale divinorum officiorum* 5.2.

116   *Editor's Note*: Jacques de Joigny de Pamèle, *Micrologus de ecclesiasticus observationibus* (1565).

117   Horace, *Satires* 2.3.326.

118   *Editor's Note*: Lorenzo Valla, "Stapulensis" (Jacques Lefèvre
d'Etaples), Desiderius Erasmus, and Juan Luis Vives were all Catholic
humanist scholars who either criticized the Vulgate Bible as inaccurate
or advocated vernacular learning.

119   Galatians 4:16.

120   Sisto da Siena, *Bibliotheca Sancta*. *Editor's Note*: Santes Pagnini, an
Italian language scholar, produced a Latin translation of the Bible that
was published in 1528. As Smith asserts, he was supported in his work
by Pope Leo X.

that *if the former Law and Testament had been sufficient, there had been no need of the latter:*[121] so we may say, that if the old vulgar had been at all points allowable, to small purpose had labour and charges been undergone about framing of a new. If they say, it was one Pope's private opinion, and that he consulted only himself; then we are able to go further with them, and to aver, that more of their chief men of all sorts, even their own *Trent* champions,[122] *Paiva* and *Vega*, and their own inquisitor *Hieronymus ab Oleastro*, and their own Bishop *Isidorus Clarius*, and their own Cardinal *Thomas a Vio Cajetan*, do either make new translations themselves, or follow new ones of other men's making, or note the vulgar interpreter for halting, none of them fear to dissent from him, nor yet to except against him. And call they this an uniform tenor of text and judgement about the text, so many of their worthies disclaiming the now received conceit? Nay, we will yet come nearer the quick. Doth not their *Paris* edition differ from the *Louvain*, and *Hentenius* his from them both, and yet all of them allowed by authority? Nay, doth not *Sixtus Quintus* confess, that certain Catholics (he meaneth certain of his own side) were in such an humour of trans*Lating* the Scriptures into *Latin*, that Satan taking occasion by them, though they thought of no such matter, did strive what he could, out of so uncertain and manifold a variety of translations, so to mingle all things, that nothing might seem to be left certain and firm in them, etc.?[123] Nay further, did not the same *Sixtus* ordain by an inviolable decree, and that with the counsel and consent of his Cardinals, that the *Latin* edition of the Old and New Testament, which the Council of *Trent* would have to be authentic, is the same without controversy which he then set forth, being diligently corrected and printed in the printing-house of *Vatican?* Thus *Sixtus* in his preface before his Bible. And yet *Clement* the Eighth, his immediate successor, publisheth another edition of the Bible, containing in it infinite differences from that of *Sixtus*, and many of them weighty and material; and yet this must be authentic by all means. What is to have the faith of our glorious Lord *Jesus Christ* with yea and nay, if this be not? Again, what is sweet harmony and consent, if this be? Therefore, as *Demaratus* of *Corinth* advised a great King, before he talked of the dissensions among the *Grecians*, to compose his domestic broils; (for at that time his Queen and his son and heir were at deadly feud with him)[124] so all the while that our adversaries do make so many and so various editions themselves, and do jar so much about the worth and authority of them, they can with no show of equity challenge us for changing and correcting.

But it is high time to leave them, and to show in brief what we proposed to ourselves, and what course we held in this our perusal and survey of the Bible. Truly, good Christian Reader, we never thought from the beginning, that we should need to make a new translation, nor yet to make of a bad one a good one; (for then the imputation of *Sixtus* had been true in some sort, that our people had been fed with gall of dragons instead of wine, with whey instead of milk;) but to make a good one better, or out of many good ones one principal good one, not justly to be excepted against; that hath been our endeavour, that our mark. To that purpose there were many chosen, that were greater in other men's eyes than in their own, and that sought the truth rather than their own praise. Again, they came, or were thought to come, to the work, not *exercendi causa*, (as one saith,) but *exercitati*, that is, learned, not to learn; for the chief overseer and εργοδιωκτης[125] under his Majesty, to whom not only we, but also our whole Church was much bound, knew by his wisdom, which thing also *Nazianzen* taught so long ago, that it is a preposterous order to teach first, and to learn after, yea that τὸ εν πιθω κεραμιαν μανθανειν[126] to learn and practice together, is neither commendable for the workman, nor safe for the work.[127] Therefore such were thought upon, as could say modestly with St. *Jerome, Et Hebreaeum sermonem ex parte didicimus, et in Latino pene ab ipsis incunabulis etc. detriti sumus; Both we have learned the Hebrew tongue in part, and in the Latin we have been exercised almost from our very cradle.* St. *Jerome* maketh no mention of the *Greek* tongue, wherein

---

121   Heb. 7:11 and 8:7.

122   *Editor's Note*: The Council of Trent was an ecumenical council of the Catholic Church which met from December 1545 to December 1563 at Trento in northern Italy. Its main object was to determine the Church's response to the rise of Protestantism.

123   Sixtus Quintus, preface to *Biblia Sacra Vulgatae* (1590).

124   *Editor's Note*: Demaratus of Corinth was an advisor to Philip II of Macedon (father of Alexander the Great); this story is retold in Plutarch, *Alexander* 9.5 and 12–14.

125   "taskmaster."

126   *Editor's Note*: The Greek phrase is glossed by the English phrase immediately following.

127   Gregory of Nazianzus, *Orationes* ("Orations") 2.47.

yet he did excel; because he translated not the Old Testament out of *Greek*, but out of *Hebrew*. And in what sort did these assemble? In the trust of their own knowledge, or of their sharpness of wit, or deepness of judgement, as it were in an arm of flesh? At no hand. They trusted in him that hath the key of *David*, opening, and no man shutting; they prayed to the Lord, the Father of our Lord, to the effect that St. *Augustine* did; *O let thy Scriptures be my pure delight; let me not be deceived in them, neither let me deceive by them.*[128] In this confidence, and with this devotion, did they assemble together; not too many, lest one should trouble another; and yet many, lest many things haply might escape them. If you ask what they had before them; truly it was the *Hebrew* text of the Old Testament, the *Greek* of the New. These are the two golden pipes, or rather conduits, where-through the olive branches empty themselves into the gold. St. *Augustine* calleth them precedent, or original tongues;[129] St. *Jerome*, fountains.[130] The same St. *Jerome* affirmeth,[131] and Gratian hath not spared to put it into his decree, That *as the credit of the old Books* (he meaneth of the Old Testament) *is to be tried by the Hebrew Volumes; so of the New by the Greek tongue*, he meaneth by the original *Greek*. If truth be to be tried by these tongues, then whence should a translation be made, but out of them? These tongues therefore (the Scriptures, we say, in those tongues) we set before us to translate, being the tongues wherein God was pleased to speak to his Church by his Prophets and Apostles. Neither did we run over the work with that posting haste that the *Septuagint* did, if that be true which is reported of them, that they finished it in seventy-two days;[132] neither were we barred or hindered from going over it again, having once done it, like St. *Jerome*, if that be true which himself reporteth, that he could no sooner write anything, but presently it was caught from him, and published, and he could not have leave to mend it:[133] neither, to be short, were we the first that fell in hand with translating the Scripture into *English*, and consequently destitute of former helps, as it is written of *Origen*, that he was the first in a manner, that put his hand to write commentaries upon the Scriptures, and therefore no marvel if he overshot himself many times. None of these things: The work hath not been huddled up in seventy-two days, but hath cost the workmen, as light as it seemeth, the pains of twice seven times seventy-two days, and more. Matters of such weight and consequence are to be speeded with maturity: for in a business of moment a man feareth not the blame of convenient slackness.[134] Neither did we think much to consult the translators or commentators, *Chaldee, Hebrew, Syrian, Greek* or *Latin*, no, nor the *Spanish, French, Italian*, or *Dutch*; neither did we disdain to revise that which we had done, and to bring back to the anvil that which we had hammered: but having and using as great helps as were needful, and fearing no reproach for slowness, nor coveting praise for expedition, we have at length, through the good hand of the Lord upon us, brought the work to that pass that you see.

Some peradventure would have no variety of senses to be set in the margin,[135] lest the authority of the Scriptures for deciding of controversies by that show of uncertainty, should somewhat be shaken. But we hold their judgement not to be sound in this point. For though *whatsoever things are necessary are manifest*, as St. *Chrysostom* saith;[136] and as St. *Augustine, in those things that are plainly set down in the Scriptures, all such matters are found, that concern faith, hope, and charity*:[137] Yet for all that it cannot be dissembled, that partly to exercise and whet our wits, partly to wean the curious from the loathing of them for their everywhere-plainness, partly also to stir up our devotion to crave the assistance of God's Spirit by prayer, and lastly, that we might be forward to seek aid of our brethren by conference, and never scorn those that be not in all respects so complete as they should be, being to seek in many things ourselves, it hath pleased God in his Divine Providence here and there to scatter words and sentences of that difficulty and doubtfulness, not in doctrinal

128   St. Augustine, *Confessions*, 11.2.3.

129   St. Augustine, *On Christian Doctrine* 3.3.7.

130   St. Jerome, *Epistles* 106.2.3 ("To Sunnia and Fretella").

131   St. Jerome, *Epistles* 71.5 ("To Lucinius"). *Editor's Note*: the *Decretum Gratiani* ("Decree of Gratian") was a 12th-century collection of Canon Law.

132   Josephus, *Jewish Antiquities*, 12.

133   St. Jerome, Epistles 48.2 ("To Pammachius").

134   See Sophocles, *Electra* 320.

135   *Editor's Note*: This refers to the translators' practice of listing alternative translations for doubtful words or phrases in the margins of the text. As this passage makes clear, this was as much a political as a scholarly decision.

136   St. John Chrysostom, *Homilies on the Epistle of St. Paul to the Thessalonians* 2.3.

137   St. Augustine, *On Christian Doctrine*, 2.9.14.

points that concern salvation, (for in such it hath been vouched that the Scriptures are plain,) but in matters of less moment, that fearfulness would better beseem us than confidence, and if we will resolve upon modesty with St. *Augustine*, (though not in this same case altogether, yet upon the same ground,) *Melius est dubitare de occultis, quam litigare de incertis:*[138] It is better to make doubt of those things which are secret, than to strive about those things that are uncertain. There be many words in the Scriptures, which be never found there but once, (having neither brother nor neighbour, as the *Hebrews* speak,) so that we cannot be holpen by conference of places. Again, there be many rare names of certain birds, beasts, and precious stones, etc. concerning which the *Hebrews* themselves are so divided among themselves for judgement, that they may seem to have defined this or that, rather because they would say something, than because they were sure of that which they said, as St. *Jerome* somewhere saith of the *Septuagint.* Now in such a case doth not a margin do well to admonish the Reader to seek further, and not to conclude or dogmatize upon this or that peremptorily? For as it is a fault of incredulity, to doubt of those things that are evident; so to determine of such things as the Spirit of God hath left (even in the judgement of the judicious) questionable, can be no less than presumption. Therefore as St. *Augustine* saith, that variety of translations is profitable for the finding out of the sense of the Scriptures:[139] so diversity of signification and sense in the margin, where the text is not so clear, must needs do good; yea, is necessary, as we are persuaded. We know that *Sixtus Quintus* expressly forbiddeth that any variety of readings of their vulgar edition should be put in the margin,[140] (which though it be not altogether the same thing to that we have in hand, yet it looketh that way;) but we think he hath not all of his own side his favourers for this conceit. They that are wise had rather have their judgements at liberty in differences of readings, than to be captivated to one, when it may be the other. If they were sure that their high priest had all laws shut up in his breast, as *Paul* the Second bragged,[141] and that he were as free from error by special privilege, as the dictators of *Rome* were made by law inviolable, it were another matter; then his word were an oracle, his opinion a decision. But the eyes of the world are now open, God be thanked, and have been a great while; they find that he is subject to the same affections and infirmities that others be, that his skin is penetrable; and therefore so much as he proveth, not as much as he claimeth, they grant and embrace.

Another thing we think good to admonish thee of, gentle Reader, that we have not tied ourselves to an uniformity of phrasing, or to an identity of words, as some peradventure would wish that we had done, because they observe, that some learned men somewhere have been as exact as they could that way. Truly, that we might not vary from the sense of that which we had translated before, if the word signified that same in both places, (for there be some words that be not the same sense everywhere,) we were especially careful, and made a conscience, according to our duty. But that we should express the same notion in the same particular word; as for example, if we translate the *Hebrew* or *Greek* word once by *purpose*, never to call it *intent*; if one where *journeying*, never *travelling*; if one where *think*, never *suppose*; if one where *pain*, never *ache*; if one where joy, never *gladness*, etc. thus to mince the matter, we thought to savour more of curiosity than wisdom, and that rather it would breed scorn in the atheist, than bring profit to the godly reader. For is the kingdom of God become words or syllables? Why should we be in bondage to them, if we may be free? use one precisely when we may use another no less fit as commodiously? A godly Father in the primitive time showed himself greatly moved, that one of newfangleness called κραββατον σκιμπους,[142] the difference be little or none; and another reporteth that he was much abused for turning *cucurbita* (to which reading the people had been used) into *hedera.*[143] Now if this happen in better times, and upon so small occasions, we might justly fear hard censure, if generally we should make verbal and unnecessary changings. We might also be charged (by scoffers) with some unequal dealing towards a great number of good *English* words. For as it is written of a certain great

---

138 St. Augustine, *De Genesi ad Litteram* 8.5.

139 St. Augustine, *On the Christian Doctrine*, 2:14.21.

140 Pope Sixtus V, preface to *Biblia Sacra Vulgatae* (1590).

141 Bartolomeo Sacchi or "Platina," *De vitis et moribus* . . .

142 Nicephorus Callistus, *Ecclesiastica historia* ("History of the Church") 8.42. *Editor's Note*: The two words in question both mean "bed."

143 St. Jerome, *Commentary on Jonah* 4.6; St. Augustine, *Epistles* 71.3.5.

Philosopher, that he should say, that those logs were happy that were made images to be worshipped; for their fellows, as good as they, lay for blocks behind the fire: so if we should say, as it were, unto certain words, Stand up higher, have a place in the Bible always; and to others of like quality, Get ye hence, be banished forever; we might be taxed peradventure with St. *James* his words, namely, *To be partial in ourselves and judges of evil thoughts.* Add hereunto, that niceness in words was always counted the next step to trifling; and so was to be curious about names too:[144] also that we cannot follow a better pattern for elocution than God himself; therefore he using divers words in his holy writ, and indifferently for one thing in nature: we, if we will not he superstitious, may use the same liberty in our *English* versions out of *Hebrew* and *Greek*, for that copia or store that he hath given us. Lastly, we have on the one side avoided the scrupulosity of the Puritans, who leave the old Ecclesiastical words, and betake them to other, as when they put *washing* for *baptism*, and *congregation* instead of *Church*: as also on the other side we have shunned the obscurity of the Papists, in their *azimes, tunike, rational, holocausts, praepuce, pasche,* and a number of such like, whereof their late translation is full, and that of purpose to darken the sense, that since they must needs translate the Bible, yet by the language thereof it may be kept from being understood.[145] But we desire that the Scripture may speak like itself, as in the language of *Canaan,* that it may be understood even of the very vulgar.

Many other things we might give thee warning of, gentle Reader, if we had not exceeded the measure of a preface already. It remaineth that we commend thee to God, and to the Spirit of his grace, which is able to build further than we can ask or think. He removeth the scales from our eyes, the veil from our hearts, opening our wits that we may understand his word, enlarging our hearts, yea, correcting our affections, that we may love it above gold and silver, yea, that we may love it to the end. Ye are brought unto fountains of living water which ye digged not; do not cast earth into them, with the Philistines, neither prefer broken pits before them, with the wicked Jews.[146] Others have laboured, and you may enter into their labours. O receive not so great things in vain: O despise not so great salvation. Be not like swine to tread under foot so precious things, neither yet like dogs to tear and abuse holy things. Say not to our Saviour with the *Gergesites,* Depart out of our coasts;[147] neither yet with *Esau* sell your birthright for a mess of pottage.[148] If light be come into the world, love not darkness more than light: if food, if clothing, be offered, go not naked, starve not yourselves. Remember the advice of *Nazianzene, It is a grievous thing* (or dangerous) *to neglect a great fair, and to seek to make markets afterwards:* also the encouragement of St. *Chrysostom, It is altogether impossible, that he that is sober (and watchful) should at any time be neglected:*[149] lastly, the admonition and menacing of St. *Augustine, They that despise God's will inviting them shall feel God's will taking vengeance of them.*[150] It is a fearful thing to fall into the hands of the living God;[151] but a blessed thing it is, and will bring us to everlasting blessedness in the end, when God speaketh unto us, to hearken; when he setteth his word before us, to read it; when he stretcheth out his hand and calleth, to answer, Here am I, here we are to do thy will, O God. The Lord work a care and conscience in us to know him and serve him, that we may be acknowledged of him at the appearing of our Lord JESUS CHRIST, to whom with the Holy Ghost be all praise and thanksgiving. Amen.

144 Eusebius, *Praeparatio Evangelica* 12.8. The original source is Plato, *Statesman* 261e.
145 *Editor's Note*: Smith is here referring to the ways in which translators from different Christian denominations inflected their translations to suit their own particular notions of Church organization and worship.
146 Gen. 26:15, Jer. 2:13.

147 Matt. 8:34.
148 Heb. 12:16.
149 St. John Chrysostom, *Homilies* 26.4.
150 *Editor's Note*: Smith attributes this phrase to St. Augustine, but subsequent scholarship has disproved this.
151 Heb. 10:31.

Gazetteer of Classical and Early Modern Names and Places

Achilles: a legendary ancient Greek warrior, son of the mortal King Peleus and the immortal sea-nymph Thetis. In Homer's *Iliad*, he is depicted as the most powerful hero on the Greek side in the Trojan War, and the whole poem is made to revolve around his anger at Agamemnon and refusal to fight. Achilles is an ambiguous figure in both Homer and later treatments of him: divinely blessed with tremendous courage and fighting skill, he is also selfish, self-indulgent, and prone to letting his emotions control him. As such, he embodies all the contradictions of the heroic way of life.

Actaeon: a mythical hunter who came upon the goddess Artemis/Diana while she was bathing; in her anger, she turned him into a stag and he was torn to pieces by his own hounds.

Adonis: a beautiful youth in Greek mythology, son of the king of Cyprus and his daughter, Myrrha. Ovid relates how the gods transformed Myrrha into a myrrh tree when the king was about to kill her, and how the baby Adonis emerged from the tree. The most commonly told myth about Adonis is that Aphrodite fell in love with him, but that he was killed while hunting wild boar. Out of his blood grew the flower anemone. Shakespeare retold this story in *Venus and Adonis*.

Aegis *see* Athena.

Aeneas: a Trojan hero who fled Troy at the end of the Trojan War with his father Anchises (his mother was the goddess Venus) and son Ascanius. He is the hero of Virgil's *Aeneid*, which relates his journey west to Italy and his mission to found the city which would later become Rome.

Aeneid: a 12-book epic poem by Virgil. In it, the Trojan hero Aeneas flees the destruction of his native Troy and journeys west to Italy. After many adventures during his voyage, numerous interventions by the gods, and a successful war against the inhabitants of Latium, he founds the city of Lavinium. The

founder of Rome, Romulus, was considered to be a distant descendant of Aeneas. Among the incidents in the text which have attracted the most attention from later writers and readers are Aeneas' narration of the fall of Troy (Book 2), his doomed love affair with Dido, the queen of Carthage (Book 4), and his journey to the Underworld with the help of the Sibyl of Cumae (Book 6). Although heavily indebted to Homer's texts as models, Virgil's epic moved away from the themes of martial heroism to explore the ideology of Rome's foundation and helped bring epic subject matter out of myth and into something like history.

Aeschylus (525–456 BC): ancient Greek tragic dramatist, and the earliest one whose work survives. His plays include *The Persians*, *The Seven Against Thebes*, *The Suppliants*, and, most famously, the three plays that have come to be known as the *Oresteia*: *Agamemnon*, *The Libation Bearers*, and *Eumenides* ("the Kindly Ones"). These plays relate the murder of King Agamemnon by his wife Clytemnestra and her lover Aegisthus after the king returns home to Argos. His son Orestes returns to Argos in the second play and kills his mother and her lover (having been commanded to do so by the Oracle at Delphi). The third play finds Orestes in the temple of Athena in Athens, having been pursued there by the Furies. Orestes is tried and acquitted for the crime of killing his mother, and the indignant Furies are mollified by the promise of a place of honor in Athenian society. The trilogy as a whole is read as a representation of the movement from clan-based vendettas to an organized, impartial form of justice.

Aesop: the legendary Greek author of a collection of fables (most involving anthropomorphized animals) which began to be attributed to him in the fifth century BCE. The stories were very well known and frequently retold in Early Modern Europe. The surviving accounts of Aesop's life are clearly fanciful, and we cannot be sure about either his existence or his connection to the tales.

Agamemnon: in Greek legend and literature, especially Homer's *Iliad*, the King of Argos who led the Greek army against the city of Troy. His brother was Menelaus, King of Sparta. After his return home to Argos, he was murdered in his bath by his wife Clytemnestra and her lover Aegisthus.

Aganippe: a spring sacred to the Muses on Mt. Helicon.

Alcides: a common literary name for Hercules. It means "descendant of Alcaeus," who was Hercules' grandfather.

Alexander the Great (356–323 BC): King of Macedon and the greatest military conqueror of the ancient world. Expanding upon his father's (Philip II) control over Greece, he invaded Asia Minor in 334 BCE and spent most of the rest of his lifetime at war. He conquered all of the former Persian empire and ruled a territory from Macedonia to northern India. After his death, his generals carved it up into several successor kingdoms. His bravery and skill as a soldier were remarkable, but his reputation in later periods was compromised by his despotic and arbitrary mode of government and personal dissipation; he was admired and excoriated with equal strength. His tutor was the philosopher Aristotle, and he was a great admirer of literature, especially Homer.

Amphion: a mythical Greek poet, whose singing caused stones to move by themselves to form the walls of the city of Thebes.

Antonius, Marcus (*c.*83–31 BC): Roman statesman and general, better known as "Mark Antony." Along with Lepidus and Octavian (later the emperor Augustus), he became one of the triumvirs appointed to restore Rome in the aftermath of Caesar's assassination in 44 BCE. After ruthlessly eliminating their enemies, the three men fell out, leading to a civil war which ended with Octavian's defeat of Antony at the battle of Actium (31 BCE). Antony committed suicide soon after, and Octavian was left undisputed ruler of the empire. His relationship with Cleopatra, the queen of Egypt, with whom he had several children, cost him a lot of popular support in Rome.

Apelles: a fourth-century BCE Greek painter who was usually praised as the greatest exponent of his art in the ancient world. He painted Alexander the Great, who is said to have allowed no other artists to paint him. He is cited as a paragon of artistic skill by many Early Modern writers.

Aphrodite: (Latin, "Venus") goddess of love, beauty, and fertility, often symbolized by doves (who are sometimes represented pulling her chariot); she is strongly associated with the island of Cyprus, and is sometimes called "Cypris" or "the Cyprian" in literary texts. She is also named "Cythera" and associated with the town of Paphos. She is the mother of Eros (Latin, "Cupid"), who personifies physical desire, and of the mortal hero Aeneas (whom she bore to the mortal Anchises).

Apollo: (also called "Phoebus," which means "the bright") god of healing, prophecy, and music. He is the son of Zeus and the mortal Leto, the twin sister of Artemis, and is represented iconographically by the bow, the lyre, and the laurel tree (hence the laurel wreath as reward for poetic skill). He is also represented as the god of plagues and sometimes associated with the sun. His most important shrine was at Delphi, where the god killed the monster Python and where an oracle foretold the future (albeit in a cryptic message) to mortals. There are many myths surrounding this god.

Ares: (Latin, "Mars") god of war; his cult was not a popular one, and there are relatively few myths surrounding him. He is the son of Zeus and Hera. He was the lover of the goddess Aphrodite, and was trapped in bed with her by her husband Hephaestus who ensnared them in an invisible net.

Aristotle (384–322 BCE): ancient Greek philosopher from Stagira, who studied with Plato at the Academy until the latter's death, but evolved very different views from his former teacher. For several years, he was tutor to the future Alexander the Great of Macedonia. His numerous surviving works cover fields as diverse as logic, metaphysics, biology, natural history, ethics, politics, literature, and art. He was, beyond any dispute, the single most widely read and taught philosopher in medieval and Renaissance Europe, where he was often referred to simply as "the philosopher." His *Rhetoric* and, especially, *Poetics*, were enormously influential on Renaissance literary scholars and writers alike.

Atalanta: a mythical Greek huntress who was famous for her disinterest in marriage. Along with a prince named Meleager, who loved her, she killed the Calydonian boar. She was a famously swift runner, and promised to marry any man who could beat her in a race (in which the penalty for failure was death). She was defeated and married by Hippomenes who, advised by Aphrodite, dropped three golden apples in Atalanta's path during the race. By stopping to retrieve them, she lost.

Atlas: in Greek mythology, the Titan who holds up the heavens on his shoulders. In later literature, he therefore became a common symbol for anyone with an intolerable burden to bear. His brother was Prometheus.

Artemis: (Latin, "Diana") goddess of the hunt and of woodlands; she is also (rather paradoxically) a virgin and the goddess who helps women in childbirth. In her Latin incarnation as Diana, she is also associated with the moon. The best-known myth involving Artemis concerns the hunter Actaeon who, after surprising the goddess while she was bathing, was turned into a stag and devoured by his own hounds. Because she was born on Mt. Cynthus, she is sometimes called "Cynthia."

Athena: (Latin, "Minerva") also commonly called "Pallas," a virgin goddess associated with wisdom, war (in defence of the city that bears her name) and the city of Athens. In mythology, she sprang fully grown out of Zeus' forehead. In her role as a war god, she is frequently represented wearing the aegis (a garment or shield bearing the image of the gorgon's head).

Atreus: in ancient Greek myth, King of Argos and the father of Agamemnon and Menelaus. He served his brother Thyestes the flesh of his own children in a banquet, thus bringing a curse on his family that manifested itself for generations.

Bacchus: an alternate name, commonly used in Latin, for the god Dionysus.

Basilisk: an imaginary species of reptile with the power to kill by breathing on or merely looking at its prey.

Boccaccio (1313–75): Italian poet and prose writer, best known as the author of the vernacular story collection *The Decameron*.

Boethius (*c.*476–524): late Roman philosopher and politician whose most famous work, *The Consolation of Philosophy*, was composed while the author was in prison and was widely read in Early Modern Europe. It is a dialogue with Philosophy personified in a mixture of prose and poetry, and aims to justify divine providence (although not in explicitly Christian terms). He also produced philosophical works and translations. He was executed in prison.

Brutus, Lucius Junius (6th/5th century BC): in Roman tradition, the leader who encouraged the Romans to expel their kings, the Tarquin dynasty, after the murder of Lucretia (the Tarquins had also killed his brother). This story is retold in Shakespeare's *The Rape of Lucrece*, and Lucius became a symbol of republican liberty in opposition to corrupt monarchy. Marcus Junius Brutus, one of Caesar's assassins, claimed descent from him.

Brutus, Marcus Junius (*c.*85–42 BC): Roman statesman who conspired to assassinate Julius Caesar in 44 BCE in order to protect the Roman republic against Caesar's dictatorial ambitions. He is a leading character in Shakespeare's *Julius Caesar*, and he also features in several of Cicero's dialogues (one of which is named for him). Recent scholarship suggests that was not, in reality, the high-minded defender of tradition that Shakespeare portrays.

Cassandra: daughter of King Priam of Troy and his wife Hecuba. According to myth, the god Apollo was in love with her and tried to win her by offering any gift she wished. She asked for the gift of true prophecy, but when she still refused his love he added the curse that no-one would believe her prophecies. She was raped in the temple of Athena during the sack of Troy, and given to King Agamemnon as a prize. Upon his homecoming, she was killed with him by his wife Clytemnestra.

Catiline (died 62 BC): Lucius Sergius Catilina was a Roman politician who gained widespread support for his proposed economic reforms and support for the poor. When he was defeated in the consular elections, he organized a conspiracy to seize power by force that was thwarted by Cicero. For Early Modern Europe, he became the type of blind ambition and is represented as an unscrupulous demagogue who will do anything to gain power.

Cato "the Censor" (234–149 BC): an important Roman politician who was used in later literature as the type of severe, inflexible probity in public office. He is popularly supposed to have hated all things Greek until he learned the language in old age.

Caesar, Gaius Julius (100–44 BC): Roman general and politician, whose ambitions to become sole ruler of Republican Rome eventually alienated his fellow nobles and led to his assassination. He is one of the greatest generals in Western history, winning many battles against Rome's enemies and his fellow citizens in civil wars, and was also an accomplished orator. His ambition was limitless, and he was actually deified shortly before his death. Later judgments of him have had to reconcile his immense personal ability with the reality that he had no new ideas for governing Rome. The civil strife which his ambition began led ultimately to the establishment of the imperial system of government.

Centaur: a mythical beast with the head and torso of a man and the body of a horse. They were proverbially wild and lecherous. *See also* Lapiths and Centaurs.

Ceres: a Roman agricultural fertility goddess, who was identified with the Greek goddess Demeter.

Charybdis: in Greek myth, a whirlpool that threatens shipping in the Straits of Messina. Across the same strait lived the sea monster Scylla. Their most famous appearance in literature is in *Odyssey* 12, where they threaten Odysseus' ship.

Cicero, Marcus Tullius ("Tully") (106–43 BC): a Roman orator and statesman who served in many public offices in the Roman republic and was the greatest of the Roman orators. He published many rhetorical and philosophical works which were enormously influential in Early Modern Europe. Among them are *De oratore* ("On oratory"), a dialogue about the methods and motives of public speaking; *Brutus*, a history of Roman oratory; *Orator* ("The Orator"), a portrait of an accomplished speaker; *De finibus bonorum et malorum* ("On the supreme good and evil"); and the *Tusculan Disputations*, on views of happiness. His Latin prose was considered by many to be the finest in that language, and it was read and studied by almost every secondary school pupil in Renaissance Europe. He was a staunch defender of the Roman republic against the possibility of dictatorship; this led him to be a vigorous opponent of Julius Caesar, and he was executed by Mark Antony's soldiers in the civil strife following Caesar's assassination.

Clytemnestra: the wife of King Agamemnon of Argos. After Agamemnon was forced to sacrifice their daughter Iphigenia, Clytemnestra plotted revenge against her husband: upon his return from the Trojan War, she slaughtered him in his bath. She was in turn killed by her son, Orestes.

Cockatrice: an imaginary species of serpent that was supposed to be able to kill its prey by merely looking at it. Often confused with a basilisk (qv).

Constantine the Great (*c*.272–337): emperor of Rome who reunited the empire in 324 and ruled it until his death. He was the first Christian emperor (although he only formally converted on his deathbed), and proclaimed official tolerance for the Christian faith in 313; he also was a strong supporter of a unified Christian Church, and tried to encourage the eradication of heresies such as Arianism and Donatism. He founded the city of Constantinople (modern Istanbul) in 330.

Cronus: (Latin, "Saturn") the son of Uranus ("Heaven") and Gaia ("the Earth") and the leader of the Titans, the gods who preceded Zeus and the Olympians. He was married to his sister Rhea. The myths around Cronus center on a cycle of father–son violence. Uranus had fathered many children, but prevented many of them from being born. Cronus castrated him with a sickle, which released the rest of the Titans from within the Earth; the drops of his blood that hit the ground formed various monsters and his genital organs (which were thrown into the sea) produced a foam out of which emerged the goddess Aphrodite. Cronus, in turn, ate all of his children as they were born, knowing that one of them would supplant him. When Zeus was born, Rhea gave him a stone wrapped in a blanket instead of the baby, and Zeus eventually grew up to release his siblings from within his father's body and banish him and the Titans from heaven. Rather paradoxically given this violent history, Cronus' period of rule, after he supplanted Uranus, is often represented in poetry as a Golden Age, in which all of creation lived in harmony; no one needed to work, no one strove for wealth or power, and no laws were needed to discipline humanity. This ended when Zeus became the ruler of the gods.

Cupid: the son of Venus and Mars, and a Roman god of love in his own right, Cupid's name derives from the Latin word meaning "desire." He is represented as a small child with wings, a bow, and a quiver full of arrows. His golden-headed arrows cause those they hit to fall in love, while the lead-tipped ones inspire hatred. In classical and Early Modern literature, the sensation of falling instantly in love is often likened to being struck with Cupid's arrow. He is often represented as being mischievous, cruel, and unpredictable in his use of his powers. In English literature, he is sometimes referred to simply as "Love."

Cyclopes: a race of one-eyed giants in Greek mythology who appear, in various incarnations, in Homer (*Odyssey* 9), Theocritus, and Hesiod. Homer's cyclops is called Polyphemus, and is said to be a son of Poseidon; elsewhere, the cyclopes are depicted as the assistants of the god Hephaestus (qv).

Cynthia *see* Diana.

Cyrus the Great (died 530 BC): an emperor of ancient Persia, who, from his small inherited kingdom, conquered all of present-day Iran and much of central Asia and built the Persian empire. His idealized life story, told by the Greek historian Xenophon (*c*.428–*c*.354 BCE), made him the type of a just ruler for Early Modern Europe.

Danae: the daughter of a king of Argos who was imprisoned in a tower to prevent her from conceiving any children. Zeus came to her in the form of a golden shower and she bore a son, Perseus.

Daphne: in *Metamorphoses* 1, a mythical nymph who, pursued by the god Apollo, prayed to her river-god father to be saved. She was turned into a laurel tree. From that moment on, Apollo designated the laurel wreath as one of his personal symbols, and also as the sign of martial victory, celebration and poetic accomplishment.

Dante (1265–1321): Florentine poet and prose writer, best known for his long three-part poem the *Commedia* (*The Comedy*; known, after the seventeenth century, as *The Divine Comedy*). The poem describes Dante's poetic journey through hell (*Inferno*), purgatory (*Purgatorio*) and heaven (*Paradiso*). He is accompanied by the ghost of the poet Virgil for most of his journey, and together they encounter the souls of many famous dead people. Dante also wrote an early and important prose treatise in Latin on literature in the vernacular (*De vulgari eloquentia*) and the series of lyric poems known as the *Vita nuova* ("The New Life").

Delphi: a city in central Greece and the site of the Delphic Oracle, which was sacred to the god Apollo.

There, the priestess of Apollo provided prophecies to those who wished to know the future. Her answers were often indirect and difficult to comprehend. The oracle appears often in classical and Early Modern literature, most famously as the source of the prediction that Oedipus will kill his father and marry his mother.

Demeter: (Latin "Ceres") goddess of agriculture and the daughter of Cronus and Rhea. With Zeus, she had a daughter Persephone (Latin "Proserpina"), who was carried off to the Underworld to be the consort of Hades.

Destinies *see* The Fates.

Diana: the Roman goddess of the hunt who is conflated with the Greek goddess Artemis.

Dido: in Virgil's *Aeneid* 1–4, the queen of Carthage. She is made to fall in love with Aeneas by the goddess Venus and kills herself when he leaves her to found Rome. In Early Modern literature, she became a symbol for those victimized by an irresistible love.

Dionysus: (Latin "Bacchus") the god of wine, ecstasy, and (to some extent) the theater; he was the son of Zeus and a mortal woman, Semele. His symbols are a bunch of grapes and the *thyrsos* (a wooden rod topped with ivy leaves), and he is often represented riding a panther or tiger. Zeus' wife, Hera, tried to kill him in the womb by suggesting to his mother that she look at Zeus in all his glory (a sight no mortal could stand). Zeus rescued the unborn child and brought it to term in his thigh. There are many myths surrounding Dionysus, especially about his struggles to be recognized as a god by skeptical mortals. He is often accompanied by intoxicated followers both male (*bacchi*) and female (*bacchae* or maenads) who were prone to being violently destructive as well as joyful (see Orpheus).

Dis: one of the names given to the Roman god of the Underworld, who is conflated with the Greek Hades. The word is a contraction of "Dives," which means "wealth."

Echo: the most commonly told myth about a character with this name concerns a nymph who was punished by the goddess Hera for obstructing the latter's attempts to spy on her unfaithful husband, Zeus. Echo was made completely dumb, except for the ability to repeat the last word spoken to her by anyone else. She later fell in love with Narcissus and was transformed to an immaterial voice after he died.

Elysium: the mythical Islands of the Blest, where the gods sent certain heroes for a happy after-life instead of to the Underworld. In literature, they became a common classical analogue to the Christian heaven.

Erasmus, Desiderius (*c.*1467–1536): Dutch humanist scholar, editor, and writer. He is best known for his edition of the New Testament in Greek (1516), which was the first to apply humanist editing and textual principles to the scriptures; *The Praise of Folly*, a satire on dogmatic theology; several popular devotional manuals; and the great compendium of classical proverbs known as the *Adagia* (1500). While never a Protestant, Erasmus was keenly interested in reform of the Catholic Church. He was highly regarded as a scholar in his own day, and was viewed by subsequent eras as the prototypical humanist.

Eros: a Greek god of love, with whom the Roman Cupid was conflated.

Fates, The: The Fates were three ancient goddesses, sometimes called the "Destinies," who were thought to determine the length of human lives: one spun the thread of an individual life, one measured the length, and the third cut it. Often, they were depicted as having the power to determine all aspects of mortal existence.

Flora: an ancient Roman goddess of flowering plants. Her cult celebrations included sexually explicit dramas, and this made her into a symbol for lasciviousness for later writers.

Furies, The: in Greek mythology, three ancient spirits of revenge which appear to punish those who commit crimes against their own family; they also appeared to punish perjury and violations of the laws of hospitality. Their most important appearance in literature is in the *Eumenides* ("The Kindly Ones"), which is the last play in Aeschylus' group of plays known as the *Oresteia*. There, they appear to punish Orestes for the murder of his mother, but are propitiated by the offer of a shrine in Athens and the acceptance of a justice system based on law rather than vendetta. The name "Kindly Ones" was applied to them out of respect and fear.

Galen (129–*c.*200): classical Roman physician, who eventually became court doctor to the Emperor Marcus Aurelius. He wrote many works on medicine and was highly esteemed as a philosopher as well. Along with the ancient Greek physician Hippocrates, he was one of the two most influential medical theorists in Early Modern Europe.

Ganymede: English form of the Greek "Ganymedes," a beautiful Trojan prince who was abducted by Zeus, who took the form of an eagle, to be his wine steward. In later classical and Early Modern literature, their relationship was often used as a metaphor for male homosexual desire (see, for example, Christopher Marlowe's play *Dido, Queen of Carthage*).

Hades: (Latin "Pluto" or "Dis") the god of the dead and ruler of the Underworld. Because precious metals come from under the ground, he is also associated with wealth. He acquired his wife Persephone by kidnapping her from the surface world.

Hecate: a Titan who became a goddess of the Underworld in Greek mythology; she is associated with witchcraft, black magic, and malevolent spirits which walk the earth. Her appearance is usually heralded by the sound of barking dogs.

Hector: in Greek legend, the son of King Priam and Queen Hecuba and the most powerful warrior in the ancient city of Troy. He was killed by Achilles. In contrast to Achilles, Hector has come to personify martial courage combined with compassion and dutifulness.

Helicon: mountain in ancient Greece where the Muses lived.

Helen of Troy: usually represented as the daughter of Zeus and Leda, she was the wife of King Menelaus of Sparta. There are many contrary versions of the myths surrounding her, but all agree that she was the epitome of mortal female beauty. The best-known story about her concerns her abduction by (or voluntary flight with, depending upon which version of the story one consults) Paris, a prince of Troy. To get her back, Menelaus and his brother Agamemnon summoned all of their allies, and began the ten-year-long Trojan War. In later literature, Helen is the type of physical beauty, but sometimes also a sinister figure, responsible for all the soldiers killed during the war to recover her.

Hephaestus: (Latin, "Vulcan") the god of fire and of the forge. He was the son of Zeus and Hera and was married to Aphrodite, and was born with a limp or club foot. Either because he was crippled, or because he sided with Hera against Zeus in an argument, he was physically thrown out of Olympus, but managed to win his way back. He is famous for his great artisanal skill, forging the armor of Achilles (*Iliad* 18) and the invisible net which trapped Ares and his wife Aphrodite in bed together. After this last feat, he invited the other gods to come and view their trapped colleagues. He is sometimes represented in a workshop under a volcano (usually Mt. Etna in Sicily) with cyclopes as assistants.

Hera: (Latin, "Juno") the goddess of marriage; she was the sister and wife of Zeus, and the daughter of Cronus and Rhea, by virtue of which she is often called the "queen of the gods." Most of the myths concerning Hera involve her attempts to punish or kill her husband's paramours and/or the children which those unions produced. She is strongly associated with the island of Samos and her iconographic bird is the peacock.

Heracles: the original Greek name for the demigod known in Latin as Hercules.

Hercules: son of Zeus and Alcmena, and the most famous hero in Greek mythology. The legends of his life and deeds are innumerable, but the best known involve the Twelve Labors, imposed upon him by Eurystheus to expiate Hercules' murder of his own wife and children. He also killed the centaur Nessus, who was trying to rape his second wife, Deianeira. While dying, Nessus told her to keep some of his blood and that, if a garment was dipped in it and placed on Hercules, it would win back his love. She subsequently did so, but the blood turned out to be a poison which caused Hercules immense pain.

Hermes: (Latin "Mercury") the messenger of the gods, and the god of merchants, thieves, negotiation, and oratory. He was also the *psychopompos*, the god who led the souls of the dead to the Underworld. The son of Zeus and the Titan Maia, he is usually represented with winged sandals, a winged hat, and a staff with two serpents wound around it (the *caduceus*).

Herodotus (*c*.490–*c*.425 BCE) was called by many ancient writers "the father of history" because his *History* of the Greek wars with Persia was written on a larger scale than any previous historical work. His work was divided into nine books, each of them named for one of the Muses.

Hesiod (eighth century BCE): ancient Greek poet, author of the *Theogony*, an account of the origins of the Greek gods, and the *Works and Days*, which describes agricultural life.

Hesperides: the mythical female guardians of a tree of golden apples, given by the Earth to Hera as a wedding present. The tree was also guarded by a dragon (Ladon) which was later killed by Hercules. The garden of the Hesperides was supposed to be at the western edge of the Ocean.

Hippocrene: a spring on Mt. Helicon, the home of the Muses, the waters of which gave poetic inspiration.

Hippodamia *see* Lapiths and Centaurs.

Homer: the traditionally ascribed author of the two earliest Greek epic poems, the *Iliad* (describing the Trojan War) and the *Odyssey* (describing the hero Odysseus' prolonged journey home from the Trojan War). The legends associated with Homer as a person include his blindness and that he lived a poor, wandering life. His mere existence is now a matter of scholarly dispute.

Humors: Early Modern physiology identified four cardinal fluids, or "humors," of the body (blood, phlegm, choler, and black bile or melancholy). The relative proportions of these fluids in the body was thought to determine a person's physical and psychological dispositions. Comic drama in this period often identified exaggerated characters with an excess of a particular humor, and traces of humor psychology remain in our language through adjectives like "sanguine," "choleric," "bilious," and "phlegmatic."

Hymen: the god of marriage in ancient Roman literature. The name came originally from a line in Greek wedding songs which did not refer to a god at all, but it was taken to refer to a divinity as time went on.

Iliad, The: a 24-book epic poem on the subject of the Trojan War (the title refers to Ilium, the name of a later city on the site of Troy which is often used synonymously with Troy). The poem revolves around the greatest of the Greek heroes, Achilles, and his angry refusal to continue fighting after a slave-girl, awarded to him as a share of the booty, is taken from him and given to King Agamemnon. In his absence, the Trojans, led by Hector, almost drive the Greeks back into the sea. Only after his friend Patroclus dies at the hands of Hector (and after his sea-nymph mother has obtained a new set of armaments for him from the god Hephaestus) does he return to the fighting. In the poem's climax, Achilles kills the honorable Hector and deliberately degrades his body. The poem treats many subjects and a vast array of characters, but perhaps the salient theme is the conflict between the individualistic, heroic mode of action (exemplified by Achilles) and the corporate, political model of leadership (exemplified by King Agamemnon).

Itys *see* Philomela.

Jove: a common English name for the Roman god Jupiter (the Greek "Zeus").

Juno: the Roman goddess of marriage and childbirth, and the consort of Jupiter; she was conflated with the Greek goddess Hera.

Jupiter: the Roman god of the sky, conflated with the Greek Zeus.

Justinian: eastern Roman emperor from 527 to 655. He is most famous for sponsoring a massive three-volume codification of Roman law. In medieval Europe, Justinian's code became the basis for most European legal education, and as such its influence has been immense.

Lapiths and Centaurs: a mythical tribe which held a famous wedding feast for their king, Pirithous, and his bride Hippodamia. They invited the neighboring centaurs, who tried to carry off the bride and the other women present at the feast. The battle of the Lapiths and the centaurs was often represented in classical and Early Modern art, and resulted in the defeat of the centaurs.

Leda: one of Zeus's many mortal paramours, she was raped by the king of the gods while he was in the form of a swan. The children of that union were the future Helen of Troy and the twins Castor and Polydeuces (Latin "Pollux"). She was the wife of King Tyndareus of Sparta, and their daughter was Clytemnestra.

Livy: common English nickname for Titus Livius (59 BC–AD 17), a Roman historian. He wrote a history of Rome in 142 books that was widely read in his own day and in Early Modern Europe.

Lucretia (sixth century BCE): in Roman legend, she was the chaste wife of the Roman general Lucius Tarquinius Collatinus; after being raped by the King of Rome's son, Sextus Tarquinius, she told her husband (in order to inspire him to revenge) and then committed suicide. In doing so, she became the literary model of the honorable wife who preferred death to dishonor. The story is narrated by Shakespeare in *The Rape of Lucrece* (1594).

Mars: the Roman god of war, who was conflated with the Greek Ares.

Menelaus: in ancient Greek legend and literature, the King of Sparta who married Helen of Troy. Her abduction by Paris, a Trojan prince, led to the Trojan War, as Menelaus and his brother Agamemnon led an army of Greeks to recover her. In later literature, he becomes a type of the cuckolded husband.

Mercury: the Roman messenger god, conflated with the Greek god Hermes.

Metamorphoses: a 15-book epic poem by the Roman poet Ovid. Although clearly indebted to Virgil's model of the epic, Ovid combined it with the more episodic style of Callimachus' *Aetia* to produce something wholly original. It presents itself as a mythic history of the Mediterranean world from the creation of the earth until Augustan Rome (Ovid's own day), but prior literature and historical fact are idiosyncratically reworked into a framework for an encyclopedic collection of myths unified by the theme of transformation (hence the title). The *Metamorphoses'* importance for later writers as a compendium of classical myth is impossible to exaggerate, and it was widely read throughout Early Modern Europe.

Midas: mythical king of Phrygia who was given a wish by a god and wished that everything he touched be turned to gold. He asked to have the gift withdrawn when he realized that his food would turn to gold too, and was told to bathe in the River Pactolus. The other principal myth about Midas depicts him as judge in a music contest between Apollo and Pan, the god of shepherds. Midas judged against Apollo, who promptly gave him the ears of an ass to indicate his stupidity.

Minerva: the Roman goddess of crafts who became identified with the Greek goddess Athena. Like Athena, she was also sometimes represented as a war god.

Morpheus: the ancient Roman god of dreams. According to Homer and Virgil, dreams come from the Underworld, where they leave through one of two gates: true dreams go through a gate of horn, and false dreams through one of ivory.

Musaeus: (1) mythical singer and associate of Orpheus, who is himself the subject of many myths; often confused with (2) a late classical Greek poet (fifth/sixth century) who wrote *Hero and Leander*, which was in turn the source for Christopher Marlowe's poem of the same name.

Muses: a group of ancient Greek goddesses, the daughters of Zeus and Mnemosyne ("Memory"), who inspired mortals in intellectual, poetic, and artistic endeavors. They are associated with Pieria and Mt. Helicon, and also with Mt. Parnassus. Beginning with Hesiod in the *Theogony*, it was conventional for all classical poets beginning a work of great length or ambition to invoke the Muses' aid in composition. Our notion of "divine inspiration" comes from the classical convention that great poetry does not begin in the mind of the poet, but that the Muses speak through the poet as their vehicle. Although their names and number vary in classical accounts, they are most commonly thought of as nine in number, with each having a particular province of the arts: Calliope (epic poetry), Clio (history), Erato (lyre music and lyric poetry), Euterpe (flute music, and the poetry accompanied by it), Melpomene (tragedy), Polyhymnia (hymns to the gods), Terpsichore (dancing and choral accompaniments), Thalia (comedy and pastoral poetry) and Urania (astronomy).

Narcissus: a beautiful mythological youth who was loved by the nymph Echo. When he rejected her, Aphrodite caused him to fall in love with his own reflection in a pool of water; unable to capture the beautiful image of himself, he pined away and died. In some later versions of the story, he drowns while trying to reach for his reflection in the pool.

Neptune: the Roman god of the sea, who was conflated with the Greek god Poseidon.

Nestor: one of the Greek heroes at the Trojan War even though he was very old. He is portrayed in mythology and literature as the type of the wise old counsellor and, in the *Iliad*, he is one of King Agamemnon's chief advisors.

Niobe: the daughter of Tantalus and the wife of Amphion, she boasted to the goddess Leto, mother of Apollo and Artemis, that she had produced more children than the goddess. Artemis and Apollo promptly killed her six children and Niobe wept for them until she was turned into a column of stone. She was frequently used by early modern writers as a symbol of maternal grief and/or mortal presumption in challenging the gods.

Odysseus: a mythical Greek hero, ruler of the island kingdom of Ithaca and a central figure in the Trojan War. Homer's *Odyssey* is the story of his 20-year attempt to return home after the war. The first line of the *Odyssey* describes him as a man of "many turns," and Odysseus exemplifies the type of hero who uses his wits as well as his strength to get what he wants. This has made him a popular subject for writers in every age: sometimes, his cunning is depicted as admirable cleverness, and sometimes as dishonorable deceit and cowardice. He is often referred to in later literature by his Latin name "Ulysses."

Odyssey: a 24-book epic poem which treats the hero Odysseus' attempts to return from the Trojan War to his home at Ithaca. Odysseus is aided by the goddess Athena, and has innumerable adventures with gods, monsters, and mortals during his travels. In a parallel plot, his wife Penelope is being wooed by a large group of suitors who think Odysseus is dead and wish to become ruler of Ithaca in his stead; as well, his son Telemachus escapes a plot to kill him and travels to Greece to get news of his father. The second half of the poem relates how Odysseus arrives at Ithaca in disguise, meets Telemachus, and then reclaims his home in a bloody battle with the suitors.

Oedipus: a mythical Greek King of Thebes and the tragic protagonist of Sophocles's *Oedipus the King* and *Oedipus at Colonos*. He gained his throne by solving the riddle of the Sphinx and was ruler; he later learned through the prophet Tiresias that he had unknowingly killed his father and married his mother. After blinding himself, he wandered Greece as an outcast. His story has fascinated writers for centuries, among them Sigmund Freud (who used the name "Oedipus Complex" for one of his most important concepts).

Orestes: the son of Agamemnon and Clytemnestra, he killed Clytemnestra after she killed his father. He was pursued by the Furies to the temple of Apollo at Delphi, and from there went to Athens, where he was acquitted by the court of the Areopagus (with the assistance of Athena). The story is narrated in Aeschylus' trilogy of plays *The Oresteia.*

Orpheus: a mythical Greek poet who is often described in literature as the first poet in human history. There are many myths about him concerning his origins (as the son of a Muse) and his skill at playing the lyre (he could charm wild animals and make inanimate objects move with his poetry). Most widely told of all is the story of his journey to the Underworld to recover his dead wife, Eurydice. His music charmed Persephone, who allowed Eurydice to return to the upper world with him as long as he did not look back at her during the journey up. He could not resist looking back to make sure she was following him, and she was taken back to Hades. He himself died after being torn to pieces by the maenads, the god Dionysus' female followers. His head continued to sing even after it was severed from his body and thrown into a river.

Ovid (43 BC–AD 47): Roman poet whose surviving works include: the *Amores* (a three-book collection of love elegies to a mistress named Corinna), the *Ars amatoria* ("Art of Love," a poetic manual on how to seduce women), the *Remedia amoris* ("Cures of Love," a manual on how to get rid of an unwanted mistress), the *Heroides* (a collection of verse epistles from mythical heroines to their husbands or lovers), and the *Metamorphoses* (an epic poem on the theme of transformation). In AD 8, he was banished by the emperor Augustus to Tomis on the Black Sea for what Ovid called *carmen et error* ("a poem and a mistake"). The poem was the *Ars amatoria*, which affronted Augustan official morality, and the mistake has been speculated to be something connected to the emperor's adulterous daughter Julia. From Tomis, he wrote the *Tristia* ("Sorrows"), a long poem about life in exile. Although never as respectable a figure as Virgil, his poetic influence on future generations is almost as great, and nearly all Western literary conventions concerning sexual mores derive ultimately from his works.

Pallas: a commonly used name for Athena or Minerva.

Pan: (Latin, "Faunus") the Greek god of shepherds. He is represented with a human torso, head, and arms, but the legs, hooves, and horns of a goat. Native to Arcadia in Greece, he features prominently in pastoral poetry and mythology. He made the first pan pipes out of reeds as a memento of the nymph Syrinx, who was changed into reeds as she fled from his unwanted sexual advances. The sensation of blind fear known as "panic" is associated with him.

Paris: a prince of Troy, son of King Priam and Queen Hecuba, and often described as the handsomest man on earth. From birth, it was prophesied that he would bring about the destruction of the city, so he was exposed to die. Shepherds rescued him and he was eventually restored to his place. As well as abducting Helen of Troy from her husband King Menelaus, he is famous for judging a beauty contest between the goddesses Aphrodite, Athena, and Hera. Each offered Paris a reward, and he chose Aphrodite (who had offered him the most beautiful woman in the world as a wife). The other two goddesses, who had offered him success in battle and power respectively, never forgave him, and the whole city of Troy suffered as a result. He was a famously skilled archer (and killed Achilles with an arrow), but is also represented as unwilling to fight in hand-to-hand combat.

Parnassus: a mountain sacred to the Muses in Greece; on it is the spring of Castalia, which was often associated with poetic inspiration by later writers.

Penelope: in Homer's *Odyssey*, Odysseus' proverbially faithful wife. During her husband's 20-year absence, she stayed at their home on Ithaca. In time, her house was overrun with suitors who believed that Odysseus was dead, but she claimed that she could not remarry until she had finished weaving a funeral shroud for her father-in-law, Laertes. To delay this moment, she would undo at night all that she had woven the previous day. Odysseus eventually returned home, slaughtered the suitors, and was accepted by Penelope.

Persephone: the daughter of Zeus and Demeter, she was kidnapped by Hades and became Queen of the Underworld. Demeter pleaded with Zeus for her release, but since Persephone had eaten with Hades (albeit only a few pomegranate seeds) she had implicitly consented to stay. An agreement was reached whereby she spent eight months of the year on earth and four with Hades.

Petrarch (1304–74): Italian humanist scholar and poet, who helped to establish the possibility for a secular (rather than clerical) life of letters and scholarship; his best-known poems are the sonnets and songs collected in the *Rime sparse,* which popularized the sonnet form in all European vernaculars. Many of the love poem conventions used by Shakespeare, Spenser, Sidney, and others were popularized by Petrarch. In addition, he published several scholarly works, volumes of letters, and an epic poem in Latin.

Phaethon: in Greek mythology, the son of the sun god Helios (in some versions of the story, he is the son of Phoebus Apollo). As a favour begged from his father, he asked to drive the chariot of the sun for a day. After he lost control of the horses, the sun's course became erratic and it veered too close to the earth, burning the surface and creating deserts in its wake. Zeus killed Phaethon with a thunderbolt in order to stop the whole planet from being consumed with fire. His sisters, crying for his death, were turned into poplar trees, with the tears represented as amber.

Philomela: the daughter of a king of Athens, she was the sister of Procne and sister-in-law to Procne's husband, King Tereus of Thrace. Tereus raped Philomela, cut out her tongue, and imprisoned her so that she could not reveal his crime. She wove a tapestry representing her plight which she managed to smuggle to her sister, who in turn used a disguise to free her sister from prison. In revenge, Procne killed her son by Tereus, Itys, and served his flesh to her husband; when he realized what had happened, he tried to kill both sisters but was transformed into a hoopoe bird. In the most common versions of the myth, Philomela was changed into a nightingale and Procne into a swallow; the early Greek versions of the myth reverse these transformations. This myth is often used as a reference for female suffering at the hands of men, and was joined with the Early Modern beliefs that nightingales sang only at night and that they pressed a thorn to their breasts to keep themselves awake.

Phoebus: a common name for the Greek god Apollo.

Phoenix: a mythical Arabian bird, which looked like an eagle but with fiery red and gold feathers. It was said to live for 500 years, whereupon it made itself a pyre and burned up; a new phoenix immediately emerged out of the ashes of the old one and the cycle repeated itself. Early versions of this myth (in Herodotus and Tacitus) are somewhat different, but the version retold here appealed to the Christian world as a pagan analogue of Christ's resurrection.

Plato (427–347 BC): ancient Greek philosopher from Athens, and an abiding influence on all Western philosophy since. He wrote about 25 philosophical dialogues (including the *Republic,* the *Phaedrus* and the *Symposium*), most of which feature his teacher Socrates and one or more interlocutors. He mounted a famous critique of poetry and its role in his utopian state in *Republic* 3.392ff. His school in Athens was called the Academy.

Plutarch (*c.*46–120): Greek historian and philosopher. His surviving writings include *Parallel Lives* (English translation 1579), a series of biographies of prominent Greeks and Romans, and the *Moralia* (English translation 1603), a series of short treatises on rhetoric and moral philosophy. He was widely read and very influential in Early Modern Europe: three of Shakespeare's plays take their plots from the *Parallel Lives,* and the *Moralia* were used as the models for the modern essay form by Montaigne and Francis Bacon.

Pluto: a Latin form of a common Greek name for Hades, god of the Underworld; it means "giver of wealth."

Poseidon: (Latin "Neptune") the god of the sea; he is also often called the "earth shaker," and has the power to cause earthquakes. He was the brother of Zeus and Hera, and one of his sons was the sea god Triton. His symbol is the trident. In Homer, he is represented as the implacable enemy of Troy (because he and Apollo were tricked into building the walls of the city) and of Odysseus (because Odysseus blinded his son Polyphemus, the cyclops).

Procne *see* Philomela.

Prometheus: a Titan, or pre-Olympian Greek god. The myths surrounding him usually depict him as a divine advocate for mortals; in some versions of the stories, he created man out of clay. After Zeus took back the gift of fire from humanity, it was Prometheus who smuggled it back down to earth; he also taught mankind many different arts and sciences. After he incurred Zeus' displeasure (either over the gift of fire or other causes), Zeus chained Prometheus to a rock in the Caucasus, where an eagle came every day to peck out his liver. At night, his liver regrew. Some myths say that the eagle was shot by Hercules; others, that Prometheus was released when he submitted to Zeus.

Proserpina: Latin name for Persephone.

Proteus: a minor sea god, also known as the "Old Man of the Sea," whom Menelaus encounters in *Odyssey* 4. He was able to see into the future and also had the power to assume any outward form he wished; he would only tell his interlocutor the truth if he was bound and prevented from changing his shape. His name has given us the adjective "protean," and he has become emblematic of the power to change shape.

Pygmalion: a legendary King of Cyprus and devotee of the cult of Aphrodite. Early versions of the myth describe how he fell in love with a statue of the goddess in a temple, but Ovid depicts the king carving the statue himself and then falling in love. This statue was subsequently animated by Aphrodite and became his wife. It is Ovid's version that has become the most widely known.

Pythagoras (*c*.580–*c*.500 BCE): ancient Greek mystic and mathematician from the island of Samos. As a mystic, he founded a widespread religious cult and introduced the doctrine of metempsychosis (transmigration of the soul) into Greek culture. As a mathematician, he is credited with discovering the geometric theorem that is named for him and the ratios which are used to set the string lengths on musical instruments. He is described by ancient writers as possessing a golden thigh, as a sign of his superhuman nature.

Sabines: an Italian tribe living near ancient Rome. In Roman mythology, the founder of the city (Romulus) invited the Sabines to watch some games in Rome; while this happening, the Sabine women were carried off to provide wives for Roman men. This led to a war in which the Sabines besieged Rome, but ended with a peaceful reconciliation between the two peoples.

Saturn: the father of Jupiter and other Roman gods, who was identified with the Greek god Cronus. Like Cronus, the period of his rule is represented as a Golden Age in life on earth.

Satyrs: (Latin "fauni") male attendants on the god Dionysus. They are represented as human, but with the legs of a goat, and are proverbially lustful. They also appear frequently in pastoral poetry as denizens of the woods.

Scylla: in Greek myth, a female sea monster with six heads which lived in a cave across the Straits of Messina from the whirlpool Charybdis. She would devour sailors from any passing ship, and is best known from her encounter with Odysseus in *Odyssey* 12. Some versions of her story assert that she was a beautiful woman before being changed into a monster by a rival in love.

Seneca (4 BCE–65CE): a Roman philosopher and dramatic poet whose tragedies were the models for Early Modern vernacular tragedy. He was an advisor to the notoriously corrupt emperor Nero, and this compromised his reputation as a moralist with some later readers.

Sibyl: the name given to various female seers and prophetesses in the ancient Greek and Roman world; perhaps the best-known is the Sibyl of Cumae, whom Aeneas visits in the *Aeneid* 6.

Sinon: in the Trojan War, the Greek soldier who persuaded the Trojans to take the wooden horse into their city. For later writers, he was the type of the liar and deceiver.

Sirens: mythical monsters who lived on a Mediterranean island; they are usually represented with women's heads and the bodies of birds of prey. Their singing bewitched men, and lured passing sailors to their deaths. In *Odyssey* 12, Odysseus defeats them by plugging his crew's ears with wax and having himself tied to the mast of his ship. In later literature, they come to represent female seductiveness and the dangers of obeying one's lusts.

Sisyphus: the mythical founder of the Greek city of Corinth, and the subject of many myths. He is best known for the punishment inflicted upon him in the Underworld, which was to perpetually roll a rock to the top of a hill only to see it roll down again.

Solomon (*c*. tenth century BC): king of Israel. The son of King David and Bathsheba, Solomon ruled Israel wisely and built the great temple in Jerusalem (see 1 Kings). For later Judeo-Christian cultures, he was a by-word for wisdom, just rule, and sagacity as a lawgiver.

Sophocles (*c*.496–*c*.406 BCE): Greek tragic dramatist. He was reputed in ancient times to have written over 120 plays, but only seven of them survive today. These include *Oedipus the King*, *Oedipus at Colonos*, *Antigone*, *Electra*, and *Philoctetes*. According to Aristotle, it was Sophocles who was responsible for adding the third actor on stage; previously, the limit in any one scene was two. His direct influence on the writing of Early Modern plays was slight, owing to the limited knowledge of Greek in Europe, but his work has been widely translated and read from the seventeenth century onward.

Syrinx: a mythical nymph; *see* Pan.

Tacitus (*c*.56–*c*.120): a Roman historian who wrote the *Histories* (on the Roman empire between the years 69 and 96 CE) and the *Annals* (on the period between 14 and 68). Both texts survive only in fragments, and were widely read in Europe from the late sixteenth century onward.

Tantalus: a mythical Greek king who offended the gods by serving them his son Pelops to eat in a banquet (other versions of the myth describe how he stole nectar and ambrosia from the table of the gods). There are two versions of his punishment in the Underworld: one sees him set, perpetually hungry and thirsty, in a pool which receded when he tried to drink from it and under fruit trees with fruit he could not reach. The other places him at a table covered with food and drink, but under a huge stone which threatened to fall on him at any moment; because of his terror, he was unable to eat or drink.

Terence (*c*.193–159 BCE): Roman comic dramatist who, along with Plautus, brought Greek New Comedy to Roman (and later) culture.

Tereus *see* Philomela.

Thebes: a city in ancient Greece with a long and tragic history that is recounted in many myths. Its mythical founder, Cadmus, was directed to the site of the city by the Delphic Oracle. There he slew a dragon and, directed by Athena, sowed some of the teeth into the ground. These sprang up as armed men, which immediately began fighting each other until only five were left. These five helped Cadmus build the citadel of the city. Later myths surrounding this city involve the Sphinx, a monster with a woman's head and torso and the body of a lion, who terrorized the city until its riddle was solved by

Oedipus. After Oedipus' banishment, the city lapsed into civil war between Oedipus' sons, Eteocles and Polyneices. After this ended with the accession of Creon, there was yet more internecine violence as Oedipus' daughter Antigone was killed for burying her brother Polyneices against Creon's orders. Creon's son, Haemon, hanged himself upon hearing of his fiancée Antigone's death. The Roman poet Statius wrote an epic poem about the city called the *Thebaid*. In later literature, Thebes came to be the emblematic example of a society that tears itself apart from within.

Theseus: a mythical king of Athens and a hero about whom innumerable myths were told. The most famous of these involves his fight against King Minos of Crete, who had imposed a yearly tribute of seven youths and seven girls on Athens; these were sent to Crete to be eaten by the Minotaur, a monster with a human body and the head of a bull which lived in the labyrinth beneath Minos's palace. Theseus slew the Minotaur and negotiated the labyrinth with the help of Minos' daughter Ariadne (whom he abandoned on the island of Naxos). He is also famous for defeating the Amazons, a nation of warrior women, and marrying their queen, Hippolyta.

Trojan War: the name given in Greek legend to the ten-year conflict in which the Greek army besieged the city of Troy in order to recover Queen Helen of Sparta, who had been abducted by the Trojan prince Paris. The war ended when the Greeks pretended to leave and left behind a large wooden horse, ostensibly as an offering to Athena. A Greek soldier named Sinon was left behind and persuaded the Trojans to take the horse into the city and, while the Trojans celebrated, the Greek soldiers hidden in the horse emerged and opened the gates of the city. The rest of the Greek army, which had returned under cover of night, flooded in and the city was utterly destroyed.

Troy: the ancient city in the region of Troas (or Dardania) on the coast of Asia Minor which, in Greek legend, was fabulously wealthy. When the Trojan prince Paris abducted Helen, Queen of Sparta, it provoked the Trojan War. Its existence as a real historical city was in some doubt until a German amateur archaeologist named Heinrich Schliemann excavated it in the years 1870–90. The city is also known by the name Ilium, which provides the title of Homer's *Iliad*.

Tully: a common English nickname for Cicero.

Ulysses: the Latin form of the Greek name "Odysseus," who is the hero of Homer's *Odyssey*. Many Early Modern writers used the Latin form of this name in preference to the original Greek.

Uranus: the personification of the heavens in Greek mythology. He is one of the original forces in the universe, and his unions with the earth ("Gaia") began the generation of all the future Greek gods.

Venus: a Roman fertility goddess, who was identified with the Greek goddess Aphrodite. She was sometimes called "Erycine," and her symbols were doves, swans, sparrows, and the myrtle plant.

Vesta: the Roman goddess of the hearth and home. Her shrine at Rome was tended by the Vestal Virgins, the only female priesthood in Rome.

Virgil (70–19 BCE): more correctly spelled Vergil, and short for P. Vergilius Maro, the most widely admired of all the Roman poets. His major works are the *Eclogues* (c.39–38 BCE), a collection of ten pastoral poems; the *Georgics* (29 BCE), a didactic poem on agriculture; and the *Aeneid* (29–19 BCE), an epic poem describing the mythical origins of Rome. Respect for his work bordered on reverence in later generations, and a tradition arose of predicting the future by reading randomly chosen passages of his poems (*sortes Virgilianae*).

Vulcan: the Roman god of the forge, who was identified with the Greek god Hephaestus.

Xenophon (c.428–c.354 BCE): an ancient Greek soldier and writer from Athens who was an admirer of Socrates in his youth. He served as a mercenary under the Persian emperor and, after his master was defeated in 401 BCE, led 10,000 Greek soldiers back to Byzantium from near present-day Baghdad; his written account of this action, *Anabasis*, is one of his most famous works. He wrote many other books, but is best known for the *Cyropaedia*, a fictionalized account of the Persian emperor Cyrus the Great that was widely cited in Renaissance Europe.

Zeus: (Latin, "Jupiter" or "Jove") the king of the Olympian gods and the god of the sky. He was the son of Cronus, whom he killed to assume his position. The most commonly repeated myths about him involve his innumerable adulterous encounters with mortal women and the fate of their offspring (Hercules, Helen of Troy, Perseus, Amphion, and many others); he also has to deal with the jealous rages of his wife, Hera. This aspect of his character should not obscure his immense power and the fear in which he was held by the other gods. His symbol is the thunderbolt.

Bibliography

Ackroyd, Peter. *The Life of Thomas More* (London, 1998).

Allen, J. W. *A History of Political Thought in the Sixteenth Century* (London, 1928).

Alpers, Svetlana. *The Art of Describing* (Chicago, 1983).

Alvares, Francisco. *The Prester John of the Indies*, ed. C. F. Beckingham and G. W. B. Huntingford. 2 vols. (Cambridge, 1961).

Aubrey, John. *Brief Lives*, ed. R. Barber (Woodbridge, Suffolk, 1982).

Ault, Norman (ed.) *Elizabethan Lyrics from the Original Texts* (New York, 1949).

Bacon, Francis. *The New Organon*, ed. Lisa Jardine and Michael Silverthorne (Cambridge, 2000).

——*The Works of Francis Bacon*, ed. James Spedding, Robert Leslie Ellis, and Douglas Denon Heath (Boston, 1863).

Barnfield, Richard. *The Poems of Richard Barnfield*, ed. Montague Summers (London, 1936).

Bates, Catherine. "Astrophil and the Manic Wit of the Abject Male," *Studies in English Literature*, 41:1 (2001), 1–24.

Beer, Anna. *Sir Walter Ralegh and His Readers in the Seventeenth Century: Speaking to the People* (New York, 1997).

Beilin, Elaine V. *Redeeming Eve: Women Writers of the English Renaissance* (Princeton, NJ, 1987).

Berry, Edward. *The Making of Sir Philip Sidney* (Toronto, 1998).

Boehrer, Bruce Thomas. *"The Fury of Men's Gullets": Ben Jonson and the Digestive Canal* (Philadelphia, 1997).

Bond, Ronald B. (ed.) *Certain Sermons or Homilies and A Homily against Disobedience and Wilful Rebellion* (Toronto, 1987).

Book of Common Prayer (Charlottesville, VA, 1976).

Booty, John E. *The Godly Kingdom of Tudor England: Great Books of the English Reformation* (Wilton, 1981).

Brown, Nancy Pollard. "Paperchase: the Dissemination of Catholic Texts in Elizabethan England," *English Manuscript Studies 1100–1700* (1989), 1:120–43.

Burckhardt, Jacob. *The Civilization of the Renaissance in Italy: An Essay* (New York, 1965).

Bush, Douglas. *English Literature in the Earlier Seventeenth Century* (Oxford, 1945).

Butler, Martin (ed.) *Re-presenting Ben Jonson: Text, History, Performance* (New York, 1999).

Buxton, John. *Sir Philip Sidney and the English Renaissance* (London, 1954).

Campion, Thomas. *The Works of Thomas Campion*, ed. Walter R. Davis (New York, 1967).

Cardwell, Edward. *A History of Conferences and Other Proceedings Connected with the Revision of the Book of Common Prayer from the Year 1558 to the Year 1690* (Oxford, 1849).

Carey, John. *John Donne: Life, Mind, and Art* (London, 1981).

Carrell, Jennifer Lee. "*Urania's* Magic Mirror of Romance," *Studies in English Literature*, 34:1 (1994), 79–107.

Carthell, Ronald J. "'The Secrecy of Man': Recusant Discourse and the Elizabethan Subject," *English Literary Renaissance*, 19:3 (1989), 272–90.

Cary, Elizabeth. *The Tragedy of Mariam*, ed. Stephanie Hodgson-Wright (Toronto, 2000).

——*The Tragedy of Mariam the Fair Queen of Jewry*, ed. Barry Weller and Margaret W. Ferguson (Berkeley, CA, 1994).

Certaine Sermons or Homilies (Gainesville, FL, 1968).

Chambers, R. W. *On the Continuity of English Prose from Alfred to More and his School* (London, 1957).

Cheney, Patrick. *Marlow's Counterfeit Profession: Ovid, Spenser, Counter-Nationhood* (Toronto, 1997).

Child, Francis J. (ed.) *English and Scottish Popular Ballads* (New York, 1956).

Craig, Hardin. *The Enchanted Glass: The Elizabethan Mind in Literature* (New York, 1936).

Daileader, Celia R. "When a Sparrow Falls: Women Readers, Male Critics, and John Skelton's *Phyllyp Sparowe*," *Philological Quarterly*, 75 (1996), 391–409.

Daniell, David. *William Tyndale: A Biography* (New Haven, 2000).

Davis, Walter R. *Thomas Campion* (Boston, 1987).

Dearmer, Percy, R. Vaughan Williams, and Martin Shaw (eds.) *The Oxford Book of Carols* (London, 1928).

Dickens, A. G. *The English Reformation* (London, 1964).

Di Cesare, Mario A. (ed.) *George Herbert and the Seventeenth-Century Religious Poets* (New York, 1978).

Docherty, Thomas. *John Donne Undone* (London, 1986).

Dollimore, Jonathan. *Radical Tragedy: Religion, Ideology, and Power in the Drama of Shakespeare and his Contemporaries*, 2nd edn. (Chicago, 1989).

Donne, John. *The Anniversaries*, ed. Frank Manley (Baltimore, MD, 1963).

——*Devotions* (Ann Arbor, MI, 1959).

——*John Donne*, ed. John Carey (Oxford, 1990).

——*Selected Poetry and Prose*, ed. T. W. Craik and R. J. Craik (London, 1986).

Donaldson, Ian. *The Rapes of Lucretia: A Myth and Its Transformations* (Oxford, 1982).

Dubrow, Heather. *Echoes of Desire: English Petrarchism and Its Counterdiscourses* (Ithaca, NY, 1995).

Duffield, G. E. (ed.) *The Work of William Tyndale* (Appleford, 1964).

Eisenstein, Elizabeth. *The Printing Press as an Agent of Change*. 2 vols. (Cambridge, 1979).

——*The Printing Revolution in Early Modern Europe* (Cambridge, 1983).

Eliot, Thomas. *The Book Named The Governor*, ed. S. E. Lehmberg (London, 1962).

Eliot, T. S. "The Metaphysical Poets," in *Selected Essays* (New York, 1950), pp. 241–50.

Elizabeth I, Queen of England. *Collected Works*, ed. Leah A. Marcus, Janet Mueller, and Mary Beth Rose (Chicago, 2000).

Elizabethan Sonnets, ed. Sidney Lee. 2 vols. (Westminster, 1904).

England's Helicon, ed. Hugh Macdonald (Cambridge, MA, 1962).

Evans, Maurice. *English Poetry in the Sixteenth Century* (London, 1955).

Evans, Robert C., and Barbara Wiedemann (eds.) *"My Name Was Martha": A Renaissance Woman's Autobiographical Poem* (West Cornwall, CT, 1993).

Fellowes, E. H. *English Madrigal Verse, 1588–1632* (Oxford, 1920).

Fenlon, Iain. "Music and Society" in *The Renaissance: From the 1470s to the End of the 16th Century*, ed. Iain Fenlon (Englewood Cliffs, NJ, 1989), pp. 1–62.

Ferguson, Wallace K. *The Renaissance in Historical Thought: Five Centuries of Interpretation* (Boston, 1948).

Fineman, Joel. *Shakespeare's Perjured Eye: The Invention of Poetic Subjectivity in the Sonnets* (Berkeley, CA, 1986).

Fish, Stanley. *John Skelton's Poetry* (New Haven, 1965).

——*Living Temple: George Herbert and Catechizing* (Berkeley, CA, 1978).

Foucault, Michel. *The Order of Things* (New York, 1973).

Fox, Alistair. *Thomas More: History and Providence* (Oxford, 1982).

Foxe, John. *Actes and Monuments* (London, 1837–41).

——*Foxe's Book of Martyrs*, ed. Marie Gentert King (Westwood, NJ, 1968).

Freeman, Rosemary. *English Emblem Books* (London, 1948).

French, Peter J. *John Dee: The World of an Elizabethan Magus* (London, 1972).

Friedman, Donald M. "The Mind in the Poem: Wyatt's 'They Flee from Me,'" *Studies in English Literature*, 7 (1967), 1–13.

Frye, Northrop. *The Anatomy of Criticism* (Princeton, NJ, 1957).

Gascoigne, George. *The Green Knight: Selected Poetry and Prose*, ed. Roger Pooley (Manchester, 1982).

——*A Hundreth Sundrie Flowres*, ed. G. W. Pigman (Oxford, 2001).

Goldberg, Jonathan. *Endlesse Worke: Spenser and the Structures of Discourse* (Baltimore, MD, 1989).

Grafton, Anthony, and Lisa Jardine. *From Humanism to the Humanities* (Cambridge, MA, 1986).

Grantley, Darryl, and Peter Roberts (eds.) *Christopher Marlowe and English Renaissance Culture* (Aldershot, 1996).

Greenberg, Noah (ed.) *An Anthology of English Medieval and Renaissance Vocal Music* (New York, 1961).

Greenblatt, Stephen. *Renaissance Self Fashioning: From More to Shakespeare* (Chicago, 1980).

——*Sir Walter Ralegh: The Renaissance Man and His Roles* (New Haven, 1973).

Greenblatt, Stephen (ed.) *New World Encounters* (Berkeley, CA, 1993).

Greene, Richard Leighton (ed.) *The Early English Carols* (Oxford, 1977).

Greene, Thomas. *The Light in Troy: Imitation and Discovery in Renaissance Poetry* (New Haven, 1982).

Greg, W. W. "Principles of Emendation in Shakespeare" (The Annual Shakespeare Lecture), *Proceedings of the British Academy* (1928).

Grossman, Marshall (ed.) *Æmilia Lanyer: Gender, Genre, and the Canon* (Lexington, KY, 1998).

Griffiths, John (ed.) *The Two Books of Homilies* (Oxford, 1859).

Hadfield, Andrew. *Spenser's Irish Experience* (Oxford, 1997).

Hakluyt, Richard. *The Principal Navigations, Voyages, Traffiques, and Discoveries of the English Nation*. 12 vols. (Glasgow, 1903–5).

Hale, John. *The Civilization of Europe in the Renaissance* (Toronto, 1994).

Hamilton, A. C. *The Structure of Allegory in "The Faerie Queene"* (Oxford, 1961).

Hamilton, A. C. (ed.) *The Spenser Encyclopedia* (Toronto, 1990).

Hanham, Alison. *Richard III and his Early Historians, 1483–1535* (Oxford, 1975).

Hannay, Margaret P. *Philip's Phoenix: Mary Sidney, Countess of Pembroke* (New York, 1990).

Hardison, O. B., Jr. *Prosody and Purpose in the English Renaissance* (Baltimore, MD, 1989).

Harp, Richard, and Stanley Stewart (eds.) *Ben Jonson* (Cambridge, 2000).

Haselkorn, Anne M., and Betty S. Travitsky (eds.) *The Renaissance Englishwoman in Print: Counterbalancing the Canon* (Amherst, MA, 1990).

Haydn, Hiram. *The Counter-Renaissance* (New York, 1950).

Helgerson, Richard. *The Elizabethan Prodigals* (Berkeley, CA, 1976).

——*Forms of Nationhood: The Elizabethan Writing of England* (Chicago, 1992).

Henry VIII, King of England. *Miscellaneous Writings*, ed. Francis Macnamara (Waltham, MA, 1924).

Hexter, J. H. *More's Utopia: The Biography of an Idea* (Princeton, NJ, 1952).

Hibbert, Christopher. *The Virgin Queen: The Personal History of Elizabeth I* (Reading, MA, 1991).

Hill, Christopher. *The Intellectual Origins of the English Revolution* (Oxford, 1965).

Hollander, John. *The Untuning of the Sky: Ideas of Music in English Poetry 1500–1700* (Princeton, NJ, 1961).

Hough, Graham. *A Preface to The Faerie Queene* (London, 1962).

Howard, Henry, Earl of Surrey. *Poems*, ed. Emrys Jones (Oxford, 1964).

Hughes, Felicity A. "Gascoigne's Poses," *Studies in English Literature*, 37:1 (1999), 1–19.

Hulse, Clark. *Metamorphic Verse: The Elizabethan Minor Epic* (Princeton, NJ, 1981).

Hulton, Paul (ed.) *America 1585: The Complete Drawings of John White* (London, 1984).

Hutson, Lorna. *Thomas Nashe in Context* (Oxford, 1989).

Jardine, Lisa, and Alan Steward. *Hostage to Fortune: The Troubled Life of Francis Bacon* (London, 1998).

Johnson, Samuel. *Lives of the Poets* ("Abraham Cowley") in *Selected Poetry and Prose*, ed. Frank Brady and W. K. Wimsatt (Berkeley, CA, 1977), pp. 337–84.

Jonson, Ben. *Poems*, ed. Ian Donaldson (Oxford, 1975).

Kerman, Joseph. *The Elizabethan Madrigal: A Comparative Study* (New York, 1962).

Kermode, Frank. *Shakespeare, Spenser, Donne: Renaissance Essays* (London, 1971).

Kermode, Frank (ed.) *English Pastoral Poetry from the Beginnings to Marvell* (London, 1954).

Kerrigan, William, and Gordon Braden. *The Idea of the Renaissance* (Baltimore, MD, 1985).

Kindall, Paul Murray. *Richard III* (New York, 1956).

King, John N. *English Reformation Literature: The Tudor Origins of the Protestant Tradition* (Princeton, NJ, 1982).

Kinsman, Robert S. (ed.) *The Darker Vision of the Renaissance* (Berkeley, CA, 1974).

Knox, John. *The First Blast of the Trumpet Against the Monstrous Regiment of Women*, ed. Edward Arber (Westminster, 1895).

Lancashire, Ian. "Elizabethan Homilies 1623: Editor's Introduction," http://www.library.utoronto.ca/utel/ret/homilies/elizhmi.html.

Lanyer, Æmilia. *The Poems of Æmilia Lanyer*, ed. Susanne Woods (New York, 1993).

Lehmberg, S. E. *Sir Thomas Elyot, Tudor Humanist* (Austin, TX, 1965).

Lestringant, Frank. *Cannibals: The Discovery and Representation of the Cannibal from Columbus to Jules Verne* (Berkeley, CA, 1997).

Lever, J. W. *The Elizabethan Love Sonnet* (London, 1956).

Lewalski, Barbara Kiefer. *Writing Women in Jacobean England* (Cambridge, MA, 1993).

Lewis, C. S. *The Allegory of Love* (Oxford, 1936).

——*The Discarded Image* (Cambridge, 1964).

——*English Literature in the Sixteenth Century Excluding Drama* (Oxford, 1954).

Linton, Joan Pong. "The Humanist in the Market: Gendering Exchange and Authorship in Lyly's Euphues Romances." In *Framing Elizabethan Fiction: Contemporary Approaches to Elizabethan Narrative Prose*, ed. Constance Relihan (Kent, OH, 1996), pp. 73–97.

Lowinsky, Edward E. *Music in the Culture of the Renaissance and Other Essays* (Chicago, 1989).

Lyly, John. *The Complete Works*, ed. R. W. Bond (Oxford, 1902).

Maley, Willy, *Salvaging Spenser: Colonialism, Culture and Identity* (New York, 1997).

Marius, Richard. *Martin Luther: The Christian Between God and Death* (Cambridge, MA, 2000).

——*Thomas More: A Biography* (New York, 1984).

Marlowe, Christopher. *The Complete Works of Christopher Marlowe*, ed. Fredson Bowers (Cambridge, 1981).

Marotti, Arthur F. "'Love Is Not Love': Elizabethan Sonnet Sequences and the Social Order." *English Literary History*, 49:2 (1982), 396–428.

——"Southwell's Remains: Catholicism and Anti-catholicism in Early Modern England." In *Texts and Cultural Change in Early Modern England*, ed. Cedric C. brown and Arthur F. Marotti (New York, 1997), pp. 37–65.

Marston, John. *Poems*, ed. Arnold Davenport (Liverpool, 1961).

Martz, Louis. *The Poetry of Meditation* (New Haven, 1954).

Matthiessen, F. O. *Translation: An Elizabethan Art* (Cambridge, MA, 1931).

Mattingly, Garrett. *The Armada* (Boston, 1959).

McCanles, Michael. "Love and Power in the Poetry of Sir Thomas Wyatt," *Modern Language Quarterly*, 29 (1968), 145–60.

Miller, Naomi J., and Gary Waller (eds.) *Reading Mary Wroth: Representing Alternatives in Early Modern England* (Knoxville, TN, 1991).

The Mirror for Magistrates, ed. Lily B. Campbell (Cambridge, 1938).

Montaigne, Michel de. *The Essays of Michel de Montaigne* (1603), trans. John Florio, ed. L. C. Harmer. 3 vols. (London, 1965).

More, Thomas. *Dialogue of Comfort Against Tribulation*, ed. Leland Miles (New York, 1985).

More, Thomas. *Utopia*, ed. David Harris Sacks (Boston, 1999).

——*The Yale Edition of the Complete Works of St. Thomas More*. 21 vols. (New Haven, 1963–97).

Morris, Christopher. *Political Thought in England: Tyndale to Hooker* (Oxford, 1953).

Muir, Kenneth. *The Life and Letters of Sir Thomas Wyatt* (Liverpool, 1963).

Mulcaster, Richard. *Positions* (New York, 1971).

Murphy, Andrew (ed.) *The Renaissance Text: Theory, Editing, Textuality* (Manchester, 2000).

Nash, Thomas. *Works*, ed. R. B. McKerrow and F. P. Wilson (Oxford, 1966).

——*The Unfortunate Traveller and Other Works*, ed. J. B. Steane (Harmondsworth, 1985).

Nauert, Charles Garfield. *Humanism and the Culture of Renaissance Europe* (Cambridge, 1995).

Neale, J. E. *Queen Elizabeth I: A Biography* (London, 1934).

Nohrnberg, James. *The Analogy of "The Faerie Queene"* (Princeton, NJ, 1976).

Norbrook, David, and H. R. Woudhuysen (eds.) *The Penguin Book of Renaissance Verse 1509–1659* (London, 1993).

Opfell, Olga S. *The King James Bible Translators* (Jefferson, NC, 1982).

Orgel, Stephen. *Impersonations: The Performance of Gender in Shakespeare's England* (Cambridge, 1996).

Panofsky, Erwin. *Renaissance and Renascences in Western Art* (New York, 1960).

Partridge, A. T. *English Biblical Translation* (London, 1973).

Pattison, Bruce. *Music and Poetry of the English Renaissance* (London, 1948).

Peltonen, Markku (ed.) *The Cambridge Companion to Bacon* (Cambridge, 1996).

Penrose, Boies. *Tudor and Early Stuart Voyaging* (Washington, DC, 1962).

Percy, Eustace. *John Knox* (London, 1937).

Peterson, Richard S. *Imitation and Praise in the Poems of Ben Jonson* (New Haven, 1982).

Petrarch, F. *Rime e Trionfi*, ed. Ferdinando Neri (Turin, 1960).

The Phoenix Nest, 1593 (London, 1973).

Pollet, Maurice. *John Skelton, Poet of Tudor England*, trans. John Warington (Lewisburg, PA, 1970).

Pomeroy, Elizabeth M. *The Elizabethan Miscellanies: Their Development and Conventions* (Berkeley, CA, 1973).

Porter, Roy. *London: A Social History* (Cambridge, MA, 1994).

Power, Michael J. "John Stow and his London" in *Imagining Early Modern London*, ed. J. F. Merritt (Cambridge, 2001), pp. 15–32.

Quinn, D. B. *The Roanoke voyages 1584–1590* (London, 1955).

Quinn, D. B. (ed.) *The Hakluyt Handbook*. 2 vols. (London, 1974).

Ralegh, Walter. *The Poems*, ed. Martin Dodsworth (London, 1999).

——*The Poems of Sir Walter Ralegh: A Historical Edition*, ed. Michael Rudnick (Ithaca, NY, 2000).

——*Selected Writings*, ed. Gerald Hammond (Manchester, 1984).

Ratcliff, Edward C. *The Book of Common Prayer of the Church of England: Its Making and Revisions* (London, 1949).

Reitenbach, Gail. "'Maydes are simple, some men say': Thomas Campion's Female Persona Poems." In *The Renaissance Englishwoman in Print: Counterbalancing the Canon*, ed. Anne M. Haselkorn and Betty S. Travitsky (Amherst, MA, 1990), pp. 108–32.

Reynolds, L. D., and N. G. Wilson. *Scribes and Scholars: A Guide to the Transmission of Greek and Latin Literature* (Oxford, 1974).

Rhodes, Erroll F., and Liana Lupas (eds.) *The Translators to the Reader: The Original Preface of the KING JAMES VERSION of 1611 Revisited* (New York, 1911).

Richardson, David A. "The Golden Mean in Campion's Airs." *Comparative Literature*, 30:2 (1978), 108–32.

Ridley, Florence. *The Aeneid of Henry Howard, Earl of Surrey* (Berkeley, CA, 1963).

Rollins, H. E. (ed.) *A Handful of Pleasant Delights* (New York, 1965).

Rowse, A. L. *The England of Elizabeth* (New York, 1950).

Rupp, E. G. *Studies in the Making of the English Protestant Tradition* (Cambridge, 1947).

Said, Edward. *Orientalism* (New York, 1978).

Sanders, Julie, Kate Chedgzoy, and Susan Wiseman (eds.) *Refashioning Ben Jonson: Gender, Politics, and the Jonsonian Canon* (New York, 1998).

Schibanoff, Susan. "Taking Jane's Cue: *Phyllyp Sparowe* as a Primer for Women Readers," *PMLA*, 101 (1986), 832–47.

Screech, M. A. *Montaigne and Melancholy: The Wisdom of the "Essays"* (Lanham, MD, 2000).

Sessions, W. A. *Henry Howard, Earl of Surrey* (Boston, 1986).

Seznec, Jean. *The Survival of the Pagan Gods: The Mythological Tradition and Its Place in Renaissance Humanism and Art*, trans. Barbara F. Sessions (New York, 1953).

Shakespeare, William. *The Complete Sonnets and Poems*, ed. Colin Burrow (Oxford, 2002).

——*The Poems*, ed. J. C. Maxwell (Cambridge, 1965).

Shuger, Debra Kuller. *The Renaissance Bible: Scholarship, Sacrifice, and Subjectivity* (Berkeley, CA, 1994).

Sidney, Philip. *Miscellaneous Prose of Sir Philip Sidney*, ed. Katherine Duncan-Jones and Jan van Dorsten (Oxford, 1973).

——*Poetry*, ed. William Ringler (Oxford, 1962).

Sidney, Philip. *The Psalms of Sir Philip Sidney and the Countess of Pembroke*, ed. J. C. A. Rathmell (New York, 1963).

Sidney, Robert. *The Poems of Robert Sidney*, ed. P. J. Croft (Oxford, 1984).

Skelton, John. *The Complete English Poems*, ed. John Scattergood (New Haven, 1983).

Smith, Bruce R. *Homosexual Desire in Shakespeare's England: A Cultural Poetics* (Chicago, 1991).

Smith, Hallett. *Elizabethan Poetry* (Cambridge, MA, 1952).

Southwell, Robert. *The Poems of Robert Southwell, S.J.*, ed. James H. McDonald and Nancy Pollard Brown (Oxford, 1967).

Speght, Rachel. *The Polemics and Poems of Rachel Speght*, ed. Barbara Kiefer Lewalski (New York, 1996).

Spencer, Theodore. *Shakespeare and the Nature of Man* (New York, 1949).

Spenser, Edmund. *Books I and II of The Faerie Queene*, ed. Robert Kellogg and Oliver Steele (New York, 1965).

——*The Poetical Works of Edmund Spenser*, ed. J. C. Smith and E. de Selincourt (London, 1912).

——*A View of the State of Ireland*, ed. Andrew Hadfield and Willy Maley (Oxford, 1997).

——*The Works of Edmund Spenser, a Variorum Edition*, ed. Edwin A Greenlaw et al. 10 vols. (Baltimore, MD, 1932–40).

Stapleton, M. L. "Nashe and the Poetics of Obscenity: The Choise of Valentines," *Classical and Modern Literature*, 12:1 (1999), 29–48.

Stow, John. *The Survey of London* (London, 1912).

Summers, Joseph H. *George Herbert: His Religion and Art* (London, 1954).

Thomson, Patricia. *Sir Thomas Wyatt and His Background* (London, 1964).

Tilley, M. P. *A Dictionary of Proverbs in England in the Sixteenth and Seventeenth Centuries* (London, 1950).

Tillyard, E. M. W. *The Elizabethan World Picture* (London, 1943).

——*The Renaissance: Fact or Fiction?* (London, 1952).

Tottel, Richard (ed.) *Tottel's Miscellany*, ed. Edward Arber (London, 1870).

——*Tottel's Miscellany (1557–1587)*, ed. Hyder Edward Rollins. 2 vols. (Cambridge, MA, 1965).

Tuve, Rosemond. *Allegorical Imagery: Some Medieval Books and their Posterity* (Princeton, 1966).

——*Elizabethan and Metaphysical Imagery* (Chicago, 1947).

Tyndale, William. *The Obedience of a Christian Man*, ed. David Daniell (London, 2000).

——*Tyndale's New Testament*, ed. David Daniell (New Haven, 1989).

Urbach, Peter. *Francis Bacon's Philosophy of Science: An Account and a Reappraisal* (La Salle, IL, 1987).

Vendler, Helen. *The Poetry of George Herbert* (Cambridge, MA, 1974).

Vickers, Brian (ed.) *Francis Bacon* (Oxford, 1996).

Vickers, Nancy. "'The Blazon of Sweet Beauty's Best': Shakespeare's Lucrece." In *Shakespeare and the Question of Theory*, ed. Patricia Parker and Geoffrey Hartmann (New York, 1985), pp. 95–115.

Waller, Gary F. *The Sidney Family Romance: Mary Wroth, William Herbert, and the Early Modern Construction of Gender* (Detroit, 1993).

Waller, Greg. *John Skelton and the Politics of the 1520s* (Cambridge, 1988).

Walton, Izaak. *The Compleat Angler*, ed. John Buchan (London, 1954).

Wharton, T. E. "'Furor Poeticus': Marston and His Contemporaries," *Explorations in Renaissance Culture*, 19 (1993), 73–84.

White, John. *The Birth and Rebirth of Pictorial Space* (Cambridge, MA, 1987).

Wilcox, Helen (ed.) *Women and Literature in Britain, 1500–1700* (Cambridge, 1996).

Williamson, George. *The Senecan Amble* (Chicago, 1951).

Wind, Edgar. *Pagan Mysteries in the Renaissance* (London, 1958).

Wilson, F. P. *Elizabethan and Jacobean* (Oxford, 1945).

Wilson, H. B. *History of the Merchant Taylors School* (London, 1964).

Wither, George. *A Collection of Emblemes, Ancient and Moderne (1635)* (Columbia, SC, 1975).

Woods, Susanne. *Lanyer: A Renaissance Woman Poet* (New York, 1999).

Woolf, Virginia. *A Room of One's Own* (New York, 1929).

Woudhuysen, H. R. *Sir Philip Sidney and the Circulation of Manuscripts, 1558–1640* (Oxford, 1996).

Wright, Louis B. *Middle-Class Culture in Elizabethan England* (Chapel Hill, NC, 1935).

Wroth, Mary. *The First Part of the Countess of Montgomery's Urania*, ed. Josephine A. Roberts (Binghamton, NY, 1995).

——*The Poems of Lady Mary Wroth*, ed. Josephine A. Roberts (Baton Rouge, LA, 1983).

Wyatt, Thomas. *The Complete Poems*, ed. R. A. Rebholz (New Haven, 1981).

Yates, Frances. *The Art of Memory* (Chicago, 1966).

——*Astraea* (London, 1975).

——*Giordano Bruno and the Hermetic Tradition* (Chicago, 1964).

——*John Florio: The Life of an Italian in Shakespeare's England* (Cambridge, 1934).

——*The Theatre of the World* (Chicago, 1969).

Zagorin, Perez. *Francis Bacon* (Princeton, NJ, 1998).

Index of Introductions and Notes

Index of Titles and First Lines